MOON

CHILE

DISCARD

STEPH DYSON

Contents

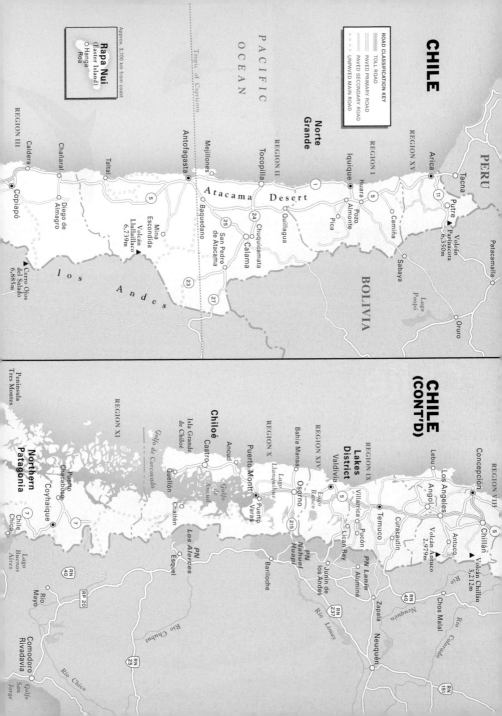

DISCOVER

Chile

Superlative in beauty and scale and at times utterly wild, Chile is a truly unique South American nation, where you can venture from desert to glacier and from pristine coastline to soaring mountaintop, all in one trip. Those seeking an unforgettable adventure will not be disappointed.

Chile is a place that, in many ways, doesn't make an awful lot of sense, defined as it is by huge contrasts. It's bookended to the east and west by the snow-cloaked Andes Mountains and the freezing waters of the Pacific Ocean. The dry desert north and the lush Patagonian south are different in every conceivable way, from the colors of the landscapes to the traditions and ethnic makeup of the people—but both somehow still represent Chile.

When I head to a national park or drive out into the mountains, there is always something new that delights me. I stumble on a bewitching glacial lake or watch in awe as the stars light up the sky above a soothing hot spring tucked away in a mountain valley.

Chile is the ideal place to stray from the main roads. Go wilderness camping in a silent forest in Patagonia. Stargaze in the Atacama Desert. Ski down the flank of a snow-covered volcano. Peel back Chile's layers and see the world from a new perspective.

Clockwise from top left: Torres del Paine; dolphins; Ahu Tahai on Rapa Nui; Santiago's Plaza de Armas; the national flower of Chile, the *copihue*; Glaciar O'Higgins.

10 TOP
EXPERIENCES

1 **Trek Through Parque Nacional Torres del Paine:** In Chile's top hiking destination, you'll encounter precarious glaciers, milky blue lakes, and iconic granite spires (page 522).

2 **Road-Trip Down the Carretera Austral:** Experience the northern part of Patagonia by car, and you'll pass through some of the country's wildest lands and its least visited national parks (page 422).

3 **Admire Chilote Architecture:** Even though it's not far from the mainland, Chiloé is culturally distinct from the rest of the country. See multicolored *palafitos* (houses on stilts) perched above the water and check out the archipelago's ingeniously assembled churches (page 381).

> > >

4 **Stargaze in the Atacama Desert:** Northern Chile has some of the globe's darkest skies. There's no better way to behold the heavens than on a star-gazing tour (page 143).

5 **Spot Chilean Wildlife:** Keep your eyes peeled for some of the most interesting animal species in the country, like penguins, whales, and pumas (page 26).

6 **Venture to the Ends of the Earth:** Take a boat cruise through the labyrinthine Chilean fjords and visit Cape Horn. It may not literally be the ends of the earth, but the remote and windswept area certainly feels that way (page 571).

7 **Go Wine-Tasting:** Visit Valle de Casablanca (page 130), Valle de San Antonio (page 133), and Valle de Colchagua (page 266) to explore Chile's top wineries and vineyards. If you're short on time, you can even do a quick day trip from Santiago to Valle de Maipo (page 88).

8 **Set Foot on Rapa Nui:** You may have heard of it as **Easter Island.** This Polynesian island far from the mainland is like nowhere else on the planet (page 573).

9 **Explore Charming Cities:** Eat at world-class restaurants in cosmopolitan **Santiago** (page 61) and ride the *ascensores* of bohemian **Valparaíso** (pictured, page 99).

10 **Get an Adrenaline Rush:** Sandboarding, surfing, and white-water rafting are just some of the nearly endless adventures possible in Chile (page 28).

Planning Your Trip

Where to Go

Santiago

In the country's most modern city, **fine-dining restaurants** rub shoulders with typical Chilean bistros and spirited **live music venues.** Historic buildings host **museums** and **cultural centers** remembering Chile's colorful history. The capital city's backdrop of the snowcapped Andes means **skiing, hiking,** and remote weekend escapes are never far away.

Valparaíso and Viña del Mar

On the coast west of Santiago is a cooler climate and crisper air, housing the seductive **beach resort** towns of hilly **bohemian** Valparaíso and **modern** Viña del Mar, where Chile's rich and famous kick back during the summer.

Picture-perfect **coastal towns** surround the two cities to the north and south, boasting glorious **sun-drenched beaches.** Nearby, the **Valle de Casablanca** is laced with long-standing **vineyards.**

Norte Grande and the Atacama Desert

Stretching from the border with Peru, the seemingly barren plains of the Norte Grande fold into the spine of the Andes. The region is home to the **mummies** of Arica, colossal waves beloved by **surfers,** and abandoned **mining towns.** The gateway to the Atacama Desert is **San Pedro de Atacama,** a place that promises lunar landscapes, otherworldly **salt flats,** and unparalleled **stargazing.**

San Pedro de Atacama

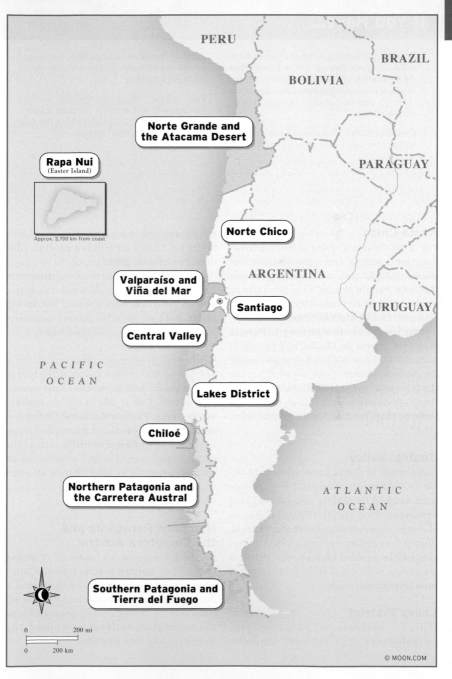

PERU

BRAZIL

BOLIVIA

PARAGUAY

Norte Grande and the Atacama Desert

Rapa Nui
(Easter Island)

Approx. 3,700 km from coast

Norte Chico

ARGENTINA

Valparaíso and Viña del Mar

Santiago

URUGUAY

Central Valley

PACIFIC OCEAN

Lakes District

Chiloé

Northern Patagonia and the Carretera Austral

ATLANTIC OCEAN

Southern Patagonia and Tierra del Fuego

0   200 mi

0   200 km

© MOON.COM

If You Have...

- **Five Days:** Visit high-altitude geyser fields and flamingo-flecked salt flats in **San Pedro de Atacama,** get lost in the graffiti-daubed streets of coastal **Valparaíso,** and dine in the country's most innovative restaurants in modern **Santiago.**

- **One Week:** With a full week, explore the highlights of the Lakes District by hiking volcanic **Parque Nacional Conguillío,** lounging in hot springs in **Pucón,** and exploring the quaint Germanic **Frutillar.**

- **Two Weeks:** Fly or take the ferry down to **Patagonia** to encounter penguin colonies and millennia-old glaciers, and hike in **Parque Nacional Torres del Paine.**

Norte Chico

The Norte Chico is a region of inviting coastlines, green valleys, and wilderness that sees few international visitors. The unsung **Parque Nacional Pan de Azúcar,** a reserve of remote beaches and wildlife, is one of the region's greatest draws. **Chañaral de Aceituno** is the country's top spot for **whale-watching.** In **Parque Nacional Llanos de Challe,** rare periods of rainfall lead to one of Chile's strangest sights: the *desierto florido* (flowering desert), when the otherwise barren land blooms with wildflowers in countless hues. Inland, the verdant **Valle de Elqui** produces Chile's national spirit, pisco.

Central Valley

Sliced in half by Chile's main highway, the fertile Central Valley is crisscrossed by grapevines and framed by **ski resorts** on the shoulders of **volcanoes.** But the Central Valley has more to offer than just **wineries** and **adventure sports.** Coastal Concepción, the largest city in the region and the capital of **Chilean rock music,** is the gateway to a range of fascinating **historical monuments** and towns.

Lakes District

With its backdrop of perfectly conical **volcanoes,** lush Valdivian temperate rainforest, and shimmering lakes, the Lakes District is Chile's **adventure capital.** Hike through **national parks** populated by unique flora and fauna, including the iconic *araucaría* (monkey puzzle tree). Summit the active **Volcán Villarrica,** relax in natural **hot spring pools,** and learn about the region's indigenous Mapuche people in this beautiful region.

Chiloé

The Chiloé Archipelago dances to the beat of its own drum, with a traditional and relaxed pace of life. This is one of Chile's **lushest ecosystems. Parque Nacional Chiloé** and **remote Parque Tantauco** are excellent places to encounter **endemic wildlife** such as the *pudú* (pygmy deer). The area is known for its architecture, which includes **historic wooden churches** and **colorful *palafitos*** (houses on stilts).

Northern Patagonia and the Carretera Austral

Northern Patagonia is a landscape of **dense forests** and **hidden glaciers.** Drive Chile's greatest road trip on the Carretera Austral, a mainly unpaved highway. It traverses the region, snaking through barely populated land and **world-class national parks** filled with quiet trails and **rare wildlife.**

Southern Patagonia and Tierra del Fuego

The emblematic granite spires of **Parque Nacional Torres del Paine** have made this South America's **hiking capital.** It's also a **wildlife haven,** home to **penguin colonies** and waters rich in **marinelife.** Tierra del Fuego is perhaps Chile's least-explored area, a landscape of steppe and **snowcapped mountains** that attracts hikers, adventurers, and fly-fishers.

Rapa Nui (Easter Island)

Over three thousand kilometers from the mainland, Rapa Nui is Chile's most enigmatic island, home to massive and awe-inspiring *moai* statues. Occupying most of the island is **Parque Nacional Rapa Nui,** Rapa Nui's biggest draw, where you can see the *moai* and other monuments of this early culture. Relax in the laid-back town of **Hanga Roa,** or join in the celebration of the Rapa Nui culture during the annual **Tapati Rapa Nui** festival.

When to Go

Seasons in Chile are reversed from the seasons in the northern hemisphere. **December-February** is **summer,** and **June-August** is **winter. September-November** is **spring,** and **March-May** is **fall.** Unlike most South American destinations, Chile doesn't have a specific rainy season, although most areas see more rainfall **April-September.**

    Orcas and **humpback, blue,** and **sei** whales appear off the Pacific coast and in the Chilean fjords late November-April. **Magellanic** and **Humboldt penguins** breed on small islets off the coast September-March.

High Season

Summer offers warm days and warmer nights across the country and sees crowds in Patagonia, Rapa Nui, San Pedro de Atacama, and the Lakes

early fall in Patagonia

District. **Easter Week (Semana Santa)** and the school holidays during the **last two weeks of July** are also high tourist season. Expect crowds and high prices at the ski resorts during this period.

Hotel prices, airfares, and bus fares soar during these periods. Booking in advance, in some cases up to two months ahead, is necessary. This is also the case for Chile's 17 or so **public holidays,** when most restaurants and shops are closed. Many of the country's main **festivals** and **celebrations** take place during summer.

Shoulder Seasons

Patagonia is best experienced in the shoulder seasons, **October-November** and **March-April,** when the weather is still warm and the fierce summer winds die down. While there is a growing trend toward accommodations and other tourist businesses opening earlier and staying open later in the season each year, some may not be open at the ends of these windows. In the rest of the country, these months are also a good time for tourist-free beaches. **Independence Day celebrations** are September 18-19 nationwide.

Before You Go

Passports and Visas

Visitors from the United States must have a **valid passport** to enter Chile. No visa is required, but your airline may ask you for **proof of onward travel** before you board. Upon arrival, travelers are normally given an entry stamp for 90 days. Australian nationals must pay a **reciprocity fee** at the airport. All visitors are given **paper entry receipts,** which must be presented at departure.

Advance Reservations

To travel in Patagonia during the December-February high season, book **accommodations** a few months in advance. For lodgings along the W and O routes in **Parque Nacional Torres del Paine,** prebooking is compulsory; expect to book your lodgings at least **three months** in advance.

Overland **bus transportation** can be booked on the day of departure, but if you're traveling in Patagonia, it's best to reserve a few days in advance. **Boat transport** can normally be arranged up to the week of travel.

Vaccinations and Insurance

No vaccinations are required for travel to Chile, but routine vaccinations should be up to date. The U.S. Centers for Disease Control and

Prevention (CDC) recommends vaccinations against hepatitis A and typhoid. Rabies shots are recommended for those traveling to remote destinations.

Medical care in Chile is of a high standard, but buying **health insurance** before traveling is recommended, as private medical treatment can be expensive.

Transportation

Car rental is easy to arrange in cities across the country. Rates are more favorable when you book in advance, particularly during the high season, when demand can often exceed supply in parts of Patagonia and around San Pedro de Atacama.

GETTING THERE

Most travelers arrive by air to Santiago's modern **Arturo Merino Benítez International Airport.** Other international airports include **Aeropuerto Internacional El Tepual** in Puerto Montt, and **Aeropuerto Internacional Presidente Carlos Ibáñez del Campo** in Punta Arenas.

The main overland routes into Chile are from **Mendoza** and **El Calafate,** Argentina. Crossing into Arica from Peru in the far north is also common.

If You're Looking For...

FINE DINING

- Try out innovative contemporary Chilean cuisine in **Santiago.**

WATER SPORTS

- Surf the waves in **Iquique** or **Pichilemu.**
- Go white-water rafting on **Río Futaleufú.**

HIKING

- Explore **Patagonia** at its most wild and stark along the dramatic W or O routes in **Parque Nacional Torres del Paine.**
- Trek up **Volcán Villarrica** in the Lakes District.

WILDLIFE

- Head to **Chañaral de Aceituno** for **whale-watching.**
- Visit **Parque Pingüino Rey** or **Reserva Nacional Pingüino de Humboldt** to see **penguin** colonies.
- Find **flamingos** in the **Atacama Desert.**

WINE-TASTING

- Sample Chile's signature carménère grape in the **Valle de Colchagua** or the **Valle de Casablanca.**

SKIING

- Day-trip into the mountains for soft white powder close to Santiago at **Valle Nevado.**
- Venture into the Central Valley to ski the slopes at **Nevados de Chillán.**

INDIGENOUS CULTURE

- Visit the **Museo Mapuche de Cañete** in the Central Valley.
- Stay overnight in a traditional **Mapuche** *ruka* on the shores of Lago Budi.

GETTING AROUND

Domestic flights are the most comfortable means of covering large distances in Chile and are becoming increasingly affordable. **Long-distance buses** are slower but comfortable. For budget travelers, they are often the most practical form of transport. **Renting a car** allows far more flexibility and provides access to national parks that are otherwise difficult to reach. Budget plenty of time for car travel, as driving distances are vast.

Public transportation is very reliable across the country. In Santiago, the metro and bus systems are affordable and easy to use. Taxis are reliable and generally safe.

It's possible to take a **boat** along the Patagonian coasts and fjords, with local passenger ferries and upmarket cruise ships offering a unique perspective of Chile. Adventurous travelers can also cover the full length of the country by **bicycle.**

What to Take

For hiking in Patagonia, **waterproof jacket, hiking boots,** and **pants** are a good idea, along with **trekking poles.** A **waterproof camera bag** or **dry bags** are useful to protect electronics from the rain. A 60-liter **backpack** for long-distance trails in Parque Nacional Torres del Paine provides enough space for camping equipment and food.

Motion sickness pills can be a welcome antidote to rough ferry journeys. Binoculars for whale-watching or bird-watching are useful. To protect against the sun, a **wide-brimmed hat** and high-SPF **sunblock** are essential. Pack plenty of **light layers** for cold nights.

The Best of Chile

Chile's sinewy length is matched by a wealth of places to visit. It's no mean feat to pack in the country's highlights in a two-week trip. Stand in awe of some of its most jaw-dropping landscapes and remotest national parks while soaking up history and culture. This itinerary is selective and fast-paced. It requires a number of domestic flights to cover the necessary long distances between attractions.

Santiago
DAY 1
Arrive in the morning into Santiago's **Aeropuerto Internacional Arturo Merino Benítez** and take a taxi to the city center. Drop your luggage at the stylish boutique hotel **The Aubrey,** in the heart of **Barrio Bellavista.**

In the vibrant **Barrio Lastarria,** take the paved path to the top of **Cerro Santa Lucía** for dazzling panoramas across the city to the mountains beyond.

Head to the **Plaza de Armas,** Santiago's main square. Visit the 18th-century **Catedral Metropolitana** before spending an hour or so in the superb **Museo Chileno de Arte Precolombino,** exploring the underground room dedicated to pre-Colombian Chilean textiles, ceramics, and religious artifacts.

For dinner, get acquainted with the country's diverse organic wines and creatively plated Chilean dishes at **Polvo Bar de Vinos.**

Valparaíso and Valle de Casablanca
DAY 2
Take the 1.5-hour bus ride west to the **wine region** of **Valle de Casablanca** and rent a taxi to take you around the nearby wineries. Drop in for a tasting and vineyard tour at **Viñamar** and **Emiliana,** then have lunch at **Tanino,** the on-site restaurant at **Casas del Bosque.**

Hop back on the public bus; it's an hour-long journey to **Valparaíso,** where you can stay the night in **Winebox,** a hotel owned by the former winemaker of Casas del Bosque.

DAY 3
Start early for the 1.5-hour bus ride to **Casa Museo Isla Negra,** the sea-inspired home of poet Pablo Neruda, south of the city. Dine on baked parmesan razor clams at the museum's restaurant, **El Rincón del Poeta,** before returning to Valparaíso.

Spend the afternoon visiting viewpoints in the graffiti-daubed hills of **Cerro Alegre.** Pop into the **Museo Municipal de Bellas Artes** for a history lesson about the city. Be sure to ride on a couple of the creaky *ascensores,* historic funiculars that transport passengers up the city's steep hills.

Southern Patagonia
DAY 4
Catch the bus to the Santiago airport and take an early-morning flight to **Aeropuerto Internacional Presidente Carlos Ibáñez del Campo** (3.5 hours), the main airport in **Patagonia.** From the airport, a bus (3.25 hours) runs north to **Puerto Natales,** where you can wander among historic weatherworn buildings and watch birds from the banks of the mountain-fringed sound on which the town is situated. Note that it's possible to **fly directly** to Puerto Natales from Santiago during high season. This will allow enough time for a half-day **horseback tour** at a nearby ranch.

Rent a car for the following day's drive. Have dinner at the innovative **Lenga** (make a reservation ahead of time) before getting a good night's sleep in elegant **VinnHaus.**

DAY 5
Leave early for the 2.5-hour drive to the southern entrance of **Parque Nacional Torres del Paine.** Take a three-hour **boat tour** with **Turismo Lago Grey** to the snout of the dazzling **Glaciar Grey.**

Have dinner at **Hotel Lago Grey,** where you'll get views of bobbing icebergs on the lake. This is also a good spot to spend the night.

DAY 6

From your hotel, take the road through the national park to the Centro de Bienvenida. From here, take the trail to **Mirador Las Torres** (15km round-trip, 4 hours), a viewpoint of the park's eponymous towers. It's a steep climb up a rocky valley to reach the lake and granite peaks. Return the way you came.

Drive back to **Puerto Natales.** Treat yourself with a night in the gorgeous fjord-side hotel **Simple Patagonia.** Dine next door in **The Singular Patagonia,** with its lavish wine menu and gourmet Patagonian-inspired cuisine.

DAY 7

It's time to visit Argentinean Patagonia. Board a bus (5hr) for **El Calafate, Argentina.** Continue on to **Parque Nacional Los Glaciares,** 1.5 hours by bus from El Calafate. In this park of extreme contrasts, you can get within a few hundred meters of **Glaciar Perito Moreno,** one of only three glaciers in the world that's growing.

When you get back to El Calafate, dine on steak and sip malbec at classy **La Zaina** before spending the night at the quirky **Patagonia Rebelde** or the friendly midrange **Kau Yatún.**

DAY 8

Return to Puerto Natales by bus (5-8 hours). Transfer to a Punta Arenas-bound bus (3.25 hours). Once you arrive in **Punta Arenas,** try the king crab at the beautifully situated **La Yegua Loca,** which is also an inn. Spend the night here or at the affordable **Hotel Lacolet.**

DAY 9

From Punta Arenas, it's possible to take a day tour of two different penguin colonies. The closer of the two is the **Monumento Natural Los Pingüinos** on **Isla Magdalena.** After a ferry or speedboat ride, you'll disembark on an island occupied by thousands of chattering Magellanic penguins.

Glaciar Grey in Parque Nacional Torres del Paine

Best Hikes and Treks

Parque Nacional Cerro Castillo

SANTIAGO

The trail to the peak of **Cerro Manquehue** (2km one-way, 3hr) is a great introductory hike within the city. You'll be rewarded with striking Santiago views. For a shorter and gentler route, hike up the lower **Cerro Manquehuito.**

CENTRAL VALLEY

Passing glorious viewpoints of the seven teal pools for which Parque Nacional Radal Siete Tazas is named, the trail to **Cascada Siete Tazas** and **Salta de Leona** (1.5km one-way, 30 min) is an easy and rewarding hike.

LAKES DISTRICT

The trek up **Volcán Villarrica** (7km one-way, 6hr) climbs an active volcano. At the top are striking views of half a dozen other volcanoes and even lava in the crater.

In Parque Nacional Conguillío, **Sendero Sierra Nevada** (10km one-way, 3hr) has striking views of volcanoes and the region's iconic *araucaria* (monkey puzzle) trees.

CHILOÉ

Embark on the challenging **Sendero Transversal** (52km, 4-5 days), a trek through the pristine evergreen forests of Parque Tantauco to encounter 800-year-old cypress trees and timid *pudú.*

NORTHERN PATAGONIA

Visit Parque Nacional Cerro Castillo to do the **Cerro Castillo Traverse** (51km, 4-5 days), a trek through mountain scenery past gleaming lakes and craggy mountains.

SOUTHERN PATAGONIA

In **Parque Nacional Torres del Paine,** the **W route** is an 80-km, four- to five-day hike that passes through spellbinding Patagonian scenery.

Near Puerto Williams, a challenging 53-km, five-day trek circumnavigates the **Dientes de Navarino.** This is quite possibly the world's southernmost trek, traversing staggering landscapes at the very ends of the earth.

The other option is to take a tour from Punta Arenas to the **Parque Pingüino Rey,** in **Tierra del Fuego.** This private reserve protects a small colony of king penguins—the only colony in the Americas.

DAY 10

Visit the **Museo Regional de Magallanes** to learn about a prominent Punta Arenas wool merchant family. Wander the promenade that parallels the Strait of Magellan for potential **dolphin** sightings.

Take an afternoon flight to **Puerto Montt** (2.25hr), then transfer from the airport to lakeside **Puerto Varas,** just 20 minutes away. Dine at **La Olla** for a feast of traditional Chilean seafood and stay overnight at hostel **Compass del Sur** to best appreciate the town's homespun charm.

Lakes District

DAY 11

Rent a car in Puerto Varas and drive an hour to **Lago Todos Los Santos** in **Parque Nacional Vicente Pérez Rosales.** Check out the superb on-site **museum,** then take a short wander along the lake's **black-sand beach.** On your way out of the park, stop to take in views of the majestic **Saltos del Petrohué** waterfalls.

On the road back to Puerto Varas, stop at the boutique hotel **AWA** and treat yourself with gourmet dining and a luxurious stay on the shores of Lago Llanquihue.

DAY 12

Rise early and return to Puerto Varas, where you can either drive or rent a bike and pedal north around the lake to quaint **Frutillar.** Catch a show at the glorious **Teatro del Lago** followed by afternoon tea overlooking the lavender fields at **Lavanda Casa de Té.**

Back in Puerto Varas, enjoy Patagonian craft beer and pizza with exquisite lake views at **La Mesa Tropera.** Check into a lodging in town and get a good night's rest.

DAY 13

Catch a bus north to **Pucón** (5hr) and spend the afternoon sunbathing on the black volcanic sand of **Playa Grande** or relaxing in the hot spring water of the Japanese-inspired **Termas Geométricas.** You may feel like you're in Europe thanks to the authentic Italian dishes at **Andiamo.** Bed down for an early night in one of the cozy hobbit holes at **Chili Kiwi.**

DAY 14

Wake before dawn for the challenging full-day ascent of **Volcán Villarrica.** Alternatively, catch a bus to **Parque Nacional Huerquehue** for a gentler hike along one of the park's trails.

Return to Pucón and toast your Chilean adventures with Mapuche-inspired dishes at **La Fleur de Sel** and a night at **Maison Nomade B&B,** with its startling volcano views. In the morning, you'll fly to Santiago, then back home.

With More Time

From Santiago, it's a 6-hour flight to **Rapa Nui (Easter Island).** Budget at least three full days on the island to best experience its awe-inspiring stone *moai.* On your first day, visit the **Museo Antropológico P. Sebastián Englert** and catch sunset at **Ahu Tahai.** The next morning, watch sunrise at **Ahu Tongariki,** then take a trip to the **Orongo ceremonial village** and the **Rano Kau volcanic crater.** On your last day, explore **Rano Raraku,** the quarry where the *moai* were carved, or climb **Maunga Terevaka** for panoramic views across the island.

Wildlife Encounters

Chile is rich in wildlife. Bird-watchers will find over 430 species, while the coasts teem with penguin colonies. The forests of the Lakes District and Patagonia are abundant in land mammals, including pumas, guanacos, and the exceptionally rare *pudú* (pygmy deer).

PENGUINS

- Find the Americas' only colony of king penguins at Tierra del Fuego's **Parque Pingüino Rey.**

- Surround yourself with a chattering 120,000-strong colony of Magellanic penguins at the **Monumento Natural Los Pingüinos** near Punta Arenas.

- Encounter 80 percent of the global population of Humboldt penguins at **Reserva Nacional Pingüino de Humboldt** near La Serena.

WHALES

- Encounter the extraordinary species that is the blue whale in the waters surrounding **Chañaral de Aceituno.**

- Boat out to the protected **Parque Marino Francisco Coloane** for a glimpse of elegant humpback whales.

PUMAS

- Watch for this elusive big cat in **Parque Nacional Patagonia** and **Parque Nacional Torres del Paine.**

DEER

- Encounter the *pudú,* a timid miniature deer species, on the slippery trails of **Parque Tantauco** or scampering through the dense forests of **Parque Nacional Pumalín Douglas Tompkins.**

- Sector Valle Chacabuco and Sector Tamango of **Parque Nacional Patagonia** provide two of the final habitats of the 1,500 elusive and seriously endangered *huemul.*

GUANACOS AND VICUÑAS

- Grazing **guanacos** are a common sight on the grassy plains of Sector Valle Chacabuco in **Parque Nacional Patagonia** and on the

a rare huemul deer

windswept steppe of **Parque Nacional Pali Aike,** near Punta Arenas.

- The stark landscapes of the high-elevation **Parque Nacional Lauca** provide a welcome sanctuary for the delicate cinnamon-hued **vicuña,** which is prized for its fine coat that is turned into luxurious, expensive wool.

BIRDS

- The leggy **rhea,** a member of the emu family, can be spotted racing through the grasslands of **Parque Nacional Patagonia** in Sector Valle Chacabuco and **Parque Nacional Torres del Paine.**

- Vast groups of James's, Andean, and Chilean **flamingos** can be spotted in the saline **Laguna Chaxa** near San Pedro de Atacama and flocking in the salty waters of the **Salar de Surire** in Reserva Nacional Las Vicuñas.

- With its prized eggs playing a revered role in the ceremonies of the historical birdman cult, the tropical **sooty tern** breeds just off the coast of **Rapa Nui.**

- The three-meter wingspan of the sacred **Andean condor** can be spotted in the skies above the **Cajón del Maipo** and **Parque Nacional Torres del Paine.**

Explore the Atacama Desert

The north of Chile promises dreamlike land-scapes of volcanoes and geysers, plus some of the country's oldest history. Distances are long and the aridity of the desert extreme, so it's far more pleasant to take buses or tours than to drive your-self, although a vehicle allows you to stop at some hidden gems en route.

Day 1

Take the two-hour flight from Santiago to **Aeropuerto Internacional El Loa** near Calama. From here, take a shuttle (1.5 hours) to **San Pedro de Atacama,** the region's most pop-ular tourist town. Jump directly on an **Atacama Desert tour,** where you'll see the flamingos of **Laguna Chaxa,** take a salty dip in **Laguna Cejar,** and watch the glorious sunset at **Laguna Tebinquinche.**

Freshen up for dinner back at the cozy adobe bedrooms of **Ckuri Atacama** or blow your budget on the elegant, all-inclusive **Tierra Atacama.** Sample the local llama burg-ers and beers brewed from endemic plants at **Cervecería St. Peter.**

Day 2

Start early with a tour out to the volcanic pave-ment of the **Piedras Rojas** and the **Salar de Talar salt flats.** Stop at the gleaming blue **Lagunas Altiplánicas** and have a picnic lunch.

Spend the afternoon **sandboarding** down the dunes of the otherworldly **Valle de la Muerte.** Return to San Pedro for an early din-ner at unpretentious **Las Delicias de Carmen** for its famous *pastel del choclo* (beef and corn pie). If it's not the full moon, join an evening **stargazing tour.**

Day 3

Rise at 4am for an early-morning tour to the **Géiseres del Tatio,** a two-hour drive from town. This is the third-largest geyser field in the world, with 80 active spouts.

From San Pedro, take the airport shuttle (1.5 hours) back to Calama, then hop on an overnight bus to **Iquique.**

Day 4

Spend the morning in Iquique taking a **surfing lesson** at the beach or a **sandboarding class** on the sand dunes above the city.

In the afternoon, catch the public bus out to **Oficina Humberstone.** Spend the afternoon wandering the ruins of this nitrate mine that has been partially reclaimed by the desert.

Back in Iquique, dine at the **Casino Español** and stay overnight the comfortable **Hotel Terrado Suites.**

Day 5

Take the three-hour bus ride north to **Arica,** just below the border with Peru. Start with a trip to **Museo de Sitio Colón 10** to see 7,000-year-old Chinchorro mummies, discovered in this exact spot in 2004. Grab a local *micro* (30 min) to **Museo Arqueológico San Miguel de Azapa** to learn more about the Chinchorro people.

Fall asleep to the sound of the waves at the lovely **Hotel Apacheta.** Take a flight back to Santiago (2.75 hours) the next morning.

With More Time

With three additional days, you can head into the altiplano and visit two stunning parks. From Arica, head east to **Putre,** a three-hour bus ride. Check into the **Terrace Lodge.** You're at high el-evation, so take a day to acclimate. Take a **guided tour** of the **Reserva Nacional Las Vicuñas,** which houses **Monumento Natural Salar de Surire,** a vast salt flat. The next day, drive your-self out to **Parque Nacional Lauca** to admire the wildfowl at **Lago Chungará.**

High-Adrenaline Adventures

Chile is the ideal destination for adventure activities. If you're in search of an adrenaline rush, this overview can help you decide what to do.

SURFING

- In **Pichilemu,** the self-proclaimed capital of surf, **Playa La Puntilla** boasts Chile's longest wave. Just south is **Punta de Lobos,** which has swells up to six meters.

- **Maitencillo** is a lesser-known surfing hot spot. Here, **Playa Aguas Blancas** and **Playa Larga** have consistent surf and good-quality waves.

- **Iquique** has some of the best waves in the country. **Playa Cavancha** is home to **El Colegio,** considered one of Chile's best right-hand waves. **La Bestia** is one of the world's top 20 breaks, attracting professional surfers.

SKIING

- **Valle Nevado,** just a few hours' drive from Santiago, is the most accessible ski resort. It's also the largest resort in the country and has plenty of advanced runs.

- **Centro de Esquí Volcán Osorno,** near Puerto Varas, has a long ski season and marvelous vistas from its mostly intermediate and advanced ski runs.

- In Malalcahuello, the little-known **Centro de Esquí Corralco** boasts striking landscapes.

- The **Nevados de Chillán** includes backcountry stretches formed long ago by lava flows.

CLIMBING VOLCANOES

- **Volcán Villarrica** is the best-known volcano that you can climb. It often has lava bubbling at the crater.

- In **Parque Nacional Pumalín,** you can hike to the jagged crater of **Volcán Chaitén.**

- Summit the **Ojos del Salado,** the world's highest active volcano, on a challenging 14-day expedition.

WHITE-WATER RAFTING AND KAYAKING

- **Río Futaleufú** has some of the most exciting Class III-V white-water rapids in the world.

- Kayak through Chiloé's spectacular **Valle de Chepú.** Look for birds and otters as you paddle.

- Paddle close to the calving, powder-blue snout of **Glaciar Grey** in **Parque Nacional Torres del Paine.**

DIVING

- Clear warm water teems with fish at **Bahía Inglesa** in the Norte Chico.

- The protected marine park around **Hanga Roa** on Rapa Nui boasts great visibility and 142 endemic marine species.

ICE TREKKING

- Clamber across glacial crevasses on the 18-kilometer-long **Glaciar Exploradores.**

- Appreciate **Parque Nacional Torres del Paine** from a different angle by taking an ice-trekking tour on **Glaciar Grey.**

- Hike over the top of the breathtaking **Glaciar Perito Moreno** in Argentina's **Parque Nacional Los Glaciares.**

SANDBOARDING

- Glide down the slopes of the sand dunes in **Valle de la Muerte,** one of the otherworldly landscapes of the **Atacama Desert.**

- **Iquique** is home to the golden sands of **Cerro Dragon,** which offers spectacular city and ocean views, particularly at sunset.

Carretera Austral Road Trip

For the drive of a lifetime, hop on the Carretera Austral, the highway through Northern Patagonia. Along the way, you'll see remote national parks dotted with glorious lakes and glaciers clinging to cliffs. There are also opportunities to spy rare endemic wildlife. Paved in some parts, the Carretera Austral is a real adventure, requiring a high-clearance vehicle and plenty of patience.

Day 1

Pick up a rental car from **Aeródromo Balmaceda** near **Coyhaique** and drive one hour to **Villa Cerro Castillo.** Organize a **horseback tour** or hike the steep but rewarding **Sendero Mirador Laguna Cerro Castillo** (14km round-trip, 6-8hr) in Parque Nacional Cerro Castillo for spectacular views.

Stay overnight at the comfortable domes at **La Araucaria** back in Villa Cerro Castillo. Bring food with you for cooking or buy basics from the local shops.

Day 2

Drive south to **Puerto Río Tranquilo** (3hr). In **Parque Nacional Laguna San Rafael,** you can take a 30-minute hike to reach a lookout for the 18-kilometer-long **Glaciar Exploradores.**

Return to Puerto Río Tranquilo and book a tour to the **Capillas de Mármol** (Marble Caves) for the next morning. Bed down at the smart **El Puesto** inn and get a rustic dinner at the unpretentious **Mate y Truco.**

Day 3

For the best light and least wind, take a morning **boat** or **kayak tour** out to the Capillas de Mármol. Or take a day tour by car and boat out to the **Ventisquero San Rafael** (San Rafael Hanging Glacier). Return to your lodgings in Puerto Río Tranquilo for the night.

Day 4

Start early and drive south to **Parque Nacional Patagonia** (3hr). Hike one of the park's many trails like **Lagunas Altas** (23km loop, 6-8hr). Dine at **El Rincón Gaucho** and stay overnight in the luxurious **Lodge at Valle Chacabuco;** if you have camping equipment, camp overnight in **Los West Winds Campground.**

Day 5

Continue south to **Caleta Tortel** (4.5hr), one of the most magical settlements along the Carretera Austral. Take an excursion to the mysterious Isla de los Muertos via **boat tour.** Spend the night at the cozy **Entrehielos Lodge,** with log fires and home-cooked dining.

Get an early start tomorrow for the 10-hour drive back to Aeródromo Balmaceda, where you'll return your rental car and board a flight back to Santiago.

Caleta Tortel

Getaway to the Lakes District and Chiloé

Stunning hiking, intriguing architecture, and more than a few volcanoes make the leafy Lakes District and the surrounding area an interesting alternative to the arid north or icy south of the country. Plenty of hot springs and cute cafés make this route ideal for those also seeking less high-adrenaline activities.

Day 1

Catch the overnight bus from Santiago (10hr) to arrive in **Pucón** early in the morning. Go on a **canyoneering** or **kayaking tour** for the day, then come back for an early night because you'll be up early the next morning. Stay in a charming hobbit hole at lakeside **Chili Kiwi.**

Day 2

Spend the day on a tour of the area's best hot springs, like the riverside **Termas Los Pozones** or the Japanese-inspired **Termas Geométricas.** Return to Pucón and sample innovative cuisine at **La Fleur de Sel** (make reservations in advance), then head back to your lodging.

Day 3

Take the bus to **Valdivia** (3hr). Take a tour of **Museo Submarino O'Brien,** a submarine docked just off the fish market, where you can also meet the local sea lion colony.

Hop on a bus to reach the **Kunstmann brewery** for their 90-minute tour, followed by tastings in the bar. Head back to Valdivia for the night and stay in the cozy but exquisitely decorated **Tejas del Sur.**

Day 4

Take the bus to **Puerto Varas** (2.75hr), then catch a local minibus to **Frutillar,** on Lago Llanquihue.

Pucón

Best Beaches

BEST FOR SURFING
Punta de Lobos near Pichilemu has six-meter swells and is considered the best left point break in the country.

BEST FOR SUNBATHING
The white sand of **Playa Las Machas** just across the bay from the town of **Bahía Inglesa** is perfect for swimming and basking in the sun.

BEST FOR UNTOUCHED SANDS
Playa Blanca inside **Parque Nacional Llanos de Challe** has white sand and is one of the country's most pristine beaches.

MOST PHOTO-WORTHY
North of Valparaíso, picture-perfect **Playa Cachagua** has glorious white sand, azure water, and even a Humboldt penguin colony on a nearby islet.

BIGGEST PARTY
Right in the heart of **Viña del Mar, Playa El Sol**

Anakena on Rapa Nui

brims with bronzing bodies during the day that spill into the nearby clubs and bars at night.

MOST TROPICAL
White sands and palm trees make **Anakena** on Rapa Nui the country's most tropical paradise.

Hang out on the **beach** or check out the **Museo Colonial Alemán** to learn about the region's German heritage.

Take afternoon tea in the picturesque **Lavanda Casa de Té,** just above town, and catch a musical performance at the striking **Teatro del Lago.** Return to Puerto Varas for the night and lodge at **Compass del Sur,** a friendly hostel-cum-guesthouse.

Day 5
Take a public bus to **Puerto Montt** and connect with a bus to **Castro** in **Chiloé,** a 3.5-hour journey in total. Spend the afternoon photographing the *palafitos* (houses on stilts) in the Gamboa neighborhood and peek into the **Iglesia San Francisco de Castro** to admire the local Chilote architecture.

Pop into the **Feria Artesanal** down by the waterfront for a little shopping. Stay overnight in the familial **Palafito Hostel,** with its views across the waterfront.

Day 6
Take a local bus to the village of **Cucao** (1.5hr), on the western coast of Chiloé's Isla Grande. Drop your belongings at **Palafito Cucao Hostel,** your lodging for the evening, and head into **Parque Nacional Chiloé** for a day's hiking, ending at **Playa de Cucao** for sunset.

Day 7
Organize a **horseback tour** or **hiking** trip to **Playa Cole Cole** for some of the region's most untouched scenery. Return to Castro by public bus and spend the night here, ready to catch an early bus to Puerto Montt and the two-hour flight back to Santiago.

Santiago

In their pursuit of adventures elsewhere in the country, few visitors stick around long enough to discover South America's best-kept secret: Santiago. It still takes prompting to get locals to admit how cool the Chilean capital city, flanked by the majestic snow-drizzled Andes Mountains, really is.

Over the decades, Santiago has quietly become a force in contemporary Latin American dining, with a growing number of restaurants on "world's best" lists. Modern Chilean gastronomy is more than just upscale grub—more traditional local eateries are scattered across a host of trendy, dynamic neighborhoods where live music reverberates in buzzing bars in the evening.

This chaotic metropolis straddles its South American and European

Highlights

Look for ★ to find recommended sights, activities, dining, and lodging.

★ **Museo Chileno de Arte Precolombino:** This museum contains one of South America's finest collections of indigenous ceramics and textiles (page 40).

★ **View from Cerro Santa Lucía:** On a clear day, the views from this hill in the heart of Barrio Lastarria are dazzling (page 44).

★ **La Chascona:** Learn about the tumultuous life and death of Nobel Prize-winning poet Pablo Neruda in his eccentric Santiago home (page 45).

★ **Museo de la Memoria y los Derechos Humanos:** This museum poignantly documents the human rights abuses that occurred during the Pinochet dictatorship (page 49).

★ **Ski at Valle Nevado:** Hit the world-class slopes of this ski resort, just an hour's drive from the city (page 82).

★ **Cajón del Maipo:** In this verdant canyon just beyond the city limits, visit small towns, take a dip in thermal springs, and hike trails through glacial landscapes (page 83).

★ **Wine-Tasting at Viña Santa Carolina:** Tour the historic wine cellar at this vineyard and pick up a bottle of award-winning cabernet sauvignon (page 88).

Santiago

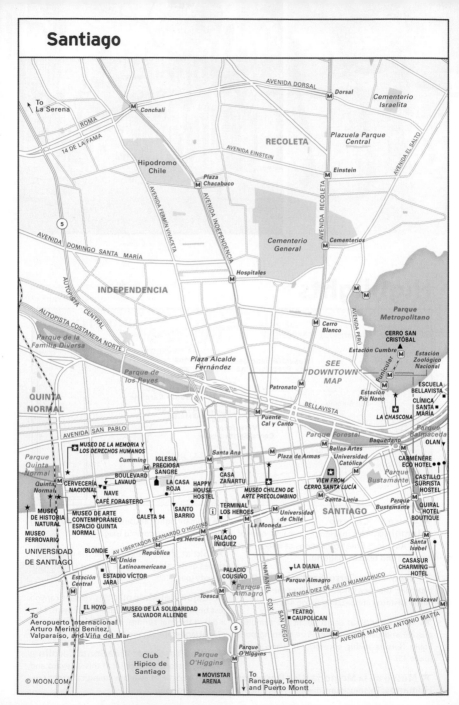

To La Serena

ROMA
14 DE LA FAMA

Conchali

AVENIDA DORSAL

Dorsal

Cementerio Israelita

RECOLETA

Plazuela Parque Central

AVENIDA EINSTEIN

Einstein

Hipodromo Chile

AVENIDA FERMÍN VIVACETA

Plaza Chacabuco

AVENIDA INDEPENDENCIA

AVENIDA DOMINGO SANTA MARÍA

Cementerio General

AVENIDA RECOLETA

Cementerios

AVENIDA EL SALTO

INDEPENDENCIA

AUTOPISTA CENTRAL

AUTOPISTA COSTANERA NORTE

Parque de la Familia Diversa

Parque de los Reyes

Hospitales

Plaza Alcalde Fernández

Cerro Blanco

AVENIDA PERÚ

Parque Metropolitano

CERRO SAN CRISTÓBAL

Estación Cumbre

Estación Zoológico Nacional

SEE DOWNTOWN MAP

QUINTA NORMAL

AVENIDA SAN PABLO

Patronato

Estación Pío Nono

ESCUELA BELLAVISTA

CLÍNICA SANTA MARÍA

Parque Quinta Normal

MUSEO DE LA MEMORIA Y LOS DERECHOS HUMANOS

Cumming

BELLAVISTA

Puente Cal y Canto

Parque Forestal

Baquedano

LA CHASCONA

Parque Balmaceda

OLAN

IGLESIA PRECIOSA SANGRE

Santa Ana

Plaza de Armas

Bellas Artes Universidad Católica

CARMÉNERE ECO HOTEL

Quinta Normal

CERVECERÍA NACIONAL

BOULEVARD LAVAUD

LA CASA ROJA

HAPPY HOUSE HOSTEL

CASA ZAÑARTU

Parque Bustamante

CASTILLO SURFISTA HOSTEL

NAVE

CAFÉ FORASTERO

CALETA 94

SANTO BARRIO

MUSEO CHILENO DE ARTE PRECOLOMBINO

VIEW FROM CERRO SANTA LUCÍA

Santa Lucía

Parque Bustamante

QUIRAL HOTEL BOUTIQUE

MUSEO DE HISTORIA NATURAL

MUSEO FERROVIARIO

MUSEO DE ARTE CONTEMPORÁNEO ESPACIO QUINTA NORMAL

TERMINAL LOS HÉROES

Universidad de Chile

SANTIAGO

UNIVERSIDAD DE SANTIAGO

AV LIBERTADOR BERNARDO O'HIGGINS

Los Héroes

La Moneda

Santa Isabel

BLONDIE

República

Unión Latinoamericana

PALACIO ÍÑIGUEZ

CASASUR CHARMING HOTEL

Estación Central

ESTADIO VÍCTOR JARA

PALACIO COUSIÑO

NATANIEL COX

LA DIANA

Parque Almagro

EL HOYO

Toesca

Parque Almagro

AVENIDA DIEZ DE JULIO HUAMACHUCO

Irarrázaval

To Aeropuerto Internacional Arturo Merino Benítez, Valparaíso, and Viña del Mar

MUSEO DE LA SOLIDARIDAD SALVADOR ALLENDE

SAN DIEGO

TEATRO CAUPOLICAN

Matta

AVENIDA MANUEL ANTONIO MATTA

Club Hípico de Santiago

Parque O'Higgins

Parque O'Higgins

MOVISTAR ARENA

To Rancagua, Temuco, and Puerto Montt

© MOON.COM

AUTOPISTA VESPUCIO NORTE EXPRESS

To Club Amanda

MUSEO RALLÍ

MUSEO DE LA MODA

AVENIDA AMÉRICO VESPUCIO NORTE

AVENIDA VITACURA

PARQUE BICENTEN

AVENIDA PRESIDENTE KENNEDY

To Los Dominicos, Cajón del Mapocho, and Ski Areas

Parque Urbano Mahuidahue

Parque Metropolitano de Santiago

VINOLIA

FABA

PARQUE ARAUCANO

Club de Golf Los Leones

Manquehue

To Pueblito Los Dominicos

Jardín Mapulemu

AVENIDA PRESIDENTE RIESCO

AVENIDA APOQUINDO

LES DIX VINS

MARGO

ECONORENT

PIZZERÍA TIRAMISÚ

Escuela Militar

LAS CONDES

DOUBLETREE BY HILTON

EUROPCAR CAFÉTIN

El Golf

Alcántara

LOS CONQUISTADORES

FLANNERY'S IRISH GEO PUB

HAPPENING

BANCO INTERNACIONAL

Tobalaba

AUTOPISTA COSTANERA NORTE

BLUESTONE

BACO

AMBROSIA BISTRO

FEDEX

99 RESTAURANTE

EL HUERTO

ELADIO

Los Leones

AVENIDA TOBALABA

AVENIDA CRISTÓBAL COLÓN

AVENIDA AMÉRICO VESPUCIO

VILAFRANCA PETIT HOTEL

Pedro de Valdivia

Plaza Loreto Cousiño

Cristóbal Colón

HERTZ

LIGURIA

Manuel Montt

AVENIDA LOS LEONES

Plaza Río de Janeiro

Francisco Bilbao

Prince of Wales Country Club

Río Mapocho

ELIODORO YÁÑEZ

PROVIDENCIA

Salvador

TANDEM SANTIAGO

BAO BAR

AVENIDA POCURO

AVENIDA FRANCISCO BILBAO

ELIECER PARADA

Príncipe de Gales

AVENIDA OSSA

Inés de Suárez

Parque Inés de Suárez

AVENIDA MANUEL MONTT

AVENIDA ANTONIO VARAS

AVENIDA PEDRO DE VALDIVIA

THE JAZZ CORNER

CAFÉ DE LA CANDELARIA

ESTACIÓN ITALIA

SILVESTRE BISTRÓ

ÓBOLO

Simón Bolívar

LA FABBRICA

EL CACHAFAZ

XOCO POR TI

MOSSTOW BREWFOOD

ÑUÑOA

To Aeródromo Tobalaba

Plaza Egaña

Monseñor Eyzaguirre

AVENIDA IRARRÁZAVAL

Ñuñoa

Chile España

LA BATUTA

Villa Frei

Nuñoa

TEATRO UC

To Parque por la Paz (Villa Grimaldi)

AVENIDA GRECIA

Estadio Nacional

0   0.5 mi

0   0.5 km

WINE TASTING AT VIÑA SANTA CAROLINA

To Estadio Nacional Julio Martínez Prádanos

To Barrio Ecológico

Los Orientales

Two Days in Santiago

DAY 1

Head straight to the **Plaza de Armas** for a view of old Santiago. Wander over to the **Museo Chileno de Arte Precolombino** for a dose of indigenous Chilean ceramics and other artifacts.

For lunch, shuffle in behind the office workers for a table at tiny **Salvador Cocina y Café** to sample traditional Chilean cooking with a modern flair. Hop on the metro to spend the afternoon in sober reflection at the **Museo de la Memoria y los Derechos Humanos.** Return to **Barrio Lastarria** for dinner and a lesson in Chilean wine at **Bocanáriz.**

DAY 2

If the weather is clear, clamber up **Cerro Santa Lucía** for views across the city. Hop on the metro to Cal y Canto station; **La Vega Central** is a few blocks away. Here you'll have a sensory experience browsing the vibrant stalls of the city's biggest market. Head south to the **Mercado Central** to chow down on a fish lunch in one of the small restaurants in the corridors beyond the gaping central atrium.

Take the metro east for an afternoon of browsing the stalls of **Pueblito los Dominicos** and purchase a few traditional Chilean souvenirs. Be sure to book a table for dinner at **Restaurant 040** to end with an innovative Spanish-Chilean fusion meal. Finish the night with late-night cocktails at the speakeasy **Room 09** on the top floor of the restaurant.

heritage. Note the lavish European mansions and centuries-old churches of Downtown, the smoke-spluttering diesel buses that race through its streets, against the sparkling high-rises of "Sanhattan," the ironic sobriquet given to the city's eastern financial districts. This juxtaposition is seen in the city's museums, which cover prehistory and the country's not-so-long-ago dictatorship, seen in visceral detail in the excellent Museo de la Memoria y los Derechos Humanos.

Spend an afternoon taking the funicular up to Parque Metropolitano on the expansive green hill above the Bellavista neighborhood, root for treasures in the eclectic antiques shops in tree-lined Italia, or explore the endless stands of the chaotic but irresistible La Vega Central, the city's largest food market.

During the winter you'll quickly discover the one downside to Santiago: an unpleasant layer of smog. Luckily, when it all gets too much, vineyards in the Valle de Maipo and world-class skiing are just an hour away.

PLANNING YOUR TIME

To cover the main sights, you'll want **two days** in Santiago. You can wander the **Plaza de Armas,** drop into the Museo Histórico Nacional to see the view from the clock tower, then nip into Correos Central and the Catedral Metropolitana. From here, it's a short walk to the **Museo Chileno de Arte Precolombino.** Spend the afternoon in the **Museo de la Memoria y de los Derechos Humanos,** then take some time to watch the ducks in Parque Quinta Normal before dining in Barrio Bellavista or Barrio Lastarria.

With **four days,** you can head out to Barrio Italia to browse the **craft and antiques shops.** Catch the funicular to the top of **Parque Metropolitano** and be rewarded with sensational panoramas. The views from **Cerro Santa Lucía** are a good alternative closer to the city center. Add a **day trip** to one of the **vineyards** in the southern suburbs, accessible by metro or taxi, or head out to the **Cajón del Maipo,** an hour's drive

---

Previous: the Plaza de Armas; ceramics from Pomaire; a Santiago neighborhood.

east, for a hike and a few hours' relaxation in **hot springs.** In winter, hit **ski resorts** like Valle Nevado or El Colorado; one day is enough for the Andean slopes.

ORIENTATION

Santiago is on the banks of the Río Mapocho. The main historic neighborhoods, from east to west, are **Downtown** (Centro Cívico), **Barrio Bellas Artes, Barrio Lastarria, Barrio Brasil,** and **Barrio Yungay.** On the eastern side of the city is **Providencia. Barrio Italia** is on the south side of the river, and **Barrio Bellavista** on the north. Farther east, **Las Condes** is an affluent residential area; within it is **Barrio El Golf.** North of Las Condes, **Vitacura** is the most fashionable and expensive part of the city, home to manicured gardens, fine dining, and designer boutiques.

HISTORY

Spanish conquistador Pedro de Valdivia founded Santiago de la Nueva Extremadura on February 12, 1541. The original city was flanked by two channels of the Río Mapocho; the southern channel has since been drained and is now Avenida Alameda. The city was designed around a checkerboard of streets emanating from the Plaza de Armas, with significant administrative and religious buildings in this central point.

The city faced constant attack from the indigenous Mapuche people. Earthquakes were also a significant threat, and the city was rebuilt on multiple occasions. It survived the Independence Wars of 1810-1818 unscathed and was named the capital of the new republic in 1818. The following century saw extensive growth, particularly at the hands of provincial governor Benjamin Vicuña Mackenna. From 1872 onward, he conducted a series of urban infrastructure projects to remodel Cerro Santa Lucía, canalize the Río Mapocho, and establish Parque O'Higgins.

The early 20th century saw rapid increase in the city's population, with numbers doubling between 1907 and 1920 to 510,000 inhabitants as the city became the country's financial center. Further infrastructure projects, including the construction of the metro, were begun during the 1960s. The period of Pinochet's dictatorship saw accelerated economic growth that resulted in a real estate boom. In the early 1990s, construction began on the shopping malls and skyscrapers that now dominate the city's increasingly highrise skyline.

Sights

Walking tours are a great way to get to know the city. **Tours 4 Tips** (tel. 2/2570 9939, http://tours4tips.com) is a reliable option run by young, knowledgeable guides. Tour groups meet outside the Museo de Bellas Artes at 10am and 3pm daily. You don't need to book a spot in advance. The tour is free, but a tip is expected. **Santiago Street Art Tours** (tel. 9/4021 5628, www.stgostreetart.com, from CH$14,000) is a great option to learn more about the city's street art; you can try your hand at making your own. Advance reservations are necessary.

DOWNTOWN
Plaza de Armas

The cavernous **Plaza de Armas** (Monjitas and 21 de Mayo) is the administrative and social core of the city. The square features pretty gardens and groves of jacarandas and cockspur coral trees, plus 36 soaring Chilean palms. During the day its paved walkways bustle with street performers, shoe shiners, and stray dogs, while tour groups weave their way among shady benches. You might come across a calm protest, more often than not accompanied by bands of police officers.

Best Restaurants and Accommodations

RESTAURANTS

★ **Ambrosia:** Chef Carolina Bazán brings sophistication to the Santiago dining scene with her take on modern Chilean cuisine in this unpretentious restaurant (page 61).

★ **Boragó:** Explore the length and breadth of the Chilean territory in this tour de force that serves the country's most distinctive ingredients (page 61).

★ **99 Restaurante:** Expect sophisticated yet casual dining at this innovative eatery serving exceptional nine-course tasting menus (page 62).

★ **Restaurant 040:** Experience experimental Spanish-influenced food at this top-dollar restaurant (page 62).

★ **Salvador Cocina y Café:** This humble Downtown eatery offers more than meets the eye with unusual Chilean dishes (page 62).

★ **Bocanáriz:** Sample the country's finest vintages without leaving the city at this swanky wine bar (page 62).

★ **Liguria:** Sit down for lunch with the locals at this authentic but marvelously trendy three-floor Chilean bistro (page 63).

★ **Peumayen:** Chilean food sourced from indigenous communities defines the menu at this innovative restaurant (page 64).

★ **Polvo Bar de Vinos:** This slick restaurant wouldn't look out of place in New York, with creatively plated Chilean dishes and the city's most extensive organic wine list (page 64).

★ **Boulevard Lavaud:** This quirky gem in an eccentric setting specializes in French fare (page 66).

On the northeast corner of the square is a **bronze statue** of Santiago and Chile's founder, Pedro de Valdivia, clasping a scroll as he sits astride his horse. The statue was a gift to the city from Spain on the 150th anniversary of Chilean independence in 1963.

Catedral Metropolitana

The oldest surviving building on the Plaza de Armas is the neoclassical 1748 **Catedral Metropolitana** (Catedral and Bandera, tel. 2/2787 5600, 11am-7pm Mon., 10am-7pm Tues.-Sat., 9am-7pm Sun.). On the northwest corner of the plaza, an elaborate stone facade, designed by Italian architect Joaquín Toesca and dating to the 1700s, marks the exterior of this impressive seat of the Chilean Catholic Church. The cathedral also reflects the Tuscan and Roman styles of architect Ignacio Cremonesi, who restored the structure and added two extra towers around the turn of the 20th century. Step inside to see religious frescoes painted on the ceiling of the nave and the splendid main altar, made of white marble and inset with lapis lazuli and bronze.

Museo Histórico Nacional

The **Museo Histórico Natural** (Plaza de Armas 951, tel. 2/2411 701, www.mhn.gob.cl, 10am-6pm Tues.-Sun., free) is in the Palacio de la Real Audiencia. The museum does a reasonable job of charting the history of Chile,

★ **Ambrosia Bistro:** Try modern Chilean cuisine infused with French influence at this smaller informal version of the award-winning Ambrosia (page 66).

★ **Pizzería Tiramisú:** Find honest Italian food at this chaotic restaurant in the heart of Las Condes (page 68).

★ **La Diana:** Expect charm alongside delicious seafood and cocktails in this former monastery attached to an amusement arcade (page 68).

★ **La Fabbrica:** Dine on authentic Italian pizza or pasta with a side of jazz in the home of the legendary Club de Jazz (page 68).

ACCOMMODATIONS

★ **Happy House Hostel:** Find acres of space in this restored mansion in Barrio Brasil with a pleasant sunny garden and a swimming pool (page 69).

★ **Castillo Surfista Hostel:** Good vibes, a friendly dog, and exceptionally affordable lodgings make this a great budget choice (page 70).

★ **Hostal Río Amazonas:** Stay in a mock-Tudor mansion just a stone's throw from Plaza Italia (page 70).

★ **Carménère Eco Hotel:** Study Chilean wine without ever leaving your hotel at this boutique lodging with a wine cellar (page 70).

★ **Casa Sur Charming Hotel:** Make yourself at home in this charmingly personal hotel at the heart of trendy Barrio Italia (page 70).

★ **Cabañas Nogalia:** Sleep beneath the trees at these comfortable cabins tucked deep in the Cajón del Maipo (page 86).

although discussion of indigenous people is limited, and discussion of the Pinochet dictatorship is nonexistent.

Several rooms present artifacts from the conquistadores and their battles with the Mapuche people, with accompanying information showing how the indigenous group upheld strategic resistance through the early 19th century by leveraging their superior knowledge of the country's geography. Displays also depict early Chile's fiercely tiered social classes, juxtaposing the daily lives of the upper-class Spanish descendants against the mestizos (children of mixed Spanish and indigenous heritage) and enslaved Africans, who were brought to toil in the gold and silver rushes. The final rooms upstairs re-create the economic climate that preceded the 1973 coup in which president Salvador Allende was overthrown by the military. The broken frames of the glasses that Allende was wearing at the time are a sobering display.

Don't miss the views of the Plaza de Armas from the top of the 1868 **Reloj de la Torre,** the clock tower that crowns the building. For a guided tour (20min) of the tower, queue at the designated spot on the internal balcony on the 2nd floor. The tours leave every 10 minutes 10am-5pm.

★ Museo Chileno de Arte Precolombino

In the portico-fronted Ex Casa de la Real Aduana (Former Royal Customs House), the **Museo Chileno de Arte Precolombino** (Bandera 361, tel. 2/2928 1500, www. precolombino.cl, 10am-6pm Tues.-Sun., CH$6,000 adults, CH$3,000 children) is easily the country's most respected museum covering indigenous civilizations, with a particular focus on pottery from across Latin America.

In a subterranean room, the museum's oldest objects are seven-sided lithic stones that date to around 11,000 BC and are thought to have had a ceremonial function. The most striking objects are towering wooden funerary statues used by the Mapuche. A couple of the Chinchorro mummies from the far northern city of Arica represent the oldest mummified remains in the world. The Chinchorro are fascinating in that their funerary rituals were so democratic: All of their dead were mummified, regardless of social status.

Upstairs, the collection turns to wider Latin America. The largest subset of artifacts is Mesoamerican and Andean ceramics, including wonderful swollen-cheeked *coquenos* (individuals chewing coca leaves) made by the Capulí people, displayed alongside a spectacular array of gold and copper masks crafted by the Moche and Chimú peoples of Peru. There's also a large stone stela from Aguateca, a former Maya temple in modern-day Guatemala. A smaller collection of textiles, mostly from arid regions of the Peruvian and Chilean coast, complete the displays.

Inside the entrance in the courtyard, a coffee shop offers a welcome chance to rest. The museum's gift shop is an excellent place for English-language books about indigenous Chilean cultures.

Basílica and Museo La Merced

The **Basílica La Merced** (Mac Iver 341, 10am-1pm and 3pm-7:30pm Mon.-Fri.) is an incongruous sight on the edge of a busy thoroughfare. This grand claret-colored building is the third iteration of this church. Two previous structures suffered earthquake damage in 1647 and 1730. The present building was inaugurated in 1760.

Next door, the **Museo La Merced** (Mac Iver 341, tel. 2/2664 9189, http:// museolamerced.cl, 10am-6pm Tues.-Sat., 10am-2pm Sun., CH$500) is the church's religious museum, in the former cloister. Inside, a tranquil sun-splashed courtyard lures you into a false sense of isolation; except for the occasional rumble of traffic, you could be outside the city. The museum hosts a large collection of Rapa Nui spiritual carvings, including one of only 29 *rongorongo* wooden tablets that remain in the world, whose meaning has yet to be deciphered. Upstairs, an eclectic selection of religious artwork completes the museum's small collection.

Mercado Central

The **Mercado Central** (San Pablo 967, no phone, www.mercadocentral.cl, 6am-5pm Sat.-Thurs., 6am-8pm Fri.) is a cavernous building hosting Santiago's liveliest fish market. Just three blocks north of the Plaza de Armas, the neoclassical cast-iron building dates to 1872. It was designed and built in the United Kingdom before being shipped to Chile, which explains its resemblance to a Victorian train station.

The market's corridors are packed with stalls with piles of sea urchins, *centolla* (king crab), and *congrio* (eels) on ice. At the center of the building a gaping atrium is filled with restaurants serving Chilean classics of *pastel de jaiba* (cheesy crab stew), seafood empanadas, and Pablo Neruda's favorite, *caldillo de congrio* (conger eel soup). Don't be enticed by the larger restaurants; the smaller ones along the edges of the central hall are more affordable and generally better quality, with dishes costing as little as CH$4,000.

For a tamer experience, head to **Mercado de Abastos Tirso del Molina** (Av. Santa

---

1: Palacio de la Moneda 2: chess players in the Plaza de Armas 3: stall in the Mercado Central 4: Catedral Metropolitana

Downtown

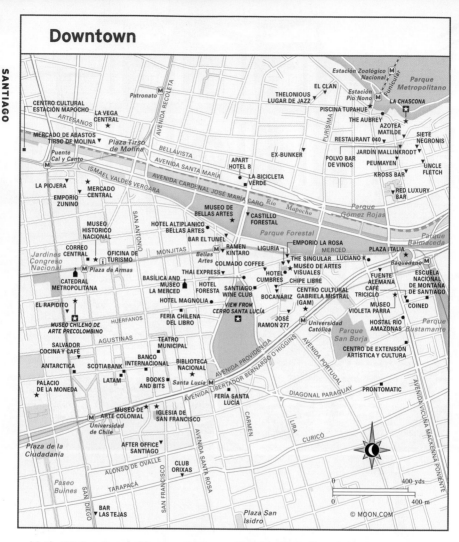

María 409, 6am-9pm daily), across the street from Mercado Central. On two floors, this market has vegetable stalls and juice stands on the bottom and a selection of restaurants upstairs, serving a range of international cuisine.

Palacio de la Moneda

A striking figure with its white neoclassical design, the **Palacio de la Moneda** (Plaza de la Constitución, 10am-6pm Mon.-Fri., free) was originally the city's mint, built in 1784 by Italian architect Joaquín Toesca to convey a sense of strength and stability, explaining its resemblance to a fortress. In 1846, President Manuel Bulnes became the first and only president to reside here. He also turned the palace into the seat of the presidency, a role that continues today.

La Moneda is one of the city's most symbolic buildings due to its role in the 1973 military coup. Military aircraft bombed the building on the orders of the four leaders of

Transforming a Street into Art

Few parts of Santiago are quite as picture-perfect as the dazzling **Calle Bandera** (from Compañía to San Diego). In December 2017, Chilean visual artist Dasic Fernández and architect Juan Carlos López turned the street into a four-block art installation, including paintings directly on the asphalt. It took 30 days and 120 artists to complete the piece, a chronology of Chile from pre-Colombian times to the future.

When the project was first designed, it was thought that Bandera would be reopened to vehicles and the installation dismantled. By the end of 2018, however, the installation was allowed to remain indefinitely. In 2019, the installation was extended a block south to Calle San Diego, passing beneath the busy Avenida Alameda via a tunnel that accommodates small fairs and events (9am-9pm daily) throughout the year. The work now covers 7,000 square meters, making it the largest mural in Latin America.

the armed forces, including General Augusto Pinochet. The same day, military forces stormed La Moneda and claimed to have discovered Allende dead by suicide. An autopsy has since supported the military's claim, but supporters of Allende have long alleged Allende was executed by military forces.

It's normally possible to walk into the building's front courtyards, but to tour some of the private rooms, you must complete a **reservation form** on the website of the Dirección Administrativa del Palacio de la Moneda (http://visitasguiadas.presidencia.cl) and book one of the four daily tours (free) at least a week in advance. English-language tours can be requested through the reservation form.

Outside the main entrance on Plaza de la Constitución, the **changing of the presidential guard** takes place every other day (odd-numbered days Apr.-May, Aug., and Nov.-Jan., even-numbered days Feb.-Mar., June-July, and Sept.-Oct.) at 10am Monday-Friday and 11am Saturday-Sunday, lasting 40 minutes.

Biblioteca Nacional

The **Biblioteca Nacional** (Av. Alameda 651, tel. 2/2360 5272, www.bibliotecanacional.cl, 9am-7pm Mon.-Fri., 9am-2pm Sat.) was built to commemorate the first centenary of Chilean independence in 1913, although its roots date to the early 19th century, when

the country's first national library was created by the government. It existed at various sites before finding its way here. Built in neoclassic style by Chilean architect Gustavo García del Postigo, the structure heavily features concrete in its design. It hosts the national archives and a reading room, as well as rotating literature, photography, and history exhibitions.

Iglesia de San Francisco

The **Iglesia de San Francisco** (Londres 4, 9am-1pm and 4pm-8pm daily) is the oldest surviving building in Chile, dating to 1618. A simple temple had been here as early as 1583, built by the Franciscans to house a 29-centimeter-tall wooden statue of the Virgen del Socorro, an idol lugged into the country by Pedro de Valdivia that was believed to have helped protect his men from harm.

The tiny Virgen del Socorro is still kept here, in the middle of the *retablo* above the main altar. She is most noticeable thanks to the gold leaf that covers her gown. The building itself is striking for its five-meter-high cypress doors and extravagantly carved cypress choir stalls.

For centuries, the Franciscans owned much of the land surrounding the church, although a financial crisis at the turn of the 20th century forced them to sell most of it. The **Museo de Arte Colonial** (Londres 4, tel. 2/2639

8737, http://museosanfrancisco.com, 9:30pm-1:30pm and 3pm-6pm Mon.-Fri., 10am-2pm Sat.-Sun., CH$1,000 adults, CH$500 children) is on the 1st floor of the convent, attached to the church. It houses some of the immense collection of art accumulated by the Franciscan order, including 42 paintings from the 17th-century Cusco School, which depict the life of Saint Francis of Assisi.

Palacio Cousiño

Several blocks south of Avenida Alameda, close to the Autopista Central, is **Palacio Cousiño** (Dieciocho 438, tel. 2/2386 7448, 9:30am-1:30pm and 2:30pm-5pm Tues.-Fri., 9:30am-1:30pm Sat.-Sun., CH$3,000 adults, CH$1,000 children), a decadent 27-bedroom mansion and the only 19th-century residence on Calle Dieciocho that hasn't been transformed into an apartment block or a school.

Designed in 1878 by Paul Lathoud, the interior of the neoclassical mansion is a striking array of Italian, French, and Moorish styles. Gilt curtains, textured velvet wallpaper, and a central staircase made of 20 types of marble hint at the enormous wealth of its former residents. Luis Cousiño made his fortunes in coal and silver mines; he ordered the construction of the palace in honor of his wife, Isidora Goyenechea. Cousiño died before the 13-year project was complete; Goyenechea then became the first businesswoman in the country and one of the top-10 richest women in the world.

The palace was the first home in the country to have electricity and a primitive type of central heating, still operating today, in which copper tubes carry hot water through the ground floor of the building. The grand 24-seat walnut dining table gives a sense of the lavish parties once thrown here.

The palace was donated to the municipal government of Santiago in 1940 and was used to host state visitors, including Charles de Gaulle and even Mahatma Gandhi. Preparations for a 1968 visit of Queen Elizabeth II caused a fire on the upstairs floor, leaving few of the original decorations and furnishings intact. Before it was turned into a museum in 1977, the final state visitors included the military presidents of Brazil and Uruguay, invited by then-president Pinochet.

Guided tours in English and Spanish every hour or so take you around the property, including the restored upstairs bedrooms, which now contain period furniture salvaged from other mansions that have since been demolished. Advance reservations aren't possible; you have to sit in the waiting room at the front of the building until a guide is available.

BARRIOS BELLAS ARTES AND LASTARRIA
★ View from Cerro Santa Lucía

Cerro Santa Lucía (bounded by Santa Lucía, Victoria Subercaseaux, and Avenida Alameda, 9am-7pm daily) is the city's loveliest green space, a perfectly rounded hill that marks the western edge of Barrio Lastarria. From its northern access point, where Santa Lucía and Victoria Subercaseaux meet, it's a 10-minute walk up paved pathways to the first of two overlooks. A statue of Pedro de Valdivia presides over the first viewpoint, where pretty Moorish tiled water fountains are surrounded by benches. On a clear day, absorb the city's finest views east across the high-rises of the financial district to the Andes. Steps carved in the rock at the center of the hill lead to the higher viewpoint—a yellow turret popular for selfies. It's a crammed space, but it boasts the clearest panoramas of Santiago.

Access the hill either from Avenida Alameda in the south, where grand stone steps climb around the Plaza Neptuno fountains, or from the north at the intersection of Santa Lucía and Victoria Subercaseaux. Visitors are sometimes required to sign in at this entrance using their passport number. There's a glass elevator (free) at the intersection of Santa Lucía and Huérfanos that's occasionally functioning.

Museo de Bellas Artes

The oldest art museum in South America, the **Museo de Bellas Artes** (Barra 650, tel. 2/2499 1600, http://mnba.gob.cl, 10am-6:45pm Tues.-Sun., free) is housed within the sumptuous Palacio de Bellas Artes, a dizzying neoclassical building designed by Chilean-French architect Émilio Jécquier and inspired by the Petit Palais in Paris. The building was inaugurated in 1910 with a 126-ton, Belgian-built dome containing 2,400 glass panes that crowns the central hall.

The museum has permanent exhibitions dedicated to surrealist Roberto Matta, among other Chilean artists. In the Central Hall, the Museo de Copias contains 40 reproductions in bronze or marble of 19th-century Renaissance statues that were commissioned by the government in 1901.

In the western wing of the palace, the Parque Forestal branch of the **Museo de Arte Contemporáneo** (Vergara 506, tel. 2/2977 1752, www.mac.uchile.cl, 11am-7pm Tues.-Sat., 11am-6pm Sun., free) belongs to the arts faculty of the Universidad de Chile and showcases modern and contemporary art, with a heavy focus on audiovisual exhibitions. Its most famous work is outside, a distinctive sculpture representing the Trojan horse by Colombian artist Fernando Botero.

Museo de Artes Visuales

Just off the pedestrianized stretch of Calle Lastarria, the **Museo de Artes Visuales** (MAVI, Lastarria 307, tel. 2/2664 9337, www.mavi.cl, 10:30am-6:30pm Tues.-Sun., CH$1,000 adults, CH$500 children) was designed in modern minimalist style by Chilean architect Cristián Undurraga. Four floors are packed with contemporary photography, sculpture, and audiovisual installations by the country's finest talents. The museum holds regular exhibitions featuring artists from across the continent. The 5th floor is home to the **Museo Arqueológico de Santiago,** which has a small display of Mapuche baskets, ceramics, and metalwork. Entrance is included with MAVI admission.

Centro Cultural Gabriela Mistral

One of the city's most important cultural centers, the **Centro Cultural Gabriela Mistral** (Av. Alameda 227, tel. 2/2566 5500, www.gam.cl, hours and cost vary), also known as **GAM,** has had a turbulent history. In 1972, President Salvador Allende rallied supporters from across the country to donate their labor to construct what would be the meeting place for a United Nations conference. Less than a year later, the building was complete, with sculptures and other artwork from 30 Chilean artists. A year after that, the building became the military headquarters of the Pinochet dictatorship, and many of the works of art were vandalized or removed. After a fire razed the building in 2006, it was restored, with new murals and other artwork.

Downstairs in the central atrium, the 1972 mural *Chile* by Italian-Chilean artist José Venturelli avoided destruction during the military dictatorship. Also on this floor, note the bronze door handles of the conference rooms, forged by Chilean sculptor Ricardo Mesa, that show the imprint of a raised fist—a symbol that represents Chilean workers.

The center is open to the public, with a small café, occasional exhibitions, and cultural performances. You can find a list of events on the website.

BARRIO BELLAVISTA
★ La Chascona

Although it's less architecturally imaginative than his two other properties in Valparaíso and Isla Negra, Pablo Neruda's Santiago home, **La Chascona** (Márquez de la Plata 192, tel. 2/2777 8741, http://fundacionneruda.org, 10am-7pm Tues.-Sun. Jan.-Feb., 10am-6pm Tues.-Sun. Mar.-Dec., CH$7,000 adults, CH$2,500 children) evokes the eccentric style of the Nobel laureate. It also provides a good introduction to the tumultuous political and personal life of Chile's best-loved poet.

Tucked down a quiet, winding street, the land was bought by Pablo Neruda's third wife, Matilde Urrutia, and construction began in

1952 on the house that would become La Chascona, a name that refers to Urrutia's wild curly red hair. Neruda took residence in 1955, living here and in his other two houses until his death in 1973.

Urrutia lived in the house until her death in 1985. Inside, you can see the desk where she wrote her memoir, *My Life with Pablo Neruda*. You can also see Neruda's Nobel Prize, awarded in 1971. The dining room was designed to feel like the inside of a ship. Don't miss the painting by Mexican muralist Diego Rivera in the living room, which depicts Urrutia with two heads—and Neruda's face hidden in her hair, a reflection of their once clandestine romance.

Cerro San Cristóbal and Parque Metropolitano

On a forested hill above Santiago is **Parque Metropolitano** (Pío Nono 450, tel. 2/2730 1331, www.parquemet.cl, 8:30am-9pm daily Nov.-Mar., 8:30am-7pm daily Apr.-Oct.). Not only does it promise the best views across the city, it is the largest urban park in the world. **Cerro San Cristóbal** marks the southern tip of the park, the place for photos of Santiago. Note that in winter, a dense layer of smog detracts from the view, so for clear skies, plan your visit following a day of rain. At the very peak of San Cristóbal is an iconic 12-meter **Virgin Mary statue,** weighing 47,000 kilos. It was built in Paris and inaugurated in 1908.

A popular way to reach the top of the hill leaves from the northern terminus of Calle Pío Nono at Plaza Caupolicán. The 1925 **Funicular San Cristóbal** (no phone, http://funicularsantiago.cl, 1pm-8pm Mon., 10am-7:45pm Tues.-Sun. summer, 1pm-6:45pm Mon., 10am-6:45pm Tues.-Sun. winter, one-way CH$1,500-2,000 adults, CH$1,000-1,500 children) rattles up a 240-meter, practically vertical route to the top of Cerro San Cristóbal. There are hiking routes that zigzag to the top, but they are unsafe, due to a spate of armed robberies.

Get another perspective on the park on the *teleférico* (10am-7pm Tues.-Sun. winter, 10am-8pm Tues.-Sun. summer, one-way to Tupahue CH$1,910 adults, CH$1,240 children, one-way to Cumbre CH$1,310 adults, CH$850 children), a gondola that stretches partway across the park. From city level at Estación Oasis, close to the park's eastern entrance (Calle Pedro de Valdivia Norte and Av. El Cerro), the *teleférico* shuttles passengers to Estación Tupahue. From here, you can walk (15min) or hop onto the gondola southwest to Estación Cumbre, the station just below the summit of Cerro San Cristóbal.

In summer, the park is a favorite among city residents, who come in droves for the refreshing waters of the two outdoor **public swimming pools** (10am-6pm daily mid-Nov.-mid-Mar.), **Piscina Tupahue** (near Estación Tupahue, CH$6,000 adults, CH$3,500 children) and **Piscina Antilén** (in the northwest of the park, CH$7,500 adults, CH$4,000 children). If you choose a weekday outside January-February, you're guaranteed to be sharing the waters with significantly fewer people.

Safety in the park remains a pressing issue. Exploring the park on foot is only safe on weekends, when you are among many other pedestrians, runners, and cyclists. Stick to Avenida Abate Mollina, one of the principal roads; it originates near the park's eastern entrance (Pedro de Valdivia Norte and Av. El Cerro).

To get to the *teleférico* at Estación Oasis, or to hike into the park along Avenida Abate Mollina, take an eastbound 409 or 502 bus (every 5 min, CH$700) from the intersection of Pío Nono and Bellavista. It drops you a five-minute walk from the entrance.

Cementerio General

Home to all but two of Chile's deceased presidents, the sprawling **Cementerio General** (Av. Profesor Alberto Zañartu 951, tel. 2/2637 7803, www.cementeriogeneral.cl, 7:30am-7pm

1: view from Cerro Santa Lucía 2: Palacio Cousiño 3: memorial sculpture by Francisco Gazitua at the Cementerio General

daily) occupies an 86-hectare plot north of La Vega Central. Many tombs are in disrepair following the 2010 earthquake, but it's a fascinating place to see the gravesites of Santiaguinos (Santiago residents) throughout history. For those interested in the country's checkered past, it's an important focal point for remembrance of those lost during the dictatorship.

Plot 102, near the eastern entrance on Avenida Recoleta, is the site of a vast slab of marble carved with the names of all the people who were disappeared or executed by the military regime 1973-1989. The size of the monument gives a sense of the gravity of the loss. Another significant grave is the fortress-like white-stone tomb of former president Salvador Allende. Just outside the southern entrance (Profesor Zañartu and La Paz), **Plaza de la Paz** is worth a stop to admire the colonnades that housed the stables of the 7th Regiment of the Line who passed through here during the 19th-century War of the Pacific.

Nighttime tours (90min, CH$3,000) of the cemetery usually run Thursday-Saturday and can be booked through the website. The closest metro stop is Cementerios, on Línea 2.

La Vega Central

Heaving masses of Santiaguinos laden with shopping bags converge on the roads surrounding the mammoth **La Vega Central** (López de Bello 743, tel. 2/2737 6161, http://vegacentral.cl, 4am-7:30pm Mon.-Sat., 9am-2:30pm Sun.), Santiago's largest market, covering 9.5 hectares in one block. More than a thousand stalls are in this metal-roofed warehouse, with narrow walkways between the rows of vendors and sacks of produce, where cats sleep among piles of onions and the delicious scent of empanadas is in the air. Over 60,000 visitors come here each day.

La Vega offers an authentic South American market experience. You'll find all sorts of produce, cheeses, and a small number of restaurants. Plan an hour or two to get lost between piles of produce and hawkers—and keep an eye on your valuables, as pickpocketing can be an issue. If you'd prefer to visit in the hands of an experienced market-goer, **La Bicicleta Verde** (Loreto 2, tel. 2/2570 9939, http://labicicletaverde.com) organizes morning bike tours of the market (US$41).

BARRIOS BRASIL AND YUNGAY
Plaza Brasil

The center of Barrio Brasil is pretty **Plaza Brasil** (bounded by Compañía, Av. Brasil, Huérfanos, and Maturana), a square dominated by a children's play area and landscaped lawns filled with lounging families on weekends. A mix of aging elegant three-story buildings and modern concrete high-rises line the plaza, many with welcoming matchbox-size cafés on the ground floor. On the northwest corner of the plaza, the maroon **Iglesia Preciosa Sangre** (Compañía 2226, open for mass) is an eye-catching sight with elaborate cornices above grand columns and two bell towers.

Parque Quinta Normal

An urban park covering 35 hectares, tranquil **Parque Quinta Normal** (main entrance Av. Matucana, 7:30am-8:30pm daily summer, 7:30am-7:30pm daily winter) is dotted with mature *araucarías,* towering California redwoods, and Chinese weeping cypress trees surrounded by lawns and winding flower-lined paths. At the center, a lagoon with ducks and paddleboats makes an excellent place to escape the frenetic energy of the city.

Within the grounds of the park lies the **Museo Ferroviario** (tel. 2/2681 6022, www.corpdicyt.cl, 10am-5:50pm Tues.-Fri., 11am-5:50pm Sat.-Sun., CH$1,000 adults, CH$700 children), a rail museum with 16 historic steam locomotives, including a 1909 English engine that worked the Transandino line that connected Los Andes, Chile, with Las Cuevas, Argentina. On weekends, there are free tours that allow visitors to enter the railway carriages.

Museo de Arte Contemporáneo Espacio Quinta Normal

The **Museo de Arte Contemporáneo Espacio Quinta Normal** (Av. Matucana 464, tel. 2/2977 1765, www.mac.uchile.cl, 11am-6:30pm Tues.-Sat., 11am-5:30pm Sun. Mar.-Jan., free) is in a striking neoclassical building named the Palace of Versailles for its outward similarities to the original in France. This branch is in Parque Quinta Normal (the other is in Parque Forestal in Barrio Bellas Artes) and is run by the Universidad de Chile's fine arts department. Its 12 rooms feature modern and contemporary art, with a focus on audiovisual displays. A handful of permanent pieces include Santiago-born plastic artist Eugenio Téllez's to-scale *Tanque (Tank)*. The museum is within the grounds of the park but accessed from Avenida Matucana, 200 meters south of the park's main entrance.

Museo de Historia Natural

In Parque Quinta Normal, the **Museo de Historia Natural** (Parque Quinta Normal, tel. 2/2680 4600, http://mnhn.cl, 10am-5:30pm Tues.-Sat., 11am-5:30pm Sun., free) is in an elegant 1875 neoclassical building designed by Paul Lathoud—the architect of the equally sumptuous Palacio Cousiño—that has survived more than a century of earthquakes; it is one of the oldest museums in Latin America.

Excellent re-creations of six of Chile's ecological regions provide an introduction to the country's biodiversity. The museum contains a replica of the Plomo Mummy, the well-preserved remains of an Inca child discovered in 1954 at the top of 5,400-meter Cerro El Plomo, a mountain in the Andes east of Santiago.

In the central atrium, a 15.9-meter, 57-vertabra sei whale named Greta is the star attraction. Equally enthralling are the two glass-walled workstations, where you can watch researchers undertaking taxidermy and other activities.

★ Museo de la Memoria y los Derechos Humanos

The harrowing yet unmissable **Museo de la Memoria y los Derechos Humanos** (Matucana 501, tel. 2/2597 9600, ww3.museodelamemoria.cl, 10am-8pm daily Jan.-Feb., 10am-6pm Tues.-Sun. Mar.-Dec., free) presents a sensitive analysis of the human cost of the Pinochet dictatorship, when more than 40,000 people were imprisoned,

Museo de la Memoria y los Derechos Humanos

The Horrors of a Secret Police Force

The Dirección de Inteligencia Nacional (DINA) was the espionage agency and secret police formed and overseen by General Manuel Contreras following the military coup that overthrew the government of Salvador Allende. Those accused of harboring political opponents of the dictatorship were "disappeared" and taken to torture centers around the country. DINA agents attempted to extract confessions about supposed crimes. Horrific methods of torture were employed, including electrocution, sexual assault, sleep deprivation, and psychological abuse. Contreras was put on trial for some of his crimes in 2004. He faced a combined sentence of 500 years for crimes against humanity. He died in prison in 2015 at age 86.

For a visceral experience of the harrowing methods employed by DINA, head to the cobbled streets of Barrio Paris-Londres, home to graceful European-style town houses built in the 1920s. Despite its picturesque facade, the neighborhood is home to **Londres 38** (Londres 38, http://londres38.cl, 10am-1pm and 3pm-6pm Tues.-Fri., 10am-2pm Sat., donation), a town house used by the military junta as a torture center for dissidents. The house remains in the same state it was during its use by DINA. The paint on the walls is flaking off and burn marks on the wooden floors hint at some of the atrocities that happened here. Information in Spanish about the people who were detained here is displayed in several rooms. The cobbles outside are inlaid with plaques bearing the names of dozens of victims of the dictatorship.

An equally horrific torture and detainment center was **Villa Grimaldi** (José Arrieta 8401, tel. 2/2292 5229, http://villagrimaldi.cl, 10am-6pm daily, donation), a country mansion that was the most important of DINA's torture centers; 4,500 political prisoners passed through. Former Chilean president Michele Bachelet is among those who were held here. Prisoners were confined in metal closets barely large enough to sit in and subjected to psychological and physical torture; a couple of reconstructed cells show their scale. A tiled cube structure near the entrance houses the site's most disturbing artifacts: iron rails used to weigh down the bodies of victims thrown into the sea to be "disappeared." The site has been transformed into the **Parque por la Paz Villa Grimaldi** (Villa Grimaldi Park for Peace), a national monument and symbol of the fight against human rights abuses. To get here, take Línea 3 of the metro to Plaza Egaña, then take a taxi or one of the buses (227, 513, or D09) heading east.

tortured, or killed. You could easily spend an afternoon taking in the horrors of the 17 years of military rule, especially with the **audio guide** (in English, French, German, and Spanish, CH$2,000), an invaluable resource for better understanding the human rights violations committed by Pinochet and his followers.

A sobering display in the main entrance hall of the three-floor building maps 200 memorial sites, many of which are mass graves dug during military rule. On the 1st floor, an audio exhibit plays President Salvador Allende's final words to the country, broadcast over Radio Magallanes, as planes began bombing the Palacio de la Moneda, the presidential seat.

The museum examines the role of the media in spreading propaganda during the dictatorship. Video testimonies reveal macabre details of the over 1,000 detention and torture centers set up around the country. People who were detained and tortured recount how they were subject to electrocution, burning, asphyxiation, sexual assault, and mock executions to force them to reveal information about dissenters. Through videos and photography, the final room on the 2nd floor narrates the last years of the dictatorship, when a decade of protests finally caused a referendum on Pinochet's leadership.

The 3rd floor hosts temporary exhibitions that shed light on human rights violations across Chile and the world. Recent displays include one on the indigenous Mapuche people in Chile's south.

Museo de la Solidaridad Salvador Allende

Created in 1971 as a call to artists across the world by President Salvador Allende, the **Museo de la Solidaridad Salvador Allende** (Av. República 475, tel. 2/2689 8761, http://mssa.cl, 10am-6pm daily Apr.-Nov., 11am-7pm daily Dec.-Feb. 3, CH$1,000, free on Sun.) houses a collection of contemporary art, most donated by left-leaning artists.

The works of 34 artists went missing during the dictatorship, although 43 pieces were returned to the museum in 2017. Among the most notable works are those by Roberto Matta, Robert Motherwell, Joan Miró, and Tetsuay Noda. Look for the intriguing display about the disappearance of Armando Gonzaléz's *La Niña y La Paloma,* a sculpture last seen in the footage of a documentary that was recorded in the office of Admiral José Toribio Merino during the military rule.

PROVIDENCIA

Plaza Italia

Considered by many Santiaguinos the center of the city, Plaza Italia is a chaotic junction where multilane traffic converges around the statue of General Manuel Baquedano, the commander in chief of the army during the 19th-century War of the Pacific. This monument marks where Avenida Alameda becomes Avenida Providencia. Across the road is the landmark Torre Telefónica, headquarters of Spanish telecommunications company Movistar. It was built in 1993 to resemble a cell phone—which today looks very dated.

This square is the regular focal point of protests; it's best avoided when these demonstrations get going. *Guanacos* (water cannons) are regularly used by the police to quell protesters.

Museo Violeta Parra

Two blocks south of Plaza Italia, the small museum and cultural space **Museo Violeta Parra** (Av. Vicuña Mackenna 37, tel. 2/2355 4600, http://museovioletaparra.cl, 9:30am-6pm Tues.-Fri., 11am-6pm Sat.-Sun., free)

was built in honor of the folk singer and visual artist (1917-1967). From a family of poets and folk singers, Parra became a cultural icon, widely considered the mother of Latin American folk music, pioneering the reinvention of Chilean folk music known as Nueva Canción Chilena (New Chilean Song Movement). Her music compiled the songs of peasants of the Central Valley region and demonstrated a leftist political attitude. Parra died by suicide at age 49.

Somewhat surprisingly, the museum focuses on Parra's artistic achievements rather than her music. After hepatitis forced a long period of bed rest in 1959, she began embroidering rural-themed tapestries, describing the work as "songs that are painted." Five years later she became the first Hispanic artist to exhibit her work individually at the Louvre Museum in Paris. Tapestries from this exhibition and earthy mosaics that use materials like dried beans, lentils, and rice are on display here. Some of Parra's musical instruments are exhibited. In the auditorium, the museum hosts puppet shows and talks, often associated with Parra's life. Most events are on weekends.

Museo Vicuña Mackenna

The **Museo Vicuña Mackenna** (Av. Vicuña Mackenna 94, tel. 2/2222 9642, http://museovicunamackenna.gob.cl, 9:30am-5:30pm Mon.-Fri., 10am-2pm Sat., free) remembers journalist turned politician Benjamín Vicuña Mackenna, who served as a senator and mayor of Santiago before running for president in 1875, an election he lost to Federico Errázuriz Zañartu. The museum is on the site of his former home. He was a prolific writer, and you can visit the study where he penned over 190 books. Four rooms of the museum cover his political and personal life.

LAS CONDES

Barrio Alonso de Córdova, an exclusive shopping district of Las Condes, is between Calle Kennedy and Parque Bicentenario and home to elite international fashion brands as well as the city's most expensive restaurants and bars. It's also home to two wonderful little museums.

Museo de la Moda

Appealing to die-hard fashionistas, the **Museo de la Moda** (Av. Vitacura 4562, tel. 2/2219 3623, www.museodelamoda.cl, by guided tour only, CH$3,000 adults, CH$1,500 children) has an eclectic collection of artwork by surrealist artist Roberto Matta and contemporary furniture designed by his brother Mario Matta Echaurren. The real highlight is the displays of clothing worn by celebrities, from a headdress worn by Lady Gaga to a Jean Paul Gautier bra worn by Madonna on

her Blond Ambition tour in 1990. Visits are by guided tour only and reservations must be made in advance.

Museo Rallí

Boasting one of the largest private collections of contemporary Latin American art in the world, the **Museo Rallí** (Sotomayor 4110, tel. 2/2206 4224, http://museoralli.cl, 10:30am-5pm Tues.-Sun. Mar.-Jan., free) was created by the late Harry Recanati, a Greek banker who spent decades collecting art. A small selection by Salvador Dalí and Roberto Matta are permanent; the rest of the 16 rooms are a rotating collection shared with other locations of the museum, scattered across the globe.

Entertainment

Thanks to its status as the cultural heart of Chile, and its ample student population, Santiago is the best place in the country for spirited nightlife and live music, theater, and cultural events. A veritable feast of jazz, *cumbia,* rock, and folk music is performed most evenings.

NIGHTLIFE

Bellavista has the densest selection of bars and venues. The main thoroughfare, Pío Nono, and more mature options in the northeast of the neighborhood are packed with students and budget bar-goers. Barrio Brasil offers a more relaxed scene, while Barrio Italia is home to jazz dens and craft beer bars with a hip vibe. Barrio Lastarria is a classier affair, while Downtown is home to Santiago's classic watering holes. Chileans start the party late: Bars get going around 10pm, and few nightclubs have much atmosphere until at least 2am. Cover charges are common at nightclubs, with reduced rates or free entry common before midnight.

Downtown

Graffiti-daubed walls and sawdust on the

floor: Welcome to **La Piojera** (Aillavilú 1030, tel. 2/2698 1682, http://lapiojera.cl, noon-midnight Mon.-Sat.), an iconic dive bar and one of *the* places to sample the devilishly strong cocktail *terremoto,* a mix of fermented wine, grenadine, and pineapple ice cream. It's so strong that you're only allowed one. Next, the bartender supplies an aftershock, a half-size *terremoto.* Packed with working-class locals and the occasional curious visitor, this spot guarantees an interesting evening.

Barrio Lastarria

Rub shoulders with Chile's moneyed elite at 9th-floor **The Singular** (Merced 294, tel. 2/2306 8820, http://thesingular.com, 5pm-12:30pm Tues.-Sat., 4pm-10pm Sun.), an exclusive bar in the five-star hotel of the same name. From its prime position, you can see Cerro San Cristóbal and the Santiago skyline while sipping exclusive wines by the glass, or choosing expertly crafted cocktails alongside cheese boards, oysters, and king crab empanadas.

The two-room dance floor of **Bar El Tunel** (Santo Domingo 439, tel. 2/2639 9714, 11pm-4am Thurs., 11am-5am Fri.-Sun., CH$10,000) gets crammed with students and other late-night revelers dancing to reggaeton, rock, R&B, or funk, depending on the evening.

Barrio Bellavista

Despite crowds of partygoers, Bellavista does have its insalubrious areas. Avoid walking the backstreets at night; it's better to call a taxi directly to your location. Armed robberies and muggings on the streets west of Calle Pío Nono have become increasingly common at night.

Owned by the Chilean craft brewery of the same name, **Kross Bar** (Dardignac 127, tel. 2/759 5434, www.kross.cl, 12:30pm-1am Mon.-Wed., 12:30pm-2am Thurs.-Sat., 6:30pm-12:30am Sun.) has half a dozen brews on tap. Try the refreshing golden, the strong and hoppy K5, or one of their specialty beers. Their pizzas and burgers are a great way to soak up the alcohol.

On the upper floor of the Patio Bellavista restaurant and bar complex, the unsigned **Red Luxury Bar** (Patio Bellavista, tel. 9/6908 2378, 7:30pm-1am Mon.-Wed., 7:30pm-2:30pm Thurs.-Sat., noon-1am Sun.) is a slick space specializing in expertly crafted cocktails using any of 300 spirits. Absorb the atmosphere from the balcony and try the Peewee for a sweet twist on a pisco sour, or the Santiago sour, which is a mixture of pisco and red wine.

The pint-size bar and club **El Clan** (Bombero Núñez 363, tel. 2/2735 3655, http://elclan.cl, 10pm-3:30am Wed.-Thurs., 10pm-4:30am Fri.-Sat., CH$5,000) promises live hip-hop, samba bands, and '80s and '90s classics. Its young clientele comes in droves. There's no sign, so you have to look for the number on the door.

You'll want the elevator to get to **Azotea Matilde** (Bello 118, tel. 2/2986 0186, www.azoteamatilde.cl, 6pm-2am Mon.-Thurs., 1pm-2am Fri.-Sat., noon-5pm Sun.), a covered terrace on the roof of a residential building with great views of the city. It's a wonderful place for sipping a cocktail or sharing a bottle of wine as the sun sets. The food is average, so get here for an early drink or later at night.

Grab a chair at the bar to watch the action: The bartenders at **Siete Negronis** (Malinkrodt 180, tel. 9/5408 8251, www.sietenegronis.cl, 6pm-2am Tues.-Thurs., 6pm-3am Thurs., 6pm-4am Fri.-Sat.) know their way around a cocktail. Negronis are the star, with seven variations available, and they change on the 7th of every month. The ambience is classy, with mood lighting and exposed brick walls. Expect to pay at least CH$7,000 per cocktail.

The intimate **Thelonious Lugar de Jazz** (Bombero Núñez 336, tel. 2/2735 7962, www.theloniouschile.com, 8:30pm-2am Tues.-Sat., CH$3,000-5,000) is one of the city's best places for live traditional, contemporary, and experimental jazz by Chilean and international acts. Reservations are essential on weekends. Two performances each night generally start at 9pm and 11pm.

Barrio Brasil

In the heart of Barrio Brasil, **Santo Barrio** (Av. Brasil 109, tel. 2/2696 7292, noon-midnight Mon.-Wed., noon-2am Thurs.-Sat., 5pm-11:30pm Sun.) is a slightly dingy watering hole with walls lined with satirical political posters. Four fridges are stacked with dozens of bottles of beer, most imported. A smaller selection of Chilean craft beer is on tap. Their mountainous *chorrillanas* (chips loaded with onions, steak slices, and a fried egg on top) are great post-beer nibbles.

At **Cervecería Nacional** (Compañía de Jesús 2858, tel. 9/184 6752 or 2/681 4713, http://cervecerianacional.cl, 6:30pm-12:30am Mon.-Thurs., 6:30pm-1:30am Fri.-Sat.), 10 Chilean craft beers are on tap and four dozen from Chilean breweries are available by the bottle. This is an unmissable stop for beer lovers. It's jammed on weekends with a young, hip crowd who come for the beer and tasty thin-crust pizzas or beer-cooked *mechada* sandwiches.

Barrio Italia

Although its liquor license dictates that you can only get a drink if you buy food, **Mosstow Brewfood** (Av. Condell 1460, tel. 2/2791 8603, http://mossto.cl, 1pm-midnight Mon.-Wed., 1pm-1am Thurs., 1pm-2am Fri.-Sat.) is a great place to sample lesser-known craft beer, with up to 20 on tap, including interesting options using cilantro seeds and cucumber, and imperial stout with *merkén* (roasted Chilean chili). You can't go wrong with the menu of pizzas and burgers (CH$5,000-11,000), many of which feature beer as an ingredient, while the small snacks are good for nibbling.

The Jazz Corner (Santa Isabel 451, tel. 2/2274 9941, www.thejazzcorner.cl, 11am-1am Tues.-Wed., 11am-Thurs.-Sat., noon-11pm Sun., CH$5,000 cover for performances), a cramped, atmospheric spot, is an intimate, lesser-known live music venue that hosts big names in Chilean jazz (music starts 9:30pm Tues.-Thurs., 10pm Fri.-Sat., 7pm Sun.). Seats are packed around a small central stage. Booking ahead is essential; get here early for the best seats.

Owned by Argentinean actor and comedian Jorge Alis, **El Cachafaz** (Av. Italia 1679, tel. 9/7386 1881, www.elcachafaz.cl, 2pm-10pm Mon.-Tues., 2pm-2am Wed.-Sat.) has an eclectic mixture of events, from tango classes (8pm Mon. and Wed., CH$5,000) and regular tango shows to burlesque and clown workshops and theater classes for children. It's also a bar where you can chow down on Chilean classics such as *chorrillanas* (fried beef, eggs, and onions mixed with french fries).

Greater Santiago

Bar Las Tejas (San Diego 236, tel. 2/2699 2789, 12:30pm-11pm Mon.-Fri., 12:30pm-5pm Sat.) has a festive atmosphere that's absolutely contagious. An old theater packed to the rafters with university students chugging pint-size *terremotos* or sharing jugs of the highly alcoholic drink, the atmosphere is rowdy but welcoming, featuring live *cumbia*

and dancing. Expect to find yourself joining in. Get here before 9pm for a seat.

La Fabbrica (Av. Ossa 123, La Reina, tel. 2/2830 6208, http://la-fabbrica.cl, 12:30pm-midnight Sun.-Thurs., 12:30pm-1am Fri.-Sat., CH$5,000 cover for performances), in Plaza Egaña, is home to the legendary live-music Club de Jazz de Santiago, which has hosted jazz heavyweights such as Louis Armstrong and Herbie Hancock. These days it welcomes exciting new jazz musicians, with music starting at 10pm. You'll want a reservation.

One of the city's best-loved live music clubs, **La Batuta** (Washington 52, Nuñoa tel. 2/2274 7096, www.batuta.cl, 11pm-4am Thurs., 11pm-5am Fri.-Sat., cover from CH$4,000) is a classic haunt in Barrio Nuñoa, south of the city center. It packs an enthusiastic crowd for live rock, ska, and *cumbia* bands, featuring local and international acts.

On the top floor of a car park, **After Office Santiago** (San Francisco 75, 9th Fl., Paris-Londres, tel. 9/9820 2573, http://aos.cl, 6pm-2am Tues.-Thurs., 7pm-4am Fri.-Sat., cover CH$0-10,000) is a bar-cum-club that oozes cool and packs in salsa, international pop, and live DJs. On the outdoor terrace, they sell *choripanes* for hungry revelers. Entry is free until 10pm and CH$7,000-10,000 afterward.

If you fancy trying your hand at salsa, **Club Orixas** (Tarapacá 755, San Isidro, tel. 2/2638 0561, www.orixas.cl, 7:30pm-midnight Wed., 8pm-3am Thurs., 9pm-3am Fri., 9pm-5am Sat., cover varies) has classes (CH$2,000) from 7pm Wednesday, plus *bachata* and casino (a Cuban-influenced style of salsa) the rest of the week. They also have regular dance shows and DJ events.

There's an Irish bar in every city, and Santiago's is **Flannery's Irish Geo Pub** (Encomenderos 179, Las Condes, tel. 2/2233 6675, http://flannerys.cl, noon-2am Mon.-Fri., 6pm-2am Sat.-Sun.). It's popular among the expat crowd, who come to drink the owner's craft beer on tap and watch international sports on huge TVs.

The 20-something crowd at **Club Amanda** (Doussinague 1767, Vitacura, tel. 2/3223 0000, http://amanda.cl, 9:30pm-4:30am Thurs.-Sat., cover CH$10,000) comes for the eclectic mix of live techno DJs with occasional salsa. It's a 20-minute drive from Downtown.

LGBTQ CLUBS
One of the city's most popular LGBTQ events is **Barcelona,** held Saturday nights at event space **Ex-Bunker** (Bombero Núñez 159, no phone, www.superfiestabarcelona.com, midnight-6am Sat., cover varies), a guaranteed wild night featuring drag acts, go-go dancing, and thumping tunes spanning the last few decades.

Be ready to queue for the student and gay favorite **Blondie** (Av. Alameda 2879, no phone, http://blondie.cl, 11:30pm-5am Thurs.-Sat., cover CH$3,000), whose four floors offer up everything from classic '80s and '90s tunes to indie rock and techno.

THE ARTS
Cultural Centers
For a list of upcoming cultural events, consult Santiago Cultural (www.santiagocultura.cl).

Centro Cultural Gabriela Mistral (Av. Alameda 227, tel. 2/2566 5500, www.gam.cl, hours and cost vary), also known as **GAM,** is one of the city's most important cultural spaces, with an extensive program of contemporary drama and dance, classical and popular music performances, and visual art exhibitions.

Beneath the Palacio de la Moneda, the **Centro Cultural La Moneda** (Plaza de la Ciudadanía 26, tel. 2/2355 6500, www.ccplm.cl, 9am-7:30pm daily, free) has a cavernous atrium around which small galleries contain artifacts on loan from regional museums. Other exhibition rooms, often showing photography, are CH$3,000 admission—but you can enter for free before noon.

Originally known as the Estadio Chile, the **Estadio Víctor Jara** (Godoy 275, no phone, http://fundacionvictorjara.org) was renamed in memory of the Chilean singer-songwriter who was detained, tortured, and killed here during the military dictatorship.

A memorial space for those lost in the dictatorship, the stadium today hosts mostly Chilean folk and rock concerts, dance performances, and sports games throughout the year.

The **Centro Cultural Estación Mapocho** (Plaza de la Cultura s/n, tel. 2/2787 0000, www.estacionmapocho.cl) near the Mercado Central, hosts photography and art exhibitions as well as large events like the annual Feria del Libro (Book Fair) in November, plus yoga classes. **NAVE** (Libertad 430, no phone, http://nave.io) in Barrio Yungay hosts contemporary dance, theater, and music performances, often with political or activist themes.

Art Galleries
Dating to 1983, **Aninat Galería de Arte** (Córdova 4355, Vitacura, tel. 2/2481 9870 or 2/2481 9871, www.aninatgaleria.org, 11am-8pm Mon.-Thurs., 11am-7pm Fri., 11am-2pm Sat., free) claims to be the oldest gallery in the city. It showcases the contemporary work of Chilean artists, often in audiovisual exhibitions and photography.

Theater
Teatro UC (Washington 26, Nuñoa, http://teatrouc.uc.cl) is a theater operated since the 1940s by the prestigious Universidad Católica. It has hosted important Chilean performance artists, such as Victor Jara and Paulina Urrutia. Performances are mostly modern or experimental. It hosts many productions during January's Santiago A Mil theater festival.

Live Music and Opera
The lavish 1857 neoclassical **Teatro Municipal** (Agustinas 794, tel. 2/2463 1000, www.municipal.cl), home to the Opera Nacional de Chile, is the country's most prominent theater, hosting ballet, opera, and classical music. Go if only to admire the spectacular architecture; it cuts a dramatic figure with its gleaming white facade. Occasional **guided tours** (free) and **private tours** (in

Art in the Metro

Don't just use the metro for transport; jump out every now and then to admire the artwork. The MetroArte project has transformed the walls of subway stations across the city. Over 40 murals, mosaics, and photographs by Chileans have been installed since 2003. Disembark at the following stations—the art sometimes extends beyond the platforms.

- **Universidad de Chile:** The most famous artwork in the metro is Mario Toral's mural *Memoria Visual de una Nación (Visual Memory of a Nation)*. It covers 1,200 square meters and six panels on platforms at this busy station. Its two sections, *Pasado (Past,* 1996) and *Presente (Present,* 1999), reflect the complex history of Chile, from its indigenous roots to 20th-century conflicts.

- **La Moneda:** On the platforms and in the warren of corridors are 14 landscapes of *Chile Hoy (Chile Today,* 2005). They depict snow-crusted mountains, the blue snout of a glacier, and *araucaría* trees at dawn. They look like photographs but are the work of realist Guillermo Muñoz Vera.

- **Bellas Artes:** The hallmark primary colors and thick black outlines of acclaimed muralist Alejandro "Mono" González and the equally recognizable woman and child by muralist Inti Castro decorate the entrance. Venture inside for Jennifer Díaz's mosaic *La Infancia Que Debe Ser (Childhood as It Should Be,* 2018), a vivid portrayal of what it means to be a child.

- **Quinta Normal:** On 55 polychrome ceramic panels by one of Chile's most acclaimed artists, the seminal 20th-century expressionist and surrealist Roberto Matta, *Verbo América (The American Verb,* 1997) depicts the roots and cosmology of pre-Colombian civilizations.

- **Franklin:** Opened in 2018, this metro station bears Rodrigo Estay's mural *Retrato de un Matarife (Portrait of a Butcher,* 2018), which reflects on the neighborhood's economic and cultural roots as the city's principal slaughterhouse district.

English, up to four people, CH$40,000) are available.

The Ballet Nacional Chileno and the Orquesta Sinfónica de Chile perform at the **Centro de Extensión Artística y Cultura** (Av. Providencia 43, tel. 2/2978 2480, http://ceacuchile.cl), a performance venue operated by the Universidad de Chile. Expect choral performances, solo pianists, orchestral music, and classic guitar.

Celebrated national acts and international acts such as New Order and Alice Cooper have graced the stage of **Teatro Caupolicán** (San Diego 850, tel. 2/2699 1556, www.teatrocaupolican. cl). The **Estadio Nacional** (Av. Grecia 2001, Nuñoa) and the **Movistar Arena** (Parque O'Higgins, tel. 2/2770 2300, http://movistararena.cl) are the city's largest concert venues, hosting acts such as the Red Hot Chili Peppers, Jamiroquai, and Shakira.

EVENTS

There's always an event going on in Santiago. Advertisements on metro platforms are among the best places to find event information, and websites **Cívico** (www.civico.com), **Toliv** (http://toliv.io), and **Agenda Revolver** (www.agendarevolver.cl) have up-to-date event listings. The websites for the city's papers, *El Mercurio* (http://digital.elmercurio. com) and *The Santiago Times* (http://santiagotimes.cl), also have listings.

Santiago A Mil

Held annually for most of January, **Santiago A Mil** (www.santiagoamil.cl) is a performing arts festival that attracts international musicians and theater and dance troupes to venues and parks across the city. Performances also take place in other cities across Chile. Many acts include English subtitles. Tickets can be found on the website.

Lollapalooza

The Chilean version of the alternative music festival from the United States, **Lollapalooza Chile** (www.lollapaloozacl.com) is held for three days in March every year in the **Movistar Arena** (Parque O'Higgins, tel. 2/2770 2300, http://movistararena.cl), with high-profile international acts such as Florence and the Machine, Arcade Fire, and Chance the Rapper, and Chilean bands such as Villa Cariño. Tickets generally sell out quickly.

Santiago Festival Internacional de Cine

For a week in August, independent films from across the world are screened in cinemas around the city at one of Latin's America's most prestigious film festivals, the **Santiago Festival Internacional de Cine** (www.sanfic.com), also known as **SANFIC.**

Fiesta del Roto Chileno

Held on the bustling streets of Barrio Yungay the third week in January, the **Fiesta del Roto Chileno** (www.elsitiodeyungay.cl) dates back 100 years. It started as a memorial for those who died in the Battle of Yungay. Nowadays it includes popular and classical music performances, folkloric dance, theater, and yoga workshops.

We Tripantu

Held on the winter solstice (June 21), **We Tripantu** is the largest celebration in the Mapuche calendar. It celebrates the rebirth of the sun and the moon at the start of the new year. Festivities are lively in Santiago, where the largest number of Mapuche people live, with concerts across the city featuring Mapuche folk musicians such as Beatriz Pichi Malen and even Mapuche rap and hip-hop artists. These are supplemented with poetry readings and unmissable gastronomic fairs, where you can try traditional Mapuche dishes. *Sopapillas* (deep-fried pastries), *muday* (a drink made from fermented wheat or corn), and meat stews are cooked in big street gatherings across the city, with new revelers always welcome to join the celebrations. Expect the party to continue long into the night.

Shopping

SOUVENIRS

The streets of **Barrio Bellavista** are known for bars and restaurants, but the commercial precinct of **Patio Bellavista** (Bellavista, between Pío Nono and Constitución, http://patiobellavista.cl, 11am-10pm daily) is packed with small shops specializing in *artesanía* (handicrafts): Chilean textiles, Mapuche-inspired copper jewelry, silver inset with lapis lazuli, and even some rare *rarí* (dyed horsehair) crafts. Prices here are high; head to **Pueblito Los Dominicos** (Apoquindo 9085, tel. 9/9253 3863, www.plosdominicos.cl, 10:30am-8pm daily Oct.-Apr., 10:30am-7pm Tues.-Sun. May-Sept.) in Las Condes for the best prices and a wider choice of goods.

A number of small **jewelry shops** mostly specializing in lapis lazuli are along **Bellavista** between Pío Nono and Magallanes. Elsewhere in the city, **Bluestone** (Los Araucanos 2020, Providencia, tel. 2/2232 2581, http://bluestone.cl, 9:30am-7pm daily) and **FABA** (Alonso de Córdova 4355, tel. 9/3262 5074, www.lapislazuli.cl, 10am-6pm Mon.-Fri., 10am-2pm Sat.) specialize in elegant lapis lazuli jewelry.

Find textiles, lapis lazuli, and other souvenirs in the small **Feria Santa Lucía** (Av. Alameda 510, 10am-8pm daily), a craft market just south of Cerro Santa Lucía. On **Calle Lastarria,** between Merced and Rosal, a small **antiques fair** (10am-8pm Thurs.-Sun.) hosts a smattering of sellers.

Best Souvenirs

Promising the full gamut of Chilean handicrafts in one browsable place, **Pueblito de los Dominicos** (Apoquindo 9085, tel. 9/9253 3863, www.plosdominicos.cl, 10:30am-8pm daily Oct.-Apr., 10:30am-7pm Tues.-Sun. May-Sept.) in Las Condes should be the first stop for souvenirs. Like a small rural village, it has 200 stores selling handicrafts from across Chile. It's an excellent spot for lapis lazuli jewelry and delicate Mapuche-inspired silverware. Pottery from Pomaire and ornamental stonework are also available; the quality is excellent.

Below are some items to consider bringing home from your trip to Chile.

- **Lapis Lazuli:** A startlingly blue semiprecious gemstone, lapis lazuli is found in Afghanistan and a handful of other countries. It's highly prized for the intensity of its color. In Chile, mining began in 1905 in the village of Tulahúen near Ovalle in the Norte Chico. Lapis lazuli became the Chilean national stone in the 1980s. You'll find it crafted into sterling silver jewelry and ornaments.

leather goods on sale at Pueblito de los Dominicos

- **Combarbalita:** This rare, polished stone is found in colors from white to rose and black and is similar to marble in its mottled pattern. It's soft enough to be worked by hand but durable enough that it doesn't crack when used in thin or delicate pieces. Unique to Combarbalá, a town close to Ovalle, it was favored by the indigenous Diaguita and El Molle peoples, whose artisans carved it into decorative pendants and utilitarian arrowheads. In markets in Norte Chico and Santiago, it's fashioned into decorative ornaments and added to jewelry, often combined with lapis lazuli.

- *Crin:* One of the country's stranger souvenirs, brightly dyed horsehair reinforced with strands of *ixle* (a cactus from Mexico) is crafted into intricate butterflies, brooches, and even *brujas* (small dolls of witches), all in shocking pinks and blues. This colorful handicraft stems from the one-street village of **Rari** (page 280).

- *Greda:* If you order a pie in a small restaurant, it's likely to come in a heavy clay pot. Known as *greda*, these smoky brown ceramics are fired in the workshops of Pomaire, just outside of Santiago, and are a staple in Chilean kitchens. Plates, bowls, and even three-footed *chanchitos* (piggy banks) can be found in markets across the city.

- **Chilean Wine:** Grapevines have been cultivated in Chile since the Jesuits planted them in the mid-1500s to make sacramental wines. The country's signature grape, carménère, along with robust cabernet sauvignons, pinot noirs, and sauvignon blancs, have made Chile a global wine powerhouse. To buy from boutique wineries, head to the knowledgeable **Santiago Wine Club** (Rosal 386, Lastarria, tel. 2/2639 3085, http://santiagowineclub.cl, 11am-9pm Mon.-Tues., 11am.-9:30pm Wed.-Sat., noon-8pm Sun.).

- **Pisco:** Chile's grape cultivation doesn't end with wine. In Norte Chico, muscat is distilled into pisco, a smooth floral liquor. It's combined with lime juice and sugar for the ubiquitous pisco sour but can also be added to a variety of cocktails or drunk neat. All supermarkets stock the large Chilean pisco brands; for more boutique options, head to **CAV** (Costanera Center, Av. Andrés Bello 2447, Local 1206, tel. 2/2618 9707, https://cav.cl, 10am-10pm daily).

With branches in the airport and in the Pueblito de los Dominicos, **Fundación Artesanías de Chile** (Centro Cultural La Moneda, Av. Alameda, no phone, http://artesaniasdechile.cl, 9am-7:30pm daily) is a fair-trade nonprofit that supports artisans across the country. It sells an extensive collection of textiles, including ponchos, rugs, and scarfs from the Atacama and Araucanía regions, Mapuche wicker baskets, ornaments carved from rare Chilean stone, and ceramics from Pomaire. It hosts craft workshops noon-4pm on weekends.

Barrio Italia is a shopper's dream, with independent boutiques selling fashionable clothing, furniture, and bric-a-brac. It's easy to spend hours browsing the galleries along **Avenida Italia,** between Calles Santa Isabel and Caupolicán. With 50 boutiques, **Estación Italia** (Av. Italia 1439, tel. 9/5235 5355, www.estacionitalia.cl, 11am-8pm daily) is great for browsing leather goods, clothes, and quirky crafts. They host regular events, including wine tastings and live music. Downstairs, don't miss **Autóctona** (Local 2S, tel. 9/9432 8572, 11am-8pm Tues.-Sat., 11am-7pm Sun.), with unique cutting boards handcrafted from Chilean wood.

Don't miss chocolate-maker **Óbolo** (Av. Italia 1584, no phone, http://obolochocolate.cl, 11:30am-8pm daily), who specializes in bean-to-bar chocolate, working with a cooperative of cacao growers in the Peruvian Amazon.

For fashion from high-end Chilean and international designers, head to the exclusive **Barrio Alonso de Córdova** and Calle Alonso de Córdova.

WINE

Santiago Wine Club (Rosal 386, Lastarria, tel. 2/2639 3085, http://santiagowineclub.cl, 11am-9pm Mon.-Tues., 11am-9:30pm Wed.-Sat., noon-8pm Sun.) specializes in wine from independent boutique wineries and unusual varietals such as carignan, viognier, and petit verdot, as well as wine from newer regions such as Itata.

Stocking a small selection of wine from the best wineries in the Colchagua, Casablanca, and Maipo valleys, **Vinolia** (Alonso de Monroy 2869, Vitacura, tel. 2/2604 8528, http://vinolia.cl, 11am-11pm Mon.-Sat.) also offers virtual tours of featured vineyards, with tastings guided by the winemakers themselves. Before the tasting, you can visit a smelling room, where you learn to identify the different notes of the wines you'll be trying. Tastings cost CH$32,500 with five pours and nibbles. Reservations are necessary.

In Las Condes, **Les Dix Vins** (Av. Vitacura 2935, Las Condes, tel. 2/2247 4705, www.lesdixvins.cl, 4pm-midnight Mon.-Tues., 11am-1am Wed.-Sat.) sells a selection of boutique Chilean and French wines and offers regular wine tastings, often with food, as well as a bar space where wine can be purchased by the glass.

BOOKS

It's hard to find English-language books in Santiago. The chain bookstore **Antártica** (www.antartica.cl) has shops across the city, mostly in malls. Another good bet is **Feria Chilena del Libro** (Huérfanos 670, tel. 2/2345 8316, www.feriachilenadellibro.cl), among a plethora of small Spanish-language bookshops on Calle Huérfanos. Two blocks south of Feria Chilena, **Books and Bits** (Tenderini 60, local 114, tel. 2/2632 7637, www.booksandbits.cl) also stocks some English titles.

Recreation

PARKS

South of Downtown, **Parque O'Higgins** (Av. Beaucheff, Tupper, Av. Viel, and Gral. Rondizzoni, no phone, 8am-9pm daily Nov.-Mar., 8am-8pm daily Apr.-Oct.) is the city's second-largest public park, with vast lawns, an ornamental pond, and picnic tables filled with locals on weekends. It hosts the indoor **Movistar Arena** (tel. 2/2770 2300, http://movistararena.cl). There's also a rickety theme park, Fantasilandia, on the grounds.

Popular with joggers, yoga clubs, and families, **Parque Araucano** (bounded by Alonso de Cordoba, Cerro Colorado, Av. Manquehue Norte, and Av. Presidente Riesco, Las Condes, tel. 600/500 0011, 7am-9pm daily) is a charmingly manicured green space in the heart of Las Condes. Landscaped lawns and a pretty rose garden make a great spot for a sunny day. It's home to a small amusement park for kids and a range of cafés, albeit overpriced.

On the banks of the river in Vitacura, **Parque Bicentenario** (Av. Costanera Sur and Bicentenario, Barrio Alonso de Córdova, tel. 9/6365 6750, 24 hrs daily) presides over a flamingo colony, plus various promenades and lush, well-maintained lawns. It's a popular spot for sunset and is within walking distance of a range of high-end restaurants. To get here, take a taxi (CH$4,000) or catch bus 405 from the nearest metro stop, Tobalaba. The bus takes 20 minutes and drops you on Avenida Vitacura, in the center of the neighborhood; it's a 15-minute, four-block walk northwest along Calle Alonso de Córdova to the main entrance.

HIKING

With 360-degree views of Santiago, the 1,620-meter peak of **Cerro Manquehue** (2km one-way, 3hr) is a worthy prize for the steep, sweaty climb required to get here. The trail is short, but the exceptionally steep gradient of the second half makes it challenging. Trekking poles are helpful, as the trail can be slippery. Plan for two hours to climb up and an hour to get down. Robberies have been known to take place along the trail, particularly in the early morning and late afternoon; don't go alone, and be sure to leave valuables in your

view from Cerro Manquehue

hotel. There are more hikers on the trail on weekends, so this is the safest time to go. You can also hike the shorter and gentler route up **Cerro Manquehuito** (Little Manquehue), from the same trailhead, although the views are less dramatic from the 1,316-meter peak. To get to the start of the hike from Vía Roja in Vitacura, take the metro to Manquehue on Línea 1, then flag down a taxi for the rest of the way.

On the eastern edge of where Las Condes meets the commune of La Reina, **Parque Natural Aguas de Ramon** (Álvaro Casanova 2583, La Reina, tel. 2/2750 112 or 2/2750 171, 8am-7pm daily summer, 8am-6pm daily winter, CH$3,000 adults, CH$2,000 children) has short, easy trails that range 1-6km round-trip. The park is also home to the popular and well-signed **Sendero Salto de Apoquindo** (17.5-km loop, 5hr), which starts from the administration building. Moderate in difficulty, this circuit climbs through the canyon of Río San Ramón to the pretty Salto de Apoquindo, a 30-meter waterfall that's most impressive in spring, when the water is more plentiful and the path is lined by flowers. In winter, hikers must be on the trail by 9am; children younger than 15 are not permitted

to hike this route. From the Francisco Bilbao metro stop on Línea 4, take bus 412 or D08 heading east and get off at Plaza La Reina. From here it's a 20-minute walk or 5-minute taxi ride.

On the east side of La Reina, **Parque Mahuida** (Av. Alcalde Fernando Castillo Velasco 11095, tel. 2/2273 4301 or 2/2275 1527, www.parquemahuida.cl, CH$3,500 per vehicle, CH$500 pedestrians, 9am.-7:30pm Tues.-Thurs. and 8am-7:30pm Fri.-Sun. summer, 9am-5:30pm Tues.-Thurs. and 8am-5:30pm Fri.-Sun. winter) has two main trails. The first is **Sendero Quebrada Guayacán** (8km one-way, 3.5hr), which climbs into the dusty foothills of the Andes for views across La Reina, and if the weather's clear, across the city. The second trail is the challenging **Sendero Cerro La Cruz** (14km one-way, 10hr), a thigh-destroying steep climb up to Cerro La Cruz (2,400m), where panoramic views across the city are your reward. Watch for condors above. Note that in summer, the path becomes compacted and slippery with dust. There is no protection from the sun. Bring plenty of water, as there is none along the route. Trekking poles can help with the steepest sections.

Food

TOP EXPERIENCE

FINE DINING IN SANTIAGO

Chile has long remained under the radar for fine dining, but Santiago is making a mark on the international scene. These restaurants make regular appearances on lists of Latin America's best restaurants, and each offers fine dining and innovative flavors.

★ **Ambrosia** (Pamplona 78, tel. 2/2217 3075, www.ambrosia.cl, 12:30pm-4:30pm and 7:30pm-11:30pm Mon.-Sat., CH$13,000-19,000): From Chilean chef Carolina Bazán, this has long been touted as one of the best

restaurants on the continent. Her modern Chilean food is inspired by her training at critically acclaimed French restaurants and is sophisticated and unpretentious, featuring veal sweetbreads, prawn tartare with squid ink, and lamb medallions with bean puree. Hidden on a residential street with a sun-drenched patio, Ambrosia offers fine dining with a comfortable, relaxed air. For a more affordable lunch, check out **Ambrosia Bistro** (page 66) in Providencia.

★ **Boragó** (Nueva Costanera 3467, Vitacura, tel. 2/2953 8893, www.borago.cl, 7pm-11:45pm Mon.-Sat., CH$55,000-68,000) astounds with its earthy, delicate flavors that celebrate Chile's diverse natural heritage. Chef Rodolfo Guzman forages for sea algae on the rocks at Isla Negra, incorporating them into an experimental 6- or 16-course menu featuring guanaco jerky and nine-hour barbecued lamb. Book well in advance and expect the spectacle to take at least three hours.

★ **99 Restaurante** (Fuenzalida 99, Providencia, tel. 2/2335 3327, http://99restaurante.com, 1pm-3pm and 8pm-10pm daily, CH$25,000-70,000, *menú del día* CH$12,900): Under the watchful gaze of owner and head chef Kurt Schmidt, this spot has a casual atmosphere, with an open kitchen and tables made of reclaimed wood. There's nothing casual about the dining experience; Chilean ingredients are decadently presented in outstanding flavors, such as pears cooked three ways or oven-braised lamb with an edamame bean puree, followed by decadent chocolate tarts. Blow your budget on a nine-course tasting menu with wine pairings, or go affordable with the excellent-value three-course lunch menu.

★ **Restaurant 040** (López de Bello 40, Providencia, tel. 2/2732 9214, http://040.cl, 7:30pm-midnight Tues.-Sat., CH$39,500): Experimental Spanish chef Sergio Barros refined his craft across Europe before opening this spot, known for its offbeat flavors and creative presentation. Not for picky eaters, the 12-course tasting menu changes daily but can include salmon and tomato *nigiri* or raw sea urchin. Booking ahead is essential. Finish the evening with a trip to their speakeasy, Room 09, a rooftop bar decorated in an industrial style that's open only to diners.

DOWNTOWN

Prices are generally cheaper in the unpretentious and often historic restaurants and cafés Downtown.

Chilean

The **Mercado Central** (San Pablo 967, no phone, www.mercadocentral.cl, 6am-5pm Sat.-Thurs., 6am-8pm Fri.) has classic Chilean fish dishes from CH$4,000. Across the river,

the **Mercado de Abastos Tirso de Molina** (Av. Santa María 409, 6am-9pm daily) is a covered food market with small kitchens on the 2nd floor serving breakfast and lunch (CH$4,000-7,000) and oodles of exotic fruit juices; ask for *poco azucar* (little sugar) if you don't want to lose your teeth.

Hidden down a side street, the award-winning ★ **Salvador Cocina y Café** (Ossa 1059, tel. 2/2673 0619, 8:30am-7pm Mon.-Fri., CH$7,700-11,000, *menú del día* CH$9,900) is an unexpected foodie haven. The daily menu includes several starters and mains, all showcasing Chilean ingredients with modern flair. Dine on pumpkin and wheat kernel salad, homemade pâté of chicken hearts, or pigs' feet on a bed of lentils. Get here early for lunch, as it quickly fills up with local businesspeople. They also serve cakes, coffee, and breakfast sandwiches.

With its horseshoe-shaped bar that makes it impossible not to chat with the white-hatted servers, **El Rapidito** (Bandera 347, tel. 2/2672 2375, 9am-8pm Mon.-Fri., 10am-4pm Sat., CH$1,800-4,000) is a Chilean institution dating to the 1960s, the city's most popular *picada* (small family-run restaurant). The quick service lives up to the name and the selection of soups, *churrascos, completos,* and empanadas are cheap and tasty.

At **Emporio Zunino** (Paseo Puente 801, tel. 2/2698 8895, www.empanadaszunino.com, 9:30pm-11pm Mon.-Fri, 9:30am-3pm Sat., CH$1,100-1,400), which dates to 1930, join the business types holding meetings over empanadas and coffee at one of the high tables. The classic choice is the *empanada de pino,* filled with minced beef, onions, and a solitary olive. They also sell cheese-filled empanadas and fresh pasta to cook at home.

BARRIOS BELLAS ARTES AND LASTARRIA

Chilean

Packed to the rafters with over 340 bottles, ★ **Bocanáriz** (Lastarria 276, tel. 2/2638 9893, http://bocanariz.cl, noon-midnight Mon.-Wed., noon-12:30pm Thurs.-Sat.,

7pm-11pm Sun., CH$7,000-15,000) is one the best places to experience Chilean viticulture. The sommeliers offer a full explanation of the wine menu and can recommend flights to sample from the dozen options by geography, varietal, or style. The food is excellent (if pricey): ceviches, seaweed salads, beef empanadas spiced with *merkén,* and a three-course menu with wine pairings (CH$39,000). The exposed brick walls and tall designer chairs lend the place a modern vibe.

★ **Liguria** (Merced 298, tel. 2/3263 4340, www.liguria.cl, noon-1am Mon.-Sat., CH$5,000-10,000) is Santiago's most quintessential bistro and an unmissable stop; it has hosted international celebrities like Kate Moss. The menu runs the gamut of traditional Chilean dishes, from lamb shank with mashed potatoes and gravy to *carne mechada* (braised beef) with pasta. They don't accept reservations, so get here early for a table. Three sister locations are in Providencia (Av. Providencia 1353, Av. Pedro de Valdivia 47, and Av. Ojeda 19) provide a cozier experience.

A pisco jug marks the entrance of **Chipe Libre** (Lastarria 282, tel. 2/2664 0584, 12:30pm-12:30am Mon.-Wed., 12:30pm-1am Thurs.-Sat., CH$7,000-10,000), a restaurant that declares itself the "Independent Republic of Pisco." There is a long-standing dispute as to whether Peru or Chile birthed this brandy-like alcohol, but Chipe Libre is considered neutral territory. Start with a frothy pisco sour or check out the pisco flights. The food, heavy on fancy, well-presented Chilean dishes, is excellent.

Down a backstreet behind the GAM building, **José Ramon 277** (José Ramon 277, tel. 9/4258 1689, www.joseramon277.cl, 9am-midnight Mon.-Fri., noon-midnight Sat.-Sun., CH$6,000-7,000) is a hip spot with epic *sanguches*—crusty white rolls stuffed with traditional Chilean fillings such as *pernil* (boiled ham hock), *prieta* (blood sausage), or *lengua* (cow's tongue), all slathered with avocado, green beans, and green chili. Three house beers join a handful of Chilean craft beers on tap, plus a selection of cocktails, making it a great place for a drink.

If you ask any Santiaguinos where to go for a quick *lomito* (steak sandwich), they'll send you to **Fuente Alemana** (Av. Alameda 58, tel. 2/2639 3231, http://falemana.cl, 10:30am-10:30pm Mon.-Sat., CH$7,000-9,000). With its horseshoe-shaped bar, hordes of hungry diners, and pinafore-wearing staff, it's a dive into a traditional Chilean lunch. Slow-cooked shavings of pork or beef combine with

Liguria is a quintessential Chilean bistro.

avocado, tomato, and mayonnaise in a huge bun, washed down with a local beer. Expect to get your hands messy and your hunger satiated.

International

Only a dozen seats are in tiny **Thai Express** (Merced 493, tel. 9/6178 9672, 12:45pm-4pm and 5:30pm-10pm Mon.-Wed., 1pm-4pm and 6pm-midnight Thurs.-Sat., CH$5,000-8,000, *menú del día* CH$4,900). It's full of office workers at lunchtime, when there's always a queue outside for affordable and authentic Thai food, with service as quick as its name suggests. Tuck into pad thai and creamy curries. Dining is more relaxed in the evening, when the menu expands, with plenty of vegetarian and vegan options.

Always buzzing with Chileans and travelers, **Ramen Kintaro** (Monjitas 460, tel. 2/2638 2448, www.kintaro.cl, 1pm-3pm and 6pm-10:30pm Mon.-Fri., 1pm-11pm Sat., CH$7,000-8,000) has Japanese food served fast. They specialize in pork or tofu ramen, although there's a handful of yakisoba noodles and curries available. The *tantan kintaro* ramen and *gyoza* are excellent, and they serve their own beer on tap. Expect to wait for a table.

In a French-inspired château in Parque Forestal, the sumptuous **Castillo Forestal** (Av. María Caro 390, tel. 2/2664 1544, http://castilloforestal.cl, 10am-11pm Mon.-Thurs., 10am-midnight Fri.-Sat., 10am-8pm Sun., CH$8,000-15,000, *menú del día* CH$16,000) offers decadent French cuisine, best eaten on the upstairs terrace. Classics such as French onion soup, boeuf bourguignon, and orange confit of duck pair with an outstanding wine menu featuring fine Chilean wines. Booking is necessary on weekends.

Come for French-inspired dining at stylish **The Singular** (Merced 294, tel. 2/2306 8820, http://thesingular.com, 12:30pm-10:30pm daily, CH$17,000-23,000 mains), where steaks of guanaco reared in Tierra del Fuego can be ordered alongside eggplant *canelones* and hare seasoned with fennel and orange. With an expansive menu and expert waitstaff, you'll find a delicious wine to match. They offer lighter sandwiches and salads and high tea in the afternoon. Booking is essential on weekends.

Budget and Light Bites

Set back from Barrio Lastarria's central thoroughfare, Calle Merced, **Colmado Coffee** (Merced 346, tel. 2/2664 2317, 9am-9pm Sun.-Mon., 9am-10pm Tues.-Thurs., 9am-11pm Fri.-Sat., CH$3,000-6,000, *menú del día* CH$5,900) is a great spot for a quick breakfast of *tostadas con palta* (avocado toast), affordable nutritious lunches, or a specialty filtered coffee matched with a deliciously rich brownie. Live jazz, electronic, and rock bands play in the upstairs bar on weekends.

A Chilean institution, **Emporio La Rosa** (Merced 291, tel. 2/2638 9257, www.emporiolarosa.cl, 9am-9:30pm Sun.-Thurs., 9am-10:30pm Sat.-Sun.) offers the creamiest ice cream in the most interesting flavors. Try an exotic flavor such as cherimoya and orange or tart *maqui* with strawberry. Stop for a coffee, cake, or sandwich too, but expect to wait in line; this place is popular.

BARRIO BELLAVISTA
Chilean

★ **Peumayen** (Constitución 134, www.peumayenchile.cl, 1pm-3pm and 7pm-midnight Tues.-Sat., 1pm-4pm Sun., CH$9,000-14,000), "dream place" in Mapudungun, the Mapuche language, focuses on indigenous Chilean dishes, offering Aymara, Rapa Nui, and Mapuche gastronomy. Dishes feature unfamiliar ingredients: *luche* (seaweed), *piñones* (nuts from the monkey puzzle tree), and *huacatay* (an herb similar to cilantro). Enthusiastic servers speak fluent English to explain this dining revelation; tasting menus allow you to appreciate a wide selection of the dishes.

Exuding slick ambience that wouldn't be out of place in New York, exquisite ★ **Polvo Bar de Vinos** (Constitución 187, tel. 2/2233 128, http://polvobardevinos.cl, 12:30pm-4pm and 7pm-midnight Mon.-Sat., 12:30pm-4pm Sun., CH$12,000-14,000, *menú del día* CH$8,000) is one of the neighborhood's top dining options. Expect creatively presented dishes of sea urchin, roasted pork, and slow-cooked beef that draw on typical Chilean ingredients and preparations at prices far lower than you'd expect. The wine list is similarly impressive, with 30 biodynamic, organic, and natural wines from across Chile by the glass. The sommelier will let you try a couple before you commit.

Argentinean

It's not just the Argentineans who worship meat: See for yourself at **Eladio** (Nueva Providencia 2250, tel. 2/2231 4224, www.eladio.cl, 1pm-midnight Mon.-Sat., 1pm-4pm Sun., CH$10,000-16,000), a popular and inexpensive place to experience the Chilean art of the *asado*. Servers with bow ties move between the grill and your table; you'll want to order a couple of sides with your meat. Try the gently grilled *entrañas* (skirt steak), succulent and lightly salted, or the *bife chorizo* (sirloin strip steak). Locals ask for their meat *a punto* (medium rare) or *medio* (medium)—you'll get a strange look if you want it cooked more.

International

Jardín Mallinkrodt (Mallinkrodt 170, tel. 9/5906 6635, 6pm-2am Tues.-Wed., 6pm-3am Thurs.-Fri., 1pm-3am Sat., 1pm-11pm Sun., CH$6,000-11,000) is one of Bellavista's trendiest dining places: an outdoor patio lined by half a dozen food trucks that serve Chilean *choripanes,* stuffed spicy tortillas, Peruvian tiraditos, and excellent ceviche. The service is helpful and enthusiastic, if somewhat hampered by too few servers, but the sun umbrellas and heaters compensate for whatever the weather throws at you. Choose from the same truck if you want your food to arrive at the same time. There's an excellent array of Chilean craft beer and wine from Chile's most awarded vineyards. In the evening, it's busy with a mix of diners and drinkers.

Burgers

With the best Chilean beers and American-style hamburgers in town, it's no wonder **Uncle Fletch** (Dardignac 192, tel. 2/2777 6477, http://uncle-fletch.com, 12:30pm-midnight Mon.-Wed., 12:30pm-1am Thurs.-Sat., 1pm-4pm Sun., CH$6,000-10,000) is a local favorite. Find 16 *schops* (beers on tap) plus dozens of Chilean and international bottled beers and an extensive range of hamburgers—vegetarian options included. Go with the chef's recommendation: the Blue Cheese Supreme (caramelized onions, blue cheese, and a handmade beef patty), and wash it down with a glass of local beer, either a light Kross Golden or a fuller, hoppier Jester IPA.

BARRIOS BRASIL AND YUNGAY
Chilean

Identifiable by two large barrels above the door, **El Hoyo** (San Vicente 375, tel. 2/689 0339, http://elhoyo.cl, 11am-11pm Mon.-Fri., 11am-8pm Sat., CH$4,500-9,500) became popular with travelers after the late Anthony Bourdain feted their pork dishes, which include *pernil con papas* (boiled ham hock with potatoes) and *arrollada* (cured pork rolled and wrapped with pork skin). El Hoyo is the originator of the *terremoto,* the hyper-sweet combination of *pipeño* (sweet fermented wine), pineapple ice cream, and grenadine.

On the ground floor of swanky Squella Restaurant and barely big enough for half a dozen tables, the informal **Caleta 94** (Ricardo Cumming 94, tel. 2/2699 3059, 11:30am-11:30pm Mon.-Sat., 11:30am-6pm Sun., CH$6,000-10,000) has some of the freshest seafood in the city. The house specialty is live scallops, kept in an aerated concrete pond at the back of the restaurant and eaten either lightly fried or doused in parmesan cheese and baked. The menu changes daily depending on what other seafood they have on hand. Expect abalone ceviche, seafood stews, and simple grilled fish dishes. Get here early, as it's a popular lunch spot.

International

Packed to the rafters with curios, including hood-style hair dryers that serve as lampshades, the ★ **Boulevard Lavaud** (Compañía 2789, tel. 2/2682 5243, http://boulevardlavaud.cl, 9am-1am Mon.-Thurs., 9am-2am Fri.-Sat., CH$6,000-14,000) shares its space with a barbershop that faces the street. Extending deep into the adjoining building, this labyrinthine restaurant offers French fare and a lengthy Chilean wine menu. Pop in for boeuf bourguignon, quiche lorraine, or coffee and a tarte tatin. Reservations are necessary on weekend evenings.

Coffee

The sizeable **Café Forastero** (Huérfanos 2917, tel. 9/7799 9115, www.cafeforastero.cl, 7:30am-9pm Mon.-Fri., 9:30am-9pm Sat.-Sun.) impresses with its setting in a sensitively restored 19th-century mansion, as well as the know-how of its baristas. Brewing options include V60 and Chemex, and they serve cold brew and nitro coffee. Sandwiches and a selection of delicious cakes, many of which are available gluten-free, make this place extra linger-worthy. Grab a chair on their pretty balcony.

PROVIDENCIA

Peruvian

There's a reason the deceptively large **Olan** (Av. Condell 200, tel. 2/2223 9342, www.restaurantolan.com, 1pm-11:45pm Mon.-Sat., 1pm-3:45pm Sun. CH$6,500-9,000) is crammed with business types at lunch: The service is rapid and the Peruvian food affordable and authentic. Dig into the special ceviche, southern ray bream mixed with prawns, or the *lomo saltado* (beef sautéed with vegetables and fries) for a guaranteed tasty lunch or dinner.

Fine Dining

Join Santiago's well-heeled for a glass at **Baco** (Nueva de Lyon 113, tel. 2/2231 4444, http://elbaco.cl, 12:30pm-12:30am Mon.-Sat., 12:30pm-11:30pm Sun., CH$7,000-14,000), an elegant wine bar and bistro serving French dishes and a wide selection of Chilean wine by the glass. Don't miss the punchy Pérez Cruz cabernet franc or the light coastal sauvignon gris from Casa Marin. The menu features gourmet French favorites plus intriguing Chilean classics such as *locos* (sea snails with mayonnaise). Booking ahead is essential.

Oozing contemporary decor and a youthful, classy atmosphere is the eight-table ★ **Ambrosia Bistro** (Nueva de Lyon 99, tel. 2/2233 4303, www.ambrosiabistro.cl, 12:30pm-midnight Mon.-Sat., CH$14,000-16,000). The small menu boasts exceptional food. Feast on lightly seasoned ceviche seeped in grapefruit and ginger, pan-fried hake, or delicate skirt steak fried in butter. Dishes can be ordered in taster sizes, and you can sit at the bar to watch chef Carolina Bazán. Reservations are essential for the evening. There is a more formal version, the critically acclaimed Ambrosia, in Las Condes.

Vegetarian

Decorated with colorful oil paintings, **El Huerto** (Luco 54, tel. 2/2231 4443, www.elhuerto.cl, 12:15pm-11pm Mon.-Wed., 12:15pm-11:30pm Thurs.-Sat., 12:30pm-4:30pm Sun., CH$6,000-8,000, *menú del día* CH$8,900) is a hit among hip young Santiaguinos and tourists alike. This vegetarian restaurant has an interesting array of seaweed ceviche, combining kelp with Peruvian corn, peanuts, and roasted pumpkin, or with cilantro, avocado, and tomato. Lighter bites include quinoa salad bowls and vegan falafels; there's a selection of hearty burritos packed with tasty beans and cheese.

Budget and Light Bites

Snug **Cafétin** (Don Carlos 3185, tel. 2/2880 9608, www.cafetin.cl, 8am-2am Mon.-Fri., 10am-6pm Sat.-Sun.) is a popular place to linger over a coffee or brunch. They have a great selection of cakes (don't miss the cinnamon buns) and specialty coffees. On the weekends, this spot transforms into a bar, with live music and DJs.

The blink-and-you'll-miss-it **Café Triciclo** (Av. Vicuña Mackenna 38, tel. 9/9543 0623, 8am-9pm Mon.-Fri., 10am-8pm Sat.-Sun.) is neatly concealed from the street by a newsstand. It buzzes with customers throughout the day, who'll stop by to sip on über-cool coffee brews in the stone-and-brick upstairs room or on the airy back terrace.

BARRIO ITALIA
Chilean
Down a side street, **Silvestre Bistró** (Caupolicán 511, tel. 9/9156 9974, 1pm-5pm and 8:30pm-1am Tues.-Sat., 12:30pm-4pm Sun., CH$12,000-16,000) is the place to be seen in Barrio Italia, as much for the food as for its bohemian alternative ambience. An antiques-stuffed dining room leads to a quirky garden filled with chipped sinks overflowing with plants, as jazz music provides a relaxed backdrop. Farm-to-table meets foraging in the streamlined menu, with dishes such as flank steak or wild octopus served with millet or seasonal vegetables, plus an exceptional brunch menu.

International
At the über-trendy **Bao Bar** (Manuel Montt 925, tel. 2/3267 4334, http://baobar.cl, 6pm-1am Mon.-Thurs., 6pm-2:30am Fri., 12:30pm-2:30am Sat., CH$2,500-6,000), choose from a delicious selection of tapas, ranging from Spanish tortilla and tuna tartare to pork *tonkatsu* with chimichurri sauce and steamed *bao* buns stuffed with osso buco or pulled pork. Leave space for the creamy crème brûlée or hang around for specialty gin cocktails—they're half price before 9pm. With dim lighting and snug nooks, it's easy to chat for hours.

Budget and Light Bites
Dainty cast-iron furniture lines the checkerboard-tiled patio of pretty **Café de la Candelaría** (Av. Italia 1449, tel. 2/2880 4127, http://cafedelacandelaria.cl, 10:30am-9pm Mon.-Sat., 10am-8pm Sun., CH$4,000-8,000), deep inside one of Barrio Italia's trademark galleries. This is the perfect place to nurse a

cup of chai tea. Affordable lunches of *charquican* (dried meat) made from pork heart or Thai curry with quinoa sit alongside sandwiches and cakes. It's a fine place for breakfast, particularly for an extensive brunch, with fruit, juice, eggs, granola, and croissants (CH$9,500 weekends); a smaller selection is offered during the week.

Serving five types of hot chocolate from across South America, **Xoco Por Ti** (Av. Italia 1634, tel. 9/5774 2673, http://xocoporti.com, 11:30am-8:30pm daily) is the ultimate café hangout for chocoholics. Options range from 55 percent cocoa to 100 percent, accompanied by various vegetable milks. Hot chocolate is the star, but ice cream is a close second. There's a cute patio.

LAS CONDES
Chilean
With slick decor and its own brand of cookbooks, **Margo** (Goyenechea 3000, Barrio El Golf, tel. 2/2385 0178, http://margo.cl, 8:30am-11:30pm Mon.-Fri., 9:30am-11:30pm Sat., 9:30am-10:30pm Sun., CH$7,000-12,000) is the third installation of a successful family-run chain. Pumpkin salads lavished with serrano ham and a balsamic vinegar glaze accompany filet steak on mushroom rice, plus a plethora of vegetarian, pasta, and fish dishes, on the extensive menu, which draws inspiration from across Chile and beyond.

Argentinean
Argentineans know how to cook their steak, so it's no surprise that Argentinean-run **Happening** (Av. Apoquindo 3090, Barrio El Golf, tel. 2/2362 1092, http://happening.cl, 12:30pm-12:30am Mon.-Sat., CH$14,000-20,000) is one of the city's top *asado* (barbecue) restaurants. Fine leather place mats and menu holders match the classy coffee-colored decor, with waistcoated servers providing recommendations in English on the best cuts. The *ojo de bife* (rib eye) or *entraña* (skirt steak) are reliable options. The extensive wine list covers the country's best vineyards.

Italian

Started in 2001 as a five-table restaurant, ★ **Pizzería Tiramisú** (Goyenechea 3141, Barrio El Golf, tel. 2/2519 4900, www.tiramisu.cl, 12:45pm-4pm and 7pm-midnight daily, CH$7,000-12,000) today occupies a large, jumbled space with dingy but cozy rooms reminiscent of a tiny Italian eatery and modern high tables complete with blaring music and powerful spotlights. The red-and-white checked tablecloths hint at the restaurant's humble roots, and the quality and authenticity of its pizzas and pastas hasn't changed.

GREATER SANTIAGO
Chilean

"Whimsical" is the best way to describe the dinosaur murals at ★ **La Diana** (Av. Arturo Prat 435, tel. 2/2632 8823, http://ladiana.cl, 1pm-1am Tues.-Sat., 1pm-6:30pm Sun. summer, 1pm-1am Fri.-Sat., 1pm-6:30pm Sun. winter, CH$6,000-11,000), whose nooks encourage lingering and make it a favorite among locals. It's in a former monastery and adjoins an old-school amusement arcade, which adds to its kooky charm. It specializes in seafood but also has burgers, salads, and an extensive liquor, cocktail, and wine menu, making it a great spot day or night. Be sure to book ahead for dinner.

Italian

Few restaurants in Santiago can match the history of ★ **La Fabbrica** (Av. Ossa 123, La Reina, tel. 2/2830 6208, http://la-fabbrica.cl, 12:30pm-midnight Sun.-Thurs., 12:30pm-1am Fri.-Sat., CH$5,000-8,000), housed in a building that dates from the 1920s in the southern neighborhood of La Reina. Serving authentic Italian cuisine (the *quattro stagioni* pizza and *tortino de cioccolato* are to die for) alongside an excellent selection of Chilean wines, La Fabbrica is the home of the legendary Club de Jazz de Santiago, a live music institution.

Accommodations

Santiago's higher-end accommodations are concentrated in bohemian Barrio Lastarria. International luxury and business chains such as the W Santiago, Doubletree by Hilton, and the Novotel are mostly in Las Condes and Vitacura. Budget and midrange options cluster around Providencia and Barrio Brasil. Take caution while walking in Brasil at night.

Thanks to the city's excellent metro and bus network, most accommodations are within easy access of the center. Prices tend to drop during January-February, when most travelers are on the coast and in the south of the country.

BARRIOS BELLAS ARTES AND LASTARRIA
CH$40,000-60,000

Thanks to details like a full coat of arms on display, **Hotel Foresta** (Subercaseaux 353, tel. 2/2639 6261, http://forestahotel.cl, CH$54,000 d) feels old-fashioned compared to the surrounding boutique hotels, but it's a solid bet. The standard rooms are suites, with a living area and double bed included. For a quieter sleep, ask for a room facing away from the main road, at no extra cost. The hotel is in a great location across from Cerro Santa Lucía. There's also private parking.

Over CH$80,000

A five-minute stroll across the river from Parque Forestal, **Apart Hotel B Santiago** (Bellavista 234, tel. 2/2732 6229, http://aparthotelb.cl, CH$100,000 d) is a great choice for self-catering, as all 10 bedrooms include a full kitchen. Breakfast is included in the rate. There's a pleasant outdoor terrace at the back of the hotel. Rates include IVA.

You can't miss the 70-room **Hotel Cumbres** (Lastarria 299, tel. 2/2496 9000, www.cumbreslastarria.com, CH$130,000 d) and its eye-catching geometric white exterior. The modern rooms are artistically decorated, combining grandeur with minimalist design. A small gym and on-site Mediterranean restaurant mean you don't have to leave, although the location on the main street of Barrio Lastarria will tempt you out. There's a rooftop pool and bar, plus slick communal spaces.

Steps from Cerro Santa Lucía, **Hotel Magnolia** (Huérfanos 539, tel. 2/2664 4043, www.hotelmagnolia.cl, CH$167,000 d) is in a striking neo-Gothic mansion where dramatic spiral staircases contrast with a modern extension. The 42 rooms are modern and light-filled thanks to large windows. Most rooms are quiet, but upper-floor rooms provide the most peaceful sleep. Views from the rooftop bar across the hill are breathtaking.

The light, airy rooms of the boutique **Hotel Altiplanico Bellas Artes** (Santo Domingo 526, tel. 2/3224 2371, www.altiplanico.cl, CH$170,000 d) match the elegance of the 1918 four-story building, thanks to slick open-plan bath suites with marble walls and large windows. Rooms on the 3rd floor have small balconies overlooking the road. For park views, opt for one of the three superiors (CH$200,000), or six suites (CH$220,000). Bilingual staff can advise on tours and dining options.

Within the bustle of Barrio Lastarria, exclusive **The Singular** (Merced 294, tel. 2/2306 8820, http://thesingular.com, CH$277,000 d) is possibly Santiago's finest boutique hotel. Sumptuous Louis XV furniture contrasts with modern fittings in sophisticated rooms, reflecting the artistic vibe of the area. A rooftop pool and spa are available to guests. It's worth dining in the restaurant or checking out the views from the top-floor bar—both of which are open to the public.

Named after an acclaimed Chilean architect, **Luciano K** (Merced 84, tel. 2/2620 0900, www.lucianokhotel.com, CH$158,000 d) is a stylish art deco hotel overlooking Parque Forestal. Its 38 rooms feature plush king-size beds and modern bath suites. A stunning rooftop bar—also open to the public—wows with kaleidoscopic floor tiles and striking views across the neighborhood. It's the perfect place to relax with a pisco sour.

BARRIO BELLAVISTA
Over CH$80,000

Set in a stylish restored 1930s mock-Tudor mansion, the boutique 15-room **The Aubrey** (Constitución 299, tel. 2/2940 2800, http://theaubrey.com, CH$173,000 d) is one of Barrio Bellavista's most sought-after accommodations. Expect exposed hardwood floors, kooky-chic design elements, and large attractive rooms. Service is exceptionally attentive. With pretty patios and a swimming pool, this is a tranquil oasis within striking distance of all of Bellavista's most notable sights.

BARRIO BRASIL
CH$40,000-60,000

With high-ceilinged hallways and a plethora of terraces and seating areas, the spacious ★ **Happy House Hostel** (Moneda 1829, tel. 2/2688 4849, http://happyhousehostel. com, CH$16,000 dorm, CH$40,000 d shared bath, CH$50,000 d private bath) is one of the city's top budget options. Its 28 rooms in a restored mansion are sizeable and attractively furnished, while the outdoor terrace with swimming pool and barbecue area is welcome in summer. Breakfast is ample, and there's a kitchen for guest use.

The building might look tired from the outside, but the rambling **La Casa Roja** (Agustinas 2113, tel. 2/2695 0600, http://lacasaroja.cl, CH$20,000 dorm, CH$40,000 d shared bath, CH$45,000 d private bath) carries its years well. Rooms are on two floors. The size of the kitchen is like a professional restaurant. There's even a dining room perfect for a banquet. A huge back garden contains a large pool and an outdoor bar.

Over CH$80,000

The former residence of Don Miguel Zañarta, one of the ministers who signed the Chilean proclamation of independence, has been converted to the regal **Casa Zañartu** (Compañía de Jesús 1520, tel. 2/2697 4590, www. casazanartu.cl, CH$89,000 d). This three-story 19th-century mansion has 18 elegantly furnished bedrooms dressed in sumptuous antique furniture and modern baths. Original tiled floors and gilt-framed portraits of the country's presidents add a splash of history.

PROVIDENCIA

Under CH$25,000

In a large colonial-style house on a quiet backstreet, ★ **Castillo Surfista Hostel** (Maria Luisa Santander 329, tel. 2/2893 3350, CH$8,000 dorm, CH$20,000 d shared bath) has good vibes thanks to a relaxed owner and friendly resident dog. Expect a hearty breakfast of waffles and a quality mattress in a cozy room. Room 3 is the largest double and has its own balcony. Guests have use of a large patio for barbecues and a shared kitchen. The owner can recommend surfing spots across Chile.

CH$40,000-60,000

The eight rooms at the 1940s town house **Vilafranca Petit Hotel** (Pérez Valenzuela 1650, tel. 2/235 1413, http://vilafranca.cl, CH$50,000 d) speak of a bygone era. Rooms are freshly decorated and full of character, with heavy wooden furniture and a charming living room with a library. There's a sunny courtyard for breakfast. Rooms are quiet, offering a reprieve from the busy roads nearby.

Claiming to be the oldest hostel in Santiago, labyrinthine ★ **Hostal Río Amazonas** (Av. Vicuña Mackenna 47, tel. 2/2635 1631, www. hostalrioamazonas.cl, CH$51,000 d) has been a favorite since the late 1990s. The 31 spacious rooms in this higgledy-piggledy mock-Tudor mansion feature sturdy wooden furniture.

Rooms are quiet, despite the location on a main road. Single-occupancy rooms are small but serviceable. The kitchen is too tiny for the number of guests, but the rates are cheap and the owners are lovely.

Over CH$80,000

Just a 10-minute walk southeast from Plaza Italia, the charming **Quiral Hotel Boutique** (Av. Condell 376, tel. 2/3221 7690, www. quiralhotelboutique.com, CH$80,000 d) blends comfort and tranquility in a restored neoclassical townhouse. Gleaming wood parquet floors and creaky antique furniture provide a place to wind down, aided by the welcoming attention of the hotel staff. A shady back garden is the cherry on top.

For a Chilean wine experience without leaving your hotel, lodge at sustainable ★ **Carménère Eco Hotel** (Santander 292, tel. 2/2993 5040, www.hotelcarmenere.com, CH$179,000 dh). Solar panels and a vegetable garden are just some of their eco-friendly credentials. Chilean wine tastings are held in the wine cellar beneath the main house. Five rooms take the names of the country's wine valleys and feature elegant antique furniture and 600-thread-count Egyptian cotton sheets. Book well in advance.

BARRIO ITALIA

Over CH$80,000

Engineers Eduardo and Catalina have effortlessly created ★ **Casa Sur Charming Hotel** (Eduardo Hyatt 527, tel. 2/2502 7170, http:// casasurchile.com, CH$113,000 d), an oasis of calm in up-and-coming Barrio Italia. The hotel has just six bright and airy bedrooms, designed after the owners' international travels, with high-thread-count cotton sheets, powerful hot showers, and an extensive breakfast of fruit, eggs, granola, and fresh coffee. For a small but sunny balcony, opt for the deluxe room (CH$147,000). It's hard to find fault with this charm-packed boutique hotel. Book well in advance.

Information and Services

VISITOR INFORMATION

SERNATUR and the municipal government have a number of **tourist information points** across the city. Both the municipal and national services have English-speaking personnel and can provide good-quality maps, many of which include a metro map.

The most central tourist office is the municipal-run **Oficina de Turismo** (Plaza de Armas s/n, tel. 2/2713 6745, www.santiagocapital.cl, 9am-6pm Mon.-Fri., 10am-4pm Sat.-Sun.). The Oficina de Turismo also has a **smaller booth** (tel. 2/2386 7185, 9am-6pm Mon.-Thurs., 9am-5pm Fri.) next to the Plaza Neptuno fountains at the southern entrance to Cerro Santa Lucía. Staff at both locations can advise on destinations in the city, and there are plenty of maps.

The central **SERNATUR Oficina Turística** (Av. Providencia 1550, tel. 2/2731 8336, 9am-6pm Mon.-Fri., 10am-2pm Sat.) and the smaller **Oficina Turística Centro Cultural Gabriela Mistral** (GAM, Av. Alameda 227, tel. 2/2731 8627, 9am-6pm Mon.-Fri., 10am-2pm Sat.) can supply regional maps as well as information about destinations elsewhere in the country. They also have an office in the **airport** (tel. 2/2731 8364, 9am-6pm Mon.-Fri., 9am-5pm Sat.).

National Parks

The office of **CONAF** (Bulnes 285, tel. 22/2663 0125, www.conaf.cl) can provide information on parks throughout the country.

TELEPHONE AND INTERNET

The city code for Santiago is 2, which precedes the seven- or eight-digit local number. If you're calling from a mobile phone, 0 must be added before the initial 2. Call centers are few, so you're better off getting a local *chip* (SIM card), which can be purchased from Entel, Claro, or Movistar, the main cellular

network companies. A 3G or 4G data connection is common throughout the city. Hotels, hostels, and guesthouses tend to have free Wi-Fi with a fast connection.

Emergency Numbers

Dial 103 for an ambulance, 132 for the fire department, and 133 for police. Few operators speak English, and they will require a street name, house number, and neighborhood.

SPANISH-LANGUAGE COURSES

Chileans have their own distinct way of speaking, which is possibly why Santiago isn't considered one of the main Spanish-learning hubs in Latin America. Expect to pay upward of US$190 per week for four hours of group instruction per day; longer courses are often cheaper. Private lessons are double this price. Packages including hostel or apartment accommodations, or a homestay with a Chilean family, can also be arranged for an additional fee. Below are a few options for Spanish-language instruction.

- **Tandem Santiago** (Triana 853, Providencia, tel. 2/2364 241, www.tandemsantiago.cl)
- **Bridge Chile** (Los Leones 439, Providencia, tel. 2/2233 4356, U.S./Canada tel. 303/4955 963, www.bridgechile.com)
- **COINED** (Paseo Bulnes 79, Oficina 60, tel. 2/2222 6371, U.S. tel. 800/8979 631, http://coined.cl)
- **Escuela Bellavista** (Arzobispo 605, Providencia, tel. 2/2732 3443, http://escuelabellavista.cl)

MONEY

Most of Santiago's shops, restaurants, and hotels accept credit cards, although you will need cash for public transport, taxis, and smaller purchases. ATMs are abundant, although most collect a surcharge on foreign cards. Generally, withdrawals are free if you use a bank on the same network as your card.

Banco Internacional (Moneda 810, Downtown; La Pastora 128, El Golf) generally doesn't charge a fee; **Scotiabank** (Moneda 906) has plenty of branches and doesn't charge fees for most cards. **Banco de Chile** charges the biggest fee: up to CH$7,000. It's wise to stock up on cash in Santiago, as banks that don't charge a fee can be hard to find elsewhere.

Most banks will exchange dollars for pesos. **Exchange houses** are in the Downtown area, along **Calle Agustinas** (between Calles Bandera and Ahumada). Most malls and large shopping centers have exchange offices. The airport generally offers the poorest conversion rate. For large transactions, you may be required to show your passport.

VISAS AND OFFICIALDOM

To extend your visa beyond the 90 days granted upon arrival, it's easiest to leave the country for either Argentina or Peru and return the next day, a practice known as "border hopping." However, a cheaper method is to visit the **Departamento de Extranjería y Migración** (Matucana 1223 or Fanor Velasco 56, tel. 600/4863 000, www.extranjeria.gob.cl, 8:30am-2pm Mon.-Fri.). You'll need to make a reservation for an appointment online (http://reservahora.extranjeria.gob.cl). Take your passport (the original and a photocopy), and the PDI slip given to you at the border, plus US$100 in the equivalent pesos.

If you have lost your PDI slip, which is required for leaving the country, you can get another one for free at a different office of the **Departamento de Extranjería y Migración** (Eleuterio Ramírez 852, 8am-2pm Mon.-Fri.); take your passport.

HEALTH

Tap water is drinkable in Santiago, although it's wise to drink it in small doses for a couple of days to give your body time to adjust. Santiago has the highest quality—and most expensive—medical services in the country, and it's very easy to get an appointment to see a doctor. Emergency medical care is of a very high quality.

Hospitals, Clinics, and Pharmacies

Private hospital and clinic **Clínica Alemana** (Vitacura 5951, Vitacura, tel. 2/2210 1111, www.clinicaalemana.cl) is highly regarded and excellent in an emergency, but it's very expensive. **Clínica Santa María** (Av. Santa María 500, Providencia, tel. 2/2913 0000, www.clinicasantamaria.cl) can provide swift assistance in an emergency.

The semiprivate **La Católica** (Marcoleta 367, Lastarria, tel. 2/2354 3000, http://redsalud.uc.cl) offers more affordable care. The best public hospital is **Hospital Clínico Universidad de Chile** (Av. Santos de Durmont 999, Independencia, tel. 2/2978 8000, www.ucchristus.cl), which offers excellent and even cheaper health care.

NEWSPAPERS

The Santiago Times (http://santiagotimes.cl) is the only English-language newspaper in the city. For satirical takedowns of Chilean and world politicians, *The Clinic* (www.theclinic.cl) is an entertaining weekly magazine. The very right-wing *El Mercurio* (http://digital.elmercurio.com) offers international news along with business, culture, and travel coverage. *La Tercera* (www.latercera.com), a conservative tabloid, is its closest competitor.

LAUNDRY

There are laundry services Downtown at **Bilbao Express** (Merced 712, tel. 2/2633 0518, http://bilbaoexpress.cl, 9:30am-7:30pm Mon.-Fri., 9:30am-1:30pm Sat.). **Prontomatic** (www.prontomatic.cl) has several laundry shops around the city, including at Diagonal Paraguay 168 (tel. 2/2799 4055,

9am-2:30pm and 3pm-9pm Mon.-Thurs., 10am-2:30pm and 3pm-8pm Fri.-Sun.), a block south of the Universidad Católica metro stop on Línea 1.

In Providencia, in the Jumbo supermarket at the Costanera Center mall, there's a location of **5asec** (Av. Vitacura and Nueva Tobalaba, Local 1121, tel. 9/4407 1942, www.5asec.cl, 8:30am-9:30pm daily). It's near the Tobalaba metro stop on Línea 1. Near the Santa Ana metro stop is **La Plancheria** (Compañía 1788, tel. 2/2702 8151, 7:30am-8:30pm Mon.-Fri., 10am-7pm Sat.).

MAIL

The **Correos Central** (Plaza de Armas 989, www.correos.cl, 9am-8:30pm Mon.-Fri., 10am-2pm Sat.) is the central post office for Santiago—worth a visit for its beautiful architecture. Check the website for other locations around the city. Postal services are excruciatingly slow for both domestic and international mail; package delivery times of over three months are not uncommon.

FedEx (Av. Providencia 2519, Providencia, tel. 2/2361 6000, www.fedex.com, 10am-1pm and 2pm-5pm Mon.-Fri.) offers reliable domestic and international shipping.

Transportation

GETTING THERE
Air
The modern **Aeropuerto Internacional Arturo Merino Benítez** (SCL, tel. 2/2690 1752, www.nuevopudahuel.cl), also known as **Aeropuerto Nuevo Pudahuel**, is 16km northwest of central Santiago. It's the largest in the country although it's small compared to most capital cities. A new international terminal is expected to be complete in 2020. The expansion will increase the number of gates from 16 to 67.

For onward domestic travel, **LATAM** (Huérfanos 926, tel. 600/5262 000, www.latam.com) has the widest selection and most frequent flights, although **Sky Airline** (Huérfanos 81, tel. 2/2632 9449, www.skyairline.com) is a close second. Budget carrier **JetSmart** (tel. 600/600 1311, http://jetsmart.com) has limited departures but offers the cheapest prices.

Check-in desks for national and international flights are on the 2nd floor of the airport. Various bars, restaurants, and coffee shops are in the departures and arrivals halls, as well as inside the terminal. Most are closed midnight-6:30am. There is a currency exchange shop in the arrivals hall, on the first floor of the building.

International carriers, including LATAM, Air Canada, American, Delta, United, Avianca, British Airways, Iberia, Copa, KLM, Air France, and Alitalia connect the Americas and Europe with Santiago.

The following **rental car companies** are in the arrivals hall of the airport: **Europcar** (tel. 2/2432 8420, www.europcar.cl, 24 hr daily), **Econorent** (tel. 2/2299 8920, http://econorent.cl, 24 hr daily), **Hertz** (tel. 2/2360 8714, www.hertz.com, 6:30am-midnight daily), **Sixt** (tel. 2/2513 6000, www.sixt.cl, 7am-midnight Sun.-Mon., 24 hr Tues.-Sat.), and **Alamo** (tel. 2/3601 132, www.alamo.com, 6:30am-11pm daily).

AIRPORT TRANSFERS
A taxi should cost CH$20,000-25,000 for destinations in central Santiago, and should take 30-60 minutes, depending on traffic. The main taxi services at the airport are **Taxi Official** (tel. 2/2601 9880, http://taxioficial.cl), **Delfos** (tel. 2/2913 8800, http://transferdelfos.com), and **TransVIP** (tel. 2/2677 3000, www.transvip.cl). Note that TransVIP can be unreliable. You'll pay a fixed price at the counters just after customs or inside the arrivals hall for all three services; you'll then be provided with a receipt that you give to the taxi driver.

Airport Taxi Scam

Once you get through customs at the airport, you will be approached by various taxi services offering to take you into town. Accepting a ride from one of these services is not recommended, as there is an increasing incidence of unlicensed drivers posing as official taxi drivers, complete with official-seeming documents. Although robberies are rare, it's not worth the risk: Exorbitant fares are often expected, with travelers being forced to pay CH$150,000 and above in some cases—for a ride that should cost only CH$25,000.

Be aware of scammers calling your name if you have prebooked an official taxi—they have seen your name written on a board by the official company. The person will direct you to a cab, where you'll be required to pay a second time for the trip.

To be safe, book directly with the main taxi firms recommended in this guide. If you're accosted by a driver without a sign with your name or who can't prove their credentials, head to the desk of the taxi service to speak with an official employee of the company, who will direct you to the official vehicles.

A queue for taxi services operated by each company is outside the airport and accessed through the Door 3 exit. **Miles and Smiles** (tel. 9/9148 2832, http://milesandsmiles.cl) is a reliable private taxi service but must be arranged in advance. Another reliable option is English-speaking Roberto of **RS Transit** (tel. 9/6366 1350).

In addition to private taxis, Delfos and TransVIP run **airport shuttle services** (CH$7,000). These companies also offer an inexpensive option to return to the airport—but be aware that your shuttle may pick up more passengers after you, which can mean that the journey takes more than an hour. Make a reservation for this service at least one day in advance.

Buses to the city pull up just outside the terminal. These include blue **Centropuerto buses** (tel. 2/2601 9883, www.centropuerto.cl), which leave every 10 minutes (6am-11:30pm) during the day and every 30 minutes (11:30pm-5:30am) overnight. They cost CH$1,800 each way and take around 40 minutes to reach central Santiago. For the return journey to the airport, these buses depart every 10 minutes 5:55am-11:15pm from an unmarked stop at the Plazoleta Central, next to the Plazoleta Los Heróes (southern side of Av. Alameda), above the Los Heróes Metro stop.

TurBus (http://turbus.cl) runs daily airport service with departures every 10 minutes 5am-midnight daily, and every 30 minutes 12:30am-4:30am daily. Buses stop at Terminal Alameda (Av. Alameda 3750). From the terminal, it's another 15 minutes via Línea 1 of the metro into the city center.

Bus

Santiago has four main bus terminals, all clustered south of Parque Quinta Normal on Avenida Alameda. Bus fares fluctuate depending on the day of the week and the season, spiking over long public holidays. Competition among bus companies is fierce and fares can often be found for lower than those quoted in this guide.

TERMINAL SANTIAGO

The **Terminal Santiago** (Av. Alameda 3850, tel. 2/2376 1750), also known as the **Terminal de Buses Sur,** has arrivals from southern and eastern destinations as well as international destinations. The closest metro station is Universidad de Santiago on Línea 1.

Buses to this terminal arrive from **Chillán** (every 30 min, 5.5hr, CH$7,000/CH$11,000), **Concepción** (every 30 min, 7hr, CH$8,000/CH$15,000), **Temuco** (every 30 min, 8pm-3pm daily, 8hr, CH$10,000/CH$18,000), **Villarrica** (at least 9 daily, 9hr, CH$15,000/CH$35,000), **Valdivia** (several daily, 10hr, CH$14,000/CH$18,000), and **Puerto Montt** (hourly, 12hr, CH$20,000/CH$25,000).

TERMINAL ALAMEDA

With a fleet of modern buses, **Tur Bus** (tel. 2/822 7500, http://turbus.cl) and **Pullman Bus** (no phone, www.pullmanbus.cl) have a joint terminal next door to the Terminal Santiago called the **Terminal Alameda** (Av. Alameda 3750). This terminal serves destinations across the country, including **Valparaíso** or **Viña del Mar** (every 15 min, 2hr, CH$3,000), **La Serena** (every 30 min, 6hr, CH$13,000/CH$18,000, premium seat CH$22,000), **Concepción** (hourly, 7hr, CH$13,000/CH$18,000, premium seat CH$24,000), and **Puerto Montt** (6 daily, 12hr, CH$25,000/CH$31,000, premium seat CH$50,000).

The **TurBus** airport service arrives departs this terminal every 10 minutes 5am-midnight, every 30 minutes 12:30am-4:30am daily.

TERMINAL SAN BORJA

Buses from northern and western destinations head to **Terminal San Borja** (San Borja 235, tel. 2/2776 0645). The closest metro station is Estación Central on Línea 1. Buses to this terminal arrive from **Valparaíso** or **Viña del Mar** (every 10 min, 2hr, CH$3,000), **La Serena** (every 30 min, 6hr, CH$10,000/CH$15,000, premium seat CH$20,000), **Copiapó** (hourly, 12hr, CH$14,000/CH$18,000, premium seat CH$33,000), **Antofagasta** (hourly, 20hr, CH$31,000/CH$60,000), **San Pedro de Atacama** (several daily, 24hr, CH$25,000/CH$50,000), **Iquique** (several daily, 24hr, CH$38,000/CH$51,000), and **Arica** (several daily, 30hr, CH$31,000/CH$48,000). Departures for local destinations include Casablanca (hourly, 1.5hr, CH$3,000) and Pomaire (75min, CH$1,700), the latter with **Autobuses Melipilla** (tel. 2/2776 2060).

TERMINAL PAJARITOS

The most frequent arrivals from and departures for **Valparíso** and **Viña del Mar** leave from **Terminal Pajaritos** (Av. Gral. Oscar Bonilla 5600). Routes from this terminal can sometimes be faster, as it's away from the traffic along Avenida Alameda. The Tur Bus airport bus stops here on its route from the Terminal Alameda to the airport.

AIRPORT BUSES

Some of the buses from the other three terminals pick up and drop off at the **Terrapuerto Los Heróes** (Jiménez 21, tel. 2/2420 009, metro station Los Heróes on Línea 1), just around the corner from the Plazoleta Central, where the blue **Centropuerto buses** (tel. 2/2601 9883, www.centropuerto.cl) for the airport depart every 10 minutes 5:55am-11:15pm daily. Other buses from the airport are operated by Tur Bus from the Terminal Alameda.

GETTING AROUND

Walking

Walking around Downtown Santiago and among nearby neighborhoods Barrios Bellas Artes, Italia, and Bellavista can be a great way to get to know the city. Many streets Downtown have been pedestrianized. Intersections are the safest places to cross; you can rely on traffic stopping at red lights, although be aware that vehicles can generally still turn even if pedestrians are walking—and many won't stop for you.

Biking

Santiago's fearless drivers make the city less than ideal for cyclists, although there are a growing number of cycle paths. The government has installed orange bikes docked in racks across the city; a Chilean ID card is required to use them.

On Sunday, stretches of Santiago's busiest streets welcome cyclists, pedestrians, and runners thanks to the **Ciclo Recreovia project** (www.ciclorecreovia.cl). Predetermined roads bar vehicle traffic 9am-2pm, including stretches of Calle Andrés Bello (from Tobalaba to the Museo de Bellas Artes) and Calle Monjitas and Calle Catedral (from the Bellas Arts metro stop until Ruta 5).

La Bicicleta Verde (Loreto 6, Recoleta, tel. 2/2570 9939, http://labicicletaverde.com,

Metro de Santiago

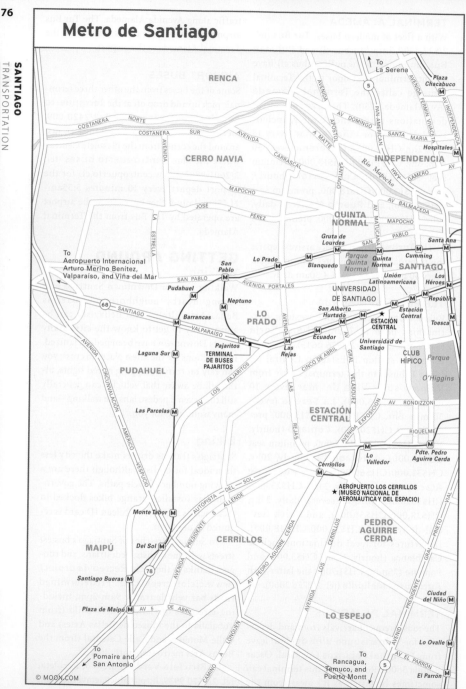

© MOON.COM

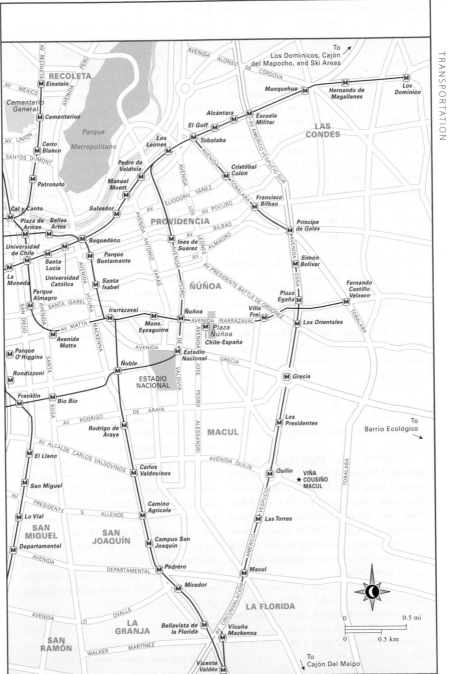

9am-6pm daily) operates cycling tours around the city and offers bike rentals (half day from CH$5,000).

Metro

The **Metro de Santiago** (tel. 600/600 9292, http://metro.cl) is an efficient, if crowded, underground transportation system, with six lines offering a hassle-free means of getting around the city. It is the most extensive line in South America, measuring 100km. For most visitors, **Línea 1,** which passes beneath Avenidas Alameda and Providencia, is the most useful. **Línea 6** connects with Línea 1 at Baquedano (on Plaza Italia) and takes you to the Plaza de Armas and Parque Quinta Normal. Download a metro map to your cell phone or pick up a city map from the tourist information center; network maps are few once you enter the metro.

A rechargeable **Tarjeta BIP** (http://tarjetabip.cl) is required to ride the metro. The card costs CH$1,500 and can be purchased from one of the booths in the metro. It can be shared between more than one person by passing it back across the turnstile after the first person has passed through. If you're only staying for a short period, you may prefer to buy single-use tickets, which are fed into the turnstiles and swallowed; neither the BIP nor the single-use ticket is required to exit the metro.

Trains run 5:30am-11pm Monday-Friday, 6:30am-11:35pm Saturday, and 8am-11pm Sunday. Some lines have slightly earlier closing times. Fares depend on the time of day. Peak fares, called *horario punta* (7am-9am and 6pm-8pm), cost CH$780. Midday fares, or *horario valle,* cost CH$700; low-period fares, *horario baja* (early morning and late night), cost CH$650.

To add money to your card, there are machines that accept credit and debit cards as well as booths where you can pay cash. You can also add to your card in affiliated convenience stores that have a BIP sign in the window.

Bus

Santiago's excellent network of buses offers the speediest way to destinations out of the center that aren't near a metro stop. Buses run 24 hours daily. Destinations are marked on signs in the front window of the vehicle, and the route is defined by the bus's number. The "Directions" feature of Google Maps offers the best means of identifying the route you need.

Santiago buses are operated by **Transantiago** (http://transantiago.cl). To ride, you need a **Tarjeta BIP** (http://tarjetabip.cl), a refillable card that allows you to travel on both buses and the metro. The card must be pressed against the ticket reader when you board a bus. If you're traveling on more than one bus or on the bus and metro in the space of two hours, you will be charged a single fare, which costs CH$650-700, depending on the time of day. The Tarjeta BIP can only be purchased at a metro station, not on a bus; the card costs CH$1,550. Some convenience stores sell cards (for CH$2,800) and can refill cards, indicated by a BIP sign. Metro stations also offer the card refill service.

Taxi

Yellow-roofed taxis have meters that start at CH$300 and generally charge an additional CH$130 per minute (or per 200 meters, whichever is first). Make sure they turn the meter on *("ponga el taxímetro, por favor").* If you're traveling a long distance, like to the airport, agree on a fixed rate before getting into the cab. Watch your money carefully when you pay; it's not uncommon for drivers to claim you paid with a fake bill—when they've actually swapped in a fake bill themselves. Most locals use either Uber or EasyTaxi apps instead of flagging a taxi off the street. Note that Uber remains illegal in Chile and passengers are not insured if there is an accident. Tipping taxi drivers is not common.

Driving

Driving around Santiago, with its furious traffic and even more furious drivers, is not for the faint of heart. Santiago has the cheapest **car rentals** in the country; offices are scattered across the city. There are also several companies at the airport. Companies with offices in the city include:

- **Europcar** (Goyenechea 3051, tel. 2/2334 6460, www.europcar.cl, 8am-1pm and 2pm-6pm Mon.-Fri.)

- **Econorent** (Isidora Goyenechea 2897, tel. 2/2299 894, http://econorent.cl, 8am-8pm Mon.-Fri., 9am-7pm Sat., 9am-7pm Sun.)

- **Hertz** (Av. Bello 1469, tel. 2/2360 8617, www.hertz.com, 8am-8pm Mon.-Fri., 8am-6pm Sat.-Sun.)

- **Alamo** (Av. Bilbao 2856, tel. 2/2225 8524, www.alamo.com, 9am-9pm Mon.-Fri., 9am-7pm Sat.-Sun.)

- **Seelmann** (Dublé Almeyda 1506, tel. 2/2346 3500, www.seelmann.cl, 8am-8pm Mon.-Fri., 9am-4pm Sat., car drop-off available)

- **Sixt** (Av. Bilbao 2245, tel. 2/2513 6000, www.sixt.cl, 9am-6pm Mon.-Fri., car drop-off available)

Tolls for the biggest highways in Santiago are charged to a device attached to your rental car's windshield. These charges are occasionally covered by the rental company, although this is not always the case; you may be required to pay a set fee. Confirm this when picking up your vehicle.

Tours

The tour agency **Miles and Smiles** (tel. 9/9148 2832, http://milesandsmiles.cl) operates private walking tours within the city. They can also organize private transfers and tours to destinations outside the city, including vineyards and ski resorts, and to the coast in Valparaíso.

Turistik (inside the Municipal Oficina de Turismo, Plaza de Armas, tel. 2/2820 1000, www.turistik.com) operates double-decker

hop-on/hop-off buses (9:30am-6pm daily, CH$23,000 adults, CH$11,500 children) around Santiago. They also run trips to ski resorts, wineries, and Valparaíso.

ONWARD TRAVEL

From **Terminal Santiago** (Av. Alameda 3850, tel. 2/2376 1750), there are at least five daily **buses** for Mendoza, Argentina (9hr, CH$21,000/CH$26,000). These buses are operated by **El Rápido Internacional** (no phone, www.elrapidoint.com.ar), **Andesmar** (no phone, www.andesmarchile.cl), and **Buses Nevada Internacional** (tel. 2/2764 1958).

Most international departures leave from **Terminal Los Héroes** (Jiménez 21, tel. 2/2420 0009). **Buses Ahumada** (tel. 2/2784 2519, http://busesahumada.cl) has one daily bus for Mendoza at 9am. Cheaper and faster **minibuses** to Mendoza (7hr, CH$20,000) and are operated by **Chi Ar Autos** (tel. 2/7760 048) and **Radio Movil** (Argentina tel. 0800/122 282). From Mendoza, there are connections onward in Argentina and to Paraguay, Brazil, and Uruguay.

Also departing from the Terminal Los Héroes are buses operated by Andesmar that leave at 8:45pm Tuesday-Sunday for **Bariloche, Argentina** (19.5hr, CH$40,000/ CH$50,000), via Osorno. There are nine weekly buses to **Lima, Peru** (54hr, CH$65,000), operated by Andesmar, **Cruz del Sur** (tel. 2/2778 7872), and **Ormeño** (tel. 2/7793 443, http://grupo-ormeno.com.pe). Buses from Ormeño also leave at 10am Friday for Guayaquil, Ecuador, continuing to Quito and to Bogota, Colombia.

EGA (http://ega.com.uy) runs weekly buses from Terminal Los Héroes to **Montevideo, Uruguay** (30hr, CH$114,000), departing at 8:30am Saturday. **Chile Bus** (tel. 2/2776 5557) offers buses to Brazil. Their buses go to **São Paulo** (56hr, CH$100,000) and **Río de Janeiro** (62hr, CH$115,000) at 8am Thursday.

Vicinity of Santiago

The capital's environs are worthwhile during the winter months for a cluster of ski resorts high in the Andes. South of the city, vineyards and wineries follow the winding Río Maipo, where globally acclaimed cabernet sauvignon tempts visitors from Santiago. This is a popular excursion; to do a tour without crowds, head elsewhere. Farther along the river, Pomaire is the home of the country's most beloved ceramics, a fitting souvenir.

Upriver, Cajón del Maipo is a favorite weekend getaway for Santiaguinos. Rustic cabins are a good place to relax after a day hiking in the mountains, in scenery reminiscent of the glacial landscapes farther south.

TRES VALLES SKI RESORTS

One of the city's biggest draws in winter is the nearby ski resorts of **Valle Nevado, La Parva,** and **El Colorado** in the area known as the **Tres Valles,** an hour east of Santiago. The road to the ski resorts is snakelike, and it's not uncommon to need snow chains. Police officers are often stationed along the road and only let vehicles with chains pass. On weekends and public holidays in season, the road is one-way: Cars can go uphill only 8am-2pm, and downhill only 4pm-8pm.

The snow season generally runs mid-June-September. Avoid mid-July, the high season, as prices are high and waits for the lifts are long. Lift passes and hotel rates are marginally cheaper during the week. It's a good idea to purchase tickets for your chosen resort online. You'll need to pay for the rechargeable pass card that gives you access to lifts at a kiosk once you enter the resort.

For rental equipment, it's cheapest to stop at one of the rental shops along Avenida Las Condes, the road east from the city toward the ski resorts. **La Pica del Ski** (Av. Las Condes 8668, tel. 2/2886 1147, www.lapicadelski.com, 10am-8pm Mon.-Sat., 10am-7pm Sun.) has

affordable prices. Equipment is available to rent at the resorts, but expect long queues and elevated prices.

Skitotal (Av. Apoquindo 4900, Local 30-46, tel. 2/2246 0156, http://skitotal.cl, 7am-8pm daily) sells lift tickets and rental gear from their office in Las Condes. They also offer a daily **shuttle service** (CH$18,000 round-trip) that leaves from their office for Valle Nevado, La Parva, and El Colorado. Book a spot in advance or get there before 8am, as the bus fills fast. **Ski Van** (tel. 9/7499 4509, http://skivan.cl) offers a similar shuttle service with departures from Plaza Italia and the Tobalaba metro stop. For larger groups, **Miles and Smiles** (tel. 9/9148 2832, http://milesandsmiles.cl) can organize private transfers for CH$60,000 each way.

Ski Van and Skitotal can also arrange tours to the ski resorts. **Servitour** (tel. 9/94425 6671, http://servitour.cl) runs ski-themed day trips as well as organizing trips to the Cajón del Maipo and the vineyards of Casablanca and Colchagua.

El Colorado

The closest resort to Santiago, **El Colorado** (El Colorado s/n, tel. 9/7897 7534, www.elcolorado.cl, CH$49,500 adults, CH$38,000 children) has 70 slopes and is 3,333 meters above sea level. Many of the trails are for beginner or intermediate skiers, who will enjoy the long cross-country trail that weaves through woods back down to the main hotel. In addition to your entry ticket, you'll need to purchase the rechargeable **Tarjeta Skipass** (CH$5,000) at a ticket booth at the entrance to the resort; this card gives you access to the ski lifts.

The nearby resort town of **Farellones** offers affordable accommodations and a veritable feast of late-night parties, making El Colorado a hit among young and budget-conscious travelers. The **Hotel Posada de**

Vicinity of Santiago

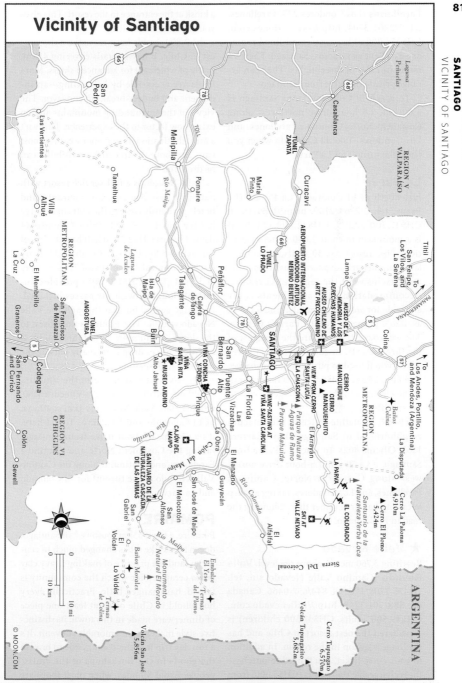

Laguna Peñuelas

66

San Pedro

78

Casablanca

68

Las Vertientes

Melipilla

TÚNEL ZAPATA

Río Maipo

TOLL

María Pinto

Curacaví

REGION V VALPARAISO

Tantehue

Pomaire

To San Felipe, Los Vilos, and La Serena

Tiltil

Villa Alhué

La Cruz

REGION METROPOLITANA

Laguna de Aculeo

El Membrillo

Peñaflor

Isla de Maipo

Calera de Tango

Talagante

AEROPUERTO INTERNACIONAL COMODORO ARTURO MERINO BENÍTEZ

Lampa

TÚNEL LO PRADO

68

MUSEO DE LA MEMORIA Y LOS DERECHOS HUMANOS

MUSEO CHILENO DE ARTE PRECOLOMBINO

Colina

5

REGION METROPOLITANA

PANAMERICANA

Graneros

La Cruz

Codegua

To San Fernando and Curicó

5

Colón

Sewell

REGION VI O'HIGGINS

San Francisco de Mostazal

TÚNEL ANGOSTURA

Buin

Alto Jahuel

MUSEO ANDINO

VIÑA SANTA RITA

VIÑA CONCHA Y TORO

San Bernardo

Puente Alto

Pirque

78

TOLL

SANTIAGO

VIEW FROM CERRO SANTA LUCÍA

LA CHASCONA

WINE-TASTING AT VIÑA SANTA CAROLINA

CERRO MANQUEHUE

CERRO MANQUEHUITO

Parque Natural Aguas de Ramo

Parque Mahuida

La Florida

Las Vizcachas

La Obra

El Arrayán

El Manzano

Río Clarillo

CAJÓN DEL MAIPO

SANTUARIO DE LA NATURALEZA CASCADA DE LAS ÁNIMAS

San Gabriel

El Volcán

Guayacán

San José de Maipo

El Melocotón

San Alfonso

Baños Morales

Lo Valdés

Termas de Colina

Río Maipo

Monumento Natural El Morado

Río Colorado

Cajón del Maipo

LA PARVA

SKI AT VALLE NEVADO

EL COLORADO

Santuario de la Naturaleza Yerba Loca

El Alfalfal

Embalse El Yeso

Termas del Plomo

Sierra Del Cortonal

La Disputada

Baños Colina

To Los Andes, Portillo, and Mendoza (Argentina)

57

Cerro La Paloma 4,910m

Cerro El Plomo 5,424m

Volcán Tupungato 6,570m

Cerro Tupungato 5,682m

Volcán San José 5,856m

ARGENTINA

0 10 km
0 10 mi

© MOON.COM

Farellones (Los Cóndores 225, Farellones, tel. 2/2201 3704, http://skifarellones.com, CH$254,000 d) has cozy wood-lined rooms and excellent views across Santiago. There's a minimum stay of three nights. They can arrange private transfers from Santiago.

To reach El Colorado from Santiago is a 60-km, 1.5-hour drive northwest along Costanera Norte, Camino a Farellones, and Los Condores. Take El Colorado when you reach the turnoff for La Parva.

La Parva

Just north of El Colorado, **La Parva** (La Parva, tel. 2/2964 2100, http://laparva.cl, CH$47,500 adults, CH$32,500 children) is a mountain town at 2,650 meters elevation. This resort has 30 trails, of which a large number are advanced runs. This is the most exclusive of the region's ski resorts. Accommodations are apartments, only available for weeklong rentals; find a list of available properties on La Parva's website. The weekday lift passes are the cheapest of the three resorts. In addition to your entry ticket, you'll need to purchase the rechargeable **ParvaPass** (CH$5,000) at a ticket booth at the entrance to the resort to get access to the ski lifts.

There's a satellite office in the Vitacura neighborhood of Santiago (Luis Carrera 1263, Oficina 402). To reach La Parva from Santiago, it's a 59-km, 1.5-hour drive northwest along Costanera Norte, Camino a Farellones, and Los Condores, taking a sharp left along La Parva rather than following the road to El Colorado.

★ Valle Nevado

Reaching 3,760 meters above sea level, **Valle Nevado** (Camino Valle Nevado s/n, tel. 2/2477 7705, U.S. tel. 844/657-0466, Canada tel. 888/301-3248, http://vallenevado.com, CH$49,500 adults, CH$37,500 children) is considered the best resort in Chile and has the longest season in the region. In addition to your entry ticket, you'll need to purchase the rechargeable **Valle Plus** (CH$5,000) from

a kiosk at the entrance to the resort. This gives you access to the ski lifts.

Its 2,800 skiable hectares make it the largest in Chile. It has 44 trails covering 45km, many of which are for advanced skiers. More trails are accessible by heli-skiing—an indulgent and budget-breaking endeavor. The views of the surrounding mountains add an extra wow factor to the experience. This isn't a great destination during poor weather; most runs are above the tree line, so visibility can be dreadful.

Valle Nevado is a full-service resort with bars that have live music, restaurants, and hotels perilously close to the cliff edge. Three luxury hotels—**Hotel Valle Nevado** (4 days, 3 nights CH$2,710 d half board), **Hotel Puerta del Sol** (4 days, 3 nights CH$2,000 d with two meals), and **Hotel Tres Puntas** (4 days, 3 nights CH$1,450 d)—provide comfortable lodging, with lift passes included. All three can be booked through the Valle Nevado website. Tres Puntas is the closest to the slopes. A minimum stay of three nights is required; prices drop marginally outside the mid-July high season.

There's a satellite office in the Vitacura neighborhood of Santiago (Av. Vitacura 5250, Oficina 304). Valle Nevado is 4km southeast of El Colorado and La Parva. To get here, it's a 65-km, 1.5-hour drive from Santiago, taking the Costanera Norte and Camino a Farellones, and continuing along the Camino Valle Nevado at the turnoff for El Colorado and La Parva.

POMAIRE

Pomaire, a town 65km southwest of Santiago, doesn't look like it has changed much in centuries, and the practice of making heavy clay *greda* ceramics, for which the community is famed, has changed little. Practically every household in Chile owns at least one piece of dinnerware made in this town; its distinctive style makes it a memorable souvenir. It's a fun day trip into the countryside to browse the goods in the workshops of the craftspeople. Avoid Monday, when most shops are closed. The rest of the week, most shops open at 11am. This is a popular weekend escape for Santiaguinos, so weekends are when the town comes to life.

The rich orange and smoky-brown bowls and other dinnerware made in Pomaire are used for serving traditional Chilean pies such as *pastel de choclo* (corn and meat pie) or *pastel de jaiba* (crab pie). In town, rows of shops and workshops sell *greda* pottery at good prices. To ensure the quality of your purchases, head to **Ceramic Badi** (Roberto Bravo 49, tel. 2/2831 2778, gredabadi@gmail. com, 9am-6pm daily) on the main road. The owners have a workshop behind their storefront and can show you how to identify a well-made product. They also have plates, bowls, and three-legged piggy banks (a good-luck charm) for sale. Prices are marginally cheaper at shops along the side streets.

On the west side of town, **Taller Barros** (Guillermo Barros 150, tel. 9/5043 2417, tallerbarros@yahoo.es,10am-5pm Mon.-Fri., 10am-7pm Sat.-Sun.) specializes in beautifully glazed flower pots and jugs, all handmade by the owner—a third-generation ceramicist. He also runs one-hour and full-day classes to make your own ceramics, but you'll need to be able to return a few days later when they've been fired and cooled.

Pomaire's high street, **Calle Roberto Bravo,** is packed with restaurants serving traditional Chilean *pernil de cerdo* (boiled ham hock), *mote de huesillo* (a sugary drink of peaches and husked wheat), and even one-kilogram empanadas.

Getting There

From Santiago, it's a 65-km, one-hour drive southwest along Ruta 78, Camino El Marco, Camino a El Tránsito, and Camino a Pomaire. **Autobuses Melipilla** (tel. 2/2776 2060) run buses to Pomaire (75min, CH$1,700) every half hour (in theory; actual departures can be erratic) 10:30am-1:30pm weekends and public holidays. Buses depart from **Terminal San Borja** (San Borja 235, tel. 2/2776 0645) in Santiago. An alternative is the half-hourly bus to Melipilla (75min, CH$1,500), where you can take a local minibus (20min) to Pomaire, 10km northeast.

★ CAJÓN DEL MAIPO

The deep **Cajón del Maipo,** whose steep sides are dusted with vegetation, has been carved through the foothills of the Andes by the rushing Río Maipo. A paved road winds deeper into the mountains, whose glacier-topped peaks stand next to snow-covered Volcán San José.

Cajón del Maipo is a favorite weekend getaway for Santiaguinos, offering cobalt-blue glacial lakes, trails for hiking and horseback rides, chaotic white-water rafting, and rustic hot springs for a post-activity soak. The facilities and the lone road through the canyon, which becomes one lane in places, can become crowded in the summer and on weekends, particularly December-March. Outside these months, it's more tranquil for a day trip or a couple of days relaxing and exploring the area.

The canyon has a few small towns and remote settlements, with most lodging and services around San José de Maipo, 26km from Puente Alto, in the south of Santiago, where the road begins. The road passes through a series of hamlets, including San Alfonso and San Gabriel, just after which is the turnoff to Embalse El Yeso, before terminating in Lo Valdes, the final settlement along the canyon, in the shadow of Volcán San José and closest to Monument Natural El Morado.

There's just one **ATM** and one **gas station** in the canyon, in San José del Maipo. It's worth stocking up on cash and fuel before departing Santiago, particularly in summer. The easiest way to reach the canyon is with a rental car or on a tour from Santiago, as public transport is sporadic and rarely goes beyond San José de Maipo. From Puente Alto, 19km south of the city center, the **G-25,** or Camino al Volcán, passes through all the villages. This can be slow going any day of the week thanks to trucks and day-trippers from Santiago. Police occasionally check documents at San

Gabriel, so make sure you have your passport and the necessary documents for your vehicle.

Tours

A tour from Santiago is an efficient way to visit the valley. Santiago-based tour agencies have a variety of tours: **EcoChile Travel** (Alberto Reyes 27, http://ecochile.travel, tel. 2/2235 2990, US tel. 650/614-1691) has expert-guided full-day hiking trips to Monumento Natural El Morado, with a hot-springs soak in Termas Valle de Colina and a wine picnic (CH$110,000), as well as full-day snowshoe expeditions (CH$82,000). **Miles and Smiles** (tel. 9/91482832, http://milesandsmiles. cl) takes visitors to the Embalse el Yeso or Monumento Natural El Morado (both CH$75,000). All tours require minimum two passengers and include hotel pickup and all entrance fees.

San José de Maipo

The small town of **San José de Maipo** is the main hub in the canyon, an hour's drive southeast of Santiago. It's not a lively town but gets jammed with visitors looking for lunch on summer weekends. It's home to a pretty **adobe church** on the main Plaza de Armas, but otherwise its main appeal is its cash machine and gas station.

A branch of **Banco Estado** (Uno Sur 56) with an ATM offers the only opportunity for withdrawing cash in the canyon. The same goes for gas: A **COPEC fuel station** is on the southern edge of town, but it's wise to fuel up in Santiago before heading up into the mountains.

ACCOMMODATIONS

In the hamlet of Melocotón, 7km south of San José de Maipo, the modern, beautifully furnished **Haiku Cabañas** (Camino al Volcán, Melocotón, tel. 9/5779 8421, http:// cabanasdelmaipo.cl, CH$110,000 d) are luxurious lodgings with views of the gushing

Río Maipo. Each of the nine rooms is *palafito* style, perched on stilts almost over the river. There's a barbecue or fire pit on each terrace. Each room has an open-plan kitchen. The boutique rooms (CH$140,000) have a separate cooking and sleeping area. Staffers speak English. Breakfast is included in the rates. Booking at least a week ahead is essential.

Just across Puente El Toyo, 6km south of San José de Maipo, **Camping El Sauce** (Estero el Sauce, tel. 9/9834 8781, CH$8,000-12,000 camping pp, CH$50,000 d cabin) offers inexpensive campsites and basic rustic cabins on six hectares of hammock-studded land on the bank of Río Maipo. They can arrange horseback and rafting trips. They also have swimming pools, designed to mimic natural pools, for guests.

GETTING THERE

To get here in your own vehicle from Santiago is a 56-km, one-hour drive on Ruta 5, Ruta 70, Acceso Sur, Avenida Eyzaguirre, Camino a San José de Maipo, and Camino Al Volcán or the G-25.

By bus, take the **Metrobús 72** (every half hour 7am-10pm daily, 1.75hr, CH$1,200) to San José de Maipo (signed "San Alfonso" or "San Gabriel"), which departs from the Terminal Intermodal bus station (look for signs for "Conexión Intermodal"; La Florida s/n) at the Bellavista de la Florida metro stop (Línea 5). It's operated by **Tur Maipo** (tel. 2/2861 1518, http://turmaipo.cl). Passengers are dropped at the Plaza de Armas. The bus doesn't accept the Tarjeta BIP, so the fare must be paid in cash.

A marginally more expensive but quicker option is the *taxi colectivo* (1.5hr, CH$1,200) from Santiago's Las Mercedes (no. 4029) or Plaza Puente Alto (no. 4010 and no. 4014) metro stops. These taxis leave when full.

San Alfonso

Eleven kilometers south of San José del Maipo, **San Alfonso** is a settlement with a small collection of restaurants and lodgings, mostly in the form of cozy, rustic cabins. Just beyond

---

1: skiers in the Andes Mountains above Santiago
2: Cajón del Maipo

the southern edge of the village, the Cascada de la Ánimas is a private reserve with outdoor activities such as kayaking, hiking, and horseback riding. It has the feel of a resort: All hiking activities require a guide, making it somewhat less enticing for independent travelers.

SANTUARIO DE LA NATURALEZ CASCADA DE LA ÁNIMAS

One of Chile's first private reserves, the **Santuario de la Naturalez Cascada de la Ánimas** (CH$14,000 adults, CH$10,000 children) came into being after a controversial gas pipeline from Argentina to Santiago was successfully defeated by the land's owners, who have demonstrated their commitment to conservation and low-impact tourism by opening the reserve to visitors. Named after the on-site waterfall, the reserve is a central destination for hikers, horseback riders, and white-water rafters and kayakers. The best months for these activities are November-March. Rates are halved in low season. The site is extensive and includes an outdoor swimming pool, use of which is included in admission.

Organize a guide at the park's entrance to hike the Sendero Cascada de las Ánimas (CH$7,000 pp), a short trail to the park's namesake waterfall. The two- to three-hour climb to the summit of Cerro Pangal (CH$25,000 pp, including guide) is another option for hikers. Horseback trips (up to 12 days) into the backcountry of the Andes start from CH$66,000 pp. Beginner riders should be cautious, as the terrain is steep. Some visitors have voiced concerns about the upkeep of the horses. Kayak and rafting tours (from CH$23,000 pp) traverse Class II-IV rapids on Río Maipo.

Accommodations are luxurious suites in the main lodge (CH$145,000 d), cozy dome "lofts" with kitchens (CH$200,000 d), basic cabins with full kitchens (CH$111,000 d), basic rooms (CH$60,000 d), and campsites (CH$22,000 d). They can arrange various packages, including transfers from Santiago.

Be aware that heating can be an issue in

some of the freestanding lodgings. Most activities require extra payment. The on-site restaurant isn't the best quality; it's closed during the week March-December, so it's worth cooking for yourself or bringing a car so that you can venture to restaurants in nearby San Alfonso and farther afield in San José de Maipo.

ACCOMMODATIONS

The seven light and airy cabins at ★ **Cabañas Nogalia** (O'Higgins 95, San Alfonso, tel. 9/9100 4456, www.nogalia.cl, CH$75,000 d) are modern and functional. The setting, among honey blossom and walnut trees, is divine. Each has a private terrace with a barbecue and a kitchen for self-catering, plus use of the communal swimming pool and access to the hot tub at additional cost. Discounts are available for stays longer than one night. Rates include IVA.

GETTING THERE

To get here from Santiago is a 68-km, 1.5-hour drive along Ruta 5, Ruta 70, Acceso Sur, Avenida Eyzaguirre, Camino a San José de Maipo, and Camino Al Volcán or the G-25. The town is a 15-minute drive south of San José del Maipo.

It's possible to take a *taxi colectivo* (1.75hr, CH$1,800) to San Alfonso from Santiago's Las Mercedes (no. 4029) or Plaza Puente Alto (no. 4010 and no. 4014) metro stops. These taxis leave when full.

Embalse El Yeso

Thirteen kilometers south of San Alfonso, just after the village of San Gabriel where the paved road ends, the road forks. The left fork heads north toward crystalline **Embalse El Yeso,** a reservoir on the dammed Río Yeso.

At 3,000 meters elevation, the cobalt reservoir is surrounded by serrated snowcapped peaks. The path on its banks is ideal for sweeping views and dramatic photographs. It's also a great location for a roadside picnic. There are no facilities here but plenty of rocks to perch on and enjoy the scenery.

Because of its altitude and the rough unpaved road, getting here can be tough. Although the route is only 28km from San Gabriel, it can take two hours to drive. Extreme caution is recommended in good weather. In poor weather and throughout winter, a 4WD vehicle is essential. Snowfall can make the reservoir inaccessible; landslides can also pose a serious danger. On weekends and during summer, cars trying to pass one another on the final stretch of road to the reservoir can cause serious traffic jams. It's often quicker to park on the side of the road and walk the final few kilometers.

At the end of the road, 20km northeast of the main viewpoint for the reservoir, rustic **Termas del Plomo** (8am-10pm daily, CH$6,000) are for the truly adventurous. These two naturally heated hot springs boast spellbinding scenery that makes the trip worth the effort. There are very basic facilities here. A 4WD vehicle is essential to get here, as a river crossing is often required.

It's possible to trek to nearby Laguna Negra and Laguna de Encañado, two striking lakes. A guide is recommended, as trails are not well-marked. The **Escuela Nacional de Montaña de Santiago** (Simpson 77, Santiago, tel. 2/2220 888, http://enam.cl) can connect you with licensed guides. Day trips to the reservoir are offered by most agencies in Santiago (from CH$20,000, transportation included).

GETTING THERE

From Santiago, it's an 80-km, 1.5-hour drive along Ruta 5, Ruta 70, Acceso Sur, Avenida Eyzaguirre, Camino a San José de Maipo, and then along the Camino Al Volcán or the G-25 to San Gabriel. Two kilometers beyond this village, take the signposted left fork northeast along Camino Embalse El Yeso; it's 25km and one hour's drive from here.

Lo Valdés

From the right-hand fork after San Gabriel, the paved but washboard road continues southeast to the hamlet of **Lo Valdés,** where there is lodging. From here, you can cross the river to Baños Morales and Monumento Natural El Morado, with excellent hiking to nearby glaciers, or continue along its southern bank deeper into the valley to beautiful hot springs. All accommodations in the area are either overpriced or offer dreadful service, so it makes sense to visit for the day from lodgings closer to Santiago.

MONUMENTO NATURAL EL MORADO

Just 200 meters across the river from Lo Valdés, Baños Morales is a clutch of houses. The perpetual sulfurous smell from three murky hot-spring pools make it less than attractive, but you'll find the picturesque trail for the Monumento Natural El Morado, a protected area of dramatic mountain scenery. Expect landscapes that are snowier and more majestic than those at lower altitudes farther down the canyon.

The **trail** (8km one-way, 3hr) begins at the **CONAF visitors center** (8:30am-6pm daily, last entry 1pm Oct.-Apr., 8:30am-5pm daily, last entry noon May-Oct., CH$5,000 adults, CH$2,500 children) on the western edge of Baños Morales, where admission for this park is charged. This moderate hike gains 600 vertical meters to reach Laguna El Morado, where sublime views of the Glaciar San Francisco and the peak of Cerro El Morado are the rewards. The trail is well marked, and although it starts with a steep incline for the first half hour, it levels off. There is no shade, so bring a sun hat and plenty of water.

Horses are sometimes available to rent cheaply from the locals of Baños Morales (ask at the visitors center for information). Camping is not permitted around the lake due to the risk of landslides. In winter, the trail is regularly closed due to weather. Contact the **Carabineros** (tel. 2/2922 3315) in San Gabriel for up-to-date information. The Santiago office of **CONAF** (Bulnes 285, tel. 22/2663 0125, metropolitana.oirs@conaf.cl) can also provide guidance.

TERMAS VALLE DE COLINA

Far superior to those in Baños Morales are the hot springs 10km beyond Lo Valdés, past the mine. The picturesque **Termas Valle de Colina** (tel. 2/2985 2609, http://termasvalledecolina.com, 24 hr daily, CH$8,000 adults, CH$4,000 children) is worth the effort of getting here. Nine pastel-blue geothermal pools are naturally heated to different temperatures ranging 25-55°C. The dramatic mountain scenery is a serious part of the appeal; the pools are crammed with visitors on weekends. There are restrooms and showers but no lockers, so leave anything of value hidden in your vehicle.

GETTING THERE

By car, it's a 56-km, one-hour drive along Ruta 5, Ruta 70, Acceso Sur, Avenida Eyzaguirre, Camino a San José de Maipo, and Camino Al Volcán or the G-25 to San José de Maipo. Continue along the G-25 for 42km (1 hour) to a bridge north to Baños Morales (1km) at the entrance to Lo Valdés, or continue along this road to reach Termas Valle de Colina, 10km southeast.

To get to Baños Morales from Santiago on public transit, take the **Metrobús 72** (7:30am daily Jan.-early Mar., 7:30am Sat.-Sun. mid-Mar.-Dec., 2.5hr, CH$8,400 round-trip), operated by **Tur Maipo** (tel. 2/2861 1518, http://turmaipo.cl). It leaves from the Terminal Intermodal Bellavista de la Florida (La Florida s/n), a metro and bus station, with a return departure from Baños Morales at 6pm.

Turismontaña (tel. 2/2850 0555) runs buses to Baños Morales (2.5hr, 8:30am daily Jan.-Feb., Thurs.-Sun. Mar.-Apr. and Oct.-Dec., CH$10,000 round-trip) from the Vicente Valdés metro stop (Línea 5 and Línea 4). Consult the driver for the return departure times.

WINE-TASTING IN VALLE DE MAIPO

Valle de Maipo is one of the best-known international wine valleys. It's also the most accessible expanse of vineyards from Santiago, just south of the capital. Valle de Maipo is home to the biggest and most established Chilean wineries. Vines have been cultivated here since the arrival of the Spanish, but with greater fervor and focus in the last 150 years, with the strength of the valley in robust, full-bodied cabernet sauvignons. For wine lovers with only a day to spare, the Valle de Maipo is ideal.

Efficient public transport links to most wineries to make it possible to visit most on a half-day independent trip. To combine several, it's easier to take a tour from Santiago. **Miles and Smiles** (tel. 9/9148 2832, www.milesandsmiles.cl) visits two wineries for CH$69,000 pp (min. 2 people, includes hotel pickup, tours, and tastings). **Uncorked Wine Tours** (tel. 2/2981 6242, www.uncorked.cl) can organize a personalized tour of the area.

★ Viña Santa Carolina

If there's one vineyard to visit, it's the award-winning **Viña Santa Carolina** (Til Til 2228, tel. 2/2450 3000, http://santacarolina.cl, CH$12,000 tour and tasting). In 1875, Chilean founder Luis Pereira Cotapos planted French grapes here and named the vineyard for Carolina Iñiguez, his wife. In 1889 their wine was the first to receive international recognition, winning a gold medal at the Exposition Universelle in Paris. A copy of this certificate can be seen in the wine cellar.

The vineyards remained here until the 1970s, when the city grew to absorb the land on its outskirts. Nowadays, Viña Santa Carolina has vineyards across the country. The winery is still a sight to behold, however. Palm-flanked colonial-style buildings date to its founding, and the **winery tour** (in English, 10:30am, 11:30am, 3pm, and 4:30pm Mon.-Fri., noon Sun.) takes you into the cellar, built using the unusual *cal y canto* technique of joining bricks with clay using egg white. You'll visit the gaping stone outbuildings once used in production. The tour ends in the **wine shop** (9am-6pm daily); pick up a bottle of signature cabernet sauvignon or do a tasting.

Viña Santa Carolina is within the city limits, a 10-minute walk from metro stop Rodrigo de Araya on Línea 5. It can easily be visited as a half-day trip from the center.

Viña Santa Rita

A winding dirt road through rows of vines leads to the 19th-century colonial-style, terracotta-roofed buildings of **Viña Santa Rita** (Camino Padre Hurtado 695, Alto Jahuel, tel. 2/2362 2524, www.santarita.com, 10:30am-4pm Tues.-Sun., CH$14,000 tour and tasting). According to local legend, independence hero Bernardo O'Higgins and his men took cover in the wine cellar here during the fight for independence in the early 1800s.

Santa Rita offers **vineyard tours** (in English, 10am and 2:45pm Tues.-Sun.) on foot or by bicycle that culminate in the wine cellar for a tasting. An alternate tour is aboard the mobile **pedal bar** (min. 8 people). Stop in the **wine shop** (10am-6pm Tues.-Sun.) for a stand-alone tasting. Also on the property are a restaurant and hotel and the superb Museo Andino, worth a visit even if you're not interested in wine.

Arrive by public transit on Línea 4 of the metro and the Puente Alto stop. Continue on bus 81 in the direction "Alto Jahuel-Buin."

You can combine a visit with a tour of Viña Concha y Toro in Puente Alto; a whole day is necessary to see both. To get here by car, it's a 45-km, 45-minute drive south along the Acceso Sur highway.

MUSEO ANDINO

In a modern white-and-gray stone building overlooking the Santa Rita vineyards, the **Museo Andino** (www.museoandino. cl, 10:30am-5:30pm Tues.-Sun., free) contains outstanding Chilean and other South American ceramics, wood carvings, and gold work from the private collection of Ricardo Claro Valdés, a lawyer and business magnate. Among Chileans, he's better known for his unwavering support for the Pinochet dictatorship.

The museum boasts a spectacular collection of *moai kava kava* wooden statues from Rapa Nui—probably the largest collection in all of Chile—and pottery that surveys the entire indigenous history of Chile. Look for the ceremonial *kero* vessels, used by the Inca for drinking *chicha,* and the museum's oldest piece, the geometric stone *litos* that date to the Huentelauquén culture, circa 11,000 BC.

The Mapuche room, containing heavy silver riding spurs and carved wooden *capucho*

indigenous pottery in the Museo Andino

stirrups, is also impressive. Information panels in English are a useful addition. The on-site shop is an excellent location for English- and Spanish-language books on Rapa Nui, the Mapuche people, and wine.

Viña Concha y Toro

Viña Concha y Toro (Victoria Subercaseaux 210, tel. 2/2476 5000, http://conchaytoro.com, 9:30am-6:30pm daily), in the Santiago suburb of Pirque, is Chile's largest producer and exporter of wine, making 600,000 bottles per day. One of the country's oldest wineries, dating to the late 19th century, its cabernet sauvignon, sauvignon blanc, and merlot grapevines were brought from France.

Although the company has vineyards across Chile, this is the only winery open to the public. **Guided tours** (in English, 10am, 1:30pm, 3:20pm, and 4:20pm daily, CH$16,000) visit the vineyards, gardens, and wine cellar, and end with a tasting. Reservations are recommended, but not required. They also have a **wine bar** (9:30am-6:30pm daily) where you can sample wine alongside tapas and charcuterie or lunch (noon-4:30pm daily).

This is the most visited winery near Santiago, so serious wine buffs or those looking to avoid crowds might want to go elsewhere. By car, it's a 30-km, 30-minute drive south along Ruta 5, Ruta 70, and Acceso Sur to Puente Alto, where you take Sargento Menadier, Presidente Salvador Allende, and Avenida Concha Y Toro to the winery. Via public transit, take Línea 4 of the metro to Plaza de Puente Alto. From there, a taxi is the quickest means of getting to the winery, and a couple of hours are plenty of time here. You can combine a visit with a tour of Viña Santa Rita, accessed by bus from Puente Alto; a full day is necessary to see both.

Valparaíso and Viña del Mar

With a cool climate and fresh air, the coastal cit- ies west of Santiago offer a welcome escape from the capital's long, hot summers. Valparaíso, with its iconic hills and artistic graffiti-daubed streets, has a scruffy bohemian air. Just north, the modern high-rises and golden sands of manicured Viña del Mar attract wealthy holiday-ing Santiaguinos.

Connecting these cities with the capital is the vineyard-laced Valle de Casablanca, home to lush plantations of sauvignon blanc and char-donnay grapes. Ruta 68 carves through the sun-scorched contours of the coastal cordillera, where neat rows of grapevines cascade toward the town of Casablanca. To the south, Valle de San Antonio, mere ki-lometers from the coast, is for wine-tasting with ocean views.

Highlights

Look for ★ to find recommended sights, activities, dining, and lodging.

★ **Ride the *Ascensores* of Valparaíso:** The historic funiculars that transport passengers up Valparaíso's steep hills are now considered national treasures (page 99).

★ **Museo Municipal de Bellas Artes:** Marvel at the opulence of 19th-century Palacio Baburizza, containing European art and intriguing Chilean work (page 100).

★ **Museo Mirador Lukas:** Learn about the life and works of Viña resident and Italian-born "Lukas" Renzo Pecchenino, cartoonist and caricaturist of the eccentricities of life (page 100).

★ **Tour La Sebastiana:** The hilltop home of revered Chilean poet and Nobel Prize-winner Pablo Neruda, this museum contains the poet's eclectic collection amassed during his travels as a Chilean ambassador (page 102).

★ **Quintay:** With restaurants serving the best seafood on the coast and a long, quiet beach, this fishing village south of Valparaíso makes a fantastic day trip (page 112).

★ **Casa Museo Isla Negra:** Pablo Neruda's favorite coastal home shows his love of the ocean in its marvelous collection of ship figureheads (page 114).

★ **Museo de Arqueología e Historia Natural Francisco Fonck:** With informative displays about Rapa Nui and an authentic *moai* statue out front, this museum is the best place to learn about the Polynesian island without actually going there (page 118).

★ **Surfing:** Popular surf town **Maitencillo** has consistently large swells, combined with long beaches, comfortable accommodations, and a youthful vibe (page 125).

★ **Wine-Tasting in Valle de Casablanca and Valle de San Antonio:** Drop in for tours and gourmet dining in the home of Chile's premier white wine (pages 130 and 133).

South of Valparaíso are eclectic seaside residences. A popular day trip is to the home of Nobel Prize-winning poet Pablo Neruda, overlooking the Pacific from its rocky vantage point in the seaside village of Isla Negra. Tiny Quintay is a blissfully uncrowded spot for a fish lunch at a picturesque harbor-side eatery or after scuba diving.

For a quieter escape, head north to the exclusive resorts of Cachagua and Zapallar, and more egalitarian Papudo, with the prettiest beaches in the country. For adventure seekers, increasingly popular Maitencillo is the place to surf and paraglide, while Parque Nacional La Campaña, due east from beachside Concón, has steep hiking trails with some of the best viewpoints of the Andes Mountains.

PLANNING YOUR TIME

Base yourself in **Valparaíso** during your time on the Central Coast. The city has the widest range of accommodations, best-quality dining, and bus connections throughout the region. **Three days** is enough time to explore the city and take a **day trip** to the surrounding beach towns or wine country. If you have a car, take a trip to **Isla Negra,** south of Valparaíso, for an afternoon of fresh fish and lounging on a quiet beach in **Quintay.**

More polished **Viña del Mar** also works as a base for sightseeing, as the metro connects it quickly with Valparaíso. Viña deserves a **half-day visit** for its museums, parks, and beaches, while the **northern coast** makes an excellent day trip or overnight hangout.

The **Valle de Casablanca** requires a day to explore properly by bus or car. A rental vehicle or a tour is necessary to visit lesser-known **Valle de San Antonio.** If you want to do some hiking in under-the-radar **Parque Nacional La Campana,** it's a long day from Valparaíso either by metro or by rental car. For a chance to hike the longer trails, you'll need **camping equipment** and at least **two days.**

HISTORY

Modern-day Valparaíso and Viña del Mar are at the mouth of Valle de Quintil, which was inhabited long before the arrival of the conquistadores by the Chango people, small fishing communities that fell under the domain of the Inca Empire. Valparaíso was founded in 1536 when Spaniard Juan de Saavedra docked in the bay. Soon designated the country's official port, it became a harbor for transporting gold north to Lima and on to Madrid. Sensing an opportunity, pirates such as Francis Drake and Joris van Spilbergen looted the town more than once, razing buildings to the ground.

After Chilean independence in 1810, the importance of the Strait of Magellan to global shipping made Valparaíso an obligatory stop between the Atlantic and the Pacific, leading to a dramatic thirtyfold increase in the city's population. English, German, Italian, and American immigrants arrived, running shipping companies and saltpeter businesses and constructing the city's lavish European-style architecture and bringing technological advancements such as gas and electricity.

In 1906 a violent earthquake laid waste to the city's commercial district, forcing businesses and families to move north to growing Viña del Mar, founded in 1878. Earlier part of the Hacienda Las Siete Hermanas—land granted to the Carreras, one of the founding families—the land on which Viña was built was sold off in small parcels to individuals, creating a rapidly developing modern city that became an elegant beach resort for the wealthy.

The opening of the Panama Canal in 1914, followed by the collapse of the saltpeter industry, severely damaged Valparaíso's port-based economy, but the importance of copper and fruit exports allowed the city to recover. For much of the region, tourism is the main source of income, aided by the World Heritage status of Valparaíso's historic center, granted in 2003.

Previous: view of Valparaíso; Valparaíso's port; surfers in Maitencillo.

Valparaíso, Viña del Mar, and the Central Coast

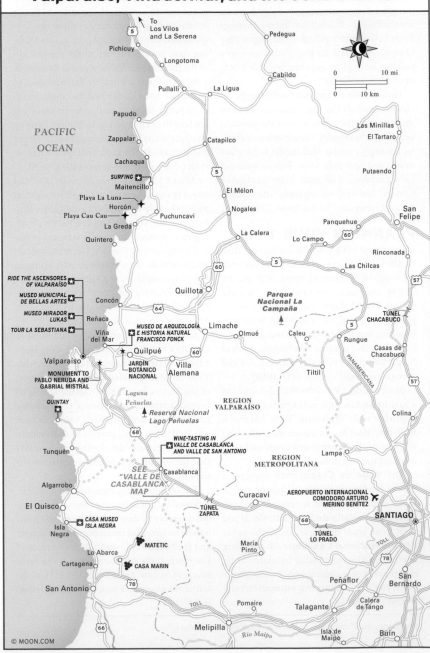

© MOON.COM

Two Days on the Central Coast

DAY 1

Start the morning in Valparaíso with a trip up the Ascensor El Peral for views of the port and a trip to the Museo Municipal de Bellas Artes. Take the steps across to Cerro Concepción and get lost in the graffiti-filled streets before lunching at Fauna, along Paseo Dimalow, where you can photograph some of the most iconic views of the city.

Head up to Cerro Alegre to take in the views, then spend an hour visiting Pablo Neruda's Valparaíso residence, La Sebastiana, at the top of Cerro Florida. In the evening, head to one of the old bars in the port area and get dinner in one of the city's trendiest restaurants, either in Cerro Concepción, Cerro Alegre, or Cerro Bellavista.

DAY 2

Rent a car from neighboring Viña del Mar or take a bus and head out to the Valle de Casablanca wine region to tour and taste at Chile's finest white wine producers. Have lunch in a French-style château or terra-cotta-roofed hacienda-style restaurant. With your own car, head south to continue wine-tasting in Valle de San Antonio. Loop back north via Isla Negra and Neruda's favorite house as you drive northward back to Valparaíso.

An alternative is to head north to the leafy seaside village of Zapallar for a morning at the beach, followed by lunch at El Chiringuito for its views and fresh fish, unloaded at the harbor next door. Return south for an afternoon of surfing in sleepy Maitencillo or relax and catch the sunset at Playa Cachagua in nearby Cachagua. Return to Valparaíso for beer and live jazz at Altamira.

Valparaíso

Occupying a sweeping curve of Pacific coastline 100km northwest of Santiago, Valparaíso is an edgy bohemian metropolis of brightly colored ramshackle 19th-century buildings cluttering 42 hills and lining the bay below. The historic quarter is a fascinating collection of 19th-century palaces and mansions, rickety funiculars that grumble up the hillsides, cobbled passageways, and steep staircases. Much of the city's architecture is faded and crumbling, which enhances its photogenic qualities. Visitors come in droves on sunny weekends to admire the cityscape.

With its proximity to the ocean, the fish is fresh in Valparaíso restaurants. Locals call the city Valpo, and call themselves *porteños* (people of the port). Ten universities and 100,000 students here and in Viña del Mar give the area a lively nightlife scene, mixing modern hangouts with century-old bars. The New Year's Eve celebration is the largest in the country, with the bay acting as a spectacular mirror for the fireworks display. During summer, Valpo is a good base for exploring neighboring Viña del Mar and the region's beaches.

Orientation

The **historic quarter** encompasses the area around Plaza Sotomayor and Plaza Echaurren in El Plan, as well as Cerro Alegre and Cerro Concepción. Historic and industrial buildings and Valparaíso's five squares are on the flat coastal section known as **El Plan,** divided into **Barrio Puerto** (the port) and **El Almendral.** In the hills, **Cerro Alegre** and **Cerro Concepción** offer the most upscale lodgings and restaurants, many with spectacular views of the bay. **Cerro Pantéon, Cerro Bellavista,** and **Cerro Florida** are where you'll find the city's extensive cemeteries, graffiti-clad streets, and houses belonging to famous former residents.

Valparaíso

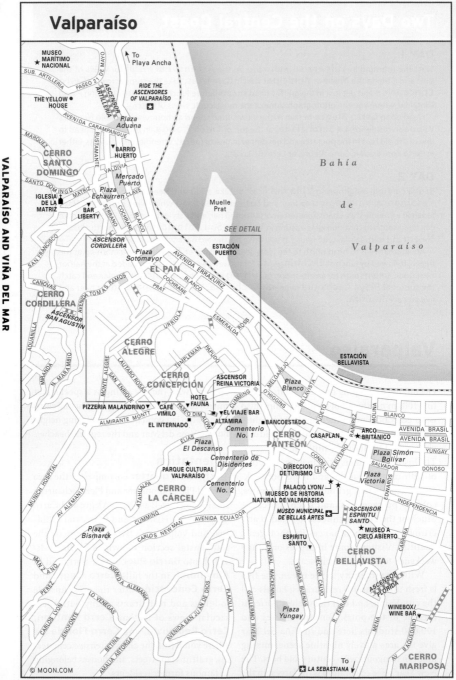

MUSEO MARÍTIMO NACIONAL

SUB. ARTILLERIA

PASEO 21 DE MAYO

ASCENSOR ARTILLERIA

THE YELLOW HOUSE

AVENIDA CARAMPANGUE

RIDE THE ASCENSORS OF VALPARAÍSO

To Playa Ancha

Plaza Aduana

MARQUEZ

CERRO SANTO DOMINGO

BUSTAMANTE

VALDIVIA

BARRIO HUERTO

SANTO DOMINGO

Mercado Puerto

Plaza Echaurren

CLAVE

IGLESIA DE LA MATRIZ

MATRIZ

BAR LIBERTY

SERRANO

COCHRANE

BLANCO

SAN FRANCISCO

CANOVAS

CERRO CORDILLERA

AQUANILLA

ASCENSOR SAN AGUSTÍN

MIRANDA

N. MARAMBIO

ASCENSOR CORDILLERA

Plaza Sotomayor

EL PAN

AVENIDA ERRAZURIZ

ESTACIÓN PUERTO

AVENIDA TOMAS RAMOS

COCHRANE

PRAT

BLANCO

URRIOLA

ESMERALDA

ROSS

MONTE ALEGRE

LAUTARO ROSAS

SAN ENRIQUE

CERRO ALEGRE

TEMPLEMAN

PAPUDO

Bahía

de

Valparaiso

Muelle Prat

SEE DETAIL

CERRO CONCEPCIÓN

ASCENSOR REINA VICTORIA

ESTACIÓN BELLAVISTA

PIZZERIA MALANDRINO

CAFÉ VIMILO

PASEO DIM

HOTEL FAUNA

CUMMING

MELGAREJO

O'HIGGINS

Plaza Blanco

BELLAVISTA

ALMIRANTE MONTT

EL INTERNADO

ALTAMIRA

EL VIAJE BAR

BANCOESTADO

Cementerio No. 1

CERRO PANTEÓN

CASAPLAN

RAMIREZ

PUDETO

BLANCO

AVENIDA BRASIL

ARCO BRITÁNICO

AVENIDA BRASIL

ELÍAS

Plaza El Descanso

Cementerio de Disidentes

DIRECCION DE TURISMO

CONDELL

ELEUTERIO

Plaza Simón Bolívar

SALVADOR

YUNGAY

DONOSO

PARQUE CULTURAL VALPARAÍSO

Cementerio No. 2

PALACIO LYON/ MUSEO DE HISTORIA NATURAL DE VALPARAISO

Plaza Victoria

EDWARDS

INDEPENDENCIA

ATAHUALPA

CERRO LA CÁRCEL

AVENIDA ECUADOR

MUSEO MUNICIPAL DE BELLAS ARTES

ASCENSOR ESPIRITU SANTO

MUSEO A CIELO ABIERTO

MUNICH HOSPITAL

CUMMING

CARLOS NEW MAN

ESPIRITU SANTO

GENERAL MACKENNA

YERBAS BUENAS

HECTOR CALVO

CARRERA

CERRO BELLAVISTA

ASCENSOR FLORIDA

Plaza Bismarck

AV. ALEMANIA

PEREZ

AVENIDA ALEMANIA

LO VENEGAS

AVENIDA SAN JUAN DE DIOS

PLACILLA

GUILLERMO RIVERA

R. FERRARI

MENA

Plaza Yungay

WINEBOX/ WINE BAR

MANZANO

CARLOS LYON

JENOFONTE

BETINA

AMALIA ASTORGA

AV. BAQUEDANO

CERRO MARIPOSA

To LA SEBASTIANA

© MOON.COM

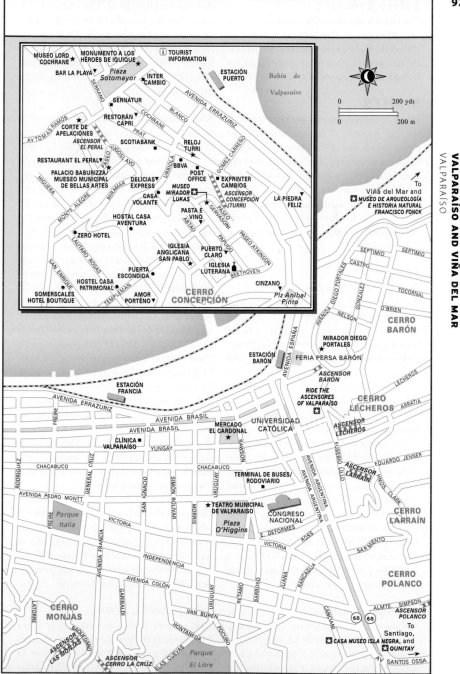

Safety Concerns

The historic quarter is the safest part of the city, although care should be taken in El Plan after dark. It's fine to venture beyond the central tourist attractions during the day, but not at night, due to the possibility of being robbed.

SIGHTS

Plenty of companies run **walking tours** of the city, stopping at historic buildings and pretty viewpoints while narrating the city's history and modern-day life. The best options include the tip-based **Tours 4 Tips** (tel. 2/2570 9939, www.tours4tips.com), which leaves twice daily from Plaza Sotomayor, and **Valpo Street Art Tour** (www.valpostreetart. com), which tours the best graffiti spots on foot or by bike.

El Plan
PLAZA SOTOMAYOR

One of the main hubs of the northern edge of El Plan is **Plaza Sotomayor** (bounded by Av. Errázuriz, Sotomayor, and Prat), with the imposing marble **Monumento a los Héroes de Iquique** at its northeastern end. Designed by French architect Norbert Maillart, the monument depicts various scenes from the 1879 Battle of Iquique and houses the remains of Arturo Prat (a naval officer who died in the battle) in a subterranean tomb.

On the southwestern end of the square, the **Armada de Chile** has its headquarters in the former **Intendencia Regional**, a 1910 French-inspired five-story building painted in pastel blues. Two blocks northeast of the plaza, **Muelle Prat** has a small municipal-run **tourist information booth** (no phone, 10am-6pm daily). You can take a 30-minute tour around the harbor (CH$4,000 pp) in a local fishing boat. Approach the boat's captain directly to arrange for a tour.

IGLESIA LA MATRIZ

Among the faded elegance and derelict buildings of El Plan is the **Iglesia La Matriz** (Santo Domingo 71, tel. 32/2214 876, open daily for mass), where the history is more interesting that the building itself. The white church stands on the site of a 1559 adobe chapel that was looted and burned by English pirate Francis Drake in 1578. It was later destroyed at least five times by earthquakes and tsunamis, being rebuilt each time. The current building dates to 1837.

ASCENSOR ARTILLERÍA

From the intersection of coastal Calle Errázuriz and Plaza Wheelwright, the 1893-built **Ascensor Artillería** (7am-10pm daily, CH$300 one-way) takes a slow, shuddering journey to the top of Cerro Artillería. It's known for its paint jobs: In the past, it has depicted Jesus on its roof, flanked by a series of winged mermaids; today it's a more subdued yellow and red. From the top station, exit onto **Paseo 21 de Mayo,** with panoramic views of the busy port and the beach town Reñaca to the northeast.

MUSEO MARÍTIMO NACIONAL

The **Museo Marítimo Nacional** (Paseo 21 de Mayo, tel. 32/2537 018, www.mmn.cl, 10am-5:30pm Tues.-Sun., CH$2,000 adults, CH$300 children) has a grand residence above the harbor on Cerro Artillería. The museum dedicates much of its extensive floor space to the 1879-1884 War of the Pacific and naval hero Arturo Prat. Display cases of postcards of Valparaíso in the 19th and 20th centuries show Plaza Sotomayor on the seafront, demonstrating how much of the city was built atop once low-lying marshland.

A small exhibition is dedicated to Thomas Cochrane, the daring Scottish-born admiral who commanded frigates in the Napoleonic Wars before arriving in Valparaíso in 1818 to lead a squadron for Chile in the campaign for independence. He later fought for independence for Peru, Brazil, and Greece.

ASCENSOR EL PERAL

Half a block from the west end of Plaza Sotomayor is the lower entrance to the red, white, and green 1902-built **Ascensor El Peral** (Plaza de la Justicia, 7am-10pm daily,

☆ Ride the *Ascensores* of Valparaíso

With its steep hills, Valparaíso has always been exhausting on foot. The solution was the hydraulic *ascensor* (elevator). Despite the name, most were actually funiculars, or cable-based railways. The first was Ascensor Concepción in 1883, connecting El Plan with the densely populated Cerro Concepción, saving locals and future tourists a lot of effort. Thirty more funiculars were built across the expanding city during the late 1800s and early 1900s, but an economic downturn in the early 1900s forced many funiculars into disuse; others were completely dismantled.

Only 16 are intact today, and just 7 still operate, shuttling passengers between El Plan and the hills. The journey is a test of the nerves, as the car rattles and creaks up and down the hillsides. Each *ascensor* has two brightly colored cabs that can carry 6-10 passengers.

To ride one of the *ascensores,* pay in cash when you arrive at the station, either at the top or bottom of the hill. Ascensor Artillería is the most picturesque route, with sweeping views south across the Valparaíso skyline and the sea. All of the operational funiculars lead to viewpoints with remarkable ocean panoramas.

These *ascensores* are the most central:

- **Ascensor Artillería** (page 98)
- **Ascensor El Peral** (page 98)
- **Ascensor Concepción** (page 100)
- **Ascensor Reina Victoria** (page 100)
- **Ascensor Polanco** (page 103)
- **Ascensor Barón** (page 103)

CH$100). To find the entrance, look for a signed doorway on the south side of Plaza de Justicia that contains the colonnade-fronted **Corte de Apelaciones** (Court of Appeals). The funicular chugs up a hill between multistory buildings to the northern side of Cerro Alegre.

At the exit is **Paseo Yugoslavo,** where the view to the port is choked with modern high-rises. This is a good place for souvenirs: Local craftspeople sell leather purses, T-shirts printed with the Valparaíso skyline, and oil paintings depicting the city.

RELOJ TURRI

Sitting between Calles Prat and Cochrane is the **Reloj Turri** (Clock Tower, Cochrane 893), an emblematic Valparaíso landmark described as the "Big Ben of Valparaíso." Despite its name, the structure isn't a freestanding tower—it's a part of a narrow building that spans the block from the corner of Prat and Cochrane northwest to Calle Urriola.

ARCO BRITÁNICO

Make your way to El Almendral to find the **Arco Británico** (Av. Brasil and Av. Ramírez), Valparaíso's own Arc de Triomphe on a smaller scale. Presiding over a stretch of grass in the median of Avenida Brasil, the white marble-covered arch features bas-reliefs of the four British men who aided the Chilean cause for independence: Bernardo O'Higgins, Thomas Cochrane, Robert Simpson, and Jorge O'Brien. A bronze sculpture of a lion sits atop the arch.

MUSEO DE HISTORIA NATURAL DE VALPARAÍSO

In Palacio Lyon, a restored Victorian-style mansion dating from 1881, **Museo de Historia Natural de Valparaíso** (Condell 1546, tel. 32/2544 840, www.mhnv.cl, 10am-8pm Tues.-Sat. Jan.-Feb., 10am-6pm Tues.-Thurs., 10am-8pm Fri.-Sat. Mar.-Dec., free) is the second-oldest museum in Chile. Despite severe earthquake damage in 2010, the museum offers a well-presented display of regional flora and fauna from Rapa Nui (Easter Island) to the Andes.

Cerro Alegre

★ **MUSEO MUNICIPAL DE BELLAS ARTES**

The sumptuous art nouveau **Palacio Baburizza,** one of Cerro Alegre's historic mansions, houses the **Museo Municipal de Bellas Artes** (Paseo Yugoslavo 176, tel. 32/2252 332, http://museobaburizza.cl, 10:30am-7pm Tues.-Sun. Jan.-Mar., 10:30am-6pm Tues.-Sun. Apr.-Dec., CH$4,000 adults, children free, free 2nd Sun. of the month). Built in 1916 by Italian immigrant Ottorino Zanell, this palace was the main residence of saltpeter and agriculture magnate Pascual Baburizza.

It's worth a visit for the architecture, and Baburizza also had an eye for European art: The ground floor contains his personal collection of impressionist, realist, and romantic art. Upstairs, rambling rooms display works by local artists from the 19th-20th centuries, including landscapes by English painter Thomas Somerscales, who began his career in Valparaíso. The 2nd-floor balconies offer impressive views of the city. In the more luxurious modern extension of the building is a hand-carved American oak and Oregon pine chimneypiece with Turkish marble.

It merits asking for the 45-minute English-language tour or the free audio guide (available in English), where you learn as much about the history of Valparaíso as about the art.

Cerro Concepción

★ **MUSEO MIRADOR LUKAS**

Showcasing the life and works of "Lukas" Renzo Pecchenino, an Italian-born cartoonist and caricaturist who spent most of his life in nearby Viña del Mar, **Museo Mirador Lukas** (Paseo Gervasoni 448, tel. 32/2221 344, www.lukas.cl, 10:30am-6:30pm Tues.-Fri., 11am-7pm Sat.-Sun., CH$1,500 adults, CH$500 children) is a superb museum with an extensive collection of Lukas's entertaining and insightful cartoons. His work reflected on Chilean society and appeared from the 1950s to the 1970s in Chilean newspapers.

A free audio guide is available in English, but his forthright and occasionally politically incorrect social commentary can get lost in translation. The collection of cartoons about Valparaíso offers a splendid insight into the idiosyncrasies and chaos of life in this unique city of streets and hills. Non-Spanish speakers can enjoy his sketches, including a humorous collection depicting Rapa Nui (Easter Island).

ASCENSOR CONCEPCIÓN

Cerro Concepción is accessed by **Ascensor Concepción** (Prat and Carreño, 7am-10pm daily, CH$300), the oldest of the city's antique funiculars that climbs 69 meters. Dating back to 1883, it had a facelift in 2019. Access is via a signed iron gate from Calle Prat. The funicular's top station leads onto Paseo Gervasoni, with pretty views toward Reloj Turri and the bay.

ASCENSOR REINA VICTORIA

The tiny **Ascensor Reina Victoria** (7am-11pm daily, CH$100), named in homage to the British monarch and constructed in 1902, links Paseo Dimalow with Avenida Elias, granting a shorter route down to Plaza Anibal Pinto and El Plan. At the top, the views from Paseo Dimalow across the city are sensational. The funicular has a capacity of only seven people.

Cerro Pantéon

Cementerios No. 1 (Cumming and Dinamarca, 8:30am-5pm daily) and **No. 2** (Dinamarca and Av. Ecuador, 8:30am-5pm daily) house intricate mausoleums and tombs of Catholic families. The **Cementerio Disidentes** (Dinamarca 217, 8:30am-5pm

---

1: Ascensor El Peral **2:** Reloj Turri **3:** Museo Municipal de Bellas Artes

daily) has its entrance directly opposite the entrance of Cementerio No. 1 and was reserved for non-Catholics; English, Scottish, Germans, and Americans are the main residents.

PARQUE CULTURAL VALPARAÍSO

Parque Cultural Valparaíso (Calle Cárcel 472, tel. 32/2359 400, http://parquecultural. cl, 9am-7pm Tues.-Sun.) is an arts and cultural space in what was once a prison. Contemporary concrete structures accompany the formidable facade of the restored cell block. The cells have been adapted into workshop spaces. Concerts, theater, and dance performances happen regularly. Arts and crafts fairs, usually on weekends, are worthy for souvenirs.

Cerro Florida and Cerro Bellavista

It's a steep climb to Cerro Florida from Calle Aldunate in El Plan, but the white cabs of the restored **Ascensor Espíritu Santo** (Aldunate, accessed through a signed iron gate, 7am-11pm daily, CH$100) connect with Calle Rudolph and can get you there much quicker.

★ LA SEBASTIANA

La Sebastiana (Ferrari 692, tel. 32/2256 606, www.fundacionneruda.org, 10am-7pm Tues.-Sun. Jan.-Feb., 10am-6pm Tues.-Sun. Mar.-Dec., CH$7,000 adults, CH$2,500 children) was the home of Chile's most famous poet, the Nobel Prize-winning Pablo Neruda, and is perhaps the most famous of his three residences. He bought the building in 1961. It's rambling but carefully designed, with a famous view of Valparaíso from the 2nd-floor living room. Neruda would enjoy the New Year's Eve fireworks from here.

Elements of Neruda's whimsical personality are evident throughout the house, with a wooden horse from a French merry-go-round embodying his oft-cited refrain that "the man who does not play has lost the child within him." The multicolored stone mural above the stairs depicts an ancient map of Antarctica and Patagonia and was assembled by his friend and co-owner of the house, Marie Martner; it's just one of many installations that the Chilean sculptor gifted to Neruda.

An informative audio guide, available in English, narrates the poet's time at La Sebastiana and highlights his extensive collection of art, maps, and trinkets picked up

entrance to the Museo Mirador Lukas

during his travels as a professional diplomat. Admission is first come, first served; in summer and on weekends, this can lead to lines later in the day.

MUSEO A CIELO ABIERTO

The **Museo a Cielo Abierto** (bounded by Ferrari, Rudolph, Paseo Quimera, and Aldunate) is an open-air collection of 20 murals on houses by some of Chile's biggest artists, including Roberto Matta and Nemesio Antúnez.

The project was started in 1973, but the military coup that year prevented it from coming to fruition until 1991. Time and vandalism have left many murals in poor condition. The easiest way to get here is to climb the Subida Pasteur stairway from the intersection of Aldunate and Hiuto, or take Ascensor Espíritu Santo. The municipal tourist information office on Calle Condell has a map labeling the different murals.

Other Neighborhoods

As with most of the hill neighborhoods, aside from the most touristed, keep an eye on your belongings and don't wander around after dark.

CERRO POLANCO

For a look at gritty untouristed Valparaíso, head southwest of Plaza O'Higgins along Calle Victoria to Calle Simpson, where a dingy 150-meter-long tunnel leads to the 1916-built **Ascensor Polanco** (7am-10pm daily, CH$100). Unique in that it's a lift, not a funicular, this *ascensor* takes you up to **Cerro Polanco,** with 360-degree views of the city at the top.

Wander back down along Calle Simpson, where over 70 **murals** are tucked into the side streets of this working-class neighborhood. Most were painted during the Primer Festival Latinoamericano de Graffiti Mural in 2012.

CERRO BARÓN

Another worthy hillside neighborhood is **Cerro Barón,** high above Avenida España

along the coast. At the top, the striking 1931 neo-gothic **Universidad Técnica Federico Santa María,** one of the most prestigious engineering universities in Latin America, overlooks the Pacific Ocean.

Accessed from narrow Pasaje Barón, just off the intersection of Avenida España and Avenida Errázuriz, **Ascensor Barón** (Av. España, 7am-10pm daily, CH$100) was the city's first electric funicular, built in 1906. It carries passengers up in red-and-white cars to **Mirador Diego Portales** for views across the hillside neighborhoods.

ENTERTAINMENT
Nightlife

Dating from 1908 and decorated with maritime signal flags, **Bar La Playa** (Cochrane 568, Barrio Puerto, tel. 9/9961 2207, 11am-12:30am Mon.-Thurs., 11am-4:30am Fri.-Sat., 11am-10pm Sun.) was a hit with the port's sailors—and it doesn't feel like it's changed much since. Come for cheap liter bottles of beer and a rowdy but fun atmosphere, particularly on weekends when the basement throbs to the beat of heavy rock bands and the upstairs to hundreds of dancing students.

With its cozy corners and live jazz music Friday-Saturday, trendy **Café Vimilo** (Almirante Montt 448, Cerro Alegre, tel. 32/2230 665, www.cafevinilo.cl, 9am-1:30pm Sun.-Thurs., 9am-3am Fri.-Sat.) is linger-worthy for its expansive array of piscos from the specialty bar and deeply knowledgeable bartenders. Live music starts at 10pm, but get here early for a table or a seat at the bar.

Close your eyes and you'll be in the 1950s with the aging musicians dressed in their Sunday best jamming in the corner of **Cinzano** (Plaza Anibal Pinto 1182, Barrio Almendral, tel. 32/2213 043, http://barcinzano.cl, 12:30pm-2:30am Mon.-Sat.), a classic *porteño* bar and restaurant that opened in 1896. The food isn't noteworthy, so grab a stool at the long wooden bar and share a *jarra de borgoña,* a jug of red wine mixed with strawberries and icing sugar. On weekends, join the rowdier guests late into

Valpo's Best Views

Paseo Atkinson has striking views of the city.

Valparaíso offers magnificent views of the harbor, Viña del Mar, Reñaca, and beyond. The best panoramas are from the tops of the city's many hills.

PASEO 21 DE MAYO

Take Ascensor Artillería up to Paseo 21 de Mayo, just below the looming Museo Marítimo Nacional, for panoramic views of the busy port and the towns north of Viña del Mar.

PASEO YUGOSLAVO

From the top of Ascensor El Peral, Paseo Yugoslavo offers vistas of the port below, with high-rises in El Plan in the foreground. The views are even better from the 2nd floor of the nearby Museo Municipal de Bellas Artes.

MUSEO LORD COCHRANE

The views from Museo Lord Cochrane (Merlet 195, no phone, 10am-2pm and 3:30pm-11pm Tues.-Fri., 9:30am-6:30pm Sat., free), at the edge of Cerro Cordillera, are special: At sunset, its cannon-ornamented terrace is a sensational place to watch the clouds turn pink.

PASEO ATKINSON AND PASEO GERVASONI

The residential Paseo Atkinson is a quaint street, with 19th-century corrugated metal-fronted houses in bright primary colors and street dogs slumbering in the shade. There are low wooden benches to appreciate the views along palm-lined Avenida Errázuriz. Get here by climbing the steep Calle Concepción from Calle Esmeralda in El Plan, or by taking Ascensor Concepción to Paseo Gervansoni, a great place for photos of Reloj Turri and the port below.

AVENIDA ALEMANIA

The 40-minute walk along Avenida Alemania to La Sebastiana from Plazuela San Luís is sweltering in summer but offers sensational bay and city views, particularly from Plaza Bismark (Av. Alemania and Cumming), 10 minutes into the walk, and Mirador Camogli (Av. Alemania and Guillermo Rivera), 500 meters west of La Sebastiana.

MIRADOR DIEGO PORTALES

For wider panoramas of the city, head up Ascensor Barón in Cerro Barón to Mirador Diego Portales (Diego Portales and Caupolicán), also known as Mirador Barón, where you can look back across El Plan, the train station, and the hills farther north.

the night, when the tables are pulled aside to form a dance floor. There's live music Wednesday-Sunday.

The ever-popular **El Viaje Bar** (Cumming 93, tel. 9/7488 9513, elviajebar@gmail.com, 8pm-4am Mon.-Sat.) has live jazz, salsa, and *cueca* bands, a dance floor, good beer, great mojitos, and even an old trolleybus inside where you can enjoy a drink. **La Piedra Feliz** (Errázuriz 1054, tel. 9/8262 7607, 9pm-4am Thurs., 9:30pm-5am Fri.-Sat., CH$10,900), right on the waterfront, is the place to party in Valparaíso. The crowd is older than that downtown. There are three rooms of music, often with live '80s rock and DJs playing salsa and modern international and Latin music. It gets going late.

You can't beat the wine selection or the views across Valparaíso's rooftops at **Winebox Wine Bar** (Baquedano 763, Cerro Mariposa, tel. 9/9424 5331, http://wineboxvalparaiso.com noon-10pm daily Dec.-Mar., 5pm-10pm daily Apr.-Nov.). Over 340 varietals—30 by the glass—are on offer at this funky rooftop bar, with sommelier-led wine-tastings and flights available. It's part of the Winebox hotel.

The Arts

The **Teatro Municipal de Valparaíso** (Av. Uruguay 410, tel. 32/2214 654, www.teatromunicipal.cl) on Plaza O'Higgins is one of the city's main venues for drama and live music.

The library at **La Sebastiana** (Ferrari 692, tel. 32/2256 606, www.fundacionneruda.org) plays host to literary workshops, poetry readings, and theater performances throughout the week. The library is accessed by a ramp just below the main house.

On Paseo Dimalow, **El Internado** (Paseo Dimalow 167, Cerro Alegre, tel. 32/3354 153, http://elinternado.cl) has a complete range of arty events, including tango, magic and comedy shows, live bands, theater, and ceramic workshops. Sunday is cinema night, with Chilean and international films on the big screen.

CasaPlan (Av. Brasil 1490, tel. 32/2593 450, 8:30am-8:30pm Mon.-Fri., 10am-2:30pm Sun.) has a printing workshop on the 1st floor, a 2nd-floor gallery with rotating monthly exhibitions of photography and modern art, plus a subterranean space where dance and music performances and festivals are held throughout the week.

Festivals and Events

Pomp and ceremony descend upon Plaza Sotomayor annually on May 21, the **Día de las Glorias Navales,** where regimented rows of army, navy, and air force members parade through Valpo's streets, commemorating the Battle of Iquique.

NEW YEAR'S EVE

The **Año Nuevo** (New Year's Eve) fireworks over the bay are a serious event in the city's calendar, when hundreds of thousands of revelers descend on the port to watch the display in double as it reflects on the ocean. Make hotel reservations at least six months in advance.

CARNAVAL MIL TAMBORES

Held annually on the first Friday-Sunday of October, the **Carnaval Mil Tambores** (www.miltambores.cl) is a colorful celebration of Valparaíso's artistic liberty, with parades of partygoers dressed in vibrant outfits or naked except for elaborate paintings on their bodies. This aspect of the festival started as a protest against the municipal government's negativity toward the original celebrations. Participants make their noisy way through the city's streets, banging drums and other percussion instruments in a friendly, arty affair. It's a spectacle to watch.

SHOPPING

In El Plan, the chaotic, noisy, and captivating **Mercado El Cardonal** (Av. Brasil, Rawson, Yungay, and Uruguay, http://elcardonal.cl, 5am-6pm daily) is the city's main market, where carefully stacked fruit and vegetables, along with absolutely anything else you could hope to buy, weight down streetside stalls.

Valparaíso has a wealth of handmade arts and crafts, found most easily wandering the streets of Cerro Alegre and Cerro Concepción, where you'll discover artisan-made jewelry and artwork. For antiques, the **Feria Antigüedades** (flea market, 10am-7pm daily), mostly at Plaza O'Higgins but sprawling along Calle Pedro Montt on Saturday-Sunday, is your best bet. **Paseo Yugoslavo** (no fixed hours), near the upper end of Ascensor El Peral, is a good place for souvenirs. Local craftspeople sell leather purses, T-shirts printed with the Valparaíso skyline, and oil paintings depicting the city.

Caleta Portales

There's no fresher fish in Valparaíso than at traditional market **Caleta Portales** (Av. España 2351, 7am-4pm Tues.-Sun.), on the eastern outskirts of the city, where gleaming piles of razor clams and scallops and pots of ceviche are on sale in the main market. Buy fish to cook in your lodging's kitchen. Look for what's in abundance, as this suggests seasonality.

At the market is a separate complex with small restaurants serving battered conger eel and crisp deep-fried seafood empanadas, although the quality is somewhat lower than in the established restaurants in Valparaíso. Wander out toward the pier to watch the catch being unloaded, and look for sea lions sunning or fighting with pelicans for first dibs on fish remains. Get here early for the fullest market experience; the metro stop Estación Caleta Portales drops you right outside.

RECREATION

The **Santiago Wanderers** (www.santiagowanderers.cl), the oldest soccer team in Chile, were founded by British immigrants in Valparaíso. The team plays in the **Estadio Elías Figueroa Brander** in Barrio Playa Ancha, northwest of Barrio Artillería. Although the rivalry between the Wanderers and Viña del Mar's team, Everton, makes for a thrilling match, fans can get rowdy and sometimes violent. You're better off watching a game between the teams at the Estadio Sausalito in Viña, where the atmosphere is calmer.

FOOD

El Plan

Prepare to fall in love with the slick new ★ **Barrio Huerto** (Blanco 038, tel. 9/9588 8249, www.barriohuerto.com, 10:30am-5pm Sun.-Wed., 11:30am-11:45pm Thurs.-Sat., CH$7,900-11,900, *menú del día* CH$6,900), on an otherwise grimy street next to the port. Inside a converted storehouse, the bare brick walls and heavy black girders give a sense of the restaurant's historical roots, while the menu uses only seasonal produce from the harbor or the local market. Devour playful, elegant dishes of boneless short ribs slow-roasted in a red wine sauce or pan-toasted gnocchi with sautéed mushrooms and parmesan foam. Meals can be prepared vegetarian or vegan. A six-course tasting menu is CH$25,000.

The simply furnished **CasaPlan** (Av. Brasil 1490, tel. 32/2593 450, 8:30am-8:30pm Mon.-Fri., 10am-2:30pm Sun.), inside a restored 1916 building, is a welcome spot for breakfast, coffee, tea, sandwiches, or cakes if you're exploring El Almendral. They have their own gallery and a downstairs theater.

Ignore the exterior: **Restorán Caprí** (Cochrane 664, tel. 32/2594 193, www.restorancapri.cl, 12:30pm-4:45pm Mon.-Sat., CH$6,000-8,500) is an award-winning Valpo *picada* in a class of its own for authentic local food in an authentic setting. Shuffle in behind the locals for a menu of fish: huge portions of lightly battered *reineta* and *merluza*, ceviche, and an unmissable Valpo favorite, conger eel soup, are for lunch.

The oldest bar in Chile, **Bar Liberty** (Almirante Riveros 9, Barrio Puerto, tel. 32/2234 100 or 9/9170 0171, 10am-late Thurs.,

1: military parade during the Día de las Glorias Navales **2:** crabs for sale at Caleta Portales

10am-6pm Fri.-Wed., CH$5,000-9,000) was historically popular among artsy bohemian types and sailors. Now it's a family-friendly daytime affair. Get serenaded with live local music as you dine on simple seafood dishes of *paila marina* (seafood soup) and empanadas. It's also a good spot for *pepiño* (sweet white wine) mixed with strawberries or combined with ice cream and grenadine to make the Chilean classic *terremoto*. In Valparaíso, this drink often goes by the name "tsunami." Thursday is live *cueca* night from 9pm.

Cerro Alegre and Cerro Concepción

For a cheap, tasty, lightning-fast lunch, tiny **Delicias Xpress** (Urriola 358, tel. 32/2237 438, 10am-6pm Mon.-Sat., CH$1,500-2,500) has 80 flavors of fried and baked empanadas to take out. Try the *queso cabra* (goat cheese), *camaron* (shrimp), and *cebollin* (chives) empanadas.

Part of the clutch of modern restaurants serving seasonal local produce, **Puerto Claro** (Papudo 612, tel. 2/2792 8196, Cero Concepción, www.puertoclarovalpo.cl, 12:30pm-4pm and 7:30pm-11pm Tues.-Sat., 12:30pm-5pm Sun., CH$12,500-14,000) has a tiny but dynamic menu with starters and mains that change regularly. You might find rib-eye steak with seasonal vegetables or duck magret with beetroot confit. The vibe is youthful and the location, in a 19th-century building stripped to its brick walls, entirely *porteño*. The seven-course tasting menu is CH$27,000.

Hip ★ **Fauna** (Paseo Dimalow 166, Cerro Alegre, tel. 32/3270 719, 1pm-10:30pm daily, CH$6,000-12,000) is always packed, for good reason. The wraparound outdoor terrace has lovely views of the bay and it serves standout braised beef with eggplant mash and sandwiches stuffed with prosciutto, apple, and camembert on wafer-thin bread. Service is fast, and the place is consistently packed, particularly after 9pm; they don't accept reservations on weekends.

The 12-table **Pasta e Vino** (Templeman 352, Cerro Concepción, tel. 32/2496 187, http://pastaevinoristorante.cl, 1pm-3:30pm, 7pm-11pm Tues.-Sat., 1pm-4pm Sun., CH$12,500-14,500) is the only place to go for fresh pasta in Valparaíso. The muted gold and brown decor contributes to warm, elegant atmosphere. Ravioli is the house special, filled with duck, smoked salmon and coconut, or scallops. The white wine selection is excellent. Booking is essential for lunch and dinner on weekends.

You'll find locals queueing out of the door at **Pizzeria Malandrino** (Almirante Montt 532, Cerro Alegre, tel. 32/3184 827, 1pm-4:30pm and 7pm-11pm Tues.-Thurs., 12:30pm-5:30pm and 7pm-midnight Fri.-Sat., 12:30pm-5:30pm Sun., CH$6,000-8,500), where you can watch wood-fired pizzas being slipped into the oven behind the bar. It's an authentic pizzeria, with a few gingham tablecloths thrown in.

A favorite watering hole among Valparaíso's 20- and 30-somethings, ★ **Altamira** (Av. Elías 126, tel. 32/3193 619, http://cerveceraaltamira.cl, 6pm-11:30pm Mon.-Thurs., 6pm-12:30am Fri., 1pm-12:30am Sat., CH$6,000-9,000) is a brewery, pub, and beer museum with origins in the city's first brewer, Irish immigrant Andrés Blest. House beers are pale, amber, stout, and strong ale, although more inventive specials are sometimes on tap. Their food isn't bad, combining pub grub (burgers, *chorrillanas,* and pizzas with beer-infused dough) and typical Chilean dishes, with a few German *crudos*. There's live jazz at 7:30pm Tuesday-Thursday and 8:30pm Saturday; you'll need dinner reservations to get a spot. They also run tours of the beer museum and brewery with prior reservations.

To the right of Ascensor El Peral, in a quiet spot behind Palacio Baburizza, ★ **Restaurant El Peral** (El Peral 182, tel. 32/3361 353, 11:30am-4:30pm daily, CH$9,000-11,000, *menú del día* CH$8,000) charms with its lovely shaded terrace and harbor views. The menu is small and changes regularly; try the *machas a la parmesana* (razor clams with parmesan) with a touch of blue cheese, local fish fresh from the harbor and lightly cooked, or *pastel de jaiba* (crab stew). Drink specials of pear daiquiris and prickly pear pisco sours change daily.

Wandering the streets of this undulating city is hot work. Sit for an ice cream or grab a cone to go in flavors like *arroz con leche* (rice pudding) or vegan chocolate at **Amor Porteño** (Almirante Montt 418, tel. 32/2216 253, 10:30am-8:30pm Tues.-Sun.).

Cerro Bellavista

It's a detour to Cerro Bellavista, but ★ **Espiritu Santo** (Héctor Calvo 392, tel. 32/3270 443, www.hosteriaespiritusanto.cl, 1:30pm-3pm Wed., 1:30pm-3pm and 8pm-11pm Thurs.-Sat., 1pm-4pm Sun., CH$12,500-16,500), run by a mother-and-son team, is worth it. The restaurant specializes in *pescado de roca* (fish that live along rocky shorelines and are caught using harpoons) prepared as ceviche or *tiraditos,* served with pureed lima beans and roasted kale or in a broth of langoustines and cherry tomatoes. The sweetbreads and grilled octopus are similarly first-rate. Booking ahead is advised.

ACCOMMODATIONS
Cerro Alegre and Cerro Concepción
UNDER CH$25,000

On a backstreet in Cerro Concepción, **Hostel Casa Aventura** (Pasaje Gálvez 11, Cerro Concepción, tel. 32/2755 963, www.casaventura.cl, CH$10,500 dorm shared bath, CH$24,000 d shared bath) is a comfortable backpacker-style hostel with six large bedrooms, three of which are shared dormitories. Communal space is limited, and the kitchen is more of a corridor, but the reasonable rates come with a relaxed and friendly atmosphere. Rates include IVA.

The warren-like **Casa Volante** (Escalera Fischer 27, Cerro Concepción, http://casavolantehostal.com, CH$10,990 dorm shared bath, CH$30,000 d shared bath, CH$37,000 flat, cash only) is a quirky hostel with multiple chill-out areas in various

high-ceilinged old buildings. Deep, comfy armchairs and a roof terrace make a welcoming choice on a budget. Options for couples include sizeable doubles and a self-sufficient flat with a kitchen. A large communal kitchen is on the 2nd floor. Dorm rooms don't include breakfast, which costs an additional CH$2,000. It can be noisy until late. Rates include IVA.

CH$25,000-40,000

The dated rooms at old-fashioned **Hostal Casa Patrimonio** (Lautaro Rosas 493, Cerro Alegre, tel. 32/2492 320, CH$28,000 d shared bath, CH$48,000 d private bath) are themed with unusual decorations; the Elvis room has floor-to-ceiling posters. For cheap digs with a view, you can't argue with the rates. Breakfast isn't offered, but the sunny terrace, with patio furniture and panoramic views across the bay, compensates. Rates include IVA.

CH$40,000-60,000

In the heart of Cerro Concepción, seven bright and airy bedrooms decorated in soothing blue or yellow are the options at superb ★ **Puerta Escondida** (Templeman 549, Cerro Concepción, tel. 32/3283 369, http://puertaescondida.cl, CH$48,000 d). This pint-size B&B has everything for a comfortable stay, but it lacks views. For a warm welcome, a large breakfast, and excellent value, you can't go wrong. Book well in advance.

OVER CH$80,000

English painter Thomas Somerscales spent 20 years in the building that's now the elegant **Somerscales Hotel Boutique** (San Enrique 446, Cerro Alegre, tel. 32/2331 006, www.hotelsomerscales.cl, CH$108,000-170,000 d). Little remains from his time, but the owners have tastefully decorated with antiques, plus cast-iron bed frames and English-style furniture. A pleasant checkerboard-tiled terrace dripping with fuchsias adds to the ample charm.

This egg-blue 1880s house was converted in 2007 into chic ★ **Zero Hotel** (Lautaro

Rosas 343, Cerro Alegre, tel. 32/2113 113, www.zerohotel.com, CH$203,000 d, suite CH$288,000 d) and has established itself as Valparaíso's top lodging. The four suites have sea views, but the five standard rooms don't. Every room has lots of space. Downstairs is a pretty terrace looking toward the bay.

Understated modernity with clear views of a pastel-hued church are at trendy **Hotel Fauna** (Paseo Dimalow 166, Cerro Alegre, tel. 32/3270 719, http://faunahotel.cl, CH$93,000-104,000 d). The original adobe walls of this 1830s house are still intact. Murals by local graffiti artists add a personal touch. It's worth the extra money for the upgrade to superior for the views of Iglesia Luterana. The only downside is the complete lack of living space, but Fauna is in the heart of Cerro Alegre's restaurants and cafés, including the hotel's restaurant next door.

Other Neighborhoods

Painted in shocking colors to match its name, **The Yellow House** (Capitán Muñoz Gamero 91, Cerro Artillería, tel. 9/8137 0839, www.theyellowhouse.cl, CH$30,000 d shared bath, CH$35,000 d private bath) on Cerro Artillería has sweeping vistas of the rickety hillside houses of Valparaíso. Opt for one of the rooms at the front of the house (CH$10,000 extra) for these magnificent views; all seven rooms are well proportioned and neat. Owner Ana and her English-speaking children are on hand to offer tips for exploring the city. Take a taxi at night to get to the main tourist neighborhoods. For an authentic taste of Valpo, there's nowhere better. Rates include IVA.

Just across a ravine from Cerro Florida, Cerro Mariposa is home to the distinctive ★ **Winebox** (Baquedano 763, Cerro Mariposa, tel. 9/9424 5331, http://wineboxvalparaiso.com, CH$77,000 d), built from 25 recycled shipping containers and brightly painted to match the character of the city. The 21 mini apartments are named for grapes and come with kitchens and floor-to-ceiling windows and balconies. A spectacular rooftop terrace has exceptional panoramas. Six graffiti artists have added their stamp to each room. This is just one of the quirky features of the hotel, masterminded by Grant Phelps, the former winemaker of Casas del Bosque in Valle de Casablanca. Phelps runs tours of his urban winery, the first in Valparaíso, in the basement of the hotel. The rooftop **Winebox Wine Bar** is open to nonguests.

INFORMATION AND SERVICES

Municipal-run **Dirección de Turismo** (Condell 1490, tel. 32/2939 262, www.vlpo.cl, 8:30am-2pm and 3:30pm-5:45pm Mon.-Thurs., 8:30am-2pm, 3:30pm-4:30pm Fri.) has enthusiastic staff who speak competent English. They have maps for the Museo Cielo Abierto and the city in general. Additional branches are at **Muelle Prat** (no phone, 10am-6pm daily) and the **Terminal de Buses** (Av. Pedro Montt 2860, no phone, 9am-1pm and 2pm-7pm daily). SERNATUR (Plaza Sotomayor 233, tel. 32/2236 264, 9am-6pm Mon.-Fri., 9am-5pm Sat.-Sun.), just off Playa Sotomayor, is equally helpful. For useful downloadable maps, check out **Valparaíso Map** (http://valparaisomap.cl), with a virtual map of the city and suggested walking routes.

For withdrawing cash downtown, Avenida Prat in Barrio Puerto is the best option, with **BBVA** (Prat 804), **Scotiabank** (Prat 762), and **BancoEstado** (Prat 656, ATM 24 hr daily) just a few streets apart. Banks are generally open only until 2pm Monday-Friday, and many ATMs close at this time. To **exchange money,** head to **Inter Cambio** (Plaza Sotomayor 11, Local 8) or **Exprinter Cambios** (Prat 895); rates are better in Santiago. You'll find the post office, **Correos** (Prat 856, 9am-6pm Mon.-Fri., 10am-1pm Sat.), in the downtown area.

The best hospital in the city is **Clínica Valparaíso** (Av. Brasil 2350, tel. 32/3818 100, www.redsalud.cl), which has urgent care services and English-speaking staff.

GETTING THERE

Getting to Valparaíso is only possible by bus or car. The nearest commercial airport is in Santiago. Most buses leave from **Terminal Rodoviario** (Av. Pedro Montt 2860, tel. 32/2939 695), half a block south of Plaza O'Higgins. Arriving at night, call a taxi, as the area is not safe after dark.

Car

To get to Valparaíso from **Santiago,** it's a 115-km, 1.5- to 2-hour drive west via Ruta 68. On Friday evening and public holidays, expect congestion around the El Prado tunnel, 46km into the drive. From Plaza Vergara in **Viña del Mar,** it's a 9-km, 15- to 30-minute drive west along Calle Álvarez, which becomes Avenida España when it reaches the coast.

Bus

The **Terminal Rodoviario Valparaíso** (Pedro Montt 2860, tel. 32/2939 695) is the main bus terminal for both regional and long-distance routes.

REGIONAL BUSES

For **Viña del Mar,** catch any bus numbering 602-604 or 606-611 (20min, CH$250-300); these leave from Avenida Errázuriz, heading south. For the beaches north of Viña, including **Maitencillo** (1.5hr), **Zapallar** (1.75hr), and **Papudo** (2hr), buses from **Sol del Pacífico** (tel. 32/2213 776) leave every 30 minutes from the Terminal Rodoviario and cost CH$2,500 to all destinations. For the return journey, buses pick up from the Plaza Papudo (bounded by Esmeralda, Miraflores, Fernández Concha, and Chorillos) in Papudo, from the intersection of the E-30-F road and 28 de Mayo in the south of Zapallar, and from Avenida del Mar, just opposite Tío Tomato (Av. Del Mar 695) in Maitencillo.

Tur Bus (www.turbus.cl) operates multiple daily buses to and from **Zapallar** (1.5hr, CH$3,000), and **Papudo** (2hr, CH$3,500), which depart from their offices in Papudo (Esmeralda 260, tel. 33/2791 377) and

Zapallar (Olegario Ovalle 128, Zapallar, tel. 33/213 8275) and terminate in the Terminal Rodoviario in Valparaíso. Tur Bus and **Pullman Bus Lago Peñuelas** (tel. 35/2287 531 or 35/2216 163) shuttle 6am-10pm daily between Valparaíso and **Isla Negra** (1.5hr, CH$3,600), dropping you a block north of Casa Museo Isla Negra. Buses pick up from the same location. **Pullman Bus** (tel. 32/2596 690, http://pullmanbus.com) and Tur Bus have the most frequent departures from **Santiago** (1.75hr, CH$6,000), with buses leaving as regularly as every 10 minutes.

LONG-DISTANCE BUSES

The main carriers bringing passengers from the north of the country to Valparaíso include **Pullman Bus** and **Tur Bus,** also recommended from destinations in the south, in addition to **Condor Bus** (tel. 32/2133 101) and **EME Bus** (tel. 32/2596 665, www.emebus.cl); EME Bus and Tur Bus offer full 180-degree *cama* (reclining) seats to some destinations. Buses from destinations in the north that do not pass through Santiago arrive every two hours. These include buses from **La Serena** (7hr, CH$10,000/CH$20,0000), **Copiapó** (12hr, CH$15,000/CH$25,000), **Antofagasta** (20hr, CH$23,000/CH$35,000), and **Iquique** (27hr, CH$28,000/CH$40,000). There are less frequent daily services from **Arica** (32hr, CH$32,000/CH$52,000). There are also eight daily departures from **Calama** (24hr, CH$28,000/CH$45,000).

Multiple buses daily run from destinations in the south, most of which pass through Santiago. These include **Talca** (6hr, CH$7,400), **Chillán** (9hr, CH$9,000/CH$14,000), **Concepción** (9.5hr, CH$10,000/CH$16,000), **Temuco** (10hr, CH$11,000/CH$15,000), **Valdivia** (11hr, CH$12,000/CH$15,000), **Pucón** (12hr, CH$14,000/CH$18,000), **Osorno** (13hr, CH$14,000/CH$17,000), and **Puerto Montt** (15hr, CH$14,000/CH$17,000).

GETTING AROUND

A car isn't necessary in the city, particularly as the narrow, hilly roads present challenges for parking. It's easy to get around on foot and using the funiculars.

Trolleybus

A truly *porteño* way of seeing the city is aboard the historic **trolleybus** (known as *troles* by locals), the only remaining in Chile, which travels an 8-km route between Edificio Aduana in Barrio Puerto and Avenida Argentina in Almendral. Visit the **Dirección de Turismo** (Condell 1490, tel. 32/2939 262, www.vlpo.cl) for a map of the routes. Look for number 814, which is officially the oldest working trolleybus in the world. It costs CH$300; bring exact change.

Metro

It's called the metro, but Valpo's commuter train looks nothing like the underground system in Santiago. The **Metro Regional de Valaparaíso** (tel. 32/2527 633, www.metrovalparaiso.cl, 6:15am-10:30pm Mon.-Fri., 8:30am-10:30pm Sat.-Sun.) runs from Estación Puerto (Av. Errázuriz 711) north along the coast to Viña del Mar and beyond. It's a useful way to get quickly to different parts of El Plan and to Viña. You'll need a rechargeable Metroval card, which can be bought for CH$2,000 from any metro station. Fares depend on the time of day; expect to pay CH$388-430, regardless of distance.

Taxis, *Taxis Colectivos*, and *Micros*

Taxis are plentiful in Valpo; you'll find taxi stands at most squares, or flag one down on the street. *Taxis colectivos* look like standard taxis, black with yellow roofs, but feature a sign indicating their destination. They run specific routes around the city and can be an excellent way of getting around without breaking a sweat.

Micros are small buses that run throughout El Plan and up into the hills. Number 612 (known by locals as the O) runs between the Congreso Nacional and Cerro Alegre. *Micros* are operated by various companies; you can get full routes on the website **TMV** (www.tmv.cl).

SOUTHERN BEACHES

The stretch of beach towns and villages south of Valparaíso, accessible by bus or car, are home to the region's finest seafood, picturesque empty beaches, and poet Pablo Neruda's most interesting former residence.

Renting a car is useful to visit this area. **Rosselot** (Victoria 2675, Valparaíso, tel. 32/2352 365, 9am-7pm Mon.-Fri., 10am-1pm Sat.) is the only company with an office in Valparaíso. Be aware that their insurance normally doesn't cover beyond third-party liability. There are more options in Viña del Mar and at Santiago's airport.

★ Quintay

One of the prettiest seaside settings on the central coast, **Quintay,** 42km south of Valparaíso, is a charming fishing village with pelicans in the harbor, Caleta Quintay. Its mellow pace makes it a worthwhile day trip from Valparaíso. Scuba-dive in clear water with local PADI-certified **Buceo Quintay** (Caleta Quintay s/n, tel. 9/9358 7382, www.buceoquintay.com), with classes in English (from CH$26,250).

A 200-meter **pedestrian path** (northwest from the end of Av. Jorge Montt) runs along the coast; watch for rare *chungungos* (marine otters) in the waves and on the rocks. The path is the site of a **craft market** (noon-6pm Sat.-Sun.) where jewelry made from rare black coral is an unusual item.

Ex-Ballanera de Quintay (tel. 32/2362 511, www.fundacionquintay.cl, 11am-6pm Wed.-Mon., CH$800), at the northwestern end of the pedestrian path, was once a whaling station where whales were butchered on the concrete floor. It's now an open-air museum dedicated to protecting these animals,

1: the fishing village of Quintay **2:** Casa Museo Isla Negra

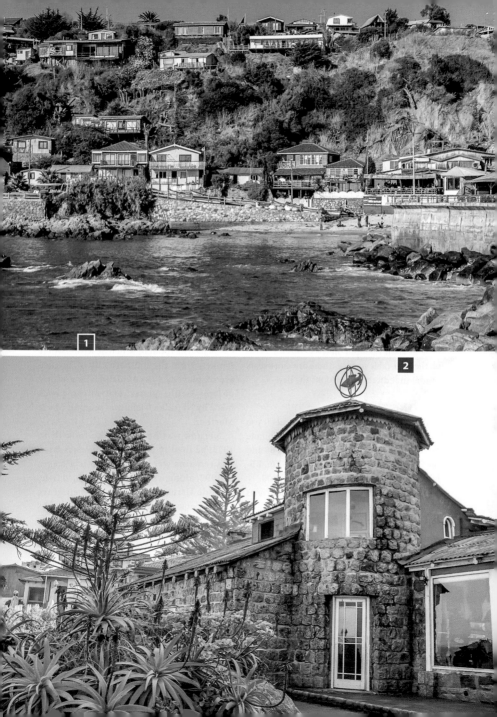

with exhibitions on the history and folklore of whales in different countries, plus an expansive collection of whalebones.

Three kilometers northwest of the village, **Playa Grande** is a kilometer-long beach bookended by sheer forested cliffs. A line of high-rise apartments sits back from the beach, but the area remains otherwise undeveloped. The beach is extremely popular in January-February, but outside these months, particularly during the week, it's not uncommon to find it serenely empty. To get here, take the potholed turnoff to the left along the F-802, just past the last few houses, and follow it to its end.

FOOD

One of the village's biggest draws is the exceptional ★ **Miramar** (Caleta Quintay s/n, tel. 32/2362 046, noon-6pm daily, CH$8,000-12,000), with the best platters of razor clams cooked in parmesan, deep-fried conger eel, and *pastel de jaiba* (crab stew) in the entire country. They don't take reservations; arrive no later than 12:30pm on weekends for a seat on their 10-table terrace (there are more seats inside) that directly overlooks the bay.

GETTING THERE

Getting to Quintay is significantly easier if you have your own vehicle. It's a 42-km, 40-minute drive south from **Valparaíso** on Ruta 68 and the F-800. From **Santiago,** it's a 125-km, 1.5-hour drive west via Ruta 68 and the F-800.

There are occasional *taxis colectivos* (40min, CH$2,000-3,000) that leave when full from the corner of Avenida Argentina and Avenida Pedro Montt in Valparaíso, half a block east of the Terminal de Buses. **Buses GR Quintay** (tel. 9/9220 7076) shuttle between Valparaíso and Quintay every two hours or so; they leave from the corner of Calles 12 de Febrero and Chacabuco, half a block north from the Terminal de Buses in Valparaíso.

★ Casa Museo Isla Negra

Pablo Neruda's favorite of his three houses, the scenic beachfront **Casa Museo Isla Negra** (Poeta Neruda s/n, tel. 35/2461 284, http://fundacionneruda.org, 10am-7pm Tues.-Sun. Jan.-Feb., 10am-6pm Tues.-Sun. Mar.-Dec., CH$7,000 adults, CH$2,500 children), is 84km south of Valparaíso, making it an easy day trip. Bought in 1938, the house faced extensive alterations that continued over 20 years; Neruda himself described the house as "growing, just like people, just like trees." It's where he finished his epic poem *Canto General.*

What sets it apart from his other homes is the sheer scale of items on display. Neruda was a keen collector of whimsical souvenirs from his travels: Moorish figures bought in Venice flank the entrance to the building, while his 600-strong shell collection is on display in an extension of the original building. Perhaps the most famed items are 16 ship figureheads that Neruda salvaged from boatyards and antiques shops and which adorn the living area and study. This house offers a strong sense of Neruda's southern Chilean roots, particularly in the Covacha, the room in which he wrote, where trinkets from the southern city of Temuco are displayed. Also on display is a mural of lapis lazuli, quartz, and volcanic rock made by Neruda's friend and sculptor Marie Martner.

Neruda was here when he took ill in 1973; he died in Santiago three days later. His remains were returned to Isla Negra in 1992, along with those of his third wife, Matilde Urrutia. You can visit their grave at the back of the house, where it looks out to sea, as was his request in the poem "Disposiciones."

An excellent audio guide in English and other languages is included in admission. Entry to the house is staggered to avoid overcrowding; arrive early so you don't have to wait in line. It's not possible to purchase tickets in advance.

FOOD

There is an excellent restaurant attached to Casa de Isla Negra. **El Rincón del Poeta** (tel. 35/2461 774, http://elrincondelpoeta.cl,

10am-5:15pm daily, CH$8,000-10,000) over-looks the beach and specializes in seafood. The *machas estrelladas* (razor clams cooked in a parmesan and white wine sauce) are particularly special. Make a reservation on summer weekends, as the restaurant gets packed.

INFORMATION AND SERVICES

A small **information kiosk** (10am-5:15pm daily) run by the municipality is on Avenida Dubournais, next to the pedestrian path to Casa Museo Isla Negra. They have information about transportation and other local attractions.

GETTING THERE

To drive to Isla Negra from **Valparaíso,** the most direct way is Ruta 68 south and the F-90 west; this 85-km drive takes just over an hour. To take the scenic route, go south on Ruta 68, then southwest on the F-800, which becomes the F-818, F-814, and G-98-F. This 70-km drive takes 1.5 hours.

It's possible to get to Isla Negra by bus. **Tur Bus** (tel. 32/2133 104, www.turbus.cl) and **Pullman Bus Lago Peñuelas** (tel. 35/2287 531 and tel. 35/2216 163) run 6am-10pm daily between Isla Negra and **Valparaíso** (1.5hr, CH$3,600), dropping you a block north of Casa Museo Isla Negra.

Viña del Mar

The smaller, more modern, and cleaner sister of Valparaíso, Viña del Mar is known as La Ciudad Jardín (The Garden City) thanks to its tidy parks, palm-lined boulevards, and pleasant beaches. Viña, as it's known to locals, doesn't attract many international tourists; instead it's a holiday destination for Santiaguinos. Many of the city's historic palaces and mansions are now museums that merit a visit.

Viña's tidy white-sand beaches are its biggest attraction; hordes of Chilean and Argentinean visitors descend on the city in the height of summer. A quieter beach experience is farther north toward Papudo. The city's nightclubs and casino allow hedonistic nights brushing shoulders with Santiago's most well-to-do. An hour's drive inland, Parque Nacional La Campana is worth a visit for its splendid views and its groves of Chilean palm trees.

ORIENTATION

Viña del Mar is 5km northeast of Valparaíso, although it's hard to pinpoint where Viña starts and Valpo ends. **Avenida España** connects the two cities, winding between ocean and hills.

Viña's streets follow a conventional grid, making it easy to navigate. It's divided into north and south by the **Estero Marga-Marga,** a sludgy estuary; bridges connect the two sections. The center of the city's commercial district is **Plaza Vergara,** where some of the old mansions are. **Avenida Libertad,** Viña's main street, runs north from the plaza, crossing the estuary. This avenue acts as the center of the grid, with roads numbered and named Norte (north), Oriente (east), and Poniente (west). Most restaurants and bars are clustered around waterfront **Avenida San Martín,** between 1 Norte and 8 Norte, with a high concentration on 6 Norte. Avenida San Martín becomes **Avenida Jorge Montt** as it heads north toward Reñaca and a series of pretty beaches.

SIGHTS

In the manicured **Plaza Vergara** (Arlegui and Valparaíso), a bust of the city's founder, José Francisco Vergara, has pride of place. The square is home to the **Teatro Municipal** (Plaza Vergara s/n, tel. 32/2681 739, www.culturaviva.cl), built in the 1930s in Greco-Roman style.

A few blocks south of the plaza, **Iglesia**

Viña del Mar

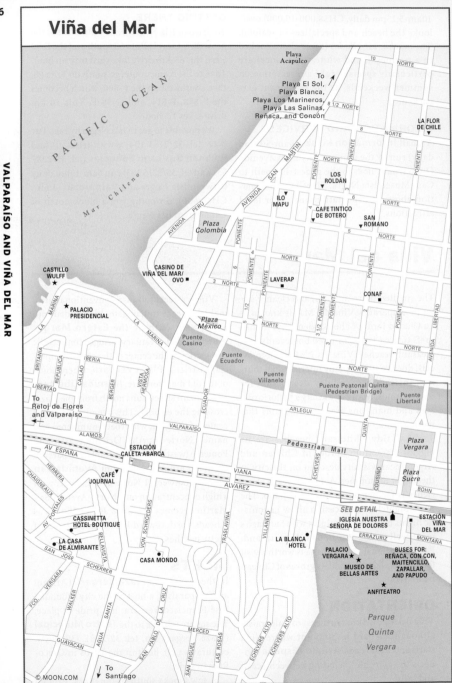

PACIFIC OCEAN

Mar Chileno

Playa
Acapulco

To
Playa El Sol,
Playa Blanca,
Playa Los Marineros,
Playa Las Salinas,
Reñaca, and Concón

10   NORTE

8 1/2 NORTE

LA FLOR
DE CHILE
▼

8   NORTE

LOS
ROLDÁN
▼

NORTE

6   NORTE

ILO
MAPU
▼

CAFE TINTICO
DE BOTERO
▼

SAN
ROMANO
▼

NORTE

Plaza
Colombia

CASTILLO
WULFF
★

★ PALACIO
PRESIDENCIAL

CASINO DE
VIÑA DEL MAR/
OVO ■

4   NORTE

6

3   NORTE

LAVERAP
■

CONAF
■

NORTE

1/2

Plaza
México

5   NORTE

3 1/2 PONIENTE

2

NORTE

Puente
Casino

Puente
Ecuador

1   NORTE

Puente
Villanelo

Puente Peatonal Quinta
(Pedestrian Bridge)

Puente
Libertad

To
Reloj de Flores
and Valparaíso
←

BRITANIA
REPÚBLICA
IBERIA
CALLAO
BERGER
VISTA
HERMOSA

LIBERTAD

BALMACEDA

ALAMOS

ECUADOR

VALPARAÍSO

ARLEGUI

QUINTA

Plaza
Vergara

AV ESPAÑA

ESTACIÓN
CALETA ABARCA

Pedestrian Mall

ECHEVERS

Plaza
Sucre

BOHN

HERRERA

CHAIGNEAUX

AV PORTALES

CAFÉ
JOURNAL
▼

VON SCHROEDERS

VIANA

ÁLVAREZ

VILLANELO

COUSIÑO

SEE DETAIL

CASSINETTA
HOTEL BOUTIQUE

BELAVISTA

TRASLAVIÑA

IGLESIA NUESTRA
SEÑORA DE DOLORES

ESTACIÓN
VIÑA
DEL MAR
■

LA CASA
DE ALMIRANTE ●

SAN JOSE

CASA MONDO

LA BLANCA
HOTEL

ERRÁZURIZ

MONTAÑA

PALACIO
VERGARA ★

BUSES FOR:
REÑACA, CON CON,
MAITENCILLO,
ZAPALLAR,
AND PAPUDO

VERGARA
FCO.
WALKER
SCHERRER
SANTA
AGUA
GUAYACAN

SAN PABLO
DE LA CRUZ
SAN MIGUEL
MERCED
LAS ROSAS
ECHEVERS ALTO
ECHEVERS ALTO

MUSEO DE
BELLAS ARTES

ANFITEATRO
★

Parque

Quinta

Vergara

To
Santiago
↓

LA MARINA

LA MARINA

PERÚ
AVENIDA
PONIENTE
PONIENTE
SAN MARTÍN
PONIENTE
PONIENTE
PONIENTE
PONIENTE
PONIENTE

AVENIDA
LIBERTAD

© MOON.COM

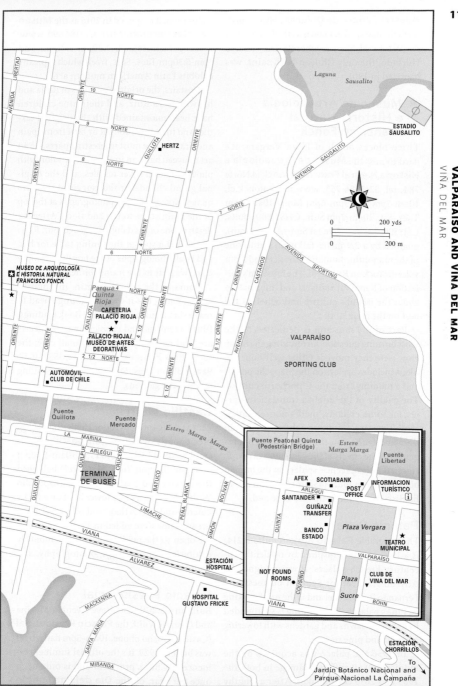

Nuestra Señora de Dolores (Álvares 662, open for mass), also known as the **Parroquia de Viña del Mar,** is where Saint Alberto Hurtado, the only Chilean-born saint, was baptized in 1901.

★ Museo de Arqueología e Historia Natural Francisco Fonck

Three blocks north of Plaza Vergara, it's hard to miss the **Museo de Arqueología e Historia Natural Francisco Fonck** (4 Norte 784, tel. 32/2686 753, www.museofonck.cl, 10am-2pm and 3pm-6pm Mon., 10am-6pm Tues.-Sat., 10am-2pm Sun., CH$2,800 adults, CH$500 children, free 1st Sun. of the month), guarded by a 2.9-meter-tall *moai* statue, one of the monolithic human figures carved from volcanic rock on Rapa Nui. The museum's collection of Rapa Nui artifacts and information about the island's culture and beliefs is the best on the mainland.

Part of the museum is dedicated to the most burning question surrounding the *moai*: How were they moved? Other well-done exhibits include displays on the Mapuche people and a mummy from the Chinchorro culture. The quality of the English translations varies; for some exhibits, there's no translation at all. Upstairs, among an exhibit on Chilean flora and fauna, is a chilling series of photographs of the effects of the venomous *araña de rincón* (Chilean recluse spider) on the human body. Museum tours (45min) are available in English and Spanish; tips are expected.

Palacio Rioja

The venerable **Palacio Rioja** (Quillota 214) is a 1907 mansion inspired by opulent 18th-century French palaces. It was designed by Alfredo Azancot for Spanish businessman Fernando Rioja Medel and is the most striking of Viña's palaces. The building is surrounded by a series of lawns and gardens with towering coconut and pine trees.

In 1956 the palace was acquired by the municipality; it suffered damage in both the 1985 and 2010 earthquakes. After a lengthy restoration, it reopened in 2016 as the **Museo de Artes Decorativa** (tel. 32/2184 690, www. museopalaciorioja.cl, 9:30am-1:30pm and 3pm-5:30pm Tues.-Sun., free), which typically exhibits Latin American modern art.

Upstairs, the original quarters of Rioja and his wife, Sara Ruiz, and their nine children have been maintained with the original textiles and furniture brought by boat from Spain and France. The most interesting parts are an art nouveau bath, an imperial-style salon with plush pink and silver textiles, and the original grand chandelier that survived the 2010 quake. Note the family photographs at the top of the main stairs to the 2nd floor. After the death of one of his daughters at age four, Rioja always left a spot at the dining table for her, and in all photographs of the family, an empty chair was left in the frame for her.

Tours of the palace (30min, in English) are available, but it's worth calling ahead to make sure a guide is available. Book readings, film screenings, and classical music concerts are held regularly. There's a small café, the **Cafetería Palacio Rioja** (tel. 9/4557 3627, 9am-8:30pm Tues.-Sun.), with tables spilling out into the gardens.

Castillo Wulff

An extravagant neo-Tudor castle that hangs precipitously over the ocean, **Castillo Wulff** (Av. Marina 37, tel. 32/2185 751, 10am-1:30pm and 3pm-5:30pm Tues.-Sun., free) belonged to saltpeter and coal mogul Gustavo Adolfo Wulff Mowle. An extra tower built on a rocky outcrop and a glass floor to allow a view of the ocean below were added in 1920. Two rooms are open to the public; they feature monthly exhibitions of paintings, photography, and sculpture.

Palacio Presidencial

Built on the hill just above Avenida Marina and Castillo Wulff, the **Palacio Presidencial** (Castillo 398, no phone, 10am-5pm daily, free) was built in 1929. It's the official summer residence of Chile's president and is only open once per year, on the **Día del Patrimonio**

Nacional (National Heritage Day, last Sun. of May, www.diadelpatrimonio.cl), when queues extend around the block. The palace's landscaped grounds are otherwise open to the public. Consult the website for information about open hours and tours.

BEACHES

After crossing the Estero Marga Marga, Avenida San Martín follows the coast and Viña's stretch of golden beaches. **Playa Acapulco,** just south of the Muelle Vergara, the old pier, is the closest to the city center. It's the most popular beach in summer, although the fringe of apartment blocks is less than picturesque. Heading north, **Playa El Sol, Playa Blanca, Playa Los Marineros,** and **Playa Las Salinas** are indistinguishable from one another but heave with sunbathers in summer. Small kiosks sell snacks and cold drinks where the beach meets the road; there are public restrooms. Playa Las Salinas is a good place to swim, if you can stand the water's cold temperature, as it's protected from ocean currents by a rocky outcrop at the southern end of the beach.

About 12 blocks south of Muelle Vergara, where Avenida España turns east to become Álvares, **Playa Caleta Abarca** lies opposite the city's iconic Reloj de Flores (a working clock made from live flowers). It's set in a small cove hemmed in by bars and a garden, protecting it from the road.

ENTERTAINMENT

Viña has a reputation as a gambling resort. The city's 1910 neoclassical **Casino de Viña del Mar,** operated by **Enjoy** (tel. 600/7006 000, www.enjoy.cl, noon-7am Mon.-Sat., noon-3:30am Sun., free), has casino games that include bingo, card tables, and slot machines. Most sections are open 1pm-5am; bingo starts at 6pm. Formal dress is preferred. It's also home to **OVO** (Av. San Martín 199, hours vary), a huge performance venue that hosts pop music concerts, dance performances, and even comedy nights.

Nightlife

Viña has a more upmarket nightlife than neighboring Valparaíso, boasting a number of flashy nightclubs, all of which charge covers. As with all nightlife in Chile, clubs don't start to get busy until at least 1am.

A historic music venue in the southwest of Viña, **Café Journal** (Av. Agua Santa 4, tel. 32/2666 654, 5pm-3:30am Mon.-Thurs., 5pm-4:30am Fri.-Sat., CH$3,000) has live local bands from 9:30pm weekends. Over three dance floors, DJs play house, electronic, and techno music from 11pm.

Inside the casino, the flashy **OVO** (Casino de Viña del Mar, Av. San Martín 199, tel. 600/7006 000, www.ovonc.com, midnight-4am Sun. and Wed.-Thurs., midnight-5am Fri.-Sat., CH$10,000) is Viña's biggest club. It hosts live DJs, and there's space for up to 600 revelers, with the party going on until dawn.

A 20-minute taxi ride northeast of the city, **Club Divino** (Camino Internacional 537, tel. 9/5708 4660, http://clubdivino.cl, 11:30pm-5am Fri.-Sat., CH$10,000) claims to be the largest gay club in Latin America. It plays host to drag queens, cabaret performances, and live DJs.

The Arts

The **Teatro Municipal** (Plaza Vergara s/n, tel. 32/2681 739, www.culturaviva.cl) has long been the heart of cultural events in the city, hosting classical music performances, ballet, and the annual Festival Internacional de Cine de Viña del Mar (Viña del Mar International Film Festival). Following damage in the 2010 earthquake, the building underwent restoration with a planned reopening in 2020. Until that point, performances are split between the **Club de Viña del Mar** (Plaza Sucre s/n, www.clubvina.cl) and the **Palacio Rioja** (Quillota 214, tel. 32/2184 690, www.museopalaciorioja.cl). At the Palacio Rioja, book readings, international and Chilean film screenings, and classical music concerts are held in the Sala Aldo Francia; book fairs and other cultural events take place in the gardens.

Festivals and Events

The annual **Festival Internacional de la Canción** (International Song Festival, www.festivaldevinachile.cl) is the biggest event in Viña and the oldest and largest in Latin America. It's broadcast on TV around the globe. The third week in February in Parque Quinta Vergara's **Anfiteatro** (amphitheater), international artists rub shoulders with Latin performers. Past acts have included Elton John and Ricky Martin. The festival hosts a mix of established and up-and-coming artists, and features a competition for new artists; 16-year-old Shakira performed in 1993 and came in third. Over 15,000 spectators descend on the city, so booking lodging a few months in advance is a necessity. Tickets start at CH$25,000 and can be bought online. The amphitheater also hosts other popular and classical music events through the year.

RECREATION

Parks

PARQUE QUINTA VERGARA

Three blocks south of Plaza Vergara, **Parque Quinta Vergara** (entrance on Calle Quinta, tel. 32/2185 900, 7am-7pm daily mid-Sept.-Easter, 7am-6pm daily Easter-mid-Sept., free) is the city's prettiest park and perhaps one of the most beautiful in the country. The land originally belonged to the Hacienda Las Siete Hermanas, passing through the hands of the Carreras family before eventually being donated to the city in 1979. The gardens contain exotic plants from across the Americas, Asia, and Europe, including fan palm and phoenix palm trees and a couple of local *araucarías*. It's a great spot to enjoy a summer afternoon.

Also in the park is the 1907 **Palacio Vergara,** built in a Venetian style. The palace now houses the **Museo de Bellas Artes** (Errázuriz 563, tel. 32/2269 431), with collections from the 17th-century Italian and 16th-century Venetian schools, plus works from Chilean artists. The palace suffered

---

1: Palacio Rioja 2: monument to Pablo Neruda and Gabriela Mistral at Parque Quinta Vergara

significant damage in the 2010 earthquake; repairs are not yet finished. At the center of the park, the 15,000-capacity **Anfiteatro** (amphitheater) is the venue of the annual Festival Internacional de la Canción (International Song Festival).

JARDÍN BOTÁNICO NACIONAL

Six kilometers east of the city center, the **Jardín Botánico Nacional** (Camino El Olivar, tel. 32/2675 091, www.jbn.cl, 10am-6pm Mon.-Thurs., 9am-6:30pm Fri.-Sun., CH$2,000 adults, CH$1,000 children) is a 395-hectare park created in 1931 after Valparaíso businessman and philanthropist Pascual Baburizza donated the land. Only 32 hectares are open to the public. The botanical garden has more than 1,100 plant species, including rare plants from Rapa Nui and the Juan Fernández archipelago. Thanks to a series of interpretive paths, picnic tables, and a lagoon, the garden feels more like a large park.

Visiting the garden is a worthwhile trip out of the city. It's a 15-minute taxi journey from the center. Alternatively, take the eastbound number 302 bus that passes along Calle Álvares every 20 minutes; the end of its route is a short walk from the garden's entrance.

Soccer

Viña's soccer team, **CD Everton** (www.everton.cl), plays at the **Estadio Sausalito** (Av. Alemania s/n) on the northeast side of the city. They have a fierce rivalry with Valparaíso's Santiago Wanderers. Nicknamed Los Ruleteros (The Roulette Players) in homage to the casino, which provided financial support when the club was founded in 1909, they're a worthy team to watch when they play at home on weekends. Tickets start at CH$2,000 and rarely sell out in advance.

FOOD

A restaurant serving indigenous Mapuche-inspired cuisine could feel out of place in a city packed with high-rise buildings, but **Ilo Mapu** (6 Norte 228, tel. 32/2691 564, http://ilomapu.cl, 10am-4pm and 7pm-11pm

Wed.-Fri., 12:30pm-5pm and 7pm-11:30pm Sat., 12:30pm-5pm Sun., CH$8,500-15,000) focuses on seasonal grains and vegetables alongside meats cooked in traditional ways, such as slow-smoked pork ribs with *pastel de choclo* (corn pie). It's a little pricey, but much of the produce comes from Mapuche communities in the Araucanía region, which justifies the higher cost. Leave room for dessert: The delightful three-dessert tasting dish includes Chilean flavors such as *maqui,* chestnut mousse, and a blackberry, walnut, and hazelnut layer cake.

Blink and you'll miss the authentic hole-in-the-wall pizza joint **San Romano** (5 Norte 303, tel. 32/3199 747, http://sanromano.cl, 11am-11pm Sun.-Mon, 11am-midnight Tues.-Thurs., 11am-1am Fri.-Sat., CH$5,000-7,000). Its thin-crust pizzas feature ingredients imported from the mother country—you can taste it in the gorgonzola. With only two tables, you might have to queue. Dinner here is a cozy, intimate affair.

Decorated with the rotund figures of Colombian sculptor and artist Fernando Botero Angulo, ★ **Café Tintico de Botero** (5 Norte 461, tel. 32/2183 580, 9:45am-9:30pm Mon.-Sat., 10am-10pm Sun.) buzzes with a local crowd throughout the day, peaking in the late afternoon for *once* (high tea). The menu includes coffees mostly from Colombia using Chemex and AeroPress filters, plus some of the best cakes in the city.

The classic Viña lunch spot **La Flor de Chile** (8 Norte 601, tel. 32/2689 554, 1pm-midnight Mon.-Sat., CH$3,500-7,000, CH$4,900 *menú del día*) serves huge *chorrillana* (fries with shredded beef, sliced sausage, onion, and two fried eggs on top). The dish is made for sharing, so bring a friend or two. There are plenty of other Chilean dishes on the lunchtime menu. It's an atmospheric place to find a taste of Viña.

Eating a deep-fried seafood empanada is a must this close to the ocean. Takeout-only **Los Roldán** (6 Norte 317, tel. 32/3114 779, 11am-9pm daily, CH$1,400-2,000) has the best, featuring mixed seafood, scallops, crab, or even razor clams. Most are made with a generous portion of melted cheese. They even have sweet options for dessert.

ACCOMMODATIONS

Popular among those on a budget, the modern digs at **Not Found Rooms** (Paseo Cousiño 12, tel. 9/3054 885, www.notfoundrooms.com, CH$15,000 dorm, CH$30,000 d shared bath) have all the necessary features, including a huge kitchen, dining, and lounge area complete with Netflix and an Xbox, plus 24-hour reception and included breakfast. The only downside is that it's on the same floor as a strip club. Ask for a room at the back to avoid the noise. Rates include IVA.

A solid budget choice, **Casa Mondo** (Anwandter 52, tel. 32/2111 064, http://casamondohostel.com, CH$12,000 dorm, CH$31,500 d shared bath) is the definition of *buena onda* (good vibes), with its laid-back but helpful staff and communal spaces built for lounging. It's well placed for both Playa Caleta Abarca and downtown, in a relaxed residential neighborhood in the southwest of the city. Rooms are basic but very clean, with locks, plenty of space, and lots of baths. There are also two terraces and kitchen access. Rates include IVA.

Down a charming alleyway west of Parque Quinta Vergara, **La Blanca Hotel** (Echevers 396, tel. 32/3204 121, www.lablancahoteles.cl, CH$53,000-85,000 d) is in a rambling century-old house that once belonged to Blanca Vergara, daughter of the city's founder. The cheapest room, the standard, has no windows; you're better off opting for the superiors at the front of the house, which are larger and have big windows onto the street. All are decorated in black and white, with heavy satin and velvet. Room service, parking, and a small terrace are included.

Rooms are less historic in **Cassinetta Hotel Boutique** (José Francisco Vergara 227, tel. 32/2667 777, http://hotelcassinetta.cl, CH$75,000-89,000 d) than the grand brick facade of this 1950s building might lead you to expect, but the facilities are slick. Bedrooms, particularly on the top floor, are large, with mini fridges and brand-new baths. Rates include IVA.

In a lovingly restored 1920s building, seven-bed ★ **La Casa de Almirante** (Pasaje El Hogar, Casa 3, tel. 9/6710 5470, http://lacasadelalmirante.com, CH$103,000 d) has luxurious bedrooms, each decorated in individual style, and pretty views of Playa Caleta Abarca across the city's oldest neighborhood. Service is friendly and efficient. The breakfast showcases homemade breads, cakes, and jams.

INFORMATION AND SERVICES

Municipal-run **Información Turístico** (Plaza Vergara 715, tel. 21/2185 5710, 9am-9pm daily mid-Sept.-Easter, 9am-2pm and 3pm-7pm Mon.-Fri., 10am-2pm and 3pm-7pm Sat., 10am-6pm Sun. Easter-mid-Sept.) has helpful English-speaking staff. It stocks maps and has information about local cultural events. An additional branch is in the **Terminal de Buses** (9:30am-5:30pm Mon.-Fri., occasionally Sat.-Sun.).

Scotiabank (Plaza Vergara 103), **Santander** (Plaza Vergara 108), and **Banco Estado** (Plaza Vergara 105) are on the edges of the main square. Most **ATMs** are not open 24 hours. To **exchange money,** visit **Guiñazú Transfer** (Arlegui 686). For mail and shipping, head to **Correos** (Acceso Poniente Arlegui 32, 9am-7pm Mon.-Fri., 10am-1pm Sat.). **Hospital Gustavo Fricke** (Álvares 1532, tel. 32/2577 602) has emergency medical services.

GETTING THERE
Car
To get to Viña from **Valparaíso,** it's a 9-km, 20-minute drive northeast on Avenida España. To Viña from **Santiago,** it's a 130-km, 1.5-hour drive west on Ruta 68.

Bus
The **Terminal de Buses de Viña** (Av. Valparaíso 1055, tel. 32/2752 000, http://rodoviario.cl), also known as the **Terminal Rodoviario,** is a short three blocks east of Plaza Vergara.

REGIONAL BUSES
From **Valparaíso,** catch any bus numbered 602-604 or 606-611 (20min, CH$490), which leave from the south side of Avenida Errázuriz, with many continuing directly to Plaza Vergara.

Daily departures from **Santiago** (2hr, CH$3,000) leave every 10 minutes 6:15am-8:30pm from **Terminal Pajaritos** (Av. General Oscar Bonilla 5600) and **Terminal Santiago/Terminal de Buses Sur** (Av. Alameda 3850, tel. 2/2376 1750, metro stop Universidad de Santiago on Línea 1), dropping passengers at Viña's Terminal de Buses. **Buses Romani** (http://busesromani.cl), **Pullman Bus** (tel. 32/2752 022, www.pullmanbus.com), and **Tur Bus** (tel. 32/2138 455, http://turbus.cl) have the most departures. From Santiago's international airport (2hr, CH$6,000), Tur Bus has daily departures at 9:50am and 2:30pm, with departures to return to the airport at 5am, 10:25am, and 12:55pm daily; book these in advance, as tickets sell out.

LONG-DISTANCE BUSES
The main carriers connecting Viña del Mar with the north include **Pullman Bus** and **Tur Bus,** while those recommended for journeys from the south include both Pullman and Tur, as well as **Condor Bus** (tel. 32/2752 027, www.condorbus.cl), **EME Bus** (tel. 32/2714 087, www.emebus.cl), and **Buses ETM** (tel. 32/271 0701, www.etm.cl). EME Bus, Buses ETM, and Tur Bus offer full 180-degree *cama* (reclining) seats to some destinations.

Journeys from the north, which bypass Santiago, run about every two hours between Viña del Mar and **La Serena** (7hr, CH$13,000/CH$20,0000), **Copiapó** (12hr, CH$15,000/CH$25,000), and **Antofagasta** (20hr, CH$23,000/CH$35,000). There are also eight daily departures from **Calama** (24hr, CH$28,000/CH$45,000), where there are direct transfers to San Pedro de Atacama.

Buses from the south, which pass through Santiago, run about every two hours between Viña del Mar and **Talca** (6hr, CH$7,400), **Chillán** (9hr, CH$11,000/CH$17,000), and **Concepción** (8hr, CH$11,000/CH$17,000). There are around 10 daily departures from **Temuco** (10hr, CH$12,000/CH$16,000) and **Valdivia** (11hr, CH$13,000/CH$16,000), and five daily buses from **Pucón** (12hr, CH$14,000/CH$18,000), **Osorno** (13hr, CH$15,000/CH$18,000), and **Puerto Montt** (15hr, CH$15,000/CH$18,000).

Metro

The **Metro Regional de Valaparaíso** (tel. 32/2527 633, http://metro-valparaiso.cl, 6:15am-10:30pm Mon.-Fri., 8:30am-10:30pm Sat.-Sun.) is a commuter train that runs between Estación Puerto (Av. Errázuriz 711) in Valparaíso and Estación Viña del Mar (Álvarez s/n, Plaza Sucre). It's a quick and easy way to get between the two cities. You'll need a rechargeable Metroval card, which can be bought for CH$2,000 from any metro station. Fares depend on the time of day; expect to pay CH$388-430, regardless of distance.

GETTING AROUND

Most of the city is concentrated within the three blocks south and eight blocks north of Plaza Vergara, making it easy to navigate on foot. To get to Viña's beaches, hop on any bus headed north toward Reñaca.

Rental Cars

Europcar (inside the Viña del Mar Sheraton Miramar, Av. Marina 15, tel. 32/2177 593, www.europcar.com, 8:30am-7pm Mon.-Fri., 9am-1pm and 2pm-6pm Sat.-Sun.) offers car rentals. There are more options at Santiago's airport.

NORTHERN BEACHES

North of Viña del Mar, a series of picturesque and exclusive resort towns stretch up the coast. The high-rise-lined beaches of easy-to-reach **Reñaca** and **Concón** cede to quieter beaches backed by large private homes in **Cachagua, Zapallar,** and **Papudo,** a relaxing escape for a day or two. Most locals choose one beach town in which to spend their time. Water sports such as surfing are drawing increasing numbers of foreign travelers to tiny **Maitencillo.** The chilly waters of the Humboldt Current mean swimming is very cold at any of these beaches.

Reñaca

Scattered high-rise apartments hug the cliff of the town of Reñaca, 4km north of Viña del Mar. Avenida Borgoño carries traffic and pedestrians 6km north of Viña to the town's white-sand beach, the kilometer-long **Playa Reñaca.** One of the most immaculate beaches in the country, it's very popular among young Chileans and Argentineans. Restaurants and bars are concentrated on Avenida Carrera Pinto, bookended by Avenida Borgoño.

Most of Reñaca's restaurants and bars are on streets east of the beach. For tasty and cheap fried empanadas, head to the Reñaca branch of **Los Roldán** (Av. Borgoño 14770, tel. 32/3114 779, 11am-8:30pm daily, CH$2,000-4,000), which has a selection of sweet and savory options.

The city has plenty of nightlife, but the trendiest spots change with the season, so it's best to ask around. There are few lodging options, so it makes more sense to stay in Viña and day-trip here.

Concón

A popular holiday destination with a high-rise skyline, Concón is part seaside resort and part gritty fishing village, 10km north of übermodern Reñaca. It's a popular day trip from Viña (15km south) for its beach, which is marginally quieter in summer than those closer to Viña.

Avenida Borgoño follows the coast, passing a rocky promontory next to the Facultad de Ciencias del Mar building where sea lions slumber and can be heard barking late into the night. Five kilometers farther north, Concón's main stretch of beaches begins. The most pleasant is **Playa Amarilla** (between Barros and Labarca), a long stretch of golden sand for sunbathing and swimming. Restaurants and bars line Avenida Borgoño along the full length of the beach.

Northeast of the beaches, **La Boca** is the old dock and commercial center of Concón. Lying at the mouth of the Río Aconcagua, which marks the northern edge of Concón, it is surrounded by small shabby buildings where you can find fresh fish for sale, plus stalls selling fried seafood empanadas.

With picturesque views from its balcony overlooking pelican-filled Caleta Higuerillas, the harbor in the south of Concón, **El Faro de los Compadres** (San Pedro 2585, tel. 32/2815 087, http://elfarodeloscompadres. cl, noon-11pm daily, CH$7,000-14,000) specializes in fish and seafood. Try the ceviche to start, delicately deep-fried conger eel, or grilled *reiñeta* (southern ray bream) with a huge salad or potatoes.

Horcón

The traditional fishing village of Horcón, 28km north of Concón and 44km north of Viña, has a reputation as a hippie stronghold, particularly as the country's only nude beach, Playa La Luna, is 3km north. The village occupies the northern part of a promontory. With few tourist facilities beyond its handful of beaches, it's best visited as part of a day trip from Viña to the more developed beach towns farther north.

With few crowds and almost empty out of season, **Playa Cau Cau** is a lovely white-sand beach on the northernmost part of the promontory, popular for its calm water and surrounded by rocky cliffs covered in pines and eucalyptus. Get here by taking Calle Cau Cau west from Avenida Principal (the main road through the village) to its end, where there is paid parking. From here, it's a very steep and unstable path down to the beach.

Follow the main street, Avenida Principal, to its northern end by the coast to a collection of **waterfront restaurants** and stalls selling fresh fish. From here, Calle Costanera Horcón turns west to picturesque wooden

Puente de Los Deseos (Bridge of Desires), where you can buy a colored ribbon for a few hundred pesos to tie to the bridge, which allegedly grants wishes. Just before the bridge, there's a **small craft market** (hours vary daily), founded in the 1970s by two members of the Chilean rock band Los Jokers.

Maitencillo

The long sandy beaches of sleepy fishing town Maitencillo, 60km north of Viña and 20km beyond Horcón, are responsible for an increasing wave of international tourism. Modern apartment high-rises are shooting up on the edges of the town, but Maitencillo, with its little houses perched precariously on the coast, is largely undeveloped. There are plenty of exclusive restaurants along the waterfront, but the real allure is surfing or unwinding on the town's numerous beaches. Maitencillo makes an excellent place to spend a day or two.

The region is also known for its favorable paragliding conditions. Experienced Belgian paraglider **Paul Peter D'Herlog** (tel. 9/5092 1692) runs 25-minute flights from nearby hills (CH$50,000 pp), with all equipment included. He speaks English, French, and Spanish. **Andes Paraglide** (Av. Del Mar 595, local 15, tel. 9/9 9199 8857, http://pabloruiztagle. wixsite.com/andesparaglide) offers similar services.

★ SURFING

One of the biggest draws of this part of the coast is its reliable surf. Both **Playa Aguas Blancas,** south of town for 1km from where Calle Aguas Blancas turns 90 degrees north, and **Playa Larga,** from Avenida del Mar and Pasaje Frutillar to the Catapilco estuary 1km north, are easily accessible from the road and have consistent surf, with an exposed river break forming quality waves. **Surf hire shops** are along **Playa El Abanico,** which becomes Playa Larga farther north.

Escuela de Surf (Av. Del Mar 1442, http:// escueladesurfmaitencillo.cl, 9am-9pm daily Dec.-Mar., 10am-7pm daily Apr.-Nov.) rents gear and runs 90-minute group lessons (up to 12 students, CH$16,000) and private surf classes (CH$28,000). The water is cold year-round; wetsuits are advised.

ACCOMMODATIONS

Hands-down the best place to stay is ★ **Hostal Maitencillo** (Ricardo 134, tel. 9/8832 6908, www.hostalmaitencillo.cl, July-Apr., CH$60,000 d, cash only), a cozy modern guesthouse a few blocks from the ocean. Amiable Álvaro welcomes guests into a spotless house with large bedrooms (those with a terrace cost only a little more), a kitchen and dining room, and free use of surfboards and wetsuits. Rates include IVA.

Cachagua

Cachagua, 12km north of Maitencillo and 65km north of Viña, is a neat village of stylish million-dollar houses for wealthy holidaymakers from the capital. It is a picturesque stop on a day trip to more developed Zapallar and Papudo, farther north, and is home to tiny but pretty **Playa Las Cujas,** a sandy beach surrounded by a rocky protective bay famed for its crystalline waters. From this beach there's access along a beautiful path around the cliffs to reach an ocean viewpoint for sunset. The beach receives fewer visitors than those farther north and is almost deserted outside January-February. To get here, take Avenida Del Mar from the E-30-F road on the northern edge of the village to Plaza de Cachagua, where you can park and take the steep steps on the square's northwestern side down to the beach.

Directly south of the village, the 3-km white-sand **Playa Cachagua** is much larger, more popular, and perfectly picturesque thanks to its clear water. It lies across from the Monumento Natural Isla Cachagua, an island with 2,000 resident Humboldt penguins—bring binoculars if you want to see them. The beach is a good spot for surfing, although you'll need to bring your own gear, as there's nowhere to rent. The beach hosts the **Cachagua Surf Festival** every year in early February. To get here, take Calle Federico Kohnenkampf west from the E-30-F road for 1km to its end, where there is a car park.

Zapallar

Verdant **Zapallar** (http://munizapallar.cl), 4km north of Cachagua and 70km north of Viña in a protected bay, is one of the most exclusive seaside resorts. Once part of Hacienda Catapilco, the land the town stands on was

Zapallar

inherited by Olegario Ovalle from his father, who founded Zapallar in 1889. He gifted land to his friends, with the agreement that they build houses within two years. Wealthy families from the capital obliged, constructing colonial-style houses interspersed with slick modern mansions that now dot the forested hills surrounding the bay.

A popular weekend beach getaway, Zapallar is a tranquil coastal refuge, perfect for a day or two. Eucalyptus-lined streets run along the coast, and Avenida la Playa leads to horseshoe-shaped **Playa Zapallar.** The immaculate golden sands are for tanning in summer, while the calm waters beyond are excellent for swimming and kayaking; you can rent equipment from the harbor.

Southwest around the bay, **Caleta Zapallar** (northern end of Francisco de Paula) is a small fish market selling plastic net bags full of fresh razor clams. Preening pelicans watch closely, awaiting their lunch. From the fish market, follow the **Rambla,** a footpath that curves around the coast, ascends a series of steps carved into the rock, and climbs the **Santuario Naturaleza Cerro La Cruz** for views of the coast.

FOOD AND ACCOMMODATIONS

Reached by the Rambla path or the road that runs seaward from Avenida Zapallar, **El Chiringuito** (Caleta Zapallar s/n, tel. 33/2741 024, 12:30pm-1am daily summer, 12:30pm-5pm Mon.-Thurs., 12:30pm-6pm and 8pm-1am Fri.-Sun. winter, CH$14,000-20,000) is somewhat overpriced but has the best views of the beach from its long outdoor terrace that is very popular in summer. The menu comprises fish directly off the boats in the harbor next door. Open hours are erratic, particularly off-season. Make a reservation or get here early for an outdoor table.

Accommodations are expensive in Zapallar, but splurging allows you to stay in one of the town's original properties. The charming ★ **Casa Wilson** (Francisco de Paula 191, tel. 9/97423 964, www.casawilson. cl, CH$180,000 d) was built by one of Zapallar's first families and combines an exclusive enchanting location overlooking the bay with a sun-soaked veranda and large bedrooms, complete with antique furniture and tons of character. All rooms include sea views. Owner Samuel breakfasts with guests and speaks perfect English. Rates include IVA and drop by a quarter outside summer.

Papudo

Nine kilometers north of Zapallar and 78km north of Viña, the orderly and historic beach town Papudo is more welcoming than its upscale southern neighbor. It was described by Pedro de Valdivia in a letter to Carlos V of Spain in 1545 as "like God's paradise." Papudo was originally a port town that became a beach resort in the late 1800s. It makes an excellent day trip from Valparaíso or Viña del Mar, or an overnight stay. The resort has avoided the development of beaches farther south, although the ugly seven-floor condominium right on Playa Grande hints at the future.

Papudo and its two beaches get packed with vacationing families during summer. The smaller sandy and pebbly **Playa Chica** (between the intersection of E-30-F and 21 de Mayo and the intersection of E-30-F and Blanco) is just below the E-30-F road along the coast as it passes through the town; this beach has calmer waters for swimming. Expansive **Playa Grande** (intersection of E-30-F and Blanco) has white sands that stretch a few kilometers north.

FOOD AND ACCOMMODATIONS

In a grand old mansion stripped bare inside, **La Maison Des Fous** (Blanco 132, tel. 9/5006 2874, 1pm-5pm and 8pm-1am Mon.-Thurs., 1pm-5pm and 6pm-5am Fri., 1pm-5pm and 8pm-5am Sat., 1pm-5pm and 6pm-midnight Sun., CH$10,000-14,000) has a focus on seafood (try the ceviche or octopus). A wide range of alternatives includes fillet steak, smoked pork ribs, and pasta. Service can be slow, but it's the place to go on a weekend in summer, as they host cover bands Friday-Sunday. Book a table if you're coming for dinner or music.

The only options for lodging include no-frills but affordable **Residencial La Plaza** (Chorrillos 119, tel. 33/2791 391, CH$20,000 d), with breakfast and somewhat small bedrooms. A more upscale alternative is four-room **Casapapudo Boutique Hotel** (Riquelme 194, tel. 33/2790 161, www.casapapudo.cl, CH$85,000 d), more like a fashionable B&B, with spotless modern bedrooms (CH$13,000 extra for sea views), one of which has its own private balcony. The English-speaking owners are friendly. It's overpriced in summer, but rates drop by 10 percent off-season.

Getting There

A rental car can be useful for visiting this area. **Europcar** (inside the Viña del Mar Sheraton Miramar, Av. Marina 15, tel. 32/2177 593, www.europcar.com, 8:30am-7pm Mon.-Fri., 9am-1pm and 2pm-6pm Sat.-Sun.) offers car hire. **Rosselot** (Victoria 2675, Valparaíso, tel. 32/2352 365, 9am-7pm Mon.-Fri., 10am-1pm Sat.) is the only company with an office in Valparaíso. Be aware that the insurance normally doesn't cover beyond third-party liability. There are more options at Santiago's international airport.

From Viña, **Avenida Bordgoño** becomes the **F-30-E** road on the other side of Concón and transitions into the **E-30-F** road north of Maitencillo. This route is frequented by trucks, making it slow at times. The drive time to Reñaca is 20 minutes, and to Papudo 1.5 hours. The best sea views are between Zapallar and Papudo.

It's easy to reach all of the northern beaches by bus. From **Viña** (Calle Grove, opposite Iglesia Nuestra Señora de Dolores), small buses depart for Maitencillo, Zapallar, and Papudo (1.5-2hr, CH$1,500) roughly every 30 minutes. Buses for Reñaca and Concón (30-40min, CH$1,500) leave more frequently. From **Valparaíso** (Terminal de Buses), **Sol del Pacífico** (tel. 32/2213 776) runs buses to Maitencillo, Zapallar, and Papudo (1.5-2hr, CH$2,500) roughly every 30 minutes; departures for Reñaca and Concón (50min-1hr,

CH$2,500) are more frequent. For the return journey, buses pick up from the Plaza Papudo (bounded by Esmeralda, Miraflores, Fernández Concha, and Chorillos) in Papudo, from the intersection of the E-30-F and 28 de Mayo in the south of Zapallar, and from Avenida del Mar, just opposite Tío Tomato (Av. Del Mar 695) in Maitencillo.

Tur Bus (www.turbus.cl) has multiple daily buses to and from **Zapallar** (Olegario Ovalle 128, Zapallar, tel. 33/213 8275) and **Papudo** (Esmeralda 260, tel. 33/2791 377), which depart from the Terminal Rodoviario Valparaíso and travel via the Terminal de Buses de Viña (1.5-2hr, CH$3,000).

PARQUE NACIONAL LA CAMPANA

Within the coastal cordillera southeast of Quillota, 78km east of Viña del Mar, **Parque Nacional La Campana** (tel. 33/2441 342, www.conaf.cl, valparaiso.oirs@conaf.cl, 9am-4:30pm Fri., 9am-5:30pm Sat.-Thurs., CH$4,000 adults, CH$2,000 children) is an 8,000-hectare protected area comprising scrubland and the largest surviving forests of Chilean palm, which can live up to 400 years. The park's namesake and star attraction is **Cerro La Campana,** a peak that Charles Darwin famously climbed in 1834.

The park's rugged topography includes elevation changes of 1,800 meters (from 400 meters at the entrance to the 2,222-meter peak of Cero El Roble), meaning that hiking can be challenging. The views of the Andes—some of the most spectacular in the country—compensate the effort. The park is divided into three distinct areas: **Sector Granizo** and **Sector Cajón Grande** are accessible from the town of Olmué, southwest of the park; **Sector Ocoa,** the northern section, is reached from the town of Hijuelas. A useful map is available from the CONAF ranger station at each of the entrances.

It's possible to visit on a day trip from Valparaíso or Viña if you have your own vehicle, but a more leisurely appreciation of the park and its trails takes two days. You can stay in the CONAF-run campgrounds. For safety purposes, you are required to be off the trails by 5:30pm.

Bring plenty of drinking water (tap water in the park is chlorinated), a sun hat and sunscreen, plus sturdy hiking shoes with grip. In winter, a raincoat can help with the usual rain showers. In summer, the park gets very hot, and wildfires are not uncommon. The best time to visit is spring or fall, when daytime temperatures drop. The campgrounds are occasionally closed to visitors; contact CONAF prior to your visit to confirm their status. Open fires are not permitted, so bring a stove. A privately operated website (http://parquelacampana.weebly.com) is the best place for up-to-date information. CONAF's website also has a topographical map of the park.

Sector Granizo

The most visited part of the park, Sector Granizo has the trail to the summit of Cerro La Campana, **Sendero Andinista** (14km round-trip, 8hr). This hike is a tiring slog that follows in the footsteps of Charles Darwin, who visited in 1834. The trail starts at the Sector Granizo entrance and ascends to the 1,880-meter summit of Cerro La Campana, an elevation gain of 1,507 meters. The final stretch is a rocky scramble that you'll feel in your hands. Park rangers don't allow hikers to start later than 9:30am. Three water sources en route mean carrying lots of water isn't necessary. Hiking shoes with good grip are essential for the path, which is often dusty and dry, making it extremely slippery, particularly on the way down. The latter half of the trail, from Mina La Prosticada upward, is often closed June-August.

Sendero Los Peumos (2.5km one-way, 3.5hr) climbs up very steeply through woodland to the Portezuelo Ocoa (Ocoa Pass), where you'll find the Sendero Los Robles, which leads steeply back down to the Cajón Grande entrance and Sendero Amasijo, which continues north across the mountains to Sector Palmas Ocoa.

A **ranger station** is at the entrance of Sector Granizo. Rangers can provide information about trekking routes. A 300-meter path (accessible by 4WD) leads to the CONAF-run campsite **Segundo Puente** (CH$6,000 per site), with space for 23 tents, plus restrooms and cold showers.

Sector Cajón Grande

This part of the park is due south of Sector Granizo. The two are connected via **Sendero Los Robles** (7km one-way, 3hr), also called **Sendero Portezuelo Ocoa**, which meets Sendero Los Peumos at Portezuelo Ocoa and has a series of viewpoints. Hiking between the two trails is possible in a day, resulting in a 12.5-km, six- to seven-hour trek. The trail can is hard going as it's constantly uphill, whichever side you walk, to reach the saddle of Portezuelo Ocoa.

A **ranger station** is at the entrance of Sector Cajón Grande. Rangers can provide information about trekking routes. They run **Camping Cajón Grande** (CH$6,000 per site), 150 meters into the park. It has space for 23 tents, with restrooms and cold showers. Spots are available on a first-come, first-served basis.

Sector Ocoa

The prettiest trek in the park is **Sendero La Cascada** (8km one-way, 3hr), which ends at a picturesque 30-meter waterfall. **Sendero Amasijo** (7km one-way, 5hr) climbs through a valley south to Portezuelo Ocoa, where it's possible to connect with the downhill Sendero Los Peumos or Sendero Los Robles, finishing at Sectors Cajón Grande or Granizo.

A **ranger station** is at the entrance of Sector Ocoa. Rangers can provide information about trekking routes. The CONAF-run campsite **Camping La Buitrera** (CH$6,000 per site), with space for 23 tents, plus restrooms and cold showers, is 800 meters from the entrance, accessible by 4WD.

Getting There

To reach Sector Granizo from Valparaíso is a 50-km, one-hour drive. Cajón Grande is 4km farther. Take the F-668, signposted west from Olmué. On public transport from Valparaíso, take the metro to the last stop in Limanche (CH$388-430). From the right-hand side of the station, the number 45 bus goes directly to Olmué (CH$2,000) every hour or so until around 5pm, terminating 1km before the entrance to Sector Granizo and 2km west of the entrance for Sector Cajón Grande; you'll need to walk back here to get picked up for the return journey. Due to later opening hours of the metro on weekends, if you plan on hiking to the summit of Cerro La Campana, it's better to go on a weekday, when service begins earlier.

The best way to get to the park from Santiago is by car; Sector Ocoa is the most accessible. Take Ruta 5 to Ocoa and continue south on the F-300 and F-304, a drive of 1.5 hours and 111km. To get to the park using public transportation from Santiago, any northbound bus (1.5hr, CH$2,000) from the capital can drop you at the town of Hijuelas, where you can walk the 12km south to the entrance, or ask around for a taxi service.

Valle de Casablanca and Valle de San Antonio

Just 40 minutes southeast of Valparaíso and an hour's drive west of Santiago, Valle de Casablanca is Chile's best-known white wine region. Lush low hills grow neat ridges of vines, and the valley is thick with fog in early morning. This unique climate allows chardonnay and sauvignon blanc to flourish, along with pinot noir, syrah, gewürztraminer, and even cabernet franc and malbec.

Directly south and spreading toward the coast, Valle de San Antonio is Casablanca's less visited cousin, characterized by a cool coastal climate and clay soils. Varietals such as sauvignon gris have taken root, although the valley's specialty remains distinctive pinot noir and sauvignon blanc.

Most of the grapes are a short distance from Ruta 68, which connects Santiago with Valparaíso. Many of these accessible wineries and vineyards offer restaurants and lodging in addition to tours and tasting rooms. The lack of public transport means a rental car or a day tour from Santiago is a far easier way to explore. Chile's zero tolerance for driving under the influence means you should have a designated driver.

Note that although the day normally starts with low-lying clouds, it's usual for them to burn off after midday, so bring sunscreen and a hat, as temperatures can rise quickly.

TOP EXPERIENCE

★ VALLE DE CASABLANCA
Wine-Tasting

Vineyards and wineries flank Ruta 68, which connects Santiago with Valparaíso, in the Valle de Casablanca, centered on the small town of Casablanca. The coastal mountains create a jagged natural barrier between inland Santiago and the coast. An hour's drive from the capital and 30 minutes from Valparaíso, the wineries are a day trip from either city. More tour operators depart from Santiago, with many able to drop you off in Valparaíso at the end of the tour.

Santiago-based **Miles and Smiles** (http://milesandsmiles.cl) offers private tours (CH$90,000 pp, min. 2 people), that visit two wineries, with pickup from your Santiago hotel included. **Uncorked Wine Tours** (tel. 2/2981 6242, www.uncorked. cl) offers a three-winery small-group tour (CH$135,000 pp) with a lunch that includes wine pairings, plus pickup from

Valle de Casablanca

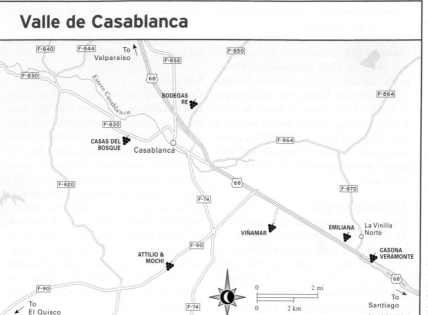

your Santiago hotel. From Valparaíso, **Wine Tours Valparaíso** (tel. 9/8428 3502, www.winetoursvalparaiso.cl) offers a two-winery tour (CH$85,000 pp) or a three-winery tour (CH$185,000 pp) with a lunch that includes wine pairings. All include winery tours and tastings.

The following wineries and vineyards are listed in order of their proximity to Valparaíso; visit them in the opposite direction from Santiago. All have their own shops with reduced prices on wines. International shipping is generally not available.

BODEGAS RE

On the western edge of the valley, slick, modern **Bodegas RE** (Camino a lo Ovalle, tel. 32/2741 234, http://bodegasre.cl, 10am-6pm daily, tour and tasting CH$17,000) gives a sense of the pioneering nature of this small family vineyard: They use antique terra-cotta amphorae to store their wines, as the Romans and Greeks did, combined with cutting-edge

winemaking practices and unusual blends such as chardonnoir, a mix of chardonnay and pinot noir. English-language tours are available, as are tastings (CH$10,000 for two wines); you'll get a detailed explanation from their on-site experts. Reservations are required for tours.

CASAS DEL BOSQUE

Just west of the town of Casablanca, picturesque **Casas del Bosque** (Hijuelas 2, Centro Ex Fundo Santa Rosa, tel. 2/2480 6941, www.casasdelbosque.cl, 10am-6pm daily, tour and tasting CH$13,500) is a green-roofed winery visible through neat rows of vines, specializing in sauvignon blanc and riesling. Awards include Chilean Vineyard of the Year in 2013 and 2014. Tastings (CH$8,500 for 2 wines) are on a fixed schedule at 11am, 1:15pm, 3:30pm, and 5pm daily. Take a tour and wine-tasting at their restaurant, Casa Mirador (CH$30,000, prior reservation required), with views of the vineyard. Accessing this part of the winery requires a car. Tours leave at 10:30am, 12:15pm, 3pm, and 4:30pm.

For lunch, the contemporary **Casa Mirador** (tel. 2/2480 946, noon-4:30pm Sat.-Sun.), on a hill overlooking the vineyards, includes the terra-cotta-roofed restaurant **Tanino** (tel. 2/2480 6946, noon-4:30pm daily, CH$13,000-20,000), in front of the main winery building on a sun-soaked terrace. A four-course set menu (CH$40,000) includes outstanding food and wine pairings. Both require reservations 48 hours in advance for weekends.

ATTILIO & MOCHI

Beyond the town of Casablanca, 6km down the F-90, **Attilio & Mochi** (Ruta F-90, tel. 9/7388 2671, http://attiliomochi.com, by appointment only, tour and tasting CH$30,000) is a boutique winery run by two Brazilian expats who focus on red wine, including cabernet franc, grenache, malbec, and pinot noir, plus unfiltered orange wines. Tours are run by the winemakers, who speak perfect English and take you around their small modern winery and vineyards for the ultimate intimate visit.

VIÑAMAR

Off the southern side of Ruta 68, a few kilometers past Casablanca, the approach to the elegant château-style buildings of **Viñamar** (Camino Interior Nuevo Mundo s/n, tel. 32/2754 300, www.vinamar.cl, 10am-6:30pm daily, tour and tasting from CH$15,000, tasting from CH$10,000) feels like the south of France. The building was inspired by the Palacio Vergara in Viña del Mar, and the views of the vineyards from the tasting rooms and restaurant across a large pond are sublime—no wonder this vineyard plays host to so many weddings. They specialize in sparkling wines made using the Champenoise and Charmat methods.

English-language tours and tastings are available on request. Their restaurant, **Macerado** (tel. 9/7831 4823, CH$7,000-10,000), has a sunny veranda and is more affordable than most in the valley but matches the quality. Dishes include duck confit in a stewed fruit sauce, baked rabbit, and fish from the Juan Fernández islands.

EMILIANA

On the north side of Ruta 68, about 12km past Casablanca, **Emiliana** (Km 60.7 Ruta 68, tel. 62/2353 9130, www.emiliana.cl, tour and tasting CH$16,000) is an organic, sustainable winery, the first in Latin America to produce certified biodynamic wine. Visiting the main vineyard is enhanced by their menagerie of animals, including a herd of friendly alpacas. For tours on summer weekends, advance reservations are required; the rest of the time you can generally arrive without a reservation. They offer tastings in the slate-roofed main building, starting from CH$2,000 per wine, plus "make your own wine" classes and organic picnics (reservations required).

VERAMONTE

Fourteen kilometers east of Casablanca, **Casona Veramonte** (Km 66 Ruta 68, tel. 32/2329 924 casonaveramonte.com, 9:30am-5pm daily, tasting CH$12,500, tour and tasting CH$14,000) offers hour-long tours (in English and Spanish, 9:45am, 11am, 12:30pm, 2pm, 3:30pm, and 4:30pm daily) of the 1,000-hectare vineyard. You can opt to take the tour on a bicycle instead of on foot. Tastings must be reserved in advance. Primus, a blend of carménère and cabernet sauvignon, is the vineyard's forte.

Transportation

Buses from **Valparaíso** (1hr, CH$1,000) depart for Casablanca from the Terminal de Buses and drop you in the central square of Casablanca. From here a taxi stand can provide onward travel to the vineyards, with a fixed rate per kilometer. Taxis should cost no more than CH$10,000 to reach the farthest vineyards; it's also possible to set a flat rate with your driver for visiting a number of wineries.

Buses leaving the **Terminal Santiago/ Terminal de Buses Sur** (Av. Alameda 3850, tel. 2/2376 1750, metro station Universidad de Santiago on Línea 1) in the direction of Valparaíso or Viña del Mar travel Ruta 68 next to Casablanca (1.5hr, CH\$3,000); you can ask to be dropped off here. Direct **minibuses** for Casablanca (1.5hr, CH\$3,000) leave hourly from platform 66 at **Terminal San Borja** (San Borja 235, tel. 2/2776 0645, metro station Estación Central on Línea 1).

★ VALLE DE SAN ANTONIO
Wine-Tasting

Valle de San Antonio, south of Valle de Casablanca, was long considered a poor location for growing grapes due to its arid soil and cold weather. The region's pioneers began planting here in 1999 and were soon compensated with the production of high-acidity wines, whose distinct mineral character is the result of the region's unique microclimate.

Contiguous with Valle de Casablanca, this wine valley lies due south, stretching within a few kilometers of the Pacific Ocean and comprising 2,000 hectares of vineyards. San Antonio is an easy addition to a tour of better-known Casablanca, or it can be part of a day trip to Pablo Neruda's Casa Museo Isla Negra, 30 minutes north of the wineries. Public transport is practically nonexistent, so taking an organized tour from Santiago or having your own vehicle is essential.

MATETIC

The stylish, family-run **Matetic** (Fundo El Rosario, Lagunillas, tel. 2/2611 1520, http://matetic.com, 9am-6pm daily by reservation only, tour and tasting CH\$14,000) winery is in a scenic location, built into a hillside to avoid visual pollution and designed so that gravitational flow allows the winemaking process to use less energy. They produce a range of whites, including chardonnay, sauvignon blanc, riesling, and gewürztraminer, plus a handful of reds.

Ten kilometers away but still on-site, the restaurant **Equilibrio** (tel. 9/8920 2066, 12:30pm-4:30pm Tues.-Sun., CH\$10,000-14,000) offers an excellent range of beef and fish on a lovely outdoor terrace. A four-course menu with wine pairing is CH\$42,000. The 10-room **La Casona** (tel. 2/2611 1519, CH\$417,000 d with 2 meals), a hotel within

wine from Casa Marín in Valle de San Antonio

a remodeled colonial house, has large bedrooms with hardwood floors, elegant communal spaces, a wraparound terrace, plus an outdoor pool. They offer two-meal and three-meal options that include a tour of the vineyard. You'll need a car to get to the different parts of the vineyard.

CASA MARÍN

In the village of Lo Abarca, 4km from the Pacific, **Casa Marín** (Lo Abarca, tel. 9/8777 6786, www.casamarin.cl, 9am-noon and 1pm-5:30pm Mon.-Fri., 10am-5pm Sat., by reservation only, tour and tasting CH$14,000) is owned by Chile's first female winemaker, María Luz Marín, who runs the winery with her son Felipe. From their 41 hectares, the main crop is sauvignon blanc, although their sauvignon gris, introduced using vines from Casa Silva in the Colchagua Valley, is particularly special. All the grapes are single-vineyard and consistently win high praise from international wine pundits.

The setting for the vineyard is spectacular and merits visiting to dine in their superb **Cipreses Winebar** (tel. 9/7748 5346, www. cipreseswinebar.cl, 12:30pm-5:30pm Wed.-Sat., CH$8,000-10,000), where you can do tastings without a reservation (CH$10,000 for 3 wines) or dine on the inventive menu of Chilean barbecued sirloin, salmon steaks, and steaming seafood soups.

Their **Villa Miramar** (tel. 9/8777 6786, CH$115,000 d) is a comfortable two-bedroom guesthouse deep in the vineyard, surrounded by sauvignon blanc grapes and with views from the terrace across the vineyards to the Pacific. It's within walking distance of the restaurant and wine cellar and has its own kitchen and barbecue.

Norte Grande and the Atacama Desert

The dusty Norte Grande region stretches from
Peru in the far north of Chile through Chile's Arica and Parinacota, Tarapacá, and Atacama regions. On the east, this vast desert—the world's driest—is hemmed in by the 6,000-meter-plus heights of the Andes Mountains, while on the west a scattering of coastal cities edge the Pacific.

Although it might appear a barren wasteland on first inspection, this vast region is rich in indigenous history and natural landmarks. The most famous are around Reserva Nacional Los Flamencos, accessible from the oasis town San Pedro de Atacama, close to the Bolivian border, where clear skies and observatories make the stars seem closer than ever, and flamingo-speckled saline lakes are fringed

Highlights

Look for ★ to find recommended sights, activities, dining, and lodging.

★ **Stargazing Tours:** Some of the world's clearest skies outside San Pedro de Atacama await (page 143).

★ **Valle de la Luna:** Marvel at the other-worldly landscape of the rugged mountains and sand dunes of this bewitching valley (page 152).

★ **Piedras Rojas and Salar de Talar:** Wander over natural lava cobblestones on the edges of a picturesque, volcano-ringed salt lake (page 155).

★ **Observatorio Cerro Paranal:** Discover the secrets of the night skies at the home to one of the most powerful telescopes on the planet (page 166).

★ **Surfing:** Rub shoulders with the pros and surf world-class waves along Iquique's white-sand coast (page 171).

★ **Sandboarding:** Power down the largest urban dunes in the world on a tour of Iquique's Cerro Dragon (page 171).

★ **Oficina Humberstone:** Pore over relics of the saltpeter industry in former nitrate refineries and ghost towns (page 178).

★ **Geoglifos de Cerros Pintados:** Marvel at 450 figures etched into the desert floor at this historically significant ancient site (page 183).

★ **Laguna Roja:** Get off the beaten path with a day excursion to the surreal blood-red waters of this lake (page 185).

★ **Chinchorro Mummies:** Learn about the funerary rites of the Chinchorro people at two outstanding museums showcasing the remains of the oldest mummies in the world (page 188).

★ **Parque Nacional Lauca and Reserva Nacional Las Vicuñas:** Observe diverse mammal and bird species in these two remote protected areas (pages 199 and 202).

with dormant volcanoes and steam rises from high-altitude geysers.

Those who venture farther east are rewarded with state-of-the-art telescopes. Head north for ghostly abandoned nitrate refineries. Near the border with Peru, discover the world's oldest mummies, enthralling relics of the ancient Chinchorro people, who once inhabited the coast.

The climate is hot, but it's never hard to escape the desert. Lush beaches and world-class surf make Iquique and Arica irresistible for adrenaline seekers. Decent local transport makes it easy to combine relaxation with high altitude adventures. Spot rare wildlife in Parque Nacional Lauca and Reserva Nacional de los Vicuñas from the sleepy town of Putre in the precordillera.

PLANNING YOUR TIME

A **week** is enough for Norte Grande's main highlights. Decent bus services connect the major cities and smaller towns, but for those tight on time, the most efficient, and sometimes most economical, way is with your own vehicle. With a week, you can visit San Pedro de Atacama and Arica, where you can fly back to Santiago.

The airports in Calama and Iquique have frequent flights from Santiago and can be your starting point. From **Calama,** most visitors go directly to **San Pedro de Atacama. Three or four days** allows for visits to the volcanoes and salt flats of unmissable Reserva Nacional Los Flamencos.

Iquique merits **1-2 days,** more if you're an avid surfer, with day trips to nearby Oficina Humberstone and Laguna Roja. Farther north, **Arica** has two museums containing the Chinchorro mummies, which deserve at least **one day.** To visit the **altiplano,** high in the eastern mountains, without succumbing to altitude sickness, **three days** is recommended. Close to the southern fringes of the region, the mining city of **Antofagasta** attracts few

international visitors; an **afternoon** or a day here is plenty.

Ruta 5, the Pan-American Highway, connects the cities of the north and is the fastest way across the desert, but the coastal vistas of **Ruta 1** offer an alternative to the tedium and trucks of the main highway. Stock up with gas where possible, and keep plenty of water and a spare wheel in your car; it could be some time before help reaches you if your vehicle breaks down.

Thanks to its year-round warm climate and near absence of rainfall, the Norte Grande makes the ideal escape from cool or rainy weather farther south.

HISTORY

Although it might look uninhabitable, human settlement in the Norte Grande dates to 10,000 BC, when the Chinchorro people, a fishing culture, settled along the coast of modern-day Arica. Leveraging the convergence of the two river valleys, the Azapa and Lauca, and an ocean rich in seafood, they prospered for 8,000 years. Later, their descendants began trading with their altiplano cousins, whose domestication of the llama and the alpaca from the wild guanaco and vicuña allowed them to transport goods over large distances, leaving geoglyphs as signposts.

Between AD 500 and 1000, the Tiwanaku and later the Inca expanded their territories into the region; the Inca reached the Río Maipo in Central Chile. The arrival of the Spanish conquistadores in 1532 and their unquenchable thirst for silver and gold saw the region expand, with coastal settlements becoming busy ports to cope with the rush of silver back to Europe, while indigenous people and enslaved Africans provided the labor.

In the late 1880s, the discovery of nitrates in the Atacama Desert, a region initially in Peruvian and Bolivian territory, sparked the War of the Pacific, the result of which

Norte Grande and the Atacama Desert

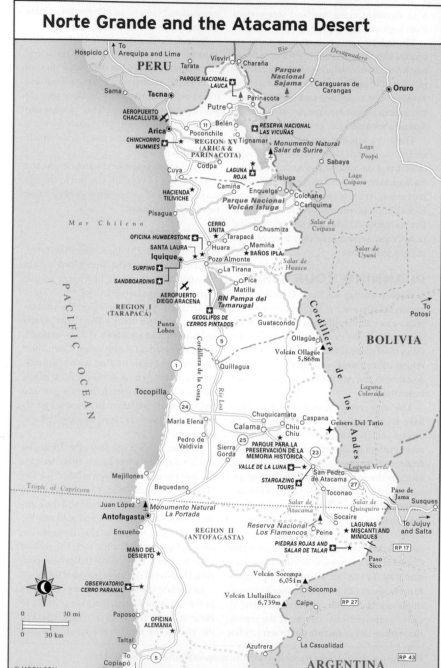

© MOON.COM

Two Days in the Norte Grande

Two days is enough time to head to **San Pedro de Atacama.**

DAY 1

Jump on a tour to **Piedras Rojas** and the **Salar de Talar** with a stop at the gleaming blue **Lagunas Altiplánicas** for an introduction to the startling beauty of the **Reserva Nacional Los Flamencos.**

Return to your hotel in San Pedro and dress warmly before heading out on a **stargazing tour** in the darkness of the desert. Peer through telescopes and contemplate the mysteries of the night skies.

DAY 2

The next day starts early with a trip to **Géiseres del Tatio** and a drive up into the mountains where a chilly sunrise illuminates the swirls of soft white steam that escape from the earth's crust.

Have a relaxed lunch at one of the many restaurants along **Calle Caracoles,** or opt for an afternoon's exercise **sandboarding** down the steep dunes of the otherworldly **Valle de la Muerte.** Finish the day in the neighboring **Valle de la Luna** as the sunset turns the colors of the undulating Cordillera del Sal and the Andes Mountains into a bewitching pastel hue.

expanded Chilean land by one-third and put the richest parts of desert into Peruvian hands. The resulting economic boom lasted until World War I, when the nitrate market collapsed due to mass production of synthetic fertilizers.

As the golden age of saltpeter ended, workers in the 200 nitrate towns gradually moved to the region's expanding copper mines, represented by the vast Chuquicamata, the largest open-pit copper mine in the world. Nowadays, the industry employs tens of thousands of people and accounts for 10 percent of global production.

San Pedro de Atacama

Nothing quite prepares you for the approach to San Pedro de Atacama. The undulating monotony of the sand-dune landscape suddenly blooms in a kaleidoscope of colors. The jagged caverns of the Cordillera del Sal rise out of the desert, brown and dusted with salt to the south. This oasis town, at 2,433 meters elevation, seems a mirage. The vast landscape is dwarfed by the snowy 5,916-meter peak of Volcán Licancabur on the Bolivian border, providing contrast against the cloudless azure sky.

The surrounding landscape is the reason for the influx of tourism to this tiny adobe town. Thousands take tours to El Tatio, the world's highest geysers, and head out to the saline lakes of Salar de Atacama to admire the pastel-pink flamingos, or sink into a high-altitude hot-spring pool, or shred the desert dunes on a sandboard. Due to the focus on the region, the town is approaching saturation, particularly during peak months of December-March, when it's bursting with visitors.

Note that the tap water is not safe to drink here or in surrounding altiplano towns, as it contains traces of arsenic. Higher-end hotels provide bottled water; otherwise expect to stock up at local shops.

Orientation

San Pedro de Atacama is a compact town of narrow dirt streets, whitewashed adobe

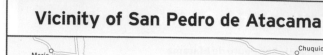

Vicinity of San Pedro de Atacama

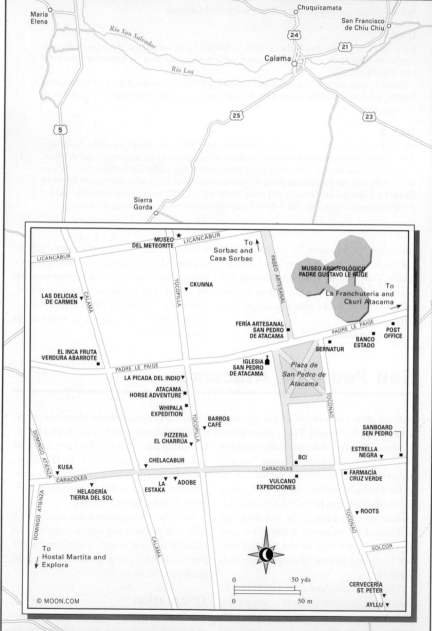

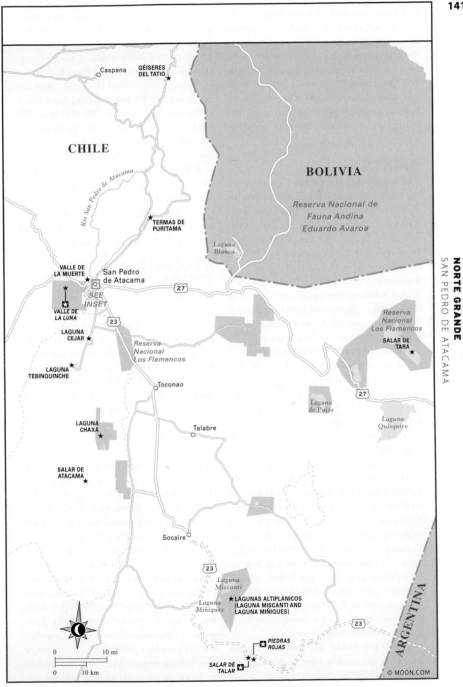

Caspana

GÉISERES DEL TATIO

CHILE

Río San Pedro de Atacama

TERMAS DE PURITAMA

BOLIVIA

Reserva Nacional de Fauna Andina Eduardo Avaroa

Laguna Blanca

VALLE DE LA MUERTE

San Pedro de Atacama

SEE INSET

VALLE DE LA LUNA

LAGUNA CEJAR

Reserva Nacional Los Flamencos

Reserva Nacional Los Flamencos

SALAR DE TARA

LAGUNA TEBINQUINCHE

Toconao

Laguna de Pujsa

Laguna Quisquiro

LAGUNA CHAXA

Talabre

SALAR DE ATACAMA

Socaire

Laguna Miscanti

LAGUNAS ALTIPLÁNICOS (LAGUNA MISCANTI AND LAGUNA MIÑIQUES)

Laguna Miñiques

PIEDRAS ROJAS

ARGENTINA

0   10 mi
0   10 km

SALAR DE TALAR

© MOON.COM

buildings, and lots of street dogs. Volcán Licancabur, due east, is visible throughout town. The streets are a less ordered version of the grid system of most Chilean cities; expect to spend the most time along main thoroughfare **Caracoles,** where you're unlikely to get lost. Most restaurants and other services are here, while other options, including the bulk of the accommodations, are rarely more than a 10-minute walk away.

SIGHTS

The **Museo del Meteorito** (Tocopilla 101, tel. 9/8360 3086, http://museodelmeteorito. cl, 10am-1pm and 3pm-7pm Tues.-Sun., CH$3,500 adults, CH$2,500 children) offers fascinating insights into the arrival of objects from space. In two large geodesic domes, it was born from the passion of two local brothers and now displays 77 of a collection of over 3,200 meteorites that have landed in the Atacama Desert; some have been dated at 4.5 million years old. A free 45-minute audio guide, available in five languages, provides technical descriptions of the meteorites; most of the fun is admiring the rocks on display. Two plastic cases with holes allow you to inspect the rocks close up and even touch them.

The **Museo Arqueológico Padre Gustavo Le Paige** (tel. 9/4005 8263 or 55/2851 002, reservasmuseospa@ucn.cl, 9am-10am, 11am-noon, 2:30pm-4pm, and 5pm-6pm daily, CH$2,500 adults, CH$1,000 children) was closed in 2017 for restoration; in 2019 a small selection of artifacts was put on temporary display (Universidad Católica del Norte, R. P. Gustavo Le Paige 380) in a shipping container on the grounds of the Universidad Católica del Norte. Its exhibitions chart the region's cultural and historical development, from the initial settlers around 11,000 years ago to the invasion of the Spaniards in the 1700s. Follow signs for the university and ask for the museum when you reach the university grounds.

The leafy **Plaza de San Pedro de Atacama** (bounded by Toconao, Vilama, and Gustavo Le Paige) is shady in the fierce desert sun. On the west side the simple 17th-century adobe **Iglesia San Pedro de Atacama** (Vilama 362, no phone, 9am-8pm daily) has a high-vaulted wooden ceiling made of algaroba planks strapped together with leather.

To learn more about the region, join the two-hour **San Pedro Walking Tour** (meet at Plaza de Armas, tel. 9/5000 9144 or 2/2570 9338, 10am and 3pm daily, tips-based), in English or Spanish. Look for the guides dressed in red-and-white-striped T-shirts.

A Bite of Atacama (meet at Plaza de Armas, tel. 9/8743 6085, www.abiteofatacama. com, 9:30am Mon.-Fri., CH$35,000 adults, CH$15,000 ages 5-13) is a 4.5-hour walking tour with stops at various restaurants around town. Booking ahead is required.

ATACAMA DESERT TOURS

Although the roads are in adequate condition to reach the attractions in the Atacama Desert and the Reserva Nacional Los Flamencos in private vehicles, visitors generally travel with one of the many tour agencies in San Pedro. Brazilian tourists are the largest group in San Pedro, so a host of Portuguese-speaking agencies exist. Unfortunately the English-speaking offerings have little competition and quality is variable, particularly at the budget end.

Established **Whipala Expedition** (Tocopilla 418A, tel. 9/5740 7836, www. whipalaexpedition.cl) and newcomer **Sorbac** (tel. 9/4294 2468, www.sorbac.com) form the top end of English-language tours to all the main sights. Sorbac also offers 4WD excursions to lesser-visited Salar de Tara and Laguna Balinache. They also give discounts for multiple bookings and to those staying in their friendly and spacious hostel, **Casa Sorbac** (Tikayki 53, Ayllu de Quitor, CH$12,000 dorm, CH$45,000 d shared bath).

123 Andes Chile Conectado (Caracoles 101 C, tel. 9/5238 6850 or 9/6678 5602, www.chileconectado.com.br) is another well-regarded operator that can organize full excursions and day tours, mainly in Spanish or Portuguese. For volcano

Desert Observatories

Thanks to a fortuitous blend of high altitude, clear skies, and little light pollution, the Atacama Desert is the best place on earth to see the stars, and astro-tourism has taken off. Cutting-edge observatories also conduct astronomical research. The largest radio telescope in the world, the **Atacama Large Millimeter/Submillimeter Array,** aka ALMA, is a collaboration among observatories in Europe, North America, East Asia, and Chile. As ALMA captures signals from the farthest and oldest galaxies, the data is analyzed by a team of astronomers in Santiago.

Research is at two locations, and a **visitors center** is at ALMA's Operations Support Facility (R-23, www.almaobservatory.org), at 2,900 meters elevation 50km east of San Pedro de Atacama. The observatory offers a four-hour **tour** (9am-1pm Sat.-Sun., free). Demand is high, so requests must be made at least a month in advance online. Visitors are required to bring a passport.

The second location, not accessible to the public, is the **Chajnantor Plateau,** used for centuries by the indigenous Atacameños or Likan Antai, in whose language "Chajnantor" means "launch site." At 5,000 meters elevation, 66 high-precision antennae form the equivalent of a radio telescope 16km in diameter, obtaining images with higher resolution than the Hubble Space Telescope.

ascents, including Volcán Licancabur, contact **Vulcano Expediciones** (Caracoles 317, tel. 55/2851 023 or 9/5333 621, www.vulcanochile. com). Tour operators normally offer hotel pickup; confirm this when you make your booking.

Tour prices are similar across the agencies. Expect to pay the following per person:

- Valle de la Luna: CH$15,000
- Laguna Cejar: CH$20,000
- Laguna Chaxa: CH$22,000
- Lagunas Altiplánicas, including Piedras Rojas and Salar de Talar and Laguna Chaxa: CH$55,000; without Piedras Rojas and Salar de Talar: CH$35,000
- Salar de Tara: CH$70,000
- Termas de Puritama: CH$12,500
- Géiseres del Tatio: CH$28,000

Consider booking multiple tours with one company to get a significant discount. Tours rarely include the entrance fee charged by CONAF, Chile's national park service. Admission fees for different parts of Reserva Nacional Los Flamencos range from free to CH$15,000. Verify whether entry fees are included when you book, and if not, bring extra cash to cover the fee.

★ Stargazing Tours

The Atacama Desert has 330 clear nights annually, so there are few better places on the planet to appreciate the night sky. The best conditions are in October-November; avoid January-February, which can see electric storms and clouds, and August-September, when high winds cause dust storms.

Unrivaled for their expert staff, the agency for stargazing tours is **San Pedro de Atacama Celestial Explorations (SPACE)** (Caracoles 400-2, 55/256 6278 or 9/5217 3959, www.spaceobs.com, office 10:20am-7pm daily summer, 10:20am-9pm daily winter, tours 7pm-9pm winter, 9pm summer, CH$25,000), with English, Spanish, and French 2.5-hour guided night tours at their outdoor observatory. They have 15 telescopes on-site, including a 720-centimeter telescope, the largest public telescope on the continent.

After leaving San Pedro (Domingo Atienze and Caracoles) and a 15-minute journey to the observatory, 6km south of town along Ruta 23, the tour starts beneath the stars with an informative and entertaining overview, including beliefs of our ancestors and how stars got their names. Visitors are then shepherded toward the telescopes and told about what they're trained on. A cup of hot chocolate and a Q&A

session end the tour, with the return trip to San Pedro included.

Most of the tour is outside. Temperatures drop 1 degree every 15 minutes after the sun sets; the difference between day and night can be up to 30 degrees, so wear plenty of layers. Blankets are also available. Reserve a tour at least a week in advance via email (info@ spaceobs.com) or at their office, at least two weeks in advance for groups of six or more. There are some same-day cancelations; check by visiting the office before 4pm. Tours don't run the three days before and after the full moon and can be suspended for weather.

Sandboarding Tours

Sandboarding in the dunes of Valle de la Muerte is a highlight of the region. A handful of decent agencies offer these trips. You're unlikely to be whizzing down the dunes as fast as the pros, but a 3.5-hour tour with **Sandboard San Pedro** (Caracoles 362-H, tel. 9/8135 1675, www.sandboardsanpedro.com, 10am-10pm daily) in the Reserva Nacional Los Flamencos is excellent cardio. Tours are for beginners and up. For CH$20,000 you get equipment that includes a helmet, an English-speaking guide, a souvenir video, and transport to the sand dunes from their office, leaving at 9am and 4pm daily (reservation required). During the full moon and occasional Saturdays, they run nighttime excursions at 9pm (CH$25,000). Tours focus on the dunes in Valle de la Muerte; those to Valle de la Luna have been suspended due to erosion.

Wine Tours

A tour of the indigenous Toconao community is an unexpected wine experience. At 2,468 meters elevation, these vineyards are the highest in the country. Neat rows of vines grow out of parched sand against the backdrop of the Salar de Atacama. Organized by tour agency **FlaviaBia Expediciones** (Callejón Reales 402B, tel. 9/4251 7683, www.flaviabiaexpediciones.com) and **Ayllu** (Toconao 479, tel. 9/6496 9163, www.aylluatacama.com.br), a cooperative of 12 wine producers of indigenous Likan Antai origins, these tours include a visit to a vineyard, a winery, and a tasting room. The tours cost CH$70,000, including transportation, plus the CH$10,000 vineyard entry fee. The tours stop at Laguna Chaxa. Tours are only in Portuguese or Spanish.

Horseback Tours

Horseback tours of up to 10 days through the desert are available with knowledgeable, mostly Spanish-speaking **Atacama Horse Adventure** (Tocopilla 406, tel. 55/2851 956 or 9/9084 5518, www.atacamahorseadventure. com) starting at CH$68,000 for a three-hour trip for two people to Valle de la Luna. They also run desert-camping trips. All guides speak Spanish; some interns speak English.

EVENTS

Celebrating their patron saint, San Pedro, the local community floods the streets June 28-29 for the **Fiesta de San Pedro y San Pablo.** Religious parades begin early in the morning, descend on Iglesia San Pedro de Atacama at 11am for mass, and continue well into the night. The next morning, dancing and processions continue through the streets, with a closing mass at 6pm. Visitors are welcome to join in. Streets around the church are closed to vehicles, while most town services remain operational.

Traditional **Carnaval celebrations** (Feb.-Mar.) begin seven days before Good Friday. Visitors can watch the colorful parades from the side of the road. Similarly riotous **New Year's Eve** is marked with the burning of straw dolls in the middle of Calle Caracoles and large, rowdy celebrations in restaurants that become clubs for the event. Expect restaurant and lodging costs to double for the days on either side of December 31.

1: wine from Ayllu 2: sandboarding in Valle de la Muerte

SHOPPING

Although many markets, including the **Feria Artesanal San Pedro de Atacama** (Paseo Artesanal, northern side of Plaza de Armas, 10am-9pm daily), claim to sell authentic crafts, the only one where all of the merchandise is manufactured by local craftspeople is the **Pueblo de Artesanos** (Tumisa 620, next to the bus station, 10:30am-7pm Wed.-Mon.), a series of stalls around a small square where the best crafts produced in nearby indigenous towns are available. Items include copper and bronze jewelry, ceramics, textiles, and, bizarrely, beautiful shoes made from salmon skin.

Cerámica Tatané Durán (Caracoles 101D, tel. 9/8219 0627, 9am-2pm and 5pm-9pm Wed.-Mon.) is a tiny shop selling the works of local contemporary ceramist Tatané Durán and other craftspeople, whose beautiful paintings, sculptures, and drawings are influenced by the altiplano.

FOOD

When it comes to dining, this tiny desert town punches above its weight. You'll find traditional Chilean dishes and gourmet dining, although prices are significantly higher than in the rest of the Norte Grande region. For plentiful portions at cheaper prices, *menús del día* (lunch menus) are a reliable option. Most are served noon-3pm, but some places offer them in the evening.

The *ley seca* (dry law) makes it illegal for restaurants to serve alcohol without food, so there's only one bar in town. Alcohol is served until 1am during the week and 1:30am weekends.

Andean and Chilean

Serving the best home cooking in town, ★ **Las Delicias de Carmen** (Calama 370 B, tel. 9/9089 5673, www.lasdeliciasdecarmen. cl, 8:30am-10:30pm daily, CH$8,000-19,000, *menú del día* CH$6,000) is a good choice for a relatively inexpensive meal. Service can be slow, but the friendly, unpretentious atmosphere and hearty food are worth the wait,

with portions so big they can be shared. Their *pastel de choclo* (a beef and sweet corn pie) is deservedly famous, but the *menú del día,* with a side salad and traditional main course, is always a winner.

The crème de la crème of San Pedro, ★ **Adobe** (Caracoles 211 A, tel. 55/2851 132, noon-midnight Wed.-Mon., 6:30pm-midnight Tues., CH$10,000-13,000, *menú del día* CH$9,000) has elegant plates of Andean-Chilean fusion such as the *lomo roquefort* (fillet of beef with roquefort) and *risotto de quinoa* showcasing local produce. The dining area is atmospheric, with simple adobe tables around an open fire, and live Andean music from 8pm nightly.

Under the same ownership as Adobe, **La Estaka** (Caracoles 219, tel. 55/2851 286, 9:30am-noon daily, CH$10,000-13,000, *menú del día* CH$10,000) is beautifully decorated, blending modernity and Andean roots with adobe walls, an open fire, and bright wall-hangings. The food melds Chilean and Peruvian with a local twist, with local ingredients such as quinoa and fish paired expertly with award-winning Chilean wines.

Don't be fooled by the basic decor; **La Picada del Indio** (Tocopilla 418, no phone, noon-4pm and 6:30pm-11pm Thurs.-Tues., CH$4,000-20,000, *menú del día* CH$5,000) is a must for meat lovers. Its huge *parrilladas* (mixed platters of barbecued cuts) prove the chef knows meat. The *menú del día,* which includes beef, pork, or chicken plus a starter and dessert, makes an exceptionally good value.

Ckunna (Tocopilla 359, tel. 55/2980 093, www.ckunna.cl, 12:30pm-11pm daily, CH$12,000-15,000, *menú del día* CH$10,000) is a decent place with a pleasant and sunny outdoor patio. The filling lunch menu makes use of regional ingredients such as quinoa and llama. The quality makes up for the slow service.

International

Cozy **Pizzeria El Charrúa** (Tocopilla 442, no phone, 1pm-midnight daily, CH$5,500-11,000) has only four tables, so arrive early for dinner. Service is fast and the pizzas are large, with De La Casa (garlic, bacon, and mushrooms) and the Iberica (tomato, serrano ham, peppers, and oregano) as popular choices.

Vegetarian restaurant **Estrella Negra** (Caracoles 169, no phone, 9am-11pm daily, CH$2,500-4,700, *menú del día* CH$4,000) specializes in cheap healthy fare. All dishes can be made vegan. Sizeable empanadas are the main draw, although soy burgers, pizzas, and tacos are superb. The *menú del día* is popular, so arrive early for lunch.

Bright, airy **Barros Café** (Tocopilla 429 B, tel. 55/2256 931, 8:30am-midnight daily, CH$5,500-8,000) is warm and welcoming. Heaters on the patio ensure diners stay warm too, even on the coldest nights. The large menu includes sweet and savory pancakes and a selection of vegetarian dishes. There's live music from 8:30pm every evening.

Budget and Light Bites

Slightly off the main thoroughfare, **Roots** (Toconao 492, tel. 9/5993 3679, 8am-11pm daily, CH$4,500-7,000) is a quirky seven-table café serving whole-wheat pizzas named after famous bands and celebrities (the back wall has photos of everyone from Albert Einstein to Charlie Chaplin), good coffee, and Chilean craft beer. The menu includes vegetarian sandwiches and gluten-free crepes. The atmosphere is chill, with jazz, blues, and reggae music and board games.

A slice of France in the desert, **La Franchuteria** (Gustavo le Paige 527 B, tel. 9/6660 1122, 7am-8:30pm daily, CH$2,000) has the best croissants in Chile. Traditional varieties rub shoulders with *manjar* (condensed milk spread), figs, and roquefort. Baguettes with unusual fillings, such as goat's cheese and oregano, complete the offerings. The outdoor seats are perfect for a sunny breakfast.

Heladería Tierra del Sol (Caracoles 169, no phone, 11am-10pm daily, CH$1,700-2,600) serves authentic Andean ice cream with unusual flavors that offer a real taste of the Atacama Desert. The most unusual include *hoja de coca* (coca leaf), *chañar* (a tree known for its medicinal properties), and *rica-rica* (similar to mint). More common flavors are available if you're not feeling adventurous.

Unpretentious food truck **Kusa** (corner of Ignacio Carrera Pinto and Caracoles, no phone, 7:30am-5:30pm daily, CH$3,000) has simple but delicious sandwiches and rolls, a range of vegetarian and meat fillings, cakes, juices, and coffee.

Drinking Establishments

Under the tagline "The desert isn't so dry anymore," ★ **Cervecería St. Peter** (Toconao 479 B, tel. 9/4287 9893, contacto@ cervezasaintpeter.cl, noon-midnight daily, CH$4,000-10,000) is San Pedro's only brewpub. The bar is accessed from gates that open to the street. The microbrewery is behind it, producing innovative flavors such as quinoa, *chañar*, and *rica-rica*. If you come only for a pint, they sidestep the dry law by bringing small baskets of sopaipillas (fried pastries) with every drink. The food is unexpectedly good and includes llama meat in steaks, burgers, and empanada fillings. For a tour of the brewery (CH$15,000), pop into tour operator **Ayllu** (Toconao 479, 9/64969163, www. aylluaytacma.com.br) next door, under the same ownership.

Lively **Chelacabur** (Caracoles 212, tel. 9/9489 8191, 11am-midnight daily) is so crowded you'll have to loiter to get a seat, but they have Chilean beers on tap and bottled, with popular 1.6-liter sharing pitchers.

ACCOMMODATIONS

Few accommodations are more than a five-minute walk from Caracoles. High rates reflect demand but not value for money. That said, budget accommodations can be found, while those seeking top quality will not be disappointed. There are no public buses and few taxis, so expect to walk from your lodging unless the hotel can provide transportation. Rates include a private bath, Wi-Fi, and breakfast unless stated otherwise.

Under CH$25,000

The cheapest rooms in town are at **Hostal Martita** (Palpana 4, tel. 9/7882 6688, CH$24,000 d shared bath, CH$35,000 d private bath, cash only). Organized around a huge parking area, the minimalist rooms contain a bed and a side table—and nothing else. The showers are hot, the Wi-Fi slow but passable, and there's a small communal kitchen and some plastic furniture for lounging in the car park. Breakfast is not included. Rates include IVA.

Budget-friendly **Hostal Eden Atacameño** (Toconao 49, tel. 55/2590 819, CH$24,000 d shared bath, CH$40,000 d private bath, cash only) is around a series of large patios with hammocks between trees, a communal barbecue, and a kitchen. Breakfast is only included for rooms with private baths. Bedrooms are spacious, with large windows, and range from singles to quadruples. The reception is as lukewarm as the showers, but the convenient location and price make it a good bet. Rates include IVA.

CH$40,000-60,000

A 10-minute walk to the main street, charming ★ **Ckuri Atacama** (Los Laureles 170, tel. 9/9531 9706, ckuriatacamma@sanpedroatacama.com, CH$48,000 d, cash only) is in traditional adobe buildings furnished with weavings and adobe furniture. Each room has a large en suite bath and adjoining seating area, where a kettle, toaster, cutlery, plates, and a fridge make self-catering breakfast possible. The attentive owners have thought of everything, including portable heaters in each room and comfortable beds, as well as bikes that can be borrowed.

The quiet and immaculate bed-and-breakfast **La Casa de Matilde** (28 de Agosto 529, tel. 9/8725 3555 or 9/8214 5919, casa.matilde01@gmail.com, CH$13,000 dorm, CH$50,000 d, CH$55,000 suite, cash only) offers superb value. Its dormitory has single beds rather than bunks, and the family suite can sleep four people in two bedrooms with a private kitchen. Breakfast is served in a cozy dining area, and a shady outdoor space has comfortable chairs. Rates include IVA.

Backpacker favorite **Mama Tierra** (Pachamama 615, tel. 55/2851 418 or 9/9410 2066, www.hostalmamatierra.cl, CH$16,000 dorm, CH$55,000 d shared bath, CH$72,000 d private bath, cash only) has 14 basic comfortable rooms around a shady patio with a number of hammocks and access to a large, well-stocked kitchen. A handful of rooms share baths. An ample buffet breakfast is included and can be packed to go for early tours. Rates include IVA.

CH$60,000-80,000

The 11 rooms at quiet **Hostal Quinta Adela** (Toconao 624, tel. 55/2851 27 or 9/7141 6758, www.quintaadela.com, CH$65,000 d) are spacious and clean, if sparsely furnished, but include central heating. The solar showers are backed up with a boiler to provide hot water 24 hours, and each room has a private bath. The large communal outdoor space has hammocks, a barbecue area, and a covered terrace where a simple breakfast is served. There's ample parking. Rates include IVA.

Over CH$80,000

The central **Hotel Pat'ta Hoiri** (Domingo Atienza 352, tel. 55/2895 720, www.pattahoiri.cl, CH$92,000 d) is an intimate hotel with modern, simple bedrooms. A small stream runs through the property, and there's a beautiful seating area with a thatched roof to relax, although proximity to Calle Caracoles means it can get noisy. Breakfast is large and can be boxed to go.

Casa Atacama (Tocopilla 8E, tel. 55/2551 360, www.noihotels.com, CH$185,000 d) is an upscale sustainable hotel and spa with spacious, stylish rooms with wooden flooring and modern decor, some with private terraces. There's a small pool surrounded by sun loungers, and access to the on-site sauna and steam room are included, as is a buffet breakfast in the restaurant, **La Romeria** (1pm-3pm and 7:30pm-10pm daily); it's also open to non-guests for gourmet fixed-price lunches and dinners.

★ **Explora** (Domingo Atienza, tel. 2/3244 2000, www.explora.com, US$1,760 d) comprises 50 luxurious rooms, some with a panoramic view of Volcán Licancabur. The 17-hectare site includes three swimming pools, a massage room, a barbecue area, and an observatory. In the dining room, an award-winning chef serves dishes made with local ingredients. Included in the price are customized excursions led by local guides.

The chic boutique hotel **Tierra Atacama** (Calle Séquitor, tel. 55/2555 977, www.tierraatacama.com, US$1,500 d all-inclusive, US$600 d breakfast only) has 32 tasteful rooms with romantic four-poster beds, air-conditioning, and central heating. Private terraces are in east-facing rooms. Excursions, including guided horseback rides, are included in the rates, but you may not want to leave the two swimming pools, jetted tub, and sauna.

INFORMATION AND SERVICES

The **Oficina de SERNATUR** (Toconao 401, tel. 55 2851 420, sanpedrodeatacama@sernatur.cl, 9am-9pm daily), Chile's official tourism service, is a useful starting point for local information and maps. Some staff speak some English. They can also provide a list of registered tour operators.

Only two banks exist in town: **BCI** (Caracoles 101, 8am-2pm Mon.-Sat., ATM 24 hr daily) and **Banco Estado** (Gustavo Le Paige, ATM only, 24 hr daily), next door to the SERNATUR office. Both regularly run out of money, so bring Chilean pesos or U.S. dollars with you. U.S. dollars can be exchanged at the shops on the southern end of Toconao. Most restaurants and hotels accept credit cards, but some services are discounted if paid in cash.

At the center of town is a pharmacy, **Farmacia Cruz Verde** (Caracoles 140, 9am-10pm daily), and a post office, **Correos Chile**

(365 Gustavo Le Paige, 9am-1:30pm and 3:30pm-6pm Mon.-Fri., 10am-noon Sat.). Laundry can be requested at most hotels.

There is no hospital, but the **Posta Médica** (Gustavo Le Paige 377, tel. 55/2851 010, 24 hr daily), a small clinic, deals with medical emergencies. The nearest hospital is **Hospital de Calama Dr. Carlos Cisternas** (Av. Grau 1490, tel. 55/2599 628, www.hospitalcalama.gob.cl) in the north of Calama, a 100-km, 30-minute drive.

A number of mini markets around town sell fresh fruit, vegetables, meat, and toiletries. **El Inca Fruta Verdura Abarrote** (Gustavo Le Paige and Calama, 10am-10pm daily) and **Supermercado Int Sol** (Domingo Atienza, 8am-9pm daily) are two of the best stocked. **Pueblo San Pedro de Atacama** (Caracoles, 10am-8pm daily) is a small farmers market selling cheap fruit and vegetables.

COPEC (Toconao, a block south of Caracoles) is the only gas station in San Pedro. Demand for fuel means long queues here, particularly in the morning. Its location, down a backstreet, can cause chaos for vehicles trying to get in and out of the pumps.

TRANSPORTATION
Getting There
BUS

All buses arrive at the **Terminal de Buses** (Ignacio Carrera Pinto 647), in the southeast part of town, an 800-meter walk from the plaza. Within the terminal are a number of small cafés with internet access, restrooms, and ticket offices (most of which keep erratic hours) that offer connections to various domestic and international destinations.

Tour Magic (tel. 9/9456 8916) runs six daily buses to **Calama Airport** (2hr, CH$8,000). **TRANSVIP** (tel. 55/2267 7300, www.transvip.cl), **Transfer Andino** (tel. 9/8792 912, transandino@sanpedrodeatacama.net), and **Transfer Pampa Expedition** (tel. 9/5256 0722 or 9/52260 720, www.transferpampa.cl) offer private and shared transfers in minivans to and from the airport and hotels in town (CH$12,000 one-way, CH$20,000 round-trip), a two-hour ride; pickup is from your hotel three hours before your flight departs.

SRTCIELO Interurbano (tel. 9/6679 3847) buses arrive from **Iquique** (2 daily, 7hr, CH$15,000) and **Arica** (1 daily, 10hr, CH$15,000) via Calama. **Tur Bus** (tel. 55/2688 704, www.turbus.cl) offers services from **Valparaíso** (6pm and 11pm daily, 26hr, CH$30,000/CH$55,000), **Santiago** (4 daily, 24hr, CH$25,000/CH$50,000), and **Antofagasta** (7 daily, 5hr, CH$9,000/CH$10,000). All buses leaving San Pedro de Atacama stop at the bus terminal in **Calama** (2hr, CH$3,000), from where taxis to the airport can be found.

CAR

It's a winding 94-km, 1.5-hour drive from Calama, the nearest domestic airport, to San Pedro de Atacama along the paved Ruta 23. The only gas station after Calama is a COPEC located in San Pedro, on Toconao about a block south of Caracoles.

Getting Around

San Pedro is compact enough that most places are within walking distance, but the main attractions are spread out, so taking a tour or organizing your own transport are the best options for getting around.

CAR AND VAN RENTAL

A rental vehicle can offer more flexibility and work out cheaper in a group, although prices are significantly higher to pick up in San Pedro than at the airport in Calama. **Europcar** (Rio Pacsa 98, tel. 55/257 8380, www.europcar.com, 8:30am-1pm and 2pm-6:30pm daily) has a range of regular and 4WD vehicles, with prices from around CH$70,000 per day. A 4WD vehicle isn't necessary for visiting any of the nearby attractions, but be careful driving on dirt roads to avoiding getting stuck.

Wicked Campers (Laskar 1, tel. 9/4207 3790, www.wickedsouthamerica.com, 9:30am-2pm and 3pm-6pm Mon.-Fri., from CH$71,000 per day) has a range of regular and 4WD campervans with 2-5 seats, while Chilean-run **Soul Vans** (tel. 9/5417 3743, www.soulvans.com, from CH$40,000 per day) has campervans with 2-3 seats.

BICYCLE RENTAL

Cycling is a good way to reach nearby Valle de la Luna and Valle de la Muerte. Take plenty of water, sunscreen, and a hat to avoid heatstroke. Bike rental costs around CH$3,000 for six hours or CH$6,000 to return at close-of-business. Most rental shops are on Toconao, south of Caracoles. Look for mountain bikes, as road bikes are of little use in the sandy conditions. Some shops include maps with rental.

Crossing into Uyuni, Bolivia

It's not recommended to drive a car into Bolivia due to safety issues. The better options are to take a bus, or, if available, go by guided tour.

VIA GUIDED TOUR

Tours from San Pedro de Atacama to El Salar de Uyuni—the world's largest salt flats—have become increasingly popular thanks to San Pedro's proximity to Uyuni and popular Reserva Nacional de Fauna Andina Eduardo Avaroa, which contains high-altitude lakes and huge flocks of migrating flamingos. The most reliable and safety-centered tours are run by the Chilean **Cruz Andina Travel** (Caracoles 419, tel. 9/6217 5033, www.cruzandinatravel.com) and Bolivian **Estrella del Sur Expeditions** (Caracoles 238 A, tel. 55/2852 109 or 9/9289 5853, www.travelestrelladelsur.cl). Both offer three- and four-day tours that stop at Laguna Verde, Laguna Colorada, El Salar de Uyuni, and the Termas de Polques hot springs. Tours end in Uyuni (from CH$125,000) or back in San Pedro de Atacama (CH$150,000) and include all food, lodging in shared hostel dormitories, and an English-speaking guide. These tours are more expensive than those from Uyuni, but they're the most convenient way to visit the salt flats from Chile.

VIA BUS

Daily buses connect San Pedro de Atacama with Uyuni. These include **Cruz del Norte** (tel. 9/7964 0819 or 9/7757 0379; 3am daily, 10hr, CH$15,000/CH$20,000) and **Trans Salvador** (tel. 9/7292 8233; noon Mon.-Fri. and 8pm Mon., Wed., and Sat.). From Uyuni, it's easy to arrange a tour to El Salar, although you're unlikely to save much compared with taking a tour from San Pedro. This method is also less time-efficient than taking a tour from San Pedro.

Crossing into Salta, Argentina
VIA BUS

The border of Argentina is only 157km from San Pedro, and many travelers cross to visit Salta. Buses leave Tuesday-Sunday for Salta (12hr, CH$30,000/CH$35,000) with **Geminis** (tel. 55/2892 049, www.geminis.cl; 9am Tues., Fri., and Sun.), **Andesmar** (tel. 55/2893 665, www.andesmarchile.cl; 8am Wed., Fri., and Sun.), **Pullman Bus** (no phone, www. pullmanbus.cl; 9:30am Wed., Fri., and Sun.), and **Frontera del Norte** (tel. 55/3214 320; 9am Thurs.).

VIA CAR

The crossing to Salta is at **Paso de Jama** (8am-11pm daily), 157km from San Pedro de Atacama along Ruta 27. From San Pedro de Atacama, the drive is around 1.5 hours; from the pass it takes another 7-8 hours to drive the 442km on Ruta 52 to Salta. You'll need to organize the insurance documents that allow you to cross into Argentina with your car rental company at least 10 days prior to your departure.

RESERVA NACIONAL LOS FLAMENCOS

Comprising more than 73,000 hectares in seven sections south and southeast of San Pedro, the spellbinding **Reserva Nacional Los Flamencos** (tel. 55/2851 608) contains the region's most breathtaking sights. The Salar de Atacama isn't as big or as blindingly white as the salt flats across the border in Bolivia, but it's a staggering landmark dotted with saline lakes that abound with flamingos. The jagged rocks of Valle de la Luna, dusky waters of the Lagunas Aliplanicas, ocher lava pavement at Piedras Rojas, and the salty lagoon of Salar de Talar are among the attractions.

Most of the reserve's seven sections have their own entrance station. There is no general park admission fee. Some sights charge individual entry fees that must be paid in cash at the CONAF ranger station at the entrance.

Planning Your Time

To see the top sights of Valle de la Luna, Géiseres del Tatio, Laguna Cejar, Laguna Chaxa, the Lagunas Altiplánicas, Termas de Puritama, and stargazing tours, at least **three days** in San Pedro de Atacama are required, although in your own vehicle you can squeeze them into two days. Each attraction charges a separate entry fee. On tours at elevations above 3,000 meters, such as to Géiseres del Tatio, Piedras Rojas, and Salar de Tara, visitors may experience altitude sickness. To avoid getting ill, it's best to work your way from the lowest- to the highest-elevation sights, particularly if you're driving, as the effects of altitude can cause accidents.

GUIDED TOURS

Most visitors take organized excursions from San Pedro-based tour agencies. **Whipala Expedition** (Tocopilla 418 A, tel. 9/5740 7836, www.whipalaexpedition.cl) and **Sorbac** (tel. 9/4294 2468, www.sorbac.com) offer English-language day tours to the main sights. Tour prices are similar at both; expect to pay the following per person:

- Valle de la Luna: CH$15,000

- Laguna Cejar: CH$20,000

- Laguna Chaxa: CH$22,000

- Lagunas Altiplánicas, including Piedras Rojas and Salar de Talar, and Laguna Chaxa: CH$55,000; without Piedras Rojas and Salar de Talar: CH$35,000

- Salar de Tara: CH$70,000
- Termas de Puritama: CH$12,500
- Géiseres del Tatio: CH$28,000

Consider booking multiple tours with one company to get a significant discount. Tours rarely include the entrance fee charged by CONAF, which can range CH$2,000-15,000; a few sections are free. Verify whether entry fees are included when you reserve, and if not bring extra cash to cover the entrance fee.

GETTING THERE

Most main sights are accessible with your own vehicle. Ruta 23 is paved until Socaire, 90km from San Pedro de Atacama, past the turnoff for Lagunas Cejar, Tebinquinche, and Laguna Chaxa. At this point a high-clearance vehicle is essential, and 4WD an added bonus, to reach Lagunas Altiplánicas, 21km from Socaire, and Piedras Rojas and Salar de Talar, 59km from Socaire.

Salar de Tara, off Ruta 27 about 130km east of San Pedro, can be visited without a tour, but this is not recommended, as the lack of marked tracks leading to the salt flat make finding it almost impossible.

Orientation

Ruta 23 runs alongside the main segments of Reserva Nacional Los Flamencos, including Valle de la Luna in the north and Lagunas Cejar and Tebinquinche (accessible by dirt roads off the main road into the Salar de Atacama), before reaching the small indigenous settlement of Toconao, 35km southeast of San Pedro. Laguna Chaxa is 25km west of Toconao, via the B-355 and B-373. The Lagunas Altiplánicas are 75km south of Toconao along Ruta 23, and the Piedras Rojas and Salar de Talar are 110km south of Toconao along Ruta 23. From San Pedro to Piedras Rojas and Salar de Talar is 150km, a two-hour, 40-minute drive.

Ruta 27, the main highway into Argentina, is the road to Salar de Tara. The Monjes de la Pakana rock formations, 103km and one hour's drive from San Pedro de Atacama, signal the entry point for the eastern section of Reserva Nacional Los Flamencos, where a confusing network of dirt tracks lead 30km to Salar de Tara.

★ Valle de la Luna

Ten kilometers west of San Pedro de Atacama, the **Valle de la Luna** (Valley of the Moon, CH$3,000 adults, CH$500 children) is a jarring set of red and white rock formations created by tectonic forces four million years ago. This is easily the most popular of the region's attractions, thanks to its proximity to San Pedro. These canyons are special at dawn or dusk, when the shadows lengthen and the soft light paints this bizarre lunar landscape and the Andes beyond in hues of pale pink.

About 5km west of San Pedro, a viewpoint along Ruta 23 offers excellent views of the valley. To explore the salt caverns and climb the sand dunes, take Ruta 23 toward Calama on the northwest edge of town and turn left 600 meters after the bridge over the Río San Pedro. Follow the signs to Valle de la Luna and a toll booth where you pay the entrance fee (often not included in tours). The popularity of this location means you'll be sharing the sunset with at least a few other travelers. It's relatively quiet during the day, so consider visiting earlier to avoid the crowds. Tours normally involve walking through the valley, visiting some of the vast salt caverns, and sitting atop a sand dune to watch the sunset.

Hiring a bicycle and pedaling to the valley is a low-cost alternative, possible during the day (bring plenty of water) or, better still, on nights with a full moon, as the main highway lacks street lamps. Take plenty of layers as the temperature drops rapidly at night. From San Pedro, it's a 30-minute ride to the ticket booth and another 15 minutes to the caverns. Rent a bike from one of the agencies in San Pedro (along Toconao, south of Caracoles). Rentals cost CH$3,000 for six hours or CH$6,000 until close of business; ask to keep the bike overnight for an additional CH$6,000.

Valle de la Muerte

Two kilometers north of Valle de la Luna, the undulating Cordillera de la Sal continues to become **Valle de la Muerte** (Valley of Death, CH$3,000), a name derived from confusion over a French accent. It was originally named Valle de Marte—Mars Valley— by a Belgian man living in the region. His accent was misunderstood and it became known as Valle de la Muerte. With its slopes of golden sand and strips of red rock, it's as otherworldly as Valle de la Luna, but significantly quieter, with fewer visitors. Most come as part of sandboarding and horseback tours from town.

Salar de Atacama

Stretching south from San Pedro over 100km, the **Salar de Atacama** is the largest salt flat in Chile and the third largest on the globe. It was formed by water deposits from the Andes Mountains collecting in this natural basin and evaporating to leave a crust of salt. The sediment—dirty and resembling dead coral—is significantly less impressive than across the border in Bolivia's El Salar de Uyuni. However, the real attractions here are Lagunas Cejar, Tebinquinche, and Chaxa, the saline lakes that dot the surreal landscape.

LAGUNA CEJAR

Just under 20km south of San Pedro de Atacama on Ruta 23 (a 30-minute drive), **Laguna Cejar** (9am-6pm daily, CH$10,000 before 2pm, CH$15,000 after 2pm) is a sinkhole with a salt concentration of 28 percent. Swimmers who enter this surprisingly cold water float weightlessly. Organized tours hit this lake around 4pm on the way to sunset at Laguna Tebinquinche, so aim to arrive at 6pm to see the sunset in peace. It's possible to persuade the people at the gate to let you enter for free for 30 minutes to take photos. The chemicals in sunblock have done damage to the fragile ecosystem of the water, so you're not allowed to enter the water with any chemicals on your skin. There are changing rooms with cold showers and modern restrooms on-site, but no lockers. To reach Laguna Cejar on your own, take Ruta 23 south from San Pedro for 17km, then take a sharp right along the dirt track.

LAGUNA TEBINQUINCHE

Laguna Tebinquinche (CH$2,000) is the ultimate destination for sunset. This large saline lake is bordered by stretches of hardened salt that turn a soft pink as the light drops. The view is made even more magical by the orange hue on the mountains in the east. Tours generally include a pisco sour and nibbles to toast the dusk, but remember to wrap up warm when the sun finally sinks behind the Cordillera de la Sal. Access the lake by continuing a couple of kilometers along the dirt track heading south from Laguna Cejar.

LAGUNA CHAXA

Laguna Chaxa (CH$2,500 adults, CH$800 children) is one of the best destinations for spotting flamingos, as it's home to large colonies of all three altiplano species: James's, Andean, and Chilean. The best time to see the birds at their most active is at sunrise, when they're busy slurping the water for algae. Laguna Chaxa is reached by taking Ruta 23 out of San Pedro south to the settlement of Toconao; continue 3.5km south of the town and take the dirt B-355 west for another 20km.

Lagunas Altiplánicas

In the southernmost section of the reserve, the heart-shaped **Laguna Miscanti** and smaller **Laguna Miñiques** make up the **Lagunas Altiplánicas** (CH$3,000 adults, CH$500 children). The lakes are surrounded by looming Volcán Miñiques and Cerro Miscanti; combined with the deep blue water, the scene is surreal. It's an excellent spot for lunch. Watch for an Andean foxes and guanacos in the surrounding scrub. The lakes are a 110-km, 1.5-hour drive south of San Pedro de Atacama on Ruta 23.

★ Piedras Rojas and Salar de Talar

Few parts of the Atacama Desert are as colorful as the **Salar de Talar** (Talar Salt Flats, free). Flanked by purple, yellowy-white, and deep-brown dormant volcanoes, the valley floor is a mass of striking white salt, contrasting the mottled blue salt lagoon and the brick-red **Piedras Rojas** (Red Rocks, free), a strip of lava pavement rich in iron. Part of the fun is clambering on the rocks and marveling at the scale and pretty pastels of the surrounding mountains.

Popular with day-trippers, Salar de Talar and Piedras Rojas are normally the end of tours to Laguna Chaxa and the Lagunas Altiplánicas, with an hour or so at the salt flats; this is enough time for independent visitors too.

Both attractions are reached along Ruta 23, a 40-km, 1.5-hour drive beyond the Lagunas Altiplánicas. From San Pedro, it's 150km and three hours to Piedras Rojas. Be careful driving up to the salt flats, as braking too hard can cause damage. At an elevation of 4,000 meters, it's wise to take it easy exploring the area to avoid altitude sickness.

Salar de Tara

The **Salar de Tara** (free), 130km east of San Pedro on Ruta 27 (which crosses into Argentina a short while later), is a breathtaking salt flat at 4,300 meters elevation, although some sections of this eastern part of Reserva Nacional Los Flamencos are as high as 4,800 meters. At the center of the salt flats is a vast salt-rimmed lagoon, home to an array of wildlife, including breeding flamingos, vicuñas, Andean foxes, and birds such as the puna plover and Andean goose.

Most tours stop on the way to admire the **Monjes de la Pakana** (the Pakana Monks), a series of rock pillars weathered by wind erosion to resemble the silhouettes of monks, although they are also known as the Moais

of Tara, a reference to their similarity to the monolithic *moai* statues found on Rapa Nui. Farther along the route to the salt flats, look for the splendid **Catedrales de Cenizas** (Ash Cathedrals), formed by an eruption of Volcán Llaima.

Tours to Salar de Tara leave San Pedro at 8am and return by 4pm. Tour groups visit Salar de Tara as an independent destination, as it's not easy to combine with the region's other attractions in the same day. It's about 120km to the salt flats from San Pedro, a 2.5-hour drive. Visiting on your own, it's possible to combine a visit here with sunset in Valle de la Luna or Laguna Tebinquinche.

Take warm clothing and plenty of water for the high altitude. Coca leaves can be bought from the markets in San Pedro; when chewed or added to water, it helps to relieve some of the effects of altitude. Inquire with your tour agency whether their vehicles carry oxygen for severe altitude sickness.

TERMAS DE PURITAMA

Eight hot springs pools are 30km north of San Pedro on the road toward Géiseres del Tatio. The **Termas de Puritama** (9am-5:30pm daily, CH$14,000, CH$7,000 after 2pm Mon.-Fri.) have a temperature of 25-30°C. The water purportedly relieves rheumatism and arthritis due to the high concentration of sodium sulfate. When the air temperature is warm, they can feel less than refreshing. The pools are in graduated sections of the valley and connected by small waterfalls. Each pool is accessible via a wooden walkway. The entrance fee is fairly high; it's worth spending an entire morning or afternoon to get your money's worth—or arrive after 2pm when the price drops. Changing rooms and restrooms are on-site.

GÉISERES DEL TATIO (TATIO GEYSERS)

With 80 active geysers on 10 square km, this geyser field is the third largest in the world, and at 4,320 meters elevation, it's the highest. Rising before dawn is the prerequisite to see

---

1: Laguna Tebinquinche at sunset 2: Piedras Rojas and the Salar de Talar

the **Géiseres del Tatio** (Tatio Geysers, 5am-5pm daily, CH$10,000) at their most photogenic, worth the bone-rattling two-hour journey on an unpaved road. If you time it right, as the early light of dawn saturates the night sky, the fumaroles (steam from the geysers) are visible as they escape the earth in huge puffy columns, some of which can reach six meters in height. Get here too late and the steam doesn't contrast as noticeably, making it less impressive.

The prime attraction is the spurting steam, but wildlife is also plentiful, and more observable after the deluge of tourists has departed. Vicuñas, viscachas, Andean foxes, and birdlife such as Andean gulls, black-billed shrike-tyrants, and the bright yellow black-hooded sierra finch are found here.

There's also a rustic thermal bath that's heated by the geysers, albeit at a cooler temperature. The hot water arrives through shafts in the bottom of the pool, meaning the water is not a consistent temperature, nor is the ambient air particularly warm. There are often long queues to use the changing facilities.

Wrap up warmly, as temperatures are well below 0°C before dawn. It can be difficult to find the route in your own vehicle in the dark, but since all the traffic leaves San Pedro at the same time to reach the geysers for dawn, it's not too hard to follow the line of vehicles. The road is unpaved, so a high-clearance vehicle is essential. Experience driving in high-altitude conditions is recommended, as the road weaves up into the mountains and gains significant altitude quickly from San Pedro de Atacama.

Safety Precautions

After a series of fatal accidents, where a number of tourists fell through the thin crust of salt that surrounds the geysers, the size of the area open to the public has been reduced significantly. Stick to the signed pathways and be careful about getting too close to the edges, as the water can reach 85°C and contact can cause serious burns—or worse.

Calama

An attractive sprawl of squat houses in the dust, Calama is the regional hub for the 67,000 miners at the nearby Chuquicamata mine. For travelers, it's the main gateway to San Pedro de Atacama and a place for a night's sleep before flying out of El Loa International Airport. There's not much to do here, but a number of pretty parks offer respite from the sun. The mine is the major attraction.

Orientation

Calama is on a grid, in a strip from north to south, with **Avenida Granaderos** and **Latorre** the principal driving routes and backbone of the town. Most facilities are on or parallel to these streets. **Plaza de Armas** (bounded by Av. Granderos, Sotomayor, Abaroa, and Ramírez) is the starting point for pedestrianized **Eleuterio Ramírez,** running east, where most shops are located.

Many places in town are named after Río Loa, Chile's longest river, which cuts a 440-km horseshoe through the desert from the foot of Volcán Miño through Parque El Loa, in the south part of the city, providing water to the inhabitants and to the Chuquicamata mine.

SIGHTS

Marking the original heart of town before it expanded outward, **Plaza de Armas** (bounded by Av. Granderos, Sotomayor, Abaroa, and Ramírez), also known as **Plaza 23 de Mayo,** is a pretty square with a bandstand, a large fountain, and benches. On the western edge of the plaza is the **Catedral San Juan Bautista,** a wall of which bears a mural of traditionally dressed Andeans.

On the western side of Río Loa, **Parque El Loa** (Av. O'Higgins and Lincoyán, 10am-6pm daily, free) is a leafy escape from the heat, offering boat rentals on the river. Across a rickety bridge is a sandy beach with thatched sun umbrellas and barbecues. Just beyond the picnic area is the **Museo de Historia Natural y Cultural del Desierto** (Museum of Natural and Cultural History of the Desert, Parque El Loa, Av. Bernardo O'Higgins s/n, tel. 55/2711 150, www.muhncal.org, 10am-1pm and 3pm-6:30pm Tues.-Sun., CH$500 adults, CH$200 children) with exhibitions on minerals, fossils, flora, fauna, and cultural artifacts.

FOOD

The bright **Tesoro del Inca** (Vicuña Mackenna 2292, tel. 9/4273 2159 or 9/6753 4480, noon-11pm Mon.-Sat., noon-6pm Sun., CH$5,000-15,000, *menú del día* CH$3,500) specializes in huge portions of tasty if overpriced Peruvian dishes like ceviche and *tiraditos* (strips of raw fish in lemon juice and spicy sauce). More Chilean in flavor, the *menú del día* provides better value, making it the pick of the miners who come for lunch.

Opposite Parque de los Lolos, the upmarket but welcoming **Maderos Bar** (Av. Granaderos 2575, no phone, 12:30pm-4pm and 7:30pm-midnight Mon.-Wed., 7:30pm-1am Thurs.-Sat., 12:30pm-4pm Sun., CH$4,900-13,000, *menú del día* CH$5,900) specializes in Chilean-style ceviche and large *parrilladas* (platters of barbecued meat).

Next door to Maderos Bar and under the same management is Calama's swankiest option, ★ **Patagonia** (Av. Granaderos 2549, tel. 55/2341 628, noon-4pm and 7:30pm-11:30pm Mon.-Sat., noon-4pm Sun., CH$11,000-20,000). Inside its cozy dark-wood interior, meats such as *cordero al palo* (roast lamb) are prepared in the Patagonian style. It's a busy during the week, so make a reservation for dinner; it's quieter Friday-Sunday.

ACCOMMODATIONS

Lodging in this stopover town is underwhelming and rarely good value. Rates listed include a private bath, Wi-Fi, breakfast, and IVA, unless stated otherwise.

Under CH$25,000

The small and plain **Nativo Hostal** (Sotomayor 2215, tel. 55/2310 377 or 9/6909 7390, www.nativo.cl, CH$13,000 s shared bath, CH$24,000 s private bath, CH$23,000 d shared bath, CH$34,000 d private bath) is an excellent value conveniently one block from Plaza de Armas. Rooms have large beds but the decor is tired. All rooms have windows to a central courtyard—in other places this would be noisy, but here the atmosphere is relaxed and quiet. The eight rooms that don't have en suite baths share just two baths between them, but you'll struggle to find the same amount of space and cleanliness at this low rate elsewhere.

CH$25,000-40,000

The superb **Alto Carmen Hostal Suite** (Serena 1137, tel. 9/8309 2671 or 9/9214 9827, CH$30,000 d, cash only) has 19 bright, airy rooms, each with a fridge, large bath, and portable hot and cold air-conditioning. Standard rooms are slightly smaller than the executive rooms but have a private balcony. A communal kitchen and breakfast room are the best self-catering facilities in the city. It's a short walk to a supermarket with an ATM and one-day laundry service.

Though not much from the outside, impeccable family-run ★ **Hostal 914** (Av. Bernardo O'Higgins 914, tel. 55/2316 767, www.hostal914.cl, CH$35,000 d) has 14 lovely rooms with wooden floors and tasteful furnishings, including a beautiful wall hanging made by the owner.

CH$40,000-60,000

The business hotel **Geotel Apart Calama** (Cobija 2273, tel. 55/2551 000, http://en.geotelcalama.com, studio CH$59,000 s or d) has 170 modern, simply decorated bedrooms in blocks with landscaped gardens. Rooms are studios (bedroom and bath) and suites (1-2 bedrooms, bath, kitchen, living room). The studios in blocks A-D include a kitchen for no additional cost. There's no air-conditioning, but guests can request a portable heating or cooling unit. Prices are normally lower and the hotel quieter on weekends.

INFORMATION AND SERVICES

In an emergency, **Hospital de Calama Dr. Carlos Cisternas** (Av. Grau 1490, tel. 55/2599 628, www.hospitalcalama.gob.cl) is the only option, a 2.7-km drive north of the Plaza de Armas. For laundry, head to **Terrano** (Vicuña Mackenna 2068 B, tel. 9/6102 8808, 9am-9pm Mon.-Fri., 9am-8pm Sat.) where washing costs CH$1,800 per kilo. Just down the street, **Correos Chile** (Vicuña Mackenna w/ Av. Granaderos, 9am-6pm Mon.-Fri., 10am-noon Sat.) provides mail services.

TRANSPORTATION
Getting There

The main entry point for travelers heading to neighboring San Pedro de Atacama and a major hub for mine employees commuting from Santiago, Calama is served by an international airport and bus terminal.

AIR

Six kilometers south of the city center, **Aeropuerto Internacional El Loa** (CJC, tel. 55/2344 897, www.cacsa.cl) offers a dozen daily flights from Santiago with **LATAM** (www.latam.com), **Sky Airline** (www.skyairline.com), and budget carrier **JetSmart** (www.jetsmart.com), none of which have offices in Calama. The average cost is CH$33,000 for the 2.25-hour flight.

Within the arrivals hall, minibus operators **TRANSVIP** (tel. 55/2267 7300, www.transvip.cl), **Transfer Andino** (tel. 9/8792 912, transandino@sanpedrodeatacama.net), and **Transfer Pampa Expedition** (tel. 9/5256 0722 or 9/5226 0720, transferpampa@gmail.com) offer shared transfers to and from hotels in San Pedro de Atacama, 1.5 hours

away, for a fixed rate of CH$12,000 one-way and CH$20,000 round-trip. The minibuses are timed to flight arrivals and departures, so avoid lingering too long at baggage claim.

BUS

At the **Terminal de Buses** (Av. Granaderos 3051), 2km north of the Plaza de Armas, keep an eye and a hand on your belongings, as theft has been known to happen. Taxis should cost no more than CH$3,000 from here to hotels in the center of town.

Pullman Bus (tel. 55/2365 744, www.pullmanbus.cl) and **Tur Bus** (tel. 55/2688 704) have regular buses from **Antofagasta** (every 15 min, 2hr, CH$5,000), **Copiapó** (hourly, 9hr, CH$15,000/CH$23,000), and **La Serena** (every 2 hr, 12hr, CH$18,000/CH$25,000), and around six buses per day from **Santiago** (22hr, CH$25,000/CH$48,000). Pullman Bus also has buses from **Iquique** (6hr, CH$9,000/CH$17,000) leaving twice daily, and from **Arica** (8hr, CH$12,000/CH$19,000) once a day.

CAR RENTAL

Renting a car from the airport is significantly cheaper than in San Pedro de Atacama. It's essential to book in advance, as prices rise dramatically and demand exceeds supply December-February.

All rental companies have a desk in the arrival hall of the airport, including **Econorent** (tel. 55/2311 325, 7am-11pm Mon.-Fri., 8:30am-8:30pm Sat., 8:30am-11pm Sun.), **Europcar** (tel. 55/2578 170, 7am-11pm daily), **First** (tel. 55/2319 833, 8am-10pm daily), and **Avis/Budget** (tel. 55/2311 325, 8am-8pm Mon.-Fri., 9am-7pm Sat., 2:30pm-8pm Sun.).

Europcar has another office (Parque Industrial Apiac Sitio 1C, tel. 55/2578 300, 8:30am-6:30pm Mon.-Fri.) on Ruta 25 in the south of Calama, 1.6km before the turnoff for the airport. **Econorent** (Latorre 2507, tel. 55/2341 076, 8:30am-6:40pm Mon.-Fri., 9am-1pm Sat.) also has a location in central Calama.

Getting Around

Services are somewhat scattered around the city, and the constant heat and dust can make it tiring on foot. **Taxi Tur Calama** (Terminal de Buses, Av. Granaderos 3051, tel. 55/2829906) has reasonable rates, with a standard CH$3,000 fare around the center or CH$4,000 farther south. The 20-minute journey to the airport costs CH$8,000. Call to arrange a pickup. Another taxi company, **LM Calama** (tel. 55/2541010 or 9/8444 5430), offers airport pickup and drop-off.

A cheaper, if more complicated, way to get around the city is with *taxis colectivos*. These shared five-door sedan taxis generally head south down Avenida Granaderos and north up Latorre, costing CH$700 for the journey, regardless of the distance you travel. Their routes are indicated on roof-top signs, although most pass alongside Plaza de Armas.

Crossing into Bolivia

It's not recommended to drive a car into Bolivia due to safety issues. The better options are to take a bus or go by guided tour.

Cruz del Norte (Av. Balmaceda at Bañados Espinoza, tel. 9/8224 8119, www.tu risticointernacionalcruzdelnorte.com) has buses to Uyuni at 5am daily (7hr, CH$12,000) leaving from its office. **Trans Salvador** (tel. 9/6821 4736, www.trans-salvador.com) buses leave from the Terminal de Buses in Calama for Uyuni (7hr, CH$12,000), Oruro (13hr, CH$18,000), and La Paz (16hr, CH$23,000) at 2pm daily and to Santa Cruz (32hr, CH$35,000) at 11pm Monday, Wednesday, and Saturday. Once over the border, you are required to change to a Bolivian bus, which is included in the ticket price.

Tours of the Salar de Uyuni, the world's largest salt flats, leave from San Pedro de Atacama, ending in Uyuni or returning to San Pedro de Atacama.

Crossing into Argentina

At Calama's Terminal de Buses on Avenida Granaderos, **Frontera del Norte** (tel. 55/3214 320) has buses to Salta, Argentina (12hr, CH$30,000), departing at 7am Monday and Thursday in summer. By car, the 700-km drive from Calama to Salta takes 8-9 hours. Take Ruta 23 to San Pedro de Atacama, then Ruta 27 to the border crossing at **Paso de Jama** (8am-11pm daily). It's another 442km to Salta from the border.

CHUQUICAMATA

Located 16km north of Calama, Chuquicamata is the world's largest open-pit copper mine, measuring 4.2km by 3km and 900 meters deep. It's so colossal you can't actually see the bottom.

The mine takes its name from the indigenous Chuqui people who once used copper for weapons and tools. The U.S.-based Guggenheim family first began mining here in 1915. Chuquicamata continued to grow, with a city built to house 2,500 workers and their families. The mine is one of the largest known deposits of copper on earth, with an annual output of 300,000 tons, 10 percent of global production.

Employees lived at Chuquicamata until 2007, when concerns over the impact of dust and pollution caused by the extraction process forced their relocation to Calama, leaving a modern-day ghost town.

Tours

The only way to enter the mine complex is on a 3.5-hour **guided tour** (meet at Av. Granaderos 4025, 1pm Mon.-Fri., free), in Spanish or English, operated by Codelco, the company that runs the mine. Tours must be booked via email (visitas@codelco.cl) a few days in advance of your desired date. Indicate your name, number of people in your group, and a contact phone number. You must send an email the day before your tour to avoid losing your spot.

After a 20-minute bus journey to the site, the tour begins with an educational video in the now deserted workers town, then moves to a viewpoint overlooking the pit, where a fleet of 120 trucks give a lesson in scale. Each is 7.85 meters tall and carries 400 tons—but still looks tiny compared to the enormous mine.

Before entering the site, visitors are required to sign a liability waiver and must bring an ID. Appropriate clothing—long sleeves, trousers, and closed shoes—is required.

PARQUE PARA LA PRESERVACIÓN DE LA MEMORIA HISTÓRICA

Leaving Calama, Ruta 23 heads southeast toward San Pedro de Atacama. Around 15km from the city, a dirt track just beyond some wind turbines gives access to **Parque Para La Preservación de la Memoria Histórica.** This simple yet moving monument rises out of the dust, with 34 red columns and a white cross honoring the 26 men and women who were executed and buried here in 1973 by the Caravan of Death led by General Sergio Arellano Stark. The infamous government squadron operated during the dictatorship, killing political prisoners who were then buried in unmarked mass graves.

Those commemorated here were found in 1990 after a 17-year search by their female relatives. The book *Flowers in the Desert: The Search for Chile's Disappeared* by Paula Allen, a photographer who joined the women as they dug through the desert sands, tells their story. The monument was inaugurated in 2004, on the 31st anniversary of the killings.

Antofagasta

With a sprawling coastline and role as an important port, Antofagasta deserves more attention from travelers than it receives. Known as the Pearl of the North, it's one Chile's richest cities, where modern highrises and casinos flank a handful of surviving Victorian and Georgian buildings. British influence is visible in city landmarks, reflecting the influx of foreign businesses after saltpeter was discovered in the Salar de Carmen, 40km from the city, in 1866. Spend a night or two here for the city's high-quality restaurants and hotels.

Orientation

Stretching along the coast, Antofagasta is one of Chile's largest cities. The **Barrio Histórico** (Historic District) runs from Bolívar to Plaza Colón, the main square, and northwest to the **Muelle Salitrero,** the historic pier built in 1870 and restored in 2015. It hosts cultural events like the annual **Contemporary Art Week** (www.proyectosaco.cl). Older, more-established accommodations and restaurants spread from this zone. Three kilometers south, surrounding the **Balneario** Municipal artificial beach, modern apartment blocks tower over the seafront. You'll find bars and restaurants where trendy middle-class locals eat and drink.

SIGHTS
Barrio Histórico

The **Barrio Histórico** is home to Antofagasta's most interesting buildings. **Plaza Colón** (bounded by Prat, Washington, José de Sucre, and San Martín) is the city's main square and excellent for people-watching. Take in the **Torre Reloj,** a 1911 clock tower donated by the British community and decorated in enameled tiles bearing British and Chilean flags.

On the southeastern edge of the plaza, neo-Gothic **Catedral de Antofagasta** (San Martín 2634, tel. 55/2221 175, mass 8:30am, 11am, 12:30pm, and 8pm daily), with its needle-like spires, dates from 1917. Its central altar was built in Paris, and its beautiful stained glass windows, only visible from the inside, were imported from Munich. One block northwest, **Casa Gibbs** (Baquedano 108, closed to the public) bears murals

Antofagasta

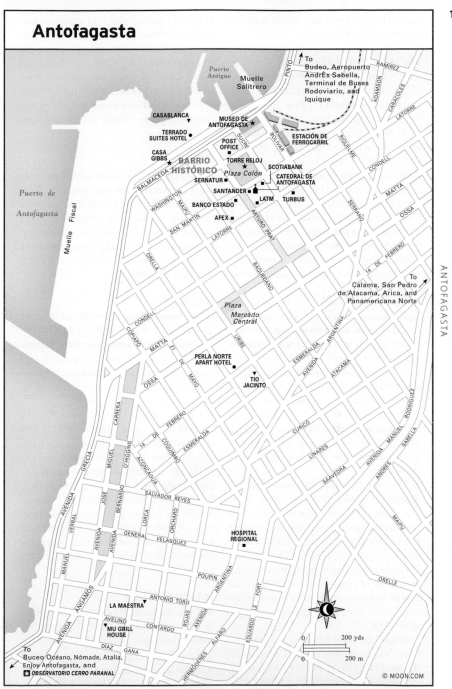

Puerto Antiguo

Muelle Salitrero

To Budeo, Aeropuerto Andrés Sabella, Terminal de Buses Rodoviario, and Iquique

PINTO

RAMIREZ

ADAMSON

CARACOLES

LATORRE

CASABLANCA

MUSEO DE ANTOFAGASTA ★

TERRADO SUITES HOTEL

SUCRE

BOLIVAR

ESTACIÓN DE FERROCARRIL

RIQUELME

CONDELL

POST OFFICE

CASA GIBBS ★

BALMACEDA

BARRIO HISTÓRICO

TORRE RELOJ

Plaza Colón

SERNATUR

SCOTIABANK ★

CATEDRAL DE ANTOFAGASTA

MATTA

OSSA

SANTANDER

LATM

TURBUS

SERRANO

Puerto de Antofagasta

Muelle Fiscal

WASHINGTON

MAIPU

BANCO ESTADO

ARTURO PRAT

AFEX

SAN MARTIN

LATORRE

ORELLA

BAQUEDANO

14 DE FEBRERO

To Calama, San Pedro de Atacama, Arica, and Panamericana Norte

ARGENTINA

CONDELL

COPIAPO

MATTA

21 DE MAYO

Plaza Mercado Central

URIBE

ESMERALDA

AVENIDA

ATACAMA

RODRIGUEZ

SABELLA

PERLA NORTE APART HOTEL

OSSA

CARRERA

DE FEBRERO

ESMERALDA

TIO JACINTÓ

CURICO

LINARES

AVENIDA MANUEL

ANDRES

MIGUEL

O'HIGGINS

14 DE

COQUIMBO

ACONCAGUA

SAAVEDRA

GRECIA

JOSE

BERNARDO

SALVADOR REYES

MAIPU

AVENIDA

VERBAL

AVENIDA

AVENIDA

LORCA

ORCHARD

GENERAL VELÁSQUEZ

HOSPITAL REGIONAL

MANUEL

POUPIN

ARGENTINA

ORELLE

ANGAMOS

ANTONIO TORO

LA MAESTRA

AVELINO

CONTARDO

ROJAS

AVENIDA

LE FORT

ALFARO

EDUARDO

MU GRILL HOUSE

DIAZ

GANA

HERMOGENES

To Buceo Océano, Nómade, Atalia, Enjoy Antofagasta, and
★ OBSERVATORIO CERRO PARANAL

0   200 yds

0   200 m

© MOON.COM

painted by local artist Luis Núñez depicting Antofagasta's industrial past.

Museo de Antofagasta

The **Museo de Antofagasta** (Balmaceda 2786, tel. 55/2227 016, www.museodeantofagasta.cl, 9am-5pm Tues.-Fri., 11am-2pm Sat.-Sun., CH$2,000 adults, CH$1,000 children) houses permanent exhibitions about the Changos, people who practiced a maritime way of life in this region, and the various cultures that evolved in this harsh, arid climate. On the main floor, look for replicas of fishing rafts made of sea lion skin.

Upstairs, exhibits trace the history of Antofagasta, the potassium nitrate boom, and the subsequent War of the Pacific. Free audio guides in English and Spanish are available by scanning a QR code with your smartphone.

RECREATION

In the second week of July each year is the **Antofagasta Bodyboarding Festival** (www.budeo.cl, July, free) at **Playa Llacolén**, 9km south of the Barrio Histórico on Ruta 1. Over 150 international bodyboarders face the might of the La Cúpula reef break, riding the crest of the waves, performing 360-degree spins, backflips and other complicated maneuvers on bodyboards (also known as boogie boards). Enjoy food, drinks, and live music as you watch the awe-inspiring athletes from the beach.

Tour outfitter and bodyboarding school **Budeo** (Av. Pérez Zujovic 5000, Playa Trocadero, no phone, www.budeo.cl) offers two-hour bodyboarding classes (CH$20,000) that include instruction and use of a bodyboard, wetsuit, and flippers. They also run five-hour snorkeling tours (CH$35,000) that include use of a wetsuit and snorkeling mask as well as transportation to and from the beach in the south of the city, with pickup at their office.

Buceo Océano (Balneario Municipal Local 15, Av. República de Croacia 155, tel. 9/7108 9888 or 9/8324 7880, www.buceooceano.cl, 10am-2pm and 4pm-9pm

Mon.-Sat.) has introductory scuba sessions for those without prior experience; the 3.5-hour tour (CH$65,000) includes equipment, an English-speaking guide, and photos and video. Certified divers can take two-hour guided tours to Isla Santa María (CH$60,000), which include all equipment and an English-speaking guide. Tours in Spanish cost CH$15,000 less.

FOOD

In Antofagasta, the fish is extremely fresh. Most restaurants are due south of Plaza Colón. Avenida Croacia south of the Balneario Municipal is home to the newer and trendier dining options. The older, established restaurants are closest to the center, around 12 blocks south. Consider taking a taxi if you're staying in the center.

Seafood

Casablanca (Baquedano 15, tel. 57/2363 134, 12:30pm-midnight daily, CH$10,000-13,000), on the ground floor of the Terrado Suites Hotel, specializes in octopus, although a wide range of other fish and meat is available. With sea views and a terrace, it's an excellent place to watch the sunset.

Unpretentious family-run ★ **Tio Jacinto** (Luis Uribe 922, tel. 55/2228 486, www.tiojacinto.cl, 12:30pm-4pm and 8pm-10:30pm Tues.-Fri., 12:30pm-4pm Sat.-Sun., CH$12,000-18,000) has been serving the simplest, freshest fish since the 1970s and regularly appears on lists of Chile's top restaurants. Sample the octopus *al pil pil* (cooked in garlic, chili, and olive oil) or langoustines with *merkén* (smoked chili peppers) alongside a glass of Chilean wine. Arrive early; space is limited.

International

Right on the beach, **Nómade** (Av. República de Croacia 26, tel. 55/2923 794, 7pm-3am Mon., 1pm-3am Tues.-Thurs. and Sun.,

---

1: view over Antofagasta 2: the sculpture *Mano del Desierto* by Chilean sculptor Mario Irarrázabal

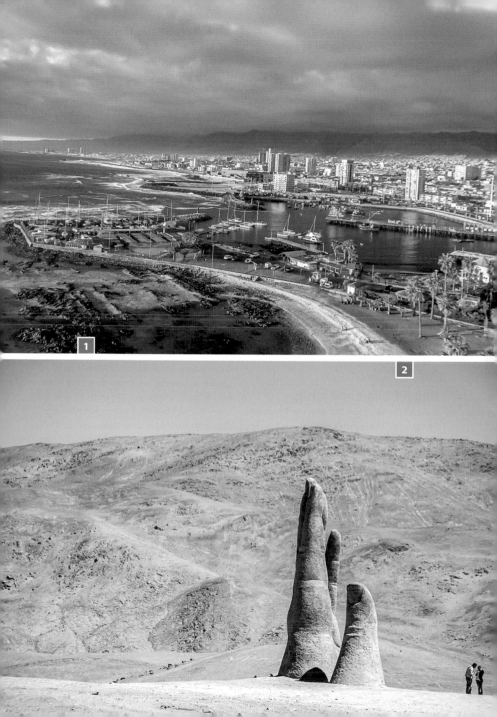

1pm-5am Fri.-Sat., CH$3,200-10,900, *menú del día* CH$5,000) is a trendy bar appealing to a young, hip crowd. Specialties include pizza and beer, with 20 beers available in *schop* (on tap) and 60 bottles from around the world, with a detailed menu separated into flavors. Beer tasting allows you to sample seven of those on tap as well as a beer-themed cocktail; you can even fill a growler to take away. Their menu is extensive, with tasty thin and crispy pizzas the top choice. The spacious upstairs terrace overlooking the beach is great for people-watching or sunset.

Carnivores should head to **Mu Grill House** (Avelino Contardo 908, tel. 55 2488783, www.mugrillhouse.cl, 8pm-11:30pm Mon., 1:30pm-3:30pm and 8pm-midnight Tues.-Sat., 1pm-3:30pm Sun., CH$8,000-18,000), with carefully selected Angus, Hereford, and *wagyu* steaks. It's pricier than most places in Antofagasta and is a favorite of the English-speaking expat crowd. Deep-red walls in the dining room, decorated with animal skins and antlers, and an extensive wine cellar lend a sense of class.

Budget and Light Bites

Around the bay from the pier, the **Terminal Pesquero** (fisherman's market, La Cañada 15, 6am-8pm daily) is filled with stalls where gleaming swordfish, shellfish, and octopus are watched over by the resident cat population. Try the deep-fried empanadas—especially the *jaiba/queso* (crab and cheese).

Fruits and vegetables are piled high at the traditional **Mercado Central** (bordered by Ossa, Sotomayor, Maipú, and Luis Uribe, 9am-9pm daily). The restaurants on the north side have *menús del día* for CH$3,000. They're also open for breakfast and dinner; fancier dishes such as ceviche and *paila marina* (fish soup) cost more.

Servings are huge, service is fast, and *churrascos* (sandwich buns filled with pan-seared or grilled steak) are delicious at popular **La Maestra** (Antonio Toro 1026, tel. 55/2280 550, www.lamaestra.cl, 12:30pm-4pm and 4:30pm-12:30am Mon.-Sat.,

CH$4,900-8,000). For lunch, one sandwich and a side can be shared between two people. Expect a wait, particularly on weekends.

ACCOMMODATIONS

Hotel rates in Antofagasta reflect the wealth of the city, but most are good value. Many are a few blocks south of the plaza; some are farther south around the Balneario Municipal beach or opposite the Ruinas de Huanchaca. Accommodations are busier during the week when local miners are in town, so it is necessary to prebook.

CH$25,000-40,000

Decorated with beautiful Andean wall hangings and with sea-facing terraces, ★ **Atalaia** (Navidad 105, tel. 55/2895 660 or 9/8293 7801, www.hotelatalaia.cl, CH$40,000 d), its name Arabic for "a place to see the waves," is a beautifully decorated hotel on a quiet street near the Balneario Municipal. All nine bedrooms have private baths with spacious modern showers and access to a cozy patio downstairs where an extensive breakfast buffet is served. It's worth booking one of the handful of doubles with private terraces and sea views (CH$47,000 d). The property has a garage with secure parking. Rates include IVA.

CH$40,000-60,000

One of the best values in town, **Perla Norte Apart Hotel** (14 de Febrero 2267, tel. 55/2223 714, www.perlanorteaparthotel.com, CH$45,000 d) is a block from Mercado Central and a five-minute walk to the Barrio Histórico. Rooms are sizeable and have a stove, fridge, and kettle. Rooms facing the main road are slightly more spacious and get a lot more natural light. The complex contains two sizeable terraces, one downstairs and one on the 4th floor with views across the city. Rates include IVA.

CH$60,000-80,000

With its prime position overlooking the main harbor, **Terrado Suites Hotel** (Baquedano 15, tel. 55/2712 801, www.

terrado.cl, CH$80,000 d) has the best views in Antofagasta. This modern hotel is part of a small Chilean chain and provides the city's most stylish accommodations. All rooms are bright, airy, and large, with air-conditioning (desirable in summer) and balconies overlooking the bay. There's an unheated infinity pool overlooking the water. A basement spa includes a gym, pool, and sauna (included) as well as various treatments (additional cost). The hotel has secure parking.

Over CH$80,000

Five-star **Enjoy Antofagasta** (Av. Angamos 1455, tel. 55/2653 000, www.enjoy.cl, CH$104,000 d) is part of the Enjoy chain of casinos, offering luxury rooms on the southern tip of the city. Each room has an ocean view with a balcony, a minibar, and 24-hour room service. Guests have access to the spa and swimming pools (including a heated rooftop pool). The on-site nightclub **Ovo Discoteque** (tel. 55/2653 000, midnight-4:45am Fri.-Sat., cover charge varies) is the most popular in the city, with live DJs and an open-air terrace with sea views. The lower-level rooms can get noisy in the evening thanks to proximity to the casino and the nightclub. Parking is included for guests.

INFORMATION AND SERVICES

The main **tourist office** (Arturo Prat 348, tel. 55/2451 818, 8:30am-6pm Mon.-Fri., 10am-2pm Sat. Mar.-Nov., 8:30am-6:30pm Mon.-Fri., 10am-6:30pm Sat. Dec.-Feb.) is on Plaza Colón. Run by SERNATUR (the national tourism organization), the office has useful information about the city and the surrounding area.

ATMs for banks, including **Santander** (San Martín 2600), **Scotiabank** (San Martín 2688), and **Banco Estado** (Prat 400), are around the square and Arturo Prat, the main pedestrianized street. For mail, **Correos Chile** (Jorge Washington 2601, 9am-6pm Mon.-Fri.) has an office on the western corner of Plaza Colón. **AFEX** (Latorre 2522, www.

afex.cl) can exchange dollars and currencies from Bolivia, Peru, and Argentina. The **Hospital Regional de Antofagasta** (Av. Argentina 1962, tel. 55/2656 729) has an emergency department. It's about 2.5km south of Plaza Colón.

GETTING THERE
Air
Aeropuerto Andrés Sabella (ANF, www.aeropuertoantofagasta.cl), also known as Aeropuerto Cerro Moreno, is 10km north of the city. No local buses serve the terminal. Taxis and airport shuttles can deliver you to your hotel in town. Around 18 flights daily from Santiago are operated by **LATAM** (www.latam.com), with an office in Antofagasta (Prat 445); **Sky Airline** (www.skyairline.com); and budget carrier **JetSmart** (www.jetsmart.com). Two flights daily arrive from Concepción with LATAM and JetSmart.

AIRPORT TRANSFERS
Shuttle and taxi services are in the foyer just outside of arrivals. To prevent visitors from getting ripped off, the maximum rates for services are listed on a board here. **Shuttle minivan transfers** to the north and center of Antofagasta cost CH$6,000 (one-way) and to the south cost CH$7,000 (one-way) with **Transfer Transvip** (tel. 2/2677 3000, www.transvip.cl), located in the arrivals hall.

Taxis cost CH$13,000 to the north of the city, CH$15,000-17,000 to the center, and CH$20,000-24,000 to the south and take roughly 30 minutes to Plaza Colón and 35 minutes to lodgings around the Balneario Municipal.

Bus
Located 3.5km north of the Barrio Histórico, 10 minutes by taxi or *taxi colectivo* from the city center, **Terminal de Buses Rodoviario** (Pedro Aguirre Cerda 5750, tel. 55/2484 502) has buses to all the main cities in the north. Buy tickets at the offices on the ground floor; the platforms are upstairs.

Buses connect to **Calama** (every 15 min, 2hr, CH$5,000), **Iquique** (hourly, 5.5hr, CH$14,000/CH$20,000), **Caldera** (5 daily, 6.5hr, CH$14,000/CH$20,000), **Copiapó** (hourly, 10hr, CH$16,000/CH$30,000), **La Serena** (hourly, 12hr, CH$20,000/ CH$40,000), and **Santiago** (hourly, 20hr, CH$31,000/CH$60,000). Companies that include **CikTur** (tel. 55/2590 794, www.ciktur. cl), **Turbus** (tel. 55/2644 900, www.turbus. cl), and **Pullman Bus** (tel. 55/2482 092, www.pullmanbus.cl) serve these destinations. Pullman also has *semi-cama* services to Salta (16hr, CH$46,000) at 5am Wednesday, Friday, and Sunday; due to high demand, it's worth booking in advance. In addition to its office in the terminal, Tur Bus has a location downtown (Latorre 2751, tel. 55/2644 921).

Car

Antofagasta is on Ruta 5, a 217-km, 3-hour drive south from Calama and a 590-km, 6.5-hour drive north from Copiapó. Coming from Copiapó, the more scenic Ruta 1 and B-710 along the coast (540km, 6hr) is marginally shorter than taking Ruta 5, which adds 40km and an additional 20 minutes to the drive. The coastal route links up with Ruta 5 about 50km south of the city, but is along roads in poorer condition. It's possible to get to Antofagasta from Iquique via Ruta 1. It's a 416-km, 5-hour drive that takes you through a series of picturesque seaside towns.

GETTING AROUND

Everything in the Barrio Histórico is within walking distance, but you'll want to take a local taxi to reach the bars, hotels, and beaches in the south of the city.

To get to the bus terminal, you have two options: *Micros* (public buses), most of which pass along Santos Ossa beside the Mercado Central, cost CH$400. The faster and cozier option is one of the numerous *taxis colectivos* (shared taxis), whose route is indicated on signs on the roof; these cost CH$750 regardless of distance.

Driving

Ruta 1, along the coastal edge of the city, makes it easy to drive between the Barrio Histórico and the beaches, bars, and restaurants farther south. Parking, however, can be a real issue in Antofagasta, with few accommodations offering off-street parking and on-street spaces difficult to find, particularly around the Barrio Histórico.

Just outside the airport's arrivals section, on the right side, are the car rental companies, including **Europcar** (tel. 55/2578 175, www. europcar.com, 7am-11pm daily), **Econorent** (tel. 55/2227 017, www.econorent.cl, 7am-10:30pm Mon.-Fri., 7am-10:30pm Sat.), **First** (tel. 55/2289 568 or 55/2225 777, http://first.cl, 9am-7:30pm daily), **Hertz** (tel. 55/2262 754, www.hertz.com, 7am-11pm daily), and **Avis/ Budget** (tel. 22/7953 977, www.avis.com, 7am-11pm Mon.-Fri., 9am-2pm Sat.-Sun.).

THE COASTAL CORDILLERA

From sea level at Antofagasta, the land quickly rises to become the Coastal Cordillera, the mountain range that hugs the coast from El Morro, a hill in Arica, until Isla de Chiloé, just over 3,000km south. The stretch near Antofagasta is a series of valleys and peaks. Ruta 1 and Ruta 5 are the main highways through this region.

Mano del Desierto

One of the Atacama Desert's iconic landmarks, *Mano del Desierto* is a giant cement sculpture of a hand reaching 11 meters out of the ground. Designed by Chilean sculptor Mario Irarrázabal and installed in 1992, it's a popular Instagram shot due to the striking contrast it makes with the desolate moonscape. It's accessible via a dirt track on the western side of Ruta 5, just after the turnoff for the B-710 toward Cerro Paranal; the drive is 71km south of the city and takes around an hour.

★ Observatorio Cerro Paranal

Run by the European Southern Observatory

(ESO), **Observatorio Cerro Paranal** makes the most of the clear night skies and high elevation (2,660 meters above sea level) to peer into the unknown depths of the universe. It has some of the strongest telescopes on the planet, including the descriptively named Very Large Telescope, composed of four Unit Telescopes, each with 8.2-meter diameters. They work together to capture images of objects four billion times dimmer than what you can see with the naked eye.

The observatory is 130km south of Antofagasta via Ruta 5 and the B-710 (watch for signs) and takes just over 1.5 hours.

Three-hour **guided tours** (tel. 9/9839 5312, www.eso.org, register online, 10am and 2pm Sat., free) begin at the visitors center with a video about the site. The tour continues with a stop at a viewing platform, where you can marvel at the sheer size of a telescope, and a visit to the control room, and then ends at the architecturally distinctive Paranal Residencia, an on-site hotel for employees, where scenes from the James Bond movie *Quantum of Solace* were filmed. Register for the tour on ESO's website well in advance and reconfirm your reservation via email or phone the week before your visit.

Iquique

The "Miami of Chile," as Iquique is known, has little in common with the Florida city, except for its trademark high-rise condos and modern hotels that glimmer against a backdrop of sand dunes. White-sand beaches stretch for miles, and the average temperature hovers around a pleasant 24°C. Despite the retail frenzy inspired by the duty-free Zona Franca, the city is relaxed, embodying the attitude of the surfers who come to take on the world-class waves.

Beyond the surf and the skyscrapers, there's plenty to do in Iquique for a handful of days in any season. It's famed for adventure sports, most notably paragliding and sandboarding from Cerro Dragon, a hill above the city. Architecture buffs will appreciate the Georgian and Victorian mansions in the historic center, which date to the late 19th century.

Orientation

The oldest and most historic buildings are along **Paseo Baquedano,** a pedestrianized road that runs north-south from Plaza Arturo Prat to Plaza 21 de Mayo and the coastal road, Avenida Arturo Prat Chacón. Housed in these colonial mansions are many of the city's museums, restaurants, and hotels. Newer offerings

are farther south along the coastal road and never far from the beach. High-rise condos, upmarket restaurants, and trendy bars are clustered in the **Península de Cavancha.** The neighborhoods east of the coast toward the sand dunes are unsafe for travelers, due to a higher risk of crime, and are not recommended as places to stay or visit at night.

SIGHTS

At the center of **Plaza Arturo Prat** (bordered by Pinto, Tarapacá, Baquedano, and Thompson), the city's main square, the 25-meter **Torre del Reloj** (Clock Tower) is an elegant structure built from Oregon pine transported from Canada and England in 1877. Designed by Don Eduardo de Lapeyrouse, the white landmark has a clock-face on each of its four sides and refined pointed arches.

Opposite the tower on the southern side of the plaza, the **Teatro Municipal** (Municipal Theater, Thomson 269, no phone, 10am-6pm Mon.-Fri., 10am-2pm Sat., free) opened in 1889. Four niches on the front facade each contain a female statue representing one of the four seasons. Inside are three floors of seating and a hand-painted domed ceiling. Beneath the stage are large wooden wheels used to

Iquique

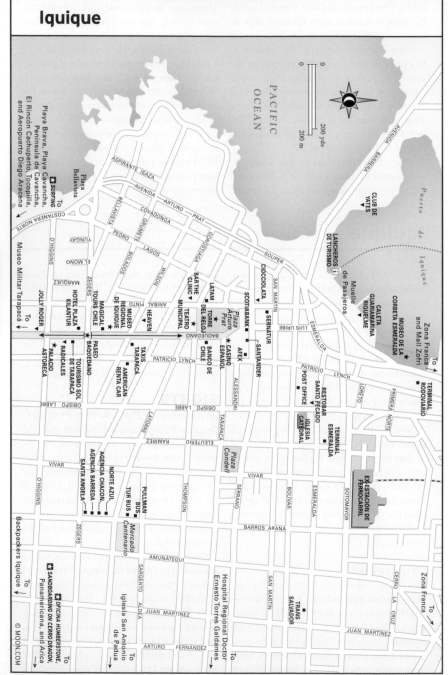

PACIFIC OCEAN

Puerto de Iquique

CLUB DE YATES

LANCHEROS DE TURISMO

Muelle de Pasajeros

CALETA GUARAMARINA RIQUELME

MUSEO DE LA CORBETA ESMERALDA

Zona Franca and Mall Zofri

To

Playa Bellavista

SURFING To
Playa Brava, Playa Cavancha, Peninsula de Cavancha, El Rincón Cachupuerto, Tocopilla, and Aeropuerto Diego Aracena

ASPIRANTE ISAZA

AVENIDA ARTURO PRAT

COVADONGA

BELLAVISTA

GRUMETE

O'HIGGINS

PEDRO LAGOS

YUNGAY

BOLADOS

EL MONO

MÁRQUEZ

ZEGERS

WILSON

ANIBAL PINTO

SOUPER

SAN MARTIN

CHOCOLATA

SCOTIABANK

LATAM

BAR THE CLINIC

MUSEO REGIONAL DE IQUIQUE

HEAVEN

TEATRO MUNICIPAL

TORRE DEL RELOJ

Plaza Arturo Prat

SERNATUR

AFEX

CASINO ESPAÑOL

BANCO DE CHILE

SANTANDER

ALESSANDRI

TARAPACA

LUIS URIBE

ESMERALDA

PATRICIO LYNCH

POST OFFICE

RESTOBAR SANTO PECADO

IGLESIA CATEDRAL

TERMINAL ESMERALDA

LORETO

PRIMERA

NORTE

TERMINAL RODOVIARIO

To

Museo Militar Tarapacá

To

HOTEL PLAZA KILANTUR

TOURS CHILE

MAGICAL

PASEO BAQUEDANO

BAQUEDANO

TAXIS TARAPACA

TURISMO SOL DE TARAPACA

RADICALES

PALACIO ASTORECA

TOURS CHILE

AMERICAN RENTA CAR

PATRICIO LYNCH

OBISPO LABBE

LATORRE

ELEUTERIO RAMIREZ

PATRICIO LYNCH

O'HIGGINS

OBISPO LABBE

VIVAR

AGENCIA CHACON

AGENCIA BARREDA

SANTA ANGELA

NORTE AZUL

PULLMAN BUS

TUR BUS

Plaza Condell

THOMPSON

VIVAR

SERRANO

BOLIVAR

ESMERALDA

SOTOMAYOR

EX-ESTACIÓN DE FERROCARRIL

Zona Franca

To

ZEGERS

Mercado Centenario

AMUNÁTEGUI

SARGENTO

ALDEA

SAN MARTIN

JUAN MARTÍNEZ

Iglesia San Antonio de Padua

BARROS ARANA

Hospital Regional Doctor Ernesto Torres Galdames

TRANS SALVADOR

CERRO LA CRUZ

JUAN MARTÍNEZ

To

Backpackers Iquique

SANDBOARDING ON CERRO DRAGON, Panamericana, and Arica

OFICINA HUMBERSTONE, Panamericana, and Arica

ARTURO FERNÁNDEZ

© MOON.COM

0   200 yds
0   200 m

change the scenery above. Restoration work is ongoing, with the theater expected to re-open in 2020.

On the northeast corner of Plaza Prat, the stunning two-story **Casino Español** (Plaza Prat 584) was designed by the architect Miguel Retornano. The exterior is a display of delightful symmetry, with five horseshoe arches on each floor and delicate blue tiling to the lower windows. Inside is exquisite Moorish architecture, with painted murals and rich patterns of gold, blue, and red, extravagant keyhole arches, and an intricately carved wood-panel ceiling. Now a **restaurant** (tel. 57/2760 630, www.casinoespanoliquique.cl, 12:30pm-3:45pm Sun.-Mon., 8am-10:45pm Tues.-Sat., CH$7,000-10,000), beyond the main dining area are shimmering chandeliers in a banquet hall that also houses 20th-century oil paintings.

Four blocks north of the plaza at the old passenger pier, one-hour **boat tours** operated by **Lancheros de Turismo** (Muelle Prat, tel. 57/2470 287, lanchasturismomuelleprat@gmail.com, 10am-5pm Mon.-Fri., 10am-6pm Sat.-Sun., CH$2,000-3,000) take visitors out to Isla de los Lobos, a small island with a resident sea lion colony. On weekends, boats require minimum 10 people to set sail; during the week it's 8 people.

Paseo Baquedano

A surprising number of houses along pedestrianized **Paseo Baquedano** (Plaza Prat to Plaza 21 de Mayo) have survived several natural disasters, including an 8.2-magnitude earthquake and various tsunamis and fires. Constructed 1880-1920, sumptuous Georgian mansions of Oregon pine with wide verandas and wooden balustrades make the street the prettiest in the city. Most tour agencies and the city's older restaurants and bars are here. An **electric tram** runs the length of Paseo Baquedano. Although it's supposedly designed for children, it's free to ride—jump on when it stops.

Close to the southern end of the street, the informative **Museo Militar Tarapacá** (Baquedano 1396, tel. 57/2412 891, 9:30am-2pm and 3pm-5:30pm Tues.-Fri., 10am-2pm Sat., free) charts Iquique's history from Peruvian port to Chilean city, documenting the main battles fought in the region with a sizeable collection of war memorabilia. One room is dedicated to the *Esmeralda,* a steam corvette sunk by Peruvian forces during the War of the Pacific. Repairs on the naval museum's original building, the Edificio de Aduana, are ongoing, with the completion date a moving target.

Museo Regional de Iquique

The **Museo Regional de Iquique** (Baquedano 951, tel. 57/2523 655, 9am-5:50pm Mon.-Thurs., 9am-4:50pm Fri., 10am-1:50pm Sat., free) houses an eclectic display of Chile's geological, anthropological, and zoological history, including a small exhibition on the 7,000-year-old Chinchorro mummies. The highlight is a display of traditional textiles from Iluga, an Aymara community.

Palacio Astoreca

Taking up most of the north side of Bernardo O'Higgins between Baquedano and Patricio Lynch, **Palacio Astoreca** (O'Higgins 250, tel. 57/2526 890, 10am-2pm and 3pm-6pm Tues.-Fri., 11am-2pm Sat., free) is an imposing cream-colored Georgian mansion built for Spanish merchant and saltpeter magnate Juan Higinio Astoreca, who died in 1908, before the building was completed. Today, the city's most spectacular mansion is furnished with period pieces that evoke the life of the city's elite in the early 20th century. Stately high-ceilinged rooms contain pieces of neo-Louis XVI and French Neo-Renaissance furniture and gleaming chandeliers. In the vestibule, look up to admire the art nouveau stained glass ceiling.

Museo de la Corbeta *Esmeralda*

Museo de la Corbeta *Esmeralda* (Paseo Lynch, off Av. Arturo Prat, tel. 57/2530 812, www.museoesmeralda.cl, 10am-12:15pm and 2pm-5pm Tues.-Sun., CH$3,500 adults, CH$1,500 children) exists within a life-size re-creation of the *Esmeralda*, a wooden-hulled steam corvette sunk by the Peruvian *Huáscar* in 1879 during a key battle in the War of the Pacific. Captain Arturo Prat's futile, ultimately fatal attempt at boarding the enemy's ship as the *Esmeralda* sank saw him go down in history as a national hero.

Inside, the ship includes separate living quarters for different ranks of sailors, and the deck comprises replicas of the 20 cannons that were used to defend the *Esmeralda* that fateful day. All visits are by **guided tour** (50min, Spanish only), which leave every 15 minutes. Priority is given to people with advance reservations (make them online at least one day prior), but walk-ins are also accepted. On Sunday, no reservations are possible, so arrive early to reserve a space on a tour.

Sightseeing Tours

To learn more about Iquique's history and architecture, **Mitour** (tel. 9/8475 9920, mitouriqq@gmail.com) offers a two-hour English-language walking tour, **Tour a Iquique** (tip-based) which starts from Muelle Prat and finishes in the Museo Militar Tarapacá. The same company runs three-hour **Bohemian Iquique** (around CH$28,000, includes hotel pickup and drop-off, food and drink extra), where you're taken by vehicle with a local guide to sample typical food and drink from a range of bars and restaurants, selected based on your interests.

ENTERTAINMENT
Nightlife

Most of Iquique's nightlife is along Paseo Baquedano. Things don't get going until at least midnight or later in clubs, so entry and drinks are often seriously discounted before 1am.

Iquique's top hip hangout is **Radicales** (Paseo Baquedano 1074, tel. 57/2766 626, 4pm-2:30am Wed., 4pm-3:30am Thurs., 4pm-5am Fri.-Sat., no cover), a bar that gets extremely crowded with a young and trendy crowd,

particularly on weekends, when a live DJ plays everything except reggaeton.

At the **Jolly Roger** (Paseo Baquedano 1125, tel. 9/4267 9805, 8:30pm-4am Tues.-Sat., no cover), a pub turned club, expect blaring reggaeton music to dance to, or enjoy weekly karaoke nights. Just off Paseo Baquedano, **Heaven** (Wilson 230, tel. 9/8157 2236, 11pm-4am Thurs.-Sat., CH$5,000) is popular among younger clubbers and often has costume events with free entry for those in a costume.

Two blocks southwest of Plaza Arturo Prat, **Bar The Clinic** (Pedros Lagos 881, tel. 57/241 3044, www.barthecliniciquique.cl, 11am-5pm Mon., 11am-2am Tues.-Thurs., 11am-4am Fri.-Sat.) is run by the owners of the satirical political magazine *The Clinic*. The menu, filled with witty jibes at the political elite, contains a good selection of beers on tap as well as burgers and sharing platters. Live bands start playing from 11pm Friday-Saturday. Get here early for a table.

The liveliest part of town is 2km south of Paseo Baquedano, along the boardwalk to the Península de Cavancha. **Casino Dreams** (Av. Arturo Prat 2755, tel. 600/626 0000, www.mundodreams.com, 10am-7am daily) has live music from 10pm Friday-Sunday. **Bulldog Sports Bar** (Filomena Valenzuela 230, tel. 9/4263 7465, 11am-4am daily) has huge screens showing sports and a prolonged happy hour to satisfy the young crowd of locals and foreigners on weekends and most weeknights. Across the street, **Zona Zero Pub Lounge & Bar** (Juan Antonio Ríos 2898, 5pm-4am Tues.-Sun., cover CH$5,000, includes 1 drink) has salsa, karaoke, '90s music nights, live DJs, and a slightly older crowd.

Festivals and Events

Iquique's **Carnaval Andino** celebrations are on a weekend in February. Tens of thousands form a procession of traditionally attired dancers from across northern Chile and Peru and Bolivia, parading to the rhythms of Andean folkloric music and the delighted applause of the spectators. Events kick off around 8:30pm and last until the early hours both Saturday and Sunday, with the procession starting at the western corner of Libertad, marching along Avenida Arturo Prat and the length of Paseo Baquedano, and ending at the Teatro Municipal. Stadium seating is set up along the roads for spectators.

RECREATION
Beaches
The allure of Iquique's beaches is their soft white sand. The largest, **Playa Cavancha,** starts just off the southerly point of Paseo Baquedano and ends at Península de Cavancha. The calm waters make it ideal for swimming, although most beachgoers come to sunbathe or relax. During summer, expect a struggle to find a spot among the bronzed Chilean and Argentinean holidaymakers.

Just 4km south, **Playa Brava** isn't suitable for swimming but attracts surfers and sunbathers. It's significantly less crowded than Playa Cavancha. Avoid getting too close to the skate park, as travelers have reported muggings in this area. Five kilometers south of the city, **Playa Huayquique** is an excellent location for watching the sunset.

★ Surfing
World-class waves have made this city a haven for surfers. Advanced surfers paddle into the ocean in droves, but there are also gentler waves for beginners. **Playa Brava,** home to an exposed beach break, is popular and has some spots for beginners.

Toward the northern edge of **Playa Cavancha, El Colegio** (named for its location opposite Colegio Don Bosco) is a reef break considered one of Chile's best righthand waves. It reaches 2.5-6 meters, making it better suited to advanced surfers, although it has good spots for beginner and intermediate surfers. More accessible but significantly smaller, the surf at **Playa Huayquique,** 5km south of the city, is consistent, with its righthand breaks better surfed in winter. Only accessible via boat or Jet Ski from Península de Cavancha, **La Bestia** is one of the top 20

breaks in the world, attracting professional surfers.

Vertical (Av. Arturo Prat 580, opposite Playa Cavancha and El Colegio reef break, tel. 9/9886 8631) rents boards and wetsuits, starting at CH$15,000 for four hours (10am-2pm or 4pm-8pm). During the summer, **group surfing classes** (1.5hr, equipment and English-language instruction included) leave from the shop at 11:30am. **Private classes** (CH$25,000 pp) can be arranged in advance. Pricing for group classes depends on the number of people but is cheaper than the private classes. The shop has showers and lockers.

Surf school **Uma Jaqi** (Obispo Labbé 159, tel. 57/215 774 or 9/6727 9145, www.umajaqi.cl) offers two-hour stand-up paddleboarding classes (CH$25,000, including equipment) as well as full-day bodyboarding and surfing tours (CH$30,000, including equipment, transportation, and lunch).

Paragliding
With perfect flying conditions 360 days of the year, it's unusual not to see paragliders launching from the peak of Cerro Dragon or Alto Hospicio. Tandem flights last 20 minutes, with thermals allowing the paraglider to soar gracefully toward the ocean and land on Cerro Dragon or one of the main beaches, depending on weather.

Hotel pickup, English instruction, and photos are normally included in the CH$45,000 cost. The most established paragliding operator is **Puro Vuelo** (Prat 1050, tel. 57/2311 127, www.purovuelo.cl). All of their pilots have at least 10 years of experience of flying tandem. They also run three-day courses (4:30pm-7:30pm, CH$180,000) where you learn to take short solo flights. Another option is **Iquique Parapente** (Diego Portales 920, tel. 9/7865 8445, www.iquiqueparapente.cl), who employ experienced pilots and have 20 years of experience running tours.

★ Sandboarding
Boasting some of the largest urban dunes in the world, Iquique has become Chile's number

one sandboarding destination. Groups ride the golden sand of **Cerro Dragon,** the 550-meter-tall, 4-km-long dune in the southwest of the city, with spectacular views. Hit the dunes at sunset, when cooler sand means faster speeds.

Two-time global champion José Martínez teaches budding boarders through **Sandboard Iquique** (tel. 9/8371 5040, classes 9am-noon and 4pm-7pm daily). Three-hour classes (CH$25,000) include boards, instruction, photographs, and transport to and from your hotel. **Munay Sandboard** (tel. 9/8292 6766, www.munaysandboardiquique. webnode.cl) provides similar service for the same cost; it also rents boards (CH$10,000 for 2hr). Both outfits are suited to beginners, and there is no minimum number for a tour.

Excursion Tours

For excursions to Oficina Humberstone, La Tirana, and Pica, generally covered in the same day, book with **Turismo Sol de Tarapacá** (Paseo Baquedano 1024, tel. 9/4041 7322 or 57/2467 910, www.turismosoldetarapaca.com). These trips usually cost CH$17,000, which includes hotel pickup, transportation, and lunch. Turisma Sol de Tarapacá also organizes full-day tours to Mamiña (CH$25,000) and Laguna Roja (CH$75,000). **Magical Tours Chile** (Casa Matriz Baquedano 997, tel. 57/2763 474, www.magicaltour.cl) is another established operator running similar tours at similar rates. **Dragon Adventure** (tel. 9/5845 3009) offer trips to the same destinations; check their Facebook page for more information.

Místico Outdoors (Eleuterio Ramírez 1535, tel. 9/9541 7762, www.chileresponsibleadventure.com), an outfitter that focuses on responsible travel and works directly with local communities, can arrange longer excursions into the precordillera and altiplano. Options include homestays with Aymara families and trips to five national parks in the Atacama Region (from CH$277,000). They also offer trekking itineraries, including a 10-day ascent of Volcán Ojos del Salado and 4-day tours of El Salar de Uyuni (Uyuni Salt Flat) in Bolivia. For each traveler who tours with them, they a plant a tree as part of their carbon-neutral initiative.

FOOD

At the **Caleta Guariamarina Riquelme** (Av. Arturo Prat, 200 meters south of Museo de la Corbeta Esmeralda, no phone, 7am-6pm daily), fresh fish, ceviche, and empanadas are sold under a watchful statue of San Pedro (Saint Peter), the patron saint of fishermen. Upstairs, a variety of typical, if pokey, Chilean restaurants sell cheap fish-based *menús del día*. The **Mercado Centenario** (between Arana, Aldea, Ammunátegui and Latorre, no phone, 10am-5pm daily), also known as the **Mercado Central,** is a covered indoor market surrounded by small restaurants offering cheap and filling lunches. This is a great place to buy fresh fish, meat, vegetables, and dried goods. Beware of pickpockets in both locations.

Chilean

In the Gavina Sens Hotel, **Terrazas del Mar** (Arturo Prat Chacón 1497, tel. 57/2393 030, noon-11pm daily, CH$7,500-12,000) proves that Chileans know how to cook seafood. Chilean-style dishes specialize in fresh tuna and salmon ceviche. Staff are attentive, and the real attraction is the uninterrupted view across Plaza Cavancha through the floor-to-ceiling windows, making it the perfect place to watch the sunset with a drink in hand.

Tucked away opposite the Catedral, one of the hippest places in town is **Restobar Santo Pecado** (Ubispo Labbé 223, tel. 57/2278 135, 9am-4:30pm Mon.-Sat., CH$4,000-6,000, *menú del día* CH$5,500). It has a relaxed, youthful atmosphere and a wide selection of sandwiches and large platters of empanadas to share. The *menú del día* is regional fare, including plenty of seafood. It gets popular noon-2pm, so get here early.

1: Museo de la Corbeta *Esmeralda* 2: Iquique's Playa Cavancha

Family-run ★ **El Rincón de Cachuperto** (Filomena Valenzuela 125, tel. 57/2329 189, 11:30pm-4pm Tues.-Sun., CH$1,000-5,000) is a great option on Península de Cavancha. Look past the unassuming exterior to find Iquique's top *empanaderia*. Try the *empanada de mariscos,* brimming with seafood, oysters, crab, prawns, and cheese, or the swordfish sandwich. Arrive before 12:30pm or call ahead to reserve your empanadas before they run out.

Attentive service by smartly dressed waiters and tasty meat are on offer at **Restaurant Rayú** (Filomena Valenzuela 125A, tel. 57/2435 441, rayu.gourmet@gmail.com, 8:30pm-11:30pm Tues.-Sat., 1pm-4pm Sun., CH$10,000-20,000), on Península de Cavancha. This upmarket steak house attracts celebrities and politicians with Japanese *wagyu* and Chilean-Peruvian fusion ceviche and *pastel de choclo,* all elegantly presented. Book ahead, particularly on weekends.

International

With an ample menu and an outdoor patio, **Santorini** (Av. Aeropuerto 2808, tel. 57/2225 392, reservas@santorinirestobar.cl, noon-midnight daily, CH$4,900-15,500) has every dish you could ever want, including Greek antipastos and pizza variations that include Peruvian and Thai flavors. The cheapest (and messiest) dishes are the gyros, which make a sizeable dinner.

For a quick and inexpensive lunch or dinner, head over to **Tikva Shauwarma** (Barros Arana 699, tel. 57/2339 109, 2pm-midnight daily, closes earlier on cold evenings, CH$3,000-5,500) for delicious authentic kebabs to take away or eat in—there's a handful of plastic furniture on the street out front. Food is ready fast, the owner and staff are friendly, and the falafel and hummus are special.

It's possible to take in the sumptuous Moorish decor of the exquisite historic ★ **Casino Español** (Plaza Prat 584, tel. 57/2760 630, www.casinoespanoliquique.cl, 12:30pm-3:45pm Sun.-Mon., 8pm-10:45pm Tues.-Sat., CH$7,000-12,000, *menú del día*

CH$9,900) without dining here, but the food's so good that it enhances the experience. The menu is mostly Spanish-inspired meaty tapas and Spanish tortillas; the pisco sours, which use lemons from nearby Pica, are famous in Iquique.

With tables in a beautiful, peaceful garden and top-notch Thai cuisine, **El Tercer Ojito** (Patricio Lynch 1420, tel. 57/2413 847 or 57/2426 517, 12:30pm-5pm and 7:30pm-12:30am Tues.-Fri., 1pm-5pm and 7:30pm-1am Sat., CH$8,000-13,000) should not be missed. The Thai curries and pad thai are impressively authentic, and they offer ample vegetarian dishes. The daily happy hour (7:30pm-10pm) sweetens the deal. It's down a backstreet one block east of Paseo Baquedano.

The Peruvian-Japanese fusion at **Restaurant La Mulata** (Av. Arturo Prat 902, tel. 57/2473 727, www.lamulata.cl, 2:30pm-4pm and 5:30pm-midnight Mon.-Sat., 12:30pm-5pm Sun., CH$6,000-13,000) is a hit with visitors and locals alike thanks to delicious sushi platters and the standout *atún de yen,* a combination of tuna with local quinoa and rustic potatoes. The cocktail menu is ample and the terrace light and airy, with views across the ocean, although the ambience is impaired by the constant traffic.

With sweeping views of the bay from the 19th floor of Hotel Terrado Cavancha, **Skybar** (Tadeo Haenke 1010, tel. 57/236 4613, 7pm-midnight daily, CH$10,000-18,000) is overpriced compared to similar restaurants. The menu is unusually large, offering Asian-Peruvian fusion sushi, sashimi, and catch of the day, but the views, and the boozy mango sours, are divine.

Budget and Light Bites

An Iquique classic, **Cioccolata** (Anibal Pinto 487, tel. 57/2532 290, 8:30am-10:30pm Mon.-Fri., 11am-10:30pm Sat., CH$4,100-5,000, *menú del día* CH$5,000) offers traditional Chilean sandwiches and cakes in a charming café setting. It's a popular choice for *once* (afternoon tea) and serves an ample *menú del día;* try to arrive before the 1pm lunch crowd.

ACCOMMODATIONS
Under CH$25,000

With brand-new furnishings and a site near the beach, sociable **El Faro** (Barros Arana 1820, tel. 57/2427 509 or 9/79358 936, elfarohostel.iquique@gmail.com, CH$7,000 dorm, CH$35,000 d private bath, cash only) is popular among backpackers. Rooms are large. The small indoor TV area and outdoor terrace with sun umbrellas allow plenty of space for socializing, which can get loud. A communal kitchen makes it easy to self-cater. They can accommodate cars on the driveway with advance notice. Rates include IVA.

The Hostelling International-affiliated ★ **Backpackers Iquique** (Amunategui 2075, tel. 57/2320 223, www.hosteliquique. com, CH$10,000 dorm, CH$27,000 d shared bath, CH$35,000 d private bath) is a backpacker favorite thanks to its almost beach-side location. The private rooms are tiny but comfortable and clean. Huge social areas include a TV room, a large full kitchen, a bar, and a terrace for barbecuing. Breakfast isn't included but is available from the adjoining café at a discount (CH$4,000). There's on-street parking outside. You can book excursions, such as sandboarding, paragliding, and surfing, at reception. Rates include IVA.

CH$25,000-40,000

The rooms at **Hostal Restaurante Virgilio** (Libertad 823, tel. 57/227 6700, CH$10,000 dorm, CH$25,000 d shared bath) are huge, if basic, although there are only two shared baths for the two floors. Service is warm, and breakfast is better than most in this price range; expect toast, eggs, avocado, yogurt, fruit, juice, and coffee, served in the attached café, whose kitchen is open until 8pm. Rooms facing the rear of the building can be noisy at night thanks to a nearby hostel, but the location, one block from Playa Cavancha, makes up for it. Rates include IVA.

Located on Paseo Baquedao, **Hotel Plaza Kilantur** (Baquedano 1025, tel. 57/2417 172 or 57/2419 339, info@kilantur.cl, CH$30,000 d) has a surprising lack of character for its location

among historic mansions, but the rooms are large enough and spotless. All have windows facing a central open-air patio. Rooms on the 3rd floor have more natural light, but it's a favored spot for smokers. Rates include IVA.

The family-run **Andina Hostel** (Benigno Posadas 1835, tel. 57/2245 647, CH$35,500 d shared bath, CH$43,000 d private bath) is an excellent choice for small budgets, boasting a perfect location nearly on Playa Brava and within walking distance of Península de Cavancha. The 14 basic rooms range from reasonably sized doubles to quintuples; only four rooms don't have private baths. The main downside is that windows open onto a central stairwell; noise from the reception area below can carry upward at night. Rates include IVA.

Over CH$80,000

On the lively Península de Cavancha, overlooking Playa Cavancha, **Hotel Terrado Suites** (Capitán Roberto Pérez 126, tel. 57/2363 901, www.terrado.cl, CH$88,000-146,000 d) is a large hotel fit for holidaymakers during summer, although it tends to attract a business crowd during the week off-season. Rooms are functional if uninspiringly decorated. The cheapest bedrooms don't have balconies. Outside are two swimming pools and various sunny terraces.

Although it's one of the priciest options in Iquique, the 82-room **Gavina Sens** (tel. 57/2393 030, www.gavina.cl, CH$110,000-120,000 d) has sweeping vistas of Playa Cavancha. All rooms have a balcony, but those with full sea views cost an additional CH$10,000. Luckily, the saltwater swimming pool and in-house bar and restaurant, both open to nonguests, have an equally stunning vantage over the coastline. The on-site entertainment center hosts regular events, so rooms on lower floors are noisier than the upper floors.

INFORMATION AND SERVICES

The **Hospital Regional Doctore Ernesto Torres Galdarnes** (Av. Heroes de la

Concepción 502, tel. 57/2405 700, www. hospitaliquique.cl) is 15 blocks east of Plaza Arturo Prat. The **Carabineros** (Chilean national police) can be found at José Joaquin 330.

SERNATUR (Anibal Pínto 436, tel. 57/2419 241, 9am-6pm Mon.-Fri., 10pm-2pm Sat.), the national tourism organization, has an office one block from Plaza Arturo Prat. Staff are unusually knowledgeable on activities and tours in the region.

The highest concentration of **ATMs,** including **Scotiabank** (Luis Uribe 530) and **Santander** (Serrano 301), are just off Plaza Arturo Prat. **Banco de Chile** (Baquedano 626) has an ATM on Plaza Arturo Prat. To exchange money, **AFEX** (Lynch 467, www. afex.cl) is centrally located.

Lavaseco Marazul (Juan Martínez 2025, tel. 57/2475 263, 9am-8pm Mon.-Sat., 9:30am-5:30pm Sun., CH$2,000/kg) has same-day laundry service. **Correos Chile** (Bolívar 458, 9am-6pm Mon.-Fri., 10am-noon Sat.) handles postal services.

GETTING THERE
Air

Around 50km south of the city, on Ruta 1, **Diego Aracena International Airport** (IQQ, tel. 57/2473 473, www. aeropuertodiegoaracena.cl) offers daily flights from Santiago, Antofagasta, and Arica as well as La Paz, Bolivia, and Asunción, Paraguay. Carriers include **Sky Airline** (www.skyairline. com); **LATAM** (www.latam.com), with an office on the western edge of Plaza Arturo Prat (Anibal Pinto 699, tel. 600/5262 000, 9am-1:30pm and 3:30pm-6:15pm Mon.-Fri., 10:30am-1pm Sat.); and **Amaszonas** (www. amaszonas.com), whose office (San Martín 428, tel. 57/2266 211 or 57/2266 212, 9:30am-1:30pm and 3:30pm-6:30pm Mon.-Fri., 10am-1pm Sat.) is two blocks northeast of Plaza Arturo Prat.

AIRPORT TRANSFERS
From outside the arrivals area, **Transfer Intipaka** (tel. 57/2434 300 or 57/2431 347, www.intipaka.cl) and **Transfer Manquehue**

(tel. 57/2311 184) offer shuttle buses to your hotel, which take 40 minutes and cost CH$5,000 each way. Advance reservations are required.

Taxis Tarapacá (tel. 57/2419 004 or 57/2415 916, www.taxistarapaca.cl) and **Taxis Aeropuerto Diego Aracena** (tel. 57/2413 368 or 57/2415 036) charge a standard fee of CH$18,000 from the airport to town; it's best to book in advance to ensure availability. Taxis can be arranged from the companies' booths in the arrivals hall.

Tur Bus (Esmeralda 594, tel. 57/2736 652, www.turbus.cl) operates a bus connecting the airport with their private bus terminal, Terminal Esmeralda (1hr, CH$3,000). Buses leave twice daily, synced with flight arrivals and departures.

Bus

Iquique's main bus station, **Terminal Rodoviario** (Patricio Lynch 50, tel. 57/2416 315) is 1km (a 10-minute walk) north of Plaza Arturo Prat. The terminal sells tickets for all major national departures.

Tur Bus offers frequent departures from Terminal Rodoviario and also has its own private terminal, **Terminal Esmeralda** (Esmeralda 594, tel. 57/2736 652, www. turbus.cl), plus a downtown office (Barros Arana 898, tel. 57/2736 161) opposite Mercado Centenario. **Pullman Bus** (Barros Arana 825, tel. 57/2425 280) also has an office opposite Mercado Centenario.

Buses connecting Iquique arrive and depart to **Arica** (hourly, 5hr, CH$6,000/CH$14,000), **Antofagasta** (every 2 hr, 7hr, CH$14,000/CH$21,000), **Calama** (5 daily, 7.5hr, CH$14,000/CH$24,000), **La Serena** (every 1.5 hr, 18hr, CH$20,000/CH$30,000), **Santiago** (hourly, 23hr, CH$38,000/CH$51,000), and **Valparaíso** (10am and 5pm daily, 27hr, CH$22,000/CH$38,000), offered by **Pullman Bus** (tel. 57/2429 852, www.pullmanbus.cl), **Ciktur** (tel. 57/2241 264, www.ciktur.cl), **Nuveo Fichtur VIP** (tel. 57/2429 852), and **Tur Bus** (tel. 57/2736 677, www.turbus.cl).

Car

There are two main routes into the city: From the south, Ruta 1 follows the coast from Antofagasta, 420km away. The more impressive and hair-raising approach is Ruta 16, which leaves Ruta 5 about 5km north of Pozo Almonte and passes through Alto Hospicio before it drops in wild zigzags to the city. In the morning and evening, fog makes visibility poor, so drive with caution.

GETTING AROUND

Most lodgings are within walking distance of Paseo Baquedano and Playa Cavancha. There's a dearth of public transportation along the coastal road, Avenida Arturo Prat, so renting a taxi is your only option. **Taxis Tarapacá** (corner of Baquedano and Wilson, tel. 57/2419 004 or 57/2415 916, www.taxistarapaca.cl) has a stand on Paseo Paquedano. Within the city, a journey shouldn't cost more than CH$1,000. Request that your driver turn the meter *(taxi-metro)* on.

As a city oversaturated with vehicles, driving in Iquique—and particularly driving out along the mountain road—is an experience, with congestion and queues a standard feature. With most lodgings south of Paseo Baquedano and in newer neighborhoods with wider streets and less traffic, on-street parking isn't difficult to find. Don't leave anything of value in your vehicle when you park.

Car Rental

To reach Oficina Humberstone, La Tirana, Mamiña, and Pica, renting a car is often the cheapest and quickest option. Outside the arrivals at Iquique's airport are counters for **Hertz** (tel. 57/2410 924, 7:30am-11:30pm Mon.-Fri., 9am-9:30pm Sat.-Sun.), **Europcar** (tel. 57/2548 790, 7am-11pm daily), **Avis** (tel. 2/2795 3975, 7:30am-11pm Mon.-Fri., 9am-5pm Sat., 2pm-11pm Sun.), and **Econorent** (tel. 57/2418 407, 7:30am-11pm Mon.-Fri., 7:20am-11pm Sat., 8am-10pm Sun.).

In town are offices of **Europcar** (Manual Bulnes 542, tel. 57/2548 780, 8:30am-6:30pm Mon.-Fri., 9am-11:30am Sat.), **Avis** (Manuel Rodríguez 730, tel. 2/2795 3961, 8:30am-6:30pm Mon.-Fri., 9am-2pm Sat.), **American Rent a Car** (Patricio Lynch 898, tel. 57/2472 612, 8:30am-7pm Mon.-Fri., 9am-2pm Sat.), and **Econorent** (Hernán Fuenzalida 1058, tel. 57/2423 723, 8:30am-7pm Mon.-Fri., 9am-1pm Sat.).

Local Buses

Local *micros* (public buses) ply the roads between the dunes and coast, with a fixed price of CH$450 per trip. Look for their destinations in the front window. All go past the corner of Tarapacá and Obispo Labb, two blocks east of Plaza Prat.

To local destinations, including Oficina Humberstone (40min, CH$2,000), La Tirana (75min, CH$2,500), and Pica (2hr, CH$3,000), departures are every 15 minutes from the offices of **Norte Azul** (Barros Arana 945, tel. 57/2578 086 or 57/2523 820, reservasnorteazul@gmail.com), **Agencia Chacón** (Barros Arana 953, tel. 57/2416 691 or 9/8181 0897), **Pullman Santa Angela** (Barros Arana 971, tel. 57/2423 751), and **Agencia Barreda** (Barros Arana 965, tel. 57/2414 938). Agencia Barreda also offers services to Mamiña (8:30am and 5pm Mon.-Sat., 2.5hr, CH$4,000). All offices are half a block south of the Mercado Centenario.

ONWARD TRAVEL

International bus departures for the Bolivian cities of **La Paz** (1pm and 7pm Mon.-Fri., 2pm Sat., CH$15,000, 18hr, via Tambo Quemado-Chungará border crossing) and **Santa Cruz** (5:30am daily, CH$38,000, 23hr, via Pisiga-Colchane border crossing) are operated by **Trans Salvador** (Esmeralda 1000, tel. 57/2425 939 or 9/7820 7355, www.trans-salvador.com). **Andesmar** (Terminal Rodoviario, tel. 57/2471 646, www.andesmarchile.cl) offers Sunday, Wednesday, and Friday buses directly to **Salta, Argentina** (12:10am, 20hr, CH$70,000-90,000).

Vicinity of Iquique

A short bus ride beyond Iquique, some of the best-preserved relics of the saltpeter age give a sense of the city's history and its role in the nitrate boom of the 1800s. Former refinery town Oficina Humberstone, 50km east of Iquique, is the most fascinating for a day trip. A 30-minute drive southeast of these historic ruins, the dusty streets of La Tirana are an explosion of Andean dance, music, and celebrations for four days in mid-July.

Farther inland, Mamiña and Pica are two verdant towns of fruit groves that have sprung up from the desert thanks to natural hot springs; they make a tranquil escape around two hours' drive from the coast. An hour's drive south along Ruta 5 from Iquique, the region's ancient human history is exposed at the striking Geoglifos de Cerros Pintados, geoglyphs (motifs etched into the ground) that date to as early as AD 700.

★ OFICINA HUMBERSTONE

The ruins of the former saltpeter refineries and attached worker towns at **Oficina Humberstone** and **Oficina Santa Laura** (A-16, tel. 57/2760 626, www.museodelsalitre.cl, 9am-7pm daily summer, 9am-6pm daily fall-spring, CH$3,000 adults, CH$1,000 children) are the closest you can get to learning about life during the golden age of saltpeter (1880-1930).

Founded in 1872, Oficina Humberstone was one of 200 nitrate towns that sprang up to process the largest deposit of saltpeter in the world. The mineral was so profitable that it came to be known as "white gold." Unlike many of the towns that collapsed after World War I, when the creation of synthetic nitrate effectively ended Chile's monopoly, Oficina Humberstone continued operating until 1960, manufacturing 4.5 million kilograms of nitrate per month at the height of production.

At its peak, Oficina Humberstone had a population of 3,700, while neighboring Santa Laura, built in 1872, was home to 750 people. Conditions were challenging, particularly as workers were paid in vouchers, only redeemable in company shops, meaning it was virtually impossible for families to move away.

Both sites suffered the same fate when declining global markets caused them to shut down in 1960. The government was focused on profit rather than protecting the two sites: Buildings were demolished and raw materials sold off. Both sites were given UNESCO World Heritage status in 2005, which has helped focus resources on conservation. These are the best-preserved refineries in the region, containing the most complete collections of artifacts. At Santa Laura, the industrial features are far better preserved than at Humberstone, where a greater proportion of residential and service areas remain.

Sights

Most tourists visit on a tour from Iquique. **Turisma Sol de Tarapacá** (Paseo Baquedano 1024, tel. 9/4041 7322 or 57/2467 910, www.turismosoldetarapaca.com) and **Dragon Adventure** (tel. 9/5845 3009) both include a visit to Oficina Humberstone as part of a tour to La Tirana and Pica (CH$17,000).

At the entrance to Humberstone, it's possible to join a free Spanish-language guided tour on Wednesday and Sunday (no set departure times), run by local volunteers. Tickets for Oficina Humberstone also include entry to the Santa Laura site, 1.8km west from the car park, accessible on foot or by car via a dirt road.

HUMBERSTONE

Thanks to the detailed map available at the ticket office, visitors can explore Humberstone at their own pace. Most striking are the different sizes of houses available to workers and their families. A good example is the first building on the right when you enter. Built using calamine, zinc, and cement to keep the interior cool during the day, it was inhabited by professional workers, such as the mechanical engineer and school director. Inside, a display of period furniture and toys gives a sense of what life was like for this stratum of society.

Opposite the professional housing are semidetached houses for mid-ranking employees and their families, with living and dining rooms, an indoor bath, and a yard. Compare them with the basic accommodations on the southeastern corner of the site: Built using adobe, they haven't survived the passage of time.

On the central square, the 1935 **Teatro La Palma** had seating for 300, including boxes for wealthier theatergoers; it was restored to its former glory in 2009. On the southern edge of the central square, restored **Iglesia Jesús Obrero** sits next to a quirky **museum** filled with hundreds of wooden doors and frames from saltpeter works across the country. On the eastern side of the square, the **former hotel** is a cavernous building containing upper-class dining rooms as well as the pergola, where lower-ranking workers could drink and dine on weekends.

At the northern corner of the residential site, the 1883 **Casa de Administración** showcases nitrate advertisements from across the globe. Look for the defunct **train engines** used to transport the saltpeter.

SANTA LAURA

At the Santa Laura site, the best-preserved relics are the huge industrial installations used to process the saltpeter, as well as buildings and machinery for manufacturing iodine. The residential areas were built using more precarious materials, such as adobe and sheet metal; most were sold for scrap or removed by locals.

Getting There

Though most people visit as part of a tour, arriving independently is easy enough. Take one of the shared minivans (CH$2,000) offered by **Norte Azul** (Barros Arana 945, tel. 57/2578 086 or 57/2523 820, reservasnorteazul@gmail. com), **Agencia Chacón** (Barros Arana 953, tel. 57/2416 691 or 9/8181 0897), **Pullman Santa Angela** (Barros Arana 971, tel. 57/2423 751), or **Agencia Barreda** (Barros Arana 965, tel. 57/2414 938). The vans leave every 15 minutes from half a block south of Iquique's Mercado Centenario in the direction of Pozo Almonte. Make sure you request that the driver drops you at the site; the vans stop at a footbridge that'll take you over the highway to a short road that leads to Oficina Humberstone.

To get here by car, take Ruta 16 inland for 50km. The turn for Oficina Humberstone is only accessible from the westbound direction, so as you approach the overpass to join Ruta 5 toward Arica, stay in the right lane to take the *retorno* back to Iquique. The turn for Oficina Humberstone is a few hundred meters back toward Iquique, on the right.

MAMIÑA

Scattered across the lower folds of the Andes at 2,800 meters elevation, tiny Mamiña is an oasis surrounded by alfalfa and fruit trees. In summer it's busy with day-trippers from Iquique, who come for its famed hot springs, but off-season it is a dusty ghost town.

The police station is on the left as you enter town. The first right turn takes you along a cobblestone road that ends at the square and the church. Opposite the church, on the northern edge of the plaza, is a small **Oficina de Turismo** (Tourism Office, no phone, 8:30am-5:20pm Wed.-Sun.). Next door you'll find public restrooms. A cobblestone road heads west from the north side of the plaza, becoming a gravel track as it runs southeast toward hotels and hot springs.

Baños Ipla

The 41°C water at **Baños Ipla** (no phone, 8:30am-1pm and 3pm-7:30pm daily, CH$2,000), piped directly from underground hot springs, is sought for relief from rheumatism, arthritis, and spinal pain. Four self-contained private tubs, big enough for two, are available to visitors in 30-minute increments. To get here, take the left at the fork in the road just after Restaurant Las Chacras de Pasquito. The sign for the baths is on the left, a few meters down the road.

Just past the entrance to Baños Ipla on the left, the **Vertiente de los Ojos** fountain is famed for its purported healing powers. Legend says the daughter of a high-ranking Inca leader was cured of blindness after washing her eyes in the spring, giving this place the name Mamiña, which in Quechua means "daughter of my eyes."

Close to the fountain is the **Barros Chinos** (no phone, 9am-4pm daily, CH$3,000), where visitors slather themselves in mud, sunbathe until it's dry, and then dip into the hot spring pool, with temperatures at 25-30°C. To get to the mud baths from the fountain, head back to the fork in the road and follow it east and then south; look for signs for the community of Macaya. After 500 meters, turn onto the driveway on the right, which is the entrance to the baths.

Food and Accommodations

There are a small number of restaurants in Mamiña, most open only for lunch on weekends. A handful of mini markets sell basic rations.

Restaurant Bacian (1 block north of the church, no phone, 6am-3pm daily, CH$4,000) serves hearty soups and other dishes accompanied by meat and rice. They also have simple rooms (CH$25,000 d shared bath) with cable TV and a (slow) Wi-Fi connection. Breakfast is included.

Hotel Tamarugal (Alto Ipla, behind the Baños Ipla, tel. 9/8777 768, hotel.tamarugal25@gmail.com, CH$50,000 d, CH$60,000 cabin, cash only) has dated but comfortable rooms and cabins that provide better value. All have large private baths with showers. Breakfast is included; lunch and dinner cost extra. Rates include IVA.

Despite dark rooms and unusual carpeted walls, **Hotel La Coruña** (Santa Rosa 687, two blocks east of the church, tel. 9/9543 0370, CH$35,000 d, CH$50,000 cabin, cash only) offers the best lodgings in town. Its huge open-air swimming pool is fed by hot spring water. Cabins have fully equipped kitchens. Request a room with a bathtub. Breakfast is included, but there's no lunch or dinner. To get here, take the road from the northeast edge of the plaza. Rates include IVA.

Getting There and Around

From Iquique, buses leave for Mamiña (8:30am and 5pm Mon.-Sat., 2.5hr, CH$4,000) from **Agencia Barreda** (Barros Arana 965, Iquique, tel. 57/2414 938) twice daily. The bus back to Iquique generally leaves from the church at 8am and 6pm daily, although it's worth confirming these times with your driver before you get off in Mamiña.

Turisma Sol de Tarapacá (Paseo Baquedano 1024, Iquique, tel. 9/4041 7322 or 57/2467 910, www.turismosoldetarapaca.com) has a full-day tour (CH$25,000) of Mamiña, which includes visits to Baños Ipla and Barros Chino (admission cost not included), a traditional lunch, and a guided tour of the village, plus transportation to and from your hotel.

By car from Iquique, it's a two-hour, 130-km drive on Ruta 16 and the A-65. There are few street signs, but locals are helpful and can give directions.

PICA

Verdant Pica offers a reprieve from the dusty desert. The town is best known for its plantations, with lush citrus groves that most notably produce lemons, a prized ingredient in pisco sour cocktails. The relaxed ambience— expect children riding tricycles around the square, and couples taking nighttime strolls— plus the warm year-round climate make it a popular weekend and holiday destination for Iquiqueños. At these times, accommodations fill and prices rise significantly.

Sights

On the southwestern corner of the floral **Plaza de Armas** (bounded by Maipú, Riquelme, and Balmaceda), the **Iglesia de**

Fiesta de La Tirana

For the annual **Fiesta de la Tirana** (July 12-16), pilgrims descend on the tiny town of La Tirana, swelling its population from 250 to 250,000. The streets explode with a mosaic of colors, folkloric music, and enthusiastic dance. Indigenous Andean culture meets Afro-Caribbean, mestizo, and creole traditions, making the event as much a cultural exchange as a religious festival. Tireless celebrations continue outside **Iglesia de La Tirana** (Plaza de La Tirana, bounded by 16 de Julio, Carlos Ibáñez, Obispado, and Ramírez, 9:30am-8pm daily), day and night, reaching a climax on the final day. Inside the church, the **Museo de la Vivencia Religiosa del Norte Grande** (Iglesia de La Tirana, tel. 9/7321 4079, 3:15pm-6:15pm Tues., 10am-2pm and 3pm-6:15pm Wed.-Sun., CH$1,000 adults, CH$500 children) explores the festival's roots.

The origins of the festival are debated. Some believe it celebrates the patron saint of Chile, the Virgin Mary, as Our Lady of Mount Carmel; others connect it to Ñusta Huillac, an Inca princess and warrior who earned the title "Tirana de Tamarugal" (Tyrant of Tamarugal) after conquering this pampa region. Ñusta fell in love with a Portuguese explorer who persuaded her to convert to Christianity. When their affair was discovered, the pair were slaughtered in a shower of arrows.

PRACTICALITIES

During the festival, every inch of floor in La Tirana is rented out to the highest bidder. It's virtually impossible to get a room without a local contact. Another 100,000 pilgrims set up camp in the desert south along the A-665. To secure a site, arrive a couple of days in advance. The easiest option is to **find a room in Iquique** and take one of the **hourly shuttle buses** that run to La Tirana day and night. Iquique lodgings fill up quickly, so book well in advance. **Restaurants** are open for hungry pilgrims throughout the celebrations.

La Tirana is 75-km, one-hour drive from Iquique via Ruta 16, Ruta 5, and the paved A-665. From Iquique, shared minivans (CH$2,500) leave every 15 minutes from **Norte Azul** (Barros Arana 945, Iquique, tel. 57/2578 086 or 57/2523 820, reservasnorteazul@gmail.com), **Agencia Chacón** (Barros Arana 953, Iquique, tel. 57/2416 691 or 9/8181 0897), **Pullman Santa Angela** (Barros Arana 971, Iquique, tel. 57/2423 751), and **Agencia Barreda** (Barros Arana 965, Iquique, tel. 57/2414 938), half a block south of the Mercado Centenario. A minivan ride to La Tirana takes one hour and 15 minutes.

San Andrés (Balmaceda, no phone, 9am-1pm and 3pm-8pm daily) is a large church with a white-and-gold-painted altar and an installation of *The Last Supper.*

Just under 2km east of the Plaza de Armas, **Cocha Resbaladero** (Av. Gral. Ibáñez, tel. 57/2741 173 or 57/2741 253, 8am-8pm daily, CH$3,000) has two swimming pools carved from volcanic rock and fed by hot springs (typically 27-30°C). There isn't much shade except in late afternoon, the best time to visit. Only one of the two pools is public. There are on-site changing rooms, showers, and a non-secured place to leave bags. It's busy on weekends, particularly in summer.

Valle de Los Dinosaurios (A-685, 1.8km southwest of Pica, 24 hr daily) has full-scale models of dinosaurs that once roamed this region, including a towering *Titanosaurus* and *Kritosaurus.* Fossilized footprints of both species were found in a nearby canyon; reproductions can be seen at the **Oficina Comunal de Turismo Pica** (Pica Tourism Office, no phone, 9am-1:45pm Mon.-Fri.).

Food and Accommodations

For cheap, fast meals, there is a row of juice shops and fast-food joints on Avenida General Ibáñez, just before Cocha Resbaladero.

Tentaciones de Pica (Av. Gral. Ibáñez, tel. 9/8839 3493, www.tentacionesdepica. cl, 10am-7:30pm daily) sells homemade fruit jams, ciders, and syrups. No-frills **El Paraiso del Sabor** (also known as Tropical, Esmeralda 444, tel. 57/2741 162, noon-midnight daily, CH$2,500-7,500, *menú del*

día CH$3,500) serves enormous plates of simple but delicious regional food. Their two-course lunch menu can easily satisfy two people. Specials include *llama a lo pobre* (llama steak with fried potatoes and a fried egg). Upmarket but still cozy **El Pomelo** (Maipu 19, 12:30pm-5:30pm daily, CH$5,000-8,000, *menú del día* CH$6,000) is only open for lunch but has well-presented dishes, including llama steaks. Enjoy fresh lemonade on the small outdoor patio.

Despite its cramped rooms, **Hostel Wintata** (Simón Bolívar 22B, tel. 57/2741 460, www.hostelwintata.cl, CH$25,000 d shared bath, CH$35,000 d private bath, CH$50,000 cabin, cash only) is the best lodging option, with friendly hosts and a large tree-filled patio. Breakfast isn't included, but a small kitchen is available. They also have a five-person cabin, complete with a private kitchen. Rates include IVA.

Information and Services

There are two **ATMs** on the eastern corner of the Plaza de Armas, although it's worth bringing cash in case they run out. There is a **COPEC gas station** on the left as you enter town, one block southeast of the Plaza de Armas.

Getting There and Around

Pica is 120km east of Iquique. In Iquique, shared minivans leave every 15 minutes from **Norte Azul** (Barros Arana 945, tel. 57/2578 086 or 57/2523 820, reservasnorteazul@gmail. com), **Agencia Chacón** (Barros Arana 953, tel. 57/2416 691 or 9/8181 0897), **Pullman Santa Angela** (Barros Arana 971, tel. 57/2423 751, www.santaangela.cl), and **Agencia Barreda** (Barros Arana 965, tel. 57/2414 938), half a block south of the Mercado Centenario. The trip takes two hours and costs CH$3,000. Minivans depart with the same frequency from the eastern edge of the Plaza de Armas

starting at 5:45am Monday-Friday, 6:45am Saturday-Sunday, until 7:30pm daily.

To get to Pica from Iquique by car, follow Ruta 16, then Ruta 5. Continue 45km along the A-665 from La Tirana, passing through Matilla and arriving in Pica in 40 minutes. Pica is small enough to explore on foot.

★ GEOGLIFOS DE CERROS PINTADOS

The 100,650-hectare **Reserva Nacional Pampa del Tamarugal** (22km south of Pozo Almonte, tel. 57/2751 055, reserva. pampadeltamarugal@conaf.cl, 24 hr daily, free) protects groves of flowering trees that once covered the pampas. The main reason for this day trip from Iquique is the spectacular geoglyphs, designs that have been marked into the earth or built atop it—usually on a large scale. Most people explore this remarkable site via a guided day trip from Iquique, but it's easy enough to visit independently with your own wheels.

The **Geoglifos de Cerros Pintados** (R-5, turnoff 49km south of Pozo Almonte, tel. 57/2751 055, 9:30am-5pm Tues.-Sun., CH$4,000 adults, CH$2,000 children) are the second most important set of geoglyphs in Latin America after Peru's Nazca Lines. This site contains 450 geometric, anthropomorphic, and zoomorphic figures etched onto the desert floor by the indigenous people who inhabited this region AD 700-1500.

A small **museum** describes the key patterns and theories about the region's previous inhabitants. Patterns include fish, llamas, and human figures. Although their exact purpose is unknown, a popular hypothesis is that they acted as signposts guiding people from the mountains across the desert to the coast to trade goods. From the back of the museum, a 1-km trail passes along the foot of the hills, offering different vantage points.

The Geoglifos de Pintados are signposted from Ruta 5. A 2-km paved road leads to the gated entrance of the reserve and then onward to the museum and the geoglyphs.

1: Oficina Humberstone 2: outside the hot springs at Cocha Resbaladero

Practicalities

CONAF operates a **campground** (R-5, 22km south of Pozo Almonte, tel. 57/2751 055, reserva.pampadeltamarugal@conaf. cl, CH$4,000 pp) with four sites for up to 25 people each. The campground has restrooms, showers, and electricity. It's on the same site as the **Centro de Educación Ambiental Pampa del Tamarugal** (Pampa del Tamarugal Environmental Education Center, tel. 57/2383 537, www. cedampampadeltamarugal.cl, 8:30am-6pm daily, free), which has information about the reserve. The center's website has a map of the services in the area.

Getting There and Around

The entrance to the reserve is a 105-km, 1.5-hour drive from Iquique via Ruta 16 and Ruta 5 and is well signposted.

A small car park is just outside the museum. For those without transport, all tours depart from Iquique; **Místico Outdoors** (Eleuterio Ramírez 1535, Iquique, tel. 9/9541 7762, www.chileresponsibleadventure.com) visits the Geoglifos de Cerros Pintados as part of their full-day English-language tour to Oficina Humberstone and other nearby sights (2-person min., CH$70,000, including hotel pickup and lunch). **Magical Tours Chile** (Casa Matriz Baquedano 997, Iquique, tel. 57/2763 474, www.magicaltour.cl) has a similar trip with a stop in Pica (CH$25,000).

PISAGUA

More than 100km north of Iquique, Pisagua was once a bustling port town of 15,000, but its population is now closer to 200. Clinging to the coast with only the vertigo-inducing main road for access, it's practically impossible to reach without your own vehicle. This isolated coastal settlement is barely a ghost town during the week and only a little busier on weekends, when day-trippers arrive from Iquique. A visit offers a sobering insight into Chile's history.

The grand mansions along the seafront have been ransacked by the elements since the collapse of the nitrate industry in the mid-1900s. What ultimately sealed Pisagua's fate was its role during the Pinochet dictatorship, when buildings were used as concentration camps for political prisoners. In 1990, the ghastly discovery of 19 bodies in a mass grave in the old cemetery added another layer of grisly history.

Sights

From its vantage point on the road into Pisagua, the blue-and-white **Torre Reloj** (clock tower), built in 1887, stands sentinel over the town. The once grandiose neoclassical 1892 **Teatro Municipal** (Esmeralda, 10:30am-3pm and 3:30pm-6pm daily) has fallen into disrepair but still hosts occasional performances. The back of the stage hangs over the Pacific, which is visible through gaping holes in the walls. To tour the inside, collect the key from the library next door.

Opposite a small square overlooking the ocean, the imposing 1910 **Cárcel Pública de Pisagua** (Videla) became notorious for housing 1,500-2,500 political prisoners in squalid conditions during the military dictatorship. Many were beaten and tortured. Men were held here; women were housed in the old market next to the theater.

A turnoff on the right just before the Torre Reloj takes you down a treacherous sand track that skirts the side of a dune (and has no guardrails), continuing around the coast for 3km before it reaches the **Cementerio Municipal.** Wooden crosses mark the graves of Pisagua's dead. On the far side of the cemetery, a **monument** remembers those who died under Pinochet's dictatorship. The hole from the mass grave where the bodies were found remains, accompanied by a plaque with a poignant quote from poet Pablo Neruda: "Although steps may tread this place for thousands of years, they will never remove the blood of those who fell here."

Food and Accommodations

Restaurant Lina Mar (Arturo Prat 20, tel. 57/2731 507 or 9/8906 8103, 9am-8pm daily,

The Nitrate War

Before the discovery of nitrates in the Atacama Desert, the borders between Chile and Bolivia had been vaguely defined. But in 1874, once the extent of the exploitable minerals in the region became apparent, the two countries agreed to an official border, upon the condition that Chile would drop claims to a sizeable chunk of the Atacama Desert and that Bolivia wouldn't raise taxes on the Chilean and British nitrate companies that were operating on its territory.

But Bolivian dictator Hilarión Daza, emboldened by a secret treaty with Peru, did raise taxes on the nitrate companies. Chileans were incensed, pushing their president, Aníbal Pinto, into declaring war. In February 1879, Chilean troops occupied Bolivian soil at Antofagasta. Two weeks later, Bolivia declared war against Chile. In April 1879, the War of the Pacific—or the Nitrate War, as it came to be known—began.

By November 1879, Chile had advanced into Peruvian territory, capturing Pisagua and Iquique. Despite heavy losses in the Battle of Tarapacá, Chilean forces continued pushing north, planting the country's flag on El Morro in Arica in July 1880. Chilean forces finally reached the Peruvian capital, Lima, in January 1881, but there a stalemate ensued for three years.

In October 1883, Peru and Chile signed a peace treaty granting Chile rights to the Tarapacá region as well as Arica and Tacna, with a referendum planned 10 years later to decide the latter cities' final ownership. In April 1884, Chile signed a truce with Bolivia that granted Chile rights to the Antofagasta region and gave Bolivia freedom of transit through the port at Antofagasta. Chile gained access to huge stocks of saltpeter (sodium nitrate), which would bolster its economy until the development of synthetic fertilizers during World War I and the onset of the Great Depression sounded the industry's death knell.

menú del día CH$4,500) is an excellent option for a filling seafood lunch or dinner. Try the huge seafood empanadas or fish-and-chips—plenty for two people. Half a block south of the prison, **La Pica Pisagueña** (Angamos s/n, no phone, 8am-8pm daily, CH$5,000-10,000) offers large and cheap empanadas, *paila marina* (fish soup), and ceviche.

Just around the corner as you head into town from the Torre Reloj, **Hostal La Roca** (Rodríguez, tel. 9/9271 7742 or 57/2731 502, CH$28,000 d, cash only) is run by French-speaking Caterine Salaña Suárez, a local historian and author who's an excellent source of information about the history of the town. The five rooms are basic and equipped with a TV and Wi-Fi. Breakfast is included. Rates include IVA.

Getting There and Around

Pisagua is a 2.5-hour, 165-km drive north of Iquique via Ruta 16, Ruta 5, and the twisting, paved A-40. No buses serve Pisagua, and it is not featured on any tours from Iquique.

The town is tiny enough to explore on foot.

The dirt track to the Cementerio Municipal is not a drive for the fainthearted because of the narrow cliffs. It's a flat 45-minute walk along this same track if you'd rather not take the risk.

★ LAGUNA ROJA

With blood-colored water, **Laguna Roja** (free) looks like a wound etched in the landscape. Its waters were believed to hold supernatural powers by the local Aymara people. The intense red, surrounded by a contrasting ring of milky white salt, certainly looks otherworldly. It isn't a work of magic: Microscopic algae that live in its 40°C water combine with a layer of sediment to produce the intense hue.

Located 250km inland from Iquique on private land, Laguna Roja is best visited on a guided tour, as the location is remote, the route is unmarked, and it's easy to get lost. Tours normally start at 5am from Iquique, stopping after a few hours for breakfast at a small village in the mountains. Another hour's drive along a potholed dirt track brings you to the three lakes: Laguna Roja, yellow Laguna Amarilla, and green Laguna Verde. On the way back to Iquique, the group stops at a number of geoglyphs, reaching the city late in the evening.

Turisma Sol de Tarapacá (Paseo Baquedano 1024, Iquique, tel. 9/4041 7322 or 57/2467 910, www.turismosoldetarapaca. com), **Magical Tours Chile** (Casa Matriz Baquedano 997, Iquique, tel. 57/2763 474, www.magicaltour.cl), and **Dragon Adventure** (tel. 9/5845 3009) all run tours to Laguna Roja (CH$75,000 pp). Tours require

a minimum of four people and include hotel pickup, breakfast, and lunch. Tours are more likely to reach the required minimum on weekends than during the week.

Tourism outfit **Místico Outdoors** (Eleuterio Ramírez 1535, Iquique, tel. 9/9541 7762, www.chileresponsibleadventure.com) runs a two-day tour that includes an overnight stay in a local community to adjust to the altitude (Laguna Roja is at 3,700 meters elevation). The group then hikes to the three lakes the following morning. Prices start at CH$174,000 for two people.

Arica

With an annual average temperature of 22°C, a subtropical desert climate, and average rainfall of only 0.76 millimeters, it's no wonder Arica has branded itself the "City of Eternal Spring." Wedged between the Lluta and Azapa Valleys, Chile's northernmost city feels like a coastal oasis—despite the fact that it's officially the driest city in the world.

Founded in 1541 as Villa San Marcos de Arica, it soon became an important port on the highway for silver from the mine in Potosí, Bolivia. Later, Arica was the site of a bloody battle between Chilean and Peruvian forces in the War of the Pacific. As a result, there are a number of intriguing historical sites in a city that feels like a backwater.

Arica is principally a beach resort. Golden-sand bays with warm water for swimming and surfing give it a year-round holiday atmosphere. The 2004 discovery of the 7,000-year-old Chinchorro mummies in the city center has garnered more international attention. What's more, Arica is the gateway to the altiplano, with Parque Nacional Lauca and Reserva Nacional Las Vicuñas just a day or two away.

Orientation

The historical area of the city is southeast of the harbor and Avenida Comandante San Martín, which runs parallel to the coast. Plaza Vicuña Mackenna, Plaza Cristóbal Colón, and Parque Manuel Baquedano mark the western corner of the center. Many tour agencies, restaurants, and shops line the pedestrianized Bolognesi and 21 de Mayo. Along Bolognesi, a small **artisans market** (11am-9pm daily) showcases a selection of local craftwork, from leather belts to textiles.

SIGHTS

The **Ex Aduana de Arica** (Former Customs House, Parque Manuel Baquedano) was prefabricated in the French workshops of Alexandre Gustave Eiffel—of Eiffel Tower fame—before being shipped to Arica, where construction finished in 1874. Each brick carries Eiffel's logo. Inside, you can see the original sketches of the building's design. Today, the building operates as the **Casa de la Cultura** (hours vary), with exhibitions in its gallery.

Catedral de San Marcos (Bolognesi, southern side of Plaza Cristóbal Colón, 9am-7pm daily) is a riot of pastel shades, with its parabolic arches edged in maroon and the rest of the structure painted light pink.

The 1913 **Estación de Ferrocarril Arica-La Paz** (Arica-La Paz Train Station, 21 de Mayo, northeastern side of the Plaza del

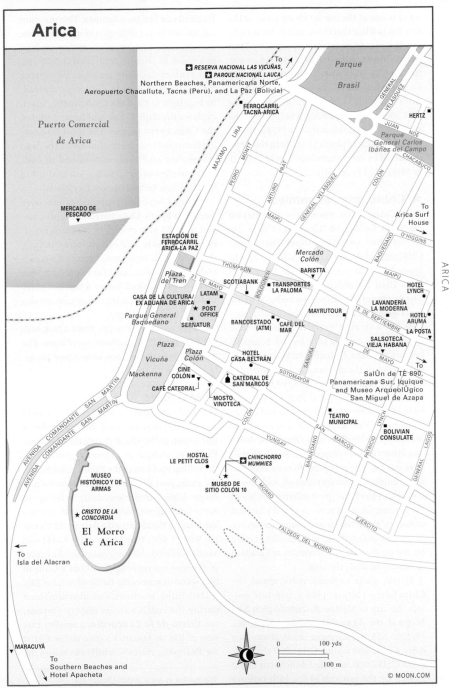

Arica

Puerto Comercial
de Arica

Parque
Brasil

To
RESERVA NACIONAL LAS VICUÑAS,
PARQUE NACIONAL LAUCA,
Northern Beaches, Panamericana Norte,
Aeropuerto Chacalluta, Tacna (Peru), and La Paz (Bolivia)

FERROCARRIL
TACNA-ARICA

HERTZ

JUAN NOÉ

Parque
General Carlos
Ibáñez del Campo

GENERAL VELÁSQUEZ

CHACABUCO

MERCADO DE
PESCADO

To
Arica Surf
House

O'HIGGINS

ESTACIÓN DE
FERROCARRIL
ARICA-LA PAZ

MÁXIMO LIRA

PEDRO MONTT

ARTURO PRAT

MAIPU

GENERAL VELÁSQUEZ

BAQUEDANO

Mercado
Colón

MAIPU

THOMPSON

Plaza
del Tren

21 DE MAYO

SCOTIABANK

BOLOGNESI

BARISTTA

TRANSPORTES
LA PALOMA

HOTEL
LYNCH

CASA DE LA CULTURA/
EX ADUANA DE ARICA

LATAM

POST
OFFICE

MAYRUTOUR

LAVANDERÍA
LA MODERNA

18 DE SEPTIEMBRE

HOTEL
ARUMÁ

Parque General
Baquedano

SERNATUR

BANCOESTADO
(ATM)

CAFÉ DEL
MAR

LA POSTA

SALSOTECA
VIEJA HABANA

21 DE MAYO

Plaza
Vicuña

Plaza
Colón

HOTEL
CASA BELTRÁN

SANGRA

To
SalÚn de TÉ 890,
Panamericana Sur, Iquique
and Museo ArqueolÚgico
San Miguel de Azapa

Mackenna

CINE
COLÓN

CAFÉ CATEDRAL

CATEDRAL DE
SAN MARCOS

SOTOMAYOR

MOSTO
VINOTECA

COLÓN

YUNGAY

TEATRO
MUNICIPAL

LYNCH

BOLIVIAN
CONSULATE

AVENIDA COMANDANTE SAN MARTÍN

AVENIDA COMANDANTE SAN MARTÍN

HOSTAL
LE PETIT CLOS

CHINCHORRO
MUMMIES

MUSEO
HISTÓRICO Y DE
ARMAS

MUSEO DE
SITIO COLÓN 10

EL MORRO

SAN MARCOS

BAQUEDANO

PATRICIO LYNCH

GENERAL LAGOS

CRISTO DE LA
CONCORDIA

El Morro
de Arica

EJÉRCITO

FALDEOS DEL MORRO

To
Isla del Alacran

MARACUYÁ

To
Southern Beaches and
Hotel Apacheta

0   100 yds

0   100 m

© MOON.COM

Tren) is one of the few surviving relics of the 440-km rail line that connected Arica with La Paz, Bolivia. A tourist train operated by **Tren Arica Poconchile** (tel. 2/2585 5360, www. tren.cl) now transports visitors from here to Poconchile in the Lluta Valley, on Saturday twice monthly. The return journey costs CH$7,000 and can be bought online or at the station. Opposite this station, a 1924 locomotive takes pride of place in the **Plaza del Tren** (bordered by Av. Comandante San Martín, 21 de Mayo, and Pedro Montt).

★ Chinchorro Mummies

The Chinchorro mummies in **Museo de Sitio Colón 10** (Cristóbal Colón 10, tel. 58/2205 041, 10am-6pm Tues.-Sun., CH$2,000 adults, CH$1,000 children) date to around 5050 BC—an incredible 2,000 years older than the oldest uncovered in Egypt. The display of 49 mummified bodies is in the exact spot they were discovered in 2004, protected by a sheet of reinforced glass, because they were too delicate to be moved. Scientists believe that the Chinchorro people originally lived in the altiplano before moving to the coast, which would mean the highlands have been inhabited for at least 10,000 years by hunter-gatherers who domesticated llamas and alpacas. Visitors can get a close look at the mummies and the vegetable fiber mats, shells, and other funerary trappings with which they were buried. The museum offers an excellent audio guide (English and Spanish, included in the ticket price) that gives information about the mummification process and the ancient culture of these fishers and hunter-gatherers. It's widely believed that other bodies remain buried on the site; the University of Tarapacá continues to study the area.

If you want to learn more about the Chinchorro culture, plan a trip just outside the city to **Museo Arqueológico San Miguel de Azapa** (Camino Azapa, tel. 58/2205 555, www.masma.uta.cl, 10am-6pm daily, CH$2,000 adults, CH$1,000 children, extra CH$2,000 for Sala Chinchorro audio guide), on the grounds of the 16th-century

Hacienda de San Juan Bautista. This museum has its own larger collection of mummies, but they are harder to appreciate as they are kept in a room in climate-controlled conditions, and visitors can only see them by peering through a glass door in the corner. Instead, its highlight is the **Sala Chinchorro,** which explores the daily rituals and funeral rites of the Chinchorro people. The most fascinating feature of their interactions with the dead is that they artificially mummified all bodies, regardless of social status—in contrast to other ancient people like the Egyptians.

Various types of mummification were employed by the Chinchorro; the most complex and oldest is evident in the black mummies. Their skin and organs were carefully removed, their bones reinforced with sticks, and the skin reattached. Clay would have been used to fill the skull before a wooden mask was added and the entire corpse covered in a layer of black manganese.

To get to Valle de Azapa from Arica, take the A-27 for 12km southeast out of town. The museum is to the left, 500 meters past the intersection with the A-33.

El Morro de Arica

With its panoramic vantage point, it should come as no surprise that **El Morro de Arica** was a strategic headland during the War of the Pacific. From here, on a clear day, you can see the rolling breakers of the Pacific crash below, the main port dotted with fishing boats and cargo ships, and the low, dusty buildings of Arica fanning out in a regulated grid. The on-site **Museo Histórico y de Armas** (El Morro, tel. 9/8625 484, 10am-8pm daily, CH$1,000 adults, CH$500 children) examines the causes of the war—surprisingly without a Chilean bias—and describes the Battle of Arica of July 7, 1880. Rifles, machetes, and other arms used during the conflict are on display. Outside, the *Cristo de la Concordia,* a smaller version of Rio de Janeiro's iconic statue *Christ the Redeemer,* stares wistfully out across the

---

1: a market in Arica 2: Hotel Apacheta

Pacific, a symbolic representation of peace between Chile and Peru.

To reach El Morro, from the southwestern end of Cristóbal Colón, a path leads first to a monument dedicated to the "Heroes del Morro" with maps pointing out Arica's main buildings. Take the left path from the bottom of the monument for a steep, lung-busting 10-minute climb to the top of El Morro.

BEACHES AND SURFING

Arica's picturesque beaches have warm water for swimming—as well as some dangerous rip currents. **Playa Chinchorro,** 1.6km north of the city center, has 1.5km of golden sand close to trendy restaurants and bars, making it the top choice for locals. At its northern edge, **Las Machas** is popular with surfers thanks to plentiful waves.

Isla del Alacrán, the artificial peninsula that juts out 500 meters south of Plaza Vicuña Mackenna, is home to **El Gringo,** widely considered the best surfing spot in the country— but only for experts. In the mornings waves can reach 4.5 meters; most surfers enter the water wearing helmets. Some 500 meters farther south, along the coastal road, Avenida Comandante San Martín, **Playa El Laucho,** with its sun umbrellas, calm water, and beach bars, appeals to a young crowd. Farther down, next door to Hotel Apacheta, **Playa La Lisera** is in a small cove frequented by families. Two hundred meters beyond, **Playa Brava** has consistent surf, best during winter; beware of the strong rip current.

Nine kilometers south of the center, sandy **Playa Corazon** merges into rocky coastline. Marine birds, include cormorants, pelicans, and Humboldt penguins, perch on the rocks in the afternoon. A 3-km hiking trail follows the water's edge.

Magic Chile (Playa Chinchorro at the 2nd pier, tel. 9/8790 6124, www.surfschool. cl, 9:30am-6pm daily) rents boards and wetsuits (CH$10,000 until close of business), with three-hour surfing classes (CH$20,000 pp) available at 9:30am and 1:30pm daily in summer and by prearrangement in winter.

ENTERTAINMENT
Nightlife

Arica has a growing nightlife scene. Many bars and clubs are along Playa Chinchorro, with a handful around the two main plazas, Plaza Vicuña Mackenna and Plaza Cristóbal Colón.

Along the pedestrianized Paseo Bolognesi, wine bar **Mosto Vinoteca** (7 de Junio 196, tel. 9/4172 636, 7pm-4am Tues.-Sun.) has a wide selection of wines, sharing platters, and pizzas, with an outdoor space spilling onto Plaza Cristóbal Colón. Four blocks northeast, **Salsoteca Vieja Habana** (21 de Mayo 487, tel. 9/9849 1236, 8:30pm-10:30pm Mon.-Thurs., 10pm-4am Sat.-Sun., salsa classes CH$3,000, no cover) offers salsa classes during the week from 7pm and turns into a full-blown salsa club on weekends.

Bar and restaurant **La Posta** (18 de Septiembre 547, tel. 9/8127 1954, http://la-posta-arica.business.site, 8pm-2am Tues.-Thurs., 8pm-3am Fri.-Sun., no cover) has a medical theme: Waitstaff are dressed as doctors and nurses, and the bar is adorned with medical paraphernalia. To enter, you'll need the password: *"¡Vengo por una urgencia!"* ("I have an emergency!").

Let loose on the dance floor at **Soho** (Buenos Aires 209, tel. 9/8905 1806, 11pm-4am Tues.-Sat., CH$8,000 cover), which overlooks the beach and hosts DJ sets and live bands. Farther north, dance the night away at lively **Mojito Arica** (Ingeniero Raul Pey 2861, 7pm-3am daily, CH$8,000 cover, including 1 beer), which has an expansive open-air dance floor, a seafront terrace, and plenty of drink deals.

Festivals and Events

The third-largest carnival celebration in South America, the **Carnival Andino Con La Fuerza del Sol** (www.aricafuerzadelsol. cl) sees 70,000 revelers descend on the otherwise tranquil city for three days of parades that feature 10,000 dancers. Troupes dressed in lavish traditional costumes and masks perform to Andean music. The festivities take place over a long weekend in late January-early February; dates change yearly to avoid overlapping with the Oruro Carnival in neighboring Bolivia. It's not necessary to buy tickets: Spectators are welcome to join in the processions by buying and spraying one another with silly foam. Accommodations should be booked weeks in advance; expect to pay peak prices. Most of the city's services have reduced hours or are closed for the duration.

The **Virgen de Las Peñas Pilgrimage** occurs over three days, culminating on the first Sunday of October, when 40,000 pilgrims hike 16km through canyons and across rivers to reach the shrine of Nuestra Señora de las Peñas, in the precordillera Quebrada de Livílcar in the Valle de Azapa. Upon arrival, the pilgrims dance to folkloric music using traditional instruments. Taxis and minivans leave regularly from Arica for the duration of the festival to reach the end of the road, 40km from San Miguel de Azapa, where the pilgrimage begins.

FOOD

Arica's dining scene is experiencing a reawakening, with restaurants and cafés springing up around the main plazas, as well as farther afield along Playa Chinchorro and toward the southern beaches. The city's enviable location between the two fertile valleys of Azapa and Llauca mean that restaurant menus are festooned with exotic fruits; its place on the coast means fresh seafood.

At the Puerto de Arica, the **Mercado de Pescado** (Fish Market, Av. Comandante San Martín, no phone, 6am-3pm) has stalls lined with fresh fish. The leftovers feed a colony of sea lions and pelicans demanding breakfast. Keep an eye on your belongings in this area. Access is from across the northwestern side of the train station. It's a working port, so watch for trucks to the right of the main entrance.

Chilean

The main selling point of **Maracuyá** (Av. Comandante San Martín 321, tel. 58/2227 600, 12:30pm-3:30pm and 8pm-12:30am daily, CH$9,000-14,000) is its sea view. For a prime table on the ocean-side terrace, reserve in advance; otherwise, there's plenty of room in the dining rooms. Smartly dressed waiters provide good service, and the menu has a wide range of local fish.

Classy **Rayú** (Ingeniero Raúl Pey 2590, tel. 58/2216 446, rayu.gourmet@gmail.com, 8am-2am Wed.-Mon., CH$9,000-30,000) has an Italian-Peruvian gourmet menu by a Peruvian head chef. It's some of the priciest food in the city, but worth the expense; the local seabream is excellent. The outside terrace is a few meters from Playa Chinchorro. Reservations are advised.

★ **Café Catedral** (7 de Junio 188, tel. 9/7755 3026, 10am-10:30pm daily, CH$4,000-14,000, *menú del día* CH$6,000-7,000) has made a mark as a trendy café and as a steak house. Its *menú del día* is unique: Choose from a selection of Chilean barbecued meat or local swordfish. All staff are certified baristas, so you'll get a decent cappuccino here.

International

Dimango (Ingeniero Raúl Pey 2592, tel. 58/2211 419, 11am-2am Mon.-Sat., 11am-11pm Sun., CH$7.200-11,500) serves reliable decently priced pizzas and pastas. Ice cream, in 18 different flavors, is available from the adjoining shop.

Budget and Light Bites

Baristta (18 de Septiembre 295, tel. 9/4533 1042, www.baristta.cl, 8:30am-10pm Mon.-Sat., CH$2,500-5,000) has a huge upstairs terrace with modern furnishings and incongruous rap music. The filtered coffee is some of the best in town, with five different types of beans. Ample breakfasts, cakes, and sandwiches make this a good pit stop for a light meal.

Surprisingly spacious **Salón de Té "890"** (21 de Maro 890, tel. 58/2256 643 or 9/4921 0458, www.890.cl, 5pm-noon daily, CH$3,000-5,300) has a large menu of snacks and mains, including empanadas, sandwiches, and crepes, although it's most popular for *once* (afternoon tea).

Local favorite **Milkhouse by Lacteos Lauca** (Caupolicán 1096, tel. 58/2324 182, 3pm-10pm Mon.-Fri., 1pm-10pm Sat.-Sun., CH$3,400-4,800) offers traditional *onces*, include *tostadas con palta* (avocado toast) as well as heartier hot and cold sandwiches served in a large covered outdoor seating area. Ice cream comes in memorable flavors made with local ingredients, such as passionfruit. It gets busy 7pm-10pm.

On the pedestrian walkway one block east of Plaza Cristóbal Colón, **Café del Mar** (21 de Mayo 260, tel. 58/2231 936, 10am-20:30pm Mon.-Sat., CH$4,000-7,000, *menú del día* CH$4,800) has surprisingly good food if you can look beyond the dingy interior and plastic furniture. The fish of the day, pizzas, salads, burgers, and kebabs are delicious.

ACCOMMODATIONS

The cheapest accommodations are a few blocks southeast of Plaza Cristóbal Colón. More expensive options are in the residential neighborhoods around Playa Chinchorro and the southern beaches.

Under CH$25,000

It's in need of some attention, but **Hotel Lynch** (Patricio Lynch 589, tel. 58/2231 581, reservashotelynch@hotmail.com, CH$17,000 d shared bath, CH$30,000 d private bath) offers the cheapest digs in town. Rooms are on two floors with dated but comfortable furnishings. Check that your window, which opens to a central terrace, locks properly. Expect to hear street noise on the 2nd floor. Rates include IVA.

Cheerful and unpretentious **Hostal Sunny Days** (Tomás Aravena 161, tel. 58/2241 038, www.sunny-days-arica.cl, CH$11,000 dorm, CH$26,000 d shared bath, CH$30,000 d private bath, cash only), two houses converted into one hostel, is packed with communal lounges, kitchens, and terraces. It's in a quiet residential area a 10-minute bus ride north of the center, and two blocks from the bus

terminal. Rooms are large, and none of the dorms have bunk beds. Rates include IVA.

Five blocks from Paseo Bolognesi, centrally located **Arica Surf House** (O'Higgins 661, tel. 58/2312 213 or 9/9843 4227, www. aricasurfhouse.cl, CH$12,000 dorm, CH$27,000 d shared bath, CH$33,000 d private bath) has clean, simple rooms with access to a large kitchen and communal space out back, which converts into a bar during summer. Doubles are spacious, while the large dorm feels like a hospital ward. Surfing lessons, board rental, scuba diving, and parasailing can all be arranged through the hostel. Rates include IVA.

CH$25,000-40,000

French-Canadian **Hostal Le Petit Clos** (Cristóbal Colón 7, tel. 58/2323 746 or 9/65855573, www.lepetitclos.cl, CH$27,000 d shared bath, CH$32,000 d private bath) has only nine spacious, clean rooms, which gives it a homey feel. Room 4 offers views across the port. Upstairs, a shady terrace and communal kitchen offer city views. A small apartment with three bedrooms and a kitchen is a steal at CH$48,000. Rates include IVA.

The friendliest service in town is at **Guest Home Valto and Ziron** (Inca de Oro 178, tel. 9/7466 8325 or 9/5625 7096, www.valtoyziron. cl, CH$30,000 d). The 12 rooms are compact but pleasantly decorated, with comfortable beds and large private baths. A large roof terrace acts as a social area and breakfast room. The owners go out of their way to make you feel at home. On-site parking and bicycles are available for guests; it's a 10-minute taxi ride from the center. Advance reservations are essential. Rates include IVA.

CH$40,000-60,000

A 20-minute bus or 10-minute taxi ride from the center, **Hotel Avenida** (Av. Diego Portales 2422, tel. 58/2583 656, www. hotelavenida.cl, CH$47,000 d) offers excellent value in its 29 identical white rooms, the best of which are on the ground floor with access to an enclosed patio. The hotel's biggest draw is its large grassy terrace, complete with comfy chairs and a large swimming pool. Rates include IVA.

CH$60,000-80,000

The location overlooking famed surfing spot El Buey makes trendy ★ **Hotel Apacheta** (Av. Comandante San Martín, tel. 58/2494 470, www.hotelapacheta.com, CH$69,000 d) one of the best lodgings in town. Designed by architect and surfer Marco Polidura, the hotel has simple wooden architecture and ample outdoor space—including a terrace protected from the elements by a wall of glass—and direct access to the ocean. All 18 rooms have large windows and terraces that look out on the sea. Expect to be awakened by the calls of gulls. Rates include IVA.

Just 150 meters from Playa Chinchorro, pricey **Hotel & Spa Las Taguas** (Edmundo Pérez Zujovic 280-286, tel. 58/2425 166, www. hotelspalastaguas.cl, CH$64,000 d) features its own spa, a covered indoor pool, a sauna, and a jetted tub. Rooms are small but comfortable, each with a minibar, private bath, and king bed. The on-site restaurant offers breakfast, lunch, and dinner 365 days a year. Rates include IVA.

Modern **Hotel Casa Beltran** (Rafael Sotomayor 266, tel. 58/225 3839, www. hotelcasabeltran.cl, CH$70,000 d) has 18 tasteful, decently sized rooms that include private baths, fast internet, and air-conditioning. Some rooms are smaller but have balconies. The restaurant downstairs serves a gourmet *menú del día* (CH$5,600). Rates include IVA.

Over CH$80,000

Stylish boutique **Hotel Aruma** (Patricio Lynch 530, tel. 58/2250 000 or 58/2252 176, www.aruma.cl, CH$90,000 d) is the only officially recognized sustainable accommodation in Arica, equipped with solar panels. The 16 large rooms are beautifully decorated with Italian furnishings and altiplano textiles. Two superior rooms boast king beds. Air-conditioning is included and

double-glazed windows block out street noise. There's a rooftop pool and terrace where breakfast and snacks are served. Rates include IVA.

INFORMATION AND SERVICES

On the corner of Parque Baquedano, **SERNATUR** (Calle San Marcos 101, tel. 58/2252 054, info@sernatur.cl, 9am-6pm Mon.-Fri., 10am-4pm Sat.) staff can be a little standoffish but will provide general information about the city and the altiplano. A **free walking tour** in both English and Spanish departs at 10am Wednesday from the office; register the day before. For money, **Banco Estado** (21 de Mayo 260) and **Scotiabank** (21 de Mayo 187) are central options. Exchange dollars and Peruvian and Bolivian currency at **Casas de Cambio,** along the pedestrianized part of Calle 21 de Mayo.

For medical services, **Hospital Dr. Juan Noé** (18 de Septiembre 1000, tel. 58/2204 592, www.hjnc.cl) is in the city center, as are the **Carabineros** (police, Esmeralda between Av. Santa María and Salvo). **Lavandería La Moderna** (18 de Septiembre 457, tel. 58/2232 006, 9:30am-2pm and 4:30pm-9pm Mon.-Fri., 9:30am-2pm Sat.) is one of the few laundry services in the center. For mail services, head to **Correos de Chile** (Arturo Prat 305, 9am-7pm Mon.-Fri., 10am-12:30pm Sat.), also in the center of town.

For U.S. citizens continuing to Bolivia, the **Bolivian Consulate** (Lynch 298, tel. 58/2583 390, consuladoboliviaarica@gmail.com) can advise on visas, which can be obtained at the border.

GETTING THERE

As the gateway to Peru, only 200km from the border with Bolivia, Arica has both international and national connections via air, bus, *taxi colectivo,* and train.

Air

Aeropuerto Internacional Chacalluta (ARI, Ruta 12, tel. 58/2213 416, www.

chacalluta.cl) is 18km north of Arica, with around five nonstop flights daily operated by **Sky Airline** (www.skyairline.com) and **LATAM** (www.latam.com) from Santiago and daily flights from Antofagasta. LATAM also has an office in the city (Arturo Prat 391, tel. 600/526/2000, 9am-1:15pm and 3:30pm-6:30pm Mon.-Fri., 9am-1pm Sat.).

AIRPORT TRANSFERS

Transfer Arica (tel. 9/5678 8255 or 9/8582 1493, www.transferarica.cl) offers airport shuttle services in shared minivans (CH$6,000) and private taxis (CH$12,000) from outside the airport. **Radio Taxi Nueva Sol** (tel. 58/2255 000 or 58/2234 000) offers airport transfers (CH$14,000) and pickups from hotels in Arica. It's a 30-minute drive from the airport into the city.

Bus

Terminal Rodoviario (Av. Diego Portales 948, 58/2225 202) is Arica's main domestic bus terminal, although some international services also leave from here. An obligatory CH$200 terminal fee must be paid at the booth in the center of the terminal before boarding your bus. Next door, the **Terminal Internacional** (Av. Diego Portales 951) offers services to Peru and Bolivia.

Domestic bus routes include **Iquique** (hourly, 5hr, CH$7,000/CH$16,000), **Calama** (8 daily, 8hr, CH$11,000/CH$30,000), **Antofagasta** (every 2 hr, 10hr, CH$14,000/CH$30,000), **La Serena** (10 daily, 20hr, CH$22,000/CH$50,000), and **Santiago** (5 daily, 30hr, CH$40,000/CH$75,000). The most frequent connections are offered by **Pullman Bus** (tel. 58/2223 837, www.pullmanbus.cl), **Nuevo FichTur VIP** (tel. 58/2241 972), and **Turbus** (tel. 58/2225 202).

Local buses to **Putre** (3hr, CH$4,500) are operated by **La Paloma** (tel. 58/2222 710), with one connection at 7am daily, and **Transportes Gutiérrez** (tel. 58/2229 338), with one connection at 6:30am on Monday, Wednesday, and Friday.

Car

Most travelers arrive in Arica via Ruta 5 from the south as it edges the Tiliviche, Suca, Miñimiñi, Carsa, and Azapa Valleys before reaching the coast at Arica. From Arica, Ruta 5 continues north to Paso Concordia at the border with Peru. To get to Arica from Iquique, it's a 310-km, four-hour drive north on Ruta 5.

Crossing into Peru

Arica's **Terminal Internacional** (Av. Diego Portales 951) has two buses to cross to Tacna, Peru. On the left side as you enter the terminal are buses (CH$2,000) that take 1.5 hours, including the border crossing. On the right side, quicker *taxis colectivos* (shared taxis, CH$3,500) take 1 hour, including the border crossing, for the same trip. The taxis depart the terminal once they're full. Heavy traffic at the border on weekends can make this journey take twice as long.

Another option to reach Tacna, Peru, is the 48-passenger train (CH$3,200) that leaves from the **Ferrocarril Arica-Tacna** (Av. Comandante San Martín 799, no phone). The train departs Arica at 6am and 4:30pm daily in winter and 7am and 5:30pm daily in summer, and leaves Tacna for Arica at 6am and 4:30pm Peruvian time daily. The trip, including border procedures, takes one hour and 15 minutes. Tickets can only be bought at the station, and the train is often out of service for repairs. Note that time in Peru is two hours earlier than in Chile mid-September-mid-April, and one hour earlier the rest of the year.

Crossing into Bolivia

From Arica's **Terminal Internacional** (Av. Diego Portales 951), you can get to La Paz, Bolivia (8hr, CH$12,000). **Buses Trans Salvador** (tel. 58/2228 547 or 9/7825 2540) offers four buses daily. **Pullman Ayca** (tel. 58/224 8465) has one bus at 7am daily. If you're headed to Putre and then on to La Paz, buy the tickets from the Terminal Internacional before you leave Arica, as there's nowhere to buy tickets in Putre.

GETTING AROUND

The historic center of town is easily walkable. Away from the center, near the southern or northern beaches, it's easy to use local transportation to get around. Car rental is an inexpensive way of exploring the coast, the altiplano, Parque Nacional Lauca, and Reserva Nacional Las Vicuñas.

Car Rental

Europcar (www.europcar.com) has an office in the arrivals terminal of the airport (tel. 58/2578 510, 7am-11pm daily) and in the center of town (Chacabuco 602, tel. 58/2578 500, 8am-1pm and 2:30pm-6:30pm Mon.-Fri., 9am-11:30am Sat.). **Hertz** (www.hertz.com) also has an office in the airport (tel. 58/2219 186, 6am-11pm daily) and in the center (Baquedano 999, tel. 58/2231 487, 8:30am-7:30pm Mon.-Fri., 9am-1pm Sat.).

Local Buses

Buses 12 and 14 leave from the corner of Baquedano and 18 de Mayo for Playa Chinchorro. The covered market El Agro is the last stop for buses 1N and 113 and one of the last for bus 16. Each journey costs CH$400, regardless of distance.

The Altiplano

Vast lakes, sharp volcanoes, and a wealth of wildlife await on the altiplano, just 2-3 hours' drive north from Arica. Much of this region is a designated UNESCO Biosphere Reserve, reflecting its exceptional diversity of Andean flora and fauna. One of the highlights is the high-elevation Parque Nacional Lauca, where dramatic ice-capped volcanoes reflect in pearly Lago Chungará. Adjoining the southern end of the park, Reserva Nacional Las Vicuñas is a surreal landscape of snowy peaks, scrubby steppe, wetlands, and the glaring white salt flats of the Monumento Natural Salar de Surire. These areas are a bird-watcher's paradise, home to 140 endemic and migratory species.

The gateway town of Putre is a 2.5-hour, 141-km drive inland from Arica. It's at a lower elevation than the surrounding national parks, making it the ideal spot to stay to acclimatize, and then day-trip to the nearby attractions. The drive on international Ruta 11 eases you into the elevation as it climbs inland, with previews of the surreal drama that awaits in the mountains above. This road travels 200km east from Arica to the border with Bolivia. Because it's the only route for the trucks from Arica's port, heavy traffic and accidents caused by dangerous driving are common.

TOUR OPTIONS

Many visitors explore Parque Nacional Lauca on a day tour from Arica. This is certainly the cheapest option, but you may suffer the effects of altitude sickness if you haven't had time to acclimatize to the elevation. Consider a two- or three-day tour, or use Putre as a base to see the region. Multiday tours include overnight stays in Putre. Only tours that are three days or longer visit Reserva Nacional Las Vicuñas, due to the poor state of the reserve's roads.

Independent travelers can organize tours from Putre, which can be cheaper if you're traveling in a group of two or more. Various tour operators, many of which work out of lodgings here, provide experienced guides. Note that many accept cash or bank transfers only. A period of at least three days is sufficient to allow for acclimatization and time to both visit the highlights of the national park and go deep into the national reserve.

Having your own vehicle allows the freedom to explore the national park at your own pace, although this is only recommended if you've had a day to acclimatize first in Putre,

The Route of the Missions

a 16th-century church in the altiplano

The **Ruta de las Misiones** (Route of the Missions) is a collection of 36 historic 16th-century Andean churches from Arica inland. Built from stone, adobe, and Peruvian feather grass, they remain important centers of Aymara communities. The best way to explore these villages and gain access to the churches is with the knowledgeable local guides of **Fundación Altiplano** (www.fundacionaltiplano.cl), offering one- to three-day (CH$255,000 pp, min. 2 people, including food, transportation, and lodging) tours of Ruta de las Misiones. Reservations must be made 15 days in advance.

A downloadable guide to the villages along the route is at www.rutadelasmisiones.cl, which also includes detailed information on dining and lodging. Many of the churches aren't open to visitors except during religious festivals. For those that are open, you'll need to find someone in the village who can lend you the key if you want to look inside. Opt to go on an official tour with Fundación Altiplano to be sure of gaining access.

as driving when suffering from the effects of high elevation can be dangerous.

Arica-Based Tours

With some of the best knowledge of the region, **Arica Unlimited Tours** (tel. 9/9844 7269, www.aricaunlimitedtours.com) is run by experienced local guide Iván Guerra. The outfitter leads private bird-watching, photography, and trekking tours into the altiplano. Many of the tours include an overnight in an indigenous Aymara community; all can be adapted depending on your interests. Tours start at CH$150,000 per day, with all

transportation, food, lodging, and park entries included. Groups need a minimum of two people; maximum group size is eight. Iván speaks Danish, English, and Spanish.

Aventura South America (tel. 9/9676 1306, www.aventurasouthamerica.com/site) arranges English-, French-, and Dutch-speaking tours around the altiplano, as well as to destinations farther afield, including Santiago, southern Peru, and Patagonia.

Orange Travel (Paseo Bolognesi 421, tel. 58/2256 693 or 9/8869 3991, www.orangetravel.cl, 9am-9pm Mon.-Fri.) runs large bus tours to Parque Nacional Lauca

PUTRE

At 3,400 meters elevation, Putre is an Aymara settlement surrounded by agricultural terraces growing oregano. It sits in the shadow of the two-pronged Nevados de Putre, formed by two adjoining volcanoes, Taapacá and Ancoma. The town's name means "sound of the water" and has Aymara roots: It refers to the channels that slice through its streets, carrying fresh water from the mountains above.

Tourism is growing in this dusty town, a gateway for day trips to Parque Nacional Lauca and Reserva Nacional Las Vicuñas. It is a good place to acclimatize to the high elevation before moving on to the parks. With a two-season climate (rainy and dry), typical of the altiplano, Putre is best avoided January-February, when seasonal rains make the paved roads dangerous—and the unpaved roads virtually impassable.

ORIENTATION

On the main road as you enter town, the **Monumento al Arrieno** is a statue of the nomadic traders who, until a few decades ago, traveled hundreds of kilometers across Arica and Parinacota with herds of llama, donkeys, and mules. The town is set around the central **Plaza de Putre** (bordered by Carrera, Latorre, Cochrane, and Arturo Prat), home to the pretty adobe **Iglesia de San Idelfonso de Putre** (closed to visitors). Most services are around the Plaza de Putre or on Baquedano, although a handful of accommodations are west down an unlit road that's in poor condition.

Food

Cantaverdi Restobar (Arturo Perez 339, no phone, putre.cantaverdi@gmail.com, 12:30pm-3pm and 6:30pm-10pm daily, CH$3,200-7,500) is Putre's most expensive restaurant. The food doesn't necessarily live up to the elevated prices, but the atmosphere is cozy, the welcome is warm, and the open fire is even warmer. Expect Chilean staples: pizzas, sandwiches, and fish, as well as llama steaks and quinoa.

(CH$30,000, full day) as well as multiple-day tours via Putre to Parque Nacional Lauca (CH$155,000, two days) and Las Vicuñas (CH$240,000, three days). Tours are conducted only in Spanish.

Mayrutour (Baquedano 411, tel. 9/8582 1493 or 9/8844 6568, www.mayurutour.com) can organize tours to the parks directly from Putre or arrange pickup from Arica. Rates for one-day excursions to Lauca from Putre start at CH$40,000 pp; from Arica, from CH$80,000 pp. Tours to Reserva Nacional Las Vicuñas generally cost CH$75,000 pp (min. 2 people).

Many other tour agencies in Arica's city center offer general-interest bus trips with little personalization. Beware of "vomi-tours," the nickname for one-day excursions to Lago Chungará, where the elevation of 4,570 meters can cause altitude sickness.

Putre-Based Tours

The expert on the altiplano, **Terrace Lodge** (Circunvalación 25, tel. 58/2230 499, www.terracelodge.com) offers full-day excursions in English (min. 2 people) into both parks, including Lago Chungará (CH$45,000), Monumento Natural Salar de Surire (CH$72,000), and north to Suriplaza and Volcán Taapacá (CH$45,000), as well as the Jurasi Mountains and hot springs (CH$34,000). Their vehicles always carry oxygen masks in case of altitude sickness. They also have a map of the region for sale, for those with their own vehicles and looking to take self-guided excursions to some of the area's lesser-known destinations. Guests planning on staying for several days can stay at their lodge in Putre.

Also based in Putre, **Tour Andino** (Baquedano 340, tel. 9/9011 0702, www.tourandino.com) leads guided tours into the parks, plus trips focused on climbing, hiking, and other adventure activities. They're the best option for summiting any of the volcanos; two-day ascents of Volcán Parinacota start at CH$450,000 for 1-2 people, including technical gear, camping equipment, and food.

How to Avoid Altitude Sickness

Reaching some of the highest elevations found in Chile, the mountains in the Norte Grande can cause the serious, and in some cases life-threatening, onset of altitude sickness. Symptoms range from mild nausea, headaches, and fatigue to more severe effects, such as shortness of breath, vomiting, and confusion. There is no way to predict how your body will respond to the change in altitude; health and age have no bearing on susceptibility to altitude sickness.

The best way to stay safe is to **give yourself time to acclimate.** Staying at the same elevation for 24 hours is recommended for 3,000 meters and higher. If you climb more than 300 meters in one day, **return to a lower altitude at night** to give your body a chance to recuperate. The mantra to remember this is "Climb high but sleep low."

Drink plenty of **water,** limit **alcohol,** and eat **light meals** to stave off altitude sickness. The over-the-counter drug **acetazolamide** can be a preventative measure.

Before signing up for high-elevation tours or treks, check with the agency to see if they carry **oxygen** for those suffering altitude sickness.

Local favorite **Walisuma** (Baquedano 300, no phone, 8am-10pm daily, CH$1,800, *menú del día* CH$3,500) has no-frills Andean cuisine, including hearty soups and huge meat and avocado sandwiches. Similarly cheap home-cooked Andean dishes like alpaca meat and rice are served at **Restaurant Hantit** (Baquedano 269, tel. 9/9836 9377, 7am-10pm daily, *menú del día* CH$2,000).

Accommodations

Although there are plenty of lodgings in Putre, many cater exclusively to local miners and don't accept private bookings. It gets cold in the altiplano at night, so check ahead about the heating facilities.

Italian-run ★ **Terrace Lodge** (Circunvalación 25, tel. 58/2230 499, www. terracelodge.com, CH$45,000 d, 2-night min.) has modern comforts in five spacious bedrooms, each with a heater. Breakfast here is substantial and included. Day excursions can be arranged with owner Flavio, who's an experienced guide and has designed a detailed road map of the region that is essential for self-guided trips.

Along the road that goes due west, 1km out of town, **La Chakana** (tel. 9/97459519, www. hotelenputre.cl, CH$44,000 d, cash only) has two-, three-, and four-person cabins, all including hot water, breakfast, Wi-Fi, and access to a large communal dining area. The heaters in the bedrooms are lackluster. Transfer from the center of Putre is occasionally available but must be organized in advance. Otherwise, it's a 10-minute walk, unlit at nighttime. Rates include IVA.

Putre's cheapest lodgings are at **Hostal Cali** (Baquedano 399 A, tel. 9/8536 1242 or 9/8518 0960, www.alojamientoenputre.com, CH$25,000-35,000 d, cash only). This small guesthouse has half a dozen basic rooms that are clean, if slightly dark, and all share a bath. Breakfast can be arranged for a fee. Heating is available on demand; catch the attention of the owners, who aren't always available. Rates include IVA.

Information and Services

The **Oficina de Información Turística** (Plaza de Putre, Latorre, next to the church, hours vary Mon.-Sat.) posts its erratic opening hours on the door the day before. The **CONAF** office (Teniente del Campo 301, 3 blocks west of the plaza, tel. 58/2585 704, luis.araya@ conaf.cl, hours vary) has information about the parks, road conditions, and camping options at Lago Chungará and Guallatire.

The **Posta Medical** (Baquedano 261, tel. 58/2594 740) is a clinic that can help with altitude sickness. After 7pm, ring the bell for attention. **Banco de Estado** (Plaza de Putre, corner of Arturo Prat and Cochrane) has a **24-hour ATM.**

There are no large shops in Putre, and only basic supplies can be acquired; the most equipped mini market is on Baquedano, opposite Walisuma restaurant.

Getting There

Two bus companies offer buses to Putre (3.5hr, CH$4,500) from the domestic bus terminal in Arica. **Transportes La Paloma** (Av. Diego Portales 948, Arica, tel. 58/2222 710, www.translapaloma.cl) leaves from Arica at 7am daily and departs Putre at 2pm daily from their office on Calle Baquedano. **Transportes Gutiérrez** (Ríos 2140, Arica, tel. 58/2229 338) offers departures at 6:30am Monday, Wednesday, and Friday from Arica. Buses return the same day, departing at 5pm from the Plaza de Putre.

To get to Putre from Arica, it's a 141-km drive inland along Ruta 5 and Ruta 11. Alternatively, via San Miguel de Azapa, you can join Ruta 11 by taking the A-19 and then the A-143, reached by a left turn 1km beyond the town. A 4WD vehicle is not necessary unless you plan to drive into Reserva Nacional Las Vicuñas, as both routes from Arica are fully paved. The drive takes 2.5 hours, although heavy truck traffic and regular accidents can slow the journey. Stay hydrated and take breaks when necessary if you start to feel the effects of the altitude.

CROSSING INTO BOLIVIA

Only 70km from the Lago Chungará border, Putre is a sensible stop before continuing on to La Paz, allowing for a period of acclimatization before reaching the Bolivian city's heady heights of 3,640 meters. It's not recommended to drive a car into Bolivia, due to safety issues. The better options are to take a bus, or, if available, go by guided tour.

Buses Trans Salvador (tel. 58/2228 547 or 9/7825 2540; 4 daily) and **Pullman Ayca** (tel. 58/224 8465; 9:30am daily) have buses to La Paz (5hr, CH$12,000). Buses do not depart from Putre, but from the turnoff for the village on the A-147, 5km from the village. There's nowhere to buy bus tickets in Putre,

so you'll need to purchase them from Arica's **Terminal Internacional** (Av. Diego Portales 951, Arica) before you leave town.

★ PARQUE NACIONAL LAUCA

Parque Nacional Lauca (tel. 58/2585 704 or 58/2201 201, 24 hr daily, free), 145km east of Arica, feels like a different world, with soaring volcanic peaks over the border in Bolivia, vast highland steppes, and *bofedale* peatlands. It is a designated UNESCO World Biosphere Reserve, together with bordering Reserva Natural Las Vicuñas to the south, and the Monumento Natural Salar de Surire, in the very south of the reserve.

Activities are limited; come to admire the scenery and the rich flora and fauna, including the chinchilla-like viscacha, wild camelids, guanacos, the rare vicuña, and 150 bird species. Lago Chungará is the jewel; you can admire it via a short trail that offers panoramic views.

The scenery is breathtaking, and the elevation even more so; Lago Chungará, the region's top attraction, is at a lung-upsetting 4,570 meters elevation, so take it easy and avoid physical exertion. If you can, it's worth spending a day or two acclimatizing in Putre rather than coming directly from Arica. UV radiation increases by 50 percent above 3,500 meters, so bring strong sunblock and plenty of water—4-6 liters per day are recommended.

There is no official entrance to the park; its territory straddles Ruta 11 as it continues east toward the border with Bolivia. A **CONAF ranger station** (no phone) is located at km 65, with a car park, restrooms, and access to a 1.6-km trail along the southwestern edge of the lake.

Sights

The **Termas de Jurasi** (tel. 9/5871 5520, 9am-7pm daily, CH$2,000 adults, CH$1,000 children) are a series of hot spring pools that reach 37°C. One large outdoor pool, two smaller indoor pools, and three outdoor mud pools receive visitors. Reach the pools from Putre by taking the A-149 out of town and then Ruta 11. The dirt track to the pools is on the right, about 3km after you turn onto Ruta 11.

Las Cuevas (20km beyond Termas de Jurasi, Ruta 11) is one of the best places to see the chinchilla-like viscachas, who emerge from the rocks to dine on peat in the early morning and afternoon. A small car park next to a CONAF ranger station gives access to an easy 1-km trail, as well as a hot spring.

On the right, just after Las Cuevas, a dirt road leads up to **Chacu Las Cuevas,** a stone structure formerly used to capture vicuñas. The dirt road, suitable only for 4WD vehicles, continues 11km to **Cerro Milagro** (4,800 meters), a picturesque landscape of rainbow-colored rock.

Beyond the turnoff for Chacu Las Cuevas, 50 meters farther along Ruta 11 is the main access point for Reserva Nacional Las Vicuñas and Monumento Natural Salar de Surire.

Among huge altiplano steppes and occasional boggy patches, look for herds of grazing llamas, alpacas, and vicuñas. A turnoff from Ruta 11 leads to the adobe settlement of **Parinacota,** a small group of white-washed buildings with thatched roofs. The most interesting sight is the 1738 **Iglesia de Parinacota** (closed to visitors), with its separate bell tower. The turnoff for the village is 16km beyond Chacu Las Cuevas.

From the village, an 11-km round-trip trek reaches nearby **Lagunas de Cotacotani,** where birds can be spotted. From the main highway, these interconnected wetlands are visible on the left, a patchwork of water surrounded by a scattering of *bofedal.* Major roadwork along Ruta 11 is underway, blocking access to the viewpoints for the lakes. Work is not expected to be completed until 2020 at the earliest.

Just before the road passes into Bolivia, mirror-like **Lago Chungará** appears out of the steppe, reflecting the snowy peak of the dormant stratovolcano Parinacota. Its name means "mossy stone" in Aymara, referring to its emerald waters. It's home to plentiful birdlife, including the black-crowned night heron, white-tufted grebe, and black-faced and puna ibis. The main draw is the view. Looking east, the K'isi K'isini volcano (5,536 m) straddles the Bolivian and Chilean border, while Sajama (6,542 m), the ninth-highest volcano on the planet, is visible in Bolivia. A **CONAF ranger station** (no phone, 8:30am-5:30pm daily) is located at km 65, with a car park, restrooms, and access to a 1.6-km trail along the southwestern edge of the lake.

Many trails in the region are ancient trade routes that have been used by locals for hundreds of years—some even in precolonial times. Notice (but don't touch) the stone cairns, called *apachitas* in Aymaran, used to mark paths and the presence of Pachamama (Mother Earth).

Practicalities

The CONAF ranger station at Lago Chungará is normally staffed year-round and can provide some information about the park. Information boards detailing the birdlife of Lago Chungará are along the trail. **Camping** was formerly available at the CONAF ranger station at Lago Chungará; now it's essential to visit the **CONAF office** in Putre (Teniente del Campo 301, 3 blocks west of the plaza, Putre, tel. 58/2585 704, luis.araya@conaf.cl) to see whether it's possible to camp. Bring water with you, as there are no sources of freshwater available. Accommodations are scarce within the park. **Albergue Don Leonel** (Parinacota, tel. 58/2261 526, leonel_parinacota@hotmail.com) has room for four people, with hot water and food prepared on request. It's essential to call before arriving, as the owners are often not here.

Getting There and Around

Many people visit the park on tours from Arica or Putre. Parque Nacional Lauca is easily navigable using your own vehicle, as the entirety of Ruta 11 is paved. Use caution, and

---

1: Parque Nacional Lauca 2: Reserva Nacional Las Vicuñas

a high-clearance vehicle, or in some cases a 4WD, for any routes off the main highway.

Get a map of the region from **SERNATUR** (Calle San Marcos 101, tel. 58/2252 054, info@sernatur.cl, 9am-6pm Mon.-Fri., 10am-4pm Sat.) in Arica. A more detailed and more accurate map is the updated *Road & Nature Map* sold at **Terrace Lodge** (Circunvalación 25, tel. 58/2230 499, www.terracelodge.com) in Putre.

★ RESERVA NACIONAL LAS VICUÑAS

Reserva Nacional Las Vicuñas (tel. 58/2585 704 or 58/2201 201, 24 hr daily, free) is even wilder and more surreal than its neighbor. It's a vast wilderness of high-altitude steppe cut through by gushing glacier meltwater streams and surrounded by 6,000-meter-high volcanos. At its southernmost point, it culminates in the blinding salt flats of Monumento Natural Salar de Surire.

It's less accessible than Parque Nacional Lauca but far more rewarding. Not only are you likely to see fewer travelers, you'll likely be treated to a glimpse of the reserve's most delicate residents: guanacos, vicuñas, *ñandús* (the greater rhea), and three types of flamingo. Day trips here, best done through a tour agency in Putre or as part of a multiple-day excursion from Arica, focus on exploring the reserve by vehicle, stopping at a range of overlooks, wetlands, and the Monumento Natural Salar de Surire to observe the native wildlife.

From the right turn signed for "Guallatire" after Las Cuevas in Parque Nacional Lauca on Ruta 11, which is 20km from Putre, the paved road becomes the A-211. In 17km south this turns into the A-235, a dirt track and the main route through the vast, treeless reserve. It heads southwest from Ruta 11, reaching the reserve after 85km at Guallatire, continuing beyond this village south to the salt pans of the Monumento Natural Salar de Surire.

A 4WD vehicle isn't essential, but it's recommended, and a vehicle with high clearance is a must. January-March should be avoided, as roads get washed out by rain, and lightning storms can be dangerous for those in vehicles. Due to the lack of phone communications and the isolated roads, taking a tour instead of going independently is strongly advised.

Sights

Guallatire, at the foot of its namesake volcano, is a 50-house town inhabited by two permanent residents. It is roughly halfway between Ruta 11 and the Monumento Natural Salar de Surire and takes 1.5 hours to reach from the turnoff from Ruta 11, which is 50 meters after Las Cuevas in Parque Nacional Lauca. Guallatire's white church was painted using borax from the nearby mines and is only open for the San Juan celebrations on June 24. If driving, you must stop at the Carabineros (national police) checkpoint here (24 hr daily) to register your vehicle to enter the park.

Nearly 130km southeast of Putre and 2km west of the border with Bolivia, the vast, blinding-white **Monumento Natural Salar de Surire** is at 4,245 meters elevation, a mass of sheer salt flats that contrast with the dusky blue saline pools. The salt flats are an important breeding ground for all three types of Andes-dwelling flamingos: Andean, James's, and Chilean. Up to 10,000 of the birds can be spotted feeding in the shallows at any given time. As you arrive to the salt flats from the north, the one-lane A-253 takes a 60-km loop around the entire protected area. Along this road are a number of viewpoints at which to park and watch the flamingos from a distance (don't get too close).

It's hard not to notice the trucks and the road through the center of the flats. In 1989, just before the end of the dictatorship, 4,560 hectares of land were opened to borax mining on the northwest side. Despite ruining some of the sublime beauty of the location and disturbing the nesting flamingos, the presence of the mine keeps the roads accessible and well maintained.

At the southern edge of the salt flats, the **Termas de Polloquere** (24 hr daily, free) are possibly the most magical hot springs you'll find in Chile, thanks to their complete desolation and stark views across the salt flats. The water is a searing 66°C where it emerges above ground, but becomes more palatable for swimmers where it forms a river to larger bodies of water. Backcountry camping here means you can enjoy a sublime sunrise over the snowcapped Andes, although the extreme altitude can make for a sleepless night if you're not properly acclimatized. No permits are required to camp here; bring water, as there are no potable sources.

Practicalities

A mobile phone tower next to the village of Guallatire, 60km north of the salt flats, provides coverage in the immediate vicinity.

A **police station,** which can assist in an emergency, is in Guallatire, as is a small **CONAF ranger station** that allows camping on its property; the station is seldom occupied by rangers, so it's necessary to book ahead via the CONAF office in Putre (Teniente del Campo 301, 3 blocks west of the plaza, Putre, tel. 58/2585 704, luis.araya@conaf.cl) to ensure that you will be allowed to stay here.

The small **Albergue Familia Sanchez**

(tel. 9/4248 3436 or 58/2242 452) mainly caters to hungry miners but offers beds and food on request. It is closed during the wet season, January-March.

Getting There and Around

To reach the reserve from Putre, join Ruta 11 heading east and drive to the signposted turn south for Guallatire, 20km later. At Guallatire, the main road through the reserve, the dirt A-211, which turns into the A-235 after 17km, begins. The official entrance of the national park is 15km beyond where the road becomes the A-235. It's a 2.5-hour drive to this point. From the ranger station on the shores of Lago Chungará in Parque Nacional Lauca, it's a 45-minute, 30-km drive to the turnoff for the A-211, a 2-hour drive in total.

Although this dirt track is well maintained, the maze of other tracks makes the route to the salt flats difficult to navigate unless you're visiting with a local tour guide or with GPS. The maps sold at **Terrace Lodge** (Circunvalación 25, tel. 58/2230 499, www. terracelodge.com) in Putre indicate the current state of all of the roads in the reserve and will help you stick to those in better condition.

Norte Chico

The glorious white-sand beaches and pristine

coves that dot the coast of the Norte Chico never fail to enrapture visitors. But this region is far more than inviting coastlines and year-round sunshine. Majestic La Serena is the gem in the Norte Chico's crown. Nearby, the town of Andacollo fills with revelers in December for one of the country's largest religious celebrations, showcasing traditional dances.

Another side of Chile can be found in the Valle de Elqui, home to Latin America's first Nobel Prize-winning poet, Gabriela Mistral, and where the national spirit, pisco, is produced. The region's cloudless night skies are ideal for stargazing.

Unparalleled whale-watching opportunities are at the fishing village Chañaral de Aceituno. Nearby and accessible by boat, the Reserva Nacional Pingüino de Humboldt provides sanctuary for 80 percent of the world's Humboldt penguins.

Highlights

Look for ★ to find recommended sights, activities, dining, and lodging.

★ **See Penguins at Reserva Nacional Pingüino de Humboldt:** Jump on a boat to observe 25,000 waddling Humboldt penguins (page 214).

★ **Whale-Watching at Chañaral de Aceituno:** Half a dozen species, including blue and fin whales and orcas, are present November-April (page 216).

★ **Museo Gabriela Mistral:** This museum is filled with correspondence and books once belonging to Latin America's first Nobel Prize-winning poet (page 218).

★ **Pisco-Tasting in the Valle de Elqui:** Sample the nation's favorite tipple, pisco, at boutique distilleries (page 226).

★ **Parque Nacional Llanos de Challe:** Be dazzled by the spectacular colors of the rare flowering desert that occurs every 5-7 years in this remote national park (page 240).

★ **Parque Paleontológico Los Dedos:** At this open-air museum, 16-million-year-old shark teeth protrude from the earth, giving important clues about the region's underwater origins (page 253).

★ **Parque Nacional Pan de Azúcar:** Hiking trails run among cacti and scattered wildflowers in this national park, also home to a small colony of Humboldt penguins (page 253).

Norte Chico

NORTE CHICO

Isla
Chañaral

**SEE PENGUINS
AT RESERVA
NACIONAL
PINGÜINO DE
HUMBOLDT**

Isla Damas

Isla
Charos

Taltal

Cifuncho

To
Antofagasta

**REGION II
(ANTOFAGASTA)**

**PARQUE NACIONAL
PAN DE AZÚCAR**

Chañaral

Diego de
Almagro

El Salvador

Salar de
Pedernales

Río Salado

**SANTUARIO DE
LA NATURALEZA
GRANITO ORBICULAR**

**REGION III
(ATACAMA)**

5

Potrerillos

31

Caldera

Bahía Inglesa

**PARQUE
PALEONTOLÓGICO
LOS DEDOS**

Puerto Viejo

**MIÑA
SAN JOSÉ**

Parque Nacional
Nevado Tres Cruces

Paso de San
Francisco
4,726m

COPIAPÓ

Tierra
Amarilla

**PN
Nevado
Tres
Cruces**

Cerro Tres
Cruces
6,749m

Cerro Ojos
del Salado
6,887m

RN
60

Río Copiapó

Laguna del
Negro Francisco

To
Catamarca
and La Rioja

Carrizal Bajo

**PARQUE NACIONAL
LLANOS DE CHALLE**

Huasco

Río Huasco

Freirina

Vallenar

Alto del
Carmen

Villa San
José de Vinchina

**WHALE-WATCHING AT
CHAÑARAL DE ACEITUNO**

**SEE
DETAIL**

ARGENTINA

**SEE PENGUINS AT RESERVA
NACIONAL PINGÜINO DE HUMBOLDT**

San
Félix

Villa Unión

Caleta de Choros

**OBSERVATORIO
LA SILLA**

RN
40

Caleta Los
Hornos

**MUSEO
GABRIELA
MISTRAL**

de los Andes

LA SERENA

Río Elqui

**SEE
"VALLE DE ELQUI"
MAP**

Coquimbo

41

Vicuña

JUNTAS DEL TORO

Río Bermejo

Guanaqueros

Tongoy

Andacollo

Pisco Elqui

**PISCO-TASTING IN THE
VALLE DE ELQUI**

Paso del
Agua Negra
4,765m

Pismanta

Rodeo

43

**Monumento
Natural Pichasca**

RN
150

Los
Flores

San José
de Jáchal

**Parque Nacional
Bosque de Fray Jorge**

R. Limarí

Ovalle

**VIÑA
TABALI**

**Monumento
Arqueológico
Valle del Encanto**

**REGION IV
(COQUIMBO)**

Cordillera

Río Jáchal

5

Combarbalá

RP 436

RN
40

Río Choapa

Illapel

Salamanca

Calingasta

Río

RP 12

Río San Juan

SAN JUAN

Los Vilos

RP 412

Pichidangui

RP 39

0   60 mi

0   60 km

La Ligua

To
Santiago

**REGION V
(VALPARAÍSO)**

To
Mendoza

© MOON.COM

P A C I F I C   O C E A N

Despite the fierce aridity of the Atacama Desert, this region is rich in national parks. Parque Nacional Pan de Azúcar has remote beaches and wildlife. Visit Parque Nacional Llanos de Challe during a rare period of rainfall and you'll find one of Chile's strangest sights: the *desierto florido* (flowering desert), when the otherwise barren earth blooms with wildflowers in a thousand hues.

HISTORY

Headed by Diego de Almagro, 500 Spanish soldiers first set foot in Chile in the Copiapó Valley; they had crossed the Andes at 4,726-meter Paso de San Francisco into the desert. They were received by the Diaguita people, part of the Inca Empire and who stemmed from Las Ánimas (AD 800-1000) and earlier El Molle (AD 300-800). These indigenous groups cultivated crops in the fertile river valleys of the lowlands and the precordillera. Many were enslaved by the Spanish, who continued south. The Spanish failed to find any gold and returned to Peru.

The area was colonized on the second Spanish mission into Chile. La Serena became Chile's second city in 1544, three years after Santiago was founded. A long battle began between the invaders and the local groups, who ransacked the new city within four years; it was later left in ruins by pirates from Europe.

The discovery of silver in 1832, close to modern-day Vallenar, and copper deposits defined the region's fortunes. This led to accelerated development of new cities in the Andes foothills and along the coast. Mining remains the main industry today, along with exotic fruits and pisco production.

In August 2010, the region made international headlines when 33 miners became trapped underground at the Mina San José. After 69 days, all of the men were rescued. In the last decade, the region faced extensive flash floods caused by uncommonly heavy El Niño rainfall, which wiped out huge sections of towns and cities. In 2015, a cataclysmic tsunami, triggered by a magnitude 8.4 earthquake off the coast of Tongoy, destroyed beaches, homes, and businesses and left the tourism industry devastated.

PLANNING YOUR TIME

To visit the Norte Chico, **2-3 days** is sufficient for the main sites; basing yourself in La Serena or Valle de Elqui is most practical. With a full **week,** a vehicle or some long bus rides can take you north of La Serena and up to the white-sand coastline of Bahía Inglesa, with a stop at the penguin colony of Punta Choros en route.

Most visitors arrive at **La Serena,** the region's most attractive city and a good base for exploring. La Serena merits **1-2 days** for its **colonial churches** and golden-sand beaches. Heading north, the **Reserva Nacional Pingüino de Humboldt,** accessed from tiny Punta Choros, is a **day trip** from La Serena. Staying overnight and arriving in your own vehicle, **Chañaral de Aceituno** is an unmissable spot on the migration route for several whale species. Afterward, it's possible to stay overnight in Vallenar.

A **two-day** trip into **Valle de Elqui** on excellent public transport or with a rental car allows visits to historic **pisco distilleries,** the region's first solar-powered brewery, and an observatory. **Two days** is adequate for the sun, sea, and atmosphere on the gorgeous white-sand beaches of **Bahía Inglesa.** The coastal town of **Caldera** makes the best base in this area.

Both hard-to-reach **Parque Nacional Llanos de Challe,** in Valle de Huasco, and **Parque Nacional Pan de Azúcar,** north of Caldera, offer spectacular coastal scenery and can be appreciated as a **day trip** or an overnight **camping** trip. In Pan de Azúcar it's possible to stay in a cabin, but you'll need your own transport or local taxis.

NORTE CHICO

Previous: Playa Blanca in Parque Nacional Llanos de Challe; Andacollo's Templo Antiguo; humpback whale.

Two Days in the Norte Chico

DAY 1

Start with a morning exploring the colonial heart of **La Serena,** stopping at the **Museo Arqueológico** to learn about the region's last pre-Hispanic inhabitants, the Diaguita people. Hop in a taxi over to admire the **Faro Monumental de La Serena,** the city's landmark lighthouse, and take a walk along the coast, finishing in **Picá Mar Adentro** for fresh seafood.
    Catch a bus to **Pisco Elqui** for an afternoon exploring the **pisco distilleries.** Return to **Vicuña** and **Museo Gabriela Mistral** to learn about the 20th-century poet. Join an **observatory tour** at El Pangue, south of the town, to learn about the night sky from professional astronomers. Return to La Serena and stay overnight at the modern **Terra Diaguita,** with design influences from the region's indigenous peoples.

DAY 2

Hop on the public bus to Punta Choros and board a speedboat to circle the offshore islands of **Reserva Nacional Pingüino de Humboldt,** home to the Humboldt penguin. Keep your eyes peeled for bottlenose dolphins playfully following the boat. If driving, continue north into the Atacama Region for an afternoon of whale-watching at **Chañaral de Aceituno,** where blue and fin whales and orcas are common. Return to La Serena.

La Serena

The second-oldest city in the country, La Serena is a thriving and attractive colonial city that doubles as a summer beach resort thanks to its kilometers of golden sand. It's calmer in winter, but the weather is still warm. The city's many churches, cathedrals, and convents date to the 17th century; its archaeological museum is a window into older cultures.

In 1946, President Gabriel González Videla remodeled the city, introducing neocolonial architecture and establishing La Serena as competitive with Santiago. It remains one of the prettiest cities in the country.

SIGHTS

The historic center of La Serena, bounded by Almagro, Vicuña, Aguirre, and Pablo Muñoz, overflows with historic buildings and some of Chile's oldest streets. It is well worth walking. The streets surrounding the main **Plaza de Armas** (bounded by Prat, Los Carrera, Cordovez, and Matta) contain most of the 19th- and 20th-century structures. The plaza is studded with high Chilean palms,

jacarandas, laurels, and cedars. In the center, the **Pileta Plaza de Armas** is a striking stone fountain carved with four stylized women to represent the seasons. It was created in 1948-1952 by Chilean sculptor Samuel Román Rojas as part of the Plan Serena.

Iglesia Catedral

On the east side of the Plaza de Armas, the neoclassical **Iglesia Catedral** (Los Carrera s/n, open for mass) was built in 1844 by French architect Juan Herbage on the site of the city's original 1559 church. The limestone construction contains a lavish marble altar. It's also home to the **Museo Sala de Arte Religiosa** (Los Carrera 450, tel. 51/2218 543, ext. 226, 9:30am-1pm and 3pm-6pm Mon.-Sat., 9:30am-1pm Sun., free), with 18 ecclesiastical paintings from the 16th and 17th centuries.

Iglesia San Francisco

A block southeast of the Plaza de Armas, **Iglesia San Francisco** (Av. Balmaceda 640,

La Serena

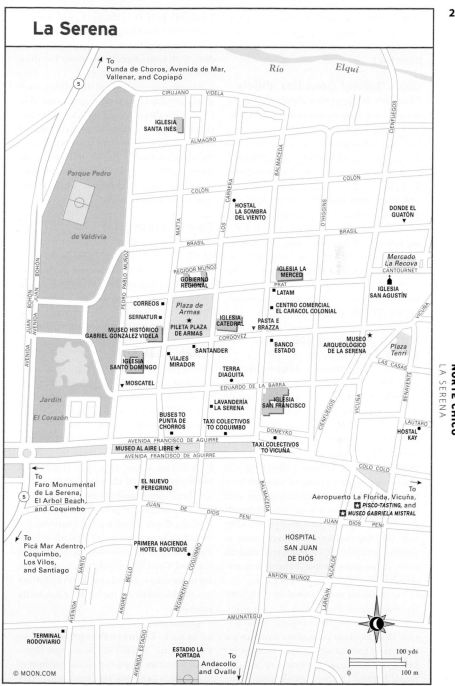

To
Punda de Choros, Avenida de Mar,
Vallenar, and Copiapó

Río   Elqui

CIRUJANO VIDELA

IGLESIA
SANTA INÉS

ALMAGRO

Parque Pedro

COLÓN   CARRERA   COLÓN

MATTA   LOS   HOSTAL
LA SOMBRA
DEL VIENTO   O'HIGGINS   DONDE EL
GUATÓN

de Valdivia   BRASIL   BRASIL

Mercado
La Recova
CANTOURNET

REGIDOR MUÑOZ   IGLESIA LA
MERCED

GOBIERNO
REGIONAL   PRAT   IGLESIA
SAN AGUSTÍN

CORREOS   LATAM

SERNATUR   Plaza de
Armas   CENTRO COMERCIAL
EL CARACOL COLONIAL   VICUÑA

MUSEO HISTÓRICO
GABRIEL GONZÁLEZ VIDELA   PILETA PLAZA
DE ARMAS   IGLESIA
CATEDRAL   PASTA E
BRAZZA   Plaza
Tenri

CORDOVEZ

IGLESIA
SANTO DOMINGO   SANTANDER   BANCO
ESTADO   MUSEO
ARQUEOLÓGICO
DE LA SERENA   LAS CASAS

VIAJES
MIRADOR   BENAVENTE

MOSCATEL   TERRA
DIAGUITA

EDUARDO DE LA BARRA

Jardín   LAVANDERÍA
LA SERENA   IGLESIA
SAN FRANCISCO   LAUTARO

El Corazón   BUSES TO
PUNTA DE
CHORROS   TAXI COLECTIVOS
TO COQUIMBO   HOSTAL
KAY

DOMEYKO   VICUÑA   CIENFUEGOS

AVENIDA FRANCISCO DE AGUIRRE   TAXI COLECTIVOS
TO VICUÑA

MUSEO AL AIRE LIBRE ★   COLO COLO

AVENIDA FRANCISCO DE AGUIRRE

To
Faro Monumental
de La Serena,
El Arbol Beach,
and Coquimbo   EL NUEVO
PEREGRINO   To
Aeropuerto La Florida, Vicuña,
PISCO-TASTING, and
MUSEO GABRIELA MISTRAL

JUAN   DE   DIOS   PENI   BALMACEDA

To
Picá Mar Adentro,
Coquimbo,
Los Vilos,
and Santiago   JUAN   DIOS   PENI

PRIMERA HACIENDA
HOTEL BOUTIQUE   HOSPITAL
SAN JUAN
DE DIÓS

ANFIÓN MUÑOZ

AMUNÁTEGUI

TERMINAL
RODOVIARIO

ESTADIO LA
PORTADA   To
Andacollo
and Ovalle

0   100 yds

0   100 m

© MOON.COM

open for mass) is the oldest stone church in the city. Construction began in 1563 but only finished in 1627. Its limestone walls are a meter thick.

Casa Gabriel González Videla

Casa Gabriel González Videla was the La Serena home of the former president of Chile. He granted women the right to vote in 1949 and was the first president in the world to visit Antarctica to claim territory. Today, his two-story home is the **Museo Histórico Gabriel González Videla** (Matta 495, tel. 51/2206 797, 10am-6pm Mon.-Fri., 10am-1pm Sat. and public holidays, free), a regional history museum with personal objects once belonging to the president, including the thermal suit he used on his voyage to Antarctica, plus a display about Plan Serena. An art exhibit contains a permanent collection of works by 18th- to 20th-century Chilean artists, including Juan Francisco González.

Museo Arqueológico de La Serena

The excellent **Museo Arqueológico de La Serena** (Cordova and Cienfuegos s/n, tel. 52/2672 210, http://museoarqueologicolaserena.cl, 9:30am-5:50pm Tues.-Fri., noon-5pm Sat., 11am-2pm Sun., free) specializes in the Diaguita culture. The Diaguita people inhabited the Elqui, Huasco, and Copiapó valleys from AD 1000 and were incorporated into the Inca Empire. Their final recorded interaction with the Spanish conquest was in 1548. Although they were thought to have disappeared after 1570, the Diaguita were finally recognized as an ethnic group by the Chilean government in 2006. Today, many people in the valleys surrounding the city identify as Diaguita.

The museum was founded in 1943, with the majority of displays on the Diaguita, with excellent English-language information. Designs in the collection's ceramics are thought to have come from the artisans inhaling hallucinogenic substances during shamanic rituals. The most emblematic of the Diaguita's pottery is the *jarro pato,* a duck-shaped pitcher with a globular body and head. The influence of the Inca on the pottery is evident, with later Diaguita ceramics blending human and animal forms.

The most famous item in the collection is a *moai* from Rapa Nui, taken from the island in 1951. It was allegedly a gift to La Serena to celebrate Roberto Parragué Singer's completion of the first-ever flight from South America to the island. Before its display in the museum, the monolith traveled to Italy and other parts of Europe for an exhibition, where it was cracked in transportation.

Faro Monumental de La Serena

At the northern end of Avenida del Mar, where it joins Avenida Francisco de Aguirre, is the 1951 lighthouse **Faro Monumental de La Serena** (not open to visitors). Known as **El Faro** to locals, its white tower and red turrets help make it the city's emblematic landmark.

NIGHTLIFE

During summer, **beach bars** spring up along the coast, disappearing again at the end of the season. Most in the downtown area are around O'Higgins and La Barra. The clientele is generally a lively student crowd.

Moscatel (Muñoz 580, tel. 51/2219 843, www.moscatel.cl, 9:30am-11pm Mon.-Wed., 9:30am-1am Thurs.-Fri., 7pm-2am Sat.), a block southwest of the plaza, can't decide whether it's an elegant café or a bar. You can't beat its selection of pisco, with 60 options from the Elqui, Huasco, and Limarí Valleys, including many you won't find elsewhere. They offer a guided pisco tasting (reservation required, CH$12,000) with three types. There are interesting regional craft beers and wines too. Sit downstairs at the bar for a less stuffy experience.

Candlelit and with portraits of musicians on its walls, **El Nuevo Peregrino** (Andrés Bello 886, tel. 51/2483 519, 9am-11pm Mon.-Wed., 9am-3am Thurs.-Sat.) is the epicenter of live music in La Serena. Jazz, blues, and poetry are usually held Thursday-Saturday. Dance along or just spectate with a pisco sour.

SHOPPING

On Sunday, locals looking for a bargain make their way to Calle Cirujano, where an informal **flea market** occupies the full length of the street.

Mercado La Recova

La Serena's central market is **Mercado La Recova** (bounded by Cienfuegos, Peatonal La Recova, Rengifo, and Cantournet, 9am-8pm Mon.-Sat., 9am-3pm Sun.), which covers an entire city block. The main entrance on Cienfuegos leads into two courtyards piled with local handicrafts. You'll find stalls stacked with ornaments carved from local *combarbalita* stone and studded with lapis lazuli. Diaguita-style pottery is on sale, along with jam, juice, and pastries.

RECREATION

Beaches

A 6-km strip of 12 beaches connects La Serena with the city of Coquimbo around the amphitheater-shaped Bahía Coquimbo. These beaches are connected by Avenida del Mar along the coast from El Faro south to where it becomes Avenida Costanera. A promenade and a cycle path make this an ideal spot for a stroll, particularly at sunset. The beaches are known to locals by their individual names, but there's practically nothing to distinguish them from each other.

Swarming with sunbathers and picnicking families during summer, La Serena's beaches are a hot spot for holidaying Argentineans. The coastal mist doesn't burn off until midday, and you'll have the beach to yourself if you visit in the morning. These golden sands are relatively empty outside summer. Public restrooms are few and often closed outside December-March.

The water is not safe for swimming due to fierce rip currents. Surfing is only recommended on the stretch known as **Playa Los Fuertes** (from Av. del Mar and Amunátegui Poniente to Av. del Mar and Los Nísperos), where surf schools are located.

Surfing

Surfing is best in winter, when waves can reach six meters along **Playa Los Fuertes** (from Av. del Mar and Amunátegui Poniente to Av. del Mar and Los Nísperos). In late summer, wave heights of 2.5 meters are more common. Experienced surfers head out to the right-hand break at **Punta de Teatinos,** 7km north of La Serena. **Totoralillo,** 17km south of Coquimbo, has four of the finest waves in the region for advanced surfers March-June.

On Playa Los Fuertes, adjoining Cafetería Poisson, **Escuela Surf Poisson** (Av. del Mar 1001, tel. 9/6848 7854, 10am-9pm daily, shorter hours Apr.-Sept.) is a surf school that offers one-hour classes (CH$20,000 pp), as well as boards and wetsuits to rent (CH$7,000/hr). Instructors speak English.

Guided Tours

The tour companies **Central Tour** (Av. Cuatro Esquinas 560, tel. 9/3094 4304, http://centraltour.cl) and **Viajes Mirador** (Matta 518, office 10, tel. 51/2218 554, http://viajesmirador.com) can organize trips to Valle de Elqui (from CH$35,000), southern beaches and Parque Nacional Bosque Fray Jorge (from CH$45,000), Valle del Encanto (from CH$90,000), or Reserva Nacional Pingüino de Humboldt (from CH$52,000). Both companies employ English-speaking guides. Highly recommended **AlfaTour** (Los Geranios 140, Coquimbo, tel. 9/3198 3483, www.alfatour.cl) is based in Coquimbo but offers hotel pickup from La Serena.

FOOD

For fresh seafood and fine dining at significantly higher prices than elsewhere in the city, **Avenida del Mar** is the place. Restaurants in the downtown area around the Plaza de Armas (3km east of Av. del Mar) are lacking in flair. It can be hard to find restaurants open in the evening, and only a handful serve on Sunday night.

The roads lining **Mercado La Recova** (bounded by Cienfuegos, Peatonal La Recova, Rengifo, and Cantournet) are packed with tiny snack restaurants serving empanadas and *churrascos*. On the 1st floor of the market, accessed from Peatonal La Recova, slightly larger restaurants sell cheap and filling Chilean stews, soups, and fish.

Despite its name, which means "fish" in French, there's no fish on the menu at **Cafetería Poisson** (Av. del Mar 1001, no phone, 10am-9:30pm daily, CH$2,500-7,000). They do have deep-fried shrimp and scallop empanadas with cheese (CH$2,500 each). There's nowhere better for a coffee or a cold juice on a sunny day than this beachside shack slung with surfboards; it's practically on the waves.

On the coast road and almost in Coquimbo, in a building damaged by the 2015 tsunami, ★ **Picá Mar Adentro** (Rengo 4629, Población Los Pescadores Peñuelas, tel. 51/2240 121, 12:30pm-11:30pm daily, CH$7,500-16,000) has been restored with a rustic *picada* dining area. The seafood selection is wider than most in this strip. Opt for the delicately cooked corvina or *reiñeta* (southern ray bream) or the cheesy prawn, scallops, and razor clam stew. Portions are huge, and servers can help with the extensive menu.

Decorative gourds line the walls and waiters wear black *huasco* hats and checkered shirts, but **Donde El Guaton** (Brasil 750, tel. 51/2211 510, 12:30pm-midnight Mon.-Sat., 12:30pm-10:30pm Sun., CH$6,000-12,000) is authentic. They specialize in meat cooked in front of you over a barbecue in the dining room. (Ask for your steak slightly less cooked than your usual preference, as they tend to overcook it.) Plenty of other traditional Chilean dishes are available.

Just off the Plaza de Armas, **Pasta e Brazza** (Gregorio Cordovez 444, tel. 51/2664 181, 8am-10pm Mon.-Tues., 8am-midnight Wed.-Sat., CH$6,000-10,000) serves excellent pisco sours along with classic Italian pastas and pizzas, all of which can be consumed in the lovely palm-fringed terrace or stylish slate-floored main dining room. Friday is karaoke night and happy hour.

ACCOMMODATIONS

Lodging rates in La Serena rise significantly January-February, and you'll need to make reservations a few months in advance to secure a room at the better places. Outside these months, prices are around 10 percent lower.

The hugely popular ★ **El Arbol Beach** (Los Nísperos, Parcela 34, Sitio 10, tel. 51/2227 824, www.hostalelarbol.cl, CH$11,000 dorm, CH$38,000 d shared bath, CH$42,000 d private bath, CH$38,000 cabin, cash only) draws a mixed crowd of Chilean families and foreign backpackers to its slick modern bedrooms and fun, welcoming atmosphere. A hammock-adorned garden is surrounded by 8- and 10-bed dorms, private doubles, and a kitchen-equipped cabin. All have access to a spacious kitchen and common area where substantial breakfast is served. The location is excellent, just a 10-minute walk from the beach and 20 minutes to the bus terminal. Book a month in advance in summer. Rates include IVA.

The French-owned ★ **Hostal La Sombra del Viento** (Los Carrera 224, tel. 51/2484 775, http://lasombradelviento.cl, CH$38,000 d, cash only) is a tasteful and minimalist converted colonial mansion with seven bedrooms around a welcoming hammock-slung courtyard. Large patio doors ensure rooms are light and airy, while modern baths are an added bonus. Owner Marielaure is a delight and speaks excellent English. There's no parking available. Rates include IVA.

A home-away-from-home two blocks south of the archaeology museum, the excellent ★ **Hostal Kay** (Calle Laurtaro 835, tel. 9/5731 0440, hostalkay@gmail.com, CH$40,000 d shared bath, CH$45,000 d private bath) has new beds and furnishings. Rooms line a cozy glass-roofed corridor that leads out to a garden with a swimming pool. Owners Katerine and Robert are exceptionally friendly and helpful. Ask for a room at the garden end of the corridor to avoid the noise of the doorbell at night. It's overpriced during summer. Rates include IVA.

On the grounds of an 1840s house, ★ **Terra Diaguita** (La Barra 440, tel. 51/2216 608, www.terradiaguita.cl, CH$37,000 d shared bath, CH$45,000 d private bath) combines modern fixtures and fittings with authentic local style. Most rooms are in the extension of the original house. Sizeable rooms offer superb value; the new wing across the road has larger, more modern, and slightly more expensive rooms. The welcoming staff, along with the spa and massage facilities, set this hotel apart. Rates include IVA.

A favorite among foreign dignitaries, the classy **Primera Hacienda Hotel Boutique** (Coquimbo 979, tel. 51/2488 932, http:// primerahacienda.cl, CH$105,000 d) is in a fully restored and extended 1700s colonial building. Rooms in the oldest part are largest, decorated with antique floor tiles and rocking horses, although work is underway to extend all rooms. A cozy lounge and breakfast area gives way to a sunny cactus-studded courtyard and swimming pool, with a guests-only restaurant in the garden.

INFORMATION AND SERVICES

On the west side of the Plaza de Armas, helpful **SERNATUR** (Matta 461, tel. 51/2225 138, 9am-8pm Mon.-Fri., 10am-6pm Sat.-Sun. summer, 9am-6pm Mon.-Fri., 10am-2pm Sat. fall-spring) has maps and information about the region. There is a small **tourist information booth** on the plaza in front of Iglesia La Merced that's only open in summer.

The **Hospital San Juan de Dios** (Av. Balmaceda 916, tel. 51/2333 424, www. hospitalserena.cl) can deal with medical emergencies. To withdraw money, **Santander** (Cordovez 351) and **Banco Estado** (Av. Balmaceda 506) have 24-hour ATMs. To change money, the **Centro Comercial El Caracol Colonial** (Av. Balmaceda 460, shop hours vary) has several currency exchange shops offering good rates.

Wash your clothes at **Lavandería La**

Serena (Los Carrera 652, tel. 9/4678 0304, 9am-6pm Mon.-Fri.). There are mail services at **Correos** (Matta 401, 9am-2pm and 3pm-6pm Mon.-Fri., 10:30am-1pm Sat.).

GETTING THERE

La Serena has some of the most regular transportation links in the Norte Chico.

Air

Eight daily flights connect Santiago with **Aeródromo La Florida** (LSC, Camino a Vicuña s/n, tel. 51/2270 353, http:// aeropuertodelaserena.cl), just east of La Serena. Flights are operated by **LATAM** (Balmaceda 406, tel. 600/5262 000, www. latam.com, 9am-1:45pm and 3:20pm-6pm Mon.-Fri., 10:30am-1:15pm Sat.), **Sky Airline** (www.skyairline.com), and **JetSmart** (http:// jetsmart.com). JetSmart also operates three flights a week from Iquique, Antofagasta, and Calama, as well as two flights weekly from Concepción. There are also three flights a week from both Mendoza and Córdoba, Argentina, to La Serena.

AIRPORT TRANSFERS

Sol del Valle (Av. Cuatro Esquinas 55, tel. 51/2484 848, www.taxisoldelvalle.cl) is the official airport transfer service, charging CH$3,000 pp for a shared transfer to your hotel or CH$7,000 for a private taxi. You can usually walk up and get a ride once you land. A cheaper method is *taxi colectivo* number 71 (CH$700), which passes outside the airport on its way into the center of La Serena. This option is not recommended if you have a lot of luggage.

Bus

Regional and long-distance buses pull into La Serena's **Terminal Rodoviario** (Amunátegui 107, tel. 51/2224 573). **Tur Bus** (tel. 51/2213 060, http://turbus.cl), **Pullman Bus** (tel. 51/2218 251, www.pullmanbus.com), and **Pluss Chile** (tel. 51/2674 286, http:// plusschile.cl) run buses every 10 minutes to La Serena from **Santiago** (Terminal San

Borja, 6hr, CH$10,000/CH$15,000). Tur Bus and Pluss Chile offer *cama* (reclining) seats (CH$20,000) on this route.

These companies plus **Buses Expreso Norte** (tel. 51/2546 886, www.expresonorte. cl) have regular connections from the north. There are hourly arrivals from **Copiapó** (4hr, CH$9,000/CH$12,000) and **Antofagasta** (10.5hr, CH$20,000/CH$30,000, *cama* CH$40,000). There are also six daily routes from **Calama** (14hr, CH$25,000/CH$35,000) and four daily from **Arica** (23hr, CH$35,000/ CH$40,000).

Car

To get to La Serena, it's a 472-km, six-hour drive from Santiago north along Ruta 5, a reasonably picturesque journey that mostly follows the coast. Be aware that, as the old saying goes, *"Entre Los Vilos y Tongoy, no hay nada."* (Between Los Vilos and Tongoy, there's nothing.) Be sure to fuel up before passing Los Vilos, as there are few options farther north.

GETTING AROUND

Central La Serena is compact enough to be walkable, but few transportation options reach the beach. Your best bet is any **Coquimbo-bound** *micro* (CH$500) along Ruta 5. Get off where you want and walk the 500 meters west to Avenida del Mar. From the center of La Serena, a taxi to the beach shouldn't cost more than CH$2,000.

To reach Coquimbo, take one of the *taxis colectivos* (24 hr daily, 15min, CH$1,000) that leave when they're full from the northern side of Avenida Aguirre, between Avenida Balmaceda and Los Carrera.

Rental Car

You won't need a car to get around La Serena, but it's a good idea to have one if you want to explore surrounding areas, like Valle de Elqui. The following rental companies are in the arrivals hall of La Serena's airport: **Econorent** (tel. 51/2270 882, http://econorent.com, 11am-9pm daily), **Salfarent** (tel. 9/5382 3302, www. salfarent.cl, 11am-9pm daily), **Europcar** (tel.

51/2568 275, www.europcar.com, 11am-9pm daily), and **Hertz** (tel. 51/2560 432, www. hertz.com, 11am-9pm daily).

The following companies have offices in downtown La Serena: **Econorent** (Av. Francisco de Aguirre 141, tel. 51/2220 113, 8:30am-6:40pm Mon.-Fri., 9am-1pm Sat.), **Salfarent** (Huanhuali 191, tel. 9/7416 1911, 8:30am-8:30pm Mon.-Fri., 9am-1pm Sat.), **Europcar** (Av. Francisco de Aguirre 15, tel. 51/2568 280, 8:30am-1:30pm and 2:30pm-6:30pm Mon.-Fri., 9am-1pm Sat.), and **Hertz** (Av. Francisco de Aguirre 409, tel. 2/2360 5770, 8:30am-6:30pm Mon.-Fri.).

★ RESERVA NACIONAL PINGÜINO DE HUMBOLDT

From September through March, Isla de Choros teems with 25,000 waddling Humboldt penguins—around 80 percent of the global population. They are protected as part of the **Reserva Nacional Pingüino de Humboldt** (tel. 51/2244 769, www.conaf.cl, coquimbo.oirs@conaf.cl, 8:45am-2pm daily Dec.-Mar., 8:45am-2pm Wed.-Sun. Apr.-Nov., CH$6,000 adults, CH$3,000 children), which is composed of three main islands: 301-hectare Isla de Choros, 71-hectare Isla Damas, and 516-hectare Isla Chañaral.

Orientation

Punta de Choros is a tiny fishing village, 114km north of La Serena, flanked by low coastal hills. It is the main gateway to the reserve. Tours of the reserve leave from its two piers. The village is home to the reserve's CONAF-run **Centro de Información** (Muelle San Agustín, 8:45am-5:30pm daily). This visitors center has information about the reserve's vegetation and fauna. Tickets for the park are sold in the **CONAF headquarters** (8:45am-5:30pm daily) next door. Payment is cash only.

1: whale-watching at Chañaral de Aceituno
2: colorful building in La Serena **3:** Faro Monumental de La Serena **4:** Reserva Nacional Pingüino de Humboldt

Tours

The only way to visit the reserve is by boat tour. The three-hour tours cost CH$10,000 and leave from **Muelle Los Corrales,** Punta de Choros's southern harbor, and from **Muelle San Agustín,** a 10-minute walk north. The latter has more frequent tours, departing roughly every half hour, depending on weather.

Tours pass Isla Choros close enough to see the penguins and other marine wildlife before continuing to Isla Damas for an hourlong excursion on the island. Isla Damas is home to 49 species of plants, including the *añañuca amarilla,* a yellow wildflower; Peruvian lilies; and various cactus species. Three short **trails** dotted with information boards allow you to inspect the island's fragile semiarid desert ecosystem.

Visitors cannot land on Isla Choros, where the mating penguin colony is joined by **Peruvian diving petrels,** an endangered species; **blue-footed boobies;** and **Inca terns.** Barking **South American sea lions** and **marine otters** are occasionally visible in the water. Another star attraction is the **bottlenose dolphin;** the reserve hosts their southernmost colony. **Minke, blue, and fin whales** also pass through November-March.

December-March, visitors can land daily on Isla Damas; April-November, CONAF only permits landings Wednesday-Sunday. For all visits, boats must reach the island before 2pm. A maximum of 750 people are allowed daily onto the island. In the peak months of January-February, it's essential to buy tickets before 9:30am to secure a spot for a boat later that day.

Boats don't depart if conditions are too windy. You must first buy tickets for your tour before paying the park admission fee at the CONAF headquarters. Bring plenty of cash, as there are no ATMs.

Food and Accommodations

Both Punta de Choros's piers have excellent seafood empanadas as well as larger, more substantial fish meals. Most visitors come for the boat tour, though overnight accommodations do exist in the village. Lodging is basic and overpriced, but it's possible to negotiate prices outside January-February.

Getting There

The bus for Punta de Choros, aptly named **Punta de Choros** (tel. 9/8970 3499 or 9/9717 0122, www.puntachorotransporteyturismo. com, 2.25hr, CH$4,500), leaves from the Panaderia El Griegos (Francisco de Aguirre 314) at 9am and returns at 4pm daily. The bus driver will wait if the boat is late. There's another departure back to La Serena at 9am the following morning for overnight visitors.

Several agencies in La Serena offer tours to the island with an English-speaking guide, starting from CH$52,000 pp. These include **Central Tour** (Av. Cuatro Esquinas 560, tel. 9/3094 4304, http://centraltour.cl) and **Viajes Mirador** (Matta 518, office 10, tel. 51/2218 554, http://viajesmirador.com). **AlfaTour** (Los Geranios 140, Coquimbo, tel. 9/3198 3483, www.alfatour.cl) is based in Coquimbo but offers hotel pickup from La Serena.

By car it's a 1.5-hour, 117-km drive north of La Serena along Ruta 5 and the D-110 and D-116. In Punta de Choros, the roads are sandy and unpaved. Most traffic picks its way through the sand dunes at will.

★ Whale-Watching at Chañaral de Aceituno

The dusty village of **Chañaral de Aceituno** lies across from **Isla Chañaral,** the third and northernmost of the three islands that form the Reserva Nacional Pingüino de Humboldt. This island hosts a smaller colony of Humboldt penguins, South American sea lions, fur seals, and Peruvian diving petrels.

Boats from Chañaral de Aceituno can take you around the island (they are not permitted to land on it), but the most interesting sights are the whales, an exceptional number of which pass close to the shore. The water is deeper, so the chances of spotting **blue whales** are increased. **Fin, sei, humpback,** and **minke whales** and orcas are common too, making this stretch of water one of the best places in the country for whale-watching.

Whales are here from the end of November to mid-April, although the best time is mid-January-March. Tour companies claim a 90 percent likelihood of seeing a whale during these months. For whale and dolphin tours around Isla Chañaral, the highly recommended **Orca Turismos** (tel. 9/9640 4844, http://turismosorca.cl) is run by local expert and photographer Luis González, with 2.5-hour tours (CH$13,000) departing from the bay in Chañaral de Aceituno. They also offer lodging in the village.

There is no transportation directly from La Serena to Chañaral de Aceituno, in the Atacama Region. From **Vallenar** (3hr, CH$3,000), buses leave at 3pm Wednesday

from the corner of Catorce de Julio and San Ambrosio. A much easier way is driving yourself or taking a tour from La Serena with a company like the recommended **Whale Watching Chile** (tel. 9/6138 5166, http://whalewatchingchile.com) or Coquimbo-based **AlfaTour** (Los Geranios 140, Coquimbo, tel. 9/3198 3483, www.alfatour.cl), which offers pickup from La Serena.

It's a 2-hour, 140-km drive north from La Serena along Ruta 5 and the D-110 and D-116 to Punta de Choros. From here, take the road leading north of the village (C-536) until its end and turn left onto the C-500 along the coast to Chañaral de Aceituno.

Continuing north, a consolidated dirt track that's fine for regular vehicles continues northeast from the village, paved for 38km before joining Ruta 5.

Valle de Elqui

Lush groves of papaya and cherimoya are joined by fringes of pisco vines in the contours of the mountains as the road heads east from La Serena. The gushing Río Elqui provides water to cultivate the subtropical fruits. Enchanting Valle de Elqui is peerless in scenic beauty, particularly during the lush green summer. The striking umber of the landscape was described by poet Gabriela Mistral as "a heroic slash in the mass of mountains . . . this little place can be loved as perfection."

The valley is best known for its main crop, the muscat grape, used for distilling pisco. The first grape harvest was recorded in 1553. The valley also boasts clear night skies. While the *camanchaca* (coastal fog) often caps La Serena until noon, the valley is hot and dry year-round, making it ideal for stargazing.

Locals say this is a place known for mystical energy, and considered a hot spot for UFO activity. There are stories of Tibetan monks finding their way here on the hunt for the region's magnetic energy. Regardless of what you're in

search of, you'll be hard pressed not to find yourself seduced by the valley's charms.

VICUÑA

As Ruta 41 leaves La Serena, it climbs past fertile fields of fruit and rises to pass the shores of Embalse Puclaro, a reservoir specked with windsurfers on windy days. It hosts the National Kitesurfing Championships on January 12-13 each year.

Farther east by 15km is Vicuña, the largest town in the Valle de Elqui and a good base for nighttime observatory tours. Vicuña's most famous former resident is the Nobel Prize-winning poet Gabriela Mistral.

Vicuña is compact, with most facilities within a few streets. At the center, the leafy **Plaza Gabriela Mistral** (bounded by Mistral, Prat, Chacabuco, and San Martín) includes a striking sculpture of Gabriela Mistral's face, created by artist Samuel Román Rojas. Geometric patterns, replicating those used by the Diaguita culture, adorn concrete planters around the square.

Valle de Elqui

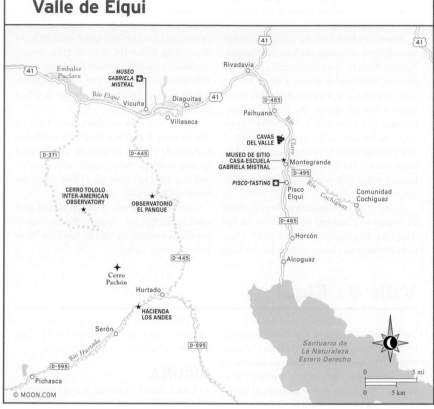

© MOON.COM

★ Museo Gabriela Mistral

Built on the site of the home that Mistral lived in with her family until age three, the **Museo Gabriela Mistral** (Gabriela Mistral 759, tel. 51/2411 223, www.mgmistral.gob.cl, 10am-7:45pm Tues.-Fri., 10:30am-6pm Sat., 10am-1pm Sun. Mar.-Dec., 10am-7pm Tues.-Fri., 10:30am-8pm Sat.-Sun. Jan.-Feb., free) gives a sense of a poet admired around the world. The museum contains thousands of books from her personal library as well as the simple plank of wood she used for writing. Mistral's humble origins and the poverty that shaped her early life are evidenced here. She once wrote, *"La mesa de escritorio nunca me servio de nada, ni en Chile ni en Paris, ni*

en Lisboa." (The writing desk is of no use to me, not in Chile, nor in Paris, nor in Lisbon.)

The museum is a collection of the author's few worldly possessions presented in glass-fronted cabinets. With few English translations, its real interest lies in something less tangible. Compared to time spent in the three houses that belonged to Chile's other Nobel Prize-winning poet, Pablo Neruda, the difference could not be starker. This museum will make you reflect on the legacy of a woman who is significantly less celebrated in Chile.

Pisco Distilleries

Capel (Camino a Peralillo s/n, tel. 51/2554 337, http://centroturisticocapel.cl, 10am-6pm daily), a cooperative of pisco producers dating to 1938, is Chile's largest pisco distillery. Now, Capel represents 1,000 local producers on 6,000 hectares of land, producing a third of all Chilean pisco. The **tour** (departs hourly, CH$4,000) of the distillery and factory includes a visit to the on-site Museo del Pisco Capel, with original distilling machinery. The tour ends in the *restobar,* where you can make a pisco cocktail for an additional CH$4,000. Most of the tours are in Spanish. Call ahead for English tour hours.

Stargazing Tours

With an average of 300 clear nights per year, the Valle de Elqui is one of the best places in the world for stargazing. September-May promises the clearest skies. Most nights are cloudy during June-July, but these months are when the Milky Way should be most visible in the night sky.

OBSERVATORIO EL PANGUE

Widely considered the best option for a thorough scientific experience, **Observatorio El Pangue** (http://observatoriodelpangue. blogspot.com) is 17km south of Vicuña, a 30-minute drive. It's led by a team of international astronomers and has a 71-centimeter telescope, the largest public telescope in Chile. At 1,478 meters elevation, the observatory is not affected by light pollution.

Expert astronomers lead two-hour tours (9pm daily summer, 6pm daily winter, CH$25,000) in English, French, and Spanish. Group sizes are capped at 10. The observatory is closed July-August and during the full moon. Make reservations at least a week in advance at their office in Vicuña (San Martín 233, tel. 51/2412 584). The tour cost includes transportation to the observatory from Vicuña.

OBSERVATORIO MAMALLUCA

The municipal **Observatorio Mamalluca** (no phone) is 9km northeast of Vicuña in the mountains at 1,150 meters elevation. It's the most visited observatory in the world, with

60,000 annual visitors. Two-hour observatory tours (8:30pm daily summer, 6:30pm daily winter, CH$7,000 adults, CH$2,500 children) are led by local guides. While the guides' scientific knowledge can vary, all offer interesting insights into indigenous beliefs about astrology and cosmology. The size of the tour groups can reach 25, and 200 visitors may be on the site at once. Tours happen even when cloud cover makes observing conditions poor. The observatory's location, close to Vicuña, means that light pollution can interfere with the sky view.

Tours are available in Spanish or English. You must reserve a spot at least a day ahead, three days ahead for long weekends, by phone, email, or in person at the office in Vicuña (Gabriela Mistral 260, tel. 51/2670 331 or 51/2670 330, 9am-1pm and 3pm-last tour Mon.-Fri., 11am-2pm and 4pm-last tour Sat.-Sun.). Transportation to the observatory is not included in the cost but can be arranged with the Vicuña office for CH$3,000 pp. You can also book a tour through a La Serena or Vicuña tour agency.

CERRO TOLOLO INTER-AMERICAN OBSERVATORY

Funded by U.S. bodies, the **Cerro Tololo Inter-American Observatory** (Km 50 Camino Centro Astronomico, tel. 51/2205 200, www.ctio.noao.edu/noao, free) is open for tours every Saturday, but you must reserve your spot a month in advance. Three-hour tours start at 9am and 1pm and are limited to 20 people each. You'll need your own vehicle to get to the observatory, 48km south of Vicuña.

Festivals and Events

Vicuña's largest celebration is the **Carnaval Elquino** (mid-Jan.-Feb. 22). Live music, folkloric dancing, and activities related to the grape harvest draw thousands of revelers. The Plaza Gabriela Mistral is the epicenter of these free events, which culminate with young women competing to be crowned festival queen on February 22, the town's anniversary.

Gabriela Mistral, Nobel Prize-Winning Poet

EARLY LIFE

Born in Vicuña, Lucila Godoy Alcayaga, better known as Gabriela Mistral, moved to Montegrande with her mother and half-sister at age three, after her father abandoned the family. Her sister took the role of schoolmaster in the village and the family installed themselves in the tiny room attached to the main classroom.

Mistral began writing in her teens, sending articles to two La Serena newspapers, *La Voz de Elqui* and *El Coquimbo,* to help support her family. She worked as a teaching assistant in the nearby village of La Compañía. Mistral was refused entry to the Escuela Normal, a prestigious school for teachers in La Serena, because her writing demonstrated pantheist ideas that ran against the Christian ideals that should be held by educators.

monument honoring Gabriela Mistral

TEACHING CAREER

Through independent hard work, Mistral acquired her teaching qualification in 1910 and was posted to schools around the country, an experience that would profoundly impact her writing, leading her to reflect on the lives of Chileans. During this period she met the aspiring poet Pablo Neruda, who was studying at the Liceo de Hombres (Boys' School) in Temuco.

GETTING PUBLISHED

Mistral was an impassioned feminist, writing in an article for a local paper in 1906 *"Instrúyase a la mujer, no hay nada en ella que la haga ser colocada en un lugar más bajo que el hombre."* (Let women be educated; nothing in them requires that they be set in a place lower than men.) She was committed to aiding the poor and vulnerable, both in her work as an educator and through her poetry. Her work often showed deep compassion for the lot of Chileans.

Mistral was first published in the Parisian literary magazine *Elegancias* in 1913, using Gabriela Mistral as her pen name to avoid her poetry being associated with her work in education. In 1922 she was invited to Mexico, beginning her stint of educational work outside Chile. Her first collection of poetry was published by Spanish teachers from the United States under the title *Desolación*. It included some of her most famous poems, including "Los sonetos de la muerte" (The Sonnets of Death), a series of three poems considered to reflect on the suicide of Romelio Ureta, a former friend and lover.

MISTRAL'S LEGACY

Mistral traveled extensively around the world and was recognized as an important literary figure in Latin America, Europe, and the United States. She taught Latin American literature at universities and gained honorary degrees from institutions around the world.

She won the Nobel Prize for Literature in 1945, although the event was overshadowed by the death of her nephew, who had lived with her since he was four. Juan Miguel Godoy Mendoza, who Mistral called Yin Yin, had died by suicide at the age of 17 just two years earlier.

When Mistral died in 1957, she left the prize money and the proceeds from the sale of her books to the children of Montegrande, a town in the Valle de Elqui where she lived for much of her life.

Shopping

On the north side of Plaza Gabriela Mistral, **Pueblo de Artesanos** (Gabriela Mistral 359, 11am-6pm daily) has mostly local handicrafts, including Diaguita-inspired leatherwork, jewelry, and textiles woven from wool and cotton. Directly opposite, across the square, the **Centro Artesanal y Comercial** (Chacabuco s/n, 11am-6pm daily) is a larger covered market with an interesting array of souvenirs, including quartz jewelry and beautiful relief panels with petroglyphs of camelids.

Recreation

The highly recommended **Elki Magic** (San Martín 472, tel. 9/6877 2015, www.elkimagic.com) specializes in self-guided **bike tours** (CH$6,000 per day) of the region, as well as round-trip cycling excursions to Alcohuaz or Pisco Elqui (from CH$15,000). They also operate **van tours** of the Valle de Elqui, including visits to Horcón and Pisco Elqui (CH$20,000) and the Paso Agua Negra and nearby thermal springs (CH$45,000, min. 4 people). Guides speak English and French. **Elqui Experience** (Gabriela Mistral 479, tel. 9/4573 0319, www.elquiexperience.com) runs similar tours, plus kayaking on the Puclaro reservoir (CH$18,000, including transportation and equipment) and 30-minute flights over the Valle de Elqui in light aircraft (CH$82,500 pp, min. 3 people).

Food

Cervecería Guayacán (Gabriela Mistral 485, no phone, http://guayacan.cl, 1pm-midnight daily, CH$5,000-8,500) is a local outpost of the Diaguitas brewery, the valley's first. It has a welcoming bar area with furniture made from recycled crate pallets and beer barrels. The large back garden is the most appealing. Stop by for its selection of eight craft beers, a tasty pizza, or a loaded salad. As one of Vicuña's few bars, it gets lively in the evenings.

Pass the tables in ★ **Chivato Negro** (Gabriela Mistral 565, tel. 9/7862 9439, www.chivatonegro.com, 9am-11pm Sun.-Wed.,

9am-1am Thurs.-Sat., CH$4,000-9,000, *menú del día* CH$4,000), an old shoe shop, and head directly to the back garden to lounge at a patio table in the shade of low-hanging Peruvian peppercorn trees. Delicious build-your-own pizzas fill the menu alongside meat and fish dishes, plus hearty sandwiches made with local cheeses and spices. Feminist talks, magic shows, live music, and other events are held weekday evenings.

Accommodations

Three blocks west of Plaza Gabriela Mistral, no-frills **Valle Hermoso Hostal** (Gabriela Mistral 706, tel. 51/2411 206, www.hostalvallehermoso.com, CH$40,000 d, cash only) is Vicuña's most welcoming budget option. Set around a central courtyard, the nine sizeable rooms have varying degrees of light (those on the northern side have the most), comfortable beds, and spotless baths. Breakfast is substantial, and parking is available. Book ahead. Rates include IVA.

The small but perfectly cozy bed-and-breakfast ★ **El Solar de los Madariaga** (Gabriela Mistral 683, tel. 51/2411 220, www.solardelosmadariaga.com, CH$47,400 d) is run by the affable Mitzi. Three large, modern bedrooms line a central courtyard and an avocado-planted garden. The 140-year-old house also contains a museum, only open to guests, that showcases the history of the Madariaga family. There is an extensive library of texts about Gabriela Mistral and other Chilean writers. Rates include IVA.

Information and Services

The **Oficina de Turismo** (San Martín 275, tel. 51/2670 308, www.vicunacapitalastronomica.cl, 9am-6pm daily Jan.-Feb., 8:30am-5:30pm Mon.-Thurs., 8:30am-6pm Fri., 9am-6pm Sat., 9am-2pm Sun. Mar.-Dec.) can provide maps for the region and advise on getting to the villages of the Valle de Elqui.

On the south side of Plaza Gabriela Mistral, **Banco Estado** (Chacabuco 384) has a 24-hour **ATM** and can exchange dollars and euros. One of the few **gas stations** in the valley is here in Vicuña, a **COPEC** (Av. Las Delicias 20, 24 hr daily) on the southwestern edge of town.

Getting There and Around

To reach Vicuña from **La Serena,** it's a 64-km, one-hour drive east along Ruta 41; it can be slow due to trucks. From **Santiago,** it's a 472-km, five-hour drive north along Ruta 5 to La Serena, where you take Ruta 41 east.

The **Terminal de Buses de Vicuña** (Prat 142, no phone) is where all buses from La Serena drop passengers. Buses leave **La Serena** (1.25hr, CH$2,000) every 10 minutes 7am-9pm daily. **Via Elqui** (tel. 51/2312 422) is one of several companies that operate buses between La Serena and Vicuña and onward to Pisco Elqui. Faster *taxis colectivos* (1hr, CH$2,500) leave from Calle Domeyko in La Serena.

Buses Expreso Norte (tel. 51/2546 890, www.expresonorte.cl) has twice-daily buses to and from **Santiago** (7hr, CH$10,000/CH$15,000). Buses bound for **Pisco Elqui** (1hr, CH$2,000) leave every 20 minutes, stopping at Montegrande. *Taxis colectivos* for the Capel pisco distillery (CH$800) and to Diaguitas (CH$1,000) leave when full from the bus terminal.

Villaseca

Across Río Turbio south of Vicuña, Villaseca is a curious village powered entirely by solar energy—apparent from the fields of solar panels. It's also known for its *cocinas solares* (solar kitchens), a novel type of restaurant where all the food is cooked by the heat of the sun.

The project started in the 1990s to leverage the abundant solar energy and help local women cook without costly gas. Since then it has become a tourist attraction, with various restaurants now cooking using the flower-shaped metal ovens that channel the sun's energy. Inside, a pan slowly cooks goat casseroles, *pastel de choclo* (corn and beef pie), and chicken stews over several hours. The food emerges tender and juicy.

Among the oldest of the restaurants, **Solar Elqui "Donde Martita"** (Magallanes 15, tel. 9/93121926 or 9/4987 537, solarelqui@yahoo.es, 11am-5pm Tues.-Sun., *menú del día* CH$8,000) serves meals cooked with this unique method as a fixed-price menu. Different types of meat are served with mashed potato or rice, plus a starter, dessert, and drink. The family-run restaurant overlooks muscat grape vines from its shaded terrace. It's a unique example of typical home cooking from the valley.

To get to Villaseca from Vicuña, it's a 4.5-km, 10-minute drive on Ruta 41 and the D-357 and D-399. From La Serena, it's a 66-km, one-hour drive on Ruta 41, the D-357, and the D-399.

Diaguitas

Sharing the name of the indigenous people who resided in the valley AD 1000-1470, the village of **Diaguitas** lines the northern bank of the Río Turbio with a strip of dusty adobe-brick housing along one of its few roads. Reflecting the settlement's ancestral roots, some of the walls have been painted to reflect the tricolor patterns used in the ceramics of the Diaguita culture.

The village's main draws are both alcohol-related. Almost all the yield at **Pisquera Aba** (Fundo San Juan, D-289 s/n, tel. 51/2411 039, www.piscoaba.cl, 10am-7pm daily summer, 10am-6pm daily winter) goes straight to export, so the only place you can buy this pisco is at the distillery. Still using traditional copper pots for distillation, this boutique distillery offers free tours around its attractive grounds and free samples of their pisco. Try it neat or combined with mango or *maqui* to make fruity sours. To get here, take the signed left turn 3km after joining Ruta 41 from Vicuña.

★ **Cervecería Guayacan** (Principal 33, tel. 9/9239 5981, http://guayacan.cl, 9am-7pm daily, CH$5,000-8,500) was the

1: Plaza Gabriela Mistral in Vicuña **2:** Cervecería Guayacan

valley's first brewery. Note the solar panels on the roof: The brewing process is entirely powered by solar energy. Take a tour with a tasting (CH$1,000) or just hang out in the sunny beer garden. In this shabby-chic collection of packing crates turned into tables and benches, you can try eight craft beers by the pint or pitcher. Don't miss the Chañar, a beer brewed using the sap of the tree of that name. The thin-crust pizzas use malted barley in the dough and are topped with local ingredients, including goat cheese and sauce made from *chañar*.

To get to Diaguitas from Vicuña, it's a 6-km, 10-minute drive east along Ruta 41 and the D-333. From La Serena, it's a 68-km, one-hour drive east along Ruta 41 and the D-333.

MONTEGRANDE

Where the road forks south from Ruta 41 at Rivadavia, it passes into a gradually widening valley lined by immaculate rows of grapevines. After 7km is the village of Paihuano, site of an alleged UFO crash in 1998, before the road continues south to Montegrande.

Just a few houses line the main road through Montegrande, a slip of a village best known for its famous resident, Gabriela Mistral. The neoclassical **Iglesia Nuestra Señora del Carmen** (Plaza de Montegrande) dates from 1870, making it the oldest in the valley. It has a powder-blue painted ceiling studded with stars and an intricate if gaudy gold-painted wood altar, dominated by a statue of the Virgen del Carmen.

Museo de Sitio Casa-Escuela Gabriela Mistral

Montegrande's most famous resident, Gabriela Mistral, spent her childhood in the village school, now the **Museo de Sitio Casa-Escuela Gabriela Mistral** (Montegrande s/n, 10am-1pm and 3pm-6pm Tues.-Sun., CH$500). Mistral and her family moved to Montegrande when she was three years old. Her sister worked as the village

schoolmaster, and the family lived in the tiny room attached to the main classroom. Both rooms remain as they would have been at the time, with the family's bedroom evidencing a humble, frugal existence.

The classroom contains some original pencil manuscripts of Mistral's poems, the original furniture used by the village children, and the Chilean flag that covered Mistral's coffin upon her death in 1957. The ticket office for the museum is the original mail room, where Mistral and her sister worked to bring in extra money for the family.

Outside, 300 meters along the road toward Pisco Elqui, on the right side, a staircase turns into a paved pathway and is adorned with information boards about the poet. It climbs to the **Mausoleo Gabriela Mistral** (10am-1pm and 3pm-6pm daily, CH$1,000 adults, CH$500 children). Mistral's tomb lies within a shady grove of trees and is inscribed with words that reflect a deep bond with her former home: *"Lo que el alma hace para su cuerpo es lo que el artista hace para su pueblo."* (That which the soul does for the body is what the artist does for their town.)

Wineries

Just 2km north of Montegrande, **Cavas del Valle** (Km 14.5 D-485, tel. 9/6842 5592, www. cavasdelvalle.cl, 9am-8:30pm daily Jan.-Feb., 9am-6:30pm daily Mar.-Dec., tour and tasting free) is a boutique family-run vineyard and the first to introduce grapes such as syrah, cabernet sauvignon, and malbec to the region. They also make a range of late-harvest wines from both syrah and muscat grapes. The local climate allows for an elongated harvest, January-May, meaning the winemakers produce up to three different wines from a single harvest. All the grapes are organic and harvested by hand. Production is tiny, at only 45,000 bottles a year, and the winery is the only place where you can buy the wine. The 20-minute tours (free) are available in English if you reserve in advance. Bottles start at CH$6,500.

Getting There and Around

From **Santiago,** it's a 472-km, 6-hour drive north along Ruta 5 to La Serena. From **La Serena,** take Ruta 41 east to Rivadavia and then Avenida Balmaceda (the D-485) south into the Valle de Elqui to Montegrande, a further 97-km, 1.5-hour drive.

All Pisco Elqui-bound buses from **La Serena** (2hr, CH$4,000) pass through Montegrande. Buses are run by a handful of companies, including **Via Elqui** (tel. 51/2312 422). All leave every 20 minutes from the **Terminal Rodoviario** (Amunátegui 107, La Serena, tel. 51/2224 573) in La Serena. They stop to drop and pick up passengers at the Plaza de Armas, near the Museo de Sitio Casa-Escuela Gabriela Mistral. You can catch these same buses as they stop at **Terminal de Buses de Vicuña** (Prat 142, Vicuña, no phone) in Vicuña (1hr, CH$2,000).

PISCO ELQUI

With 300 days of sunshine per year, Pisco Elqui is the prettiest and largest of the villages in the Valle de Elqui and near some of the oldest pisco distilleries. The relaxed ambience and the friendly, chatty demeanor of the local people, who take great pride in their home, leads many travelers to stay longer than expected. This is helped by the fact that the lodgings here rank among the best in the Norte Chico. Founded in 1800, the village was originally called La Unión but formally changed its name in 1936 to reflect its main industry, pisco.

Sights

The heart of Pisco Elqui is lively **Plaza Pisco Elqui** (O'Higgins), normally populated by conversing or flute-playing locals and backpackers selling handcrafted jewelry. The iconic 1922 **Iglesia Nuestra Señora del Rosario** (Plaza Pisco Elqui, 2pm-6pm daily), its blue-and-cream wooden steeple peeling but resplendent in the sunshine, is staffed by chatty guardians. The entrance is flanked by two earthenware pisco jugs;

inside the church, the central nave is hung with religious art of French origin.

Pisco Distilleries

The largest distillery around Pisco Elqui, the **Destilería Pisco Mistral** (O'Higgins 746, tel. 51/2451 358, www.destileriapiscomistral.cl, 11:30am-9pm daily Jan.-Feb., 11:30am-6pm Tues.-Sun. Mar.-Dec.) lacks the artisanal charm of other producers in the valley, but its location on the main square makes it the most accessible. The **tour** (Spanish hourly noon-7pm daily Jan.-Feb., noon-5pm Tues.-Sun. Mar.-Dec., English 3:30pm daily Jan.-Feb., 3:30pm Tues.-Sun. Mar.-Dec., CH$6,000 with tasting) takes you around the low adobe buildings crammed with antique machinery, ending with a pisco tasting and a cocktail in the bar.

A short walk south of Pisco Elqui, **Doña Josefa de Elqui** (Km 1 Camino a Horcón, tel. 9/6201 5414, 10:30am-9pm daily Jan.-Feb., 10:30am-8pm daily Mar.-Dec.) is a family-run artisanal pisco producer with 25 years of experience. It offers **tours** (Spanish only) on which you can request a free pisco tasting. It's accessed by a steep dirt road, about 200 meters south of the main road leaving town.

The oldest distillery in Chile, artisanal **Fundo Los Nichos** (Km 4 Camino a Horcón, tel. 51/4510 85, contacto@fundolosnichos.cl, 11am-6pm daily), is just 4km south of Pisco Elqui. **Tours** (Spanish only, 4 daily, CH$1,000 with tasting) take you from a shady courtyard filled with orange trees to the distillery, where organic and traditional methods are still used. They make two distinct types of pisco: Fundo Los Nichos red label and their signature Espiritú de Elqui, aged three years in French oak barrels and with a flavor similar to brandy. The tour also includes a trip into the subterranean wine cellar. Producing only 180,000 bottles annually, you won't find this pisco outside the distillery; bottles start at CH$5,000.

☆ Pisco-Tasting in the Valle de Elqui

the oldest pisco distillery in the country, Fundo Los Nichos

The origins of the grape brandy known as pisco are far from confirmed. Peru fiercely defends its claim as the original producer; in 2013, the town of Ica, Peru, was officially ruled by the European Commission to be the geographical origin of pisco. However, researchers claim to have found a 1733 inventory from the Hacienda Latorre in Pisco Elqui that refers to three jars of "pisco"—which may prove that Chile's claim dates to far earlier than Peru's.

Each country's version of pisco is different in taste and production. Peruvian pisco can only be distilled once and must be bottled directly. Chilean pisco can be distilled up to three times. During the distilling process, the "head" and the "tail," the low-quality alcohols, are removed through evaporation, leaving just the "heart," the best-quality pisco, which is blended with water to reduce the alcohol content.

In 1931, a Denominación de Origen (Name of Origin) for Chile was implemented, meaning that pisco can only officially be produced in the Atacama and Coquimbo regions. Both have climates with low rainfall and hot sunshine, making them excellent for cultivating the muscat grapes used to make pisco. Pisco comes in three forms: *transparente* (unaged), *de guarda* (stored for six months in an oak cask), and *envejecido* (stored for a year in an oak cask).

WHERE TO TRY IT

Visiting a pisco distillery, or *pisquera*, is much like visiting a winery. You'll see steel or concrete tanks where the grape juice is fermented into wine before being introduced to copper stills where the alcohol is then distilled. Most distilleries will show you around the cellar and finish with a grand pisco tasting. You can usually try the liquor neat, choosing from aged and unaged varieties and blends with different alcohol percentages. Expect to notice fruity and floral scents. Below are distilleries in the area that offer guided tours or tastings.

- **Capel** (page 218)

- **Pisquera Aba** (page 222)

- **Destilería Pisco Mistral** (page 225)

- **Doña Josefa de Elqui** (page 225)

- **Fundo Los Nichos** (page 225)

Shopping

Opposite the Plaza Pisco Elqui, on the south side, a small **handicrafts market** (11am-7:30pm daily) is a good spot for local crafts, including crystals, tie-dyed garments, leatherwork, and delicious jams and ice creams featuring local flavors like papaya and pisco sour.

Recreation

Turismo Migrantes (O'Higgins s/n, tel. 51/2451 917, www.turismomigrantes.cl) organizes tours across the valley. They can arrange a visit to local distilleries and the Cavas del Valle winery (CH$25,000), including entry and transportation. They also organize treks into Valle de Cochiguaz and Valle de Elqui to pretty waterfalls or hot springs near the Embalse La Laguna. They offer **self-guided bike tours** (from CH$18,000, includes transportation and bike rental, min. 2 people), where they drop you off and you cycle back. Guided **horseback riding tours** (2hr, CH$28,000 pp, includes transportation) are also available. The most interesting option combines a horseback ride with their Elqui Experience tour (CH$38,000), where you ride to a telescope in the mountains. You can also do this tour by car (CH$18,000 pp, min. 4 people). They also run multiple-day horseback trips and can organize tours to the meditation pyramids in Cochiguaz.

Food and Accommodations

Reliable **Restaurant Durmiente Elquino** (Los Carreras s/n, tel. 9/8906 2754, eldurmienteelquino@gmail.com, 1pm-midnight Tues.-Sun., CH$5,000-8,000) has an ample menu and a pretty terrace surrounded by bamboo. Inside, the dining room is carpeted with quartz. Quinoa risottos, roasted pork ribs, and rib-eye steaks plus salads are on offer, while their luridly colored piscos, flavored with mint, ginger, *merkén,* guava, or basil, are not to be missed.

The valley's top dining option is ★ **Hacienda Miraflores** (Km 3 Camino a Horcón, tel. 9/7742 9690, www.haciendamiraflores.cl, 1pm-5pm Tues.-Sun.,

CH$11,000-14,000), with sumptuous views along the valley from its pergola-shaded patio and inside its adobe-walled restaurant. An open grill cooks meat exquisitely, and all come with salads or potatoes as sides.

Those on a budget will be happy to find the relaxed **Camping Refugio del Angel** (eastern end of Carrera, tel. 51/2451 292, http://campingrefugiodelangel.cl, CH$10,000 pp). The campground's 90 sites dot two hectares in a leafy grove on the banks of the Río Claro. The sites can feel close together, but the ban on loud music maintains a quiet setting. Hot showers, a small kitchen, and a barbecue for each campsite are supplied; you'll need a gas stove if you plan to self-cater. To get here, follow Carrera to its eastern end and take the right-hand fork down to the river.

Pisco Elqui's most comfortable budget option, a five-minute walk from the plaza, is **Hostal Trishel** (Baquedano 90, tel. 9/9419 8680, http://hostaltriskel.cl, CH$15,000 pp, cash only). Seven lime-green and yellow rooms are in the main house and a separate block; those in the main house are tiny. A large communal kitchen leads to an extensive hammock-slung garden, where the only sounds you'll hear are the brook and birds. The only thing missing is a swimming pool.

Few places in the region can compare with the value of the ★ **Cabañas Elquimista** (Pasaje Aurora de Chile s/n, tel. 9/8904 5570, www.elquimista.com, CH$50,000 d without kitchen, CH$75,000 d with kitchen), in a prime location overlooking the valley. Unusually, all rooms and cabins have terraces or balconies with views. The vibe is modern but retains a homespun friendliness (the owners live on-site). There are two large pools. The cheapest rooms have facilities just for making breakfast, while the mid-price rooms have full kitchens. The two VIP cabins (CH$118,000) have rooftop terraces with private pools. Book two months in advance for December-April.

From a vantage point on a hillside above the road, 2km south of Pisco Elqui, the seven cabins of luxurious ★ **Cabañas Caballieri** (tel. 51/2412 636, http://caballieri.cl,

Crossing the Border at Paso Agua Negra

East from La Serena or Vicuña, if you continue along Ruta 41 rather than turning south for Pisco Elqui at Rivadavia, a drive of 150km leads to the border crossing **Paso Agua Negra** (no phone, entry to Argentina 7am-5pm daily, entry to Chile 7am-9pm daily Dec.-Mar.). From Rivadavia, the road is paved for 3km to Varillar. After Varillar it's in poor condition and you'll need a high-clearance vehicle on the winding but spectacular route to the border. At 4,779 meters elevation at the pass, this road can leave you with serious altitude sickness, particularly if you're driving directly from La Serena. A full tank of gas is essential, as you won't find it again until Las Flores, 38km into Argentina.

CH$60,000-110,000) have enchanting views across the valley. Each is unique. For the finest valley views and unique architecture, opt for Aire, the stone cabin at the top of the hill, or Quartz, built from striking rose quartz. Two smaller, cheaper cabins don't have terraces or views. All have modern kitchens and access to a blue-tiled swimming room that overlooks the Río Claro. Book well in advance.

Information and Services

An **Oficina de Turismo** (Plaza Pisco Elqui, 10:30am-8pm daily Jan.-Feb., 10:30am-6:30pm daily Mar.-Dec.) operated by the tour agency Ruta del Pisco can provide information about getting to local distilleries. For more information about the town, visit the website http://piscoelqui.com.

The only **ATM** east of Vicuña is Pisco Elqui's **Banco de Chile** (O'Higgins and Carrera), just off the main square. There are no currency exchange facilities.

Getting There and Around

From **Santiago,** it's a 472-km, 6-hour drive north along Ruta 5 to La Serena; from **La Serena,** take Ruta 41 east to Rivadavia and then Avenida Balmaceda (the D-485) south to Valle de Elqui to reach Pisco Elqui, 100km farther, a 1-hour, 40-minute drive.

The bus company **Via Elqui** (tel. 51/2312 422), along with a handful of others, runs buses every 20 minutes from **La Serena** (2.5hr, CH$4,000) to Pisco Elqui. Buses depart from the **Terminal Rodoviario** (Amunátegui 107, La Serena, tel. 51/2224 573) in La Serena. For the return journey to La Serena, buses depart from the eastern side of the Plaza Pisco Elqui. The final bus leaves for La Serena at 8pm daily.

To get between the villages in the valley without a car, **hitchhiking** is easiest and commonly used by locals. If you're driving, you may want to consider giving a hitcher a lift, as they may be going just to the next village. Cycling is another recommended option, as the roads are reasonably quiet and very scenic. **Tour Misticos** (Rodríguez s/n, tel. 9/8330 2741) rents bikes for CH$7,000 per day.

Horcón

Eight kilometers south of Pisco Elqui, Horcón is home to the **Pueblito Artesanal de Horcón** (Horcón Craft Village, 10:30am-6pm daily Jan.-Feb., noon-6pm daily Mar.-Dec.), a collection of stalls selling local delicacies of organic *manjar* and *lucuma* jams, plus wood and leatherwork, crochet and textiles, and even massages and tarot reading. The craft village is busiest Thursday-Sunday.

By the river, 300 meters from the craft village, the excellent **Las Terrazas Doña Mely** (tel. 9/8594 0057, 1:30pm-8pm daily, CH$7,000-9,000) is the place to sample regional cuisine such as *conejo escabechado* (rabbit marinated in an onion and garlic sauce) and *cabra* (oven-roasted goat), with portion sizes for two. Get here early, as they often run out. They also have local craft beers Guayacán and Cactus by the bottle, and pisco sours made from Los Nichos pisco.

Alcohuaz

South of Horcón, the road is a one-lane washboard track with steep curves and a vertical drop on one side. It continues through the valley to the southernmost village, Alcohuaz. For a real escape from civilization, you won't find better than this picturesque village, which started life as a farm estate. Nowadays it's a cluster of adobe buildings and grapevines that slope to the Río Claro below. The village is home to a clutch of restaurants and lodgings.

At the end of the road in the valley, the beautifully preserved **Casona Distante** (tel. 9/9226 5440, www.casonadistante.cl, CH$86,000 d) is in the adobe *casona* of a former estate. The pisco plantations still surround the house. Half-meter-thick walls keep the eight rooms cozy, if a little dark, with few windows, but king beds with crisp white linens ensure comfort. Meals, pisco sours, and wine can be requested from the small guests-only restaurant. There are terraces and a swimming pool. This is a real escape in a remote part of Valle de Elqui, with no internet access. The credit card processor can be slow, so cash is advised. Rates include IVA.

COMUNIDAD COCHIGUAZ

Just south of Montegrande, an eastern spur road follows the fork of the Río Cochiguaz into Valle de Cochiguaz, a patchwork of pisco vines and scorched earth. The narrow road climbs gradually into the Andean foothills to **Comunidad Cochiguaz,** a collection of cabins, campgrounds, and hotels with dramatic highland scenery.

The settlement was founded in the 1960s, and a stream of hippies and mystics has found their way here for quartz crystals, positive energy, and UFO sightings, establishing Comunidad Cochiguaz as a destination for holistic therapies and spiritual tourism.

Sights

On the left as you approach Cochiguaz is the **Observatorio Cancana** (Km 11.5 Camino a Cochiguaz, tel. 9/9047 3859, www.cancana.

cl). Tours (9:30pm and 11:30pm daily summer, 7pm and 9pm daily winter, CH$15,000 adults, CH$7,000 children) of the observatory are in Spanish for up to 40 people. Transportation to and from the observatory isn't included; it's best visited on a tour from Pisco Elqui.

Food and Accommodations

Down by the river and a set of natural pools, **Luz de Luna** (Km 3 Camino a Cochiguaz, tel. 9/8419 6923 or 9/8428 4546, http://campingluzdeluna.cl, CH$8,000 camping pp, CH$65,000 cabin, cash only) is a very relaxed campground near gushing waterfalls with sites right at the water. There are cabins for 4-5 people that include breakfast. Meals can be provided by the owners. The campground has six meditation pyramids, wooden structures large enough for half a dozen people to sit inside, which are popular among health tourism groups visiting from Pisco Elqui. You can visit for the day (CH$5,000), including access to the river, waterfalls, and the mediation pyramids. There are no advance reservations for camping. Rates include IVA.

North of Cochiguaz 500 meters, **Spa Cochiguaz** (Parcela 8-B, tel. 9/85012 680 or 9/8502 2723, www.spacochiguaz.cl, CH$34,000 d, CH$60,000 cabins) offers lodgings in tired and simple cabins that don't meet the quality of those in the same price range in Pisco Elqui. The draw is the therapies, including clay and herbal baths, Reiki, and quartz crystals. An on-site pool and vegetarian restaurant mean you don't need to leave the spa. Cabins have kitchens; bedrooms don't. There's no Wi-Fi. Rates include IVA.

Getting There and Around

From **Santiago,** it's a 472-km, six-hour drive north along Ruta 5 to La Serena; from **La Serena,** take Ruta 41 east via Vicuña to Rivadavia and then Avenida Balmaceda (the D-485) south into the Valle de Elqui to reach Montegrande, where the Camino a Cochiguaz (the D-487) turns east into the Valle de

Cochiguaz and eventually reaches Cochiguaz, a 108-km, 2-hour drive. From **Vicuña,** it's a 45-km, 1-hour drive.

There is no public transit into the valley. Instead, **hitchhiking** is the locals' transportation of choice. You'll almost certainly get a ride if anyone is passing. You can also **rent a bike** from agencies in Vicuña or Pisco Elqui that drop you off at the farthest point of the valley to pedal back.

South of La Serena

Ruta 5 hugs the coast as it wiggles southward to Los Andes, Valparaíso, and Santiago in central Chile. The landscape south of La Serena is river gullies and gently rolling coastal mountains. These gradually become greener, a striking contrast to the sunbaked mountains farther north.

All traffic runs on Ruta 5, and getting into the towns deep in the valleys requires more effort. It's worth your while, with curious stretches of semitropical forest at Parque Nacional Bosque de Fray Jorge, mountain lodges in the blissfully untouched backcountry of Valle Hurtado, and at Monumento Arqueológico Valle del Encanto, millennia-old petroglyphs from the region's indigenous cultures.

Along the coast, unassuming fishing villages Guanaqueros and Tongoy are popular for quiet, sunny white-sand beaches and casual seafood restaurants.

COQUIMBO

Joining La Serena to the south in an urban area of 438,000, the city of Coquimbo has profoundly English roots, houses notable landmarks, and offers beach resorts farther down the coast. Founded in 1550 by Pedro de Valdivia on the southernmost tip of Bahía Coquimbo, it became a chaotic mining city 300 years later, where immigrants from France, the United States, and England flocked. They put up buildings that reflected the architecture of their homelands, today part of the historic Barrio Inglés (English Quarter). After the boom came a bust, which left a rundown aspect that remains today and contrasts strikingly with the gleaming elegance of colonial La Serena.

Coquimbo is a sprawling city on a hilly peninsula at the cusp of Bahía Coquimbo and Bahía La Herradura. Residential areas spread south, bordering Coquimbo's main beach, Playa La Herradura. Barrio Inglés and downtown Coquimbo are close to the eastern coast of the peninsula. Other facilities such as the bus station are a few blocks south; the Cruz del Tercer Milenio, the highest point on the peninsula, is 10 steep blocks west of Barrio Inglés.

Sights
BARRIO INGLÉS

Barrio Inglés, where the English immigrants built their homes in the 1800s, is worth walking around. **Calle Aldunate,** between **Plaza Vicuña Mackenna** (bounded by Buenaventura Argandoña, Av. Costanera, Buenaventura Argandoña, and Aldunate) and the **Plaza de Armas** (bounded by Las Heras, Juan Melgarejo, and Aldunate) is dotted with aging but still grand 19th-century buildings. At night, these streets transform into the city's de facto nightlife hot spot, a livelier alternative to sedate La Serena, although a bit dead outside summer.

The **Casa Novella** (Aldunate 569), built from Oregon pine and American oak in 1940, its balconies propped up with wooden columns, is the second-oldest house in the city. Next door, **Casa Chesney Cosgrove** is now the **Centro Cultural Palace** (Aldunate 599, tel. 51/2256 418), a cultural center that hosts art exhibitions, music, and readings in its two rooms. Free **guided tours** (in Spanish,

12:30pm Tues.-Fri.) of the Barrio Inglés leave from here.

In a glass-roofed dome on the **Plaza de Gabriela Mistral** (adjacent to the Plaza de Armas, bounded by Las Heras, Aldunate, and Juan Melgarejo), the **Museo de Sitio Cultura Las Ánimas** (Las Heras s/n, tel. 51/2317 006, 8:30am-5:30pm Mon.-Fri., free) is a small museum on the site of a cemetery thought to date to AD 900-1000 and the indigenous Las Ánimas people. Construction on the square uncovered 36 tombs, three of which are on display. Ceramics decorated with black geometric designs on red, pink, and yellow backgrounds were found buried with the bodies.

CRUZ DEL TERCER MILENIO

Conspicuous from its position on top of a hill, the **Cruz del Tercer Milenio** (Cross of the Third Millennium, tel. 51/2327 935, http://cruzdeltercermilenio.cl, 8:30am-9:30pm daily Dec.-Mar., 9:30am-8pm daily Apr.-Nov., CH$2,000 adults, CH$1,000 children) is the highest monument in Latin America, rising 93 meters in the shape of a cross. Spectacular 360-degree views are available on a clear day. At the base of the cross, a small museum contains liturgical items, including a silver chalice donated by Pope John Paul II in 2000, as well as photographs of the dramatic building's equally dramatic construction.

Beaches

South of downtown Coquimbo along the full length of Bahía Herradura, **Playa La Herradura** has golden sand and is a cheaper and quieter beach than La Serena. It's also one of the few beaches in the region that is safe for swimming. For the more adventurous, it's a popular spot for stand-up paddleboarding and windsurfing. Access the beach from practically any of the side streets heading north off Ruta 5. Public restrooms and kiosks selling snacks and drinks are located along the beach.

La Serena-based **Herradura Experience** (Camino Cayetano Almeida s/n, La Serena, tel. 9/9033 2870, http://herraduraexperience.cl) runs stand-up paddleboarding classes (1.5hr, CH$35,000) and windsurfing classes (1.5hr, CH$35,000) from the **Club de Yates de La Herradura** (La Marina 281, Coquimbo). Both require advance reservations.

The town of **Totoralillo,** on an arrow-shaped peninsula 17km south of Coquimbo, just a 20-minute drive along Ruta 5, has four of the finest waves in the region. It's best for advanced surfers March-June, with rentals (from CH$15,000 for 2hr) and classes (from CH$30,000) available with local instructors **Surf Totoralillo** (Playa Totoralillo, tel. 9/9741 6149, www.surftotoralillo.cl).

Food and Accommodations

Lodging is cheaper but lower quality in Coquimbo than in La Serena. However, there are a couple of reasonable and affordable places during the peak summer months when La Serena is packed and rooms are scarce.

Two blocks south of the bus terminal and seven blocks from the Plaza de Armas, **Hostel Del Puerto** (Aldunate 1577, tel. 51/2311 171, http://hosteldelpuerto.cl, CH$12,500 dorm, CH$35,000 d private bath) has warm and welcoming staff. There's a superb rooftop terrace for lounging in the sun with views of the Cruz del Tercer Milenio, plus ample bedrooms with clean if dated furniture. Free parking is available.

The wood-paneled rooms are dated and there's an overwhelming use of magenta at **Hotel San Juan** (Capri Sur 151, La Herradura, tel. 51/2260 114, www.hotelsanjuan.cl, CH$36,000 d), but you can't beat the location, a stone's throw from Playa La Herradura. This spot is very affordable, even in the height of summer. Rooms are large and have modern white baths.

Information and Services

The employees at **Corporación Municipal de Turismo de Coquimbo** (Aldunate 699, 2nd Fl., tel. 51/2310 655, http://coquimboturismo.cl, 9am-1pm and 2pm-6pm

Mon.-Fri.) are helpful. There's another **tourist information booth** open only in summer on Plaza Vicuña Mackenna. For money, head to **Banco de Estado** (Juán Melgarejo 890). **Hospital San Pablo de Coquimbo** (Av. Videla s/n, tel. 51/2336 702, www.hospitalcoquimbo.cl), just off Ruta 5, is the public hospital.

Getting There and Around

It's a 13-km, 20-minute drive south along Ruta 5 from **La Serena** to Coquimbo. From **Santiago,** it's a 461-km, five-hour journey north along Ruta 5.

The **Terminal Rodoviario** (Varela 1300, tel. 51/2314 340) receives *micros* (25min, CH$600) from **La Serena,** which pass along Avenida Aguirre before taking Ruta 5 south. *Taxis colectivos* (15min, CH$1,000) from La Serena leave when full from Avenida Aguirre (between Los Carrera and Av. Balmaceda) 24 hours daily.

Long-distance buses to Coquimbo have similar schedules to those bound for La Serena. **Tur Bus** (tel. 51/2213 060, http://turbus.cl), **Pullman Bus** (tel. 51/2218 251, www.pullmanbus.com), and **Pluss Chile** (tel. 51/2674 286, http://plusschile.cl) have frequent departures from **Santiago** (Terminal San Borja, every 10 min, 6hr, CH$10,000/CH$15,000) to Coquimbo, which continue on to La Serena. Tur Bus and Pluss Chile offer *cama* seats (CH$20,000) on this route.

These companies, plus **Buses Expreso Norte** (tel. 51/2546 886, www.expresonorte.cl), offer hourly departures from **Copiapó** (4hr, CH$9,000/CH$12,000) and **Antofagasta** (10.5hr, CH$20,000/CH$30,000, *cama* CH$40,000). There are also six daily buses from **Calama** (14hr, CH$25,000/CH$35,000) and four daily from **Arica** (23hr, CH$35,000/CH$40,000).

From **Guanaqueros** (50min, CH$1,800) and **Tongoy** (1.25hr, CH$1,900), buses operated by **Serena Mar** (tel. 51/2323 422, www.serenamar.cl) leave every 20 minutes for Coquimbo, then continue to La Serena. **Alfamar Taxis Colectivos** (tel. 51/2323

719) has faster shared taxis (CH$2,500) from these two towns to Coquimbo, leaving 6am-8:30pm daily. **Buses Palacios** (tel. 51/2321 489) has routes from **Andacollo** hourly (1.25hr, CH$2,500).

GUANAQUEROS

On the southern edge of sweeping Bahía Guanaqueros, the town of Guanaqueros, 37km south of Coquimbo, is a popular beach resort for Chileans. Multicolored concrete houses cling to the hill overlooking the bay as **Playa Guanaqueros** stretches an impressive 10km around the coast. This crescent of golden sand and calm water perfect for swimming is chockablock with sun umbrellas and lazing families in January-February, but for the rest of the year, it's mostly empty. Kick back for a couple of days here in a beachside cabin or for the day from La Serena. A clutch of small restaurants along Avenida Linderman, the main road through town, are the only facilities for visitors, although you may spot an enterprising vendor on the beach selling ice cream and cold drinks.

Food and Accommodations

At local favorite **Centro Gastronomic El Suizo** (Av. Linderman 2427, tel. 51/2395 408, 10am-10pm daily Jan.-Feb., shorter hours Mar.-Dec., CH$4,000-7,000), matching black metal chairs and tables sit in a courtyard surrounded by half a dozen matchbox-size kitchens serving up delicious shellfish or razor clam empanadas with cheese (CH$2,000). Plates piled high with fried or grilled hake, conger eel, or steaming seafood soups will fill you up.

Although it's aimed at families with young children, **Bahía Club** (Av. Guanaqueros 2880, just off the traffic circle at the entrance to town, tel. 51/2395 818, www.bahiaclub.cl, CH$35,000 campsite, CH$60,000-65,000 cabin) is worth staying at even if you don't have kids, thanks to the sea views from cabins on the beach. All 16 large cabins have barbecue areas on the balcony and fully equipped kitchens. The camping spots are overpriced, with 60 spaces in a grove of eucalyptus, each with a picnic table and barbecue and their own private bath. Rates include IVA.

Getting There

From **La Serena,** it's a 45-km, 40-minute drive south on Ruta 5, turning west onto the signposted D-410, which becomes Avenida Guanaqueros as it approaches town from the east. From **Santiago,** it's a 4-hour, 40-minute drive 436km north on Ruta 5, taking the signposted D-410 heading west after 4.5 hours.

From La Serena's **Terminal Rodoviario** (Amunátegui 107, tel. 51/2224 573), buses from **Serena Mar** (tel. 51/2323 422, www.serenamar.cl) head to Guanaqueros (1.5hr, CH$2,000) every 20 minutes. Before reaching Guanaqueros, these buses pass through Coquimbo's **Terminal Rodoviario** (Varela 1300, tel. 51/2314 340). From Coquimbo (CH$1,800), it's a 50-minute ride. From **Tongoy** (20min, CH$200), you can take one of Serena Mar's buses in the direction of Coquimbo and La Serena to reach Guanaqueros. These run every 20 minutes.

Also running out of the Terminal Rodoviario in Coquimbo, **Alfamar Taxis Colectivos** (tel. 51/2323 719) have faster **shared taxis** (30min, CH$2,500) to Guanaqueros that run 6am-8:30pm daily.

TONGOY

Sleepy Tongoy, 15km south of Guanaqueros, is a peninsula town with long beaches of exquisite white sand on both sides. The most easily accessed beach is the location of the town's main harbor, **Playa Grande,** southeast of town. A prettier beach is **Playa Socos,** a sweeping curve separated from the eastern edge of Tongoy by the estuary of the Río Tongoy. Neither beach has facilities but both are within walking distance of the town's array of small no-frills restaurants.

It's quieter here than in Guanaqueros, perhaps because on some days a slightly sulfuric smell emanates from the red seaweed dotting Playa Grande. Playa Socos is spared this fate and is a quieter, pleasanter place to enjoy the

ocean. The calm water looks tropical, but it's cooler than you might expect.

Tongoy and Guanaqueros can be visited together or separately; a day trip from La Serena can easily include both. They make a scenic overnight stop to break up the long drive from Santiago to La Serena.

Food and Accommodations

On the northern end of Playa Grande, most restaurants are on the sand or within a block of it. The **Caleta Pescadores de Tongoy** (9am-5pm daily Jan.-Feb., 9am-5pm Sat.-Sun. Mar.-Dec.) has stalls selling scallops and oysters, as well as conger eel and freshly caught fish. The small restaurants lining the market specialize in *paila de mariscos* (soupy seafood stew) and dishes featuring fresh *erizo* (sea urchin) for CH$4,000-8,000.

It feels like staying with kind relatives at welcoming **Agua Marina** (Fundación Sur 93, tel. 51/2391 870, contaproff@yahoo.es, CH$40,000 d, cash only). Elsa and her husband have a clutch of small en suite doubles surrounding a sunny courtyard a two-minute walk from the beach.

Information and Services

There is a 24-hour **Banco de Chile ATM** (Fundación Norte s/n) in Tongoy, but it's wise to bring cash with you. A **COPEC gas station** (next to the police office on the main road into town, 24 hours daily) is the only place for gas in the area.

Getting There and Around

From **La Serena,** it's a 56-km, 50-minute drive south on Ruta 5 to the D-410, heading west to Guanaqueros, where the road bends due south for 4km before continuing west to reach Tongoy. The D-410 to Guanaqueros is paved; the road connecting Guanaqueros and Tongoy is unpaved and takes around 30 minutes. **From Santiago,** it's a 427-km, 4.5-hour drive north on Ruta 5, where a signpost indicates the way on the paved D-440.

From La Serena's **Terminal Rodoviario** (Amunátegui 107, tel. 51/2224 573), **Serena**

Mar (tel. 51/2323 422, www.serenamar.cl) buses leave every 20 minutes for **Tongoy** (1.75hr, CH$1,900), passing through Coquimbo's **Terminal Rodoviario** (Varela 1300, tel. 51/2314 340). From **Coquimbo** (CH$1,900) it's a 1.25-hour ride; these buses pass through Guanaqueros (20min, CH$500) and pick up additional passengers.

Alfamar Taxis Colectivos (tel. 51/2323 719) have faster **shared taxis** (50min, CH$2,500) from Coquimbo's Terminal Rodoviario, leaving 6am-8:30pm daily.

ANDACOLLO

High in the mountains southeast of La Serena, the copper- and gold-mining town of Andacollo fills with 100,000 pilgrims for the annual Fiesta de la Virgen de Andacollo, held December 24-26. The town has a basilica and a smaller church that become the focal points of the festivities. A lack of good-quality lodging and dining options means Andacollo makes a far better day trip from Coquimbo or La Serena than an overnight stay.

Sights

The Roman-Byzantine **Templo Grande** or **Basílica de Andacollo** (Plaza Andacollo s/n, 9am-6pm daily), designed by Italian architect Eusebio Celli, took 20 years to build, with work starting in 1873. Part of it was built from Oregon pine brought from California; the outside walls are adobe covered in sheets of galvanized iron. The basilica is 70 meters long and includes five naves. The main cupola is 45 meters high, with the towers reaching 53 meters. The church can hold 10,000 worshippers.

Across Plaza Andacollo to the west, the **Templo Antiguo** or **Templo Chico** (Plaza Andacollo s/n, 9am-8pm daily) was built to replace the town's first church, built in 1580. The present structure was inaugurated in 1789 and restored in 2016. It houses the Virgen del Rosario when she isn't being paraded through the streets for the Fiesta de la Virgen de Andacollo. Attached to the church is the intriguing **Museo de Ofrendas de la Virgen** (no phone, 10am-1:30pm and 3pm-6:30pm Mon.-Sat., 9am-5pm Sun., donation), which contains photographs of the Fiesta de la Virgen de Andacollo and a fascinating collection of offerings made to the Virgin, including resplendent ceramics from China and other parts of the world.

Festivals and Events

FIESTA DE LA VIRGEN DE ANDACOLLO

Over 3,000 dancers from across Chile move through the streets December 24-26 in what is known as the **Fiesta Grande** or the **Fiesta de la Virgen de Andacollo.** The main religious procession sees the statue of the Virgin carried from the Templo Chico to the Templo Grande. Over three days, *bailes chinos* (groups of male dancers) perform choreographed routines to drums and flutes of pre-Columbian origin. This style of dance, unique to the Norte Chico region, is considered an Intangible Cultural Heritage of Humanity by UNESCO.

The festivities date to the 16th century, when the carved image of the Virgen del Rosario was hidden in the mountains near present-day Andacollo when La Serena was under attack. It was later discovered by an indigenous man seeking firewood, who brought it back to his house and began to worship it. The original statue was lost in the 17th century, and a statue carved from cedar was sent from Peru as a replacement.

On the first Sunday of October, the **Fiesta Chica** is a smaller version of the December festivities, with 3,000 attendees.

Getting There and Around

From **La Serena** to Andacollo is a 55-km, one-hour drive south on Ruta 43 and the D-51. The final 16km are characterized by several 90-degree bends as the road curls into the mountains and should be taken with caution. From **Santiago,** it's a 481-km, five-hour drive north on Ruta 5, turning east onto the D-427 (signposted for "Tambillos"), and north on Ruta 43 to join the D-51 into the mountains.

Several **buses** run to Andacollo from the Terminal Rodoviario (Amunátegui 107, tel. 51/2224 573) in **La Serena** (1.25hr, CH$2,500). **Buses Palacios** (tel. 51/2431 664) and **Buses Vía Andacollo** (tel. 51/2431 664) offer hourly departures. The final bus back to La Serena on Sunday departs at 2:30pm; it leaves at 8pm Monday-Saturday. There are also *taxis colectivos* (1hr, CH$3,000) to Andacollo from La Serena, departing from Calle Domeyho.

VALLE DE LIMARÍ

The Valle de Limarí is known for its spectacular greenery in summer, contrasting the scrubby, arid hillsides surrounding the deep river canyon. It's one of Chile's northernmost farming regions, producing white wine. Many of the country's top vineyards harvest their chardonnay here, making the most of the region's distinctive cool, arid conditions and limestone soil.

Rich in agriculture, particularly tropical fruits, the area boasts unique natural and historical sites. It contains the northernmost patch of Valdivian temperate rainforest as well as petroglyphs by the El Molle people and dramatic scenery as backroads climb into increasingly remote precordillera.

Ovalle

Capital of Limarí province, the city of Ovalle is an oasis at the convergence of the Río Grande and Río Hurtado. Dubbed the Pearl of the Limarí, Ovalle has a pleasant and sunny climate year-round and is known for the lively **Festival de La Vendimia,** the wine harvest, in March. The main draw is convenience. Stopping here overnight shaves time off a trip to Valle de Encanto, a 30-minute drive from here rather than a 1.5-hour journey from La Serena.

WINERIES

Most of the large winemakers have vineyards in Valle de Limarí, but just one small-scale producer is open to visitors. **Viña Tabalí** (Quebrada del Durazno, between Ovalle and Valle Encanto, tel. 2/2352 6800, www.tabali. com, by reservation only, CH$10,000 tasting) is a state-of-the-art winery built into a deep ravine, where they produce single-vineyard wines that include chardonnay, syrah, malbec, and viognier. The winery offers tastings only; advance reservations are essential. Tastings run four times daily Monday-Friday. The winery is about 20km southwest of Ovalle, a 20-minute drive. Tours of the nearby Monumento Arqueológico Valle del Encanto usually include a tour of this winery.

FOOD AND ACCOMMODATIONS

The **Mercado Municipal** (Victoria and Independencia, tel. 53/262 9510, 8am-7pm Mon.-Sat., 8am-4pm Sun., CH$4,000-8,000) is the city's central market. Aside from locally crafted lapis lazuli jewelry and *combarbalita* stone ornaments, you can find inexpensive meals at half a dozen cheap and cheerful restaurants dishing up local favorites of chicken stew with *chuchoca* (mashed corn) and *charquicán* (potato, pumpkin, and beef jerky stew).

Ovalle's most affordable lodging is **Aloja Express** (Av. La Feria 80, tel. 9/8538 3752, CH$29,750 d shared bath, cash only). The owners do their best to understand other languages and are welcoming at this very basic but clean and centrally located hostel. Rates include IVA.

A midrange lodging is the art deco **Gran Hotel Ovalle** (Vicuña Mackenna 210, tel. 53/2621 084, www.granhotelovalle.cl, CH$42,500 d), which is past its prime but has 28 nicely painted bedrooms and a good buffet breakfast. For a deeper sleep, request a room facing away from the noisy street. Rates include IVA.

GETTING THERE

From **La Serena,** it's a 1.25-hour, 89-km drive south on Ruta 43. From **Santiago,** it's a 405-km, 4.5-hour drive north on Ruta 5 and east on Ruta 45.

Ovalle's **Terminal de Buses** (Ariztía Poniente 849, no phone) is well connected with **La Serena.** Hourly direct buses run from

Vallenar (4.5hr, CH$8,000/CH$13,000) and Copiapó (7hr, CH$8,000/CH$13,000). There are less frequent buses from Antofagasta (14hr, CH$17,000/CH$21,000) and Calama (17hr, CH$21,000/CH$26,000). There are also hourly buses from the Terminal Borja in Santiago (6hr, CH$9,000/CH$12,000).

Buses operated by Tur Bus (tel. 53/2624 960, http://turbus.cl), Pullman Bus (tel. 53/2620 427, www.pullmanbus.com), Buses Serena Mar (tel. 53/2625 687, www.serenamar.cl), and Expresso Norte (tel. 53/2631 593, www.expresonorte.cl) leave every half hour from La Serena and Coquimbo (1.75hr, CH$2,000). There are six daily buses from Combarbalá (2hr, CH$300) operated by Expreso Rojas (tel. 9/6897 8737).

Monumento Arqueológico Valle del Encanto

Halfway between Ovalle and Ruta 5 is the 4,000-year-old collection of petroglyphs, pictographs, and *piedras tacitas* (grinding stones) that line the shallow river canyon of the Monumento Arqueológico Valle del Encanto (8:30am-8pm daily Jan.-Feb., 8:30am-6pm daily Mar.-Dec., CH$1000 adults, CH$500 children). Granite slabs the size of cars are strewn along the river's course, many etched with symbols by the indigenous El Molle people, who inhabited the region AD 300-800. They are thought to have been influenced by cultures as far south as central Chile and as far north as the Amazon.

A map of the site provided at the entrance shows the route along the river, between and over rocks interspersed with cacti and waxy-leaved shrubs. Most of the carvings are about water—hardly surprising in such an arid environment—as well as human figures, with clearly defined eyes and noses but no mouths. Most striking are the depictions of semicircular headdresses, interpreted as crowns and as alien-like antennae.

Many of the *piedras tacitas* are covered with 10- to 15-centimeter-wide holes used for grinding maize and other grains; they likely also had a ceremonial function. The small river in the canyon has a series of pools known as Baños del Inca, presumably used for bathing. Many of the petroglyphs have faded; noon is the best time to see them in relief. Be sure to bring a hat and sunscreen.

The easiest way to get here is with your own vehicle or on a tour from Ovalle or La Serena. From La Serena, Tembeta (Andres Bello 870, tel. 2/2215 553 or 9/9012 8608, www.tembeta.cl) employs guides that speak excellent English and have extensive knowledge about the indigenous people who once inhabited the valley. Viajes Mirador (Matta 518, office 10, tel. 51/2218 554, http://viajesmirador.com) and AlfaTour (Los Geranios 140, Coquimbo, tel. 9/3198 3483, www.alfatour.cl) are in Coquimbo but offer hotel pickup from La Serena. Tours generally include hotel pickup and lunch, plus a tour of nearby winery Viña Tabalí, for CH$90,000 pp.

From Ovalle, it's a 25-km, 30-minute drive west on Ruta 45, where you take the signposted D-589 south. From La Serena, it's 122km and 1.5 hours south on Ruta 5 before turning onto Ruta 45 heading east; take the signposted D-589 south.

Parque Nacional Bosque de Fray Jorge

Rainforest is not what you'd expect to find in a semi-desert region, but coastal Parque Nacional Bosque de Fray Jorge (tel. 51/2244 769, www.conaf.cl, coquimbo.oirs@conaf.cl, 9am-4pm daily Dec.-Mar., 9am-5:30pm Thurs.-Sun. Apr.-Nov., last entry 3pm, CH$6,000 adults, CH$3,000 children) contains the northernmost Valdivian temperate rainforest, normally found 1,200km south.

Lying 90km west of Ovalle, the park exists in the coastal cordillera, the Aktis de Talinay, which rise up to 666 meters above the desert plain. Thick morning fog rolls in, explaining how the high-elevation Valdivian temperate rainforest survives in otherwise arid conditions. This water nurtures *canelo, boldo,* and *olivillo,* which give way to ferns, lichens, and mosses. At lower altitudes, cacti and flowering trees such as *Vachellia caven* and *guayacán,* as well as species of desert wildflowers, provide colorful vegetation.

Birdlife is prominent, with two species of owl, Chilean tinamous, partridges, and the long-tailed meadowlark in residence. Chinchillas, hog-nosed skunks, and rare Chilean iguanas scuttle through the undergrowth.

Admission is collected at a wooden booth 200 meters beyond the park entrance, which is 28km from Ruta 5 along the D-540 and an unnamed road that is signposted for the park. The CONAF-run **headquarters** and **Centro de Interpretación** is 2.5km south of the entrance and has a small display on the park's unique flora.

No camping is permitted in the park. A small picnic area 200 meters from the headquarters has tables and restrooms. There are no other services; bring food and water with you, plus a jacket, as the fog and wind can be cold. Entry is limited to 50 cars daily, so get here early.

HIKING

The park has a handful of trails, the most popular being the **Sendero Bosque Hidrófilo** (1-km loop, 30min), which covers both of the park's principal ecosystems: the semiarid desert and the Valdivian temperate rainforest. The trail is often encased in thick fog in the early morning and late afternoon. It begins 6.5km southwest of the park headquarters, along a road with sections that are in poor condition, for which a 4WD vehicle is strongly recommended; drive time is 20 minutes, and you may have to wait for other vehicles to return, as only a dozen are allowed in at one time.

GETTING THERE

From La Serena, it's an 85-km, one-hour drive on Ruta 5 to the junction at km 387, where you leave the highway and head north a short distance on the D-540 before it heads west. Look for signs reading "Fray Jorge Cerrillos." The first 15km are along the washboard D-540; at km 15, a sign for the national park points down an unnamed road that continues for 10km, past the scattered settlement of Peral Ojo de Agua, to the park entrance and the admission booth. Ignore turnoffs signposted for "Hacienda El Arrayán." The road is in a reasonable condition for most vehicles and should take 40 minutes from Ruta 5. An alternative route west from Ruta 5 along the D-560 is shown on the map, but this road is now closed to vehicles.

From Ovalle, it's a 65-km, 1.5-hour drive to the park. Drive west on the D-505 and the D-535 to cross Ruta 5 and join the D-540. Look for signs reading "Fray Jorge Cerrillos." The next 15km are on the washboard D-540. At km 15, follow the sign for the national park down an unnamed road and continue for 10km, past the settlement of Peral Ojo de Agua, to the park entrance and the admission booth. Ignore turnoffs signposted for "Hacienda El Arrayán." The road is in a reasonable condition for most vehicles and should take 40 minutes from Ruta 5.

VALLE HURTADO

Northeast of Ovalle, connected to Vicuña and the Valle de Elqui, Valle Hurtado is a rugged landscape of cacti-scattered mountains and groves of willows and *olivillo* along Río Hurtado. The D-595 leads into the valley 5km north of Ovalle and is paved for 60km, until 15km before Hacienda Los Andes.

Just northwest of the village of San Pedro Viejo, the **Monumento Natural Pichasca** (tel. 9/8923 0010, monumento.pichasca@conaf.cl, 9am-4pm daily Dec.-Mar., 9am-4pm Thurs.-Sun. Apr.-Nov., CH$6,000 adults, CH$3,000 children) houses fossilized 66-million-year-old *araucaría* trees. Sadly, the area was plundered before it came under CONAF protection, so not many of the trees remain. Fossilized dinosaur bones have also been found. A small cave known as the Casa de Piedra contained human remains around 9,000 years old along with petroglyphs thought to be made by El Molle people. The reserve is accessible by a bridge from San Pedro Viejo.

The estate that contains ★ **Hacienda Los Andes** (tel. 53/2691 822, http://haciendalosandes.com, CH$72,000 d,

Side Trip for Semiprecious Souvenirs

Reached by a picturesque drive through Valle Hurtado, following the Río Cogoti south of Ovalle, with the cacti-scuffed mountains giving way to the Andes, the town of **Combarbalá** is best known for its unique ornaments made from *combarbalita* **stone.** A semiprecious volcanic rock only found in this part of Chile, it often contains traces of clay, quartz, copper, and silver. It was named the Chilean national stone in 1993.

Workshops in town produce delicate jewelry, ornaments, and other souvenirs from the rock. From the main road into town, take the first left onto Calle Juan Ignacio Flores and, 450 meters later, turn left to find the shop **Artesanía Frívola** (Dr. Aguirre Perry 668, tel. 53/2741 118, hours vary), full to the rafters with handicrafts, including animal figurines, clocks, and ashtrays. **Artesanía Castillo** (Juan Ignacio Flores 552, tel. 53/2741 081, http://entrepiedras.cl, hours vary) has a fancier array of merchandise, with pestle-and-mortar sets and even tables, all carved entirely from *combarbalita*.

The town is home to the **Observatorio Cruz del Sur** (tel. 53/2741 854, www.observatoriocruzdelsur.cl, tour CH$5,000 adults, CH$4,000 children) on a hill 3.5km south of town. This observatory has four specially designed domes fitted with telescopes, and while it's certainly not worth going out of your way for, the low levels of light-pollution can prove decidedly fruitful for stargazing. You must reserve your space for the observatory in their office in Combarbalá (on the Plaza de Armas, 10am-2pm and 4pm-11pm daily). There are generally two tours (2hr) per night, the first at 9:30pm in summer and 7pm in winter. The office can help you organize a taxi to the observatory.

ACCOMMODATIONS

The town has a range of budget *residenciales* (B&B-style lodgings) and restaurants. It's important to book lodgings ahead of time, particularly outside summer, to ensure that there is someone to receive you. The **Hostal Apuwara** (Alonso de Ercilla 179, tel. 53/2741 690, http://apuwara.cl, CH$31,000 d) is the town's most upscale option, with sizeable rooms with beautiful *combarbalita* sinks set around a sunny central patio with a swimming pool. Rates include IVA.

GETTING THERE

There are two ways to get to Combarbalá from Ovalle. The quicker route is via the road that passes through Monte Patria and Chañaral Alto. This route is 112km, takes 1.75 hours, and is fully paved. The slower route, through Punitaqui, is technically shorter, at 88km, but takes 2.25 hours because the road is unpaved south of Punitaqui. You can also reach Combarbalá from the south via the paved road through Canela Baja. From Ruta 5, it's 74km to Combarbalá and takes 1.25 hours.

Buses from **Ovalle** (2.5hr, CH$8,000), operated by **Expreso Rojas** (tel. 9/6897 8737), leave six times daily from the Terminal de Buses (Ariztía Poniente 849).

CH$113,000 suite, CH$6,000 camping) offers a fine escape into one of the region's least visited areas, in a rustic colonial-style lodge with views of the snowcapped Andes. The larger suite has phenomenal views. All stays can include meals for an additional CH$16,000 pp per day, served in the restaurant. Campsites line Río Hurtado, and campers can add breakfast for CH$7,000 pp. The hacienda offers a range of backcountry trips (by horseback or 4WD vehicle), access to Diaguita cave paintings, and stargazing tours in their private observatory. They can pick you up from La Serena, Vicuña, or Ovalle at additional cost.

At least three daily buses depart Ovalle's Feria Modelo through the Valle Hurtado, which can drop you off just before the Monumento Natural Pichasca and at the lodge (2.5hr, CH$2,400). Departures are listed on the lodge's website. From the lodge, it's 48km along a compacted dirt road to the turnoff onto Ruta 41 for Vicuña, through remote Andean scenery. It's a stunning backcountry way to the Valle de Elqui.

Valle de Huasco

North of La Serena, Ruta 5 heads inland into the folds of the coastal cordillera and back out the other side. Here the deep trough of the Valle de Huasco is known for its olives and river shrimp. This is pisco country, and in September-October, it's a good base to see the extraordinary *desierto florido* (flowering desert) phenomenon, particularly striking in the dry river valleys and exquisite beaches of Parque Nacional Llanos de Challe.

VALLENAR

Nearly 200km north of La Serena, Vallenar is in the river basin of the Río Huasco. A dusty, run-down city, it dates to 1789. After a period of extensive rebuilding, it's now a base for workers in local silver, copper, and iron mines and agricultural industries in surrounding valleys.

Vallenar is best used as a stopping point on the drive from Santiago north, or as a gateway for nearby Parque Nacional Llanos de Challe. Both the national park and the highway out of Vallenar are hot spots for the increasingly frequent *desierto florido* (flowering desert) phenomenon, making this a good day trip to see the most spectacular blooms.

The small **Museo del Huasco** (Prat 1542, tel. 51/2618 586, http://museodelhuascoenvallenar.blogspot.com, 9am-1pm and 3:30pm-6pm Mon.-Fri., CH$800 adults, CH$450 children) contains exhibits on minerology, archaeology, and the history of the region, including photographs of the damage caused by the 1922 earthquake.

Food and Accommodations

Much nicer than the outside might suggest, **Club Social Vallenar** (Prat 899, tel. 9/8204 8612, www.clubsocialvallenar.cl, noon-midnight Mon.-Sat., noon-5pm Sun., CH$6,000-14,000) dates to the late 19th century, although the menu has kept pace with modern times. Tasty pizzas, scallops baked with parmesan, and *causa* (a Peruvian dish of mashed potato stuffed with avocado and crab or chicken) are highlights. Live jazz performances are on Saturday (no cover).

The lime-green **Hotel Esmeralda** (Ramírez 341, tel. 51/2612 977, http://hotelesmeraldavallenar.cl, CH$41,650 d) is the place for a short stay in Vallenar, with 29 simple, small rooms with cool tile floors, parking, and breakfast. It's a popular lodging for mining companies, so it's worth booking in advance. Rates include IVA.

Six kilometers west of Vallenar, crossing the Pan-American Highway on the way to Huasco, **Hotel Orígenes** (Llanos de Ferrera 2, tel. 9/6208 609 or 51/2672 580, www.hotelorigenes.cl, CH$95,000 d) is Vallenar's only quality hotel. It's used for mining conferences, but with a swimming pool in attractive gardens and 18 welcoming, modern rooms, all with spacious baths, TV, and strong Wi-Fi, it's a good choice. You can arrange meals from the guests-only restaurant, which has well-presented steaks, burgers, and more. Rates include IVA.

Information and Services

The **Oficina de Turismo** (Teatro de Vallenar, Prat 1099, 1st Fl., tel. 51/2656 417, www.vallenar.cl, 8:30am-2pm and 3pm-5:20pm Mon.-Fri., occasionally open Sat.) has friendly staff who speak basic English and can advise on tours to nearby observatories and to Parque Nacional Llanos de Challe. **CONAF** (Merced 731, tel. 51/2611 555, 9am-2pm and 3pm-5pm Mon.-Fri.) also has an information office and can advise on the best places to see the flowering desert when it's occurring. A **24-hour ATM** is available at **Banco Estado** (Prat 1201). This bank can also exchange dollars.

Getting There and Around

From **La Serena,** it's a 195-km, 2.25-hour

drive to Vallenar, north on Ruta 5. From **Copiapó,** it's a 147-km, 1.25-hour drive south on Ruta 5. From **Santiago,** it's a 665-km, 7.5-hour drive north on Ruta 5.

Vallenar's small **Terminal de Buses** (Prat 137, tel. 51/2611 431) has frequent buses from **Condor Bus** (tel. 51/26144 74, www.condorbus.cl). and **Buses Expreso Norte** (tel. 51/2546 677, www.expresonorte.cl), which offers the most departures. Next door, **Pullman Bus** (Prat s/n, tel. 51/2619 587, www.pullmanbus.com) has its own terminal, as does **Tur Bus** (Prat 32, tel. 51/2611 738, http://turbus.cl) across the road.

Buses that operate at these terminals come from northern destinations like **Copiapó** (hourly, 2hr, CH$5,000/CH$8,000), **Chañaral** (every 2 hr, 4hr, CH$10,000/CH$12,000), **Calama** (10 daily, 12hr, CH$17,000/CH$35,000), **Iquique** (8 daily, 15hr, CH$23,000/CH$38,000), and **Arica** (5 daily, 21hr, CH$28,000/CH$41,000). Buses come from southern destinations that include **La Serena** (every 30 min, 2.5hr, CH$6,000/CH$10,000) and **Santiago** (hourly, 10hr, CH$12,000/CH$16,000).

Observatorio La Silla

Run by the European Southern Observatory, which also operates the Observatorio Paranal near Antofagasta, **Observatorio La Silla** (Santiago tel. 2/2463 3000, www.eso.org) provides a unique perspective into some of the world's most accurate telescopes. At 2,400 meters elevation in the foothills of the Andes, 137km south of Vallenar and 154km north of La Serena, the state-of-the-art telescopes measure up to 3.6 meters in diameter. Free guided tours (3hr) introduce the research done here, which focuses on detecting exoplanets around other stars. The tours take place at 9:30am and 1:30pm Saturday and include two of the most important telescopes. You must register online for a tour at least a month in advance, as space is limited. Bring plenty of drinking water and food.

No transportation is offered to the observatory, so you'll have to drive yourself.

The views across the desert hills as the road climbs to the observatory are Mars-like, getting you in the mood for learning about the universe. To get here, take Ruta 5 south from Vallenar. You want to take the C-541 turnoff heading west, 75km beyond Vallenar, but it's only accessible to vehicles heading north, so you must continue on Ruta 5 for 15km to a turnaround, where you can return northbound to the turnoff. It's a 137-km, 2-hour drive each way. From La Serena, it's a 155-km, 2.25-hour drive north on Ruta 5 and the C-541. For both journeys, fill your tank before leaving Vallenar, as there are no gas stations en route to the observatory.

Ecoturismo La Serena (Av. Francisco de Aguirre 76, La Serena, tel. 51/2219 500 or 9/7615 2371, www.ecoturismolaserena.cl) can arrange transportation to and from the observatory, with stargazing from the road outside the compound using a small telescope included after the main observatory tour. However, with prices starting at CH$217,000 pp (min. 2 people), you're better off renting a car from La Serena and driving yourself.

★ PARQUE NACIONAL LLANOS DE CHALLE

With empty white-sand beaches that wouldn't look out of place in the Caribbean, the 45,708-hectare **Parque Nacional Llanos de Challe** (Copiapó tel. 52/2213 404, www.conaf.cl, atacama.oirs@conaf.cl, 8:30am-12:30pm and 2pm-7pm daily, CH$5,000 adults, CH$1,500 children) is one of the region's star attractions. Along the coast northwest of Vallenar, it's also the epicenter of the spectacular *desierto florido* (flowering desert), when torrential rainfall transforms the arid landscape into a carpet of multicolored blooms. The most noteworthy of these is the *garra de león* (lion's claw), a deep-red or yellow flower endemic to the Atacama coast and an endangered species.

The best way to visit the park is with your own vehicle, but you can take a **day tour** from Vallenar (from CH$40,000 pp), arranged through the **Oficina de Turismo** (Teatro de

The Flowering Desert

the *desierto florido* in full bloom

The Atacama Desert, the driest on earth, gets just 15 millimeters of rain annually. But every 5-7 years, El Niño brings warmer and wetter weather, transforming the dusty, barren landscapes of the Valle de Huasco into magnificent blooms of pink, white, red, and yellow wildflowers. Because of the desert's aridity, seeds can lie dormant in the soil for years until rainfall triggers them to sprout in great clusters, a phenomenon known as the *desierto florido* (flowering desert), or super bloom. The event can last up to two months, depending on the rain.

Rains normally arrive in mid-August, although the bloom can happen any time after June. The best spots to observe this rare and striking event are in Parque Nacional Llanos de Challe and anywhere along the 150-km stretch of Ruta 5 that connects Vallenar and Copiapó. Typical blooms include the *garra de león* (lion's claw) and the delicate *añañuca*, both of which can bloom in red or yellow, plus white *Leucocoryne*, purple *Pasithea*, and powder-pink *Cistanthe grandiflora*, with different species germinating at different times. All have special adaptations to the extreme climate of the desert. Many are pale to better reflect the sun's rays and heat, while others collect moisture directly from the fog.

The largest flowering desert in 20 years was in 2015 and 2017. Thousands flocked to northern Chile to admire the spectacle. While the increase in El Niño can be good for tourism, it's had a devastating effect on the region's residents. In 2015, flash flooding and mudslides inundated Chañaral and Copiapó, when rivers burst their banks and lashed urban areas, taking everything in their path. Around 25 people died and 11,000 were displaced. President Michelle Bachelet declared a state of catastrophe in the regions of Atacama, Antofagasta, and Coquimbo. Climate change is considered the cause of the uptick in El Niño events.

NORTE CHICO
VALLE DE HUASCO

Vallenar, Prat 1099, 1st Fl., tel. 51/2656 417, www.vallenar.cl, 8:30am-2pm and 3pm-5:20pm Mon.-Fri., occasionally open Sat.).

Tour operators based in Caldera, Bahía Inglesa, and even La Serena run trips during peak *desierto florido* season. From Caldera and Bahía Inglesa, **Geoturismo Atacama** (Av. El Morro 840, tel. 9/9331 8763 or 9/5647 1513, www.geoturismoatacama.com) is recommended. From La Serena, you can go with **Central Tour** (Av. Cuatro Esquinas 560, tel. 9/3094 4304, http://centraltour.cl). From Coquimbo, there's **AlfaTour** (Los Geranios 140, Coquimbo, tel. 9/3198 3483, www.

alfatour.cl), which also offers pickup in La Serena.

The park has two sectors and three main entrances. In the south, the paved C-470 follows the coast; 31km past Huasco Bajo it reaches the park boundary and the small eastern **Sector Los Pozos**. A **CONAF ranger station** (C-470 s/n, no phone) 1.5km north of the boundary collects admission year-round.

Sector Administración is the northern part of the park and has two entrances: from the west via the gravel C-440 (6km southeast of Carrizal Bajo) or the C-440 entering the park from the east, 38km northwest of where it leaves Ruta 5. A second **CONAF ranger station** (C-440 s/n, no phone) is situated equidistant between the two entrances and collects admission December-March.

Sector Los Pozos

Accessed by a road opposite the ranger station, the enchanting fine-white sand of the blissfully undeveloped **Playa Blanca** is washed by the turquoise Pacific. You'd be forgiven for feeling like you've been transported to tropical climes. It's frequented in summer by sunbathers, but the waters aren't safe for swimming. Bring your own shade as the sun can be fierce.

If you continue driving north of the park toward Carrizal Bajo, a handful of unnamed and somewhat less aesthetically spectacular beaches are farther north. They're teeming with a dozen species of marine birds, including neotropical cormorants and American oystercatchers.

Sector Administración

This part of the national park has fewer defined sites but is a great place for blooms on the side of the road during the *desierto florido*. The C-440 runs east-west through this sector before joining with the C-470 on the coast, which you can take south to enter Sector Los Pozos, before continuing to Huasco and taking the C-46 back to Ruta 5.

Accommodations

Camping is possible at **Punta Los Pozas** (C-470 s/n, Sector Los Pozos, opposite the CONAF ranger station, no phone, CH$4,000 pp), where campers are provided 20 liters of drinking water daily and there are paid showers (CH$1,000 adults, CH$200 children). Shade is limited due to a complete lack of vegetation, so bring umbrellas. The campground operates on a first-come, first-served basis.

Getting There

From Vallenar, it's a 46-km drive west along the C-46 to reach the village of Huasco Bajo. The road passes north through low flat-topped hills and a fertile river valley known for its olives. At Huasco Bajo, take the C-470 as it heads north along the coast, passing fishing villages and empty stretches of sand, to the boundary of Sector Los Pozos in 31km. In total, it's a 77-km, one-hour journey.

To reach Sector Administración, continue on the C-470 north through Sector Los Pozos and take the C-440 that runs west-east through this sector, a 16-km drive in total. Alternatively, from Vallenar it's a 55-km, 40-minute journey along Ruta 5 and the C-440. Take Ruta 5 north and turn onto westbound C-440 at the turnaround 20km later. From here, it's a 38-km, 30-minute drive to the eastern entrance of the park.

A 4WD vehicle isn't necessary to get to the park, as most roads are paved and in good condition. Come with a full tank of gas and plenty of food and water. The desert can be unforgiving if your vehicle breaks down, and the chances of other vehicles passing are low.

During summer, daily public transportation to and from the park is sometimes available. Confirm with Vallenar's **Oficina de Turismo** (Teatro de Vallenar, Prat 1099, 1st Fl., tel. 51/2656 417, www.vallenar.cl, 8:30am-2pm and 3pm-5:20pm Mon.-Fri., occasionally open Sat.).

Copiapó

In a valley surrounded by umber hillsides, Copiapó (population 172,000) is a grimy mining city with an interesting historic center. Pedro de Valdivia officially took possession of Chile here in 1540 under the flag of Spanish king Charles V. Debate continues over the origins of the city's name, but it likely originates from the word *copayapu,* "cup of gold" in the indigenous Aymará language—a reflection of the region's rich mineral resources.

The city has a few points of interest for visitors, including museums, but the real draw is nearby Mina San José, which made international headlines in 2010 when 33 miners became trapped and were rescued after 69 days. Tours of the site allow you to imagine some parts of that experience.

Rather than staying here, most visitors find a far more pleasant base in picturesque beach towns Caldera and Bahía Inglesa, just 74km west, and visit Copiapó and the mine on a day trip. Women traveling alone may find themselves the subject of unwelcome attention from the city's disproportionately male population.

SIGHTS

Copiapó's historic center is on the north bank of Río Copiapó. After the discovery of silver nearby, in the 1830s it became the most important mining enclave in the country. The **Plaza de Armas Arturo Prat** (bounded by Los Carrera, Colipi, Bernardo O'Higgins, and Chacabuco), with its towering Peruvian pepper trees, reflects Copiapó at its boom. In the center of the plaza, *La Minería* is a two-level neoclassical fountain carved from Carrara marble and installed in 1863. It depicts a female figure, symbolizing the local mines, standing on a pedestal supported by the heads of condors, an allegory for Chile.

The **Museo Mineralógico** (Colipi 587, tel. 52/2206 606, 10:30am-1pm and 3:30pm-6pm Mon.-Tues. and Thurs.-Fri., CH$1,000

adults, children free) has the largest mineral collection in Chile. Damaged in the devastating flash floods in 2015, the museum was restored and reopened in 2018. Around 150 samples of minerals and rocks are on display, each with information about their distinctive features. The museum's meteorite collection is also impressive.

Museo Regional de Atacama

Four blocks west of the Plaza de Armas, **Museo Regional de Atacama** (Casilla 134, tel. 52/2212 313, http://museodeatacama.gob.cl, 9am-5:45pm Tues.-Fri., 10am-12:45pm and 3pm-5:45pm Sat., 10:30am-1:15pm Sun., free) has extensive information about the Mina San José, where 33 miners were trapped for more than two months in 2010. On display is the original *Fénix II* capsule, which rescued one miner at a time over a 24-hour period. Inside a plastic case is the note that carried the now-famous words *"Estamos bien en el refugio, los 33"* (We are well in the shelter, the 33). The note was attached to a drill bit that had bored into the part of the mine where the men were sheltering.

Other collections focus on Diaguita pottery, the region's gold mining history, and writer, politician, and founder of the Radical Party Manuel Antonio Matta, in whose lavish neoclassical home the museum is located.

ENTERTAINMENT

Sparkling modern **Centro Cultural Atacama** (Av. Matta 260, tel. 52/254 3540) hosts concerts and theater and dance performances.

Held annually for two weeks before February 2, the **Festival de la Virgen de La Candelaria** attracts 50,000 Catholic pilgrims to the **Iglesia de La Candelaria** (Los Carrera and Figueroa). The festival celebrates the alleged discovery of the image of the Virgin in the nearby mountains and pays homage to the

The Disaster at Mina San José

On August 5, 2010, disaster struck at Mina San José, a copper and gold mine in operation since the 1800s. A block of diorite as tall as a 45-story building broke off within the mine, plugging the main shaft in two locations and trapping 33 miners some 680 meters below.

Rescue attempts began immediately, but it wasn't until 17 days later that a probe used to drill boreholes into the collapsed mine found the men. A note reading *"Estamos bien en el refugio, los 33"* (We are well in the shelter, the 33) came back attached to the drill, giving the first indication that all 33 of the miners were alive.

Modeled on successful rescue efforts in other mining disasters, plans were proposed to drill three boreholes for the miners to be winched to safety in specially designed capsules. Food, water, videos, and other essentials were winched down to the miners while they awaited rescue.

The first borehole to reach the miners was the shaft used for the rescue. The first miner to be rescued was Florencio Antonio Avalos Silva, at 12:11am on October

Mina San José

13. The miners had spent 69 days trapped in the mine, the longest time spent underground ever recorded. Shift foreman Luis Alberto Urzúa Iribarren was the final miner rescued, 22.5 hours after the extractions began. President Sebastian Piñera camped out for the duration of the final efforts and embraced each miner as they hit the surface, an event broadcast to 1.5 billion television viewers around the globe.

The rescued miners were flown around the world, appearing on television. Some attended the star-studded release of the film about the catastrophe, *33*. Many felt that they were exploited by the media and politicians, however, as well as the lawyers that they hired to sue the mining company. After a three-year investigation into the disaster, no charges were filed against the company. Many of the rescued miners have since returned to work in other mines in the region.

The mine closed down the day the miners became trapped. Today it's possible to visit the mine (10am-6pm Thurs.-Sun.), where flat mounds of excavated dirt contrast with the golden horizon. The 33 Chilean flags on the hill above the car park were put up during the rescue and still flutter in the wind. Jorge Galleguillos, the 11th miner to be rescued from the catastrophe, now runs tours (CH$5,000) on demand around the scarred earth that bears few traces of the event. He will show you the drill holes used to search for the miners and the now-covered shaft used to bring them out using *Fénix II*, the capsule on display in the Museo Regional de Atacama in Copiapó. The emptiness and barrenness of the site are powerful. As you reach the car park, Jorge or a family member will greet you.

At the mine is a small information center (tel. 9/8990 0593, 10am-6pm Thurs.-Sun., free) where the stages of the disaster are charted through video footage of the prolonged rescue efforts. *Fénix III*, the third capsule built for the rescue but ultimately not used, stands next to the visitors center. A ceremony is held annually every August 5 and October 13 to mark the day of the catastrophe and the day of rescue, with Chile's president often in attendance.

It's a 50-km, 1.25-hour drive from Copiapó northwest to Mina San José. From Ruta 5, take the turnoff to the north and follow signs for "Mina Gallegoso" for 31km to a junction, where you should follow the sign for "Caldera" and head west. From this point, the road is unpaved for 17km to the mine, which is clearly signposted from the road.

patron saint of mines. It's a noisy event combining religious fervor with folkloric dances, processions, and blessings. Accommodations are fully booked for these days.

RECREATION

A handful of tour agencies offer excursions into the Upper Copiapó Valley, west to the Mina San José and Bahía Inglesa, north to Parque Nacional Pan de Azúcar, and to more remote destinations west, including Parque Nacional Nevado Tres Cruces and Ojos del Salado. **Copayapu Travel** (Los Carrera 464, tel. 9/5219 0549, copayaputravel@gmail.com) and **Chillitrip** (Los Carrera 464, tel. 9/8190 9019, www.chillitrip.cl) are both highly recommended. **Geo Adventures** (Martínez 635, tel. 9/6131 426, www.geoadventures.cl) conducts highly recommended trips to Parque Nacional Nevado Tres Cruces and offers pickups from Caldera.

FOOD AND ACCOMMODATIONS

On the edge of a car park a block and a half west of Plaza de Armas Arturo Prat, **Pizza Piero** (Gana 451, tel. 52/2524 910, http://pizzapiero.cl, 12:30pm-10:30pm daily, CH$5,000-8,000) doesn't look like much but has the best pizza in Copiapó. Authentic thin-crust pizzas are loaded with four dozen toppings. There's a reasonable selection of Chilean beer and wine.

Most lodgings in Copiapó cater to mining companies, so solo female travelers may prefer to pay for midrange or better accommodations to avoid feeling uncomfortable. There are 11 rooms at **La Casona** (O'Higgins 150, tel. 52/2217 277, www.lacasonahotel.cl, CH$49,600 d), a cozy midrange guesthouse in a historical building. A shady patio garden decorated with flowering vines is perfect on a hot day. The rooms are simply furnished, in keeping with the setting. The only downsides are a lack of air-conditioning and a nearby bar playing loud music on weekends.

Four blocks northwest of the Plaza de Armas, the friendly **Hostal El Cactus** (Portales 451, tel. 9/8262 3253, CH$29,000 d, cash only) offers superb budget lodging. The walls are thin but the beds are comfortable, and there's a small cactus-lined patio for hot days. Breakfast is not included, but a small kitchenette with a fridge, kettle, and toaster means you can prepare your own.

INFORMATION AND SERVICES

SERNATUR (Av. Los Carrera 691, tel. 52/2212 838, infoatacama@sernatur.cl, 8:30am-6pm Mon.-Fri.) has a helpful information office on the Plaza de Armas and can advise on tours and transportation. **CONAF** (Martínez 55, 52/2213 404, atacama.oirs@conaf.cl, 8am-5:30pm Mon.-Thurs., 8am-4:30pm Fri.) can advise on conditions in the Parque Nacional Nevado Tres Cruces.

The **Hospital Regional de Copiapó** (Los Carrera 1320, tel. 52/2231 580, http://hospitalcopiapo.cl) has the most extensive medical facilities in the region. **Scotiabank** (Atacama 540) has a 24-hour ATM. For mail, head to **Correos** (Los Carrera 691, 9am-2pm and 3pm-6pm Mon.-Fri., 9:30am-1pm Sat.). **Lavanorte** (Chañarcilo 612, http://lavanorte.negocio.site, 9am-8pm Mon.-Fri., 10am-4pm Sat.) handles the laundry.

GETTING THERE
Air

The nearest airport is **Aeródromo Caldera** (Km 860 R-5, tel. 52/2523 600, www.aeropuertodecaldera.cl), also known as the Aeropuerto Desierto de Atacama, 54km west of Copiapó on Ruta 5 and a 20-minute, 25-km drive south from Caldera. There are six daily flights from Santiago on **LATAM** (Colipí 484, tel. 600/5262 000, www.latam.com, 9am-2pm and 3pm-6pm Mon.-Fri., 10:30am-1pm Sat.), **Sky Airline** (www.skyairline.com), and **JetSmart** (http://jetsmart.com). Flights between Caldera and Cusco in Peru are planned.

Rental car companies at the airport are **Europcar** (tel. 52/2528 880, 8:30am-8:30pm Mon.-Fri., 10:30am-6pm Sat., 10:30am-8:30pm Sun., www.europcar.com) and **Hertz**

(tel. 52/2216 259, 8:30am-9pm Mon.-Fri., 9am-6pm Sat., 8:30am-9pm Sun., www.hertz.com).

AIRPORT TRANSFER

Transfer Casther (tel. 52/2235 891 or 52/2218 413, http://casther.cl) offers minivan transfers from the airport to Caldera (CH$5,500), Bahía Inglesa (CH$5,500), and Copiapó (CH$7,000). They have a desk in the arrivals hall; you can walk up to the desk to book a ride.

A taxi stand outside the airport has taxis to Copiapó, or book ahead with **RCK** (tel. 9/9100 1839, rchuartk@gmail.com) or **Taxi Turismo J.R.** (9/9371 4689, juanrosastaxitour64@gmail.com); the journey should cost no more than CH$20,000.

Tur Bus (Chañarcillo 560, tel. 52/2212 629, http://turbus.cl) operates buses into Copiapó (45min, CH$3,000) that coordinate with flight arrivals. Advance reservations aren't possible; buy tickets from the desk in arrivals.

Car

Copiapó is 807km north of **Santiago** along Ruta 5, which runs along the southern edge of the city. The drive from Santiago takes nine hours. From **Vallenar,** it's a 148-km, 1.75-hour drive north on Ruta 5.

Bus

Copiapó's **Terminal de Buses** (Chañarcillo 680, no phone) mostly serves **Buses Expreso Norte** (tel. 52/2231 176, www.expresonorte.cl), the cheapest operator. **Buses Casther** (tel. 51/2218 889, http://casther.cl) and **Buses Caldera** (tel. 9/9207 6848) offer frequent buses to and from **Caldera** (1hr, CH$2,500), where *taxis colectivos* connect with Bahía Inglesa.

Across the road from the city's terminal, **Tur Bus** (Chañarcillo 560, tel. 52/2212 629, http://turbus.cl) operates from a swanky terminal. They have the most regular routes and often have the newest buses, some of which have *cama* seats. The terminal for **Pullman Bus** (Colipi and Av. Copayapu s/n, tel. 52/2238 612, www.pullmanbus.com) is one block south.

Among the three companies, there are buses from **Antofagasta** (hourly, 7hr, CH$14,000/CH$25,000), **Calama** (10 daily, 9hr, CH$15,000/CH$40,000), **Iquique** (10 daily, 13hr, CH$19,000/CH$32,000), and **Arica** (10 daily, 18hr, CH$20,000/CH$35,000). Most pick up passengers in **Chañaral** (2hr, CH$5,000/CH$10,000). From the south, buses depart hourly from **Vallenar** (2hr, CH$5,000/CH$8,000), **La Serena** (5hr, CH$9,000/CH$12,000), and **Santiago** (12hr, CH$14,000/CH$18,000, *cama* CH$33,000).

GETTING AROUND

In addition to their airport locations, **Europcar** (Río Copiapó Sur 194, tel. 52/2528 860, www.europcar.com, 8:30am-6:30pm Mon.-Fri., 9am-1pm Sat.) and **Hertz** (Av. Copayapu 173, tel. 52/2213 522, www.hertz.com, 8:30am-7pm Mon.-Fri., 9am-12:30pm Sat.) have downtown offices. The rental car company **Rodaggio** (Av. Colipí 127, tel. 52/2212 153, www.rodaggio.cl, 8:30am-1pm and 3pm-8pm Mon.-Fri., 9am-1pm Sat.) is downtown.

PARQUE NACIONAL NEVADO TRES CRUCES

In the Andes northeast of Copiapó, high-altitude puna grasslands form much of the 59,000-hectare **Parque Nacional Nevado Tres Cruces** (tel. 52/2213 404, www.conaf.cl, atacama.oirs@conaf.cl, 9:30am-5pm daily Oct.-May, hours depend on weather June-Sept., CH$5,000 adults, CH$1,500 children). Ranging 3,800-4,200 meters elevation, the park is in the basin between the Cordillera Domeyko and Cordillera Claudio Gay, two branches of the Andes that mark the eastern edge of the Atacama Desert.

This vast arid plateau is characterized by sweeping salt flats and saline lagoons dotted with pink flamingos. The park's most famous sights include the imposing 6,749-meter **Nevado Tres Cruces,** a dormant stratovolcano complex towering over the park, and the salt flats of **Salar de Maracunga.** Wildlife is minimal, although the delicate vicuña and hardier guanaco breed here.

Climbing Ojos del Salado

Straddling the border with Argentina, 6,893-meter **Ojos del Salado**, South America's second-highest peak, is the world's highest active volcano. It hasn't erupted since 1956; sulfuric gasses are as much activity as you'll likely see. A crater lake close to the summit is probably the highest lake of any kind in the world.

Ascending the volcano requires serious planning and bureaucracy. Before attempting the climb, all climbers must get permission from the **Dirección de Fronteras y Límites** (DIFROL, Administration of Borders, http://difrol.gob.cl). The main climbing season is November-March. Expeditions are a minimum of 14 days and include ascents of nearby mountains in preparation for climbing Ojos del Salado.

The easiest way is to go with a tour agency based in Copiapó. The agency can organize the necessary permissions and equipment. Both **High Mountain** (Av. Salvador 838, Santiago, tel. 2/2209 6175, www.highmountainla.com) and **Andes Contact** (www.andescontact.cl) organize expeditions on set dates each year. For departures outside these dates, speak to **SERNATUR** (Av. Los Carrera 691, Copiapó, tel. 52/2212 838, infoatacama@sernatur.cl, 8:30am-6pm Mon.-Fri.) in Copiapó.

You can visit the park in your own vehicle, but it's highly recommended to explore it with a tour from Copiapó or Bahía Inglesa. Most tours visit both sectors, continuing almost to the border with Argentina to turquoise **Laguna Verde,** a saline lake ringed by some of the region's highest mountains. **Geo Adventures** (Martínez 635, Copiapó, tel. 9/6131 426, www.geoadventures.cl), based in Copiapó, is a particularly good option, as is **Geoturismo Atacama** (Av. El Morro 840, Bahía Inglesa, tel. 9/9331 8763 or 9/5647 1513, www.geoturismoatacama.com) in Bahía Inglesa. Both operators offer tours in English.

Orientation

Bumpy Ruta 31 heads northeast from Copiapó, climbing among colorful bare mountains, a dramatic contrast to the electric-blue cloudless sky. After 183km, this road reaches an unmarked dirt road and the **unmarked main entrance** to the park and its northern section, **Sector Laguna Santa Rosa.** Next to the lake of that name is a **CONAF ranger station** (9:30am-5pm daily Oct.-May, hours depend on weather June-Sept.), where admission is collected.

From Laguna Santa Rosa, the dirt road exits the park and continues south 77km as it circuits Volcán Copiapó to the **unmarked main entrance** of **Sector Laguna Negro Francisco.**

Sights and Recreation

Flanked by volcanic calderas on the southwest boundary of Sector Laguna Santa Rosa is the gleaming blue **Laguna Santa Rosa,** dotted with flamingos feeding on crustaceans and plankton. The birds are present in small numbers year-round, with up to 8,000 migrating in summer.

This picturesque lake is the southern boundary of the **Salar de Maricunga,** a vivid streak of white across the landscape from Ruta 31 to the lake. It's both the southernmost salt flat in Chile and distinctly whiter than the more famous Salar de Atacama near San Pedro de Atacama—and blissfully free of crowds. Both the lake and the salt flat are reached along the dirt track heading southwest and labeled for "Copiapó" that branches of Ruta 31, 183km after you leave Copiapó. It's only suitable for 4WD vehicles.

The southern Sector Laguna del Negro Francisco, reached by passing the Mina Marta along the unmarked dirt C-347, is home to the **Laguna del Negro Francisco.** Similar to Laguna Santa Rosa, it's also an

NORTE CHICO
COPIAPÓ

important breeding ground for vast numbers of flamingos in summer, along with horned coots, Andean geese, and crested ducks.

Accommodations

Near Laguna Santa Rosa, a set of **cabins** (tel. 9/9051 3202 or 52/2520 112, erciomettifogo@gmail.com or reservas@wara.cl) with basic facilities are available to rent. The **Refugio Laguna del Negro Francisco** (CH$10,000 pp) is a very basic lodge with a dorm with bunks, electricity, restrooms with hot showers, and kitchen facilities, but no drinking water. You'll also need your own gas stove. Make reservations for the *refugio* at the Copiapó **CONAF office** (Martínez 55, 52/2213 404, atacama.oirs@conaf.cl, 8am-5:30pm Mon.-Thurs., 8am-4:30pm Fri.).

Information and Services

Get helpful information about the park, including maps, from the Copiapó **CONAF office** (Martínez 55, 52/2213 404, atacama.

oirs@conaf.cl, 8am-5:30pm Mon.-Thurs., 8am-4:30pm Fri.) or the **ranger station** in Sector Laguna Santa Rosa.

Getting There

The entrance for Sector Laguna Santa Rosa is a 183-km, three-hour drive from Copiapó on Ruta 31. With you own vehicle, 4WD and a GPS receiver are essential. There are no gas stations after leaving the city, so fill a couple of extra gas cans to avoid running out. The rapid increase in elevation from Copiapó may affect your ability to drive—another reason a tour is a good option.

East of the park, on the northern edge of the Salar de Maracunga, a customs and immigration post marks the border for those continuing into Argentina's La Rioja and Catamarca provinces via the 4,748-meter **Paso San Francisco** (8:30am-6:30pm daily, closed winter). All vehicles must stop and present passports, even if you don't plan on crossing the border.

Caldera

The fog lingers well into the morning, but port town Caldera promises year-round sunshine, an abundance of history, and fresh seafood. Scallops, the local delicacy, are best sampled from the seaside shacks lining the road south out of town. The best beaches are south of Caldera, at Bahía Inglesa.

SIGHTS

Most of the town's sights are in the four blocks northwest of spacious **Plaza Caldera** (bounded by Gallo, Cousiño, Carvello, and Ossa Cerda), with vine-covered pergolas and wooden booths selling cheap jewelry and other trinkets. Beware of locals selling shark teeth, which are taken illegally from fossils in Parque Paleontológico Los Dedos.

Pedestrianized **Paseo Gana** leads to the harbor and the Costanera, Caldera's coast

road. It contains some of the town's oldest buildings, built using Oregon pine and American oak from the United States. The structures are notable for their corrugated iron facades painted in bold colors.

Casa Tornini Museo Centro Cultural

The **Casa Tornini Museo Centro Cultural** (Paseo Gana 210, tel. 52/2317 930, http://casatornini.cl, guided tour only, noon-8pm daily Jan.-Feb., 11:30am-4:30pm daily Mar.-Dec., CH$2,500) was variously occupied by British consul Henry Beazley and Italian consul Bernardo Tornini Capelli, in whose family's hands it remained until 2009. It's now a private museum of the archaeological and ethnographic history of the house, the Tornini family, and the Atacama Region, with seven rooms crammed with period furniture. It's only possible to visit on a guided tour, available in English, Spanish, and German.

Estación de Ferrocarril

Right on the harbor between two piers, the **Estación de Ferrocarril** (Wheelwright s/n, no phone, 9am-6pm daily) is Chile's oldest railway station, built in 1850. It was fully restored in 1999 and contains a series of historical artifacts, including an old train carriage and two penny-farthing bicycles. Behind the station is a statue of railway and steamship pioneer William Wheelwright. The building now functions as an events and cultural center, the setting for Caldera's annual film festival, and the **Museo Paleontológico de Caldera** (tel. 52/2535 604, 10am-1:30pm and 3pm-5:30pm Tues.-Sun., CH$1,000 adults, CH$500 children). The Caldera area contains several archaeological sites with fossils of whale, dolphin, penguin, and shark species—many well preserved—dating back nine million years. The objects in the museum's 15,000-piece collection are professionally displayed. The most famous is the 18-million-year-old cranium of a whale found in a bay south of Caldera.

Behind the station, **Muelle Pescador** is the covered **local fish market.** Scallops are the specialty, but eel, *reiñeta* (southern ray bream), and swordfish are fresh from the sea. Continue south to a **boatyard** where you can watch the fishers cleaning and repairing their boats and see the rest of the vessels bobbing in the bay.

BEACHES

Ten kilometers north of Caldera, **Playa Ramada** is a glimmering strip of white-sand beach, protected by a peninsula to the south. There are no facilities, and it's not suitable for swimming due to rip currents, but it is an escape from the heaving beaches of Bahía Inglesa during summer.

A few kilometers north of Playa Ramada, **Santuario de la Naturaleza Granito Orbicular** is a small protected area named for exceptionally rare Jurassic-era rocks of orbicular granite, formed from magma slowly cooling beneath the earth's surface. This process leaves unusual spherical patterns, earning them the nickname "the rocks with eyes." The area has a pretty white-sand beach that's popular among snorkelers, although the rocky coastline means you need to be careful. A path leads north to a lookout for a sea lion colony.

To get to these beaches, ask the driver of any Chañaral-bound bus to drop you at the turn for the beach or the reserve. Both are a 1-km walk west from Ruta 5.

FOOD AND ACCOMMODATIONS

Few restaurants are as cozy as local favorite **El Vecino Otto** (Gallo 203, tel. 52/2317 730, 9:30am-8:30pm daily, CH$2,000-5,000), operating in the owner's home. The food is hearty Chilean *cazuelas* (stews), *humitas* (steamed corn cakes), and *pastel de choclo* (corn and beef pies).

The scallops and fish at **El Delfín** (just before Muelle Pescador, no phone, 9am-7pm Mon.-Fri., 9am-8pm Sat.-Sun., CH$3,000-7,000) travel just a few meters from the fish market to be served in inexpensive, delicious dishes. Scallops baked in cheese are the specialty (they sell them on ice if you want to cook them yourself). The ceviche is excellent too.

Reserve early for the wonderful ★ **Casa Hostal El Faro** (Pasaje Alcalde H. Gigoux 504, tel. 9/7369 6902, www.casahostalelfaro. com, CH$30,000 d), a lovely guesthouse west from the center of town, around the bay, with homespun charm thanks to warm and welcoming Mariela. Rooms have cozy beds and small baths. The sun-splashed rooftop terrace has sea views and a heated swimming pool. There's a communal kitchen and a sizeable breakfast.

INFORMATION AND SERVICES

The **Municipal Oficina Turística** (Plaza Caldera, tel. 52/2535 761, 9:30am-6:30pm daily Jan.-Feb., 9:30am-6:30pm Mon.-Sat.

Mar.-Dec.), in a concrete building on Plaza Caldera, has maps and transportation information.

TRANSPORTATION
Air

The nearest airport is **Aeródromo Caldera** (also known as the Aeropuerto Desierto de Atacama, km 860, R-5, tel. 52/2523 600, www.aeropuertodecaldera.cl), 25km south of Caldera, a 20-minute drive. There are six daily flights from Santiago on **LATAM** (Colipí 484, tel. 600/5262 000, www.latam.com, 9am-2pm and 3pm-6pm Mon.-Fri., 10:30am-1pm Sat.), **Sky Airline** (www.skyairline.com), and **JetSmart** (http://jetsmart.com). Flights between Caldera and Cusco in Peru are planned.

Rental car companies at the airport are **Europcar** (tel. 52/2528 880, 8:30am-8:30pm Mon.-Fri., 10:30am-6pm Sat., 10:30am-8:30pm Sun., www.europcar.com) and **Hertz** (tel. 52/2216 259, 8:30am-9pm Mon.-Fri., 9am-6pm Sat., 8:30am-9pm Sun., www.hertz.com).

AIRPORT TRANSFER

Transfer Casther (tel. 52/2235 891 or 52/2218 413, http://casther.cl) offers minivan transfers from the airport to Caldera (CH$5,500), Bahía Inglesa (CH$5,500), and Copiapó (CH$7,000). They have a desk in the arrivals hall; walk up to book a ride.

A taxi stand outside the airport has taxis to Caldera, or book ahead with **RCK** (tel. 9/9100 1839, rchuartk@gmail.com) or **Taxi Turismo J.R.** (9/9371 4689, juanrosastaxitour64@gmail.com); the journey should cost no more than CH$15,000.

Car

From **Copiapó,** it's a 77-km, one-hour drive northwest on Ruta 5 to Caldera. From **Bahía Inglesa,** it's a 6-km, 10-minute drive north along the C-354.

1: Estación de Ferrocarril **2:** rare granite at Santuario de la Naturaleza Granito Orbicular near Caldera

Car rental is available at the airport and through **Mar Atacama** (Los Tulipanes 869, tel. 9/50094428 or 9/6900 0910, 9am-7pm Mon.-Fri., by appointment Sat.-Sun.).

Bus and *Taxi Colectivo*

Buses from Copiapó and other destinations stop at the **Terminal de Buses** (Ossa Varas and Cifuentes, no phone), a collection of ticket booths and a bus stand on the southern side of the Plaza Las Americas, three blocks southwest of the Plaza Caldera.

Buses Caldera (tel. 52/2316 680) and **Buses Casther** (tel. 52/2315 308, http://casther.cl) have a booth in the terminal and have half-hourly buses to Copiapó (1hr, CH$2,500). **Tur Bus** (Paseo Gana 241, tel. 52/2205 016, http://turbus.cl) has an office in the city center, but buses arrive and depart from the Terminal de Buses. They have the most regular routes and often the newest buses, some of which offer *cama* seats. Departures with **Pullman Bus** (Gallo 160, tel. 52/2315 227, www.pullmanbus.cl) leave from their office, three blocks north of Plaza Caldera.

Tur Bus and Pullman Bus offer routes from southern destinations, including **Vallenar** (9 daily, 3hr, CH$7,000/CH$13,000), **La Serena** (7 daily, 6.5hr, CH$12,000/CH$18,000), and **Santiago** (4 daily, 14hr, CH$18,000/CH$26,000, *cama* CH$33,000). The same companies have buses from the north, including **Antofagasta** (9 daily, 6.5hr, CH$12,000/CH$24,000), **Calama** (5 daily, 9.5hr, CH$16,000/CH$35,000), **Iquique** (4 daily, 12hr, CH$19,000/CH$32,000), and **Arica** (4 daily, 17.5hr, CH$20,000/CH$30,000). All of these buses pass through **Chañaral** (1.25hr, CH$4,000/CH$8,000), where they will drop off and pick up passengers.

Taxis colectivos (CH$1,000) for Bahía Inglesa depart when full from Calle Gallo on the north side of the Plaza Caldera.

Getting Around

It's possible to get to the beaches north and south of Caldera by bicycle. **Tiska Bicicletas**

(Zuiderste s/n, roundabout southwest of Caldera on the road to Bahía Inglesa, tel. 9/9716 2746, hours vary) rents bikes for CH$10,000 per day.

BAHÍA INGLESA

With a strip of white sand and black rocks contrasting the picturesque turquoise ocean, it's no wonder that the town of Bahía Inglesa has become the beach resort of choice for wealthy Chileans. Unfortunately, this means that the town loses much of its charm when the crowds descend on the beach and choke the streets with cars.

Outside January-February, expect to have the place virtually to yourself, with some of the prettiest beaches in the area within walking distance. All facilities, including good lodgings, restaurants, and tour agencies, are clustered on the waterfront.

Recreation

BEACHES

Bahía Inglesa's main beach has gorgeous white sand, aptly named **Playa Blanca** (White Beach). It continues from the main part of town south around the coast to become the larger, still heavenly white **Playa Las Machas.** At both beaches, swimming is not permitted, but there are kayaks available to rent on the beachfront.

DIVING

Bahía Inglesa is known as a good spot for **diving,** thanks to clear water teeming with fish. The water is cold; divers have to wear wetsuits. You can arrange to dive with team at the PADI-accredited **Bahía Mako** (Av. El Morro 610, tel. 9/5358 0487, bahiamako@gmail.com), one of the diving schools housed in wooden shacks along the main waterfront. Prices start at CH$35,000 per dive for those already certified, with equipment included. You can also arrange a dive for the same price with PADI-certified **AtacamaBuceo** (tel. 9/9488 3425, https://atacamabuceo.cl).

GUIDED TOURS

The highly recommended **Geoturismo Atacama** (Av. El Morro 840, tel. 9/9331 8763 or 9/5647 1513, www.geoturismoatacama.com) operates tours of the coast south of Bahía Inglesa and to Parque Nacional Pan de Azúcar, the Mina San José, and Parque Nacional Nevado Tres Cruces. Tour prices start at CH$20,000.

Food and Accommodations

Most of the lodgings in Bahía Inglesa are overpriced in summer due to high demand. Prices drop dramatically outside mid-December-mid-March. Many restaurants close early during the week outside these months.

In an unassuming shack on the main beach, **Ostiones Vivas** (Av. El Morro 1038, noon-8:30pm daily summer, hours vary rest of the year, CH$500-7,000) sells ocean-fresh scallops either raw with a squeeze of lemon juice and salt or oven-baked with a parmesan crust. They'll likely be the best you've ever tasted, with incredible views across the bay to boot.

At the beachside **Nautel Hospedaje** (Copiapó 549, tel. 9/9824 4688, http://nautel.cl, CH$60,000 d), the eight rooms are simple but clean, with modern baths. You'll pay an extra CH$20,000 for views of the sea; the other rooms look onto a road. There's a lovely outdoor patio with squishy sofas, a covered kitchen, and a barbecue for evenings. Prices drop by 50 percent outside summer.

On the beachfront, **K Hotel Boutique** (Av. El Morro 416, tel. 9/98314 617, www.khotelboutique.cl, CH$80,000-130,000 d) has four smart rooms, the largest of which has its own balcony with spectacular views. The other rooms have slight or no views of the sea. All rooms have soft cotton sheets and modern baths. You'll feel looked after by the owners.

Getting There and Around

From **Caldera,** it's a 6-km, 10-minute drive south along the C-345, which leaves town at the roundabout in the south of Caldera. Bahía Inglesa doesn't have a bus terminal. The only transport is *taxis colectivos* (10min, CH$1,000) that connect Bahía Inglesa with Caldera. They depart when full from Calle Gallo on the north side of the Plaza Caldera. Another option is to hire a bicycle from **Tiska Bicicletas** (Zuiderste s/n, roundabout southwest of Caldera on the road to Bahía Inglesa, tel. 9/9716 2746, hours vary) for CH$10,000 per day.

★ PARQUE PALEONTOLÓGICO LOS DEDOS

Spanning 371 hectares of eroded landscapes of scorched sand that looks straight out of a *Star Wars* film, the municipal-run open-air **Parque Paleontológico Los Dedos** (tel. 52/2535 604 or 9/7616 0891, aolivares@caldera.cl, by guided tour only, 10am-5pm Tues.-Sun., free) is the most important collection of fossils in Chile and one of the top paleontological sites on the continent. Vertebrae from 70 different species have been found here, including prehistoric birds such as the *Pelagornis*, megalodon sharks, gharial crocodiles, and giant ground sloths, with bones dated to 16 million years ago.

Still a working excavation site, the park opened to the public in 2011. Half a kilometer of paths lead through a small section that can be visited by guided tour in Spanish only. Most of the fossils are still buried; you can spot whale bones and razor-sharp shark teeth jutting out of clearly defined layers of volcanic ash and phosphorous, which sit above layers of sedimentary rock, all of which have preserved the remains for millions of years.

The theft of fossils from the park, particularly shark teeth, which turn up in local handcraft jewelry, is a problem. If you see jewelry in Caldera or Bahía Inglesa that's made of shark teeth, don't buy it.

Getting There

It's a 15-minute, 12-km drive south along the C-345 to the roundabout just before Bahía Inglesa, where you take the road southeast that's signed for "Copiapó" for 1km and turn south onto the C-302, which passes in front of the park entrance after 6km (5min). From Bahía Inglesa, it's a 7-km, six-minute journey east of the village.

BEACHES SOUTH OF BAHÍA INGLESA

The coast south of Bahía Inglesa is largely untouched; a wealth of picturesque empty beaches await those with their own transportation to sunbathe or paddle in the cool, calm water.

Pretty **Playa El Morro,** 7km south of Bahía Inglesa, is on the southern edge of the scooping bay of the same name, offering pretty views. It's the strip of sand across the coast road from the Parque Paleontológico Los Dedos. Seven kilometers south of Playa El Morro, accessed by a packed dirt road, **Playa Chorillos** is a rocky beach overlooked by steep dramatic cliffs layered with sedimentary rock.

Popular among Chileans, **Playa Virgen,** 32km south of Playa Chorillos, lies beyond the oldest port in the region, Puerto Viejo. Famed for twinkling turquoise water that is exceptionally calm, it is one of the few beaches in the region that is safe for swimming. The growing popularity of the bay has brought piles of rubbish that destroy the magic of the area.

Other hidden beaches exist, but you'll need local knowledge or a local guide to find them. Agencies in Bahía Inglesa, such as **Geoturismo Atacama** (Av. El Morro 840, tel. 9/9331 8763 or 9/5647 1513, www.geoturismoatacama.com), organize day trips starting from CH$20,000.

★ PARQUE NACIONAL PAN DE AZÚCAR

The fog clings to the coastal cordillera, veiling it in dense clouds in the early morning and watering the low vegetation of the stark **Parque Nacional Pan de Azúcar** (tel. 52/2213 404, www.conaf.cl, atacama.

oirs@conaf.cl, 8:30am-12:30pm and 2pm-6pm daily, CH$5,000 adults, CH$1,500 children). The park straddles the Atacama and Antofagasta regions and contains stunning coastal campsites and an array of hiking trails.

The national park is along the coast and home to 20 cactus species, mainly of the genus *Copiapoa*. Marine wildlife is extensive, particularly around Isla Pan de Azúcar, the sugarloaf-shaped island that gives the park its name, with marine otters and South American sea lions. In the higher reaches of the park, up to 900 meters elevation, the odd guanaco is visible.

The main entrance is from Chañaral in the south, a 20-km, 30-minute drive along the signposted C-120. From here, 10 minutes north brings you to **CONAF headquarters** (8:30am-12:30pm and 2pm-6pm daily), where admission is collected. Access into the park is also possible from the east, where a signed turn at Las Bombas, 45km northwest of Chañaral, takes you along the Quebrada Pan de Azúcar to the coast, passing through the park's trademark sloping ravines covered with a thin layer of vegetation. Admission is rarely charged at this entrance.

Bring a sun hat, plenty of sunscreen, and enough water for your stay; there's nowhere to buy them in the park. Chañaral, the town south of the park, is a good base for a day trip. Those with more time and a vehicle can camp overnight or stay in cabins on one of the park's trademark white-sand beaches.

Sights

One kilometer north of the signposted entrance to the park (admission is collected farther north) along a smooth unpaved track, the **Sendero Quebrada Castillo** (9km round-trip, 2hr) is a trail into the Castillo gully, one of the finest places to see the flowers of the *desierto florido*. Fog droplets cling to the gorge and create a diverse array of blooms. It's one of the main sites for Copao de Saint-Pieana, a species of cactus that grows up to seven meters tall. A kilometer north of this trailhead, **Playa Blanca** is a broad, gleaming white-sand beach that's not suitable for swimming but has awe-inspiring views of the ocean.

Four kilometers north of Playa Blanca, most of the park's services are at **Playa Piqueros,** with CONAF headquarters, camping, and cabins. Playa Piqueros, beneath the looming Cerro Soldado and bordered by guano-splattered rocks, is not suitable for

Parque Nacional Pan de Azúcar

swimming. Neighboring **Playa Soldado,** a few hundred meters south and accessible by a walking path, is a good spot for a dip.

From the CONAF station, the **Sendero Aguada Los Sapos** (5km one-way, 2hr) passes through a deep ravine home to the Atacama toad. The **Sendero Mirador Chico** (11km-loop, 4hr) reaches a viewpoint across the bay.

The most popular trail is the **Sendero El Mirador** (2.5km one-way, 1hr) a flat hike along a gentle gradient to the park's finest panoramic viewpoint, across the bay and toward the island. The path is bordered by huge cacti and flowering vegetation. It's possible to see guanaco and *culpeo* foxes. This trail gets exceptionally busy in summer, so get here early.

ISLA PAN DE AZÚCAR
One of the park's most popular excursions is the boat ride to **Isla Pan de Azúcar,** a sanctuary for Humboldt penguins, Peruvian blue-footed boobies, brown pelicans, Inca terns, and red-legged cormorants, among other seabirds. There are also breeding colonies of South American sea lions. Launches from the pier in Caleta Pan de Azúcar, the 20-family fishing hamlet in the park, are frequent in summer and on weekends, but far fewer the rest of the year.

The excursions are run by the local fishing association, **Embarcación Pan de Azúcar** (tel. 9/8664 0463). Ten passengers are required for the boat to leave. It normally costs CH$10,000 pp, although smaller groups can pay the full price of CH$100,000. The journey takes around 1.5 hours, getting close enough to the islands to admire the wildlife, although landing is prohibited.

Food and Accommodations
Food is available from the collection of fish restaurants at **Caleta Pan de Azúcar,** which specialize in dorado and other local fish, which you can normally buy directly from fishing boats.

Right on Playa Piqueros, the park's only lodging is **Camping and Cabañas Pan de Azúcar** (tel. 9/9844 7375 or 9/8802 1299, www.pandeazucarlodge.cl, CH$65,000 2-person cabin with private bath, CH$8,500 camping pp). It feels like heaven, with a beachside setting overlooking the crashing waves. The five cabins are simple but clean, with kitchens and hot showers, although there's no electricity. Camping is basic, with cold showers. They stock some basics in the shop during summer, but it's better to bring all your food with you; a camping stove is essential, as fires are not permitted in the park. The campground gets packed in summer but is virtually empty the rest of the year.

Information and Services
All of the park's paths are well marked, although you can find basic maps at CONAF's **Centro de Información Ambiental** (opposite Playa Piqueros, tel. 9/7950 5662, jose. gutierrez@conaf.cl, 8:30am-12:30pm and 2pm-6pm daily), where you must stop to pay the entrance fee. A cactarium here identifies the different cacti in the park, while the small museum inside explains different flora and fauna and the history of the park's early inhabitants, the Chango people.

Getting There and Around
From Caldera, it's a 105-km, 1.25-hour drive north on Ruta 5 and the C-120. From Copiapó, add an extra 74km and 45 minutes.

Nearly all buses northbound from Copiapó and Caldera pass through Chañaral (2hr, CH$5,000/CH$10,000), the town just south of the park, where you can negotiate a taxi, but you'll pay at least CH$15,000 each way. The easiest way to the park is a rental car, which allows you to explore at your own pace.

Taking the eastern route out of the park, it's possible to rejoin Ruta 5, and then take the road toward the coast 21km later, signed for "Cifunche." This spectacular road passes the fishing town and seaside resort Cifunche and passes the larger settlement of Taltal as it makes its slow, winding way along the coast and through ravines north to Antofagasta. At times, the earth looks to be carpeted in low green vegetation, but it's an illusion caused by the leaching of copper. Wooden houses line the edges of the hills and the coasts.

CHAÑARAL

The grimy town of Chañaral, 167km northwest of Copiapó, is a stop for buses heading south and north. It's a good base for a day trip into Parque Nacional Pan de Azúcar. Sadly, half the town washed away in the 2015 floods, when water surged through the middle, flattening houses and other buildings. The town is slowly rebuilding.

Accommodations

You can't go wrong with **Hostal Pan de Azúcar** (Doctor Herrara 1527, tel. 56/2480 754, http://hostalpandeazucar.wordpress. com, CH$30,000 d), the town's nicest lodgings. Owners Willy and Fernando make the perfect hosts and can help you arrange trips into the nearby national park. Various seating areas on the terrace offer sea views, while an ample breakfast is served downstairs in the kitchen. The inn boasts large rooms, all with en suite baths and comfortable beds. The Wi-Fi only reaches the rooms closest to the reception area.

Getting There

From **Caldera,** it's a 90-km, one-hour drive north on Ruta 5. Nearly all buses northbound from **Copiapó** and **Caldera** (2hr, CH$5,000/CH$10,000) pass through Chañaral. These include **Tur Bus** (Merino Jarpa 1187, Chañaral, tel. 52/2481 012, http://turbus.cl) and **Pullman Bus** (Merino Jarpa 577, Chañaral, tel. 52/2480 213, www.pullmanbus.cl), which have their own terminals in Chañaral, one block east of Ruta 5. They also bring passengers from destinations in the north, including nine daily buses from **Antofagasta** (5hr, CH$10,000/CH$15,000), four daily from **Calama** (8hr, CH$20,000/CH$26,000), and three daily from **Iquique** (12.5hr, CH$14,000/CH$25,000) and **Arica** (16hr, CH$20,000/CH$35,000).

Central Valley

The Central Valley is Chile's breadbasket—its agricultural heart, home to fertile alluvial soils and a pleasant Mediterranean climate, where kiwis and nectarines grow on trees that line the highways.

The region extends from Rancagua to the banks of the Río Bío Bío, some 450km south, and is best known for its viticulture. Six distinct wine valleys include the internationally renowned Valle de Colchagua and Valle de Maule. Here, historic terra-cotta-roofed wineries are open for tastings, dining, and even as luxurious lodgings.

To the west are empty white-sand beaches, with waves up to six meters tall providing some of Chile's best surfing in places such as Pichilemu. In the mountains to the east, the ski resort Nevados

Highlights

Look for ★ to find recommended sights, activities, dining, and lodging.

★ **Museo Colchagua:** The country's largest private museum covers the history of Chile (page 265).

★ **Wine-Tasting:** Sample the finest carménère in Chile's most celebrated wine valley, **Valle de Colchagua** (page 266).

★ **Museo de la Artesanía Chilena:** Learn about Chile's diverse handicrafts traditions in the picturesque colonial town of Lolol (page 271).

★ **Surfing:** Take on Chile's longest wave in **Pichilemu** (page 271).

★ **Parque Nacional Radal Siete Tazas:** See crystalline waterfalls in this spectacular national park (page 275).

★ **Handicrafts in Rari:** Buy unique souvenirs from this village that specializes in delicate jewelry and ornaments made from dyed horsehair (page 280).

★ **Reserva Nacional Altos de Lircay:** Rugged volcanic scenery dazzles in this high-altitude national reserve on the edges of the Andes (page 282).

★ **Escuela Mexico:** See Chilean and Mexican history at its most dramatic in the murals of David Alfaro Siqueiros (page 285).

★ **Ski at Nevados de Chillán:** Hit the slopes at this resort on the side of three active

volcanoes, then get your après-ski fix in the adjoining hot springs (page 287).

★ **Mina Chiflón del Diablo:** Take a tour of the world's only undersea mine (page 295).

de Chillán entices adrenaline seekers. Throughout the region, national parks with rare wildlife and volcanic landscapes provide unforgettable sights for hikers.

Scattered across the Central Valley are historic towns that bear the marks of colonial battles between the Spanish and the indigenous Mapuche people. Also evident is the destruction caused by multiple earthquakes. The lively university city Concepción remains standing, with metropolitan ambience and fame as the birthplace of Chilean rock music.

PLANNING YOUR TIME

The Central Valley is an often overlooked part of Chile, but the incomparable **vineyards** are growing in popularity. **Santa Cruz** is the most sensible base for a day or two of tastings, vineyard tours, and lunch in the **Valle de Colchagua.** The vineyards of the **Valle del Cachapoal** and **Valle de Curicó** can be visited as short detours from Ruta 5. The **Valle de Maule,** home to some of the country's oldest vines, has a number of pleasant vineyards and luxurious lodgings, making it worth an overnight trip.

The mellow coastal hangout **Pichilemu** is Chile's capital of surf, with enough six-meter waves to keep you occupied for a day or two. If quiet beaches with rarely another human in sight are more your style, the coastal road from **Constitución to Cobquecura** offers a day's drive with an array of charming hidden coves.

The Central Valley's main hiking destinations offer volcano-studded scenery and far fewer visitors than the more popular national parks farther south. Among them, **Parque Nacional Radal Siete Tazas** and **Reserva Nacional Altos de Lircay** are the most compelling; you'll want at least two days in each.

For skiing, the slopes of the snow-topped **Nevados de Chillán** can be visited in a day from **Chillán,** although an overnight stay at this resort allows for an evening dip in the region's famed hot springs.

Concepción has lively student-led **nightlife,** but not much else for visitors. A two-day stop allows for exploring the nearby **Lota mine and park,** the Mapuche museum in **Cañete,** and the **pretty beaches** north of the city.

HISTORY

Agriculture was introduced to the Central Valley by the indigenous Chiquillane and Pehuenche people, two branches of the Mapuche. The first invaders were the Inca, but the Spanish would eventually oust the indigenous Mapuche in brutal battles from the 1500s to the late 1800s. The Spanish divided this new territory among themselves, effectively enslaving the indigenous people to work the land. The mass clearing of forests allowed for the cultivation of fruits and vegetables. Grapevines were introduced by missionaries, with the first recorded vintage produced in 1551.

In the late 1800s the coal mines of Lota, near Concepción, aided the expansion of steam trains across the region. East of Rancagua, the El Teniente copper mine, the largest underground mine in the world, is still an important part of the local economy. Despite the colonial origins of many of the region's towns, the Central Valley's susceptibility to earthquakes means that a large proportion of original buildings have been lost.

Previous: surfing in the Central Valley; Parque Nacional Radal Siete Tazas; turkey vulture in Parque Pedro del Río Zañartu.

Central Valley

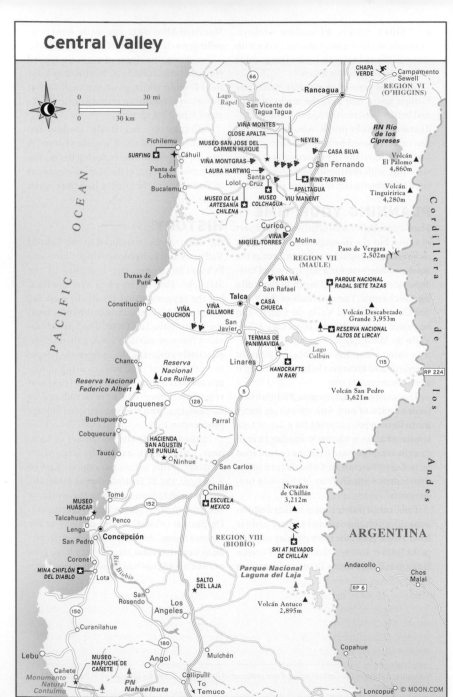

0   30 mi
0   30 km

Rancagua

CHAPA VERDE
Campamento Sewell
REGION VI (O'HIGGINS)

66

Lago Rapel
San Vicente de Tagua Tagua

RN Río de los Cipreses

VIÑA MONTES
CLOSE APALTA
NEYEN
CASA SILVA

Pichilemu
MUSEO SAN JOSE DEL CARMEN HUIQUE
SURFING
Cáhuil
VIÑA MONTGRAS
LAURA HARTWIG
Punta de Lobos
Lolol
Santa Cruz

Volcán El Palomo 4,860m

San Fernando

WINE-TASTING

APALTAGUA

Volcán Tinguiririca 4,280m

Bucalemu
MUSEO DE LA ARTESANÍA CHILENA
MUSEO COLCHAGUA
VIU MANENT

Curicó

VIÑA MIGUEL TORRES
Molina

Paso de Vergara 2,502m

REGION VII (MAULE)

Dunas de Putú
VIÑA VIA
San Rafael

PARQUE NACIONAL RADAL SIETE TAZAS

Constitución
Talca
CASA CHUECA

VIÑA BOUCHON
VIÑA GILLMORE
San Javier
Volcán Descabezado Grande 3,953m

RESERVA NACIONAL ALTOS DE LIRCAY

TERMAS DE PANIMAVIDA

Chanco
Reserva Nacional Los Ruiles
Linares
Lago Colbún

Reserva Nacional Federico Albert
HANDCRAFTS IN RARI

115

RP 224

Volcán San Pedro 3,621m

Cauquenes
128
5

Buchupureo
Parral

Cobquecura
HACIENDA SAN AGUSTÍN DE PUÑUAL

Taucú
Ninhue
San Carlos

Tomé
Chillán
Nevados de Chillán 3,212m

MUSEO HUÁSCAR
152
ESCUELA MEXICO

Talcahuano
Penco
Lenga
San Pedro
REGION VIII (BIOBÍO)

SKI AT NEVADOS DE CHILLÁN

ARGENTINA

Concepción

Coronel
MINA CHIFLÓN DEL DIABLO
Lota
Río Biobío
SALTO DEL LAJA

Parque Nacional Laguna del Laja

Andacollo
Chos Malal

RP 6

San Rosendo
Los Angeles
Volcán Antuco 2,895m

150
Curanilahue

Lebu
180
Angol
Mulchén

MUSEO MAPUCHE DE CAÑETE
Cañete
Monumento Natural Contulmo
PN Nahuelbuta
Collipulli
To Temuco

Copahue

Loncopué

PACIFIC OCEAN

Cordillera de los Andes

© MOON.COM

Two Days in the Central Valley

DAY 1
Join a **morning tour** for a trip to the **vineyards** of the **Apalta and Colchagua Valleys,** stopping at **Viu Manent** and **Clos Apalta,** and ending with an extravagant lunch at specialty barbecue restaurant **Fuegos de Apalta** in **Viña Montes.**

Head to **Santa Cruz** and spend a few hours admiring the incredible collection of artifacts in the **Museo Colchagua** before catching a cab to **Colchagua Camp** for a night in cozy geodesic domes with a hot tub overlooking a grove of citrus trees.

DAY 2
Hop on the bus to **Pichilemu** on the coast for a day enjoying the town's relaxed ambience, with a few hours on the beach watching the surfers catching the waves at **Punta de Lobos.**

Enjoy a sundowner and dinner on the terrace at **La Casa Verde** before spending the night in the enchanting forest hideaway of **Tripanko Lodge & Bungalows,** up the hill from Punta de Lobos.

Valle del Cachapoal

Stretching from Rancagua, 56km south of Santiago, to the town of San Fernando, the Valle del Cachapoal is home to a few wineries in the south, but it's more notable as the site of the annual rodeo in the regional capital Rancagua. Outside of the city, the Andean backcountry is typified by the little-known Reserva Nacional Río de Los Cipreses and the abandoned mining village of Campamento Sewell, tucked into the mountains.

RANCAGUA
The historic roots of Rancagua go deep. Founded in 1743, it was the site of the 1814 Desastre de Rancagua (Rancagua Disaster), where Bernardo O'Higgins's pro-independence forces lost a brutal battle to royalist Spanish troops. Apart from a few colonial buildings surrounding the central plaza, the city shows little of its role in history. Now the heart of farming country, it is surrounded by fruit groves. It's also host to the national rodeo championships, which welcome thousands of participants and spectators from across the country.

For most visitors, Rancagua merits just a brief stop as part of a day trip to surrounding attractions, which include the Sewell mining town and the rugged, parrot-filled Reserva Nacional Río de los Cipreses.

Sights
Rancagua was designed on a grid surrounding its unusual circular and well-tended **Plaza de Héroes** (bounded by Estero). At the center of the plaza is a bronze statue of independence leader Bernardo O'Higgins.

Three blocks south along pedestrianized Paseo Estado, two colonial adobe houses, both national monuments, make up the **Museo Regional de Rancagua** (tel. 72/2221 524, http://museorancagua.cl, 10am-6pm Mon.-Thurs., 10am-5pm Fri., 10am-2pm Sat., free). The grander of the two is the **Casa del Pilar de Esquina** (Paseo Estado 684), named after its quirky pillar where Paseo Estado meets Calle Ibieta. It has small exhibitions in one room of local photography and art, but more interesting is the back garden, where the original centuries-old adobe walls of the building are visible, propped up with bricks and cement following earthquake damage. Across the road, the **Casa Ochavo** (Paseo Estado 685) is larger inside than it looks, with pretty palm-lined patios surrounded by rooms dressed in 19th-century furniture. There's a section dedicated to the events of the Desastre de Rancagua.

Entertainment
CAMPEONATO NACIONAL DE RODEO

The most important tournament of its kind in the country, the **Campeonato Nacional de Rodeo** (National Rodeo Championships, Medialuna Monumental de Rancagua, Av. España and Ibarra, tel. 72/2221 286), held the first weekend in April, draws crowds of up to 50,000 for the official Chilean sport. The most capable *huasos* (Chilean cowboys) compete on Chilean Corraleros (one of the oldest horse breeds in the Americas) in the city's *medialuna,* a circular corral used for the rodeo.

Rodeo is a male-dominated event, although women are starting to compete. The men dress in typical *huaso* clothing, including brightly colored woven ponchos, broad-brimmed straw hats known as *chupallas,* and glimmering silver spurs on heavy leather boots.

The main event is the *atajada,* where two competitors work together on their horses, which are specially trained to run sideways, to herd a calf around the ring twice before pinning it against a marked area on the wall. Held the same weekend as the rodeo championships, the lively **Fiesta Huasa** (Plaza de Héroes) celebrates rural traditions, with local food and wine, regional handicrafts, and folkloric music and dancing.

Food and Accommodations

At **La Pamplona** (Almarza 495, tel. 9/5329 2830, www.lapamplona.cl, noon-11pm Mon.-Thurs., noon-1am Fri.-Sat., CH$4,500-11,000), a slick hamburger joint, triple-decker burgers and thin-crust pizzas accompany craft beer on tap.

A reliable lodging 2km east of the center, **Hotel Manquehue Rancagua** (Av. Alberto Einstein 290, tel. 72/2352 000, www. hotelmanquehuerancagua.cl, CH$55,000 d)

is part of a Chilean chain of hotels and is the city's main conference center. The rooms are modern and include air-conditioning. English-speaking staff are helpful, and mountain views from upper-floor bedrooms and the restaurant terrace are the cherry on top.

Information and Services

The **SERNATUR office** (Germán Riesco 350, Edificio Gobernación, tel. 72/2227 261, inforancagua@sernatur.cl, 9am-2pm and 3pm-6pm Mon.-Thurs, 9am-1pm and 2pm-5pm Fri.) has helpful regional maps. The **Hospital Regional** (Av. O'Higgins 3095, tel. 72/2982 715, http://hospitalrancagua.cl) can deal with most medical emergencies. For mail services, head to **Correos** (Campos 322, tel. 600/9502 020, 9am-2pm and 3pm-6pm Mon.-Fri., 10:30pm-1pm Sat.).

Getting There and Around

From **Santiago** by car, it's a one-hour, 86-km drive south on Ruta 5, then Ex-Ruta 5 just before the city, which continues into the center.

Rancagua is a stop on most southbound buses leaving **Terminal Santiago** (Av. Alameda 3850, tel. 2/2376 1750) and the **Terminal Alameda** (Av. Alameda 3750, no phone) in **Santiago** (1hr, CH$2,400), which drop off at Rancagua's **Terminal O'Higgins** (O'Higgins 484, tel. 72/2225 425). **Pullman Bus** (tel. 72/2222 540, www.pullmanbus.cl) and **Condor Bus** (tel. 72/2222 542, www. condorbus.cl) have the most regular departures from Santiago. **Tur Bus** (O'Carrol 1175, tel. 72/2230 341, http://turbus.cl) has its own terminal where most of their Santiago buses arrive.

Bus company **Nilahue** (tel. 72/2238 567) offers hourly departures from **Pichilemu** (4.5hr, CH$6,000), plus buses every 30 minutes from **San Fernando** (50min, CH$3,000) and **Santa Cruz** (2.25hr, CH$5,000). From the south, hourly buses arrive from **Chillán** (3.75hr, CH$10,000), often stopping at Curicó and Talca. There are buses every 15 minutes from the **Terminal Rodoviario** (Dr. Salinas 1165, tel. 72/2225 425) to **Machalí** (30min,

CH$1,000) for onward travel to Chacayes and the Reserva Nacional Río de Los Cipreses.

From Estación Alameda in Santiago, **trains** (1.5hr, CH$2,290) depart every two hours for the **Estación Rancagua** (Av. Estación s/n, tel. 2/2585 5000, www. trencentral.cl), with slightly fewer trains on weekends. Rancagua is the final stop on the Metrotrén route; TerraSur trains continue south to Talca and terminate in Chillán. From Talca, the Buscarril narrow-gauge train line runs west to Constitución.

CAMPAMENTO SEWELL

Former mining town **Campamento Sewell** retains an air of its former existence in timber buildings painted bright red, green, and yellow. Residents once worked at the nearby El Teniente copper mine, the largest underground mine of its type in the world.

After the mine opened in 1905, owner William Branden established infrastructure to connect it with Rancagua, 55km west. Roads, worker housing, and even a railway were built in this remote Andes outpost. The town had 15,000 inhabitants by 1960 and came to be known as the Ciudad de las Escaleras (City of Steps) for its mountainside position; too steep for cars, the entire town was pedestrianized.

By the late 1960s, the company decided it was cheaper to bus its employees from Rancagua. Demolition began but was eventually halted to conserve the site. In 2006, Campamento Sewell became a UNESCO World Heritage Site.

Campamento Sewell and El Teniente mine can be visited as part of a day tour. Stops generally include employee houses, the social club, and the church as well as a visit to the entrance of the still-operating mine. The tour ends with a visit to a museum about the mine and a late lunch. Tours are available in Spanish or English. The agency **VTS** (Manuel Montt 192, Rancagua, tel. 72/2952 692, www.vts.cl) offers tours Saturday-Sunday (CH$47,000 pp from Santiago, CH$42,000 from Rancagua, lunch included). Sturdy shoes for climbing plenty of steps and a jacket are advised, as the town is at 2,200 meters elevation and temperatures can be cold.

RESERVA NACIONAL RÍO DE LOS CIPRESES

Southeast of Rancagua, the 36,882-hectare **Reserva Nacional Río de Los Cipreses** (tel. 72/2297 505, reserva.cipreses@conaf.cl, 8:30am-8pm daily summer, 8:30am-5:30pm daily winter, CH$5,000 adults, CH$2,500 children) was established to protect the endangered *ciprés de la cordillera* (Andean cypress), which live up to 1,000 years. Most of these trees are in the park's hard-to-reach Sector de Maitén. You're more likely to see *peumo* (Chilean acorn) and *canelo* (winter's bark), which form dense evergreen forests lining the steep sides of the Río Cachapoal. Most of the park's trails and campgrounds are along this river.

This thick woodland harbors interesting native fauna, including viscachas, reintroduced pumas, the elusive *gato colocolo,* plus skittish lizards and iguanas. At higher altitudes near the Río Ciprés are guanacos. The star attraction is the breeding colony of burrowing parrots, Chile's largest species. The park is one of the remaining habitats for this bird, whose distinctive blue-and-yellow plumage can be seen in the sky—although it's their screeching that normally gives them away. Keep your eyes peeled for Andean condors too.

Bring all the food you need with you, including drinking water. Pack all rubbish out. Only gas stoves are allowed. There are a few small shops in Chacayes, the gateway to the park, but many keep erratic hours.

Orientation

The entrance to the park is on the southeastern tip of Chacayes, down a gravel road that leads to the park's headquarters, **Administración,** which marks the northern edge of the protected area. Admission is collected here. Next door, the small **Centro de Visitantes** offers a thorough introduction, with displays on park flora and fauna and the handful of archaeological sites. Small and somewhat confusing maps of the hiking trails are handed out at entry.

The park is divided into two sections. The first is between **Administración** and the **Guardia Ranchillo,** a ranger station and campsite 4km south; this sector has no official name and borders Río Cachapoal. The second is striking and barely touched **Sector de Maitén,** only accessible by an 11-km day hike or bike ride from where the road ends at Guardia Ranchillo. The valley is coated in Andean cypresses and small lakes that flock with *cauquenes* (upland geese) in summer.

Hiking and Camping

The first sector of the park has several short trails, including **Sendero Los Tricahues,** a 200-meter trail that's good for seeing the resident parrots.

There are two campgrounds (first come, first served, CH$5,000 pp) in the first sector: **Tricahues** (5km from Administración) and **Ranchillo** (6km from Administración), both accessible by vehicle and with cold showers but no electricity or drinking water. There

are basic campgrounds in Sector de Maitén, but you must visit with a guide. Contact **Lara Angel** (tel. 9/7796 2706 or 9/8345 1199), based in Chacayes, who can arrange hikes or horseback rides to this part of the reserve.

Getting There

East from Machalí, the H-25 climbs a series of switchbacks into the foothills of the Andes, with splendid views of Rancagua and the valley beneath, becoming the H-265 just before the village of Coya, after 40 minutes. Just past the village, with signs for the national park, it becomes the H-33, a gravel road for 14km through the hamlet of Chacayes to the park entrance. In total, it's a 29-kilometer, 40-minute drive. All roads in the national park are gravel. A 4WD vehicle isn't necessary, but high clearance is advised. A speed limit of 20km/h is enforced in the park.

From **Machalí** (1hr, CH$2,000), buses operated by **Bus Machalí** (no phone) leave from opposite the municipal swimming pool (just south of Plaza de Machalí) at 7am, noon, and 5pm Monday-Friday and 8am and 4pm Saturday. Boarding priority is given to residents of Chacayes, so you may not be allowed on if the bus reaches capacity.

Reserva Nacional Río de Los Cipreses

WINE-TASTING

The Valle del Cachapoal has 35,000 hectares of wine-producing grapevines in the fertile precordillera east of Ruta 5 along Río Cachapoal. Wines here are mostly cabernet sauvignon and carménère reds. You'll find many big-name wineries with terrain here, but few are open to visitors. The Valle del Cachapoal has yet to develop an official wine-tasting route. The best bet for finding wineries is Google Maps or the tourist office in Rancagua.

The standout is **Viña San Pedro** (tel. 9/7518 6554, www.sanpedro.cl, tours 10:30am, 12:30pm, and 3:30pm Mon.-Sat., CH$50,000 tour and tasting), the premier arm of one of Chile's largest wineries. This modern winery was founded in 2000 and has a picturesque location in the Andes piedmont, where the brand's top wines are processed and aged, including iconic, award-winning Altaïr. For a 1.5-hour tour of the vineyards, which includes a tasting in their spectacular bar cut into the hillside, reservations must be made a few days in advance. Picnics, hikes, and bike tours of the vineyards can be arranged. The winery is difficult to find. Ask for a map from the vineyard when booking, or use Google Maps. From Rancagua, it's a 40-minute, 32-km journey.

Valle de Colchagua and Vicinity

South of Rancagua, just beyond the nondescript town of San Fernando, are vineyards, the region's main draw. The low hills mark the northern edge of the Valle de Colchagua, home to Chile's most prized grape: carménère. Vineyards spread east to the foothills and west beyond the town of Lolol, but the most interesting ones are around Santa Cruz. Wineries and shops stocking exceptionally cheap bottles are signposted at regular intervals along Ruta 90 as you approach the town.

On the coast, beyond the vineyards, the tatty but mellow surfing town of Pichilemu has long beaches with world-class waves. A fashionable getaway for broke Chilean university students and, increasingly, wealthy families, it's a pleasant location for a day or two of surfing or just clean salt air.

SANTA CRUZ

Regional hub Santa Cruz is an attractive town with a Mediterranean climate, making it one of the best places in the country for red wine—specifically carménère. Its success as a wine destination is thanks to Carlos Cardoen, a controversial local resident and arms dealer whose investment has put the town on the international tourism map.

Sights

Within the shade of palms and *araucaría* trees, the **Plaza de Armas** (Plaza de Armas and General del Canto), close to the southern edge of the town, provides a reprieve from the heat during summer.

★ MUSEO COLCHAGUA

Two blocks southeast of the Plaza de Armas, Chile's largest private museum is the huge **Museo Colchagua** (Av Errázuriz 315, tel. 72/2821 050, http://museocolchagua.cl, 10am-7pm daily, CH$7,000 adults, CH$3,000 children). The 21 sizeable rooms cover the gamut from Chile's geological origins to the 2010 rescue of the miners from Mina San José.

There's enough to occupy hours (your ticket is valid for 24 hours, so you can return later). The most linger-worthy room is the collection of indigenous pottery, with an array of 2,000-year-old ceramics depicting different illnesses such as toothache and hernias from the Tumaco-La Tolita people of Ecuador and Colombia. Upstairs, the *Joyas de los Andes* room is similarly enthralling. Glass cases brim with Mapuche silverware and precious, priceless *Spondylus* shell-encrusted ornaments from the tombs of the Moche ruler El Señor de Sipan, considered one of the finest archaeological finds in South American history.

Festivals and Events

With 150 wines from vineyards across the valley, plus a festival of local cuisine, popular music, and *cueca* dance performances, the **Fiesta de la Vendimia de Colchagua** is one of the region's largest celebrations. Traditionally held the first weekend of March in the Plaza de Armas, it attracts 40,000 revelers.

Food and Accommodations

Next door to the Laura Hartwig winery, **Ristorante Vino Bello** (Camino Barreales s/n, tel. 72/2822 755, www.ristorantevinobello.com, 12:30pm-10:30pm daily Jan.-Mar., 12:30pm-3:30pm and 7:30pm-10:30pm Mon.-Fri., 12:30pm-10:30pm Sat.-Sun. Apr.-Dec., CH$9,000-11,000) is an impressive authentic Italian restaurant. Its fine setting only adds to the ambience: Dining tables are in a converted hacienda slung with chandeliers made from farm machinery. A wide, sunny terrace at the back is an excellent place for a sundowner. Homemade pastas are of particular note. Service can be variable, particularly when it's busy. Reservations are essential in summer.

Don't be fooled: The pretty *casona* of **Hotel TerraViña** (Camino a los Boldos s/n, tel. 72/2821 284, http://terravina.cl, CH$106,000 d), with its whitewashed walls and terra-cotta roof, only dates to 2010. Its charming location means all 19 rooms overlook rows of vines from cast-iron balconies. Take a dip in the swimming pool on the main lawn, or wander over to the Laura Hartwig winery, reached by a short vine-lined path.

Run by a young Swiss-Canadian couple, the cozy **Casa Suiza** (Los Libertadores 199, tel. 9/7578 7240, www.casa-suiza.com, CH$14,000 dorm, CH$35,000 d shared bath) is a great budget option, although the cheapest two-bed dorms are tiny. Beds and mattresses are new, and there are plenty of places to unwind, including a grassy garden. The owners run bike tours to local boutique wineries.

They also rent mountain bikes, complete with panniers for the return trip. Rates include IVA.

Swap vineyards for orange and lime trees at wonderful ★ **Colchagua Camp** (El Arrayán s/n, Palmilla, tel. 9/9812 0068, http://colchaguacamp.cl, CH$130,000 d), 15km northwest of Santa Cruz. Six geodesic domes come with heating, minibars, private hot tubs, and patios for enjoying the view; dome 1 has the best view. A circular swimming pool, ringed by palms and sun loungers, has equally splendid views. Note that the private baths are separate from the domes. Dinner can be arranged at additional cost with advance warning, as can on-site wine-tastings with local oenologists. A taxi to Santa Cruz costs around CH$15,000.

Information and Services

In an antique bell tower on the Plaza de Armas, **Información Turístico** (no phone) keeps erratic hours but can advise on taxi services to get to nearby wineries.

Getting There and Around

From **Santiago,** it's a 181-km, 2.25-hour drive south on Ruta 5 and west on Ruta 90.

The main bus terminal is the **Terminal de Buses de Santa Cruz** (Av. Rafael Casanova 480, tel. 72/282 2191). From the **Terminal Santiago** (Av. Alameda 3850, tel. 2/2376 1750) in **Santiago** (3hr, CH$7,000), buses operated by **Nilahue** (tel. 72/2238 567) shuttle to Santa Cruz, picking up in **Rancagua** (1.5hr, CH$4,000) and **San Fernando** (30min, CH$3,000) every 30 minutes. Other buses operated by Nilahue depart from **Pichilemu** (1.5hr, CH$3,500) for Santa Cruz, generally continuing to Santiago.

TOP EXPERIENCE

★ WINE-TASTING

The Valle de Colchagua is the trendiest of Chile's wine regions and the most awarded internationally. Carménère is the region's signature grape, although cabernet sauvignon is the most planted, and the territory continues to expand south toward Lolol and west to where cool-climate white grapes are made into some of the newest wines.

Laura Hartwig

In Santa Cruz, **Laura Hartwig** (Camino Barreales s/n, Santa Cruz, tel. 72/2823 179, http://laurahartwig.cl, 10am-7pm daily Sept.-Apr., 9am-6pm daily May-Aug., tour with tasting CH$12,000) is a boutique winery with only 80 planted hectares. Most of the 144,000 bottles produced each year are sold for export; you'll struggle to find this wine outside the vineyard. The quality of the yield can be variable, but the merlot and the cabernet franc are normally very good. September-April, tours involve a horse-drawn carriage ride around the vineyard. It's also possible to taste on the patio overlooking their polo fields; tastings start at CH$1,000.

Viu Manent

Eight kilometers east of Santa Cruz, **Viu Manent** (Carretera del Vino, km 37, tel. 2/2840 3160, http://viumanent.cl, 10am-6pm daily, tour with tasting CH$15,000) was founded in 1966 on a hacienda with 150-year-old vines. The focus is on reds in a number of varietals, with signature carménère and malbec. The **tour** (four times daily, in Spanish or English) consists of a horse-and-carriage ride through the vineyards followed by a tasting in their shop, La Llavería. You can also organize tastings of seven wines (CH$12,000) or a 2.5-hour winemaking course where you blend your own. Chilean chef Pilar Rodríguez leads cooking classes in the **Food and Wine Studio.** If you arrive without a booking, it's possible to buy some wines by the glass, as well as snacks, from the **Winery Café,** which overlooks the vineyards.

On-site restaurant ★ **Rayuela Wine & Grill** (tel. 9/7136 6147, 1pm-4pm and 8pm-10:30pm Fri.-Sat. Oct.-Apr., 1pm-4pm Sun.-Thurs. May-Sept., CH$9,000-14,000) focuses on simply prepared gourmet Chilean food. Options include succulent rib-eye or

tenderloin steaks, grilled conger eel or salmon, and slow-roasted lamb chops. Service is attentive but can be leisurely. With views across the vineyard, it's worth taking your time.

Viña MontGras

Ten kilometers northwest of Santa Cruz, **Viña MontGras** (Camino Isla de Yáquil s/n, Palmilla, tel. 72/2822 845, http://montgras.cl, 9am-5pm daily, tour with tasting CH$15,000) produces wine mostly for export, growing from modest beginnings in 1993 to vineyards across the country. The main grapes are carménère, cabernet sauvignon, and syrah in a variety of blends. They have an interesting line of sparkling wines, harvested from cool-climate vineyards. **Tours** (in Spanish or English, 4 daily Mon.-Fri., 3 daily Sat.-Sun.) and tastings include food pairings. You can organize a class to blend your own wine.

Casa Silva

Northeast of Santa Cruz, vinicultural giant **Casa Silva** (Hijuelas Norte s/n, tel. 72/716 519, http://casasilva.cl, 10am-6:30pm daily, tour with tasting CH$19,000) is the most award-winning winery in Chile. After sampling their signature micro-terroir carménère, it's not hard to see why. Their comprehensive range of grapes includes pinot noir, chardonnay, syrah, and cabernet sauvignon with more unusual sauvignon gris and sparkling wines from Lago Ranco in the south of Chile. The vineyard **tour** (5 daily, in English and Spanish) includes the colonial wine cellar, the owner's antique car collection, and the wine shop. Reservations for the tour are essential. You can also try wines in the shop (from CH$1,000).

It's worth combining your tour with the winery's excellent restaurant, ★ **Polo Club House** (tel. 72/2716 519, 12:30pm-6pm daily, closed Sun. in winter, CH$10,000-14,000). The building overlooks the polo field where the family's team plays in summer. The food is spectacular: delicate trout ceviche starters and mains of roasted lamb ribs, succulent *lomo vetado* (rib-eye), barbecues of mixed meat for two, and subtly seasoned crab ravioli. Grab a table in the main clubhouse, decorated with polo team photographs and medals, or out on the terrace.

The Silva family's original home has been converted into the boutique **Hotel Casa Silva** (CH$135,000 d), where elegant rooms with heavy antique furnishings are set around a living area of plush sofas overlooking a sunny courtyard. Service is excellent, and the hotel oozes history; the downside is the lack of vineyard views from the rooms. An adjoining **wine bar** (12:30pm-6pm daily, closed Sun. in winter, CH$10,000-14,000), attached to the wine cellar, serves a distilled version of the menu in the Polo Club House; it's open to nonguests. Hotel guests get a 25 percent discount on the vineyard tour.

Valle de Apalta

On the northern banks of serpentine Río Tinguiririca, which runs east-west between Santa Cruz and San Fernando, the **Valle de Apalta,** a crescent-shaped subvalley of Colchagua, is the richest terrain for carménère in the country and is home to some of the most acclaimed wineries. It also contains the most exclusive restaurants in the region, with bookings necessary well in advance throughout summer.

The valley is a mere 10-minute drive from Santa Cruz on Ruta 90; you can easily hire a taxi for the day to explore. This can be arranged with the help of your hotel or the **Información Turístico** (Plaza de Armas, Santa Cruz, no phone). **Ruta del Vino de Colchagua** (Plaza de Armas 298, tel. 72/2823 199, http://rutadelvino.cl) can organize full- and half-day trips to local wineries. Alternatively, it's an 8-km pedal. Rent mountain bikes, complete with panniers, from **Casa Suiza** (Los Libertadores 199, tel. 9/7578 7240, www.casa-suiza.com) in Colchagua.

CLOS APALTA

Just 6km east along Ruta 90 from Santa Cruz and a short distance along the I-350, a 2-km dirt track between the vines leads to **Clos**

Apalta (Km 4 I-350, Apalta, tel. 72/2953 350, www.lapostollewines.com, by appointment only, tour with tasting CH$20,000). The winery is one arm of the mammoth Lapostolle brand, opened by a descendant of the Grand Marnier dynasty. Only the high-end Clos Apalta blend of carménère, cabernet sauvignon, and merlot is made here, in a modern six-story cylindrical winery built into the side of the valley. **Tours** (in English and Spanish, 4 daily Sat.-Sun., fewer during the week) focus on the state-of-the-art technology and the use of gravity in the winemaking process. Reservations are essential. If you're short on time or don't have a reservation, you can visit the **wine shop** (Km 36 Ruta 90, Santa Cruz, tel. 72/2953 339, 10am-6pm daily) to purchase discounted bottles.

The best views of the Valle de Apalta are here, although you'll have to grab a table at the exclusive seven-table Relais & Châteaux-run **Clos Apalta Residence** (tel. 72/2953 360, 1:30pm-2:30pm daily, CH$40,000 two-course menu with wine pairings) on the winery's roof terrace. A set menu of seasonal dishes, including Rapa Nui tuna and short ribs, is paired with Lapostolle wine. Make reservations at least two weeks in advance in summer.

VIÑA MONTES

Just 2km east of Clos Apalta, **Viña Montes** (Millahue de Apalta, tel. 72/2817 815, www.monteswines.com, tour with tasting CH$10,000) was one of the pioneering vineyards in the Valle de Apalta, starting with their iconic cabernet sauvignon but also with a strong focus on carménère and syrah. The wine is aged to the sound of Gregorian chanting in an amphitheater-shaped cellar. The state-of-the-art winery follows feng shui concepts, and the production process uses low-energy gravity-assisted methods. Alongside the **tours** (in English and Spanish, 4 daily) you can also do tastings in the wine shop (from CH$2,000 per pour).

1: Hotel TerraViña **2:** Viu Manent **3:** wine-tasting at Casa Silva **4:** vineyards in the Valle de Colchagua

Opposite the winery, renowned Argentinean chef Francis Mallmann's ★ **Fuegos de Apalta** (tel. 72/2605 190, 12:30pm-4:30pm daily, reservas@fuegosdeapalta.com, CH$20,000-24,000) is outstanding in every way. At the center of the restaurant is a circular iron grill where all the cooking is done. Expect expert *lomo liso* (sirloin), *entraña* (skirt steak), and fish, all succulent and with a delicious smoky flavor. You can watch the chefs at work; only a glass partition separates them from the dining room.

APALTAGUA

A short distance beyond Viña Montes, **Apaltagua** (Millahue s/n, tel. 72/2976 6300, www.apaltagua.com, tour with tasting CH$14,000) isn't as modern as other wineries in the valley, but it's a personal favorite for its inexpensive yet excellent wines, including carménère and cabernet sauvignon.

NEYEN

At the end of the Apalta vineyards, on the eastern edge of the valley, picturesque **Neyen** (Km 11 Camino Apalta, tel. 9/8527 4411, www.neyen.cl, tour with tasting CH$22,000) has the oldest wine cellar in Apalta, dating to 1890, when their original cabernet sauvignon vines were planted. The modern winery contrasts with beautiful colonial buildings in a grove of eucalyptus trees and produces just one wine, a blend of cabernet sauvignon and carménère. They also arrange hiking tours of the estate, with optional picnics or more formal lunches. All tours must be arranged a day in advance.

Getting There and Around

All the wineries can be visited by hiring a taxi from Santa Cruz to get you between vineyards; expect to pay around CH$40,000 for a visit to three wineries, including waiting time. It's also possible to arrive in your own vehicle, but Chile has a zero-tolerance policy on alcohol and driving, so if you plan to taste, be sure to spit. A heavy police presence is common on the main roads through the valley.

Alternatively, **Ruta del Vino de Colchagua** (Plaza de Armas 298, tel. 72/2823 199, http://rutadelvino.cl) can organize full- and half-day trips to the local wineries in their association of vineyards. For a tour of two wineries, including transportation from their office in Santa Cruz, prices start at CH$40,000 pp. Private tours, plus lunch, are available; transport from Santiago can be arranged.

Huique

A worthy detour between Santa Cruz and Pichilemu is **Museo San José del Carmen del Huique** (Av. El Huique s/n, tel. 9/9733 1105, www.museoelhuique.cl, 9:30am-noon and 2pm-5pm Tues.-Sun., CH$3,000 adults, CH$2,000 children). This old adobe hacienda dates from the 1600s and belonged to the family of Chilean president Federico Errázuriz Echaurren, in office 1896-1901.

In its heyday, the hacienda employed most workers in the Valle San José del Carmen, one of the first agricultural zones in the country. It was an impressive sight, with 22 patios scattered with living space for the family and their many servants. Nowadays, the main patio is the only one accessible to visitors due to structural damage from the 2010 earthquake. Surrounding the patio are several bedrooms with their original furniture to showcase how the family lived.

Above the patio on the southern side, the baby-pink balustrade and 23-meter bell tower of the chapel miraculously survived the earthquake. If you look closely, you'll see the meter-thick adobe walls, which probably have something to do with why it was unscathed.

To get here, take Ruta 90 west toward the coast for 10 minutes, then the signposted I-352 for the museum; it's a 16-km, 19-minute drive.

Lolol

A half-hour's drive southwest of Santa Cruz through grapevines is Lolol, a pretty traditional village founded as Hacienda Lolol. The fringes of the settlement contain low houses with gated gardens with fruit trees. At its heart are elegant single-story adobe houses with terra-cotta roof tiles and delightful covered corridors.

These colonial homes line Lolol's three oldest streets, Las Acacias, Los Aromos, and Las Achiras, which form a triangle around Plaza Lolol and Iglesia Natividad de María. Unfortunately, many of the homes were damaged by the 2010 earthquake; only those along Los Aromos, opposite the museum, have been restored. The crumpled remains of the houses on Las Acacias and Las Achiras evidence the severity of the devastation.

★ MUSEO DE LA ARTESANÍA CHILENA

Across from the houses on Los Aromos, the **Museo de la Artesanía Chilena** (Los Aromos 95, tel. 72/2941 085, artesanias@ fundacioncardoen.cl, 10am-6pm Tues.-Sun., CH$3,000 adults, CH$1,500 children) is the main reason for a detour to this side of the valley. It houses a fine collection of contemporary crafts in diverse materials produced by hand across the country. Display items include traditional *mimbre* (wicker) furniture and baskets from Chimbarongo, models of buildings carved from the Mexican *cardón* cactus from San Pedro de Atacama, and unusual scented clay ceramics crafted in Talagante, south of Santiago. You won't see these crafts elsewhere unless you visit the individual villages.

PICHILEMU

Sprawling along the coast and several rocky promontories, beachside Pichilemu is a popular summer destination for Santiaguinos fleeing the heat of the capital. A welcome cool breeze makes the hot weather bearable. In peak summer, the fine black sand of lengthy Playa Principal, which wraps around the western edge of town, heaves with sun umbrellas and tourists.

For international visitors, Pichilemu's greatest appeal is the waves—it's the self-appointed Chilean capital of surf. In reality, the best breaks are 4km south at Punta de Lobos, part of the Circuit Chileno de Surf (Chilean Surf Circuit) every November.

Wherever you jump in, the water is rarely warmer than 15°C, so wetsuits are essential.

Despite its origins as an aristocratic beach resort, the town has a welcoming charm and a split identity. Wind-battered houses dot the coastline on its northern edges, while on the road south to Punta de Lobos, development is plush cabins and hotels, hinting at the future of this modest town.

The oldest part of Pichilemu is the northeast, a dozen blocks after crossing the Estero San Antonio from the north. Plaza Arturo Prat and access to the main beach are here. Continuing south, the road leaves Pichilemu, continuing to Punta de Lobos. There are plenty of one-way roads in town, so keep an eye on traffic signs.

Sights

Landscaped **Plaza Arturo Prat** (bounded by Arturo Prat, Daniel Ortúzar, Federico Errázuriz, and Ángel Gaete) is home to a bust of navy war hero Arturo Prat. The plaza is the focus of events, including live music and craft and food fairs on weekends year-round.

Just beneath the square, following Calle Ortúzar downhill, **Playa Principal** (also known as **Playa San Antonio**) is a long, wide stretch for a horseback ride (you pay for the distance you travel, from CH$3,000). It connects with La Puntilla, a rocky headland to the west.

A third of the way to the headland, **Parque Ross** takes the name of the town's founder, Agustín Ross Edwards, and is far more pleasant than the bare main square, with shade from 100-year-old palms.

★ Surfing

Pichilemu has several beaches for surfing. **Playa La Puntilla** is south of La Puntilla headland and boasts Chile's longest wave, an exposed point break that goes for 800 meters. It's best in March and November, although it's reliable year-round and makes a good spot for beginners.

Within walking distance north, on the edges of **Playa Las Terrazas,** are most of the rental shops and surf schools, including **Waitara Escuela De Surf** (Av. Costanera 1039, tel. 722 843004, http://waitara.cl, 9am-8pm daily), renting boards, wetsuits, and boots for CH$16,000 per day. They teach 1.5-hour classes (from CH$12,000), including equipment and an English-speaking teacher.

Just south, **Playa Infiernillo** has a left break but is rougher than its neighbor and is best on days when there's not as much swell. Waves can reach four meters.

Food and Accommodations

Meals and lodging can be on par with Santiago in terms of cost. For a quick, cheap lunch, plenty of *completo* and empanada stands line the road on the descent to Playa Principal.

On the southern flanks of Pichilemu, **Racha** (Av. Comercio 2865, tel. 9/3194 6403, www.racharesto.cl, 1pm-11pm Wed.-Mon., CH$7,000-12,000) has a hip, youthful feel with superbly welcoming service and a great outdoor terrace for sunny days. The menu includes falafel burgers and healthy salads, but locally caught fish is the specialty, with bean and seafood stews and grilled fish of the day with quinoa.

On the southeast corner of Plaza Arturo Prat, **La Casa Verde** (Daniel Ortúzar 215, tel. 72/2841 163, 1pm-11pm daily, CH$5,000-8,000) is a relaxed restaurant specializing in sizeable sandwiches. Seven fillings include tomato and aioli or gouda cheese with caramelized onions, combined with fried of grilled fish, *mechada,* or vegetarian burgers. There's craft beer on tap, including the local Etnica. The terrace, with views of the sea, is a perfect spot for sunset.

Pichilemu Surf Hostal (Eugenio Díaz Lira 164, tel. 9/7492 6848, http://surfhostal. com, CH$45,000 d), run by friendly English-speaking Dutch owner Marcel, has the vibe of a guesthouse more than a hostel, as there are limited social areas. Rooms are tiny, but it's clean, smartly decorated, and has great ocean views. Breakfast is on the ocean-side terrace of the restaurant across the way, which has saltwater heated baths and great panoramas across Playa La Puntilla. On weekends, the nightclub next door can be noisy. They offer discounted rates with local surf schools. Rates include IVA.

Information and Services

Información Turístico (Ángel Gaete 365, tel. 72/2976 530, www.pichilemu.cl, 8am-1pm and 2pm-5:50pm Mon.-Fri.), inside the municipal buildings, can provide some information about local beaches and transportation.

Getting There and Around

Driving, it's a two-hour, 180-km journey south on Ruta 5 and Ruta 90 from Santiago to Santa Cruz. Buses from **Santiago** (3.5hr, CH$8,000), often stopping at **Rancagua** (2.75hr, CH$7,000), **San Fernando** (2hr, CH$5,000), and **Santa Cruz** (1.5hr, CH$3,500), arrive at the **Terminal Rodoviario de Pichilemu** (Millaco 534, tel. 72/2980 504), five blocks south of Parque Ross. **Nilahue** (tel. 72/2842 042) has hourly buses between the four locations, while **Pullman del Sur** (tel. 72/2842 425, http://pdelsur.cl) has hourly direct buses from Santiago. **Tenobus** (tel. 72/2312 637) has five daily buses from **Curicó** (2.5hr, CH$4,000).

Taxis colectivos shuttle between Pichilemu and **Punta de Lobos** (10min, CH$1,000) every 10-30 minutes 24 hours daily. Otherwise, it's a 10-minute drive or an hour's walk along the main road to Punta de Lobos.

Punta de Lobos

An urban sprawl of tourist cabins and pricey condos connects Pichilemu with Punta de Lobos, a beach and town 4km south. Consistent swells up to six meters produce a steep left point break, considered the best in Chile. From the cliffs above, various trails lead down to the beach, where there are plenty of surf schools renting equipment and offering surfing and kitesurfing classes. The road continues to the end of the headland, where a parking lot plays host to hip **food trucks** and **craft stalls** in summer and on weekends. The beach is also suitable for swimming and fishing.

The perfect surfer hangout is **La Sirena Insolente** (Camino Punta de Lobos 169, tel. 9/5856 5784, http://sirenainsolentehostel.cl, CH$12,000 dorm, CH$35,000 d private bath, CH$50,000 d apartment), a short stroll from the Punta de Lobos beach. The communal spaces are worn, but the range of sizeable dorms and private rooms are modern, with large, comfortable beds. In two sprawling buildings, the hostel has plenty of social space in geodesic domes stuffed with hammocks and convivial fire pits. A communal kitchen and a TV room add to the *buena onda* (good vibes) here. You can rent boards and suits (CH$15,000 daily) as well as bikes (CH$7,000 daily). They run group surfing classes (from CH$25,000), comprising a 1.5-hour lesson followed by 3 hours of board rental time.

Built with a focus on sustainability, **Tripanko Lodge & Bungalows** (Catrianca, tel. 9/5608 8351, www.tripanko.cl, CH$80,000 d private bath, CH$90,000 2-person bungalow, cash only) is some distance from the beach, in the woods above Punta de Lobos. A car or taxi is the only way to get here, but it's a slice of paradise. Lodgings are self-contained stylish wooden bungalows with kitchens, or simple bedrooms with balconies in the main lodge, all on raised platforms in the heart of a eucalyptus forest. Breakfast is included for guests in the lodge; the terrace on top of the lodge has splendid views. Rates include IVA.

Valle Curicó

Most travelers make a beeline for the vineyards of the Colchagua Valley, but vineyards spread farther south on the fertile plains and coastal hills of the Valle Curicó, 200km from Santiago. Unlike nearby Colchagua, this valley has yet to fully embrace tourism; despite being home to some of the oldest vines in the country, few wineries are open to visitors. Instead, the most captivating sights are the bewitching waterfalls of the Parque Nacional Radal Siete Tazas in the foothills of the Andes, most easily accessed from the orderly city of Curicó, distinguished by its magnificent square.

CURICÓ

Founded in 1743, the small city of Curicó makes expedient place to break the journey south to the ski regions of Chillán or the remote beach towns north of Concepción. The city is also a good base to visit the nearby national park and the few wineries that allow tours.

Sights

Curicó's most notable sight is its **Plaza de Armas** (bounded by Merced, Carmen, Estado, and Yungay), a national monument and splendid forest of 60 towering Canary Island date palms, among other exotic species from around the world. On the southern edge of the plaza is a 1906 wrought-iron bandstand in New Orleans style, typical of the era. A late 19th-century French fountain features three nymphs, contrasting with a statue of fearless Mapuche leader and warrior Lautaro, carved from a tree trunk.

Festivals and Events

The Plaza de Armas is the site of the lively four-day **Fiesta de la Vendimia** (Wine Harvest, Mar. or Apr.), the largest of the harvest festivals in the Central Valley, with around 200,000 visitors. Events include election of the Queen of the Wine Harvest, grape treading, plus the blessing of the first grape juice. It's hosted by Chilean TV stars and includes live music and dancing.

Food and Accommodations

The restaurant at **Viña Miguel Torres** (Km 195 Panamericana Sur, tel. 75/256 4110, http://migueltorres.cl, 12:30pm-4pm and 8:30pm-11pm Fri., 12:30pm-4pm Sat.-Thurs., CH$10,000-14,000), a 10-minute drive south of Curicó, is the best bet for a reliable if expensive meal.

The English-speaking hosts of **Homestay Chile** (Argomedo 448, tel. 75/2225 275, www.homestaychile.cl, CH$35,000 d, cash only) make guests feel like part of the family at this friendly matchbox-size guesthouse a few blocks south of the Plaza de Armas. The three rooms are sizeable and have access to a cozy living room downstairs. The breakfast spread is enough to keep you going. Rates include IVA.

The small town of Molina, 18km south of Curicó, has an excellent hotel in stylish, modern ★ **Hotel Lagar Boutique** (Membrillar 1217, tel. 75/2395 778, http://lagarhotel.com, CH$55,000 d), with neutrally painted rooms around a sunny central courtyard. Friendly, chatty English-speaking owner Francisco is passionate about good food and wine (he's a trained chef and sommelier), which he serves in the attached café (10:30am-7pm Mon.-Sat., CH$3,000-7,000), where he also runs the occasional wine-tasting night. Rates include IVA.

Information and Services

The staff at the municipal-run **Oficina de Turismo** (Av. Manso de Velasco 449, tel. 75/2547 690, turismo@curico.cl, 8:15am-5:15pm Mon.-Fri.) speak English and can provide information about vineyards, visiting the Parque Nacional Radal Siete Tazas, and the Fiesta de la Vendimia.

The **Hospital San Juan de Dios** (Chacabuco 121, tel. 75/2566 200, www. hospitalcurico.cl), also known as the **Hospital de Curicó,** is the more central of the two hospitals. The **Banco Estado** (Carmen 600) is just off the northeast edge of the Plaza de Armas. **Correos de Chile** (Carmen 556) is on the eastern side of the plaza.

Getting There and Around

It's a two-hour, 196-km drive south on Ruta 5 from Santiago to Curicó. Buses from **Santiago** (2.5hr, CH$5,000) stop at **Terminal Curicó** (Arturo Prat 780, tel. 75/2558 118), four blocks west of the Plaza de Armas, every 15 minutes, with the most regular buses by **Nueva Andimar VIP** (tel. 75/2312 000, http://nuevaandimar.cl) and **Pullman del Sur** (tel. 75/2328 090, http://pdelsur.cl). **Aquelarre** (tel. 75/2326 404) has minibuses every five minutes to **Molina** (35min, CH$600), where you can find transport onward to Parque Nacional Radal Siete Tazas. Somewhat inconveniently located in the south of the city, just off Ruta 5, **Tur Bus** (Manso de Velasco and Castellon s/n, tel. 75/2414 834, http://turbus.cl) has its own terminal, with buses from Santiago and **Chillán** (3hr, CH$6,000/CH$8,000).

At the **Estación de Trenes** (Maipú 657, tel. 600/5855 000, http://trencentral.cl), opposite the Terminal Curicó, TerraSur trains arrive from **Santiago** (2.25hr, CH$4,000), continuing to Molina, Talca, and terminating in Chillán. Trains depart the Estación Central in Santiago at 8:30am and 5:30pm daily.

WINE-TASTING

The Valle de Curicó is among the country's larger wine regions, growing sauvignon blanc and other white varietals; cabernet sauvignon is also common. Unfortunately for oenophiles, most wineries aren't open to visitors.

Viña Miguel Torres

Six kilometers south of Curicó and part of Ruta del Vino de Curicó, **Viña Miguel Torres** (Km 195 Panamericana Sur, tel. 75/256 4110, http://migueltorres.cl, 10am-8pm Mon.-Fri., 10am-6pm Sat.-Sun. summer, 10am-6pm daily winter, tour with tasting CH$15,000) is one of the country's largest wine producers. It's named for its founder, a Spanish vintner and pioneer of the region who began cultivating grapes here in 1979.

Tours of the vineyard explore the range of vines grown here and in the company's other vineyards, which include 100-year-old cabernet sauvignon grapes, carménères and merlots, interesting old grapes such as país, carignan, and muscat, as well as sparkling brut pinot noir from Valle de Curicó. Tours are on a drop-in basis; to visit the vineyards by bicycle (CH$16,000), you'll need to reserve in advance.

Reservations are necessary, particularly on weekends, for the excellent ★ **Restaurant Viña Torres** (12:30pm-4pm and 8:30pm-11pm Fri., 12:30pm-4pm Sat.-Thurs., CH$10,000-14,000), in modern buildings that contrast beautifully with the old wine cellar. The menu is Chilean food with a recommended wine pairing. Slow-cooked ribs in cabernet sauvignon sauce, fried conger eel with a serrano ham crust, and delicate soups of shrimp, monkfish, and coconut milk are among the highlights. It's worth a stop for lunch as it's right next to the highway.

The winery and restaurant are just south of Curicó, a 5-km, seven-minute drive on Ruta 5. A taxi to the winery should cost no more than CH$7,000.

★ PARQUE NACIONAL RADAL SIETE TAZAS

In the precordillera of the Andes Mountains southeast of Curicó, the 5,026-hectare **Parque Nacional Radal Siete Tazas** (tel. 71/2224 461, parque.radalsietetazas@conaf.cl, 9am-7pm daily Dec.-Apr., 9am-5:30pm daily May-Nov., CH$5,000 adults, CH$2,500 children) lines the northern banks of the Río Claro. Heavily visited by Chileans, few foreign travelers make it here because of its inaccessibility. Pristine deciduous forest and scenic trails, combined with the star attraction Siete Tazas (Seven Cups), deep pools in the basalt with splendid waterfalls emerging, make this an unforgettable place.

The spectacular waterfalls are the main draw, but hiking trails with significantly fewer visitors, even on busy summer weekends, are wonderful. Expect glimpses of Andean condors, peregrine falcons, burrowing parrots, and Magellanic woodpeckers. The thick forests provide excellent cover for the park's land-bound fauna, which is much harder to spot. *Pudús, culpeo* foxes, and Molina's hog-nosed skunks are here, with several species of small lizards.

The park normally closes June-September due to snowfall; at other times, trails may be partially closed due to weather.

Orientation

The park's entrance is just past the village of El Radal, home to a police checkpoint. If the weather is poor, you'll be turned away here. An unnamed gravel road, signposted for the national park, runs southwest from here, entering the unnamed western side. After 3km is Salto Velo de la Novia; 3.5km farther is a **parking lot** for the Cascada Siete Tazas and a CONAF **ranger station,** where you buy the entry ticket.

The road continues east through the park for 4.5km to **Sector Parque Inglés,** the eastern section, where the **park headquarters,** called Administración, also sells entry tickets. There are two **campgrounds** here.

Sights and Recreation

SALTO VELO DE LA NOVIA

The park contains a range of accessible waterfalls and more adventurous hiking trails. By car and with little exertion, it's possible to visit the first waterfall, picturesque 40-meter **Salto Velo de la Novia.** Surrounded by a shroud of spray as it pours into the pool below, the viewpoint is next to the main road, 3km from the entrance, and does not require an entry ticket. Parking can be an issue on busy summer days.

CASCADA SIETE TAZAS

The **Cascada Siete Tazas,** a delightful series of seven teal-hued pools carved out of black basalt by thousands of years of water in Río Claro, are the park's focal point. A 300-meter boardwalk from the car park brings you to a series of viewpoints and a staircase to the last of the seven pools, although expect to be elbowing selfie sticks out of the way. The pools are 6.5km from the entrance; the parking lot is along the main park road.

From the pools, a 1.2-km trail continues through the woods to a viewpoint of the **Salta**

de Leona, a continuation of the Río Claro that erupts from the rock as a 25-meter fall above a crystalline lake. You can reach the edge of the pool via a 500-meter trail down to the riverbank.

HIKING

The main hiking trails leave from the Administración building in **Sector Parque Inglés.** The shortest is the **Sendero El Coigüe** (1.5km loop, 1hr), an interpretive trail through heavy forests of Patagonian oak to a viewpoint south across the park.

One of the prettiest trails is **Sendero Chiquillanes** (7km round-trip, 4hr), named after the original indigenous settlement in the valley. The trail climbs steeply from behind Administración through woodlands lined with towering 100-year-old Patagonian oaks and *coigüe*. It reaches a viewpoint across the park, and, farther on, splendid views of Volcán Descabezado Grande southeast.

Heading southeast through the park, the **Sendero Mala Cara** (8km round-trip, 1.5hr) passes eroded pools in Río Claro. For fit hikers, it can be combined with additional trails, one of which climbs steeply into the mountains, gaining 900 vertical meters in only a few kilometers to emerge above the tree line into barren landscapes punctuated by *coiron* grasses, with exceptional views across the full basin of the Claro River.

Accommodations

The park's **campgrounds** (CH$4,000), **Camping Los Robles** and **Camping Rocas Basalticas,** are in Sector Parque Inglés and operate on a first-come, first-served basis. Both have cold showers and areas for cooking with a gas stove; open fires are not permitted in the park. They close in June-July.

Near the main entrance of the park and accessible from the police checkpoint on the road that continues along the river, rather than the road into the park, **Cabañas Doña Goya**

1: Lolol 2: Pichilemu 3: Parque Nacional Radal Siete Tazas

(tel. 9/8957 7676, http://cabañasdoñagoya.cl, rmart.araya@gmail.com, CH$40,000) has six cozy two-person cabins. Each has a full kitchen, a living area, and even a TV. The grounds are home to ducks, chickens, and a couple of horses. The cabins come with gas heaters but get cold during winter.

Information and Services

The staff at **Administración** (9am-1pm and 2pm-5:30pm daily) and the rangers at the Siete Tazas trailhead can advise on trail conditions. CONAF employees are responsive to emails. There is a **shop** supplying basic dried foods, cheese, and ham just west of the bridge in Radal. A handful of places sell coffee, lunch, and snacks near the Administración building during summer. It's best to buy all your food in Curicó or Talca before you arrive.

Getting There and Around

The park is a 67-km, 1.5-hour drive from Curicó, on Ruta 5, the K-19 through the town of Molina, and the K-175, signposted for the park. Note that the paved road becomes a compacted gravel road 24km from the entrance, and a vehicle with high clearance is recommended.

To get to the park with public transport, you'll first need to get to the town of Molina, 22km south of Curicó. Buses from Curicó arrive at the **Aquelarre bus station** (Luis Cruz Martínez 3580, tel. 9/9479 3264) at the entrance to the town from Ruta 5. Hourly buses from **Santiago** (3hr) with **Pullman del Sur** (tel. 75/2491 366, http://pdelsur.cl, CH$6,000) and **MT Bus** (tel. 2/2764 3968, CH$6,300) stop at the **Terminal de Buses** (Maipú 1738, no phone).

Buses travel through the park to terminate at Sector Parque Inglés from Molina's Terminal de Buses (1.75hr, CH$3,000). **Buses Radal 7 Tazas** (tel. 9/95926 311) runs buses January-mid-March at 12:30pm, 6:16pm, and 8:15pm, returning at 7:10am, 10:30am, and 3:45pm Monday-Thursday, with an additional departure at 11:30am and return at 6:30pm Friday-Saturday. On Sunday, buses leave at

7am, 2pm, 7:30pm, and 10pm, returning at 10:30am, 1:30pm, 3:30pm, and 6:45pm.

Mid-March to December, buses depart Molina at 7pm Monday-Friday; departures in the other direction leave the park at 7:30am. Buses depart Molina at 9am Saturday and depart the national park at 7:30am. On Sunday, buses leave Molina at 9am, returning from the park at 5pm. The winter route only goes to Radal, the police checkpoint.

Buses Hernández (tel. 75/2521 303 or 9/6911 206/) also operates five daily buses (four on Sunday) between Molina and Sector Parque Inglés, but only January-March.

Valle del Maule

Grapevines were introduced by Catholic priests to the Valle de Maule in the mid-1500s, making the vineyards from Talca to the Río Perquilauquén the oldest in the country. A clutch of wineries has embraced the ancient roots of the winemaking tradition, cultivating varietals found in few other places. The area also has an interesting craft tradition, and a breezy, practically deserted coastline offers surfing without the crowds found farther north.

TALCA

Talca is a quiet, unassuming city, famed as the location of the signing of the Chilean declaration of independence by liberator Bernardo O'Higgins in 1818. In 2010, an 8.8 magnitude earthquake struck 100km west of the city; many areas were heavily damaged and abandoned for good.

Talca is relatively compact, with Ruta 5 on the east and Río Claro on the west. Its streets follow a numbered grid, according to their direction, beginning at 1 Norte (1 North), 1 Sur (1 South), 1 Poniente (1 West), and 1 Oriente (1 East) from their starting point at the Plaza de Armas.

With practically the entire historic core wiped out by the earthquake, Talca has little to attract visitors but makes a good base to explore the Reserva Nacional Altos de Lircay or the wineries of the Valle del Maule, the oldest wine territory in the country. Summers here are hot, and winters can be icy.

Sights

The center of the city is the **Plaza de Armas** (bounded by 1 Norte, 1 Oriente, 1 Sur, and 1 Poniente). On the northeast edge of the plaza is the 2016 **Monumento Bernardo O'Higgins,** a life-size bronze of the first governor of Chile in the act of signing the Chilean Declaration of Independence.

On the northeast edge of the city, the **Jardín Botánico** (Km 4.56 Av. Lircay s/n, Campus Universidad de Talca, tel. 71/2200 263, pegomez@utalca.cl, 10am-8pm daily summer, 10am-6pm winter, free), located on the campus of the Universidad de Talca, is a pleasant place for a wander. One half of the botanic garden is filled with lakes and a chaotic ensemble of noisy wildfowl, goats, and even a beaver, while the other side is an arboretum filled with native Chilean plant species. Free guided tours are available, but you must reserve in advance.

Festivals and Events
CHANCHO MUERTO

The city's most important festival is the **Chancho Muerto** (Dead Pig), a traditional pork festival held in mid-winter, the first or second weekend of August, in the Plaza de Armas. Expect 40 food stalls from across Chile, Argentina, and Peru cooking pork barbecued, stewed, and in pasta. The *anticuchos* (hearts) and *chicharrónes* (deep-fried pork) are delicacies; *longanizas* (sausages) are a tradition of the Maule region. Local wines and craft beer are also for sale.

Food and Accommodations

★ **Restaurante Caupolicán** (4 Sur 1392, tel. 71/2357 040, noon-4pm and 7pm-11pm Mon.-Sat., noon-4pm Sun, CH$4,000-8,000) is a no-frills restaurant that serves possibly the best pork you've ever eaten, in mammoth portions. Dishes include ribs and *arrollados* (rolled pork), plus more unusual offerings such as blood sausages and trotters. Sandwiches, burgers, and shareable barbecue platters are available for the less adventurous. It's a friendly, family-run affair that's also a butcher shop, so the meat is fresh.

Offering some of Talca's cleanest and most affordable lodgings, **Hostal del Puente** (1 Sur 407, tel. 41/2131 091, http://hostaldelpuente.cl, CH$31,000 d) has 16 neat rooms around a floral courtyard with plenty of parking. It's a popular spot for foreign travelers and is a five-minute walk from the Plaza de Armas. Staff are very friendly. While the facilities are basic, it's excellent value for the money. Rates include IVA.

A 20-minute drive from Talca, ★ **Casa Chueca** (Viña Andrea s/n, tel. 71/1970 097, www.trekkingchile.com, CH$15,500 dorm, CH$58,000 d, CH$90,000 apartment) has comfortable, rustic lodgings on a six-hectare plot. Lodging options include dorms, private rooms, and modern two-person apartments with kitchens and jetted tubs. All guests have access to the large, sunny terrace and swimming pool. The atmosphere is familial; the knowledgeable staff are happy to help plan activities. Casa Chueca is closed from after Easter Week to September.

Information and Services

Visitor information is provided by helpful **SERNATUR** (1 Oriente 1150, tel. 71/2233 669, infomaule@sernatur.cl, 8:30am-7pm Mon.-Fri., 10am-1pm Sat. Jan.-Feb., 8:30am-5:30pm Mon.-Thurs., 8:30am-4:30pm Fri. Mar.-Dec.). They have maps and information about Talca and the Maule region. **CONAF** (4 Norte 1673; 6 Norte 1240, tel. 71/2209 517, talca.oirs@ conaf.cl) has maps and information for the Reserva Nacional Altos de Lircay.

Talca is a good place to withdraw cash. There are several banks, including **Banco Santander** (1 Sur 829), **Banco Estado** (1 Sur 971), and **Banco de Chile** (1 Sur 1191), in the first few blocks east of the Plaza de Armas. **Correos** (1 Oriente 1150, 9:30am-6:30pm Mon.-Fri., 10am-12:30pm Sat.) deals with the post, and the **Hospital de Talca** (1 Norte 1951, tel. 71/2747 000, http://hospitaldetalca. cl) deals with emergencies.

Getting There

Talca is the main transportation hub for the Maule region, with bus and rail connections.

CAR

Talca is a 1-hour, 67-km drive south on Ruta 5 from **Curicó**. From **Santiago,** it is 2.5 hours and 256km. Public transport to rural regional destinations is practically nonexistent, so a rental car can provide flexibility for visiting the nearby national reserve and the remote beaches to the south. Rental agencies in town include **Europcar** (21 Oriente 790, tel. 71/2523 970, http://europcar.cl, 8:30am-1:30pm and 3pm-6:30pm Mon.-Fri., 9am-11:30am Sat.) and **Rent a Car Maule** (2 Norte 22, tel. 71/2401 552, http://rentacarmaule.cl, 9am.-5pm Mon.-Fri.).

BUS

Talca is a stopping point for buses between Santiago and Concepción and serves a handful of destinations farther south. Most buses arrive at the **Terminal Rodoviario** (2 Sur 1920, tel. 2/2243 270). **Tur Bus** (2 Sur 1920, tel. 71/2414 801, http://turbus.cl) has its own terminal, although occasional Tur buses arrive and depart from Terminal Rodoviario. Buses from Santiago and Concepción arrive every 30 minutes.

From **Concepción** (3.5hr, CH$6,000/11,000), buses leave every 30 minutes with **Linatel** (tel. 71/2614 464, www.linatel.cl) and **Condor Bus** (tel. 71/2245 920, www.condorbus.cl), which also has three daily departures from **Valdivia** (8hr, CH$17,000/CH$25,000) and two daily departures from **Puerto Montt** (10hr, CH$19,000/ CH$29,000). From their own terminal, **Tur Bus** has five departures from Concepción and the most regular departures from **Santiago** (8 daily, 3hr, CH$6,000/CH$12,000) and **Puerto Montt** (2 daily, 10hr, CH$24,000/ CH$34,000).

TRAIN

TerraSur trains depart Estación Central in **Santiago** (8:30am and 5:30pm daily, 3hr, CH$5,000) and stop at the **Estación de Ferocarriles de Talca** (11 Oriente 900, tel. 2/2585 5000, http://trencentral.cl). Trains continue south to Chillán.

The **Buscarril,** the final remaining narrow-gauge *ramal* train in the country, follows an 88-km route to Constitución. It's a slow but interesting journey skirting the Río Maule through pastures and farmland. You'll ride across an early 20th-century railway bridge designed by Gustave Eiffel of Eiffel Tower fame. Locals have priority for tickets, but travelers can buy them if available. Daily departures leave for Constitución (3.25hr, CH$2,250) at 7:40am and 4:10pm, but in summer, you'll need to get here around 6:30am to be sure of acquiring a ticket.

VICINITY OF TALCA

Lago Colbún

Southeast of Talca, as the road climbs into the precordillera, **Lago Colbún** is a reservoir with year-round sunshine even when it's cloudy in the valley below. During summer, when the water level is highest, it is an idyllic getaway for a dip.

On the edge of the reservoir, **Chez L'Habitant** (tel. 9/9132 4064, http:// lodgecolbun.com, CH$105,000 d) is a paradisiacal place for a weekend, offering affordable options. Stay in a modern room with a panorama of the lake or a slightly older cabin with a kitchen in the forest. The owners are experts on the region, specializing in mountain biking

and trekking, and can arrange winery and village tours through their sister tour agency. Massage services are available in high season, and the property has a hot tub and a swimming pool. There's a reason you need to book months in advance.

There is no public transport, so you'll need your own vehicle to get here. From Talca, it's a 1.25-hour, 62-km drive southeast along Avenida Huamachuco and the K-25, L-11, and L-391. The hotel is on the lake's southern periphery.

Panimávida

Panimávida is a pretty village 57km southeast of Talca. Just off the leafy square, the **Termas de Panimávida** (Panimávida s/n, tel. 73/2211 743, http://termasdepanimavida. cl, 3pm-9pm daily, CH$17,500 adults, CH$12,500 children) is a historical spa and hotel complex dating to 1822. It was rebuilt in the early 2000s, although it doesn't feel like it's been updated much. Despite its elderly appearance, it merits a half-day visit to sink into its three indoor pools, naturally heated to 37°C.

★ Handicrafts in Rari

Made from brightly dyed horsehair reinforced with cactus fiber, the colorful crafts of the one-street village of **Rari,** 1km southeast of Panimávida, are truly unique. The fiber is made into brooches and intricate butterflies, among other things. Most of the community's 160 families continue to work with this traditional handicraft, which dates back 200 years and is recognized by UNESCO as a Living Cultural Monument.

Prices start from CH$2,500. The majority of shops are just after crossing Puente Rari to enter the main village. For more upmarket jewelry, don't miss **Chilean Crafts: Tienda Boutique** (tel. 9/9622 722), a showroom down a dirt track just after the bridge. Ring the bell to be let in.

1: surfers near Cobquecura **2:** view of the central coast

★ RESERVA NACIONAL ALTOS DE LIRCAY

Encompassing the forests of the Río Lircay valley and the foothills of the Andes, the **Reserva Nacional Altos de Lircay** (tel. 71/2209 517, talca.oirs@conaf.cl, 8:30am-7pm daily summer, 8:30am-5:30pm daily winter, last entry 2 hr before closing, CH$5,000 adults, CH$2,500 children) has fine hiking through old-growth forests with dramatic vistas of deep canyons and crater lakes ringed by snow-topped volcanic peaks. Burrowing parrots and Magellanic woodpeckers frequent the park, while pumas have been reintroduced through a conservation project.

This reserve is south of Parque Nacional Radal Siete Tazas, protecting the deciduous forests skirting the slopes of the Andes heading south. The entrance, marked by the CONAF-operated **Centro de Información Ambiental,** where admission is collected, is from the west, 4km beyond Vilches Alto, the reserve's closest settlement. **Camping Antahuara** is 800 meters beyond the entrance, east along a dirt road.

Summers are hot and dry, so bring plenty of drinking water. Winters are frigid, often with heavy snowfall that leaves many of the trails closed. It's always best to contact CONAF directly for information on current conditions. Campfires are not permitted; you may be asked to show your gas camping stove on arrival.

The best part about visiting this park is that you can expect to be practically alone on the trails, particularly outside of January and February. The road into the park is unpaved, so it's best visited October-May, when conditions are good.

Trekking Chile (http://trekkingchile.com), based in **Casa Chueca** (Viña Andrea s/n, Talca, tel. 71/1970 097), has the best maps of the area.

Hiking

Close to the CONAF-operated **Centro de Información Ambiental,** vestiges of the park's indigenous former inhabitants are visible in *piedras tacitas,* smoothly carved rocks used for grinding corn. The rocks are accessible by a short trail.

Several short interpretative trails depart from the CONAF office, including the **Sendero Mirador Antahuara,** a 20-minute hike that passes a 500-year-old Patagonian oak tree 2.4 meters in diameter. The **Sendero Mirador El Peine** (3km round-trip, 1hr) climbs through dense Patagonian oak forest to an overlook where, on a clear day, it's possible to spot Andean condors.

The most popular hikes continue east. **Sendero El Enladrillado** (10km round-trip, 7hr) is the jewel in the reserve's crown, reaching El Enladrillado, an area of flat hexagonal rocks. Beyond, the 3,830-meter peak of Volcán Descabezado Grande and the Andes provide a breathtaking backdrop. This rewarding hike can be made into a circuit that includes a trip to a viewpoint across the crystalline Laguna del Alto, although it's a long day with 800 meters of ascent.

Accommodations

The CONAF-run **Camping Antahuara** (CH$3,000) is 800 meters east of the park entrance and has spots for 30 tents, picnic tables, hot showers, and even electricity (though it can be temperamental). Camping is first come, first served. Other campsites and simple cabins are on the road connecting the hamlet of Vilches Alto and the entrance to the park.

Getting There

From Talca to the park is a 66-km, 1.5-hour drive southwest; you'll need your own car. The final 20km are gravel roads; travel can be difficult following heavy rain. Roads in the park are dirt and require a high-clearance vehicle.

An alternative is four daily **buses** (Jan.-Feb., 2hr, CH$1,900) operated by **Buses Vilches** (tel. 9/5909 0748) between the Terminal Rodoviario in Talca and Vilches Alto, 2km short of the entrance to the reserve. March-December, there are three departures a day. There is no office in the bus terminal; buy your ticket on the bus.

WINE-TASTING

Despite having some of the oldest grapevines in the country, the Valle de Maule has yet to fully develop the tourism potential of its wineries. For interesting varietals, the valley is home to país, a grape thought to descend from those brought to Mexico in 1520 by the Spanish conquistador Hernán Cortés. Carignan, which was previously used only in blends, is also now being bottled here in its own right.

Viña Gillmore

About 50km southwest of Talca, on a road that runs to the coast, family-run boutique **Viña Gillmore** (Km 20 Camino a Constitución, tel. 73/1975 539, http://gillmorewines.cl, 9:30am-6pm Mon.-Sat., tour with tasting CH$6,000) was founded in 1990 and cultivates a range of cabernet franc, cabernet sauvignon, merlot, and carignan grapes, with the harvest done by hand. No reservations are necessary for tastings (from CH$2,000) or to visit the shop, which also sells local crafts, but booking for their vineyard tour is necessary.

Viña Bouchon

The family that owns **Viña Bouchon** (Fundo Mingre, km 30 Camino a Constitución, tel. 9/7477 4878, http://casabouchon.com, 8am-6pm Mon.-Fri., hours vary Sat.-Sun., tour with tasting CH$15,000) has been making wine here for four generations. Their oldest vines date from the late 19th century and include país, carignan, and cabernet sauvignon. Their most interesting wine is made in tiny quantities from organic wild país grapes. Tours, which must be organized in advance, cover the winery's early 20th-century adobe buildings and clay fermentation pots. There's a wine shop on-site with house brands and bottles from small vineyards nearby.

The owners operate the exclusive **Casa Bouchon** (CH$266,000 d), in 180-year-old adobe buildings with colonial elements like scrubbed stone floors along with elegant modern baths and central heating, all with a personal cozy atmosphere. Room 3 is the largest of the standard rooms and has the best views of the surrounding vineyards. Soak in the hot tub and dine on lavish gourmet meals in the guests-only restaurant. Horseback riding, hiking, and tours of the vineyards can be organized. Prices drop by around US$100 May-August.

Viña Via

About 20km northeast of Talca, just off Ruta 5, **Via Wines** (Fundo La Esperanza, tel. 2/2355 9900, http://viawines.com, tour with tasting CH$14,000) has over 1,000 hectares of vineyards at the Viña San Rafael estate. Interesting blends include cabernet franc and merlot. Tours of their vineyards end with a tasting at the winery building, in a majestic setting overlooking a swan-filled lake.

CONSTITUCIÓN TO COBQUECURA

The 126-km coastal road that connects Constitución and Cobquecura is a scenic drive through some of the region's wildest beaches and desolate coast, in the midst of which is excellent off-the-beaten-path surfing and pleasant ocean-side lodgings, all but deserted outside January-February.

A car is the easiest way to explore this untouched stretch of black-and-white-sand beaches. It is possible to take public transportation; take one of the hourly minibuses from Chillán's **Terminal la Merced** (Maipo 890, Chillán, tel. 42/2423 814, www.terminallamerced.cl) with **Buses Petoch** (no phone) or **Via Itata** (tel. 42/2211 196) to Cobquecura (2hr, CH$2,300). Eight daily departures (four in winter) continue north to Buchupureo (2.25hr, CH$2,600).

Constitución

The pretty fishing town of Constitución lines the southern side of the mouth of the Río Maule as it meets the ocean. On the southern edge of town are a series of picturesque freestanding granite stacks, known as Piedra de la Iglesia, Piedra el Obelisco, and Arco de los Enamorados.

Buchupureo

The route south of Constitución passes a long strip of coastline framed by pine forests and desolate black-sand beaches. Some aren't a good place to swim but make for a wonderful place to disconnect. Most villages have a number of rustic cabins for lodging.

About 26km south of Constitución, **Costa Blanca,** just beyond the scattering of houses that make up Los Pellines, is a long stretch of black sand popular among fishing enthusiasts. Another 47km south, the slightly larger village of **Pelluhue** has a series of black-sand beaches between rocky coves accessed from the main road. Sixteen kilometers north of Buchupureo, **Playa Tregualemu** is a long, thick stretch of sand and dunes.

In **Buchupureo, Playa La Boca** is another beautiful crescent of sand. It isn't suitable for swimming, but the river directly behind the beach allows for a dip. The area is known to surfers for its consistent long left breaks. The best waves are reached from the top of the hill as the road continues south.

Cobquecura

Continuing south from Buchupureo, the road passes the **Iglesia de Piedra,** a hollow rock formation, just south of the headland. It's accessible by a path from the main road.

Following the coastline, **Cobquecura** is a fishing village of small, low houses and a long black beach. Surfers come from across the country for the mighty waves up to six meters. Look for the colony of 2,500 barking South American sea lions that live on four islets 1km out to sea. Don't miss the local delicacy, papaya—the southernmost found in the country.

South of Cobquecura, the hamlet of **Taucú** is home to **Playa Rinconada** and an excellent left-hand wave (a local secret) and rugged cliffs that hide myriad small desolate beaches and caves.

Ruka Antu Eco Lodge (Camino Colmuyao, Taucú, tel. 9/6811 0895, http://rukaantu.cl, CH$98,000 d) has the best views of the beach from its 2nd-floor rooms and from the hot tub on the hammock-slung front terrace. A unique escape from civilization, this lodge is just a minute's walk from Taucú's harbor. Small, simple wooden rooms have crisp white sheets and modern baths, plus access to a private balcony or the main terrace. Sound carries easily between the rooms. Staff lead fun tours: stand-up paddleboarding, hiking along the coast, and horseback riding on the beach. They also have surfboards and wetsuits to rent. There's a restaurant with inventive dishes and boutique wines from the Valle de Maule.

Chillán

About 400km south of Santiago, Chillán is the capital of the Ñuble region. For many just a stop on the way to nearby Nevados de Chillán ski resort, the home of liberator Bernardo O'Higgins has an intriguing array of museums and a series of murals painted by renowned Mexican artist David Alfaro Siqueiros.

The central part of Chillán, known as Las Cuatros Avenidas, is bounded by Avenida Ecuador in the north, Avenida Argentina in the east, Avenida Collín in the south, and Avenida Brasil in the west. At the center is the Plaza de Armas, also known as Plaza Bernardo O'Higgins.

SIGHTS

At the center of Chillán's **Plaza de Armas** (bounded by Av. Libertad, Arauco, Constitución, and 18 de Septiembre), national hero Bernardo O'Higgins is immortalized with a statue. On the northeast corner, the modernist **Catedral de Chillán** (Arauco 505, no phone, 10am-7pm daily) is a national monument with a striking design: a single nave and a roof shaped by 10 parabolic arches.

★ Escuela Mexico

Among the city's most famed sights are the murals of **Escuela Mexico** (O'Higgins 250, tel. 42/2212012, muralescuelamexicochillan@gmail.com, 10am-12:30pm and 3pm-6pm Mon.-Fri., free). The Mexican fresco painter David Alfaro Siqueiros and muralist Xavier Guerrero established their names in the Mexican Mural Renaissance in the early 1920s, working alongside artists such as Diego Rivera. In 1941, Siqueiros and Guerrero were jointly commissioned to paint a series of murals on the walls of this school.

Siqueiros's communist leanings can be identified in the dramatic, vivid murals that adorn the walls and ceiling of the Pedro Aguierre Cerda Library on the school's 2nd floor. The *Muerte al Invasor (Death of the Invader),* in two distinct murals, *Sur de Chile* and *Norte Mexico,* took a year to complete. The southern wall covers Chilean history. At the center, Galvarino, a Mapuche warrior, is launched from a cannon during a battle for his people. Note the gruesome details of his bleeding arms—his hands were cut off by Chilean governor García Hurtado de Mendoza. Caupolicán and Lautaro, two other Mapuche leaders, join in the fight, accompanied by Luis Emilio Recabarren, father of the worker's movement in Chile.

The mural on the north wall is dominated by the form of Cuauthémoc, the final Aztec emperor. He is shooting arrows at a cross to symbolize what the introduction of Christianity meant to his people's way of life. Other important revolutionary figures, including Miguel Hidalgo, priest and leader of the Mexican independence movement, and Emiliano Zapata, leader of the peasant revolution, also feature in the work.

Guerrero's murals are less vivid and expressionist in style. On the staircase ceiling, just inside the main entrance, his mural *México a Chile (From Mexico to Chile)* signifies the aid offered to Chile by Mexico following the 1939 earthquake. The school is private, but the library is open to the public.

Museo Claudio Arrau

The **Museo Claudio Arrau** (Claudio Arrau 558, tel. 42/2433 374, 8:30am-1:30pm and 3pm-7pm Tues.-Fri., 10am-1pm and 4pm-7:30pm Sat., 10am-2pm Sun., free, donation) is a museum dedicated to the world-renowned 20th-century classical musician Claudio Arrau. A child prodigy born in Chillán, he learned to read music before words. Eventually he studied at the Stern Conservatory in Berlin, Germany, and spent his life performing throughout Europe and the United States. The museum is on the site of what was left of the pianist's childhood home after the 1939 earthquake.

The 25-minute compulsory tour shows you the interactive exhibits, including a piano driven by light, and a small room with rotating art exhibitions. Unfortunately, not many of Arrau's personal items are on display; some were lost to earthquake damage and others are part of collections abroad.

Casa Gonzalo Rojas

Three blocks southeast of the Plaza de Armas, the **Casa Gonzalo Rojas** (El Roble 1051, no phone, www.gonzalorojas.org, 10:30am-1pm and 2pm-7pm Mon.-Fri., free) is the former home of celebrated Chilean poet Gonzalo Rojas, who lived here until his death in 2011. Rojas was awarded the National Prize for Literature for his lyrical poetry, which focused on the lives of the people affected by the 1973 military coup.

The house contains little more than a collection of photographs and quotations from Rojas's poetry, but the Seussian blue and turquoise of the building evidence his whimsical nature. The house connects with a tower where he would write at night overlooking the lights of the city. At the back, a rose garden that Rojas lovingly tended contains 100 species, a particularly pretty sight in September-October when they start to bloom. The house now plays host to poetry readings and lectures for the local literary community.

SHOPPING

Plaza Sargento Aldea (bounded by Maipón, Isabel Riquelme, Arturo Prat, and 5 de Abril) is home to the octagonal **Feria de Chillán** (7am-7pm daily), a huge craft market featuring Mapuche woven baskets, leather purses, and hand-carved wooden ornaments between stalls selling funerary wreaths and dried fruits and spices. This is a good place to stock up on the local smoked chili pepper *merkén*. It's easy to get lost in the market's spoke-like avenues.

FOOD AND ACCOMMODATIONS

Three blocks southeast of the Plaza de Armas is **Mercado de Chillán** (5 de Abril, between El Roble and Maipón, 9am-7pm daily), also known as the **Mercado Techado,** one of the most interesting in the Central Valley, as farmers flog fruit and vegetables beneath the domed, corrugated iron roof. In the meat hall is regional specialty *longanizas* (sausages), hanging in rows. The best are sold by **Villablanca** (Stand 62), **Emanuel** (Stand 41), and **Cecinas Pincheira** (Stand 65). In the middle of the market, small kitchens sell steaming bowls of *cazuela de pavo* (turkey stew) and other local dishes (around CH$2,500).

The popular **Fuente Alemana** (Arauco 661, tel. 4/2423 565, 8am-10:30pm daily, CH$3,000-7,000) feels like a school cafeteria, but ignore the layout. This is a top choice for hearty Chilean *churrasco* or *lomo* with sauerkraut, avocados, or homemade mayonnaise. Service is fast, and if you sit near the door, you can watch the meat being cooked on the grill. If you want your loaded sandwich to take away, **Fuente Alemana Express** next door has a fast-moving queue.

One of Chillán's more upmarket lodging options, **Hotel Las Terrazas Express** (Constitución 633, tel. 42/2437 004, www.lasterrazas.cl, CH$51,000 d) has 20 rooms with white baths, white linens, and white walls. It's comfortable and just half a block from the Plaza de Armas. If you want to be able to open the window for air, ask for a street-facing room.

INFORMATION AND SERVICES

Tremendously helpful and with English leaflets about many nearby destinations, the **Oficina de Turismo** (Teatro Municipal, Dieciocho de Septiembre 510, 1st Fl., tel. 42/2255 770, www.biobioestuyo.cl, 10am-7pm Mon.-Sat.) should be your first stop for queries. **SERNATUR** (Bulnes 847, no phone, infochillan@sernatur.cl, 9am-1pm and 3pm-6pm Mon.-Fri., 10am-2pm Sat.) has maps and information on the whole of the Ñuble region.

For money, **Banco Estado** (Constitución 500), **BBVA** (Constitución 580), and **Santander** (Constitución 595) have **24-hour ATMs** within a few blocks of the Plaza de Armas. The **Hospital Clínico Herminda Martín** (Av. Francisco Ramírez 10, tel. 42/2586 400, http://hospitaldechillan.cl) is on the eastern edge of Las Cuatros Avenidas. **Lavandería Lavaseco Chillán** (Arturo Prat 637, tel. 42/2230 435) offers laundry services.

TRANSPORTATION
Car

Chillán is a 405-km, 4.5-hour drive south on Ruta 5 from **Santiago.** From **Talca,** it's a 152-km, 1.75-hour drive, also on Ruta 5. From **Concepción,** it's a 98-km, 1.5-hour drive east along Ruta 150, Ruta 152, and Ruta 5.

Chillán is reached by Avenida O'Higgins, three blocks from the plaza, which acts as the entrance road into Chillán from Ruta 5 and the exit to rejoin the highway farther south. If you're headed west to Nevados de Chillán, the cheapest gas is in Chillán and the final option is in Pinto, 47km before Las Trancas.

Bus

Chillán has three bus terminals, all with specific destinations and departures. Long-distance buses use the modern **Terminal de Buses María Teresa** (Longitudinal Sur 10, tel. 42/2272 151) on the northern edge of town. There are at least four departures daily from **Puerto Montt** (11hr, CH$15,000/CH$28,000) with **Pullman Bus** (tel. 42/2270 913, www.pullmanbus.cl), **Jac** (tel. 42/2424 182, http://jac.cl), and **Turbus** (tel. 42/2205 702, http://turbus.cl). Many pass through **Temuco** (4hr, CH$10,000/CH$14,000), **Valdivia** (6hr, CH$13,000/CH$22,000), and **Osorno** (7.5hr, CH$15,000/CH$24,000). Turbus also has hourly service from Temuco and two daily direct buses from **Pucón** (1:50pm and 3:55pm daily, 6hr, CH$11,000/CH$15,000). From **Santiago** (every 30 min, 3.5hr, CH$6,000/CH$9,000) to Chillán, all three companies run buses, as does **EME Bus** (tel. 42/2270 137, http://emebus.cl). Departures for Los Ángeles (1.5hr, CH$4,000/CH$6,000) to change to buses for Antuco and Parque Nacional Laguna del Laja also leave from this bus terminal every 30 minutes.

From **Concepción** (1.5hr, CH$3,000/CH$7,000), there are buses every half hour from the Terminal de Buses María Teresa; even more regular departures can be found at the **Terminal del Centro** (Brasil 560, tel. 42/2226 095) on the west of the city, a few hundred meters south of the train station.

Terminal La Merced (Maipo 890, tel. 42/2423 814, www.terminallamerced.cl), half a block east of Plaza Sargento Aldea, has hourly minibuses to **Cobquecura** (2hr, CH$2,300) and eight daily to **Buchupureo** (2.25hr, CH$2,600), on the coast.

Train

Chillán's **Estación de Ferrocarriles** (Brasil 487, tel. 600/5855 000, http://trencentral.cl) is the final stop on the twice-daily TerraSur train from **Santiago** (depart 8:30am and 5:30pm daily, 4.5hr, CH$11,900).

Getting Around

Within the city, it's rarely necessary to use anything other than your own feet for getting around the main sights and bus terminals.

A hired car is useful if you're heading west to the coast or east to Nevados de Chillán. You can rent a vehicle from **MV Rent a Car** (Los Benedictinos 2105, tel. 9/9959 8091, http://empresasmv.cl, 9am-5pm daily). Be sure to ask for snow chains if you're going to Nevados de Chillán in winter. Depending on weather conditions, the police may prevent you from continuing to the resort without chains.

★ NEVADOS DE CHILLÁN

On the snowy flanks of three stratovolcanoes, **Nevados de Chillán** (tel. 600/6000 170, http://nevadosdechillan.com, day passes from CH$48,000) is considered the Central Valley's best ski resort. Skiing down the often ash-littered runs that crisscross the southern side of the 3,122-meter Volcán Chillán is a unique experience. Annual snowfall averages 10 meters, and the resort offers a good mix of beginner and intermediate runs. Many backcountry stretches were formed long ago by lava flows. These volcanoes are among the most active in Chile, but recent eruptions have been little more than plumes of ash and small earthquakes, with the last major event in 1973.

The resort is known for its high-quality facilities, including 30 runs on 35km of skiable terrain and 13 lifts, with an elevation change of around 1,000 meters. The highest lifts are often closed due to winds. You can rent gear on-site, although prices are more affordable from rental shops in the settlement of Las Trancas, which lines the main road to the resort, 8km west. The ski season normally runs June-October. In summer, hiking and horseback-riding excursions are also possible. Take plenty of cash with you, as not all places at the resort accept cards.

Parque de Agua

The **Parque de Agua** (tel. 42/2206 100, 9am-9pm daily July, 9am-5pm Mon.-Fri., 9am-8pm Sat.-Sun. Aug.-June, CH$11,000 adults, CH$6,000 children) is a group of four hot springs pools beside Hotel Nevados de Chillán. The resort's greatest attraction after the slopes, the water soothes tired limbs after a day of skiing. The pools are open to non-guests and have changing facilities on-site. There's a poolside bar, so you don't even have to leave the water to buy a drink.

Rental Gear

Pick up cheap, good-quality ski equipment at **Ski Motion** (Km 71.3 Camino a Nevados de Chillán, tel. 9/9678 9550, www.skimotion.cl, 8:30am-8:30pm daily) in La Trancas. Expect to pay CH$8,000-10,000 for skis, boots, a jacket, and a snowsuit. Prices are much higher at the ski resort.

Food and Accommodations

There are three hotels beneath the slopes: **Hotel Nevados** (CH$294,000 d), **Hotel Alto Nevados** (CH$225,000 d), and **Departamentos Valle Hermoso** (CH$87,000 apartment). All three can be booked by phone or online (tel. 600/6000 170, www.nevadosdechillan.com). A plethora of cheaper but comfortable accommodations are available in Las Trancas, 8km west of the resort.

For a post-ski meal, you can't go wrong with the ski shack-inspired **Restaurant Chil'in** (Km 72 Camino a Termas de Chillán, tel. 42/2247 075, www.chil-in.com, 1pm-10:30pm daily, CH$6,000-12,000) in Las Trancas. Better-than-average pizzas and cheap beer are the biggest draw, although the hot chocolate and outdoor tables are an added bonus.

Easily Las Trancas's most interesting lodging is **Ecobox Andino** (Km 0.2 Camino a Shangri-La, tel. 42/2423 134, http://ecoboxandino.cl, CH$80,000 d). The five-person cabins are built from reused shipping containers. Another option is one of the seven rooms in the hexagonal Refugio de la Luna, each with a private balcony, a large kitchen, and a living room. Central heating and a hearty breakfast are included. There's a hot tub, but you'll pay a fee to use it. Prices drop by half September-June.

Twelve kilometers west of Las Trancas, the modern **Nordic Lodge** (Km 56 Camino a Las Trancas, tel. 9/6100 1414, http://nordiclodge.cl, CH$95,000) has four Scandinavian cabins

skiing in Nevados de Chillán

in the forest. It's an ideal spot winter or summer, with large terraces, a swimming pool, a hot tub, and a sauna. All cabins sleep four and have spacious dining and living areas, plus fully equipped kitchens. The owners are effusively friendly.

Getting There

It's an 80-km, 1.5-hour drive along the N-55 to the resort. Snow chains are generally required in winter for the last few kilometers to the resort, and you may be stopped and turned back by the police if you don't have them.

While a rental car offers far more flexibility, you can reach the ski resort on public transport. From Chillán's **Terminal la Merced** (Maipón 890, tel. 42/2423 814, www.terminallamerced.cl), **Rem Bus** (tel. 42/2229 377, www.busesrembus.cl) leaves at 7:50am, 8:20am, 1pm, and 1:30pm daily. Buses go directly to the Hotel Nevados de Chillán (2hr, CH$3,300); they return at 9:30am, 9:40am, 4:30pm, and 4:45pm. Buy tickets in advance, as demand is high, particularly on weekends in winter. In summer, departures drop to twice daily.

To get to **Las Trancas** (1.75hr, CH$2,200), there are hourly departures from Chillán 8am-6pm daily. From here, transfer services like **Volcán Chillán** (Calle Los Cofré, Recinto s/n, tel. 9/8411 0903, transfervolcanchillan@gmail.com) can shuttle you to the ski resort. The Las Trancas **Oficina de Información Turística** (Km 73 Camino a Termas de Chillán, no phone, 9am-5pm daily winter) can provide assistance.

Concepción

Conce, as it's fondly called by its residents, is a busy university city, home to lauded educational institutions and considered the birthplace of Chilean rock—bands such as Los Tres and Los Bunkers hail from here. While it's not exactly cosmopolitan, Concepción has a liberal, friendly vibe.

Concepción is 520km south of Santiago on the eastern bank of the Río Bío Bío where it meets the sea. Despite its population of 223,000, Concepción is compact, centered on the Plaza de la Independencia. Bordering the plaza are Parque Ecuador and Cerro Caracol to the south, Plaza Perú and the Universidad de Concepción to the east, and the Río Bío Bío to the west. Most of the main attractions are within this area.

SIGHTS

At the heart of the city, **Plaza de la Independencia** (bounded by Barros Arana, Anibal Pinto, O'Higgins, and Caupolicán) is crowned by a bronze water feature, the **Pileta de la Plaza.** On a pedestal stands Ceres, goddess of agriculture, with four sirens beneath her. In the square, another monument stands in honor of Mapuche leader Lautaro, who led the resistance against the Spanish.

Chile's third-oldest university, **Universidad de Concepción** (Av. Chacabuco s/n), which borders Plaza Perú, is a landmark that opened in 1919 and one of the most prestigious schools in the country. Its most distinguishable feature is the **Arco de Medicina,** which grants access to the campus from Avenida Chacabuco. It features a stone frieze, created in 1950 by Mario Francisco Ormezzano, that depicts ancient Greeks in pursuit of knowledge and learning.

The **Casa de Arte** (Av. Chacabuco 1343, tel. 41/2203 835, 10am-6pm Tues.-Fri., 11am-5pm Sat., 11am-2pm Sun., free), also called the **Pinacoteca,** is a small art museum known for Mexican artist Jorge González Camarena's 1965 *La Presencia de Latino America,* a large mural inside the main entrance. The work depicts the fraternity among the peoples of Latin America, narrating the history of the continent; it is "read" from left to right.

Concepción

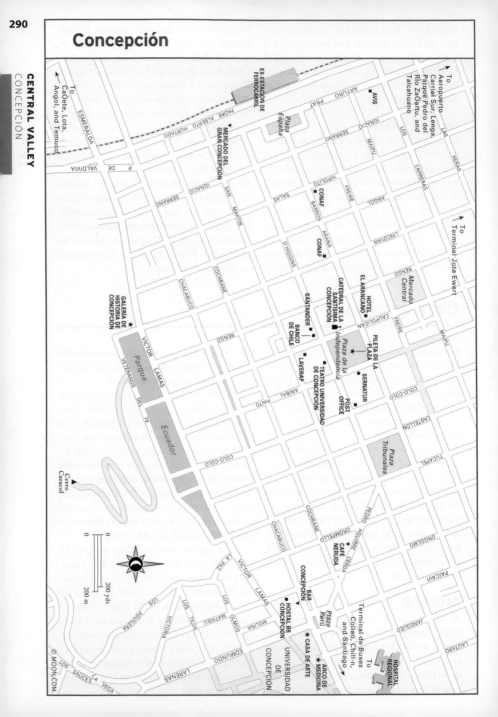

EX-ESTACIÓN DE
FERROCARRIL

To
Aeropuerto,
Carriel Sur, Lenga,
Parque Pedro del
Río Zañartu, and
Talcahuano

To
Cañete, Lota,
Angol, and Temuco

AVIS

Plaza
España

MERCADO DEL
GRAN CONCEPCIÓN

To
Terminal Jota Ewert

CONAF

CONAF

Mercado
Central

CATEDRAL DE LA
SANTÍSIMA
CONCEPCIÓN

HOTEL
EL ARANCANO

SANTANDER

BANCO
DE CHILE

PILETA DE LA
PLAZA

Plaza de la
Independencia

POST
OFFICE

SERNATUR

LAVERAP

TEATRO UNIVERSIDAD
DE CONCEPCIÓN

GALERÍA DE
HISTORIA DE
CONCEPCIÓN

Parque
Ecuador

Plaza
Tribunales

Cerro
Caracol

CAFÉ
NERUDA

BAR
CONCEPCIÓN

HOSTAL BB
CONCEPCIÓN

Plaza
Perú

CASA DE ARTE

ARCO DE
MEDICINA

UNIVERSIDAD
DE
CONCEPCIÓN

To
Terminal de Buses
Collao, Chillán,
and Santiago

HOSPITAL
REGIONAL

0   200 yds

0   200 m

© MOON.COM

(street labels) PADRE ALBERTO HURTADO, ESMERALDA, P. DE VALDIVIA, IGNACIO SERRANO, SAN MARTÍN, SERRANO, CHACABUCO, COCHRANE, RENGO, SALAS, BARROS, ARANA, O'HIGGINS, ANÍBAL PINTO, COLO-COLO, CHACABUCO, COCHRANE, OROMPELLO, PEDRO AGUIRRE CERDA, ARTURO PRAT, IGNACIO SERRANO, MAIPÚ, LOS HERAS, CARRERAS, ANGOL, LINCOYÁN, CAUPOLICÁN, FREIRE, MAIPÚ, COLO-COLO, CASTELLÓN, TUCAPEL, ONGOLMO, PAICAVÍ, JANEQUEO, LAUTARO, VÍCTOR LAMAS, VETERANOS DEL 79, LA PAZ, VÍCTOR LAMAS, LOS AGUILERA, LOS SAUCES, LA VEGA, VICTORIA, LOS OLMOS, MATHIEU, MOLINA, EDMUNDO, LARENAS, HIPÓLITO, FREIRE

Parque Ecuador

Stretching 11 blocks, almost a kilometer in length along the southern edge of the city, the narrow, landscaped gardens of **Parque Ecuador** (Victor Lamas, between Arturo Pratt and Tucapel, 24 hr daily) are studded with pines, palms, and other trees. It's immensely popular among joggers, lounging university students, and families playing football or taking a late afternoon stroll. At the southern edge, **Cerro Carracol** rises above the park, with paved trails leading to viewpoints across the city.

In the park's western half is the **Galería de História de Concepción** (Hospicio 40, tel. 41 285 3759, www.ghconcepcion.cl, 11am-8pm Tues.-Sun. summer, 11am-7pm Tues.-Sun. winter, free). Upstairs, a collection of ceramics displays the notable pottery of the Bío Bío region. The most interesting are those of the Cerámica Lota collection, a form of handmade pottery depicting religious and modern cultural themes—note the bust of Evita Perón.

Parque Pedro del Río Zañartu

On the north shore of the mouth of the Río Bío Bío, the pleasant grounds of the 552-hectare Parque Pedro del Río Zañartu (Fundo Hualpén s/n, tel. 41/2426 399, www.prz.cl, 8am-11:30pm daily, CH$3,000 per vehicle) have an abundance of *araucaría,* palms, and evergreen species from across Chile, crisscrossed with short paths with views of the coast and Concepción.

Built in 1870, the **Museo Pedro del Río Zañartu** (9am-5:40pm Mon.-Fri., 10am-6:40pm Sat.-Sun. Sept.-Mar., 9am-5:40pm daily Apr.-Aug., free) was once the home of avid globe-trotter Pedro del Río Zañartu. Today it contains his collection of objects picked up on his explorations. One of his trips lasted two years, visiting 298 cities and towns. Highlights include an Egyptian mummy and a collection of coins from around the world.

There's no public transport to the park. Instead, catch a **bus** (50min, CH$470) from Calle Freire, a block north of the Plaza de la Independencia. Get off at Avenida Los Golondrinas; from here it should be no more than a CH$3,000 taxi ride to reach the park. Alternatively, take Avenida Costanera north along the riverbank and turn onto Ramuntcho at the suburb of Hualpén; the road is signposted for the park. It's a 12-km, 20-minute journey.

Universidad de Concepción

Lenga

A tiny fishing village on the tip of the peninsula, **Lenga** is a great place to watch the sunset, although the factory on the other side of the bay is unsightly. The empanadas and fresh fish from the various *picadas* that line the shore are great for a cheap and tasty bite.

On public transit, take Buses Puchacay 71 or 480, which leave from Avenida Los Carrera, near Plaza Acevedo. In your own vehicle, take Avenida Costanera north along the riverbank until it intersects with the Camino a Lenga heading west to the bay. It's a 15-km, 20-minute drive.

Museo Huáscar

The industrial town of Talcahuano, 15km northwest of Concepción, is home to the Segunda Zona Naval, one of the largest naval bases in Chile and home to **Museo Huáscar** (Base Naval Talcahuano, tel. 41/2745 520, http://huascar.cl, 9:30am-11:45am and 2pm-4:30pm daily, CH$1,000 adults, CH$500 children), a museum that houses the restored ironclad turret ship *Huáscar.* This vessel belonged to the Peruvian navy; Chilean war hero Arturo Prat, who died aboard the vessel after it sank his ship, the *Esmeralda,* during the War of the Pacific, is honored throughout the museum. Only small groups are allowed to board the ship at one time, so arrive early on weekends to guarantee a spot.

To get here, *micros* (30min, CH$470) with signs for "Base Naval" depart in a westerly direction from any intersection along Calle O'Higgins (between Paicaví and Arturo Prat) and drop passengers at Plaza el Ancla in Talcahuano, a 700-meter walk to the museum. With your own vehicle, it's a 16-km, 25-minute drive along Calle Paicaví, Ruta 154, and Calle Peréz Gacitúa, which becomes Blanco Encalada, and ultimately Jorge Montt.

ENTERTAINMENT

The **Teatro Universidad de Concepción** (O'Higgins 660, tel. 41/2243 536, http://corcudec.cl), on the Plaza de la Independencia, is Concepción's most important cultural space, with regular classical music, art, theater, and dance performances. Consult their website for the full program.

Nightlife

The greatest concentration of bars is along Calle Diagonal. A favorite among the university crowd, **Café Neruda** (Diagonal Pedro Aguirre Cerda 1134, tel. 41/2218 835, 5pm-11pm Mon.-Sat.) is always heaving as groups of students swarm around the wooden tables for long discussions into the night. Make sure you get a jug of the local tipple, *borgoña,* a mix of red wine, ice, sugar, and strawberries—it's sweet enough to leave your teeth tingling.

Half a block from the Pinoteca and attracting a youthful crowd, **Bar Concepción** (Av. Chacabuco 1124, tel. 41/2198 111, 4pm-1am Sun.-Mon., 4pm-2am Tues., 4pm-3am Wed.-Sat.) has a great selection of craft beer on tap and blaring rock music. Drink specials and live music (folk, jazz, swing, and rock) a few days a week make this a top choice any day.

FOOD AND ACCOMMODATIONS

Concepción is an affordable city for dining. Some of the cheapest spots are along Calle Diagonal, with sun umbrellas and plastic tables tumbling onto the street in summer. **Mercado del Gran Concepción** (O'Higgins 50, no phone, 10:30am-7pm daily) specializes in cheap eats, selling *cazuelas* (stews), fried fish, empanadas, and, during the summer, *porotos granados* (stew made from cranberry beans, squash, and maize).

In a rough-around-the-edges neighborhood and run by owner-chef Andrés, **40 Sillas** (Lientur 905, tel. 9/6620 8714, 8:30pm-midnight Mon.-Sat., by reservation only, CH$18,500, cash only) is a unique spot in Concepción: It operates purely by reservation, with a set four-course menu of inventive pairings such as steak with pureed beans served with local wines. Ask for a seat at the bar to watch and chat with Andrés and his assistant chef.

A solid lodging choice in Concepción, **Hotel El Araucano** (Caupolicán 521, tel. 41/2740 606, http://hotelaraucano.cl, CH$60,000 d) has 160 rooms, all spacious if a little dated. Guests have access to a swimming pool and jetted tub. This hotel is an excellent value as it's right on Plaza de la Independencia—the noise of which you don't hear in the rooms. The staff speaks English.

Just a block from Plaza Perú, the superb **Hostal BB Concepción** (Ongolmo 62, tel. 41/3189 308, http://hostalboutiqueconcepcion. com, CH$39,000 d, cash only) is Concepción's top affordable option. Everything is smart and simple, although the rooms are somewhat cramped. On weekends, the music from neighboring Bar Concepción can be heard throughout the hotel. Breakfast is insubstantial, but the downstairs café has great cakes and sandwiches. Choose a room on the 1st or 2nd floor for the best Wi-Fi signal. Parking can be an issue, as there is only space for a few vehicles. Rates include IVA.

INFORMATION AND SERVICES

On the Plaza de la Independencia, **SERNATUR** (Aníbal Pinto 460, tel. 41/2741 337, infobiobio@sernatur.cl, 9am-7pm Mon.-Fri., 10am-2pm Sat. summer, 9am-6pm Mon.-Fri., 10am-1pm Sat. winter) is well supplied with maps. Staff have an exhaustive knowledge of transportation options to local and regional attractions. There is also a municipal **Oficina de Turismo** (Barros Arana 544, 4th Fl., tel. 41/2208 916, http://concepcion.cl, 8:45am-1:45pm Mon.-Fri.).

For money, **Banco de Chile** (O'Higgins 598) and **Santander** (O'Higgins 560) are within a few blocks of the Plaza de la Independencia. **Correos** (O'Higgins 799) handles the mail. Get your clothes washed at **Laverap** (Caupolicán 334, tel. 41/2234 826). The **Hospital Regional** (San Martín 1436, tel. 41/2722 500, http://hospitalregional.cl) can deal with medical emergencies.

GETTING THERE

Concepción has well-developed transportation infrastructure, including an airport and regular buses between Santiago in the north and Puerto Montt in the south.

Air

Aeropuerto Carriel Sur (CCP, Jorge Alessandri s/n, tel. 41/2732 000, http:// carrielsur.cl) is 5km north of the city, on the road toward Talcahuano. **LATAM** (Av. Alessandri 3177, tel. 600/526 2000, http:// latam.com, 10am-9pm Mon.-Fri., 11am-8:30pm Sat.-Sun.) has eight daily flights between Santiago and Concepción and one daily flight between Antofagasta and Concepción. Low-cost carrier **Sky Airline** (http:// skyairline.com) has three daily flights from Santiago. **JetSmart** (http://jetsmart.com) has daily flights between Concepción and Santiago, Antofagasta, Iquique, and Calama.

AIRPORT TRANSFER

Various companies, including **TaxVan** (tel. 9/5079 4136, www.taxvan.cl) and **Transfer Concepción** (tel. 9/9303 5218, www. transferconcepcion.cl), are in the arrivals hall of the airport; book in advance or just walk up for a **shuttle transfer** (around CH$5,000) or **private taxi** (around CH$8,000) to hotels in the center of Concepción. You can also take a taxi (CH$8,000) from the stand outside arrivals.

RENTAL CARS

Europcar (tel. 41/2178 835, http://europcar. com, 7:30am-10pm Mon.-Fri., 9am-8pm Sat.-Sun.) and **Avis** (tel. 2/2795 3979, www.avis. com, 8am-9:30pm Mon.-Fri., 9am-8pm Sat., 9am-9:30pm Sun.) both have rental locations at the airport. Avis also has a downtown office (Av. Arturo Prat 750, tel. 2/2795 3966, 8:30am-7pm Mon.-Fri., 9am-12:30pm Sat.).

Car

From **Chillán,** Concepción is a 99-km, 1.5-hour drive southwest on Ruta 152, which is usually blissfully quiet, most likely because of the hefty toll ($4,240). From **Santiago**, it's a 500-km, 5.5-hour drive south on Ruta 5 and southwest on Ruta 152.

Parking can be an issue in the city due to strict rules about on-street parking during daylight hours. These are generally indicated clearly on signs on the affected streets, but plan on parking in lots or garages when possible to avoid the hassle of learning the rules or getting a ticket.

Bus

Most buses use the **Terminal de Buses Collao** (Tegualda 860, tel. 41/2749 002, www.terminalcollao.cl), five blocks southeast of the Universidad de Concepción. **Tur Bus** (tel. 41/2316 989, http://turbus.cl) and **Eme Bus** (tel. 41/2320 094, http://emebus.

cl) have departures every 30 minutes from **Santiago** (6.5hr, CH$8,000/CH$15,000), generally stopping at **Chillán** (1.5hr, CH$2,5000) and **Talca** (4hr, CH$5,000) en route. Some of these buses originate in **Valparaíso** and **Viña del Mar** (8.5hr, CH$9,000/CH$16,000).

For the south, including **Valdivia** (6hr, CH$9,000/CH$15,000) and **Puerto Montt** (10hr, CH$10,000/CH$20,000), **Tur Bus** and **Pullman Bus** (tel. 41/2320 309, www.pullmanbus.cl) have the most regular arrivals and departures.

The **Terminal Jota Ewert** (Lincoyán 1425, tel. 41/2855 673) has buses to and from long-distance destinations such as **Angol** (3hr, CH$5,000) with **Buses Bío Bío** (http://busesbiobio.cl). Half of their buses use the Terminal de Buses Collao.

Vicinity of Concepción

The coastline north of Concepción is picturesque and largely empty of residents or visitors, making it a paradise of untouched bays and mellow fishing villages granting escape from the chaos of the city. Just south, Chile's industrial past is seen in the town of Lota, where a gorgeous hilltop park and the dank, dark corridors of a former mine show two sides of its history of coal mining.

Farther inland, the low coastal cordillera promises views of the distinctive umbrella-shaped *araucaría* trees at Parque Nacional Nahuelbuta, in the former territory of the Mapuche people, whose history and modern culture is shown at the fascinating Museo Mapuche de Cañete.

NORTHERN BEACHES

The coastline north of Concepción is difficult to reach but offers quiet, picture-perfect coves that make for a pretty half-day trip. Outside of the peak summer season, you can expect to be more or less alone.

The most accessible beaches are along the coast of sprawling fishing town **Tomé**, 30km north of the city. Its two main beaches are **Playa Bellavista**, on its southern edge, with a large expanse of sand overlooked by lemon-yellow apartment blocks, and **Playa El Morro**, a much smaller sandy beach in the center of town. *Micros* (50min, CH$900) bound for Tomé from Concepción leave every five minutes from Avenida Chacabuco heading east.

Seven kilometers before Tomé and accessed by a side road, **Playa Punta de Parra** is a picturesque and sheltered beach. It requires a vehicle entry fee (CH$5,000 Mon.-Fri., CH$7,000 Sat.-Sun.), although out of season you may not be required to pay. There's also a beachside restaurant here that opens in summer.

With a long sandy beach where pelicans and surfers bob in the waves, the quiet fishing village of **Colcholgüe** makes a scenic stop; it's quiet even in summer. A good place for a fish lunch is Caleta Chica, the town's harbor. Surfboards and bodyboards are available to rent from a handful of places. *Taxis colectivos* signed for "Colcholgüe" shuttle between Tomé and the village, 3.5km northwest.

Thirteen kilometers north of Tomé, **Coliumo** is a relaxed fishing village on a hilly peninsula where colorful houses are stepped into the hill above the bay. Its prettiest beach is **Playa Coliumo,** on the western edge of town, overlooking wooden fishing boats and the pebble beach on the north of the peninsula. To get here by public transit from Tomé, take one of the buses signed for "Coliumo."

From the turnoff for Coliumo, in 4km the town of **Dichato** lines a crescent of sand. At the northern edge you can watch fishing boats bringing in catches. On the main stretch of **Playa Dichato** are plenty of fish restaurants and empanada shops. *Micros* bound for Dichato leave from Tomé.

One of the prettiest beaches along this coast, surrounded by forested hills that slide into dark, rocky outcrops in the ocean, **Playa Merquinche** is 10km north of Dichato. Crashing waves and rocks mean it's not safe for swimming, but it's an idyllic and uncrowded place to spend a few hours. You'll need your own vehicle to get here. From Dichato, head north, and take the left fork when you reach the dirt road.

LOTA

Forty kilometers south of Concepción, a clutter of colorful tin buildings speckle a headland sandwiched between two bays. Lota was historically a coal mining town, from 1840 until finally closing in 1997. The town has struggled since then, noticeable in its disheveled look, but the incongruously bucolic Parque de Lota Isidora Cousiño, and the experience of going down beneath the sea in the tunnels of the Mina Chiflón del Diablo, make Lota a worthwhile day trip from Concepción.

Parque de Lota Isidora Cousiño

On the southern side of town, the botanic garden **Parque de Lota Isidora Cousiño** (Av. El Parque s/n, tel. 9/5402 6183 or 41/2870 934, http://lotasorprendente.cl, 10:30am-7pm

daily, CH$2,700 adults, CH$1,800 children) bears the name of the wife of a 19th-century coal magnate. Covering 14 hectares, the park was planted with trees from across the world. Its most interesting aspect is its collection of 27 cast-iron sculptures of French origin. Guides in traditional 19th-century dress, complete with parasols, take visitors around the park, although you're welcome to wander on your own.

★ Mina Chiflón del Diablo

On the north end of the peninsula, in the area known as Lota Alto, the **Mina Chiflón del Diablo** (Devil's Blast, tel. 9/5402 6183 or 41/2870 934, http://lotasorprendente.cl, 10:30am-7pm daily, final tour 5:30pm daily), formerly known as the Mina Chiflón Carlos, extracted coal from the first and only mine built under the sea. Tunnels up to 580 meters long were dug under the Golfo de Arauco.

Nowadays it's a tourist attraction where visitors can go into the mine to learn about the awful conditions faced by the miners who once worked here. Guided **tours** (Spanish only, 1.5hr, CH$8,700), leaving from the ticket office at the mine entrance, are run by the charismatic grandsons of former miners, although non-Spanish speakers may want to give the tour a miss. Hard hats and head-mounted lights are provided. Arrive early in the day to get a spot on the first-come, first-served tour, as summer weekends can mean long queues.

Buses (50min, CH$900) bound for Lota leave Concepción every 20 minutes from the corner of Los Carrera and Tucapel.

SALTO DEL LAJA

About 100km southeast of Concepción, the **Salto del Laja** is a dramatic thundering waterfall where the Río Laja tumbles 50 meters down a wide lip into the river below. It's a popular stop for a swim for Chileans. Although it can feel like a tourist trap thanks to the shacks touting low-quality souvenirs surrounding the waterfall, it's a good spot for a picnic lunch.

Mapuche Heritage in Cañete

Museo Mapuche de Cañete

A worthy detour south of Concepción is the town of Cañete. One-fifth of the population is of Mapuche heritage. Cañete's excellent **Museo Mapuche de Cañete** (Camino Contulmo, tel. 41/2611 093, http://museomapuchecanete.cl, 9:30am-5:30pm Mon.-Fri., 11am-5:30pm Sat., 1pm-5:30pm Sun. March-Dec., 10am-6pm Mon.-Fri., 11am-6pm Sat., 1pm-6pm Sun. Jan.-Feb., free) gives insight into Mapuche culture.

An impressive array of audiovisual displays at the museum focuses largely on the Lafkenche (People of the Sea), a Mapuche group that inhabited the southern coast of Chile. Five rooms cover geography, history, ritual ceremonies, and daily life, centered on the hearth in the traditional *ruka*, made from straw and wood; one stands on the hill behind the museum. Perhaps most interesting is the room about *nometulafken*, the Mapuche concept of death, where a laurel canoe symbolizes the belief that the soul ventures across the ocean after death. A small shop on the premises displays local art, textiles, and pottery made by local Mapuche women.

To get here from Concepción, it's a splendid 137-km, two-hour drive south through low coastal mountains and dense forests of introduced eucalyptus along Ruta 160 and the P-60-R road. The museum lies on the southern edge of Cañete.

The best views are from the bottom of the falls, reached by a climbing path. To see them at their most forceful, visit outside summer, when water levels are highest. Ruta 5 used to pass the falls directly, but today it's a short signposted detour east, with parking on the road where the path begins.

ANGOL

Founded in 1553, former frontier town Angol suffered serious damage in the ongoing battles between the Mapuche people and the Spanish. At the feet of the Cordillera Nahuelbuta, the location of Parque Nacional Nahuelbuta, Angol makes a good base for hiking in rarely visited forests of *araucaría*.

The town is known for its annual folk festival, **Brotes de Chile,** held the first two weeks of January, featuring competing folk bands from across the country in addition to traditional dancing and local gastronomy. The only worthwhile sight in town is the **Museo**

Dillman Bullock (Escuela Agrícola El Vergel, tel. 45/2711 142, 8am-1pm and 2pm-5:30pm Mon., 8am-1pm and 2pm-7pm Tues.-Fri., 10am-1pm and 1:30pm-6:30pm Sat., 1pm-5:30pm Sun., CH$1,000 adults, CH$500 children), at Escuela Agrícole El Vergel, an agricultural school. Born in Michigan in 1878, Dillman Bullock was a Methodist missionary and one of the first foreigners to study Mapuche culture, even learning the language. Bullock died in 1971 and bequeathed to the school his collection of archaeological and natural history artifacts from across the Americas, now displayed across three rooms. It's a 5-km drive from town to the museum. Catch a *taxi colectivo* (CH$500) from the south side of Angol's Plaza de Armas (bounded by Lautaro, Chorrillos, Prat, and Bunster).

Food and Accommodations
One block west of the Plaza de Armas, the incongruously stylish **Hotel Duhatau** (Arturo Prat 420, tel. 452714320, http://hotelduhatao. cl, CH$59,500 d) has smartly decorated bedrooms with Mapuche textiles, shiny baths, and heavy rustic wooden furniture. Room 213 has a nice balcony; Rooms 210 and 211 have the most space. Downstairs, the large café and restaurant (11am-10pm Mon.-Sat., CH$5,000-8,000) wouldn't look out of place in Santiago, serving a great selection of main dishes, including an affordable lunch menu. Rates include IVA.

Information and Services
On the **Plaza de Armas** (bounded by Lautaro, Chorillos, Arturo Prat, and Bunster), the **Oficina de Turismo** (Chorillos s/n, tel. 45/2990 840, http://angol.cl, 8:30am-2pm and 3pm-7pm Mon.-Fri., 8:30am-1pm Sat.-Sun. Jan.-Feb., 8:30am-2pm and 3pm-5:30pm Mon.-Fri., occasional Sat. Mar.-Dec.) has a useful map of Parque Nacional Nahuelbuta and can advise on transportation options. **CONAF** (Arturo Prat 191, 2nd Fl., tel. 45/2711 870, jorge.salvo@conaf.cl, hours vary) can

provide more detailed advice on hiking trails and weather conditions. There is a **Banco Estado** (Chorrillos 390) with a 24-hour **ATM** just off the Plaza de Armas.

Getting There and Around
From **Concepción,** take Ruta 156 and then Ruta 180 heading south, a 2.25-hour, 148-km drive. Buses from **Concepción** (3.5hr, CH$4,900) depart from the **Terminal de Buses Collao** (Tegualda 860, tel. 41/2749 002, www.terminalcollao.cl), five blocks southeast of the Universidad de Concepción, and from the **Terminal Jota Ewert** (Lincoyán 1425, tel. 41/2855 673) with **Buses Bío Bío,** arriving at Angol's **Terminal de Buses Bío Bío** (Sepúlveda 55, no phone). There are also buses from **Valdivia** (every 20 min, 4hr, CH$5,000) and **Temuco** (every 10 min, 2hr, CH$3,900).

PARQUE NACIONAL NAHUELBUTA
Rising from the coastal cordillera east of Angol up to 1,530 meters, the 6,832-hectare **Parque Nacional Nahuelbuta** (tel. 2/2840 6845 or 9/9643 6927, parque.nahuelbuta@ conaf.cl, CH$5,000 adults, CH$3,000 children, prices drop by half in winter) is a great place to see majestic *araucaría* trees. They hover above the rest of the dense forest, some over 1,000 years old. Pumas are known to prowl here, but you're far more likely to spot a Darwin's fox or the various species of parakeet and woodpecker in the treetops. From the tops of some of the higher peaks, sensational views of the Andes can be spied to the east.

There are three entrances to the park. Driving yourself, the quickest route is via the unpaved road that passes Vegas Blancas west of Angol and enters the park from the east via the ranger station **Guardería Portones.** A few kilometers east of Vegas Blancas, the gravel road becomes a dirt track.

Another entrance, from the west, allows access from the town of Cañete. This lesser-traveled and significantly worse-for-wear dirt track heads east from Cañete to enter the park at **Guardería Pichinahue.** A third entrance, from the northeast via **Guardería Cotico,** is not recommended due to the poor state of the road.

Admission is only collected at these three ranger stations. At **Guardería Pehuenco,** the park's headquarters, 5km west of Guardería Portones, a small **Centro de Informaciones Ecológicas** provides some information on the flora and fauna of the park.

Hiking

The park has six main trails. The most popular is the **Sendero Piedra del Aguila** (4.5km loop, 2hr), which starts from the Guardería Pehuenco and takes a winding loop west among *araucaría,* including the oldest tree in the park (age 1,500 years), to reach the summit of the 1,379-meter **Piedra del Aguila,** with the best views of the Andes to the east.

Reaching 1,400 meters, the **Mirador Cerro Anay** has similar views and provides an excellent overview of the park. It's possible to reach the overlook either by vehicle and a short hike, or by taking the **Sendero Estero Los Gringos** (5km one-way, 2hr), which joins the **Sendero Cerro Anay** for the final 0.8-km stretch to the peak.

Camping

Next to the Guardería Pehuenco, **Camping Pehuenco** (CH$16,000 per site, CH$8,000 in winter) has 11 basic campsites with picnic tables and cold showers. You'll need to bring all food into the park and a gas camping stove; fires are not permitted.

Getting There

The easiest route is from Angol, a 31-km, 1.5-hour drive west via the R-226 and R-150-P roads. Both roads have signposts for the national park and the Guardería Portones entrance. From Cañete, it's a harder 50-km, 1.5-hour drive east on a poorly maintained dirt road to the Guardería Pichinahue entrance. Annual rainfall in the park averages 150 centimeters, mostly May-September. Toward the end of this period, snow isn't uncommon, and access can be difficult without a 4WD vehicle. There is no direct public transport to the park.

Full-day **tours** (starting from CH$35,000) and **taxis** (starting from CH$20,000-30,000 including waiting time) can be arranged through Angol's **Oficina de Turismo** (Chorillos s/n, tel. 45/2990 840, http://angol.cl, 8:30am-2pm and 3pm-7pm Mon.-Fri., 8:30am-1pm Sat.-Sun. Jan.-Feb., 8:30am-2pm and 3pm-5:30pm Mon.-Fri., occasional Sat. Mar.-Dec.).

Lakes District

With its backdrop of perfectly conical volca-
noes and hiking trails leading through dense forests to vast, shimmering lakes, the Lakes District encompasses the Araucanía and Los
Ríos regions in addition to the namesake Los Lagos.

In Chile's self-proclaimed adventure capital, you can summit a
2,800-meter volcano to peer into its bubbling crater and ski your way
back down again, paddle in surging white water, or kayak through hidden fjords to crystalline lakes deep in the mountains. For a slower pace,
take a dip in volcano-adjacent hot springs and relax beneath the stars.

Stretching down from the foothills of the Andes are lush Valdivian
temperate rainforests. At higher elevations are the umbrella-shaped
boughs of the ancient *araucaría* (monkey puzzle tree).

Highlights

Look for ★ to find recommended sights, activities, dining, and lodging.

★ **Ski at Centro de Esquí Corralco:** Ski on the slopes of a volcano at one of Chile's most highly regarded resorts (page 313).

★ **Parque Nacional Conguillío:** Wander along black lava flows that join forests of ancient *araucaría* trees and feel as if you've stumbled back in time (page 315).

★ **Hot Springs:** Near **Pucón**, luxuriate in Chile's most lavish hot springs or opt for a more rustic experience with a nighttime dip beneath the stars (page 328).

★ **Parque Nacional Huerquehue:** Hike through a forest to a series of powerful waterfalls and gleaming mountaintop lakes in this picture-perfect national park (page 335).

★ **Trek to Volcán Villarrica:** Conquer the summit of the lofty volcano by hiking to its lava-filled crater and sliding back down the snowy slopes on a sled (page 337).

★ **Kunstmann Brewery Tour:** Savor the region's Germanic influence with a tour of Valdivia's best-known brewery (page 343).

★ **Frutillar:** Explore the German influence of this charming small town near Puerto Varas (page 360).

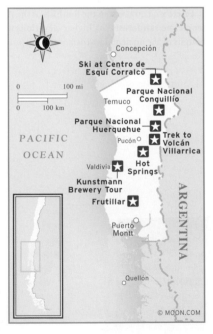

Cultural assets include chances to learn about the region's indigenous Mapuche people, who live in small subsistence communities and are renowned for their expert craftsmanship in silver jewelry, woolen textiles, and sculptures. Around Lago Llanquihue, traces of the German settlers who came here 150 years ago can be noted in the orderly feel and dramatic colonial mansions of their towns and the tradition of beer-making.

PLANNING YOUR TIME

Because this region covers **400km** from north to south, it's best to focus on only a few destinations, like those close to Pucón or Puerto Varas. Otherwise you'll need at least **five days** to spend time in the main highlights. Most of the towns and cities can be visited in one day, while the surrounding national parks and protected areas require more time. In most cases, excellent accommodations and dining options make it easy to spend a night in a remote town.

Pucón offers access to Volcán Villarrica and Parque Nacional Huerquehue. **Puerto Varas** is well-placed for visiting Parque Nacional Vicente Pérez Rosales and the slopes of Volcán Osorno. Both towns make a good base. Cities with less tourist infrastructure, such as Puerto Montt, Osorno, and Temuco, are better as brief lunch stops.

Frequent and affordable flights from Santiago to several regional airports are an easy way to cut down on travel time. Regular flights run to Puerto Montt in the far south. From here, it's easy to rent a car to explore the region, although a developed bus network connects all cities, towns, and many villages. Buses in rural areas can be infrequent and slow; hitchhiking is sometimes the only option for getting around without your own vehicle.

Infrastructure is generally well developed in the Lakes District, with the artery-like Ruta 5, the Pan-American Highway, running through the middle. Plenty of bus companies ply this route, offering regular cheap connections, with the exception of the region's national parks. Outside summer, when bus frequency drops, you'll need your own car. The farther you are from Ruta 5, the more dirt roads you'll encounter. Most are passable in any vehicle during the summer, but may require a 4WD or high-clearance vehicle during the rainy and snowy winter.

The region is a popular summer holiday destination for Chileans fleeing the capital. Expect high prices and increased congestion along roads, beaches, and hiking trails December-February. The weather outside January-February can be incessantly rainy, but the shoulder seasons (Sept.-Nov. and Mar.-May) guarantee a quieter experience, with lodging rates dropping considerably. Outside the peak summer months of January-February, it's easy to travel without making advance reservations.

HISTORY

The land that covers the modern-day Araucanía, Los Ríos, and Los Lagos regions has been inhabited since around 12,800 BC. One settlement may date to 16,500 BC, making it the oldest known archaeological site in the Americas. The inhabitants were hunter-gatherers who subsisted on both marine and land products.

Little is known about the later groups who inhabited the region. They formed small dispersed settlements from the Andes to the coast and comprised different cultural groups, including the Pichunche, Araucanos, Pehuenche, and Huilliche, all part of the Mapuche culture. Fearsome in war, they were successful in fending off the advance of the Inca, ending the latter's attempt at southern colonization in the 15th century AD.

Previous: Lago Llanquihue at sunset; *araucaría* trees; Mapuche statue.

Lakes District

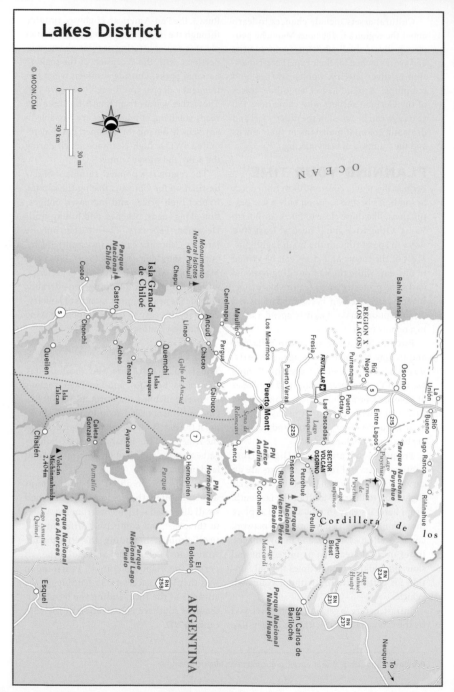

© MOON.COM

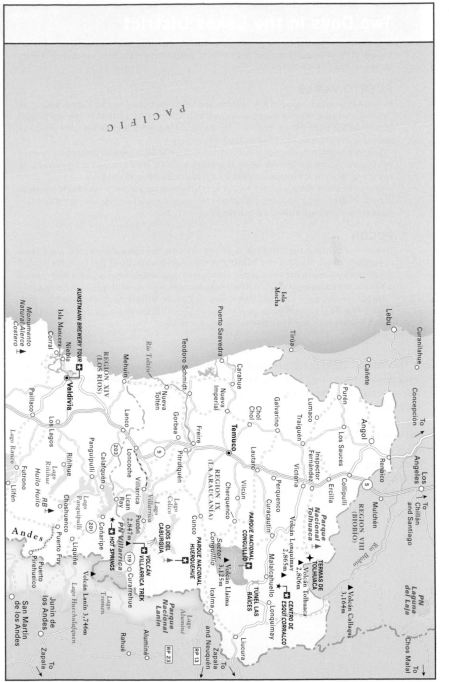

PACIFIC

Monumento
Natural Alerce
Costero

KUNSTMANN BREWERY TOUR

Isla Mancera
Corral
Niebla
Valdivia
Paillaco

REGIÓN XIV
(LOS RÍOS)

Mehuín
Río Toltén

Los Lagos

Lago Ranco

Lago
Riñihue
Riñihue

Futrono
Llifén

Andes

Huilo Huilo
RB

Choshuenco
Puerto Fuy
Pirehueico
Puerto
Pirehueico

San Martín
de los Andes

To
Zapala

Junín de
los Andes

Volcán Lanín 3,746m

Parque
Nacional
Lanín

Rahué

Aluminé

Lago
Tromen

Curarrehue

RP 23

RP 13

To
Zapala
and Neuquén

Liucura

Lago
Aluminé

Lago
Aluminé

Lago Huechulafquen

Lonquimay
Malalcahuello

TÚNEL LAS
RAÍCES

CENTRO DE
ESQUÍ CORRALCO

Icalma

Volcán Tolhuaca
2,806m

Volcán Lonquimay
2,865m

TERMAS DE
TOLHUACA

Parque
Nacional
Tolhuaca

Volcán Callaqui
3,164m

PN
Laguna
del Laja

REGIÓN VIII
(BIOBÍO)

Río Biobío

To Chos Malal

Mulchén

Renaico

To
Chillán
and Santiago

To
Los
Ángeles

To
Concepción

Angol

Los Sauces

Collipulli

Ercilla

Purén

Cañete

Lebu

Isla
Mocha

Tirúa

Carahue
Nueva
Imperial

Puerto Saavedra

Teodoro Schmidt

Nueva
Toltén

Gorbea

Lanco

Loncoche

Panguipulli

Calafquén

Coñaripe

Liquiñe

Lago
Panguipulli

Lago
Panguipulli

Choshuenco

Villarrica

Lican
Ray

PN Villarrica

Pucón

VOLCÁN
CABURGUA

OJOS DEL
CABURGUA

HOT SPRINGS

119

VILLARRICA TREK

VOLCÁN

Cunco

Cherquenco

Curacautín

Lago
Colico

Volcán Villarrica
2,847m

Volcán Llaima
3,125m

PARQUE NACIONAL
HUERQUEHUE

Sector
Conguillío

PARQUE NACIONAL
CONGUILLÍO

REGIÓN IX
(LA ARAUCANÍA)

Vilcún

Lautaro

Perquenco

Victoria

Inspector
Fernández

Traiguén

Galvarino

Lumaco

Chol
Chol

Temuco

Freire

Pitrufquén

Villarrica

203

201

5

5

Río Toltén

Two Days in the Lakes District

Because of the vast size of the region and the fact that activities are scattered widely, this itinerary focuses on Puerto Varas and Pucón.

PUERTO VARAS

Fly into Aeropuerto El Tepual in Puerto Montt and head directly for **Puerto Varas,** where you can walk along the edges of the aquamarine **Lago Todos Los Santos** in nearby **Parque Nacional Vicente Pérez Rosales.** Up the adrenaline with a **kayaking tour** down the raging Class III and IV rapids of **Río Petrohué.**

Sink your teeth into exceptional seafood dishes at **La Olla** or soak up sensational views of Volcán Osorno from the lakeside tables of trendy **La Mesa Tropera,** and sleep easily in the *palafito*-style cabins at tranquil **Gracias a La Vida** outside Puerto Varas.

On your second day, cycle or take the bus to **Frutillar** to catch a performance at the glorious lakeside **Teatro del Lago.** Enjoy afternoon tea or German kuchen overlooking the lavender fields at the charming **Lavanda Casa de Té.**

PUCÓN

Take an overnight bus from Santiago to arrive in **Pucón,** the Lakes District's self-proclaimed adventure capital. Spend a day **hiking** in the beautiful forests of **Parque Nacional Huerquehue,** which has views across dense green trees and shimmering lakes from various overlooks. Spend the night at **Chili Kiwi,** in a cozy tree house overlooking Lago Villarrica.

For your second day, it's an early start to summit **Volcán Villarrica,** but it's worth the challenging hike. By lunchtime, you'll be at the crater, peering down into the bubbling pit of lava, before heading back down toboggan-style on a plastic sled.

The conquistadores posed a far more serious threat, and the long-running Arauco War with the Mapuche started in the mid-1500s. During this time, the indigenous groups attempted to reclaim their ancestral land from Spain by attacking colonial cities such as Valdivia and Osorno. The Spanish responded by building extensive fortifications.

In the 1800s, with Chilean independence from Spain, the newly established Chilean government initiated the military campaign known as the Pacification of Araucanía, resulting in the deaths of around 100,000 Mapuche people. Hundreds of thousands of Mapuche were forced off their lands, which were gifted to European families that colonized the region. With the new settlers, many of whom were German, a wave of industry and development swept the region.

Temuco

The capital of the Araucanía region, Temuco is a quiet city with an unfinished quality, with a central jumble of ramshackle tin-roofed buildings. It lies at the heart of what was once Mapuche territory and is home to a large indigenous population.

Temuco is a comfortable, mellow, and friendly place to spend a day or two to break up a journey from Santiago. Two good museums include one of the country's best about the Mapuche people. At the energetic and convivial SERNATUR office, staff can help with planning your travel in the region. Many of Chile's best national reserves and parks are within striking distance; both Reserva Nacional Malalcahuello-Nalcas and Parque Nacional Conguillío are served by regular bus routes.

SIGHTS

At the center of Temuco's main square, **Plaza Aníbal Pinto,** also known as the **Plaza de Armas,** the **Monumento a la Araucanía** consists of five statues representing Temuco's population: a Machi (Mapuche shaman), a soldier, a European settler, the Spanish poet Alonso de Ercilla, and renowned Mapuche warrior and leader against the conquistadores, Caupolicán.

Museo Regional de la Araucanía

The **Museo Regional de la Araucanía** (Av. Alemania 84, tel. 45/2747-948 or tel. 45/2747-949, www.museoregionalaraucania. cl, 9:30am-5:30pm Tues.-Fri., 11am-5pm Sat., 11am-2pm Sun., free), nine blocks from the plaza, is the most comprehensive museum in the Araucanía region and provides a good introduction to the Mapuche culture. Permanent exhibitions in the imposing 1924 mansion cover the history of Araucanía's indigenous peoples, and temporary exhibitions disseminate cultural or historical themes such

as photography and Mapuche textiles, silverware, and crafts.

For fair-trade Mapuche crafts, **Rakizuam** (museum entrance hall, tel. 45/2592 676, tienda@cholchol.org, 9:30am-2pm and 3pm-5pm Tues.-Fri., 11am-2pm and 3pm-5pm Sat.) is a small shop selling everything from *fajas* (belts) and *mantas* (blankets) to delicate leatherwork.

Museo Nacional Ferroviario Pablo Neruda

Indoor-outdoor **Museo Nacional Ferroviario Pablo Neruda** (Barros Arana 565, tel. 45/2973 940 or tel. 45/2973 941, www. museoferroviariodetemuco.cl, 9am-6pm Mon.-Fri., 10am-6pm Sat.-Sun., free) details the region's railway history in an early 1900s railway complex. Restored buildings include the 1930s *casa de máquinas* (roundhouse) and a building with scale models detailing the history of Chile's rail system. Two exhibition spaces host changing Chilean art, sculpture, and photography installations.

The highlight is the 45-minute **guided tour** (depart every 45 min, CH$1,000 adults, CH$300 children) inside five restored train cars, including the Presidential Car, with bronze bed frames and leather upholstery, used by eight Chilean presidents.

Take *colectivo* (shared minivan) 2A, 7A, or 10A to be dropped within a couple blocks of the museum.

Feria Aníbal Pinto

Feria Aníbal Pinto (bounded by Miraflores, Av. Barros Arana, Lautaro, and Anibal Pinto, with additional stalls on Balmaceda, 8am-5pm daily), also known as the **Feria Libre,** is a disorderly metal-roofed open-air market of produce and handicrafts. Head to the central corridor, marked by murals, to find a dozen stalls selling empanadas, *churrascos* (meat sandwiches), and a tasty Mapuche

Temuco

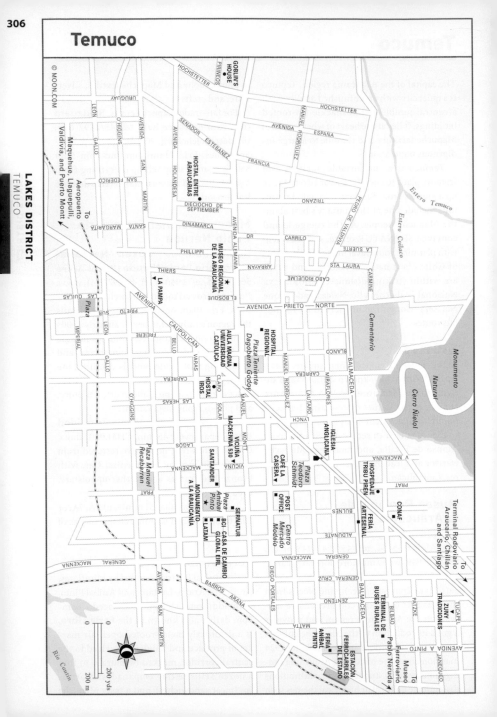

© MOON.COM

To Maquehue, Llaguepulli, Valdivia, and Puerto Montt

To Aeropuerto Araucario, Chillán and Santiago

To Terminal Rodoviario Araucario, Chillán and Santiago

GOBLIN'S HOUSE

HOSTAL ENTRE ARAUCARIAS

MUSEO REGIONAL DE LA ARAUCANIA

LA PAMPA

AULA MAGNA UNIVERSIDAD CATOLICA

Plaza Teniente Dagoberto Godoy

HOSPITAL REGIONAL

HOSTAL IROS

Plaza Manuel Recabarren

VICUÑA MACKENNA 530

SANTANDER

MONUMENTO A LA ARAUCANIA

Plaza Anibal Pinto

SERNATUR

BCI CASA DE CAMBIO GLOBAL EIRL

LATAM

CAFE LA CASERA

POST OFFICE

Centro Mercado Modelo

IGLESIA ANGLICANA

Plaza Teodoro Schmidt

HOSPEDAJE TRIBU PIREN

FERIA ARTESENAL

CONAF

TERMINAL DE BUSES RURALES

ZUNY TRADICIONES

FERIA ANIBAL PINTO

ESTACION FERROCARRILES DEL ESTADO

Museo Ferroviario Pablo Neruda

Estero Temuco

Estero Coilaco

Cementerio

Monumento Natural

Cerro Ñielol

Rio Cautín

0   200 yds

0   200 m

Mapuche Handicrafts

The Mapuche people, who live in small communities across the Araucanía and Los Ríos regions, are known for their beautiful craftsmanship. Most striking is their silverwork, with intricately detailed *trapelachuca* (decorative breast pieces), *quipus* (pins with large trapezoid hanging pendants), and *tarilonco* headpieces, all of which are highly valued and worn at ceremonial events. The most impressive pieces are in museums, but it's possible to purchase Mapuche-made *chawi* (earrings) in small artisanal fairs such as those in Villarrica.

The artisans' stalls of Villarrica are a good place to find **Mapuche wood carvings,** which include kitchen utensils, polished bowls, and decorative wall hangings depicting Mapuche daily life. Small *chemamüll* ("wooden person") are miniature versions of the two-meter-high wooden funerary totems used by the Mapuche to mark their graves. The most striking *chemamüll* stand in the Plaza de Armas in Pucón and downstairs in the **Museo Chileno de Arte Precolombino** in Santiago.

Mapuche artisans hand-weave sheep's wool **ponchos** and other clothing, *mantas* (blankets), rugs, and *fajas* (belts or sashes) on upright looms. The best are for sale in markets in Villarrica and Temuco, where you can also buy **Mapuche baskets,** originally used for fishing and agriculture. These are woven using *chupón*, a highly elastic fiber native to Chile.

Mapuche handmade crafts are sold at **Rakizuam** (entrance hall of the Museo Regional de la Araucanía, Temuco, tel. 45/2592 676, tienda@cholchol.org, 9:30am-2pm and 3pm-5pm Tues.-Fri., 11am-2pm and 3pm-5pm Sat.).

LAKES DISTRICT
TEMUCO

snack: boiled *piñones* (*araucaría* nuts). South of the food stands, the rest of the market is less bustling. You'll see cuts of beef hanging from hooks and piles of mussels next to whole *merluza* (hake) and *sierra* (barracuda).

SHOPPING
Mapuche Crafts
The **Centro Mercado Modelo** (Gral. Adunate 341, 9am-6:30pm daily) has the best range of Mapuche crafts in the city, with delicately shaped wooden and clay bowls, woolen wall murals, and local *loganizas* (sausages) and cheeses. Three blocks north along Balmaceda is the **Feria Artesenal** (between Manuel Bulnes and Gral. Adunate, 9am-6:30pm daily), with a smaller collection of crafts, including woven baskets and textiles.

FOOD
Temuco is a cheaper place to get a meal than most cities in the region. No-frills fast-food restaurants and cheap bars line Avenida Alemania, home to the Universidad de Católica and Universidad Mayor, catering to the city's students and getting rowdy on weekend nights. For more refined—and more expensive—cuisine, head to the blocks around the main square or San Martín, which runs parallel to Avenida Alemania.

Chilean
Down a side street a dozen blocks northeast of the plaza, ★ **Zuny Tradiciones** (Tucapel 1374, tel. 9/7922 295, zunytradiciones@gmail.com, noon-4pm Mon.-Sat., CH$5,000) is a wonderland of traditional Mapuche woven baskets and woolen tapestries serving traditional Mapuche cuisine. The server will inform you of the options for the day, which include healthy dishes of slow-cooked meat with a range of salad and grains (there's no fried food here). Make sure you leave room for dessert—they always have two delicious options, such as quinoa with raspberries. To find Zuny, look for the colorful bird mural on its exterior.

Considered Temuco's best restaurant, ★ **La Pampa** (San Martín 137, tel. 45/2329 999, www.lapampa.cl, noon-4pm and 7pm-midnight Mon.-Sat., noon-4pm Sun., CH$10,000-16,000) proves that it's not just the

Argentineans who know a thing or two about barbecuing beef. Stylish wood and leather decor is complemented by attentive waiters. Try the juiciest cut, *bife chorizo* (sirloin), or the range of pan-fried fish dishes, and wash it down with a glass of Chilean carménère.

International

With exposed brick, a rusted exterior, and a shabby-chic interior, **Vicuña Mackenna 530** (Vicuña Mackenna 530, tel. 45/2620 512, 8:45am-11pm Mon.-Fri., 10:30am-11pm Sat., CH$6,000-10,000) feels like a cross between a European dive bar and an upmarket restaurant. The food is a range of pizzas and pastas, quinoa risottos, and burgers. It's particularly popular for a work lunch, so you'll need a reservation noon-3pm.

Cafés and Light Bites

Although it looks more charming from the outside, **Café La Casera** (Diego Portales 785, tel. 45/2740 150, www.lacasera.cl, Mon.-Fri. 9am-11pm, Sat. 10am-7pm, CH$4,500-7,000, *menú del día* CH$7,800) has a warm atmosphere and is all about coffee and cake any time of day. Breakfasts are wholesome and reasonably priced, cake portions are enormous (try the *quatro leches*), and it's a top local choice for *once* (afternoon tea). The three-course lunch menu is also good value. On Thursday, some of the tables get whipped away for tango classes (9pm-11pm).

ACCOMMODATIONS

The handful of decent lodging options in Temuco are mostly around Avenida Alemania or a few blocks north of the plaza. Temuco is generally safe, but avoid staying in the rundown northeast, toward the Terminal de Buses Rurales and the Museo Nacional Ferroviario Pablo Neruda. All lodgings include breakfast, Wi-Fi, and IVA in the rates unless otherwise stated.

The best budget choice is cozy family-run **Hospedaje Tribu Piren** (Arturo Prat 69, reservas@tribupiren.com, tel. 45/2985 711, CH$30,000 d shared bath, CH$35,000 d private bath), which lacks a bit of attention but offers a warm welcome in an excellent city-center location. Eight upstairs rooms are large, and the double and twin rooms at the front include small balconies overlooking the street. Downstairs is a small communal area with a dining table and a sofa. Call ahead to reserve gated parking.

Set within a residential home a block from the bars and restaurants of Avenida

Zuny Tradiciones

Chile's Mapuche People

The Mapuche people are the largest indigenous group in Chile, accounting for 4 percent of the population. In 1991, the Indigenous Law was passed to protect Chile's indigenous groups. Today, around 70 percent of Mapuche live in urban areas such as Santiago, many in extreme poverty. Long-running disputes over former Mapuche land have turned increasingly violent, particularly toward the timber companies that now have a monopoly on land ownership in the region.

To learn more about Mapuche life, visit the welcoming community of **Llaguepulli** (Km 13 Ruta Puerto Domínguez a Hualpin, tel. 9/9808 1559, www.lagobudi.cl), on the shores of Lago Budi, one of around 120 Mapuche communities in the Araucanía region. Visitors can spend the night in a traditional *ruka* (CH$60,000), a wooden dwelling built with *coigüe* trunks and Peruvian feathergrass, or a comfortable cabin (CH$57,000). Homestay rates include breakfast and dinner. Workshops and tours let you sample and cook Mapuche cuisine, learn how to play *palín* (a Mapuche sport), or discover the medicinal properties of the plants that they grow. Don't miss the talk on Mapuche worldviews and spirituality, held around a fire in one of the *rukas*. Tours and workshops start at CH$5,000. Advance booking is required and can be organized through the website.

a *ruka*, a traditional Mapuche dwelling

Alemania, **Hostal Entre Araucarias** (18 de Septiembre 690, tel. 45/2607 009 or 9/7238 0876, CH$48,000 d) has six small rooms, each with wide windows for plenty of light. The best features are the ample communal living and kitchen areas and vast back garden, which compensate for the modest bedrooms. There's a large driveway with parking.

The pub sign in the front garden and the narrow corridors give a sense of the former identity of Irish-inspired **Goblin's House** (Pirineos 841, tel. 45/2320 044 or 9/7388 6624, CH$55,000 d), a modern boutique hotel with 14 bedrooms, each with central heating, fans, and huge, clean baths. If you want outdoor space, opt for one of the smaller rooms at the back with its own balcony. The breakfast room on the top floor has a spacious communal terrace. Parking is secure, and Goblin's is often full, so book well in advance.

Blink and you'll miss the narrow **Hostal Iros** (Claro Solar 310, tel. 9/5338 5417, www.hostaliros.cl, CH$40,000 d), which packs in seven bedrooms back from the road and accessed by a staircase. The double at the front of the house is the roomiest, but all are ample and freshly painted in neutral shades. There's a small seating area on the upper floor and portable electric heaters available if you need one.

INFORMATION AND SERVICES

The wonderfully helpful **SERNATUR office** (Manuel Bulnes 586, tel. 45/2406 215, 9am-8pm daily Jan.-Feb., 9am-6pm Mon.-Thurs. and 9am-7pm Fri. Mar.-Dec.) is on the northeastern corner of Plaza Aníbal Pinto and can provide maps of the city and hiking maps for the nearby national parks. The English-speaking employees can contact the rangers in the parks to get up-to-date road conditions, as many are closed due to snow outside summer. **CONAF** (Bilbao 931, tel. 45/2981 000, www.conaf.cl) has an office seven blocks north that can also supply you with maps.

For medical attention, head to the **Hospital Regional** (Manuel Montt 115, at Blanco, tel. 45/2559 000, www.hhha.cl). A clutch of **24-hour ATMs** are on Plaza Anibal Pinto, including **BCI** (northeast corner), **Santander** (northwest corner), **Scotiabank** (southeast corner), and **Banco de Chile** (southwest corner). **Casa de Cambio Global Eirl** (Manuel Bulnes 655, 9:30am-7pm Mon.-Fri., 10am-1pm Sat.) exchanges money. For mail services, **Correos** (9am-7pm Mon.-Fri., 10am-1pm Sat.) is at the corner of Portales and Prat.

GETTING THERE

Air

About 20km south of Temuco along Ruta 5, **Aeropuerto Araucanía** (ZCO, tel. 45/2201 901, www.aeropuertoaraucania.cl) has seven flights per day with **LATAM** (www.latam.com), **Sky Airline** (www.skyairline.com), and **JetSmart** (www.jetsmart.com) from Santiago, with a flight time of 1.5 hours. LATAM (Manuel Bulnes 687, tel. 600/5262 000, 9am-1:30pm and 3pm-6:30pm Mon.-Fri., 10am-1pm Sat.) is the only airline with an office in Temuco.

Beyond the arrivals area, look for the desk of **Transfer Temuco** (tel. 45/2334 033, 45/2722 970, or 9/9324 9597, www.transfertemuco.cl). They offer a shared minivan service that can drop you off at your hotel or at the Terminal Rodoviario (Temuco's long-distance bus terminal) for CH$5,000-6,000. An **official taxi** at the taxi stand outside costs CH$12,000-15,000. Both options take around 30 minutes.

Bus

Long-distance buses arrive and leave from Temuco's **Terminal Rodoviario** (Reyes Católicos 1420, tel. 45/2225 005), 3km northeast of Plaza Aníbal Pinto. **Pullman Bus** (tel. 45/2322 1301, www.pullmanbus.cl) and **Tur Bus** (tel. 45/201 1521, www.turbus.cl) offer the lion's share of connections with **Santiago** (every 40 min-1 hr daily, 8hr, CH$10,000/CH$18,000) and within Los Lagos. **Buses Jac** (tel. 64/2553 300, www.jac.cl) has service

every half hour to and from **Pucón** (1.75hr, CH$2,800).

Alongside **Condor Bus** (tel. 45/2201 526, www.condorbus.cl), these companies offer buses to and from **Valdivia** (10 daily, 2hr, CH$4,000/CH$7,000), **Villarrica** (10 daily, 1.5hr, CH$4,000/CH$7,000), and **Puerto Varas** (6 daily, all after 5pm, 4hr, CH$6,000). **Cruz del Sur** (tel. 45/2730 310, www.buscruzdelsur.cl) runs buses from **Puerto Montt** (5.5hr, CH$7,000) and **Concepción** (5 daily, 4hr, CH$7,000).

Most local buses leave from the **Terminal de Buses Rurales** (Aníbal Pinto 32, tel. 45/2210 494). Local service to and from **Curacuatín** (8 daily, 2hr, CH$3,700) and **Lonquimay** (up to 10 daily, 2.5hr, CH$3,100-4,700) is offered by **Buses Bio Bio** (tel. 45/2464 425, www.busesbiobio.cl) and **Erbuc** (tel. 45/2210 960). Buses also connect every half hour to **Curacautín** (CH$1,400) with **Buses Curacautín Express** (tel. 56/2993 525), while **Nar Bus** (tel. 45/2407 740) has hourly connections to **Melipeuco** (2hr, CH$1,900).

International connections with **Bariloche, Argentina** (5:30am daily to Bariloche, 2pm daily to Temuco, 10.5hr, CH$27,000/CH$35,000), are offered by **Andesmar** (tel. 45/2258 626, www.andesmarchile.cl).

Car

From **Concepción,** it's a 293-km, 3.25-hour drive south via Ruta 146 and Ruta 5 to reach Temuco. To get here from **Puerto Montt,** it's a 353-km, 4-hour drive north up the Pan-American Highway.

GETTING AROUND

Most sights in Temuco are within walking distance of one another. For the farther-afield Museo Nacional Ferroviario Pablo Neruda and Terminal Rodoviario, all the *micros* (minibuses, CH$250) pass along Rodríguez, between General Aldunate and Manuel Bulnes, while all *colectivos* (shared taxis, CH$350) travel along Manuel Montt (between Gral. Aldunate and Manuel Bulnes).

The excellent website **Que Micro Me Sirve** (www.quemicromesirve.cl) indicates the path of each of the city's *micros* and *colectivos* if you enter your starting point. *Colectivos* 2A, 7A, and 10A leave from the center of town to the Museo Nacional Ferroviario Pablo Neruda; 7A and 10A continue to the Terminal Rodoviario.

Temuco is easy to drive in, and having a car provides more freedom and quicker travel time to the national parks around Curacautín and Melipeuco in the Bío Bío region.

Just outside arrivals in the airport terminal are **Alamo** (tel. 45/2422 700, www.alamochile.com, 8:30am-9pm Mon.-Fri., 9am-8:30pm Sat.-Sun.), **Avis/Budget** (tel. 2/2795 3978, www.avis.cl, 9am-9pm Mon.-Fri., 9:30am-8:30pm Sat.-Sun.), **Econorent** (tel. 45/2918 927, www.econorent.cl, 9am-9pm Mon.-Fri., 9am-2pm and 4pm-9pm Sat.-Sun.), **Ecarent** (tel. 9/7139 8960, www.ecarent.cl, 9am-8pm daily), **Europcar** (tel. 45/2918 940 or 45/2918 941, www.europcar.com, 9am-9pm Mon.-Fri., 9am-8pm Sat.-Sun.), and **First Rent a Car** (tel. 9/8819 3028, www.firstrentacar.cl, 9am-7pm daily).

Taxis can be flagged down in the street, but a safer option is the taxi stand a few meters from the SERNATUR office (Claro Solar and Manuel Bulnes). Taxis to Avenida Alemania should cost no more than CH$2,000; to the Terminal Rodoviario, CH$3,000.

Bío Bío

A glimpse of two snow-topped volcanoes on the horizon is your introduction to the magnificent landscapes of the Bío Bío: Volcán Lonquimay and Volcán Llaima are in Reserva Nacional Malalacahuello-Nalcas and Parque Nacional Conguillío, respectively, the two main draws of the region.

From Ruta 5 just north of Temuco, the S-11 from Lautaro veers east, flanked on each side by meadows of wildflowers, interspersed with groves of eucalyptus and small farms. In winter, skiers and snowboarders come in droves; in summer it's hikers and campers.

CURACAUTÍN

On the way to the nearby national parks, the drab and empty streets of Curacautín offer little more than a good hostel and a tour agency that can help with onward travel and tours in Parque Nacional Conguillío.

A favorite among backpackers, the friendly, family-run hostel **Epu Pewen** (Manuel Rodríguez 705, tel. 45/2881 793 or 9/9401 8502, www.epupewen.cl, CH$8,000 dorm, CH$20,000 d shared bath, CH$33,000 d private bath, including IVA) has six bright and airy bedrooms, most with private baths and all with central heating, plus a huge fully equipped kitchen. There's a barbecue area outside and a lovely sheltered seating area for relaxing.

The hostel is affiliated with the **Epu Pewen tourist agency** (Miguel Rodríguez 705 B, tel. 45/2881 793 or 9/7877 3952, www.agenciaepupewen.cl, 10am-1pm and 3pm-6pm daily Mar.-Dec., until 9pm Jan.-Feb.) next door, which offers full-day trekking excursions into Parque Nacional Conguillío (CH$55,000 pp), including transport to and from the park, as well as full-day trekking excursions in Reserve Nacional Malalcahuello-Nalcas (CH$40,000 pp, including transport). They also run full-day ascents of Volcán Sierra Nevada, Volcán Lonquimay, and Volcán Llaima (from CH$70,000, including transportation and food), plus half-day rafting trips along the Río Cautín (from CH$25,000, including all equipment), with Class II to Class IV waters. All excursions require a minimum of two people.

Information and Services

The English-speaking **Oficina de Turismo** (Manuel Rodríguez, opposite Plaza de Armas, tel. 45/2374 519, 8:30am-6pm daily Jan.-Mar., 8:30am-6pm Mon.-Sat. Apr.-Dec.) can help with maps and information about activities in the region, as well as bus timetables for reaching Malalcahuello and Parque Nacional Conguillío.

The **CONAF office** (Junay 240, tel. 45/2881 184, jaime.videla@conaf.cl, 9am-2pm Mon.-Fri.) provides up-to-date information about the conditions in the national parks plus maps. For money, there is a 24-hour ATM at **Banco Estado** (O'Higgins and Calama). Basic emergency medical services are provided by **Hospital Curacautín** (Serrano s/n, between Prat and Chorrillos, tel. 45/2551 802).

Getting There

From Temuco to Curacautín is an 85-km drive north on Ruta 5 and east on the S-11, which takes just over an hour. **Buses Bio Bio** (tel. 45/2464 425, www.busesbiobio.cl) offers connections with **Temuco** (8 daily, 2hr, CH$3,700), departing from the **Terminal Rodoviario** (Reyes Católicos 1420, Temuco, tel. 45/2225 005). These buses stop four blocks northwest of Curacautín's Plaza de Armas on Ruta 181. Also from Temuco, **minibuses** (CH$1,400) run by **Buses Curacautín Express** (tel. 56/2993 525) depart every half hour from the **Terminal de Buses Rurales** (Aníbal Pinto 32, Temuco, tel. 45/2210 494). From the same terminal, **Erbuc** (tel. 45/2210 960, www.erbuc.cl) runs minibuses to Curacautín five times a day.

Tur Bus (tel. 2/822 7500, www.turbus.cl) runs direct overnight buses from **Santiago** (9:55pm and 10:10pm daily, 8hr, CH$21,000/CH$35,000) that depart from the Terminal Alameda. They have an office in Curacautín (Serrano 101, tel. 45/2686 629).

Onward to Parque Nacional Conguillío

The drive to La Administración ranger station along Ruta 925, via the park entrance and ranger station at Laguna Captrén, is 40km and takes about an hour. **Buses Curacautín**

Express (tel. 45/2258 125) runs a **summer-only service** (30min, CH$1,000). Buses leave several times a day Monday-Friday from the main road in Curacautín, dropping passengers off 5km before the Laguna Captrén CONAF ranger station; walk or hitchhike from here.

Taxi Letrero Blanco (tel. 45/2881 880) and **Taxi Letrero Amarillo** (tel. 45/2881 920) can drop you off at La Administración for around CH$25,000, a journey of just over an hour. Find one at the taxi stand on the north side of the Plaza de Armas.

MALALCAHUELLO

Malalcahuello, 31km east of Curacautín along Ruta 181, feels more isolated than most towns in the Araucanía Region. This side of the mountains is quieter and less touristed than neighboring Parque Nacional Conguillío—a big part of its appeal. But this small town, surrounded by dense forests of distinctive *araucaría,* has seen a quiet explosion in tourism over the past decade, as it's a perfect base for a day or two of hiking in the Reserva Nacional Malalcahuello-Nalcas or skiing on Volcán Lonquimay.

The two **high seasons** are January-February and June-August, when lodging rates rise significantly. January-February are busiest, when Chileans descend for the holidays. Outside these peak seasons, it's a silent paradise, but some services are closed, so always call ahead to check.

Reserva Nacional Malalcahuello-Nalcas

With trails through dense oak and beech forests and towering 30-meter *araucaría* as you reach higher altitudes, **Reserva Nacional Malalcahuello-Nalcas** (CH$2,000 adults, CH$1,500 children) is a stunning slice of native forest and sooty trails of hardened lava. The reserve is open year-round, but most of the trails are closed from July to mid-November due to snow and rainfall. All are accessible January-March, depending on weather conditions.

Most visitors enter via the more accessible **Reserva Nacional Malalcahuello,** 500 meters past the turnoff into the village of Malalcahuello, where a **CONAF ranger station** (tel. 9/9656 4455, 8:30am-1pm and 2pm-6pm daily) acts as the park's **headquarters** and where visitors must register before entering this section of the park. Most trails start from this entrance and are marked on the reserve's official map; rangers can give you a copy and advise on which are open. A second entrance, also marked by a **CONAF ranger station** (no phone, 8:30am-6pm daily), is in the eastern part of the reserve, a 20-minute drive from Malalcahuello. You likely won't be charged an admission fee at this entrance.

Leaving from the reserve headquarters, one of the most popular trails is **Sendero Piedra Santa** (7.5km one-way, 5hr). It climbs 700 meters through towering *araucaría, lenga,* and *coigüe* to reach a series of overlooks with views of the snow-cloaked peaks of Volcán Lonquimay and Volcán Llaima. Return the way you came.

Reserva Nacional Nalcas is on the northern limit of Reserva Nacional Malalcahuello. Its main access is via the **Sendero Laguna Blanca** (trailhead at end of Sendero Piedra Santa), a challenging multiday trek that follows the edges of Volcán Lonquimay, offering views of the lava fields that have formed over the centuries. It's a total distance of 80km and 3-4 days of hiking, for which a guide is strongly recommended. There are no official campgrounds; pitch your tent in places that have previously been used to avoid further damage to the vegetation.

GETTING THERE

There are no taxi or local bus services from Malalcahuello to the reserve, but the ranger station closest to Malalcahuello is within walking distance from the town. To get to the second entrance from the village of Malalcahuello, drive east along Ruta 181. After 3km, take the left fork north into a valley that skirts the edges of the reserve. Veer left again

after 4km to reach the entrance, just before the Centro de Esquí Corralco ski resort.

★ Centro de Esquí Corralco

With 1,800 acres of skiable terrain, 29 runs to suit all levels, and six lifts, the **Centro de Esquí Corralco** (Reserva Nacional Malalcahuello, tel. 2/2206 0741, www.corralco.com, full-day CH$37,000 adults, CH$28,000 children) is a ski resort along the southeastern slopes of Volcán Lonquimay. It is considered one of the best places to ski in the country, and its striking volcanic surroundings and curiously shaped *araucaría* trees add to its charm. If you visit outside the school holidays in July, you'll be practically the only person on the slopes.

This is one of the best places in the world for *randonée* (where you hike up and then ski back down the mountain, using specially designed skis) and splitboard (a snowboarding-skiing hybrid). There's a school at the ski resort (all classes are conducted in Spanish). You can rent gear from the resort, but prices are half as much at the rental shops on the road to the resort.

The attached **Hotel Corralco** (CH$108,000 d) comprises 54 smart rooms. Rates include use of the spa facilities, outdoor pools, and guided outdoor excursions. They can also arrange a direct transfer from Temuco (CH$80,000 pp, min. 2 people).

There are no taxi or local bus services connecting Malalcahuello with the ski center, so the only way to get here is with your own vehicle. The entrance is just a few minutes' drive beyond the second entrance to the Reserva Nacional Malalcahuello, reached by taking Ruta 181 east from Malalcahuello and the left fork after 3km. After 4km, take the left fork again to climb 5km into the foothills of the volcano, with the reserve entrance marked by a ranger station, and the resort entrance shortly after.

Food

As a burgeoning tourism destination, Malalcahuello has a wealth of good accommodations mostly along Ruta 181, the main highway between Curacautín and Malalcahuello. A small collection of others is on Ruta 89, the road toward the Centro de Esquí Corralco, while the ski resort also has a cafeteria and restaurant.

From slow-cooked beef sandwiches to locally made sausages, the **Sandwichería Fuente Araucania** (Km 0.2 R-89 Camino a Corralco, tel. 9/9313 7499, 11am-9pm Tues.-Sat., 11am-7:30pm Sun, CH$3,000-7,800) is a popular stop for a quick meal, with some picnic seating outside on a small wooden terrace.

Specializing in fish dishes, **MYA** (Rinconada 550A, tel. 9/8358 6322 or tel. 9/7488 0047, restaurantmyamalacahuello@gmail.com, 1pm-11pm daily winter and summer, 1pm-9pm daily other months, CH$6,000-9,000, *menú del día* CH$12,000) is a cozy restaurant with unexpectedly good food and is one of the few in town open year-round. Their salmon or tuna ceviche comes in huge portions, along with kuchen and other cakes.

Accommodations

Unless otherwise stated, rooms include breakfast, Wi-Fi, and IVA.

UNDER CH$25,000

Kingo Camping (Km 91.5 Ruta 181, tel. 9/8383 2625, year-round, CH$5,000 camping, CH$15,000 pp) has a small grassy area for tents, with access to hot showers and baths. The owner's house has a handful of very basic rooms, but they're small and dingy and not good value compared with other nearby options. Breakfast is not included.

CH$25,000-40,000

An economical choice in Malalcahuello, **Hostal Ruta 181** (Km 88.9 Ruta 181, tel. 9/5003 3923 or 45/2917 502, www.hostalruta181.com, CH$15,000 dorm, CH$45,000 d private bath) has smallish rooms, but the staff are skiers and can help with information and finding a guide. There's

a large bar and common room with local beer on tap and a shared kitchen, making this the most popular local backpacking hostel.

CH$40,000-60,000

In a beautiful wooden cabin surrounded by eucalyptus and pines, charming guesthouse **Estación Benedicto** (Km 69 Ruta 181, tel. 9/7422 2792, www.estacionbenedicto.cl, CH$47,000-56,000 d private bath, CH$75,000 cabin, CH$95,000 dome) has two elegant rooms with wooden furnishings and Mapuche weavings, a five-person dome a few meters from the river, and a four-person cabin; both the dome and cabin have kitchens. Wood-burners and electric heaters keep everything toasty during the winter, when there's two hot tubs to use. The downstairs café (noon-8pm daily, sometimes closed Mon., CH$4,000-5,000) has sandwiches and salads, as well as hot chocolate and delectable pisco sours.

Comfortable Swiss-owned 40-bedroom **Suizandina Lodge** (Km 83 Ruta 181, tel. 45/21973 725 or tel. 9/9884 9541, www.suizandina.com, CH$26,000 dorm, CH$50,000 d private bath, camping CH$8,000, not including IVA) is a huge wooden lodge and six-spot campground. Rooms are simpler than other options in this price range, but the owners' extensive knowledge of skiing and horseback riding (tours CH$19,000 per hour) make it a good choice. They also have a small restaurant (1:30pm-4:30pm daily, CH$4,000-9,000), open to non-guests, with Swiss favorites such as *rosti* and cheese fondue.

CH$60,000-80,000

With only three rooms, charming ★ **Casa Verde Hostal Ecológico** (Km 1.5 Camino a Corralco, tel. 9/9526 2609 or 9/5662 3101, www.casaverdemalalcahuello.cl, CH$65,000 d, not including IVA) has wonderful touches such as a rustic living room and kitchen with exposed brickwork. Guests can request a homemade dinner using local ingredients, eaten around a large dining table with the owners and other guests. The rooms are tastefully decorated, and the place feels far from civilization.

OVER CH$80,000

In a wooded area with a restaurant on-site, **Vortice** (Km 69.5 Ruta 181, tel. 9/9549 4858 or 45/2897 594, www.vorticechile.com, CH$80,000 d, including breakfast and lunch) is an extensive adventure resort with hiking, zip lines, climbing, rappelling, and a swimming pool on-site. They can organize excursions into Parque Nacional Conguillío. The best lodging is in five domes on platforms in the treetops with views across the river and of the stars. Each has a kitchen and a bath downstairs in a separate small cabin; unfortunately, they get very hot in summer.

Information and Services

In a squat building on the right just after the main turn to enter the village, the **Oficina de Turismo** (tel. 9/7608 3176, 9am-6pm Wed.-Fri., 9am-1pm Sat.) has information about accommodations and restaurants in Malalcahuello, as well as about reaching the various local hot springs.

There's no ATM or gas station in Malalcahuello. While many hotels and restaurants accept credit cards, make sure you withdraw cash and fuel up in Curacautín. The **Posta de Salud Rural** (tel. 600/360 7777, 8:30am-1pm and 1:45pm-5:30pm daily) handles basic medical emergencies.

SKI HIRE AND EXCURSIONS

IsoTerma Cero (R-89 and R-181, tel. 9/5832 9882, 9am-9pm daily winter, 10am-8pm summer) rents ski jackets and bibs, skis and poles, snowboards, *randonées,* splitboards, and crampons and ice axes for volcano ascents, with prices for full ski gear starting at CH$12,000 per day, significantly cheaper than at the resort. They also run full-day ascents of Volcán Lonquimay (CH$85,000, min. 2 people), with ice axes, helmets, and crampons

included. There's a small market with basic food items here.

Getting There and Around

The easiest way to visit this region is with a rental car, as there are no taxi or local bus services connecting Malalcahuello with the ski center or the national park. From **Temuco,** it's a two-hour, 110-km drive via Ruta 5, S-11, and Ruta 181 to Malalcahuello.

Buses Bio Bio (tel. 45/2464 425, www. busesbiobio.cl) and **Erbuc** (tel. 45/2210 960) have service to Malalcahuello from Temuco's **Terminal Rodoviario** (Reyes Católicos 1420, tel. 45/2225 005; up to 10 daily, 2.5hr, CH$3,100-4,700). From **Santiago** (10:10pm daily, 10hr, CH$14,000/CH$28,000), **Tur Bus** (Terminal Alameda Tur Bus, tel. 2/2822 7500) has daily buses to Lonquimay that stop in Malalcahuello.

If you're staying in accommodations farther along Ruta 785, the road to the ski center, you'll need to arrange transfers when you book. It's possible to hitchhike in the peak seasons, when there is plenty of traffic along Ruta 181.

★ PARQUE NACIONAL CONGUILLÍO

In the stunningly beautiful **Parque Nacional Conguillío** (tel. 2/2840 6818, parque. conguillio@conaf.cl, 8:30am-6:15pm daily, CH$6,000 adults, CH$3,000 children), ancient forests of *araucaría* and *coigüe* contrast with the dusty jet-black lava flows from the 40 smoldering craters of Volcán Llaima, the park's centerpiece. There are also shimmering midnight-blue lakes in the folds of the mountains. This a popular destination for hikers and draws busloads of tourists.

Tourism to the park is increasing, which means more crowds on its dirt roads and hiking trails. An average of 35,000 people visit in January-February each year. To avoid the crowds, visit in November-December, when the weather is warming up, or in April to see the autumn yellows and golds.

The park is generally open from southern Melipeuco north to La Administración year-round. Snowfall between La Administración and the ranger station at Laguna Captrén, a bit north, sometimes prevents access from Curacautín, the northernmost entrance. During summer, the roads are passable in a standard vehicle. Much of the section between Laguna Arco Iris and Laguna Captrén is dirt track and must be taken slowly and carefully by low-clearance vehicles. In winter, it's not possible to enter without a 4WD vehicle.

Trails are mostly marked. While ranger stations carry trail maps, they often run out. For those considering serious hiking in the park, it's worth getting a copy of the topographical **AndesProfundo Conguillío Map** (www.andesprofundo.com), sold in shops in the Araucanía region and in Santiago.

Although most of the park's trails have access to fresh-running glacier water, it's essential to bring sufficient provisions.

Orientation

The town of Curacautín is north of the park, and the town of Melipeuco is south. Unpaved Ruta 925 connects the two towns directly through the park. Outside January-February, snowfall sometimes closes the Curacautín entrance.

Sector Volcán Llaima, surrounding the eponymous volcano, is the most widely visited. Enter in the south via **Truful-Truful CONAF ranger station** (12km north of Melipeuco along R-925, no phone, 8:30am-6:15pm daily) or in the north at **Laguna Captrén CONAF ranger station** (34km south of Curacautín along R-925, no phone, 8:30am-6:15pm daily). At both stations you're required to sign in and pay the entrance fee. From the Truful-Truful entrance it's 17km north along the park's only road, or 12km from the Laguna Captrén entrance, to reach a signed turnoff for **La Administración ranger station** (500 m from the main road,

tel. 2/2840 6818, parque.conguillio@conaf. cl, 8:30am-6:15pm daily), on the southwestern shore of Laguna Conguillío in the heart of the park. It has the best-informed rangers plus picnic areas, restrooms, and access to the black sands of Playa Curacautín.

Sector Los Paraguas is on the western slopes of Volcán Llaima and attracts skiers to its two resorts. The paved road from Temuco to Cherquenco, 19km east of Sector Los Paraguas, is the main route. A **CONAF ranger station** just before the road forks to access the two ski centers is open year-round.

Sector Volcán Llaima

Perfectly conical in shape, the double-cratered **Volcán Llaima** is flanked by ashy lava flows. One of Chile's most active volcanoes, with over 37 eruptions recorded since 1852, Llaima forced dozens of local people and tourists to be evacuated from the region in 2008 when an eruption saw huge columns of smoke and lava spewing down its eastern slope.

Just beyond the ranger station at Truful-Truful, the **Sendero Truful-Truful** (1.2km one-way, 30min) runs along lava flows to reach a gushing waterfall and river. From the Truful-Truful ranger station, 12km along a gravel road brings you to the picturesque **Laguna Arcoiris**, whose rainbow-colored waters can be appreciated from the short **Sendero Colonia** (1.2km one-way, 1hr) or the viewing platform next to the road.

For some of the best views in the park, take the **Sendero Sierra Nevada** (10km one-way, 3hr) from Playa Linda on the eastern edge of Lago Conguillío. This trail scales the initial flanks of Volcán Sierra Nevada to reach a ridge with astounding vistas across the lake. It's not uncommon to see condors in the sky. From here, only experienced trekkers can continue along the **Traversía Río Blanco** (5km one-way, 5hr), a highly challenging trek that passes along the Sierra Nevada Ridge, crossing a glacier before ascending to the peak of the volcano.

1: Centro de Esquí Corralco **2:** Parque Nacional Conguillío

Sector Los Paraguas

On the western slopes of Volcán Llaima, Sector Los Paraguas has very little for hikers, except the short **Sendero Lan Lan** (200m one-way, 20min) to a waterfall.

This section of the park attracts mostly winter tourists, thanks to its two ski resorts. **Centro de Esquí Las Araucarias** (tel. 52/2741 41 or 45/2562 313, www.skiaraucarias.cl, full-day lift pass CH$25,000-30,000 adults, CH$20,000-22,000 children), 8km east of Temuco, has the better facilities, although the skiing here, with three lifts and 350 skiable hectares, doesn't match other nearby ski resorts such as Malalcahuello.

Rent skis, poles, and boots for CH$15,000 per day. Basic lodging is available in shared dorm rooms (CH$12,000) and in three double rooms (CH$30,000); you'll pay CH$80,000 more for three meals per day.

Food and Accommodations

Accommodations are in the towns that flank the park—Curacautín in the north and Melipeuco in the south—and on the southern stretch of Ruta 925 toward Melipeuco. Lodging rates cited include IVA.

WITHIN THE PARK

The only company allowed to operate within the park, **Sendas Conguillío** (tel. 2/2840 6852, www.sendasconguillio.cl, CH$10,000 pp, CH$35,000 tent site, CH$115,000 3-person cabin) provides lodging year-round, most of which is around La Administración, 31km from Melipeuco and 39km from Curacautín. Eleven fully equipped cabins include hot water, kitchens, and a private hot tub, and camping is at five sites; the closest to the hiking trails are Camping Ñirres and Camping Carpinteros, for up to eight people, which can be booked in advance, and Camping El Estero, for individuals or couples, which cannot be booked in advance but normally doesn't fill up.

Next to the main office at La Administración, **Cafetería Pewen** is open in January-February, serving sandwiches and other light dishes, while a small market is also open November-March with basic food items and essentials such as camping gas.

MELIPEUCO

The traditional **Los Troncos** (Aguirre Cerda 352, 45/2581 088, 9am-10pm daily, CH$4,000-6,000) doesn't have a menu; instead diners are offered home-cooked dishes such as *cazeulas* (stews) and cuts of meat with local vegetables. The bread is home-baked, and most of the dishes are sourced from the owner's farm. The wooden interior and large open fire make it a warm and pleasant place for dinner. The friendliness of your reception depends on how the host is feeling.

Located on the eastern edge of Melipeuco as the road leaves the village, **Hospedaje y Camping Relmucura** (Camino Internacional S-61, tel. 9/9424 2454 or tel. 9/9659 1462, www.relmucura.cl, CH$15,000 pp private bath, CH$5,000 camping) offers a warm welcome from its owner, María, who also bakes delicious bread and kuchen for a hearty breakfast—the best you'll find in this price range—with astounding views of Volcán Llaima from the breakfast room. The walls are thin but the beds are comfortable. Prices are charged per person, so individual travelers will find themselves in a double room. The camping spots out of the back have access to cold showers, or for CH$1,000 you can use the hot showers in the house.

Running entirely on solar and wind energy, ★ **La Baita** (Km 18 Camino Melipeuco a Laguna Verde, tel. 45/2581 073, www.labaitaconguillio.cl, July-May, CH$93,000 d, cabin CH$75,000) is an attractive choice for its eco credentials, the six modern bedrooms with slate-tiled baths—all of which have mountain views—and the six cabins with kitchens. The open-plan common room, with a central wood burner and squishy seating, makes the perfect hangout. They also cook up pizzas and *menús del día* in the kitchen and can arrange guided treks and transfers from Melipeuco. La Baita is a 25-minute drive from town.

Expect a warm welcome from seasoned hotelier Miguel at **Vista Hermosa** (Km 10 Camino Melipeuco a Laguna Verde, tel. 9/9444 1630, www.vistahermosaconguillio. cl, CH$62,000 d), with stunning views of Volcán Llaima from the eastern shores of Río Truful-Truful. Accessed by a dirt track (you need a 4WD in winter), the four double rooms are like cabins as they're self-contained and separate from the main house, where a small menu of food can be ordered to eat on the large volcano-facing terrace. Staff can arrange transfers from Melipeuco.

Information and Services

Most of the park's services are around Playa Curacautín and La Administración, where there's a picnic area, public restrooms, and a large car park. All buses departing the park leave from this car park. In January-February, **Ruka Witran,** a small kiosk selling Mapuche crafted products, is open.

Before you take the turn for La Administración, there's a **Centro de Información** with a lengthy series of displays on everything from the trekking routes to the flora, fauna, and seismic history of the park.

The northern access from Curacautín has problems with snow during winter; check with the SERNATUR or CONAF offices in Temuco for the most up-to-date information. There are no trash bins in the park; take your rubbish with you.

Getting There and Around

Trailheads are widely spread, so renting a car from Temuco is the easiest way to get around this area. Bus access to the park is infrequent in summer and nonexistent the rest of the year, but it is possible to arrive by public transport, particularly if you plan to spend a couple of nights in the park. In January-February, **Nar Bus** (tel. 45/2407 740, www.narbus.cl) offers one departure daily to Parque Nacional Conguillío from Temuco's **Terminal de Buses Rurales** (Aníbal Pinto 32, Temuco, tel. 45/2210 494; 9am daily, returning at 4:15pm Mon.-Sat. and 6pm Sun., 2.5hr, CH$4,000). The bus arrives at La Administración ranger station and returns to Temuco immediately. Bus schedules change regularly, so confirm at the bus station the day before you intend to travel.

Buses Curacautín Express (tel. 45/2258 125) runs a **summer-only service** (30min, CH$1,000) to the park. Buses leave several times a day Monday-Friday from the main road in Curacautín, dropping passengers off 5km before the Laguna Captrén CONAF ranger station (expect to walk or hitchhike from here). The return bus leaves an hour after it arrives.

A **taxi** from Curacautín to the park costs around CH$25,000 and takes around one hour. Be sure to arrange your return journey before you get dropped off, as cell reception is limited in the park.

There are no public transport connections to Sector Los Paraguas. **Vogabus** (tel. 45/2910 134) runs six daily buses from Temuco's **Terminal de Buses Rurales** (Aníbal Pinto 32, tel. 45/2210 494) to Cherquenco, 19km before the ski resorts. You can sometimes organize onward transport by emailing the resorts directly. Otherwise, a rental car is necessary, and during winter, a 4WD vehicle with snow chains is essential. From Vilcún, 35km east of the park, it's a 20-km drive to Cherquenco on a paved road, after which it is gravel (a difficult drive in winter) to reach a narrow, unpaved road that leads to the entrance to the two ski resorts.

Villarrica

Villarrica, often overlooked for its bigger sibling Pucón to the east, is set on the southwest edge of picturesque Lago Villarrica, over which the looming peak of Volcán Villarrica towers. Becoming a destination in its own right, the city offers a string of golden sand, artificial lakefront beaches, and a colorful history. Like much of the Araucanía region, it is a stronghold of Mapuche culture and life.

Those who linger for a day or two will find an emerging food scene and locals keen to prove that Villarrica is an excellent alternative to Pucón. Unfortunately, good-quality accommodations are few.

For those with a vehicle, Villarrica may be a better choice than Pucón as a base. It's quieter and has better access to the region's top hot springs. If you plan to drive to the national parks east of Pucón, the road connecting Villarrica and Pucón, which normally takes 20 minutes, can become a three-hour ordeal in summer.

SIGHTS

There are few tourist attractions in Villarrica; it's easy to see them in an afternoon. Make a beeline for the **Costanera Pucará,** a 1.8-km stretch of pavement that follows the shoreline of Lago Villarrica from Playa Pucará, a 400-meter-long beach in the west, to the harbor and Pueblito Artesanal in the east. It has the best views of the volcano, making it the ideal spot for sunset when the snow-draped slopes turn red. At the **harbor** (Gral Komer and Bernardo O'Higgins), **kayaks** (CH$3,000 pp/30min) and *pedalos* (CH$2,000 pp/30min) are available to rent.

Tour outfitters **Entrenciones Acuáticas Aedo** (tel. 9/8357 1240, http://aedoturismo.cl) and **Aillaquillen** (tel. 9/8357 1240) take daily trips to **Playa Chillan** (CH$13,000), a hidden beach on a small island, only accessible by boat, where you can swim. Trips include a 1.5-hour speedboat trip out to the island plus time to relax on the beach. Bring food and drink, as there are no amenities on the island. In January-February, there are multiple departures per day 10am-sunset. The rest of the year, call ahead to make reservations.

Three kilometers north of town along the S-69, **Playa Blanca** is a small black-sand beach with sweeping views of the volcano and shallow waters for swimming. There's no sign; the beach is accessed down a small passageway on the right side of the road. Look for vehicles parked along the street, particularly on weekends, when it's a popular picnicking spot.

Museo Leandro Penchulef

Museo Leandro Penchulef (Bernardo O'Higgins 401, tel. 45/22354 7367, www.museoleandropenchulef.uc.cl, 9am-12:30pm and 2pm-5:30pm Mon.-Fri., free) contains a collection of Mapuche objects, including metal stirrups, wicker baskets, silver jewelry, and belts, enhanced by quotations from local Mapuche people, situating each within the social and religious context of the culture. Two canoes carved out of thick *coigüe* trunks dominate the center of this small but interesting museum. Find it on the campus of the Pontificia Universidad Católica de Chile, on the right side below the large main staircase into the Señor Paul Wevering W building.

Museo Histórico y Arqueológico Municipal

Packed into an attic room above the city library, the **Museo Histórico y Arqueológico Municipal** (Pedro de Valdivia 1050, entrance on the left side of the library, tel. 45/2415 706, 9:30am-1pm and 2:30pm-6:30pm Mon.-Fri., free) is a storeroom-cum-museum with a collection of Mapuche objects, including textiles and silverware. Most interesting is the display of traditional bamboo cane *pinkulwes* (flutes), hollowed-out pumpkin *wadas* (maracas), and other musical instruments.

Villarrica

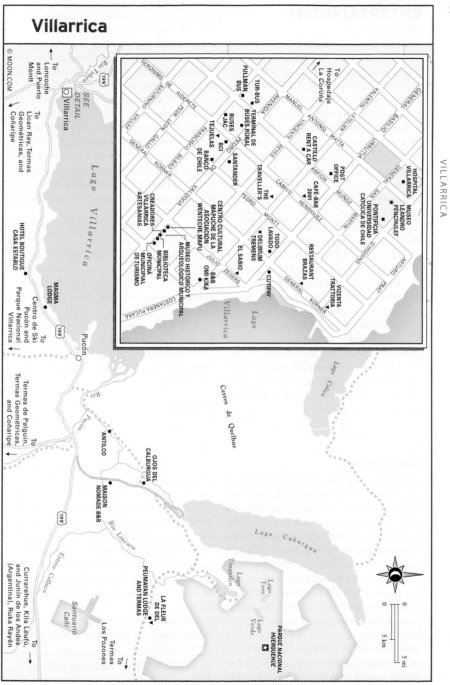

© MOON.COM

To Loncoche and Puerto Montt

To Lican Ray, Termas Geométricas, and Coñaripe

Río Toltén

199

SEE DETAIL

Villarrica

Lago Villarrica

HOTEL BOUTIQUE CASA ESTABLO

MAGMA LODGE

199

Pucón

To Centro de Ski Pucón and Parque Nacional Villarrica

To Termas de Palguín, Termas Geométricas, and Coñaripe

Río Pucón

ANTILCO

OJOS DEL CALBURGUA

MAISON NOMADE B&B

199

Río Liucura

Estero Coilaco

Cerros de Quelhue

Lago Caburgua

Lago Colico

Lago Tinquilco

Lago Toro

Lago Verde

PARQUE NACIONAL HUERQUEHUE

Santuario Cañi

To Currarehue, Kila Leufú, and Junín de los Andes (Argentina), Ruka Rayén

PEUMAYAN LODGE AND TERMAS

LA FLEUR DE DEL

To Termas Los Pozones

N

0   5 km
0   5 mi

DETAIL:

To Hospedaje La Coruña

GERÓNIMO DE AIDERETE

PEDRO LEÓN GALLO

EPULEF

GENERAL GALLO

GENERAL KORNER

FRANCISCO BILBAO

PEDRO DE VALDIVIA

PULLMAN BUS

TUR-BUS

TERMINAL DE BUSES RURAL

BUSES JAC

TEJUELAS

BANCO DE CHILE

BCI

SANTANDER

AVENIDA

MANUEL ANTONIO MATTA

VICENTE REYES

VALENTÍN LETELIER

GENERAL URRUTIA

GENERAL BASILIO

CASTILLO RENT A CAR

POST OFFICE

CAFÉ-BAR 2001

ANFIÓN MUÑOZ

CAMILO HENRÍQUEZ

SAN MARTÍN

O'HIGGINS

ARTURO PRAT

PEDRO MONTT

JULIO ZEGERS

GENERAL KORNER

THE TRAVELLER'S

TODO LAVADO

CENTRO CULTURAL MAPUCHE DE LA ASOCIACIÓN WENTECHE MAPU

DELIRIUM TREMENS

EL SABIO

B&B OMI KIKA

CUTIPAY

CREADORES VILLARRICA ARTESANÍAS

MUSEO HISTÓRICO Y ARQUEOLÓGICO MUNICIPAL

BIBLIOTECA MUNICIPAL

OFICINA MUNICIPAL DE TURISMO

RESTAURANT BRAZAS

VIZENTA TRATTORIA

PONTIFICIA UNIVERSIDAD CATÓLICA DE CHILE

HOSPITAL VILLARRICA

MUSEO LEANDRO PENCHULEF

COSTANERA PUCARÁ

Lago Villarrica

Lago

ENTERTAINMENT
Nightlife

The nightlife in Villarrica isn't half as wild as in Pucón, but a handful of bars along Valentín Letelier are busy on weekends. A Villarrica institution, **The Travellers** (Valentín Letelier 753, tel. 45/2413 617, 11am-1am Mon.-Wed., 11am-3am Fri.-Sat.), with its London Underground-style sign outside, New York skyline above the bar, and international food, pays homage to the owners' extensive travels. The terrace, lit by fairy lights, has a great atmosphere in the evenings. It gets crammed with locals and tourists later, particularly on Friday. The food is not bad and includes Chilean, Thai, Indian, and Mexican; it's a good place to snack on empanadas with a pint or a mojito, the house specialty.

Just down the road from The Travellers, **Delirium Tremens** (Valentín Letelier 836, tel. 59/8448 4111, 6pm-3am Tues.-Fri., 8pm-5am Sat.) draws a younger crowd in its cozy living room-style interior. Pick from a mind-boggling selection of beer by the bottle as well as their own craft beer, Bravía, on tap. It's popular as an after-work hangout during the week, and it's the number one stop for indie and rock fans on Saturday, with tunes blaring out of the sound system and the occasional live band—although things don't get going until late.

SHOPPING

Villarrica has the largest selection of Mapuche souvenirs in the Araucanía Region. Most of the stalls are clustered along Pedro de Valdivia, between General Komer and Aviador Acevedo. The **Centro Cultural Mapuche de la Asociación Wenteche Mapu** (Pedro de Valdivia 1041, no phone, 10am-6pm daily winter, 10am-11:30pm daily summer) not only has a number of stalls run by local Mapuche women selling everything from decorated wooden kitchen utensils to ornaments, they have a *ruka* (a traditional Mapuche dwelling made from *coigüe* wood and thatched using straw) inside to prepare Mapuche-style dishes, such as tortillas cooked over an open fire. The

ceremonial area, adorned with wooden statues, is the site of ancestral rituals and spiritual events on summer evenings.

Next door, eastward along Pedro de Valdivia, **Creadores Villarrica Artesanias** (10:30am-6pm daily winter, 10:30am-midnight daily summer) has a collection of wooden ornaments, key chains, and chopping boards, plus textiles. Around the corner along General Komer between Pedro de Valdivia and Vicente Reyes, **Huerto Esperanza** (no phone, 9:30am-7pm Mon.-Sat., some shops open Sun.) is another small market with a selection of crafts, mainly wooden carvings and wool textiles.

Feria Mapuche

With a mass of stalls selling Mapuche ponchos, textiles, wooden sculptures and tableware, leather, and food, the **Feria Mapuche** (location varies, no phone, 10am-11pm daily last week of Jan.) is the best place to pick up Mapuche-crafted souvenirs if you're in Villarrica the last week of January. The location changes every year; visit the Oficina Municipal de Turismo for up-to-date information.

FOOD

Villarrica doesn't have the same variety of restaurants as Pucón, but a growing focus on quality dining and an upsurge in view restaurants means a new era in dining along General Komer, in front of the harbor. To explore the city with your stomach, **Caminatas Gourmet** (tel. 9/6249 6894, www.caminatasgourmet.cl, departs 11am Mon.-Sat., CH$50,000) offers a three-hour walking tour to guide you through Mapuche and Chilean dishes, including wild fruits and vegetables, at a variety of restaurants. Book 48 hours in advance to confirm the meeting location.

Best known for its range of pizzas and vegetarian dishes, **El Sabio** (Julio Zegers 393,

---

1: booth selling Mapuche handicrafts **2:** Café-Bar 2001

tel. 9/7125 8957, 12:30pm-4pm and 6:30pm-10pm Mon.-Sat., CH$4,000-6,000) hits the spot when it comes to a healthy and filling meal. Pizzas range from Spanish chorizo with mozzarella to a vegetable feast of sweet corn, mushrooms, and capers, while the glass cabinet at the cash register displays different types of empanadas and sweet pastries. The owner is hugely welcoming and speaks a little English. To keep up with demand, the restaurant opens an adjoining covered terrace in summer.

Opened in 1978, ★ **Café-Bar 2001** (Camilo Henríquez 379, tel. 45/2411 470, 9am-noon Mon.-Sat., 10am-11pm Sun., CH$4,000-8,000) is *the* hangout for breakfast, lunch, *onces,* and even dinner. The menu covers homemade burgers wrapped in warm pita bread, traditional *mechadas* (slow-roasted beef sandwiches), and Chilean and American breakfasts. The place hasn't lost its charm, and you'll likely bump into the owner, Nancy, who's decorated the inside walls with keyrings donated by passing travelers. Service is excellent, and the outside terrace is a great place to sit during the summer.

Upmarket and trendy, **Restaurant Brazas** (Gral. Korner 145, tel. 45/2411 631, 12:30pm-2am daily summer, 12:30pm-2pm and 7:30pm-11pm Mon.-Sat., 12:30pm-5pm Sun. winter, CH$9,000-16,000) is superior in the quality of its service—and its meat. Every cut of beef imaginable includes the exquisite confit beef ribs and fish dishes such as eel in an abalone sauce. The large covered terrace has prime views across the lake toward the volcano and explains part of the restaurant's appeal; in February it's essential to reserve, and outside summer, lunch is the busiest time.

Run by the same owners as neighboring Restaurant Brazas, **Vizenta Trattoria** (Bernardo O'Higgins 890, tel. 45/2726 373, 10am-2am daily summer, 11:30am-2am daily winter, CH$6,000-10,000), has red gingham tablecloths that manage to re-create a sense of Italy on Lago Villarrica. They pride themselves on having the best and cheapest pasta and Chilean-influenced pizzas in town and an excellent selection of Chilean wine to wash it down.

ACCOMMODATIONS

Lodging is cheaper than in Pucón, although there are far fewer options. For good views and proximity to restaurants and bars, look close to the Costanera Pucará, although few accommodations are more than a 10-minute walk to the lake. Wi-Fi and IVA are included in the rates, but not breakfast, unless stated.

The cheapest digs in town, the great **Hospedaje La Coruña** (Oscar Lagos 570, tel. 45/2413 659, rod_galaz@hotmail.com, CH$22,000 d shared bath) has only three rooms in a small terrace house on a residential street 10 blocks from the Costanera Pucará. The bedrooms are larger than expected for this price range, with access to a large downstairs sitting area and kitchen, where the owners (who live in rooms at the back of the house) sit around to chat in the evening, creating a convivial and welcoming vibe.

With its pleasant location next to a stream, **B&B Omi Kika** (Valentín Letelier 1055, tel. 9/6836 5197, CH$30,000 d shared bath, CH$40,000 d private bath) has rooms with thick feather duvets. The rooms on the top floor that share a bath are much lighter than the option on the ground floor. The upstairs breakfast room and communal space (breakfast costs an additional CH$3,000) have views across the volcano.

With bedrooms in a separate two-story cabin and the communal areas within owner Roberto's house, **Cutipay** (Gral. Korner 240, tel. 9/7580 0498, CH$25,000 d shared bath, CH$30,000 d private bath) can feel chaotic, but it's near the harbor and has the best views of the lake from its large, sunny terrace. Guests have access to a huge communal kitchen. Opt for a bedroom with a private bath (the shared-bath setup is a little odd). Rooms are basic but clean, and all have electric heaters.

Four kilometers north of Villarrica along Ruta 199 toward Temuco, **Cabañas Quilamalen** (Ruta 199, tel. 9/9886 6509,

The Call of the Wild

Answer the call of the wild with a day mushing with Siberian huskies. **Aurora Austral** (tel. 9/8901 4518, www.auroraaustral.com) runs a husky farm 19km south of Villarrica occupied by more than 50 of the adorable animals. During winter, spend a full day learning the ropes (CH$80,000 pp), with the option to extend to a two- or three-day adventure into the mountains to learn how to care for the dogs. In summer, the sleds have wheels (CH$33,000 pp) or opt to just enjoy a trek with one of the dogs (CH$38,000 pp). All packages require a minimum of two people, and transport to the farm is not included. The farm also rents cabins (from CH$40,000).

To get here from Villarrica, it's a 25-minute, 21-km drive south along the S-95-T towards Licanray, branching off onto the S-239-T as you follow signposts for Panguipulli.

www.quilamalen.cl, CH$50,000 d tree house, CH$100,000 cabin) has three beautiful grass-roofed cabins, designed to stay warm in winter and cool in summer, amid extensive lawns and gardens. Built from adobe, the cabins are light and airy with sizeable kitchens. The tree house is slightly smaller, with no kitchen, but it has a table built around the tree below for alfresco dining. There's a swimming pool on-site.

INFORMATION AND SERVICES

The meticulously organized and helpful **Oficina Municipal de Turismo** (Pedro de Valdivia 1059, tel. 45/2206 619, www. visitvillarrica.cl, 8:30am-6pm Mon.-Fri., 9am-1pm and 2:30pm-5:30pm Sun. winter, 8:30am-11pm daily summer) has an endless stock of pamphlets with historical and logistical information about the city and maps for the nearby national parks. The staff speak fluent English.

Find a cluster of **24-hour ATMs,** including **Santander, BCI, BBVA,** and **Banco de Chile,** on Pedro de Valdivia between Pedro Montt and Camilo Henriquez. For laundry, head to **Todo Lavado** (Gral. Urrutia 614, tel. 45/2414 452, 9:30am-1:30pm and 3pm-7pm Mon.-Sat.). The post office, **Correos** (Anfión Muñoz 315, 9am-2:30pm and 3:30pm-7pm Mon.-Fri., 10am-1pm Sat.), is on Anfión Muñoz. For medical emergencies, the **Hospital de Villarrica** (San Martín 460, tel. 45/2555 252) can assist.

GETTING THERE

Bus

Local buses arrive and leave from Villarrica's **Terminal de Buses Rural** (Pedro de Valdivia 599, no phone), a few blocks west from the harbor. **Bipurey** (tel. 9/6835 5798) has service from **Pucón** (30min, CH$900) every 7 minutes during the week and every 15 minutes on weekends. **Buses Coñaripe** (tel. 9/7178 3803) has frequent service from **Coñaripe** (every 15 min, 1hr, CH$2,100). Next door to the Terminal de Buses Rural, **Buses JAC** (Francisco Bilbao 629, tel. 45/2467 775, www. jac.cl) has its own terminal. Buses arrive from **Temuco** (every 10 min daily, 1.5hr, CH$2,000), **Valdivia** (7 times daily, 2.5hr, CH$4,500), and **Puerto Montt** (around 6 daily, 4hr, CH$9,300).

Across the road from the Terminal de Buses Rural, **Pullman Bus** (Francisco Bilbao 598, tel. 45/2414 217, www.pullmanbus.cl) runs twice daily from **Santiago** (9hr, CH$16,000/CH$26,000). They also shuttle once daily between **Concepción** (4.5hr, CH$10,000/CH$15,000) and Villarrica. Next door to Pullman Bus, **Tur Bus** (Anfión Muñoz 657, tel. 45/2204 105) has four daily arrivals from **Santiago** (9hr, CH$15,000/CH$35,000).

Car

Villarrica is a one-hour, 80-km drive south from Temuco via Ruta 5 and Ruta 199. Villarrica is 25km west of Pucón via Ruta 199, a 30-minute drive. During the peak season, expect to add a few hours to journey times due to the volume of traffic.

GETTING AROUND

There's little need to hire a taxi to get around. For trips beyond the city, such as to Playa Blanca, **Taxis Premium** (Pedro Montt 470, tel. 45/2411 444) or **Taxis Villarrica** (Pdte Ríos 815, tel. 45/2414 141 or 45/2419 072) can get you there for around CH$4,000.

Rental Car

Options for car rental from Villarrica are limited; try **Rent A Car** (Anfión Muñoz 415, tel. 45/2411 618, 9am-1pm and 3pm-7pm Mon.-Sat.).

Pucón

Pucón is a compact town along the edge of Lago Villarrica. Achingly cool and painfully expensive, Pucón is the self-proclaimed adventure capital of Chile and the closest town to active Volcán Villarrica, which dominates the landscape. After catching a glimpse, few travelers can fight the urge to summit it. Pucón is also a short bus ride from the breathtaking Parque Nacional Huerquehue.

Pucón has a playful, young, and hip small-town vibe. Waves of Chileans and foreigners come year-round for adventure activities, many of which revolve around the volcano: hiking, canyoneering, horseback riding, and skiing. After a long day of adventure are the many restaurants and small but buzzing nightlife spots. The town's popularity means it's one of the region's most expensive places to visit.

Pucón is best avoided during January-February, when its narrow streets are practically gridlocked with visitors. November and March, the shoulder seasons, see the tide of people recede, while the weather is still dry enough for volcano ascents. When it rains here, it pours, so be prepared for poor weather to disrupt your plans, and visit one of the many nearby hot springs, which are too hot on a sunny day but a real treat at night.

ORIENTATION

The majority of the action takes places on Pucón's crowded central thoroughfare, **O'Higgins,** which runs east-west through the heart of the town. Atypical for Chilean towns, the large **Plaza de Armas** (bounded by Linconyán, Holzapfel, Ansorena, and Pedro de Valdivia) is not at the center of the town but lies three blocks north of O'Higgins. It's a pleasant mix of statues of Mapuche chiefs, decorative pools, concrete chessboards, and plenty of benches beneath the boughs of laurel, *araucaría*, roble, and myrtle.

SIGHTS

Playa Grande

The crunchy black volcanic sand of **Playa Grande,** on the north side of Pucón, mere blocks from the Plaza de Armas, teems with umbrellas and sunbathers during summer, when the waters of Lago Villarrica are pleasantly warm and restaurants spring up along the beach. The beach is a romantic place to watch the sun set. The sand is coarse and can be painful underfoot, so bring flip-flops. October-February, rentable **kayaks** (around CH$2,000 per half hour) are moored along the beach.

ENTERTAINMENT AND SHOPPING

Nightlife

An old favorite with the locals, **Mama's and Tapas** (O'Higgins 581, tel. 45/2449 002, www.mamasandtapas.cl, 6pm-3am Sun.-Thurs., 6pm-4:30am Fri.-Sat., after 11pm CH$10,000 entrance) has everything from passable Mexican food (served until 2am) and nightly drink deals (6pm-11pm) to live sports broadcasts and a DJ playing electronic music until

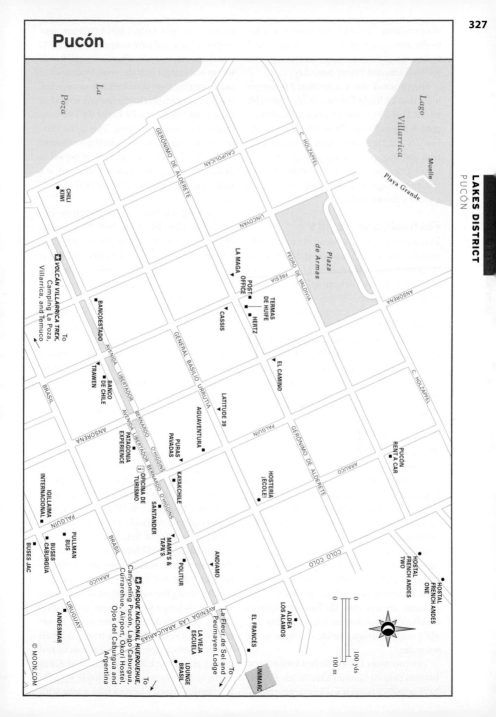

Pucón

Lago
Villarrica

Muelle

Playa Grande

La
Poza

GERÓNIMO DE ALDERETE

CAUPOLICÁN

C. HOLZAPEL

CHILI
KIWI

LINCOYÁN

FRESIA

Plaza
de Armas

PEDRO DE VALDIVIA

ANSORENA

C. HOLZAPEL

LA MAGA

POST
OFFICE

TERMAS
DE HUIFE

HERTZ

VOLCÁN VILLARRICA TREK,
Camping La Poza,
Villarrica, and Temuco

To

BANCOESTADO

CASSIS

AVENIDA LIBERTADOR BERNARDO O'HIGGINS

GENERAL BASILIO URRUTIA

EL CAMINO

GERÓNIMO DE ALDERETE

PUCÓN
RENT A CAR

BRASIL

TRAWEN

BANCO
DE CHILE

LATITUDE 39

AGUAVENTURA

PALGUÍN

ARAUCO

ANSORENA

AVENIDA LIBERTADOR BERNARDO O'HIGGINS

PATAGONIA
EXPERIENCE

PURAS
PAVADAS

HOSTERÍA
¡ECOLE!

PALGUÍN

IGUILLAIMA
INTERNACIONAL

OFICINA DE
TURISMO

KAYAKCHILE

SANTANDER

COLO COLO

HOSTAL
FRENCH ANDES
TWO

HOSTAL
FRENCH ANDES
ONE

BRASIL

PULLMAN
BUS

BUSES
CABURGUA

MAMA's &
TAPA'S

POLITUR

ANDIAMO

ARAUCO

La Fleur de Sel and
Peumayen Lodge

To

ALDEA
LOS ÁLAMOS

BUSES JAC

URUGUAY

PARQUE NACIONAL HUERQUEHUE,
Canyoning Pucón, Lago Caburgua,
Cuñrarehue, Airport, Okori Hostel,
Ojos del Caburgua and
Argentina

To

AVENIDA LAS ARAUCARIAS

LA VIEJA
ESCUELA

EL FRANCÉS

ANDESMAR

LOUNGE
BRASIL

UNIMARC

© MOON.COM

0
0

100 yds
100 m

the early hours. It's a bit dingy, but that adds to the divey atmosphere. You're guaranteed to find this place lively any summer night; in winter it's busiest Friday-Saturday.

High-backed velvet-upholstered furniture hints that **La Vieja Escuela** (Colo Colo 450, tel. 45/2444 039, www.laviejaescuelacultobar. com, 8:30pm-3:30am Mon.-Thurs., 8:30pm-5am Fri.-Sat.) is a classy affair. Its elderly pool table and stage promise a good night out. Live bands grace the stage on weekends, and the terrace seating is the place to sip cocktails on a warm summer night.

Festivals and Events

Throughout summer, Pucón thrums to the sound of live music, theater, and film, most of which is free. For a full list of events, head to the Oficina de Turismo for the January-February programs.

Shopping

For a taste of Pucón's artsy side, head to the row of colorful cabins at **Aldea Los Alamos** (Colo Colo 361, no phone, 10am-7pm daily summer), each featuring the ceramics, stonework, and paintings of a local Pucón artist, which can be purchased for reasonable prices.

RECREATION
★ Hot Springs

The area surrounding Volcán Villarrica is rife with hot springs, especially northeast of Pucón, clustered around Río Liucura and the S-907. Many have been developed to create luxury experiences, but some remain closer to the natural state. Although many Pucón-based tour companies take visitors by the busload during the day, the hot springs are far better visited at night, when the steam accents the starry sky, and the cool air makes a welcome reprieve from the heat. Hot springs are also the ideal destination on a rainy day, when cold raindrops provide a contrast to the hot water.

The two pools at **Peumayen Lodge and Termas** (Km 20 Camino a Huife, tel. 45/2197 0060 or 9/7778 0285, www.termaspeumayen.

cl, 10:30am-5pm daily, CH\$14,000) are next to Río Liucura and have temperatures of 36°C and 22°C, respectively. There's a small beach where you can get into the river. Peumayen is much smaller than the other hot springs but it feels exclusive. Packages include a meal at the on-site restaurant, **La Fleur de Sel,** considered the best in the area. This is the closest hot springs to Pucón. Take the bus bound for Termas Los Pozones and ask to get off at Peumayen Lodge. Because it's so small, it's worth calling ahead to make sure they have room.

The most popular spot for nighttime visits, **Termas Los Pozones** (S-907, 34km east of Pucón, tel. 45/1972 350, 11am-3am daily, last entry at midnight, CH\$8,000-10,000) is a set of five open-air hot pools ranging 25-45°C. The river flows alongside the pools for a soothing backdrop. It's a more rustic experience than at nearby hotels but also sports unsightly concrete installations. Take a refreshing plunge in the river when you get too warm. There are basic changing rooms and cubbyholes next to each pool for storing your things; leave valuables in your hotel room. Stays are capped at three hours. Los Pozones is 6km east of Peumayen Lodge. Take the **Pullman Bus** (Palguín 555, tel. 45/2443 331) **minibus** (7 daily, final bus leaves hot springs at 7:30pm Mon.-Sat., 5pm Sun., 1hr, CH\$1,500), which drops you off right outside.

In a river canyon, Japanese-inspired **Termas Geométricas** (15km east of Coñaripe, tel. 9/7477 1708, www. termasgeometricas.cl, 11am-8pm Sun.-Thurs, 11am-11pm Fri.-Sat., CH\$21,000-25,000 adults, CH\$12,000 children) has 17 slate-lined pools with a 500-meter walkway between giant *nalca* plants to a gushing waterfall. During the week and outside summer, you'll likely have a pool to yourself. Changing rooms are dotted throughout; you'll be assigned a locker and given a towel. A small cafeteria with a wood fire serves snacks and drinks at reasonable prices. Located 82km south of Pucón, it is not reachable by public transport, so it's best to take a tour with

Aguaventura Expediciones (Palguín 336, tel. 45/2444 246, www.aguaventura.com) that includes Termas Geométricas (12:30pm or 2pm daily, CH$35,000, 6pm on weekends, CH$30,000). Rates include transport and hot springs entry. They also offer four-hour night trips to Los Pozones (CH$20,000) leaving their office at 8pm.

Hiking

For ascents of nearby **Volcán Villarrica** (CH$85,000-100,000, including all equipment), **Patagonia Experience** (O'Higgins 461, tel. 45/2444 36, www. patagoniaexperience.cl) and **Summit Chile** (Urrutia 585, tel. 45/2443 259, www. summitchile.org) have solid safety records, quality equipment, and English-speaking guides. Summit Chile also offers other challenging volcano ascents, starting at CH$170,000 for Volcán Llama and Lonquimay, including guides and transportation, plus trekking in Parque Nacional Huerquehue. **Aguaventura Expediciones** (Palguín 336, tel. 45/2444 246, www. aguaventura.com) has a variety of trips and can provide information on solo treks as well as renting out hiking gear.

Canyoneering

Canyoning Pucón (Blanco Encalada 185, tel. 9/9294 6913 or tel. 9/4455 9901, www. canyoningpucon.cl) is the only outfit to explore the interesting Pillan and Nevado canyons. Pillan is at the bottom of Volcán Villarrica and is best explored October-December. The tour involves plenty of rappelling and zip-lining. Nevado, deeper in the Andes, is best visited from December, when it has plenty of water for waterslides and cliff jumping.

The company has an impeccable safety record, and the owner, Miguel, is a safety expert for Red Bull when the company holds events in Chile. Six-hour tours to either canyon cost CH$35,000 and include all safety equipment and insurance, plus hotel pickup and drop-off. There are no age or experience restrictions, although minors must have permission from their legal guardians.

Kayaking

For kayaking Class II-IV rapids, check out English-speaking **Kayak Chile** (O'Higgins 524, tel. 45/2441 584, www.kayakchilepucon. com) for tours along the Río Liucura, northeast of Pucón. On the **double kayak tour** (2hr, from CH$40,000), you're in the front of the kayak and the guide is in the back. They also have **ducky tours** (from CH$25,000), where you crash through rapids in an inflatable kayak. No experience is required. Kayakers of all levels will benefit from their full-day lesson (CH$60,000), which starts on Lago Villarrica and ends on the river, where you put into practice what you've learned. They also run stand-up paddleboard tours (3hr, CH$30,000) on the same river. Transport from their office and use of a life vest are included.

Horse Trekking

The most established company for horseback trekking is **Antilco** (Km 7 Carhuello, tel. 9/9713 9758, www.antilco.com), whose English-speaking guides have years of experience in tourism and who match riders individually to one of their 20 horses. Half-day treks to a local Mapuche community, 4km from Pucón or into the mountains in Parque Nacional Villarrica, cost CH$30,000. Other tours range from one-day (CH$60,000) to four-day treks in Parque Nacional Huerquehue and Parque Nacional Villarrica (from CH$460,000). For more experienced riders, ask about nine-day rides into Argentina (from CH$1,960,000).

FOOD

Restaurants in Pucón reflect the town's popularity: The food is of excellent quality, there's almost every style of cuisine to pick from, and it's far more expensive than dining out in other towns. Most restaurants are along O'Higgins and are open year-round, with longer hours in summer. Reservations at most are essential during peak season, although a number of places only accept walk-ins, so you just have to wait for a table.

For a taste of the city's culinary roots, **Caminatas Gourmet** (tel. 9/6249 6894, www.caminatasgourmet.cl, CH$50,000, departs 2pm Mon.-Sat.) take you around the city's restaurants to sample local ingredients and dishes on a three-hour walking tour. Book 48 hours in advance to get the meeting location.

Chilean

Specializing in fancy organic Chilean dishes and set right on the main drag, **Trawen** (O'Higgins 311, tel. 45/2442 024, www.trawen. cl, 8am-11:30pm Mon.-Sat., 9am-11:30pm Sun,, until 12:30am summer, CH$8,000-16,000) uses only local ingredients, many sourced from its own organic farm. Expect quinoa, homemade ravioli, and fish. This is the only restaurant in Pucón with a list of biodynamic and unfiltered Chilean wine.

Vegetarian food has never tasted as good as at bohemian ¡**Ecolé!** (Gral. Urrutia 592, tel. 45/2441 675, 8am-11pm daily summer, 8am-10:30pm daily winter, CH$2,500-5,000), with tasty, wholesome dishes at affordable prices. Homemade lasagna and veggie burritos—with lashings of Mapuche hot sauce—are the stars of the menu, but the *"poder de la hora" (menú del día)* is a steal at CH$5,000, while breakfast, with eggs, juice, and homemade granola, is a great way to start the day.

Decorated with ponchos, stirrups, and saddles, **La Maga** (Gerónimo de Alderete 276, tel. 45/2444 277, www.lamagapucon.cl, 1pm-11:30pm daily, CH$14,000-22,000) makes no illusions about its specialty, rib-eye steaks and short ribs, with an extensive wine menu. Sit out front, where you can watch your meat being cooked over an open fire. Reservations are essential on weekends.

Home to Pucón's most innovative cuisine, the Basque-French chef of ★ **La Fleur de Sel** (Peumayen Lodge and Termas, km 28 Camino a Huife, tel. 45/2197 0060 or 9/7778 0285, www.termaspeumayen.cl, 1pm-4pm and 7:30pm-9pm daily summer, 1pm-4pm Tues.-Sun. and by reservation only 7:30pm-9pm winter, CH$10,000-16,000) cooks up a storm with Mapuche ingredients: *merkén, piñon,* regional potatoes, *maqui,* quinoa and other seeds, and wild fruits, much of which is grown at the owners' farm. A three-course *menú del día* (CH$15,000) changes seasonally; the food is exquisitely prepared and served in the rustic circular dining room, with knotted wooden doors and a huge fire at its center. It's a 40-minute drive east of Pucón, so you'll need a car.

Light Bites

The relaxed and slightly grungy **El Camino** (Miguel Ansorena 212, tel. 45/2444 078, 1pm-1am Wed.-Mon., CH$5,000-8,000) is all about the simple Chilean sandwich. Customize the seven basic styles, such as chicken, veggie, and *churrasco* (steak), with a long list of extras. Kick back with a local beer and the alternative crowd on the wooden outdoor benches with reggae music. It gets busy from 7pm Friday-Saturday.

Kooky ★ **Puras Pavadas** (Palguín 370, tel. 9/9158 7910 or 9/9696 8099, puraspavadaspucon@gmail.com, 10:30am-9pm daily, open later in summer, CH$1,700-2,000), with only a handful of seats, is easily the top *empanaderia* in the region. Service can be hit or miss, but it's worth it. A dozen varieties of huge empanadas, stuffed with fresh ingredients and deep fried, are served with homemade sweet and sour sauces. They even do takeout.

International

Both modern and authentically Italian, ★ **Andiamo** (O'Higgins 630, tel. 45/2441 559, www.andiamoristorante.cl, 12:30pm-11:30pm daily, CH$6,000-9,000) specializes in house-made pasta with 10 or so options for sauces. The pozotti with salmon and prawns will leave you licking your plate clean. Pick a

---

1: Termas Geométricas **2:** a "hobbit hole" at Chili Kiwi **3:** La Maga **4:** hiking up Volcán Villarrica

table on the terrace to enjoy the sunset over the volcano in the distance.

Californian-run **Latitude 39** (Urrutia 436, tel. 9/7430 0016, noon-11:30pm Mon.-Sat. summer, noon-9:30pm Mon.-Sat. winter, CH$5,000-7,000), with its "gringilicious grub," has the Grand Prix burger (peanut butter, caramelized onions, and bacon) plus an array of burritos, tacos, and salads. The walls are decorated with license plates from the United States. It's possible to pick up local and international beer, guaranteed to make you feel at home.

Cafés

With tables and sun umbrellas spilling out onto the street, **Cassis** (Fresia 233, tel. 9/8151 9358, www.chocolatescassis.com, 8am-midnight daily, CH$2,000-8,000) is the ultimate place for satisfying your sweet cravings. The 50 types of cakes are legendary, although not all are offered at once. The range of sweet and savory crepes, sandwiches, and traditional Chilean dishes make this a pit stop any time of day. They don't take reservations, so there's always a wait.

ACCOMMODATIONS

Pucón has a host of first-rate hostels and hotels, mostly around O'Higgins. To avoid some of the chaos of Pucón in the summer, stay at one of the plush, modern accommodations outside the city. A car is almost essential for reaching these places; most can arrange transfers, but it's far easier to bring your own transport. All lodgings include breakfast, Wi-Fi, and IVA, unless otherwise stated.

Within Pucón
UNDER CH$25,000

With 50 tent sites in a wooded and grassy area, **Camping La Poza** (Roberto Geiss 769, tel. 9/7848 9944 or 45/2444 982, CH$8,000 pp) is one of Pucón's few campgrounds. Each site has a table, lights, an electrical socket, and access to a barbecue. There's an indoor kitchen for poor weather, plus hot showers, lockers, and Wi-Fi in the reception area. During the

first week of February, call ahead to make sure there's room; otherwise you don't need advance reservations.

CH$25,000-40,000

Set up by two veteran backpackers, ★ **Chili Kiwi** (O'Higgins 20, tel. 45/2449 540, www.chilikiwihostel.com, CH$16,000 dorms, CH$40,000 d shared bath) has spacious dorms, three "hobbit hole" rooms, and two tree houses with unrivaled lakeside views. Get to know other guests in the social areas and on-site craft beer bar with outdoor seating. Two daily information sessions offer recommendations on things to do in the area; the owners' skiing knowledge is peerless. Breakfast isn't included in the rates.

CH$40,000-60,000

Better known for its delectable breakfasts and lunch, **Hostería ¡Ecolé!** (Gral. Urrutia 592, tel. 45/2441 675, CH$12,000 dorm, CH$32,500 d shared bath, CH$49,000 d private bath) has 23 bedrooms. Those in the building with the restaurant are dated, so get a more modern, spotlessly clean room in the newer cabin out back. There's no breakfast included, and rates don't include IVA.

In two locations about 20 meters apart, **Hostal French Andes** (Pasaje Tinquilco 3, tel. 45/2443 309; Pasaje Luck 795, tel. 45/2443 324; www.french-andes.com, CH$10,000 dorm, CH$25,000-55,000 d) has a range of lodging that includes minuscule Japanese-style "capsules," with just a bed and a locker in the corridor, as well as more traditional rooms. Ask for the room at French Andes One with views of the volcano and a private bath. Rooms aren't large, but this sociable hostel has atmosphere and a pleasant back garden. Rates don't include IVA.

OVER CH$80,000

With seven king-bed rooms, **Lounge Brasil** (Colo Colo 485, tel. 45/2947 482, www.cafeloungebrasil.com, CH$120,000 d) is a cute, cozy, chic boutique hotel, with high ceilings, quirky furniture, and plenty of wood. Downstairs are communal areas such as a small library and a café-bar that's open to nonguests. Rates don't include IVA.

Outside Pucón
CH$40,000-60,000
In a woodland opposite the airport, **Okori Hostel** (Km 5 R-199, tel. 9/6752 8686 or 9/9821 9442, www.okorihostelpucon.com, CH$16,000 dorm, CH$56,000 d shared bath, CH$65,000 d private bath) wows its backpacker clientele with a huge communal area with comfortable seating, an enormous kitchen, and a quiet setting just beyond Pucón. Three light and airy private rooms are popular with couples. There's central heating plus hammocks in the trees. Rent a bike to cycle into town, or take the buses that pass right outside.

CH$60,000-80,000
Run by a friendly Chilean-French couple, ★ **Maison Nomade B&B** (Km 15 Camino a Caburgua, tel. 9/8293 6388, www.nomadepucon.com, closed May-June, CH$74,000 d) is recognized as a sustainable tourist business thanks to a focus on renewable energy, recycling, and composting. First-class views of the volcano from expansive gardens, home-baked bread, housemade honey, and the wooden interiors built by local Mapuche builders make this place stand out. There's also a swimming pool and communal kitchen. The owners can help guests plan activities in the area. Rates don't include IVA.

OVER CH$80,000
Amid pretty lawns and flower beds in a forest clearing, **Peumayen Lodge and Termas** (Km 28 Camino a Huife, tel. 45/2197 0060 or 9/7778 0285, www.termaspeumayen.cl, CH$81,000 d, CH$107,000 suite) feels more exclusive than its rates suggest. The eight standard rooms at this hot springs lodge are spacious, and four suites tucked into the trees overlook the river. Inside are polished wooden furniture and private terraces. Meals are served in their renowned restaurant, **La Fleur de Sel,** with its Basque-French chef and Mapuche-inspired cuisine. Rates don't include IVA.

Hotel Boutique Casa Establo (Km 6 Camino a Pucón, tel. 45/2443 084, www. casaestablo.com, CH$101,000 d) has views across the lake from 10 stylish rooms; those on the 3rd floor have the best views. The hotel resembles a barn, most noticeable in the huge wooden doors at the entrance. Rooms combine modern furnishings with sheepskin rugs and old-fashioned cast-iron stoves. Attentive staff and the self-service bar make this an excellent escape. Getting here can be hair-raising; the turnoff from Ruta 199 is 6km west of Pucón and leads up a steep dirt track. Rates don't include IVA.

Despite its location on the busy road to Pucón, the 11 domes at **Magma Lodge** (Km 0.3 Camino a Pucón, tel. 45/2442 005, www. magmalodge.cl, CH$116,000 d) are hidden in a forest of pine and poplar. Each dome is built on a raised wooden platform; the two-person domes are closest to the private beach and have the best views across the lake from their terraces. Domes have a skylight for watching the stars. Furniture is funky and modern, and each dome has air-conditioning and heating. Rates don't include IVA.

INFORMATION AND SERVICES
The post office, **Correos** (Fresia 183, 9am-1pm and 2:30pm-6pm Mon.-Fri., 9am-12:30pm Sat.), is two blocks north of the main street. **Banco de Chile** (O'Higgins 318) and **Santander** (O'Higgins 311) have **24-hour ATMs. Banco Estado** (O'Higgins 240) has the best **currency exchange** rates in town. The **Hospital San Francisco Pucón** (Uruguay 325, tel. 45/2290 400, www. hospitalpucon.cl) offers medical attention.

The **Oficina de Turismo** (O'Higgins 483, tel. 45/2293 002, 8:30am-7pm daily) has maps of Pucón and can advise on transport to local attractions. There's an **information booth** (Pedro de Valdivia and Fresia) that springs up in the Plaza de Armas in summer. There are various supermarkets around the town. Pucón is plastic bag-free; bring a reusable shopping bag.

GETTING THERE
Bus

Pucón doesn't have a central bus terminal. Operators have their own offices, mostly at the corner of Palguín and Uruguay. **Pullman Bus** (Palguín 555, tel. 45/2443 331, www.pullmanbus.cl) has three daily buses from **Santiago** (10hr, CH$17,000/CH$22,000). Just around the corner from Pullman, **Buses JAC** (Uruguay 505, tel. 45/2993 181, www.jac.cl) has the best selection of routes, with buses from **Villarrica** (every 30 min daily, 20min, CH$1,000), **Temuco** (every 30 min daily, 1.75hr, CH$2,800), **Valdivia** (6 daily, 3hr, CH$4,700), **Osorno** (5 daily, 2.5hr, CH$8,400), **Puerto Varas** (4 daily, 5hr, CH$9,500), and **Puerto Montt** (5 daily, 5.5hr, CH$9,800). They also have six daily buses from **Santiago** (10hr, CH$30,000/CH$69,000).

Air

Aeropuerto Pucón (ZPC, Ruta 199, no phone), 5km east of Pucón, has flights in January-February from Santiago with **LATAM** (www.latam.com) and **Sky Airline** (www.skyairline). Expect a taxi from the airport into town to cost CH$3,000.

GETTING AROUND

If you're staying in town, everything can be reached on foot. If you're staying farther out, taxi companies **Radio Taxi Pucón** (Miguel Ansorena 190, tel. 45/2442 222) and **Radio Taxi Tour** (Palguín 615, tel. 45/2442 323) are the best way to get into Pucón; have your lodging call for you.

To travel independently to the hot springs or national parks, rent a car from **Hertz** (Gerónimo de Alderete 324, tel. 45/2441 664, 9:30am-5:30pm Mon.-Fri., 10am-1pm Sat.), which only operates January-March, or **Pucón Rent a Car** (Pedro de Valdivia 636, tel. 9/8998 0294, www.puconrentacar.cl, 9am-1:30pm and 3:30pm-6:30pm Mon.-Sat., 12:30pm-1:30pm and 6:30pm-7:30pm Sun.) year-round.

Chile Campers (www.chile-campers.com), with the same owners as Aguaventura Expediciones and French Andes, rents two-person fully equipped camper vans with double beds, cooking equipment, and even a shower, starting at CH$55,000 per day, with a limit of 250km daily.

Crossing into Argentina

About 80km southeast of Pucón along Ruta 199, **Paso Mamuil Malal,** also known as **Paso Tromen,** is the main border crossing from Pucón to Argentina. The road is paved until the halfway point, a few kilometers after the town of Curarrehue. From here it becomes a gravel road passable with any type of vehicle.

From the border, it's 110km to **San Martín de los Andes. Buses Igillaima Internacional** (Uruguay and Palguín, tel. 45/2444 762, www.igillaima.cl) have departures for San Martín (10am Mon.-Sat., noon Sun., 4.5hr, CH$13,000), from where it's possible to make a connection with **Bariloche** (6pm daily, 5hr, CH$32,000). **Andesmar** (Uruguay 627, tel. 45/2442 798, www.andesmarchile.com) has a direct bus to Bariloche (9hr, CH$28,000/CH$31,000), which leaves daily at 8:15am.

Vicinity of Pucón

Although Pucón is an ideal base, the real highlights are in the surrounding countryside. Hiking is the region's specialty: the thickly vegetated virgin forests of *coigüe, mañio,* and *araucaría* in Parque Nacional Huerquehue and the lava- and ash-covered slopes of Volcán Villarrica in Parque Nacional Villarrica combine challenging trekking with electrifying scenery. Skiing is possible in winter. Homestays in Mapuche communities or in luxurious lodgings in the Reserva Biológica Huilo Huilo offer a taste of the region's cultural identity.

Many of the attractions closest to Pucón are accessible by public transport. The area's technical adventures require expert guides.

OJOS DEL CABURGUA

Ojos del Caburgua (9am-6pm daily, CH$1,000), 15km northeast of Pucón, are a set of three waterfalls spilling into the crystal waters of a natural pool in the Río Caburgua. Boardwalks and paths run between the falls, with a number of picnic tables. It's not possible to swim in the pools, but the cool breeze and surrounding vegetation are a good respite from Pucón. You'll be sharing the site with dozens of other holidaymakers in summer. Take the second signed entrance from the road from Pucón; from here, there are a number of trails and viewpoints to admire the waterfalls.

To get here, take the Caburgua-bound bus (every 30 min, last bus leaves Caburgua at 7pm, CH$700) operated by **Buses Caburgua** (Uruguay 540, tel. 9/9838 9047). Ask to be dropped off at Ojos del Caburgua. It's also possible to rent a bike (around CH$5,000 per half-day) in Pucón from any one of the many companies along O'Higgins and cycle to the falls; it's about 2.5 hours.

★ PARQUE NACIONAL HUERQUEHUE

In the foothills of the Andes 35km east of Pucón, few national parks are quite as accessible and beautiful as **Parque Nacional Huerquehue** (tel. 9/6157 4089, parque. huerquehue@conaf.cl, 8:30am-8pm daily Nov.-Mar., 8:30am-6pm daily Apr.-Oct., CH$5,000 adults, CH$3,000 children).

Several hiking routes wind between lofty *mañio* and *coigüe* trees and into forests of *araucaría* at higher elevations, and charming panoramic views across the lakes and volcanoes litter the landscape. The park is easily accessed from Pucón for a day trip, although campsites and other accommodations make it possible to spend a night here. Most companies based in Pucón offer full-day trekking excursions into the park.

The park is open year-round, although many trails aren't fully open April-November due to snowfall and heavy rain. Inquire about conditions at the CONAF ranger station at the entrance to the park, where you sign in and pay. There are public restrooms about 100 meters past the ranger station.

Orientation

The entrance to the park and the **CONAF ranger station** are on the southern side of Lago Tinquilco. From the ranger station, two paths lead into the park: **Sendero Quinchol** and **Sendero Ñirrico,** the latter of which connects with **Sendero Los Lagos.**

A car park and a campsite, both run by CONAF, are located at the entrance. A handful of lodges are accessible either by hiking 2km along Sendero Los Lagos, or continuing along the 4WD-only road that passes the ranger station.

Hiking

The park is a popular trekking destination. Most trails are best suited to hikers in good shape; practically all feature steep stretches.

The most popular trail is the **Sendero Los Lagos** (13km one-way, 3hr). To reach it, first take the short, flat **Sendero Ñirrico** (1km one-way, 20min), which passes the edge of a lake. Los Lagos gains height quickly with a series of switchbacks to reach two waterfalls, Nido de Aguila and Salto Trufulco, as well as viewpoints back across Lago Tinquilco and Volcán Villarrica if the sky is clear. The route continues climbing, eventually reaching several lakes, colorful meadows, and evergreen trees. It's a round-trip of six hours.

From the ranger station heading east, **Sendero Quinchol** (5km loop, 3.5hr) climbs steeply through woods of stubby *coigüe* and *araucaría* with views of six volcanoes, as well as a viewpoint looking over Lago Tinquilco and Lago Caburgua. It's best on clear days.

Food and Accommodations

There are no restaurants in the park. About 2km from the park entrance, a collection of small kiosks serve empanadas, *sopapillas* (deep-fried pumpkin dough), and drinks during the summer.

The **CONAF campground** (CH$15,000/site, up to 6 people) at the park entrance has 22 tent sites. In summer, reservations are necessary. Facilities include hot showers, a covered dining area, and a washing-up station.

Two kilometers along the Sendero Ñirrico, **Refugio Tinquilco** (tel. 9/9278 9831 or 9/9539 2728, www.tinquilco.cl, Sept.-May, CH$20,000 tent site for 2 people, CH$35,000-43,000 d) is a charming rustic cabin decorated with vibrant nature-themed murals by Chilean artists. Rooms are cramped and slightly dingy, but a private beach suitable for bathing and a terrace outside the main house make up for it. Dinner (not included) is a communal feast of nutritious food. Four camping spots, hidden in the forest, provide absolute peace and quiet.

Getting There

The park entrance is accessed by taking the road northeast toward Caburgua and following the signs for the S-911 shortly before reaching the village. From Pucón, it's a 35-km, 45-minute drive.

To get here by public transit from Pucón, take one of the buses run by **Buses Caburgua** (Uruguay 540, tel. 9/9838 9047; 4 daily, final bus leaves the park at 7:30pm, 1hr, CH$1,000). Passengers are dropped off and picked up outside the ranger station.

PARQUE NACIONAL VILLARRICA

The gently smoking conical stratovolcano Villarrica dominates the landscape around Pucón and the western edge of **Parque Nacional Villarrica** (tel. 45/2443 781, http://parquenacionalvillarrica.blogspot.com, parque.villarrica@conaf.cl, CH$8,000). The volcano last erupted in 2015, spewing fountains of smoke and orange flames into the sky and causing 3,000 people to evacuate the area. It's Pucón's ultimate adventure attraction.

In summer, lines of hikers dressed in heavy jackets and thick boots clamber up the snow-dusted northern flanks of the volcano, hoping for a glimpse of bubbling lava in the crater. More experienced mountaineers can be seen farther east on the quieter but more challenging traverse between Volcán Villarrica and Volcán Quetrupillán.

In winter, the snowy slopes of the volcano transform into a ski resort that offers dramatic views across a landscape of volcanoes and deep-blue lakes. Watch for peregrine falcons in the sky and for skunks and foxes—and even rare *pudú* deer or pumas—in the undergrowth.

Bring plenty of food and water; there are no shops in the park, and finding clean water in Sector Rucapillán can be a challenge. Bring camping equipment if you're attempting a multiday hike on your own. Permits are not required for camping, but try to camp on a spot that has been used previously to avoid damaging the undergrowth.

Orientation

Situated 10km north of Pucón, Parque Nacional Villarrica covers 63,000 hectares. Most people visit the very western side of the park, **Sector Rucapillán,** where Volcán Villarrica, the principal entrance, and the CONAF ranger station are located.

Two additional ranger stations are found in **Sector Quetrupillán,** southeast of Sector Rucapillán, accessed by the S-941, and **Sector Puesco,** the easternmost part of the park, accessed by Ruta 199 from Curarrehue.

Hiking

VILLARRICA TRAVERSE

The most popular route through the park is the **Villarrica Traverse,** a route starting at the CONAF ranger station at the base of the volcano in Sector Rucapillán, where you must register and pay an additional fee of CH$5,000. It links **Sendero Challupen Chinay, Sendero Estero Mocho,** and **Sendero Las Avutardas** as it crosses the park to form a challenging 81-km, six-day trek that climbs around Volcán Villarrica and Volcán Quetrupillán to end at the ranger station in Sector Puesco. At the end of the hike, you have to walk to reach Ruta 199, the road back to Pucón, where you can find public transportation.

Pucón-based **Travel Aid** (Asorena 425, local 4, tel. 45/2444 040 or 9/9353 6886, www.travelaid.cl) can organize transfers (up to 4 people, CH$45,000) from the end of the trek. They also rent out GPS devices and sell trekking maps of the park from their shop in Pucón. Carolyn McCarthy's *Trekking in the Patagonian Andes* hasn't been updated for years but still provides useful route information. The Spanish-language *Trekking Por Chile* by María Jesús Ossandón and Juan Pablo Gardeweg is the most recent description of the trek and can be purchased from Travel Aid. They can also help organize guides, which start from around CH$400,000, not including transfers, equipment, or food.

It's not recommended to attempt this hike outside December-March due to the chance of rainy or snowy weather. Before leaving, check in with the CONAF office in Pucón for updates on weather conditions and for a map of the route.

★ VOLCÁN VILLARRICA TREK

If you're fiercely adventurous, it's hard to pass up the opportunity to climb Volcán Villarrica, one of Chile's most active volcanoes. The ascent of this 2,847-meter stratovolcano is challenging but doesn't require technical expertise. Essential gear for the climb includes sturdy hiking boots, an ice ax, and a gas mask to avoid inhaling the noxious gases at the crater, so hikers should make the trip with one of several agencies based in Pucón.

Tours leave early in the morning from Pucón, driving to the Sector Rucapillán entrance. From the ranger station at the entrance, a 6-km drive winds up to the Centro de Ski Pucón, where a dusty trail of volcanic rock signals the beginning of the ascent. Climbers are offered the option of taking the ski lift (additional CH$10,000), if it's working, to save an hour's hiking time and 400 vertical meters.

From the top of the lift, it's a steep, grueling, six-hour clamber to the summit, where molten lava can be spied in the crater. The views from the top are startling: On a clear day, 360-degree panoramas take in at least seven other volcanoes and miles of countryside beyond. Unfortunately, bad weather is common and can force groups to turn back, particularly when high winds, snow, or poor visibility make continuing too dangerous. Elevated activity levels inside the crater also cause route closures.

Getting back down is significantly more pleasant: You'll slide down on a plastic sled along toboggan-style chutes through the snow, steering with your ice ax.

January-March, the number of people attempting the climb can reduce the fun of the experience, as queues of hikers 50 deep slog their way to the summit. Summer months have better weather and an increased chance of reaching the top, but September-October, when there's more residual snow, make the climb and the descent more interesting.

Tour prices range CH$85,000-100,000, including all equipment. An ice ax, gas mask, helmet, crampons, sturdy hiking shoes, thick waterproof pants and jacket, and a sled are included, as is insurance, the park entrance fee, and round-trip transportation. Drop by the office of your tour agency the night before to get fitted for your equipment. You will not be refunded if your group is forced to turn around before the summit. **Summit Chile** (Urrutia 585, tel. 45/2443 259, www.summitchile.org), **Patagonia Experience** (O'Higgins 461, tel. 45/2444 369, www.patagoniaexperience.cl), and **Aguaventura Expediciones** (Palguín 336, tel. 45/2444 246, www.aguaventura.com) have solid safety records, good-quality equipment, and English-speaking guides.

Skiing

CENTRO DE SKI PUCÓN

Only 20 minutes from Pucón on the northern slopes of Volcán Villarrica, the **Centro de Ski Pucón** (tel. 45/2441 901, www.skipucon.cl) offers the chance to ski down the edge of a steaming volcano. The 17 runs are best suited to beginners and intermediate skiers, and the sweeping views are sensational. The six lifts aren't all operational throughout the season. Bad weather at the top can regularly close the slopes, but the season is long, June-October. Prices start at CH$38,000 for a full-day lift pass, expensive for the quality of the services and the number of runs that are normally open. It's also possible to go snowshoeing (book through the resort). There's a café and lovely outdoor terrace at the main lodge that also boast terrific views.

It's easy to get here from Pucón, but you need your own vehicle with snow chains. In winter, a shuttle bus is sometimes available from Pucón to the lodge. For gear rentals, **Aguaventura Expediciones** (Palguín 336, tel. 45/2444 246, www.aguaventura.com) has good-quality skis and snowboards.

El Francés (O'Higgins 755) has slightly newer equipment, but that is reflected in the prices. Be aware of the quality of the equipment rented by other outfits, as many places haven't updated their gear since the 1970s.

Getting There

There is no public transport into the park. It's a 16-km, 30-minute drive or taxi ride (CH$20,000-25,000) from Pucón to the ranger station at the Volcán Villarrica entrance.

RESERVA BIOLÓGICA HUILO HUILO

A 98-km drive southeast from Villarrica, along breathtaking country roads that hug the forested shorelines of Lago Calafquén and Lago Panguipulli, **Reserva Biológica Huilo Huilo** (tel. 56/2335 5938, www.huilohuilo.com, CH$5,000-15,000 adults, CH$2,500-2,750 children) boasts a number of family-friendly outdoor activities. The landscape is enchanting and fragile. The reserve protects the increasingly rare Valdivian temperate rainforest and the resident fauna. The world's smallest deer, the *pudú,* is a possible sight here, alongside 81 species of bird and the endangered Darwin's frog.

Orientation

The reserve contains the villages of Neltume in the west and Puerto Fuy in the east, and Ruta 203 runs through the middle. Most services, including accommodations and the central visitors center, are on the road between Neltume and Puerto Fuy.

Sights

The surprisingly good **Museo de los Volcanes** (CH$3,000) has display cabinets brimming with maté gourds, plates, silverware, and riding equipment made and used by Mapuche craftspeople, alongside artifacts from 11 other indigenous cultures. The museum itself is a work of art, built into a hill and topped with a glass roof.

Learning about the Mapuche

The Araucanía region is home to some Mapuche communities that have opened themselves to tourism, providing a unique window into the heritage and ancestral traditions of this indigenous group.

The working Mapuche farm **Hostería Kila Leufú** (Km 23 Palguín Bajo, tel. 9/9876 4576 or 9/8791 1455, agrokilaleufu@gmail.com, from CH$12,000 pp dorm, CH$30,000-40,000 d, cash only) is owned by friendly matriarch Irma Epulef. Guests can take part in a variety of farm activities, including horseback riding and a traditional Mapuche cooking class. Irma only speaks Spanish and Mapudungun. Lodgings come in the form of dorms and private rooms, with breakfast included. Traditional Mapuche meals and other lunch and dinner options are available (CH$8,000 per meal); expect to dine with Irma and her family. Rates include IVA. The farm is 23km east of Pucón on Ruta 199, just beyond Palguín Bajo. Buses (every 20 min, 45min, CH$1,000) operated by **Trans Curarrehue** (Palguín 550, tel. 9/9273 1043) and **Buses Vipu-Ray** (Palguín 550, tel. 9/6835 5798) pass directly outside the farm on their way to Curarrehue.

Operating from Curarrehue, 38km east of Pucón, **Rutas Ancestrales Araucarias** (tel. 9/9541 2805, http://raaraucarias.com) is a cooperative of 30 Mapuche families. Take a weaving or traditional medicine class, spend the afternoon in the organic vegetable gardens learning about Mapuche farming, or take a multiday excursion into the nearby national parks. For multiday programs, lodging is in comfortable guesthouses in Mapuche communities. Prices start at CH$119,000 pp (min. 2 people), including transportation and lunch, although you will need to get to Curarrehue. Buses from Pucón (45min, CH$1,000) operated by **Trans Curarrehue** (Palguín 550, tel. 9/9273 1043) and **Buses Vipu-Ray** (Palguín 550, tel. 9/6835 5798) connect with Curarrehue every 20 minutes.

Recreation

The reserve has several easy self-guided hiking trails, all of which run 1-4km. The **Sendero Truful** (3.9km loop, 2hr) follows the Río Truful through a pristine forest. The picturesque and impressive Salto del Huilo Huilo, a waterfall that crashes into a series of turquoise pools, is reached by the **Sendero Huilo Huilo** (0.5km one-way, 15min), an easy hike along the Río Fuy. Watch for birds like the orange throated *chucao* and the red- or black-headed Magellanic woodpecker.

The **Teléferico Cóndor Andino** (noon-7pm Sat.-Sun., CH$10,000-12,000 adults, CH$5,000-6,000 children) is a cable car with sweeping views across the reserve and the snowy summit of Volcán Choshuenco. The trip takes 15 minutes.

Organized through the reserve, **horseback riding tours** with experienced guides range from one hour to all day, with no prior experience required. **Mountain bike rental** is available, with three trails for experienced riders, as well as easier trails for all

ages. Other reserve activities include **rafting** on the Río Fuy and **kayaking** on Pirihueico.

More extreme activities, such as climbing to the peak of Volcán Choshuenco, ice trekking on a glacier, or snowshoeing, can also be organized through the reserve. The reserve also has a spa that offers several treatments.

Food and Accommodations

For smaller budgets, Neltume and Puerto Fuy have affordable options, as well as a range of small restaurants with cheap *menús del día*. The nearest ATM is in Panguipulli. Services run by the reserve accept credit cards, but smaller accommodations and privately owned restaurants only accept cash.

The beer house and restaurant **Cerveceria Petermann** (Km 59 Ruta 203, no phone, 12:30pm-10:30pm Sun.-Thurs., 12:30pm-1am Fri.-Sat. summer, 12:30pm-7:30pm daily winter, CH$14,000) has a lovely sunny terrace with shade umbrellas, fairy lights, and rustic tree-trunk furniture. The simple menu has seven pizzas using local wild boar, trout, and cheese, plus four types of beer brewed on the premises. Service is variable.

One of the less pricey and less kitschy hotel offerings, **Hotel Marina del Fuy** (tel. 63/2672 111, http://huilohuilo.com, CH$135,000-155,000 d) is next to the port in Puerto Fuy and has 22 rooms. Standard rooms have views of the volcano, while superior rooms have views of the lake from a private balcony. All have modern furnishings of slate and wood. Service is good, but staff speak limited English. Breakfast and the on-site restaurant are disappointing for the price.

On the main road through Neltume, the privately owned domes at **Karü Domos del Fuy** (R-203, 429 Neltume, tel. 9/7758 7603, www.domosdelfuy.com, CH$45,000 d) have smart slate floors, polished wooden furniture, and windows at the top to allow the air to circulate—essential in summer. Each of the six domes has a private terrace, some looking onto Río Fuy, and comes with a fully equipped kitchen and board games for passing quiet evenings.

Just down the road out of Neltume, privately owned **Río Fuy** (R-203, Neltume, tel. 9/1330 230 or tel. 9/8426 7762, CH$5,000) has campsites, including some with wooden roofs to keep out the rain, as well as hot showers, barbecue facilities, and extremely friendly owners.

Few places can boast views like ★ **Cabañas Borgolafquén** (Km 16 R-203, tel. 9/4461 6902, www.borgolafquen.com, CH$145,000), outside the park on the banks of Lago Panguipulli. Cabins have large sunny terraces overlooking the lake, private barbecues, fully equipped kitchens, fireplaces, and modern decoration. Kayaks can be rented, and it's possible to bathe in the lake. Prices drop by 50 percent outside summer. Rates include IVA.

Getting There

It's easiest to get to the reserve with your own car. The most direct route from Villarrica is the road south to Panguipulli (50km, 50min), then east along Ruta 203, around the eastern banks of Lago Panguipulli. After 55km (50min) is the main entrance of the reserve. The total drive is 105km and takes about two hours. The reserve also operates its own expensive shared transfer service from the airports in Temuco and Puerto Montt; contact them for a quote.

Cabañas Borgolafquén

Valdivia and Vicinity

A small city at the confluence of Río Calle-Calle, Río Cruces, and Río Valdivia, Valdivia was founded by the Chilean governor Pedro de Valdivia. An important port during the colonial period, it was razed in the late 16th century by a Mapuche uprising, then became part of independent Chile in the 19th century. Many of the city's older buildings were destroyed in a 1960 earthquake.

Capital of Los Ríos, Valdivia is a pleasant and lively university city best known for its beer, courtesy of the German immigrants who settled the region, and is home to one of the country's largest breweries, along with a growing assortment of craft breweries. Along the coast north and south, pristine temperate rainforest and skeletal ruins of forts can be explored on day trips.

Valdivia is divided by the calm waters of the Río Valdivia. On the eastern bank, the Costanera, a pedestrianized walkway, is home to the lively **Feria Fluvial,** where fresh fish, fruit, and vegetables can be purchased from vendors. North of the market is a wooden plinth occupied by a colony of sea lions. They're most visible in the mornings and evenings, sunbathing or facing off against bold dogs.

Many restaurants, bars, and banks are near the **Plaza de la República** (bounded by O'Higgins, Letelier, Camilo Henríquez, and Maipú).

SIGHTS

West of the river, Isla Teja (Tile Island, where bricks and tiles were once produced) hosts Valdivia's main museums, including the **Museo Histórico y Anthropológico Mauricio Van de Maele** (Los Laureles, tel. 63/2293 840 or 63/2212 872, www.museosaustral.cl, 10am-1pm and 2pm-6pm Tues.-Sun., CH$1,500, joint ticket with the Museo de la Exploración R. A. Philippi CH$2,500). Head upstairs to see European,

Mapuche, and other indigenous pottery side-by-side; don't miss the stone flutes from the Pitrén people, dated to 300-1100 AD. Downstairs is dedicated to important figures from Valdivia's history, including Karl Anwandter, a German immigrant whose home this once was.

Next door, the **Museo de la Exploración R. A. Philippi** (Los Laureles, tel. 63/2293 840, www.museosaustral.cl, 10am-1pm and 2pm-6pm Tues.-Sun., CH$1,500, joint ticket with the Museo Histórico y Anthropológico Mauricio Van de Maele CH$2,500) explores the life and work of renowned German naturalist Rodolfo Amando Philippi, as well as relics from early German settlers.

Covering 30 hectares on the northern edge of Isla Teja, **Parque Saval** (Los Lingues, tel. 9/8856 9672 or 9/9690 1434, 8am-7pm daily, free) is a favorite among picnicking families on weekends and makes for a pleasant stroll through grassy woodlands and the Laguna de los Lotos, a pretty lake filled with blooming lilies. Across the road, the **Jardín Botánico** (Campus Isla Teja UACH, www.jardinbotanicouach.cl, 9am-7pm daily, free) is a well-maintained series of gardens within the campus of the Universidad Austral de Chile. Established in 1955, it contains over 950 plant species from all over the country.

Museo Submarino O'Brien

South of the Feria Fluvial and across a small wooden bridge, the excellent **Museo Submarino O'Brien** (Costanera, tel. 63/2219 690, 10:30am-12:50pm and 3pm-7pm daily Oct.-Apr., 10:30am-12:50pm and 3:10pm-6:20pm daily May-Sept., by tour only, CH$2,000 adults and children) is a decommissioned submarine submerged in the waters of the Río Calle-Calle. During the 40-minute guided tour (mostly in Spanish; some guides speak English) you learn about the vessel, constructed in 1971, which once contained

Valdivia

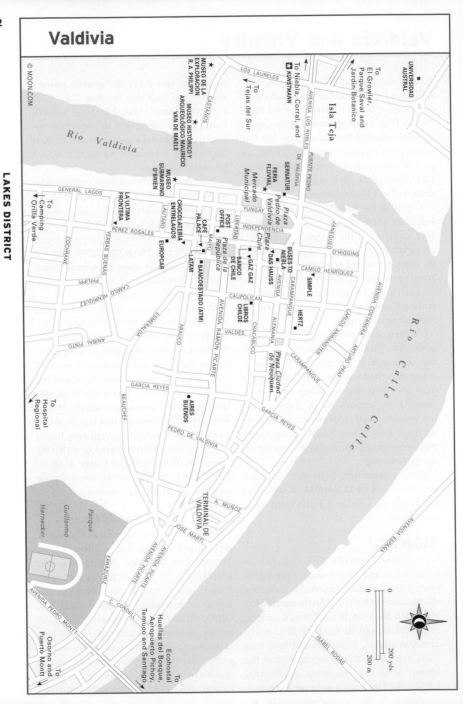

To Niebla, Corral, and
El Growler,
Parque Saval and
Jardín Botánico

UNIVERSIDAD
AUSTRAL

LOS LAURELES

KUNSTMANN

MUSEO DE LA
EXPLORACIÓN
R. A. PHILIPPI

CASTAÑOS

To
Tejas del Sur

AVENIDA LOS ROBLES

Isla Teja

MUSEO HISTÓRICO Y
ARQUEOLÓGICO MAURICIO
VAN DE MAELE

Río Valdivia

DE VALDIVIA

PUENTE PEDRO

MUSEO
SUBMARINO
O'BRIEN

SERNATUR

FERIA
FLUVIAL

Mercado
Municipal

Pedro de
Valdivia

Plaza

Plaza de
la
República

JANEQUEO

O'HIGGINS

GENERAL LAGOS

LA ULTIMA
FRONTERA

LAUTARO

YUNGAY

INDEPENDENCIA

CHILE

LIBERTAD

AVENIDA

CAMARINGUE

CAMILO HENRÍQUEZ

SIMPLE

HERTZ

To
Camping
Orilla Verde

CHOCOLATERÍA
ENTRELAGOS

CAFÉ
PALACE

POST
OFFICE

MAIPÚ

DAS HAUS

GAZ GAZ

BANCO
DE CHILE

ALEMANIA

CHACABUCO

PÉREZ ROSALES

EUROPCAR

LATAM

YERBAS BUENAS

CAUPOLICÁN

LIBROS
CHILOÉ

CARAMPANGUE

COCHRANE

BANCOESTADO (ATM)

ARAUCO

ESMERALDA

VALDÉS

Plaza Ciudad
de Neuquen.

AVENIDA COSTANERA

CARLOS ANWANDTER

ARTURO PRAT

Río
Calle
Calle

ANIBAL PINTO

PHIL.IPPI

CAMILO HENRÍQUEZ

AVENIDA RAMÓN PICARTE

GARCÍA REYES

GARCÍA REYES

BEAUCHEF

AIRES
BUENOS

PEDRO DE VALDIVIA

To
Hospital
Regional

Parque
Guillermo
Harnecker

A. MUÑOZ

TERMINAL DE
VALDIVIA

JOSÉ MARTÍ

AVENIDA PEDRO MONTT

ENRRAZURIZ

AVENIDA PICARTE

AVENIDA PICARTE

C. CONDELL

To
Osorno and
Puerto Montt

To
Ecohostal
Huellas del Bosque,
Aeropuerto Pichoy,
Temuco and Santiago

AVENIDA ESPAÑA

ISABEL RODAS

0   200 yds

0   200 m

a crew of 75. You'll visit the torpedo room, where still-active missiles are housed. This is not an experience for the claustrophobic. In summer it's a popular attraction, so get to the ticket office at 10am to get a spot on a tour later that day.

ENTERTAINMENT
Nightlife

The oldest café in Valdivia, **Café Palace** (Rosales 580, tel. 63/2213 539, 8am-4am Sun.-Thurs., 8am-5am Fri.-Sat.) offers breakfast through early-morning post-beer snacks. The sandwiches are enormous, but most folks come to drink beer, wine, and an extensive selection of spirits around the curved bar beneath the glitter ball.

Busy from around 12:30am, **Gaz Gaz** (Camilo Henríquez 436, no phone, 11pm-3:30am Weds.-Sat., CH$2,000) is the club of choice for the younger crowd, with two rooms offering different types of music. Expect everything from old-school classics to electronic music, cumbia, and live bands.

★ Kunstmann Brewery Tour

Valdivia's best-known brewery and one of Chile's longest established, **Kunstmann** (Ruta T-350 950, tel. 63/2292 969, www.cerveza-kunstmann.cl, noon-midnight daily) started in the back garden of the owners' house in 1991, before opening its present location in 1997. They now have 15 types of beer and regular beer tastings in the restaurant, plus hourly brewery tours from 12:15pm.

The two tours are Historia (CH$10,000), on the history of the brewery, and Elaboración (CH$15,000), to see the processes used to make the beer, from harvesting hops to the final product, with a tasting included. The restaurant has gone downhill in recent years; visit for a pint or to sample the beer flights, but skip the overpriced food.

Festivals and Events

Valdivia plays host to regular concerts, live music, theater, and cinema. Look for ads or pop into the tourist office to see the board with the week's events.

One weekend in October, a German-inspired **Oktoberfest** grips the city, when stalls with food and local craft beer, live music, and even classes on brewing spring up in Parque Saval. On the final weekend in January, it's **Bierfest Kuntsmann** (www.bierfestkunstmann.cl), an even more German-themed event, with German dancing, music, and food in Parque Saval, but this time with the beer of this Valdivian brewery giant dominating the bar.

FOOD

German heritage can be seen in the beer and the food in Valdivia, and the influence of the student population is felt in the prices. Many older restaurants and cafés are located within a few blocks of Plaza de la República, while cheaper student favorites are along Esmerelda and Caupolicán.

Chilean

Always jammed with students in the afternoon and evening, **La Ultima Frontera** (Vicente Pérez Rosales 787, tel. 63/2235 363, laultima_frontera@hotmail.com, 10am-2am Mon.-Thurs, 10am-3am Fri.-Sat., CH$4,000-6,000) is Valdivia's coolest café-bar, with three different rooms decorated with eclectic art, including dream catchers and Japanese parasols. There are picnic tables out front for the overflow, and it can be a scrum to get a table on weekends. Plenty of local beer and cheap eats include a range of sandwiches.

A classic Valdivian bar-diner, **Das Haus** (O'Higgins 394, tel. 63/2213 878, www.dashaus1959.cl, 8am-10pm Mon.-Sat., CH$2,000-4,000) serves the classic Valdivian snack *crudo,* basically meat tartare with onions. If you're unsure, start with the smaller 70-gram portion. They also have plentiful breakfasts, kuchen, hot dogs, and burgers served with the uniquely German-Chilean mix of sauerkraut and avocado. The booths and the sweeping bar on the right as you enter are the original 1959 section.

Expect to queue for a table after 8pm at the ever-popular ★ **El Growler** (Saelzer 99, tel. 63/2229 545, www.elgrowler.cl, 9am-1am daily, CH$6,000-12,000). It's an upmarket pub with 15 local beers on tap, which you can taste in a flight. The menu rangers from huge *baldes,* buckets of fish or sausages and fries to share, to seafood sautéed in beer. The bar staff are knowledgeable about the beer and can offer suggestions. You can reserve before 8pm daily; after that, it's first come, first served.

Light Bites

The decor is old-fashioned, but **Chocolatería Entrelagos** (Pérez Rosales 622, tel. 63/2218 333, 9am-10pm Mon.-Fri., 10am-10pm Sat., 11am-10pm Sun., CH$3,000-10,000), which opened in 1976, is a classic Valdivian café with sharing platters of meat, Peruvian-style fish, and specialty sandwiches and cakes (displayed next door in the chocolate shop and workshop). Here you can be served biscuits, truffles, pastries, or cakes by women in red dresses with white lace-edged pinafores.

With only a handful of seats, **Simple** (Camilo Henríquez 266, tel. 9/9590 8987, 7:30am-7pm Mon.-Sat., CH$2,000-5,000) lives up to its name, with a selection of decadent cakes, sandwiches, wraps, and empanadas in a modern, minimalist, but cozy setting. Service is friendly, and there are often deals on cakes and coffee. The selection of creamy and delicious artisanal ice creams is not to be missed.

ACCOMMODATIONS

The best of the few options in Valdivia are a short walk from the Plaza de la República and the Costanera. Wi-Fi, breakfast, and IVA are included, unless otherwise stated.

With good-size bedrooms on three floors and sustainable permaculture practices, ★ **AiresBuenos** (Garcia Reyes 550, tel. 63/222 2202, www.airesbuenos.cl, CH$12,000 dorm, CH$32,000 d private bath) is a gem of a hostel, with a laid-back vibe and helpful staff with local knowledge. Breakfast is a cut above normal hostel fare, including oats with yogurt, fruit, and freshly baked brown bread and jam. Communal areas include a music corner with guitars and a large kitchen overlooking the shady garden that's home to the resident duck.

In the owner's family home on the southern edge of Isla Teja, charming ★ **Tejas del Sur** (Las Arrayanes 490, tel. 9/9378 3389, CH$68,000 d) has two suites offering exceptional value. The house is beautifully decorated—note the Mapuche silverware on the stairway and the intricately weaved wall hangings. Service is warm and personal, with breakfast served in your room. Watch the hummingbirds sipping from the flowers in summer on the patio and garden out back.

A small number of campsites, each with a picnic table and access to a kitchen and dining area, can be found at **Camping Orilla Verde** (E Lillo 24, tel. 63/2433 902, CH$6,000), overlooking Río Valdivia. There are restrooms, hot showers, Wi-Fi, and a small space for parking. It's open year-round, and breakfast is not included. It's a short five-minute walk into town.

On the outskirts of Valdivia in pristine temperate rainforest, **Ecohostal Huellas del Bosque** (Parcela 14 Los Maitenes, tel. 63/2277 944 or 9/9553 0081, www.huellasdelbosque.cl, CH$54,000 d) has six large, simple bedrooms with magnificent oak beds and plenty of natural light. An ample buffet breakfast includes house-made free range eggs, butter, bread, jam, and cakes, and the fruit is picked from their own organic farm. They also offer *once* (additional fee), which sometimes includes wild-boar ham.

INFORMATION AND SERVICES

The SERNATUR-run **Oficina de Turismo** (Av. Arturo Prat, next to the Feria Fluvial, tel.63/2239 060, tel. www.descubrelosrios.cl, 9am-6pm Mon.-Fri, 10am-4pm Sat.-Sun., longer hours in summer) can advise on local festivals and events as well as transport to Niebla.

Banco de Chile (Letelier 300) and **Banco Estado** (Camilo Henríquez 562)

German Influences in Los Ríos and Los Lagos

Teatro del Lago in Frutillar

With the *colonización* law signed in 1845 by President Manuel Bulnes, Chile sought to attract skilled professionals to the region between Valdivia and Puerto Montt. From 1846 to 1875 there were 66 ships that sailed from Hamburg, Germany, a five-month trip across the Atlantic and around the dreaded Cape Horn. The first arrivals settled around Valdivia. An expedition led by German expatriate Bernard Eunom Phillip into the rainforest northeast of what is now Puerto Montt opened new lands, including Lago Llanquihue, and the next wave of German families set up cattle ranches and farms as well as the new towns of Puerto Octay and Frutillar on its shores.

The legacy of these settlers remains in Los Ríos and Los Lagos in the beer—Valdivia's first brewery, Cervecería Anwandter, was started by a German farmer in 1851—and in the desserts and cakes such as kuchen found in many good cafés.

Their influence can also be seen in architecture, with many notable buildings dating from the period, and the musical scene in the towns around Lago Llanquihue, culminating in the **Teatro del Lago** (Av. Philippi 1000, tel. 65/2422 900, www.teatrodellago.cl, performances starting at CH$15,000), Chile's top theater.

Learn more about the new arrivals and the machinery they brought with them from Europe at **Museo Colonial Alemán** (Av. Vincente Pérez Rosales, tel. 65/2621 142, 9:30am-7:30pm daily summer, 9:30am-5:30pm daily winter, CH$2,000 adults, CH$500 children) in Frutillar, with replica buildings of those constructed by the settlers, and the **Museo Histórico Municipal de Osorno** (Antonio Matta 809, tel. 64/2238 615, 9:30am-6pm Mon.-Fri., 2pm-6pm Sat.-Sun., free) in Puerto Octay, with excellent displays and English-language descriptions of life in the colonies.

have **24-hour ATMs.** The post office, **Correos** (O'Higgins 575, 9am-7pm Mon.-Fri., 9:30am-1pm Sat.), is on the southwestern corner of the Plaza de Armas. The **Hospital Regional** (Bueras 1003, tel. 63/2263 300, www.hbvaldivia.cl), 2km south of the Plaza de Armas, deals with medical emergencies.

GETTING THERE
Air

Situated 30km north of Valdivia along Ruta 202, **Aeropuerto Pichoy** (ZAL, San José de la Mariquina, tel. 63/2272 294) has daily flights from Santiago (1.5hr) with **LATAM** (tel. 600/5266 000, www.latam.com) and **Sky**

Airline (www.skyairline.com). LATAM has an office in Valdivia (Maipú 271, 9:30am-1:30pm and 3:30pm-6:30pm Mon.-Fri., 10am-1pm Sat.).

AIRPORT TRANSFER

From outside the terminal, **Transfer Aeropuerto Valdivia** (tel. 63/2225 533, www.transfervaldivia.cl) and **TPT Valdivia** (tel. 63/2218 133, www.tptvaldivia.com) run shared minivans to your hotel, costing CH$4,000 pp. Reservations are recommended. It's a 30-minute drive to the city center.

Car

To get to Valdivia from **Santiago,** it's a 900-km, 9-hour drive south on Ruta 5. From **Villarrica,** it's a 130-km, 2-hour drive southwest on Ruta 5 and Ruta 202. From **Osorno,** it's a 110-km, 1.5-hour drive north on Ruta 5 and Ruta 206.

Bus

The **Terminal de Valdivia** (Anfión Muñez 360, tel. 63/2220 498, www.terminalvaldivia.cl) is the main bus station in the city. Buses to Valdivia from **Osorno** (1.75hr, CH$3,800/CH$4,500) are operated by **Cruz del Sur** (tel. 63/2213 840, http://web.busescruzdelsur.cl) and **Buses Jac** (tel. 63/2268 404, www.jac.cl). Cruz del Sur also runs buses from **Puerto Montt** (every 1.5 hr, 3.5hr, CH$5,500), most of which stop in **Puerto Varas** (2.75hr, CH$5,000). Buses Jac have six daily connections with **Pucón** (3hr, CH$4,700). From **Santiago** (11hr, CH$15,000/CH$20,000), **Pullman Bus** (tel. 63/2224 669, www.pullmanbus.com), **Tur Bus,** and **Cruz del Sur** have around 13 daily departures, most of which leave after 7pm.

ONWARD TRAVEL

Buses from **Andesmar** (tel. 63/2207 948, www.andesmarchile.cl) leave for **Bariloche, Argentina** (5.5hr, CH$20,000/CH$30,000), at 8:15am daily.

GETTING AROUND

Valdivia is a compact city. Buses or taxis are only necessary to reach attractions southwest at Niebla. It's possible to flag down a taxi on the street, or call taxi company **Sagredo Transportes** (tel. 9/7381 9999, sagredotransporte@gmail.com). Rides should cost no more than CH$3,000.

Local buses, known as *micros,* cost CH$450 per journey, and those bound for Niebla can be picked up from Avenida Alemania just before the bridge onto Isla Teja.

Parking is difficult in the city. Cheaper accommodations don't offer on-site parking, but you can find gated parking spots in people's back gardens, where you'll be charged around CH$4,000 to store your car overnight.

Car Rental

Europcar (tel. 63/2558 670, www.europcar.cl, noon-4pm daily) and **Hertz** (tel. 63/2272 273, www.hertz.cl, 9:30am-5pm daily) offer car rental at Aeropuerto Pichoy. Rental offices within Valdivia include **Hertz** (Carampangue 488, tel. 63/2218 316, 8am-8pm Mon.-Fri., 9am-2pm Sat.), **Europcar** (Vicente Pérez Rosales 674, tel. 63/2558 660, 8:30am-1:30pm and 3pm-7pm Mon.-Fri., 9am-12:30pm Sat.), and **Assef y Mendez Rent a Car** (Gral. Lagos 1335, tel. 63/2213 205, www.assefymendez.cl, 9am-7pm Mon.-Sat.).

NIEBLA

Southwest of Valdivia on the coast, **Niebla** is a small community perfect for a day trip from Valdivia. Its once extensive fortifications were built to protect against English and Dutch privateers who ransacked coastal settlements.

The fortresses provide an interesting diversion for a couple of hours. Visiting in summer or on the weekend in winter, make sure to stop off for a crisp deep-fried prawn-and-cheese empanada or freshly cooked fish at the **Feria Costumbrista** (main road north out of Niebla, noon-11pm daily summer, noon-9pm

1: Feria Fluvial **2:** sea lion **3:** Museo de Sitio Fuerte Niebla **4:** Das Haus

Sat.-Sun. winter, CH$2,000), a covered food market that has delicious fresh seafood.

Accessed down a small dirt road opposite the Feria Costumbrista, **Playa Grande de Niebla** is a stunning strip of black sand that makes a perfect place for a quiet walk or a picnic, although the winds can be cold outside summer.

Museo de Sitio Fuerte Niebla

On the westernmost point of Niebla, with uninterrupted views of the sea, **Museo de Sitio Fuerte Niebla** (tel. 63/2282 084, www.museodeniebla.cl, 10am-6:30pm Tues.-Sun., free) is the remains of a fortress built by the Spanish to protect Valdivia, the "capital of the south seas," from the English and other European navies. Nowadays, only a few of the battlements remain, with a clutch of cannons in situ, but the views of the Pacific and south toward Corral give a good sense of its strategic location.

Metal walkways above the grass and the ruins allow you to explore the site, while the museum has information about the arrival of the Spanish and their interaction with the indigenous population, including a number of scale models of soldiers. The final room features a display of traditional handicrafts from Los Ríos, including wicker baskets, ponchos, and brooches. Guides dressed as Spanish admirals or pirates are on hand to give fascinating tours of the site (free) in Spanish and English; tips are expected.

Isla Mancera

Isla Mancera is a small, tranquil island just off the coast of Niebla that's accessed by boat. It was once the site of the city of Valdivia and is now home to 40 permanent residents.

There are no roads on the island, so it's only possible to explore on foot. On the northern tip of the island, the fort, **Castillo San Pedro de Alcántara** (tel. 63/2212 872, 10am-8pm daily in summer, 10am-1pm and 2pm-6pm Tues.-Sun., CH$700 in summer, free in winter), dates from 1645. Like the others in the region, it was built from volcanic *cancagua*

rock. Historic reenactments are held here on the grass in summer.

From the signposted **Muelle de Pasajeros** (passenger ferry terminal), 1km before you reach Niebla on the road from Valdivia, the **L/M Aylin** (10min, CH$300) leaves every 1.5 hours Monday-Saturday. **Local fishing boats** also offer the trip (10min, CH$1,000) roughly every 10 minutes, less frequently outside January-February. Boats leave less frequently Sunday. Buy tickets on board. You'll be dropped at the jetty on the island; it's a 300-meter walk up to the fort.

Corral

Across the Bay of Corral from Niebla, Corral is a smaller settlement with the **Castillo San Sebastián de la Cruz** (tel. 63/2471 824, 9am-5pm daily, CH$1,500), also built in 1645, with additional bulwarks added in later centuries, including the **Batería de la Argolla,** a cannon battery used to defend the fortress, and **La Cortina,** a large wall that helped join the fortress, making it the most impenetrable in the bay. In summer, daily reenactments depict an important part of Valdivia's history: the conflict for independence in which Chilean forces defeat the Spanish, with actors dressed in period outfits.

From the **Muelle de Pasajeros,** 1km before you reach Niebla on the road from Valdivia, **passenger boats** (20min, CH$1,000) with a capacity of 40 leave every 30 minutes. They drop you at the jetty in Corral, from where it's a 200-meter walk south along Calle Esmeralda to reach the entrance to the fort.

Getting There

To get to Niebla from Valdivia, take orange bus no. 20 from Avenida Alemania, just before the bridge to Isla Teja (every 15 min, 30min, CH$450). It'll drop you at the main road in Niebla. You can also ask to be dropped at the passenger ferry terminal, 1km before town, but don't confuse it with the car ferry terminal. The passenger ferry terminal also has a car park for those arriving by vehicle.

Osorno and Vicinity

Not to be confused with the volcano of the same name, Osorno is a busy city, 110km south of Valdivia, that acts as a transport hub for buses running north-south. It's also the backbone for transportation for local farmers. There's a surprising clutch of good restaurants and a pretty main plaza, but for visitors it's a good point from which to explore nearby Parque Nacional Puyehue and travel onward to lakeside Frutillar, Puerto Octay, and Puerto Varas, farther south.

The city's most recognizable building is the **Catédral San Mateo** (Antonio Matta, no phone, 8am-7pm daily) with a magnificent mosaic facade of the apostles in bright colors and vast stained glass windows above the doors. Inside, the two stones beneath the statue of Saint Matthew in the entrance are the only ones that survived when the original 1573 structure was razed in the 1604 Mapuche-led attacks that destroyed Osorno.

The **Museo Histórico Municipal de Osorno** (Antonio Matta 809, tel. 64/2238 615, www.extensioncultural.imo.cl, 9:30am-6pm Mon.-Fri., 2pm-6pm Sat.-Sun., free) has a room dedicated to archaeological and paleontological discoveries from the region and artifacts charting the history of the Huilliche, the southernmost culture of the Mapuche. Across the road, **Museo Artes Visuales Surazo** (Antonio Matta 812, tel. 64/2313 264, www.museosurazo.cl, hours vary Mon.-Fri., free) is an exhibition space for art, photography, and sculpture that holds regular cultural events such as book launches and live music.

FOOD AND ACCOMMODATIONS

While lodging options are severely limited, the food scene in Osorno is surprisingly good.

Combining the Chilean love of the sandwich with a hipster twist, **Gallardia Sambuchería Gurmé** (O'Higgins 1220, tel. 64/2221 011, 1pm-1am Tues.-Sat., 1pm-4pm Sun., CH$5,000-7,000) cooks tasty sandwiches with ingredients such as cilantro mayonnaise, turkey breast with a fizzy wine sauce, or salads with goat cheese, mango, and a pear balsamic vinegar. Housed in a large turquoise cabin with plenty of tables and cozy nooks for a comfortable lunch or dinner, the restaurant also has a front terrace with sun umbrellas.

In a large converted family house, **Hostel Vermont** (Toribio Medina 2020, tel. 64/2247 030, www.osorno.hostelvermont.cl, CH$15,000 dorm, CH$37,000 d shared bath) is the best budget option in town and a favorite among backpackers. There's a lovely outdoor roof terrace, ample communal areas that include a kitchen, and a much cozier vibe than is typical in this price range. There's central heating and the bedrooms are sizeable, but the hostel closes April-October. Rates include IVA.

INFORMATION AND SERVICES

The SERNATUR-run **Oficina de Turismo** has a room on the ground floor of the Edificio Gobernación (O'Higgins 667, tel. 64/2234 105, 9am-6pm Mon.-Fri.) that can supply maps and information about reaching Parque Nacional Puyehue, as well as information about the city. The municipal-run **Oficina de Turismo** (Plaza de Armas, 8:15am-2pm and 3pm-5:15pm Mon.-Fri., 10:30am-1:30pm Sat.) is less helpful, but it's open Saturday.

The post office, **Correos** (O'Higgins, next door to Edificio Gobernación, 9am-7pm Mon.-Fri., 9am-1pm Sat.) is on the Plaza de Armas. **BBVA** (Av. Mackenna 879), **Santander** (O'Higgins 707), and **Banco de Chile** (Antonio Matta 700) all have **24-hour ATMs** nearby. The **Hospital Base** (Antonio Matta 448, tel. 64/2336 200, www.hospitalbaseosorno.cl) in the south of town can provide medical attention.

TRANSPORTATION

Osorno is fairly compact, with most services a few blocks from the Plaza de Armas. While it's easy to get most places on foot, you can flag down taxis in the street.

Air

Aeropuerto Cañal Bajo Carlos Hott Sieber (ZOS, Ruta 215, tel. 64/2247 555) is 5km southeast of Osorno and has one daily connection with Santiago (1.5hr) via **LATAM** (www.latam.com) or **Sky Airline** (www.skyairline.com). LATAM has an office on the Plaza de Armas (9am-1:30pm, 3pm-6:30pm Mon.-Fri, 9:30am-1pm Sat). To get to the airport, **Vemoll** (tel. 64/2224 901) should charge no more than CH$3,000 for the 15-minute journey.

Bus

Osorno's **Terminal de Buses** (Errazuriz 1400, tel. 642/2234 149) offers regular connections to many cities and is a useful transport hub. Hourly buses from **Temuco** (3.5-4hr, CH$5,700/CH$6,500) and **Valdivia** (1.75hr, CH$3,800/CH$4,500) are offered by **Buses Jac** (tel. 64/2553 300, www.jac.cl) and **Cruz del Sur** (tel. 64/2232 777, http://web. busescruzdelsur.cl). From **Pucón** (2.5hr, CH$8,400), Buses Jac runs five daily buses. Cruz del Sur also has six departures daily from **Frutillar** (1.5hr, CH$1,800/CH$3,000) and hourly services from **Puerto Varas** (1.5hr, CH$2,000) and **Puerto Montt** (2hr, CH$2,200). **Turbus** (tel. 64/2234 170, www. turbus.cl) and **Buses ETM** (tel. 64/2207 903, www.etm.cl) have the most regular services from **Santiago** (10 daily, 10.5hr, CH$17,000/ CH$29,000) and **Valparaíso** (2 daily, 12hr, CH$20,000/CH$35,000). There are also small minibuses from **Puerto Octay** (every 20 min, 1hr, CH$1,500) offered by **Vía Octay** (tel. 64/2237 043) and from **Puerto Montt** (every 10 min, 1hr, CH$2,000), which are run by **Thaebus** (tel. 64/22207 038).

The small **rural bus terminal** within the Mercado Municipal (Errázuiz 1300), just down the street from the main terminal, has buses to Termas Aguas Calientes and Sector Agues Calientes of **Parque Nacional Puyehue** (1.5hr, CH$2,200). **Expresso Lago Puyehue** (tel. 64/2243 919, http:// expresolagopuyehue.wixsite.com/buses-expreso) depart more or less every hour daily.

Crossing into Argentina

From Osorno, it's 120km along the paved Ruta 125 to **Paso Cardenal Antonio Samoré** at the border with Argentina. It's open 8am-8am in summer and 8am-7pm in winter; it's 125km from there to reach **San Carlos de Bariloche.** To get to Bariloche via bus, **Andesmar** (tel. 64/2233 050, www. andesmarchile.cl) has 10am and 10:30am daily departures (4hr, CH$17,000/CH$25,000).

PARQUE NACIONAL PUYEHUE

Parque Nacional Puyehue (tel. 64/1974 572 or 64/1974 573, loslagos.oirs@conaf.cl, 9am-1pm and 2pm-6pm daily, admission varies by sector), located in the pre-cordillera and cordillera of the Andes Mountains 80km east of Osorno, is best known for the hot springs at the Termas Aguas Calientes resort. However, the park's glacial valleys, volcanoes, and Valdivian temperate rainforest provide rich scenery.

Volcán Puyehue and Volcán Casablanca, the park's two volcanoes, have left a savage mark: In 2011, Volcán Puyehue erupted after 51 years of dormancy, causing thousands of people to evacuate. Ash billowing out of the crater forced flight cancellations as far away as Australia. The sheer quantity of ash radically changed the face of the park, producing dust flows that left many formerly lush sections barren.

Hikers should take safety precautions for rainy and sometimes snowy conditions. Register with the CONAF offices at Sector Aguas Calientes and Sector Anticura, and heed the advice of park officials on weather conditions.

Orientation

The park's three main sectors are **Sector Aguas Calientes,** in the west, closest to Osorno; **Sector Antillanca,** south of Aguas Calientes; and **Sector Anticura,** northeast of the other two. Sector Anticura has the greatest range of hiking trails, including some long and challenging multiday treks.

In Sector Aguas Calientes, 4km after the turnoff from Ruta 215, the **CONAF ranger office** (next to Termas Aguas Calientes, tel. 64/1974 572 or 64/1974 573, loslagos.oirs@conaf.cl, 9am-1pm and 2pm-6pm daily, free) marks the entrance to the park and is the administrative center for Sector Aguas Calientes and Sector Antillanca. It has a useful **information center** and a museum about the region's fauna and flora.

In Sector Anticura is a **CONAF ranger office** (Km 90 Ruta 215, no phone, 9am-1pm and 2pm-6pm daily). Across the road is the **Centro Turístico Anticura** (tel. 9/9104 8061 or 9/7215 0060, www.anticura.com), where the CH$1,500 entrance fee for this part of the park is charged.

Hot Springs

Next to the ranger station are the **Termas Aguas Calientes** (Km 76 R-215, tel. 64/2331 700 or 64/2331 785, www.termasaguascalientes.cl, 8:30am-8pm daily, CH$7,000-17,000). You might feel like a sardine in a tin during summer; these crowded hot springs lack the rustic charm or finesse of those around Pucón. They are more pleasant outside January-February, both for the cooler weather and the lack of other bathers. An indoor and an outdoor pool are in a scenic spot beside the river and naturally heated to 38-39°C. They are popular with families and those seeking relief from arthritis. There's a small café on-site serving basic but overpriced sandwiches and snacks, and a more formal, even more expensive restaurant across the road. You're better off bringing your own food and drink.

Hiking

Before hiking along any of the park's trails, you must register with a ranger at the **CONAF ranger office** (next to Termas Aguas Calientes, tel. 64/1974 572 or 64/1974 573, loslagos.oirs@conaf.cl, 9am-1pm and 2pm-6pm daily, free) in Sector Aguas Calientes, which can also provide you with maps and information about the routes.

Shorter trails in Sector Anticura, which start from the Centro Turístico Anticura, include **Sendero del Indo** (2km round-trip, 1hr), an easy walk that brings you to a breathtaking waterfall on the Río Golgol, and **Sendero La Princesa** (1.6km, 30min), an easy meander through the rainforest to a small set of waterfalls.

Skiing

Small in size but scenic, **Ski Antillanca** (tel. 64/2612 070, www.antillanca.cl, full-day lift ticket CH$35,000 adults, CH$20,000 children) is on the slopes of Volcán Casablanca in Sector Antillanca. Its 400 skiable hectares have 14 mostly intermediate runs, but backcountry routes ascend to the summit for spectacular views across the surrounding mountains. With far fewer visitors than other nearby ski resorts, many come here to appreciate the peacefulness as much as the snow, which is variable in quality due to the low elevation. The ski season generally runs mid-June-September.

Ski equipment can be rented and there's a cafeteria serving snacks, a more formal restaurant, and the rustic and overpriced Hotel Antillanca. During summer, short trails are good for hiking or mountain biking, while nearby lakes provide fly-fishing opportunities.

In winter, the resort can organize **private shuttles** from Osorno (tel. 9/7997 4731, CH$160,000, up to 16 passengers). In your own vehicle, from the ranger station at Aguas Calientes (78km, 1hr from Osorno), it's 18km (30min) south along the gravel road, for which you will need a high-clearance vehicle and snow chains.

Food and Accommodations

Turística Aguas Calientes is the concession-aire in Sector Aguas Calientes, and its lodgings are all overpriced. Lodgings in Sector Anticura are more reasonable, but you need a vehicle to get here. If traveling with your own vehicle, it's worth staying outside the park to avoid the crowds and the inflated prices.

A popular weekend getaway from Osorno, German-owned **Cervecería Armin Schmid** (R-215 10480, tel. 9/8294 1818, 1:30am-10:30pm Tues.-Sat., CH$6,000-8,000) has a large beer garden and classic German dishes and pizzas to eat with the house-made brews. The indoor dining area is snug, so be sure to reserve ahead for the evening. Look for the Chilean flags on the right side coming from Osorno, then turn onto a gravel road at the red metal building.

A few hundred meters from the hot springs, 17 geodesic domes are hidden in the woods at **Domos Termas Aguas Calientes** (Km 76 R-215, tel. 64/2331 700 or 64/2331 785, www.termasaguascalientes.cl, CH$70,000 d shared bath, CH$90,000 d private bath), giving them far more privacy than the cabins near the main office. They're also the most reasonably priced, and the rates are halved during the week. Although the furniture is not the quality you'd expect at these rates, rooms include a fridge, a heater, and a fan—essential during summer—and a king bed with views across the river. Rates include IVA. Within the same grounds is expensive **Camping Chanleufuâ** (Km 76 R-215, tel. 64/2331 700 or 64/2331 785, www.termasaguascalientes.cl, Dec.-May only, CH$30,000/site), with access to hot water and picnic tables. RVs are welcome. Rates include IVA.

In Sector Anticura at the Centro Turístico Anticura, **Cabañas Anticura** (Km 90 R-215, tel. 9/9104 8061 or 9/7215 0060, www.anticura.com, CH$45,000) are fully equipped cabins with woodstoves and kitchens. On the same grounds is the 200-site **Camping Catrue** (CH$15,000/site for 1-2 people), in the forest and with 24-hour hot showers and fire pits. Rates include IVA.

Ecolodge & Cabañas Las Juntas (Km 58 Ruta 215, tel. 9/5148 4767 or 9/9802 1059, www.lasjuntas.com, CH$74,000 d) is a charming hotel on the banks of Lago Puyehue. Three of the double rooms have lake views, and the wide terrace is a quiet place to absorb the peak. Rooms are simply furnished but spotless. The owners live on-site and are welcoming, with a shot of homemade wheatgrass liquor and an hour of kayaking included. Rates include IVA.

Information and Services

The **CONAF ranger office** (next door to Termas Aguas Calientes, tel. 64/1974 572 or tel. 64/1974 573, loslagos.oirs@conaf.cl, 9am-1pm and 2pm-6pm daily, free) is the best place for information about the trails and to get maps for longer hikes.

Patagonia Expeditions (tel. 9/9104 8061) helps administer Sector Anticura, offering guided treks to Volcán Puyehue (CH$60,000 pp) and Volcán Casablanca (CH$40,000 pp), including lunch and pickup from your hotel in Osorno.

Getting There

It's an 80-km, one-hour drive to the park from Osorno. Take Ruta 215 east for 75km, then turn right at the signposted road for Termas Aguas Calientes and Sector Aguas Calientes, 4km farther. The road continues to Sector Antillanca, 18km south. For Sector Anticura, continue along Ruta 215 for 17km to the park entrance. Osorno's small **rural bus terminal,** within the Mercado Municipal (Errázuiz 1300), just down the street from the Terminal de Buses, has departures for Termas Aguas Calientes and Sector Agues Calientes with **Expresso Lago Puyehue** (tel. 64/2243 919, http://expresolagopuyehue.wixsite.com/buses) that leave more or less every hour daily (1.5hr, CH$2,200). To reach Sector Anticura by public transport, take the turnoff for Aguas Calientes and hitchhike the final 17km.

Puerto Varas

On the banks of Chile's second-largest lake, Lago Llanquihue, with views of Volcán Osorno and Volcán Calbuco, Puerto Varas is the most vibrant and most visited of the towns in Los Lagos. It is home to an artsy crowd of expats and ex-Santiaguinos and has long been a popular destination for Chileans in summer, when you'll have book rooms and restaurants in advance.

This picturesque town, with German-inspired architecture and pretty lakeside surroundings, has recently become the tourist hub of Los Lagos, usurping drab Puerto Montt, which is strategically better located for traveling on to the Carretera Austral or Chiloé in the south, or north to Los Ríos.

Puerto Varas is alive with events and festivals, and its restaurants offer some of the south's best dining. Within day-trip distance are the village of Frutillar and Parque Nacional Vicente Pérez Rosales, Chile's oldest national park.

ORIENTATION

Puerto Varas is on the southwestern shore of the Lago Llanquihue. Most services are within a few blocks of the small **Plaza de Armas** and along Del Salvador. From Ruta 225, which starts as Gramado in the west and becomes San José through the center of town, Puerto Varas gradually climbs into hilly residential neighborhoods, where most of the accommodations are. This road continues east toward Parque Nacional Vicente Pérez Rosales and the border with Argentina.

SIGHTS

The **Plaza de Armas** (bounded by Santa Rosa, San José, San Juan, and Del Salvador) is underwhelming, but the covered section of Santa Rosa hosts music and other cultural events year-round. From here it's one block east to the **Costanera,** the paved walkway that runs the length of the town, with Vicente Pérez Rosales (Ruta 225) on one side and the lake on the other. Lots of traffic passes alongside, but the artificial beaches of black sand are crowded in summer. The beaches extend from where Santa Rosa and Turismo meet on the northern edge of the lake to the point where the road leaves town.

The eccentric **Museo Pablo Fierro** (Ruta 225, tel. 9/6703 447, www.pablofierro.cl, 9:30am-1pm and 3pm-8pm Mon.-Sat., donation) showcases bric-a-brac by the owner, Pablo Fierro, a local artist. Housed in a former pump house, the collection features random objects, from traffic lights to carriage wheels and scales. Check out the interactive rooms, where the artist's own paintings of birds are displayed while a soundtrack of birdsong plays and a huge wooden ibis peers from a hole in the wall.

Puerto Varas is home to some beautiful Germanic buildings, including the 1914 **Casa Kuschel** (Kenner 299), a dramatic wooden mansion with a domed turret; the modest 1905 **Casa Götschlich** (Otto Bader 701), with wooden tiles; and the two-story 1932 **Casa Yunge** (San Ignacio 711), also in wooden tiles. The **Paseo Patrimonial,** a two-hour self-guided walking tour, takes you to these and other historic buildings, many of which are now private residences that have explanatory signs outside. Pick up maps from the **Oficina de Turismo** (Del Salvador 320, tel. 65/2361 175, 8:30am-9pm daily summer, 8:30am-7pm Mon.-Fri., 10am-2pm and 3pm-7pm Sat.-Sun. winter).

The **Iglesia del Sagrado Corazón de Jesús** (San Francisco and María Brunn) is Puerto Varas's most recognizable building but is not open to the public. Built in 1915 in a Romanesque Revival and baroque style, the church's red steeple spears the sky, while the edges of its windows are lined with iron plates that contrast the sheer white of the main building.

Puerto Varas

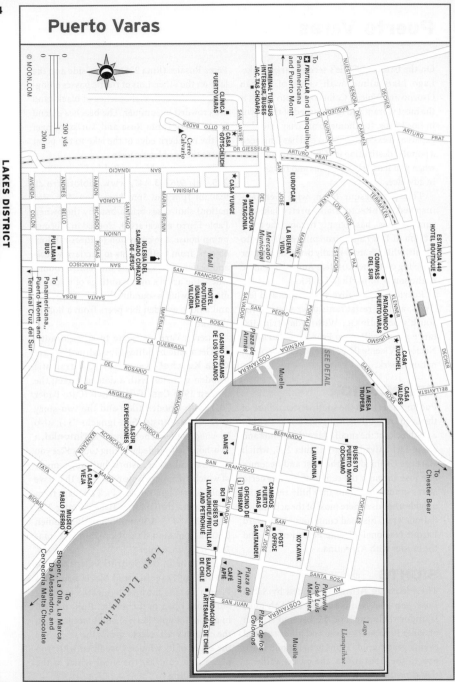

© MOON.COM

0   200 yds
0   200 m

To FRUTILLAR and Llanquihue,
Panamericana and Puerto Montt

TERMINAL TUR-BUS
(INTERSUR, BUSES
JAC, TAS CHOAPA)

CLINICA
PUERTO VARAS

CASA
GOTSCHLICH

Cerro
Calvario

DR OTTO BADER

SAN JAVIER

DR GIESSELER

ARTURO PRAT

DECHER

ARTURO PRAT

NUESTRA SEÑORA DEL CARMEN

BAQUEDANO

QUINTANILLA

ESTANCIA 440
HOTEL BOUTIQUE

SAN IGNACIO

PURISIMA

CASA YUNGE

MARGOUYA
PATAGONIA

MARIA BRUNN

DEL SALVADOR

SAN JOSÉ

EUROPCAR

LA BUENA
VIDA

Mercado
Municipal

MARTINEZ

ESTACION

LOS TILOS

WALKER

LA PAZ

TERRAPLEN

KLENNER

COMPASS
DEL SUR

PATAGÓNICO
PUERTO VARAS

CASA
KUSCHEL

AVENIDA

ANDRES

COLON

BELLO

RAMON

RICARDO

SANTIAGO

FLORIDA

ROSAS

UNION

SAN FRANCISCO

SANTA
ROSA

PULLMAN
BUS

IGLESIA DEL
SAGRADO CORAZON
DE JESUS

Mall

SAN FRANCISCO

HOTEL
BOUTIQUE
IGNACIA
VILLORIA

SANTA ROSA

IMPERIAL

CASINO DREAMS
DE LOS VOLCANOS

SAN
PEDRO

SAN
SALVADOR

PORTALES

Plaza de
Armas

AVENIDA COSTANERA

Muelle

SEE DETAIL

To
Panamericana,
Puerto Montt, and
Terminal Cruz del Sur

LA QUEBRADA

DEL ROSARIO

LOS ANGELES

MIRADOR

CONDOR

ALSUR
EXPEDICIONES

ACONCAGUA

MANZANA

ITATA

LA CASA
VIEJA

MAIPO

BIOBIO

MUSEO
PABLO FIERRO

To
Shoper, La Olla, La Marca,
Da Alessandro, and
Cervecería Malta Chocolate

COMPASS DEL SUR

SANTA
VALDÉS

SANTA
ROSA

BELLAVISTA

DECHER

LA MESA
TROPERA

To
Chester Bear

Lago Llanquihue

DETAIL

SAN BERNARDO

DANE'S

LAVANDINA

SAN FRANCISCO

BUSES TO
PUERTO MONTT/
COCHAMÓ

CAMBIOS
PUERTO
VARAS

OFICINO DE
TURISMO

DEL SALVADOR

BCI

BUSES TO
LLANQUIHUE/FRUTILLAR
AND PETROHUE

SANTANDER

SAN JOSÉ

POST
OFFICE

KOYAKAK

SAN
PEDRO

PORTALES

BANCO
DE CHILE

CAFÉ
APIE

Plaza de
Armas

SANTA ROSA

AV COSTANERA

Plazuela
José Luis
Martínez

FUNDACIÓN
ARTESANÍAS DE CHILE

SAN JUAN

Plaza de
los Colomos

Muelle

Lago
Llanquihue

ENTERTAINMENT

Many of the town's cultural events are held in the larger hotels, such as **Patagonico Puerto Varas** (Klener 349, tel. 65/2201 000), which has ample exhibition space for food and drinks events. In the center of town, on the western side of the Plaza de Armas, the **covered section of Santa Rosa,** once a food court, is used year-round, peaking in February, for music, theater, and food and beer events, many of which are free to enter. Municipal-led events, including craft fairs, are held in the building that houses the restaurant Mesa Tropera.

Casino Dreams de los Volcanes (Del Salvador 21, tel. 65/2249 2000) has regular live concerts and rotating art displays on the 2nd floor.

Nightlife

Puerto Varas has calmer nightlife than tourist destinations like Pucón. Skip the food and go straight for the beer at **Shoper** (Vicente Pérez Rosales 1117, tel. 65/2235 534, noon-midnight daily summer, 4pm-midnight daily winter), where there's an unrivaled selection. It's a favorite watering hole for locals, as its covered terrace has romantic views for sunset. Inside, there's a big-screen TV for sports.

Try four award-winning beers on tap at **Chester Beer** (Camino Línea Nueva 93, tel. 9/4287 2341, www.chesterbeer.cl, 3pm-7pm daily summer), a makeshift bar behind a shipping container. There are few places to sit but great lake views, and you can snap photos of the owners' VW vans. In summer, their "beer bus" has a couple of daily departures from the old train station (Estación Trenes, Klener 348-350) in Puerto Varas to the brewery.

Busy from midnight onward, **La Buena Vida** (Walker Martínez 551, tel. 9/9700 8843, 7pm-1:30am Tues.-Wed., 8pm-3:30am Thurs., 8pm-4:30am Fri.-Sat.) is Puerto Varas's main live music venue, with karaoke Tuesday. Thursday-Saturday feature jazz, blues, electronic music, or rock. It feels a bit formal, with tables in the middle and sofas on the edge, but after a couple of drinks you'll be up dancing.

SHOPPING

Part of a fair-trade nonprofit network around Chile that creates opportunities for craftspeople and artisans across the country, the **Fundación Artesanías de Chile** (Del Salvador 109, tel. 65/2346 332, www.artesaniasdechile.cl, 9am-9pm daily in summer, 10:30pm-7pm daily in winter) has pottery, wooden crafts, woven ponchos and other textiles, and silverware made by Chilean artisans.

RECREATION

Puerto Varas has become a top outdoor adventure destination, with activities on the lake, on the slopes of Volcán Osorno, and in Parque Nacional Vicente Pérez Rosales and Valle de Cochamó. Conditions are best September-April; outside these months is persistent rain and sometimes snow.

CYCLING

From Puerto Varas it's possible to cycle the old railway north to Frutillar, a tough 32-km slog through Llanquihue, a small settlement between the two towns, along mainly dirt roads with excellent views. From the east side of town, take the cycle path along Ruta 225 to Ensenada, a village just before the turnoff for Petrohué, where you cycle the Paso Desolación trail that connects the northern slopes of Volcán Osorno with Lago Todos Los Santos. For avid cyclists, it's also possible to loop Lago Llanquihue, a distance of 100km.

Rent mountain bikes at **Austral Bikes** (Centro Comercial Doña Ema 32, tel. 65/2868 228, 10am-8pm daily), on the eastern edge of town, from CH$6,000 for two hours, and at **La Comarca** (Vicente Pérez Rosales, tel. 9/9799 1920, www.pueloadventure.cl, 9am-7pm Mon.-Fri., 9am-1:30pm Sat.) for CH$10,000 per half day. La Comarca runs cycle tours (CH$77,000), starting at their offices and including bike rental, the tour guide, and transportation back to Puerto Varas.

HIKING

Nearby **Parque Nacional Vicente Pérez Rosales** and **Valle de Cochamó** offer the best hiking trails. Although they're easily hiked on your own, various agencies in Puerto Varas offer guided tours. It's also possible to do a guided ascent to the 2,652-meter summit of **Volcán Osorno,** a challenging climb requiring technical ice climbing expertise or an experienced guide.

Well-established **ALSUR Expediciones** (Aconcagua and Imperial, tel. 65/2232 300 www.alsurexpeditions.com) has an excellent safety record, qualified guides, good quality equipment, hotel pickups, and insurance; it's a one-stop shop for most adventure activities in the region. They offer half- and full-day hikes in Parque Nacional Vicente Pérez Rosales as well as trips to summit Volcán Osorno (CH$192,000 pp). ALSUR also runs full-day ascents of **Volcán Calbuco** (CH$192,000 pp) on horseback and on foot, with hostel pickup, transportation to the trailhead, and lunch.

RAFTING AND KAYAKING

The best agencies for water sports are **Ko'Kayak** (San Pedro 311, tel. 65/2233 004, www.kokayak.cl) and **ALSUR Expediciones** (Aconcagua and Imperial, tel. 65/2232 300 www.alsurexpeditions.com), and the most popular water sport is **rafting** (CH$35,000, including a snack) through the Class III and IV rapids of Río Petrohué, just above the Saltos del Petrohué, where water crashes over the weathered basalt formed by ancient lava flows from Volcán Osorno. There are also half-day **ducky tours** (kayaking in an inflatable two-person kayak with your guide seated behind you) along the same stretch, for those without previous experience.

Half-day **kayaking tours** run on Laguna Escondida, a lake surrounded by dense woodland and wetlands, or a two-day trip along the Río Puelo, which connects Lago Todos Los Santos with the Estero Reloncaví and the town of Cochamó. Tours include hotel pickup, equipment rental, and a snack or full lunch. Full-day tours start at CH$70,000.

SKIING

With 10 runs, the **Centro de Esquí Volcán Osorno** (tel. 9/6679 2284, www.volcanosorno.com, 10am-7pm daily in summer, 8:30am-9pm in winter, full-day lift pass CH$26,000 adults, CH$17,000 children) on the southern flanks of Volcán Osorno makes a good winter day trip. In summer, the ski lifts operate to take you to marvelous views at the top. Ski rental (CH$20,000 per day for full equipment) and tubing and snowshoe tours (CH$15,000/30min) are available. You'll need your own vehicle to get here, 59km east of Puerto Varas, on the paved V-555 that winds up to the car park.

FOOD

The range and quality of restaurants in Puerto Varas make it a top dining hub in the country, although the food is pricier than in other local towns.

Chilean

Local consensus holds that ★ **La Olla** (just before the road bends north out of Puerto Varas, Ruta 225, tel. 65/2233 540, noon-10:30pm Mon.-Sat., CH$7,000-15,000) is Puerto Varas's top seafood restaurant, and the queue snakes out the door on weekends. It's worth making a reservation for the chance of settling down to a feast of *machas a la parmesan* (razor clams with parmesan), juicy seafood empanadas, and huge platters of fried *congrio* (conger eel) and pan-fried *merluza* (hake). The decor is stuck in the 1980s, but the food speaks for itself.

With slick service from smartly dressed waitstaff and large windows with views across the lake, **Casa Valdés** (Santa Rosa 40, tel. 9/9079 3938, 12:30pm-4pm and 7pm-11pm Mon.-Sat., 1pm-4:30pm and 7pm-10pm Sun., CH$6,500-10,000) has more fancy food and unusual dishes than most restaurants in town, with the chef reimagining Chilean seafood. The conger eel cheeks sautéed in butter are not to be missed.

Offering traditional Italian fare with no pretense, ★ **La Mesa Tropera** (Santa Rosa

161, tel. 65/2237 973, www.mesatropera.cl, 10am-2am Mon.-Sat., CH$6,000-9,000) is Patagonia-Italian fusion with pizza toppings such as spit-roasted lamb, cilantro, prawns, red onion, and *merkén*. The views are the best of any restaurant in Puerto Varas, perched *palafito*-style on wooden stilts over Lago Llanquihue with wide windows. Sample the excellent beer, Tropera. You can't make reservations, so be prepared to wait for a table.

International

With traditional Chilean dishes such as *caldillo de congrio* (conger eel soup) and *pastel del choclo* (corn and meat pie), **La Marca** (Ruta 225, east of Puerto Varas, tel. 65/2232 026, noon-11:30pm Tues.-Sat., noon-5pm Sun., CH$7,000-14,000) is better known for tenderloin, rump, and rib-eye steak. Chilean *huaso* (cowboy) stirrups and whips adorn the lofty wooden cabin and give it a rustic edge, but the English-speaking staff and excellent service make it a wonderful blend of Chilean *campo* and fine dining.

The three-beer microbrewery—one of a few in Los Lagos—**Cervecería Malta Chocolate** (Km 7 Ruta 225, tel. 9/9539 3631, 12:30pm-midnight Tues.-Sat., 12:30pm-8pm Sun., CH$7,000-12,000) is on the shore of Lago Llanquihue, 12km west of Puerto Varas. Accompanying the beer are simple wood-fired pizzas, gourmet burgers, ceviche, and meat sharing platters. There's not much seating, and it can get unpleasantly windy outside, so get here early for lunch and dinner on the weekend to get an indoor table.

With decent pizzas and pastas, **Da Alessandro** (Vicente Pérez Rosales 1156-1250, tel. 65/2310 583, 12:30pm-11pm daily, CH$7,000-12,000) combines hearty Italian food with a modern dining area of blue-and-white gingham tablecloths and good views of the lake from the terrace. The four-cheese sauce over ham-filled pasta makes a gloriously cheesy feast.

Cafés and Light Bites

With pinstriped cream and lemon walls and waiters with bow ties, **Dane's** (Del Salvador 441, tel. 65/2232 371, 7:30am-10:30pm daily, CH$1,300-4,500) is a smart little café with traditional Chilean sandwiches and juices, although it's really all about their excellent empanadas, small but oozing with cheese; order a couple.

A tiny coffee truck with a location on Plaza de Armas and another outside the mall, **Café Apié** (Santa Rosa on Plaza de Armas; San Francisco and Pío Nono, tel. 65/2237 694, 9am-9pm Mon.-Fri, 10am-9pm Sat.-Sun) has tasty roasted Colombian coffee from a proper coffee machine with plenty of syrups to add flavor, plus hot chocolate.

ACCOMMODATIONS

Puerto Varas has some of the best, and consequently most expensive, accommodations in Los Lagos. Expect prices to spike significantly in January-February, when flocks of Chileans from the drier parts of the country descend for summer holidays. There are superb options in town, but if you have your own vehicle, consider one of the cabins or hotels that line Lago Llanquihue, with better value and more spectacular views.

In Puerto Varas

UNDER CH$25,000

Tiny but very sociable and a good bet for individual travelers, **La Casa Vieja** (Imperial 632, tel. 9/5375 5311, casaviejapv@gmail.com, CH$8,000 camping, CH$12,000 dorm) has accommodations in four dormitories, each small and with shocking purple and green decor. Everything is spotlessly clean and owner Carolina speaks perfect English. She used to work as a tour guide and has comprehensive knowledge of surrounding attractions. There's space for four tents in the large back garden. Rates include IVA.

CH$25,000-40,000

There's not much communal space, but **Margouya Patagonia** (Purísima 681, tel. 65/2237 695, http://mapatagonia.cl, CH$11,000 dorm, CH$32,000 d shared bath) has sizeable rooms on two floors and a sociable atmosphere, making it popular among young backpackers. They offer kayaking, horseback riding, and rafting tours as well as trips to Volcán Osorno and Parque Nacional Vicente Pérez Rosales. They also rent out new mountain bikes at reasonable prices. Rates include IVA.

My favorite Puerto Varas hostel, and the town's most comfortable and convivial, is Swedish-Chilean-run ★ **Compass del Sur** (Klenner 467, tel. 65/2232 044 or 9/7648 6787, www.compassdelsur.cl, CH$10,000 camping, CH$14,000 dorm, CH$39,000 d shared bath, CH$46,000 d private bath), a home away from home on a quiet road a few blocks north of the main road. Most of the rooms have en suite baths, and the communal kitchen and dining spaces are sizeable. There's space for tents and parking in the back garden, and a secure luggage room. They can recommend activities, and one of the owners, Mauricio, leads hiking tours to lesser-known destinations such as Lago Cayuhue as well as day trips to Chiloé.

CH$40,000-60,000

On the hill above Del Salvador and accessed via a dirt track off Santa Rosa, **Hotel Boutique Ignacia Villoria** (Santa Rosa 714, tel. 65/2232 897, www.hotelignaciavilloria. cl, CH$48,600 d) is a small budget hotel with views across the lake from the terrace and breakfast room, where a sizeable breakfast buffet is served. Rooms are dated, with functional, old-fashioned baths. The owner is very friendly and welcoming. There's ample parking at the back of the hotel.

CH$60,000-80,000

In a traditional German mansion and decorated in homage to ranch life, **Estancia 440 Hotel Boutique** (Decher 440, tel. 65/2233 921 or 65/2555 0432, www.estancia440.cl, CH$72,000 d) marries elegant rustic decor with absolute comfort in each of its seven bedrooms. Don't miss the photos of Chilean ranch hands above the stairs, once featured in

National Geographic. Breakfast is served on the grand wooden dining table, while communal spaces such as a small kitchen, a terrace with a sun lounger, a hot tub, and a sofa room beneath the house offer plenty of places for relaxing. Exceptionally personalized service makes this feel more like a luxurious home than a hotel. Rates include IVA.

Around Puerto Varas
OVER CH$80,000

A dozen kilometers north of Puerto Varas on stilts over the banks of Laguna Pichilaguna, the four spectacular cabins of ★ **Gracias a la Vida** (Parcela 44 Pichilaguna, tel. 9/9826 1268, www.graciasalavidalodge.com, CH$93,000, 2-night min.) have bedrooms with huge windows for bird-watching from bed. Details such as the woodland scene painted into the washbasins and the views of the lake from the tub make this a superb stay. The cabins have full kitchens, or enjoy a huge breakfast (CH$6,000) in the snug communal dining area. Rates include IVA.

The most luxurious of all the hotels around Puerto Varas, ★ **AWA** (Km 27 Ruta 225, tel. 65/2292 020, www.hotelawa.cl, CH$400,000 d) has phenomenal views across the lake from huge bedrooms, stylishly decorated in rough-hewn Mapuche fabrics and with enormous baths with whirlpool bathtubs. There's a spa with a swimming pool and an excellent restaurant, open to nonguests, with sublime views across the lake. The menu uses local ingredients, like the chocolate volcano with grape sorbet, plated in front of you from the open kitchen.

Seven kilometers north of Puerto Varas and providing personalized family-friendly service, **Tulipanes del Lago** (Costanera Viento Norte, Parcela 10, tel. 9/9257 9187, CH$120,000 d, CH$145,000 cabin) has three fully equipped and stylish cabins, each with a private terrace. Large grounds include a barbecue area with panoramic views of the lake, a hot tub, a vegetable plot, and a chicken coop. Swim or kayak at the private beach. B&B is offered in the main house in the summer, with a hearty breakfast and the best views of the lake from these bedrooms. Rates include IVA.

Offering seven elegant bedrooms with attentive five-star service, **Los Caiquenes** (Km 9.5 Ruta 225, tel. 9/8159 0489, www.hotelloscaiquenes.cl, CH$305,000 d) is boutique hotel in a beautiful wooden-tiled building among extensive lawns with sumptuous lake views. Rooms are decorated with restored antique furniture and dramatic modern artwork; those on the lake side get hotter in summer. There's a large swimming pool, a hot tub, and an on-site restaurant with traditional Chilean fish and meat dishes. Rates drop by around 50 percent May-November.

INFORMATION AND SERVICES

The friendly and knowledgeable municipal-run **Oficina de Turismo** (Del Salvador 320, tel. 65/2361 175, aboegel@ptovaras.cl, 8:30am-9pm daily summer, 8:30am-7pm Mon.-Fri., 10am-2pm and 3pm-7pm Sat.-Sun winter) can advise on transportation and activities in the local national parks, Frutillar and other nearby towns, and events and services in Puerto Varas. More tourist information is at privately run **Corporación de Desarrollo Turístico y Cultural de Puerto Varas** (tel. 65/2237 956, www.puertovaras.org, 9am-6:30pm Mon.-Fri., 10am-6:30pm Sat.-Sun.) at Muelle Pideraplen on the Costanera.

Del Salvador has the majority of banking services, with **BCI** (Del Salvador 305), **Banco de Chile** (Del Salvador 201), and **Santander** (Del Salvador 399), all with 24-hour ATMs. For laundry, head to **Lavandina** (Walker Martínez 411, 10am-1pm and 3pm-7pm Mon.-Fri., 10am-1pm Sat.). **Correos** (San José 242, 9am-1:30pm, 3pm-6pm Mon.-Fri., 9:30am-12:30pm Sat.) is one block from Del Salvador. To exchange money, there's **Cambios Puerto Varas** (San Pedro 422). Just below Cerro Calvario in the west part of town, the **Clínica Puerto Varas** (Dr. Otto Bader 810, tel. 65/2333 300, www.clinicapv.cl) offers medical assistance and emergency care.

GETTING THERE
Bus

There's no central bus terminal in Puerto Varas, so companies have terminals and ticket offices around the city. Most buses from Puerto Montt do not stop in Puerto Varas. If you're struggling to find suitable departure times, it's better to head directly to the bus terminal in Puerto Montt.

In Puerto Varas, **Pullman Bus** (Andrés Bello 485, tel. 65/2252 813, www.pullmanbus.com) and **Tur Bus** (Del Salvador 1093, tel. 65/2233 787, www.turbus.cl) run 10 daily buses from **Santiago** (13hr, CH$24,000/CH$45,000). **Buses Jac** (Martínez 227, tel. 65/2383 800, www.jac.cl) shuttles between Puerto Varas and **Pucón** (4 daily, 5hr, CH$9,500). **Cruz del Sur** (San Francisco 1317, tel. 65/2236 969) has hourly departures from **Osorno** (1.5hr, CH$2,000).

From the corner of Del Salvador and San Pedro, **Thaebus** (tel. 65/2421 047, www.thaebus.cl) has a fleet of blue minibuses going hourly to **Frutillar** (1hr, CH$1,300).

Car

To reach Puerto Varas from **Osorno,** it's a 90-km one-hour drive on Ruta 5. To get to **Puerto Montt,** the quickest route is the 20-km drive along Ruta 5, which takes 30 minutes.

GETTING AROUND

To rent a car, **Europcar** (Av. Gramado 700, tel. 65/2230 872, 9am-2pm and 3pm-7pm Mon.-Fri., 9am-2pm Sat.) has an office in Puerto Varas. Rentals are far cheaper at the airport in Puerto Montt—and there's a wider range of providers.

CROSSING INTO ARGENTINA

Buses Norte Internacional (San Francisco 1317, tel. 65/2236 969, www.busnortechile.cl) has one daily departure for **Bariloche, Argentina** (8:50am, 6hr, CH$18,000).

Vicinity of Puerto Varas

Part of the attraction of Puerto Varas is its proximity to picturesque Germanic towns that are home to thriving art communities, such as cultured Frutillar and pleasant summer hangout Puerto Octay. It's also on the doorstep of the Lakes District's most accessible parks, including Parque Nacional Vicente Pérez Rosales.

The more adventurous will enjoy the challenge of reaching the lesser-known Valle Cochamó, a valley only reachable on foot that's often compared with Yosemite Valley for its domed granite sides and unspoiled forests that draw climbers and hikers.

★ FRUTILLAR

Thirty kilometers around Lago Llanquihue from Puerto Varas, the town of Frutillar is an orderly clutch of handsome German-style buildings. The town comprises **Frutillar Bajo,** the stretch of houses, restaurants, and hotels lakeside along Avenida Philippi, and **Frutillar Alto,** 2km up a slight hill, with fewer facilities.

Founded by German settlers in 1852, who brought knowledge of agriculture and baking (Frutillar reputedly has the best kuchen in the area) as well as music, Frutillar has since become known as a the "city of music" in the Los Lagos cultural scene. At its heart is the architecturally striking Teatro del Lago, next to the black sand and calm swimming waters of the main beach, both of which draws visitors in droves.

Sights
TEATRO DEL LAGO
Held above the water by wooden stilts, the **Teatro del Lago** (Av. Philippi 1000, tel. 65/2422 900, www.teatrodellago.cl) is a theater and concert hall that hosts top music, opera, and ballet, plus international acts that snub the theaters in Santiago to perform here. Inaugurated in 2010, it's the largest theater

in the country and has first-class acoustics. Designed in the image of a Chilean barn but inspired by the town's German architecture, the outside is decorated with colored wood tiles, and the copper roof symbolizes the importance of this mineral to Chile. It seats 1,178 and performances are held year-round.

Take a one-hour **guided tour** (noon daily, CH$4,500) to learn about the history and architecture; tickets are available at the box office. The only way to truly admire this important building is by watching a performance (from CH$15,000). Reserve online or at the box office on the street side.

MUSEO COLONIAL ALEMÁN
One block from the lake on the western end of Arturo Prat, **Museo Colonial Alemán** (Av. Vincente Pérez Rosales, tel. 65/2621 142, 9:30am-7:30pm daily in summer, 9:30am-5:30pm daily in winter, CH$2,000 adults, CH$500 children) is worth visiting for the beautifully tended flower gardens. On a three-hectare site with replicas of 1840s buildings, it has the best selection of artifacts brought from Germany. The **Molino de Agua** (watermill)—note the wheel outside—has information about the Ley de Colonización (colonization law) that brought the settlers, while the **Campanario** (belfry) has a display of original machinery, including a beautiful horse-drawn carriage with original leather upholstery. At the top of the **Casa de Herrero** (blacksmith's house) are lovely views of the grounds, Frutillar, and the volcanoes beyond the lake. The **Casona de Campo** (farmhouse) has been set up to re-create daily life of the period. At the far end of the site, beyond the farmhouse, a pretty lily pond blooms in January.

Festivals and Events
In the final week of January and early February, the annual two-week **Semanas**

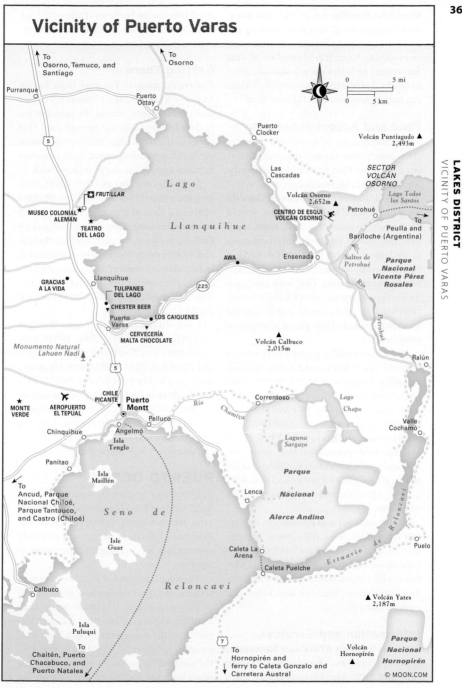

Vicinity of Puerto Varas

To Osorno, Temuco, and Santiago

To Osorno

Purranque

Puerto Octay

Puerto Clocker

Volcán Puntiagudo ▲ 2,493m

Las Cascadas

SECTOR VOLCÁN OSORNO

Lago Todos los Santos

Lago

★ FRUTILLAR

Volcán Osorno 2,652m

CENTRO DE ESQUI VOLCÁN OSORNO

Petrohué

MUSEO COLONIAL ALEMAN ★

Llanquihue

Peulla and Bariloche (Argentina)

TEATRO DEL LAGO

To

AWA

Ensenada

Saltos de Petrohué

Parque Nacional Vicente Pérez Rosales

GRACIAS A LA VIDA

Llanquihue

TULIPANES DEL LAGO

225

Río

CHESTER BEER

Puerto Varas

LOS CAIQUENES

CERVECERÍA MALTA CHOCOLATE

Volcán Calbuco 2,015m

Petrohué

Monumento Natural Lahuen Nadi ▲

Ralún

5

CHILE PICANTE

Puerto Montt

Correntoso

Lago Chapo

Valle Cochamó

★ MONTE VERDE

✈ AEROPUERTO EL TEPUAL

Pelluco

Río Chamiza

Chinquihue

Angelmó

Isla Tenglo

Laguna Sargazo

Panitao

Isla Maillén

Parque

To Ancud, Parque Nacional Chiloé, Parque Tantauco, and Castro (Chiloé)

Lenca

Nacional

Seno de

Alerce Andino

Estuario de Reloncaví

Isle Guar

Caleta La Arena

Puelo

Calbuco

Caleta Puelche

Reloncaví

▲ Volcán Yates 2,187m

Isla Puluqui

To Chaitén, Puerto Chacabuco, and Puerto Natales

7

To Hornopirén and ferry to Caleta Gonzalo and Carretera Austral

Volcán Hornopirén ▲

Parque Nacional Hornopirén

© MOON.COM

0   5 mi
0   5 km

Musicales Frutillar (tel. 65/2421 386, www. semanasmusicales.cl) sees music recitals and performances in the theater and other locations around town. It celebrated its 50-year anniversary in 2018. Concerts also take place in nearby Puerto Montt and Osorno. Tickets can be bought online or at the box office.

Food and Accommodations

Many restaurants close outside summer (Dec.-Mar.), when the vast majority of tourists disappear. Prices can spike during the Semanas Musicales Frutillar event.

The fields around ★ **Lavanda Casa de Té** (Fundo Santa Mart, km 15, tel. 9/9458 0804, www.lavandacasadete.cl, 11am-10pm daily Dec.-Mar., CH$3,000-8,000) have views to the lake and are at their most striking in summer, when they erupt in a dazzling display of purple blooms. This is an ideal spot for lunch or afternoon tea, with 21 flavors accompanied by cakes, scones, and jam served on delicate floral china, plus a selection of sandwiches.

Word has it that Frutillar's best kuchen is at the cute whitewashed tables of **Casa Rosalba** (Caupolicán 28, tel. 9/9336 9286, 9am-8pm Mon.-Fri., 11am-10pm Sat., noon-9pm Sun., CH$3,500-6,000), on a hill above the main road north out of town. The brownies and other cakes aren't bad either, and reasonably priced breakfasts, soups, salads, and sandwiches make it a good spot for lunch. It's *the* place for coffee and cake with a view of the lake and, on a clear day, the volcanoes.

All 16 bedrooms in **El Arroyo** (Av. Philippi 989, tel. 65/2421 560, CH$65,000 d) are sizeable; those at the front have lake views. It's a little creaky and dated, but right on the lakefront, with a splendid back garden with paths and seating areas. Breakfast is included, and rates include IVA.

Information and Services

There are **24-hour ATMs** with **Santander** (Philippi 555) and **Banco del Estado** (Philippi 403). The Municipalidad has a small **Oficina de Turismo** (Philippi 753, tel. 65/2421 261, 8:30am-5:30pm Mon.-Thurs., 8:30am-4:30pm Fri.).

Getting There

The fastest route to Frutillar from Puerto Varas is Ruta 5 (25km, 20min). For the more scenic route, exit at the junction for Llanquihue and take the narrow road that clings to the lake's edge, offering panoramic views of the volcano beyond, until it reaches Frutillar Bajo, 24km and 30 minutes later.

From **Puerto Varas** (1hr, CH$1,300), **Thaebus** (San Francisco 1065, tel. 65/2263 019) has a fleet of blue minibuses running hourly to Frutillar. They drop passengers on Calle Jorge Montt, between Avenida Philippi and Vicente Pérez Rosales. The destination is indicated by a cardboard sign in the front window; make sure the bus is going to Frutillar Bajo, not Frutillar Alto, which is 3.5km from the lake.

Long-distance buses from **Osorno** (roughly every 2 hr, 1.5hr, CH$1,800/ CH$3,000) and **Santiago** (8pm, 8:45pm, and 10pm daily, 12hr, CH$25,000/CH$39,000) are offered by **Cruz del Sur** (tel. 64/2232 777) and **Turbus** (tel. 64/2234 170, www.turbus. cl). They arrive at the **Terminal de Buses** (Av. Arturo Alessandri 381) in Frutillar Alto; from there, a *taxi colectivo* (5min, CH$600) can shuttle you to Frutillar Bajo.

PUERTO OCTAY

Puerto Octay is a pretty town with dramatic views of Lago Llanquihue and the volcano, but with fewer visitors than Frutillar. Península Centinela becomes a seriously popular spot for camping and swimming in summer.

The town was founded in 1852 by German settlers, and its buildings bear testament to its European origins. It is much smaller than Frutillar, although it was once the most important of the lakeside towns, as it connected the other settlements on the lake by ship with the one road to Osorno. Its industrial decline came with the decline of shipping on the lake. Nowadays, it relies on agriculture, cattle ranching, and salmon farming as its main industries.

Sights

Wander the streets to see fine examples of European-style neoclassical architecture executed by Chilean craftspeople. Notable are **Hotel Haase** (Pedro Montt 344), with a porch that extends around three sides of the building; the dramatic chalet-style 1925 **Casa Wulf** (Germán Wulf); and the neo-Gothic 1908 **Parroquia San Agustín** (Germán Wulf corner of Los Carreras) with its red steeple and ogival arches.

Housed above the library in the historic 1920 Casa Niklitschek, the small **Museo de Puerto Octay "El Colono"** (Av. Independencia 591, tel. 64/2643 327, 10am-1pm and 3pm-5pm Mon.-Sat., CH$1,000 adults, children free) is worth a visit for the history of German settlement in English and Spanish, artifacts used in the colonies such as spinning wheels, musical instruments, and shoe molds, plus a collection of plans with information about the town's historic buildings.

For beaches, head south around the bay to **Península Centinela** and the pretty black-sand **Playa Centinela,** the summer's greatest local attraction thanks to calm waters, pleasant shady areas, and views across the lake to Puerto Octay. There are some campsites nearby. Buses operated by Vía Octay leave from Osorno and terminate here in summer.

Festivals and Events

The first weekend in October sees Puerto Octay's **Oktoberfest** (Gimnasio Municipal, Germán Wulf 728, tel. 9/5947 4951, www.oktoberfestpuertooctay.cl, CH$1,000), with food trucks and craft beer stalls, live music, and Chilean dancing in on the field behind the municipal gymnasium. The same organizers run **Bierfest Puerto Octay** (Gimnasio Municipal, Germán Wulf 728) the first weekend in January.

Food and Accommodations

There are not a lot of lodging options in Puerto Octay, and dining is of significantly lesser quality than in Frutillar and Puerto Varas.

For a filling lunch in beautiful surroundings, German buffet restaurant **Espantapájaros** (Km 6 Camino a Puerto Octay, tel. 65/2330 049, www.espantapajaros.cl, 10am-5:30pm Mon.-Thurs., 10am-10pm Fri.-Sat., 10am-7:30pm Sun., CH$17,000 buffet, CH$3,500-6,000) specializes in spit-roasted meat and has an extensive salad bar. After you've had your fill, wander the large lawns outside with the obligatory volcano view. Cheap Chilean-style sandwiches and *onces* make a light bite, and local juices, condiments, honey, and woolen clothing are sold in the adjoining shop.

For cheap camping, head to **Camping El Molino** (Costanera Pichi Juan 124, tel. 9/9545 0607, CH$7,000 for 1-3 people), with 26 sites next to the lake. They don't have volcano views, but there's ample parking for campers and cars, as well as picnic tables, a covered dining area, and sinks to wash up. Boats can be rented. Unfortunately, it's only open December-March.

There are far better accommodations at this price in Puerto Varas, but **Hostal Triwe** (Germán Wulf 582, tel. 64/2391 359 or tel. 9/8259 6327, CH$43,000 d) has large airy bedrooms, some with lake views, and modern if tired furnishings. A small cafeteria, open to nonguests, does good sandwiches.

Getting There and Around

To reach Puerto Octay from **Puerto Varas** by car, it's a 50-km, 45-minute drive north on Ruta 5, turning at the junction for Frutillar. From Frutillar it's a 25-km, 30-minute drive around the north shore of the lake, with pretty views among the trees.

Drive to Puerto Octay from **Frutillar** on the paved U-55 from Frutillar Alto, a 25-km, 20-minute trip, or on the more scenic compacted-gravel road north from Frutillar Bajo that runs along the shore of Lake

Llanquihue, which adds 2km and 10 minutes to the drive time.

Via Octay (tel. 64/2237 043) runs buses every 20 minutes from **Osorno** (1hr, CH$1,500) to Puerto Octay's **Terminal de Buses** (La Esperanca and Balmaceda), half a block south of the Plaza de Armas. In summer, the bus continues on to the Península Centinela. From **Puerto Montt** (1.25hr, CH$2,000), **Thaebus** (tel. 65/2263 019) runs five buses daily.

The town is compact enough to walk; Playa Centinela is 3km from Puerto Octay along the main road.

PARQUE NACIONAL VICENTE PÉREZ ROSALES

With its centerpiece 2,562-meter Volcán Osorno, often compared to Mount Fuji because of its symmetrical cone, **Parque Nacional Vicente Pérez Rosales** (tel. 65/2486 115, loslagos.oirs@conaf.cl, 8:30am-8pm Nov.-Mar., 8:30am-6:30pm Apr.-Oct., CH$4,000 adults, CH$2,000 children) is hemmed in by the Andes and centered on the narrow Lago Todos Los Santos. One of the region's most photogenic, this lake is surrounded by dense Valdivian temperate rainforest that climbs into the mountains. Another of the park's attractions is the Saltos del Petrohué, a thunderous set of waterfalls along the Río Petrohué.

For visitors, the main attractions are the handful of hiking trails. Some of the best ways to explore the park are by boat on calm Lago Todos Los Santos and kayaking or rafting down the rapids of Río Petrohué.

Ruta 225 provides access to the Saltos del Petrohué, 55km northeast of Puerto Varas, and the village of Petrohué, 6km farther northeast. Access to Volcán Osorno and the Centro de Esquí Volcán Osorno is via the main road that circumnavigates Lago Llanquihue.

Lago Todos Los Santos

From the end of the road at Petrohué, it's possible to embark on boat trips across the glorious blue waters of Lago Todos Los Santos or on trails around the base and close to the crater of Volcán Osorno. In a deep valley surrounded by lofty mountains and rainforest, in the shadow of the ever-present volcano, this part of the park is truly breathtaking.

Don't miss the superb **Museo Pioneros Petrohué** (Km 64 R-225, tel. 9/8464 4870 or 65/2212 028, 10:30am-12:30pm and 1:30pm-6:30pm daily, CH$2,000 adults, children free), covering the pioneers of the region. Exhibits start with the inhabitants of Monte Verde, a site 80km away; they were believed to have arrived around 14,800 years ago, making Monte Verde one of the earliest archaeological sites in the Americas. The museum is next to Petrohué Lodge; get the key from Expediciones Petrohué next door if it's closed.

HIKING

The helpful **CONAF ranger station** (tel. 65/2486 115, loslagos.oirs@conaf.cl, 8:30am-8pm daily Nov.-Mar., 8:30am-6:30pm daily Apr.-Oct.), behind the museum, has hiking maps. Sign in if you'll be hiking any of the trails near Petrohué.

The easiest trail is **Sendero Rincón del Osorno** (2.5km one-way). It begins from the ranger station and follows the western shore of the lake. Return the way you came or continue north along the lake, where the path becomes the **Sendero Los Alerces,** which climbs a number of viewpoints above the lake. This path continues back to Petrohué for a total of 14km and five hours.

A more challenging trudge is **Sendero Paso Desolación** (14km one-way, 5hr), starting from the ranger station and climbing the northern folds of Volcán Osorno for views back across the volcano. If you go as part of an organized tour, you'll only walk in one direction; if you're alone, follow your path back for a hike of 28km and 10 hours.

Expediciones Petrohué (behind the Museo de los Pioneros, tel. 9/7573 1394, www.petrohue.com), owned by Petrohué Lodge, can arrange full- and half-day trekking tours around the volcano, as well as half-day rafting trips for similar rates as the agencies in Puerto Varas. They also rent out kayaks by the hour (CH$4,500).

BOAT TRIPS

A more leisurely activity is a small-boat tour along the southern shores of the lake to peer through the forest at sprawling mansions. Boats from **Turismo Sanchez** (Petrohué harbor, tel. 9/7881 8849, 10am-6pm daily) leave when they have more than five passengers for a 40-minute trip (CH$6,000).

WHITE-WATER RAFTING AND KAYAKING

Río Petrohué, with Class III and IV rapids, is a white-water rafting and kayaking destination for novices and experienced paddlers. From Puerto Varas, tour operators **Ko'Kayak** (San Pedro 311, Puerto Varas, tel. 65/2233 004, www.kokayak.cl) and **ALSUR Expediciones** (Aconcagua, Imperial and Puerto Varas, tel. 65/2232 300, www.alsurexpeditions.com) organize half-day kayaking and rafting trips (from CH$35,000 pp, min. 2 people), with English-Spanish bilingual guides, all equipment, and round-trip transport included. Half-day ducky tours (from CH$44,000 pp, min. 2 people, Oct.-Mar.) are for those without experience, with the guide in the inflatable kayak with you.

Saltos del Petrohué (Petrohué Falls)

Few waterfalls have the majesty of **Saltos del Petrohué** (R-225, 6km southwest of Petrohué, tel. 65/2486 115, loslagos.oirs@conaf.cl, 8:30am-8pm daily Nov.-Mar., 8:30am-6:30pm daily Apr.-Oct., CH$4,000 adults, CH$2,000 children), on the Río Petrohué. They're not very high, but the series is dramatic due to the volume of water and the polished black basalt. The scene is enhanced by the backdrop of Volcán Osorno.

The entrance to the falls is marked by a **CONAF ranger station** and **visitors center**, with a café and restrooms. Once you pay the entrance fee and get through the building, there are three short trails. The **Sendero Saltos del Petrohué** (600 m one-way, 20min) is the pièce de résistance, offering the best view of the falls. **Sendero Los Enamorados** (900 m one-way, 30min) heads to a pretty turquoise lake, and **Sendero Carilemu** (1.2km one-way, 45min), has boardwalks following the smaller Río Los Patos; both are worth a wander.

Sector Volcán Osorno
VOLCÁN OSORNO TREK

The 2,652-meter Volcán Osorno towers over the lake. The hiking route to the crater is a challenging ascent requiring technical equipment and a guide. The CONAF ranger station at the trailhead requires proof of gear and experience before hikers are allowed to ascend. Although previous experience isn't necessary, being in good shape is essential. Due to snowfall, the trek is only possible December-April. Even during summer, it's not uncommon for poor weather to cause cancellations.

The obvious choice for guiding volcano ascents is **ALSUR Expediciones** (Aconcagua and Imperial, tel. 65/2232 300 www.alsurexpeditions.com), with over 20 years of experience and an unblemished safety record. Full-day tours to the summit (CH$192,000 pp) include qualified guides, good quality equipment, hotel pickups, and insurance. Experienced climber and mountaineering instructor José Dattoli runs the Puerto Montt-based **Trekka** (tel. 9/9894 0820, www.trekka.cl). He guides trips up Osorno as well as other volcanoes in the area.

SKIING

The 10-run **Centro de Esquí Volcán Osorno** (tel. 9/6679 2284, www.volcanosorno.com, 10am-7pm daily summer, 8:30am-9pm winter, full-day lift pass CH$26,000 adults, CH$17,000 children) has mostly intermediate and advanced routes and one of the longest skiable seasons in the country. Infrastructure isn't great (there's no lodging at the resort), and there are only two lifts, but the road is

paved, making it significantly easier to reach (with snow chains and a high-clearance vehicle) than many other ski resorts in the region. They have Spanish-language snowboarding and skiing classes (CH$35,000), ski rental (CH$20,000 per day for full equipment), and tubing and snowshoe tours (CH$15,000/30min).

Off-season you can take the two ski lifts (CH$16,000 adults, CH$8,000 children) close to the summit for spectacular panoramic views. Even the drive to the ski center is worth it for dazzling lake views when there's clear weather.

Food and Accommodations

SECTOR PETROHUÉ

Run by CONAF and on the shore of Lago Todos Los Santos, **Camping Playa Petrohué** (tel. 65/2882 1680, perezrosales@conaf.cl, CH$10,000 per site) has sites with picnic tables, some with wooden roofs, restrooms, and access to the long black-sand beach. Open only December-March, reservations aren't taken, and rates include IVA.

The lobby of the beautiful four-star **Petrohué Lodge** (Km 64 R-225, tel. 65/2212 025 or 9/8464 4870, www.petrohue.com, July-Apr., CH$160,000-180,000 d) has a rustic flagstone floor and wooden beams, while bedrooms have polished wooden furniture. There is a sauna and hot tubs. Worth the splurge, the superior double on the top floor has a sofa, jetted tub, woodstove, and views of the lake. The good restaurant has a seasonal menu of Chilean dishes and sandwiches. Rates include IVA.

SECTOR VOLCÁN OSORNO

On a flat stretch before the ski center, **Teski Club** (Km 12 V-555, tel. 65/2566 622, www.teski.cl, CH$17,000 one person, CH$42,000 d shared bath, CH$54,000 d private bath) has cramped bunk beds packed into tiny rooms and no luxuries except the magnificent views across Lago Llanquihue. Some rooms have

a private bath but all have shared showers. There's central heating and a wood fire for winter, when it's a popular base to be first on the slopes in the morning; in summer it attracts hikers and climbers. Skip the food at the restaurant; it's a better place for a cold beer or a coffee with views across the lake, which are much better here than from the ski resort's café. Rates include IVA.

Information and Services

The Petrohué **CONAF ranger station** (Petrohué, tel. 65/2882 1680, perezrosales@conaf.cl, 8:30am-6:30pm daily), a few hundred meters from the dock and behind the museum, can provide maps and information about hiking routes and conditions. This part of the park is free, but you must register before hiking any trails. There's a second **CONAF ranger station** (Saltos del Petrohué, no phone, 9am-7pm daily) at Saltos del Petrohué, with a car park on the opposite side of the road (CH$1,000).

Getting There

From Puerto Varas, it's a 60-km, one-hour drive northeast to Petrohué. Ruta 225 runs along the southern shore of Lago Llanquihue to Ensenada, where it continues northeast, passing the Saltos del Petrohué after 10km, and Petrohué 6km after that. To reach Volcán Osorno and the ski resort from Ensenada, turn north on the road around the lake. Turn right after 2km to climb the southern side of the volcano. It's another 15km to the ski resort. The total drive from Puerto Varas to the ski resort is about 60km, and takes a little over an hour in good conditions.

Public transport to the park is straightforward and reliable, with a minibus (1.25hr, CH$2,000) that departs from Puerto Varas (main bus stop, Martínez and San Bernardo) for Petrohué every 30 minutes daily. It stops at Saltos del Petrohué en route. There is no public transport to the trailhead for Volcán Osorno.

1: Lavanda Casa de Té **2:** Saltos del Petrohué

Exploring Remote Valle Cochamó

Referred to as Chile's Yosemite, **Valle Cochamó** (www.cochamo.com) is defined by steep granite cliffs. The appeal is its remoteness—it's accessible only on foot. This beguiling backcountry destination is a must for those looking to escape in nature.

The best time to visit is November-mid-April, when rainfall is lower but there's enough water to keep the waterfalls gushing. Climbing is best in December, with 15 hours of daylight, but the weather is much drier in February. Higher rainfall and swollen rivers can make parts of the valley impassable May-October.

The detailed website contains essential information about hiking trails and lodging, along with contact information for bilingual climbing, trekking, and kayaking guides. **Southern Trips** (tel. 9/8407 2559, www.southern-trips.com) offers multiday horseback riding tours into the valley. **ALSUR Expediciones** (Aconcagua and Imperial, tel. 65/2232 300, www.alsurexpeditions.com) runs multiday trekking expeditions to Cochamó from Puerto Varas. **Trekka** (tel. 9/9894 0820, www.trekka.cl) offers four-day climbing expeditions (CH$380,000 pp, min. 2 people), including transportation from Puerto Montt.

To get into the valley, you hike 10km from the town of Cochamó. It's a gradual climb, but heavy rain can make it muddy, making progress difficult.

HIKING AND CLIMBING

Various trails include the challenging **Cerro Arco Iris** (6km one-way, 5hr). It ends with a vertical ascent assisted by climbing ropes attached to the wall. At the top are spectacular panoramic views across the entire valley. The hundreds of climbing routes in the valley all require extensive experience, with multi-pitch routes starting at 5.10c and above. You can find detailed route descriptions on the website.

ACCOMMODATIONS

Reservations for lodgings must be made at least a week in advance through the valley's website. Payment is by PayPal before arrival. The rustic **Refugio Cochamó** (La Junta, www.cochamo.com, Thurs.-Sun. Dec.-mid-Mar., CH$17,000 dorm, CH$52,000 d shared bath) has friendly communal spaces, a shared kitchen, electricity, and even internet. A basic breakfast is available for CH$4,000 pp. Organic dinners, using produce from the on-site garden, can be prepared for an additional fee. The *refugio* gets fully booked, so make your reservation early.

Camping La Junta (www.cochamo.com, mid-Sept.-Apr., CH$6,000 pp) is a basic campground with cold showers, composting toilets, and fire pits. There is nowhere to buy provisions outside the village of Cochamó, so bring all your food with you. You must take all trash with you out of the park.

GETTING THERE

Buses for Cochamó village (2hr, CH$3,500), which is 4.5km before the turnoff for the trailhead, leave from the bus terminal in Puerto Montt and pass through Puerto Varas. **Buses Estuario Reloncavi** (tel. 65/2841 200) and **Transher** (tel. 65/2254 187) run four daily buses. It's best to take the bus from Puerto Montt rather than Puerto Varas, as it is often full in January-February and does not stop to pick up more passengers. Bus schedules change regularly, so confirm before you travel.

From Cochamó, take a taxi to the trailhead or walk. It's 6km to the trailhead after the turn at the bridge over the Río Cochamó. **Leonel Delgado** (tel. 9/9665 6505) can take you from Cochamó to the trailhead. At the trailhead, you must register at the municipal office.

Crossing into Argentina

Cruce Andino (Del Salvador 72, no phone, www.cruceandino.com) runs the spectacular Andean crossing to **San Carlos de Bariloche** in Argentina, a route taken by Che Guevara. Highlights of the 12-hour trip include sailing across Lago Todos Los Santos, Lago Frías, and Lago Nahuel Huapi. The trip costs CH$173,000, including bus transportation from Puerto Varas (and the overland sections between the three lakes) and a bilingual guide. If there's bad weather, the trip can be grim, so aim to travel October-April, when conditions are better.

Puerto Montt

Puerto Montt is 22km south of Puerto Varas on the northern shore of Estero Reloncaví, a huge fjord that connects the city with the Patagonian fjords and the Pacific Ocean to the south. An industrial town and a transport hub with connections to Chiloé, the Carretera Austral, and Southern Patagonia, Puerto Montt has a busy airport, a harbor, and a bus terminal, all of which bring thousands of visitors. The handful of attractions includes the Angelmó craft market and Puerto de Angelmó, the fish market. Only 20 minutes north, Puerto Varas is a bigger draw for outdoor adventures.

SIGHTS

There's not a lot to see in Puerto Montt beyond the striking wooden 1856 **Catédral de Puerto Montt** (Benaventí 385, accessed from Urmeneta, http://arzobispadodepuertomontt.cl, open for mass), copper-domed and with Parthenon-style columns at the front. It's on the northern side of the Plaza de Armas, also known as the **Plaza Manuel Irarrázaval** (bounded by O'Higgins, Urmeneta, Quillota, and Antonio Varas).

Next door to the bus terminal, **Museo Juan Pablo II** (Diego Portales 997, tel. 65/2233 029, 9am-12:30pm and 3pm-5:30pm Mon.-Thurs., 9am-12:30pm and 2pm-4:30pm Fri., free) has exhibitions on archaeological sites, including the ancient site of Monte Verde, 35km west; the process of colonization by the Spanish and Germans; and a blow-by-blow account of the city's history.

SHOPPING

Angelmó (no phone, 10am-7pm daily), a 400-meter stretch of craft stalls along Calle Angelmó, is worth a look on your way to the Puerto de Angelmó. Plenty of stalls sell the mass-produced llama wool jumpers seen all over South America, but there are some real gems, and you can see many artisans making their wares. Look for those selling flavored liquors and leatherwork.

At the end of the road, the **Puerto de Angelmó** (no phone, 10am-8pm daily) is a higgledy-piggledy warren of small wooden booths selling cheeses and housing tiny restaurants; at the center, a covered building contains the fish stalls, where you can find good deals on locally farmed salmon, prepared ceviches, and even *longaniza* sausages. On the edges of the market are plenty of rather pricey seafood restaurants; expect to pay CH$7,000-10,000 for a meal.

FOOD AND DRINK

A surprising gem hidden 10 blocks northwest of the bus terminal, ★ **Chile Picante** (Vicente Pérez Rosales 567, tel. 9/8454 8923, noon-3pm and 7:30pm-10:30pm Mon.-Sat., CH$10,500) is as good as you'll find in Puerto Montt. The three-course fixed menu is a mouthwatering array of inventive dishes using fresh local ingredients that change daily, including Calafate berries, *nalca* leaves, crab, and other regional products. You're waited on by owner Francisco, who serves delicately presented dishes and sublime pisco sours amid glorious views of snow-topped mountains.

Full of junk collected since it opened in 1962, **Cirus Bar** (Miraflores 1177, tel. 65/2252 016, 9am-1am Mon.-Sat., CH$4,000-8,000) is Puerto Montt's best-known watering hole. Old men prop up the bar during the day, but at lunch and at night it transforms into a vibrant music venue, with folkloric music at noon and 8pm daily. It's so popular for its large selection of drinks and cheap food that it's essential to book on Friday, when it's busiest. It only accepts cash.

ACCOMMODATIONS

Despite high visitor numbers, lodging options in Puerto Montt are dismal. Some well-known chains are along the waterfront, but the quality doesn't match the rates, and the streets in this area are dangerous at night. Stay at one of the cheaper options in the hillside neighborhoods, about eight blocks northwest of the bus terminal. Breakfast and Wi-Fi are included unless otherwise stated, and all are located in safe neighborhoods.

Easily Puerto Montt's most comfortable lodging, **Austral View Hostel** (Bellavista 620, tel. 9/6284 0751, CH$15,000 dorm, CH$30,000 d shared bath, CH$35,000 d private bath, CH$35,000 cabin, CH$45,000 dome) has a four-person dome and a two-person cabin, both with kitchens, as well as large rooms with linens and dated but functional baths. There's plenty of parking in the secure garden, and a communal kitchen. Friendly policies, such as free first use of the washing machine, and the rather splendid views down to the water are the cherry on top.

The family home at **Casa Perla** (Trigal 312, tel. 65/2262 104, casaperla@hotmail.com, CH$11,000 dorm, CH$26,000 d shared bath) has been welcoming travelers since the 1980s. It's chaotic and cramped but cheap, and the owners are friendly and speak English. There's kitchen access and space for five tents on a sunny stretch of grass out back.

Popular among fishery workers, **Hospedaje Corina** (Los Guindes 329, tel. 65/2273 948 or tel. 9/82403 037, www.hospedajecorina.cl, CH$30,000 d shared bath, CH$35,000 d private bath) has 13 very clean bedrooms on two properties, all neutrally decorated. There's no central heating, but everything's clean in this slightly soulless bed-and-breakfast.

The five bedrooms at family-run **Hospedaje Vista al Mar** (Francisco Vivar 1337, tel. 65/2255 625 or tel. 9/9819 4202, www.hospedajevistaalmar.cl, CH$30,000 d

prepared ceviches at the Puerto de Angelmó

shared bath, CH$35,000 d private bath) are simple but functional. The doubles upstairs have the best sea views, and there are electric heaters in all bedrooms and a simple breakfast of bread and jam. The live-in owner is very friendly and can provide information about travel in the region.

INFORMATION AND SERVICES

SERNATUR has an **Oficina de Turismo** (San Martín 80, tel. 65/2256 999, 9am-1pm, 3pm-6pm Mon.-Fri., 9am-2pm Sat.) with information regarding onward transport along the Carretera Austral as well as trips into nearby national parks. Another desk is in the arrivals hall at the airport (no phone, 8am-5:30pm Mon.-Fri.) with maps of towns and national parks; they speak fluent English.

Hospital Puerto Montt (Los Aramos 65, tel. 65/2362 001) is on the northern exit of Puerto Montt. The post office, **Correos** (Rancagua 126, 10am-6pm Mon.-Fri., 10am-noon Sat.), is six blocks from the bus terminal. **Banco Estado** (Urmeneta 580) and **Banco de Chile** (Urmeneta 464) are centrally located. Conveniently located a couple of blocks south of the bus terminal, **Lavanderia** (Angelmo 1668, no phone, 9am-1pm and 3pm-7pm Mon.-Fri., 10am-1pm and 3pm-6pm Sat.) can wash your clothes the same day.

GETTING THERE
Air
Just under 20km northeast of Puerto Montt, **Aeropuerto El Tepual** (PMC, V-60, tel. 65/2294 161, www.aeropuertoeltepual.cl) has regular daily flights to Santiago, Concepción, Punta Arenas, and Balmaceda (Coyhaique) with **LAW** (www.vuelalaw.com), **LATAM** (O'Higgins 167, www.latam.com), **Sky Airline** (www.skyairline.com), and **JetSmart** (www.jetsmart.com).

AIRPORT TRANSFER
The quickest and cheapest way into town from the airport is with **Andrés Tour** (tel. 65/2542 161, www.andrestour.com). They offer hourly

buses (CH$2,500) that sync with flight arrivals 7am-11pm daily for the 30-minute journey between the airport and Terminal de Buses Puerto Montt. They also offer private transfers between the airport and hotels in Puerto Montt (CH$5,000) and Puerto Varas (CH$10,000). All tickets are sold from their location outside the arrivals area of the airport and at booth 38 in the bus terminal (tel. 65/2318 628).

Taxis from outside the terminal will cost about CH$12,000 to destinations in Puerto Montt.

Bus
The **Terminal de Buses Puerto Montt** (Diego Portales 1001, tel. 65/2283 000) is on the fjord in the far south of the city. **Thaebus** (tel. 65/2263 019, www.thaebus.cl) runs small minibuses from **Puerto Varas** (20min, CH$1,000). **Cruz del Sur** (tel. 65/2483 14, http://web.busescruzdelsur.cl) has hourly buses from **Temuco** (3.5hr, CH$5,600) and **Osorno** (2hr, CH$2,200), as well as connections with **Valdivia** (3.5hr, CH$5,500) every 1.5 hours. **Buses JAC** (tel. 65/2384 600, www.jac.cl) has five daily buses to **Pucón** (5.5hr, CH$9,800/CH$12,000).

Various operators run buses from **Santiago** (12hr, CH$12,000/CH$18,000); **Pullman Bus** (tel. 65/2316 561, www.pullmanbus.com) and **Tur Bus** (tel. 65/2493 402) offer hourly departures. **Queilén Bus** (tel. 65/2253 468, www.queilenbus.cl) has buses every 30 minutes from **Castro** (3.5hr, CH$5,000/CH$6,000) and **Ancud** (2.5hr, CH$5,000/CH$6,5000) in Chiloé.

Boat
Two companies offer slightly different routes into Patagonia from Puerto Montt. **Navimag Ferry** (Diego Portales 2000, tel. 2/2869 9900, www.navimag.com, 9am-1pm and 2:30pm-6pm Mon.-Thurs., 9am-5pm Fri., 3pm-6pm Sat.) sails the *Evangelistas*, a large passenger, vehicle, and cargo ship that plies the fjords to **Puerto Chacabuco** (Fri. and Sun., 24hr, CH$51,000), 450km south. The marginally

Traveling into Patagonia

Navimag Ferry

Puerto Montt is the main gateway for onward travel to Patagonia. The quickest transport is by air, with **LATAM** (www.latam.com), **Sky Airline** (www.skyairline.com), and **JetSmart** (www.jetsmart.com) offering daily departures for Punta Arenas, the largest city in Southern Patagonia, as well as seasonal flights during summer to Coyhaique along the Carretera Austral (LATAM and Sky Airline) and Puerto Natales (LATAM). If you book in advance, fares can be very reasonable and significantly cheaper than other modes.

A more adventurous trip is to take one of the passenger or cargo boats that cruise the Patagonian fjords. **Navimag Ferry** (Diego Portales 2000, tel. 2/2869 9900, www.navimag.com, 9am-1pm and 2:30pm-6pm Mon.-Sat., 9am-5pm Fri, 3pm-6pm Sat.) has the more comfortable—but not luxurious—boats to Puerto Chacabuco (24hr) on the Carretera Austral and Puerto Natales (72hr), while **Naviera Austral** (Empresa Portuaría, Agelmó 1673, tel. 600/4019 000, http://navieraustral.cl, 9am-9pm daily summer, 9am-1pm and 3pm-7pm Mon.-Fri., 10am-1pm Sat. winter) is a passenger and vehicle ferry, mostly used by locals, that takes a longer route (28hr) to Puerto Chacabuco. Both offer spellbinding scenery of the volcano-fringed fjords—but only if the weather is good. When it rains, expect to see very little of the landscape, although there's still a chance to see whales, dolphins, and sea lions, particularly on the Naviera Austral, which travels closer to shore.

Along the length of the Carretera Austral, there are expensive bus services that are busy in summer and unreliable with irregular timing in winter. Buses from Puerto Montt head to Chaitén, at the top of the Carretera Austral, with **Kemelbus** (tel. 65/2253 530, www.kemelbus.cl; 7am daily, 8.5hr, CH$20,000), while **Queillen Bus** (tel. 65/2253 468; 9:35am Wed.) and **Becker** (tel. 67/2232 167; noon Tues.) continue to Coyhaique (16hr, CH$40,000), with the latter passing via Futaleúfu (12hr, CH$20,000). From both destinations, it's possible to connect with onward travel farther south or across the border in Argentina.

With your own vehicle, the Carretera Austral is a real adventure. A 4WD isn't necessary, but high clearance for the extensive sections of the road that haven't yet been paved is important. Be sure to stock up on food, drink, and gasoline at every available opportunity, as these commodities are scare in some places.

more luxurious *Eden* continues through the Patagonia fjords to **Puerto Natales** (Fri., 72hr, CH$278,000), 1,200km south of Puerto Montt. Fares include a berth in a cabin and all meals.

The other company, **Naviera Austral** (Empresa Portuaría, Agelmí 1673, tel. 600/4019 000, http://navieraustral.cl, 9am-9pm daily summer, 9am-1pm and 3pm-7pm Mon.-Fri., 10am-1pm Sat. winter) has a passenger and car ferry with Monday, Thursday, and Friday departures for **Chaitén** (12hr, CH$17,300). Ferry service runs to Puerto Chacabuco from Quellón in Chiloé.

GETTING AROUND
Car Rental
Puerto Montt is a good place to rent a car, as it's cheaper than in other cities in the region. Outside the arrivals hall of the airport, **Hertz** (tel. 65/2268 944, www.hertz.cl, 8am-11:30pm daily), **Europcar** (tel. 65/2368 225, www.europcar.cl, 8am-11pm daily), **Econorent** (tel. 65/2481 264, www.econorent.cl, 7:30am-11pm daily), and **Avis/Budget** (tel. 2/2795 3982, www.avis.cl, 8am-10pm Mon.-Fri., 8am-9pm Sun.) have desks, as do smaller rental agencies.

It's best to take only **official taxis** with the blue sign in their windshield; around Puerto Montt, journeys should cost no more than CH$2,000. The streets around the bus terminal are not safe at night, and it's always best to call a taxi after dark. Get your lodgings to call you a taxi, or try **Radio Taxi Larch** (tel. 65/2430 100).

CROSSING INTO ARGENTINA
Trans Austral Bus (tel. 65/2270 984) has one departure four days a week for Bariloche (10:45am Mon. and Wed.-Fri., 5hr, CH$16,000). The bus continues onto **El Bolsón** (Mon. and Thurs., 6hr, CH$24,000) and **Esquel** (Mon. and Thurs., 8hr, CH$34,000).

Chiloé

Separated from mainland Chile by the Chacao

Canal, the Chiloé Archipelago dances to the beat of its own drum, with a relaxed pace of life. The fierce pride with which the islanders view their own roots—Chilote first, Chilean second—is matched by the fierce weather that bring deluges of heavy rain to batter the western coast.

Chiloé comprises several dozen islands, the largest of which is Isla Grande (Big Island), 180km by 50km. Along with the less visited, more remote islands, Isla Grande is home to lush ecosystems of Valdivian forest. Two main reserves, Parque Nacional Chiloé and the remote Parque Tantauco, grant intrepid visitors access to old-growth forests and rare native wildlife.

Highlights

Look for ★ to find recommended sights, activities, dining, and lodging.

★ **Chilote Churches:** Admire their colorful facades and traditional Chilote construction (page 381).

★ **Valle de Chepú:** Thanks to changes to the terrain caused by the 1960 earthquake, this valley is a wildlife-watcher's paradise. Kayak the river at dawn to spot otters and birds galore (page 385).

★ **Palafitos:** Castro's rainbow-painted houses on stilts still line much of the city's coast, with many converted into upscale lodgings and cafés (page 389).

★ **Museo del Acordeón:** Try your hand at playing one of the 70 accordions in the collection belonging to a renowned Chonchi musician (page 401).

★ **Queilén:** Absorb views of the mighty Volcán Corcovado rising out of the distant Andes or spot Magellanic penguins on a boat tour from this remote village (page 402).

★ **Muelle de las Almas:** Walk along an art installation on a pier that depicts part of Mapuche mythology (page 405).

★ **Parque Nacional Chiloé:** This national park is filled with native wildlife, temperate rainforest, and beautiful fine-sand beaches (page 407).

© MOON.COM

★ **Parque Tantauco:** This remote park is the best place in Chiloé to trek through primary forest and spot the rare *pudú* deer (page 411).

Chiloé

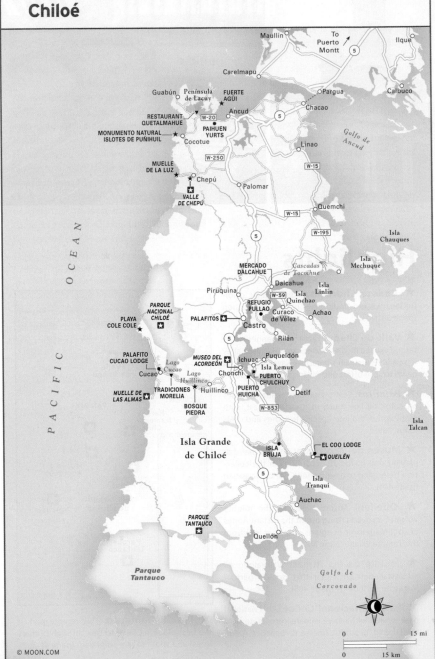

Maullín
To Puerto Montt
Ilque
5
Carelmapu
Calbuco
Guabún
Península de Lacuy
FUERTE AGÜI
Pargua
RESTAURANT QUETALMAHUE
W-20
Ancud
Chacao
5
Golfo de Ancud
PAIHUEN YURTS
MONUMENTO NATURAL ISLOTES DE PUÑIHUIL
Cocotue
Linao
W-250
W-15
MUELLE DE LA LUZ
Chepú
Palomar
VALLE DE CHEPÚ
Quemchi
W-15
Isla Chauques
5
W-195
Isla Mechuque
MERCADO DALCAHUE
Cascadas de Tocoihue
Piruquina
Dalcahue
Isla Linlin
W-59
Isla Quinchao
REFUGIO PULLAO
PALAFITOS
Curaco de Vélez
Achao
Castro
PLAYA COLE COLE
Parque Nacional Chiloé
Rilán
5
PALAFITO CUCAO LODGE
MUSEO DEL ACORDEÓN
Ichuac
Puqueldón
Lago Cucao
Isla Lemuy
Cucao
Lago Huillinco
Chonchi
PUERTO CHULCHUY
MUELLE DE LAS ALMAS
TRADICIONES MORELIA
Huillinco
PUERTO HUICHA
Detif
BOSQUE PIEDRA
W-853
O C E A N
P A C I F I C
Isla Talcan
Isla Grande de Chiloé
EL COO LODGE
ISLA BRUJA
QUEILÉN
Isla Tranqui
5
Auchac
PARQUE TANTAUCO
Quellón
Parque Tantauco
Golfo de Corcovado

0   15 mi
0   15 km

The archipelago's noteworthy architecture is seen in the main settlements that line Isla Grande's sheltered eastern coast, characterized by houses shingled in *alerce* wood. Some of these, known as *palafitos*, stand precariously on wooden stilts. Sixty charming and flamboyantly painted historic wooden churches bear evidence of Jesuit influence.

PLANNING YOUR TIME

Chiloé can be a **day trip** from northern Patagonia's Puerto Montt or Puerto Varas. For a true grasp of the island's unique character, however, **2-3 days** are necessary. **Castro** is the only city on the archipelago. It's a sensible base, especially for those without transportation, due to the network of transit links that connect it with the rest of Isla Grande, and the quality of its lodgings. Plan on staying in Castro and visiting surrounding destinations on a few day trips.

Having a **rental vehicle** can enhance your visit. Transit options to more remote areas exist but are infrequent, and some of the region's unique lodgings are in places not served by public transit. Rent a car in Puerto Montt, as prices are lower and vehicle insurance is guaranteed—not always the case from rental companies on the islands.

On the northern coast, a 30-minute drive beyond the ferry landing that transports vehicles from the mainland, **Ancud** is a pleasant overnight stop on the way south from the ferry. A good day trip from here is **Monumento Natural Islotes de Puñihuil,** with a nesting colony of Humboldt and Magellanic penguins.

With its *palafitos,* historic church, and produce market, **Castro** can be experienced in half a day. A popular day trip from Castro is to take the ferry east across to **Isla Quinchao.** Visiting the pretty churches and sampling the ocean-fresh *picadas* of the villages of Curaco de Vélez, Achao, and remote Quinchao will take about half a day. Take the ferry back to **Dalcahue** and have lunch, then return to Castro for the evening.

Many of Chiloé's most **picturesque villages** are close to Castro and make good day trips. Go north to see the churches and coastal views of **Tenaún** and **Quemchi.** Head south to visit **Queilén, Chonchi,** and **Isla Puqueldón.** All of these destinations are best explored with plenty of time or by rental car, as the narrow country lanes that crisscross Chiloé can be slow going on public transit.

The **Valle de Chepú,** on the western edge of Isla Grande, is hard to reach. The brackish waters of the Río Chepú are a paradise for **kayakers** and **bird-watchers.** It's best experienced as a day trip from Ancud, the closest major town; only a handful of basic lodgings cater to travelers.

Also on the west coast, midway on the island, accessible **Cucao** is surrounded by sloping, thickly forested hills and lined by fine sand dunes, making it a good one- or two-day getaway for hiking or horseback riding in **Parque Nacional Chiloé** or a visit to the mystical **Muelle de las Almas.** A paradisiacal sunset over the Pacific and a night spent on the tranquil waters of Lago Cucao should be included.

Quellón, the final stop along the Pan-American Highway, only merits a visit as the gateway to the private reserve **Parque Tantauco** (for which you'll want at least two days) and to Patagonia, with no-frills passenger ferries sailing south from its port.

HISTORY

Until 9,000 years ago, when the glacial ice that covered Chiloé melted, this area was part of Chile's mainland. The original inhabitants of the archipelago, the Chono people, are thought to have arrived around 2,000 years ago. Expert at fishing, they navigated the fjords in search of shellfish and inhabited the small islands off Isla Grande. The

---

Previous: fishing boat near Queilén; Iglesia Nuestra Señora de Patrocinio de Tenaún; Museo del Acordeón in Chonchi.

Two Days in Chiloé

DAY 1

Arrive by boat or plane to **Castro** and head directly to the *palafitos* on the Río Gamboa for the best light for taking photos, before dropping in at the candy-colored **Iglesia San Francisco de Castro** on the main Plaza de Armas. Catch a bus for **Dalcahue,** 20 minutes north, for a true Chilote lunch of *curanto a la olla* before hopping back on a bus to Castro and south to **Chonchi** for an afternoon wandering past the town's historic shingled houses. Don't forget to drop in at the eccentric **Museo del Acordeón** to see the accordion collection.

Head back via bus to Castro for dinner in quirky restaurant **Mercadito de Chiloé,** where the fish is as fresh as it gets and the range of pisco sours made using local fruits is enough to make your head spin—literally. Stay overnight in the affordable **Palafito Hostel.** Treat yourself to a seaside room for picturesque views in the morning.

DAY 2

Hop on a bus to **Cucao** and spend the morning hiking or on horseback to the enchanting **Muelle de las Almas.** Get a simple but delicious lunch at **Arrayán** in Cucao and spend the afternoon wandering the trails of **Parque Nacional Chiloé,** with sunset spent at Playa Cucao. Stay overnight in **Palafito Cucao Lodge** for jaw-dropping views across Lago Cucao; you might spot a southern river otter in the water.

Huilliche people, related to the Mapuche, sharing the language and growing quinoa and potatoes on coastal lands, immigrated to Chiloé around the 14th century AD. In 1567, a group of 200 Spanish settlers arrived on the islands, introducing new crops and technologies. The Mapuche rebellion drove the rest of the Spaniards north in 1598, so this small group was completely isolated for more than two centuries, eventually integrating with the indigenous people and adopting their ways of living.

From 1608 Jesuit missionaries traveled across the archipelago to build new churches, fusing European designs with traditional local construction methods. During the war for Chilean independence in 1818, Chiloé became the final battleground for Spanish loyalists and was the last part of the country to join the Chilean republic, eight years after independence.

Contemporary Chiloé remains isolated, with poverty rates as high as 25 percent on some parts of Isla Grande, significantly higher than the rest of Chile. The economy is chained to the commercial salmon industry, a precarious business due to the increased incidence of the toxic algal bloom known as *marea roja* (red tide). In 2016 the national government banned infected fish and shellfish from Chilote waters, resulting in job losses for thousands and protests that stopped tourists and Chileans alike from entering or leaving the island. *Marea roja* has become a growing concern due to rising sea temperatures caused by climate change.

A 2.5-km bridge to connect Chiloé with the mainland should be completed in 2023. The bridge is controversial among residents. Some hope that it will allow for better access to health care and education, while others fear a loss of their cultural identity and the incursion of mining companies to harvest gold and iron.

Ancud and Vicinity

Across from the mainland, on the southern side of the Canal de Chacao, the quiet town of Ancud is home to 18th-century forts, bays with migrating blue whales, and green-fringed islets occupied by noisy colonies of Humboldt and Magellanic penguins. Farther south, in the Valle de Chepú, verdant river valleys dense with rainforest are swarmed by wildfowl and offer glimpses of the rare southern river otter.

Chiloé's northwest coast is much less visited than Castro, the island's only city, but it makes for a pleasant stop for a day, particularly for kayaking or learning about the island's quirky wooden churches.

ANCUD

On a promontory into the Canal de Chacao, the harbor town of Ancud looks somewhat weathered. It can't compete with the colorful charisma of Castro, but it has an independent streak. In town and on the Península de Lacuy are remains of two Spanish fortresses that defended the settlement against pirates. There is charm in subdued Ancud, from the mythology-inspired statues in the main square to its two bustling local markets and harbor-side accommodations with pretty sunset views.

Sights

The **Plaza de Armas** (bordered by Libertad, Ramírez, Blanco Encalada, and Pudeto) is the heart of Ancud, just one block east of the coastal road. Hidden among the shrubbery are sculptures carved from *cancagua,* a hard volcanic rock used to build nearby Fuerte Agüi. The sculptures represent creatures from Chilote mythology.

The **Centro de Visitantes** of the **Fundación Amigos de las Iglesias de Chiloé** (Errázurris 227, tel. 65/2621 046, 9:30am-6pm daily Jan.-Feb., 9:30am-6pm Mon.-Fri. Mar.-Dec.) is worth a visit for an introduction to the architecture and history of Chiloé's 60 wooden churches, 16 of which gained UNESCO World Heritage status in 2000. The visitors center is in the 1875 German neoclassical and neo-Gothic **Iglesia de la Inmaculada Concepción,** which has served as a school, a convent, and interim cathedral following the destruction of the original in the 1960 earthquake.

The interior of the church houses a fascinating collection of doors and windows from Chiloé's various churches. Following restorations through the years, they have ended up slung from the ceiling here. There are scale models of some of the churches on display.

An attached shop has wooden souvenirs and some English-language books about Chiloé. It also sells **La Ruta de Las Iglesias** (The Route of the Churches, CH$2,500), a passport that you can get stamped as you visit the different churches.

From the plaza, wander north along the coastal Calle Lord Cochrane. It becomes Calle San Antonio as it passes the Spanish-built **Fuerte San Antonio** (Lord Cochrane s/n, 9am-9pm daily, free), the remains of a 16-cannon fort built in 1770. It looks out across the often stormy Golfo de Quetalmahue and played an integral part in protecting the town from invasion.

Entertainment

The **Casa de la Cultura** (Libertad 663, tel. 65/2628 164, www.ancudcultura.cl, 8am-1pm and 2pm-5:15pm daily) is Ancud's main cultural space, with one room dedicated to a monthly exhibition that normally showcases local art or sculpture. The other seven rooms play host to a rotating program of yoga, dance, and chess games.

Shopping

Bundles of dried seaweed and smoked mussels threaded onto thick strings hang from the stalls of Ancud's legendary **Feria Rural**

Municipal (Pedro Montt and Arturo Prat, 9am-5pm daily), where local farmers and fisherfolk congregate to sell their goods. The main part of the market is inside a high-ceilinged metal structure, with plenty of overflow in the outdoor passageway east from Calle Pedro Montt. Fruit and vegetable vendors (note the misshapen Chilote potatoes) lead to a secondary room where fish and shellfish are piled high on ice. Cheap restaurants specializing in grilled fish and seafood soup are on the 2nd floor, along with a small selection of stalls selling handmade crafts.

For crafts, you're better off heading two blocks west along Arturo Prat to the **Mercado Municipal** (Arturo Prat 161-195, 9am-5pm daily), which has plenty of hand-knitted woolen clothing (although much is mass-produced), small wooden ornaments carved like Chilote churches, and plenty of local jams, chocolates, and liquors.

Food

Slightly out of place in Ancud, trendy **Café Blanco** (Libertad 669, tel. 65/262 9066, cafeblancoancud@gmail.com, 9:30am-8pm Mon.-Sat.) has thick and creamy hot chocolate, fresh juices and coffees, and homemade cake and empanadas. At the back of the shop, chunky woolen throws and homemade *nalca* (Chilean rhubarb) jams and savory salsas are for sale. Their other branch (Ramírez 259, tel. 65/2620 197, 9:30am-9pm Mon.-Sat., 4:30pm-8pm Sun.) has a bigger kitchen and an affordable *menú del día* (CH$4,600) of traditional Chilean dishes.

Kuranton (Av. Prat 94, tel. 65/2623 090, noon-11pm daily summer, noon-7:30pm daily fall-spring, CH$6,000-9,500) is one of Ancud's oldest restaurants. *Cancagua* stone sculptures of Chilote mythical creatures highlight an eclectic collection of historical bric-a-brac with a soundtrack of traditional accordion music. Best-known are the hearty bowls of steaming *pulmay* (*curanto* cooked in a *perol,* or pot) that are more than enough for two people. If you're on your own, any of the seafood dishes will do.

On the road toward Fuerte San Antonio, the cute and cozy ★ **Amaranthine** (Lord Cochrane 412, tel. 65/2627 448, www.amaranthinechiloe.com, 10am-9pm Mon.-Sat. summer, 3pm-9pm Mon.-Fri. fall-spring, CH$3,500-5,500) is a rarity in a fishing town: It specializes in vegetarian food. All ingredients are locally sourced, organic, and cooked to order, so expect to wait. Hearty quinoa salads flavored with plump Chilote garlic and thick soups are pleasant on a drizzly day. There are rich homemade cakes and views of the bay.

Attached to the hostel of the same name, **Mundo Nuevo** (Av. Salvador Allende 748, tel. 65/2628 383, http://newworld.cl, 1pm-4pm and 7:30pm-11pm Tues.-Sat., CH$7,500-10,000, *menú del día* CH$5,000) has the most interesting menu in town, although it's definitely pricey. Lunch is a set menu with a starter and an eclectic range of mains, from fish curry to lamb stews and grilled steaks slathered with blue cheese. The sea views make the food taste even better.

With *alerce* wooden tiles and a bar shaped like a boat, there's nowhere that looks quite as Chilote as **Club Social Baquedano** (Baquedano 459, tel. 65/2623 633, 1pm-1am Mon.-Sat., 1pm-5pm Sun., CH$6,000-12,000), in the former social club of that name. Local craft beers are on tap, and the menu is very un-Chilote: large pizzas, burgers, sandwiches, ceviche, and chicken and octopus fajitas. Don't come in a hurry; service can be very slow.

Accommodations

Across the road from the Cruz del Sur bus terminal is ★ **13 Lunas** (Los Carrera 855, tel. 65/2622 106, http://13lunas.cl, CH$11,500 dorm, CH$30,000 d shared bath), a backpacker's favorite built in the style of a traditional Chilote house. Accommodations include large four-, five-, and six-bed dormitories with lockers as well as private rooms. Creature comforts are a huge fully equipped kitchen, a TV room with Netflix, a basement bar and barbecue area, and a sea-view terrace. The double

TOP EXPERIENCE

☆ Chilote Churches

Iglesia Nuestra Señora del Rosario de Chonchi

With the arrival of the Jesuits in 1608 came the construction of at least 150 wooden churches, a fusion of European architectural styles and Chilote building techniques, heavily influenced by the islanders' expertise with boatbuilding. Today about 60 remain, and 16 have been designated UNESCO World Heritage sites.

Most of the churches are characterized by a symmetrical tower, a gable, and an arched portico, with a vaulted ceiling inside. Outside the churches are covered in wooden shingles known as *tejuelas,* made from *alerce,* a hardwood endemic to the islands and durable in the extreme damp climate. These shingles are a hallmark of Chilote houses and are used to waterproof the walls of the *palafitos* in Castro and other villages.

The most impressive feature of the churches is that they were built without nails, which were difficult to acquire at the time. Instead, wooden dowels and joints were used for assembly. Hook-and-butt and dovetail joints reflect the islanders' skill with woodwork, adapted from a long culture of boatbuilding. The construction methods were sound; the remaining structures have survived the island's wet climate and serious earthquakes—all without a single nail.

If you plan to visit more than a couple, stop at the **Centro de Visitantes** of the **Fundación Amigos de las Iglesias de Chiloé** (Errázurris 227, tel. 65/2621 046, 9:30am-6pm daily Jan.-Feb., 9:30am-6pm Mon.-Fri. Mar.-Dec.) in Ancud to get **La Ruta de las Iglesias** (The Route of the Churches) passport. As you visit each church, you get a stamp. Note that it can be difficult to track down church caretakers, who are in possession of the passport stamps.

Dropping in on all 16 of the UNESCO World Heritage churches is quite a task, so if you're short on time, consider visiting a smaller list:

- **Iglesia Nuestra Señora de Patrocinio de Tenaún** (page 388)

- **Iglesia San Francisco de Castro** (page 389)

- **Iglesia Santa María de Loreto de Achao** (page 399)

- **Iglesia Nuestra Señora del Rosario de Chonchi** (page 401)

room is in the basement, so ask for the twin on the first floor. If you want a warm shower, wait until evening; the water is heated by solar panels. They rent out bikes and run tours to the penguin colony at Puñihuil as well as kayaking excursions. Rates include IVA.

Just one block from the Plaza de Armas, centrally located **Casa Damasco** (Errazuriz 209, tel. 9/8556 8446 or 9/7882 4232, casadamascochiloe@gmail.com, CH$40,000 d shared bath, cash only) has only three rooms but an abundance of communal spaces, including a huge kitchen and living area. The upstairs double room is the largest, but all are sizeable and decorated with handwoven textiles. Bikes are available to rent and the Chilean-German owners operate local tours around Ancud. Rates include IVA.

In a large building just off the main coastal road, the Swiss-run **Hostal Mundo Nuevo** (Av. Salvador Allende 748, tel. 65/2628 383, www.newworld.cl, July-May, CH$14,000 dorm, CH$41,000 d shared bath, CH$52,000 d private bath) feels more like a small hotel than a hostel, particularly in the 2nd-floor rooms, which are brighter and larger than those on the 3rd floor. Downstairs, the sunroom and living spaces are immaculate spots to absorb the sea views. A hot tub adds to the extensive amenities. The hostel is closed in June. Rates include IVA.

A 15-minute drive or taxi journey southwest from Ancud, ★ **Paihuen Yurts** (Camino a Lechagua, tel. 9/9158 1073, www. paihuenyurts.cl, CH$60,000 2-person yurt, cash only) have one spacious canvas yurt hidden in the forest, with its own private hot tub down a short path to the river. The setting is serene and the facilities superb, with a complete kitchen, modern bath, and a good shower. There's space for up to four people; children are not permitted. Rates include IVA.

Information and Services

The staff at **SERNATUR** (Libertad 621, tel. 65/2622 665, www.ancud.cl, infochiloe@ sernatur.cl, 8:30am-6:30pm Mon.-Thurs., 8:30am-5:30pm Fri. Jan.-Feb., 8:30am-5:30pm Mon.-Thurs., 8:30am-4:30pm Fri. Mar.-Dec.) speak some English; this is the most helpful tourism office on the island. They have maps for Chiloé and can help with transport routes to small villages, as well as provide information about *festivales constumbristas*, the traditional festivals held throughout summer in different towns.

For medical attention, head to the **Hospital de Ancud** (La Torre 301, tel. 65/2326 478). The ATMs of **Banco Estado** (Los Carrera 821) and **Banco de Chile** (Libertad 621) are open 24 hours daily. To do laundry, head to **Clean Center** (Pudeto 45, no phone, 10am-1pm and 3pm-7:30pm Mon.-Sat.). Mail services can be found at **Correos** (Pudeto 220, 9am-1:30pm and 3pm-6pm Mon.-Fri., 9:30am-12:30pm Sat.).

Getting There
CAR
From **Puerto Montt,** it's a 95-km, 2.5-hour journey to Ancud, which includes a 30-minute ferry ride. Ruta 5 runs southwest to Pargua, where **Transmarchilay** (www. transmarchilay.cl, every 15-30 min, 24 hr daily, CH$12,600 vehicle with passengers, CH$8,600 motorbike, CH$2,500 bike) operates the 30-minute ferry crossing to Chacao on Isla Grande. From here, it's a 30-km, 30-minute drive along Ruta 5 through crop fields and pastures to reach Ancud. To reach Ancud from **Castro,** it's 82km north on the one-lane Ruta 5, which takes a little over an hour.

BUS
Ancud has two bus stations. The **Terminal de Buses Cruz del Sur** (Los Carrera 956, tel. 65/2622 265) serves both local and long-distance buses operated by **Cruz del Sur** (www.webcds.cl). These include frequent services from **Castro** (every 30 min, 1.5hr, CH$2,300), **Chonchi** (6 daily, 2hr, CH$3,000),

---

1: cheese for sale at Ancud's Feria Rural Municipal
2: Paihuen Yurts

and **Quellón** (hourly, 3.5hr, CH$4,500). Cruz del Sur operates the most buses from **Dalcahue** (4 daily, 1hr, CH$1,700).

Cruz del Sur also runs buses to Ancud from the mainland, including **Puerto Montt** (every 30 min, 2.5hr, CH$5,000), **Puerto Varas** (5 daily, 2.75hr, CH$5,500), **Osorno** (10 daily, 3.5hr, CH$7,000), **Valdivia** (6 daily, 5hr, CH$9,500), **Temuco** (6 daily, 6hr, CH$12,500), **Concepción** (5 daily, 12hr, CH$23,000/CH$29,000), and **Santiago** (7pm and 7:35pm daily, 14hr, CH$30,000/CH$41,000). You can also reach Ancud by bus from **Punta Arenas** (23hr, CH$45,000). These routes travel to Puerto Montt and then through Argentina (although you can't leave the bus), departing at 8:30pm Tuesday, Thursday, and Saturday.

The smaller **Terminal Rural** (Colo Colo 318, tel. 65/2628 246) is where you'll find **minibuses** that run to and from local rural destinations, including **Chepú** (1 daily, 1.5hr, CH$2,000) and the village of **Puñihuil** (4 daily Mon.-Fri., 2 daily Sat., 40min, CH$2,000). There's also a route that runs to and from **Fuerte Agüi** (11:45pm and 2:45pm Mon.-Fri., 1pm Sat. to Fuerte Agüi; 4:30pm Mon.-Sat. to Ancud, 1.5hr, CH$1,500).

Getting Around

Ancud is small enough that distances are easily walkable. If you're staying out of town, use **Taxis Dieciocho** (tel. 65/2622 565).

Península de Lacuy

Following the coast west, the road clings to the Golfo de Quetalmahue, passing clusters of small tin-roofed houses. The northwestern edge of Isla Grande is the **Península de Lacuy,** a hilly area covered in archaeological remains from the island's first settlers. The family-run **Museo Prehistórico de Quilo** (just after the bridge, 17km northwest of Ancud, tel. 9/9245 0490, 8am-10pm daily, CH$1,000 adults, CH$500 children) has an extensive collection of stone tools used by the indigenous Huilliche people, plus two complete sperm whale skeletons.

The peninsula is a great spot for **bird-watching,** as it's on the migratory route for a number of seabirds, including sooty shearwaters, black-browed albatrosses, and southern giant petrels.

Guided tours of the peninsula can be organized through community-run **Wape** (tel. 9/4243 6079, http://wape.cl). Tour options include bird-watching across the gulf or whale-watching off the western coast through a telescope, where you'll have a far higher probability than in a boat of spying the blue, southern right, humpback, and pygmy whales that pass through these waters October-April. The staff at Wape can also connect you to their network of lodgings, tour companies, and restaurants operated by local indigenous farmers and fisherfolk.

FUERTE AGÜI

On the eastern tip of the peninsula, **Fuerte Agüi** (no phone, 24 hr daily, free), also known as **Fuerte de Ahui,** was built from native wood in 1779, then reinforced with local *cancagua* stone in the early 1900s. The fort had a strategic role in defending San Carlos de Chiloé (modern-day Ancud); its impenetrable nature allowed the island to remain the final stronghold of the Spanish during the war of Chilean independence. Each February, there are reenactments of the failed 1820 attack of Thomas Cochrane and his men, who sought to liberate the island from Spanish rule.

To get here by public transit, **buses** (11:45pm and 2:45pm Mon.-Fri., 1pm Sat., 1.5hr, CH$1,500) leave from the **Terminal Rural** (Colo Colo 318, tel. 65/2628 246) in Ancud and drop you just before the fort; the return bus leaves at 4:30pm. Driving from Ancud, take the W-20 west from Ancud, then the W-236 and the W-242. It's a 36-km, one-hour drive.

MONUMENTO NATURAL ISLOTES DE PUÑIHUIL

About 25km southwest of Ancud are three scrub-covered islets known as the **Monumento Natural Islotes de Puñihuil,** a sanctuary for nesting Humboldt and Magellanic penguins that spend their summers breeding here. It's best visited as a day trip from Ancud.

Penguin-Watching Tours

From the beach at the small settlement of Puñihuil, local fisherfolk operating under the name **Pingüineras Chiloé** (tel. 9/8317 4302, http://pinguineraschiloe.cl) take penguin-watchers in 35-seat boats for the 30-minute journey (CH$7,500 adults, CH$4,000 children) around the three islands collectively known as Islotes de Puñihuil.

From the boat, expect to see a small but noisy colony of Magellanic and Humboldt penguins lining the rocky cliffs. This is one of the only places on the planet where these two species nest together. Your English-speaking guide will show you how to distinguish between them. You may spot sea otters or even blue whales in the surrounding waters.

Boats stay a few hundred meters from the islands; landing on them is prohibited. You'll want a zoom lens for the best photos. The boats leave every 20 minutes 10:15am-5:45pm daily September-mid-March. The islands are best visited starting in December, when the full colony arrives to breed.

Booking in advance isn't necessary, although it's best to arrive early in the day in January-February, when the attraction is most popular.

Ecomarine Puñihuil (tel. 9/8317 4302) operates **wildlife-watching tours** (daily, CH$65,000 pp) that depart from Puñihuil. On these three- to four-hour tours, which visit a sea lion colony, you may also spot blue, humpback, and southern right whales, and even orcas. Poor weather can cause cancellations. Make reservations at least a few days in advance, especially if you want to want to secure an English-speaking guide.

Accommodations

Seven kilometers south of Puñihuil, the departure point for penguin-watching tours, **Vertientes de Pumillahue** (Pumillahue, tel. 9/7829 2779, www.vertientesdepumillahue.cl, CH$95,000 d cabin, cash only) has an enviable location overlooking the ocean. It's tempting to never venture out of these two-level cabins, except to take the beach path that leaves from their doorstep. Built with attention to detail, cabins have the huge windows to appreciate the ocean views. Rates include IVA.

Getting There

You can get to Puñihuil by public transit, with your own vehicle, or by joining a tour. The hostel **13 Lunas** (Los Carrera 855, Ancud, tel. 65/2622 106, http://13lunas.cl) runs four-hour **tours** (CH$15,000 pp, additional CH$5,000 for English-speaking guide) that include round-trip transportation from the hostel and passage on one of the boats operated by Pingüineras Chiloé.

From Castro, **Siempre Verde Turismo** (Blanco Encalada 50, Castro, tel. 9/5253 0540, www.siempreverdeturismo.com) and **Chiloé Natural** (Blanco Encalada 100, Castro, tel. 65/2534 973, www.chiloenatural.com) run full-day tours (CH$55,000 pp, min. 2 people) that include hotel pickup and passage on one of the boats operated by Pingüineras Chiloé.

You can also get here by taking a Puñihuil-bound **bus** (40min, CH$2,000) from Ancud's **Terminal Rural** (Colo Colo 318, Ancud, tel. 65/2628 246). There are four departures a day Monday-Friday and at 1pm and 1:30pm Saturday; these buses drop passengers and then leave for the return journey to Ancud 10 minutes later. (Plan on taking a taxi in the morning if you're going on Saturday and want to return on the bus.)

To get to Puñihuil in your own vehicle, it's a 28-km, one-hour drive west from Ancud along the W-20, W-220, and W-246.

★ VALLE DE CHEPÚ

On the western coast of Isla Grande, 40km southwest of Ancud, the village of Chepú is home to a scattering of houses along tidal Río Chepú. In 1960, when a 9.6 magnitude earthquake struck the island, the ground of the surrounding **Valle de Chepú** dropped by two meters, forming a 1,400-hectare expanse of wetlands and sunken forest through which the Río Punta and Río Chepú flow to the ocean. This impressive act of nature transformed the area into an important biodiverse environment for birds. Ringed kingfishers, black-faced ibis, Chilean swallows, and slender-billed parakeets are among the commonly spotted species.

Muelle de la Luz

On the southern side of the mouth of Río Chepú, **Muelle de la Luz** (Dock of Light) is an installation by Chilean artist Marcelo Orellana Rivera. The structure is shaped like a curved pier and faces the ocean. The artist's most famous work is Muelle de las Almas (Dock of the Souls), just south of Cucao.

Local fishing boats can take you on a two-hour **boat tour** (CH$5,000 adults, CH$4,000 children, min. 4 people), which includes an hour at the pier for photos. Motorized boats leave from the dock in Chepú, where the road descends steeply to reach the bridge over the Estuario Anguai. The Castro-based tour operator **Siempre Verde Turismo** (Blanco Encalada 50, Castro, tel. 9/5253 0540, www.siempreverdeturismo.com) runs a full-day tour to the Muelle de la Luz for CH$60,000

pp (min. 2 people) that includes hotel pickup, a bilingual guide, and a snack.

Recreation
KAYAKING

Kayaking at dawn along the Río Chepú and into the Río Puntra is the most popular activity here. You're likely to see endangered southern river otters. Organize a four-hour **kayaking tour** (including transportation, min. 3 people, CH$30,000) with the Ancud-based hostel **13 Lunas** (Los Carrera 855, Ancud, tel. 65/2622 106, http://13lunas.cl) for around two hours in the water.

BEACHES

Accessed by a path from where the road through the village of Chepú ends at the coast, the breathtaking **Playa Aulen** is flanked by sand dunes on one side and crashing waves on the other, making it one of Isla Grande's star beaches. In spring and summer, whale and even orca sightings are possible.

GUIDED TOURS

Austral Adventures (Av. Salvador Allender 904, Ancud, tel. 65/2625 977, http://austral-adventures.com) organizes day trips from Ancud to Chepú with a boat tour to birding

kayaking in Valle de Chepú

hot spot Laguna Coluco and a trek through rainforest. The trip can also be extended to include a visit to a penguin colony; prices start at CH$85,000 pp (min. 2 people) and include transportation, lunch, and a bilingual guide.

From Castro, try the tour operator **Chiloétnico** (Los Carrera 435, Castro, tel. 65/2630 951, www.chiloetnico.cl), which combines a dawn kayaking tour with a trip to the penguin colony at Puñihuil (CH$98,000 pp, min. 2 people) and includes hotel pickup and an English-speaking guide.

Food and Accommodations

With thick wooden walls and comfortable beds, **Senderos Chepú** (W-250, tel. 9/9260 2423, enriquetacs@yahoo.com, CH$25,000 full-board pp, cash only) is a simple, rustic bed-and-breakfast that makes a good base. Expect a warm welcome and excellent home-cooking (it is also possible to arrange lodging without food). They can organize kayaking tours and hikes along the coast, and have a private trail through the forest. They also run a **restaurant** across the road from the house, with sweeping views of the Chepú valley and the Río Chepú, where home-cooked dishes of salmon and meat and set lunches can be arranged; outside January-February, call to make sure it's open. Senderos Chepú is 2km west along the gravel W-250 from the dock, just after the bridge over the Estuario Anguai.

Getting There and Around

To reach Chepú by car, it's a 33-km, one-hour drive from **Ancud,** south on Ruta 5 and then southwest on the W-250. From **Castro,** it's a 76-km, 1.5-hour drive north along Ruta 5, the W-30, and the W-250.

Without your own vehicle, Chepú is difficult to reach. From Ancud's **Terminal Rural** (Colo Colo 318, Ancud, tel. 65/2628 246), Chepú-bound **buses** (1.5hr, CH$2,000) leave at 4pm Monday, Wednesday, and Friday. The only other option is the buses from Ancud to **Castro** (30min, CH$1,500), but you have to disembark after 22km (25min), where Ruta 5 intersects with the W-30, which runs west to Chepú, and hitchhike the rest of the way; vehicles are infrequent along this road.

QUEMCHI

On the eastern coast of Isla Grande, Quemchi is a lovely Chilote fishing village with a scattering of shingled houses clustered around two strips of road. On a clear day, the snow-dusted peaks of the Andes, 50km east, are visible. A former timber port, Quemchi is sustained by salmon farming and fishing.

Sights

Overlooking the main beach, the **Casa Museo Francisco Coloane** (a few doors down from Bar Lo Ventos, 9:30am-6pm daily Jan.-Feb., 9:30am-6pm Tues.-Sat. Mar.-Dec., free) is a replica of the house of the Quemchi author Francisco Coloane. The original structure was destroyed in the 1960 earthquake. A small collection of photos of the author, best known for his seafaring adventure novels, are displayed.

Food and Accommodations

Quemchi makes a good spot for lunch, particularly at ★ **Las Conchas de Sus Mares** (on the right as you enter the village from the south, tel. 9/7430 1616, 1pm-9pm daily Jan.-Feb., 1pm-9pm Wed.-Thurs. Mar.-Dec., CH$4,000-6,500, cash only), a haven of tranquility next to the sea. Tables are in a bright and airy extension with simple booths and incredible sea views. Food ranges from wood-fired pizzas topped with salmon and capers or smoked pork *longanizas* to homemade kuchen. Outside, a small garden with deep, cozy chairs allows you to enjoy the harbor-side vistas. If you can't bear to leave, two cozy bedrooms (CH$35,000 d shared bath) are upstairs. The owners live on-site.

With a breezy upstairs terrace overlooking Isla Cacahue and the mountains behind, **Barloventos** (Yungay 8, tel. 9/7873 8112 or 65/2691 239, 9am-11:30pm daily Jan.-Feb., 9am-8pm Mon.-Sat. Mar.-Dec., CH$5,000-8,000) serves simple towering plates of excellent grilled fish. Opt for a table on the outside terrace or upstairs—the downstairs rooms are somewhat dingy. They serve their own craft beer, brewed on-site.

Getting There

The coastal route from **Ancud** along the W-15, reached by taking Ruta 5 north, is in poor condition; it's far quicker to take the inland route south on Ruta 5 and then the W-15 and W-195 east. It's a 62-km, one-hour drive from Ancud via the inland route. The route to Quemchi from **Castro** is fully paved. To get here, take Ruta 5 north, followed by the W-15 and W-195. It's a 66-km drive that takes just over an hour.

The bus company **Expresos Catalina** (no phone) offers two daily departures from **Castro** (7:30am and 1pm daily, 1.75hr, CH$2,000). There are hourly buses from **Ancud** (6 departures Sat., 4 departures Sun., 1.5hr, CH$2,000) that depart from the **Terminal Rural** (Colo Colo 318, Ancud, tel. 65/2628 246).

TENAÚN

Thirty kilometers south of Quemchi, the road dips down from a hill to reach peaceful Tenaún, a fishing village surrounded by rolling hills and fields of grazing cattle. A single road connects two rows of dilapidated shingled houses, some of which are inhabited.

Sights

The village is known for the bold blue **Iglesia Nuestra Señora de Patrocinio de Tenaún** (Virgen María s/n, no phone), an unusual three-towered church that's a UNESCO World Heritage Site and second in aesthetic drama only to Castro's church. It dates to 1845 and has had hefty restoration over the past few decades. To go inside (9am-8pm daily), you'll need the keys from the caretaker, who lives in the house across the street with the white picket fence.

Local fishing boats can take you across the water to the remote **Isla Mechuque,** east of the village and part of the Chauques Archipelago. Mechuque has a population of only 200, the majority of whom are elderly and still live in seaside *palafitos*. There's a pretty baby-blue shingled church, and you can often find locals preparing *curanto* in the traditional way. To find the boats, head east from the village along the coastal road to the beach and the fishing pier. Expect to pay around CH$40,000 for the 45-minute **boat ride** (maximum of 8 people) there and back. Ask your boat captain to come back at an agreed-upon time, as there are few public boats.

CASCADAS DE TOCOIHUE

About 10km west of Tenaún, the **Cascadas de Tocoihue** (9am-8pm daily, CH$1,000 adults, CH$500 children) are three waterfalls hidden in the undergrowth of the temperate rainforest. A short set of steep steps leads to a platform with a view from above. You can also walk a few hundred meters from the entrance to stand beneath the falls. According to local legend, any young woman wishing to become a witch must bathe in these waters for 12 hours to remove the shackles of Catholicism. It's possible to camp on the banks of the river (CH$5,000 pp).

The falls are accessible from the W-195 where it intersects with the W-231, about 200 meters west of Tenaún's church. To get here with your own vehicle, take the unpaved road that forks south off the W-195 for 1km, following the signs for Cascadas de Tocoihue. This road becomes swampy after heavy rain and should only be attempted with a 4WD vehicle then. Buses from Castro bound for Tenaún can drop you off at the turnoff for the falls.

Getting There

To reach Tenaún, it's a slow amble from either Ancud or Castro. From **Ancud,** take Ruta 5 south, then the W-15 east to Quemchi, and then the W-195 south. The gravel turnoff for the waterfalls is where the W-195 takes a sharp 90-degree turn west. It's an 80-km, 1.5-hour drive. From **Quemchi,** it's 23km and 30 minutes. From **Castro,** it's a 48-km, one-hour drive north along Ruta 5, the W-55 through Dalcuhue, and the W-195. Turn south on the gravel track, which is 1km before the W-195 takes a 90-degree turn north.

Tenaún-bound **buses** (1:30pm and 7pm daily, 1.75hr, CH$2,000) depart from Ancud's **Terminal Rural** (Colo Colo 318, Ancud, tel. 65/2628 246). From Castro's **Terminal Municipal** (San Martín 667, Castro, tel. 65/2635 666), **Buses Bahmondi** (tel. 9/8330 4956) and **Expreso Tenaún** (tel. 9/7155 7796 or 9/8342 4819) have eight buses for Tenaún (1.25hr, CH$1,600) Monday-Saturday and three on Sunday (7:45am, 2:40pm, and 4:45pm). These buses drop passengers and return immediately to their point of origin.

Castro and Vicinity

CASTRO

With rainbow-colored houses on stilts along the shore and the banana-yellow church on the Plaza de Armas, Castro (pop. 40,000) is Chiloé's most colorful settlement. It's also Chiloé's only city, dating to 1567 when Martín Ruiz de Gamboa claimed it for Spain. It has survived earthquakes and looting by pirates. This lively port town has a burgeoning dining scene that attracts a growing number of travelers; the chance to spend a night in a refurbished *palafito* adds to the appeal.

The city is bounded on three sides by water: the Río La Chacra in the east, the Mar de Chiloé (Chilote Sea) to the south, and the Río Gamboa on the southwest. Both rivers are lined with crooked *palafitos* that hang over the water. Ruta 5 passes through Castro from north to west via a bridge across Río Gamboa. The Plaza de Armas is in the south of the city, two blocks before Ruta 5 reaches the southernmost tip of Castro.

Sights
IGLESIA SAN FRANCISCO DE CASTRO

Looming over the north side of the **Plaza de Armas** (bounded by Almirate Latorre, San Martín, Blanco, and O'Higgins), the two-towered **Iglesia San Francisco de Castro** (Almirante Latorre, 9:30am-12:30pm and 3:30pm-8pm daily) is startling and seemingly plucked from a candy shop thanks to its corrugated galvanized-iron facade daubed in shocking yellow and lavender. A UNESCO World Heritage Site, it stands on the site of the island's first church, built in 1567, that burned multiple times. The current building, constructed 1910-1912, was designed by Italian architect Eduardo Provasoli in neo-Gothic and neoclassical styles with Chilote construction techniques.

The impressive interior is built from native polished *raulí* and *olivillo* woods. Suspended over the altar is a replica of *El Nazareno* statue—Jesus on the cross—that was found in the Iglesia de Caguach near Achao. The church is sometimes closed Monday.

★ PALAFITOS

Hovering above the shoreline on wooden stilts, the boldly painted *palafitos* of Castro are one of the city's most iconic sights. Built with one door fronting the road and another facing the ocean, these dwellings were originally inhabited by fishing families. Although once prolific across the archipelago, many *palafitos* were lost in the 1960 earthquake. Recent years have seen the remaining houses converted into boutique hotels and cafés.

Castro has the largest number of *palafitos* in good repair. The easiest to see are in the **Gamboa neighborhood;** you'll find a viewing platform west of the bridge that crosses the Río Gamboa, on Ruta 5 before it climbs into the city. You can also admire the houses from farther away at **Mirador Chacabuco** (Gamboa and Eyzaguirre), an overlook with excellent views. Gamboa's *palafitos* are most photogenic in the morning, when the light shines on them from the east. You can find more *palafitos* on **Avenida Pedro Montt** in

Castro

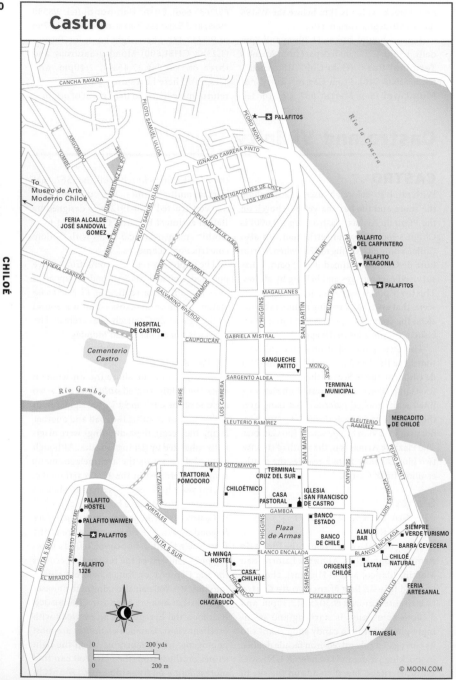

CANCHA RAYADA

PILOTO SAMUEL ULLOA

ARGOMEDO
YUMBEL
JUAN MARTÍNEZ DE VELASCO
SYSSA

IGNACIO CARRERA PINTO

★ ⊠ PALAFITOS

PEDRO MONTT

Río la Chacra

INVESTIGACIONES DE CHILE

LOS LIRIOS

To
Museo de Arte
Moderno Chiloé

FERIA ALCALDE
JOSÉ SANDOVAL
GOMEZ

MANUEL MUÑOZ

DIPUTADO FELIX GARAY

PILOTO SAMUEL ULLOA

EL TEJAR

PALAFITO
DEL CARPINTERO

PEDRO MONTT

PALAFITO
PATAGONIA

JUAN SARRAT

JAVIERA CARRERA

IQUIQUE

GALVARINO RIVEROS
ANGMOS

PILOTO PARDO

★ ⊠ PALAFITOS

MAGALLANES

O'HIGGINS

SAN MARTÍN

HOSPITAL
DE CASTRO

CAUPOLICÁN

GABRIELA MISTRAL

Cementerio
Castro

Río Gamboa

FREIRE

LOS CARRERA

SARGENTO ALDEA

SANGUECHE
PATITO

MONJITAS

TERMINAL
MUNICIPAL

ELEUTERIO RAMÍREZ

ELEUTERIO
RAMÍREZ

MERCADITO
DE CHILOÉ

SAN MARTÍN

EMILIO SOTOMAYOR

SERRANO

PEDRO MONTT

TRATTORIA
POMODORO

EYZAGUIRRE

TERMINAL
CRUZ DEL SUR

CHILOÉTNICO

CASA
PASTORAL

IGLESIA
SAN FRANCISCO
DE CASTRO

LUIS ESPINOZA

PALAFITO
HOSTEL

PORTALES

GAMBOA

BANCO
ESTADO

SIEMPRE
VERDE TURISMO

● PALAFITO WAIWEN

ERNESTO RIQUELME

O'HIGGINS

Plaza
de Armas

BANCO
DE CHILE

ALMUD
BAR

BLANCO ENCALADA

BARRA CEVECERA

★ ⊠ PALAFITOS

RUTA 5 SUR

BLANCO ENCALADA

CHILOÉ
NATURAL

PALAFITO
1326

RUTA 5 SUR

LA MINGA
HOSTEL

ESMERALDA

ORIGENES
CHILOÉ

LATAM

EL MIRADOR

CASA
CHILHUÉ

CHACABUCO

THOMSON

FERIA
ARTESANAL

EUSEBIO LILLO

MIRADOR
CHACABUCO

CHACABUCO

TRAVESÍA

0   200 yds
0   200 m

© MOON.COM

a 700-meter stretch where it intersects with Ruta 5, in the northern approach to the city.

MUSEO DE ARTE MODERNO CHILOÉ

On the northwestern edge of Castro, 4km from the Plaza de Armas, **Museo de Arte Moderno Chiloé** (Parque Municipal s/n, tel. 65/2635 454, www.mamchiloe.cl, 10am-6pm daily summer and 10am-5pm daily fall-spring during exhibitions, donation) is within a shingled barn-like building and contains a collection from over 300 Chilean artists. There is no permanent collection; the museum hosts art shows and other exhibitions. Consult the website for open days. You can get here with a *taxi colectivo* from the Plaza de Armas.

Entertainment

With a large cocktail menu, '80s music, and a young crowd, **Almud Bar** (Ignacio Serrano 325, tel. 65/2530 084, 6:30pm-1am Tues.-Thurs., 7:30pm-3am Fri., 8:30pm-3am-Sat.) is Castro's liveliest bar. Local ingredients including *murta* and *merkén* make an appearance in their cocktails and their food, which is surprisingly good for a bar. One hundred types of beer are crammed behind the bar at local favorite **Barra Cevecera** (Blanco 96, tel. 65/2533 775, 5:30pm-1am Mon.-Thurs., 5:30pm-3am Fri.-Sat.). They have local beers on tap, plus a great vantage point over the bay from the back terrace.

Castro's best-known event is the **Festival Costumbrista,** also known as the **Festival de Castro,** a weeklong celebration of Chilote food, folkloric music and dancing, and vendors selling local crafts, held the second or third week of February in Parque Municipal in the northwest of the city. Try traditional dishes and Chilote drinks such as *chicha* (apple cider) and *licor de oro* (a liqueur made from aguardiente and flavored with saffron and whey).

Food festivals and other cultural events are also held throughout the year in the **Casa Pastoral** (Almirante Latorre s/n), next to the Iglesia San Francisco de Castro.

Shopping

Castro is a great place for local souvenirs that reflect the archipelago's indigenous heritage. Some of the best items include thick woolen hats known as *gorros chilotes,* with long earpieces, and woven baskets and mythological figurines, both made from the fibers of the manila plant.

A good selection of Chilote crafts, including baskets and wall hangings, wooden boats, and thick woolen rugs are available at **Origenes Chiloé** (Thompson 295, tel. 65/2632 838, http://origeneschiloe.cl, 10am-2pm and 3pm-8pm Mon.-Sat. Jan.-Feb., 11am-1:30pm and 3:45pm-7:30pm Mon.-Fri., 11am-2pm and 4pm-7pm Sat. Mar.-Dec.).

FERIA ARTESANAL

By the waterfront, the **Feria Artesanal** (Lillo s/n, just before the harbor, 9:30am-6pm daily) has an extensive collection of crafts for sale, many of which are locally made, displayed on heaving stalls that open onto the street. Find carved wooden maté pots, miniature churches, and tasty liqueurs of mango, *maqui,* and *licor de oro.* The high-ceilinged main hall teems with local woolens. It's the biggest craft market in Chiloé and offers the most variety.

The fish vendors here attract a small group of sea lions that hang around begging for scraps. They strike poses for photographs, but are still wild animals, so give them a wide berth.

Recreation

Dan Ettinger of **Tepa Trails** (tel. 9/9815 7869, http://danieljettinger.wixsite.com/tepatrailschile) creates superb tours with a focus on bird-watching, cultural experiences, or hiking to practically any destination in Chiloé. All itineraries are private, customizable, and focus on authentic experiences with local people. Prices start from CH$70,000 pp (min. 2 people) and include transportation and lunch. One-person tours (from CH$165,000) can also be organized.

Visit some of the churches beyond Castro with **Siempre Verde Turismo**

(Blanco Encalada 50, tel. 9/5253 0540, www. siempreverdeturismo.com), **Chiloétnico** (Los Carrera 435, tel. 9/9135 3448, http:// chiloetnico.cl), or **Chiloé Natural** (Blanco Encalada 100, tel. 65/2534 973, www. chiloenatural.com). Tours start at CH$35,000 for a half-day tour to Dalcahue and Isla Quinchao, and CH$45,000 for a full-day tour to Isla Lemuy. Hotel pickup and an English-speaking guide are included. All three companies also run tours to the Puñihuil penguin colony and Parque Tantauco; Siempre Verde and Chiloétnico offer excursions to Valle de Chepú.

Highly recommended tour company **Rancho Pullao** (tel. 9/9541 7402, www. refugiopullao.cl) operates from Refugio Pullao, a remote lodge outside Castro, and specializes in half-day, daylong, and multi-day horseback tours with expert local guides who speak excellent English. A half-day tour starts at CH$35,000, including equipment and a snack. A barbecue or *curanto* lunch or additional bird-watching can be added. Standalone 2.5-hour bird-watching tours start at CH$15,000 pp. If you don't have your own vehicle, transportation to Refugio Pullao can be arranged for an additional fee. It's a 30-minute, 20-km drive along Ruta 5 and the W-55, W-65, and W-535.

Northwest of Castro, the Cordillera de Pichuén provides the backdrop for horseback tours with **Cabalgatas Chiloé** (tel. 9/9079 0722 or 9/8873 377, www.cabalgataschiloe. cl), with well-trained horses and experienced English-speaking guides. Other activity options include kayaking tours along the Río San Pedro and a day learning about farm life and helping out with the livestock. Transfers from Castro, lunch, and equipment are included. Horseback riding and kayaking cost CH$35,000 pp (min. 2 people) for a half-day.

Food

You'll find **Sangueche Patito** (San Martín 718, tel. 65/2380 028, 1pm-7:30pm Mon.-Fri., 1pm-9pm Sat., CH$2,500-3,800) by the queue out the door. This poky place specializes in enormous *mechada* (braised beef) sandwiches on tasty homemade bread. Go for braised lamb, pork, or even mushroom with a dozen types of mayonnaise and sauces to slather on your sandwich. Eat shoulder-to-shoulder with the other patrons at the tiny bar area or opt for takeout.

A guitar hangs above the door the door at the quirky ★ **Mercadito de Chiloé** (Av. Pedro Montt 210, tel. 65/2533 866, http:// elmercaditodechiloe.cl, 1pm-3:30pm and 7:30pm-10:30pm Tues.-Sun., CH$7,000-10,000), where the focus is on fresh seafood—the best in Castro. The menu changes with the seasons and what they can source from local suppliers. The red tuna, shrimp, prawn, and kiwi ceviche offers a fresh twist on a classic dish. Don't miss the *murta* sour in earthenware cups. Booking is essential on the weekend.

Castro's only specialty coffee shop, ★ **Palafito Patagonia** (Pedro Montt 651, tel. 9/5618 8933, noon-8pm Thurs.-Tues. fall-spring, 10am-8pm Thurs.-Tues. summer) is run by enthusiastic Pato, a coffee expert. Espresso and lattes are joined by specialty pour-over preparations, with beans sourced from Costa Rica, Honduras, and Peru. The views across the peninsula from the terrace are as good as the coffee. The entrance of this converted *palafito* also houses a small exhibit of works by artists from Chiloé and Patagonia.

Thin-crust pizzas at **Trattoria Pomodoro** (Sotomayor 520, tel. 9/8338 248, 1pm-11pm Tues.-Sat., 1pm-5pm Sun., CH$6,600-9,000) are second to none in this trendy Italian spot. Fresh pasta is served with a choice of nine sauces, and you're presented with a checkered bib if you pick a spaghetti dish. On weekends it's essential to book ahead.

Find top gastronomy under the guise of home cooking at **Travesía** (Lillo 188, tel. 65/2630 137, http://travesiarestaurant. blogspot.com, 1pm-11pm Mon.-Sat., 1pm-4pm Sun., CH$9,000-14,000, cash only), a

---

1: lunch at Travesía 2: Iglesia San Francisco de Castro 3: bird-watching 4: a *palafito*

modern restaurant in an old Chilote cottage. Innovative dishes offer excellent flavor combinations, such as the braised smoked pork with Chilote potato puree and murta sauce. Prices are among the highest in town, but the dining experience is worth it. Reservations on weekends are essential.

FERIA ALCALDE JOSÉ SANDOVAL GÓMEZ

The **Feria Alcalde José Sandoval Gómez** (Manuel Muñoz 611, 8am-8pm Sun.-Fri., 7am-8pm Sat.), also known as the **Mercado Municipal de Castro,** is the largest farmers market on the island, particularly on Saturday, when local vendors converge to sell an array of bulbous purple Chilote potatoes, huge cloves of Chilote garlic, honey, cheeses, juicy *cholgas* (giant mussels), and *choritos* (small mussels). Fruit and vegetable aisles accompany 30 stalls selling fish. Upstairs, small kitchens (CH$4,000-5,000) serve steaming *paila marina* (seafood soup), thick chicken and beef stews, and fried fish as well as snacks such as deep-fried potato patties filled with *chicharrones* (deep-fried pork) for CH$1,000.

Accommodations

Castro has the widest selection of affordable and upscale accommodations on the island. Be aware that few lodgings have parking.

UNDER CH$25,000

★ **La Minga Hostel** (Chacabuco 481, tel. 9/4843 5349, http://lamingahostel.com, CH$13,000 dorm, cash only) is the most sociable hostel in Castro. Rooms are tiny and there aren't many baths to go around, but the atmosphere is convivial. The owner's local knowledge is extensive. The location, just a block from the Plaza de Armas, is second to none.

CH$25,000-40,000

Expect a warm welcome at family-run **Casa Chilhué** (Chacabuco 455, tel. 65/2638 903, www.hostalchilhue.com, CH$35,000 d shared bath, CH$48,000 d private bath, cash only), a guesthouse in the center of the city. Rooms are a little dark, but everything is spotless. The breakfast comes with homemade kuchen, fruit, and cereal. Rates include IVA.

CH$40,000-60,000

In one of the converted *palafitos* in the Gamboa neighborhood, overlooking the Río Gamboa estuary, **Palafito Waiwen** (Ernesto Riquelme 1236, tel. 65/2633 888, http://palafitowaiwen.com, CH$15,000 dorm, CH$55,000 d private bath) is an excellent value. It has a young vibe thanks to the backpackers who occupy the downstairs dormitories. Private rooms upstairs are sizable but have tiny baths. The living areas are cozy. The terrace leads out to the water, as does the breakfast room, where a substantial breakfast with homemade breads and cake is served. To get estuary views from your bed, upgrade to the larger suite for an extra CH$35,000. Rates include IVA.

CH$60,000-80,000

The first *palafito*-turned-lodging in Castro, ★ **Palafito Hostel** (Ernesto Riquelme 1210, tel. 65/2531 008, http://palafitohostel. com, CH$17,000 dorm, CH$75,000 d private bath) offers large modern bedrooms in the Gamboa neighborhood. Two of the rooms have sea views and balconies. Although it looks run-down from the outside, inside are a communal lounge, kitchen, and front terrace that boast views across the estuary. The large breakfast and familial welcome keep guests coming back.

The brown-shingled **Palafito 1326** (Ernesto Riquelme 1326, tel. 65/2530 053, http://palafito1326.cl, CH$89,000-107,000 d) has the same owners as the Palafito Hostel and is decorated in slick modern style. Rooms are spacious, with crisp white linens, and those overlooking the water have a balcony. An extensive homemade breakfast is served at a long table in the cozy living room. Upstairs, a rooftop café, open to nonguests, switches to a bar in the late afternoon, serving local craft beers and killer pisco sours.

Chilote Cuisine

In near isolation for centuries, the Chiloé archipelago has distinctive cuisine, and islanders' favorite dishes showcase a wealth of local ingredients. Chiloé's wet climate is a hot spot for potatoes, with hundreds of different varieties that are easy to spot in markets, sometimes with bright purple skins. The best place to sample authentic Chilote cooking is one of the island's markets. Head to Castro's **Feria Alcalde José Sandoval Gómez** (Manuel Muñoz 611, Castro, 8am-8pm Sun.-Fri., 7am-8pm Sat.), **Mercado Dalcahue** (Pedro Montt s/n, Dalcahue, no phone, 9am-7pm daily), or **Mercado Municipal de Chonchi** (Irarrázabal s/n, Chonchi, 8am-8pm daily Jan.-Feb., 9:30am-4:30pm daily Mar.-Dec.).

CURANTO EN HOYO

Curanto en hoyo is a traditional Chilote preparation of meat, including *longanizas,* chicken, and shellfish, plus potatoes, *chapeles* (wheat and potato dumplings), and sometimes *milaco* (dumplings made from mashed potato and filled with crispy pork) cooked in a *hoyo* (hole) lined with hot rocks. The rocks are covered with *nalca* leaves and a layer of turf, which trap the steam and moisture. The process can take up to five hours, so a *curanto* is as much a social gathering as a dining experience.

It can be hard to find an authentic *curanto.* In January-February, the best option is in Quetalmahue, 12km west of Ancud, where **Restaurant Quetalmahue** (W-20, eastern fringes of Quetalmahue, tel. 9/8791 9410, 11am-8pm daily Jan.-Feb., CH$10,000) is known for authentic *curanto.* Get here before 2pm, when they often start running out of food.

Tour companies in Castro such as **Turismo Queilén** (Av. Gamboa 351, Local 116, Castro, tel. 9/7890 2625, http://turismoqueilenchiloe.cl) and lodgings throughout the region, such as **Isla Bruja Lodge** (Km 3 Camino Paildad s/n, Queilén, tel. 9/7732 3226, www.islabrujalodge.com) near Queilén, can arrange for you to take part in cooking and eating a traditional *curanto.* Turismo Queilén operates large Spanish-language-only group tours (up to 40 people, CH$30,000 pp). Included is transportation from their Castro office to Isla Mechuque, where the *curanto* is prepared, and the meal itself.

CURANTO EN OLLA

The more casual form of *curanto* is **curanto en olla,** or **pulmay,** made with the same ingredients but cooked in a large pot *(olla)* on a stove. This common form of the dish is easy to track down outside summer. Both versions are normally referred to as *curanto,* so double-check to be sure what you're getting. The best places to try *pulmay* are at **Mercado Dalcahue** (Pedro Montt s/n, Dalcahue, no phone, 9am-7pm daily, CH$6,000) and Ancud's **Kuranton** (Av. Prat 94, Ancud, tel. 65/2623 090, noon-11pm daily summer, noon-7:30pm spring-fall, CH$8,000). It's best to go for lunch, when the food is freshest.

MILCAO, CHAPALELES, AND CHOCHOCA

Milcao are fried grated and mashed potato dumplings filled with deep-fried pork. They make a great snack and are also an occasional ingredient in *curanto.* *Chapaleles* are similar to *milcao* but made from a mixture of wheat and potato with pork lard and bacon, boiled or steamed. Both dumplings can be slathered with honey for a tea-time snack. For the best *milcao* and *chapaleles,* visit Dalcahue's **Doña Lula** (stand 8, Mercado Dalcahue, Pedro Montt s/n, Dalcahue, no phone, 9am-7pm daily).

Chochoca is similar to *milcao* and *chapaleles.* Grated and mashed potatoes are combined with lard, rolled into a long piece of dough, and filled with deep-fried pork. The dough is wound around a log and cooked over coals. This snack is hard to find; you may see it sold at traditional folk festivals or other events on the island.

OVER CH$80,000

Luxurious double suites with floor-to-ceiling patio doors are at **Palafito del Carpintero** (Pedro Montt 705, tel. 9/6762 3802, CH$180,000 d). Designed by a Chilean architect, this old *palafito* has been converted into two huge modern bedrooms that are still in keeping with their traditional surroundings. Both rooms include a full kitchen and living area. Ask for the downstairs Palafito One, with a private terrace. The personalized attention and excellent local knowledge of the staff, combined with the tranquil setting looking across the water, make staying here even more comfortable. Breakfast is an additional CH$7,000; parking is available.

Information and Services

Castro's tourist information office is not very helpful. The best source is at Ancud's **SERNATUR office** (Libertad 621, Ancud, tel. 65/2622 665, infochiloe@sernatur.cl, www.ancud.cl, 8:30am-6:30pm Mon.-Thurs., 8:30am-5:30pm Fri. Jan.-Feb., 8:30am-5:30pm Mon.-Thurs., 8:30am-4:30pm Fri. Mar.-Dec.). The local **Hospital de Castro** (Ramón Freir 852, tel. 65/2530 755) has some emergency services. To withdraw cash, there are **24-hour ATMs** at **Banco Estado** (San Martín 392) and **Banco de Chile** (Blanco 201).

Getting There

AIR

The **Aeródromo Mocopulli de Castro** (MHC, km 1160, R-5), 19km north of Castro, is the only airport on the island. It has five weekly flights from Santiago December-March operated by **LATAM** (Blanco 180, Castro, tel. 65/2494 425, www.latam.com, 9am-1:15pm and 3pm-6:30pm Mon.-Fri.). This frequency drops to twice weekly April-November. **Transfer Chiloé** (tel. 9/8864 6793, http://transferchiloeoficial.com) charges CH$5,000 pp for a minivan transfer to the center of Castro.

CAR

From **Ancud,** it's an 82-km, 1.5-hour drive south along the paved Ruta 5 to Castro. It can be slow going thanks to trucking traffic. From **Quellón,** the 85-km route can be similarly slow due to freight transport. On a good day, it's a 1.5-hour drive.

BUS

Castro's **Terminal Cruz del Sur** (San Martín 462, tel. 65/2635 152) has most of the regional and long-distance buses. There are restrooms and a luggage storage area. Terminal Cruz del Sur's most regular connections are with **Puerto Montt** (every 30 min, 4hr, CH$7,000) via Ancud. Other connections include: **Puerto Varas** (6 daily, 4.25hr, CH$7,500), **Osorno** (hourly, 5hr, CH$8,500/CH$10,000), **Valdivia** (6 daily, 7hr, CH$10,500), **Temuco** (9 daily, 9.5hr, CH$12,000/CH$15,000), **Concepción** (5 daily, 13hr, CH$18,000/CH$22,000), and **Santiago** (3 daily, 16hr, CH$22,000/CH$28,000). There are also local routes to and from **Quellón** via Chonchi (every 2 hr, 2hr, CH$2,000).

Most local routes are served by the **Terminal Municipal** (San Martín 667, tel. 65/2635 666); minibuses arrive and leave from behind the company booths. Connections at Terminal Municipal include: **Achao** (every 30 min, 1.75hr, CH$1,800) at Platform 1, **Chonchi** (40min, CH$800) from Platform 2, and **Dalacahue** (40min, CH$800). **Buses Union Express** (tel. 9/6668 3531) and **Buses Ojeda** (tel. 65/2635 477) run hourly connections with **Cucao** (1.5hr, CH$2,000). Hourly connections with **Ancud** (1.5hr, CH$1,500) and Castro are operated by **San Cristobal** (tel. 9/8244 655, busessancristobal@gmail.com), and half-hourly buses to and from **Quellón** (1.75hr, CH$1,800) are run by **Quellón Express** (tel. 69/142 6644).

Long-distance carriers, including **ETM** (tel. 65/2533 759, contacto@busesetm.cl), **JAC** (tel. 65/2539 544, www.jac.cl), and **Queilén Bus** (tel. 65/2632 173, www.queilenbus.cl)

Off-the-Beaten-Path Lodges

sunset at Isla Bruja Lodge

There are plenty of places to stay outside Chiloé's main towns, many of which can organize tours and local experiences. Here are two worth a visit.

For a true Chilote experience, the fantastic **Refugio Pullao** (W-535, Quilquico, tel. 9/9895 7911, www.refugiopullao.cl, CH$163,000 d), northeast of Castro on the Peninsula Rilán, has six rooms in three single-story cabins set against a hillside with sweeping views. Host Amalia prepares homemade breakfasts and Chilote-inspired dinners (with advance notice), while Julien leads horseback rides along the beach. Rooms have king beds and sitting areas with views. Rates drop by half outside summer. They also run **Rancho Pullao,** a tour agency for bird-watching tours, horseback riding, and other activities. From Castro, it's a 20-km, 30-minute drive north along Ruta 5, then southwest along the W-55, W-65, and W-535.

Forty kilometers south of Chonchi and linked to Queilén by back roads, the divine **Isla Bruja Lodge** (Km 3 Camino Paildad, Queilén, tel. 9/7732 3226, www.islabrujalodge.com, CH$93,000 d, *palafito* CH$100,000) is Chiloé's best-kept secret. On the shores of an estuary, this guesthouse is welcoming thanks to hospitable Francisco and Marie. Four rooms are in the main guesthouse, and two *palafitos del bosque* (forest *palafitos*) are by the beach. The family dog can be borrowed for long walks through the surrounding forest. You're likely to encounter the family's domesticated sheep. Use of mountain bikes, kayaks, hiking trails, and the hot tub with estuary views are included. Lunches and dinners can be added for an extra charge. From Castro, take Ruta 5 south, then the W-853 toward Queilén, and the W-879 and W-855. The drive is magnificent.

also operate at Terminal Municipal. They have services with similar frequencies to those listed for Cruz del Sur. Queilén Bus also has hourly connections with **Queilén** (1.5hr, CH$1,600).

Getting Around

The center of Castro is small enough to be covered on foot. For excursions to other parts of the island, having a vehicle is helpful, as public transport can take a long time. The most recommendable company is **Europcar** (tel. 65/2368 390, www.europcar.com, 9am-4:30pm Mon.-Fri., 9am-4pm Sat.-Sun.), at the Aeródromo Mocopulli de Castro north of Castro. Otherwise, it's best to rent a vehicle at Puerto Montt's Aeropuerto El Tepual or one of the offices in Puerto Montt.

DALCAHUE

With its shingle-roofed craft markets and beachside food stands, laid-back Dalcahue makes a good day trip from Castro. This small town buzzes with visitors on weekends and throughout summer. It's a lunch spot for many Castro locals to admire the tiny fishing boats bobbing in the sheltered bay. It's also the gateway to Isla Quinchao, the second-largest island in the archipelago, connected to Dalcahue by ferry.

Calle Freire is the main road through the town, running southwest to northeast two blocks inland from the bay. The Plaza de Armas is one block inland. The coastal road Calle Pedro Montt leads to the traditionally designed **Mercado Artesanal** (9am-8pm daily), where artisans from across Chiloé sell their wares, with a particular focus on knitted woolens, textile wall decorations, and hand-woven baskets, as well as local liqueurs made from *arrayán* (Chilean myrtle) and *cedron* (lemon beebrush). On weekends, the stalls spill onto the surrounding square.

Iglesia de Nuestra Señora de los Dolores de Dalcahue

Standing over the **Plaza de Armas** (bounded by San Martín, Aguirre Cerda, and Bahamondes), **Iglesia de Nuestra Señora de los Dolores de Dalcahue** (Bahamondes s/n, hours vary) was built in 1858 on the site of a previous Jesuit chapel and is characterized by its nine-arched portico and soaring tower, which can be seen from the bay. Inside, an exhibition documents the church's 2015 restoration. It is a UNESCO World Heritage Site.

Food

In a restored *alerce*-shingled Chilote cottage, **Refugio de Navegantes** (San Martín 165, tel. 65/2641 128, www.refugiodenavegantes.cl, 12:30pm-9:30pm Mon.-Thurs., 1pm-10pm Fri.-Sat., 11am-8pm Sun., CH$2,000-6,500) is the most upscale restaurant in Dalcahue, with distressed wooden furniture and sunken leather armchairs. In the large room upstairs are views across the water to Isla Quichao

and the church. Coffees, handmade cakes, and *onces* are better than the mains. The staff is attentive.

Next to the Mercado Artesanal, in the boat-shaped building that houses the ★ **Mercado Dalcahue** (Pedro Montt s/n, no phone, 9am-7pm daily, CH$6,000), Chilote women spend their mornings cooking. This is the best place on the island for *curanto en olla* (*curanto* cooked on a stove), *milcao* (deep-fried mashed potato dumplings filled with crispy pork), *lloco* (beef or pork cooked in butter, with blood sausage, potatoes, and savory wheat doughnuts) and *chapaleles* (wheat and potato dumplings). **Doña Lula** (stand 8) is the favorite of locals.

A few doors down from the Mercado Artesanal, **Casita de Piedra** (Pedro Montt 144, tel. 9/9489 9050, noon-4pm Mon., noon-8pm Tues.-Sat., noon-7pm Sun., CH$3,000-4,500, *menú del día* CH$4,500) has decent espressos, ristrettos, and cappuccinos, plus a range of simple sandwiches, baked empanadas, and cakes. A changing daily three-course menu includes salmon ceviche, paella with local mussels, or seaweed soup.

Getting There

From **Castro,** Dalcahue is a 20-km, 40-minute drive north along Ruta 5 and northwest along the W-55. To get here from **Ancud,** take Ruta 5 south and the W-45 southwest for 70km, just over an hour.

By public transit, it's a 30-minute **bus ride** (CH$800) from Castro's **Terminal Municipal** (San Martín 667, Castro, tel. 65/2635 666), with departures roughly every 15 minutes. The bus drops you along Calle Freire; the return bus leaves from this same road, at the stop between Calles Camilo Henríquez and M. Eugenin.

ISLA QUINCHAO

Many of the 9,000 residents of the second-largest island of the archipelago, Isla Quinchao, are indigenous Huilliche (southern Mapuche) and Chono (nomadic seafarers) people. The traditional festivals held during summer and the photogenic wood-shingled houses show that little has changed in centuries. The island is home to two of Chiloé's UNESCO World Heritage site churches.

A series of low rolling hills with neat fields and apple orchards, the island is a 10-minute ferry ride southeast of Dalcahue. Achao is the largest town and has a handful of attractions, including its elderly church, a seafood market, and riotous spring and summer folk festivals. Two other main towns—Curaco de Vélez, a good spot for a seafood lunch and bird-watching, and Quinchao, interesting for its church—have just a few streets each.

Small minibuses ply the winding narrow road that runs the length of the island, stopping to drop off and pick up passengers at both Curaco de Vélez and Achao. To go deeper into the island, plan to drive your own car over on the ferry.

Curaco de Vélez

Nine kilometers southeast of the Rampa Isla Quinchao ferry dock, a clutch of streets on a rounded bay mark Curaco de Vélez. Among pretty shingled houses is the modern **Iglesia Santo Judas Tadeo** (Francisco Bohle, open for mass) on the **Plaza de Armas** (bounded by Plaza, Errázuriz, and Bohie), on the west side of the village, half a block from the ocean. The church's lime-green facade and sloping wooden walls make a statement; from most angles, its shingled tower looks decidedly crooked.

Calle Francisco Bohle leads southwest from the Plaza de Armas, and after it crosses a small bridge, a wooden boardwalk on the west side is a great spot for **bird-watching.** This pathway leads over an estuary and wetlands that form an important conservation area for Hudsonian godwits, back-necked swans, and other seabirds that migrate 16,000km from Alaska each year.

Artesanías Ensueño (Av. del Mar s/n, no phone, 10am-5pm daily) sells wooden spoons and buttons carved from *alerce,* plus woolen clothing and bags. The rustic but charming **Ostras Los Troncos** (Av. del Mar 8, tel.

9/6848 7102, noon-7pm daily Jan.-Feb., hours vary Mar.-Dec., CH$3,000-5,000) is the place for freshly fried seafood empanadas, oven-cooked salmon, and a delicacy: fresh oysters with a squirt of lemon. Eat outside in the covered dining area where the seats are made from tree trunks. Outside January-February, they sell fresh oysters to take out.

Achao

Achao is the largest town on Isla Quinchao, but it takes no more than 10 minutes to traverse its dozen streets, dressed in colorful shingled buildings. The W-59 connects the Rampa Isla Quinchao ferry dock to Achao and curls along the southern edge of town. The **Plaza de Achao** (bounded by Delicias, Zañartu, Progreso, and Plaza) and waterfront are a few blocks north.

The **Iglesia Santa María de Loreto de Achao** (Progreso, 10am-7pm daily) commands a view across the plaza. One of the oldest churches in the country, it is Isla Quinchao's longest-standing. Construction of this shingled structure began in 1730. The tower was built in the early 19th century; the original shingles, held in place by wooden pegs, are now covered by tiles. Inside are an unusual baroque *retablo* and an elaborately carved pulpit. The church is still used for mass; its patron saint is celebrated on December 10. The church is a UNESCO World Heritage site.

On the northwest corner of the plaza, the **Museo Municipal de Achao** (Delicias and Amunátegui, 11am-7pm daily Dec.-Feb., donation) has a small collection of artifacts from Achao, plus exhibits on local crafts such as basketry, weaving, and boatbuilding.

Right on the seafront, the **Mercado de Achao** (Paseo Arturo Prat and Serrano, 10am-8pm daily Jan.-Feb., 11am-5pm daily Mar.-Dec.) has fresh seafood. Inside the adjoining **Feria de Artesanía** (10am-8pm daily Jan.-Feb., 11am-5pm daily Mar.-Dec.), vendors sell crafts that include baskets woven from the fibers of local plants. Another **craft market** (Serrano between Pedro Montt and

Av. Curaco de Vélez, noon-6pm Mon.-Sat.) has similar wares and only operates during summer.

Achao is known for the **Encuentro Folclórico de las Islas del Archipiélago** (Folkloric Gathering of the Archipelago Islands, early Feb.), one of the most important Chilote cultural events, where folk music groups from across the island perform. The last week of October, the **Encuentro Gastronómico de Productos del Mar** (Gastronomic Gathering of Seafood) is a seafood festival held during peak shellfish season.

The unassuming **El Medan** (Serrano 618, tel. 65/2661 469, 10am-7pm Mon.-Fri., CH$3,000) is Isla Quinchao's best restaurant, serving fresh fish, soups, and meats accompanied by sides such as local potatoes with a spicy Chilote sauce. Get here early, as demand often exceeds supply. Lunch service starts at 12:30pm.

The town's most reasonable lodging is the eight-room peach-painted **Hospedaje Sol y Lluvia** (Ricardo Jara 9, tel. 65/2661 383, CH$15,000 d shared bath, CH$25,000 d private bath, cash only). Lodgings are in sizable if dated bedrooms on the upper floor, with a good breakfast included. Rates include IVA.

A few doors south of the Museo Municipal de Achao, in the municipal building, the **Oficina de Información Turístico** (Amunategui 18, tel. 65/2661 143, www.municipalidadquinchao.cl, 8:30am-5:30pm Mon.-Fri.) has maps of the island and can help with information, including homestays and transport to nine nearby islands.

Quinchao

As the island tapers southeast of Achao, its settlements become smaller, and **Quinchao** is barely more than two streets: the paved main road from the ferry dock, 30km north, and a gravel track along the shore.

On the shorefront road is the UNESCO World Heritage site **Iglesia Nuestra Señora de Gracia de Villa Quinchao** (hours vary, closed Mon. mornings), dating to 1880 and weather-beaten by constant winds. The church stands out against its modest surroundings as the largest of the traditional churches in Chiloé, 53 meters in length. Celebrations for the patron saint are held on December 8. Outside summer, you'll have to ask around for the key to look inside.

Getting There

To get to Isla Quinchao on a bus or with your own vehicle, take the **ferry** (6am-1am daily, CH$2,500 per vehicle) from **Rampa Dalcahue** (15 de Septiembre s/n, no phone) on the western end of Dalcahue. It's a 10-minute boat journey to **Rampa Isla Quinchao,** from where the paved W-59 originates. The road continues as far as Quinchao, passing Curaco de Vélez and Achao en route.

Buses from Castro's **Terminal Municipal** (San Martín 667, tel. 65/2635 666) leave every 30 minutes for **Curaco de Vélez** (1.5hr, CH$1,500), continuing to **Achao** (1.75hr, CH$1,800). The fare includes the ferry crossing. You can catch these buses in **Dalcahue** before they board the ferry at the Rampa Dalcahue. From here, it's 50 minutes to Curaco de Vélez (CH$1,000) and 1.25 hours to Achao (CH$1,200).

CHONCHI AND VICINITY

Few visitors linger in the higgledy-piggledy hillside town of Chonchi, 22km south of Castro, but it's a worthwhile visit for Chiloé's best preserved and most colorful architecture. It was one of the first locations of the Jesuit missions, founded in 1767. It gained the nickname of Ciudad de los Tres Pisos (City of Three Levels): Its steep hillsides form three distinct levels as they descend to a curved bay.

The turnoff from Ruta 5 runs to the southern edge of town, whose buildings cascade north along Calle Centenario down to the bay, where the fields and forested hills of Isla Lemuy are visible across a small harbor.

Sights

Chonchi's most appealing street is **Calle Centenario,** home to well-preserved two- and three-story 19th-century houses built from cypress and other native hardwoods. Centenario connects the bay with the UNESCO World Heritage site **Iglesia Nuestra Señora del Rosario de Chonchi** (Francisco Corral s/n, hours vary), built in 1893 of cypress wood. It has since been renovated and repainted with an eye-catching mix of robin's-egg blue on its portico and lemon yellow on the tower. Inside, a pretty blue cupola is studded with stars, and there is information on the reconstruction work of 2009.

About halfway up Centenario, **Museo de las Tradiciones Chonchinas** (Centenario 116, tel. 65/2672 802, http://museodechonchi.cl, 9:30am-1:30pm and 2:30pm-6pm daily Dec.-Feb., 10am-6pm Mon.-Fri., 9:30am-1:30pm Sat. Mar.-Nov., CH$700) is within a refurbished wooden house and contains rooms decorated with original furniture to reflect life in Chonchi between 1860 and 1935. It also operates as the town's main cultural space, holding book readings and other community-led events.

★ **MUSEO DEL ACORDEÓN**
The fantastic and informal **Museo del Acordeón** (Andrade s/n, tel. 9/9473 0364, by appointment only, donation) contains the private collection of over 70 accordions belonging to local resident and renowned player Don Sergio Colivoro Barra. Picked up during his performances across the globe, the accordions include some unique models, such as the oldest of the collection, a German 115 Bass accordion from 1915, and the sparkly Florentina, a rare Italian model and one of only a few ever made. Don Sergio allows you a chance to play the instruments and normally puts on an impromptu concert himself. To visit, you can generally call and be let in within a few minutes.

Food and Accommodations
In a dusk-blue 1927 house, **La Ventana de Elisa** (Irarrázabal 119, tel. 65/2671 242, http://laventanadeelisa.cl, 12:30pm-8pm Mon.-Sat., CH$3,000-6,000, *menú del día* CH$4,000) is a cute matchbox-size café with delicious homemade soups, salads, and braised beef sandwiches. Stop for a slice of homemade kuchen or *alfajor* cake with a coffee. The lunch menu always includes fresh Chilote-inspired dishes that feature seaweed and local potatoes, among other ingredients.

At the southeastern end of the coastal Calle Irarrázabal, sitting on stilts over the water, the grand **Mercado Municipal de Chonchi** (Irarrázabal s/n, 8am-8pm daily Jan.-Feb., 9:30am-4:30pm daily Mar.-Dec., CH$4,000-6,000) has traditional seafood restaurants on the second floor with steamy dishes of *caldo de mariscos* (shellfish soup) and *salmon a lo pobre* (grilled salmon served with fries and a fried egg) at affordable prices with excellent views. Downstairs are stalls selling Chonchi's most notable beverage, *licor de oro,* a milk- and herb-based alcohol that's considered an aphrodisiac.

On the seafront in a sprawling lime-green house, **Hostal Emarley** (Irarrázabal 191, tel. 65/2671 202 or 9/7652 3358, CH$20,000 d shared bath, CH$25,000 d private bath, cash only) is a popular 18-room guesthouse run by warm and welcoming Eliana. A scattering of spotless bedrooms are simply furnished, with acres of communal space. The room at the front of the house has sea views and a private bath. Use of the kitchen is possible outside January-February; breakfast is an additional CH$4,000.

Getting There
From **Castro,** it's a 30-minute, 22-km drive south along Ruta 5 and the W-853. From **Ancud,** it's a 104-km drive south down Ruta 5 and the W-853, which takes an hour and 45 minutes. From **Quellón,** take Ruta 5 heading north and then the W-75. It's a one-hour, 67-km journey.

All **Cruz del Sur** (Pedro Montt 233, tel. 65/2671 218) buses traveling between **Castro** (9 daily, 30min, CH$1,100) and **Quellón** (9 daily, 1.25hr, CH$1,800) pass through Chonchi. They drop passengers and sell tickets at their office a few doors east of Iglesia

Nuestra Señora del Rosario de Chonchi. Local minibuses from Castro's **Terminal Municipal** (San Martín 667, Castro, tel. 65/2635 666) drop passengers every half hour at the bus stop at the corner of Francisco Corral and Centenario; some continue on to Cucao.

Isla Lemuy

Remote and lush, undulating and forested **Isla Lemuy** receives few foreign visitors, but it's worth the effort and is considered the archipelago's most charming spot. Settlement began as a Jesuit mission in the mid-1700s with just 65 families; the population hasn't grown considerably since then.

An afternoon is plenty of time to absorb the island's fine sea air and snap photos of its three UNESCO World Heritage site churches. On the eastern edge of the island, the land narrows to a sinewy strip before widening into a sharpened spur. It's possible to take a bus from Castro to the island, but in your own vehicle you can appreciate the picturesque hillsides that roll into magnificent bays as the island's main unnamed road winds from the western ferry dock through Ichuac, Puqueldón, San Agustín, and Detif.

On the southern side of **Ichuac,** the 1880 **Iglesia Natividad María de Ichuac** (7km north of Puerto Chulchuy ferry ramp, Chonchi-Puqueldón road, hours vary) took five years and 120 workers to construct. Inside, a painted clock marks 3pm, which, according to locals, either corresponds to the hour in which Jesus died or when the 1960 earthquake occurred.

Puqueldón is the largest settlement on the island and home to the twin-towered 1845 **Iglesia San Pedro Nolasco de Puqueldón** (bounded by Blanco Encalada, Galvarino Riveros, Miguel Carrera, and O'Higgins, hours vary) that has the appearance of a fortress and sits on its main square. East of Puqueldón is the **Iglesia de San Agustín** (5km east of Puqueldón, Puqueldón-Detif road, hours vary), the only church in Chiloé

that isn't beside the sea. It sports rust-colored shingles.

Close to the southeasternmost point of the island is the lovely and exceptionally remote hamlet **Detif** and the simple **Iglesia Santiago Apóstol de Detif** (Puqueldón-Detif road). It's just after the road curves north to the bay. Ask for the key at the Mercado Particular El Gallito.

GETTING THERE

Puerto Huicha, 4.5km southeast of Chonchi, is the departure point for the **ferry** to Isla Lemuy. Ferries operated by **Naviera Puelche** (W-853 s/n, no phone, http://navierapuelche.cl, 7am-12:30am daily, CH$2,100 per vehicle) cross every 30 minutes to **Puerto Chulchuy** on Isla Lemuy. From here, it's 3km to Ichuac.

From **Castro,** it's a 40-minute, 26-km drive south along Ruta 5 and the W-853. Buses from Castro's **Terminal Municipal** (San Martín 667, tel. 65/2635 666) depart roughly every hour for Puerto Huicha, arriving at Ichuac (1hr, CH$2,000) and continuing on to Puqueldón (1.25hr, CH$2,500).

★ QUEILÉN

The paved road along the eastern coast of Isla Grande is flanked by thick evergreen forest with huge *nalca* (Chilean rhubarb) creeping out onto the road. On a small peninsula lined on both sides by a wealth of serene sandy beaches, the village of Queilén could be the island's most picturesque destination.

From the long beach that lines the village's eastern edge and tapers into a thin sandy spit at Queilén's southernmost point, the views to mainland Chile on a clear day are spectacular. The snow-dusted peak of Volcán Corcovado crowns the landscape. Pods of dolphins leaping out of the water are an even more common sight.

Penguin-Watching Tours

Queilén is the closest village to the

Magellanic penguin colony on Islote Conejo. To see them, take a tour aboard the 30-passenger *Kawesqar II* with the highly recommended **Quilun Ecoturismo Marino** (Queilén harbor, tel. 9/6918 379 or 9/9351 8288, www.quilun.cl). The 2.5-hour tours run October-March and pass around Islote Conejo for views of the penguins before returning via the southern edge of Isla Tranqui. It's not unusual to spy dolphins feeding on algae in the shallows here. The largest numbers of penguins are on Islote Conejo in January-February. Tours cost CH$15,000 pp, including seafood snacks, wine, and a Spanish-speaking guide.

The Castro-based **Siempre Verde Turismo** (Blanco Encalada 50, Castro, tel. 9/5253 0540, www.siempreverdeturismo. com) runs a half-day tour to Queilén (CH$50,000 pp, min. 2 people), with passage on the *Kawesqar II* and round-trip transportation from your hotel included. For an extra CH$15,000 pp, you can also visit the church in Chonchi.

Accommodations

At the entrance to Queilén, ★ **El Coo Lodge** (Av. La Paz s/n, tel. 9/6867 8334 or tel. 9/9545 2981, www.elcoolodge.com, CH$80,000 d) is a magnificent feat of architecture, designed by a local architect using recycled materials to mimic the style of Chiloé's *palafitos*. The three bedrooms are all modern and stylish, with the downstairs room opening onto a balcony. All the rooms share astounding sea views across to the mountains. Service is exceptional and breakfast, with homemade bread, jams, local cheeses, ham, and fruit, is noteworthy.

Getting There

From **Castro,** it's a 65-km, 1.25-hour drive south along Ruta 5 and the W-853. From **Quellón,** it's an 81-km, 1.75-hour journey north along Ruta 5, the W-879, W-851, and the W-853. **Queilén Bus** (tel. 65/2632 173, www.queilenbus.cl) runs hourly buses (1.5hr, CH$1,600) from Castro's **Terminal Municipal** (San Martín 667, Castro, tel. 65/2635 666) via Chonchi.

El Coo Lodge

Parque Nacional Chiloé and Vicinity

West of Chonchi, the landscape grows darker green and wilder, with fenced fields and clusters of tin-roofed houses giving way to dense tracts of forest and the waters of Lago Huillinco. This part of Chiloé is marked by the low forested hills of the Cordillera de Piuchén, which make up the eastern part of Parque Nacional Chiloé.

Coming from mainland Chile via Castro, the national park is the first glimpse of the archipelago's unique vegetation. A small number of hiking trails weave through the park's protected evergreen forests; others hug the coastline and grant rare views of Chiloé's gloriously untouched western beaches. In the southern part of the park, Muelle de las Almas is a popular art installation that can be reached on foot or on horseback.

The hamlet of Cucao is the gateway to the national park. All of the shortest hiking routes are accessible from the main CONAF headquarters, a two-minute walk north of Cucao. The majority of services are in and around this settlement. There are a few basic campgrounds in the park. Budget at least a day for exploring the park and at least one or two more for relaxing in this enchantingly easygoing corner of Chiloé.

CUCAO

On narrow Lago Cucao, which spills into the ocean at vast Bahía Cucao, the tiny fishing village of Cucao retains a magical atmosphere despite the gusty winds that batter the western side of the island. Cucao's 500 residents are outnumbered by wildlife: Southern river otters float in the brackish waters that drain from the lake, and the fine sand of the coastal dunes and beach that border the village provide ample opportunities to spot humpback and blue whales and dolphins.

The W-850 enters town from the east, with a T-junction in Cucao. The village is scattered loosely along an unnamed road that runs north from the W-850. About 800 meters north of the junction is a river that connects Lago Cucao with the ocean. North of the river is where the tourist services and access to the hiking trails of Parque Nacional Chiloé are. The road south of the junction leads to the trailhead for the Muelle de las Almas, 10km away.

Cucao is a cash-only place, so bring plenty with you. There's only a handful of basic mini markets in the village, so if you plan to cook, stock up on provisions in Castro. To escape to a truly remote refuge, Cucao is best visited outside the peak months of January-February.

Food and Accommodations

The quality of accommodations is surprisingly high in Cucao. Be aware that outside December-March, restaurants have limited hours.

On the right side before the bridge, **Brisas del Pacífico** (tel. 9/9815 5427, 10:30am-9:30pm daily, CH$4,000-6,000, cash only) is a reliable option, but it's not fancy. Deep-fried cheese and seafood empanadas are excellent, and the mains, such as grilled salmon, hake, and *bife a lo pobre* (cuts of beefsteak with fries and a fried egg) are substantial.

With a wider menu and more upmarket atmosphere than most, **El Arrayán** (just before the entrance to the national park, tel. 9/5771 3659, elarrayanrestorant@gmail.com, 10am-10:30pm daily Dec.-Mar., noon-8:30pm daily Apr. and June-Nov., CH$6,000-8,000, cash only) is a safe bet, with friendly waiters and well-presented plates of *bife de chorizo* (top loin), fish prepared with local seasonings, ceviche, and even pizzas. They also offer breakfast and cakes.

A few kilometers east on the W-850 is unassuming ★ **Tradiciones Morelia** (Km 25 W-850, tel. 9/9794 6594, 11am-6:15pm daily, CH$4,000-6,000), featured in news reports worldwide thanks to the refined takes on traditional dishes that chef and owner Morelia cooks. *Chancho ahumado* (smoked pork), *cazeula de machas* (razor clam and seaweed stew), and other uniquely Chilote dishes are served with sides of native potatoes. Most ingredients grow right behind the restaurant. Homespun charm exudes from every sheep's wool-covered stool and handcrafted wall hanging.

On the western shores of Lago Cucao, ★ **Palafito Cucao Lodge** (tel. 65/2971 164, http://palafitocucaolodge.cl, CH$18,000 dorm, CH$65,000 d private bath, cash only) is the town's top accommodation. The building mimics a traditional wooden-shingled *palafito*, with a stylish living room and wraparound terrace over the lake, where you may spot an otter. The 10 private rooms and six-bed dormitory feel like they should cost more. For the most sublime lake vistas, ask for the room on the northwestern side of the building. Guests have access to the kitchen, and a substantial homemade breakfast is included. Activities in the national park can be arranged through the hostel's **Palafito Trip** (tel. 9/9884 9552, http://palafitotrip.cl), which also rents out kayaks to use on the lake.

Just north of the bridge, the cozy and sociable **Parador Darwin** (tel. 9/5400 5944, www.paradordarwin.com, Sept.-Mar., CH$15,000 dorm, CH$40,000 d private bath, cash only) has five small but clean wooden-walled rooms and a **snack bar** (6pm-2am daily Dec.-Feb.) that's also open to nonguests and where live performances of folkloric music are often held. The Wi-Fi is only in communal areas. Rates include IVA.

Getting There

From **Castro,** it's a 54-km, 1.5-hour drive south along Ruta 5 and the W-80 and W-850. Take the same route to get to Cucao from **Ancud,** just under 2 hours for the 136-km journey. From **Quellón,** take Ruta 5 heading north, then the W-80 and W-850, a 93-km, 1.5-hour drive. **Buses Union Express** (tel. 9/6668 3531) and **Buses Ojeda** (tel. 65/2635 477) have hourly departures (1.5hr, CH$2,000)

from Castro's **Terminal Municipal** (San Martín 667, Castro, tel. 65/2635 666).

★ MUELLE DE LAS ALMAS

Atop a cliff at Punta Pirulil facing the churning Pacific, the **Muelle de las Almas** (Dock of the Souls, 9am-5pm daily, CH$1,500, parking CH$2,000 per vehicle) is a wooden art installation by Santiago sculptor and art professor Marcelo Orellana Rivera. Forming a walkable pier over the ocean, the installation is named for a Mapuche myth that when a person died, their soul was carried across the water by the Tempilcahue, a boatman who required a fee, normally in the form of small turquoise stones that the Mapuche buried with their dead. Not everyone was accepted; those left behind had to spend eternity at this western point of Chiloé. The voices of these unfortunate souls can sometimes be heard wailing from below the *muelle* (or maybe it's just the wind or the sea lion colony on the rocks below). It's an enchanting and contemplative spot, where frequent heavy mist and dark clouds add to the mysterious ambience.

The mythical atmosphere is missing in January-February, when hour-long queues to walk on the pier are the norm. Get here as early as possible; it's a 45-minute walk from the car park. The path is exposed to the elements, so hold onto your hat. Thick mud coats the trail, and parts of it have a steep incline. It's best on a clear day for the views of the surrounding headland. Muelle de las Almas is 11km south of Cucao via the road south from the W-850 junction.

Based in Cucao, highly recommended **Palafito Trip** (tel. 9/9884 9552, http://palafitotrip.cl) offer a guided **hiking tour** (CH$46,000 pp, min. 2 people) of the *muelle* that includes a visit to a local family. They also offer horseback riding March-December. This tour is also possible from Castro.

GETTING THERE

From Castro, it's a one-hour, 53-km journey to Cucao. Take Ruta 5 south, then west along

the W-80 and W-850 to the southern entrance of Cucao. From here, it's a 30-minute, 11-km drive south. Follow the unpaved W-848 and take the right fork along the unnamed dirt road after 4km. The road to the *muelle* is in a dreadful state. You'll need a high-clearance vehicle to make it the full 11km from Cucao to the attraction's car park.

From Castro's **Terminal Municipal** (San Martín 667, Castro, tel. 65/2635 666), **Buses Ojeda** (tel. 65/2635 477) runs four daily buses (9:15am, 10:15am, 11:15am, and 12:15pm, 1.75hr, CH$4,000) to the car park of the *muelle*. The final bus back to Castro departs at 3pm. Buses Ojeda also runs daily routes from **Cucao** (CH$3,500 round-trip) at 11:45am, 1:15pm, and 4:30pm, which return at 12:30pm, 3pm, and 5:30pm. The buses depart from their bus stop opposite the headquarters of Parque Nacional Chiloé, on the northern edge of Cucao.

Bosque Piedra

About 12km east of Cucao, the private reserve **Bosque Piedra** (Camino Cucaokm 15, tel. 9/9289 6798, http://bosquepiedra.cl, tours by reservation only, CH$10,000 pp, min. 2 people) is run by Elena Bochetti, a former Santiago resident and expert on local flora and fauna. The reserve is home to a tract of Valdivian temperate rainforest of *tepual, canelo,* and *luma.* It's one of the few remaining sections of primary forest on the entire island, and the easiest to access. It also has important biodiversity in its lichens and ferns.

Elena guides English-, Spanish-, and German-language tours of the reserve, with a focus on ecology and geology. There are 32 species of birds, best seen in March, when they change their plumage, or the September mating season. Mammals, such as the *pudú* (the world's smallest deer), and *monito del monte* (a type of opossum), are also local residents.

In summer, contact Elena two days in advance to book a tour. Tours normally begin at 11am or 3pm and take an easy 2.5-hour walk

1: Muelle de las Almas 2: Palafito Cucao Lodge

on well-maintained trails. To get here from Castro by public transit, catch any Cucao-bound bus from the **Terminal Municipal** (San Martín 667, Castro, tel. 65/2635 666) and ask to be dropped at the front gate of the reserve. In your own vehicle, it's 37km from Castro, around 45 minutes. Take Ruta 5 south to the W-80, then continue to the W-850; it's around 10 minutes west of the village of Huillinco.

★ PARQUE NACIONAL CHILOÉ

Covering 43,000 hectares, but with only 0.2 percent easily accessible to visitors, **Parque Nacional Chiloé** (tel. 65/2970 724, parque. chiloe@conaf.cl, hours and admission vary by sector) was founded in 1982 and is one of the best places on the island to encounter Chiloe's characteristic Valdivian temperate rainforest, with valleys and slopes thick with glossy-leafed *olivillo,* bamboo-like *quila,* and *luma,* with its rust-colored bark. Within this dense forest, you may encounter one of Chiloé's shyest—and rarest—species, the adorably squat *pudú* or the even more timid *monito del monte.*

The park is split into three distinct sectors: **Sector Chanquin,** easily accessed on the northern edge of Cucao; **Sector Huentemó (Cole Cole),** 10km north of Cucao; and **Sector Chepú,** south of the village of Chepú and very difficult to visit without a guide. Heavy rainfall, particularly May-September, make trails muddy and even boggy. A raincoat and sturdy waterproof hiking boots are recommended.

Tours

Activities in the national park can be arranged through the Cucao-based tour agency **Palafito Trip** (Palafito Cucao Lodge, Camino Rural s/n, tel. 9/9884 9552, http://palafitotrip. cl). They offer a day hike (CH$40,000 pp) or horseback ride (CH$75,000) to Playa Cole Cole, a six-hour horseback tour (CH$34,000) in the national park and along the beach, and kayaking (CH$25,000) in one of the rivers in the national park or on Lago Cucao. All tours include round-trip transfers, a picnic, and a bilingual guide. If you want to start your tour from Castro, add CH$20,000 to the price. Tours starting from Castro require a minimum of two people.

Sector Chanquin

On the northern edge of Cucao, Sector Chanquin is the easiest of the park's three sectors to reach. The bus from Castro drops you at the park's headquarters, the **CONAF Administración** (Camino Rural s/n, 700 m north of the bridge, Cucao, no phone, 9am-8pm daily summer, 9am-6pm daily winter, CH$4,000 adults, CH$2,000 children). Pay the entrance fee here and receive a marginally useful map. Follow the trail north from the CONAF headquarters for a few minutes to reach the small but informative **Centro de Información Ambiental** (no phone, 9am-8pm daily summer, 9am-6pm daily winter, free). This information center has displays about the geological origins and human residents of Chiloé and the national park, plus a guide to the flora and fauna that you can see on the trails.

HIKING

The most interesting trail in this sector of the national park, **Sendero Dunas de Cucao** (1km loop), begins 100 meters north of the park's headquarters, on the left side of the road. This loop trail takes a mostly flat route through dense forest with a *mirador* overlooking the beach. After a few hundred meters, it intersects with the **Sendero Playa** (1.2km), which continues to **Playa de Cucao**, a vast stretch of white sand cut through by a thin strip of slow-running river, which you have to cross to reach the ocean. The water here is not suitable for swimming due to fierce currents and surf. This is a great spot to watch a beautiful sunset, but be aware that the park is technically closed by 6pm daily in winter and 8pm daily in summer.

Starting from Sector Chanquin and continuing north to Sector Huentemó (Cole Cole), the scenic **Sendero Cole Cole** (12km one-way, 3.5hr) is a flat trail that passes alongside evergreen forest, ocean-side cliffs, and a long white-sand beach that connects Cucao with Huentemó, a small indigenous settlement. Upon reaching Huentemó, many hikers continue to the idyllic white sands of Playa Cole Cole.

There are various other, longer trails in this sector, but most are not well maintained, and you're better visiting with a local guide, like **Palafito Trip** (Palafito Cucao Hostel, Camino Rural s/n, tel. 9/9884 9552, http://palafitotrip.cl).

FOOD AND ACCOMMODATIONS

In Sector Chanquin, the CONAF-run **campground** (CH$6,000 pp) has 25 sites and is tucked in the forest on the shore of Lago Cucao, with access to baths with hot showers (8pm-11pm daily). As this section of the park is within five minutes' walk of Cucao, it's worth finding lodgings in the village, particularly when there's heavy rain.

In this part of the park, there is also the small **El Fogón** (no phone, 11am-4pm daily, CH$6,000-7,000), a cafeteria serving cakes, coffee, and meals. It's 100 meters north of the Centro de Información Ambiental.

GETTING THERE

From **Castro,** it's a 54-km, 1.5-hour drive south along Ruta 5 and the W-80 and W-850 to reach the park entrance in Cucao. Take the same route to get to the park from **Ancud,** just under 2 hours for the 136-km journey. There is a car park outside the park headquarters. **Buses Union Express** (tel. 9/6668 3531) and **Buses Ojeda** (tel. 65/2635 477) have hourly departures (1.5hr, CH$2,000) from Castro's **Terminal Municipal** (San Martín 667, Castro, tel. 65/2635 666). Buses drop passengers in the car park just outside park headquarters.

Sector Huentemó (Cole Cole)

Sector Huentemó (Cole Cole) (hours vary, CH$1,500) is located in and administered by the local indigenous community of Huentemó, 20km north of Cucao. There is no official ranger station in Huentemó, so you may not be charged for entry if no one from the community comes to collect your admission fee. The official entrance to this part of the park is on the northern tip of the village.

A dirt track connects Cucao and Huentemó. To drive, you'll need a 4WD vehicle and a local map; the route is difficult to follow, and part of it traverses the beach. A far better way is the **minibus service** offered by **Parador Darwin** (Camino Rural s/n, tel. 9/5400 5944, www.paradordarwin.com) in Cucao.

HIKING

In the village of Huentemó, 12km north of the CONAF headquarters in Sector Chanquin, is the trailhead for an undulating **coastal path** (5km one-way, 2hr) that awards intrepid hikers with unrivaled views of Chiloé's largely untouched western coast. To reach this path, head north past the *refugio* to reach an unmarked path that hugs the coast to reach the startlingly white sands and azure waters of the remote **Playa Cole Cole,** a beach that wouldn't look out of place in the Caribbean. Most visitors overnight at the campground on Playa Cole Cole.

The easy **Sendero Cole Cole** (12km one-way, 3.5hr), which most hikers take north to reach Sector Huentemó (Cole Cole) from Sector Chanquin, can also be walked south in order to return to Cucao.

FOOD AND ACCOMMODATIONS

All accommodations operate on a first-come, first-served basis. There are no shops, restaurants, or reliable freshwater sources; bring all food and plenty of water with you. At the entrance to Sector Huentemó (Cole Cole), just beyond Huemtemó village, a very basic *refugio* (CH$5,000) has four sets of bunk beds without sheets, space for cooking with your own stove, and cold showers. The *refugio* is normally open December-March.

On the grass on the southern edge of Playa Cole Cole is a 10-site **campground** (CH$2,000). Sadly, many of the beach's visitors do not take away their trash, which has spoiled the otherwise bucolic charm of this isolated stretch of coast. Pack out your own rubbish; consider taking any other garbage out with you as well.

GETTING THERE

To get to Playa Cole Cole without hiking the whole way, take a 16-seater **minibus** (CH$5,000 round-trip) run by the owner of the Cucao-based lodge **Parador Darwin** (Camino Rural s/n, tel. 9/5400 5944, www.paradordarwin.com). The minibus departs from Parador Darwin at 8:45am Monday, Wednesday, and Friday (returning at 5pm). It drops passengers off just before the village of Huentemó. From there, it's a 6-km walk to reach the beach. You can arrange to be picked up the following day if you plan to camp in the park.

Quellón and Vicinity

On the far southern end of Isla Grande, Quellón is a gritty harbor town, the largest port for fish exports in Chiloé. It's also the southern terminus of Ruta 5 at Punta de La Paz, on the southwestern edge of town. The town is made up of rows of ramshackle buildings; many of the houses along the coastal road were abandoned in the wake of the 1960 tsunami. A grid of narrow roads leads down to the port. The area is known for the blue whales that feed southwest of Quellón. It's also a gateway to Parque Tantauco and the departure point for the Naviera Austral ferry south to Patagonia.

As Ruta 5 curves west into Quellón, it gains the name Calle Ladrilleros. Most services are located along this road or on the roads leading south to the harbor.

WHALE-WATCHING

In 2003, international researchers discovered hundreds of blue whales in the Golfo de Corcovado, just off the southern coast of Chiloé. The whales come December-April to nurse their calves and feed. Smaller numbers of humpback whales also migrate through this gulf during the austral summer.

Whale-watching season runs December-April. Excursiones Quellón (Jorge Vivar 382, Quellón, tel. 9/7402 2456 or 65/2683 031, info@excursionesquellon.cl) operates 10-hour tours from Quellón, including a trip to a large colony of imperial cormorants. Sightings of austral and Chilean dolphins are also possible. If you're lucky, you may get within a few hundred meters of a blue whale. Prices start from CH$90,000 pp.

FOOD AND ACCOMMODATIONS

There are generous servings and more than just sandwiches at local favorite Sandwichería Mitos (Jorge Vivar 221, no phone, www.mitoschiloe.cl, 8:30am-10pm Mon.-Fri., 11am-10pm Sat., 11am-4pm Sun., CH$3,000-7,000, menú del día CH$5,500), in a quirky traditional Chilote cottage one block from the harbor. Watch dishes like burgers and vegetarian sandwiches being prepared from the horseshoe-shaped open bar. House-made maté is available. Lunch portions are large and feature hearty Chilote stews and soups. Four clean bedrooms (CH$56,000 d) have modern baths. Room rates include IVA.

Next to the end of Ruta 5, Restaurant Corcovado (tel. 9/9087 9333, noon-4pm and 7pm-midnight Tues.-Sat., CH$6,000-9,500, cash only) has the widest array of dining choices in a town with few options. Its extensive menu includes mixed grills for two, rib-eye steak, and salmon ceviche. The owner is welcoming, and a large window faces the sea.

Quellón's most upscale lodgings and the only one that can be described as a hotel is the Hotel Patagonia Insular (Ladrilleros 1737, tel. 65/2681 610, CH$54,000 d), on the western edge of town. There are 30 bedrooms on two floors, all with sea views; rooms 201-214 have the best views. A reasonable restaurant on-site operates as a café on Sunday, and 4pm-10pm Monday-Saturday serving standard Chilean dishes.

INFORMATION AND SERVICES

For cash, head to Banco Estado (22 de Mayo and Ladrilleros) or Banco de Chile (Ladrilleros 315), which both have 24-hour ATMs. The post office, Correos (22 de Mayo s/n, no phone, 9am-1:30pm and 3pm-5:30pm Mon.-Fri., 9am-12:30pm Sat.), is next door to the Oficina de Turismo (22 de Mayo 351, tel. 65/2686 801, http://muniquellon.cl, hours vary). The tourism office keeps erratic hours, particularly outside January-February. The small Hospital de Quellón (Doctor Ahués 305, tel. 65/2326 600, http://hospitalquellon.redsalud.gob.cl) offers medical attention.

TRANSPORTATION

Car

From Castro, it's a 1.5-hour, 85-km drive south on Ruta 5 to Quellón. From Ancud, it's a 2.5-hour, 168-km trip south on Ruta 5 through Castro.

Bus

In the Terminal Cruz del Sur (Pedro Aguirre 52, tel. 65/2681 284, www.webcds.cl), buses connect with Castro (every 40 min, 2hr, CH$2,500). There are also hourly buses from Puerto Montt (6hr, CH$8,500). Three blocks east of Terminal Cruz del Sur, in the Terminal Municipal (Ercilla 355, tel. 65/2681 284), blue minibuses run by Quellón Express (tel. 65/2327 187) shuttle between Castro (CH$1,800) and Quellón every 30 minutes.

Ferry

Naviera Austral (Pedro Montt 355, tel. 65/2682 505, www.navieraustral.cl) runs a ferry service (CH$35,800 foot passengers,

CH$231,400 vehicle) between **Puerto Chacabuco** and Quellón, a 31-hour journey with stops in Melinka, Raúl Marín Balmaceda, and Puerto Cisnes. The ferries have reclining seats on the main deck and a cafeteria, although you'll want to bring food and drinks. Warm waterproof clothing (for time spent out on deck) and a sleeping bag are recommended. It's common to spot Magellanic penguin colonies, sea lions, and even whales on the journey. The ferry leaves at 8pm Monday and noon Friday from Puerto Chacabuco; the return journey leaves Quellón at 11pm Wednesday and Saturday. You can buy tickets at Naviera Austral's office in Coyhaique (Paseo Horn 40, tel. 67/2210 727) or from **Buses Suray** (Aldea 1143, Puerto Aysén, tel. 67/2336 222, bussurayaeropuerto@gmail.com, 8am-8pm daily) in Puerto Aysén.

Naviera Austral also operates the four-hour ferry to Quellón from **Chaitén** (CH$15,000 foot passengers, CH$79,000 vehicles) that leaves at 10am Tuesday and Saturday; the return journey leaves Quellón at 7pm Sunday and 3pm Thursday. You can buy tickets from their office in Chaitén (Riveros 188, tel. 65/2731 011).

Arriving in Quellón on an early or late boat, take a taxi from the port to your lodgings, as the surrounding streets aren't safe. It should cost no more than CH$1,500. Contact **Radio Taxi Gaby** (tel. 65/2682 456).

★ PARQUE TANTAUCO

The 118,000-hectare **Parque Tantauco** (no phone, www.parquetantauco.cl, 9am-8pm daily, CH$3,500 adults, CH$500 children), 20km southwest of Quellón, is a private reserve owned by two-time Chilean president Sebastián Piñera, who was allegedly inspired by Doug Tompkins's land protection exploits in Patagonia. This park is one of Chiloé's least-visited corners, providing a refuge for pristine evergreen forests home to increasingly rare animal species.

Trails marked by the roots of snaking *tepual* trees and peat bog are lined by 800-year-old Guaitecas cypress trees. (Deeper into the forest, there are cypress trees over 2,000 years old.) There are also important populations of Darwin's frog, Darwin's fox, and *pudú*. The *pudú* is a common sight on the park's trails due to the lack of predators.

What makes this park compelling for some is how difficult it is to reach. The northern part is accessible by vehicle from a dirt road off Ruta 5; the southern section, home to the park's headquarters, can only be reached on foot, light aircraft, or a twice-weekly motor launch from Quellón.

The park is divided into three sectors, although much of it is inaccessible. **Sector Yaldad** is on the northeastern fringes of the park, 18km west of Ruta 5. This is the **main entrance** of the park, home to a visitors center and two short trails. **Sector Chaiguata** is 20km southwest of Sector Yaldad. It offers lodging, day hikes, and multiday treks. On the coast in the very south, and only accessible by boat, **Sector Inío** is home to the park's **headquarters.** It's also where the most comfortable lodging is.

The park's accommodations and facilities are exceptional for such a remote area. Gaiters and high-top hiking boots with good grip are strongly recommended. The best time for hiking in the park is in March and December, when there are fewer visitors on the trails. Trails can sometimes be closed for maintenance outside summer.

The park's **administrative office** (Ruta 5 Sur 1826, tel. 65/2633 805, 9am-6pm daily Jan.-Feb., 9am-6pm Mon.-Fri. Mar.-Dec.), where you can make reservations and get information about the park, is in Castro.

Tours

From Castro, **Chiloétnico** (Ernesto Riquelme 1228, tel. 9/9135 3448, http://chiloetnico.cl) and **Chiloé Natural** (Blanco Encalada 100, tel. 65/2534 973, www.chiloenatural.com) run tours to the park, starting from CH$80,000 pp (min. 2 people), including a bilingual guide, lunch, transportation, and a hike along one or two of the trails in Sectors Yaldad or Chaiguata.

Sector Yaldad

The most accessible sector, Sector Yaldad, is the area around Lago Yaldad. The park's main entrance is here. Pay your admission fee, which covers access to all sectors of the park, at the **Portería Parque Tantauco ranger station,** a 45-minute drive from Ruta 5 along a bumpy, potholed dirt track. This building also acts as the trailhead for two of the three hikes in this sector. Around 2km farther southwest along the same road is the **visitors center** (9am-8pm daily), with information about the reforestation work in the park and its native flora and fauna.

HIKING

All of the hikes in Sector Yaldad are easy, making them ideal for families. **Sendero Río Yaldad** (2.7km one-way, 1hr) follows the river to Lago Yaldad and the visitors center. From the visitors center, **Sendero Siempreverde** (0.5-km loop, 30min) is a circuit that passes through dense evergreen forest. Also at the visitors center is a short walk to the **Mañío Abuelo,** a 500-year-old podocarp tree that is endemic to the Valdivian temperate rainforest.

Sector Chaiguata

Twenty kilometers southwest of Sector Yaldad, along the same jolting road, Sector Chaiguata has a greater appeal for longer hikes or those wishing to spend at least two days in the park. It has both lodging and a restaurant, clustered together on the northeastern shore of Lago Chaiguata.

All trailheads in this sector are at the entrance. The lake is a playground, with sit-on-top double kayaks available to rent (around CH$5,000 per half-day). Park rangers are also stationed here.

HIKING

Starting from Camping del Lago Chaiguata, the **Sendero Bosque Hundio** (2km one-way, 1hr) offers a good representation of the park's vegetation, leading through a section of reforested land with footbridges over *tepual* roots and thick peat bog, with views of Lago Chaiguata.

Also leaving from the campground is the moderately difficult **Sendero Laguna Chaiguaco** (15.8-km loop, 2 days), which connects Lago Chaiguata with Laguna Chaiguaco. You might see southern river

a *pudú* in Parque Tantauco

otters. On the first day, the trail ends at Refugio Chaiguaco and Camping Chaiguaco, both of which are on the shore of the eponymous lake.

TREKKING

The most popular of the park's trekking trails is the **Sendero Transversal,** a 52-km four- to five-day hike that crosses the entire park. From Camping del Lago Chaiguata, the first day traverses the Sendero Laguna Chaiguaco to Laguna Chaiguaco. The path continues west to Refugio Pirámide on the second day, before turning south and arriving at Sector Inío and the coast on the fourth or fifth day. *Refugios* located between 7.5 and 15.4km apart are for overnights, with an average of six or seven hours of hiking per day.

The trail is challenging, with slippery *tepual* tree roots underfoot, often with a cap of vegetation or thick mud. Tree trunks often block the path and must be clambered over. The average annual rainfall is up to 300 centimeters, so you may find yourself hiking in thigh-deep mud. Unfortunately, trekking poles aren't useful, as they get stuck in the bog or trapped around a tree root. You'll also need to carry all food and equipment, as there is nowhere to buy any provisions on the trail.

Even more challenging is the 83-km, eight-day, out-and-back trek along **Sendero Caleta Zorra,** which follows the same route as the Sendero Transversal until Refugio Pirámide, where it continues west to Refugio Emerenciana, from where you can take a day trip to Caleta Zorra, one of Chiloé's most beautiful remote beaches (with no facilities). The trail follows the same route back to finish at Sector Chaiguata. This hike goes through some of the best preserved old-growth forests of Guaiteca cypresses in Chile.

On the final 3km of the third day, where you hike to Refugio Emerenciana, and on the fifth day, as you make your way back along the same stretch, there are sections of the trail that require nearly vertical rock climbs using tree roots and ropes. There are also a number of river crossings, which can be impossible after heavy rainfall. This trek should only be attempted by those with significant experience.

These two trails can be combined to form the **Sendero Tantauco trek,** which comes in at 93.5km and takes nine days.

FOOD AND ACCOMMODATIONS

All the facilities in this sector are together on the northeastern shore of Lago Chaiguata. In January-February, the restaurant **Fogón** serves basic lunches, dinners, and sandwiches.

Camping del Lago Chaiguata (CH$15,000 Jan.-Feb., CH$10,000 Mar.-Dec., up to 4 people per site) has 20 tent sites and hot-water showers, plus **domes** (CH$84,000 d Jan.-Feb., CH$60,000 d Mar.-Dec.) with heating and linens; baths are private but are located outside the dome. All guests have access to a *quincho* (a covered cooking area with utensils and sinks, CH$2,500 pp per day) March-December. Bring your own food, as there is nowhere to buy provisions in the park.

All camping and dome reservations must be made in advance via the park's administrative office in Castro. Rangers in this sector of the park rent out **two-person tents** with two sleeping mats for CH$10,000 per day.

Located at km 7.5 along Sendero Laguna Chaiguaco, the first *refugio* along the Sendero Transversal and Sendero Caleta Zorra is **Refugio Chaiguaco** (CH$15,000 Jan.-Feb., CH$12,000 Mar.-Dec.), which has space for only eight people. Adjacent is **Camping Chaiguaco** (CH$12,000 Jan.-Feb only, max. 2 people). For both the campground and the *refugio,* advance reservations (either through the park's administrative office in Castro or with park rangers) are required.

Along the Sendero Transversal, basic *refugios* (CH$15,000 Jan.-Feb., CH$12,000 Mar.-Dec.) contain large bunk beds without linens (bring a sleeping bag and mat) with space for eight people. There's a separate cooking area with space for a wood fire for heating the cabin; pack newspaper for kindling and bring all cooking equipment. **Refugio Chaiguaco** is located at km 7.5; **Refugio Pirámide** is at km 20; **Refugio Huillín** is at km 35.4; and **Refugio Mirador Inío** is at km 43.

The Sendero Caleta Zorra has the same-style *refugios*. **Refugio Chaiguaco** is at km 7.5; **Refugio Pirámide** is at km 20; and **Refugio Emerenciana** is at km 35.

Camping is not permitted along the Sendero Transversal or the Sendero Caleta Zorra. Take all trash with you. Before you begin hiking, book your spot in the *refugios* for each day, either at the park's office in Castro or online. As there is only space for eight hikers each night in the *refugios*, it is essential to book a few weeks in advance for January-February; you won't be allowed to start hiking if you don't have a reservation. Bring all food with you, as there is nowhere to buy supplies in the park.

Sector Inío

Sector Inío is the least accessible part of the park, allowing entry only via boat or light aircraft. Only the most intrepid find their way to this remote, remarkable frontier. Sector Inío lies along the southernmost coast of the park and of Chiloé. The gateway is the modest fishing village of Inío, within the reserve and home to 30 families. Nowadays, many of the residents are employed by the park, staffing the lodgings within the village.

Sector Inío is home to the **park headquarters** and the only airstrip in the park. It's the end point of both the Sendero Transversal and Sendero Caleta Zorra, multiday trekking trails that begin in Sector Chaiguata.

HIKING AND TREKKING

From Inío village, you can take two day hikes. The **Sendero Altos de Inío** (6.5-km loop, 3hr) traverses a rocky headland and returns along part of the Sendero Transversal

through pristine evergreen forest. The **Sendero Punta Rocosa** (4.5-km loop, 3hr) follows the edges of a rocky peninsula, with views of the Faro de Inío (Inío Lighthouse).

A more challenging option is the 22.4-km, two-day **Sendero Quilanlar trek,** a loop around the headland on which the village is located, passing through old-growth forest, archaeological sites, and a number of picturesque beaches.

ACCOMMODATIONS

In Sector Inío, there is a **campground** (CH$15,000 per site) within the forest with space for 20 tents and access to hot water. Also here is the **Casa de Huespedes** (CH$40,000-60,000 d shared bath, CH$50,000-70,000 d private bath), a cozy guesthouse with six bedrooms (two with private baths) and a small kitchen. A hearty homemade breakfast is included in the rates; you can request other meals for an additional fee. All lodgings must be booked in advance via the administrative office in Castro.

Getting There

Excursiones Quellón (Jorge Vivar 382, tel. 9/7402 2456 or 65/2683 031) offers a regular **transfer service** to the park from Quellón in January-February. Outside these months, both Excursiones Quellón and **Origenes Tour** (Santo Vargas 348, tel. 65/2683 031, http://origenestour.com) can arrange **private transfers** (CH$30,000 round-trip) to Sector Chaiguata.

From **Quellón,** it's 38km to Sector Yaldad and the park entrance. Head north along Ruta 5, then after 15 minutes and 15km take the W-890, which is signposted for the park. The final stretch from Ruta 5 to the park entrance is an unpaved, potholed dirt track that takes 45 minutes. Sector Chaiguata is 15km farther southwest along the same road. This could take an additional hour or more, depending on how carefully you drive.

To reach Sector Inío, only accessible by boat, a **motorized launch** (CH$1,000 pp) operated by Quellón local **Luís Aguilar** (tel. 9/7807 2086) shuttles passengers from **Quellón,** departing on Sunday and Wednesday. The return journey leaves on Monday and Thursday. Contact Luís for reservations and to confirm departure dates and times. The journey can take up to six hours; it can also be delayed by a day or two, depending on the weather. Look for blue whales as the boat passes through the Golfo de Corcovado.

There is also a **light aircraft** that flies from **Castro,** just behind the park's administrative office, to Inío, at a cost of CH$240,000 for two people. You can book this service directly through the administrative office.

Northern Patagonia and the Carretera Austral

Nothing quite captures the essence of Northern Patagonia like the Carretera Austral (Southern Highway). Also known as Ruta 7, the 1,240-km highway stretches south from Puerto Montt to Villa O'Higgins through lush forests, glacial valleys, and towering cliffs.

Connecting the popular Lakes District to one of the wildest extremes of Chile, this highway offers a tantalizing route into the country's least explored parts: tumbling, slumbering masses of glacial ice; lush rainforests that shelter rare animals; and South America's finest and youngest national parks and hiking routes.

Northern Patagonia is surrounded by the Southern Patagonian Ice Field, the serrated Andes, labyrinthine fjords, and lush rainforest.

Highlights

Look for ★ to find recommended sights, activities, dining, and lodging.

★ **Parque Nacional Pumalín Douglas Tompkins:** Excellent hiking trails lead to millennia-old *alerce* and dramatic volcanic craters (page 428).

★ **Rafting the Río Futaleufú:** An abundance of rapids of varying difficulty make this river the ultimate place in South America for white-water rafting (page 434).

★ **Parque Nacional Queulat:** Its picture-perfect hanging glacier has long been the region's poster child. Watching its calving, egg-blue snout leaves little doubt as to why (page 444).

★ **Parque Nacional Cerro Castillo:** Day hikes and longer treks wind through glacial scenery to cobalt-blue lakes and striking granite ridges (page 456).

★ **Capillas de Mármol:** These colorful caves made of rainbow-hued marble were created by the wild waves of Lago General Carrera (page 459).

★ **Parque Nacional Laguna San Rafael:** It's home to one of Patagonia's most rapidly retreating tidewater glaciers, as well as an easier-to-access glacier popular for ice-trekking tours (page 462).

★ **Parque Nacional Patagonia:** With sun-scorched pampas, high-altitude lagoons, and *lenga* forests, this newest national park has extensive infrastructure, hiking trails, and breathtaking views (page 468).

★ **Caleta Tortel:** This enchantingly remote community on the shores of a milky-blue sound has wooden boardwalks in lieu of roads (page 477).

★ **Villa O'Higgins:** Situated at the very end of the Carretera Austral, this matchbox-size village is the gateway to the Southern Patagonian Ice Field and Patagonia's most adventurous border crossing into Argentina (page 481).

Northern Patagonia and the Carretera Austral

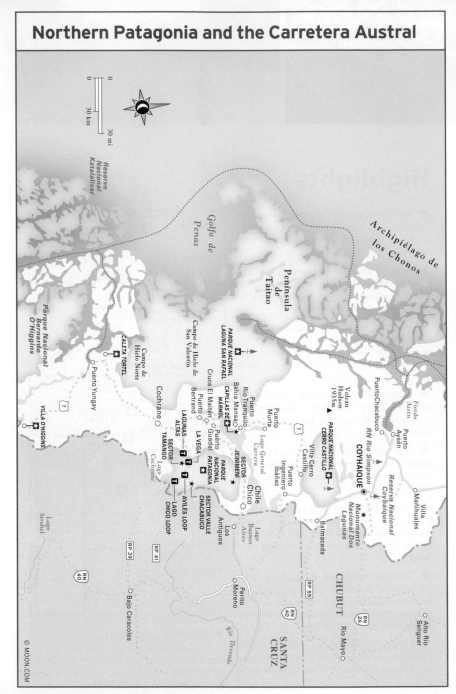

© MOON.COM

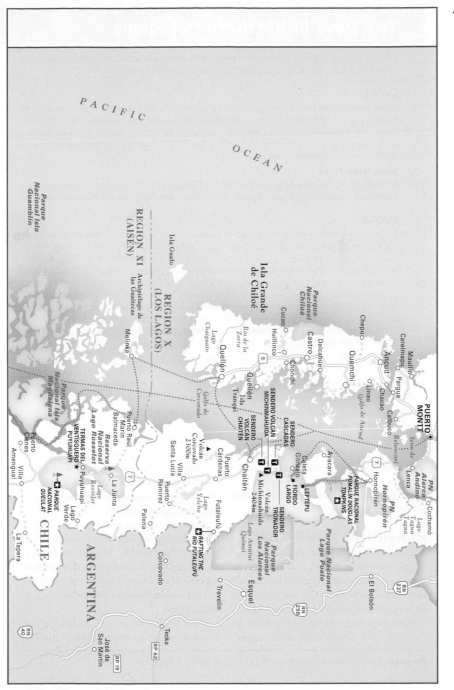

Two Days in Northern Patagonia

Take the morning flight from Santiago to Aeródromo Balmaceda (2.5hr), pick up a rental car and drive to Puerto Río Tranquilo (4hr), ready for an early start the next day.

DAY 1

Take a morning boat tour of the **Capillas de Mármol** (Marble Caves) and admire the veins of marble lit by the first rays of the sun. In the afternoon, take the one-hour drive along the Valle Exploradores to reach the flanks of Monte San Valentín—the tallest mountain in Chilean Patagonia—and panoramic vistas of the glacier at **Mirador Exploradores.** For dinner, order a pizza at **Mate y Truco** and relax for a while.

With More Time

Add an extra day for a nine-hour hike atop the ice of **Glaciar Exploradores,** a dramatic way to experience **Parque Nacional Laguna San Rafael** and the Northern Patagonian Ice Field.

DAY 2

Set out early from Puerto Río Tranquilo and continue south along the Carretera Austral, pausing for photographs at viewpoints of cobalt Lago General Carrera, whose microclimate almost guarantees sunshine. After a 2.5-hour drive is a turn into **Parque Nacional Patagonia,** within the old ranching terrain of Valle Chacabuco. Overnight in the luxurious **Lodge at Valle Chacabuco** or camp in more modest **Los West Winds Campground.**

You should have enough time to hike the spectacular 23-km, seven- to nine-hour **Lagunas Altas Trail.** Alternatively, drive another hour east to hike the popular 12-km, four-hour **Lago Chico Loop** around the lake, with dramatic rocky outcrops and scrubby grassland.

The following morning, return to Balmaceda to drop the car and fly back to Santiago or to Punta Arenas in Southern Patagonia.

Following the Carretera Austral, visitors can find striking natural rock formations, like the psychedelic caves above the fantastical Lago General Carrera, and tumultuous foaming rivers with Class V white-water rapids.

Travel on the fabled highway is slow, distances are long, and the weather is unpredictable. But venturing deep into Patagonia, still with barely a tourism footprint, is a trip that offers startling rewards.

PLANNING YOUR TIME

Northern Patagonia requires time and patience. A **rental car** from Puerto Montt or Aeródromo Balmaceda (south of Coyhaique) saves time—but be aware that rental prices are high and driving conditions challenging.

Four days is enough to visit the **glaciers,** colorful rock formations, and rugged, mountainous **national parks.** The easiest way is to fly from Santiago to Aeródromo Balmaceda and drive south to **Puerto Río Tranquilo,** then take a boat to the Glaciar Exploradores in **Parque Nacional Laguna San Rafael.** Alternatively, head north from Coyhaique to **Puyuhuapi** and the magnificent hanging glacier in **Parque Nacional Queulat.** Both journeys require at least a day's driving each way.

Most visitors don't go farther than Puerto Río Tranquilo, but for a truly authentic experience, and outstanding hiking, consider adding 2-3 days and continuing farther south to hike the wind-sculpted steppe and *lenga* forests of **Parque Nacional Patagonia,** north of Cochrane.

From Puerto Montt, an 8-10-hour bus or boat journey brings you to **Chaitén** and the

NORTHERN PATAGONIA

unmissable **Parque Nacional Pumalín,** with its millennia-old *alerce* forests, and the hike up the slopes of Volcán Chaitén to its astoundingly gigantesque crater. The park merits at least **1-2 days.** The eight-hour passenger and vehicle ferry from industrial Quellón is another possibility for creating a full circuit from Puerto Montt, via Chiloé and back along the Carretera Austral.

If you're connecting a trip to Southern Patagonia with the Carretera Austral, the 41-hour passenger, vehicle, and cargo ferry that plies the route north from Puerto Natales to **Caleta Tortel** and Puerto Yungay offers a spectacular and unique way to approach the road's southern terminus. From the picturesque cypress houses of fjord-side Caleta Tortel, it's a full day's northbound drive to Coyhaique, with stops at Cochrane and Parque Nacional Patagonia, Puerto Río Tranquilo and the marble caves, and Villa Cerro Castillo. Travelers from Argentina will find the border crossing at **Chile Chico** is the easiest and fastest.

Weather and Transportation

October-April are the best months for travel. Strong snowfall and black ice June-August leaves the roads impassable; it can snow as late as November. Expect large amounts of rain May-September, although it rains year-round. This is one of the rainiest places on the planet, with average annual rainfall reaching up to 400 centimeters. Many travel outfits, including hotels and even restaurants, close completely outside high season. During the peak months of January-February, visitors can expect to battle for seats on buses, hotel rooms, and photo ops as city-dwelling Chileans, Argentines, and Brazilians use these months for vacations. Consider traveling at the start and end of the season for lower prices, more flexibility in bookings, and a more authentic feeling of remoteness on this majestic road.

HISTORY

Human settlement in this remotest and least accessible part of Chile dates back centuries. The Kawésqar (Alcaluf) peoples long dominated the labyrinthine waterways off the western shores of Chile. The original "Patagones" spotted by European sailors in the 1520s were the Tehuelche people, hunters who lived off the guanaco and *ñandú* (lesser rhea) that roamed the grassy plains.

The Aysén region and Pacific coast were explored by the Europeans later than the southern and eastern coasts of Patagonia. The first expedition landed in 1553, commanded by Francisco de Ulloa on the orders of Chile's first governor. José de Moraleda y Montero in the late 1700s and Fitz Roy and Darwin aboard the *Beagle* in the 1830s contributed significantly to cartography of the fjords and waterways of Aysén and mainland Chiloé.

The first region to be colonized was Coyhaique, the modern capital of the Aysén region. Settlers from central Chile founded communities in these river valleys and the basin of Lago General Carrera, clearing land for agriculture by burning vast tracts of woodland. Many of these fires spread out of control and contributed to the scarcity of forest along the Carretera Austral between Coyhaique and Puerto Ibáñez.

As settlements grew, the need for a road connecting them became apparent. Although dictator Augusto Pinochet bears much of the credit for this ambitious construction project, plans actually began under president Salvador Allende. The Carretera Austral opened in the early 1980s, connecting Chaitén to Coyhaique. The road is still referred to by some residents as "Pinochet's Highway." In 1999, the final stretch connected Puerto Yungay and Villa O'Higgins, marking the end of the mammoth project. Today, road work continues in a plan to pave the entire road.

Road-Tripping the Carretera Austral

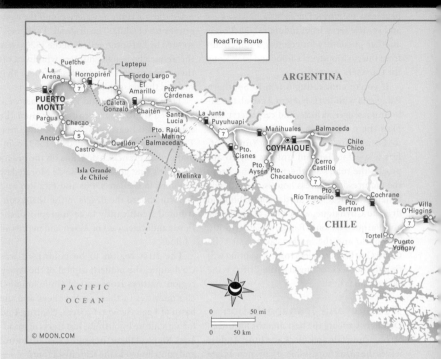

On its 1,240-km route from Puerto Montt south to Villa O'Higgins, the Carretera Austral travels through deep glacial valleys, impenetrable forest, and sheer cliffs. A journey on the Carretera Austral is equal to the destination, and you'll have some of the best experiences that Northern Patagonia has to offer.

BEST OF THE CARRETERA AUSTRAL

- **Best Wildlife-Watching:** Keep your eyes peeled for *pudú* on the roads around **Parque Nacional Pumalín.** *Huemul* sightings are possible on the final stretch of the Carretera Austral, from Puerto Yungay to **Villa O'Higgins.**

- **Best Photo Op:** It doesn't get more picturesque than bright blue ice calving from the snout of the Ventisquero Colgante, a hanging glacier in Parque Nacional Queulat. Hike the **Sendero Mirador del Ventisquero** for the best views.

- **Best Adventure Tour:** Clamber across glacial crevasses and admire the majesty of millennia-old ice with an ice-trekking tour of **Glaciar Exploradores.**

- **Best Day Hike:** For panoramic views of azure lakes and the Valle Chacabuco, take the challenging but rewarding **Lagunas Altas Trail** in Parque Nacional Patagonia.

- **Most Unique Place to Sleep:** Escape to a luxury hideout deep in the fjords, where dolphins splash right outside your window, at **Puyuhuapi Lodge & Spa.**

- **Most Unique Town:** With most of its roads consisting of wooden boardwalks, the hillside fjord settlement of **Caleta Tortel** must be seen to be believed.

- **Most Picturesque Ferry Journey:** Connecting Caleta Tortel and Puerto Yungay with Southern Patagonia, the **Transbordadora Austral Broom ferry** putters through the narrow channels of the Chilean fjords and some of the country's most pristine landscapes.

TIPS AND STRATEGY

When you drive the Carretera Austral, you should have a flexible itinerary. In Patagonia, things don't always go as planned, so leave some cushion.

Time: Two weeks is enough time to enjoy most of the Carretera Austral. Most travelers rent vehicles in Puerto Montt or Coyhaique. Because of the high cost of one-way rentals, it makes sense to hire and drop your vehicle in the same place. To do this, start in Puerto Montt and drive south to Coyhaique, or fly into Coyhaique and head north to Puyuhuapi, then drive south to Caleta Tortel. A week is enough time to drive north to Puyuhuapi and south to Cochrane, both of which are a day's drive from Coyhaique.

Vehicle rental: A 4WD vehicle is not essential but it makes the drive easier; a high-clearance vehicle and patience are necessary. Expect to pay CH$450,000 and up for a week's rental of a 4WD vehicle. Be aware that when renting a vehicle, insurance that covers driving along the Carretera Austral may not be included; be sure to confirm when booking. Hiring a campervan is also popular, allowing you to stop at will. Along the Carretera Austral, only **Recasur** (www.recasur-rac.cl) in Coyhaique rent campervans. **Wicked Campers** (www.wickedsouthamerica.com) and **Chile Motor Homes** (www.chilemotorhomes.cl) have locations in Puerto Varas and Punta Arenas. **Holiday Rent** (www.holidayrent.cl) operates in Punta Arenas.

Road conditions: Around 90 percent of the road from Puerto Montt to Puyuhuapi (about 430km) is paved. South of Puyuhuapi, you'll encounter potholed gravel roads and ample construction projects. This portion is less pleasant to drive, but the scenery and remoteness are incomparable.

Construction: Ongoing road construction, especially directly south of Puyuhuapi, Coyhaique, and Villa Cerro Castillo, can add up to an hour. Be aware that 1pm-5pm is peak time for road closures; check the status in the tourist information offices in **Puerto Montt** (Oficina de Turismo, San Martín 80, tel. 65/2256 999, 9am-1pm and 3pm-6pm Mon.-Fri., 9am-2pm Sat.) or **Coyhaique** (SERNATUR, Bulnes 35, tel. 67/2240 298, 9am-9pm daily Dec.-Mar., 9am-6:30pm Mon.-Fri., 10am-6pm Sat. Apr.-Nov.).

Safety precautions: Keeping speeds below 60km/h is wise. Possible hazards include tire punctures, chips to the windshield from gravel, and wildlife on the road. Pack food, water, and a sleeping bag in case of breakdowns. When picking up your vehicle, double-check that it has a spare tire.

Ferries: A ferry crossing is necessary in several places along the route. Bookings can be made online and must be made at least two weeks in advance during high season. You are generally required to enter the license plate number of your vehicle when booking; if you don't have this, you can inform the ferry company by email or phone when you pick up your rental car.

Where to stay: Hire a campervan or bring a tent and you can park nearly anywhere you find a spot along the Carretera Austral. Standard backcountry camping rules apply: Check if you're allowed to camp with the land's owners, and pack out all waste. Most of the national parks do not allow wild camping, but check with rangers at the main entrance.

Northern Carretera Austral: Puerto Montt to Puyuhuapi

The Carretera Austral officially begins at Puerto Montt's waterfront. The first section, from Puerto Montt to Chaitén, is a 240-km, nine-hour journey that includes two ferry rides. Just before Chaitén, the road passes through Parque Nacional Pumalín Douglas Tompkins; look for the smoking crater of Volcán Chaitén.

South of Chaitén, the highway is in a narrow forested valley that opens in points to reveal cleared plains. From here to fjord-side Puyuhuapi is a 190-km, three-hour journey, with only the village of La Junta to break up the drive. Puyuhuapi is on the western edge of Parque Nacional Queulat, the crown jewel of this region and home to a mesmerizing hanging glacier.

Budget at least two days for hiking in Parque Nacional Pumalín Douglas Tompkins, an afternoon to hike the glacier at Parque Nacional Queulat, and a half-day to wander around the Germanic village of Puyuhuapi.

Part of the fun of the northern Carretera Austral is that at two points along the road between Puerto Montt and Coyhaique, the land gives way to water, and you need to take a ferry. The first is at the Caleta Arena ferry landing, 45km south of Puerto Montt. Here, **Transportes del Estuario** (tel. 9/6191 9206, www.transportesdelestuario. cl, 24 hr daily, 45min, CH$10,000 per vehicle) operates two **car and passenger ferries** that cross every 45 minutes to the ferry landing at Caleta Puelche. Booking ahead is not possible; the service operates on a first-come, first-served basis. Expect to wait in high season. The second ferry passage, at Hornopirén, transports vehicles and passengers on the 4.5-hour journey to Caleta Gonzalo.

HORNOPIRÉN

From the Caleta Puelche ferry landing, the Carretera Austral continues south for 40km before turning northeast, reaching Hornopirén in 15km. The first official town along the Carretera Austral, Hornopirén feels separated from others to the south, enhanced by its location at the northern tip of the vast Comau Fjord. This sleepy town is a great introduction to the mellow pace of life in Patagonia. Nearby Parque Nacional Hornopirén is the town's main attraction, with hot springs and hiking trails. Most people stop to kill a few hours before boarding the southbound ferry.

The town is divided by the Río Negro; the port is on the western bank, surrounded by a number of small but adequate restaurants. The Plaza de Armas is on the east side of the river, where bus company offices are located. There is a **gas station** on the northern edge of town.

SOMARCO (Ingenieros Militares 450, tel. 65/2217 413 or 65/2217 414, www.barcazas.cl, CH$5,600 foot passenger, CH$33,600 vehicle including passengers) runs the **passenger and vehicle ferry** that connects Hornopirén with the rest of the Carretera Austral. As the highway enters town, continue south for 500 meters to the ferry ramp.

Food and Accommodations

A reliable choice and only 200 meters from the ferry ramp, **El Pescador** (Río Barcelo s/n, tel. 9/9508 9534, 10am-10pm daily, CH$6,000-10,000) serves huge fillets of fish and simple salads, fries, or potatoes. Hearty home-cooked stews and chicken dishes are alternatives.

It feels a bit like a museum at **Hotel Hornopirén** (Ignacio Carrera Pinto 388, tel. 65/2217 256, www.hotelhornopiren.cl,

Following the Carretera Austral Without a Car

Instead of driving the Carretera Austral, many visitors to this part of the country opt to go by bus, on a bicycle, or hitchhiking.

BUS

If hiring a car is out of your budget, public buses are a good alternative. Services run multiple times a week, if not daily, December-February. Outside the peak months, frequency drops dramatically. Travelers looking to cover large distances at once, like from Coyhaique to Chaitén, may find there is only one bus per week, which can sell out a few days in advance. Bus schedules change as regularly as the weather. Upon arriving in any destination, visit the bus terminal or offices of the local bus companies to confirm the schedules.

Buses are costly, except for a few subsidized services. It's always worth booking a couple of days in advance. In most cases, this requires a visit to the bus terminal or office in the town you're traveling from.

CYCLING

For the hardier traveler, going by bicycle is an increasingly popular way of navigating the Southern Highway. You'll need to bring all cycling gear from your home country, sturdy camping equipment to survive the fierce westerly winds, ample wet-weather gear, and a strong will. The poor state of the roads, rough terrain, and constant threat of rain make this quite the undertaking.

A DEDO (HITCHHIKING)

As the popularity of the Carretera Austral has increased, it has also acquired legendary status for young backpackers. It's common to find small clusters of travelers trying their luck at hitching a lift with locals, truck drivers, or other visitors. Considered safer than in most countries, hitchhiking in Patagonia is a different way to see the road and meet its inhabitants. Speaking a little Spanish to pass the journey when you get a lift enhances the experience and makes the time pass more quickly. Travel in groups of two or three—any larger and getting a lift can be problematic.

Never get into a car with someone you don't feel comfortable with. Don't hesitate to ask to be dropped off at the nearest safe place at any point on your journey. Competition between hitchers can be fierce in peak summer, December-January. Expect to wait several hours for a lift, particularly in Puyuhuapi and Puerto Río Tranquilo. This is also when the most traffic plies the road. Chances of getting a lift drop dramatically in the shoulder seasons, October-November and March-April. Consider bringing a tent, cooking equipment, and food in case you end up by the side of the road for longer than intended.

Scenic Detour to Lago Tagua-Tagua

Barranco Lodge

From Caleta Puelche, the Carretera Austral continues south toward Hornopirén, but another road heads east along a rocky cliff edge. This scenic detour leads to **Lago Tagua-Tagua,** a ribbon-shaped lake that spreads southeast to become Río Puelo.

Accessible by boat, **Parque Tagua-Tagua** (tel. 2/3263 2060, www.parquetaguatagua.cl, CH$5,000) is a little-known privately run tract of evergreen forest on the lake's southern shore. Hiking and kayaking are the main activities; rustic refuges and all-inclusive lodges provide lodgings.

Accommodations include fully sustainable **Barranco Lodge** (Lago Tagua-Tagua, tel. 9/9734 4050, www.barracolodge.com, 3D/2N US$5,000 d all-inclusive), whose restored 1940s structure is a masterclass in understated style. Perched on Lago Tagua-Tagua's northern shore, the lodge specializes in fly-fishing, kayaking, and horseback riding. All tours can include a helicopter ride. They also offer heli-skiing in winter. The food, using local ingredients, is some of the best in Patagonia.

CH$35,000 d private bath, CH$30,000 d shared bath), officially the oldest lodging in town, operating since the 1940s. This slice of history is constructed from *alerce,* a dark wood that makes it feel like the bowels of a ship. The half-dozen rooms aren't large, but the fjord views add to the charm. Those on a budget will appreciate the kitchen access and the adjoining mini market that stocks basic provisions.

A cut above other lodgings in this price range, **Hostería Catalina** (Ingenieros Militares s/n, tel. 65/2217 359, www.hosteriacatalina.cl, CH$42,900 d) is a typical Patagonian hotel with sturdy polished wooden walls, although its 10 rooms are larger than average with generous baths. Those on the 2nd floor have views across the fjord. Downstairs, a restaurant for guests offers a dinner menu—order in advance. Rates include IVA.

Getting There

From **Puerto Montt,** Hornopirén is 110km south along the Carretera Austral, about a three-hour journey, including the ferry crossing from Caleta Arena to Caleta Puelche. Once the ferry has arrived in Caleta Puelche, take the Carretera Austral for 60km to reach Hornopirén. This stretch of road is gravel and can become very muddy after rainfall.

Traveling by bus, **Kemel Bus** (O'Higgins and Portales, tel. 65/2217 272) has four daily departures from **Puerto Montt** (3hr, CH$5,000). Heading north, the bus from **Chaitén** (7hr, CH$10,000) reaches Hornopirén at around 6pm.

Continuing South on the Ferry

South of Hornopirén, the highway temporarily ends. A ferry connection from Hornopirén's dock to **Leptepu** is the next step of the southward journey. From Leptepu, a 10-km section of paved road connects to the next port, **Fiordo Largo.** You board another southbound ferry to reach **Caleta Gonzalo** and the continuation of the Carretera Austral.

SOMARCO (Ingenieros Militares 450, tel. 65/2217 413 or 65/2217 414, www.barcazas. cl, CH$5,600 foot passenger, CH$33,600 vehicle including passengers) runs the two-part **ferry service** from Hornopirén to Leptepu (3.5hr) and Fiordo Largo to Caleta Gonzalo (45min). The operator's 172-passenger vessels, the *Capitán M. Andrade* and the *Hornopirén* (Fiordo Largo to Caleta Gonzalo), accommodate both pedestrians and vehicles.

The ferries are scheduled to allow passengers traveling in either direction to connect with the second boat. There are three daily departures in high season, with timetables listed on SOMARCO's website. You can book tickets online up to 10 hours before departure and in their office up to 2 hours before departure (up to 4 hours for vehicles). During peak season, vehicle bookings need to be made at least two weeks in advance. Be at the terminal 2-3 hours before departure. The first southbound ferry (Hornopirén to Leptepu) has a cafeteria on board.

For the return voyage, you must have a printed copy of your tickets; SOMARCO's **ticket office** in Chaitén (Juan Todesco 188, tel. 65/2731 760 or 65/2731 762) can assist with this. Traveling by bus between Hornopirén and Chaitén, ferry tickets are included in the fare.

The ferry operator can change as frequently as every year. For the most up-to-date ferry information, contact Puerto Montt's **Oficina de Turismo** (San Martín 80, tel. 65/2256 999, 9am-1pm and 3pm-6pm Mon.-Fri., 9am-2pm Sat.).

Parque Nacional Hornopirén

With its forest of tall *alerce* trees and endangered flora and fauna, **Parque Nacional Hornopirén** (10km north of Hornopirén town, tel. 65/2217297 or 65/2486 115, loslagos. oirs@conaf.cl, www.conaf.cl, 24 hr daily, free) is a pleasant side trip from Hornopirén. Along with ancient forests of virgin hardwoods and dense groves of bamboo and ferns, mammals are the star residents. *Huemules,* pumas, *pudús,* and *kodkods*—the smallest species of South American cat—thrive in the untouched depths of this large reserve.

To reach the park, continue along the Carretera Austral past Hornopirén for 5km, where a dirt track signposted for Chaqueihua continues straight as the main highway veers right. From here, a high-clearance vehicle is necessary, as the 5km to the entrance of the park are in poor condition. At the end of the road, where the Fundo Chaqueihua Alto farm begins, a small car park and unattended ranger's office mark the official entrance.

HIKING

The park's main hike is to **Lago Pinto Concha** (18km round-trip, 7hr), a forest- and mountain-ringed lake tucked deep in the park. The trail starts at the gate of the Fundo Chaqueihua Alto farm, which you enter. After 300 meters you'll reach a footbridge; it's another 7km through private land to reach signs marking the boundaries of the park. From here, it's 4km to the lake, where there are basic camping facilities and two other short trails, including one that climbs the flanks of Volcán Yates for splendid panoramas.

The path to Lago Pinto Concha climbs persistently; plan for hiking 4-6 hours, depending on your pace. The route can be muddy, particularly after rain, so shoes with good grip and hiking poles are recommended. There is nowhere to buy food, although clean water is available from rivers en route; no filtering or treatment is needed. Bring your trash back with you.

★ PARQUE NACIONAL PUMALÍN DOUGLAS TOMPKINS

Offering a glimpse of Patagonia at its most unspoiled, the results of three decades of conservation on a mammoth scale, **Parque Nacional Pumalín Douglas Tompkins** (tel. 65/2299 339, www.parquepumalin.cl, 24 hr daily, free) is a unique natural treasure, protecting virgin Valdivian temperate rainforest and the steaming cone of Volcán Chaitén. Carefully planned and well-maintained trails pass waterfalls, earthy forests of southern beech, myrtle, and laurel, and dramatic viewpoints of Volcán Chaitén. Well-thought-out facilities, including campgrounds and cabins, provide comfortable spaces to spend the night.

The park stretches from the Pacific to the Andes, between the towns of Chaitén in the south and Hornopirén in the north, with the Carretera Austral bisecting it. Access is easiest from the south near Chaitén. It's open year-round. The **park office** (Klenner 299, Puerto Varas, tel. 65/2299 339) in Puerto Varas and the website have information to get you acquainted with the park before you arrive.

The first sections were acquired by late U.S. billionaire philanthropist Douglas Tompkins in 1991. The rest was acquired over the following decade. In 2018 the land was donated by Tompkins's widow, Kristine McDivitt Tompkins, to the Chilean state, and it formally became a national park.

The park's main focus is protecting millennia-old groves of towering *alerce*. This species of conifer is the largest in South America, reaching up to 70 meters and living 3,500 years. It's found from Chaitén north to around Valdivia, although many of the extant forests are secondary—the result of logging or fire. Pumalín contains significant primary forests.

Exploring the Park

The park has plenty of hiking trails and facilities, making it one of the Carretera Austral's most accessible. In one day, it's possible to hike a selection of trails. Heading south along the Carretera Austral, it's easy to stop at a number of trailheads. You'll need your own car or the services of a local guide; there's no public transport connecting the trailheads. Two or three days are ample for exploring the park.

ORIENTATION

The three main parts are **Pumalín North, Pumalín West,** and **Sector El Amarillo,** also referred to as **Pumalín South.** To access Pumalín North and visit its **hot springs,** you have to take a tour or charter a boat. Pumalín West is more accessible and offers **hiking trails,** some of which take you to **volcanoes.** The main draw of Sector El Amarillo is its **glacier.**

PLANNING TIPS

Depending on weather and road conditions, it's six hours' drive between Hornopirén (to the north) and Chaitén (to the south). The most efficient way to experience the park is with a **rental car.** There is ample parking at trailheads and campgrounds. Transportation links between these gateway towns and the park are frustratingly sparse. Without your own wheels, or if you're short on time, a **tour from Chaitén** to Pumalín West or to Sector El Amarillo is the most efficient.

The park's coastal forests receive over 590 centimeters of rainfall annually. Hiking after a brisk rain can be perilous due to exposed tree roots, thick mud, and soggy bridges. Bring **hiking boots** with good tread, **trekking poles,** and a **waterproof jacket.**

GUIDED TOURS

Local expert Nicolás runs **Chaitur Excursiones** (O'Higgins 67, tel. 65/2731 429 or 9/7468 5608, www.chaitur.com, from CH$10,000), with both the cheapest and most flexible tours. You might hike three trails in one day or hit the hot springs in

Sector El Amarillo. Expect to be transported between destinations in a rickety 16-seat minibus; prices depend on how many passengers there are and start from CH$10,000 for a day tour.

For smaller or private tours, **Nartour** (green bus, O'Higgins 166, tel. 2/2897 7638, www.natour.cl) is an excellent choice for trips to Pumalín West and Sector El Amarillo. Prices start at CH$20,000 pp for the hike up Volcán Chaitén. They also offer a half-day sea kayak tour (CH$25,000, equipment and transport to Santa Barbara included), where you paddle out to a sea lion colony. Guides speak English, Spanish, and German.

One of Chile's oldest tourism enterprises, **Altue Sea Kayaking** (tel. 9/9419 6809, www. seakayakchile.com) leads sea kayaking expeditions (6 days, 5 nights from US$1,780) that explore the fjords of the national park, including transfers from Puerto Montt airport, food, lodgings, equipment, and bilingual guides.

Pumalín North

Not accessible from the Carretera Austral, Pumalín North occupies an area south of Hornopirén. This sector is only accessible through a **kayak tour** with Puerto Varas-based outfitter **Al Sur Expediciones** (tel. 65/2232 300, www.alsurexpeditions.com) or by chartering a boat from Hornopirén. A selection of **hot springs,** including the **Termas Porcelana** and **Terma de Cahuelmó,** and hectares of virgin forest are the star attractions. There's free camping at Termas Porcelana.

Pumalín West

The most easily accessed section of the park is Pumalín West, which spans the area south from the Caleta Gonzalo ferry landing to Chaitén and is bisected by the Carretera Austral. Most of the park's hiking trails are here, as are the main accommodations. At the northernmost edge of the sector, **Caleta Gonzalo** houses a visitors center, a café, and cabins along the highway. The **Centro de Información** (Caleta Gonzalo, tel. 65/2250

079, hours vary) can provide maps of the park and information about the state of the trails.

SIGHTS AND RECREATION

The following trails have small parking lots and are signposted from the Carretera Austral.

With the most striking views and a sense of the dramatic damage caused by the 2008 volcanic eruption, challenging **Sendero Volcán Chaitén** (4.4km round-trip, 3hr) has its trailhead 24km north of Chaitén. The trail ascends steeply through lush forest and quickly climbs out of the greenery into the path of the eruption, now a landscape of charred tree trunks. A final steep climb leads to the edge of the 3.5-km-wide crater for phenomenal views of the still-steaming volcano and the destruction of the surrounding landscape. The crater is supposedly large enough to fit the town of Chaitén inside, with space left over. Look for lumps of glassy obsidian and featherweight pumice stones strewn across the path. The trail gains 600 meters elevation. Trekking poles are recommended.

One of the most popular and shortest treks in the park is the **Sendero de Alerces** (700 m loop, 40min), which starts 12.5km south of Caleta Gonzalo. It passes astounding 3,000-4,000-year-old *alerce,* some of which are over three meters thick, with informational panels along the way. This trail is accessible from the Carretera Austral. With its trailhead next to the café at Caleta Gonzalo, the moderate **Sendero Cascadas** (5.6km round-trip, 3hr) winds through the forest to arrive at a 15-meter waterfall. Almost 11km south of Caleta Gonzalo, **Sendero Tronador** (5km round-trip, 4hr) is a tough trek, starting with a series of wooden stairs that climb to a bridge that crosses Río Tronador. The trail ends at forest-fringed **Laguna Tronador,** where camping is allowed but there are no facilities. This trail is accessible from the highway.

About 14km south of Caleta Gonzalo, **Sendero Cascadas Escondidas** (1.8km loop, 2hr) climbs through dense forest to two sets of pretty waterfalls, the first of which can be appreciated from a viewpoint above or by climbing down a slippery wooden ladder to the base. This moderate trail is accessible from the Carretera Austral. About 30km south of Caleta Gonzalo, **Sendero Volcán Michinmahuida** (24km round-trip, 8-10hr) is a difficult trail that leads to the base of the volcano. This trail is accessible from the Carretera Austral.

The dramatic black-sand beach **Playa Santa Barbara** (western edge of Santa Barbara settlement, 11km northwest of Chaitén) is a great place to watch the sunset, with Commerson's dolphins frolicking in the water. Most tours of the southern sector of the park end here.

FOOD AND ACCOMMODATIONS

The only restaurant in the park, the pretty **Café Caleta Gonzalo** (Caleta Gonzalo, 9am-10pm daily Nov.-Mar., 9am-2pm and 4pm-8pm Mon.-Sat. Apr.-Oct., CH$5,000-16,000) has blond pine furniture, dramatic black-and-white photographs of the park, and a roaring log fire. All of the ingredients come from the organic farm nearby, where you can buy fruit and vegetables. This well-run little café offers huge sandwiches, soups, and homemade bread as well as boxed lunches to go. If the Centro de Información is closed, they have maps and can offer information about the park.

At Caleta Gonzalo's ferry port, the nine cabins of **Cabañas Caleta Gonzalo** (Caleta Gonzalo, tel. 65/250 079, reservas@parquepumalin.cl, CH$100,000 d) exude rustic charm with all the modern touches you need. Cabins are decorated with rough-hewn wood and thick woolen throws and come with electric heaters. On the edge of the fjord, they have sea views and private baths. Each cabin fits up to five people, with loft spaces for additional beds. There's no Wi-Fi or cell reception. Breakfast, served next door in the café, is included. Book well ahead in summer.

A footbridge 300 meters south of the ferry ramp at Caleta Gonzalo brings you to the large **Camping Río Gonzalo** (Caleta Gonzalo, CH$6,000 tents, CH$10,000 RVs), with plenty of space for tents, cooking shelters, and baths with cold showers. You can buy fruit and vegetables grown on the neighboring organic farm. It's within walking distance of Café Caleta Gonzalo and the Centro de Información. Beyond the campground, the two cabins at **Cabañas Río Gonzalo** (Caleta Gonzalo, tel. 65/250 079, reservas@parquepumalin.cl, Jan.-Feb. only, CH$65,000 2-person cabin) offer a great option to cook for yourself without camping. Cabaña Hobbit is a self-contained cottage with space for four in two bedrooms, while Cabaña Colono is a loft space with bunk beds for two; both include a kitchen and a wood fire. Minimum stay is three days; book well ahead.

The second-largest campground in the park, between Chaitén and Caleta Gonzalo, **Camping El Volcán** (28km south of Caleta Gonzalo, 29km north of Chaitén, CH$6,000 tents, CH$10,000 RVs) has 12 sites with access to roofed cooking areas, barbecues, and tap water. Baths have only cold water. This campground is accessible from the highway. With some of the best views of the eponymous lake, **Camping Lago Blanco** (24km south of Caleta Gonzalo, 33km north of Chaitén, CH$6,000 tents, CH$10,000 RVs), accessible from the highway, has campsites next to the water, covered cooking spots, and public baths. With shelters and space for a dozen tents, **Camping Cascadas Escondidas** (14km south of Caleta Gonzalo, 44km north of Chaitén, CH$6,000 tents, CH$10,000 RVs), accessible from the highway, has clean bath facilities. It is at the trailhead of the Sendero Cascadas Escondidas.

GETTING THERE

To get to Caleta Gonzalo from **Hornopirén** is a 4.5-hour journey south through the fjords aboard two different ferries. To get to Caleta Gonzalo from **Chaitén,** it's a 55-km, one-hour drive north on the Carretera Austral.

Sector El Amarillo

Sector El Amarillo occupies an area southeast of Chaitén. Most sights are accessible from the unpaved W-887, which runs east from the Carretera Austral at the town of El Amarillo.

SIGHTS AND RECREATION

The flat **Sendero Ventisquero El Amarillo** (20km round-trip, 6hr) reaches the snout of the slightly grubby but still impressive **Glaciar Michinmahuida**. A river crossing near the beginning of the trek can be dangerous when water levels are high; get updated information from rangers at the Centro de Información in El Amarillo. Start hiking early; the river rises during the day due to snowmelt. The trailhead is accessed directly from the Ventisquero campground. To get there, it's a 10-km drive off the Carretera Austral from El Amarillo's Centro de Información.

Termas El Amarillo (tel. 9/6760 8204, 8am-6pm daily, CH$7,000, cash only) has two hot springs pools in pretty surroundings. Bring a towel and a padlock to use a locker. To get here, turn onto the gravel W-887, which runs east from the highway just as you leave the town of El Amarillo.

ACCOMMODATIONS

The prettiest campground in the park, located at the trailhead for Sendero Ventisquero El Amarillo, **Camping Ventisquero** (CH$6,000 tents, CH$10,000 RVs free Mar.-mid-Dec.) has eight private sites with access to sheltered huts with benches and tables for cooking, plus toilets and very cold showers. The 10-km gravel access road, passable in a high-clearance vehicle, leaves the Carretera Austral just opposite El Amarillo's Centro de Información.

GETTING THERE

To get to El Amarillo and the W-877 from **Chaitén,** it's a 25-km, 20-minute drive southeast on the Carretera Austral. From **Coyhaique,** it's a 400-km, 7.5-hour drive north on the Carretera Austral.

CHAITÉN

All but buried under a deluge of thick ash and debris after the eruption of Volcán Chaitén in 2008, Chaitén today is a neat grid of drab houses looking out onto a thick strip of mud along the coast—the remains of the lahar that spilled through the town.

Some travelers start their trip along the Carretera Austral by flying or boating to Chaitén from Puerto Montt. Chaitén's location and transportation links make it a useful hub for trips along the Carretera Austral toward Futaleufú or Puyuhuapi. The lush, primeval forests of Parque National Pumalín can be reached in a day trip from Chaitén.

Although new buildings have been built, it's easy to get a sense of the extraordinary destruction caused by the 2008 eruption. Follow Calle Ercilla to its end at the intersection with Calle Padre Juan Todesco to find the outdoor **Museo de Chaitén** (no phone, 24 hr daily, free). The museum is a row of *alerce*-shingled wooden houses that survived the eruption and have been preserved. Lining what was formerly a residential road, some of the structures are perilously angled, while others appear to be halfway underground, submerged by ash.

Food

Bring a coat on a cold evening in the geodesic dome that houses ★ **El Rincón Del Mate** (Libertad, tel. 9/96899 464, 12:30pm-4pm and 6:30pm-11:30pm Mon.-Sat., CH$7,000-10,000). Thin-crust pizzas, enormous sandwiches and burgers, and daily specials of fresh salmon and prawn ceviche make up for the slight discomfort. Don't miss their Calafate (Magellan barberry) or rosehip pisco sours.

A stylish green bus has been repurposed to house **Natour** (O'Higgins 166, tel. 2/2897 7638, www.natour.cl, 8am-2pm and 4pm-7pm Tues.-Sun., CH$2,000-4,500), a great place for Desayuno de Campeones, a full English breakfast. For smaller appetites, standard sandwiches of cheese, ham, sausage, or avocado can be washed down with a latte, cappuccino, or hot chocolate. The Wi-Fi and free maps of the

Force of Nature

Just after midnight on May 2, 2008, smoke and ash abruptly began billowing from Volcán Chaitén, a volcanic caldera 10km northwest of Chaitén town. Neither locals nor volcanologists were aware of the existence of the volcano until this moment, but the response was swift—within a few hours, tiny fishing boats and local ferries had flocked to the shores of the town to evacuate its 4,000 residents, resulting in no human casualties. On May 6, the eruption grew in intensity, with pyroclastic flows and an eruption column 32km in the sky. The spectacular display forced residents within a 50-km radius to evacuate.

The damage was vast. Lahars of mud and ash blanketed Chaitén and filled the Río Chaitén, causing it to reroute down one of the town's main streets. The eruption continued for two months, providing fascinating insights into rhyolite magma—the first eruption of its kind to be studied in modern times. Locals were kept from their homes for almost a year, and basic facilities such as running water and electricity were not restored until 2011. Local authorities even attempted to relocate the town to Santa Barbara, 10km north, but Chaitén's residents refused.

On December 16, 2017, torrential rains caused rock and mud to dislodge from Glaciar Yelcho, resulting in a landslide that plowed along a river valley and engulfed half the village of Villa Santa Lucia, 75km south of Chaitén; 22 people were killed. A 2-km stretch of the Carretera Austral north of Villa Santa Lucia was buried beneath the mud, hampering rescue efforts. The road reopened in April 2018.

For inhabitants of the surrounding towns, both events remain raw, proving the vulnerable position of those living in a place so tangibly subject to the whims of nature.

town are welcome additions, as are the helpful owners, who also have a tour agency.

Great beer, juices, and pizzas make **Pizzeria Reconquista** (O'Higgins 298, tel. 9/7495 4442, noon-2pm and 4pm-11pm daily, CH$4,000-8,000) a popular bet for dinner, as the pizzas are big enough to share. The burgers aren't bad, and the chatty service makes you feel right at home.

Accommodations

Rooms are cramped at higgledy-piggledy **Hostel Chaitén Renace** (Valdivia 120, tel. 9/6591 761, CH$12,000 dorm, CH$24,000 d shared bath), but it is budget-conscious as the only lodging in town with kitchen access. The hostel is on two floors with two same-sex dorms and a couple of double rooms. It's cramped, but at this price, it's hard to argue. Rates include IVA.

The half-dozen bedrooms at no-frills **Hospedaje Doña Collita** (Portales 54, tel. 9/8445 7500, CH$30,000 d shared bath) are well looked after, with pretty linens and baths to share. A wood-burning stove in the breakfast room keeps the rooms upstairs toasty. The breakfast offerings at this B&B are standard and included in the rates. Host Doña Collita isn't very chatty, but she steers a well-run ship. Rates include IVA.

The well-presented rooms at **Hostal Don Carlos** (Riveros 52, tel. 65/2731 287 or 9/9128 3328, CH$30,000 d shared bath, CH$35,000 d private bath) bridge the gap between the budget and more expensive options, without the increase in price. The 23 rooms vary in size; opt for the newer wing on the west of the house for larger superior rooms, all with private baths and central heating. Rooms are plain but spotless, but wooden floors mean you can sometimes hear your neighbors. Rates include IVA.

With upmarket pretensions, **Hotel Mi Casa** (Av. Norte 206, tel. 65/2731 285, www. hotelmicasa.cl, CH$57,500 d) is on a low hill above the town with beautiful views of the bay from the breakfast rooms, but not from the guest rooms. Rooms are a mishmash of modern, inoffensive style. Double-glazed windows and central heating ensure the hotel is warm. English, Spanish, and some French are spoken; noise between bedrooms can be an issue.

Information and Services

U.S. expat Nicolás La Penna of **Chaitur Excursiones** (O'Higgins 67, tel. 65/2731 429 or 9/7468 5608, www.chaitur.com) is a font of knowledge about the area, including the geography and flora and fauna of the national park. His website has useful transportation information; he operates the best-value trips into the park and rents out bikes (CH$10,000 per day).

The English-speaking employees at the **Oficina de Turismo** (Diego Portales 141, tel. 65/2731 092, www.municipalidadchaiten. cl, 8:30am-5:30pm daily Nov.-Apr.) can help with bus and boat timetables. The tour agency **Natour** (green bus, O'Higgins 166, tel. 2/2897 7638, www.natour.cl) has free detailed maps of Chaitén and the national park.

The **Hospital de Chaitén** (Carrera Pinto 153, tel. 65/2326 704) can offer basic emergency care. **BancoEstado** (Libertad at O'Higgins) has an **ATM** and can **exchange currency,** but rates are significantly better in Puerto Montt. A **COPEC gas station** is a block and a half south of the bus terminal, along Ruta 7, the coastal road; prices are more expensive here than farther south.

Getting There and Around

Chaitén is one of the easiest places on the Carretera Austral to reach from Puerto Montt.

AIR

Twice-daily flights (CH$50,000) in 9- or 19-seat Twin Otter planes connect Puerto Montt's airport, Aeródromo La Paloma, with the **Aeródromo Chaitén** (WCH, also called Aeropuerto Nuevo Chaitén, no phone), 20km northwest of Chaitén. Flights are operated by **Aerocord** (Portales 287, Chaitén, tel. 9/7669 4515 or 65/2262 300, www.aerocord.cl) and **Pewen** (Av. Carrera Pinto 362, Chaitén, tel. 9/9403 4298, www.pewenchile.com); book in advance for summer trips. Schedules vary, but there's normally a morning and an afternoon departure, with only one daily Saturday and Sunday.

The schedule for **Transfer Fletes Chaitén** (tel. 9/5726 2794, transferchaiten@gmail.com)

is aligned with flight times for its shared van transfers (45min, CH$5,000) to and from the Chaitén airfield. **Nartour** (green bus, O'Higgins 166, tel. 2/2897 7638, www. natour.cl) can organize private transfers (from CH$10,000, min. 2 passengers).

BUS

Most buses in Chaitén use the makeshift **Terminal de Buses** outside **Chaitur Excursiones** (O'Higgins 67), opposite the Gobernación building. From **Futaleufú** (3.5hr, CH$2,500), **Buses Cárdenas** (tel. 9/4268 0432 or 9/8597 6405) for Chaitén leave at 11am daily from their stop outside Supermercado Flores (Prat s/n) on the western side of the Plaza de Armas. **Bus D & R** (Hermanos Carrera 280, tel. 9/4262 0432, www.busesdyr.cl) also has daily departures from Futaleufú (CH$2,500), leaving at 6am from its office.

From **Coyhaique** (9hr, CH$24,000), **Buses Becker** (Gral. Parra 355, tel. 67/2232 167, www.busesbecker.com) operates a weekly bus to Chaitén, departing at 10am Tuesday and departing Chaitén on the return trip at 11:30am Wednesday. Buses stop at Puyuhuapi and La Junta en route. Direct buses to Chaitén from **Puyuhuapi** (3hr, CH$6,000) are operated by **Terraustral** (tel. 67/2325 131). Buses leave from outside Puyuhuapi's Nido de Puyes mini market at 6am Monday, Wednesday, and Friday, returning to Puyuhuapi from Chaitén at 4pm.

From **Puerto Montt** (10hr, CH$20,000), **Kemelbus** (Terminal de Buses, tel. 65/2721 301, www.kemelbus.cl) has a bus to Chaitén at 7am daily. In Chaitén, tickets are sold from **Ruta Patagonia 7** (Corcovado 468, tel. 65/2731 494), opposite COPEC. Ticket prices include the cost of the two ferries connecting Hornopirén with Caleta Gonzalo. This journey is long, but with beautiful scenery.

FERRY

The ferry from Puerto Montt to Chaitén is similar in duration to the long bus trip but has the benefit of allowing you to stretch your legs. It takes around nine hours for the 246-seat *JACAF* passenger and vehicle ferry, operated by **Naviera Austral** (www.navieraustral.cl, CH$12,400 foot passengers, CH$10,200 bicycles, CH$95,100 vehicles), to travel from Puerto Montt to Chaitén. The ferry ramp in Chaitén is 1km northwest of town along Ruta 7.

Boats leave three times weekly: 11pm Monday, Thursday, and Friday from Puerto Montt; the return journey departs Chaitén at 11am Thursday, 10am Friday, and 11:50pm Sunday. Ticket price includes a *semi-cama* (partially reclining) seat in a large open area. There's a cafeteria on board, but it's poor quality and overpriced; it's better to bring your own food. The same boat plies the route between Quellón, on the southernmost tip of Chiloé, and Chaitén (CH$13,000 foot passengers, CH$71,000 vehicles), which takes four hours. For both routes, weather conditions can significantly affect the time of departures and arrivals.

There is space for 55 cars on board. Reservations must be made at least two months in advance for peak season, December-February. For foot passengers, booking a week in advance is adequate. Bookings can be made on Naviera Austral's website; print your tickets or get them printed at their offices in Puerto Montt (Angelmó 1673, tel. 65/2270 430 or 65/2270 431), Quellón (Pedro Montt 355, tel. 65/2682 207 or 65/2682 505), or Chaitén (Riveros 188, tel. 65/2731 011 or tel. 65/2731 012).

CAR

The 240-km journey from **Puerto Montt** to Chaitén, including multiple ferry transports, takes about nine hours. Chaitén is 60km south of **Caleta Gonzalo** along the Carretera Austral, a drive of about an hour.

FUTALEUFÚ

Wedged in a river basin 10km from the Argentine border and 75km east of the Carretera Austral, Futaleufú is a charming town that offers world-class white-water rafting on the Río Futaleufú, also known as the "the Fu" or "Futa." This small mountain town makes a perfect hangout: It's a hive of activity in the summer, with rafting, kayaking, hiking, horseback riding, mountain biking, climbing, and fly-fishing. Plan at least a day for an adrenaline-fueled jaunt down the Fu and a couple more for day trips and to appreciate the town's remote, picturesque setting.

In late January or early February, don't miss the annual **rodeo,** a weekend event when *huasos* (Chilean cowboys) throng to the town to compete. It's held in the half-moon-shaped arena known as the *medialuna* (eastern end of Carrera s/n), on the northeastern edge of town.

The town mostly shuts down at the start of April, with many tour guides and instructors leaving the region until the next season begins in November.

Orientation

Comprising a handful of paved streets, Futaleufú is sandwiched between the pretty azure Lago Espejo in the east and Río Espolón, which joins Río Futaleufú farther south. Most restaurants and lodgings are in the streets immediately surrounding the **Plaza de Armas.**

★ Rafting the Río Futaleufú

Futaleufú means "large river" in the indigenous Mapuche tongue of Mapundungun, and they're not kidding. With swirling features named the Inferno, Purgatory, and the Angel's Dance, the Fu tumbles through vertical basalt gorges and 47 rapids, making it a world-class destination for white-water rafting.

WHEN TO GO

The main rafting season is November-March. For the best conditions, book a tour in March, when stable weather and high water guarantee the most exhilarating rapids.

1: Sendero Cascadas Escondidas in Parque Nacional Pumalín Douglas Tompkins **2:** Futaleufú's Plaza de Armas **3:** Volcán Chaitén **4:** Chaitén town

TOURS

Outfitters offer three basic rafting tours. You'll be given an extensive safety talk and a lesson in river rescue. Safety-conscious companies also provide support kayaks and catarafts.

You don't need rafting experience for the popular four-hour **Bridge to Bridge Tour** (around CH$60,000), although reasonable swimming skills are essential; you're guaranteed a thrill. Numerous Class III-IV and the IV+ Mundaca Rapids form this 8-km stretch of foam. In high season, most companies offer morning and afternoon tours.

For more high-adrenaline fun, take the **Río Azul to Bridge Tour** (around CH$80,000). This version adds two Class V rapids (Terminator and the Himalayas) to the Bridge to Bridge trip, extending it to a 14-km, six-hour tour. The final option is the 20-km, eight-hour **Río Azul to Macul Tour** (around CH$110,000). It adds two more Class V rapids to the Río Azul to Bridge trip. Participants should have rafting experience or have previously taken the Bridge to Bridge tour.

Transportation to and from the outfitter's office and lunch or a snack are always provided. Many agencies are run by U.S. expats; bilingual guides ensure instructions are crystal clear. Outfitters have a two-person minimum for tours.

OUTFITTERS

Patagonia Elements (Cerda 549, tel. 9/7499 0296, www.patagoniaelements.com) and **Bochinche Expediciones** (Cerda 697, tel. 9/8143 4373, www.bochinchex.com) are the most popular and highly regarded tour operators in the industry. Both offer trekking tours; Bochinche Expediciones also operates river bug tours (a vessel shaped like an armchair that you sit in and use flippers attached to your hands to steer).

Kayaking

The Class III Río Espolón is ideal for beginner white-water kayaking. The expert Nate from **Hostal Las Natalias** (W-915,

Futaleufú, tel. 9/6283 571 or 9/8566 5290, www.hostallasnatalias.info) runs four- to five-hour trips (from CH$75,000 pp) on the calm Río Espolón, with all transport and equipment included. He also offers an option where he takes out experienced kayakers to gnarly stretches of water.

Hiking

There are a couple of day hikes within easy access of town, including the popular, easy **Sendero Piedra La Aguila** (7km round-trip, 2.5hr). Accessed from a path signposted on the right 2km after Hostal Las Natalias (W-915), the trail follows a gravel road to the top of the Piedra La Aguila, a 40-meter rock that juts across the valley for sweeping views of Pinto and Noroesta Lakes. Access is via private land, so you may need to cough up CH$1,000 if you see the owner. The trailhead is about 3km northwest of the Plaza de Armas.

From the east side of town, the **Sendero Mirador Torre de Agua** (1.6km round-trip, 40min) begins at the eastern edge of Laguna Espejo. This short walk brings you the best views of the Fu, flanked by sharp, snowy mountains. To reach the trailhead, follow Calle Carmona east to its end and take the path around the northern side of the lake.

Starting from the entry road to Maitén Camping is an easy hike (3km round-trip, 45min) with views east across the town and the mountains. The trail gains 250 meters to the top of **Cerro La Bandera.** Entry is through private property, so expect to pay CH$500 to the owners. To get to the trailhead, take the W-915 heading northwest out of town. It's on the right after 300 meters.

Other Activities

Patagonia Elements (Cerda 549, tel. 9/7499 0296, www.patagoniaelements.com) has **horseback day tours** to visit, meet, and dine with local *huasos* (Chilean cowboys) in their homes. It can also organize full-day and half-day **fly-fishing tours,** at the border with Argentina or in the Valle Las Escalas, known for brown and rainbow trout.

Hotels in town are good options for arranging tours; both **Uman Lodge** (Fundo La Confluencia s/n, tel. 65/2721 700, www.umanlodge.com) and **Hostal La Gringa Carioca** (Aldea 498, tel. 65/2721 260 or 9/9659 9341, www.hostallagringacarioca.cl) organize horseback rides, while **El Barranco** (O'Higgins 172, tel. 65/2721 314, www.elbarranco.cl) specializes in fly-fishing.

Food

Cooking in front of you, chatty Fabio runs the takeout-only **Pizzas de Fabio** (Isabel Riquelme and O'Higgins, tel. 9/8577 8334, noon-3pm and 6pm-10:30pm Tues.-Sun., CH$8,000-13,000). All 20 pizzas are made on thin-crust bases. The Favorita, with blue cheese and mountains of caramelized onions, is particularly good.

A pleasant locale that's popular on weekends, **El Encuentro** (O'Higgins 653, tel. 9/5201 9716, 9am-11pm daily, CH$4,000-12,000) serves abundant plates of cheese or seafood empanadas, plus mountainous dishes of *lomo a lo pobre* and grilled fish. The food epitomizes simple home cooking.

With its atmospheric dining area where tree trunks seem to hold up the ceiling, **Restaurant El Barranco** (O'Higgins 172, tel. 65/2721 314, www.elbarranco.cl, 7pm-11:30pm daily, CH$8,000-16,000), at the hotel El Barranco, is one of the best spots in Futa. It isn't cheap, but top-quality ingredients in the classic Chilean dishes include salmon ceviche, tenderly cooked Patagonia lamb, and hare with pureed carrots and chocolate sauce. Hotel guests have priority in the small dining area when it's busy, so make a reservation if you're not staying here.

A daily rotating menu featuring fresh ingredients from the owners' farm is at gourmet ★ **Martín Pescador** (Balmaceda 603, tel. 65/2721 279, 8pm-11pm daily, CH$9,000-13,000, cash only). Don't let the wooden cabin surroundings fool you; the husband-and-wife team present beautiful innovative fare, such as the *maqui* fruit, locally caught hare, and plants foraged from local forests.

Accommodations

UNDER CH$25,000

Several hundred meters beyond the western limit of town, as the W-915 drops to the Río Espolón and goes back up again, is **Maitén Camping** (tel. 9/7512 711, CH$4,000), with space for 15 tents in an apple orchard next to the owner's house. A wood-fired boiler means there's sometimes hot water in the two baths. Facilities are basic (there's no covered *quincho*) but suit a stiff budget. Rates include IVA.

At the southern end of Calle Aldea, before Calle Puerto Espolón, is the entrance for the wooded one-hectare campground **Aldea Puerto Espolón** (Aldea, tel. 9/5324 0305, www.aldeapuertoespolon.cl, CH$7,000 tent sites, *domos* CH$9,000), on the Río Espolón. Its basic facilities include a barbecue area with grills, electricity, and cooking utensils. There are only a handful of restrooms, which causes problems in peak season. Unfurnished *domos* (domed yurts) set on raised wooden platforms can sleep groups of four or more if you have your own sleeping bag. Owners Arturo and Mónica welcome guests with home-brewed beer and rental bikes. A sandy beach by the river is perfect for swimming and catch-and-release fly-fishing. The campground is open from November until the snow starts in May-June. Rates include IVA.

CH$25,000-40,000

A backpacker's paradise, American-run ★ **Hostal Las Natalias** (W-915, tel. 9/6283 571 or 9/8566 5290, www.hostallasnatalias.info, Nov.-Apr., CH$32,000-36,000 d, CH$15,000 dorm) provides cozy bedrooms in a stunning location with mountain views. Travelers mingle in the large open kitchen and the lounge with a roaring fire. Eight large bedrooms provide simple lodgings; opt for one on the south side for the best views. Some baths are shared. Owners Nate and Nancy live in a cottage on-site, offer kayaking classes and bike rentals, and are the best source of information on hiking and adventure activities. Las Natalias is just up the hill from Maitén Camping. Rates include IVA.

CH$60,000-80,000

Hostería Río Grande (O'Higgins 397, tel. 65/2721 320, CH$65,000 d) has hot water, reasonable Wi-Fi, and 12 sizeable bedrooms that are overpriced for what they are, particularly the 1st-floor rooms behind the car park, which receive the noise of the owners living above. Breakfast is sufficient and service is friendly, and there's plenty of parking. An attached restaurant specializes in all-you-can-eat buffets (CH$15,000) and is useful on a Sunday when other establishments are closed. Rates include IVA.

OVER CH$80,000

In a grand old German house with a whiff of the British countryside, the cute ★ **Hostal La Gringa Carioca** (Aldea 498, tel. 65/2721 260 or 9/9659 9341, www.hostallagringacarioca.cl, CH$89,000 d) has lovely gardens that overlook Río Espolón. Of the four rooms, the one upstairs, with a double and a single bed, has the best views. A superb breakfast (cereal, homemade bread, eggs) is the pièce de résistance. The owner is the perfect host. Rates include IVA.

With thick wooden beams and cowboy hats around the property, **El Barranco** (O'Higgins 172, tel. 65/2721 314, www.elbarranco.cl, Sept.-mid-Apr., CH$136,000 d) is a nod to the town's *huaso* culture. On two floors overlooking a swimming pool and the forest, 10 bedrooms have rough wood walls and huge squishy beds. It feels separate from the town despite being just a few blocks from the square. They can arrange tours, including fly-fishing on nearby rivers and lakes. There's a good restaurant on-site.

Six kilometers by gravel road south of Futaleufú, **Uman Lodge** (Fundo La Confluencia s/n, tel. 65/2721 700, www.umanlodge.com, Oct.-Apr., CH$388,000 d, CH$471,000 d breakfast and dinner, CH$529,000 d full-board) has a spectacular setting in the forest with mountain views from 16 modern bedrooms. A pool and spa allow for relaxation, while the on-site restaurant negates the hassle of going into town. The food

incorporates ingredients from the owners' organic farm, and the resident sommelier guides the wine pairings. They can organize whitewater rafting with companies in town, as well as horse tours. Rates include IVA.

Information and Services

The **Oficina de Turismo** (O'Higgins s/n, tel. 65/2237 629, www.futaleufu.cl, 9am-9pm daily Sept.-Mar., 10am-5pm daily Apr.-Aug.), on the southern side of the Plaza de Armas, is superbly helpful, providing up-to-date transport information, hotel and restaurant recommendations, and contacts for tour companies; English is spoken.

On the east side of the plaza, **BancoEstado** (Rodríguez s/n, at O'Higgins) has a **24-hour ATM** that works with most cards, although Visa cards can be problematic; bring cash with you. **Hostal Los Abuelos** (Cerda 436, tel. 65/2721 458) can exchange Argentine pesos and dollars. The **Hospital de Futaleufú** (Balmaceda 382, tel. 65/2721 313) provides emergency medical attention.

Getting There and Around

CAR

From **Chaitén,** Futaleufú is 150km southeast. To get there, take the Carretera Austral south to Villa Santa Lucia, where Ruta 235 heads east. From Ruta 235, turn north onto Ruta 231, which winds northeast along Río Futaleufú before reaching the town of Futaleufú. The drive takes 3.5 hours.

BUS

The major bus routes to Futaleufú run north from **Chaitén** and south from **Coyhaique.** Buses are the most regular from the north.

Serving Futaleufú, **Buses Cárdenas** (tel. 9/4268 0432 or 65/2721 214) leaves from **Chaitén** (3.5hr, CH$2,500) 4pm-5pm daily. Once in Futaleufú, buses drop passengers outside **Supermercado Flores** (Prat s/n) on the western side of the Plaza de Armas. You can buy tickets when you board the bus in Chaitén. **Bus D & R** (tel. 9/4262 0432, www.busesdyr.cl) also runs buses from **Chaitén** (noon daily) that drop passengers at its office in Futaleufú (Hermanos Carrera 280). The return journey to Chaitén leaves at 6am.

From **Puerto Montt** (12hr, CH$25,000), the fastest route is north to Osorno and south through Argentina (you are not permitted to get off the bus in Argentina) to Futaleufú. This is faster than taking the bus from Puerto Montt to Chaitén and connecting to Futaleufú from there. This service is operated by **Buses Absa** (Terminal de Buses Puerto Montt, tel. 65/2380 982, www.busesabsa.cl) and leaves at 6am Monday and Thursday from Puerto Montt, departing for the return at 7:30am Tuesday and Friday. Buses drop and pick up passengers from Futaleufú's old post office (Balmaceda 501, tel. 65/2721 360).

To get here from southern destinations like **Coyhaique,** or to continue south from Futaleufú, you'll need to plan in advance, as the only service from Futaleufú south along the Carretera Austral is **Buses Becker** (Coyhaique tel. 67/2232 167 or 9/8554 7774, www.busesbecker.com). Northbound buses leave at 8am Tuesday and Saturday from **Coyhaique** (10hr, CH$18,000), stopping and picking up passengers in **Puyuhuapi** (4.5hr, CH$12,000) and **La Junta** (4hr, CH$12,000). Tickets are sold from Futaleufú's **old post office** (Balmaceda 501). Note that these buses are often full in high season, so book your ticket a day or two in advance.

CROSSING INTO ARGENTINA

The 75-km journey to Esquel, Argentina, via the **Paso Futaleufú** (Ruta 231, 8am-9pm daily) is faster and the border formalities quicker than at the **Paso Río Encuentro** (Ruta 235, tel. 63/2765 462, 8am-8pm), 97km south of Futaleufú.

Buses Futaleufú offers service to **Esquel, Argentina** (9am and 7pm Tues.-Thurs., 2hr, CH$2,500), from Futaleufú. Buses leave from outside Hostal Los Abuelos (Cerda 436, tel. 65/2721 458). At the border, you'll board another bus and buy a ticket to take you onward to Esquel.

Taxis or *fletes* (minivans) can take you to the border for CH$25,000-30,000, where you'll find more taxis and minivans waiting. The **Oficina de Turismo** (O'Higgins s/n, tel. 65/2237 629, www.futaleufu.cl, 9am-9pm daily Sept.-Mar., 10am-5pm daily Apr.-Aug.) has a list of the local people who operate these services to the border.

LA JUNTA AND VICINITY

A small village along the Carretera Austral, **La Junta,** which means "The Junction," is literally that: a connecting point for buses that ply the Southern Highway, plus an interchange for the roads east toward Argentina or west to the port of Raúl Marín Balmaceda. It's about halfway between Chaitén to the north and Coyhaique to the south. It's also the northernmost town in the Aysén region, Chile's least populated district.

Most visitors stop in La Junta for lunch on the long drive south to Puyuhuapi or Coyhaique. An excellent café offers the best meal in town. If you're tempted to stay for the fly-fishing on the nearby Río Rosselot, there are a number of decent accommodations.

A COPEC **gas station** on the northern edge of town is a compulsory stop for motorists, as gas is cheaper here than Puyuhuapi; it is across the road from a rare lime-green monument to former dictator Augusto Pinochet. The town has no ATM; bring cash from Chaitén or Futaleufú.

Fly-Fishing

The **Reserva Nacional Lago Rosselot,** which flanks La Junta east and west, is excellent for fly-fishing thanks to the small creeks that drain into the namesake lake on the eastern side of the reserve. Its outlet river, Río Rosselot, is how trout get into other rivers downstream. The reserve has no infrastructure for visitors; for general information, contact **CONAF** (Av. Ogana 1060, Coyhaique, tel. 67/2212 225, www.conaf.cl, aysen.oirs@conaf.cl).

A number of high-end fishing lodges here

include **Chucao Lodge Rosselot** (Lago Rosselot, Santiago tel. 2/2201 8571, www.chucaolodge.com, US$4,500 7-day, 6-night fly-fishing package, CH$415,000 pp per night), outside the boundaries of the reserve, on Lago Rosselot where it empties into the Río Rosselot. Conditions for fly-fishing for brown and rainbow trout and salmon vary late November-mid-March. It's a 15-minute drive from La Junta. Rates include nights at the Chucao Rosselot and Chucao Yelcho, on the shores of Lago Yelcho, 100km north of La Junta, as well as meals, an open bar, and transportation from Puerto Montt. Activities for non-anglers are also available. Not all guides speak fluent English.

On a smaller budget or with less time, **Entre Aguas** (outside Alto Melimayu hotel, La Junta, tel. 9/8438 828, www.entreaguaspatagonia.cl) has half-day fly-fishing tours (Oct.-Mar., CH$90,000 for 2 people) with transfers and Spanish-speaking guides included. They can organize fishing licenses with advance notice.

Food and Accommodations

A charming little café on the highway, **Mi Casita de Té** (Carretera Austral s/n, tel. 67/2314 206, tel. 9/7802 0488, elypaz.cortes@gmail.com, 8:30am-1am daily Jan.-Feb., 8:30am-11:30pm daily rest of year, CH$4,500-10,000, *menu del día* CH$8,000) is usually packed with travelers for breakfast, a slice of homemade *tres leches* cake, or the three-course lunch menu. Run by chatty matriarch Eliana, who directs the show from the bar, it's an excellent place to get visitor information. Eliana also has four nicely decorated cabins (2-person cabin CH$45,000) next door, all with Wi-Fi, central heating, private baths, and breakfast—served in the café, of course. Laundry service is also available. Credit cards are accepted.

Next door and run by the same owners, **Camping Don Fede** (Carretera Austral s/n, tel. 9/4061 6432, Dec.-Feb., CH$5,000) offers no-frills tent sites with a *quincho* (covered kitchen area) and restrooms. You can pay with a credit card in the café.

The owners can be a bit surly, but you can't fault the cleanliness of the nine rooms at **Hostería Rayen** (Angamos s/n, tel. 67/2314 275, CH$28,000 d shared bath, CH$31,000 d private bath). All rooms except one share a clutch of baths. Pains have gone into keeping the rooms comfortable, with crisp white linens and bedside lamps. It is 1.5 blocks from the Carretera Austral and around the corner from the Buses Becker stop. Breakfast is basic but ample.

Spacious rooms and verdant gardens characterize superb ★ **Espacio y Tiempo** (Carretera Austral 399, tel. 67/2314 141, www.espacioytiempo.cl, Nov.-mid-Apr., CH$92,000 d). English-speaking owners Alan and Connie lovingly maintain the nine slick and modern rooms with white baths. The ground-floor rooms have terraces. Their superb **Restaurant Espacio y Tiempo** (12:30pm-2:30pm and 7:30pm-10pm daily, CH$7,000-10,000) has a simple menu of homemade pasta, steaks, cheese boards, and salads, and the bar is renowned for its pisco sour. Both the restaurant and bar are open to nonguests. Book ahead in peak season; prices at the hotel drop up to 14 percent outside January-February. Rates include IVA.

Alto Melimoyu (Carretera Austral 375, tel. 67/2314 320, www.altomelimoyu.cl, CH$82,000-88,000 d) is a reasonable option that's open year-round. Slightly cramped rooms are inlaid with thick pine for a rustic feel, with woolen decorations adorning the walls. There's a sauna and a restaurant on the premises. Rates drop by a third April-October.

Getting There and Around

From Chaitén to La Junta, it's 150km on the Carretera Austral, a drive of just over 2 hours. To La Junta from Futaleufú, it's a 150-km, 3.5-hour journey southwest on Ruta 231, Ruta 235, and the Carretera Austral. From Coyhaique, it's a 280-km, 5.5-hour drive north on the Carretera Austral.

Buses Becker (Coyhaique tel. 67/2232 167, www.busesbecker.com) offers services to La Junta from **Coyhaique** (8am and 1:30pm Tues. and Sat., 5hr, CH$12,000). At 11:30am Wednesday and Sunday, buses return from **Chaitén** (3hr, CH$15,000) to La Junta. The buses stop for lunch in La Junta at **Restaurant Teresita** (Pedro de Valdivia s/n, between Lynch and Angamos); passenger pickup is here. **Terraustral** (Manuel Montt 817, La Junta, tel. 67/2314 400, www.busesterraustral. cl) also has buses from **Chaitén** (4pm Mon., Wed., and Fri., 4hr, CH$5,000), **Coyhaique** (Coyhaique tel. 67/2254 335, 8am and 3pm daily, 6hr, CH$12,000), and **Puyuhuapi** (5hr, CH$9,000). Outside January-February, bus frequencies can drop to one daily.

Minibuses by **Entre Verdes** (Mistral s/n, tel. 9/9510 3196) shuttle between La Junta and **Puyuhuapi** (5:45pm Mon., Wed., Fri., 1 hour, CH$500). In Puyuhuapi, the minibuses stop at the mini market (also called Entre Verdes) to collect passengers heading north to La Junta. In La Junta, they pick you up from your hotel, so book your journey in advance.

PUYUHUAPI

From La Junta, the Carretera Austral runs south through thick forests enclosed by low hills. The final 10km of the highway before the charming port village of Puyuhuapi follows the western shore of Lago Risopatrón. The town is on the north end of the Fiordo Puyuhuapi (Puyuhuapi Fjord); keep your eyes peeled for *toninas* (small Chilean dolphins).

With fewer than 800 inhabitants, this sleepy little fishing village feels like rural Germany or a fairy tale, with a clutch of historic Bavarian-style wooden houses. Founded by four Germans in 1935, but only connected to the rest of Chile by road in 1977, Puyuhuapi has an alluring remoteness. It is a gateway to Parque Nacional Queulat, just a 30-minute drive away.

The original German settlers brought expertise in textiles. Opened in 1945, the **Alfombras de Puyuhuapi** (Aysén s/n) was where skillfully woven handmade rugs and carpets were manufactured until 2017, when the factory closed its doors for good.

For good views, follow Calle Otto Uebel west almost to its end and the trailhead for **Sendero Los Canelos,** a gentle, 1.5-km well-marked trail through private ground up to a *mirador* (overlook); if the owner's around, you may be required to pay a CH$500-1,000 entry fee.

Termas del Ventísquero Puyuhuapi

Intense geothermal activity in the area is responsible for the 20-40°C temperatures at the **Termas del Ventísquero Puyuhuapi** (tel. 9/7966 6805, www. termasventisqueropuyuhuapi.cl, 9am-9pm daily Dec.-Feb., reduced hours rest of year, CH$17,000 adults, CH$12,000 children), hot springs pools 6km south of Puyuhuapi. One large and three small spring-heated pools are located outdoors on the fjord and hidden from the road by forest. Changing facilities, baths, and lockers are on-site, as are a restaurant and a café. Only food and drink bought here can be consumed here. It gets crowded, particularly in late afternoon.

Recreation

Turismo Experiencia Austral (Otto Uebel 36, tel. 9/5004 4699 or 9/8744 8755, www. experienciaustral.com) offers **guided kayak excursions** (from CH$30,000) of three or six hours, with a minimum of two people, including food and equipment. They also offer kayak rentals (CH$5,000 per hour). The outfitter runs full-day guided excursions of Parque Nacional Queulat (CH$30,000, min. 4 people) with English-speaking guides. Rates include the boat trip across the lake. If you just need a ride to the park, the daily transfer service (CH$5,000 round-trip) leaves from their office at 8:30am and returns from the park at 6:30pm.

Food and Accommodations

The village springs to life December-February, when the majority of tourists arrive. The more expensive accommodations book up quickly.

Day Trip to Raúl Marín Balmaceda

On the delta of the Río Palena and Fiordo Pitipalena, the hamlet of Raúl Marín Balmaceda feels untouched and untamed. Frolicking dolphins are regular visitors, while sea lion colonies and penguins are on islands a short distance away. A day trip from La Junta is enough time to appreciate the port's charms, particularly if you arrange sea kayaking or a boat trip to the fjord. To appreciate the simple serenity of this coastal village, plan an overnight trip. There are no ATMs or gas stations, so bring plenty of cash and a full tank of fuel.

ACTIVITIES

Paddle a kayak or hire a local fishing boat for a morning trip on the Fiordo Pitipalena. Keep your eyes peeled for wildlife, including blue whales, most prevalent in February. At Isla Las Hermanas you can see a feisty colony of sea lions.

Hostería Isla del Palena can help you organize activities with locals from the village; prices start from CH$72,000 for up to four people. **Kawelyek Expeditions** (tel. 9/75429 056, www. kawelyek.cl) can organize day-kayaking tours in the vicinity. You can hike the trails into the southern beech forest that flanks the village or along the sweeping coastline without a guide.

ACCOMMODATIONS

A number of hostels and B&Bs are in the village. The best is the warm and welcoming **Hostería Isla del Palena** (Las Hermanas s/n, tel. 9/6608 9536, isladelpalena@gmail.com, CH$40,000). Its on-site restaurant (CH$8,000-12,000) excels with hearty home-cooked favorites of *pastel de jaiba* (crab pie) and grilled catch-of-the-day pulled from the sea, and even homemade ice cream using local flavors.

GETTING THERE

From La Junta, the two-hour, 75-km drive along the X-12 to Raúl Marín Balmaceda includes a 10-minute crossing aboard a small passenger and vehicle ferry (free) over the Río Palena. It doesn't operate 1pm-2pm, after 8:30pm in summer (earlier hours in winter), or following heavy rain. The best way to confirm if the boat is running is to ask one of the operators in the village.

Also from La Junta, **Heriberto Klein** (tel. 9/6607 5746) operates a Monday, Wednesday, and Friday minibus (2hr, CH$2,500), departing at 3pm outside the Oficina Municipal, dropping passengers at the port in Raúl Marín Balmaceda.

ONWARD TRAVEL

The cargo and passenger ferry **Naviera Austral** (tel. 65/2731 011, www.navieraustral.cl) offers onward transportation to Quellón (5hr, CH$7,450 foot passengers, CH$55,150 vehicles), northeast in Chiloé, or south to Puerto Chacabuco (26hr, CH$13,960 foot passengers, CH$141,000 vehicles). The ferry passes through Raúl Marín Balmaceda twice weekly in each direction (departing Quellón 11pm Wed. and Sat., departing Puerto Chacabuco 8pm Mon. and noon Fri.). The ticket office in Raúl Marín Balmaceda can update you on departure times, which can vary wildly based on weather conditions. Buy tickets at Hostería Isla de Palena, at their office in Chaitén (Riveros 188), or through the website.

The menu is small but the food is cooked to perfection at **Senderos Puyuhuapi** (Llautureo 28, tel. 9/98810 9796, 8am-10pm daily Dec.-Feb., 11am-6pm daily Mar.-Nov., CH$6,000-8,500), with a clutch of tables and a soundtrack of jazz classics. Four dishes are offered, including grilled salmon, chicken, and beef; there's a good selection of German-inspired desserts and cakes.

With grander intentions than you'd expect in a village of this size, **Misur** (Av. Otto Uebel 86, tel. 9/7550 7656, restaurant. misur.puyuhuapi@gmail.com, 1pm-3pm and 7pm-11:30pm Tues.-Sun. Aug.-May,

CH$7,500-8,000, cash only) serves imaginative dishes from its tiny menu. Fish from the fjord is transformed into beautifully presented ceviche and risotto or oven-baked with chorizo. The owners are enthusiastic and attentive.

One road back from Avenida Otto Uebel, **Hospedaje Don Luis** (Diego Portales 5, tel. 9/8839 0649, CH$30,000 d shared bath) features a warm welcome from owners Don Luís and Doña Margarita, with a handful of single and double bedrooms with shared baths, all immaculately clean. Breakfast is extensive, with homemade bread, avocado, and eggs.

There are just two cabins at cozy Swiss-Peruvian **Cabañas Turin** (Hamburgo 130, tel. 9/9931 1321, diego.turin.vagnieres@gmail.com, Oct.-Mar., from CH$44,000). One can accommodate two people; the other holds six. Kitchens are included, and woodstoves keep them toasty. The two-person cabin offers excellent value for money. Rates include IVA.

In an imposing Germanic building, family-run **Hostería Alemana** (Av. Otto Uebel 450, tel. 67/2325 118, www.hosteriaalemana.cl, CH$45,000 d) is welcoming and good value for the money, particularly if you ask for a newer room, with modern white bath suites and views of the lovely garden. Breakfast is ample, with cheese and bread plus the occasional cake or kuchen. Rates include IVA.

The sprawling **Hostal Aonikenk** (Hamburgo 16, tel. 67/2325 208, www.aonikenkpuyuhuapi.cl, CH$54,000 d) reflects Puyuhuapi's burgeoning tourism scene, with 12 bedrooms and cabins that emerge unexpectedly from a lovely untamed garden of native trees. Guest facilities include a communal kitchen and a bike shed. The best rooms are the newest ones, spacious and with electric heaters rather than the kerosene version. Book in advance for summer. Rates include IVA.

The grand old ★ **Casa Ludwig** (Av. Otto Uebel 202, tel. 67/2325 220, www.casaludwig.cl, Oct.-Mar., CH$30,000 d shared bath, CH$54,000 d private bath), listed as a historic monument for its Germanic architecture and history, is run by friendly multilingual host Luisa Ludwig. It offers sizeable bedrooms, most with private baths, on four floors. A convivial communal kitchen and grand living room make up one floor; Wi-Fi is confined to here. The attic rooms are cheapest and most cramped; ask for the double at the front of the building for fjord views. Rates include IVA.

PUYUHUAPI LODGE & SPA

Few places along the Carretera Austral can claim such a beautiful setting as exclusive ★ **Puyuhuapi Lodge & Spa** (tel. 67/2450 305, Santiago tel. 2/2225 6489, www.puyuhuapilodge.com, CH$202,000 d with breakfast, CH$272,000 d 2 meals, CH$538,000 d 3 meals). Accessible by speedboat from a signposted jetty 15km south of Puyuhuapi, the lodge is on Fiordo Puyuhuapi, where squat *toninas* (Chilean dolphins), seabirds, and other marinelife are visible. Arrive at nightfall for a more spectacular approach, when the reflections of the lights of the lodge flicker in the water. The design of the lodge mimics the *palafitos* (wooden houses on stilts) of Chiloé, with *alerce* tiles blending into the damp evergreen forests. A huge living room with creased leather sofas and rough-hewn walls has floor-to-ceiling windows to watch the weather and the mountains of the national park. At the excellent restaurant next door, gourmet Chilean dishes of tuna tartare and hake in a creamy scallop sauce are served.

Thirty bedrooms are in a handful of buildings, all elegant and modern. Almost all have fjord views; the Viento Puelche block is on the fjord, with balconies to appreciate the smell of the ocean. Three outdoor hot springs pools are down a short path through the woods, with sun loungers and views. There's also a spa with an indoor swimming pool and treatments at additional cost. Nonguests can use the spa (CH$50,000 per day). There's also a small cafeteria next to the outdoor pools. There's no Wi-Fi, TV, or cell reception. Kayaks are available to use on the fjord, and the hotel can recommend day trips in the area. The speedboat operates four times daily.

Information and Services

The municipal-run **Oficina de Turismo** (hours vary Dec.-Mar.) provides information about bus timetables and the national park. A **COPEC gas station** is at the western end of Calle Aysén.

Getting There and Around

From **La Junta,** it's a 45-km, 50-minute drive to Puyuhuapi south along the Carretera Austral. From **Coyhaique,** it's a 230-km, 4.5-hour drive north on the Carretera Austral.

By **bus,** it's a bumpy journey to Puyuhuapi from **Coyhaique** (5hr, CH$9,000). **Terraustral** (Coyhaique tel. 67/2254 335, www.busesterraustral.cl) has the most regular connections; buses leave Coyhaique at 8am and 3pm daily. The bus stops in Puyuhuapi before continuing to La Junta. These buses leave **La Junta** (1 hour, CH$2000) at 5:30am and 12:10pm daily, reaching Puyuhuapi at 6:20am and 1pm, respectively. Outside January-February, bus frequency can drop to one daily. **Buses Becker** (Gral. Parra 355, tel. 67/2232 167, www.busesbecker.com) offers service to Puyuhuapi from **Coyhaique** (8am Tues. and Sat.) on its way north to Chaitén. These buses return from **Chaitén** (4hr, CH$15,000) at 11:30am Wednesday and Sunday, dropping passengers in Puyuhuapi at the corner of Avenida Otto Uebel and Llautureo.

Minibuses operated by **Entre Verdes** (Mistral s/n, tel. 9/9510 3196) run to Puyuhuapi from **La Junta** (7am Mon., Wed., and Fri., 1 hour, CH$2,000). The pickup point can change, so call ahead and they will pick you up from your La Junta hotel. In Puyuhuapi, the minibuses drop passengers at the Entre Verdes mini market.

★ PARQUE NACIONAL QUEULAT

Dramatic egg-blue **Ventisquero Colgante del Queulat** (Queulat Hanging Glacier), clinging precariously to the mountain above the icy Laguna Témpanos, is the most famous sight in bewitching **Parque Nacional Queulat** (tel. 2/2221 7948, www.conaf.cl, parque.queulat@conaf.cl, 8:30am-5pm daily, CH$5,000 adults, CH$3,000 children), east of Puyuhuapi. The glacier's exaggerated blues are perfectly contrasted against the dark green of the forest. Evergreen southern beeches line the hills around Laguna Témpanos, the lake that captures the great hunks of ice that splinter from the glacier's snout.

The park is divided into three areas: Sector El Puma, Sector Bosque Encantado, and **Sector Ventisquero Colgante** (Hanging Glacier Sector). Ventisquero Colgante, the most accessible, is 20km south of Puyuhuapi, on an unpaved road east of the Carretera Austral. Bring food with you; there is nowhere to purchase supplies in the park.

Turismo Experiencia Austral (Av. Otto Uebel 36, Puyuhuapi, tel. 9/5004 4699 or 9/8744 8755, www.experienciaustral.com) operates kayaking expeditions (from CH$30,000) in the park, on Laguna Témpanos and Puyuhuapi Fjord. Prices include transfers from their office in Puyuhuapi and park admission.

Sector Ventisquero Colgante (Hanging Glacier Sector)

The most accessible of the three sectors is home to the most striking sight: the Queulat Hanging Glacier, visible from the Carretera Austral. Paths wind through misty temperate rainforest dripping with moss. If you're quiet, you may spot the endemic red-breasted *chucao* (similar to a robin) and the black-throated *huet huet,* named by the Mapuche people for the noise it makes.

From the main entrance, some 20km due south of Puyuhuapi, a signed turnoff down a gravel road brings you to a CONAF ranger station, a campground, a car park, and three trailheads. The most impressive trail is the moderate **Sendero Mirador del Ventisquero** (Glacier Viewpoint Trail, 6.5km round-trip, 2.5hr) that climbs through

---

1: Puyuhuapi Lodge & Spa **2:** Ventisquero Colgante del Queulat

evergreen southern beech forest to a viewpoint across from the glacier. Afternoon provides the best lighting to watch the dramatic calving.

From the sector's campground, the flat, 350-meter **Sendero El Aluvión** (1km loop, 30min) circuit begins, with interpretive signs explaining the geography of the region. **Sendero Laguna Témpanos** (1.2-km round-trip, 30min) forks off the trail toward the glacier viewpoint about 200 meters in and arrives at the lakeshore for a broader but more distant view of the glacier.

In summer, speedboats docked at the end of the Sendero Laguna Témpanos can take you across the water beneath the glacier. The 30-minute trip costs CH$3,500 adults and CH$1,500 children. A minimum of four people is required.

Camping

In the Sector Ventisquero Colgante, a 10-site **campground** (CH$5,000 adults, CH$3,000 children) with toilets and hot showers, plus roofed picnic tables, is run by park concessionaire **Turismo Experiencia Austral** (tel. 9/5004 4699 or 9/8744 8755, www. experienciaustral.com). Book in advance in summer; it fills up.

Getting There

From **Puyuhuapi** to the park's main entrance, it's a 20-km, 30-minute drive south on the Carretera Austral. The gravel entrance road is another 1.5km to the entrance to the **Sector Ventisquero Colgante.** From **Coyhaique,** it's a 233-km, 4.5-hour drive north along the Carretera Austral.

Minibus transfers (CH$5,000 round-trip) to Sector Ventisquero Colgante are run by park concessionaire **Turismo Experiencia Austral** (tel. 9/5004 4699 or 9/8744 8755, www.experienciaustral.com). The minibuses leave at 8:30am daily from their Puyuhuapi office (Otto Uebel 36); they depart the park at 6:30pm. Buses traveling between Puyuhuapi and Coyhaique can also drop you off at the turnoff for the park.

Southern Carretera Austral: Coyhaique to Villa O'Higgins

The mostly unpaved Carretera Austral is most impressive south from Parque Nacional Queulat to Coyhaique. Your car tumbles over deep trench-like potholes and noses around blind bends, spiraling up to Paso Queulat and then rushing back down again. After the turnoff for fishing village Puerto Cisnes, the next 175km to Coyhaique are perfectly paved, a tonic for frayed nerves.

From Coyhaique, the scenery changes. Narrow valleys become wider plains. The views are dominated by serrated mountains scattered with deciduous forests with glaciers above. The Northern Patagonian Ice Field, paralleling the Carretera Austral on the west between Puerto Río Tranquilo and Caleta Tortel, gives a sense of the geological forces that shaped the region. The protected lands of Parque Nacional Patagonia provide a crucial home to one of the world's rarest deer.

Traffic thins and visitor numbers drop dramatically on the very southern stretches. Unpaved for much of the final 230km between Cochrane and Villa O'Higgins, the Carretera Austral is practically empty as it reaches the fairytale village of Caleta Tortel and Villa O'Higgins, the literal end of the road. These final 560km lend themselves to deep exploration, particularly as the drive itself takes at least 14 hours. Plan for at least seven days for this part of the drive. With another day or two, you'll have an easier time reaching and making the most of Villa O'Higgins.

Flying from Santiago to Coyhaique's airport is a cost-effective way to focus on the southern half of the highway. Another option is to link a trip to Southern Patagonia with the Carretera Austral by taking the ferry that connects Caleta Tortel and Puerto Natales.

COYHAIQUE

The capital of the Aysén Region, Coyhaique dates to 1929, one of the oldest settlements along the Carretera Austral. The buildings retain the weathered aspect of much of the Southern Highway, but it's a vibrant city, with coffee shops, restaurants, and even nightlife. Coyhaique is a gateway to the southern half of the Carretera Austral.

In the Río Simpson basin with Cerro Mackay looming above, Coyhaique's paved streets are thick with traffic. If you're traveling overland, Coyhaique is an unavoidable waypoint and has the only large supermarket along the entire Southern Highway. Restaurants and accommodations are significantly higher-end than elsewhere in the region. Coyhaique is also home to the largest airport in the region, Aeródromo Balmaceda.

Orientation

Coyhaique is hemmed in by Río Simpson in the west and Río Coyhaique northeast. Ruta 7 parallels Río Simpson along the town's west side. The town sits in orderly rows of streets below its northern border, Calle Baquedano.

Most accommodations and restaurants surround the pentagonal **Plaza de Armas,** in the northwestern part of town. On the plaza's southwestern corner is the pedestrianized **Paseo Horn,** where many restaurants and transportation offices are located. Paseo Horn joins north-south **Avenida Ogana,** another main artery.

Sights

It feels like all roads lead to the vast **Plaza de Armas** (bounded by Gral. Parra, Prat, Bilbao, Eusebio Lillo, and Veintiuno de Mayo),

where a water feature dominates and artisans sell wooden and wool trinkets from a small wooden hut.

To learn more about Coyhaique's past, head to the eastern edge of town and the **Museo Regional Aysén** (Ruta 243, www.museoregionalaysen.cl, 11am-7pm Tues.-Fri., 2pm-6pm Sat.-Sun., free). Inaugurated in 2018, the interactive displays narrate the region's history of sheep ranching. It also has artifacts from the colonizers who came from England to work the land. Audiovisual presentations show every part of the process, from the sheering to sale. To get here from downtown, a taxi should cost no more than CH$3,000. It's a 45-minute walk from the Plaza de Armas.

Nightlife

With a pub feel and a reputation as a meeting place for travelers, **La Taberna D'Olbek** (Gral. Baquedano 1895, tel. 67/2239 385, 6pm-12:30am Mon.-Sat.) is the obvious choice for a quiet drink. Three beers are made in the brewery behind the bar. Try the unique *maqui* fruit beer. The food—burgers and sandwiches and German-inspired *crudos*—isn't bad.

Recreation

Specialist adventure outfit **Patagonia Adventure Expeditions** (tel. 9/8182 0608, www.patagoniaadventureexpeditions.com) has three unique hiking routes that traverse unexplored terrain where you won't see another soul. The most popular is the 10-day Aysén Glacier Trail trek (US$6,000 pp). Only 111 people per year are allowed on this isolated route in secluded, untouched sections of the surrounding mountains and valleys, skirting the edge of the Northern Patagonian Ice Field, before ending at the company's remote Sol de Mayo ranch. Camping and basic lodgings, meals, and pickup from Coyhaique or Aeródromo Balmaceda are included. Custom trips of any duration are also possible. All treks start from Puerto Bertrand, 280km south of Coyhaique.

Coyhaique

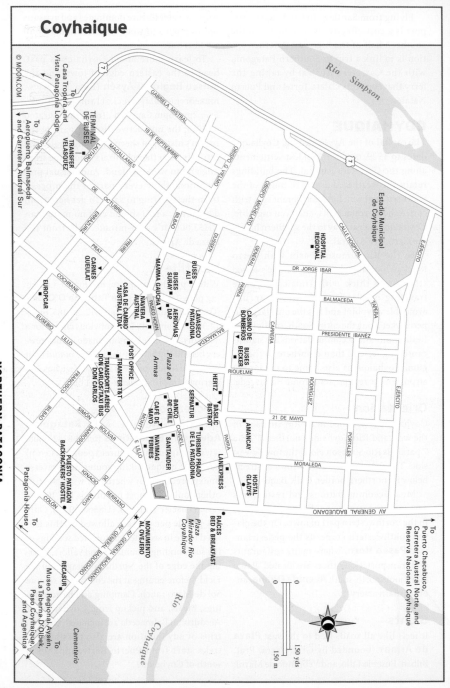

© MOON.COM

Rio Simpson

To Casa Tropera and Vista Patagonia Lodge

To Aeropuerto Balmaceda and Carretera Austral Sur

TERMINAL DE BUSES

TRANSFER VELASQUEZ

GABRIELA MISTRAL

18 DE SEPTIEMBRE

OBISPO G. VIELMO

MAGALLANES

LAUTARO (ALDEA)

12 DE OCTUBRE

ERRAZURIZ

FREIRE

OBISPO MICHELATO

GENERAL PARRA

CALLE HOSPITAL

Estadio Municipal de Coyhaique

EJERCITO

BILBAO

DUSSEN

HOSPITAL REGIONAL

DR. JORGE IBAR

BALMACEDA

TAPERA

PRAT

COCHRANE

CARNES QUELLAT

EUSEBIO

LILLO

EUROPCAR

MAMMA GAUCHA

BUSES ALI

BUSES SURAY

NAVIERA AUSTRAL

PASEO HORN

AEROVIAS DAP

LAVASECO PATAGONIA

BALMACEDA

CASINO DE BOMBEROS

CARRERA

BALMACEDA

PRESIDENTE IBANEZ

RODRIGUEZ

EJERCITO

CASA DE CAMBIO "AUSTRAL LTDA."

POST OFFICE

TRANSFER T&T

Plaza de Armas

BUSES BECKER

RIQUELME

HERTZ

BASILIC BISTROT

21 DE MAYO

PORTALES

FRANCISCO

TRANSPORTE AEREO DON CARLOS/TAXI BUS DON CARLOS

SIMON

BARROSO

21

MONTT

E. LILLO

CAFE DE MAYO

BANCO DE CHILE

SERNATUR

CONDELL

AMANCAY

PARRA

MORALEDA

PUESTO PATAGON BACKPACKERS' HOSTEL

BILBAO

IGNACIO

DE MAYO

COLON

SERRANO

BOLIVAR

SANTANDER

NAVIMAG FERRIES

TURISMO PRADO DE LA PATAGONIA

LANEXPRESS

HOSTAL GLADYS

AV GENERAL BAQUEDANO

To Patagonia House

MONUMENTO AL OVEJERO

AV GENERAL BAQUEDANO

Plaza Mirador Rio Coyhaique

RAICES BED & BREAKFAST

To Puerto Chacabuco, Carretera Austral Norte, and Reserva Nacional Coyhaique

RECASUR

Museo Regional Aysen, La Taberna D'Olbek, Paso Coyhaique, and Argentina

Cementerio

Rio Coyhaique

0   150 yds
0   150 m

To

N

Rio Simpson

Food

CHILEAN

With its windowless wood-paneled walls, the long-standing ★ **Casino de Bomberos** (Gral. Parra 365, tel. 67/2231 437, 11:30am-4pm and 8pm-11:30pm daily, CH$7,500-10,500) looks more like an old-fashioned clubhouse or gym. Join the queue out the door waiting for a table. Expect huge platters of beef, grilled salmon, and a two-course daily menu, plus juicy empanadas.

Unassuming **Carnes Queulat** (Freire 327, tel. 67/2250 507, 11am-11pm Mon.-Sat., CH$7,000-12,000), just off Calle Prat, surprises on price without disappointing on quality. The menu has Chilean cuts of beef plus huge platters of traditional Patagonian barbecued lamb, more than enough for two. The restaurant itself feels dated but the service is attentive.

INTERNATIONAL

Mama Gaucha (Paseo Horn 47, tel. 67/2210 721, www.mammagaucha.cl, 10am-2am Mon.-Sat., CH$4,900-10,000) is famed for crisp thin-crust pizza with an interesting array of toppings (goat cheese with roasted onion, *merkén,* and cilantro), and beer from nearby Casa Tropera brewery. Service can be slow; book ahead for evenings and weekends in high season.

Tricky to find, across the Río Simpson on the road to the airfield, restaurant and brewery ★ **Casa Tropera** (Km 1.5 Camino Aeródromo Teniente Vidal, tel. 9/6597 0585, noon-2am Mon.-Sat., CH$5,900-7,600) unites good hamburgers and loaded sandwiches with excellent beer, brewed in-house in the stainless steel tanks next to the tables. The vibe is young and hip. It's a 20-minute walk from the Plaza de Armas.

Coyhaique's first vegetarian restaurant, ★ **Basilic Bistrot** (Gral. Parra 220, tel. 9/7766 2784, 9am-7:30pm Tues.-Fri., 11am-8pm Sat.-Sun., CH$5,000-8,000) attracts a trendy crowd and impresses with tabbouleh-style salads, lentil and chickpea or roasted red pepper and sweet pickle burgers, thick vegetable soups, cakes, and pudding—the majority of which can be vegan on request. They offer a dish of the day (CH$7,000); service is excellent and the atmosphere inviting.

LIGHTS BITES AND COFFEE

With coffee options from ristretto to affogato and macchiato, the cutesy and hip **Cafe de Mayo** (Veintiuno de Mayo 543, tel. 67/2273 020, www.cafedemayo.negocio.site, 8am-10pm Mon.-Sat., CH$3,500-5,200) should be the first stop for coffee lovers. Dodge the tableware suspended from the ceiling and grab a table—it's hugely popular, so you may have to wait. It's a local favorite for *once* (afternoon tea).

Accommodations

UNDER CH$25,000

Attracting backpackers and budget-minded travelers, ★ **Puesto Patagon Backpackers' Hostel** (Cristóbal Colón 133, tel. 9/8198 2922, puestopatagon@gmail.com, CH$10,000 dorm, CH$32,000 d) has smallish dorm rooms and one double room with a shared bath in the newly decorated upstairs of a family home run by a welcoming and good-humored mother-daughter team. Guests have access to a kitchen and dining area downstairs. Rates include IVA.

CH$25,000-40,000

Rooms are dated and it's a 10-minute walk to the Plaza de Armas, but the welcome of the English-speaking owner at **Aumkenk Aike** (Simpson 1443, tel. 9/9670 3853, CH$25,000 d shared bath) makes this a friendly place to stay, aided by the convivial resident cat. Laundry service, a bar and games area, and kitchen access add to the budget-friendly charm of this matchbox-size B&B. Rates include IVA.

CH$40,000-60,000

Long established as one of Coyhaique's best value lodgings and two blocks from the Plaza de Armas, **Hostal Gladys** (Gral. Parra 65, tel. 67/2245 288, www.hostalgladys.cl, CH$40,000 d shared bath, CH$45,000 d private bath) has 14 bedrooms, all but two with en suite baths. Choose a street-side room to get a window; those on the other sides have skylights. Towels are not included, so bring your own. Rates include IVA.

CH$60,000-80,000

With its elegant, old-fashioned grandeur encapsulated in its heavy chandeliers and antique furniture, **El Reloj** (Baquedano 828, tel. 67/2231 108, www.elrelojhotel.cl, CH$69,000 d)—named after the owner's clock collection—feels out of place in small-town Coyhaique. The 19 rooms are more dated than other options in this price range, but crisp white sheets, king beds, and modern baths are perfectly good for a few nights. El Reloj is closed for June or July each year.

OVER CH$80,000

Offering exceptional value for the money, ★ **Raices Bed and Breakfast** (Baquedano 444, tel. 9/9619 5672, info@ raicesbedandbreakfast.com, CH$82,000-92,000 d) has personalized service and 12 beautifully adorned large rooms, cypress-paneled communal areas, and an outdoor terrace. Bilingual owner Cecilia offers information and can organize regional tours. It's worth upgrading to the superior room for more space and light.

With only four rooms and on the outskirts of a pine forest a five-minute drive from Coyhaique, **Vista Patagonia Lodge** (Camino Aeródromo Parcela 3 S-5, tel. 9/9824 2589, www.vistapatagonia.com, CH$85,000 d) oozes rustic comfort with blond pine bedroom walls, crisp white sheets, and large windows with views of Cerro Mackay. The young owners live on-site and specialize in fishing and mountain biking tours. They offer simple meals of pizza in the bar area. The lodge is down a muddy, potholed track, so a high-clearance vehicle is essential for getting here. Rates include IVA.

Built on a large piece of land overlooking Coyhaique from the south, the 12 ground-floor cabins at **Patagonia House** (Camino Campo Alegre s/n, tel. 672-211 488, www. patagonia-house.com, CH$88,000 d) have modern fittings and local decorative touches such as *alerce* headboards. All have central heating and access to a hot tub with mountain views. The superior-size rooms (CH$129,000) are much larger and have better views, reflected in the price. They also offer dinner service. It's out of town, so you need a car or to arrange transfers from Coyhaique. Rates include IVA.

Information and Services

The main tourist office for the Aysén region is **SERNATUR** (Bulnes 35, tel. 67/2240 298, www.coyhaique.cl/portalturismo, 9am-9pm daily Dec.-Mar., 9am-6:30pm Mon.-Fri., 10am-6pm Sat. Apr.-Nov.). Staff can provide information for destinations along the Carretera Austral. **CONAF** (Av. Ogana 1060, tel. 67/2212 225, www.conaf.cl, aysen.oirs@ conaf.cl, 10am-4pm Mon.-Fri.) also has a central Aysén office here, although it can be difficult to enter; they respond well to emails.

The largest hospital in the Aysén region, **Hospital Regional** (Jorge Ibar 68, tel. 67/2262 001) provides 24-hour medical attention. Banks in town include **Banco de Chile** (Carlos Condell 298) and **Santander** (Carlos Condell 184). Exchange dollars, Argentine pesos, and euros at **Casa de Cambio "Austral Ltda"** (Paseo Horn 40) and **Turismo Prado de la Patagonia** (Veintiuno de Mayo 411). Find mail services at the **Correos** (Lord Cochrane 226, 9am-6:30pm Mon.-Fri., 10am-1pm Sat.). To do laundry, head to **Lavaseco Patagonia** (Dussen 340).

To rent equipment to explore the surrounding national parks, **Rent a Tent Chile** (tel. 9/9884 3849, www.rentatentchile.com) has all the camping and cooking equipment you need for the trek; they can deliver to your hotel in Coyhaique.

Transportation

AIR

About 60km southeast of Coyhaique lies **Aeródromo Balmaceda** (BBA, tel. 2/2222 8400), with two flights daily from Santiago and two from Puerto Montt on **Sky Airline** (www.skyairline.com) and **LATAM** (www.latam.com). **Aeriovías DAP** (Arturo Prat 286, Coyhaique, tel. 67/2212 898, www.dapairline.com) offers flights from Punta Arenas once a week on Tuesday.

Transfer T&T (Cruz 63, tel. 67/2256 000) and **Transfer Velasquez** (Lautaro 145, tel. 67/2250 413) offer direct hotel transfers (CH$5,000) from outside the arrivals hall of the airport. The minivans take one hour to get into town. To get back to the airport, book your transfer a day in advance and confirm that they will collect you from your hotel.

Buses Suray (Arturo Prat 265, tel. 67/2238 387, bussurayaeropuerto@gmail.com) have twice-daily departures (CH$2,500) to and from the airport Tuesday-Sunday, leaving from their office. Book the day before if you're heading to the airport.

CAR

To get to Coyhaique from **Puyuhuapi**, it's a 235-km, 4.5-hour drive south on the Carretera Austral. About 160km south of Puyuhuapi, follow the turnoff to the right (west), signed as the X-50, which splits from Ruta 7 toward Puerto Aysén, then reconnects to Ruta 7 after 65km; this route is faster, and it's paved. From **Puerto Río Tranquilo**, it's a 220-km, 4.5-hour drive north on the Carretera Austral.

To reach Coyhaique from Río Mayo in Argentina, the easiest route is via **Paso Coyhaique** (tel. 67/2256 7099, 8am-10pm daily summer, 8am-8pm daily winter), 45km east of Coyhaique. The total drive is about 175km and takes four hours. Roads on both sides of the border are gravel but in good condition. About 60km southeast of Coyhaique and 3km from the airport, **Paso Huemules** (tel. 67/2256 7105, 8am-10pm daily summer,

8am-8pm daily winter) is paved from the Chilean border. The road that heads southwest from Río Mayo is gravel and in poor condition; drive carefully. This drive is just under 200km and takes about four hours.

Both Aeródromo Balmaceda (60km southeast of Coyhaique) and the town of Coyhaique have a wide selection of rental car companies. Prices are the cheapest you'll find along the Carretera Austral. Expect to pay at least CH$55,000 for a 2WD high-clearance vehicle. Recommended local companies with booths at the airport include **Europcar** (tel. 67/2678 640, www.europcar.com, 10am-5:30pm daily) and **Recasur** (tel. 9/9015 8550 or 9/9257 1613, www.recasur-rac.cl, 9am-7pm Mon.-Sat.); they also rent converted campervans.

In Coyhaique are **Recasur** (Moraleda 305, tel. 67/2238 990, 9am-7pm Mon.-Sat.), **Europcar** (Errazuriz 454, tel. 67/2678 652, 9am-1pm and 3pm-7pm Mon.-Fri., 9am-1pm Sat.), and **Hertz** (Gral. Parra 280, tel. 67/2272 178, www.hertz.com, 10am-5:30pm daily). Hertz can arrange rental car pickup at the airport.

BUS

Connections along the Carretera Austral mostly arrive at Coyhaique's **Terminal de Buses** (Lautaro 109), which has a heated waiting room and luggage storage. There are several options to get to Coyhaique from **Cochrane** (6hr, CH$14,000) by bus. The companies listed here run either small buses or minibuses and depart from the terminal in Cochrane. All buses to Coyhaique from Cochrane also pick up at **Puerto Río Tranquilo** (5hr, CH$10,000) and **Villa Cerro Castillo** (2hr, CH$5,000).

- **Buses Acuario 13** (Río Baker 349, Cochrane, tel. 67/2522 143, Coyhaique tel. 67/2240 990): 6:30am Tuesday, Thursday, and Saturday

- **Buses Sao Paulo** (Coyhaique tel. 67/2237 630, Cochrane, tel. 67/2522 470, www.busessaopaulo.cl): 6:30am daily

- **Buses Aguilas Patagonicas** (Coyhaique tel. 67/2112 88, Cochrane tel. 67/2523 730, www.aguilaspatagonicas.cl): 7am daily

- **Buses Don Carlos** (Cruz 73, Coyhaique, tel. 67/223 298, Cochrane tel. 67/2214 507): 9am Monday-Saturday

Terraustral (tel. 67/2254 335, www.busesterraustral.cl) offers a bus to Coyhaique from **Puerto Río Tranquilo** (4pm daily, 5hr, CH$10,000). They also run a bus from **La Junta** (5:30am and 12:10pm daily, 6hr, CH$10,000) through **Puyuhuapi** (6:20am and 1pm daily, 5hr, CH$8,000) on its way to Coyhaique. Outside January-March, bus frequencies on the La Junta-Coyhaique route can drop.

From the ferry ramp at **Puerto Ibáñez,** minibuses to Coyhaique (2hr, CH$5,000-6,000) and **Aeródromo Balmaceda** (1.5hr, CH$10,000) leave when the boat arrives from Chile Chico. These include **Buses Alejandro** (tel. 67/2236 060 or 9/7652 9546), **Miguel Acuña** (tel. 67/2411 804), **Buses Carolina** (tel. 67/2411 490, buscarolina@hotmail.com), and **Transporte Lukas** (tel. 67/2521 045 or 9/89568 6587, lukas_tur@live.com). Pay in cash; reservations can be made in Chile Chico for the journey north and are recommended if you're heading to the airport.

The fastest way between Coyhaique and **Puerto Montt** (24hr, CH$30,000) via bus is aboard the 10:30am Monday, Wednesday, or Friday departure from Puerto Montt operated by **Queilén Bus** (Coyhaique tel. 67/2240 760, www.queilenbus.cl). The bus goes north to Osorno, crosses into Argentina, travels south, and crosses back into Chile at Paso Coyhaique. Passengers can't get off in Argentina. The return route leaves at 2pm Monday, Wednesday, and Friday from Coyhaique; outside December-March, bus frequencies drop to once per week.

Buses Becker (Terminal de Buses Puerto Montt, Diego Portales 1001, www.busesbecker.com) runs the same route through Argentina from **Puerto Montt** (24hr, CH$45,000), leaving at 11am Thursday; the return journey leaves at 11:30am Tuesday December-March, with frequencies dropping to a couple of times per month the rest of the year. Buses from Puerto Montt arrive in their private terminal (Gral. Parra 355, tel. 67/2232 167). **Buses Becker** also offers buses to Coyhaique from **Chaitén** (9hr, CH$24,000) at 11:30am Wednesday and Sunday. They pick up passengers at La Junta and Puyuhuapi en route. The return journey leaves at 8am Tuesday and Saturday from Coyhaique.

From **Puerto Aysén** (1.5hr, CH$2,200), buses to Coyhaique run hourly 7am-8pm from the terminals of **Buses Ali** (Aldea 1143, tel. 67/2333 335, www.busesali.cl) and **Buses Suray** (Ibar 630, tel. 67/2336 222, bussurayaeropuerto@gmail.com), both on the northern side of the Río Aysén.

FERRY

Ferry operators **Naviera Austral** (Paseo Horn 40, tel. 67/2210 727) and **Navimag Ferries** (Lillo 91, tel. 2/2869 9908) have offices in Coyhaique. Ferries arrive and depart from **Puerto Chacabuco,** west of Coyhaique. To Coyhaique from Puerto Chacabuco, it's an 80-km, 1.5-hour drive along Ruta 240.

RESERVA NACIONAL COYHAIQUE

Easily accessible from the city on foot or by car, the 2,150-hectare **Reserva Nacional Coyhaique** (8:30am-7pm daily Oct.-Mar., 8:30am-5:30pm daily Apr.-Sept., CH$3,000 adults, CH$1,500 children) is characterized by dense forests of introduced pine, plus swaths of repopulated forests. Native species such as *lenga, coigüe,* and *ñirre* are being reintroduced.

Although the trails aren't comparable to those in the national parks farther south, they make for a good day trip from Coyhaique. Most are gentle, climbing from the entrance into the reserve through forests with occasional views across Coyhaique.

One of the highlights is the stunning **Laguna Verde.** You can hike around it in 20 minutes, and it's also reachable by vehicle.

Those looking to stretch their legs can get here by a 10-km, four-hour circuit that starts at the CONAF ranger hut at the entrance, climbing to the lake before heading west through dense forest and past slightly less picturesque lakes.

For more serious trekkers, a more challenging loop (17km, 7hr) combines five trails, starting from the main entrance and running through the reserve to the top of **Cerro Cinchao** (1,361m) via the **Sendero Los Piedras** before joining a path back to the entrance; snowfall at the top can make it impassable in winter. There are also mountain biking trails.

Getting There

From Coyhaique, drive 3.8km north on Avenida Baquedano (back toward the highway), across the bridge, and up a very steep gravel road to reach the **CONAF ranger station** (tel. 9/7432 1684, www.conaf.cl), where the entry fee is collected and maps of the park are available. Maps are also online (www.recorreaysen.cl). A taxi here costs CH$5,000.

RESERVA NACIONAL RÍO SIMPSON

Fanning out northwest from Coyhaique and split by Ruta 240 and the Río Simpson, **Reserva Nacional Río Simpson** (tel. 67/2212 109, visitors center 9am-5pm Tues.-Sun., www.conaf.cl, CH$3,000 adults, CH$1,500 children) covers 41,000 hectares but has little infrastructure. The main entrance is 36km northwest of Coyhaique on Ruta 240.

The focus of the reserve is on conservation, not tourism. This is detailed in the 2016-built, CONAF-run large wooden **Centro de Información Ambiental,** where detailed Spanish information boards highlight native fauna and flora. With a mobile phone and a QR code reader, it's possible to download English information. From outside the building, a pleasant hike (3km round-trip) runs along Río Simpson.

Getting There

It's a 36-km, one-hour drive northwest from Coyhaique via Ruta 7 and Ruta 240 to the reserve's Centro de Información Ambiental. On the drive you'll notice two pretty waterfalls, La Virgen and El Velo de la Novia, on the right side. From Coyhaique, buses heading in the direction of Puerto Aysén will drop you at the information center.

PUERTO AYSÉN

Although the word for "port" is in its name, Puerto Aysén is a misnomer. Boats no longer dock at this riverside town; you can find them at Puerto Chacabuco, the main harbor for the region, a 15-minute drive southwest. There's little reason to stop in Puerto Aysén. Lodgings and restaurants are vastly superior in Coyhaique, an hour's drive southeast. However, if you're arriving late or leaving early on the Navimag ferry or taking a day tour to Parque Nacional Laguna San Rafael, it makes sense to overnight here.

On the southern bank of the Río Aysén, the vividly painted **Patagonia Green** (Av. Lago Riesco 350, tel. 67/2336 796, www.patagoniagreen.cl, CH$75,000 d) provides comfortable lodgings amid expansive lawns surrounded by woodland. Eight large double rooms have balconies overlooking gardens. The five-person cabins (CH$110,000, discounted for smaller groups) include a kitchen and a living room. Lunch and dinner service are available; breakfast is not included for those staying in the cabins.

Run by the charming and helpful Cecilia, **Flor de Michay** (Lago Atravesado 110, tel. 9/7705 4733, CH$18,000 pp) is a spotless, budget-friendly family house with four simple rooms sharing two baths and with kitchen access. Cecilia can help you sort out transfers to Puerto Chacabuco. Rates include IVA.

Transportation

To get to Puerto Aysén by car from **Puerto Chacabuco,** it's a 15-km, 20-minute drive northeast on Ruta 240. From **Coyhaique,**

Puerto Aysén is a 65-km, one-hour drive northwest on Ruta 240.

From Puerto Chacabuco, a bus that's timed to pick up ferry passengers can drop you off anywhere along the main road through Puerto Aysén (CH$500). A taxi from the harbor at Puerto Chacabuco costs CH$6,000; you'll find them waiting, or contact **Daniel Sáez** (tel. 9/9560 7851). From **Coyhaique** (1.5hr, CH$2,200), hourly buses shuttle to Puerto Aysén 7am-8pm daily, leaving from the terminals of **Buses Ali** (Dussen 283, Coyhaique, tel. 67/26232 350, www.busesali.cl) and **Buses Suray** (Prat 265, Coyhaique, tel. 67/2238 387, bussurayaeropuerto@gmail.com). They arrive at Calle Aldea 1143 and Calle Ibar 630, respectively, both on the northern side of the river.

PUERTO CHACABUCO

Puerto Chacabuco is the main ferry port for the region. It consists of a few residential streets of low concrete and wood houses and scattered industrial buildings. Most travelers arriving by boat pass directly through on their way to Coyhaique.

Just 500 meters from the port, **Hostería Loberias del Sur** (Miguel Carrera 50, tel. 67/2351 115, www.loberiasdelsur.cl, CH$112,000 d) is a 60-room traditional hotel that feels out of place. The rooms are dated and have small baths; those ending in an odd number have better views of the mountains beyond. The hotel has a gym and sauna, a bar with harbor views, an on-site restaurant serving buffet dishes, and a cafeteria with light bites. The main reason to stay here is the tours to Parque Nacional Laguna San Rafael through **Catamaranes del Sur** (tel. 67/235 1112, Santiago tel. 2/2231 1902).

Transportation

To get to Puerto Chacabuco from **Puerto Aysén,** it's a 15-km, 20-minute drive southwest on Ruta 240. From **Coyhaique,** Puerto Chacabuco is an 80-km, 1.5-hour drive northwest on Ruta 240. To get here from Puerto Aysén, it's possible to take one of the minibuses that leave every 20 minutes from Paseo Mahuen (Ibar and Aldea). You can also flag down a taxi or call **Daniel Sáez** (tel. 9/9560 7851). Taxi rides from Puerto Aysén should cost CH$6,000 to the dock.

FERRY

The twice-weekly *Evangelistas* **ferry** (CH$51,000 bed in 4-person cabin, CH$13,000 2-person cabin, 24hr) operated by **Navimag Ferries** (Diego Portales 2000, Puerto Montt, tel. 2/2869 9900, www.navimag.com) leaves Puerto Montt at 6am Thursday and Sunday, arriving in Puerto Chacabuco 24 hours later. A no-frills passenger and cargo ferry, it's popular with locals and offers a fast, cheap, picturesque way to get to Puerto Aysén. The cargo, often cattle and machinery, is interesting to watch being loaded. Three meals are included. No snacks are sold on board, so bring anything else you might need. Showers are available but are often cold.

Tickets should be bought online at least **three months in advance** for ferries December-February. Ferries from Puerto Chacabuco to Puerto Montt often have plenty of space, particularly in March, and can be booked last-minute. Check-in is at Navimag's Puerto Montt office. For the return route, check-in at the dock in Puerto Chacabuco. Navimag has an additional office in Coyhaique (Lillo 91, tel. 2/2869 9908).

Reach Puerto Chacabuco from farther north via the more basic **Naviera Austral ferry** (Pedro Montt 355, Quellón, tel. 65/2682 207 or 65/2682 505, www.navieraustral.cl). This passenger and car ferry leaves from **Quellón** (31hr, CH$17,450 foot passengers, CH$141,000 vehicles) in Chiloé at 1am Thursday and Sunday. Buy tickets online or in their Quellón or Puerto Montt offices (Angelmó 1673, Puerto Montt). For the return journey from Puerto Chacabuco, buy tickets at their office in Coyhaique (Paseo Horn 40, tel. 67/2210 638) or in the **Buses Suray office** (Calle Aldea 1143, tel. 67/2336 222, bussurayaeropuerto@gmail.com) in Puerto Aysén.

There are no cabins on the Naviera Austral ferry; instead, you buy a seat on the main inside deck. There's a small cafeteria, but it's worth bringing all your food and drink, a sleeping bag, and warm waterproof clothing for time spent out on deck. Although it's far less comfortable than the Navimag, this boat stops at several ports en route in the fjords of the Carretera Austral, including Melinka, Raúl Marín Balmaceda, and Puerto Cisnes. Because the boat approaches the shore more frequently, it's likely that you'll see colonies of Magellanic penguins and sea lions.

On both ferry routes, minke and blue whale and even orca sightings are possible in Golfo Corcovado and Canal Moraleda November-March. Sightings of Commerson's and bottlenose dolphins, albatross, South American sea lions, and fur seals are even more likely. The landscape is reminiscent of the sweeping steppe of Southern Patagonia. As you reach lush Parque Nacional Cerro Castillo, the transition to the *Nothofagus* (southern beech) forests that visibly dominate the landscapes from here south to Tierra del Fuego is marked.

VILLA CERRO CASTILLO

In a deep river basin, the hamlet of Villa Cerro Castillo has superlative scenery, flanked in the north by Parque Nacional Cerro Castillo's sharp granite pillars, the most striking of which is the 2,675-meter three-toothed Cerro Castillo, comparable in grandeur to Parque Nacional Torres del Paine in Southern Patagonia. On a clear day, the views along the Río Ibáñez, bordered by the jagged Cordillera Castillo and Volcán Hudson, are breathtaking.

A frontier town, Cerro Castillo has dusty streets occupied by affable stray dogs and makes an ideal base for hiking in the national park. It's also devoutly *huaso* in culture: On the last weekend in January, don't miss the traditional **Fiesta Costumbrista,** with its rodeo and sheepdog displays, plus traditional dance performances. Food and *artesanía* from across the region are sold here.

On the southern edge of town, 850 meters after leaving Villa Cerro Castillo, a gravel road leads east 2km to the **Museo de Sitio Escuela Antigua** (tel. 67/2423 216, www.museoescuela-cerrocastillo.cl, 10am-5pm Tues.-Sun., CH$2,000 adults, CH$1,000). Inside the old school building, which is now a national monument, the museum has interesting exhibits accompanied by Spanish and English descriptions of the region's history. A guide (included in the fee) can take you the 10-minute walk to **Paredón de Las Manos,** a rock face that has been painted with handprints dating back 3,000 years.

Food and Accommodations

A favorite lunch venue for the truckers passing through town, the classic Villa Cerro Castillo eatery **La Cocina de Sole** (Carretera Austral, tel. 9/8398 135, 9am-5:30pm daily, CH$5,000-6,500) is two buses fastened together. Feast on the huge *churrasco* (sliced beef) sandwiches with avocado, cheese, and tomato for a delicious greasy lunch.

The village has a growing number of lodgings. Although facilities are general no-frills, prices are fair and the owners friendly. Modeled on a mountain refuge, **Senderos Patagonia** (Carretera Austral, tel. 9/6224 4725, www.aysensenderospatagonia.com, CH$10,000 dorm, CH$5,000 campsite) attracts backpackers and hikers, making it a good place to swap notes on local trails. It has basic facilities, including towering bunk beds (linens CH$2,000), a large open kitchen and living area, and shared restrooms. Campers have access to the indoor facilities. The Spanish- and English-speaking owners run high-end horse riding and trekking excursions in the national park and farther afield. Heading south, it's on the right just before leaving town. Rates include IVA.

Down a track on the southeastern edge of the village, **La Araucaria** (Los Pioneros 962, tel. 9/7661 1709, www.turismoalgalope.cl, CH$50,000 4-person cabin or 2-person dome, CH$10,000 dorm, CH$4,000 campsite) has a large grassy campground, two geodesic domes with dorm beds but no heating, a two-bed dome with a private bath and a gas heater, and four cabins, with kitchens, for four people. The catch for those in the campsites or dorms is that you only have access to hot water at certain times in the morning and afternoon. A large *quincho* (covered kitchen area) for cooking and dining almost makes up for the inconvenience. La Araucaria can organize airport transfers as well as horseback tours beyond the national park. Rates include IVA.

Information and Services

A small municipal-run **Información de Turismo** (Ruta 7, between O'Higgins and Los Pioneros, hours vary, Nov.-Mar.) is in a wooden booth on the lawns just behind the bus stop. It has basic trekking maps for the national park.

Transportation

To get to Villa Cerro Castillo from **Coyhaique** by car, it's a 100-km, 1.5-hour drive south on the Carretera Austral. From **Puerto Río Tranquilo**, it's a 125-km, 3-hour drive northeast along the Carretera Austral. Roadwork can cause long delays along the final stretch before you enter Puerto Río Tranquilo.

Buses stop in Villa Cerro Castillo (bus stop on Ruta 7, opposite La Cocina de Sole food truck) on their way between **Coyhaique** and **Cochrane. Puerto Río Tranquilo** is also on this route. From **Coyhaique** (CH$5,000), it's a two-hour journey to Villa Cerro Castillo. **Buses Acuario 13** (tel. 67/2522 143) leaves at 8:30am Wednesday, Friday, or Sunday. **Buses Sao Paulo** (tel. 67/2255 726, www. busessaopaulo.cl) departs at 9am daily. **Buses Don Carlos** (Cruz 73, tel. 67/2231 981) departs at 9:30am Monday-Saturday. All of these buses terminate in Cochrane and run the return route on the same day. Buses stop in **Puerto Río Tranquilo** (9am-11:30am daily, 2.5hr, CH$7,000) and continue to Villa Cerro Castillo.

Buses with the Puerto Río Tranquilo-based **Sagitario** (tel. 9/8327 1664) leave

Puerto Río Tranquilo at 4pm and pass through Villa Cerro Castillo at 7pm daily on their way to Coyhaique. **Terraustral** (tel. 67/2254 335, www.busesterraustral.cl) buses leave Coyhaique at 8am Monday, Tuesday, Thursday, and Friday; the return bus leaves at 6:45pm the same days.

★ PARQUE NACIONAL CERRO CASTILLO

Dubbed the "new Torres del Paine," **Parque Nacional Cerro Castillo** (tel. 9/9779 3321, www.conaf.cl, aysen.oirs@conaf.cl, hours and admission vary by sector) came into being in October 2017. The park is just north of Villa Cerro Castillo. Part of its appeal is that it's a quieter, less crowded version of Torres del Paine.

The park's metamorphic basalt rock, which reveals the region's volcanic origins, dominates the surrounding landscape in Cerro Castillo (Castle Hill)—which, yes, is shaped a bit like a castle. Cyan lagoons, Calafate bushes, *lenga* forests that turn deep red in fall, and craggy ridges make it an adventurous hikers' playground. Andean foxes, pumas, skunks, guanacos, and *huemules* skulk in dense forests, and trails offer wide vistas of glaciers and deep valleys.

Visiting the Park

There are two sectors and four entrances. **Sector Estero Parada-Las Horquetas** covers the area between **Las Horquetas entrance** (30km northeast of Cerro Castillo, accessed from the Carretera Austral, 7am-1pm daily) and the **Estero Parada entrance** (6km west of Cerro Castillo, 7am-4pm daily), which mark the beginning and the end of the **Cerro Castillo Traverse,** also known as **Travesía Las Horquetas.**

Sector Laguna Chinguay (7:30am-7pm daily Dec.-Mar., 8:30am-5pm daily Apr.-Nov) includes the zone north and west of the Carretera Austral from the **Laguna Chinguay entrance** (36km northeast of Cerro Castillo).

The popular **Sendero Mirador Laguna**

Parque Nacional Cerro Castillo

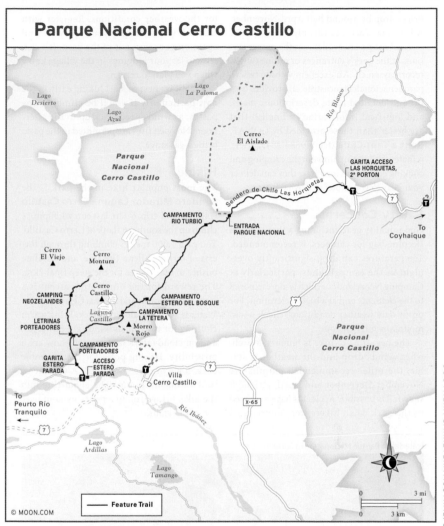

Cerro Castillo entrance (7:30am-7pm daily Dec.-Mar., 8:30am-5pm daily Apr.-Nov) is reached by passing through 3km of private land along the **Sendero Mirador Laguna Cerro Castillo.** The trailhead and **CONAF ranger station,** where entrance fees are collected, are 1km along a gravel road from the northwest edge of Villa Cerro Castillo.

Different concessionaires administer each sector, so the cost of visiting the park varies considerably. Entering through the Estero Parada entrance for a day hike costs CH$10,000 for adults, free for children; entering through the Estero Parada or Las Horquetas entrances for an overnight trek of any length costs CH$20,500 for adults, CH$1,500 for children. Fees are charged at booths at each entrance. Entering the park via Sector Laguna Chinguay costs CH$4,000 for adults, CH$3,000 for children. Entering via Sendero Mirador Cerro Castillo costs CH$7,000 for adults, CH$3,000 for children.

Prices drop by around half April-November. All entrances accept cash only.

Trail maps are available at the ranger stations at the park's entrances or online (www.recorreaysen.cl). An excellent website (www.parquenacionalcerrocastillo.cl) provides useful and detailed route descriptions, maps, and logistical information in English that are better than those provided by CONAF. **Rent a Tent Chile** (tel. 9/9884 3849, www.rentatentchile.com) hires out the camping and cooking equipment for a trek; they can deliver your gear to your hotel in Coyhaique.

Safety Concerns

Good-quality gear, including a three-season sleeping bag for campers, is recommended. Temperatures can drop significantly overnight in the campgrounds, particularly at Camping Neozelandés, which is more exposed to the elements and at a higher elevation. For up-to-date weather conditions, check www.mountain-forecast.com.

The best time to hike is January-March, when winds drop and the weather is stable; the other recommended months are November-December and April, although snowfall is possible. Accidents have occurred in the park when hikers were unprepared for the weather conditions. Register with CONAF when you pay your entry fee and again on your way out of the park. It's also wise to let your lodgings in the village know when you plan to return.

It's always best to start hiking early in the day, particularly if you'll be climbing any passes, as wind speeds pick up in the afternoon. No open fires are permitted in the park; bring a gas stove.

Hiking

The most popular hike in the park is the **Sendero Mirador Laguna Cerro Castillo** (14km round-trip, 6-8hr, last entry 1:30pm), a climb up the southern flank of Cerro Castillo. You gain 1,000 meters climbing through forests of ñirre, Chilean fire tree, and Calafate bushes to reach scree for the steep final 2km. The reward for the unrelenting ascent is a view of mountains and Laguna Cerro Castillo. Water is available along the trek. Bring warm clothing for the top, as winds are powerful, and on cloudy days rain or even snow are a possibility. Hiking poles for the scramble back down are recommended. A 600-meter trail leading off to the right, about 1km into the hike, brings you to a pretty lookout over some waterfalls.

waterfall in Parque Nacional Cerro Castillo

Cerro Castillo Traverse

For those with more time, the 51-km, four-to five-day **Cerro Castillo Traverse,** also known as the **Travesía Las Horquetas,** is a challenging trek through exposed passes, where the rewards are panoramic views of glacier-studded peaks. Only those with trekking experience and camping equipment suitable for cold, wet weather should attempt this without a guide.

Senderos Patagonia (Carretera Austral, Villa Cerro Castillo, tel. 9/6224 4725, www.aysensenderospatagonia.com) run five-day, four-night tours of the trail (from US$1,350), including food and English-speaking guides. They can also arrange other backcountry hikes.

The trail starts at Las Horquetas. After a few hundred meters is a ranger station, where the CH$20,500 overnight fee is collected. On the first day (15.4km, 5hr), hikers can camp at the **CONAF** *guardería,* 13km into the trek, or at **Campamento Turbio,** a basic campground that's 2.3km farther along the trail; both have picnic tables and toilets. The second day includes a challenging steep grade to reach **Campamento Bosque** (10km, 5-7hr) for views of Cerro Castillo and its glaciers, and a climb over 1,300-meter **Paso El Peñón** for views of Glacier El Peñón.

On the third day (8.3km, 8-9hr), hikers skirt the shores of **Laguna Cerro Castillo** before climbing a 1,670-meter pass. Camp overnight at **Camping Los Porteadores,** 8km west. The fourth day involves a climb of 300 meters and 3.6km to reach **Camping Neozelandés.** At 1,162 meters above sea level, it is the most picturesque campground and has access to Laguna Duff and viewpoints for various glaciers. Spend a night here or continue 7km down through the Valle Parada to where the hike ends, west of Villa Cerro Castillo. To finish, you'll need to hike 6km back along a gravel road to the village.

Getting There

Las Horquetas is 30km northeast of Villa Cerro Castillo, a 30-minute drive along the Carretera Austral. From Coyhaique, it's a 66-km, 1-hour drive. The entrance is on the west side of the road, indicated by a green "Sendero de Chile" sign. The Laguna Chinguay entrance is 6km beyond Las Horquetas, northeast along the Carretera Austral.

Estero Parada is a 6km, 15-minute drive west of Villa Cerro Castillo along an unnamed gravel road from the northwest edge of the town. The entrance for the **Sendero Mirador Laguna Cerro Castillo** is on this same road, 1km from Villa Cerro Castillo.

Buses between Villa Cerro Castillo and Coyhaique pass the Las Horquetas entrance. The ride costs CH$1,000-2,000 from Villa Cerro Castillo and CH$5,000 from Coyhaique. Ask the driver to drop you at the trailhead.

PUERTO RÍO TRANQUILO

In the international consciousness due to its proximity to the hypnotic rainbow of nearby Capillas de Mármol (Marble Caves), Puerto Río Tranquilo is a sleepy village. Only a few gravel streets deep, it lies on the western shore of Lago General Carrera, four hours south of Coyhaique.

Puerto Río Tranquilo feels like it's in a state of continual slow expansion. Lodgings and dining options have improved over the past decade, but if you're looking for a slice of comfort or luxury, go south to Cruce Puerto Maitén.

In January-February, due to the sheer quantity of tourists, facilities can become overstretched and lodgings fully booked; plan well in advance if you intend on traveling during these months.

★ Capillas de Mármol (Marble Caves)

The dreamlike **Capillas de Mármol** (literally "Marble Chapels," but referred to in English as the **Marble Caves**) are a collection of rainbow-hued rock caves, where softer limestone has been eroded by the wind and waves of Lago General Carrera to leave a series of grottos. Boats depart from Puerto Río

Tranquilo for 1.5-hour journeys. In summer and early fall (Apr.-June), when water levels are lower, boats can pass through passageways in the caves.

The main road in Puerto Río Tranquilo runs along the lake and is home to tour agencies that offer **speedboat tours** (CH$10,000 pp), with up to 10 people in each vessel. An additional CH$10,000 buys an extended three-hour trip across the lake to Puerto Sánchez, where there are more caves—and fewer tourists—that are more accessible by boat. Take a tour in the early morning for the best lighting, although departures depend on weather conditions, as waves in the lake can be fierce.

In your own vehicle, head to Bahía Mansa, 5km south, where the boat journey to the caves is only 10 minutes. Be aware that the road from the Carretera Austral to this bay is only recommended for 4WD vehicles.

January-April, you can visit the caves in kayak, which is the best way to pass between them. **Kayak tours** (CH$35,000-40,000, min. 2 people) normally leave in the morning, when winds are lower, departing from Bahía Mansa. It's a 20-minute paddle to the caves, and you'll spend three hours in total in the water. You'll need your own vehicle or to organize a transfer with the tour company. The cost of the tour includes a waterproof jacket and a spray skirt to protect your legs from the water. Both **Valle Leones** (Carretera Austral s/n, tel. 9/7703 1622, www.valleleones.cl) and **99% Aventura** (Carretera Austral s/n, tel. 9/4290 0802, www.99aventura.cl) lead kayak tours with experienced guides.

Food and Accommodations

The freshest meals in Puerto Río Tranquilo are enjoyed at the conversation-inducing bench tables of pint-size ★ **Mate y Truco** (Carretera Austral 121, tel. 9/9078 5698, 12:30pm-10:30pm daily, CH$5,000-14,000). The simple menu includes thin-crust pizzas whipped up on demand using whatever ingredients are in stock, fresh gnocchi and pastas, and a handful of traditional Chilean dishes. The ambience is relaxed, aided by a jazz soundtrack and a handful of artisanal beers and Chilean wines.

Service by the beret-wearing waiters matches the sluggish pace of things in Patagonia, but **Casa Bruja** (Los Chochos 332, behind the police station, tel. 9/8929 4785, 11am-1am Mon.-Sat., 1pm-5pm Sun. Dec.-Feb., 11am-11pm Mon.-Sat. Mar.-Nov., CH$7,000-13,000) has the most extensive menu in the village, offering well-cooked meat, grilled fish, and more inventive options such as lamb slow-cooked in a cilantro sauce. It has good views of the lake.

Simple but oozing friendliness, family-run lodging **Bellavista** (Población Estadio s/n, behind the stadium, tel. 9/8152 8505, www.campingbellavista.cl, CH$25,000 d shared bath, CH$12,000 dorm, CH$5,000 camping) is an excellent budget choice, with 14 rooms and 10 baths. Rooms are small but have comfortable beds; there's space for 50 tents in the back garden, with separate baths and a covered cooking space. For guests in the main hostel, the communal kitchen is small, but there's room to spill out into a larger living-dining space. Rates include IVA.

Puerto Río Tranquilo's most upscale lodging, perhaps a little overpriced, is **El Puesto** (Pedro Lagos 258, tel. 9/6297 3794, www.elpuesto.cl, CH$110,000 d), with 10 small rooms decorated in pale cypress. For more light, choose a room on the top floor; there's only one with a double bed (the rest have twins). Downstairs, a pleasant living area evokes a country cottage and is the place to spend time. There's no Wi-Fi. They offer a dinner service November-February with a fixed menu, pizzas, or salads. An onsite tour agency can arrange boat and kayak tours to the Marble Caves that visit caves the other tours don't, as well as treks on Glaciar Exploradores in Parque Nacional Laguna San Rafael.

Information and Services

There is no ATM in town; withdraw money in Coyhaique, Cochrane, or Chile Chico before arriving. You can often finagle a discount

Fly-Fishing in Patagonia

Although the Lakes District was long considered the spot for fly-fishing, lately attention has shifted south to Aysén, now ranked among the most coveted destinations on the planet, with astoundingly pure rivers and lakes ringed by virgin terrain of snowy peaks, lush native forests, and few other anglers. Part of the appeal is the absolute isolation of many spots; expect to arrive by speedboat or along a bumpy dirt track.

Trophy-size fish are the norm, from 80-centimeter brown trout to 20-kilo chinook salmon. Woolly bugger streamers and pheasant tail nymphs are effective year-round; dragonfly dry flies are useful January-early March. Fishing is catch-and-release. The main season is October-April. You'll need a license (CH$35,000 for a year), which your lodge can help you acquire, or get one online at SERNAPESCA (www.pescareacreativa.sernapesca.cl); you may also visit the tourist information office in Coyhaique for a list of stores selling them. Bring your own equipment; rental is not easy outside Coyhaique. You will be charged a small fee for your gear to be disinfected when you land in Chile as a preventative measure against didymo, an algae that causes extensive river bloom.

Lodges have sprung up along the Carretera Austral catering to a moneyed crowd. Expect to spend US$4,500-7,000 for a weeklong package, including your guide, lodging, meals, an open bar, and transportation.

FISHING LODGES

The ultra-luxurious Barranco Lodge (Lago Tagua-Tagua, tel. 9/9734 4050, www.barracolodge. com, 6 days, 5 nights US$4,204 pp) is on Lago Tagua-Tagua, 100km southeast of Puerto Montt, specializing in fly-fishing on the Río Puelo and heli-fishing trips, the latter using a helicopter to reach remote mountain lakes. Species are brown and rainbow trout and coho, Atlantic, and chinook salmon.

With a lodge a 20-km drive north of La Junta, and three glamping sites on rivers in the region, Patagonian BaseCamp (tel. 9/7999 6873, www.patagonian-basecamp.com, mid-Dec.-Apr., 7 days, 6 nights US$6,995 pp) enables anglers to explore the Palena, Rosselot, Figueroa, and Yelcho rivers. Tours include stays in multiple lodges, transfers to and from Puerto Montt, all meals, an open bar, and a fishing license. They also offer the unique Patagonia One package, which allows fishing on both sides of the Andes in the Valle Río Pico in Argentina.

Chucao Lodge Rosselot (Lago Rosselot, Santiago tel. 2/2201 8571, www.chucaolodge. com, 7 days, 6 nights US$4,500, CH$415,000 pp per night all-inclusive) is near La Junta on Lago Rosselot, where it empties into the Río Rosselot, offering varied conditions for fly-fishing brown and rainbow trout and salmon late November-mid-March. Rates include lodging at both properties—Chucao Rosselot and Chucao Yelcho (Lago Yelcho, 100km north of La Junta)—meals, an open bar, and transportation, including a charter flight to Chaitén from Puerto Montt. Activities for non-anglers are available. Not all guides speak fluent English.

Los Torreones Lodge (Km 23 Camino Aysén, tel. 9/9873 9031, www.flyfishpatagonia.com, 7 days, 6 nights US$4,950 pp) is on Río Simpson, a 40-minute drive north of Coyhaique. Their specialist bilingual guides find the best places to catch 50-centimeter rainbow or brown trout in the pristine Simpson, Manihuales, Nirehuao, and Cisnes rivers. Chinook salmon, over a meter long, swim up these rivers in February-March.

Named for its access to five rivers, Cinco Ríos Lodge (Km 5 Camino Balmaceda, tel. 67/2244 917, www.cincorios.cl, 7 days, 6 nights US$4,995) has room for only 12 guests, offering exceptionally personalized service in luxurious riverside surroundings. They claim to have the best fishing in Chile, if not the world, and the Paloma, Azul, Simpson, Desagüe, and Emperador Guillermo rivers don't disappoint, with trophy-size catches.

on tours if you pay in cash. A municipal-run **tourist information office** (Pedro Lagos and Los Arrayanes, no phone, hours vary) is in a wooden hut on the southwestern corner of the plaza. A **COPEC gas station** is on Carretera Austral along the lakeside.

Getting There and Around

From **Coyhaique,** it's a 4.5-hour, 220-km drive south to Puerto Río Tranquilo on the Carretera Austral. From **Villa Cerro Castillo,** it's a 120-km, 3-hour drive south. To get to Puerto Río Tranquilo from **Chile Chico,** it's a 165-km, 4-hour drive west on unpaved washboard Ruta 265 and north up the Carretera Austral.

South of Villa Cerro Castillo, the road to Puerto Río Tranquilo is in poor condition, so avoid going faster than 60km/h. Two stretches of construction directly south of Villa Cerro Castillo are ongoing; expect each to add a delay of about 30 minutes.

Buses stop in Puerto Río Tranquilo on the route between **Cochrane** and **Coyhaique.** There's no central terminal in Puerto Río Tranquilo; most buses pick up and drop passengers outside the Silvana café, on the corner of Exploradores and Dagoberto Godoy.

From **Coyhaique** (5hr, CH$10,000):

- **Buses Don Carlos** (Cruz 73, tel. 67/223 298): 9am Monday-Saturday

- **Buses Aguilas Patagonicas** (tel. 67/2112 88, www.aguilaspatagonicas.cl): 9:30am daily

- **Buses Acuario 13** (Río Baker 349, tel. 67/2240 990): 8:30am Wednesday, Friday, and Sunday

- **Buses Sao Paulo** (tel. 67/2237 630, www.busessaopaulo.cl): 9am daily

- **Sagitario** (Carretera Austral 269, next to COPEC, tel. 9/8327 1664): 9am daily

From **Cochrane** (2.5hr, CH$7,000):

- **Buses Don Carlos** (tel. 67/2214 507): 9am Monday-Saturday

- **Buses Aguilas Patagonicas** (tel. 67/2523 730): 7am daily

- **Buses Acuario 13** (tel. 67/2522 143): 6:30am Tuesday, Thursday, and Saturday

- **Buses Sao Paulo** (tel. 67/2522 470): 6:30am daily

Buses Marfer (tel. 9/7756 8234, transmarfer@gmail.com) offers a route from **Chile Chico** (4hr, CH$13,000) to Puerto Río Tranquilo, departing at 4pm daily.

★ PARQUE NACIONAL LAGUNA SAN RAFAEL

Comprising rugged terrain of glacial-melt fjords, woodland, and the Northern Patagonian Ice Field, **Parque Nacional Laguna San Rafael** (tel. 67/2212 109, www.conaf.cl, aysen.oirs@conaf.cl, 24 hr daily, CH$7,000 adults, CH$3,500 children) is one of the country's largest and most remote protected areas. It's also home to the highest peak in Patagonia, the 4,058-meter Monte San Valentín.

For many years the difficult-to-reach **Laguna San Rafael** was the star attraction of this UNESCO World Biosphere Reserve, where the cyan-crevassed Ventisquero San Rafael, also known as **Glaciar San Rafael,** crumbled into huge bergs. Since the early 2010s, tours to **Glaciar Exploradores,** on the northern side of Monte San Valentín, 25km northwest of Puerto Río Tranquilo, have seen tourism opening more of the park. In 2010, construction of the 77-km east-west road from Puerto Río Tranquilo to the coast at Bahía Exploradores, passing Glaciar Exploradores, made the park even more accessible.

The Northern Patagonian Ice Field is within the park's boundaries, and 19 glaciers feed from it. Areas not covered in ice contain boggy wetlands and dense deciduous beech forest, the ideal cover for small land mammals, including *pudús, huemules,* foxes, pumas, and the *guiña* or *kodkod*—the smallest cat in the Americas.

In the fjords and Laguna San Rafael, bird-life, including flightless steamer-ducks, can be spotted, as can acrobatic Chilean and Peele's dolphins, but at the lake, eyes are on the spectacle of ice calving from the Ventisquero San Rafael. From this 3-km-long, 70-meter-high wall, ice calves regularly into the lagoon—and never fails to disappoint. The booming echo of the splintering ice and crash as it is swallowed by the water is a sound few forget.

Until the 1960 Valdivia earthquake, the largest recorded on the planet, Laguna San Rafael was a lake; the tectonic movement connected it to the Golfo Elefantes and the Pacific, resulting in today's brackish lagoon. Now the closest tidewater glacier to the equator, Ventisquero San Rafael causes concern to climate scientists. In 1871, the glacier extended 10km farther into the lake than at present, a rapid retreat blamed on climate change.

The national park can be approached from two points: Puerto Río Tranquilo, where tours to Glaciar Exploradores and Ventisquero San Rafael depart; and Puerto Chacabuco, 225km northeast, where catamaran ferries ply the fjords south to reach the lake. More expensive transport is also possible from Coyhaique and Puerto Montt.

Glaciar Exploradores

Cascading in crisp waves of dense blue ice from the north side of Monte San Valentín, the 18-km-long **Glaciar Exploradores** makes a worthwhile reason to extend your stay in Puerto Río Tranquilo. In the last few years, agencies have started offering **ice-trekking tours** (CH$70,000) along the glacier. You start from Puerto Río Tranquilo with a scenic one-hour drive along the picturesque X-728, the new road that skirts the northern flanks of Monte San Valentín through Valle Exploradores. After 52km, you reach the **Mirador Exploradores,** where the ice trek begins.

To see the glacier from a greater distance, Exploradores Lookout is a wide-reaching panorama of the glacier and Northern Patagonian Ice Field beyond. El Puesto, a hotel in Puerto Río Tranquilo, owns the land that the 30-minute lookout trail traverses. They charge CH$4,000 for entry, payable in cash at the **visitors center,** which sells snacks and has restrooms.

PRACTICALITIES

Going with a qualified guide is essential; the shifting crevasses and ravines in the ice, plus the moraine boulders that you have to climb before you get there, require knowledge of safe routes. Expect to spend six hours trekking, including two hours to reach the glacier. Crampons, a wind jacket and helmet, transportation from Puerto Río Tranquilo, and a snack are included in the nine-hour tour.

Wear trekking shoes and well-fitted hiking trousers to avoid tripping over them with your crampons, and bring plenty of sunblock. Guides often take trekkers through ice caves, so you'll want a change of socks and shoes for the return drive home.

Outside December-February, opt to go with an outfit that offers kayak tours to the marble caves as well. You can often get a discount of around CH$15,000 if you pay in cash.

Ventisquero San Rafael (San Rafael Hanging Glacier)

Seeing the dramatic 30-meter **Ventisquero San Rafael** is an incomparable experience. Famed for its regular calving, watch from aboard a small vessel as shimmering chunks of ice splinter off the snout into the milky-green fjord. The waves caused by this sudden separation shake the icebergs and the boats.

To reach Bahía Exploradores, where the boats for the glacier depart, it's an 86-km, 2.5-hour drive west from Puerto Río Tranquilo along the gravel X-728. There's a small car park. At km 75 is a bridge that crosses the Río Exploradores; it's not suitable for RVs. Park entrance fees are collected at the **CONAF ranger station.** Also here is a small campground and seven-bed *refugio*.

If you're on a one-day tour, after a short walk to the remains of the Hotel Ofqui, you'll get back in the boat for lunch (and a whisky with shaved glacial ice) in front of the glacier's snout before heading back to Bahía Exploradores. On a two-day tour, you'll take a 40-minute hike to a *mirador* to see the glacier and then sail to its front wall on the second day.

From Puerto Chacabuco, it's a 5.5-hour boat ride, navigating leisurely through Seno Aysén, Golfo Tres Cruces, and along Golfo Elefantes in 94-passenger catamarans.

TOURS

The closest access point to the glacier is Puerto Río Tranquilo, where **Río Exploradores** (La Casa de Turista, Pedro Lagos at Costanera, tel. 9/6205 0534, www.exploradores-sanrafael.cl) run one- and two-day tours to the glacier (mid-Oct.-Apr., from CH$150,000 pp), departing from Bahía Exploradores with a maximum 12 people. The one-day tour includes a buffet lunch and park entry, while the two-day tour includes all food and park entry.

Destino Patagonia (Gilberta Flores 208, tel. 9/9158 6044, www.destinopatagonia.cl) has similar tours to Río Exploradores (CH$150,000 pp, min. 5 passengers) but with a boat capacity of up to 22. They also have three-day tours (CH$380,000 pp, 4-5 passengers), which add a trek to the Río Negro and take a Zodiac boat to visit Glaciar San Quintín. Transport can be arranged from Puerto Río Tranquilo for CH$15,000-20,000 pp.

From Tierra Luna Lodge in Puerto Guadal, **Patagonia Helitours** (tel. 9/9883 6285, www.terraluna.cl) has 3.5-hour flyovers of the glacier (Nov.-mid-Mar., US$3,200, maximum 5 passengers) in their Eurocopter B3 helicopter, including two hours on land. There's an extra fee for a boat navigation of Laguna San Rafael. They also offer shorter and longer flights around the region.

The luxury outfit **Skorpios** (Angelmó 1660, Puerto Montt, tel. 65/2275 646 or US tel. 305/285 8416, www.skorpios.cl) operates cruises aboard the 106-passenger M/V *Skorpios II*, remodeled in 2012. As part of their Ruta Chonos (mid-Sept.-Apr., from US$2,520

pp d) from Puerto Montt, they dock in Laguna San Rafael on the third day of the six-day, five-night cruise, approaching the glacier as weather conditions allow and with Zodiac excursions to shore or to get closer to the front wall. The cruise also docks at Dalcahue; Quemchi; the Magellanic penguin colony of Islote Conejos, near Queilén in Chiloé; Puerto Aguirre, a remote island settlement only accessible by boat in the Canal Moraleda; plus the hot springs in the Quitralco fjord.

The vessels of **Catamaranes del Sur,** operated by Puerto Chacabuco-based hotel **Loberías del Sur** (José Miguel Carrera 50, tel. 67/235 1112, Santiago tel. 2/2231 1902, www.loberiasdelsur.cl), are the only ones that depart from Puerto Chacabuco. The cost of the 13-hour journey (Mon. and Fri.-Sat. high season, once weekly winter, CH$200,000 adults, CH$100,000 children) includes transportation from Loberías del Sur, breakfast, lunch, and tea, plus a whisky with shaved glacier ice. Short Zodiac trips within Laguna San Rafael depend on weather conditions.

CRUCE EL MAITÉN

Cruce El Maitén, 50km south of Puerto Río Tranquilo, is the junction where the Carretera Austral meets narrow Ruta 265, a picturesque gravel road that runs northeast to Chile Chico. A number of lodges line the junction. With over 300 sunny days annually, this southwestern corner of Lago General Carrera is idyllic to break up the drive.

On a patch of land cleared from rosehip, ★ **Mallin Colorado Ecolodge** (Km 273 Carretera Austral, tel. 9/7137 6242, www.mallincolorado.com, Nov.-Apr., CH$101,000 d, CH$158,000 2-person cabin) offers a prime vantage point on the lake. Lodgings include the plush Casa Lenga, with six modern bedrooms around a slate-floored living room, all with floor-to-ceiling lake-view windows. Three rustic-chic cabins with similarly stunning views are among the trees for a little more privacy. Three-course lunch and dinner menus are available by request, as are horseback riding tours and hikes on the extensive grounds. The staff and owners provide personal attention. Payment is in cash or by bank transfer only. The lodge is 48km south of Puerto Río Tranquilo.

Getting There

From **Puerto Río Tranquilo,** Cruce El Maitén is 50km south on the Carretera Austral. The crossroads is where Ruta 7 meets Ruta 265.

CHILE CHICO

A frontier town just 9km from Los Antiguos in Argentina, **Chile Chico** is on the southern shore of Lago General Carrera. It feels both wide open and confined, boxed in by the lake to the north and in the south by the rocky hills that become the mountains of the striking Reserva Lago Jeinimeni. This side of the lake has an unusual microclimate that has allowed cherry farming to flourish.

Set along Avenida O'Higgins, the main artery that continues east to Argentina, Chile Chico is one of the oldest towns in the region, inhabited since the arrival of farmers in 1909. Its proximity to Argentina and the trails that crisscross the untouched mountains in between made it a haven for smuggling, with cattle and liquor the most profitable goods to traffic across the border. These days, the trails are occupied by adventurous hikers.

Most visitors just pass through this waypoint, one of the main crossings from Argentina to the Carretera Austral. On a clear day, the ferry journey across Lago General Carrera is more than worth the stop.

Food and Accommodations

As a frontier town, Chile Chico's dining and lodging options are limited and of lower quality.

The quirky **Bustaurante** (Rodríguez 387, tel. 9/4073 2624, 9am-11pm Tues.-Sun., CH$4,000-8,000) is a restaurant in an old bus. Bunting is slung from the sides, and it offers views to the lake down a less than pretty river. Bustaurante is a café in style, but the food is homemade. The charming owner

demonstrates determined commitment to regional produce. Expect whatever she's rustled up that morning (chicken, lamb stew, or a vegetarian dish) along with homemade *sopapillas* and exceptional homemade sauces. In the evening, pizzas with homemade dough take center stage.

A true backpacker hangout, **Campamento Nandú** (Av. O'Higgins 750, tel. 9/6779 3390, www.nanducamp.com, CH$40,000 d private bath, CH$30,000 s shared bath, CH$14,000 dorm) has seven rooms off a central communal area with a wood fire that keeps the place toasty. Bedrooms are huge, and there's an adjoined colossal bath block with powerful showers. A steady stream of budget travelers pass through, many lured by the large kitchen and sociable vibe. The hostel offers bike rentals and information about the nearby reserve. The owners also run **Patagonia Huts** (tel. 9/98182153, www.patagoniahuts.com).

The cheapest option in town and right on the road to the border, **No Me Olvides** (Camino International s/n, tel. 9/5692 9093, CH$11,000 pp) is overseen by the wonderful María, whose four rooms with shared baths are simple but well cared for. The house is warm thanks to wood burners, while Wi-Fi and a large kitchen for use by guests are welcome additions. Prices are per person, so this is a great option for single travelers.

The spick-and-span **Brisas del Lago** (Rodríguez 443, tel. 67/2411 204, brisasdellago@gmail.com, CH$30,000 d shared bath, CH$45,000 cabin), three blocks from the main square, is a well-run B&B with central heating and seven mostly twin bedrooms. All share three spotless baths. There are three cabins in the back garden, one with only a kettle and fridge, the others with kitchens. Rates include IVA.

With only five bedrooms, the intimate and charming ★ **Hostería y Camping de la Patagonia** (Camino International s/n, tel. 9/8159 2146, www.hosteriadelapatagonia. cl, CH$5,000 camping, CH$65,000 d) offers personal attention, delicious breakfasts, and quaint bedrooms. The grounds are a pretty garden that doubles as a campsite. Consider the boat room—literally a converted boat, although it can get cold outside summer. The restaurant has some of the best dishes in town, with set two-course menus (CH$12,500). Walk-ins are accepted, although it's often best to book ahead, particularly outside December-February, when the restaurant needs advance notice. It's located opposite No Me Olvides. Rates include IVA.

Chile Chico's most modern lodgings are the eight spacious apartments of **Costanera Apart** (Rodríguez 7, tel. 9/4095 7890, CH$56,000). Apartments feature fully equipped kitchens and have views across the lake. They were built in 2017, so furnishings are new, providing space and a little style, with central heating. Book well in advance. Rates include IVA.

Information and Services

The **Oficina de Turismo** (Av. O'Higgins 333, tel. 67/2411 303 or 67/2411 751, www.chilechico.cl, 8am-10pm Mon.-Fri., 10am-9:30pm Sat., 10am-1pm and 3pm-8pm Sun. Dec.-Mar., 8am-7:30pm Mon.-Fri., 10am-2pm Sat. Apr.-Nov.) is home to both SERNATUR and the municipal tourism office. English-speaking staff are supremely helpful, with maps of the town and Reserva Nacional Lago Jeinimeni; they can offer updates on bus services to cross the border to Argentina. **CONAF** (Gana 121, tel. 67/2411 325, aysen.oirs@conaf.cl) also has an office in Chile Chico. For useful visitor information, including up-to-date bus schedules, check out http://chile-chico.com.

The **Hospital Dr Leopoldo Ortega** (Lautaro 275, tel. 67/2411 334) can deal with basic medical emergencies. A **24-hour ATM** is attached to the **BancoEstado** (Pedro González 112). Find currency exchange at **Martín Pescador** (Av. O'Higgins 497), which trades Argentinean and Chilean pesos. **Supermercado Sur** (O'Higgins 394, tel. 67/2411 420, 9am-10pm Mon.-Sat., 10am-10pm Sun.) is a well-stocked supermarket.

Getting There and Around

Most visitors arrive from Argentina or via the passenger and vehicle ferry from Puerto Ibáñez, north of Chile Chico, mainly because there is limited transportation connecting Chile Chico with Cochrane and Puerto Río Tranquilo.

FERRY

The majority of visitors get to town on the *Tehuelche* **ferry** (2.25hr, CH$2,250 foot passengers, CH$19,500 vehicles), operated by **Naviera Austral** (Terminal Puerto Ibáñez, tel. 9/3448 8688, www.navieraustral.cl). This 250-passenger, 30-vehicle ferry plies Lago General Carrera on its way from Puerto Ibáñez south to Chile Chico. The journey is spectacular when the weather is clear, as you can appreciate the icy peaks of Reserva Nacional Lago Jeinimeni. The boat leaves from the ferry terminal in Puerto Ibáñez daily and twice on Tuesday and Wednesday, returning to Puerto Ibáñez the same day. In Chile Chico, you disembark at the ferry ramp on the northwestern end of Calle Manuel Rodríguez.

Ferry schedules change, so refer to the website for up-to-date information. From November through March, make vehicle and passenger reservations at least one week in advance. Check in at the ferry ramp an hour before departure. Tickets are only sold online and in the **Naviera Austral office** (Av. O'Higgins 209, tel. 9/3448 0131, www.navieraustral.cl, 7am-11am and 3pm-6pm Mon.-Tues. and Thurs., 8am-1pm and 2pm-6pm Wed. and Fri., 8am-2pm Sat., 1pm-5pm Sun.), inside Chile Chico's Terminal de Buses.

Villa Cerro Castillo is the closest hub to Puerto Ibáñez. Fourteen-seater minibuses (40min, CH$800) operated by **Bus Luis Morales** (tel. 9/7649 4451) leave from outside the tourist information office in Villa Cerro Castillo at 8am and 4pm Monday and Wednesday-Friday for Puerto Ibáñez,

1: Mallin Colorado Ecolodge in Cruce El Maitén **2:** Capillas de Mármol **3:** a drink with glacier ice at Parque Nacional Laguna San Rafael **4:** ferry crossing between Chile Chico and Puerto Ibáñez

dropping you in Plaza Puerto Ibáñez, 1km from where the ferry leaves for Chile Chico.

CAR

For those driving from **Puerto Río Tranquilo,** Chile Chico is a 165-km, 3.5-hour drive south on Ruta 7 and east on the scenic but unpaved Ruta 265. Its sharp curves and vertical drops are not for the fainthearted. From **Cochrane,** it's a 180-km, 4-hour drive north on Ruta 7 and Ruta 265. There are no services along Ruta 265, so fill up with gas in Chile Chico.

BUS

Buses to Chile Chico arrive at the **Terminal de Buses** (O'Higgins 209, tel. 672/431 961).

From **Coyhaique** (2hr, CH$6,000), 16-seater minivans operated by **Buses Alejandro** (tel. 9/7652 9546), **Miguel Acuña** (tel. 67/2151 579), **Buses Carolina** (Diego de Almagro 1633, tel. 9/8952 1529, www.buscarolina.cl), and **Transporte Lukas** (tel. 9/8354 1503, lukas_tur@live.com) offer connections to Chile Chico. They can pick you up from your hotel or outside the **COPEC gas station** (Ogana 1157) in Coyhaique 2.5-3 hours before the scheduled departure for the ferry from Puerto Ibáñez. Reservations must be made via telephone for companies without a physical office. Organize your pickup location when booking your ticket. Prices don't include the cost of the ferry; you will need to book this yourself.

From **Puerto Río Tranquilo** (3:30pm daily, 4hr, CH$15,000), **Martín Pescador** (Av. O'Higgins 47, Chile Chico tel. 67/2411 033 or 9/9786 5285, www.turismomartinpescador.cl) operates minivans to Chile Chico. Find the minivan along Ruta 7, opposite the COPEC gas station in town.

The minivans of **Buses Marfer** (tel. 9/7756 8234 or 9/9645 3621, transmarfer@gmail.com) run between Chile Chico and **Cochrane** (5hr, CH$15,000), leaving Cochrane at 8am Monday, Wednesday, and Friday. The schedule sometimes changes to Wednesday, Friday, and Saturday; confirm at the bus terminal.

CROSSING INTO ARGENTINA

The Chilean side of the **Paso Río Jeinimeni** (8am-10pm daily) is 4.5km east of Chile Chico. From here, it's 6.5km to reach Argentine border control. From there it's 2km to **Los Antiguos,** where there are gas stations, ATMs, and lodgings.

To cross into **Los Antiguos** (CH$3,500, 1 hour) by bus, **Martín Pescador** (O'Higgins 47, Chile Chico tel. 67/2411 033 or 9/9786 5285, www.turismomartinpescador.cl) runs minivans that leave from outside its Chile Chico office (7:45am, 10am, and 3:30pm daily) November-March, less frequently the rest of the year, dropping you at Los Antiguos's **Terminal de Ómnibus** (Av. Tehuelche 157, no phone). Minivans heading in the opposite direction leave Los Antiguos at 8:30am, 1pm, and 6pm daily.

TAQSA Marga (tel. 02966/1541 9615, www.taqsa.com.ar) also offer this journey, leaving Chile Chico at 10:30am, 1:30pm, and 5pm Monday-Friday, 1:30pm and 5pm Saturday. The return route leaves Los Antiguos at 9am, noon, and 5pm Monday-Friday and 9am and 12:15pm Saturday.

For a **taxi** to the border, contact **Mirta Vogt** (tel. 9/7756 8234), **Samuel Jimenez** (tel. 9/9443 7144), or **Francisco Silva** (tel. 9/5614 0337). They will drop you at the Chilean side; you'll need to ask them to help you contact a taxi driver on the Argentine side to drive you the 8.5km to Los Antiguos.

★ PARQUE NACIONAL PATAGONIA

Parque Nacional Patagonia (no phone, www.patagoniapark.org, hours and cost vary by sector) is one of the finest national parks along the Carretera Austral, if not all of Patagonia. You could spend weeks roaming the mountains and lakes bluer than the sky. A visit promises a unique interaction with Patagonia's fauna. Many of the region's most endangered animals have been reintroduced here and are actively protected. These include guanacos, pumas, Andean condors, pampas cats, and the emblematic *huemul,* a deer that features on the Chilean coat of arms. This zone is one of the final habitats for the 1,500 members of this species.

The park comprises three formerly separate parks and reserves: Reserva Nacional Jeinimeni (hen-ee-MEN-ee) in the north, the once privately owned Parque Patagonia in the center, and Reserva Nacional Tamango in the south. They were joined as Parque National Patagonia in 2018, forming an area 1.5 times the size of Parque Nacional Torres del Paine.

This region of Patagonia has a surprisingly dry, warm climate during summer. Bring **hiking boots** with good tread, **trekking poles,** and a **waterproof jacket,** as rainfall and high winds are always possible and weather can change rapidly. Layers and a warm sleeping bag for overnights are essential, as temperatures can drop below 10°C. Bring all food with you if you're planning to camp.

Orientation

The park is divided into three sectors. **Sector Jeinimeni,** the northernmost, is accessed via Chile Chico. Visiting requires your own vehicle, a local guide, or a transfer service; no public transit options are available. Budget a day for visiting Jeinimeni's eponymous lake. Camp here overnight or return to Chile Chico.

Sector Valle Chacabuco, the middle section, is home to a variety of **hiking trails** and the park's best facilities: a visitors center, a luxury lodge, and a restaurant. It's accessible from the Carretera Austral, north of Cochrane. There's usually no direct public transportation to this area. Take at least a day to explore the trails or venture deeper into the territory by car. You can stay overnight here or return to Cochrane.

Southernmost **Sector Tamango** is the most accessible, with proximity to Cochrane. You can combine a couple of shorter trails into a full-day hike and be back in town for dinner. This area especially is an important habitat for the endangered *huemul.*

Sector Jeinimeni

Sector Jeinimeni (tel. 67/2411 325, aysen. oirs@conaf.cl, 8:30am-7pm daily Dec.-Feb., 8:30am-5:30pm daily Mar.-June and Sept.-Nov., CH$3,000 adults, CH$1,500 children) is one of the region's best-kept secrets, offering milky lakes, glacier-scoured mountain peaks, and expanses of rough Patagonian steppe and virgin forest. Lying 50km south of Chile Chico, this sector is divided into two sections, both accessed via a gravel road only suitable for high-clearance vehicles; 4WD is recommended, and the drive shouldn't be attempted after heavy rainfall. It takes at least 2.5 hours to reach Lago Jeinimeni from Chile Chico.

SIGHTS AND RECREATION

You can access one part of the sector via the **X-753,** which has its northern terminus just east of Chile Chico. No entry fee is charged here. Follow the X-753 south for 25km. A 2.5-km 4WD-only road is signposted on the left.

Here, a moderate **hiking circuit** (7.4km loop, 4hr) begins. The trail stops at several points of interest, including **Piedra Clavada,** a 40-meter naturally formed tower of rock jutting out of the steppe; the **Portezuelo,** the highest point of the hike (1,145 m), with far-reaching views north to the lake; the **Cueva de los Manos,** which holds 10,000-year-old Tehuelche paintings of hands; and **Valle Lunar,** a viewpoint that overlooks a low moon-like landscape of rust-colored wind-and rain-sculpted rock.

If you follow the X-753 for 26km farther, you'll reach Jeinimeni's **main entrance.** The road ends at a small car park and a wooden footbridge across Río Jeinimeni. **CONAF** has a ranger here at the *guardería,* where the entrance fee is collected. This is also where the **El Silencio campground** (CH$10,000 per site, up to 10 people) is located.

A handful of short **trails,** many up to lake viewpoints, start from here. The trailhead for the **Sendero Lago Verde** (10km round-trip), is also here; it takes you along the shores of Lago Jeinimeni to Lago Verde, both of which are a similar electric blue.

At Lago Jeinimeni, the three- to four-day, 47-km trek known as the **Travesía Jeinimeni-Avilés** (Jeinimeni-Avilés Traverse) or **Sendero Valle Hermoso-Valle Chacabuco** (Hermoso Valley-Chacabuco Valley Trail) begins. The first night's camping is at **Valle Hermoso** (CH$10,000 per site). On the second night, you must camp in the upper Avilés Valley (free), as no other backcountry camping is allowed in this part of the national park. The third night, you camp in the **Stone House Campground** (CH$8,000 pp).

SMUGGLER'S TRAIL

In 2018, the four-day, 69-km **Smuggler's Trail** opened. It's equipped and managed by **Patagonia Huts** (tel. 9/98182153, www.patagoniahuts.com). Starting at Lago Jeinimeni, the path passes along Lago Verde before cutting northwest to reach Lago General Carrerea. It offers unique hiking through untouched scenery along trails that were once used to smuggle cattle between Chile and Argentina.

There are wooden huts for cooking and camping areas. Only 25 hikers a day can start the trek. The route is only accessible with one of Patagonia Huts' guides. Contact the company directly to discuss logistics to get to the trailhead and back after the trek.

TOURS

Several companies based in Chile Chico organize day tours of the park. **Patagonia Xpress** (O'Higgins 333, tel. 67/2394 757, www.patagoniaxpress.com) has flexible, mostly full-day tours that can be personalized for hiking, mountain biking, or a lakeside barbecue. Tours start at CH$53,000 pp (min. 2 people), with round-trip transportation from the Patagonia Xpress office in Chile Chico and lunch included.

Martín Pescador (Av. O'Higgins 497, tel. 67/2411 033 or 9/9786 5285, www.turismomartinpescador.cl) runs five-hour trips (CH$25,000 pp) to the northeastern portion of this sector, including a transfer from its office. They are also the best option

for transportation if you plan on trekking the Traversía Jeinimeni-Avilés. A minibus transfer to Lago Jeinimeni and the trailhead costs CH$15,000 pp.

GETTING THERE

There is no public transport to this part of the park and no cell phone reception, so organize all your transfers before leaving. To get here from Chile Chico, it's a 50-km, two-hour drive south on the unpaved X-753. River crossings are sometimes necessary after rainstorms. Confirm the state of the roads by visiting Chile Chico's **Oficina de Turismo** (Av. O'Higgins 333, tel. 67/2411 303 or 67/2411 751, www.chilechico.cl, 8am-10pm Mon.-Fri., 10am-9:30pm Sat., 10am-1pm and 3pm-8pm Sun. Dec.-Mar., 8am-7:30pm Mon.-Fri., 10am-2pm Sat. Apr.-Nov.) before departure.

Sector Valle Chacabuco

Sector Valle Chacabuco (no phone, www.patagoniapark.org, 24 hr daily Oct.-Apr., free) has some of the best hiking in the region. The result of decades of conservation work by Tompkins Conservation, a group founded by the late Doug Tompkins and now led by his widow, Kris McDivitt Tompkins, the Estancia Valle Chacabuco, one of the region's largest sheep and cattle ranches, was bought in 2004. The land had been overgrazed by intensive farming, but gradual restoration and the reintroduction of native species of flora and fauna has helped the ecosystem return to its natural state.

At the heart of the area is the east-west Río Chacabuco valley. The western edges of the park are wet and mountainous, containing southern beech forests; the eastern side, flanking the Argentine border, is home to arid steppe. This region is an important refuge for the *huemul* deer as well as guanacos, Andean foxes, and pumas. A breeding center for the Darwin's rhea, on the eastern edge of the park, has helped expand the population of this endemic species.

A dozen well-maintained trails traverse magnificent landscapes of hidden lagoons,

Creating the Route of Parks

On January 29, 2018, Chilean president Michelle Bachelet changed the face of conservation in Chile by creating the **Ruta de los Parques de la Patagonia** (Patagonian Route of Parks, www.rutadelosparques.org). This 2,400-km tourism route links 17 national parks along the length of Patagonia. Bachelet also established three new national parks, expanded three others, and reclassified a handful of national reserves.

The creation of the network came as a result of the record-breaking land donation made by Tompkins Conservation, headed by Kristine McDivitt Tompkins, whose philanthropic billionaire husband, Doug Tompkins, died in a kayaking accident on Lago General Carrera in 2015. The donation of half a million hectares of land was hailed as the largest transfer of land from a private body to a government in history, and was matched by a donation of 3.5 million hectares of government land, which together forms an area slightly larger than Switzerland.

Private parks once operated by Tompkins Conservation, Parque Pumalín and Parque Patagonia, as well as the national reserve at Cerro Castillo, have officially become national parks. The Reserva Nacional Jeinimeni and Reserva Nacional Tamango had their protection status increased when they became part of the expanded Parque Nacional Patagonia in 2018. The deal has been lauded as a crucial step in conservation in a country where logging, mining, and hydroelectricity interests have been known to dominate economic decisions.

The Tompkins' commitment to buying up land and rewilding it has historically not been received positively. Since they started in the 1990s, they have been accused of land-grabbing, threatening national sovereignty, of being CIA spies, and that they were secretly seeking to establish a Zionist state in Chile. In 2005, when they started donating land to the Chilean state, the critics fell quiet.

---

scrubby grasslands, and territory rich in recuperating plant and animal species. Campgrounds, a luxury lodge, and a restaurant are also available to visitors.

There are no trash cans, so pack out your rubbish. Fires are not permitted in the park. If you plan to cook, bring a gas stove and all your food, as there is nowhere to buy supplies in the park. There are taps in the campgrounds, but you can also drink the water from streams; filtering it before you drink is always sensible. Maps, available at the visitors center, indicate where there are water sources on the trail.

The **main entrance** to the sector is via a turnoff from the Carretera Austral, 16km north of Cochrane and signed as "Parque Nacional Patagonia." From the entrance, a gravel road runs east for 11km to the **main park headquarters,** where most services are concentrated. Here you'll find the El Rincón Gaucho restaurant and bar, the **visitors center,** and the Lodge at Valle Chacabuco. Los West Winds Campground and the car

park for the Lagunas Altas trail are 2km southwest along a gravel road.

From the park headquarters, the Stone House Campground is 25km northeast, along the X-83 that bisects the park, where the Avilés Loop begins. Alta Valle Campground is 15km farther, southeast along this same road, where you'll find another two trails. It takes around an hour to reach this campground from the headquarters.

SIGHTS AND RECREATION

In your own vehicle, the west-east drive across Valle Chacabuco, dubbed **La Ruta Escénica** (The Scenic Route), is spectacular, taking you through the different ecosystems. You'll pass grasslands filled with rheas and guanacos, the flamingo-filled waters of Laguna de los Flamencos and Laguna Seca, and views of the glacial peak Cerro Kristine.

The drive starts from the entrance, crossing through the valley along the unsigned X-83 for 74km to reach the border with Argentina. The drive should take 1.5 hours one-way. You can even continue along the X-83 to reach Paso Roballos, the border with Argentina.

HIKING

The park contains both short hikes and long, challenging ones, the majority of which are well signposted. Pick up a map in the visitors center. You need your own vehicle to reach the trails in the east of the park. In summer, when visitor numbers are higher, it is occasionally possible to hitchhike.

The easiest hike in the park is **La Vega** (7km loop, 2hr), a flat loop that starts behind the Lodge at Valle Chacabuco and passes a cemetery, where you'll see the graves of previous ranch residents and of Doug Tompkins. Continue to the cypress trees at Los West Winds Campground, where the trail skirts the edge of the road to return.

The most popular hike is the moderate **Lagunas Altas trail** (23km loop, 6-8hr), from the car park just above Los West Winds Campground, climbing the flanks of Cerro Tamanguito. The path ascends steadily and is exposed for the first few kilometers before it reaches *lenga* forest and a *mirador* on a scree ridge with striking views along Valle Chacabuco. The path also passes a series of small lakes, the first of which is a scenic spot for lunch. About 500 meters from the visitors center and restaurant, the trail joins the road, leading back to the campground for the final 2km.

Starting from the Stone House Campground, the **Avilés Loop** (16-km loop, 5-7hr) is a challenging hike that follows the Río Avilés through a narrow valley heading north toward Reserva Nacional Jeinimeni. At the hanging footbridge over the river, day hikers can cross the bridge and return south along the opposite bank.

Backpackers can continue north along the trail to end at Lago Jeinimeni, a three- to four-day, 47-km trek known as the **Traversía Jeinimeni-Avilés** (Jeinimeni-Avilés Traverse) or **Sendero Valle Hermoso-Valle Chacabuco** (Hermoso Valley-Chacabuco Valley Trail). Only experienced hikers should attempt this trek, particularly as there are several challenging river crossings. You can also hike with a guide from outfitters such as **Martín Pescador** (Av. O'Higgins 497, Chile Chico, tel. 67/2411 033 or 9/9786 5285, www.turismomartinpescador.cl). If you're planning the trek independently, you must check with the visitors center before leaving, as the daily number of hikers on the trail is limited. There is no cellular signal at either end of the trail, so organize your transfers in advance.

Seven kilometers south of Alta Valle Campground in the east of the park, another popular hike is the **Lago Chico Loop** (12km loop, 4hr), a moderate trail that circuits Lago Chico through dramatic rocky terrain and scrubby grasslands. Nearby, there's also the spectacular **Doug Tompkins Mirador,** with panoramic views of Lago Cochrane and Monte San Lorenzo (3,706 m), one of the highest peaks in Patagonia.

FOOD AND ACCOMMODATIONS

Accommodations in Valle Chacabuco are limited to five-star luxury or three campgrounds, all of which are within reach of hiking trails. If you're not staying in the lodge, your best option for food is cooking yourself using a gas stove. The on-site restaurant has excellent food, but the prices match those of the lodge.

Open throughout the day for lunch, fancy sandwiches and salads, or a gourmet evening meal, **El Rincón Gaucho** (1pm-3pm lunch service, 3:30pm-6pm light meals and drinks, 7:30pm-10pm dinner service, lunch *menú del día* CH$16,000, dinner *menú del día* CH$26,000, CH$6,500-18,000) serves the needs of most visitors. The restaurant has a cafeteria side that's open during lunch and the afternoon, while the more formal dining area is for evening service. Impressively, all of the vegetables are organic, grown just a few hundred meters away, with seasonal produce determining the content of the ever-changing menu. On Sunday, lunch is a traditional Patagonian lamb barbecue.

With eight cooking areas and a central bathhouse with showers heated by solar paneling, the **Los West Winds Campground** (Oct.-Apr., CH$8,000) is for those on a budget. As the name indicates, the site experiences westerly winds that can be fierce, so it's a good idea to camp on the eastern side of the low shrubs that provide some protection. There is space for 60 tents. Payment can be made in cash to the ranger or by credit card at El Rincón Gaucho restaurant, 2km away. Advance bookings are not accepted.

Stone House Campground (www. patagoniapark.org, Oct.-Mar. 15, CH$8,000) is at the confluence of the Río Chacabuco and the Río Avilés, a 25km, 30-minute drive east from the park headquarters. It has space for only eight tents, with covered cooking areas to provide some shelter against the wind. It marks the trailhead for the Avilés Loop and the Traversía Jeinimeni-Avilés. Register and pay for a spot at the visitors center before driving out to the campground; reservations are not accepted in advance.

Alto Valle Campground (www. patagoniapark.org, Oct.-Apr. 20, CH$8,000), 35km southeast from the park headquarters, is close to the Lago Chico Loop and the Doug Tompkins Mirador. Facilities include large, shared cooking shelters, restrooms, and showers heated by solar panels. Shrubs and trees provide some shelter for tents. Register and pay for a spot at the visitors center before driving out to the campground; reservations are not accepted in advance.

It's easy to forget that you're in the middle of a remote national park in the understated antique elegance of the exquisitely designed **Lodge at Valle Chacabuco** (no phone, www.parquepatagonia.org, CH$325,000 d). Most of its 10 rooms feature sweeping views across the steppe, while the communal living area has floor-to-ceiling windows and a terrace for guests to appreciate the scenery. Stunning photographs line the walls. Guest rooms in the annex are much larger than those in the main section and include *chimineas* (freestanding fireplaces), although the views aren't as good. Wi-Fi, unsurprisingly, is very slow, and electricity—all of which must be produced in the park—is limited to 7am-midnight.

INFORMATION AND SERVICES

The **visitors center** (tel. 65/225 0079, www. parquepatagonia.org, 9am-1pm and 2pm-5:30pm Mon.-Fri., 9am-1pm and 2:30pm-6pm Sat.-Sun.) contains a small museum and

Los West Winds Campground

is part of the park headquarters, restaurant, and lodge complex. Stop for information and maps when you arrive; the staff speak excellent English. There are cell-phone charging points for customers of the restaurant or cafeteria. There is no cell reception in this sector of the national park. Fires are not permitted anywhere in the park.

Guide services (reservas@ vallechacabuco.cl) can be organized in advance through the Lodge at Valle Chacabuco. The lodge works with expert guide Sergio Urrejola, who is particularly knowledgeable about native birds and Patagonian landscapes.

GETTING THERE AND AROUND

The easiest way to experience Valle Chacabuco is with your own vehicle. There are no public buses, and the distances between trailheads are great. From Cochrane, it's a 16-km, 30-minute drive north on Ruta 7 to El Cruce Entrada Baker, where you turn east on the unpaved washboard X-83 (unsigned) for 11km (30min).

For the most committed, it's possible to **rent a bike** from **Turismo TresMil** (inside Cafetería Naciónpatagonia, Golondrinas 491, Cochrane, tel. 9/9474 6239, www. turismotresmil.com), although it's a 27-km pedal from Cochrane to the visitors center. A **private taxi** from Cochrane will cost CH$25,000-50,000 to get to the park headquarters. Talk to Turismo TresMil for the best rates.

It's also possible to hitchhike from Cochrane or take a Coyhaique-bound bus, get off at the entrance, and hitchhike from there. **Buses Sao Paulo** (tel. 67/2522 470, www.busessaopaulo.cl) and **Buses Aguilas Patagonicas** (tel. 67/2523 730, www. aguilaspatagonicas.cl) have the most regular buses. Be aware: Outside December-February, traffic into the park is significantly less frequent, and it's a dull two-hour walk from the park entrance.

Getting out of the park for the return journey to Cochrane can be even more difficult. A unique way to cross from Sector Valle Chacabuco into Sector Tamango is with **Turismo TresMil** (inside Cafetería Naciónpatagonia, Golondrinas 491, Cochrane, tel. 9/9474 6239, www.turismotresmil.com) on a challenging 10-hour trek (CH$69,000 pp, min. 2 people). The trail is poorly marked, so it's not a good idea to attempt this trek without a guide.

Sector Tamango

With gleaming crystalline Lago Cochrane marking its southern boundary, **Sector Tamango** (tel. 67/25222 164, reservanacionaltamango@gmail.com, 8:30am-7pm daily Dec.-Mar., 8:30am-5:30pm daily Apr.-Nov., CH$5,000 adults, CH$2,500 children) is just a few kilometers northeast of Cochrane. It contains 10 well-marked trails with picturesque views across a pristine lake, plus the likelihood of spotting the critically endangered *huemul*; the park contains a stable population of around 25 of the estimated 1,500 still in existence.

Register and pay the fee at the **CONAF ranger station** at the entrance to this sector of the park. They also have maps and information.

HIKING

The most popular trails include **Los Carpinteros** (4.6km one-way, 2hr), a trek through forest that joins with **Los Coigües** (4km one-way, 2.5hr), an out-and-back path on the shore of Lago Cochrane, passing pretty beaches. These trails can be turned into a 20-km, eight- to nine-hour circuit with the addition of **Los Ciruelillos** (1.3km one-way, 45min), which climbs to join the flat **Los Huemules** (7km one-way, 2hr). This trail flanks a hill before linking with **Las Aguilas** (3.2km one-way, 1 hour), which descends back to the ranger station. This circuit is a good place to spot *huemules,* particularly in spring.

It's also possible to cross from Sector Tamango into Valle Chacabuco along **Ruta de Huemul,** heading north to reach Cerro Tamanguito, where you join the Lagunas

Altas trail. Due to trail erosion and a lack of markers, this should only be attempted with a tour agency from Cochrane, like **Turismo TresMil** (inside Cafetería Naciónpatagonia, Golondrinas 491, Cochrane, tel. 9/9474 6239, www.turismotresmil.com).

ACCOMMODATIONS

A **campground** (tel. 9/7662 2891, cgarridomoneva@hotmail.com, CH$5,000) with electricity, drinking water, a covered cooking area, and baths with hot showers is available 300 meters northeast of the *guardería*. The campground's owner offers excursions on the lake in a six-person boat (CH$30,000-40,000). You can also arrange boat pickups from hikes farther around the lake, rather than walking back.

GETTING THERE

Sector Tamango is 4km and 15 minutes northeast of Cochrane, along the X-893, which leaves Cochrane from the eastern end of Calle Vicente Previske. A taxi from Cochrane to the ranger station and the main entrance should cost no more than CH$4,000; otherwise it's easy enough to hike or hitchhike the paved road.

COCHRANE

Orderly Cochrane is the final supply stop for heading south to the end of the Carretera Austral. In a river valley surrounded by crystal-clear Río Cochrane, the town has roots in the early 1900s, when Estancia Valle Chacabuco (now part of Parque Nacional Patagonia), opened, bringing settlers to remote and uninhabited territories. The creation of Parque Nacional Patagonia is sure to put this drowsy town on the map. Its aspirations can be read in the Hollywood-style sign perched on the hill overlooking town.

Cochrane makes a great base to stock up before heading south, go hiking in nearby Reserva Nacional Tamango, or just enjoy the slow pace of life in the dramatically landscaped Plaza de Armas, with its towering cypresses and deafening chatter of the emerald-green austral parakeets that spend summer here.

Most restaurants close down March-November. During the second weekend in February, when the town celebrates the three-day **Encuentro Costumbrista** with traditional food, music, and parades, the town's hotels are packed and the ATM runs dry of cash.

Tours
WATER SPORTS

Turismo TresMil (inside Cafetería Naciónpatagonia, Golondrinas 491, Cochrane, tel. 9/9474 6239, www.turismotresmil.com) is Cochrane's only official tourism agency, formed by the combined efforts of local tour guides. October-April, depending on weather, they offer full-day **hydrospeed tours** (CH$27,000 pp for 2) and **kayaking trips** (CH$38,000 pp for 2) on Río Cochrane. Scientifically proven to be one of the clearest in the world, Río Cochrane is a unique place for water sports. Transportation from the Turismo TresMil office, specialist guides (English-speaking for kayaking but not for other tours), a snack, and neoprene wetsuits are included.

For **fishing tours,** including lunch, equipment, and transport, **Último Paraíso** (Lago Brown 455, tel. 67/2522 361, www.hotelultimoparaiso.cl) is the best local outfit. It can organize trips for a minimum of two starting at CH$251,000.

TREKKING

Turismo TresMil (inside Cafetería Naciónpatagonia, Golondrinas 491, Cochrane, tel. 9/9474 6239, www.turismotresmil.com) is also expert in leading trekking tours, including the challenging 10-hour crossing from Parque Nacional Patagonia via Cerro Tamangito to Sector Tamango (CH$69,000 pp, min. 2 people), with a specialist guide, lunch, and transportation included. They can help organize transportation to Sector Valle Chacabuco and also rent bikes (CH$9,000 half day, CH$16,000 full day).

Cochrane native Jimmy Valdez of **Lord Patagonia** (Pasaje Cerro La Cruz 557, tel. 9/8425 2419) is the best bet for **ice trekking** on the nearby Glaciar Calluqueo, on the flanks of Monte San Lorenzo. Full-day tours with equipment cost CH$65,000 pp (min. 2 people).

Food and Accommodations

Cozy **La Isla** (Prat 100 B, tel. 9/9888 5256, noon-10pm daily, CH$4,000-8,000), in a wood-lined cabin, merits the walk across town. Patagonian roast lamb accompanied by roasted potatoes is the specialty, usually only available on weekends. The array of Chilean home cooking includes *cazuelas* (meat stews), grilled fish, lasagnas, and pasta, all at very reasonable prices. The homemade desserts are also good. Follow Calle Arturo Pratt south to its end.

Just down the road from the bus terminal, tiny **Martica** (Caucahues 565, tel. 9/9410 1617, 12:45pm-10:30pm Sun.-Fri., CH$4,000-7,000) specializes in exquisitely simple and delicious Chilean dishes. Three-course menus with 2-3 options change daily, offering zucchini soup, butter bean stews, and vegetable-stuffed chicken breasts, plus simple desserts of fresh fruit or *leche asada* (Chilean-style custard). Prices are excellent, and you're served by the owners.

The charming **Naciónpatagonia** (Golondrinas 491, 9:30am-8:30pm Mon.-Sat.) feels like the Cochrane of yore. Traditional Chilean music provides the perfect backdrop to a lingering afternoon in this café enjoying thick hot chocolate or homemade kuchen. Bring a book or watch the world go by through the large windows onto the square.

Run by the charming Marlen, ★ **Hostal Beraca** (Prat 303, tel. 9/9075 9027, CH$25,000 d shared bath) is the ultimate home away from home. Occupying her old family house, the rooms are a little tired but are kept spotless and have comfortable mattresses. Marlen is a fantastic cook, and breakfast here is the best for this price range along the Carretera Austral, with *sopapillas,* homemade kuchen, bread, and jams. You can make use of the kitchen when Marlen's not cooking. Rates include IVA.

Attracting foreign backpackers and Chilean holidaymakers, **Lejana Patagonia** (Río Los Lados 521, tel. 9/7764 6669, lejanapatagonia2016@gmail.com, CH$30,000 d shared bath) is a modern, well-run bed-and-breakfast with 10 pine-decorated bedrooms, heated by wood burners and central heating. All share baths, and there's a guest kitchen and convivial communal spaces. Breakfast costs CH$6,000 per room. Rates include IVA.

Utilitarian in style, the seven pine-decorated 1st-floor bedrooms at **Último Paraíso** (Lago Brown 455, tel. 67/2522 361, www.hotelultimoparaiso.cl, CH$86,000 d) feel a bit gloomy but have large, modern baths and wood burners; this is a cut above the other options in Cochrane. The hotel can organize day tours to fly-fish on local rivers and lakes.

Information and Services

For visitor information, the **Oficina de Turismo** (Dr. Steffens 398, tel. 67/2522 115, www.municochrane.cl, 10am-1pm and 3pm-7pm Mon.-Sat. Nov.-May), in a kiosk on the southeastern corner of the Plaza de Armas, has maps and information on Parque Nacional Patagonia. There is also a **SERNATUR booth** (no phone, infocochrane@sernatur.cl, 9am-1pm and 2:30pm-6:30pm Mon.-Fri., 2pm-6pm Sat.) in the bus terminal.

This is the final place that you'll find an **ATM** or **bank** along the Carretera Austral. The **BancoEstado** (Esmeralda 460, 9am-2pm Mon.-Fri.) is on the Plaza de Armas, with a **24-hour ATM** that accepts MasterCard only. You can also exchange dollars here.

The **Hospital de Cochrane** (Av. O'Higgins s/n, tel. 67/271 337) provides 24-hour emergency care. Find mail services at **Correos** (Golondrinas 399, 9:30am-1pm and 3:30pm-7pm Mon.-Fri., 10am-1pm Sat.). A handful of **mini markets** exist around the town, but the best **supermarket** for food, camping equipment, and vehicle repairs is in

Casa Melero (Golondrinas 148). For laundry, Camping Cochrane (Dr. Steffens and Golondrinas) can offer a one-day turnaround. The COPEC gas station can be found at the corner of Avenida Pratt and Avenida O'Higgins on the south edge of town.

Getting There and Around

CAR

From Caleta Tortel, Cochrane is a 125-km, three-hour drive northeast on the Carretera Austral. From Puerto Río Tranquilo, it's a 115-km, 2.5-hour drive south on the Carretera Austral. To get to Sector Tamango or Sector Valle Chacabuco in Parque Nacional Patagonia, taxi firms Catalina (tel. 9/8429 8970) and Cordillera (tel. 9/5610 8372) can help.

BUS

The two-floor Terminal de Buses (Río Maitén 197), on the northern edge of town, is where all buses arrive and depart.

From Coyhaique (6hr, CH$14,000), Buses Don Carlos (Cruz 73, tel. 67/223 298) leave at 9am Monday-Saturday. Buses Sao Paulo (Coyhaique tel. 67/2237 630, www.busessaopaulo.cl) leave Coyhaique at 9am daily. Buses Acuario 13 (Río Baker 349, tel. 67/2240 990) leave at 8:30am Wednesday, Friday, and Sunday from their office. All buses heading from Coyhaique to Cochrane also stop and pick up passengers from Villa Cerro Castillo (5.5hr, CH$10,000) and Puerto Río Tranquilo (2.5hr, CH$7,000).

From Chile Chico (4hr, CH$13,000), Buses Marfer (tel. 9/7756 82354, transmarfer@gmail.com) leave at 4pm daily, stopping to pick up from Puerto Guadal (1.75hr, CH$6,000). Minivans from Caleta Tortel (3hr, CH$7,000) operated by Aldea (tel. 67/2638 291) leave at 3pm Tuesday-Thursday and Saturday-Sunday, and at 6pm Friday. Buses Cordillera Tortel (tel. 9/8134 4990) leave from Caleta Tortel at 8am Monday and Thursday, and at 1:30pm Saturday. Buses Katalina (tel. 67/2391 845) leave Caleta Tortel at 8pm Tuesday-Sunday. They also have

buses from Puerto Río Tranquilo (2.5hr, CH$7,000), leaving Cochrane at 8am daily.

Pachamama (Merino 499, Cochrane, tel. 9/9411 4755) operates out of its own office in Cochrane with departures from Caleta Tortel at 8am and 9pm Monday, 10am Wednesday, and 3pm Saturday. Buses Aguilas Patagonicas (tel. 67/2523 730, www.aguilaspatagonicas.cl) shuttle between Cochrane and Villa O'Higgins (5.5hr, CH$12,000), leaving Villa O'Higgins at 8:30am Tuesday, Thursday, and Sunday. They also have a bus at 9:30am daily from Coyhaique.

★ CALETA TORTEL

Nothing quite prepares you for Caleta Tortel, easily the most magical of the settlements along the Carretera Austral. Over 100km south of Cochrane, the village clings to a green-fringed hill along the turquoise waters of the sound. There are no roads; instead of pavement are 10km of cypress-wood walkways, at some points seemingly hovering above the water, which is fed by electric-blue Río Baker and glacial melt of the Northern and Southern Patagonian Ice Fields. At intervals, pretty hexagonal wooden platforms with roofs provide a welcome breather and a vantage point to appreciate the magic of this unique settlement.

Caleta Tortel's quirky boardwalks are the main attraction, and most visitors are content with a short day trip, particularly as facilities and services are minimal. Those who stay longer have the chance to visit the two nearby ice fields by boat tour.

Water and electricity are at a premium in the town, as both are supplied by a hydroelectric turbine that runs dry during summer. Most houses have an electricity generator. Trash is a significant issue here, so avoid leaving too much waste, or take it away with you.

Orientation

Overland access to Caleta Tortel is via the X-904, the unpaved spur that connects the village with the Carretera Austral. The village can be surprisingly difficult to navigate. It is divided into four sections. The **Estacionamiento** (car park) connects to the X-904 and marks the **Sector Rincón Bajo.** **Sector Centro** is the central section of the town, connected to the Estacionamiento by a steep set of stairs. Sector Centro contains the **Plaza de Armas** and a number of other small plazas and the ferry ramp. **Sector Playa Ancha** is southwest of Sector Centro and also has a number of plazas. **Sector Junquillo** is the southernmost part of the village, 2km from the car park.

Unfortunately, no signs indicate the transition between sectors. It's a good idea to stop at the **tourist office** (western side of the Estacionamiento, caletatortelpatagonia@ gmail.com, 9am-10am, noon-1pm, and 4pm-5pm Mon.-Fri., 9am-1pm and 2:30pm-5:30pm Sat.-Sun.) to pick up a map of the village.

From Sector Rincón Baja, it is a steep climb down wooden staircases to reach the bay and the paths that lead to the rest of the village. Depending on where you stay, it can be a surprisingly long and exhausting walk to your lodging, so it's a good idea to minimize your luggage. It's sometimes possible to hire a local to transport you farther around the coast in their boat.

The boardwalks can get dangerously slippery when wet. If you're arriving at night aboard the ferry from Puerto Natales, bring a headlamp.

Food and Accommodations

Up some steps from the Plaza de Armas, **El Mirador** (Sector Centro, tel. 9/8190 1923, elmiradorrestaurant@hotmail.com, 12:30pm-9pm Tues.-Sun., CH$7,000-10,000) is a solid choice for its food and views. Well-presented salmon and other freshly caught fish accompany salad and potatoes. Huge pizzas are more than enough to be shared. They have the best Wi-Fi connection in the village and serve their own dark beer on tap.

A good budget option close to the Estacionamiento and with some of the longest hours in the town, **Restaurante Bellavista** (Sector Rincón Bajo, tel. 9/6211 7430, 1pm-9:30pm Mon.-Sat., CH$5,000-8,000) has lovely views from the dimly lit living room-cum-restaurant. Dishes are uneventful, including the usual grilled salmon, *carbonada* (a hearty soup of chunks of beef, vegetables and corn), stews, and empanadas. Prices are on the lower end for the town.

On the far southern side of the town, **Residencial Brisas del Sur** (Sector Playa Ancha, tel. 9/5688 2723, CH$15,000 pp), a very clean, neat, and utilitarian family home, is the best lodging option at this price point, with pretty views across the bay. There's no kitchen access, but Wi-Fi and breakfast are included. Rates are per person, making it a good option for single travelers. Central heating ensures that rooms stay warm. The owners will pick up guests arriving by ferry. Rates include IVA.

A few hundred meters from the Estacionamiento and with only a few steps to descend, **Hostal Nunatak** (Sector Rincón Bajo, tel. 9/8113 452, CH$35,000 d) has a handful of functional bedrooms with unsightly chipboard walls but which are kept warm by a wood stove. Each room has an en suite bath with hot water available on demand and a simple breakfast put on by the friendly owners. Rates include IVA.

Caleta Tortel's most comfortable option, the five modern bedrooms at ★ **Entrehielos Lodge** (Sector Centro, tel. 9/9579 3779, www. entrehielos.cl, Sept.-May, CH$103,000 d), are far ahead in quality compared with the basic family-run guesthouses around the village. Run by Santiago native Maria, the hotel oozes style and charm. Rooms are stylish and have rain showers and central heating—welcome when the icy wind comes off the nearby glaciers. A small library and sitting area with wood fire adjoin the dining room, where gourmet Chilean dishes are prepared by the on-site chef. An extensive wine menu belies the remote setting. They also run overnight boat trips to the Steffens and Jorge Montt Glaciers. Rates include IVA.

Information and Services

There is a small **Oficina de Turismo** (western side of the Estacionamiento, tel. 9/6230 4879, caletatortelpatagonia@gmail.com, 9am-10am, noon-1pm, and 4pm-5pm Mon.-Fri., 9am-1pm and 2:30pm-5:30pm Sat.-Sun) run by the municipality. Stop here to get a map of the village and use the **public restrooms** for a nominal fee. The **Posta de Salud** (tel. 9/7398 3590 or 9/8241 609), a clinic with basic emergency facilities, is on the southwestern edge of the car park.

Getting There and Around

CAR

From **Cochrane** to Caleta Tortel is a 125-km, three-hour drive southwest along Ruta 7 and the X-904. From **Villa O'Higgins,** it's a 150-km, six-hour journey north along the Carretera Austral, which includes a short ferry ride.

BUS

Provisiones Hijo de Pioneros, the grocery store on the western edge of the Estacionamiento, sells tickets for the buses listed here. Sixteen-seater minivans operated by **Vultur Patagonia** (tel. 9/7870 1956 or 9/9350 8156) leave Caleta Tortel at 4:30pm and **Villa O'Higgins** (3.5hr, CH$4,000) at 8:30am Monday, Thursday, and Saturday; services reduce to once weekly May-October. In high season, book a day or two in advance.

Six- to 14-seat minibuses from **Cochrane** (3hr, CH$7,000) are operated by **Pachamama** (Merino 499, tel. 9/9411 4755; 6pm Sun.-Mon. and 10am Wed. and Sat.), **Aldea** (tel. 67/2393 119; 9:30am Tues., Thurs., and Sun. and 2pm Fri.), and **Buses Katalina** (tel. 67/2391 845; 5:30pm Tues.-Sun.). **Buses Cordillera Tortel** (tel. 9/8134 4990) charge the same price for the journey and have an office on the eastern side of the Estacionamiento. They leave from Cochrane at 6pm Monday, Thursday, and Saturday.

FERRY

Since 2016, **Transbordadora Austral Broom** (Av. Pedro Montt 605, Puerto Natales, tel. 61/2728 100, www.tabsa.cl) has operated the 41-hour **ferry crossing** from Puerto Natales. The route travels north from Southern Patagonia to Caleta Tortel, then loops southeast to Puerto Yungay (CH$125,160 foot passengers, CH$120,000 vehicles, plus CH$25,030 per meter for the length of the vehicle). The trip, representing the only transport connection between the regions of Aysén and Magallanes without crossing into Argentina, has become increasingly popular among foreign and Chilean tourists. It's run in the somewhat aged *Crux Australis,* a cargo boat-cum-ferry with space for 142 passengers in *semi-cama* bus-style seating.

This vessel has received few adaptations for tourists and is less comfortable than the Punta Arenas-Puerto Williams ferry operated by the same company. The ratio of passengers to showers and toilets is lower and the food quality and quantity leaves much to be desired. However, this trip feels similarly wild and provides an easy connection between Southern Chilean Patagonia and the Carretera Austral.

Unlike the Navimag ferry that covers much of the same journey between Puerto Montt and Puerto Williams, the *Crux Australis* stops for 1-3 hours in **Puerto Eden** to unload cargo. Passengers are allowed to disembark and wander this tiny settlement, home to around 170 people and the only remaining indigenous Kawésqar people. Like Caleta Tortel, this remote hamlet has only wooden walkways to connect the houses. Shoes with good grip and a waterproof coat are essential; the walkways are in poor condition and can get slippery when it rains. From the ferry ramp at Puerto Eden, take the walkway left of the harbor and the first set of stairs leading upward on your right after about 300 meters; you'll reach the top of the hill and a *mirador* that overlooks Puerto Eden and the magnificent fjord scenery. There is also cell phone signal (with the Chilean mobile phone provider Entel) at Puerto Eden.

The ferry leaves weekly from Puerto Natales at 5am, although all passengers and

Excursions from Caleta Tortel

GLACIER TOURS

One of the few excursions you can take from Caleta Tortel is to visit the nearby **Ventisquero Steffens** (Steffens Hanging Glacier), a glacier named after German explorer Hans Steffen. Taking a boat 2.5 hours northwest through the fjords brings you to an iceberg-filled bay and the glacier, within the boundaries of Parque Nacional Laguna San Rafael. Look out for *huemules* in the forest on the edges of the glacier.

Another excursion from Caleta Tortel is to **Glaciar Jorge Montt** (Jorge Montt Glacier), 1.5 hours south by boat, on the northern edge of Parque Nacional Bernardo O'Higgins. Time-lapse photography in 2010-2011 showed that this glacier retreated by an entire kilometer in a year, raising great concerns about the rapid retreat of the ice fields in the region. Visitors approach the snout of the glacier by boat, with the possibility to disembark and walk along the moraine. Due to the concentration of pack ice that accumulates here, however, boats are often unable to get closer than a few kilometers from the ice wall.

For both trips, small motorboats carrying 8-10 passengers can be arranged for a full-day tour from Caleta Tortel (CH$70,000 pp). Boats only leave with a minimum of eight passengers; this shouldn't be a problem during January-February but can be difficult the rest of the year. **Evelyn Vargas** (tel. 9/4281 9293) is a reliable choice, while **Entrehielos** (Sector Centro, tel. 9/9579 3779, www.entrehielos.cl) run overnight trips to both glaciers in their eight-person vessel. Trips are two days, one night (there are bunk beds on board) and cost CH$400,000 for up to eight people.

ISLA DE LOS MUERTOS TOURS

On the bleak **Isla de los Muertos,** 3km northwest of Caleta Tortel at the mouth of the Río Baker, 33 cypress crosses bear testament to the pioneers of the region. Workers of the Sociedad Exploradora del Baker, a forestry company, colonized the zone in 1904-1908, but all died in mysterious circumstances. Various theories abound, including that a scurvy epidemic or accidental poisoning (caused by consuming flour that had been contaminated with arsenic) was responsible for wiping out the population. The most frightening—and most believed by the local people—is that the workers were killed by the company itself, as a means of avoiding paying their wages. The graves were exhumed by archaeologists in 1998, but the cause of death has never been identified.

This mysterious, macabre island was named a historical monument in 2001. Two-hour boat tours now land here, and a path leads around the tiny cemetery. In 2018, the municipal government built walkways and a jetty to improve access to the island. There are plenty of locals offering tours in their fishing vessels. **Enrique Fernández** (tel. 9/9940 8265) is the best option; otherwise, a guided tour with **Entrehielos** (Sector Centro, tel. 9/9579 3779, www.entrehielos.cl), including an English-speaking guide, will give some history of the island. Expect to pay CH$40,000 per boat, with space for four people.

those with vehicles are required to board the previous night. Three meals per day are included, but you should bring extra snacks, as portion size and quality is not the best. All seats recline 160 degrees and blankets are provided, although it can get cold at night, so bring extra layers. Part of the fun of the trip is watching the scenery from above deck, so waterproof and windproof clothing are essential. The winds can be fierce, even if most of the journey is through the protected fjords.

Onboard, films play in the seating area late into the night. Bring earplugs and an eye mask to block out noise and light. Lockers are available for your belongings, although suitcases and backpacks must be left below deck upon boarding; bring a small day pack for the items you need for the trip.

If you're traveling December-February, book your seat or vehicle reservation in October. Outside these months, it's often possible to get a seat and even a space for your car a week or two in advance.

The arrival time of the ferry depends entirely on weather conditions, and it's not uncommon for the boat to land at Caleta Tortel in the middle of the night. Confirm with your hotel that they will come to pick you up from the harbor before you set sail.

For those traveling south from Caleta Tortel, the **Transbordadora Austral Broom office** (Sector Centro, follow signs for "El Negrito" mini market, 9am-1pm and 3pm-6:30pm Mon.-Fri., 9am-noon Sat.) can advise on scheduled boat departures, particularly when they're delayed due to weather. Be aware that the office keeps erratic hours. Theoretically, the boat departs for Puerto Natales from the ferry ramp at 11pm Saturday and arrives at 4pm Monday. The boat operates year-round.

In **Puerto Yungay,** there is another office (tel. 9/8452 7228, Sat. only) where vehicles board and disembark the ferry. The small cafeteria **El Peregrino** (tel. 9/3017 4949), which serves coffees and basic meals, is open in the hours leading up to the ferry departure, normally at 8pm Saturday.

★ VILLA O'HIGGINS

From Caleta Tortel, the gravel Carretera Austral runs southeast along the mountains as deep river valleys open up beneath. This 98-km final stretch, the most remote and wild, runs from the ferry crossing from Puerto Yungay to Villa O'Higgins, the last settlement along the Carretera Austral. It was only completed in 1999; before that it was only possible to arrive in a light aircraft.

Since its foundation in 1966, this village has grown little; in 2017 the population was just 625. The isolation and distance from the rest of the region is tangible. The perpetually iced peaks of the Southern Patagonian Ice Field loom over Villa O'Higgins's western flank, while a short distance south lies the northern shore of the grand, glacier-filled Lago O'Higgins. Few places are imbued with the same feeling of mystique as this remote village, emphasized by the fact that few of the Carretera Austral's many travelers ever make it here.

Although there's not much to see in the village, it's a gateway to hiking trails through virgin lands, boat trips and flyovers of the nearby glaciers, plus Patagonia's most extreme border crossing.

Orientation

Villa O'Higgins is a small village, and it's not possible to get lost. Coming from the north via Caleta Tortel, the Carretera Austral passes along the west edge of town, continuing 7km to **Puerto Bahamondes,** where there is a sign indicating the official end of the Carretera Austral. Those coming from the south and the border crossing with Argentina, via Lago Desierto and Lago O'Higgins, will find the boat from Candelario Mancilla docks here.

Sights

There are few sights in town. The **Plaza de Armas** is dominated by the statue of **La Pionera (The Pioneer),** a memorial to the region's early pioneers, with a particular focus on the otherwise undocumented women who came with their men. It depicts a woman with a baby riding a *baguale,* a breed of Patagonian horse notable for its small stature.

On the northern side of the plaza, the **Museo Padre Ronchi** (no phone, 8am-1pm and 2pm-6:30pm Mon.-Fri., free), a small museum set within the old church, charts the life of Italian missionary Padre Ronchi; he worked to improve rural living conditions across the region and helped build the church in 1977. It contains a collection of historic memorabilia and photographs charting the history of the village, plus the priest's simple living quarters, where you'll notice he insulated the gap-riddled wooden walls with metal taken from tin cans.

Hiking

Villa O'Higgins has a small number of trails, easily reached on foot. The most popular is the steep, muscle-busting, three-hour round-trip **Sendero La Bandera** (4km round-trip, 3hr), which climbs from the eastern end of

Excursions from Villa O'Higgins

a boat tour to the snout of Glaciar O'Higgins

With the Southern Patagonian Ice Field and its sizeable share of Chile's 24,133 glaciers only a short distance southwest of Villa O'Higgins, the village is ideal for exploring the northern part of the ice field.

A popular day trip is to the tongue of **Glaciar O'Higgins** (O'Higgins Glacier), which covers 75,000 hectares over 38km from the ice field. Difficult to access and receiving only a few thousand visitors annually, this glacier guarantees a spectacular display of ice; you'll likely to see huge bergs calving off the 80-meter snout into turquoise Lago O'Higgins. **Robinson Crusoe** (Carretera Austral, Villa O'Higgins, tel. 2/2334 1503 or 67/2431 811, www.robinsoncrusoe.com) operates tours on the 58-passeger LM *Quetru,* with an open deck to appreciate the view when it stops a few hundred meters from the snout. The ship has a cafeteria on board, and a whisky with shaved glacier ice is included in the tour.

Leaving Puerto Bahamondes, just south of Villa O'Higgins, the initial stop on the tour is at Candelario Mancilla, one of the first inhabited parts of the region, now the location of a basic refuge and the Chilean *carabineros* (police) that deal with border formalities for the crossing into Argentina. Additional passengers are collected for the voyage to the glacier, passing through a maze of icebergs to reach the snout. Finally, the boat returns to Candelario Mancilla to drop passengers continuing to Argentina, and returns to Puerto Bahamondes.

The full-day tour (CH$82,000) operates 2-3 times weekly, normally at 11:30am Wednesday and Saturday. A round-trip transfer between Villa O'Higgins and Puerto Bahamondes costs an additional CH$4,000. Bring wind- and waterproof clothing; the area is known for extreme winds that howl across the lake, causing departure delays that sometimes last for days.

An even more impressive alternative is to fly over the ice. Experienced pilot Vincente Beasley, who runs **WINGS** (tel. 9/9162 5137 or 9/9357 8196, www.wingspatagonia.com), has a six-seater GAF Nomad plane for one-hour tours over Glacier O'Higgins and the Southern Patagonian Ice Field. The route depends on weather conditions; most flights leave in early morning when the weather is more stable. You'll fly above Glacier O'Higgins, maybe catching a glimpse of ice calving into the water, and drop as low as 20 meters above the ice to see the dense blue fissures up to 60 meters deep.

Vicente maintains English and Spanish commentary on the scenery, which can include views across to Monte Fitz Roy in Argentina. For a one-hour flight, expect to pay CH$190,000 pp. Turbulence is common, and sick bags are provided.

Calle Río Pascua, where a wooden gate leads to the trail up Cerro Santiago, the 1,140-meter mountain that dominates the village. This trail zigzags to a viewpoint with a covered viewing platform, 600 meters after the trailhead, before steep switchbacks through southern beech forest lead 1.9km to the **Mirador La Bandera.** Expect panoramic views of the valley, the lake, and the glimmer of the glaciers to the west. The trail can be horribly muddy after wet weather, and steep sections make it easy to slip; good hiking boots and trekking poles are recommended.

Food and Accommodations

With a cavernous 60-seat dining area, **Restaurant Lago Cisne** (tel. 9/6673 2734, http://restaurantlagocisne.cl, 10am-10pm daily, CH$6,000-12,000) offers traditional Chilean home-cooking that's popular among locals. Owner Marilyn makes a real effort with presentation, and you'll get everything from grilled salmon with spicy potatoes to occasional specials such as *pastel de choclo.* In the evening, particularly on weekends, expect live music or karaoke.

On the northern edge of Villa O'Higgins, just before the road enters the village, **Entre Patagones** (tel. 9/4980 460, www. entrepatagones.cl, 9:30am-9:30pm daily, CH$8,000-12,000) has reliable food in a welcoming environment. There's no written menu, so you'll need to ask what's available; normally it's grilled salmon or other fish, a thick soup, or a meat dish. They often have vegetarian options, and for large groups, Patagonian roast lamb is possible. Book in advance, as they are usually only open on days when they have reservations.

The same family has cabin and yurt accommodations, mostly on the same site as the restaurant. The seven cabins at **Entre Patagones** (tel. 9/4980 460, www. entrepatagones.cl, CH$40,000-50,000 cabin, CH$65,000 yurt) are made from wood and are rustic in style, ranging from those with a small kitchen to those with only tea- and coffee-making facilities. A five-minute walk north along the road are two modern yurts hidden in the forest, with utter privacy from the road and views across the mountains. Both have beautifully designed circular bedrooms, up-to-date baths, a wood fire for heat, a fully equipped kitchen, a balcony, and a private hot tub. Rates include IVA.

A meeting place for backpackers, cyclists, and road trippers, **El Mosco** (Km 1240 Carretera Austral, northern end as it enters the village, tel. 67/2431 819, patagoniaelmosco@ yahoo.es, CH$6,000 camping, CH$9,000 dorm, CH$45,000 d), has a range of accommodations in the main house: basic dorms with chipboard walls and no lockers on the 1st floor, and six more comfortable private rooms upstairs, with private baths for the double rooms. A large kitchen and living area on the ground floor get crowded when the hostel is full. On the same land, two bright orange cabins (CH$45,000) are excellent value, with a private kitchen and bath for the same price as a private room. Outside, low shrubs provide some protection against the elements for campers, who also have access to indoor baths and the kitchen. Staff can offer a wealth of travel information, about hiking in the region and the border crossing to El Chaltén. Rates include IVA.

For a slice of unexpected luxury in the middle of nowhere, the ambitious ★ **Robinson Crusoe** (Km 1240 Carretera Austral, opposite El Mosco, tel. 2/2334 1503 or 67/2431 811, www.robinsoncrusoe.com, CH$166,000 d) is both stylish in design and decoration. The lodge's 12 ground-floor bedrooms contain comforts that include hot tubs with mountain views. The clubhouse is decorated in earthy rustic-chic style, with long benches for communal dining, plus breakout sofas around a welcoming wood-burning stove. Staffers have excellent knowledge of the region and activities. They offer boat trips to Glaciar O'Higgins as well as flights over the Southern Patagonian Ice Field. They can arrange multiday packages, including transport from Coyhaique's Aeródromo Balmaceda to the hotel. Rates drop 30 percent mid-April-October.

Border Disputes

Villa O'Higgins might feel far from Argentina due to the boundary of the Andes Mountains and the Southern Patagonian Ice Field, but this small settlement has seen its share of territorial disputes. Villa O'Higgins was founded in 1966 during a period when the Chilean government was keen to strengthen sovereignty in the region. In 1985, Argentina responded in kind, founding El Chaitén, due south across the mountains.

The mountainous nature of this terrain has made it difficult to define exact borders. It wasn't until 2007 that an agreement finally defined the border through the Southern Patagonian Ice Field. The accord left Lago O'Higgins split between the countries, bearing the name Lago San Martín for its Argentine half.

A glitch in Google's maps in 2007 once again redefined the contentious border, if only temporarily: Searches at the time showed the border having moved so that Villa O'Higgins lay in Argentina, causing the Chilean Foreign Ministry to request that the village be returned to its rightful country.

Although relations between Argentina and Chile have improved in recent decades, frustrations are still felt in Villa O'Higgins. Locals decry what they view as Argentina's intentional refusal to build bridges that would make the Paso Meyer, a border crossing 48km north, open to all vehicles. If this were to happen, the route would be the only road crossing between the Carretera Austral and Ruta 40 this far south—a move that residents believe would increase tourism dramatically. With this route, visitors could drive directly between El Chaltén in Argentina and Villa O'Higgins, rather than driving 332km north to Chile Chico, one of the most widely used border crossings along the Carretera Austral.

Information and Services

On the eastern side of the Plaza de Armas, inside the municipal office, the **Oficina de Información Turística** (tel. 67/2573 203, www.municipalidadohiggins.cl) has no fixed hours, and the staff does not speak English, but they are enthusiastic and can give you information about transportation links and services within the village. The **Posta de Salud** (Hernán Merino 45, tel. 67/2431 883) is a basic health center offering limited emergency care.

Note that there are no ATMs or banks in Villa O'Higgins. Although some of the main hotels and restaurants accept credit cards, it's essential to bring cash, particularly as there are no money-changing facilities. The **COPEC gas station,** at the northern entrance to the village, has the dubious honor of having the most expensive fuel along the Carretera Austral.

Getting There and Around

From Caleta Tortel, it's a one-hour drive along gravel roads to Puerto Yungay, the port with a free vehicle and passenger ferry crossing to Río Bravo, where the road continues south to Villa O'Higgins. **Barcaza Padre Antonio Ronchi** (tel. 9/6586 6626, www.barcazafiordomitchell.cl) operates the route, with space for 15 vehicles. November-March, ferries cross four times daily in each direction (free, 45min); April-October, the boat operates Monday-Saturday at noon and 3pm (toward Río Bravo) and 1pm and 4pm (toward Puerto Yungay). This journey takes just over six hours and covers 150km.

Aguilas Patagónicas (Lago Christie s/n, tel. 67/2523 730) has minivans that shuttle between **Cochrane** (4.5hr, CH$12,000) and Villa O'Higgins at 8:30am daily. **Vultur Patagonia** (Lago Cisnes 215, tel. 9/9350 8156) offers minivans that leave **Caleta Tortel** (3.5hr, CH$4,000) at 4:30pm Monday, Thursday, and Saturday; services reduce to once weekly May-October. In high season, book a day or two in advance.

The lodge **Robinson Crusoe** (Km 1240 Carretera Austral, opposite El Mosco, tel. 2/2334 1503 or 67/2431 811, www.

robinsoncrusoe.com) can arrange car rental through Hertz in Coyhaique, with the vehicle delivered to the hotel for you to drive back to Coyhaique. Note that a hefty one-way fee is included in the cost.

Villa O'Higgins has a tiny **airfield.** It's possible to charter flights through **Transportes Aéreos del Sur** (Adelaida Vargas 497, tel. 9/9357 8196 or 67/2393 163) between Villa O'Higgins and destinations along the Carretera Austral, including Cochrane and Balmaceda. Expect to pay around US$2,400 for up to eight passengers.

In a small office next door to the Robinson Crusoe lodge, **Hielo Sur** (tel. 67/2431 811, www.robinsoncrusoe.com) sells tickets for the 58-passenger LM *Quetru* for the boat-based Argentine border crossing to Candelario Mancilla and the onward journey by foot to El Chaltén. Boats leave 2-3 times per week, normally at 8:30am Wednesday and Saturday. It is possible to cross directly from Puerto Bahamondes (CH$36,000),

south of Villa O'Higgins, or with a visit to the foot of Glaciar Villa O'Higgins included (CH$82,000); the round-trip with glacier visit costs CH$103,000. An additional transfer (CH$2,500 one-way, CH$4,000 round-trip) between Villa O'Higgins and Puerto Bahamondes can be arranged.

Ruedas de la Patagonia (Pasaje Antonio Ronchi, tel. 9/7604 2400, www.turismoruedasdelapatagonia.cl) operates a smaller boat to Candelario Mancilla, aimed at those crossing to Argentina, leaving at 9am Tuesday, Thursday, and Friday (1.5hr, CH$36,000 one-way); the return journey is at 4:30pm Wednesday, Thursday, and Saturday from Candelario Mancilla. The transfer between Villa O'Higgins and Puerto Bahamondes is included in the price.

Bici Lájep (O'Higgins s/n, tel. 9/8253 9090, bicilajep@gmail.com) rents bikes by the hour and by the day, offering a good option for those without transport to reach the end of the Carretera Austral.

Southern Patagonia and Tierra del Fuego

Few places in Chile feel as wild, untouched, and alive as Patagonia. Covering a million hectares—the size of Venezuela—this region was long a place of legend. The name, according to some, comes from *patagones*, meaning "big feet." It was first used by Antonio Pigafetta on Ferdinand Magellan's voyage through the Strait of Magellan in 1520, ascribing gigantesque proportions to the land's indigenous inhabitants. More than four centuries later, the mythic sense of the area was heightened thanks to Bruce Chatwin's *In Patagonia* (1977), in which he wrote about his travels in search of the remains of a *Mylodon* (giant sloth).

    Southern Patagonia illustrates Chile's extremes: The region stretches from Argentina's El Chaltén, which neighbors the world's

Highlights

Look for ★ to find recommended sights, activities, dining, and lodging.

★ **Museo Regional de Magallanes:** Learn about the lives of Patagonia's indigenous peoples, the first Europeans that explored the region, and Punta Arenas's wealthy wool barons (page 494).

★ **Museo Nao Victoria:** Step on board exact replicas of the most significant ships to have sailed the Patagonian seas at this superb museum (page 494).

★ **Museo de Historia Natural Río Seco:** Watch the restoration of skeletons of marine mammals at this fascinating museum about the natural history of Southern Patagonia (page 496).

★ **Monumento Natural Los Pingüinos:** Get up close to a chattering colony of 120,000 Magellanic penguins (page 505).

★ **Trekking Torres del Paine:** Hike through this national park's dramatic glacial landscape along crystalline lakes and towering rock formations (page 522).

★ **Parque Nacional Los Glaciares:** Watch icebergs as large as buildings calve off Glaciar Perito Moreno (page 542).

★ **Parque Pingüino Rey:** Meet the only colony of king penguins in the Americas (page 564).

★ **Museo Martín Gusinde:** Learn about the lives of the indigenous seafaring Yaghan, the southernmost people on the planet, in this museum in Puerto Williams (page 566).

★ **Ferry from Punta Arenas:** Ply the Chilean fjords to Puerto Williams to see spectacular glaciers and frolicking whales (page 568).

★ **Cape Horn:** Take a plane or a boat to this remote windswept headland, the southernmost part of Tierra del Fuego (page 571).

Southern Patagonia and Tierra del Fuego

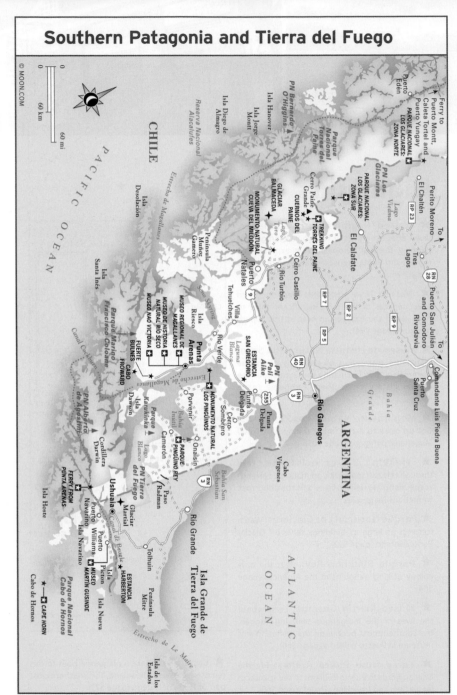

© MOON.COM

0   60 Km
0   60 mi

CHILE

PACIFIC OCEAN

Ferry to
Puerto Montt,
Caleta Tortel and
Puerto Yungay

Puerto
Edén

Puerto
Natales

Reserva Nacional
Alacalufes

Isla Diego de
Almagro

Isla Jorge
Montt

Isla Hanover

PN Bernardo
O'Higgins

Parque
Nacional
Torres del
Paine

PARQUE NACIONAL
LOS GLACIARES:
ZONA NORTE

Perito Moreno

El Chaltén

Lago
Viedma

Tres
Lagos

RP 23

To

Cerro Paine
Grande

PN Los
Glaciares

PARQUE NACIONAL
LOS GLACIARES:
ZONA SUR

El Calafate

GLACIAR
BALMACEDA

MONUMENTO NATURAL
CUEVA DEL MILODÓN

CUERNOS DEL
PAINE

TREKKING
TORRES DEL PAINE

Lago
Toro

Cerro Castillo

Río Turbio

Puerto San Julián
and Comodoro
Rivadavia

RN
28

RP 7

RP 2

RP 5

RP 9

Península
Muñoz
Gamero

Isla
Desolación

Estrecho de Magallanes

Villa
Tehuelches

Puerto
Natales

Laguna
Blanca

ESTANCIA
SAN GREGORIO

Punta
Delgada

RN
40

RN
3

Río Gallegos

ARGENTINA

Comandante
Luis Piedra Buena

Puerto
Santa Cruz

Bahía
Grande

Isla
Santa Inés

MUSEO REGIONAL DE
MAGALLANES

MUSEO DE HISTORIA
NATURAL RÍO SECO

MUSEO NAO VICTORIA

FUERTE
BULNES

CABO
FROWARD

Punta
Arenas

Isla
Riesco

Río Verde

Seno Skyring

255

Punta
Delgada

Cabo
Vírgenes

Parque Marino
Francisco Coloane

PN Alberto
de Agostini

Cordillera
Darwin

Isla
Dawson

Parque
Karukinka

Porvenir

MONUMENTO NATURAL
LOS PINGÜINOS

Bahía
Inútil

Cerro
Sombrero

Bahía San
Sebastián

ATLANTIC
OCEAN

Canal Cockburn

FERRY FROM
PUNTA ARENAS

Ushuaia

Isla
Hoste

Puerto
Navarino

Isla
Navarino

Puerto
Williams

Glaciar
Martial

Canal de Beagle

Lago
Blanco

Cameron

PARQUE
PINGÜINO REY

PN Tierra
del Fuego

Paso
Radman

Onaisín

RN
3

Tolhuin

Isla Grande de
Tierra del Fuego

Río Grande

Isla
Picton

Isla
Nueva

MUSEO
MARTÍN GUSINDE

ESTANCIA
HARBERTON

Península
Mitre

Estrecho de Le Maire

Cabo de Hornos

Parque Nacional
Cabo de Hornos

CAPE HORN

Isla de los
Estados

Three Days in Southern Patagonia

DAY 1

Get a morning flight to Aeródromo Teniente Julio Gallardo, 6km north of Puerto Natales. At the bus terminal, board the afternoon bus to **Parque Nacional Torres del Paine.** Stay at the **Refugio y Camping Torre Central.**

DAY 2

Rise early and start the steep 9.5-km, 3.5-hour hike up to the base of the park's legendary granite *torres* (towers). Spend an hour or so appreciating the view before heading back the way you came.

Make the five-hour bus journey across the border to **El Calafate.** Stay overnight in the elegant lodgings of the converted ranch **Kau Yatún** and celebrate your hiking achievements with a traditional Patagonian lamb dish at the stylish **La Zaina.**

DAY 3

Join a **kayaking tour** to the southern sector of **Parque Nacional Los Glaciares,** where the crisp blue ice of the mammoth **Glaciar Perito Moreno** awaits. At the end of the tour, spend an hour walking the boardwalks at the snout of the ice. Return to El Calafate and enjoy local craft beer, snacks, and live music at the lively **La Zorra Taprooms.** Don't stay out too late: You'll need to catch an early bus back to Puerto Natales (or onward to Buenos Aires) to catch your flight home.

second-largest contiguous ice field, to the churning ocean of the Cape Horn Archipelago. Those who venture to the southernmost edges of South America find many treasures: The granite spires of Torres del Paine have put Patagonia on the map, and Parque Nacional Los Glaciares contains accessible Glaciar Perito Moreno plus a warren of trails. Millions of hectares of fjords promise hanging glaciers and untouched forests for those patient enough to travel the waterways on slow boat journeys. The islands at the southern end are similarly wild, home to penguin colonies and rich marinelife. Tierra del Fuego, Chile's least-explored area, is a landscape of guanaco-punctuated steppes and snow-tipped mountains that attracts hikers, adventurers, and fly-fishers.

PLANNING YOUR TIME

Because of its size and lack of infrastructure, Southern Patagonia requires thorough planning before your arrival. A short weeklong trip is possible, but a lot of that time is spent on long-haul buses. In order to visit the highlights, devote 10 days. With transit time, you'll have time for two days of hiking in Parque Nacional Torres del Paine, one day exploring the Perito Moreno glacier, and three or four days hiking in Parque Nacional Los Glaciares.

The main draws of the region can be subdivided into **Parque Nacional Los Glaciares** and the nearby towns of El Chaltén and El Calafate; **Torres del Paine** and the surrounding fjords, glaciers, and gateway settlements Puerto Natales and Punta Arenas; and **Tierra del Fuego** and the southern islands.

Many visitors choose to fly to Punta Arenas via Santiago. If you have just a short time here, consider flying into Punta Arenas from Santiago and then flying out of El Calafate and on to Buenos Aires. From Punta Arenas, long overland bus connections, short flights, and multiple-day passenger ferries and cruise ships can bring you to the subregions. **December-February is high season;** book early and expect to pay at least 20 percent more than at other times of the year.

Argentina's economy has suffered rapid inflation and devaluation since 2017. It's not unusual for the currency to fluctuate by 20-30 percent in the space of six months.

Parque Nacional Los Glaciares

Parque Nacional Los Glaciares is best reached by bus from Puerto Natales (at least 5.5hr) or a 1.5-hour flight from Ushuaia to El Calafate. **One day** is enough to admire the majesty of **Glacier Perito Moreno,** either by boat or kayak, or from the boardwalks at its nose. **El Calafate** is a large town, but most travelers continue to **El Chaltén,** three hours north, as it has ample hiking and adventure sports activities; aim for at least **three days** here, including travel time.

Torres del Paine

Parque Nacional Torres del Paine is best appreciated on a **5- or 10-day trek** around its two main trails, the W and the O. Accommodations must be booked at least **four months in advance** for high season, December-February. For those short on time, the highlights can be appreciated on a **one- or two-day trip** into the park, either in a rental car or on a tour from Puerto Natales. If you have more money than time, go for an **all-inclusive package** organized by one of the nearby luxury hotels—these are expensive but efficient.

Allow **1-2 days** in **Punta Arenas** to explore sites such as **Fuerte Bulnes** or the **Magellanic penguin colony** on **Isla Magdalena,** or even go **humpback whale-watching** in **Parque Marino Francisco Coloane.**

Tierra del Fuego

The Argentinean side of Tierra del Fuego is the more easily accessed. Ushuaia sees thousands of visitors who embark on Antarctic cruises. Nearby **glaciers,** the historic **Estancia Harberton,** and **Parque Nacional Tierra del Fuego** make it a good destination for **2-3 days.** Bear in mind that overland transport takes **12 hours from Punta Arenas** in Chile or **16 hours from El Calafate** in Argentina. Flying from Punta Arenas or El Calafate significantly reduces travel time.

The 32-hour boat ride from Punta Arenas is an adventure that brings you to the southernmost town on earth, Puerto Williams, where 1-2 days is enough for short hikes and a chance to absorb the pace of life here at the end of the earth. There are expensive speedboat connections with Ushuaia that will get you back within a couple of hours.

Cabos de Hornos and the Chilean fjords can only be reached via four-day round-trip cruises or expensive one-day flyovers. Volatile weather can mean flights are delayed—sometimes by multiple days. Chilean Tierra del Fuego is only accessible via vehicle or private tour; 3-4 days are necessary to cover the more than 500km of road, where hiking opportunities and untouched wilderness are plentiful.

HISTORY

The first inhabitants of Patagonia and Tierra del Fuego arrived 14,000 to 10,000 years ago. A land bridge across the Strait of Magellan allowed these first people to cross to a barely hospitable land. As the ice caps and glaciers retreated, they moved farther south, living for millennia as hunter-gatherers. Little is left of their societies; the four distinct indigenous groups that had developed by the arrival of the first European explorers in the 1500s—the Tehuelche or Aonikenk, Yaghan or Yámana, Selk'nam or Ona, and Kawésqar or Alacalufe—were mostly wiped out by disease, starvation, and genocide in the subsequent four centuries.

Portuguese explorer Ferdinand Magellan is credited with discovering the Strait of Magellan during his circumnavigation of the globe in 1520. Later, the English privateer Francis Drake was the first European to land on Islas de Hornos, home to Cape Horn. Charles Darwin, aboard the HMS *Beagle,* introduced the world to this remote and wild region in his chronicles *The Voyage of the Beagle.*

The first European settlements of the region were attempted in 1584, along the northern coast of the Strait of Magellan. It took 300 years for permanent settlements to emerge, mainly as a way of settling disputes between Argentina and Chile over territorial boundaries. Immigrants from Chiloé inhabited the Chilean side at Fuerte Bulnes in the mid-1800s; Anglican missionaries arrived in the Falklands and later relocated to Tierra del Fuego, and the Argentinean government founded Ushuaia along the shores of the Beagle Channel in 1884.

The development of the region was later driven by a short-lived late 19th-century gold rush in Tierra del Fuego. Around this time, the introduction of sheep from the Falkland Islands by British merchants spurred a wool boom that brought settlers from across Europe, some of whom quickly became rich and prominent members of Chilean and Argentinean society. As this industry stalled in the early 20th century, fisheries, oil reserves, and tourism became important to the economy. Nowadays, both the Argentinean and Chilean sides are relatively affluent.

Punta Arenas

Along the Strait of Magellan, Punta Arenas, capital of Chile's southernmost region, doesn't have the romance or mystic appeal you might expect. The frontier town is heavily trafficked and harassed by grisly weather—there are ropes in the main square to help when the wind blows strong enough to take you with it. Look a little harder, though, and you'll find it has a certain charm.

Around the central plaza, decadent old mansions, a legacy of Punta Arenas's wool boom, spread into the side streets. Many less grandiose buildings are painted a kaleidoscope of colors, offering a sharp contrast with the gunmetal gray of sea and sky.

For many travelers, the airport is the closest they get to Punta Arenas, but it is a great place to pick up supplies before heading into Parque Nacional Torres del Paine or the wilderness of Chilean Tierra del Fuego. There are enough museums and penguin colonies to keep you occupied for several days.

SIGHTS

Plaza Muñoz Gamero

The center of the city is **Plaza Muñoz Gamero** (bounded by Muñoz Gamero, 21 de Mayo, Julio A. Roca, and Carlos Bories), the most impressive of the squares in Southern Patagonia. Named after an early governor, the plaza has towering conifers and is surrounded by opulent mansions. The square's most notable feature is the imposing bronze sculpture at its center by Chilean artist Guillermo Córdova. On a tall pedestal, it depicts Ferdinand Magellan astride a cannon in honor of the 400th anniversary of his voyage through the strait. Underneath are various figures, including an indigenous Selk'nam person. Notice that one of Magellan's toes is a different shade of bronze; according to local legend, if you kiss the toe, you will return to Punta Arenas in the future.

Palacio Sara Braun

On the northeastern side of Plaza Muñoz Gamero is the elegant **Palacio Sara Braun** (Plaza Muñoz Gamero 716, tel. 61/248840, 10am-12:45pm Mon., 10am-12:45pm and 4pm-7:30pm Tues.-Sat., CH$2,000), an imposing European-style palace and Punta Arenas landmark. Built in 1895 for Sara Braun, who took over her husband's business after his death, the building retains many original features, including the large winter garden. A handful of rooms can be visited, still adorned with the 19th-century furniture that crossed the Atlantic.

Punta Arenas

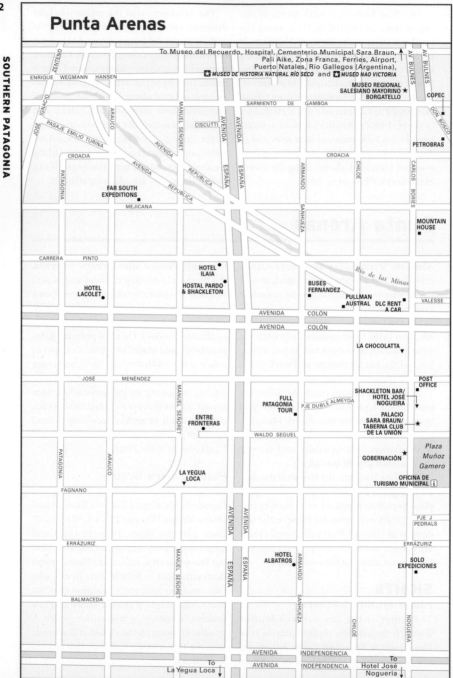

To Museo del Recuerdo, Hospital, Cementerio Municipal Sara Braun,
Pali Aike, Zona Franca, Ferries, Airport,
Puerto Natales, Río Gallegos (Argentina),
★ *MUSEO DE HISTORIA NATURAL RÍO SECO* and ★ *MUSEO NAO VICTORIA*

ENRIQUE   WEGMANN   HANSEN

ZENTENO

AV BULNES

AV BULNES

MUSEO REGIONAL
SALESIANO MAYORINO ★
BORGATELLO

COPEC

SARMIENTO   DE   GAMBOA

DON BOSCO

PETROBRAS

JOSÉ   IGNACIO

ARAUCO

MANUEL SEÑORET

CISCUTTI

AVENIDA

AVENIDA

REPÚBLICA

ESPAÑA

ARMANDO

CHILOE

CROACIA

CARLOS BORIES

PASAJE EMILIO TURINA

CROACIA

AVENIDA

AVENIDA

REPÚBLICA

SANHUEZA

PATAGONIA

FAR SOUTH
EXPEDITIONS ■

MEJICANA

MOUNTAIN
HOUSE ■

CARRERA   PINTO

HOTEL
ILAIA ●

Río de las Minas

HOTEL
LACOLET ●

HOSTAL PARDO
& SHACKLETON ●

BUSES
FERNÁNDEZ ■

PULLMAN
AUSTRAL ■   DLC RENT
A CAR

VALESSE

AVENIDA   COLÓN

AVENIDA   COLÓN

LA CHOCOLATTA ▼

POST
OFFICE ■

JOSÉ   MENÉNDEZ

MANUEL SEÑORET

FULL
PATAGONIA
TOUR ■

PJE DUBLE ALMEYDA

SHACKLETON BAR/
HOTEL JOSÉ
NOGUEIRA ■

ENTRE
FRONTERAS ■

PALACIO
SARA BRAUN/
TABERNA CLUB
DE LA UNIÓN ★

WALDO SEGUEL

PATAGONIA

ARAUCO

LA YEGUA
LOCA ▼

GOBERNACIÓN ★

Plaza
Muñoz
Gamero

OFICINA DE
TURISMO MUNICIPAL ℹ️

FAGNANO

PJE J
PEDRALS

ERRÁZURIZ

MANUEL SEÑORET

AVENIDA

AVENIDA

ESPAÑA

ARMANDO

HOTEL
ALBATROS ●

ERRÁZURIZ

SOLO
EXPEDICIONES ■

NOGUEIRA

BALMACEDA

SANHUEZA

CHILOE

AVENIDA   INDEPENDENCIA

AVENIDA   INDEPENDENCIA

To
La Yegua Loca ↓

To
Hotel José
Nogueira ↓

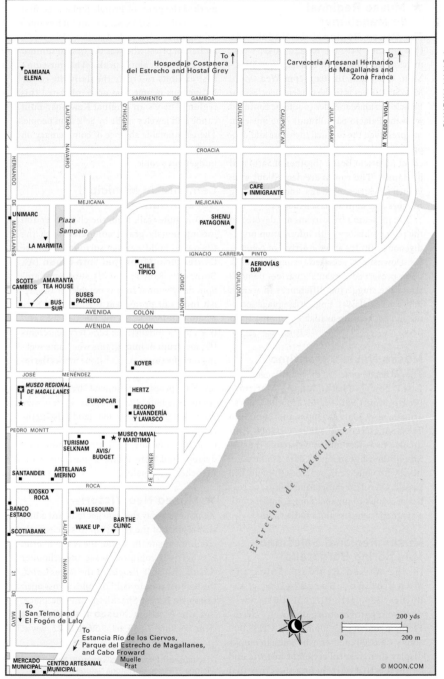

▼ DAMIANA ELENA

To ↑
Hospedaje Costanera del Estrecho and Hostal Grey

To ↑
Carveceria Artesanal Hernando de Magallanes and Zona Franca

LAUTARO

NAVARRO

O'HIGGINS

SARMIENTO DE GAMBOA

QUILLOTA

CAUPOLICAN

JULIA GARAY

M. TOLEDO VIOLA

HERNANDO

CROACIA

DE

MAGALLANES

MEJICANA

MEJICANA

CAFÉ
▼ INMIGRANTE

■ UNIMARC

Plaza
Sampaio

SHENU
PATAGONIA ●

▼ LA MARMITA

IGNACIO CARRERA PINTO

CHILE
TÍPICO ■

JORGE MONTT

■ AERIOVÍAS
DAP

SCOTT
CAMBIOS

AMARANTA
TEA HOUSE

■ BUS-
SUR

▼

■ BUSES
PACHECO

QUILLOTA

AVENIDA COLÓN

AVENIDA COLÓN

KOYER ■

JOSÉ MENÉNDEZ

✠ MUSEO REGIONAL
DE MAGALLANES
★

HERTZ ■

EUROPCAR ■

■ RECORD
LAVANDERÍA
Y LAVASCO

PEDRO MONTT

■ MUSEO NAVAL
★ Y MARÍTIMO

■ TURISMO
SELKNAM

■ AVIS/
BUDGET

PJE KÖRNER

■ SANTANDER

ARTELANAS
MERINO ■

ROCA

KIOSKO ▼
ROCA

LAUTARO

NAVARRO

■ BANCO
ESTADO

■ WHALESOUND

WAKE UP ▼

BAR THE
▼ CLINIC

■ SCOTIABANK

21

DE

MAYO

To
San Telmo and
El Fogón de Lalo

Estrecho de Magallanes

To
Estancia Río de los Ciervos,
Parque del Estrecho de Magallanes,
and Cabo Froward

Muelle
Prat

MERCADO
MUNICIPAL ■

■ CENTRO ARTESANAL
MUNICIPAL

0   200 yds
0   200 m

© MOON.COM

★ Museo Regional de Magallanes

The **Museo Regional de Magallanes** (Magallanes 949, tel. 61/2242 049, www. museodemagallanes.cl, 10:30am-5pm Wed.-Mon. Oct.-Apr., 10:30am-2pm Wed.-Mon. May-Sept., free) is in the opulent neoclassical Palacio Braun Menéndez (not to be confused with the Palacio Sara Braun). The museum has preserved the original furniture and decoration of the former residence of wool merchant Mauricio Braun (brother of Sara) and his family. The rooms are decked out with French tapestries, portraits, and even ceiling frescoes and stained glass windows.

The museum's back rooms are devoted to the region's history, with information on indigenous cultures and the arrival of colonizers. Downstairs, accessed through the back door, preserved servants' quarters demonstrate the staggering differences in wealth between the classes. English-language information packets are available from the front desk.

Museo Naval y Marítimo

The old headquarters of the Magallanes Naval Base is now the **Museo Naval y Marítimo** (Pedro Montt 981, tel. 61/2245 987, www. armada.cl, 9:30am-12:30pm and 2pm-5pm Tues.-Sat., CH$1,000 adults, CH$600 children), a two-story museum charting the history of the Chilean navy. Glass cabinets are filled with objects rescued from shipwrecked vessels. One of the museum's exhibits is a replica of a ship's command room, complete with a magnetic compass and a radio room.

Museo Regional Salesiano Maggiorino Borgatello

In the **Museo Regional Salesiano Maggiorino Borgatello** (Av. Bulnes 336, tel. 61/2221 001, www. museomaggiorinoborgatello.cl, 10am-12:30pm and 3pm-5:30pm daily, CH$3,000 adults, CH$200 children), the Salesian monks display their vast collection of historic and cultural artifacts, including the cross that marked the grave of Pringle Stokes, the first captain of the HMS *Beagle*, and items once belonging to Alberto de Agostini (1883-1960), an Italian priest who was the first to summit many of the region's peaks. The museum's best exhibits re-create the daily life of the indigenous people that once inhabited this region. There's an original Kawésqar-built canoe and jewelry made by Selk'nam people. There's a notable absence of commentary on the impact of the Salesian missions on these indigenous people.

Cementerio Municipal Sara Braun

A 20-minute walk from the city center and incongruously grand compared with the tin-roofed buildings that surround it, pretty **Cementerio Municipal Sara Braun** (Av. Bulnes 29, 8am-8pm daily summer, 8am-6pm daily winter, free) is notable for the lavish tombs of prominent townspeople Sara Braun and José Nogueira. Divided into sections by nationality, the cemetery represents the spectrum of immigrants who came seeking their fortunes. A tombstone marks the remains of the last member of the indigenous Selk'nam people, exterminated by ranch owners in the 1880s after European settlers were granted rights to indigenous land. Also in the cemetery is a somber monument of a dozen concrete columns, dedicated to those who disappeared from Punta Arenas under the Pinochet dictatorship.

★ Museo Nao Victoria

It's not every day that you get to board a life-size replica of the first ship to successfully circumnavigate the world, the *Nao Victoria*. Neither is it common to see the schooner *Ancud*, the HMS *Beagle*, or the *James Caird*, the lifeboat used to sail 720 miles across open ocean by Ernest Shackleton, in one place. But the excellent **Museo Nao Victoria** (Km 7.5 Ruta Y-565, tel. 9/9640 0772, www.

1: sculpture in Plaza Muñoz Gamero 2: Museo Nao Victoria 3: Museo de Historia Natural Río Seco

NAO VICTORIA
Ferdinand Magellan Ship, replica
Patagonia - Chile

naovictoria.cl, 9am-7pm daily, CH$4,000 adults, CH$1,500 children) offers exactly that. Each of the vessels was built using the exact dimensions of the originals. You can even go down into the ships' holds to get a sense of how claustrophobic the crews must have felt.

There's some information about the different voyages in English. It's worth tracking down the museum's owner, who's normally on-site and can give you more information about the vessels in competent English.

Museo del Recuerdo

The open-air **Museo de Recuerdo** (Av. Bulnes 1890, tel. 61/2207 051, www.museorecuerdo.cl, 8am-6pm daily Oct.-Mar., 9am-11am and 2pm-5pm daily Apr.-Sept., CH$2,500 adults, children under 14 free) makes a worthwhile stop on the way into Punta Arenas. It charts the city's history through a display of steam engines and steam cranes, rusting farm machinery, and even restored houses that were moved from across town. Pop into the garage, which contains a collection of late-1800s motorcars that belonged to businessman José Menéndez. You'll need a car to get here, or *colectivos* heading for the Zona Franca mall across the street can drop you off.

★ Museo de Historia Natural Río Seco

In a cavernous old warehouse, the truly marvelous **Museo de Historia Natural Río Seco** (Antiguo Frigorífico Río Seco, Y-565, tel. 9/5335 0707 or 9/5100 3791, http://mhnrioseco.weebly.com, ring for tours, donation) offers an astounding collection of land-based and marine animal specimens, all of which are native to the region. The main building contains a macabre but fascinating collection of skeletons, including false killer whales *(Pseudorca crassidens),* sea lions, and albatross. You can even watch the team cleaning and restoring skeletons in the workshop next door.

Located 13.5km north of Punta Arenas, a taxi is the only way to get here. Contact the museum a day in advance to arrange for an English-speaking guide to show you around.

ENTERTAINMENT

There's not a lot to do in Punta Arenas in the evening, and Sunday-Monday it can be difficult to find anything that's open.

If you're a fan of craft beer, **Cerveceria Artesanal Hernando de Magallanes** (Toledo Viola 220, tel. 61/2227 118, 10:30am-8pm Mon.-Sat., brewery tours Dec.-Feb.) is a good spot. They don't have an alcohol license, but you can buy three ales—an IPA, stout, and golden—or sample them at patio tables outside, as well as take a free tour of the brewery.

In the Hotel José Nogueri, the sumptuous **Shackleton Bar** (Bories 967, tel. 61/2711 000, www.hotelnogueira.com, 10:30am-midnight daily) has finely carved wooden furniture, ornate chandeliers, and paintings depicting Shackleton's voyage on the *Endurance,* with the chance for a quiet drink.

Decked out in chestnut furniture and wood paneling, with lowered ceilings reminiscent of an old-fashioned saloon or a ship, the **Taberna Club de la Unión** (Pedro Montt 701, tel. 61/2222 777, 7pm-3am Tues.-Sat.), in the basement of Palacio Sara Braun, gets busy on weekends. Find a shadowy nook for a pint of Patagonian beer or a pisco sour.

A meeting point for the young liberal community and decorated like an old saloon, **Bar The Clinic** (Errázuriz 970, tel. 61/2371 250, www.bartheclinicpuq.cl, 6pm-2:30am Mon.-Thurs, 6pm-3:30am Fri.-Sat.) offers good vibes and extensive beer, wine, and cocktails. With branches in Valparaiso and Santiago, the bar is named after a parodic political magazine.

SHOPPING

Artelanas Merino (Roca 848, tel. 61/2220 800, contacto@artelanosmerino.cl, 9:30am-7:30pm daily) sells beautiful sweaters and other merino wool clothing made by a weaving cooperative in the workshops out back. They also run two-hour classes (CH$15,000) where you make a small decorative piece of weaving.

Punta Arenas isn't known for its crafts, but the **Centro Artesanal Municipal** (inside Mercado Municipal, 21 de Mayo 1463) has a good selection of handmade baskets woven using indigenous Kawésqar techniques, as well as tapestries. Downstairs in the main part of the **Mercado Municipal,** you can find fish and tomato-red king crab.

A few kilometers northeast of the main plaza, the **Zona Franca** (Km 3.5 Av. Bulnes, 11am-1pm and 3pm-8:30pm Mon.-Fri., 11am-10:30pm Sat., 11am-1pm and 3pm-7:30pm Sun.) is a good place to pick up electrical items and hiking gear, although you'll likely find that prices are similar to those back home. To get here, catch the number 2 bus or any of the *colectivos* destined for the Zona Franca from Calle Magallanes.

RECREATION

For wildlife-focused tours, **Far South Expeditions** (Manuel Señoret 610, tel. 61/2615 793, www.farsouthexp.com), with expert naturalist guides, is the obvious choice. They run multiple-day excursions to destinations such as Isla Navarino, Puerto Williams, and Cape Horn, plus seven-day tours of Patagonia to different spots rich in birdlife.

Fly-fishing enthusiasts will find the trout-filled waters of the Río Penitente, north of Punta Arenas, appealing. Local experts **Magallanes Fly Fishing** (no phone, www. magallanesflyfishing.com) can organize full-day fishing tours (from US$375 pp, min. 2 people), with transport, food, an English-speaking guide, a fishing license, and fishing equipment included. They also operate full-day heli-fishing trips farther afield, plus multiple-day excursions to Tierra del Fuego. **Go Tierra del Fuego** (tel. 9/9741 5558, www. gotierradelfuego.com) specializes in multiple-day fishing trips to the Río Grande in Tierra del Fuego.

FOOD
Chilean

For Punta Arenas's specialty, king crab, head four blocks southwest of the plaza to the **Mercado Municipal** (21 de Mayo 1463, 11am-6pm daily, CH$5,000-8,000), where you'll find the freshest fish in town. Feast on plates piled high with *chupe de centolla* (thick, cheesy king crab stew), freshly fried empanadas, and the grilled catch of the day.

Eating at ★ **La Marmita** (Plaza Sampaio 678, tel. 61/2222 056, www.marmitamaga. cl, 12:30pm-11:30pm Mon.-Sat., CH$7,000-10,500, cash only), provides a sense of Punta Arenas's expansive history thanks to their library of books and magazines. They also combine innovative cooking with a charming, friendly ambience. Choose from roast guanaco, locally sourced hake with calamari spaghetti, or many vegetarian takes on classic Chilean dishes as you sip their legendary pisco sour. Reservations are recommended.

Book a table in the Terraza (a sun house in the front garden) of **La Yegua Loca** (Fagnano 310, tel. tel. 61/ 2371 734, www.yegualoca.com, 10am-10pm daily, CH$8,000-16,000) for spectacular views across Punta Arenas. The food is gourmet Patagonian cuisine of steak and fish, including many with *centolla* (king crab). Lamb dishes, such as the rich, slow-cooked lamb shank stew, are of particular note. The wine list and dessert selection are excellent; service can be variable.

Find everything from salmon to ceviche and fish stews along with meat, the highlight at local favorite ★ **San Telmo** (21 de Mayo 1502, tel. 61/2223 529, 12:30pm-3:30pm and 7:15pm-11:30pm Tues.-Sun., CH$6,000-14,000). Portions of steak are ample, with a selection of sauces and sides. The space might feel a little fussy and old-fashioned, but the pisco sours and superb, and knowledgeable servers set this place apart.

Upmarket **El Fogón de Lalo** (21 de Mayo 1650, tel. 61/2371 149, elfogondelalo@gmail. com, 8pm-11pm Mon.-Fri., 1pm-2:30pm and 8pm-11pm Sat., CH$7,000-15,000) is a grill house serving creatively plated beef and lamb.

Order steaks up to 32 ounces, cooked to perfection. An extensive wine selection completes the offerings. Oozing stylish modernity, the interior is simply decorated with memorabilia from the ranches of old Punta Arenas.

You'll need to make a reservation at the **Damiana Elena** (Magallanes 341, tel. 61/2222 818, 7:30pm-midnight daily except Mon., CH$10,000-16,000), in a grand old house and lit with elegant antique lamps. There's no fixed menu; instead, the chef rustles up different dishes each day, blending local ingredients with a modern twist. Pasta is the specialty, but there are always innovative fish and meat options, plus an expansive wine selection.

Light Bites

Channeling the vibe of an English tearoom with its cutesy decorations, **Amaranta Tea House** (Av. Colón 822, tel. 61/2371 132, 10am-9pm Mon.-Sat., CH$4,000-9,000, *menú del día* CH$5,900) is an excellent spot for British, German, and French tea. Vegetarian dishes and simple, tasty sandwiches steal the show. The lunch menu includes a main course and a cup of tea, excellent for the budget-conscious.

Inspired by New York coffeehouses, trendy ★ **Wake Up** (Errázuriz 944, tel. 61/2371 641, 7am-8pm Mon.-Fri., 9am-4pm Sat., 10am-4pm Sun., CH$2,800-6,000, *menú del día* CH$4,950) has the best coffee in town. Espresso, cappuccinos, and mochaccinos accompany specially brewed coffees made with a Chemex. Drinks are served from the recycled wooden-crate bar. Plenty of electrical sockets and fast Wi-Fi make this a good place to charge your batteries. Try one of their breakfast items, like eggs Benedict or the full English breakfast.

There's no more quintessential Punta Arenas experience than sitting at the bar at **Kiosko Roca** (Roca 875, tel. 61/2223 436, www.kioskoroca.cl, 7am-7pm Mon.-Fri., 8am-1pm Sat., CH$500-900), an award-winning *picada* (traditional family-run restaurant), and enjoying a traditional *choripán* (bread filled with a sausage and tomato paste) and a banana milk shake. This place is always packed, so ask to take it with you or hover to grab a vacated seat.

The residents of Punta Arenas take *once* (afternoon tea) seriously, and ★ **Café Inmigrante** (Quillota 599, tel. 61/2222 205, www.inmigrante.cl, 2:30pm-9pm Mon.-Thurs., 12:30pm-9pm Fri.-Sat., CH$3,500-7,000), in an early 20th-century building, is second to none, with 40 types of cake and a range of traditional sandwiches. Soak up the kitschy ambience of crotched curtains and Victorian-style photographs in garish gold frames.

An institution in Punta Arenas, **La Chocolatta** (Bories 852, tel. 61/2248 150, 10am-9pm Mon.-Sat., 10:30pm-9pm Sun., CH$4,000-8,000) is best known for its luxuriously thick hot chocolate—the perfect antidote to the city's chilly winds. They also serve decent coffee, cakes, and chocolate truffles made in house. The decor hasn't changed in years and includes fascinating black-and-white photos of the Magallanes region.

ACCOMMODATIONS
CH$25,000-40,000

A 10-minute walk from the city center, the welcoming ★ **Hospedaje Costanera del Estrecho** (Rómulo Correo 1221, tel. 61/2224 0175, hospedajecostanera2@gmail.com, CH$15,000 dorm, CH$30,000 d shared bath, CH$40,000 d private bath) is popular among backpackers and budget travelers. The kitchen is small but there's comfortable living space, plus central heating and 10 spotless baths for 12 rooms. Owners Teresa and Luís can provide information about tours and independent travel. Rates include IVA.

In the spotless **Hostal Grey** (Maipú 1186, tel. 9/6125 2007, CH$32,000 d shared bath), where you're received by the owner, Gabriela, the bedrooms are modern, if basic, with laminate wood flooring. Comfortable spaces to relax are scarce, but there's a communal kitchen and dining area where an ample breakfast—impressive for this price range—is provided. Five bedrooms share two sizeable baths. Rates include IVA.

Just five blocks northeast of the plaza on busy Avenida España, **Hostal Pardo & Shackleton** (Av. España 728, tel. 9/7767 6141, www.hostalpardoshackleton.com, CH$37,000 d shared bath) has six bedrooms on two floors. Some look onto the street but aren't plagued by traffic noise. Breakfast is very good for the cost, and a large communal kitchen, vast 2nd-floor sitting room, and friendly staff make this an excellent value. Rates include IVA.

CH$40,000-60,000

In a grand old stone-brick house, charming eight-room ★ **Hotel Lacolet** (Arauco 786, tel. 61/2222 045, CH$50,000 standard d, CH$56,000 superior d) is close enough to town but exudes peacefulness, particularly from its lovely sunny front garden. Standard doubles feel small; it's worth the extra cost for a superior with a king bed, although all the baths are small. Desk staff speak fluent English. Rates include IVA.

Everything about the friendly **Hotel Albatros** (Sanhueza 1248, tel. 61/2240 569 or 9/8223 7382, www.albatrospatagonia.cl, CH$53,000 d) is pleasant. Rooms are large and spotlessly clean, with white baths, wood laminate flooring, and bird-themed decor. Service is attentive, and breakfast better than you'd expect at these rates. There is also private parking and laundry service.

Six superbly priced apartments at **Entre Fronteras** (Waldo Segel 322, tel. 9/6404 3371, www.entrefronteras.cl, CH$60,000 for 4 people) have fully fitted open-plan kitchens, living rooms with dining tables, and two upstairs bedrooms. The owners deliver breakfast to your kitchen and offer a free daily cleaning service. This is a good option for couples visiting outside high season, as they offer a 25 percent discount for double occupancy during the off season. You can also get a discount on a rental vehicle if you book through the jointly owned DLC Rent A Car. Rates include IVA.

Over CH$80,000

The ultramodern ★ **Shenu Patagonia** (Quillota 658, tel. 61/2371 573, www.shenupatagonia.cl, CH$82,800 4-person cabin) has four stylish cabins with everything you need for your stay, thanks to a fully equipped kitchen with a breakfast bar, large baths with stone washbasins, and sizeable master bedrooms with king beds (the lounge has a pullout sofa bed). Secure parking, safes, and the welcoming owners add to the appeal. Book a month in advance in high season. Rates include IVA.

Swedish design-inspired **Hotel Ilaia** (Carrera Pinto 351, tel. 61/2723 100, www.ilaiapatagonia.com, Sept.-Apr., CH$94,000 d) is an oasis of calm four blocks northwest of the plaza. This serene eight-bed boutique hotel has larger-than-average bedrooms with equally sizeable king beds plus slick new bath suites. Breakfast is excellent—there's no going hungry here—but the real defining feature of the hotel is its beautiful 3rd-floor sitting room, where floor-to-ceiling windows grant views across the city. Secure parking is available. Massages and yoga classes are offered at additional cost. Rates include IVA.

Charmingly rustic with authentic Patagonian history, **Estancia Río de los Ciervos** (Km 5.5 Sur, tel. 61/2262 281 www.estanciariodelosciervos.com, CH$115,000 d) is the perfect place to escape. A 10-minute drive south along the Magellan Strait, this hotel was once a sheep ranch; its seven rooms are still filled with antique furniture. The spacious double at the front of the house is the comfiest. Also on the property are horse-drawn carriages and a museum offering a brief history of the Magallanes region. Rates include IVA.

With individual themes for each bedroom, luxurious ★ **La Yegua Loca** (Fagnano 310, tel. 61/2371 734, www.yegualoca.com, CH$119,000 standard d, CH$138,000 superior d) is in a league of its own. Every detail has been considered, from old-fashioned bath fittings to antique wooden furniture. The four superior rooms have views and balconies; the four standard rooms lack good views. Service is on par with the price range. The attached restaurant is superb.

A piece of living history in Punta Arenas, **Hotel José Nogueira** (Bories 967, tel. 61/2711 000, www.hotelnogueira.com, CH$134,000 d) is in the Palacio Sara Braun. Rooms have been updated with modern white baths but still contain antique furniture, including very low beds. For a quiet sleep away from the noise of the square, ask for a room on the 3rd floor. The downstairs greenhouse-cum-breakfast room contains the oldest grapevines in southern Chile, while the Shackleton Bar, with its sumptuous satin curtains, is worth a visit whether you're staying here or not. The room rates are cut in half April-September. Rates include IVA.

INFORMATION AND SERVICES

Residents of Punta Arenas enthusiastically continue the Spanish tradition of the siesta; it can be difficult to find any businesses open 1pm-3pm.

Mostly helpful, the English-speaking staff at **SERNATUR** (José Fagnano 643, tel. 61/2248 790, www.patagonia-chile.com, 8:30am-8pm Mon.-Fri., 10am-6pm Sat.-Sun.) has a wide selection of information about Southern Patagonia and can provide maps of the Dientes de Navarino trek in Puerto Williams. On the southwestern corner of Plaza Muñoz Gamero, within a picturesque restored 19th-century kiosk, the **Oficina de Turismo Municipal** (tel. 61/2200 610, www. puntaarenas.cl, 8am-8pm Mon.-Fri., 9am-7pm Sat., 9am-5pm Sun.) also provides useful tourist information.

The **Hospital Naval de las Fuerzas** (Av. Bulnes 256, tel. 61/2207 500) can deal with medical emergencies. For the mail, head to **Correos** (Bories 911, no phone, www.correos. cl, 9am-6:30pm Mon.-Fri., 10am-1pm Sat.).

A number of currency exchange shops are on Calle Navarro, between Pedro Montt and Roca. You can change Argentinean pesos and other currencies at **SCOTT Cambios** (Av.

Colón 822 D, 10am-1pm and 2pm-6pm Tues.-Sat., 10am-1pm Sun.). To withdraw cash, **Santander** (21 de Mayo 800), **Scotiabank** (21 de Mayo 1190), and **BancoEstado** (Muñoz Gamero 799) have ATMs directly on the main square or half a block away. For laundry, head to **Record Lavanderia y Lavasco** (O'Higgins 969, 9am-5:30pm Mon.-Fri., 10am-3pm Sat.).

The closest gas stations to the center of the city are **Petrobras** (Diagonal Don Bosco 464) and **COPEC** (Diagonial Don Bosco s/n). A number of other gas stations are on Avenida Presidente Manuel Bulnes, heading northeast of the city toward Ruta 9.

To stock up on groceries, head to the well-stocked central **UNIMARC supermarket** (Carlos Bories 647, www.unimarc.cl, 9am-10pm Mon.-Sat., 11am-7pm Sun.). There's another location (Av. España, no phone, 9am-10pm daily) on the road northwest out of the city.

SIG Patagon produces excellent trail maps of Torres del Paine National Park and maps for Tierra del Fuego and Isla Navarino. Buy them at **Mountain House** (Bories 655, Local 2, tel. 61/2222 219, http://mountainhouse.cl, 10:30am-1pm and 3:30pm-8pm daily).

GETTING THERE

Punta Arenas is the easiest of the Chilean cities in Southern Patagonia to reach, with frequent air links from Santiago and Puerto Montt, and onward flights to Porvenir in Chilean Tierra del Fuego and Puerto Williams on Isla Navarino. Overland buses cross the Argentinean border to Ushuaia, and ferries link the city with Chilean Tierra del Fuego and Puerto Williams. A luxury cruise ship also connects Punta Arenas with Ushuaia, with stops along the way at Cape Horn.

Air

Aeropuerto Internacional Presidente Carlos Ibáñez del Campo (PUQ, km 20.5 Ruta 9, tel. 62/2238 282) is 22km north of the city. **LATAM** (Av. Eduardo Frei Montalva

01110, no phone, www.latam.com, 11am-8pm daily), **Sky Airline** (www.skyairline.com), and **JetSmart** (www.jetsmart.com) have at least four daily nonstop flights between Santiago and Punta Arenas; a handful of others travel via Puerto Montt, while two daily nonstop flights connect Puerto Montt and Punta Arenas. LATAM also runs weekly Saturday flights between Punta Arenas and Mount Pleasant on the Falkland Isles.

Aeriovías DAP (Ignacio Carrera Pinto 1015, tel. 61/2229 936, www.dapairline.com, 8:30am-6:15pm Mon.-Fri., 9am-1pm and 3pm-6pm Sat.) has three flights (15min) Monday-Friday and two on Saturday between Porvenir and Punta Arenas. One daily flight (40min, Mon.-Sat.) connects Puerto Williams and Punta Arenas. On Tuesday, flights link the city with Aeródromo Balmaceda in Coyhaique (1.25hr). November-March, the airline offers Wednesday and Saturday departures from Ushuaia (30min).

Small minivans wait outside the airport and charge CH$5,000 pp to drop off at your hotel; **Transfer Fin Del Mundo** (tel. 61/2244 560, www.turismofindelmundo.cl) is a good option. A taxi will cost CH$7,000-10,000 to take you from the airport to your hotel in town. Try **Radio Taxi Cofrima** (tel. 61/2214 063, www.radiotaxicofrima.cl) or **Taxi Las Vertientes** (tel. 61/2230 087).

Buses between Punta Arenas and Puerto Natales generally stop at the airport on the way; confirm with the driver when you board. To continue to Puerto Natales from the airport, **Bus Sur** (www.bussur.com) has seven services that pass the airport (3.25hr, CH$8,000); you must make a reservation online as there is nowhere to purchase tickets in the terminal.

Taking marginally less time than the public bus, **private transfers** (CH$135,000 for 2 passengers) between the airport and hotels in Punta Arenas and Puerto Natales are operated by **Full Patagonia Tour** (Armando Sanhueza 974, tel. 61/2723 198, www.fullpatagoniatour.com).

Boat

Transbordadora Austral Broom (TABSA, Terminal de Ferry Tres Puentes, tel. 61/2728 100, www.tabsa.cl) runs most of the **passenger ferries** between Punta Arenas and Tierra del Fuego. There are two crossings daily in summer, one daily in winter, Tuesday-Sunday to and from **Porvenir** (2.25hr, CH$6,800 passengers, CH$43,500 vehicle including driver), leaving from the **Terminal de Ferry Tres Puentes,** 5km north of Punta Arenas center. Getting to the ferry terminal costs about CH$3,000 in a taxi or CH$800 in a *colectivo* from Calle Magallanes. The ferry docks at the **TABSA port** (Y-625) in Bahía Chilota, 5km west of Porvenir. Schedules change regularly, so consult TABSA's website or visit either ferry terminal to confirm departure times. Advance bookings, particularly for vehicles, are essential in high season.

The **passenger and cargo ferry** trip aboard the *Yaghan* (32hr, CH$151,110 full reclining seat) runs to and from **Puerto Williams.** It's operated by Transbordadora Austral Broom and departs twice weekly from the **ferry ramp** (Costanera s/n, opposite Café Luisa) in Puerto Williams and docks at the **Terminal de Ferry Tres Puentes** in Punta Arenas. Bookings must be made two months in advance in high season. It's possible to reserve a *semi-cama* (partially reclining) seat starting 24 hours before departure; before that, they're reserved for Puerto Williams residents. Three daily meals are included. Taking the ferry to Puerto Williams is vastly more spectacular than going in the opposite direction. Weather permitting, the ferry will pass along the scenic Glacier Alley during daylight hours.

For boats to and from **Ushuaia,** the only option is via the **cruise ships** *Ventus Australis* and *Stella Australis* with adventure operator **Australis** (tel. 2/2840 0100, www.australis.com). These ply the Chilean fjords of Tierra del Fuego on a four-night cruise via Glacier Alley and Cape Horn, either beginning or ending in Ushuaia. They also offer six- and eight-night options. Reservations are required in advance. Good discounts are often available in shoulder seasons (September-October and late March). Cruises start at US$5,180 for a two-person cabin with two twin beds. Passengers must present themselves at the offices of tourism agency **Tolkeyén** (Av. San Martín 409, Ushuaia, tel. 54/11 5983 9402) in Ushuaia or at **Muelle Prat** (Av. Costanera del Estrecho 1398, Punta Arenas, tel. 2/2840 0100) in Punta Arenas for check-in.

Bus

There's no central bus terminal in Punta Arenas; all buses depart and arrive from individual offices. From its upscale terminal with a waiting room and Wi-Fi, **Bus Sur** (Av. Colón 842, tel. 61/2614 224, www.bussur. com) has 10 daily buses to and from **Puerto Natales** (3.25hr, CH$8,000) September-April. **Buses Fernández** (Armando Sanhueza 745, tel. 61/2242 313, www.busesfernandez.com) has a similar number of departures.

Half a block down the street from Bus Sur, **Buses Pacheco** (Av. Colón 900, tel. 61/2242 174, www.busespacheco.com) has three weekly buses from **Ushuaia** (6am Tues., Thurs., and Sat., 12hr, CH$38,000), with a connection to a new bus in Río Grande. Two and a half blocks northwest along Avenida Colón, **Pullman Austral** (Colón 568, tel. 61/2223 359) runs the long journey from **Puerto Montt** (32hr, CH$45,000) departing at 10:30am once or twice weekly, dropping to once a week March-November.

Car

Paved **Ruta 9** connects **Puerto Natales** with Punta Arenas, a three-hour drive of 250km south through a landscape of sun-scorched grasslands and the Strait of Magellan. To get here from **Porvenir** in Chilean Tierra del Fuego, it's a 2.5-hour, 132-km drive along mostly paved road to Cruce Bahía Azul, where the ferry operated by **Transbordadora Austral Broom** (tel. 61/2728 100, www.tabsa. cl, 8:30am and 1am daily, 20min, CH$15,000 car including passengers, CH$1,700 foot passengers, cash only) crosses to Cruce Punta Delgada. From here, you connect with the paved

Ruta 255 that runs southwest, joining Ruta 9 in 115km as it continues to Punta Arenas.

To drive from **Ushuaia,** take Ruta 3, the only road north, until **Paso San Sebastián** (no phone, 24 hr daily summer, 8am-10pm daily winter) and the border crossing into Chile. You cannot bring any animal products into Chile and will be fined if you do not declare them at customs. From here, it's 45km along unpaved Ruta 257 before this road turns north, and it is paved for the final 115km to Cruce Bahía Azul and the ferry crossing to join Ruta 255 heading west to Punta Arenas.

GETTING AROUND

Within the city center, it's easy enough to get around on foot. To reach the Zona Franca or the Terminal de Ferry Tres Puentes, take a taxi *colectivo* (note the destination written on the roof). *Colectivos* pass along Calle Magallanes at regular intervals.

All taxis have **meters** (ask the driver to use the *reloj*) with a journey around the center costing around CH$2,000. Try **Radio Taxi Cofrima** (tel. 61/2214 063, www. radiotaxicofrima.cl) or **Taxi Las Vertientes** (tel. 61/2230 087).

Car Rental

There are numerous car rental options in Punta Arenas. Smaller rental agencies rarely offer roadside assistance; finding yourself stranded in the middle of remote Patagonia can be less than fun.

Inside the city, you'll find **DLC Rent A Car** (Bories 786, tel. 61/2240 0965, www. dlcrentacar.com), **Avis/Budget** (Pedro Montt 969, tel. 61/2614 381, www.avis.com, 9am-12:30pm and 2:30pm-7pm Mon.-Fri., 10am-12:30pm Sat.), **Hertz** (O'Higgins 931 tel. 61/2613 087, www.hertz.com, 9am-7pm Mon.-Fri., 9am-2pm Sat.), **Europcar** (O'Higgins 964, tel. 61/2746 580, www.europcar.cl, 9am-1pm and 3pm-7pm Mon.-Fri., 9am-1pm Sat.), and **Koyer** (José Menéndez 1024, tel. 61/2243 357, www.arriendoskoyer.com, 9am-1pm and 3pm-7pm Mon.-Fri., 9am-2pm Sat.). Most can organize airport pickup for an extra fee. In the arrivals terminal of the airport are offices of **Avis/Budget** (tel. 61/2614 381, 9am-7pm daily), **Hertz** (tel. 61/2613 087, 7:30am-11pm daily), and **Europcar** (tel. 61/2743 940, 8am-9pm daily).

A campervan can be an excellent way to explore Patagonia, allowing for greater flexibility. Outside the cities, you can park and sleep practically anywhere. **Wicked Campers** (tel. 9/4207 3790, www.wickedsouthamerica.com), **Chile Motor Homes** (tel. 9/9743 3141, www. chilemotorhomes.cl), and **Holiday Rent** (tel. 2/2409 4185, www.holidayrent.cl) offer campervan rental, including the required additional insurance for driving into Argentina.

ONWARD TO ANTARCTICA AND CAPE HORN

Excursions to Antarctica typically depart from Ushuaia in Argentinean Tierra del Fuego, farther south. If you're short on time and have substantial cash to spare, you can fly from Punta Arenas. **Aerovías DAP** (Ignacio Carrera Pinto 1015, tel. 61/2229 936, www.dapairline.com, 8:30am-6:15pm Mon.-Fri., 9am-1pm and 3pm-6pm Sat.), operating under the name **Antarctica Airways,** offers five-hour day tours and overnight trips to Antarctica, landing on King George Island and taking Zodiac boats to penguin colonies. Overnight tours include camping and a visit to an elephant seal colony. Rates start at US$5,500 for a day tour. Flights are often rescheduled due to poor weather, so the tour price includes four nights in a Punta Arenas hotel, allowing for multiple attempts if your original flight is canceled.

Aerovías DAP also offers 20-minute fly-overs of Cape Horn via charter flight. The round-trip is 3.5 hours. Flights cost US$7,470 for a six-person plane.

Vicinity of Punta Arenas

Beyond the city of Punta Arenas are a number of places of historical and geographical interest. The best way to appreciate them is by car or on a costly tour.

FUERTE BULNES

In March 1584, Pedro Sarmiento de Gamboa's fleet landed at Punta Santa Ana, 60km south of modern-day Punta Arenas. Of the 23 ships and 3,000 men that had started the voyage, only three ships and 300 men arrived, after a series of dreadful storms and disasters. After landing, the colonists constructed Ciudad del Rey Don Felipe. The Spaniards soon realized the location was too barren and remote. When English privateer Thomas Cavendish and his crew landed here three years later, all they found were the ruins of the colony and one surviving resident, Tomé Hernández. From that day, it acquired the name Port Famine, **Puerto del Hambre.** The site is not accessible to the public.

Two kilometers farther south along the Punta Santa Ana peninsula, **Fuerte Bulnes** was the next part of the Strait of Magellan to be settled, after the Chilean schooner *Ancud* sailed from Chiloé. Arriving at Punta Santa Ana on September 21, 1843, the new colony had only marginally better luck; they relocated to the site of modern Punta Arenas in 1849.

Punta Santa Ana and Fuerte Bulnes have been preserved as **Parque del Estrecho de Magallanes** (no phone, www. straitofmagellanpark.cl, 9:30am-6:30pm Mon.-Fri., 9:30am-7pm Sat.-Sun. summer, 10:30am-6:30pm daily winter, CH$14,000 adults, CH$6,000 children), an upscale private park that charges an exorbitant entry fee. A 2-km drive from the entrance gate brings you to the **Centro de Interpretación,** with a museum about the strait's first explorers, as well as a small shop and a cafeteria. The center's large rooms offer displays on the recession of Patagonia's glaciers, the region's indigenous peoples, and local flora and fauna—though all of these are light on information. The English-language tours in the Centro de Interpretación (12:30pm and 3:30pm Mon.-Fri., 12:30pm, 3:30pm, and 5:30pm Sat.-Sun.) and in the fort (11am and 5pm Mon.-Fri., 11am, 2pm, and 5pm Sat.-Sun.) help to fill in some of the gaps.

A gravel road continues through the *torreones* (guard towers) to restored Fuerte Bulnes. Inside is detailed information (in English and Spanish) about the fort's colorful history. There's also a two-story jail. The views across the strait are spectacular, though you'll have to brave the fierce winds.

Look for seabirds, whales, and even pumas on two short trails: the 300-meter Wind Forest that departs from the fort, and, 50 meters into the path, the 1.5-km Coastal Trail circuit. The weather is extremely changeable and the location exposed, so bring good footwear and warm clothing.

A taxi here will cost CH\$40,000, including 1-2 hours of waiting. Tours with companies such as **Turismo Selknam** (Pedro Montt 913, tel. 2/2254 1698, www.turismoselknam.cl) generally start at CH\$15,000 pp, excluding the park's entrance fee. It's simpler and cheaper if you have your own vehicle.

CABO FROWARD

The southernmost point of continental South America, **Cabo Froward** is the point where the Atlantic and Pacific Oceans meet. The cape is 30km southwest of where the 70-km road from Punta Arenas ends. There's no road to the cape; the only way to reach it is via a five-day round-trip trek. At the cape's highest point, 365 meters above the crashing waves, towering **Cruz de los Mare** (Cross of the Sea) commemorates Pope John Paul II's visit to the Magallanes region in 1987. If the weather is clear, there are sweeping views down and across the Strait of Magellan to the distant mountains of Isla Dawson in the east and the two-peaked Monte Sarmiento southeast.

The five-day, 78-km round-trip trek to Cabo Froward starts at the end of the road from Punta Arenas, 70km south of town. It's a challenging, poorly marked trail that passes through remote and demanding terrain of forest and peat bog. Heavy rain means a likelihood of waist- to neck-high river crossings, and there are no facilities en route, so you'll need to find a dry spot to camp. You'll also need to time your hike with the tide so that you can cross sections of the beach during low tide. **SHOA** (www.shoa.cl), the Chilean navy's hydrographic and oceanographic website, has tide tables. Only those with considerable hiking experience should do this trek; don't attempt it alone.

Trekking Tours

The Puerto Natales-based **Erratic Rock** (Baquedano 955, Puerto Natales, www.erraticrock.com) offers five-day, four-night Cabo Froward trekking tours (from US\$900); you're expected to carry all your belongings.

Getting There

Transportation to the trailhead can be arranged with help from the Punta Arenas office of **SERNATUR** (José Fagnano 643, Punta Arenas, tel. 61/2248 790, www.patagonia-chile.com, 8:30am-8pm Mon.-Fri., 10am-6pm Sat.-Sun.). Where the road ends, 70km southwest of Punta Arenas, there is space for one or two cars to park. Day-trippers from Punta Arenas can also drive here and stop to enjoy the spectacular views of the Strait of Magellan.

PARQUE NACIONAL PALI AIKE

Surrounded by arid shrubs, sharp *coirón* grass, and grazing animals, **Parque Nacional Pali Aike** (tel. 61/2360 489, parque.paliaike@conaf.cl, 8:30am-8pm daily Oct.-Apr., CH\$3,000 adults, CH\$1,000 children) is a strange volcanic landscape cut through by black, red, and gray lava flows and wide craters. Established as a national park in 1970, this 5,000-hectare reserve has a fantastical quality. Meaning "desolate place of bad spirits" in the Tehuelche language, Pali Aike is the perfect place to escape other travelers—only around 2,500 visitors make it here each year. For such a barren-seeming place, there's a wealth of wildlife; watch for armadillos, skunks, and gray foxes. The park is also known for its puma population.

The **visitors center** at the park entrance is staffed by a CONAF ranger who can provide maps and information about the park's history and geography. At the visitors center are displays of arrowheads and other lithic tools uncovered in the park, plus a collection of puma skulls. There are public restrooms here. Camping is not allowed in the park, except next to the visitors center, if you request permission from the ranger. Sturdy footwear and windproof clothing is a must for hiking.

The main sights in the park can all be reached by vehicle along a gravel road. During archaeological digs in the 1930s at **Cueva Pali Aike,** the cave was found to contain signs of early human inhabitants and local megafauna, including the *Mylodon,* a type of giant sloth, and the *Onohippidium,* a species of horse, dating back over 8,000 years. The cave is perhaps the least interesting part of the park as it lacks information to contextualize the large, empty space. Note that this isn't the cave where the *Mylodon* associated with Bruce Chatwin comes from; you can find this at the **Monumento Natural Cueva del Milodón,** northwest of Puerto Natales.

Eight kilometers from the cave, a car park marks the start of the 1.7-km hike to the **Escorial del Diablo** (Devil's Slag Heap), which approaches the rim of the volcanic crater **Morada del Diablo** (Devil's Dwelling). From here, a 2-km path heads east through crunchy lava flows to the **Pozos del Diablo,** two huge craters. Avoid getting too close to the edge of the craters, as the wind is fierce. You can also reach **Laguna Ana** via a 9-km footpath from Cueva Pali Aike or from a car park 500 meters from the water; look for flamingos, who come to breed December-January, in the water.

Getting There

The park is 200km northeast of Punta Arenas, a three-hour drive north on Ruta 9 and east on Ruta 255. From the village of Punta Delgado, take the gravel Y-405 heading north. No public transport serves the park.

Tour agencies in Punta Arenas offer park tours (from CH$40,000 pp); expect to pay more for fewer than three people. It's far cheaper to rent a car for the day in Punta Arenas. You can stay overnight in Punta Delgada, where there are a handful of passable lodgings. **Hostal San Gregorio** (Punta Delgada s/n, tel. 61/2642 636, www. hostalsangregorio.cl, CH$15,000 pp) has comfortable two- and three-bedroom cabins with baths. Meals are an additional CH$8,000.

★ MONUMENTO NATURAL LOS PINGÜINOS

Drawing huge crowds every summer when the 120,000-strong Magellanic penguin colony returns to nest, the 97-hectare **Isla Magdalena** is a great place to get close to these birds. Isla Magdalena was declared the **Monumento Natural Los Pingüinos** (Penguins Natural Monument, tel. 9/8794 9646, magallanes. oirs@conaf.cl, Oct.-Apr., CH$7,000 adults, CH$3,500 children) in 1982; the reserve is administered by CONAF.

Isla Magdalena is 35km northeast of Punta Arenas along the Strait of Magellan, reached by a two-hour ferry ride or a 30-minute speedboat trip. Visitors disembark on the east side of the island. An 800-meter path is lined by thousands of wandering penguins hooting and braying loudly to one another from their nests in the ground and squabbling over nesting materials. The path leads to Faro Magdalena (Magdalena Lighthouse).

Around 32,000 tourists visit the island each year November-March, when the birds are in residence, although a few stragglers remain into April. The best months are December-February, when the colony is at its most numerous, including newly hatched chicks.

Each group of visitors is allowed just one hour on the island, plenty of time to get close to the penguins, who have become so used to people that they'll likely wander into your photographs. Note that there are no facilities on the island; a small cafeteria and restrooms are on the ferry.

The island is home to cormorants, Chilean skuas, flightless ducks, and upland geese. The boat ride is an opportunity to spot dolphins, including the local *tonina* or Chilean dolphin. The number of penguins decreases rapidly at the end of the season, when they migrate north to Brazil for the winter.

Getting There

November-April, the ferry M/V *Malinka,* operated by **Transbordadora Austral Broom** (TABSA, Terminal de Ferry Tres Puentes, Punta Arenas, tel. 61/2728 100, www.tabsa. cl), departs twice daily from the Terminal de Ferry Tres Puentes in Punta Arenas (a 15-minute taxi journey from the city center), taking 1.5 hours to arrive at the island. The round-trip journey costs CH$50,000 adults, CH$25,000 children, with a guide. Buy tickets from TABSA or with the more conveniently located tour agency **Comapa** (Lautaro Navarro 1112, tel. 61/2200 200, www.comapa. com), in the center of Punta Arenas. Reserve a day or two in advance in high season. This is the cheapest option for visiting the penguins, but there can be up to 220 passengers disembarking onto the island at one time.

Solo Expediciones (José Nogueira 1255, Punta Arenas, tel. 61/2710 219, www. soloexpediciones.com) offers daily speedboat tours (6:30am departure, CH$63,000 pp) to Isla Magdalena and the sea lion colony on Isla Marta. Taking a speedboat cuts the journey to the island to 30 minutes each way, but if the sea is rough, the ride can be unpleasant. The boats carry up to 67 passengers and arrive at a different time from the ferry passengers, making for a far more pleasant experience on the island. Transfers to and from the boat's departure point plus tea and coffee are included in the cost.

Most journeys between Punta Arenas and Ushuaia aboard the adventure cruise ships *Stella Australis* and *Ventus Australis,* operated by **Australis** (tel. 2/2840 0100, www.australis. com), make a stop at Isla Magdalena, but at a different time of the day than the other boats.

PARQUE MARINO FRANCISCO COLOANE

Humpbacks normally migrate south to Antarctica to feed, but many remain in the Strait of Magellan during summer, making it their only nonpolar feeding location. December-May are the best months for whale-watching, especially in the waters around **Isla Carlos III,** an island in the western half of the Strait of Magellan. You can expect gymnastic displays of tail splashing and even breaching. In 1994, the 67,000 hectares of water and land that surround Isla Carlos III were protected as the **Parque Marino Francisco Coloane** (no phone, 24 hr daily, free). Plenty of species of seabirds and even orcas are seen here.

The only way to visit Isla Carlos III is via a whale-watching tour. **Whale Sound** (Lautaro Navarro 1191, Punta Arenas, tel. 61/2221 935, www.whalesound.com) is the pioneer of tourism and research in the region. From your hotel in Punta Arenas, a transfer takes you to the jetty at Punta Carrera, where a nine-hour sail aboard the 16-passenger *Tanu* brings you to Isla Carlos III. This is your home for three days and two nights, taking excursions to wildlife colonies, Glaciar Santa Ines, and to look for humpback whales. Whale Sound runs the remote Eco Camp Carlos III on the island, which offers simple accommodations in geodesic domes heated by wood-burning stoves and with separate baths. Included in the tour cost are scientific talks in English led by researchers, all food and drink, and hotel transfers. Prices start at US$1,500. Passage along the strait can be tough during poor weather, so bring anti-nausea medication.

1: aboard the *Yaghan* ferry 2: Fuerte Bulnes
3: Monumento Natural Los Pingüinos

Another option to visit the island is aboard the MN *Forrest,* a transformed cargo ship, with **Expedición Fitz Roy** (Roca 825, Oficina 3, Punta Arenas, tel. 61-2613932, www.expedicionfitzroy.com). This live-aboard trip sails from Punta Carrera, 50km south of Punta Arenas, around Isla Carlos III, with excursions by Zodiac boats to Glaciar Santa Ines and whale-watching in the surrounding waters. Guests sleep in cabins on board; for a two-night, three-day tour, rates start at US$1,070 pp d, with shared bath, including transfer to the ship. Private baths are also available.

If you're short on time, **Solo Expediciones** (José Nogueira 1255, Punta Arenas, tel. 61/2710 219, www.soloexpediciones.com) runs an exhausting 12- to 14-hour tour (CH$245,000 pp) from Punta Arenas to the outskirts of the marine park, with the chance to view resident humpback whales. Included in the rates are bilingual guides, breakfast, lunch, hot drinks, and transportation from their office to the port in Punta Arenas.

Puerto Natales

On the eastern shore of Seno Última Esperanza (Last Hope Sound), the small town of Puerto Natales has impressive views west across sprawling Peninsula Antonio Varas and the knife-edge peaks of Parque Nacional Bernardo O'Higgins. Puerto Natales was once a quiet port town that played a major role in the sheep and wool trade, when the surrounding steppe was dotted with *estancias* (ranches).

Nowadays, Puerto Natales is Chilean Southern Patagonia's most visited town, with thousands treading its streets during the windy summer as they prepare for their trekking adventures in Parque Nacional Torres del Paine. With facilities for organizing rental gear, tours, and excellent restaurants, it's ideal for a pre- and post-park stay. The vast majority of attractions are in the national park, but a number of nearby ranches and glaciers make interesting day trips.

SIGHTS

Puerto Natales is compact, centered on the large **Plaza de Armas Arturo Prat** (bounded by Carlos Bories, Arturo Prat, Hermann Eberhard, and Tomás Rogers), with towering pine trees and a large water feature. Surrounding the plaza are the town's most important buildings, including the lemon-yellow **Parroquia María Auxiliadora** (Eberhard, mass 7pm Tues.-Sat., 11pm and 7pm Sun.), built in 1918 with a 30-meter tower, one of the tallest buildings in town.

Next door, you can't miss the striking 1929 **Municipalidad,** replete with crimson wood paneling. The 2nd-floor balcony was used by town authorities to announce civil and military activities. Half a block east along Calle Eberhard and painted in similar style is the **Casa de la Familia Vidal,** one of the oldest remaining buildings in Puerto Natales. It dates to 1925-1928, built by a local Spanish family using materials brought from Spain. Note its Moorish-style turret.

One block southwest of the plaza, the well-organized **Museo Histórico Municipalidad Natales** (Bulnes 285, tel. 61/2209 534, 8am-7pm Mon.-Fri., 10am-1pm and 3pm-7pm Sat. Nov.-Mar., 8am-5pm Mon.-Thurs., 8am-4pm Fri. Apr.-Oct., CH$1,000 adults, free under 12) makes a great introduction to the indigenous cultures and people of Patagonia. Extensive displays with English translations cover the daily life, art, belief systems, and funerary rituals of the Kawésqar and the Tehuelche peoples, contextualizing the demise of their cultures, first with the arrival of the Spanish in the 15th century and the second wave of Europeans to Southern Patagonia and Tierra del Fuego.

Three blocks west of the plaza along the coastal Avenida Pedro Montt, industrial

Puerto Natales

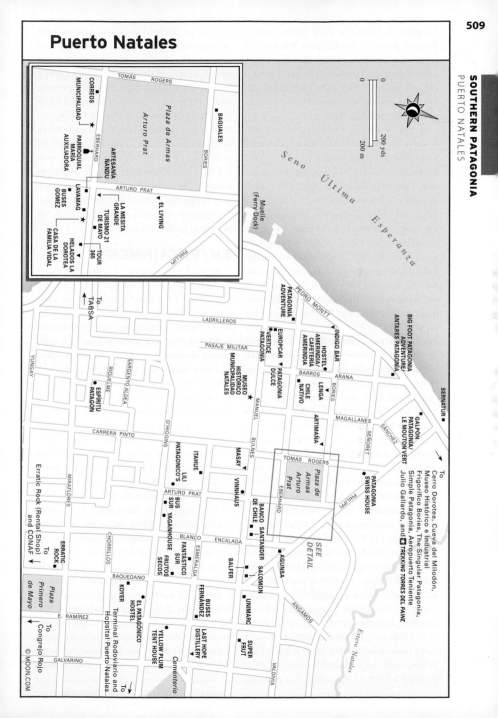

Detail map (inset):
- TOMÁS ROGERS
- CORREOS
- MUNICIPALIDAD
- BAGUALES
- EBERHARD
- Plaza de Armas Arturo Prat
- BORIES
- PARROQUIAL MARÍA AUXILIADORA
- ARTESANÍA ÑANDU
- ARTURO PRAT
- BUSES GOMEZ
- LAVAMAG
- LA MESITA GRANDE
- TURISMO 21
- TUR 365
- TOUR 365
- EL LIVING
- HELADOS LA DOROTEA
- CASA DE LA FAMILIA VIDAL
- PHILLIPI

Seno Última Esperanza

Muelle (Ferry Dock)

0 200 yds
0 200 m

Main map:
- To TABSA
- PEDRO MONTT
- PATAGONIA ADVENTURE
- LADRILLEROS
- BIG FOOT PATAGONIA ADVENTURE / ANTARES PATAGONIA
- PASAJE MILITAR
- HOSTEL AMERINDIA / CAFETERÍA AMERINDIA
- INDIGO BAR
- EUROPCAR
- VÉRTICE PATAGONIA
- PATAGONIA DULCE
- BARROS
- CHILE NATIVO
- ARANA
- LENGA
- BORIES
- MUSEO HISTÓRICO MUNICIPALIDAD NATALES
- YUNGAY
- SARGENTO ALDEA
- RIQUELME
- ESPÍRITU PATAGON
- MANUEL
- MAGALLANES
- SEÑORET
- SERNATUR
- ARTIMAÑA
- CARRERA PINTO
- O'HIGGINS
- BUILNES
- GALPÓN PATAGONIA / LE MOUTON VERT
- SÁNCHEZ
- MASAY
- ITAHUE
- LILI PATAGÓNICO'S
- TOMÁS ROGERS
- Plaza de Armas Arturo Prat
- VINNHAUS
- EBERHARD
- PATAGONIA SWISS HOUSE
- ARTURO PRAT
- BUS SUR
- YAGANHOUSE
- BANCO DE CHILE
- BANCO SANTANDER
- PHILLIPI
- SEE DETAIL
- MIRAFLORES
- BLANCO
- FANTÁSTICO SUR
- FRUTOS SECOS
- ENCALADA
- ESMERALDA
- SALOMON
- AGUNSA
- BALFER
- Erratic Rock (Rental Shop) and CONAF
- CHORRILLOS
- BAQUEDANO
- ERRATIC ROCK
- KOYER
- EL PATAGÓNICO HOSTEL
- BUSES FERNÁNDEZ
- UNIMARC
- Estero Natales
- To Erratic Rock
- Plaza Primero de Mayo
- E. RAMÍREZ
- Terminal Rodoviario and Hospital Puerto Natales
- YELLOW PLUM TENT HOUSE
- LAST HOPE DISTILLERY
- SUPER FRUT
- Cementerio
- To Congrejo Rojo
- GALVARINO
- VALDIVIA
- ANGÁMOS
- To Cerro Dorotea, Cueva del Milodón, Museo Histórico e Industrial Frigorífico Bories, The Singular Patagonia, Simple Patagonia, Aeropuerto Teniente Julio Gallardo, and TREKKING TORRES DEL PAINE

© MOON.COM

warehouses from the early 20th century are now home to the **Galpón Patagonia** (Av. Pedro Montt 16, tel. 61/2414 611, www.galponpatagonia.cl, 10am-8pm daily, free), a modern cultural center showcasing art, sculpture, and photography from Puerto Natales and the surrounding region.

In Puerto Bories, a few kilometers north of town, the **Museo Histórico e Industrial Frigorífico Bories** (Km 5 Ruta 9, Puerto Bories, tel. 61/2722 030, http://thesingular.com, 1pm-9pm daily Oct.-Apr., CH$5,000) displays machinery from the 1915 building's origins as Chile's largest abattoir, slaughtering sheep and exporting the meat. The plant closed in the late 1980s. In 2011 the structure was converted into the luxurious Singular Hotel. Inside, machines dot the corridors connecting the main lobby with the restaurant and guest rooms. Still standing are the enormous steam boilers and the engine room that supplied electricity to the rooms where the meat was stored. Outside, the building's original funicular shuttles visitors 20 meters down to the lobby. Customers of the hotel's bar or restaurant can enter the museum for free.

To visit a 19,000-hectare family-run sheep farm, sign up for the full-day tour of **Estancia La Península** (Herman Eberhard 385, Puerto Natales, tel. 9/8416 8161, www.estanciaspatagonia.com). From Puerto Natales, you travel a few kilometers north to Puerto Bories to board a covered speedboat that takes you 30 minutes northwest up Seno Última Esperanza. At the ranch, you'll watch sheepdog herding and sheep-shearing demonstrations, enjoy a lamb barbecue, and take a two-hour trek, 4WD ride, or horseback ride through windswept grasslands. Multiple-day horseback riding or trekking tours are possible; these include accommodation and meals (some options require camping gear). Prices for a full-day tour start at CH$154,700 pp.

The 549-meter **Cerro Dorotea** (Ruta 9, dawn to dusk daily, CH$5,000) is a few kilometers northeast of Puerto Natales. To get to the top is a 3-km, 1.5-hour walk. The path cuts through private land, so pay your entrance fee to owner Juan de Dios Saavedra at the house before you begin. The trail is well marked and climbs steeply. If the weather is clear, you'll be able to see across Seno Última Esperanza and north to the icy peaks of Torres del Paine and Parque Nacional Bernardo O'Higgins. Wear warm clothes, as the wind can be fierce on the exposed ridge. Taxis should cost no more than CH$4,000, or rent a bike to cover the 8km east along Ruta 9 north of Puerto Natales. The owner's house and trailhead are well signposted on the north side of the road. For the return journey, ask at the house to call you a taxi back to town.

ENTERTAINMENT

With its English pub-like atmosphere and deafening rock music, **Baguales** (Bories 430, tel. 61/2411 920, 5pm-2:30am Mon.-Sat.) is a great spot for a drink, around a wooden bar with windows looking onto the stainless steel tanks of the brewery. The food's not bad, comprising Mexican tacos, beef and lamb burgers, and even salads. Try the three beers brewed here or a diverse range of bottled beer.

The world's southernmost distillery, **Last Hope Distillery** (Esmeralda 882, tel. 9/7201 8585, www.lasthopedistillery.com, 5pm-2am Wed.-Sun.) is run by two Australian expats. Whiskey and gin, including their trademark gin distilled with Calafate berries, are made here; helpful staff will offer samples. Don't miss the superb cocktails that combine local Chilean ingredients (carménère wine, *araucano* bitters, local beer), or the small sharing platters with local seaweed, among other ingredients. Get here at 5:30pm for a free tour of the distillery.

The drinks aren't cheap, but on a clear evening, it's worth heading to the 2nd-floor **Indigo Bar** (Indigo Hotel, Ladrilleros 105, tel. 61/274 0670, www.indigopatagonia.com, noon-11pm daily) for a pisco sour and a memorable sunset view from its sound-side windows. The interior is an eyeful, with modern

---

1: Last Hope Distillery 2: horseback riding tour

furniture vying for space with a collection of antique saws on the walls.

SHOPPING

For English-language maps and books about Patagonia, Cape Horn, and the region's first inhabitants, as well as local jams, liquors, and woolen textiles, head to **Artesanía Ñandu** (Hermann Eberhard 301, no phone, 9am-11pm Mon.-Sat., 10am-10pm Sun.) on the southeast edge of the square.

Inside the Galpón Patagonia cultural center, **Le Mouton Vert** (Pedro Montt 16, tel. 9/9295 8329, www.lemoutonvert.org, 10am-8pm daily) sells handmade organic merino wool clothing and interior decorations, which you can watch being made in the workshop. All of their wool is sustainably sourced from the nearby Estancia La Península.

Outdoor Gear and Equipment

Prices for rental gear for trekking to Torres del Paine start from CH$7,500 per day for a two-person tent, sleeping bag, sleeping mat, and cooking set. The quality of the gear can vary, so it's a good idea to check for holes or damage.

Hostels in Puerto Natales often rent out camping and hiking gear. Unlike most hostels, **Erratic Rock** (Baquedano 955, no phone, www.erraticrock.com, 2pm-11pm daily) has a dedicated rental shop. They update the gear yearly and are best known for the invaluable free "3 o'clock talk" (3pm daily), where the most up-to-date information and tips for hiking in Torres del Paine are shared. **Yaganhouse** (O'Higgins 584, tel. 9/8243 0642, www.yaganhouse.cl, 10am-8pm daily) has some of the cheapest good-quality rental gear. **Lili Patagónico's** (Arturo Prat 479, tel. 61/2414 063, www.lilipatagonicos.com, 10am-8pm daily) also has an ample selection of gear.

To buy equipment, **Balfer** (Bulnes 646, no phone, 10am-8pm daily) has cheaper Chilean brands, while French brand **Salomon** (Bulnes 698, no phone, 10am-8pm daily) has its own shop; expect to pay extremely elevated prices.

RECREATION
Horseback Riding

For horseback riding tours, **Pingo Salvaje** (Estancia Laguna Sofía, tel. 9/6236 0371, www.pingosalvaje.com) offers half-day and full-day excursions around Laguna Sofía, 22km north of Puerto Natales. Condor sightings and views of Parque Nacional O'Higgins are possible. You can also stay in their basic lodge (CH$8,000 camping, CH$22,000 dorm); transfers to and from the lodge and meals are extra. Half-day rides begin at CH$40,000 pp; there's no minimum tour size.

Kayaking

Espíritu Patagón (Magallanes 158, tel. 9/7984 0285, www.espiritupatagon.com) offers a unique three-day kayak excursion, starting in Lago Grey in Parque Nacional Torres del Paine. You'll row 60km south to Puerto Bories and the Singular Hotel. Along the way are rare views of hidden glaciers, condors, and part of the national park experienced by few. The trip stops overnight in comfortable lodgings and a remote campground. Tours cost CH$650,000 pp (min. 2 people), including all meals, equipment (but not camping gear), and transfer to the national park.

Glacier Tours

October-March, **Turismo 21 de Mayo** (Eberhard 560, tel. 61/2614 420, www.turismo21demayo.com) and **Agunsa** (Blanco Encalada 244, tel. 9/9015 6433, www.agunsapatagonia.cl) run day tours to the Balmaceda and Serrano glaciers in Parque Nacional Bernardo O'Higgins, with lunch at a local ranch on the return journey. Tours start from CH$90,000 pp. Turismo 21 de Mayo also offers an extended version of this tour (from CH$145,000 pp) that continues to Hotel del Paine, 9km south of the southern entrance to Parque Nacional Torres del Paine.

FOOD

Puerto Natales has a surprisingly large number of top-quality restaurants—and you can expect to pay higher than average prices.

Reservations are essential for most places in summer. Opening hours reduce significantly April-September; some spots close completely during the off-season.

Supermarkets sell items at inflated rates, options are limited, and lines are long, so if you're planning to stock up on food for a trip into Torres del Paine, shop in Punta Arenas. Otherwise, **Super Frut** (Bulnes 849, tel. 61/2410 249, 8:30am-9:30pm Mon.-Sat., 10:30pm-1pm and 5:30pm-8:30pm Sun.) has a wide selection of fruit and vegetables; **UNIMARC** (Bulnes 742, no phone, www.unimarc.cl, 9am-10pm Mon.-Sat., 11am-7pm Sun.) has the most expansive selection of all the shops and the lowest prices. Both **Frutos Secos** (Baquedano 443, no phone, 10am-1pm and 3pm-8pm Mon.-Sat.) and **Itahue** (Esmeralda 455B, no phone, 10am-1pm and 2pm-8pm Mon.-Sat.) have a range of dried fruit and nuts. Most shops are closed noon-3pm.

Patagonian and Chilean

There's nothing flashy about the simple local favorite **Masay** (Bulnes 427, tel. 61/2415 008, masaypizza@gmail.com, 11am-midnight Wed.-Mon., CH$4,000-7,000), but you're guaranteed a wide choice of traditional Chilean-style sandwiches at cheap prices. They specialize in *churrascos* (steak sandwiches on thick toasted white bread), with the *churrasco palta* (steak and avocado sandwich) a particular favorite. Service is friendly.

A little Patagonian gem hidden off the plaza, offbeat six-table ★ **Artimaña** (Bores 349, tel. 61/2414 856, noon-10pm Tues.-Sat., CH$6,000-9,000, cash only) combines friendly service with a simple menu of fish specials, Chilean-style sandwiches, *lomo a lo pobre,* and snack-sized *bombagos* (short-crust pastry pies). A top choice for Puerto Natales's youthful and alternative crowd, it's the ideal place for an evening of impromptu harmonica and guitar jam sessions.

With a formidable wine list of carménères and cabernet sauvignons and less commonplace cabernet franc and carignan, ★ **The**

Singular Patagonia (Km 5 Ruta 9, tel. 61/2722 030, www.thesingular.com, 1pm-2:30pm and 7:30pm-10:30pm daily Oct.-Apr., CH$10,000-18,000) is peerless. It's on two floors in a repurposed industrial building on the sound, with fashionably mismatched leather sofas, antique lampstands, and luxurious dark wooden tables. The menu is a feast of gourmet Patagonian ingredients, from scallops, king crab, octopus, and salmon ceviche to veal, hare, and lamb. Reservations are required.

One of the best places to dine, matchbox-size ★ **Lenga** (Bories 221, tel. 61/2691 187, 6pm-11pm Tues.-Sun. Sept.-Mar., 6pm-11pm Fri.-Sat. Apr.-July, CH$9,000-12,000) excels in classic Patagonian with a modern twist. The menu is updated daily, with options like eel cheeks with sea asparagus, roasted guanaco, and braised lamb smoked over *lenga* wood, all impeccably presented. Servers speak fluent English and wear T-shirts with the motto "Cook Free or Die." Reservations are essential.

Seafood

You can expect some of the best seafood in Puerto Natales in the funky **Congrejo Rojo** (Santiago Buenas 782, tel. 61/2412 436, 11am-10:30pm Mon.-Sat., CH$9,000-13,000). Decorated with fishing memorabilia and serving mouthwatering *chupe de centolla* (king crab stew) and delicately pan-fried salmon, it is a bit of a walk or a short taxi ride from the center, but worth the effort. Try the seafood sharing platter, with parmesan scallops, garlic prawns, and mussels.

International

Run by English owners, the vegetarian **El Living** (Arturo Prat 156, tel. 61/2411 140, www.el-living.com, 11am-10:30pm Sun.-Fri. Nov.-mid-Apr., CH$4,000-6,000) has squishy sofas, mountains of magazines, and a wood-burning stove. Pop in for freshly ground coffee, delicious sandwiches and baguettes (don't miss the hummus with roasted red pepper and camembert), homemade cakes, and daily dishes such as vegetarian curry. It's most popular for lunch, and there is a reasonably priced wine selection, some by the glass.

La Mesita Grande (Arturo Prat 196, tel. 61/2411 571, www.mesitagrande.cl, noon-11pm Mon.-Sat., 1pm-9pm Sun., CH$4,000-8,000) means "Big Table," named for its long communal table that takes center stage. Popular with foreign travelers for a big meal after hiking, pizza is the specialty. From the 30 varieties, all named after trails in the park, try one with king crab or smoked salmon. The gnocchi and fettuccini dishes showcase local ingredients such as Patagonian lamb with *merkén*.

Light Bites

Escape the rain at cozy **Patagonia Dulce** (Barros Arana 233, tel. 61/2415 285, www.patagoniadulce.cl, 9:30am-8:30pm Mon.-Sat., CH$2,000-3,000), a charming cafeteria renowned for hot chocolate—the De Chile includes *merkén* (smoked chili pepper) and pisco and has quite a kick. There are also mouthwatering fruity cakes, ice cream, and sandwiches.

The best ice cream shop in Puerto Natales, **Helados La Dorotea** (Eberhard 577, tel. 9/4496 571, 7am-8:30pm Mon.-Sat., CH$1,900) has tasty homemade ice cream in a range of flavors, including tiramisu, watermelon, mango, and *dulce de leche,* while a selection of pastries and coffees make a good breakfast or snack.

A trendy hangout attached to the Hostel Amerindia, **Cafetería Amerindia** (Barros Arana 135, tel. 61/2411 945, www.hostelamerindia.com, 10:30am-10pm daily, CH$7,900) offers some of the best vegetarian food in Puerto Natales. Options are limited, with the main choice the "make your own sandwich" (CH$7,900 for a burger big enough for two), which includes a range of vegetarian fillings—seaweed, black beans, beet, and pumpkin and ginger. For meat eaters, the smoked lamb is special. There's a range of vegan cakes and brownies plus coffee and soy milk.

ACCOMMODATIONS

Lodging options are plentiful in Puerto Natales, and rates are mostly reasonable. Book at least 2-3 months in advance for December-February.

Under CH$25,000

It's not quite "glamping," but the excellent **Yellow Plum Tent House** (Eleuterio Ramírez 444, tel. 9/6675 9930, www.campingyellowplum.com, CH$13,000) gets close. The 15 campsites are close together, but a heated restroom and shower block with 24-7 hot water and a covered cooking area with a stove, sink, and picnic tables make up for the tight sleeping quarters. The owners speak perfect English and rent out gear; free information for planning a trip to Parque Nacional Torres del Paine is available. Rates include IVA.

The simple **Jos Mar II** (Juan Mclean 367, tel. 61/2411 685, www.josmar.cl, CH$6,000 camping) offers eight grassy, widely spaced campsites, plus a shower block with hot water, picnic tables, and a small indoor kitchen with a fridge. Rates include IVA.

CH$25,000-40,000

You'll need sunglasses for the rooms, painted vibrant shades of orange, green, and purple, but **Lili Patagónico's** (Arturo Prat 479, tel. 61/2414 063, www.lilipatagonicos.com, CH$14,000 dorm, CH$29,000 d shared bath, CH$37,000 d private bath) is a solid choice in Puerto Natales, with 10 sizeable if dated bedrooms, a handful of which have en suite baths, and a large kitchen. The vibe is convivial and the staff are knowledgeable about the area, offering information, bus tickets, and equipment rental; gear is also rented to nonguests. Rates include IVA.

Get hotel-quality bedrooms with hostel ambience in the elegant ★ **VinnHaus** (Manuel Bulnes 499, tel. 9/8269 2510, www.vinnhaus.net, CH$13,000 dorm, CH$37,000 d), a converted 1920s house with modern touches (electrical sockets fit any international plug). The five en suite rooms are lovingly dressed in antique furniture and have huge windows overlooking a grassy terrace. Dorms are sizable, with blinds for privacy and access to large, spotless baths. The small café is a communal living area; guests get a discount on the light bites and coffee. Rates include IVA.

The owners of cheerful **El Patagónico Hostel** (O'Higgins 741, tel. 61/2413 290, www.elpatagonicohostel.com, CH$15,000 dorm, CH$33,000 d shared bath, CH$38,000 d private bath, cash only) are helpful and hospitable. Rooms feel dated but have comfortable beds. The building has a huge communal kitchen and various cozy areas. There are only six rooms, sharing three large baths. Breakfast is not included, but help yourself to tea and coffee. Like most hostels in Puerto Natales, they organize trips to Torres del Paine and rent camping equipment. Rates include IVA.

Cozy, modern ★ **Yaganhouse** (O'Higgins 584, tel. 9/8243 0642, www.yaganhouse.cl, CH$15,000 dorm, CH$38,000 d shared bath, CH$45,000 d private bath) offers excellent value in a modern setting. Large, bright, airy bedrooms are decorated with woolen textiles. A huge communal kitchen and living area look out onto a small garden. Of the nine bedrooms, four have en suite baths. They rent out good-quality camping gear for some of the cheapest prices in town. Rates include IVA.

Erratic Rock (Baquedano 719, www.erraticrock.com, CH$15,000 dorms, CH$30,000 d) is a meeting point for treks into Torres del Paine and an institution in Puerto Natales. This hostel attracts a relaxed crowd with acres of communal space and five small, simple bedrooms; all rooms share baths. The facilities are dated, but the breakfast is great, and there's kitchen access. Their rental shop is one block south at Baquedano 955. Rates include IVA.

At friendly central **Isla Morena** (Roger 38, tel. 61/2414 773, laislamorena@gmail.com, CH$8,000 camping, CH$32,000 d), rooms are a little dated, with creaky wooden floors and thin walls, but you can't fault the rates.

Bedrooms have private baths with modern white fittings, TVs, and a DVD player, with access to the owner's extensive DVD collection. There's a bright reading room, plus a piano and a guitar to keep guests occupied. Budget travelers will appreciate the small camping space outside, with its own covered kitchen. Isla Morena is half a block from the main square. Rates include IVA.

CH$40,000-60,000

The backpacker favorite **The Singing Lamb** (Arauco 779, tel. 61/2410 958, www.thesinginglamb.com, CH$14,000 dorm, CH$50,000 d private bath) has a cozy, familial atmosphere. Huge dorms are great on a budget, while the wing of private rooms—all with large baths—suits couples or families. The lounge has a sun room, sofas, and a sociable dining table where an extensive buffet breakfast is served. Guests have access to a sizeable kitchen and laundry service, while the staff can organize tours and bus tickets. Rates include IVA.

Friendly English-speaking Marcela runs a tight ship at spotless **Big Bang** (Benjamin Zamora 732, tel. 61/2414 317, www.bigbangpatagonia.com, CH$48,000 d). Rooms are on two floors around a grassy garden and are simply decorated. Most have en suite baths. Wooden floorboards and thin walls can mean noise carries between rooms. An ample breakfast of home-baked bread, fruit, and eggs is served in a somewhat formal dining and living area. There's a small kitchen for guest use. The Wi-Fi only reaches communal areas.

With friendly Swiss owners and a relaxed atmosphere, **Patagonia Swiss House** (Roger 60, tel. 61/2412 698, www.patagoniaswisshouse.cl, CH$33,000 d shared bath, CH$53,000 d private bath) makes a perfect pre- or post-hiking lodging. The atrium and living area has shocking lime-green walls, but this doesn't affect the tranquility. Most bedrooms are simple but clean, large, and with en suite baths. Central heating and carpeted floors complete the offerings. Knowledgeable staff can organize tours and equipment rental. Rates include IVA.

At tidy, modern **Hostel Amerindia** (Barros Arana 135, tel. 61/2411 945, www. hostelamerindia.com, CH$48,000 d shared bath, CH$55,000 d private bath), 14 large bedrooms have individual heaters. Most have private baths, and all have comfortable beds, quirky modern decor, and access to a number of snug communal areas with squishy sofas and wood-burning stoves. The Wi-Fi doesn't reach all rooms, so opt for one close to the communal areas. There's an attached café specializing in vegetarian and vegan food. Rates include IVA.

Over CH$80,000

On clear nights, sunsets across the sound are spectacular from the vast windows of ★ **Simple Patagonia** (Ruta 9, tel. 9/9640 0512, www.simplepatagonia.cl, CH$127,000 d), 4km north of Puerto Natales. Channeling the barns that once populated the region, the buildings are simple, while inside is modern warm design, with underfloor heating, large tiled baths, and astonishing views from the living and dining area and bedrooms (best are rooms 8 and 11). The three-course dinner menu employs local ingredients to produce top-quality dishes. The breakfast buffet is similarly impressive and is included in the rates.

Just over 1km north of Puerto Natales, 30-bedroom **Weskar Lodge** (Huerto 274B, tel. 9/9162 7221, www.weskar.cl, CH$107,000-170,000 d), with sweeping views of the sound, makes an excellent escape from the bustle of town. Tastefully decorated with rough-hewn woolen wall hangings and rustic wood-panel walls, the bedrooms vary significantly depending on the rate. Skip the cramped basic interior bedrooms and opt for a superior that's roomier and with a view. Guests can rent bicycles to get into town, although the on-site restaurant's menu, featuring local ingredients such as guanaco and king crab, means you don't need to leave the property to dine well. The Wi-Fi is poor. The hotel closes

for one month during winter; closure dates change each year.

INFORMATION AND SERVICES

Right on the waterfront, the helpful English-speaking staff at **SERNATUR** (Pedro Montt 19, tel. 61/2412 125, www.patagonia-chile. com, infonatales@sernatur.cl, 8:30am-8pm daily Oct.-mid-Mar., 8:30am-6pm Mon.-Sat. mid-Mar.-Sept.) can provide information about the national park and other local destinations. **CONAF** (Baquedano 847, tel. 61/2411 843, 9am-5pm Mon.-Thurs., 9am-4pm Fri.) has information about current conditions in the park, although the free talk (3pm daily) offered by outfitter and hostel **Erratic Rock** (Baquedano 955, no phone, www.erraticrock. com) is more useful.

There are only a handful of **ATMs** in town, including at **Santander** (Bulnes 598) and **Banco de Chile** (Bulnes 596). Currency exchange houses are few, but you can try local tour operator **Tour 365** (Eberhard 545, tel. 61/2414 669, www.tour365.cl, 10am-9pm Mon.-Sat., 2pm-8pm Sun.).

For laundry, head to **Lavamag** (Hermann Eberhard 525, tel. 61/2410 930, 8am-8pm Mon.-Sat.). To mail something, go to the **Correos** (Eberhard 429, no phone, www. correos.cl, 9:30am-1pm and 3pm-8pm Mon.-Fri., 10am-12:30pm Sat.). Medical emergencies can be handled by the **Hospital de Puerto Natales** (Av. España 1650, tel. 61/2452 000, http://hospitalnatales.cl) in the east of town.

The two companies that operate the campgrounds and *refugios* along Torres del Paine's trekking circuits have offices in Puerto Natales. **Vertice Patagonia** (Bulnes 100, tel. 61/2415 716, www.verticepatagonia.cl, 9am-1pm and 2:30pm-6pm Mon.-Fri., 9:30am-noon Sat. Sept.-May) and **Fantástico Sur** (Esmeralda 661, Puerto Natales, tel. 61/2614 184, www.fantasticosur.com, 9am-1pm and 3pm-7pm daily) have mostly helpful English-speaking staff and can help with last-minute reservations or information about their facilities.

GETTING THERE

Air

Six kilometers north of Puerto Natales is the small **Aeródromo Teniente Julio Gallardo** (PNT, tel. 61/2411 980), served by flights from Santiago on **LATAM** (www.latam.com) twice weekly October-November and March, and four times weekly December-February. A taxi from the airport into town costs around CH$7,000. You can book transfers with **Onteaiken Patagonia** (tel. 9/6468 5637, www.onteaikenpatagonia.cl) for CH$7,000 pp.

Ferry

FROM PUERTO MONTT

A popular way to get to Puerto Natales from **Puerto Montt** is via a ferry operated by **Navimag** (Av. Diego Portales 2000, Puerto Montt, tel. 2/2869 9900, 9am-1pm and 2:30pm-6:30pm Mon.-Thurs., 9am-5pm Fri., 3pm-6pm Sat., www.navimag.com). The three-day, four-night journey runs once a week October-March. The ships are far from luxurious, but sailing through the Chilean fjords offers a chance at numerous wildlife sightings, including orcas, blue whales, and rare seabirds.

All food is included, along with yoga classes and lectures in English about the flora, fauna, and geography of the fjords. Be aware that the timing of the tides and poor weather often result in delayed departures from Puerto Montt.

The cheapest option is a four-bed shared cabin (from US$400 pp); private cabins start at US$600. Ferries for Puerto Natales leave Puerto Montt at 4pm Friday; these are generally fully booked a few months in advance. The ferry back to Puerto Montt from Puerto Natales leaves at 6am Tuesday (boarding occurs the night before); it's sometimes possible to get a last-minute spot. Requesting an upgrade upon arrival is sometimes possible, particularly in shoulder seasons (Oct.-Nov. and Mar.).

FROM PUERTO YUNGAY

A less-frequented way to Puerto Natales is aboard the 41-hour **Transbordadora**

Austral Broom (TABSA, Av. Pedro Montt 605, Puerto Natales, tel. 61/2728 100, www.tabsa.cl) ferry crossing from **Puerto Yungay.** The route starts in Puerto Yungay (CH$125,160 foot passengers, CH$120,000 vehicles, plus CH$25,030 per meter for the length of the vehicle), picking up passengers in Caleta Tortel before sailing south. It's run in the *Crux Australis,* a cargo boat-cum-ferry with space for 142 passengers in *semi-cama* bus-style seating.

The ferry leaves at 8pm weekly from Puerto Yungay, arriving in Puerto Natales around 4pm two days later. Three meals per day are included, but you should bring extra snacks. All seats recline 160 degrees and blankets are provided, although it can get cold at night, so bring extra layers. Part of the fun of the trip is watching the scenery from above deck, so waterproof and windproof clothing is essential. For December-February, book your seat or vehicle reservation in October. Outside these months, it's often possible to get a seat and even a space for your car a week or two in advance.

Bus

All national and international buses leave from **Terminal Rodoviario** (Av. España 1455), 10 blocks southeast of the Plaza de Armas, although some agencies have ticket offices closer to the center of town.

Bus Sur (tel. 61/2410 784, www.bussur. com) and **Buses Fernández** (tel. 61/2414 786, www.busesfernandez.com) shuttle between **Punta Arenas** and the Terminal Rodoviario in Puerto Natales (3.25hr, CH$8,000). Buses from each company leave at alternating hours throughout the day.

Routes from **El Calafate, Argentina** (5-8hours, CH$17,000), are operated by **Bus Sur** (8am Wed., Fri., and Sun., 8am and 4:30pm Tues., Thurs., and Sat. Nov.-Mar.). Buses operated by **COOTRA** (tel. 61/2412 785, www. cootra.com.ar) leave from El Calafate at 7:30am daily. Buses run by **Turismo Zaahj** (tel. 61/2411 355, www.turismozaahj.co.cl) depart El Calafate at 8am Monday, Wednesday, and Friday, and 2pm Tuesday, Thursday, and Saturday. There is a reduced frequency of departures April-October.

Car

Puerto Natales is 250km north of **Punta Arenas** via Ruta 9, a three-hour drive. You'll pass through sparse, flat grasslands devoid of human habitation. Keep an eye out for guanacos, rheas, and even flamingos, which inhabit the lakes and wetlands that line the road.

From the north, it's 70km along a mostly paved road from the **Paso Río Don Guillermo,** a principal border crossing to Argentina. From the border, it's a 10-minute drive along the unpaved Y-205 to the hamlet of Villa Cerro Castillo, where the paved Ruta 9 runs 60km (one hour's drive) south to Puerto Natales.

The southernmost entrance to Parque Nacional Torres del Paine, Portería Río Serrano, is reached by taking Ruta 9 north for 18km and then continuing northwest along the unpaved Y-290 for 93km. The entire journey takes one hour and 45 minutes. The park's northernmost entrance is reached by a turnoff at the settlement of Villa Cerro Castillo, 60km north of Puerto Natales in the direction of the Argentinean border. From Cerro Castillo, it's 53km to Portería Laguna Amarga along the gravel Y-156. The journey takes around one hour and 45 minutes.

GETTING AROUND

Puerto Natales is compact. Unless you're staying north of town, it's easy to get around on foot. Taxi journeys within Puerto Natales cost a flat rate of CH$1,500 during the day and CH$1,800-2,000 after 10pm and on weekends. To request a taxi, call **Radio Taxi Milodón** (tel. 61/2410 426) or **Radiotaxis Hoffman** (tel. 61/2411 022).

There are plenty of places offering **rental bikes** of variable quality. Expect to pay from CH$2,000 per hour or CH$12,000 for a full day.

Car Rental

Renting a car for the day to visit Torres del Paine can be cheaper than a day tour; it also allows greater flexibility to visit different sectors of the park. If you plan to cross into Argentina, written permission from your rental company must be arranged with at least a week's notice.

The best car rental options in Puerto Natales are **Europcar** (Bulnes 100, tel. 61/2414 475, www.europcar.cl, 9am-1pm and 3pm-7pm daily), **Koyer** (Baquedano 558, tel. 9/4466 7705, www.arriendoskoyer.com, 9am-1pm and 3pm-7pm Mon.-Fri., 9am-2pm Sat.), and **Magallanes Rent A Car** (Simón Bolívar 1429, tel. 9/7464 7228, www.magallanesrentacar.cl, hours vary).

MONUMENTO NATURAL CUEVA DEL MILODÓN

Northwest of Puerto Natales, the **Monumento Natural Cueva del Milodón** (Km 8 Ruta Y-290, tel. 61/2360 485, www.cuevadelmilodon.cl, 8am-7pm daily Oct.-Apr., 8:30am-6pm daily May-Sept., CH$2,500-5,000 adults, CH$500-2,500 children) inspired Bruce Chatwin to venture to Patagonia, recounted in his renowned book *In Patagonia*. Skin fragments of the *Mylodon*, a giant land sloth that roamed the Patagonian steppe during the Pleistocene era, were unearthed in this cave in 1895 by local resident Hermann Eberhard.

Swedish archaeologist Erland Nordenskiöld conducted the first excavation of the site in 1899. Fur, bones, and feces of the *Mylodon* were uncovered in the cave and have been carbon-dated to 10,400 years. Also in the cave were lithic tools and human remains of the same age, suggesting that the *Mylodon* existed alongside humans.

The site is less compelling than the history, however. The **Museo del Sitio,** the on-site museum, provides information on the first inhabitants of the region and the types of animal remains discovered in the caves. Visitors can hike to the cave complex,

Crossing into Argentina

Buses to El Calafate, Argentina, cross the border at Paso Río Don Guillermo (tel. 61/22761 167, 8am-10pm daily), 60km north of Puerto Natales. Take Ruta 9 to the small settlement of Cerro Castillo, then travel 7km east along the unpaved Y-205 to the border. The length of the border formalities process depends on the volume of travelers attempting to cross; waits of up to three hours are possible.

You'll need to hand your **PDI receipt,** which you received when you entered Chile, to the Chilean border officials. If you have a rental vehicle, you need to show **proof of permission** to travel into Argentina and your driver's license to Argentinean officials. Those traveling by bus are dropped at the Chilean border, where the bus waits to take you the 2km across to the Argentinean offices, where it'll wait again for all passengers to go through the process.

The landscape here is exposed, so winds are fierce. Dress in warm clothing, as queues mean you'll often be required to wait outside of the tiny buildings that house the officials.

Returning to Chile, officials are assiduous about checking luggage and vehicles for produce and animal products. All private cars and personal belongings will be checked with trained dogs. It is not unusual to be asked to remove all your belongings from the bus or car and have them scanned in the border office. Don't hide items in your luggage; fines for those who break the rules are high.

Having Argentinean pesos is useful if you have your own car. You can buy gas at one of the two small stations in the villages of Tapi Aike and Esperanza on the road to El Calafate. Exchange Chilean pesos and U.S. dollars at a premium at the **small shop** (8am-10pm daily) next door to Chilean border control.

which rises dramatically out of the otherwise flat plain. Three caves are accessible, including the 200-meter-deep, 80-meter-wide, 30-meter-tall Cueva del Milodón, in which you'll find a garish life-size statue of the *Mylodon*. Nearby, you can walk to the Devil's Chair, a rock formation believed to be where the devil shows himself to those searching for him.

GETTING THERE

The entrance to the Cueva del Milodón is located 26km north of Puerto Natales, 7km after the turnoff for the southern entrance of Parque Nacional Torres del Paine. Most one-day tours to Torres del Paine stop briefly at Cueva del Milodón on the return journey; entry is rarely included in the cost of the tour. It's possible to organize a half-day trip directly to the cave for CH$15,000, including transportation and a guide, but it's not worth the effort or the cost. It's possible to cycle to the cave from Puerto Natales, but it's a two-hour ride each way.

PARQUE NACIONAL BERNARDO O'HIGGINS

Northwest of Parque Nacional Torres del Paine is the far larger and less visited **Parque Nacional Bernardo O'Higgins** (tel. 61/2360 484 or 61/2360 492, magallanes.oirs@conaf. cl, 24 hr daily Oct.-Apr., CH$7,000 adults, CH$3,500 children). Receiving only 35,000 visitors annually, it is the largest national park in Chile, covering 3.5 million hectares of unconnected fjords and the majority of the Southern Patagonian Ice Field. The park's main attractions are its two glaciers, Balmaceda and Serrano.

Glaciares Balmaceda and Serrano

On the southeastern flank of serrated, snow-covered, 2,035-meter Monte Balmaceda are **Glaciares Balmaceda and Serrano.** In the most visited part of Bernardo O'Higgins, they are the most accessible glaciers from Puerto Natales. To visit the glaciers, you'll need to join a 7- or 10-hour boat excursion from

Puerto Natales. The ships sail 50km north through Seno Última Esperanza, past a cormorant colony, before arriving at a viewpoint of the rapidly retreating Glaciar Balmaceda. A few decades ago it extended far into the water; now the snout is on land, just before the shoreline, having receded 2km in 30 years.

Passengers disembark for an hour for a brief hike. The narrow path through southern beech forest terminates at a viewpoint of the chiseled Glaciar Serrano. Back on board the boat, you're treated to a whiskey or pisco sour using freshly cut glacier ice before disembarking again for lunch at a nearby ranch.

Agunsa (Blanco Encalada 244, tel. 9/9015 6433, www.agunsapatagonia.cl) and **Turismo 21 de Mayo** (Eberhard 560, tel. 61/2614 420, www.turismo21demayo.com) are the main operators running trips to the glaciers. Agunsa generally only runs boats with a maximum of 50 passengers on newer vessels; Turismo 21 de Mayo uses 130-passenger ships. The size of the vessel ultimately depends on how many spots are filled. To guarantee a smaller group, opt for a full-day tour, which includes a Zodiac ride to Parque Nacional Torres del Paine. Both outfitters' trips can include a Patagonian *asado* lunch. Prices start from CH$90,000.

Multiday Tours

One of the best options for exploring this remote park is aboard the 90-passenger MV *Skorpios III*. From their port in Puerto Natales, **Skorpios** (Camino Puerto Bories s/n, Puerto Natales, tel. 61/241 2714, US tel. 305/285-8416, www.skorpios.cl) leads four-day, three-night cruises to an impressive 15 glaciers in the park. At some, passengers can take short treks across the moraine ridges. Small expedition vessels with strengthened hulls and capacity for 20 passengers are used to get as close as possible to the glaciers.

Dolphins, arctic terns, albatross, and cormorants are common sights as you explore some of the least-visited fjords in Patagonia. The quality of the food (included, along with drinks) is notable, particularly the farewell dinner. The trips include on-board lectures about the flora, fauna, and geography of the region. Rates start from US$2,175 pp d.

Parque Nacional Torres del Paine

TOP EXPERIENCE

Soaring granite peaks and sparkling crystalline lakes with mirror-like reflections of jaw-dropping mountains—the sublime scenery of **Parque Nacional Torres del Paine** (www.parquetorresdelpaine.cl, CH$21,000 Oct.-Apr., CH$11,000 May-Sept., cash only) has become a symbol of Patagonia at its wildest and most beautiful. The 181,414-hectare park's most prominent feature is the **Paine Massif,** crooked peaks that form the Andes, around which the park's main hiking routes traverse. On the east side of the Paine Massif, beyond a deep river valley, three weathered spires of rock known as the **Torres del Paine** are what draw the vast majority of visitors.

The **entrance fee** can be paid at the Laguna Amarga, Lago Sarmiento, and Administración ranger offices; you will receive an entrance ticket valid for three consecutive days of entry. (If you're trekking the W or the O, your ticket is valid until you leave the park.) Note that May-September you can only hike in the park if you're accompanied by a certified guide.

The central section of the Paine Massif is another dramatic highlight. The craggy wedges of three horn-shaped rocks known as the **Cuernos del Paine** loom above the western shores of Lago Nordenskjöld and are visible from the southern entrance of the park. Even larger is the colossal blue-hued **Glaciar Grey,** in the northwestern edge of the park.

Parque Nacional Torres del Paine has acquired global acclaim as one of South America's best trekking destinations,

Parque Nacional Torres del Paine

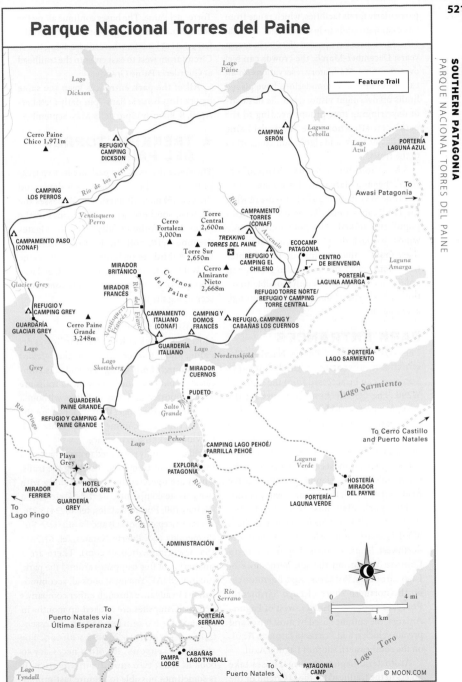

Lago Paine

Lago Dickson

Feature Trail

Lago Paine

Cerro Paine Chico 1,971m

REFUGIO Y CAMPING DICKSON

CAMPING SERÓN

Laguna Cebolla

Lago Azul

PORTERÍA LAGUNA AZUL

Río de los Perros

Río

To Awasi Patagonia

CAMPING LOS PERROS

Ventisquero Perro

CAMPAMENTO PASO (CONAF)

Glacier Grey

Cerro Fortaleza 3,000m

Torre Central 2,600m

TREKKING TORRES DEL PAINE ✪

Torre Sur 2,650m

CAMPAMENTO TORRES (CONAF)

Ascensio

ECOCAMP PATAGONIA

REFUGIO Y CAMPING EL CHILENO

CENTRO DE BIENVENIDA

Laguna Amarga

MIRADOR BRITÁNICO

MIRADOR FRANCÉS

REFUGIO Y CAMPING GREY

GUARDARÍA GLACIAR GREY

Cerro Paine Grande 3,248m

Cuernos del Paine

Río del Francés

Ventisquero Francés

Cerro Almirante Nieto 2,668m

REFUGIO TORRE NORTE/ REFUGIO Y CAMPING TORRE CENTRAL

PORTERÍA LAGUNA AMARGA

CAMPAMENTO ITALIANO (CONAF)

CAMPING Y DOMOS FRANCÉS

REFUGIO, CAMPING Y CABAÑAS LOS CUERNOS

GUARDERÍA ITALIANO

Lago Skottsberg

Lago Nordenskjöld

PORTERÍA LAGO SARMIENTO

Lago Grey

MIRADOR CUERNOS

Lago Sarmiento

GUARDERÍA PAINE GRANDE

PUDETO

REFUGIO Y CAMPING PAINE GRANDE

Río Pingo

Salto Grande

Lago Pehoé

To Cerro Castillo and Puerto Natales

CAMPING LAGO PEHOÉ/ PARRILLA PEHOÉ

Playa Grey

EXPLORA PATAGONIA

Laguna Verde

MIRADOR FERRIER

HOTEL LAGO GREY

Río Grey

HOSTERÍA MIRADOR DEL PAYNE

To Lago Pingo

GUARDERÍA GREY

Río Paine

PORTERÍA LAGUNA VERDE

ADMINISTRACIÓN

N

Río Serrano

0   4 mi

0   4 km

To Puerto Natales via Última Esperanza

PORTERÍA SERRANO

Lago Toro

Lago Tyndall

PAMPA LODGE

CABAÑAS LAGO TYNDALL

To Puerto Natales

PATAGONIA CAMP

© MOON.COM

particularly for its facilities, which range from basic campgrounds to luxury lodges. Annual visitor numbers have passed 250,000 in recent years; December-March, the crowds can feel overwhelming. Mandatory reservations for all campsites and accommodations have placed limits on overnight visitors, but the busloads of day-tripping tour groups heading to the park's star attractions, the Torres del Paine and Glaciar Grey, add significant congestion to the trails.

The shoulder seasons, September-November and March-April, are a much quieter time to visit, giving a better sense of what the landscapes were like before the park's popularity spiked. The notoriously fierce winds that lash the park are also calmer in these months than during summer. Winter treks along the O and W are also growing in popularity, although it's only possible to do this with a certified guide arranged through a tour agency.

PARK ENTRANCES

The park is north of Puerto Natales. The **southern entrance,** called **Portería Serrano,** can be accessed from the unpaved Y-290. The **CONAF headquarters** for the park, known as **Administración,** is 5km north of this entrance, on Lago del Torre. The scenic park road continues north to Pudeto, the ferry port on the eastern edge of Lago Pehoé, where the most celebrated views of the Cuernos del Paine are found. From Pudeto, the road connects with the northern entry points.

The park also has **four northern entrances,** all accessible from the settlement of Villa Cerro Castillo, where Ruta 9 continues northwest. South to north, they are **Portería Laguna Verde,** on the southern shore of Lago Sarmiento; **Portería Lago Sarmiento,** on the northern shore of Lago Sarmiento; **Portería Laguna Amarga,** west of Laguna Amarga, the entrance used by most buses and private vehicles; and **Portería Laguna Azul,** on the southeastern shore of Laguna Azul.

At Portería Laguna Amarga, buses take hikers to the trailhead for the O Circuit or the

Torres del Paine. The buses continue along the southern shore of Lago Nordenskjöld to the ferry port at Pudeto, where hikers doing the W Circuit from west to east cross to the trailhead at Guardería Paine Grande.

All of the park entrances keep the same **operating hours:** 8am-7pm daily October-April, 8:30am-6:15pm daily May-September.

★ TREKKING TORRES DEL PAINE

The major draws of the park are its two trekking routes, the **W** (80km, 4-5 days) and the **O** (115km, 9-10 days). The W passes the western, southern, and eastern sides of the Paine Massif; the O fully circumnavigates the mountain. Both trails offer sensational views. A third option is the Q, a variant on the O. Wildlife, including guanacos, Magellanic woodpeckers, and even pumas are commonly seen along the trails.

Planning Your Trek

Most visitors trek independently in Torres del Paine. Making reservations for the *refugios* and campgrounds along the routes is complicated, but both the W and the O trails are well signposted and easy to follow without a guide. Due to the longer daily distances for the O, this route is recommended for those with previous trekking experience.

Hikers are only permitted to camp or stay in the *refugios* or campgrounds along the trails, which are operated by CONAF, along with two private companies, **Vertice Patagonia** (Bulnes 100, Puerto Natales, tel. 61/2415 716, www.verticepatagonia.cl) and **Fantástico Sur** (Esmeralda 661, Puerto Natales, tel. 61/2614 184, www.fantasticosur.com). There are a smattering of free campsites around the park, run by CONAF. You must book all accommodations in advance through either company's website. Campsites are booked up months in advance; for **November-March,** it's essential to **reserve four months ahead.** For **shoulder seasons,** it's often necessary to book **at least two months in advance.** It is sometimes possible to acquire last-minute

Lightening Your Impact

With over 250,000 people visiting Parque Nacional Torres del Paine each year, concerns about environmental impact are increasing. Visitor numbers have doubled in the past decade, growing up to 10 percent annually. Due to the volume of hikers, trails have widened, eroding the surrounding land.

Impact on the trails is not the only issue. Human-caused fires have destroyed up to one-fifth of the park's land area since 1985. In 2011, a fire burned for a month, destroying 36,000 hectares of native forest, after a tourist set fire to toilet paper and didn't fully extinguish the flames. If you're caught making a fire within the park or using stoves in prohibited areas, the maximum penalty is a fine of up to CH$2 million and a jail term of three years, thanks to a law enacted after the 2011 fire.

The park is attempting to manage the increase in tourism and lighten environmental impact through several methods:

- In 2017, a **70-hiker daily limit** was imposed on the O trail. There is currently no daily limit for the W trail.

- Lodging provider **EcoCamp Patagonia** (www.ecocamp.travel) uses hydro- and solar energy and offers lodging in low-impact geodesic domes.

- The **Torres del Paine Legacy Fund** (www.supporttdp.org) leads reforestation projects, trail restoration, and maintenance. The fund also helped implement a recycling system in Puerto Natales, diverting 250,000 kilograms of waste from landfills in just the first year of the project.

- In 2018, the Awasi reserve, on the eastern edge of the park, was expanded from 600 to 4,500 hectares. The **Awasi Puma Foundation** (http://awasipatagonia.com/puma-foundation) is helping to restore the land to its original state, increasing territory for pumas and other native fauna.

Here are some ways that you can lighten your impact during your visit:

- Consider visiting during **shoulder seasons** (Oct.-Nov. and Mar.-Apr.) to help reduce overcrowding.

- **Stay on trails** at all times to avoid widening them.

- Practice **Leave No Trace** principles: Bring all rubbish out with you when you leave.

- Bring a **reusable water bottle** to fill at water taps in each of the campgrounds to reduce your use of single-use plastic bottles.

- **Don't smoke** on the trails; smoking is only permitted in designated areas.

- **Use a camp stove** only in designated parts of the campgrounds, and avoid any other type of fire.

- Consider donating to the **Torres del Paine Legacy Fund** (www.supporttdp.org) to support their restoration work and tourism infrastructure improvements, or to **Tu Mejor Huella** (www.tumejorhuella.com), a Canadian-led campaign to restore and future-proof part of the W trail.

spots by heading to the Puerto Natales offices of the two companies.

A CONAF-run **reservation site** (www.entradas.parquesnacionales.cl) allows you to book your campsites and buy your park ticket in one spot.

The W Route

The popular **W** route draws the lion's share of the park's crowds. If you don't mind sharing the trail with others, the experience retains a sense of hiking through wilderness, accompanied by surreal landscapes. The trail is named for the W shape that it traces from Lago Grey, across the northern shore of Lago Nordenskjöld and into Valle Ascencio.

The main starting point for this 80-km, four- to five-day trek is **Guardería Paine Grande,** in the west of the park. Hike east from here to see the granite towers of the Torres del Paine on your final day. In this direction, the end point of the route is the car park of the Hotel Las Torres. A 1-km hike northeast along the road toward Laguna Amarga leads to the **Centro de Bienvenida** (Welcome Center; next door to Refugio y Camping Torre Central). Here, minibuses shuttle passengers to Portería Laguna Amarga, where you can catch the bus to Puerto Natales. A benefit of going this direction is that you do the steepest climb when your backpack is at its lightest. It is possible to hike the route from east to west; you'll likely get stuck behind fewer hikers, but you'll also face a lot of oncoming traffic.

Trails are well marked, and at some points widened dramatically by the huge number of boots that pass daily. A guide is not necessary, although some people prefer going with an outfitter to avoid the hassle of reserving accommodations, which must be made online through each company's reservation system.

GETTING TO THE START

To reach Guardería Paine Grande, take the 90-passenger catamaran ferry from Pudeto operated by **Hielos Patagónicos** (Pudeto, tel. 61/2411 133, www.hipsur.com, departures 9am, 11am, 4:15pm, and 6pm daily Dec.-Mar., fewer daily departures Apr.-Nov., 25min., CH$23,000, cash only). You can't book a spot in advance; passengers pay at the ferry terminal and are accepted onto the boat on a first-come, first-served basis. In high season, get here at least 20 minutes before departure to ensure your spot on the boat.

DAY 1 (11KM)

From **Guardería Paine Grande,** take the trail north as it slices between the Paine Massif and Lago Grey, passing a series of striking viewpoints of Glaciar Grey in the distance, an hour after starting the hike. The trail arrives at **Guardería Glaciar Grey** and **Refugio y Camping Vertice Grey.** From the campsite, 1km through the forest are two viewpoints to watch bus-size chunks of ice bobbing in the water, or even calving from the glacier.

DAY 2 (11KM OR 18KM)

Retrace your steps south. Stay at **Refugio y Camping Paine Grande.** Hikers with higher fitness levels can add 3.5km each way by taking the trail heading north from the campground to reach two rope bridges hanging vertiginously over ravines gushing with water. There are breathtaking glacier views from the farther bridge.

DAY 3 (11.5KM OR 18.5KM)

From Refugio y Camping Paine Grande, the trail turns north and skirts the small Lago Skottberg before crossing the Río Francés by rope bridge to **Guardería Italiano** and the free CONAF-run **Campamento Italiano.** You can leave your bags here with the ranger before taking the spur that climbs north into the **Valle del Francés.** After an hour's steep climb up the rocky and slippery trail to **Mirador Francés,** absorb the views of Glaciar Francés.

Energetic hikers can continue to **Mirador Británico** (3.5km each way, 3hr), where lush forest leads to a ring of toothy granite peaks, including the park's second-most famous landmark, the three-horned **Cuernos del Paine.** It's one of the park's most stunning viewpoints—when the sky is clear.

From Guardería and Campamento Italiano, the path heads east along Lago Nordenskjöld. It's 30 minutes and 1.6km to **Camping y Domos Francés,** or continue 3.5km (45min) to **Refugio, Camping y Cabañas Los Cuernos.**

1: Glaciar Grey 2: hiking in Parque Nacional Torres del Paine

DAY 4 (12KM)

The path continues along the northern edge of Lago Nordenskjöld. After 8km (2.5hr), the trail forks. Take the well-signposted route north. Here begins the ascent to Mirador Las Torres. The trail enters the V-shaped Valle Ascencio, where the Río Ascencio is your constant companion. Following a bridge crossing 4km after the trail splits, Refugio y Camping El Chileno is tucked into the forest. This is the best place to stop for the night if you want to watch the sun rise across the towers at Mirador Las Torres the next morning.

DAY 5 (15KM)

The final day involves a steady climb through forested Valle Ascencio and a steep 30-minute slog through glacial moraine to Mirador Las Torres, the viewpoint of the famed towers and picturesque Laguna Torres. They're most stunning at dawn. To catch this view, leave at least two hours before sunrise, which can be as early as 4:45am in summer. Otherwise it takes 45 minutes to reach the towers from the free CONAF-run Campamento Torres (currently closed), 3km beyond Refugio y Camping El Chileno.

To finish the trek, double back and descend to the car park of Hotel Las Torres, the end point of the W trail. Take the well-signposted left fork of the trail 1.5km after leaving Refugio y Camping El Chileno. To get to the shuttles that meet the public buses at Laguna Amarga, it's a 1-km walk along the road northeast from the hotel. The bus departs from the car park of the Centro de Bienvenida.

HIKING THE W IN FOUR DAYS

It's possible to do the trek in just four days. This involves combining days one and two for a 22-km, seven-hour day by hiking to the Guardería Paine Grande and Guardería Glaciar Grey, and staying overnight at Refugio y Camping Paine Grande.

FOOD AND ACCOMMODATIONS

Vertice Patagonia (tel. 61/2415 716, www.verticepatagonia.cl) operates the basic Refugio y Camping Paine Grande (from CH$6,500 campsite, CH$34,000 dorm) and Refugio y Camping Vertice Grey (from CH$5,500 campsite, CH$22,000 dorm), situated between Guardería Paine Grande and Guardería Glaciar Grey.

Between Guardería Italiano and Mirador Las Torres, Fantástico Sur (tel. 61/2614 184, www.fantasticosur.com) has four lodgings: Camping y Domos Francés (CH$30,000 2-person camping platform, CH$83,000 dorm), Refugio, Camping y Cabañas Los Cuernos (CH$30,000 2-person camping platform, CH$83,000 dorm, CH$255,000 cabin), and the neighboring Refugio Torre Norte (CH$55,000 dorm) and Refugio y Camping Torre Central (CH$30,000 2-person camping platform, CH$83,000 dorm). At the eastern end of the route is Refugio y Camping El Chileno (CH$87,000 2-person camping platform, CH$140,000 dorm), where self-catering is not allowed; meals are included in the rates.

If meals aren't built into the rates, you can request breakfast or three meals (including a box lunch) for extra cost. All lodgings include access to hot showers. Paine Grande, Francés, Torre Norte, and El Chileno also have small shops selling basic supplies. If you plan to cook for yourself, buy all your food and gas canisters in Puerto Natales.

CONAF runs two free but extremely basic campsites, Campamento Italiano and Campamento Torres. Facilities consist of a small covered lean-to without electricity or equipment for cooking and two toilets. Campamento Torres is currently closed, with no set date for reopening. For either campsite, it's essential to make reservations on the park's website (www.parquetorresdelpaine.cl).

The O Route (The Circuit)

The official name of this route is the Circuito Macizo Paine Grande, but it's more commonly called The Circuit or just the O. It's an extended version of the W route that totals 115km and takes 9-10 days to complete. The park caps the maximum number of hikers on the O to 70 per day, making it decidedly quieter.

For fit hikers, it's possible, if challenging, to combine some sections to shorten the trek to seven days, as many sections only require five hours of hiking. The route is mostly well marked, but a GPS receiver or map downloaded onto your phone can help at points where the trail splits in different directions. The O is open to independent hikers October-mid-April, although poor weather can see it closed earlier. Outside these months, you must visit with a guide, such as **Erratic Rock** (Baquedano 955, Puerto Natales, www.erraticrock.com), which has excellent English-speaking guides and includes camping gear.

The route begins at the **Portería Laguna Amarga,** looping counterclockwise around the Paine Massif and joining the W at **Guardería Glaciar Grey.** From the trailhead, you walk 7km (1.5hr) along the road to the Centro de Bienvenida (Welcome Center), passing north through Valle Encantado. From the Refugio y Camping Torre Central next door, the trail curves west to follow the gushing meltwaters of Río Paine and takes an easy, mostly flat route along the river. Your first night's lodging is at **Camping Serón,** 13km and four hours later.

The second day is more challenging, with the trail traversing the northern foothills of the Cordillera Paine as it continues west. A steep descent leads to the southern end of Lago Dickson after 18km (5hr), a lake ringed with hanging glaciers. Camping is available on a flat grassy plain next to the lake at **Refugio y Camping Dickson.**

On day three, the path continues west, climbing steadily into the Cordillera Paine, offering viewpoints back across Lago Dickson and forward toward Glaciar Puma and the striking Glaciar Los Perros, which cling precipitously to the mountains. Stop overnight at **Camping Los Perros.**

Day four begins with a steep 4.5-km, three-hour climb over the 1,180-meter Paso John Gardner—best attempted early in the morning when the winds are calmer—for panoramic views of Glaciar Grey and, on a clear day, north across the blinding expanse of the Southern Patagonian Ice Field. After an unpleasant steep section of downhill, where trekking poles are recommended (particularly after poor weather), the trail turns south to pass alongside Glaciar Grey. **Campamento Paso** is 3.5km after the pass. Many hikers continue to **Refugio y Camping Vertice Grey,** where the lodgings are significantly more comfortable. This *refugio* marks the beginning of the W; from Paso John Gardner, it's 7km.

FOOD AND ACCOMMODATIONS

Accommodations along the O are far more basic than on the W. **Camping Serón** (CH$22,000 pp) is a large campground with multiple covered cooking areas and even hot showers. It's owned by **Fantástico Sur** (tel. 61/2614 184, www.fantasticosur.com).

Operated by **Vertice Patagonia** (tel. 61/2415 716, www.verticepatagonia.cl), **Refugio y Camping Dickson** (from CH$5,500 campsite, CH$22,000 dorm) has hot showers and geodesic domes for cooking, as well as a full-board option. It is also possible to recharge your devices here. From the same company, **Camping Los Perros** (CH$5,500 campsite) has the most basic facilities—expect only a cold shower.

Before the O joins the W, there's nowhere to buy food other than in the very basic shops at Camping Serón and Refugio y Camping Dickson. It's best to buy all your provisions in Puerto Natales. Mice can be a real problem in the park, particularly on the O, so keep food off the ground; tie it in a tree where possible.

The Q

Adding 18km to the O route, the Q requires hikers to start at **Guardería Paine Grande,** continue east along the W route, join the O at **Hotel Las Torres,** and hike the full circuit to return to Guardería Paine Grande. Rather than taking the ferry across the lake to Pudeto, continue south along the path that leads to **Administración.**

Due to restrictions imposed by CONAF, it is only possible to leave, not enter, the park via this path. If you're planning on taking the bus back from Administración, confirm with your bus company that they pick up passengers here; many buses have reduced their services because of these restrictions.

Other Hikes

Beyond the three main routes, a number of other paths promise equally stunning views with significantly fewer visitors. Only accessible with a guide, **Sendero al Pingo** (36km round-trip, 2 days) starts from Guardería Grey on the southern skirts of Lago Grey and is a tiring, six- to seven-hour climb to reach Mirador Zapata, with glorious views of Glaciar Pingo. There's camping nearby at the basic free Campamento Zapata (run by CONAF), around 1.5 hours' hike from the *mirador*.

Also starting from Guardería Lago Grey, a steep trail (2.2km one-way, 2hr) gains 600 meters of elevation as it climbs through forest to emerge at **Mirador Ferrier** for spectacular views across Lago Grey and toward Lago Pehoé and the Paine Massif. From the Pudeto ferry dock, the **Sendero Mirador Cuernos** (3km one-way, 1hr) is a lovely, easy hike with the looming, rugged peaks of the Cuernos del Paine visible throughout. The trail starts around 700 meters along the Y-158 from the ferry dock; take the signposted path heading north.

On the northeastern edge of the park, accessed from the car park at the Portería Laguna Azul, is the **Sendero Laguna Cebolla** (10km one-way, 3hr), an easy, flat hike through low scrubby bushes to the shores of the trail's namesake lake.

TOURS

Puerto Natales is where the majority of tours to Parque Nacional Torres del Paine depart from.

Day Tours

For those short on time, a day tour from Puerto Natales allows a hike on one section of the W. Most tour agencies in Puerto Natales offer 8- to 10-hour tours of the park in large buses. These tours include stops at viewpoints along Lago Sarmiento, Laguna Amarga, Lago Nordenskjöld, and Lago Pehoé, short walks to Salto Grande and along Lago Grey, plus a visit to the Cueva del Milodón. Entrance fees for the park and Cueva del Milodón and food are not included. **Patagonia Adventure** (Ladrilleros 209, tel. 61/2411 028, www.apatagonia.com) and **Comapa** (Bulnes 541, tel. 61/2414 300, www.comapa.com) offer cheap excursions (from CH$40,000). The tradeoff for the low price is a large group size. Both outfitters also offer a **hiking tour** (from CH$40,000) that takes you to the base of the Torres del Paine. The 12-hour tour includes transportation from Puerto Natales to the trailhead, a guide, and trekking poles.

Agencies in Punta Arenas also offer day trips, but with an additional three hours of driving just to get to Puerto Natales, it's an exhaustingly long tour, and you'll only spend 10 minutes at each stop in the park.

Note that in the winter (May-Sept.), visitors can only enter the park with a certified tour guide. This applies to both day hikers and multiday trekkers.

Trekking Tours

Various Puerto Natales tour agencies offer trekking tours of the W, including a guide, all meals, and equipment (except sleeping bags and trekking poles) and transfers into and out of the park. These tours start at US$1,100. A guided tour is rarely necessary because the trails are well marked, but taking one does mean you avoid the hassle of organizing your accommodations with the different companies. Far fewer companies run guided tours of the O.

Chile Nativo (Eberhard 230, tel. 61/2411 835, www.chilenativo.travel) offers tours of the W with knowledgeable English-speaking guides (US$2,000). Lodging is in dorm-style accommodations. **Erratic Rock** (Baquedano 955, www.erraticrock.com) employs excellent

English-speaking guides on its tours of both the W (from US$1,500) and the O (US$2,500). Prices include camping gear (except trekking poles and sleeping bags), meals, and transfers to and from the park. For an additional US$150 per day, Erratic Rock offers a porter service. Erratic Rock also runs the shorter and more challenging eight-day, seven-night version of the Circuit.

Ice-Trekking and Kayaking Tours

Big Foot Patagonia Adventure (Av. Pedro Montt 161, tel. 61/2414 611, www. bigfootpatagonia.com) is the only company permitted to take tours onto **Glaciar Grey.** A short Zodiac ride takes you to the edge of the glacier, where, after a 45-minute walk, you spend 2.5 hours climbing through tunnels in the ice, peering into the deep fissures, and appreciating the sunshine refracted off the deep-blue ice.

Crampons and harnesses are supplied. It's necessary to be fit for this activity, as you climb ladders over rock faces and, optionally, out of ice caves. Group sizes are capped at 15 (2-person min.); tours are CH$104,500 pp. Transfers into the park to the Big Foot Base Camp are not included in the price.

Big Foot also offers 2.5-hour kayaking tours (2-person min., CH$66,000 pp) of Lago Grey, leaving from their base camp. You paddle 500 meters from Glaciar Grey as you dodge icebergs. Tours include all equipment, a safety briefing, and a snack. The outfitter is inside the hotel Spacio Kau. Excursions run October-April.

Antares Patagonia (Av. Pedro Montt 161, inside Spacio Kau, tel. 61/2414 611, www. antarespatagonia.com) can organize four- or five-day excursions that include pickup from Punta Arenas, a shortened version of the W route, plus kayaking on Lago Grey and ice trekking on Glaciar Grey. All transfers, accommodations, food, and equipment are included. Prices start at US$1,185 (2-person min.).

Boat Tours

From the jetty at Playa Grey, **Turismo Lago Grey** (tel. 61/2712 100, www.lagogrey. com) runs the *Grey III* (3-4 times daily), a 98-passenger ferry. The ferry crosses Lago Grey to Refugio y Camping Glaciar Grey, returning via a stop in front of the western arm of Glaciar Grey to admire the dense blue color of this mammoth block of ice. One-way tickets cost CH$65,000 adults, CH$32,000 children. Round-trip tickets are CH$75,000 adults, CH$37,500 children. Round-trip tickets are only for those who don't plan to disembark from the boat.

ACCOMMODATIONS

Most hotels at the park have their own restaurants. Many of these are open to nonguests; expect high prices for both food and lodging. There's a small **café** serving sandwiches, cakes, and coffees at the Pudeto ferry dock. For accommodations along the W or O trekking routes, see the *Food and Accommodations* section for each route.

Under CH$25,000

The large, fifty-site **Camping Lago Pehoé** (tel. 2/1962 0387 or 9/7499 1958, www. campingpehoe.com, CH$90,000 dome for two with shared bath and breakfast, CH$11,000 camping pp), 10km north of Administración and a 10-minute drive from the catamaran ferry jetty at Pudeto, has 24-hour electricity, hot showers, and several small shelters with picnic tables for cooking. Five geodesic domes are bare of any furniture but are warmer and more stable against the wind than camping. They offer tent rentals too. There's also a small store on-site, with basic canned food, chocolate, and cereal, and the occasional fresh fruit and vegetables. A small restaurant, **Parrilla Pehoé** (noon-3pm and 8pm-11pm daily Oct.-Mar., CH$9,000-11,000, *menu del día* $22,000), serves steak and grilled fish, along with three-course set menus of barbecued meat or fish; portions are ample and the views are spectacular.

Over CH$80,000

Hotel Lago Tyndall burned down in 2017, but the affiliated **Cabañas Lago Tyndall** (tel. 9/4095 8332, www.explorandopatagonia.cl, Sept.-Apr., CH$110,000 4-person cabin) is still operating. On a bend in Río Serrano, the cabins are somewhat dated but spacious, with ample living space, an equipped kitchen, and robust underfloor heating, making them a good option for self-catering to avoid the extortionate dining fees in the park. Make sure to stock up in Puerto Natales, as there are no shops here. Breakfast is not available. Rates include IVA.

Next to the Portería Laguna Verde entrance, **Hostería Mirador del Payne** (Y-180, Lazo, tel. 9/7519 0351, www.miradordelpayne.cl, CH$151,000 d) has stylishly if slightly simpler bedrooms than you might expect at this price range. The beautiful, tranquil setting and views across Lago Verde and the Paine Massif make up for the lack of luxury. A number of short hiking trails with spectacular views start nearby. This working ranch with a herd of Hereford cattle provides a true sense of Patagonia far from other visitors. Breakfast costs extra, while a fixed daily menu and a box lunch can be organized. There's only electricity in the morning and evening, and no Wi-Fi. Note that it's a 1.5-hour drive to enter the park from here. It's wise to bring a spare can of gasoline to avoid the need to return to Puerto Natales to refuel your vehicle. They accept payment by cash or bank transfer only.

With minimalist design and views across Río Serrano to the Paine Massif, the nine-room **Pampa Lodge** (www.pampalodgepatagonia.com, Oct.-Apr., CH$205,000 d) is a more affordable option than most in the park. The living area and bedrooms have sweeping views. Meals are available in their restaurant—specializing in roast lamb, although various dishes are available—and they offer horseback tours to nearby lookouts. Rates include IVA.

On the southern banks of the bewitching Lago Grey is **Hotel Lago Grey** (tel. 61/2712 100, www.lagogrey.com, CH$225,000 standard d, CH$262,000 superior d). It's worth spending on one of the superior rooms that looks out on the lake for views of icebergs from your bed. Rooms are modern, with all the necessary facilities, and the restaurant offers a set menu for lunch and dinner, with decent food; the food in the bar is disappointing. This is also the check-in for Lago Grey boat crossings and glacier tours. They have an office in Punta Arenas (Lautaro Navarro 1077). Rates include IVA.

Few of the hotels in the park blend so effortlessly into the surroundings as the geodesic domes of ★ **EcoCamp Patagonia** (tel. 2/2923 5950, US toll-free tel. 888/232-3813, www.ecocamp.travel, US$3,150 d 3 nights all-inclusive), a short distance from the trailhead for Mirador Las Torres. The domes are designed after the dwellings of the indigenous Kawésqar people but include all the modern amenities for post-hike relaxation. With state-of-the-art composting toilets and hydraulic and solar energy, the domes have impressive sustainable credentials. It's worth upgrading from a standard dome with shared bath—which has no electricity, heating, or a locking door—to a superior or a suite. Suites have wood stoves, the best views of the forest, and en suite baths. Single travelers can opt to share a standard dome with a member of the same sex without paying the single surcharge. They have a yoga dome and an office in Puerto Natales (Barros Arana 166).

With its prime position on the southern shore of Lago Torre looking toward the Paine Massif, ★ **Patagonia Camp** (Km 74 Ruta Y-290, tel. 2/2594 0591, www.patagoniacamp.com, CH$426,000 d, 2-night min.) is a top choice for luxury lodgings. All 20 yurts contain rain showers and wood heaters, while the service and knowledge of the guides is exceptional. There are no TVs or Wi-Fi in the rooms, and the Wi-Fi in communal areas is spotty, but each yurt has panoramic views, a private terrace, and even a jetted tub in the suites. Energy credentials are impressive; the hotel is almost fully sustainable, with solar, wind, and small hydro turbines for electricity and composting toilets that look like normal ones. All-inclusive packages are available, including tours and meals at the superb on-site restaurant, with *cordero al palo* (spit-roasted lamb) available twice weekly. They have an office in Puerto Natales (Manuel Señoret 325, tel. 61/2415 149).

On the eastern shore of Lago Sarmiento, 30 minutes' drive from the Portería Laguna Amarga entrance, **Tierra Patagonia Hotel & Spa** (tel. 2/2207 8861, www.tierrahotels. com, Oct.-May, US$7,000 d 3 nights all-inclusive) offers luxury despite the remote setting. Low on the landscape, the wooden exterior seems to disappear into the surrounding grasslands. Rooms are decorated with local materials, although perhaps more simply than expected at this price range, with views across the lake and the national park. Dining and attention are top-notch. All packages include park excursions, use of the spa, and transfers from the airport in Punta Arenas. Packages start from three nights.

On the outskirts of the park, the secluded 14 luxury villas, each with a private hot tub, at ★ **Awasi Patagonia** (tel. 2/2233 9641, US toll-free tel. 888/880-3219, www. awasipatagonia.com, Oct.-Apr., US$7,400 d 3 nights all-inclusive) are tucked into the steppe, making them seem part of the landscape. To provide the most custom-made experience of any lodging in the park, the hotel assigns guests their own private guide and a 4WD vehicle to explore at their own pace. From the restaurant, with innovative customized cuisine with local ingredients, it's possible to see the tips of the towers, which are particularly stunning at dawn. Villas are spread out, so opt for one close to the lodge if you want to avoid a 10-miniute walk. They offer excursions within their adjoining 4,500-hectare private reserve. Minimum is three nights; transfers from and to Puerto Natales are included.

If it's views you're after, no other property matches **Explora Patagonia** (Salto Chico, tel. 2/2395 2800, US toll-free tel. 866/750-6699, www.explora.com, US$8,000 d 3 nights all-inclusive), inside the park and with panoramic vistas of Lago Pehoé and the Paine Massif from most bedrooms, the grand living area, and even the jetted tubs on the shoreline. Their Explorer's Bar makes a welcome retreat after hiking. Prices are all-inclusive, with decadent meals cooked by chefs and transfers from Punta Arenas airport.

INFORMATION AND SERVICES

Administración (tel. 61/2691 931, 8am-7pm daily Oct.-Apr., 8:30am-6:15pm daily May-Sept.) has a visitors center with information about the geography and flora and fauna of the park, plus public **restrooms** and a public **telephone.** To climb any mountain in the Paine Massif, you must obtain authorization from the rangers here.

Store your luggage with **Refugio y Camping Torre Central** (next to the Centro de Bienvenida). Rates are CH$4,000 per day for backpacks 40 liters and smaller, and CH$7,000 per day for packs larger than 40 liters. The service operates on a first-come, first-served basis.

Public **restrooms** are also at Portería Lago Sarmiento and Portería Laguna Amarga, the Pudeto catamaran dock, and at Guardería Grey. Next to the Refugio y Camping Torre Central, the **Centro de Bienvenida** (Welcome Center, no phone, www.cerropaine. com, 9am-11pm daily Sept.-Apr.) has restrooms, a large car park, and a shop that sells hiking clothing and rents camping equipment.

GETTING THERE
Car
From Puerto Natales, it's an 84-km drive north on Ruta 9 and the unpaved Y-290 to reach the park's southern entrance, **Portería Serrano.** The **CONAF headquarters** for the park, known as **Administración,** is 5km north of here. The main northern entrance, **Portería Laguna Amarga,** is 112km (1.5hr) north on Ruta 9 and northwest along the Y-150, Y-160, and Y-156.

Three lesser-used entrances are also accessible by vehicle. **Portería Laguna Verde,** on the southern shore of Lago Sarmiento, is a 112-km, 2-hour drive along Ruta 9 and the Y-180. **Portería Lago Sarmiento,** on the northern shore of Lago Sarmiento, is 111km and 1.5 hours along Ruta 9 and the Y-150. **Portería Laguna Azul,** on the southeastern shore of Laguna Azul, is via Ruta 9, continuing north on the Y-160 when it turns west toward Laguna Amarga; it's a drive of 116km and 2 hours.

There are car parks at all entrances, in addition to a large car park outside the Centro de Bienvenida, 6km west of Portería Laguna Amarga, at Administración, and at the Pudeto ferry dock. The car park outside Hotel Las Torres is only for guests of the hotel.

Note that there are no gas stations in the park or on any road from Puerto Natales. Bringing an extra can of gas is a sensible idea if you plan on driving more than one day around the national park. Hotel Las Torres can sometimes sell 10 liters of fuel, but expect to pay double what it costs in Puerto Natales.

Bus

It's possible to take a bus from Puerto Natales's Terminal Rodoviario (Av. España 1455) to three of the park entrances. The fare is CH$8,000 one-way or CH$15,000 round-trip. In high season, there are two departures from Puerto Natales, 7am and 2:30pm daily. Buses enter at the **Portería Laguna Amarga,** arriving 9am and 4:30pm, before continuing to the catamaran ferry dock at **Pudeto,** arriving 10am and 5:30pm, and ending at **Administración** (11:45am and 6pm). You are generally required to pay your park admission fee at the Portería Laguna Amarga, regardless of whether you are continuing into the park by bus. Some bus companies no longer stop at the Administración; if you're planning to get off or get picked up here, confirm this before purchasing your ticket. Leaving the park, buses pick up passengers at 12:30pm and 6pm daily from Administración, at 1pm and 7pm from Pudeto, and at 2:30pm and 7:45pm from Portería Laguna Amarga.

A number of bus companies offer routes into the park, including **JB Buses Patagonia** (tel. 61/2410 242, www.busesjb. com), **Transport Maria José** (tel. 61/2410 951, www.busesmariajose.com), **Buses Juan Ojeda** (tel. 9/8943 7808), and **Buses Gómez** (tel. 61/2415700, www.busesgomez.com). In peak season, book bus tickets at least a day in advance; the return ticket is valid for any day, although it's a good idea to confirm your intended return date when you buy the ticket.

Direct bus transfers between El Calafate and the national park (dropping off and collecting passengers at Laguna Amarga or the Pudeto ferry dock) operate daily September-April through **Always Glaciares** (Av. del Libertador 924, tel. 02902/493 961, http://alwaysglaciers.com). The journey takes 5-9 hours and starts from US$55 pp.

Boat

Turismo 21 de Mayo (Eberhard 560, tel. 61/2614 420, www.turismo21demayo.com) is the only company that runs the one-day boat journey from Puerto Natales into the park. From their office in Puerto Natales, you'll be driven to Muelle Bories to board a boat that takes you north through the Seno Última Esperanza to admire Glaciares Balmaceda and Serrano and then, via speedboat, up the meandering Río Serrano, with views of the Southern Patagonian Ice Field, to reach its confluence with Río Grey. For CH$140,000, lunch is included; your park entry fee is not. They also offer the trip in reverse.

GETTING AROUND

Beyond the twice-daily buses that shuttle hikers into the park, public transportation is nonexistent. Without a vehicle, it is difficult to get between the sectors of the park, unless you're hiking. One option is to wait for the public buses bringing hikers into the park to see if they have space to take you between Laguna Amarga and Pudeto (or vice versa); expect to pay around CH$4,000.

Once you're in the park, to reach **Guardería Paine Grande,** a few hundred meters from the start of the W trek, you'll need to board the 90-passenger catamaran ferry at the **Pudeto dock**. It's operated by **Hielos Patagónicos** (Pudeto, tel. 61/2411 133, www.hipsur.com, departures 9am, 11am, 4:15pm, and 6pm daily Dec.-Mar., fewer daily departures Apr.-Nov., 25min, CH$23,000, cash only). The service does not operate May-August. You can't book a spot in advance; passengers pay at the ferry terminal and board the boat first come, first served. In high season, get here at least 20 minutes before departure to ensure your spot on the boat.

A **minivan shuttle service** (30min, CH$5,000) runs between Portería Laguna Amarga and the car park of the Centro de Bienvenida, 11km northwest along the Y-156 and the signposted turnoff to Refugio y Camping Torre Central. You can book a spot via the Centro de Bienvenida's website (www.cerropaine.com) or try for a walk-up spot (first-come, first-served). The minivans are timed to connect with the buses arriving at Laguna Amarga and those leaving again in the afternoon.

Argentinean Patagonia

The Argentinean side of Southern Patagonia has striking natural landmarks, including the accessible El Perito Moreno, Argentina's most famous glacier, and a maze of hiking trails. This part of Patagonia is unmissable for trekkers thanks to Parque Nacional Los Glaciares.

At the southern edge of Argentinean Tierra del Fuego, lively Ushuaia gives visitors bragging rights for having reached the world's southernmost city. Cruise ships depart from here to otherwise inaccessible Chilean fjords and the ultimate adventure destination: Antarctica.

EL CALAFATE

On the milky-green waters of Lago Argentino, the town of El Calafate (pop. 24,000), has grown rapidly since the early 2000s. The town allows access to the dramatic Glaciar Perito Moreno, 56km southwest in Parque Nacional Los Glaciares. The international airport provides easy links throughout the region as well as to Buenos Aires.

El Calafate is along east-west Ruta 11, known as Avenida del Libertador General José de San Martín; locals shorten this to **Avenida del Libertador** and **Avenida San Martín.** Along the avenue are many restaurants and shops selling high-priced souvenirs and expensive outdoor equipment. Prices are among the highest you'll find in Argentina outside Ushuaia. A day or two here is sufficient, particularly if you'll be hiking in the northern part of the national park, which is better accessed from El Chaltén.

Sights

The **Museo Calafate** (Av. Brown y Bonwell, tel. 02902/492 799, 10am-8pm daily, US$8 adults, US$4 children) contains information on some of the region's first inhabitants. One exhibit sensitively covers the inhumane treatment of the indigenous Tehuelche people, many of whom were forced from their lands in the 1880s and into labor camps in naval workshops and barracks, while others were kidnapped and sent to be studied in European museums.

GLACIARIUM

Six kilometers west of El Calafate, the excellent **Glaciarium** (Km 6 Ruta 11, tel. 02902/497 912, www.glaciarium.com, 9am-8pm daily Oct.-Mar., 11am-7pm daily Apr.-Sept., US$15 adults, US$6 children) is an audiovisual museum on the Southern Patagonian Ice Field. Interactive images show the retreat of many glaciers in this ice cap; the change in the past decade in Glaciar Upsala is particularly notable. One dramatic room highlights the tremendous effects of global warming across the world.

El Calafate

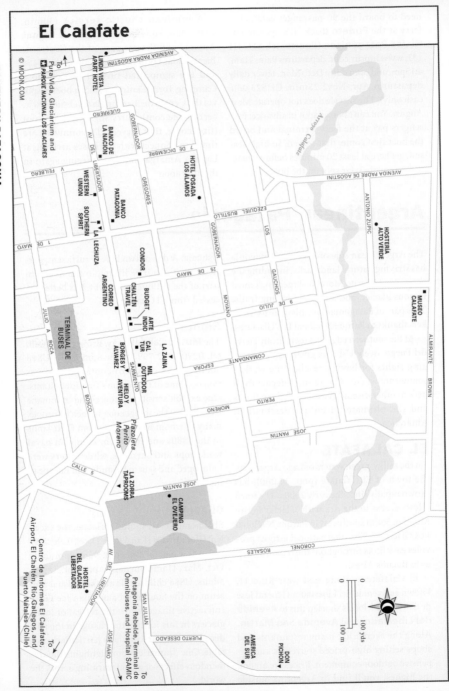

To Pura Vida, Glaciarium and ⊞ PARQUE NACIONAL LOS GLACIARES

LINDA VISTA APART HOTEL

AVENIDA PADRA AGOSTINI

GUERRERO

GOBERNADOR

7 DE DICIEMBRE

BANCO DE LA NACIÓN

HOTEL POSADA LOS ÁLAMOS

AV. DEL LIBERTADOR

V. FELBERG

GREGORES

EZEQUIEL BUSTILLO

AVENIDA PADRE DE AGOSTINI

ANTONIO ZUPIC

WESTERN UNION

SOUTHERN SPIRIT

LA LECHUZA

BANCO PATAGONIA

GOBERNADOR

LOS GAUCHOS

HOSTERÍA ALTO VERDE

1 DE MAYO

CONDOR

25 DE MAYO

MOYANO

MUSEO CALAFATE

ALMIRANTE BROWN

CORREO ARGENTINO

CHALTÉN TRAVEL

BUDGET

ARTE INDIO

9 DE JULIO

JULIO A. ROCA

TERMINAL DE BUSES

BORGES Y ALVAREZ

CAL TUR

MIL OUTDOOR

LA ZAINA

COMANDANTE ESPORA

PERITO

S J BOSCO

HIELO Y AVENTURA

SARMIENTO

MORENO

JOSÉ PANTIN

CALLE 5

Plazoleta Perito Moreno

JOSÉ PANTIN

LA ZORRA TAPROOMS

CAMPING EL OVEJERO

CORONEL ROSALES

Centro de Informes El Calafate, Airport, El Chaltén, Río Gallegos, and Puerto Natales (Chile)

HOSTEL DEL GLACIAR LIBERTADOR

AV. DEL LIBERTADOR

JOSÉ HARO

SAN JULIÁN

PUERTO DESEADO

To Patagonia Rebelde, Terminal de Ómnibuses, and Hospital SAMIC

To El Chaltén, Río Gallegos, and

AMÉRICA DEL SUR

DON PICHON

0   100 yds
0   100 m

Downstairs in the same building, **Glaciobar** (11:30am-8pm daily, US$10 adults, US$5 children) is a bar completely made from ice—the tables, the walls, even the glasses. Due to the chilly temperature, you can spend a maximum of 30 minutes here.

Food

Adorned with fairy lights, the stylishly antique ★ **La Zaina** (Gobernador Gregores 1057, tel. 02902/496 789, 5:30pm-midnight daily, US$12-16) has perhaps the best food in El Calafate. The dishes are decidedly Argentinean; it's a good place for steak, although the braised lamb in malbec and the huge lamb burgers go down well too. Despite always being filled with customers, the low lighting and small size makes it feel intimate.

A 10-minute walk west down Avenida San Martín, quirky ★ **Pura Vida** (Av. del Libertador 1876, tel. 02902/493 356, 7:30pm-11:30pm Thurs.-Tues., US$10-15) offers hearty meat stews and pies that are perfect for a cold night. Rich lasagnas and vegetarian baked eggplant are some of El Calafate's best. With a roaring fire and chirpy waiters, the space is even more inviting than the menu.

A solid if not fancy option, **La Lechuza** (Av. del Libertador 1301, tel. 02902/491 610, noon-11:30pm daily, US$10-12) offers a large menu of pizza with practically any topping you can think of. Their empanadas are excellent. Service at peak times can be slow, even by local standards.

Hip beer bars have come to Argentina in the form of the slick **La Zorra Taprooms** (Av. del Libertador 832, tel. 02902/488 042, 6am-2am Mon., noon-2am Tues.-Thurs., noon-3am Fri.-Sat., noon-2am Sun., US$5-8). Choose from 12 beers on tap, brewed here in El Calafate. Sensational food options include scotch ale-braised pork steak sandwiches, thick lamb stews, and lighter bites. The atmosphere is buzzing thanks to the cool young clientele. Get here early, as it's always packed. There's live music some nights, and half-price pints 6pm-7pm daily.

Well-established and welcoming **Don**

Pichón (Puerto Deseado 242, tel. 02902/492 577, www.parrilladonpichon.com, 6:30pm-midnight daily, US$12-15) is famed for roasted lamb and enormous meat platters, large enough for two, as well as the view from huge windows of the city and Lago Argentino. Dig into top-quality Argentinean steak with a glass of red from the ample wine menu.

Accommodations

Lodgings are expensive in El Calafate. There's not a huge variety of options, particularly at the top end. Reservations are essential December-February.

UNDER US$40

The cheapest rooms in town are at no-frills hostel **El Ovejero** (José Pantín 64, tel. 02902/493 422, campingelovejero@hotmail.com, US$5 camping, US$9 dorm). Dorm beds feature cast-iron frames. There is a very small kitchen and communal area, and outside, space for 60 tents next to a small stream. Each plot has a picnic table and barbecue area plus access to hot showers and laundry sinks.

US$40-65

Rooms line a central grassy area in the deceptively large **Hostel del Glaciar Libertador** (Av. del Libertador 587, tel. 02902/492 492, June-Apr., US$18-25 dorm, US$62 d). The dorms are cramped but all have en suite baths. Private rooms are simple but spotless; the toilet and shower both have their own individual rooms. There's a kitchen, restaurant, and tour agency, as well as bike rental and laundry service.

A 10-minute walk from the bus station and Avenida San Martín, backpacker-favorite **America del Sur** (Puerto Deseado 153, tel. 02902/493 525, http://americahostel.com.ar, US$20 dorm, US$80 d) is one of the largest hostels in town, making it feel slightly impersonal. The huge kitchen, large living and dining area with sweeping lake views, and en suite guest rooms make it feel anything but budget. Well-priced meals are available in the evenings, and there's occasional live music.

US$65-95

In the converted house of an old estancia, **Kau Yatún** (Estancia 25 de Mayo, tel. 02902/491 059, www.kauyatun.com, US$77 standard d, US$90 superior d) offers hotel rooms in a pretty rural setting 1.5km south of El Calafate. The standard rooms, smaller than the superiors, are well proportioned and charmingly decorated with wooden shutters and old-fashioned light fixtures. Guests can take a free tour of the still-functioning sheep ranch. It's easy to zip back and forth into town on the complimentary bikes.

US$95-125

Linda Vista Apart Hotel (Alberto de Agostini 71, tel. 02902/493 598, www.lindavistahotel.com.ar, US$120 d) offers 10 functional close-set cabins around a pretty floral garden. Cabins vary in size but all have living areas and kitchens, an excellent budget option to cook for yourself. Breakfast is included.

On the northern side of El Calafate, close to Lago Argentino but only a 10-minute walk to Avenida San Martín, **Hostería Alto Verde** (Zupic 138, tel. 02902/491 326, US$95 d, US$150 apartment) is in an unappealing building but with a pretty lawn and rose garden out front. Inside is a mixture of exposed brickwork and neutral decorations. Standard rooms are large and contain desks and mini fridges; the apartments have a kitchenette with kettle, fridge, microwave, and table. The staff exude friendliness.

OVER CH$125

The word *quirky* doesn't do justice to the 12 bedrooms of the grand **Patagonia Rebelde** (José Haro 442, tel. 02902/494 495, www.patagoniarebelde.com, US$130 standard d, US$263 Pullman d). Everything from the hotel's signage, which recalls a historic station platform, to the old brass carriage numbers on the doors and the dim hallway lighting resemble a 1950s Buenos Aires train station. Unfortunately, the rooms are also realistic in their small size. Downstairs, the stylish living room and bar contain antique trunks, typewriters, and other railroad memorabilia. Breakfast is on the simple side. The hostel is a 10-minute walk to the bus terminal and the main stretch of Avenida San Martín.

Four-star **Hotel Posada Los Alamos** (Ingenerio Guatti 1135, tel. 02902/491 144, www.posadalosalamos.com, US$270 standard d) is one of El Calafate's most traditional options. In four redbrick buildings with wood-framed windows and pretty window boxes, this hotel has all amenities, including a pool and spa, a nine-hole golf course, and a cocktail bar. The on-site restaurant, La Posta, is open to nonguests.

Information and Services

For information about El Calafate or the national park, visit **Centro de Informes El Calafate** (Bajada de Palma 44, tel. 02902/491 090, www.elcalafate.tur.ar, 8am-8pm daily), run by the municipal tourist board, with maps and other useful information. Staffers speak English.

Within town is **Hospital SAMIC** (Jorge Newberry 435, tel. 02902/491 889) and the post office, **Correo Argentino** (Av. del Libertador 1133, tel. 02902/491 012, 8am-4:30pm Mon.-Fri.). Most restaurants and hotels accept cards, but **Banco de la Nación** (Av. del Libertador and 7 de Diciembre) and **Banco Patagonia** (Av. del Libertador 1355) have **24-hour ATMs** that allow withdrawals using international credit and debit cards. The **Western Union** (Av. del Libertador 1133, tel. 02902/490 565, 9am-8pm Mon.-Fri., 10am-8pm Sat., 4pm-8pm Sun.) offers currency exchange. Withdrawing money can be a real issue in the city, as ATMs frequently run out of cash or do not accept foreign bank cards. Bring U.S. dollars when possible, as these can be exchanged or used to pay directly.

Condor (25 de Mayo 51, tel. 02902/491 655 or 02902/492 655, www.remiscondorcalafate.com.ar) operates taxis around the city and can provide private transfers (US$100) to and from local attractions, including Zona Sur of the Parque Nacional Los Glaciares. Rental car companies are concentrated in the arrivals terminal of the airport, including **Hertz** (tel. 02902/492 525, www.hertz.com, 8am-10m daily) and **Budget** (tel. 02902/492 829, www.budget.com.ar, 8am-8pm Mon.-Fri., 9am-6pm Sat.-Sun.). In El Calafate are **Hertz** (Av. del Libertador 1822, tel. 02902/493 033, 9am-8pm Mon.-Sat.) and **Budget** (9 de Julio 190, tel. 02902/496 200, 9am-noon and 5pm-8pm Mon.-Fri., 9am-noon Sat.).

If you're driving north to El Chaltén, fill up in El Calafate at the **YPF gas station** (Av. del Libertador and José Pantín, no phone, 24 hr daily). There is no gas station between the towns; the one in El Chaltén often runs out and is cash only. There is only one gas station between El Calafate and Puerto Natales, at the settlement of **Tapi Aike** (8am-8pm daily), 158km south of El Calafate on Ruta 40. It's cash only and can suffer gas shortages. A guaranteed final option is to take Ruta 7 east at Tapi Aike, continuing 80km to reach the village of Esperanza, where there is a **YPF gas station** (Esperanza, no phone, 24 hr daily) that always has gas but only accepts Visa credit cards. Bring backup cash regardless in case the credit card machine is down. They accept euros and U.S. dollars.

Getting There
AIR
Aeropuerto Internacional Comandante Armando Tola (FTE, tel. 02902/491 230, www.aeropuertoelcalafate.com) is 15km east of El Calafate, with three daily nonstop flights from Buenos Aires's domestic airport, Aeroparque Internacional Jorge Newbery—a flight time of three hours—and two daily nonstop flights to Ushuaia (1.5hr), both with Aerolíneas Argentinas (tel. 02901/436 338, www.aerolineas.com.ar).

From the airport, **VES Patagonia** (tel. 02902/497 355, www.vespatagonia.com.ar) is the only company that runs a **shuttle** (US$6) to hotels in El Calafate. You can buy tickets just outside the arrivals hall. **Condor** (25 de Mayo 51, El Calafate, tel. 02902/491 655 or 02902/492 655, www.remiscondorcalafate.

com.ar) operates taxis between the airport and your hotel (US$13.50). It's a 20-minute drive between the airport and the city center. **Transporte La Lengas** (tel. 02962/493 023, www.transportelaslengas.com) runs shuttles between the airport and El Chaltén (3hr, US$40).

CAR
From **Puerto Natales,** it's a 272-km drive north along Ruta 9, crossing to Ruta 40 at Paso Río Don Guillermo at the Argentinean border. Note that the stretch of Ruta 40 between the settlements of Tapi Aike and El Cerrito is a bumpy dirt track; a sensible detour is via the village of Esperanza, 80km east of Tapi Aike, where you take Ruta 5 for 67km to rejoin Ruta 40 to El Calafate. This adds 45 minutes to the journey. After 170km along Ruta 40, take Ruta 11 heading west along the southern shore of Lago Argentino. The whole journey takes 2.5-6 hours, depending on how many other vehicles are trying to cross at the border.

From **El Chaltén,** it's a 214-km drive south along Ruta 23, Ruta 40, and Ruta 11, which takes around three hours.

BUS
The **Terminal de Ómnibuses** (Antoine de Saint Exupéry 87, tel. 02902/491 476), 1.5km east of the town center, is El Calafate's regional bus terminal.

At the terminal, two companies offer buses to **El Chaltén** (3hr, US$25): **Cal-Tur** (tel. 02902/491 842, www.caltur.com.ar) has three daily buses in each direction (departs El Chaltén 8am, 1pm, and 6pm daily; departs El Calafate 8am, 1pm, and 6pm daily). Cal-Tur also has an office at Libertador 1080 (tel. 02902/491 368). **Chaltén Travel** (tel. 02902/492 212, www.chaltentravel.com) also has three daily buses in each direction (departs El Chaltén 7:30am, 1pm, and 6pm daily; departs El Calafate 8am, 1pm, and 6pm daily). Chaltén Travel also has a route to and from **Bariloche** (departs Bariloche 7:45am daily; departs El Calafate 6pm daily; 26hr, US$104). In addition to their location at the bus terminal, Chaltén Travel also has an office at Avenida San Martín 1174.

Three companies offer buses between El Calafate and **Puerto Natales** (5-8hr, US$25-32). **Bus Sur** (tel. 02902/494 250, www.bussur.com) departs from Puerto Natales daily (7:30am Tues., Thurs., and Sat. Apr.-Oct., 7:30am and 2:30pm Tues., Thurs., and Sat. Nov.-Mar.). **COOTRA** (tel. 02902/491 444, www.cootra.com.ar) departs Puerto Natales at 7:30am daily. **Turismo Zaahj** (tel. 02902/491 631, www.turismozaahj.co.cl) departs Puerto Natales at 8am and 2pm Monday, Wednesday, and Friday, and 7am Tuesday, Thursday, and Saturday. Frequency is reduced April-October.

Marga Taqsa (tel. 02902/491 843, www.taqsa.com.ar) has daily connections from **Ushuaia** (5am, change in Río Gallegos; 19hr, US$80) and **Bariloche** (6:30am, 26hr, US$104/US$121).

Direct bus transfers from Parque Nacional Torres del Paine to El Calafate are operated daily September-April by **Always Glaciares** (Av. del Libertador 924, tel. 02902/493 961, alwaysglaciers.com). The journey takes 5-9 hours with fares from US$55 pp.

EL CHALTÉN

Frontier town El Chaltén was founded in 1985 to strengthen Argentina's sovereignty. It has since transformed into one of the region's most visited towns due to its access to and magical views of Monte Fitz Roy, which rises out of the northern sector of Parque Nacional Los Glaciares. Surrounded by mountains on all sides, the town has a laid-back vibe but is full of hotels and restaurants. Outside the main October-April hiking season, the town returns to a sleepy state.

Food

For such a small place, the dining options are exceptional. Restaurants are heaving during the summer; dinner reservations are always necessary.

The vegan food at ★ **Cúrcuma** (Av. Antonio Rojo 219, tel. 02902/485 656,

10am-10pm daily, US$8-12) is a world away from the meat-centric restaurants elsewhere in town. Try the huge hummus wrap stuffed with alfalfa shoots, beetroot, salad, and seeds, or the hearty bean burger, or a lighter soup or juice. They sell great takeout lunches (reserve the night before), and vegan muffins and biscuits. There are only two tables, so get here early to eat in for lunch or dinner.

The only café that opens early, **Lo De Haydee** (Av. Lago Desierto 254, tel. 02962/493 272, 7:30am-9:30pm daily, US$3-6) is the only option for breakfast, with toast and jam, omelets and scrambled eggs, sandwiches and coffee, plus baked empanadas and cake. You can get one of the cheapest box lunches in town (CH$8), a feast of sandwiches, empanadas, *alfajores*, and fruit. Service is unfortunately slow and the Wi-Fi glacial, but this place covers what you need for an early start.

The pizzas and calzones are big enough to share at excellent ★ **La Ruca Mahuida** (Lionel Terray 55, tel. 02962/493 018, 6pm-11pm daily, US$10-15). Tucked down a side street a block from the main thoroughfare, it doesn't get the same foot traffic as other restaurants. The exterior resembles a rustic cottage; inside is even more charming, with exposed wooden beams and wool throws. The food and prices are superb. They even have a beer garden in summer.

On the northern edge of Avenida San Martín, small **El Muro** (Av. San Martín 912, tel. 02962/493 248, noon-midnight daily, US$8-12) is the best place in El Chaltén for steak and lamb, barbecue sharing platters, and roasted Patagonia lamb. Add a range of delicious sides to your meal.

With a whole wall dedicated to the wine they sell, **La Vinería** (Av. Lago de Desierto 265, tel. 02962/493 301, 3pm-2am daily) doesn't have a lot of space, but seat yourself at the bar or around a makeshift wine barrel table for an impressive array of Argentinean wines by the glass, from the traditional malbec to an unlikely carménère. Try a flight of three for a fixed fee. The staff know their stuff,

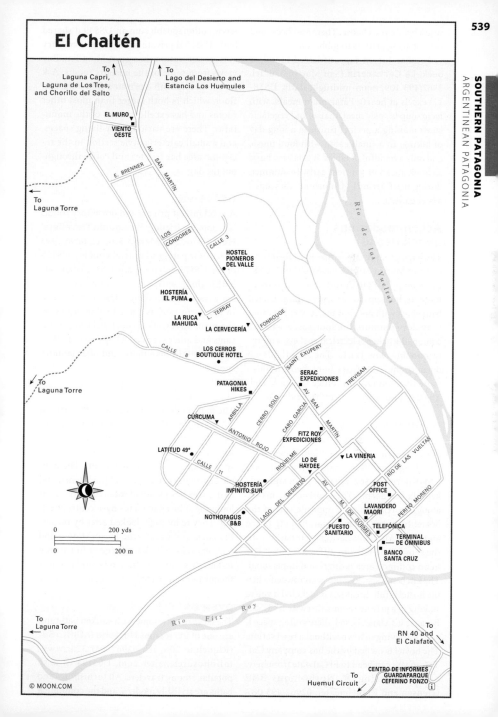

El Chaltén

To
Laguna Capri,
Laguna de Los Tres,
and Chorillo del Salto

To
Lago del Desierto and
Estancia Los Huemules

EL MURO

VIENTO
OESTE

AV. SAN MARTÍN

E. BRENNER

To
Laguna Torre

LOS CÓNDORES

CALLE 3

HOSTEL
PIONEROS
DEL VALLE

HOSTERÍA
EL PUMA

L. TERRAY

LA RUCA
MAHUIDA

LA CERVECERÍA

FONROUGE

CALLE 8

LOS CERROS
BOUTIQUE HOTEL

To
Laguna Torre

SAINT EXUPERY

PATAGONIA
HIKES

SERAC
EXPEDICIONES

TREVISAN

ARBILLA

CERRO SOLO

AV. SAN MARTÍN

CÚRCUMA

ANTONIO ROJO

CABO GARCIA

FITZ ROY
EXPEDICIONES

LATITUD 49°

CALLE 11

RIQUELME

LA VINERIA

LO DE
HAYDEE

RIO DE LAS VUELTAS

HOSTERÍA
INFINITO SUR

LAGO DEL DESIERTO

AV.

POST
OFFICE

PERITO MORENO

NOTHOFAGUS
B&B

LAVANDERO
MAORI

M. DE GÜEMES

PUESTO
SANITARIO

TELEFÓNICA

TERMINAL
DE ÓMNIBUS

BANCO
SANTA CRUZ

Rio de las Vueltas

0   200 yds

0   200 m

To
Laguna Torre

Rio Fitz Roy

To
RN 40 and
El Calafate

To
Huemul Circuit

CENTRO DE INFORMES
GUARDAPARQUE
CEFERINO FONZO

© MOON.COM

so ask before you choose. There are cheese and meat sharing platters to nibble on.

Popular for on-tap unfiltered blond or bock, **La Cervecería** (San Martín 320, tel. 2962/493 109, noon-midnight daily, US$8-12) excels at hearty Patagonian meals, with *locro* soup (a spicy meat, maize, and vegetable stew) making a perfect finish to a long day of hiking. In a small cabin with loud music and only a handful of tables, it gets very busy, so book ahead or get here early. In summer, during brief periods of sunshine, they open a beer garden.

Accommodations
UNDER US$40

The huge grounds of **Camping El Relincho** (Av. San Martín 219, tel. 02962/492 007, US$7 camping pp, US$10 dorm) have ample space for tents, hookups for RVs, and a large heated bath block with hot showers. A wooden cabin provides communal indoor space with an equipped kitchen, electrical sockets, and interminably slow Wi-Fi. The slightly damp dorm room holds three bunk beds; it looks more like a mountain refuge than a hostel. The staff also organize horseback riding tours.

US$40-65

Hostel Pioneros del Valle (Av. San Martín 451, tel. 02902/493 079, hostelpionerosdelvallechalten@hotmail.com, US$18 dorm, US$62 d) has 12 clean and well-kept six-bed dorms. The 13 private rooms are along a corridor on the opposite side of the hostel from the dorms, guaranteeing peace and quiet. All rooms have en suite baths, with the shower and toilet in different spaces. The main common area is dingy and impersonal. The kitchen is spacious but gets crowded when the hostel is full. Breakfast is included if you're staying in a private room; otherwise it's US$5. Because it's a large hostel, there's often space if you're arriving in town without a reservation. The hostel is owned by the bus company Cal-Tur, so you can head to El Calafate from here.

The charming ★ **Nothofagus B&B** (Hensen and Riquelme, tel. 02962/493 087, www.nothofagusbb.com.ar, US$49 d shared bath, US$65 d private bath), with its country cottage decoration, has great Mont Fitz Roy views from some of the upstairs rooms. Ask for the double with a private bath on the 2nd floor, which is both larger than most other rooms and has excellent views of the mountains. There are various cozy living spaces, and a small cafeteria-style section in the reception area has free tea and coffee throughout the day.

US$65-95

A good mix of private and dormitory rooms is at popular, friendly **Patagonia Travellers' Hostel** (Av. San Martín 376, tel. 02962/493 019, www.patagoniahostel.com.ar, US$25 dorm, US$75 d shared bath, US$105 d private bath), along with ample communal areas. Showers are hot and breakfast (not included in the dorm rate) is a good value. Right on the main street, it's a short walk to restaurants and other services. They rent out bikes, run mountain bike tours, and offer laundry service.

US$95-125

The four modern apartments at ★ **Latitud 49°** (Arbilla 145, tel. 02962/493 347, www.latitud49.com.ar, US$100 d) have all the conveniences you need for self-catering with more space than a standard hotel room. The double bedroom is sizeable, and the kitchen and living area has plenty of room for cooking or lounging. The apartments have central heating. They're lovingly looked after by owners Florencia and Lucas, who live next door and have encyclopedic knowledge of El Chaltén restaurants and activities, so be sure to query them when you arrive.

OVER US$125

The large rooms, some with sunken bathtubs, are one of the reasons **Hostería Infinito Sur** (Riquelme 208, tel. 02962/493 325, www.infinitosurelchalten.com, US$144 d) is so popular among travelers. All furnishings and baths are stylishly modern, and the communal living room looks at Monte Fitz Roy. Staff go out of their way to help guests and will arrange boxed lunches for hikers. Breakfast isn't varied, and low water pressure can be an issue.

The 12 bedrooms of **Hostería El Puma** (Lionel Terray 212, tel. 02962/493 095, www. hosteriaelpuma.com.ar, US$165 d) are sizeable, with laminate wood floors and large windows, although there aren't any spectacular views here. A cozy fire-warmed living room with a small attached library and a good on-site restaurant add to the appeal. It's popular with tour groups and gets booked well in advance.

The views are spectacular from the plush sofas in the living room at **Los Cerros Boutique Hotel** (Av. San Martín 260, tel. 02962/493 182, www. hoteldonloscerrosdelchalten.com, US$187 standard d, US$220 superior d). Guest rooms lack character, but the even-numbered ones have stunning mountain views for no extra cost, although they're smaller. All rooms have large baths, minibars, and safes. A small subterranean on-site spa with a jetted tub and a sauna is for guest use. Dinner and drinks are served in the main bar and restaurant, with sublime views of the mountains.

Information and Services
The **Centro de Informes El Chaltén** (Terminal de Ómnibuses, tel. 02962/493 370, 8am-10pm daily) has helpful English-speaking staff who provide information about town services, transportation, and tour agencies. They have information about hiking in the national park, but you're better off going 500 meters southeast to the **Centro de Informes Guardaparque Ceferino Fonzo** (Ruta 23, tel. 02962/493 004, pnlgzonanorte@ apn.gob.ar, 9am-5pm daily), where you can speak with park rangers directly. The **Puesto Sanitario** (Av. de Agostini 74, tel. 02902/493 033), a basic clinic, deals with medical emergencies.

Most **supermarkets** are on Avenida San Martín, although inventory is limited. If you're planning to cook, you're better off buying most items elsewhere before you arrive. Basic supplies, including some fresh fruit and vegetables, meat, cheese, and canned and dried items are available, although shelves can empty during the summer when all the hikers arrive.

Lavadero Maori (Av. Güemes 149), a block north of the bus station, has the cheapest laundry service in town, with a same-day option. If you need postal service, **Correo Argentino** (Andreas Madsen 22, tel. 02962/493 172, 9am-4pm Mon.-Fri.) has an office here, but regularly runs out of stamps.

There's only one **ATM** in town: the **Banco Santa Cruz** (Perito Moreno and Martín de Güemes) on the western side of the bus terminal. Many restaurants and hotels accept cards, but it's worth stocking up on Argentinean pesos before arriving or bringing U.S. dollars, widely accepted by businesses in the town. **Chaltén Travel** (Terminal de Ómnibuses, Av. Perito Moreno 28, tel. 02962/493 005, www. chaltentravel.com) offers currency exchange.

For equipment rental, head to **Viento Oeste** (Av. San Martín 898, tel. 02962/493 200, 11am-1pm and 3pm-7:30pm Thurs.-Tues.), **Patagonia Hikes** (Comandante Arrúa 505, tel. 02962/493 359 or 911/4418 5660, www.patagoniahikes.com, 9am-1pm and 3pm-9pm daily), or **Serac Expediciones** (Av. San Martín 175, tel. 02962/493 371, www.serac.com.ar, 10am-6pm Mon.-Fri.). Patagonia Hikes and Serac both offer guided treks in the park, plus more challenging mountain summits and expeditions in the nearby mountains.

There is a **YPF gas station** (Ruta 23, El Chaltén, 8am-10pm daily), 1km before you reach the southern edge of El Chaltén. They accept cash only. Don't count on getting gas here, as it regularly runs out; be sure to fill up in El Calafate, and carry an extra can of fuel, just in case.

Getting There
From **El Calafate,** it's a 214-km drive north along Ruta 11, Ruta 40, and Ruta 23, which takes three hours. The **Terminal**

de Ómnibuses (Av. Perito Moreno 28, tel. 02962/493 370) is on the southern edge of town, where Cal-Tur (tel. 02962/493 079, www.caltur.com.ar) has thrice-daily buses from El Calafate (8am, 1pm, and 6pm daily, 3hr, US$25). Chaltén Travel (tel. 02962/493 005, www.chaltentravel.com) has three daily buses from El Calafate (8am, 1pm, and 6pm daily). Marga Taqsa (tel. 02962/493 130, www.taqsa.com.ar) offers comfortable buses from Bariloche (6:30am daily, 23hr, US$100/US$122, includes all meals) via Los Antiguos, Perito Moreno, Esquel, and El Bolsón.

The closest airport is in El Calafate. From Aeropuerto Internacional Comandante Armando Tola (FTE, tel. 02902/491 230, www.aeropuertoelcalafate.com), Transporte La Lengas (tel. 02962/493 023, www.transportelaslengas.com) offers shuttle buses directly to El Chaltén (3hr, US$20), roughly timed to coincide with flight arrivals; this could mean waiting up to two hours for the bus to leave.

Lago del Desierto

Just under 40km north of El Chaltén, Lago del Desierto (northern end of Ruta 23, no phone, 24 hr daily, free) is where visitors can enjoy stark scenery: A turquoise-blue lake with dense *lenga* forests and spiky glacier-shrouded mountains beyond. A number of hikes start from the southern end of the lake, where most visitors arrive. Hike along the eastern edge of the lake on the path that starts the long crossing to Villa O'Higgins in Chile for pretty views. The trail can become waterlogged after heavy rainfall. It's possible to take the 40-minute hike up to milky-blue Laguna Huemul, at the base of retreating Glaciar Huemul; pay the US$8 entrance fee for this hike at the Estancia Lago del Desierto campground.

GETTING THERE

Minibuses operated by Full Patagonia (tel. 02966/385 541, 11am daily, 2hr, US$22 round-trip) and Transportes Las Lengas (tel. 02962/493 023, www.transportelaslengas.com,

4 daily, 2hr, US$20) take passengers to the lake from El Chaltén. The minibuses also stop at Hostería El Pilar (30min, US$8), the northern trailhead for the Laguna de los Tres hike, and Hostería Los Huemules (35min, US$10). Minibuses make the return journey around 10 minutes after arriving at Lago del Desierto, but your ticket is valid for later departures.

In your own vehicle, take Ruta 23 north out of El Chaltén and follow it to its end, 36km later, a drive of 1.5 hours along a mostly unpaved road.

Estancia Los Huemules

A little less than 20km north of El Chaltén, the Estancia Los Huemules (Ruta 23, tel. 011/2313 4084, www.loshuemules.com, 9am-6pm daily Sept.-Apr., US$8) is a privately operated 5,800-hectare nature reserve with 25km of well-maintained trails that lead to nearby lakes, offering views of Monte Fitz Roy, plus a visitors center with information about local flora and fauna and the indigenous people who once inhabited the region. On-site is the rustic mountain refuge Puesto Cagliero (tel. 02966/644 856, www.puestocagliero.com, US$220 d), which offers basic but warm lodging, with all meals included and optional ice-trekking excursions on Glaciar Cagliero.

To get here by car, head north of El Chaltén for 17km along unpaved Ruta 23, a drive of 45 minutes.

★ PARQUE NACIONAL LOS GLACIARES

The 726,927-hectare Parque Nacional Los Glaciares (tel. 02902/491 005, 02902/491 788, or 02962/ 493 004, 8am-6pm daily Sept.-Easter Week, 9am-4pm daily Easter Week-Aug., entry fee varies by sector) is part of the vast Southern Patagonian Ice Field. The park has extreme contrasts, sandwiched between the 3,000-meter peaks of the Andes in the west and the flat, barren steppe in the east. The park offers unusually easy access to its hulking glaciers, which are at low elevation. On a day trip from El Calafate, get close to the snout of a glacier on foot, in a boat, or in a kayak—you can even stand on one.

Shaped by glaciation in the Pleistocene epoch, which began over two million years ago and ended abruptly 10,000 years ago, the park's landscape is riven with deep trough-like valleys and dramatic—although rapidly shrinking—glaciers. Easily the most famous of the glaciers is the 25,000-hectare **Glaciar Perito Moreno,** which kneels in the gray-blue water of 160-km-long Lago Argentino. Also flowing into the lake is **Glaciar Upsala,** at 54km long and covering 29,500 hectares the third-largest glacier in South America. Upsala is rapidly retreating and thinning, having lost 2,160 hectares over 25 years. The other big-name glacier is 17-km-long **Glaciar Spegazzini,** one of the most stable in the region.

The park isn't only defined by glaciers. In the northern zone, thick granite spires of **Monte Fitz Roy** dominate the surrounding area, visible from the nearest town, El Chaltén, on clear days. The iconic shape of the 3,375-meter mountain was the inspiration for the logo for clothing brand Patagonia.

The ecosystems in the park range from high-altitude mountains to low-elevation steppe, punctuated by freshwater lakes. In the west and south are Chilean national parks Bernardo O'Higgins and Torres del Paine, making the region one contiguous protected area. As in most of Southern Patagonia, the forests are sub-Antarctic, containing varieties of southern beech that flare with color in fall, which give way to scrubland and semiarid grasslands. A wide biodiversity of fauna includes elusive pumas and Andean cats, along with the rare *huemul* deer. Birdlife includes the Andean condor at higher elevations and Darwin's rhea on lower grasslands.

The park is divided into two sectors: **Zona Sur** (Southern Zone) and **Zona Norte** (Northern Zone). Zona Sur contains most of the **glaciers** and the **best access** to them; it's best accessed from El Calafate. Zona Norte is home to the park's many hiking trails; the closest town is El Chaltén.

In the Zona Norte, the **Centro de Informes Guardaparque Ceferino Fonzo** (Ruta 23, tel. 02962/493 004, pnlgzonanorte@ apn.gob.ar, 9am-5pm daily) hosts a short talk about the rules of the park and an overview of the trails for all visitors arriving in public buses. There is a room dedicated to the flora and fauna of the park—including information about the conservation of the *huemul* and notable ascents of Monte Fitz Roy. Simple maps are available; for more detailed maps, including the crossing to Villa O'Higgins, plenty of shops in El Chaltén stock the *Chaltén Outdoor Map* (www.chalten-outdoor.com). Buses from El Calafate to El Chaltén make a 15-minute stop here.

Campfires are not permitted in the park; campers must bring a portable gas stove. If you see a *huemul* in the park, you must report it to park rangers. There are no bins around the park, so take all rubbish off the trails with you.

Zona Sur
ORIENTATION

The entrance for Zona Sur is at **Portado de Acceso** (Ruta 11, 9am-6pm daily Sept.-Easter, 9am-4pm daily Easter-Aug., US$25), 47km west of El Calafate on Ruta 11. Visitors must stop here and pay the entry fee in cash. It's 30km on Ruta 11 from the entrance to the vast **parking lot** where a network of wooden boardwalks with sublime views of Glaciar Perito Moreno resides.

The only option for food in the park is the overpriced cafeteria-style **Nativos de la Patagonia** (tel. 02902/499 144, 10am-5pm daily, US$6-15), in the Glaciar Perito Moreno parking lot. It serves sandwiches, empanadas, and variable-quality dishes—although it does have great views of the glacier. This is the only indoor seating area in the park; only food that has been bought on the premises can be consumed here. There are public baths and a small gift shop here.

GLACIAR PERITO MORENO
Glaciar Perito Moreno isn't the biggest in Patagonia, but its accessibility and the

Parque Nacional Los Glaciares

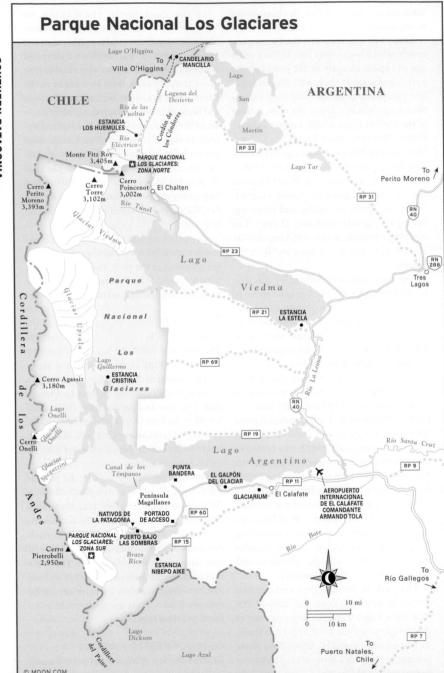

CHILE

ARGENTINA

Lago O'Higgins

To
Villa O'Higgins

CANDELARIO
MANCILLA

Laguna del
Desierto

Lago
San

Martín

Río de las
Vueltas

ESTANCIA
LOS HUEMULES

Río
Eléctrico

Monte Fitz Roy
3,405m

RP 33

Lago Tar

PARQUE NACIONAL
LOS GLACIARES:
ZONA NORTE

To
Perito Moreno

Cerro
Perito
Moreno
3,393m

Cerro
Torre
3,102m

Cerro
Poincenot
3,002m

El Chalten

RP 31

Glaciar Viedma

Río Túnel

RN
40

RP 23

RN
288

Lago

Viedma

Tres
Lagos

Cordón
de
los
Cóndores

Parque

Glaciar Upsala

Nacional

RP 21

ESTANCIA
LA ESTELA

Cerro Agassiz
3,180m

Los

Lago
Guillermo

ESTANCIA
CRISTINA

Glaciares

RP 69

Río La Leona

Lago
Onelli

Glaciar
Onelli

RN
40

Cerro
Onelli

Glaciar
Spegazzini

RP 19

Río Santa Cruz

Lago

Argentino

Cordillera de los Andes

Canal de los
Témpanos

PUNTA
BANDERA

EL GALPÓN
DEL GLACIAR

GLACIARIUM

El Calafate

RP 11

RP 9

Península
Magallanes

NATIVOS DE
LA PATAGONIA

PORTADO
DE ACCESO

RP 60

AEROPUERTO
INTERNACIONAL
DE EL CALAFATE
COMANDANTE
ARMANDO TOLA

PARQUE NACIONAL
LOS GLACIARES:
ZONA SUR

PUERTO BAJO
LAS SOMBRAS

RP 15

Cerro
Pietrobelli
2,950m

Brazo
Rico

Río
Bote

To
Río Gallegos

ESTANCIA
NIBEPO AIKE

0   10 mi

0   10 km

Lago
Dickson

Cordillera
del Paine

Lago Azul

To
Puerto Natales,
Chile

RP 7

© MOON.COM

regularity with which it calves dense-blue icebergs into Lago Argentino make it a spectacular sight. One of only three glaciers in the world that is growing, Perito Moreno's ice actually advances far enough to dam the Brazo Rico, the southern arm of Lago Argentino. This causes the lake's water levels to increase dramatically. As the pressure builds between the lake and the ice dam, fissures in the ice are created, forming an **ice bridge** through which water pours. Eventually, the bridge ruptures in a spectacular display of collapsing ice. This phenomenon occurs roughly every two to four years, with the most recent in March 2018.

Visitors can get within a few hundred meters of the ice thanks to five color-coded boardwalks offering views from different angles, with the paths ranging 500-1,700 meters in length. Most people arrive at the Glaciar Perito Moreno parking lot by tour bus in the morning; time your visit for early afternoon to avoid some of the crowds.

BOAT TOURS

From a kiosk in the Glaciar Perito Moreno parking lot, **Southern Spirit** (www.southernspiritfte.com.ar) offers hour-long **boat tours** (US$20 pp) that pass 100 meters from the northern face of the glacier. There are departures up to five times hourly December-February, fewer March-November. Boats depart from the jetty at the bottom of the boardwalk. Southern Spirit also has an office in El Calafate (Av. del Libertador 1319, tel. 02902/491 582).

Hielo y Aventura (Puerto Bajo de las Sombras, www.hieloyaventura.com) runs one-hour tours (US$20 pp) to the glacier on its 130-passenger vessel *Yaghan* (hourly departures 10am-4pm daily Oct.-May). Boats leave from Puerto Bajo de las Sombras, a port 6km east of the main car park. You can also buy tickets here. It is sometimes possible to arrange a stop at the port with one of the public buses heading to the western terminus of Ruta 11 and the Glaciar Perito Moreno parking lot; confirm this when purchasing your ticket.

Their office in El Calafate (Av. del Libertador 935, 02902/492 205) is where you can buy tickets for all tours.

KAYAK TOURS

For a unique perspective of the glacier, consider a **kayaking tour** (US$195) with experts **Mil Outdoor** (Av. del Libertador 1037, tel. 02902/491 446, www.miloutdoor.com.ar), whose guides are bilingual kayaking experts from around the world. The tour includes 2.5 hours of paddling through Lago Argentina in double kayaks, a quiet way of appreciating the glacier. With daily departures August-May, the full-day tour includes technical gear (Gore-Tex dry suits), snacks, and photographs from the trip. Transfers to and from hotels in El Calafate can be organized.

GLACIER TREKS

Hielo y Aventura (Puerto Bajo de las Sombras, www.hieloyaventura.com) offers **glacier treks** on Perito Moreno, where you can hike alongside pools and crevasses to appreciate the dense blues of the ice. The tours run daily from Puerto Bajo de las Sombras. Full-day options include accessible Mini Trekking (US$110), with 1.5 hours on the ice, or the demanding Big Ice (US$215), with 3.5 hours on the ice. Ice-trekking equipment, bilingual certified trekking guides, and a whiskey with glacier ice are included. Hotel pickup and transfer to the port from El Calafate can be arranged for an additional fee. Their office in El Calafate (Av. del Libertador 935, 02902/492 205) is where you can buy tickets for all tours.

GETTING THERE

To get from El Calafate to the entrance of the Zona Sur is a 47-km, 45-minute drive west on Ruta 11. To reach the parking lot for Glaciar Perito Moreno, it's another 30km west on Ruta 11, a drive of 50 minutes.

Public buses bound for the Zona Sur shuttle between the **Terminal de Ómnibuses** (Antoine de Saint Exupéry 87) in El Calafate, 1.5km east of the center, and the parking lot

for Glaciar Perito Moreno, although most offer hotel pickup; confirm this when purchasing your ticket. **Cal-Tur** (Terminal de Ómnibuses, tel. 02901/491 842; Av. del Libertador 1080, tel. 02902/491 368, www.caltur.com.ar) has three daily trips to and from the park (1.5hr, US$24 round-trip) October–March; departures drop to two daily April–September. **Chaltén Travel** (Terminal de Ómnibuses and Av. del Libertador 1174, tel. 02902/492 212, www.chaltentravel.com) also has two daily departures (1.5hr, US$24 round-trip) for the Zona Sur.

Zona Norte
ORIENTATION

The park's northern sector, **Zona Norte** (24 hr daily, free), has an excellent array of well-maintained **trails** for both day hikes and multiday excursions. There is no official entrance to Zona Norte, and most trails start from the small town of **El Chaltén,** a 3.5-hour drive north from El Calafate. There's no entrance fee for Zona Norte; paths are open year-round, subject to weather conditions. The **Centro de Informes Guardaparque Ceferino Fonzo** (Ruta 23, tel. 02962/493 004, pnlgzonanorte@ apn.gob.ar, 9am-5pm daily) has information about trails, including hiking maps. It's also known as the **Centro de Visitantes Ceferino Fonzo.**

DAY HIKES

Over 90,000 tourists annually visit the Zona Norte, which has branded itself Argentina's hiking capital. The park contains the most varied hiking in Patagonia and has a few advantages over neighboring Parque Nacional Torres del Paine. As most of the self-guided trails are accessible from El Chaltén, hikers can return to town at night to stay in hotels or hostels. Additionally, the trails feel much quieter than those in Torres del Paine.

Parque Nacional Los Glaciares contains a number of day-hike trails as well as the

1: Glaciar Perito Moreno 2: pizza at La Ruca Mahuida in El Chaltén 3: visitors center at Parque Nacional Los Glaciares 4: Monte Fitz Roy

demanding but worthwhile Huemul Circuit, a four-day trek. Most trails begin from near El Chaltén and are well marked. Camping facilities exist, but they're basic, with poorly maintained chemical toilets. The campgrounds do allow hikers to link trails for multiday excursions.

The park's most popular hike is to **Laguna de los Tres** (also known as the **Senda al Fitz Roy**), a 23-km, 8- to 10-hour round-trip with the best panoramic views of Monte Fitz Roy above the lake. The trail leaves El Chaltén from the northern end of Avenida San Martín, climbing sharply through *lenga* forest for 3km. The Mirador del Fitz Roy, 3.5km after the beginning of the trail, offers sweeping views of jagged Monte Fitz Roy—if the weather is clear.

From here, the trail drops slightly for a gentle, flat hike through forests and along the river before reaching the free but very basic campground Campamento Poincenot. This is a good place to stop for the night, so that you can approach Laguna de los Tres at dawn the next morning. From here, it's a 400-meter ascent over 2km through switchbacks up a scree slope to reach a moraine ridge overlooking Laguna de Los Tres, Glaciar de Los Tres, and Monte Fitzy Roy, a panorama that is one of the most spectacular in the Andes. If you continue down to the lake, you can take a 700-meter side trip to admire the gleaming waters of Laguna Sucia.

To return to El Chaltén, go back the way you came. It's possible to make the return trip on different trails by connecting with the trail to Laguna Torre via a path that passes alongside Laguna Madre and Laguna Hija, or take a quick side trip around Laguna Capri rather than past the Mirador del Fitz Roy. You can also start from Hostería El Pilar, 14km from El Chaltén, where the trail is mostly flat through the Río Blanco valley, to reach the Campamento Poincenot.

Other popular day treks include the moderate 18-km, nine-hour trek to **Laguna Torre,** a lake at the snout of Glaciar Grande. It's not uncommon to see icebergs bobbing in

The Direct Route to Villa O'Higgins

Despite being just 100km north of El Chaltén, Villa O'Higgins, which marks the southern terminus of the Carretera Austral in Chile, feels very far away. To reach the Carretera Austral from El Chaltén, it has been necessary to drive 650km north to the border crossing between Los Antiguos, Argentina, and Chile Chico. From Chile Chico, it's a 560-km journey south along the poorly maintained highway to Villa O'Higgins.

However, a growing number of adventurous tourists are opting to take the direct route: a two-day, one-night journey that combines a minibus, a boat, and hiking to cross Lago del Desierto on the Argentinean side and Lago O'Higgins in Chilean territory via the border crossing **Portezuelo de la Divisoria.** This crossing is only possible **November-April.** Bring Chilean pesos, enough food for two or three days of waiting for a boat, camping equipment, and plenty of warm waterproof clothing.

Not for the weak, as you have to carry all of your luggage on the hikes, the journey starts from El Chaltén, where **minibus transfers** to Lago del Desierto are offered by **Remis Keoken** (tel. 02966/702 814, transporteskeoken@gmail.com, US$80 up to 4 people), **Full Patagonia** (tel. 02966/385 541, 11am, 2hr, US$22 round-trip), and **Transportes Las Lengas** (tel. 02962/493 023, www.transporteslaslengas.com; 4 daily, 2hr, US$20).

The next step is a **boat crossing** (US$28, cash only, including U.S. dollars and pesos), operated by **Exploradores Lago del Desierto** (tel. 02966/1546 7103). The boat departs at 10am and 4:30pm daily from the jetty on the southern edge of Lago del Desierto. It takes one hour to reach the Argentinean border control on the lake's northern edge. The boat operator has a ticket office at the lake.

After the border formalities, it's a **6-km hike** (with a steep incline for the first 3km) to Portezuelo de la Divisoria and the border with Chile. It is sometimes possible to rent a horse (CH$40,000) for this stretch, for your luggage or yourself; speak to Argentinean border control for more information. From the Chilean border, it's **16km** along a gravel road to reach the Chilean border control at the cluster of buildings that mark the settlement of **Candelario Mancilla,** where you get your passport stamped. You can also arrange a truck to transport your luggage (CH$10,000) or you and your luggage (CH$15,000) for this stretch of the journey; book in advance by contact-

the water; it also has spellbinding views of the Cordón Adela mountains and the often cloud-covered Cerro Torre (3,102 meters). The trek to **Chorrillo del Salto,** a 20-meter waterfall, is 4km from the northern edge of El Chaltén via a path that skirts the road. It can also be reached by vehicle; there's a car park just before the final 500 meters to the waterfall.

HUEMUL CIRCUIT

The four-day, 70-km **Huemul Circuit** is an adventurous and more technically challenging alternative to the O circuit in Parque Nacional Torres del Paine, with 180-degree views of the Southern Patagonian Ice Field. January-February see the best weather conditions. During this time, the trail hosts around 40 hikers daily, while November-December mean fewer people and slightly more variable weather. The trek has two river crossings; depending on water levels, they often require use of zip lines that have been installed.

The trailhead is 500 meters south of the bus station on Ruta 23 toward El Calafate at the Centro de Informes Ceferino Fonzo. Trekking poles are recommended for several steep sections of the trail.

Wind speeds can reach up to 100km/h on the trail's two passes, so consult the weather forecast and take advice from the park rangers before departing. You must register with the park rangers and show that you have the necessary equipment (including a harness, two carabiners, a safety line, and 20 meters of rope) in order to receive your permit; rangers will also talk you through the hike and show you a short slideshow with information about the trail and the zip-line crossings. It's

ing Ricardo (tel. 9/9316 2011, ricardolevican@hotmail.com), who lives in Candelario Mancilla and operates the lodgings there. At Candelario Mancilla, you can camp, stay in one of a half-dozen basic private rooms (CH$15,000 pp), and buy meals. Reservations for camping are not necessary but are advised for the guesthouse.

Next is the **boat crossing** to **Puerto Bahamondes.** Check with the border police on when the next boat will leave, as the crossing can be delayed for multiple days due to poor weather. You can buy your ticket on the boat using a credit card. If boats are delayed, those who purchased a ticket in advance have boarding priority. You can buy tickets in advance at **Exploradores Lago del Desierto/Receptivo Chaltén** (Lago del Desierto 296, El Chaltén, tel. 02966/1546 7103 or 02962/493 081, www.exploradoreslagodeldesierto.com) or online via **Robinson Crusoe Lodge** (www.robinsoncrusoe.com). At Puerto Bahamondes, you can either pay for the minibus that connects with the boat (10min, CH$2,500) and drops you in the center of Villa O'Higgins, or you can walk the remaining 8km along the road.

Two companies on the Chilean side operate ferries. **Hielo Sur** (tel. 9/8210 3191, www.villaohiggins.com/hielosur), with the LM *Quetru* (2-3/week, glacier tour 11:30am Tues. and Sat., 9hr, CH$82,000; direct 5:30pm, 2.75hr, CH$36,000), sails between Candelario Mancilla and Puerto Bahamondes, and you can opt to visit Glacier O'Higgins en route. They also offer transfer to Villa O'Higgins from Puerto Bahamondes (10min, CH$2,000). You can book online via **Robinson Crusoe Lodge** (Carretera Austral, Villa O'Higgins, tel. 2/2334 1503 or 67/2431 811, www.robinsoncrusoe.com). **Ruedas de la Patagonia** (tel. 9/7604 2400, www.turismoruedasdelapatagonia.cl) leaves at 4pm Monday, Wednesday, and Saturday from Candelario Mancilla (1.5hr, CH$36,000). The transfer to Villa O'Higgins is included in the fare. For both, you can pay in cash or with a card.

Note that there are no ATMs in Villa O'Higgins, and few hotels and restaurants accept credit cards. Be sure to exchange money in El Calafate or El Chaltén before you leave.

A website (www.villaohiggins.com/crossing/border2.htm) allows you to make advance reservations for all the buses and boats, plus horses for cargo and the campsite at Candelario Mancilla.

helpful to take photographs of this information for reference on the trail. Trekking experience and a GPS receiver are recommended. Be aware that if you're hiking with a tour company, and the trek gets canceled or you are forced to turn back after the first day, you are unlikely to have your money refunded.

GUIDED TREKS

Several tour agencies lead guided treks of the Huemul Circuit and other trails in the park. **Fitz Roy Expediciones** (Av. San Martín 56, El Chaltén, tel. 02962/493 178, www.fitzroyexpediciones.com.ar) has tours covering most of the trails, plus ice trekking, kayaking expeditions, and rock and ice climbing excursions. **Serac Expediciones** (Av. San Martín 175, El Chaltén, tel. 02962/493 371, www.serac.com.ar) are the region's experts

when it comes to trekking and expedition-style excursions, using experienced hiking and climbing guides and top-quality equipment. **Patagonia Hikes** (Comandante Arrúa 505, El Chaltén, tel. 02962/493 359 or 911/4418 5660, www.patagoniahikes.com) also offers technical summits of two nearby mountains. Both Serac Expediciones and Patagonia Hikes rent trekking equipment from their shops.

RAFTING

Running alongside El Chaltén, the Río de Las Vuelta offers Class III and IV+ whitewater rafting on an 8-km stretch of rapids. El Calafate-based **Mil Outdoor** (Av. San Martín 1037, El Calafate, tel. 02902/491 446, www.miloutdoor.com.ar) is the local expert. A half-day tour (US$105) starts from El Chaltén and includes all necessary technical equipment, including a dry suit and a helmet. On this outing, you'll spend two hours in the cold 5°C water. You can expect stunning views of Monte Fitz Roy during the activity. Transfer to and from El Calafate is available at additional cost.

GETTING THERE

The national park flanks El Chaltén to the west, with most trails starting from the town. The trek to Laguna de los Tres starts from the northern end of Avenida San Martín, as does the trail for Chorrillo del Salto. To get to the Chorrillo del Salto trailhead by vehicle, it's a 4-km, five-minute drive north of El Chaltén on Ruta 23. The trailhead for Laguna Torre begins where Calles Llao Llao and Los Charitos meet on the town's western edge. The Huemul Circuit leaves from the Centro de Informes Ceferino Fonzo, a 500-meter walk south of the bus station.

USHUAIA

Best known as the southernmost city in the world, Ushuaia is also one of the most expensive cities in Argentina, partly due to the wealth brought daily in summer by cruise ships, many of which continue to Antarctica.

Flanked by the snowy teeth of the Montes Martiales (the Martial Mountains) on the north and the cloud-covered peaks of Isa Navarino south across the Beagle Channel, Ushuaia is a uniquely Patagonian city that reflects the extremes of this region. Restaurants and hotels are significantly better than expected in such a remote outpost. The city's museums and nearby natural attractions mean there's plenty to do beyond just boarding a cruise.

Orientation

The city is in the foothills of the Montes Martiales; the streets incline more steeply the farther you get from the water, at the south end of the city. Two blocks north of the coastal road is the central artery of Ushuaia, Avenida San Martín, which runs southwest-northeast.

This is where most shops, restaurants, and banks are located.

Museo Marítimo y del Presidio

The extensive **Museo Marítimo y del Presidio** (Yaganes and Gobernador Paz, tel. 02901/437 481, www.museomaritimo.com, 10am-8pm daily, adults US$16, free under 12) is the city's largest, a complex of five two-story pavilions where visitors can wander freely. The **Museo del Presidio** offers a history of Ushuaia's jail (the building it's in), along with information about the grisly crimes committed by its most notorious inmates. The **Museo Antártico** features memorabilia from numerous expeditions to Antarctica. The **Museo Marítimo** houses a huge collection of replicas of boats that sailed the Patagonia seas, including Magellan's *Trinidad* and the HMS *Beagle*. The **Museo de Arte Marino** (4pm-8pm Mon.-Sat.) has a collection of sea-themed Argentinean art. The **Galería de Arte** houses changing exhibitions. The most striking building in the complex is the untouched **Pabellón Histórico,** a wing of the prison left in its original state. Even on the hottest days, the flagstones and chipped plaster walls emit an iciness that helps you imagine how unbearably cold it must have been here in winter.

The museum is fascinating, but much of the exhibit information is only in Spanish or poorly translated English. If you show your passport and ticket at the entrance, you can get a stamp that allows you to return within 24 hours for free. There is a café and gift shop onsite. Optional Spanish-language guided tours occur at 11:30am, 4:30pm, and 6:30pm daily.

Museo del Fin del Mundo

Housed in two grand historic buildings on the same street, the **Museo del Fin del Mundo** (http://mfm.tierradelfuego.gov.ar, 10am-7pm Mon.-Fri., 11am-5pm Sat.-Sun., free) contains a wide collection of historical artifacts. In the **Casa Banco Nación** (Av. Maipú 173, tel. 02901/421 863), two rooms cover the history of the inhabitants of the region, with utensils

Ushuaia

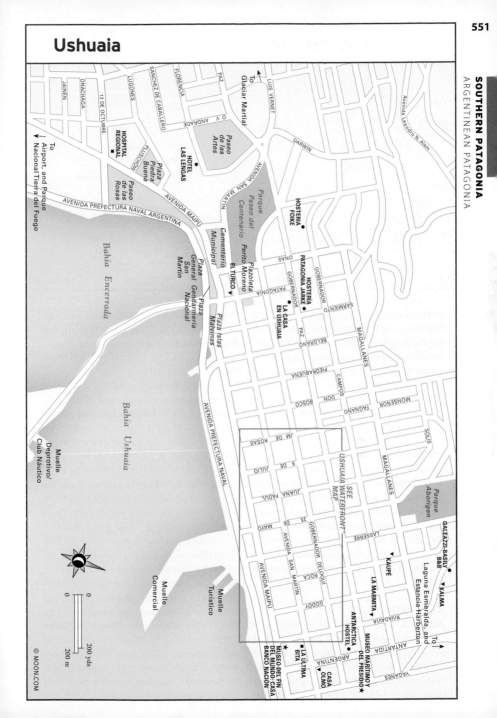

To Glaciar Martial

LUIS VERNET

O V ANDRADE

DARWIN

Avenida Leandro N. Alem

PAZ

FLORENCIA

SÁNCHEZ DE CABALLERO

LUGONES

ONACHAGA

JAINEN

12 DE OCTUBRE

PLUSCHOW

HOSPITAL REGIONAL

Plaza Piedra Buena

Paseo de las Rosas

HOTEL LAS LENGAS

Paseo de las Artes

Parque del Centenario

Paseo del Perito Moreno

AVENIDA SAN MARTÍN

AVENIDA MAIPÚ

AVENIDA PREFECTURA NAVAL ARGENTINA

To Airport, and Parque Nacional Tierra del Fuego

Bahía Encerrada

Bahía Ushuaia

Cementerio Municipal

EL TURCO

Plazoleta

Plaza General Gendarmería San Martín

Plaza Islas Malvinas

HOSTERÍA FOIKE

ONAS

PATAGONIA

GOBERNADOR

HOSTERÍA PATAGONIA JARKÉ

PATAGONIA JARKÉ

LA CASA EN USHUAIA

GOBERNADOR PAZ

SARMIENTO

BELGRANO

PIEDRABUENA

DON BOSCO

CAMPOS

FAGNANO

MONSEÑOR

MAGALLANES

SOLIS

AVENIDA PREFECTURA NAVAL

J.M. DE ROSAS

JULIO

9 DE JULIO

JUANA FADUL

25 DE MAYO

AVENIDA SAN MARTÍN

AVENIDA MAIPÚ

GOBERNADOR DELOQUI

GODOY

SEE USHUAIA WATERFRONT MAP

MAGALLANES

LASSERRE

Parque Aborigen

GALEAZZI-BASILY B&B

KALMA

Laguna Esmeralda, and Estancia Harberton

KAUPÉ

LA MARMITA

RIVADAVIA

ANTÁRTIDA ARGENTINA

ANTARCTICA HOSTEL

LA ÚLTIMA BITA

MUSEO DEL FIN DEL MUNDO-CASA BANCO NACIÓN

CASA OLMO

MUSEO MARÍTIMO Y DEL PRESIDIO

To YAGANES

Muelle Deportivo/ Club Náutico

Muelle Comercial

Muelle Turístico

0 200 yds
0 200 m

© MOON.COM

Ushuaia Waterfront

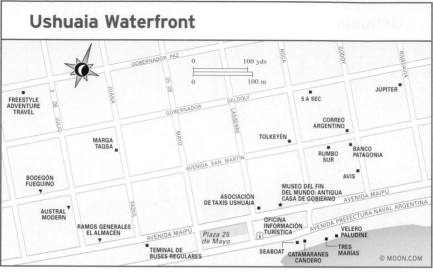

and tools used by the indigenous Yaghan and Selk'nam peoples, plus later arrivals, including the Anglican missions in 1870 and the Salesian missions in 1890. There's also an imposing collection of taxidermy birds, including two huge condors.

The most interesting section is about the shipwreck and sinking of the English *Duchess of Albany;* the vessel's impressive figurehead is suspended from the ceiling in the main room. The ship sank in 1893 in Caleta Policarpo in Tierra del Fuego, where it remains.

In **Antigua Casa de Gobierno** (Av. Maipú 465, tel. 02901/422 551), a former government building, are exhibits on Ushuaia's prison, although there is little new information from the Museo Marítimo y del Presidio. It's possible to arrange guided tours for both buildings in Spanish by asking at the reception desk.

Recreation
BEAGLE CHANNEL BOAT TOURS

One of the best aspects of Ushuaia is easy access to the mountains and the ocean. A popular excursion from the Muelle Turístico in Ushuaia is a **boat tour** along the Beagle Channel to islands such as **Isla de los Lobos,** with its southern sea lion and South American fur seal colonies; **Isla de los Pájaros,** home to a large imperial cormorant colony; and the iconic island lighthouse **Faro Les Éclaireurs.**

Several larger boats make this three-hour trip; expect a tour to cost around US$50 with operators such as **Rumbo Sur** (San Martín 350, tel. 02901/421 139, www.rumbosur. com.ar). Tour operator **Tres Marías** (Muelle Turístico, tel. 02901/582 060, www. tresmariasweb.com) has smaller vessels that do this trip, including the sailboat *If* and the 14-passenger motorboat *Yate* (10am and 3pm daily, US$80, including port taxes). These smaller vessels can get closer to the islands.

Another popular excursion is to **Isla Martillo,** a 32-hectare island and reserve that's part of the Estancia Harberton. November-March it is home to 3,000 breeding pairs of Magellanic penguins, plus a small number of gentoo and king penguins. Large vessels offer this trip, but **Velero Paludine** (Muelle Turístico, tel. 91166/716 733) and their eight-passenger sailboats are the best option, as they can get closest to the penguins. The six-hour tour, including transfers from their office and a snack, costs US$80.

GLACIAR MARTIAL

Just 7km northeast of Ushuaia, the impressive **Glaciar Martial** rises out of the Martial Mountains. From the end of Luis Fernando Martial—the road that winds up via switchbacks to the base of the mountains behind Ushuaia—a two-hour, 3-km trail climbs steeply across glacial moraine, following the route of a ski lift; this path is part of the Cerro Castor ski resort. The trail reaches an 825-meter viewpoint of Glaciar Martial and the Beagle Channel. The final climb is steep and crosses scree; trekking poles are recommended. The weather is incredibly variable, even during summer—snow is not unheard of—so carry layers. Water is available from a number of small glacial streams en route.

A taxi to the trailhead from Ushuaia costs US$10; otherwise it's a 7-km, mostly uphill hike from the center of town. There's a café at the trailhead that makes for a good spot for a post-hike drink.

LAGUNA ESMERALDA

Beautifully green and surrounded by a ring of toothy snowcapped peaks of the Sierra Alvear, the bewitching **Laguna Esmeralda,** a glacial lake 20km northeast of Ushuaia along Ruta 3, has become a very popular day trip for hikers. Threading through young *lenga* forest and areas of peat bog that can get very muddy after rainfall, a 9-km round-trip trail finds its way to this dramatic lake.

In summer, the route is packed with visitors, so it's recommended to leave Ushuaia as early as possible to avoid the crowds. Shuttle minivans (20min, US$14 round-trip) from the **Terminal de Buses Regulares** (Av. Maipú and Av. Fadul) leave hourly 9am-4pm daily January-February; service is less regular outside these months. Ask to be dropped off at the trailhead for the hike, around 100 meters before the entrance to the Valle de Lobos restaurant at km 3,037.

Food and Drinks
PATAGONIAN

Ignore the name; there's little that's Turkish about ★ **El Turco** (Av. San Martín 1410, tel. 02901/424 711, noon-3pm and 8pm-midnight Mon.-Sat., US$6-12). Instead, sample traditional Argentinean *sorrentinos* (pasta filled with salmon or vegetables) and the range of pizzas and grilled meat dishes. Friendly waitstaff can offer food and wine recommendations. Prices are very reasonable.

A favorite for dinner among visitors and locals alike, rustic **Bodegón Fueguino** (Av. San Martín 859, tel. 02901/431 972, www.tierradehumos.com, noon-12:45pm and 8pm-midnight Tues.-Sun., US$9-16) is best known for Patagonian lamb dishes. Hearty salads combine with a meaty empanada (US$1.50) or pumpkin soup (US$4). Service is excellent, even when the space is overcrowded with hungry patrons.

It's a bit of a hike up the hill to the best food in the city at ★ **Kalma** (Gobernador Valdés 293, tel. 02901 42-5786, www.kalma-resto.negocio.site, 7pm-11pm Mon.-Sat., US$20-35), but it's worth the exertion. An inventive, exquisitely presented six-course tasting menu (US$65) is made with regional ingredients, complete with wine pairings. A small menu offering ceviches, richly sauced fish, juicy steaks, and vegetarian dishes completes the options. Portions are on the small side. Reservations are recommended.

No other restaurant in Ushuaia can compete with **Kaupé** (Roca 470, tel. 02901/422 704, www.kaupe.com.ar, US$20-50) when it comes to the freshest seafood. Try the five-course tasting menu (US$60) for dishes like king crab crepes with saffron, scallop ceviche, and black sea bass with a carrot and pear *a la juliana,* with wine pairings. The small à la carte menu offers a handful of alternatives, including steak. The view at sunset is stunning, while the service matches the quality of the experience. Reservations are recommended.

LIGHT BITES AND COFFEE

The hip **Austral Modern** (9 de Julio 74, no phone, 9am-8:30pm Mon.-Sat., US$1.50-2) channels a hip vibe and offers a small menu of coffees, cakes, croissants, and simple sandwiches. Corrugated metal walls inside make you feel like you've wandered into a shipping container.

There's no better place to try traditional Argentinean empanadas than tiny ★ **La Marmita** (Rivadavia 322, tel. 02901/432 968, 9am-4pm and 7pm-midnight Mon.-Sat., 10am-3pm Sun., US$1-3), where the short-crust oven-baked delights ooze fillings like *caprese,* bacon, and onion. This is a great place to stock up for lunch if you're heading out for a day trip.

With shelves sinking under the weight of bric-a-brac (don't miss the antique underwear hanging on the bath doors), **Ramos Generales El Almacén** (Av. Maipú 749, tel. 02901/424317, www.ramosgeneralesush.com. ar, 9am-midnight daily, US$6-15) is in a former general store, catering mainly to travelers. Hearty fare comprises the *menú del día;* or try the soups, risottos, and stews, many vegetarian, plus sizable baguettes; the small bakery serves good pastries to take away. Service is slow.

Crammed with locals in the evening, trendy **Casa Olmo** (Av. San Martín 87, tel. 02901/422 824, 7pm-2am Sun.-Thurs., 7pm-4am Fri.-Sat., US$7-13) has 37 bottled beers from across Argentina. The tasting menu of beer from Cape Horn Brewery comes with a series of nibbles. Modern industrial tables contrast the rustic fishing nets hanging from the ceiling; expect a cool young crowd. Dishes include pizzas, sandwiches, and light bites, plus a range of vegetarian options.

Accommodations

US$40-65

All the large rooms at backpacker-friendly **Antarctica Hostel** (Antártida Argentina 270, tel. 02901/435 774, CH$17 dorm, US$65 d) share two blocks of baths downstairs. Wi-Fi is fast and electrical outlets are plentiful in dorms and communal areas, but the best aspects are the open-plan living area, with a shared kitchen on a platform above, and the staff's encyclopedic knowledge of activities in the region. Guests in the dorms have to walk through the kitchen and living room to use the baths; there are plans to install another upstairs bath.

US$65-95

Run by welcoming hosts who've converted their family home into the friendly ★ **Galeazzi-Basily B&B** (Gobernador Valdés 323, tel. 02901/423 213, www. avesdelsur.com, US$70 d shared bath, US$95 cabin for two people), this top-notch bed-and-breakfast has four simple, well-maintained bedrooms that share two baths, plus three cabins in the large garden, complete with kitchens and spacious bedrooms. Fluent English is spoken; the owners have a wealth of knowledge about the local area.

A stellar choice in this price range, ★ **La Casa en Ushuaia** (Gobernador Paz 1380, tel. 02901/423 202, US$80 d shared bath) is a superb little B&B with simply decorated bedrooms with crisp white sheets and views across the Beagle Channel. There's a small upstairs living room that opens onto a terrace with views of the harbor. Breakfast is basic, but this lodging is central, just two blocks uphill from Avenida San Martín.

US$95-125

Offering a warm reception, **Isla Bella** (Gómez 618, tel. 02901/579255, US$100 d shared bath, US$152 d private bath) has three well-proportioned bedrooms with comfortable mattresses and large windows; one has an en suite bath. Owners Miguel and Monica have long worked in tourism and have helpful knowledge about the region, and Monica speaks fluent English. Breakfast is better than average in this price range. It's a steep eight-block, 15-minute hike up from Avenida San Martín.

1: the hike up to Glaciar Martial 2: Antarctica Hostel

Popular for conferences and tour groups, **Hotel Las Lengas** (Goleta Florencia 1722, tel. 02901/436 100, www.laslengashotel.com. ar, US$105 d) is a good value, although the quality of the rooms doesn't quite live up to the modern furnishings of the lobby, with its views across Bahía Escondida. None of the rooms share these views; bedrooms and baths are a little tired. There's plenty of parking and an attached pizza restaurant.

OVER US$125

Rooms are slightly mismatched in furniture and style in the eco-friendly **Hostería Foike** (Gobernador Campos 1554, tel. 02901/422 475, www.hosteriafoike.com.ar, US$145 standard d, US$165 superior d), but architect Luis and his wife are the perfect hosts of this seven-room B&B. Superior rooms are on the 2nd floor and have better views of the Beagle Channel, while the two standard doubles downstairs, with private terraces, are a good option on a tighter budget. The breakfast buffet includes jams made from their fruit garden out back, while guests have access to free tea and coffee and a space with a microwave and counter to prepare simple meals. Airport transfers are offered at additional cost.

Built into the side of the hill, the light and airy **Hostería Patagonia Jarké** (Gobernador Paz 1305, tel. 02901/437 245, www.patagoniajarke.com.ar, US$195 d) has comfortable sofas and sumptuous Beagle Channel views from its elegantly decorated common areas on two floors of the building. The modern bedrooms, complete with tea- and coffee-making facilities, aren't large. Rooms 14 and 15 make up for this with the best views. A continental breakfast is served in a sunny glass-roofed breakfast room. Private parking is available. The staff speaks very little English.

A 20-minute drive from the center, **Los Cauquenes** (De La Ermita 3462, tel. 02901/441 3000, www.loscauquenes.com, US$398 standard d, US$497 superior d) has exceptional views of the Beagle Channel from the superior bedrooms; all the modern rooms have the amenities expected of a five-star property, including king beds with crisp linens, and tea- and coffee-making facilities. The on-site spa has a sauna, a jetted tub, and a gym, while the restaurant offers top-quality dining. Glacier tours and boat tours on the Beagle Channel can be arranged. The hotel is far enough from the bustle of the city that you almost feel you've escaped to a more remote part of Tierra del Fuego. The internet connection can be temperamental. The hotel operates a shuttle service every two hours to and from the city.

Information and Services

The very well organized, English-speaking **Oficina Información Turística** (Puerto Prefectura Naval Argentina 470, tel. 02901/437 666, www.turismoushuaia.com, 9am-8pm daily) can advise on bus timetables and day trips. They also offer free certificates indicating you've reached the world's southernmost city.

La Última Bita (Av. San Martín 130, tel. 02901/424 116, 10am-1pm and 4pm-9pm Mon.-Sat.) has good maps of El Chaltén, Cape Horn, and Patagonia, along with English-language books about Tierra del Fuego.

Withdrawing cash can be an ordeal in Ushuaia; the ATM network can go down for prolonged periods. The eastern end of Avenida San Martín (between Laserre and Antártida Argentine) has the majority of the banks with 24-hour ATMs. **Banco Patagonia** (Av. San Martín 302) is one of the most reliable, while Banco Tierra del Fuego rarely accepts foreign cards. To exchange money, head to currency house **Júpiter** (Rivadavia 176, no phone, 10am-6pm daily) with your passport; don't expect a good exchange rate for any currency other than U.S. dollars.

For laundry, head out early to **5 a Sec** (Gobernador Deloqui 299, no phone, 10am-8:30pm Mon.-Wed., noon-8:30pm Thurs., 10am-8:30pm Fri., 10am-4pm Sat.) to avoid competition from the cruise ships. Mail items at **Correo Argentinos** (Av. San Martín 209, tel. 02901/421 347, 9am-4:45pm Mon.-Fri.). To see a doctor or for medical emergencies, go to **Hospital Regional Ushuaia** (Av. 12 de Octubre, tel. 2901/441 000).

Getting There and Around

AIR

Aeropuerto Internacional Malvinas Argentinas (USH, tel. 02901/431 232, www.aeropuertoushuaia.com) is 5km south of the city. For destinations within Argentina, **Aerolíneas Argentinas** (Av. Maipú and 9 de Julio, tel. 02901/436 338, www.aerolineas.com.ar) has four daily nonstop flights to Buenos Aires's Aeroparque Jorge Newbury (3.5hr) and two daily nonstop flights to El Calafate (1.5hr). **LATAM** (www.latam.com) flies daily to Aeroparque Jorge Newbury.

A taxi to or from the airport should cost US$6-10. It's impossible to flag down taxis on the street of Ushuaia; you have to call the **Asociación de Taxis Ushuaia** (Av. Maipú and Laserre, tel. 02901/422 007) or **Taxi Coop** (tel. 02901/433 843). There is a taxi stand at the airport to head into the city. Tour operator **Tolkeyén** (Av. San Martín 409, tel. 02901/437 073, www.tolkeyenpatagonia.com) can arrange minibus transfers to and from your hotel for a similar price as the taxi.

BUS

Buses Pacheco offers thrice-weekly buses from **Punta Arenas** (8:30am, Mon., Wed., and Fri., 12hr, US$60), with a transfer in Río Grande. **Bus Sur** has a direct thrice-weekly service from Punta Arenas (8:30am Mon., Wed., and Fri., 12hr, US$56). You can buy tickets at the offices of tour operator **Tolkeyén** (Av. San Martín 409, tel. 02901/437 073, www.tolkeyenpatagonia.com).

To get to Ushuaia from **El Calafate** (19hr, US$80), **Marga Taqsa** (Juana Fadul 126, tel. 02091/435 453, www.taqsa.com.ar) offers daily buses, with a change in Río Gallegos. Buses depart at 3am from El Calafate.

CAR

To drive to Ushuaia from **Punta Arenas,** it's a 630-km, 9- to 11-hour drive. After two hours on Ruta 9, Ruta 255, and Ruta 257, you'll board a ferry operated by **Transbordadora Austral Broom** (www.tabsa.cl, 8:30am and 1am daily, 20min, CH$15,000 car including passengers, CH$1,700 foot passengers, cash only) at Cruce Punta Delgada, which takes you quickly across to Cruce Bahía Azul, where you'll continue south on Ruta 257, through Chilean Tierra del Fuego. The highway becomes a gravel road that eventually turns east to the border at **Paso San Sebastián** (tel. 61/2761 190, 24 hr daily summer, 8am-10pm daily winter). From here, Ruta 3 is fully paved for 295km to Ushuaia. Gas and ATMs are available in the sprawling town of Río Grande, 90km beyond the border.

To get to Ushuaia from **El Calafate,** it's an 878-km, 11- to 13-hour journey on Ruta 11, Ruta 40, and Ruta 5 to the **Paso Integración Austral** (tel. 61/2276 1122, 24 hr daily Nov.-Mar., 8am-10pm Apr.-Oct.), the border crossing with Chile. Continue south on Ruta 255 and Ruta 257 to reach the ferry crossing at Cruce Punta Delgada. Ruta 257 continues to **Paso San Sebastián** (tel. 61/2761 190, 24 hr daily summer, 8am-10pm daily winter). In Argentina, Ruta 3 is fully paved for 295km to Ushuaia. Gas and ATMs are available in the sprawling town of Río Grande, 90km beyond the border. Make sure you change money in El Calafate before departing or exchange dollars or Argentinean pesos for Chilean pesos at **Aguado Seguros** (Av. N.C. Kirchner 489) or **Luis B. Lopetegui S.R.L.** (Zapiola 469) in Río Gallegos; there are also ATMs here.

To cross between Argentina and Chile in a rental vehicle, you must have **advance written permission** from your rental company.

GETTING AROUND

To get around, your best bet is **Asociación de Taxis Ushuaia** (Av. Maipú and Laserre, tel. 02901/422 007, www.taxisdeushuaia.com.ar) or **Taxi Coop** (tel. 02901/433 843). Alternatively, rental cars are available at the airport with **Hertz** (tel. 02901/432 429, www.hertz.com, 7am-11pm daily) and **Avis** (tel.

Last-Minute Cruises to Antarctica

A trip to the White Continent is the ultimate bucket-list item for many travelers. Ushuaia is the main departure point for cruises thanks to its proximity to Antarctica. Cruises last a minimum of six days, with multiple companies departing daily December-January, when daylight can last almost 24 hours. Outside these months, companies depart 3-4 times per week. The season for cruises to Antarctica is October-mid-April. March is the optimal time for whale-watching.

Booking well in advance for a cruise to Antarctica is recommended. For budget travelers, last-minute deals exist. Ushuaia-based **Freestyle Adventure Travel** (Gobernador Paz 866, tel. 2901/609 792, www.freestyleadventuretravel.com) specializes in finding cheaper deals, both advance and last-minute. **Rumbo Sur** (Av. San Martín 350, tel. 02901/421 139, www.rumbosur. com.ar), Ushuaia's longest-running tour company, sometimes has last-minute cruise deals. Expect to pay around US$5,000 pp; January-February are the best months for these types of deals. If you turn up in Ushuaia hunting for a cheap deal, you might spend up to two weeks in town waiting for a ticket. After mid-February, daylight hours reduce dramatically, so you can expect prices to drop around 25 percent.

02901/430 269, www.avis.com.ar, 8am-8pm daily). Avis also has an office in the center of Ushuaia (Godoy 49, tel. 02901/437 373, 9am-12:30pm and 4pm-8:30pm Mon.-Sat.).

Onward Travel via Boat

Cruise ships leaving for **Antarctica** (Oct.-mid-Apr.) and **Punta Arenas** (Sept.-Mar.) dock in Ushuaia's harbor. Boarding any boat at the harbor, you have to pay an embarkation tax (ARSCH$0.80) at the port.

Australis (tel. 2/2840 0100, www.australis. com) offers one-way (4 nights, ending in Punta Arenas) and round-trip (7-8 nights) journeys sailing via Glacier Alley, Isla Magdalena, and Bahía Ainsworth and with a landing on Cape Horn (weather permitting). Reservations are required in advance. Good discounts are often available in shoulder seasons (Sept.-Oct. and late Mar.). A four-night, one-way cruise starts at US$5,180 for a 2-person cabin with twin beds.

The 40-minute **ferry crossing** between Ushuaia and Puerto Williams is run by two Argentinean companies that both offer departures once daily Tuesday-Sunday. Ferry tickets can be bought online or at the office of the organized tour outfitter **Seaboat** (Muelle Turístico, tel. 02901/603/711, 2.5hr, US$120 one-way, US$220 round-trip). Boats leave

from Puerto Williams at 9am and at 10am from Ushuaia.

On the Ushuaia side, travelers wait at the offices of Seaboat, where you're escorted through the border crossing formalities to depart Argentina before embarking. Passengers are transported overland from the dock at Puerto Navarino to the Municipalidad building in Puerto Williams, where the border crossing procedures for entry to Chile are conducted.

PARQUE NACIONAL TIERRA DEL FUEGO

With thick forests of southern beech that turn deep red as autumn sets in, **Parque Nacional Tierra del Fuego** (tel. 02901/421 315, tierradelfuego@apn.gob.ar, 8am-9pm daily, US$17), 12km west of Ushuaia, covers 70,000 hectares and is the southernmost protected area in Argentina. Heavy glacier activity in the region is responsible for the deep valleys between mountain ridges, many of which straddle the border with Chile.

Native wildlife is another attraction, including the rare black-browed albatross, Fuegian steamer duck, imperial cormorant, and kelp goose, particularly in the bays on the park's southern edge, while the distinctive Magellanic woodpecker and the thorn-tailed rayadito are present in the forests. Otters and sea lions can often be spied in the bays.

The **Centro de Visitantes Alakush** (Alakush Visitors Center, km 3,075 Ruta 3, tel. 02901/1551 9727, www.centroalakush.com.ar, 9am-6pm daily) is 8.5km west of the park entrance, on the west side of the park. It has a gift shop, restrooms, and a café, plus a small museum covering flora, fauna, and geography and information about the indigenous people who first inhabited Tierra del Fuego.

There are four free **campgrounds** with very basic facilities in the park: **Camping Bahía Ensenada, Camping Río Pipo, Camping Las Bandurrias,** and **Camping Laguna Verde.** Sites are first come, first served. Campfires are permitted, but you'll need to bring wood from town.

Orientation

Ruta 3 is the main road through the park. The park's entrance, marked by a **ranger station,** is accessed from Ruta 3. From the ranger station, it's a 2-km drive west along Ruta 3 to the unmarked and unpaved road heading south. It runs 1.5km to Ensenada Zaratiegui, a former dock, and the trailhead for Senda Costera and Senda Pampa Alta. From the turnoff, if you continue along Ruta 3 west, it's 7km to the Centro de Visitantes Alakush, where the Senda Hito XXIV and Cerro Guanaco trails begin.

Ruta 3's western terminus is at **Puerto Arias,** a former dock, where there is a car park and a handful of short trails.

Hiking

The four hiking trails in the park are the main attraction. The most popular is the **Senda Costera** (8km one-way, 4hr), an easy coastal path that starts from Ensenada Zaratiegui, passing through forests of *canelo* (winter's bark) on its way west to reach the Centro de Visitantes Alakush, with mountain views. This trail is popular for cruise ship expeditions, especially 9am-1pm; for smaller crowds, arrive later. From the same starting point, heading north, **Senda Pampa Alta** (3km one-way, 1hr) climbs up to a lookout for views of the Beagle Channel and the Valle del Río Pipo.

The jewel in the park is the seriously challenging **Cerro Guanaco trail** (8km round-trip, 8hr), which gains 973 meters in elevation in only 4km to reach the peak of Cerro Guanaco. Climbing through *lenga* forests, the trail offers several stunning panoramas of the Beagle Channel and the Darwin Mountains, passing through patches of peat bog that can

hiking the Cerro Guanaco trail

be unpleasant after heavy rains. The finale is a steep ascent along the edge of the mountain to the peak. If the weather's good, you can see for miles along the Beagle Channel. The trailhead for Cerro Guanaco is at the Centro de Visitantes Alakush.

Far less visited and with pleasant views, the **Senda Hito XXIV** (7km round-trip, 3hr) passes along the edges of Lago Acigami to the border with Chile, indicated by a metal marker and sign. This trail begins at the Centro de Visitantes Alakush.

Getting There

Minibuses (US$20 round-trip) leave hourly 9am-5pm daily from the **Terminal de Buses Regulares** (Av. Maipú and Av. Fadul) in Ushuaia. Theoretically, they also return hourly from the park's three main stops (Ensenada Zaratiegui, Centro de Visitante Alakush, and Puerto Arias), but it's best to check with the driver about the time, as the schedules are erratic. The final bus leaves the park at 7pm. It's far cheaper and more convenient, particularly for groups, to rent a car for the day.

ESTANCIA HARBERTON

The oldest estancia in the Argentinean portion of Tierra del Fuego, **Estancia Harberton** (Ruta J, tel. 02901/422 742, www.estanciaharberton.com, 10am-7pm daily Oct. 15-Mar., US$11) was founded by Anglican missionary Thomas Bridges (1842-1898). In 1886, the Argentinean National Congress gave Bridges this tract of land, 60km east of Ushuaia. Covering 20,000 hectares, the ranch is on a peninsula that stretches into the Beagle Channel. The original buildings, in English country cottage style, still stand. A working sheep ranch until the mid-1900s, Estancia Harberton is now open to visitors.

Just 500 meters from the main house, the **Museo Acatushún de Aves y Mamíferos Marinos Australes** is a working laboratory where scientists study marine mammals and birds from the region and includes a fascinating collection of over 5,000 skeletons.

English- and Spanish-language tours of the property start at midday and stop at the museum, ranch buildings, and an on-site nature reserve. A tearoom in the converted northwest wing of the old house serves a small lunch menu, as well as cakes and coffees, with views across Bahía Harberton; advance reservations are required.

You can stay overnight in the ranch's charming guesthouse, the Shepherd's House (US$400 d, includes breakfast and lunch or dinner) or the hostel, the Foreman's House (US$50 dorm, includes breakfast). Both offer access to a small kitchen; additional meals can be requested.

You can visit the ranch on one of the full-day **boat tours** that leave from Ushuaia and visit Isla Martillo, Faro Les Éclaireurs, and Isla Bridges to see South American fur seals and a colony of cormorants. **Rumbo Sur** (San Martín 350, tel. 02901/421 139, www.rumbosur.com.ar) and **Tolkeyén** (Av. San Martín 409, tel. 02901/437 073, www.tolkeyenpatagonia.com) spend 1.5 hours at the ranch (enough time to take the guided tour) for US$100, with entrance fees included. **Catamaranes Canoero** (Muelle Turístico, tel. 02901/433 893, www.hotelyamanas.com.ar) offers a 3.5-hour visit at the estancia, with entrance fees included, for US$100.

By road, it's an 82-km, 1.75-hour drive on Ruta 3 and Ruta J, which has splendid views. For more information about the ranch and its history, see the 1948 book *The Uttermost Part of the Earth* by Bridges's son, Lucas Bridges.

Chilean Tierra del Fuego

Sparsely inhabited and barely developed, Tierra del Fuego purportedly takes its name from the flickering lights of the fires of its indigenous inhabitants that were visible from the deck of Fernando Magallanes's ship in 1520. Separated from the rest of South America by the Strait of Magellan, the terrain of this 4.8-million-hectare island, split between Chile and Argentina, is less hospitable than the mainland. Most infrastructure is concentrated in the very south of Argentinean territory, around Ushuaia.

The western side of the island, the Chilean sector, is a version of Patagonia that has barely changed since the times of its original inhabitants. The steppe is made heavy with sharply defined low clouds. The terrain soon becomes ragged, with chiseled mountain ranges and deep valleys thick with peat bog, where wilderness is king.

A road trip through Chilean Tierra del Fuego is the ultimate journey. The handful of towns that dot this largely uninhabited terrain have only passing interest for most visitors; it's the landscapes that bewitch. Porvenir and Cerro Sombrero make reasonable destinations to break up the drive from Punta Arenas, but the region's real attractions are deeper in the island.

ORIENTATION

Paved **Ruta 257** is the central artery of Chilean Tierra del Fuego, running south from the ferry dock at Cruce Bahía Azul and turning due east after 115km. It continues another 40km to the San Sebastián border crossing with Argentina.

A 30-minute drive south of Cruce Bahía Azul on Ruta 257 is **Cerro Sombrero,** a seemingly abandoned town of 700 inhabitants. If you need to stop for the night, you can stay in the dated but clean 50-room **Hostería Tunkelen** (tel. 61/2212 757, www. hosteriatunkelen.cl, CH$39,500-74,000 d

shared bath), with an on-site restaurant. Advance booking is advised. There is also a **COPEC gas station** just inside the edge of town; ask around if you can't find it. Before setting out to any of the locations farther south, it is essential to fill up your tank.

One of the other few roads on the island is the **Y-65,** which leaves Ruta 257 about 10km south of its northern end at Cruce Bahía Azul. The Y-65 runs southwest to Porvenir, leaving the town as the Y-71 as it runs east across the island to rejoin Ruta 257.

From the crossroads of the Y-71 and Ruta 257, the gravel **Y-85** heads southward, hugging the western coast. It passes Bahía Inútil and the tiny fishing village of Camerón before heading inland toward Cerro Guanaco, the only settlement in this part of the island. The Y-85 terminates on the southwestern shore of Lago Fagnano, where the Camino Vicuña is being built to reach the otherwise inaccessible Parque Nacional Yendegaia and the southern shore of the island, where a proposed ferry will connect it with Puerto Williams. The road will likely be under construction through 2022.

PORVENIR

Practically a city by the island's standards, Porvenir is on a harbor that cuts sharply into the northwestern edge of Tierra del Fuego, overlooking the southern shores of the Strait of Magellan. The town originated with the island's short-lived 1879 gold rush; later, sheep estancias were founded in the surrounding windswept grasslands, bringing workers from Chiloé. Nowadays, Porvenir's economy is fueled by a nearby salmon processing plant.

There are few sights here. The town's colorful, rusted, wind-weathered houses represent an authentic version of Patagonia that's different from the large touristed cities. Pass an afternoon wandering Manuel Señoret, the *costanera* (coastal road), and admiring the

Chilean Tierra del Fuego

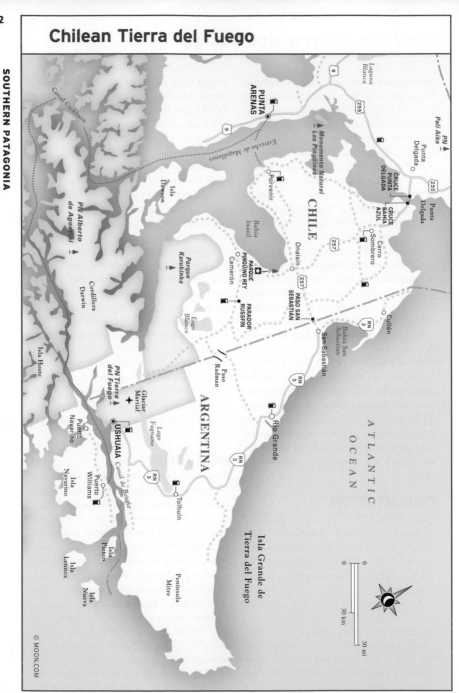

© MOON.COM

town's early 20th-century buildings, many of which bear some resemblance to European architecture.

The **Museo de Tierra del Fuego Fernando Rusque Cordero** (Jorge Schythe 71, tel. 61/2581 800, 8am-5:15pm Mon.-Thurs., 8am-4:15pm Fri., 10am-4pm Sat.-Sun., CH$1,000 adults, children free) contains a mock-up of an old Porvenir corner shop and information about the Tierra del Fuego gold rush.

The SERNATUR-run **Oficina de Información Turístico** (Manuel Señoret 770, tel. 61/2580 098, www.muniporvenir.cl, 8:30am-1pm and 2:30pm-5:30pm Mon.-Thurs., 8:30am-1pm and 2:30pm-4:30pm Fri.) can help put you in touch with local guides for exploring the area and for visiting the king penguin colony at Bahía Inútil.

There is a **COPEC gas station** in town. Fill up before leaving Porvenir, as there's only one other gas station south from here, and no other gas stations before reaching Río Grande, 232km east.

Food and Accommodations

For reliably good local dishes, head directly to **Anclamar** (Manuel Señoret 448, tel. 61/2580 191, 11am-11pm daily, CH$5,000-13,000). Well-presented dishes of *centolla* (king crab), scallops, and beautifully cooked fresh salmon are specialties in this popular restaurant; welcoming service and sea views from the coastal road are the cherry on top.

Half a block west, in a formal 1920 building, **Club Croata** (Manuel Señoret 542, tel. 61/2580 053, 11am-4pm and 7pm-10:30pm Tues.-Sun., CH$5,000-11,000) is another good option for excellent, enormous king crab and salmon, although service is sluggish. The setting is the most upscale in town. They also have fish and grilled meat, Croatian dishes, and a small wine menu.

Family-run **Hotel Espana** (Croacia 698, tel. 61/2580 160, www.hotelespana.cl, CH$30,000 d) is one of the more upmarket options in Porvenir. Rooms are warm and sizeable if somewhat utilitarian, and all have private baths. There's an attached restaurant, although service is extremely slow.

In a lovingly restored old house, **Yendegaia House** (Croacia 702, tel. 61/2581 919, http://yendegaiahouse.com, CH$58,000 d) was the first lodgings in the town and has friendly hosts, a library of books on naturalism, and neat, spacious bedrooms. A good breakfast is also included. The owners are bird specialists and work with Far South Expeditions, a tour agency based in Punta Arenas.

Getting There

There are no buses from either Punta Arenas or Ushuaia to Porvenir. The easiest option is the daily passenger ferry from Punta Arenas.

AIR

The three daily flights operated by **Aeriovías DAP** (O'Higgins 891, tel. 61/2616 100, www.dapairline.com) are the quickest route to Porvenir from Punta Arenas, constituting a mere 12 minutes in the air, landing at **Aeródromo Capitán Fuentes Martínez** (WPR), 5km northeast of town.

BOAT

The daily **passenger ferry** from Punta Arenas (2.25hr, CH$39,800 vehicle including driver, CH$6,200 foot passengers) is run by **Transbordadora Austral Broom** (tel. 61/2728 100, www.tabsa.cl). Boats depart Tuesday-Sunday from the **Terminal de Ferry Tres Puentes,** 5km north of Punta Arenas center (CH$3,000 in a taxi or CH$800 by *colectivo* from Calle Magallanes). They dock at Bahía Chilota, 5km west of Porvenir.

Schedules change regularly, so consult the website or visit the ferry terminal in Punta Arenas to confirm departure time. Advance bookings, particularly for vehicles, are essential in high season.

CAR

To get to Porvenir by car from **Punta Arenas** is a two-hour drive along Ruta 9, Ruta 255, and Ruta 257 to reach Cruce Punta Delgada, where you'll board a ferry, operated by **Transbordadora Austral Broom** (8:30am-1am daily, www.tabsa.cl, 20min, CH$15,000 car including passengers, CH$1,700 foot passengers, cash only) across to Cruce Bahía Azul. It's a 10-minute drive on Ruta 257 to the mostly paved Y-65. It's another 125km and two hours to Porvenir. On the drive, watch for flamingos in the lakes that line the road—they migrate here during the summer. The total journey is just over four hours.

From **Ushuaia,** it's a six-hour, 440-km journey. Take Ruta 3 northeast from the city and follow it to the border at **Paso San Sebastián** (tel. 61/2761 190, 24 hr daily summer, 8am-10pm daily winter). Gas and ATMs are available in the sprawling town of Río Grande, 90km before the border. From here, gravel Ruta 257 continues west, turning into the narrow Y-71 after 45km for the final 100km and 1.5 hours of the journey.

★ PARQUE PINGÜINO REY

Opened in 2011, **Parque Pingüino Rey** (Bahía Inútil, on the Y-85 to Camerón, tel. 9/9831 9211, www.pinguinorey.com, 11am-6pm Tues.-Sun. Aug.-June, CH$12,000 adults, under 12 free) is a private reserve with a growing population of around 60 king penguins. It is the only colony of king penguins in the Americas. Skeletal remains have proven that king penguins have resided in the region throughout the last few hundred years, although the 1960s and 1970s saw many of the birds packed off to foreign zoos. Luckily, an attitude shift has turned the focus toward the conservation and study of the penguins.

A modern visitors center staffed by the ornithologists who study the colony gives ample information about the penguins. A short path leads to a viewing area a few dozen meters from the group. Only 20 people are allowed into the park at once, so avoid the peak times of 1pm-3pm, when the tour groups arrive. It's possible to pay with a credit card, but the

reader is often out of service, so bring cash. Because of the daily limit, it's a good idea to reserve your trip in advance via the website.

Organize a tour with a company in Punta Arenas (from CH$65,000) such as **Comapa** (Lautaro Navarro 1112, Punta Arenas, tel. 61/2200 200, www.comapa. com) or **Full Patagonia Tour** (inside the Hotel Chalet Chapital, Armando Sanhueza 974, Punta Arenas, tel. 61/2723 199, www. fullpatagoniatour.com). Alternatively, rent a car: It's a two-hour, 130-km drive south from Cruce Bahía Azul, or a two-hour, 112-km drive southeast from Porvenir. **Far South Expeditions** (Manuel Señoret 610, tel. 61/2615 793, www.farsouthexp.com) operates two-day tours with expert guides (from US$1,962 pp) that include all transportation, food, and lodging.

For those with more money than time, **Aeriovías DAP** (O'Higgins 891, Punta Arenas, tel. 61/2616 100, www.dapairline. com) runs full-day tours from Punta Arenas (US$370, min. 2 passengers) that include the 12-minute flight across the Strait of Magellan to Porvenir, lunch, vehicle transfer, and entrance to the park.

PARQUE KARUKINKA

Established by the Chilean arm of the Wildlife Conservation Society, **Parque Karukinka** (tel. 61/2613 334, http://chile.wcs.org and www.karukinkanatural.cl, 24 hr daily, free) covers 300,000 hectares on the southwestern edge of Chilean Tierra del Fuego's temperate forest, Patagonian steppe, and peat bog ecosystems. You'll see native wildlife, from the ubiquitous crested caracara and the upland goose to the black-browed albatross, with its wingspan of up to 2.5 meters.

The park's main entrance is a 15-km drive south of Pampa Guanaco, the southernmost settlement on the Chilean side of the island. This is where the park's **ranger station** (no phone, 8am-6pm daily) and the Refugio Vicuña guesthouse and campground are; you can get maps of the park here.

Hiking

Within the park are four well-marked trails. About 1.5km after the sign indicating that you've entered the park, **Sendero Cerro Pietro Grande** (7km loop, 3hr) is a circuit that climbs steeply through *lenga* and *ñirre* to the top of Cerro Pietro Grande for all-around views across the Patagonian steppe.

Sendero Laguna del Cura (12km loop, 5hr) begins from the park's guesthouse, Refugio Vicuña, and passes through native woodland to reach Laguna del Cura. The way back offers spectacular views from the top of Cerro del Cura. Also leaving from the guesthouse, the easy **Sendero Cerro Cóndores Imaginarios** (4.6km loop, 3hr) gains 240 meters elevation to a viewpoint across the plains.

Tours

TDF Patagonia Tour (tel. 9/8636 1772, www.tdfpatagoniatour.com) is the only agency operating three-day tours to Parque Nacional Karukinka (from US$830, min. 2 people). Tours start in Porvenir, and all food, dorm-style lodging, onward transport, entry costs, and bilingual guides are included.

Accommodations

Lodgings in the region are few; dining options are even fewer, so stock up on food in Punta Arenas before you depart.

Within the park, **Refugio Vicuña** (CH$8,000 campsite, CH$30,000 dome, CH$35,000 d shared bath) has basic lodgings in a five-bedroom guesthouse with kitchen access, 10 campsites, and two-person domes on raised platforms (bring a sleeping bag and mat). The campsites and domes have access to toilets and covered areas for cooking. Bring all food and a gas stove for cooking, and make sure to reserve ahead of arrival.

North of the park on the shores of Lago Blanco, **Hostería Las Lengas** (Lago Blanco, tel. 9/4450 3252, www.hosterialaslengas.com, Oct.-Apr., CH$140,000 d, CH$83,000 cabin) is a comfortable place with six rooms and two fully equipped cabins. Constructed from local *lenga* wood, the main house comprises plain bedrooms, and the cabins have views across the lake. It's designed for people fishing the world-class Río Blanco, but it's also the perfect place to just watch the clouds go by, only an hour's drive from the park entrance. Only the cabins have kitchens; meals can be arranged with advance notice. Reserve before arrival to ensure the lodge is open and to get instructions on how to find it (it's down a dirt track, the first right turn after the police station in Pampa Guanaco).

Information and Services

Beyond Porvenir, there are no places to withdraw cash, so make sure you come with plenty, as nowhere accepts cards. The **Parador Russfin** (tel. 61/2216 748, www.paradorrussfin.cl, 7am-7pm daily), a sawmill 38km from Camerón, is the final stop for fuel. They also have a handful of rooms (CH$37,000 dorm, CH$57,000 d private bath) for overnight stays and can offer lunch and dinner in their canteen (call ahead to reserve) and even Wi-Fi.

Getting There

To get to Parque Karukinka from Cruce Bahía Azul is a 5.5-hour, 265-km drive south on Ruta 257 and the Y-85. Around 2.5 hours into the drive, the Y-85 passes through Camerón, where the road curves and continues southeast. From Porvenir, it's a 2.5-hour, 140-km drive to Camerón, then 3 hours and 105km to reach the park entrance.

PUERTO WILLIAMS

Clinging to the southern shores of the Beagle Channel on the largely uninhabited 2.5 million-hectare Isla Navarino, the town of Puerto Williams is overshadowed by the bright lights of Ushuaia 50km northwest across the water. With 2,900 people, it is the southernmost settlement in the world, although few tourists venture this far.

Puerto Williams is a small town defined by neat regimented housing. It can feel like there are more horses than people—you'll see horses foraging in people's front gardens. This remote and often rain- and windswept corner of Chilean Patagonia offers the region's wildest and most spectacular hiking in the Dientes del Navarino trek, which circumnavigates the toothy mountain ridge behind the village. For a true glimpse of untamed Patagonia, few places can compete with Puerto Williams. Getting here by speedboat, plane, or ferry is part of the adventure.

Orientation

Only seven streets deep, Puerto Williams is a neatly organized town, although a lack of road signs—and even road names in some places—can make it hard to navigate. It's small enough that you can wander from edge to edge in less than 20 minutes. Most visitors arrive either at the TABSA ferry ramp on the western edge of Costanera or at the airport, a 10-minute drive west on a small peninsula.

O'Higgins is the main street, where you'll find the municipal buildings, the Centro Comercial, a small plaza, and the hospital; it ends in the unassuming Plaza Bernardo O'Higgins on the west side of town. Most restaurants and supermarkets are on the Costanera or Piloto Pardo, and hotels are scattered around town; a few are far enough out that you'll need to organize transport or rent a bike or vehicle.

★ Museo Martín Gusinde

The modern **Museo Martín Gusinde** (Añagay, tel. 61/2621 043, www.museomartingusinde.cl, 9:30am-1pm and 3pm-6pm Tues.-Fri., 2:30pm-6:30pm Sat.-Sun., free) is unmissable. The museum opened in 1975 and was extensively revamped in 2011. It focuses primarily on the indigenous Yaghan people, offering the most complete and nuanced presentation of their culture and traditions that you'll find in Patagonia, if not all of Chile. Through vivid photography and videos, the museum gives insight into the lives of these seafaring people. Exhibits cover Yaghan mythology, their evangelization by Anglican missionaries, and a lovingly built replica of a Yaghan canoe in the atrium.

The only downside to this otherwise excellent museum is that nothing is translated into English. The focus on visual and interactive displays is enough to keep even non-Spanish speakers engaged.

Recreation

Attempting to make something good of the invasive beaver population, **Navarino Beaver** (Centro Comercial 140 B, tel. 9/9548 7365, www.barberjorge.wixsite.com/navarinbeaver2) offer four-hour beaver viewing and hunting tours (from CH$35,000 pp, min. 3 people), which can be combined with beaver meat-tasting. Transfers and equipment are included.

Explora Navarino (Centro Comercial 140B, tel. 9/9185 0155, www.exploraislanavarino.com) provides advice and guided treks of the Dientes de Navarino, plus four-hour kayak outings in the Beagle Channel (CH$50,000, min. 3 people), plus SUP tours (CH$50,000, no min.), both including transfers to and from their office, plus equipment.

Food

Thanks to its extreme southern location, food and lodging in Puerto Williams are overpriced for the service offered. There are some excellent options, however.

The simply decorated **El Resto del Sur** (Ricardo Maragaño 146, tel. 61/2621 849, 12:30pm-3:30pm Mon.-Sat., 8pm-11pm Sun., CH$5,500-13,000) feels like a cafeteria rather than a restaurant, but has good enough food from its large menu, from pizzas to pastas—though the *sorrentinos de centolla* (king crab pasta parcels) are disappointing—and well-cooked salmon dishes. On Friday, it's pizza only. Service is friendly and English-speaking, and the views across the Beagle Channel from the 2nd-floor dining room are lovely.

Specializing in Chilean-style fast food, **Onashaga** (Piloto Pardo s/n, 11am-11pm Mon.-Fri., 11am-9:30pm Sun., CH$3,000-6,000, *menú del día* CH$4,800-5,800) has some of the cheapest prices for meals on the island. Choose from *chorrillanas* (fries topped with sliced meat, onions, and a fried eggs), *pichangas* (pickled vegetables with cubes of cheese and ham), simple breakfasts, large sandwiches, and more local dishes. The local Nativa beer is on tap.

The unexpectedly excellent ★ **Pizzería Kanasaka** (Costanera 273, tel. 9/7987 5491, CH$5,500-8,500) might feed you the best pizza in Patagonia. Run in the one-tabled living room of the French owners' house, the world's southernmost pizzeria has a fixed menu, although options depend largely on what ingredients they have. Specials such as king crab accompany chicken spiced with *merkén,* salami, or vegetables. There's no alcohol license, so bring your own.

Accommodations

Run by the helpful Cecilia, **Refugio El Padrino** (Costanera, opposite Café Luisa, tel. 9/84380843, ceciliamancillao@yahoo.com.ar, CH$15,000 dorm) has very basic but impeccably clean lodgings. It has two- and three-dorm bedrooms—mostly with bunk beds—painted lime green and shocking orange, along with a welcoming if cluttered living and kitchen area. The hostel operates on the honor system; there are no locks for bedrooms or the front door, and new arrivals can let themselves in, choose a bed, and pay when Cecilia arrives in the evening. Some 350 meters west along the Costanera, **Camping El Padrino** (off Costanera before Pizzeria Kansaka, tel. 9/84380843, ceciliamancillao@yahoo.com.ar, CH$8,000) is run by the same owner and has a small garden with space for a few tents as well as a wooden cabin with a living room and an area for cooking. They can arrange horse tours around the island.

With the best Beagle Channel views in town, ★ **Miramar** (Teniente Muñoz 155, tel. 61/2621 372, CH$30,000 d shared bath, CH$40,000 d private bath) is even more appealing thanks to its affable hosts, who welcome you into their cozy, clean, and affordable bed-and-breakfast. Bedrooms are a good size.

There's kitchen access when the owners aren't cooking. They also rent bikes (CH$5,000 half day, CH$10,000 full day).

The 24-bed **Lakutaia Lodge** (Seno Lauta s/n, tel. 61/2621 721, www.lakutaia.com, CH$184,000 d) doesn't have the views that Errante Ecolodge has, but the facilities are excellent. Upstairs bedrooms have views across the Beagle Channel, elegantly furnished with driftwood lamps. Decorated throughout with Yaghan crafts, the communal areas are a large dining area and a cozy library. Staff aid guests to plan excursions, which include flights over Cape Horn, while well-presented food is available at additional cost. Guests can use the bikes for the 2-km pedal into town.

Six kilometers west along a gravel road, the excellently finished ★ **Errante Ecolodge** (Km 5.5 Ruta Y-905, tel. 9/9368 972, www.errantecolodge.cl, CH$152,320 d, CH$45,700 dorm) has truly astounding views across the Beagle Channel from the vast windows of its dining room, upstairs café and bar, and each of the seven bedrooms. Decorated with modern furnishings, the rooms aren't huge. The two dorm bedrooms with magnificent three-bed bunks attract a younger crowd. Gourmet dining for dinner costs extra, as does bike and car rental, while a transfer to the airport or Puerto Williams is included in the rates. The young owners are experts in local tourism and can arrange tours around the island, as well as boat tours to Glacier Alley. Starting in 2019, the cafeteria and a new restaurant will be open to nonguests.

Information and Services

There are few services on the island. Consider yourself lucky if the **Oficina Municipal de Turismo** (O'Higgins 189, tel. 61/2621 013, www.ptowilliams.cl, hours vary) is open when you stop by. For medical emergencies, there's the **Hospital Base Naval** (McIntyre 56, tel. 61/2621 098). To send postcards from the southernmost settlement on the planet, make your way to the **Correos** (Centro Comercial, 9:15am-12:30pm and 3pm-6pm Mon.-Fri., 11am-2pm Sat.), next door to the DAP office.

There's a 24-hour **ATM** in the **Banco de Chile** (western corner of Yelcho).

For camping equipment, GPS rental, and gas canisters, head to **Shila** (O'Higgins 240, tel. 9/7897 2005, open daily), opposite the municipal building. They also sell tickets for the crossing to Ushuaia. The two main supermarkets are **Supermercado y Panandería Temuco** (Piloto Pardo 541, 9:30am-10pm daily) and **Simon & Simon** (Piloto Pardo 254, 9:30am-11:30pm daily), both of which stock a surprisingly comprehensive range of fruit, vegetables, and canned and frozen food, plus wine and the two local beers, Nativa and the significantly better Tierra de Humos.

The **Gobernación** (Government) or **Municipalidad** (Municipality) building (O'Higgins 189, tel. 61/2621 012, www.imcabodehornos.cl) is where you handle passport formalities if you're arriving from or leaving for Ushuaia, in Argentina.

Car rental is possible through **Navarino Beaver** (Centro Comercial 140 B, tel. 9/9548 7365, www.barberjorge.wixsite.com/navarinbeaver2) and **Errante Ecolodge** (Km 5.5 Ruta Y-905, tel. 9/9368 972, www.errantecolodge.cl); prices start at CH$30,000 for half-day rental. Errante Ecolodge can also organize hiking, kayaking, and boat tours to visit Glacier Alley and Cape Horn, all of which require groups of at least six and start at around CH$200,000 pp for a full-day tour, with transfers and food included.

Getting There and Around
AIR

The tiny **Aeródromo Guardiamarina Zañartu** (WPU) on the western side of town receives the 19-seater Twin Otter planes flown by **Aeriovías DAP** (Centro Comercial, tel. 61/2621 114, www.dapairline.com) from Punta Arenas. The flight takes 1.5 hours and runs once daily Monday-Saturday. Flights book up rapidly in high season, so reserve your spot three months in advance. Arrange airport transfers with your hotel or through **Transfer Puerto Williams** (tel. 9/4267 5015).

★ FERRY FROM PUNTA ARENAS

The most picturesque way to Puerto Williams is aboard the *Yaghan* (32hr, CH$151,110 *cama,* CH$108,110 *semi-cama*), a **passenger and cargo ferry** operated by **Transbordadora Austral Broom** (tel. 61/2728 100, www.tabsa.cl) that departs twice weekly from the **Terminal de Ferry Tres Puentes** in Punta Arenas. If the weather is good, mirror-like water reflects the green islands through the fjords of Parque Nacional Alberto Agostini. You'll sail through Glacier Alley, along the western edge of the Beagle Channel, with eight striking tidewater glaciers, before arriving in Puerto Williams 32 hours later. The return journey, departing from Puerto Williams, promises stunning scenery, but the boat passes through Glacier Alley in darkness. Coming south from Punta Arenas guarantees the best views.

Significantly less luxurious than the other boats that ply Glacier Alley, the *Yaghan* is still impressive, with seats that recline fully flat, charging outlets, and three multicourse meals per day in the downstairs dining area. It's a unique way to see the most untouched parts of Patagonia without an expensive tour. The *Yaghan* is the mode used by residents of Puerto Williams. The cheapest seats are reserved for locals until 24 hours before departure.

Schedules for the journey change monthly and are often delayed due to poor weather, so consult the ferry operator's website. Bookings must be made at least two months in advance in high season; it's possible to book a cheaper *semi-cama* (partially reclining) seat beginning 24 hours before departure. Pack an eye mask and earplugs to escape the light and noise from the television screens, a towel to make use of the hot showers, and a small day pack; you're required to leave luggage in a locked room off the main deck when you board. You'll get everything back when you dock.

1: Parque Pingüino Rey 2: the end of the road in Tierra del Fuego 3: Puerto Williams 4: the *Yaghan* ferry

In Puerto Williams, you can get updates on the departure of the ferry at the office for **Transbordadora Austral Broom** (Costanera 314, tel. 61/2621 015), opposite the **Rampa Transbordador,** where the ferry arrives.

FERRY FROM USHUAIA

The 40-minute ferry crossing (US$120 one-way, US$220 round-trip) between Ushuaia and Puerto Williams counts as the most expensive boat journey in Patagonia. Two companies run the journey, leaving once daily Tuesday-Sunday. Ferry tickets can be bought in Puerto Williams at the shop **Shila** (O'Higgins 240, tel. 9/7897 2005, open daily) or from the Ushuaia offices of **Seaboat** (Muelle Turístico, Ushuaia, tel. 02901/603/711, www.sea-boat.com, 7am-4pm daily).

Passengers departing for Ushuaia need to be at the **Gobernación building** (O'Higgins 189, tel. 61/2621 012, www.imcabodehornos.cl) at 9am on the day of departure with their passport and PDI forms ready. Border crossing procedures are conducted here before you board a minibus to make the 54-km, one-hour journey to Puerto Navarino, on the far western side of island. Watch for whales and dolphins in the water. Once in Ushuaia, you'll be escorted through the equivalent border crossing procedures at the Argentinean border control at the port.

DIENTES DE NAVARINO TREK

Growing in popularity as a less crowded and more challenging alternative to the popular trails in Parque Nacional Torres del Paine, the difficult **Dientes de Navarino** is a 53.5-km,

five-day trek. It circumnavigates the Dientes de Navarino mountain range, passing through peat bog and bleak exposed rock. Throughout, hikers are treated to staggering views across the island of the jagged snow-dusted peaks, as well as numerous hidden lakes.

Hikers should not attempt the trail alone. It's best to go with a guide, as it's very remote and trails are not fully marked. Carrying a GPS receiver is recommended. Water is readily available, but avoid stagnant water around the beaver lodges. December-March are the best months for the trek. Weather can be extreme, including snowfall in summer, so check the forecast before leaving. Register with the police in Puerto Williams before you leave.

For the most up-to-date information about trail conditions, **Explora Isla Navarino** (Centro Comercial 140B, tel. 9/9185 0155, www.exploraislanavarino.com) are the undisputed experts. They also offer guided tours, including transfers to and from the start of the trail and the services of a guide with a satellite phone (from CH$200,000, min. 3 people). **Errante Ecolodge** (Km 5.5 Ruta Y-905, tel. 9/9368 972, www.errantecolodge.cl) also offers guided trekking tours (from US$1,600 pp, min. 2 people), including all transfers, food, guides, and one porter per two hikers.

For those without the time, equipment, or experience to embark on the full trek, the trail up to **Cerro Bandera** (4km one-way, 2hr) leaves from the Plaza de la Virgen on the western edge of town. After leading through a forested area, it emerges above the tree line, where a Chilean flag marks the top of the hill. Along the way, two viewpoints promise vistas across the town and the Beagle Channel; the views are most impressive from the very top.

Cape Horn and the Chilean Fjords

Few parts of Patagonia feel as remote and inaccessible as the maze-like Chilean fjords. The stark, sub-Antarctic landscapes of Tierra del Fuego, the Beagle Channel, and Cape Horn are the most dramatic and unrivaled scenery on the continent.

The area's waters remain abundant in wildlife, and it's possible to spot rare Commerson's dolphins, humpback whales, sea lions, and Magellanic penguins. The fjords are encircled by pristine terrain, including the barely visited, practically inaccessible Parque Nacional Alberto de Agostini.

What has disappeared are the southernmost people on earth, the Yaghan, who survived in the fierce climate, navigating the fjords in resilient boats made from *lenga* bark. The only clue to their presence are the middens (mounds containing waste, including mollusk shells and guanaco bones) that remain on remote beaches where they once lived.

Those who venture into the wild depths arrive by boat, mostly aboard adventure cruise ships. For those short on time but with lots of money, a chartered flight over Cape Horn from Puerto Williams is an efficient way of exploring the region from a different perspective.

Most voyages into the fjords stop at a number of wildlife colonies, including the penguin colonies of **Isla Magdalena** and **Ilotes de Tucker** (Tucker Islets), before entering the waters surrounding **Parque Nacional Alberto de Agostini** and docking at **Bahía Ainsworth** for a land-based excursion to admire the magnificent **Glaciar Marinelli** and the Darwin Mountains beyond.

GLACIER ALLEY

A stretch of hanging tidewater glaciers that plunge into the Beagle Channel, **Glacier Alley** is a dramatic sight. Spilling down from the Darwin Ice Field, these vast walls of glacial ice are easily admired from a ship; most boats pause to allow for photographs as water cascades from the ice and into the ocean, leaving a prominent difference in color between the glacial meltwater and the saltwater.

The majority of the alley's glaciers have the names of European countries: España, Alemania, Italia, and Holanda. Cruise ships also sail into Fiordo Pía to appreciate what many regard as the highlight of the journey, the 30-meter high Glaciar Pía, where it's possible to disembark and hike up the lateral moraine for views across the fjord and the icy Darwin Mountains.

TOP EXPERIENCE

★ CAPE HORN

Only 10,000 visitors a year stand on Cape Horn, the famed headland of the treeless Isla Hornos (Horn Island). Cruises that venture through the Chilean fjords normally attempt to dock here, at what has been mistakenly called the southernmost point of South America (Águila Islet of the Diego Ramírez Islands, 112km southwest, actually takes this crown). Wind conditions are crucial in deciding whether vessels are able to land.

Much of the thrill of the experience is overcoming the odds—and the often brutal winds and waves—at this remote island's shores, a feeling of conquering the might and majesty of nature's most violent and powerful forces at this point where the Pacific and Atlantic Oceans meet.

From the rocky landing beach, a short, wind-battered trail clambers up to an exposed cliff top with a seven-meter-tall steel memorial designed by Chilean sculptor José Balcell, the silhouette of an albatross to remember mariners who died "rounding the Horn." It's accompanied by a eulogy composed by Chilean poet Sara Vial. The sculpture was designed to withstand gusting winds of up to 200km/h. The rolling ocean and the incessant whistling wind howling through the scorched, scrubby moorland provide a fitting backdrop.

On the island, the only buildings include a lighthouse, in which the sole inhabitants of the island, a Chilean naval officer and his family, live, and the tiny wooden Stella Maris Chapel.

CAPE HORN AND FJORD TOURS

There are several modes of transportation—and several price brackets—for tours of the Chilean fjords and Cape Horn. However you travel, bring plenty of wind- and waterproof layers and sturdy shoes.

Australis

For a traditional cruise experience, **Australis** (Chile tel. 2/2840 0100, US tel. 800/743 0119, www.australis.com) runs fjord and Cape Horn tours aboard the 200-passenger adventure cruise ships *Stella Australis* and *Ventus Australis* September-March. Good discounts are available in shoulder seasons (Sept.-Oct. and late Mar.), although reservations should be made well in advance. Expect comfortable if not luxurious cabins with double or twin beds, closets, and hot showers, plus four-course dinners with wine pairings, an all-inclusive bar, a library, and onboard lectures about flora, fauna, and the history of the region.

It's possible to start and end your cruise in Punta Arenas or Ushuaia with the six- to eight-night options. All voyages, regardless of starting point, sail along Glacier Alley, visit Cape Horn (with an attempt to land, if conditions are favorable), and land at Bahía

Wulaia, Bahía Ainsworth, Islotes de Tucker, and Isla Magdalena. Cruises start at US$5,180 for a two-person cabin with two twin beds. To disembark in Ushuaia, in Argentina, it's necessary to go through border-crossing procedures in Puerto Navarino, west of Puerto Williams; crew members take passengers' documents to the border police office.

Yaghan Ferry

To visit Glacier Alley at a more accessible cost, take a ride on the utilitarian but equally adventurous cargo ferry *Yaghan* (32hr, CH$108,110-151,110), operated by **Transbordadora Austral Broom** (tel. 61/2728 100, www.tabsa.cl). The ferry departs twice weekly from the **Terminal de Ferry Tres Puentes** in Punta Arenas, arriving in Puerto Williams—weather permitting—32 hours later. The southward journey, from Punta Arenas to Puerto Williams, promises better views; the northbound journey goes through Glacier Alley at night. Departure schedules are weather dependent; long delays are common. A small bag is allowed onboard with you; backpacks and suitcases must be stored upon entry, with no access allowed during the trip.

Plane and Helicopter Tours

From the airport in Puerto Williams, you can board a Twin Otter plane or a helicopter for a one-hour flight over Cape Horn, passing over the rugged, remote scenery of Isla Navarino. There are normally two set departures per month between October and March. Contact **Lakutaia Lodge** (Seno Lauta s/n, Puerto Williams, tel. 9/6226 8448, www.lakutaia. com) for further information. Prices start at US$1,800 pp (min. 2 people).

Rapa Nui (Easter Island)

Thousands of kilometers west of the mainland,

Rapa Nui is Chile's most enigmatic island. The story of a civilization driven to the brink of extinction continues to attract visitors intrigued by the mystery that surrounds the 887 *moai,* the famed stone monoliths populating the coasts. Most of the statues are in Parque Nacional Rapa Nui, the island's central attraction, but there are a wealth of other examples of this early culture in the town of Hanga Roa.

If Rapa Nui feels distinctly un-Chilean, it's no wonder: The Rapa Nui people are committed to preserving their Polynesian roots, speaking both Spanish and their native language, also named Rapa Nui, which is closely related to the Tahitian and Marquesan languages and spoken by

Highlights

Look for ★ to find recommended sights, activities, dining, and lodging.

★ **Museo Antropológico P. Sebastián Englert:** Dive into Rapa Nui history and culture in this small but perfect museum (page 580).

★ **Ahu Tahai:** Watch the sun set behind a cluster of *moai* that line the coast (page 580).

★ **Tapati Rapa Nui Festival:** Watch locals take part in exciting competitions designed to showcase traditional sports and other activities (page 581).

★ **Ahu Tongariki:** The largest *ahu* on the island, with 15 *moai*, this dramatic site is the island's best spot for sunrise (page 594).

★ **Rano Raraku:** The lush slopes and crater of this volcano vent are filled with unfinished *moai* statues (page 594).

★ **Ahu Akahanga:** One of the most impressive unrestored platforms, this *ahu* is notable for its many toppled *moai*, as well as the nearby remains of traditional boat-shaped houses (page 596).

★ **Orongo Ceremonial Village:** On the edge of a volcano, the remains of this village are home to 1,700 petroglyphs (page 596).

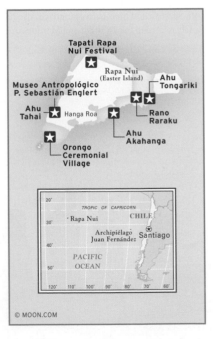

© MOON.COM

only 3,000 people. Celebrate this culture at the annual Tapati Rapa Nui festival in February.

For many the appeal of Rapa Nui is its distance from the rest of the world. It is the most remote inhabited island on earth; its nearest neighbors are on Pitcairn Island, 2,000km northwest. Mainland Chile is 3,700km to the island's east. Rapa Nui was formed by the eruption of three volcanoes: Poike, Rano Kau, and Terevaka. There are other volcanic cones dotted around the island, including the most famous, Rano Raraku.

Although better known by the moniker Isla de Pascua (Easter Island), thanks to its "discovery" on Easter Day by Dutch sailors, you can guarantee a friendlier welcome from the locals if you refer to it as Rapa Nui. Mainland Chileans still refer to it by its colonial name; you'll also see "Easter Island" used in airports.

PLANNING YOUR TIME

You'll need at least **three days** on Rapa Nui if you want to see the island's most dramatic sights. Given that it takes six hours to fly here from Santiago, add a day on each end for travel. Most accommodations, restaurants, and tourism services are in and around **Hanga Roa,** on the southwest coast. This is a good base, given that the island is only 25km long, and it takes 30 minutes to drive from Hanga Roa to the opposite end of the road at Anakena. The main sights **north of Hanga Roa** are within walking distance of the town. The island's other attractions are concentrated on the **northern coast** around **Anakena,** along the **southeastern coast,** and **south of Hanga Roa.**

Plan on **renting a car** to get around the island. In your own vehicle you can visit lesser-known destinations, particularly along the **southeastern coast.** You can rent bicycles, but the humidity, heat, and lack of shade make cycling an arduous experience during summer.

It's possible to take **tours** of the island's main sights; the knowledge of a local guide can enhance your experience. Unfortunately, these trips spend a brief amount of time at each site, and you may be following the same route as other tour groups. **Hiking tours** offer a good way to see the **Poike peninsula** and the **northern coast,** both with unique archaeological sites and few tourists.

Rapa Nui has a subtropical climate. The summer months, **December-March,** are the island's **high season.** During the first two weeks of February, the **Tapati Rapa Nui Festival** attracts up to 20,000 visitors. Summer means blue skies and mostly dry weather, but temperatures reach 30°C and can feel higher due to the humidity, and crowds at the major attractions are overwhelming. Airfares also peak during these months. Accommodations should be booked at least three months in advance, and earlier for early February.

September-November and April-May offer warm weather and fewer tourists, as well as better conditions for hiking or other physical activities. April-May are the island's rainiest months. The austral winter, June-August, sees cooler, more unsettled weather, but the almost complete lack of other visitors makes this time appealing for the solitude. The downside is that tourist sites close much earlier than during the summer, so you may feel rushed. Rainfall is possible year-round, so pack a waterproof jacket.

Mosquitos can be a problem on the island, particularly during the rainy season of April-May. Each year, there are confirmed cases of dengue fever carried by the *Aedes aegypti* mosquito. There is no vaccine against the virus, which can be fatal in serious cases. You can lower your chances of being infected by wearing long-sleeved clothing, using insect repellent, and sleeping under a mosquito net—although you'll need to bring your own, as these are rarely present in lodgings.

Previous: Ahu Tahai; red scoria rock at Ahu Akahanga; *moai* at Anakena.

Rapa Nui (Easter Island)

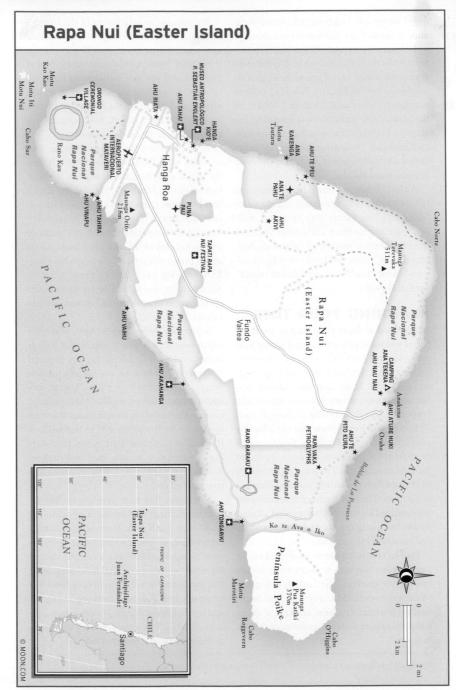

Motu Kao Kao
Motu Iti
Motu Nui

Cabo Sur

ORONGO CEREMONIAL VILLAGE

Rano Kau

Parque Nacional Rapa Nui

AEROPUERTO INTERNACIONAL MATAVERI

AHU TAHIRA
AHU VINAPU

MUSEO ANTROPOLÓGICO
P. SEBASTIÁN ENGLERT

AHU RIATA
AHU TAHAI
AHU TA PEU

HANGA KIO'E

Hanga Roa

Maunga Orito 218m

PUNA PAU

TAPATI RAPA NUI FESTIVAL

ANA KAKENGA
Motu Tautara

AHU TE PEU

ANA TE PAHU
AHU AKIVI

Maunga Terevaka 511m

Parque Nacional Rapa Nui

Cabo Norte

PACIFIC OCEAN

AHU VAIHU

Parque Nacional Rapa Nui

AHU AKAHANGA

Fundo Vaitea

Rapa Nui (Easter Island)

CAMPING
ANA TEKENA
AHU NAU NAU

Anakena
AHU ATURE HUKI
Ovahe

RANO RARAKU

RAPA VAKA PETROGLYPHS

AHU TE PITO KURA

Bahía de La Pérouse

PACIFIC OCEAN

Parque Nacional Rapa Nui

AHU TONGARIKI

Ko te Ava o Iko

Motu Marotiri

Maunga Pua Kariki 370m

Península Poike

Cabo Roggeven
Cabo O'Higgins

PACIFIC OCEAN

120° 110° 100° 90° 80° 70° 60°
50° 40° 30° 20°

PACIFIC OCEAN

Rapa Nui (Easter Island)

TROPIC OF CAPRICORN

Archipiélago Juan Fernández

CHILE
Santiago

© MOON.COM

0   2 km
0   2 mi

Three Days on Rapa Nui

Three days on Rapa Nui allows you to pack in plenty of the island's highlights, with enough time to stop by the most significant points in the national park. Buy your ticket for the national park from the booth in the arrivals hall of the airport. There's another ticket office in Hanga Roa, but the airport is more convenient.

DAY 1

Rent a car from **Hanga Roa** and drive south to the **Orongo ceremonial village** and the spectacular **Rano Kau** volcanic crater, where you have sweeping views of the small islands off the coast of Rapa Nui. Marvel at the extensive collection of **petroglyphs** depicting a strange creature known as the birdman.

Drive to the **southeastern coast** to **Ahu Vinapu** to admire the intricate stonework. Head back to Hanga Roa and take the short walk north to **Ahu Tahai** to see the sun set behind the five *moai*.

Sample local cuisine at **Haka Honu** with a dinner of tuna ceviche before bedding down at the modern bungalows of **Pikera Uri Lodge,** on the outskirts of Hanga Roa.

DAY 2

Get up early for sunrise between the statues at **Ahu Tongariki,** on the eastern side of the island. Take the road north to the petroglyphs at **Papa Vaka** and spend a few hours on the white sand at **Anakena** and the exceptionally well-preserved *moai*.

Head south and spend the afternoon wandering between the half-formed figures at **Rano Raraku,** the quarry where the majority of *moai* were carved.

Catch **sunset** from a different spot along the west coast, either at **Caleta Hanga Piko,** south of Hanga Roa, or **Te Moana,** with a pisco sour in hand. Spend the evening watching high-energy traditional Polynesian dance at the **Ballet Cultural Kari Kari.**

DAY 3

Finish your time on the island driving to **Puna Pau,** the quarry where the topknots of the *moai* were carved, and **Ahu Akivi.** Hike up to the summit of **Maunga Terevaka** for panoramic views before heading back to Hanga Roa to visit **Museo Antropológico P. Sebastián Englert.** Pop into the unassuming **Ahi-Ahi** for a quick and filling lunch of deep-fried tuna empanadas.

Another option is to start early with a **hiking tour** of the **northern coast** of the island, exploring archaeological remains that lie where they have for centuries.

HISTORY

Hotu Matu'a, the first king and spiritual leader of the Rapa Nui people, arrived by double-canoe to Anakena, on the northern coast of Rapa Nui, after a 2,000-km journey from another Polynesian island. Hotu Matu'a brought with him a band of settlers. Archaeologists debate when this happened, but the latest research dates their arrival to AD 1200. After clearing some of the extensive palm forests that covered the island, the settlers began creating the *moai*, stone statues that were carved to represent dead chiefs or other important community members. This cult of ancestor worship saw 887 *moai* constructed in the subsequent centuries.

On Easter Day 1722, Capitan Roelof Rosendaal and his Dutch crew landed on Rapa Nui. The first interactions with the islanders involved offerings of gifts, although a skirmish resulted in the Dutch opening fire and killing 10 people. The Spanish landed in 1770, Captain James Cook and his English fleet in 1774, and French explorer Lapérouse in 1786. By the time Cook arrived, some of the *moai* had been toppled. By 1838, only four were still standing, and by 1868, all had been pushed to the ground.

No one is entirely sure what caused the islanders to topple the statues. Research suggests the introduction of the Polynesian rat resulted in centuries of severe deforestation and soil erosion. This may have created food shortages, thus escalating tensions among the island's population, causing members of different communities to topple others' statues. Interactions with Europeans meant germs and venereal diseases were introduced to the island's inhabitants, leading to many deaths. The exact number is unknown, but the population of the island dropped to 111 in the 1860s, from an estimated high of 3,000.

In 1862, Peruvian slave raiders kidnapped 1,500 islanders to take back to work on the mainland. The Peruvian government eventually repatriated those who had been enslaved, but only a dozen people ever returned home. French missionaries moved to the island in 1864, followed by Frenchman Jean-Baptiste Dutrou-Bornier in 1868. He violently established himself as king and laid claim to 80 percent of the island. He was killed by locals in 1875. In 1888, Chile annexed the island.

In 1895, Valparaíso businessman Enrique Merlet purchased practically all of Rapa Nui, transforming it into a ranch and forcing the local people off their land and into modern-day Hanga Roa. Towering walls defined the boundaries of the ranch, effectively making the locals prisoners on a small strip of land. The ranch was eventually sold to Williamson, Balfour & Co., an English sheep company. Over 45 years, the sheep ranch devastated the native flora and fauna, causing extensive soil erosion that is still evident today. In 1953, control of the island was assumed by the Chilean navy, who prohibited the use of the Rapa Nui language.

In 1965, as part of a growing movement for autonomy, local teacher Alfonso Rapu forced the Chilean government to return the land to its people. In 1966 residents finally acquired Chilean citizenship, 78 years after Rapa Nui and its people became part of Chile. Nowadays, the Rapa Nui have extended some of their rights. Only people of island descent are allowed to own land, and new laws prevent outsiders from mainland Chile and beyond to move here permanently.

Hanga Roa

Rapa Nui's only town, Hanga Roa is a sprawling collection of terra-cotta-tiled palm-thatched buildings on the southwestern coast. The town is growing rapidly with hotels and restaurants. Along the main street, it's not uncommon to see locals selling handcrafted wares as fresh fish hang from hooks over makeshift stalls or are sold out of the backs of trucks. The laid-back, tropical vibe is contagious.

In the first two weeks of February, this otherwise relaxed little town is choked with traffic and tourists during the annual Tapati Rapa Nui Festival. Events include parades and boisterous dancing and singing competitions on the main ceremonial green.

Most visitors base themselves at one of Hanga Roa's many hotels, bungalows, and campgrounds. Many of the island's most famous sights, including Ahu Tahai, can be accessed easily from town. For trips farther afield, a car or bike is necessary.

ORIENTATION

Hanga Roa is small and easy to navigate. The airport is at the town's southern edge, along which **Calle Hotu Matu'a** runs, connecting the town with the northern and eastern sides of the island. Hanga Roa's main road, **Atamu Tekena,** runs north-south. Paralleling the coast a block west is **Policarpo Toro.** These two roads are where you'll find most tour

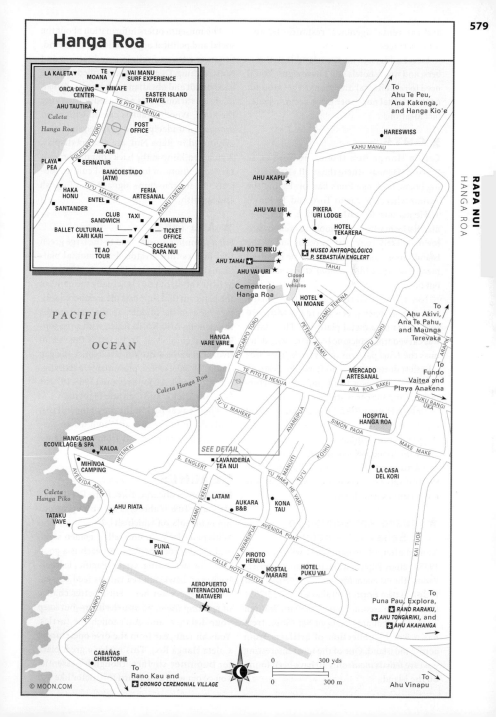

and car rental agencies, restaurants, and other services.

Street addresses on the island lack numbers, and many hotels don't have signs. You'll need to rely on local directions to get around; neither digital nor paper maps accurately depict locations.

SIGHTS

Caleta Hanga Roa (Policarpo Toro at Te Pito o Te Henua), where the swell jostles fishing boats, is Hanga Roa's harbor. Facing the harbor where Policarpo Toro and Te Pito o Te Henua intersect, **Ahu Tautira**, a ceremonial platform with a *moai* looking back toward town, is likely your first introduction to the island's most famous residents. One hundred meters north, another *moai* stares stoically out to sea.

North along Calle Policarpo Toro from the harbor is an open green where the **Moai de la Paz** sits on a metal platform. This statue was carved from volcanic basalt in 1992; don't miss the relief patterns on its back. This area is busiest during the Tapati Rapa Nui Festival, when it becomes a focal point for performances and the coronation ceremony.

Caleta Hanga Piko (Apina, 2km south of Caleta Hanga Roa) is the harbor where cargo ships from the mainland dock. On a slope just above the harbor, a *moai* stands on the expansive **Ahu Riata**. This is a good place to watch the sun set, as it gets less crowded than the more famous Ahu Tahai.

★ Museo Antropológico P. Sebastián Englert

Named after a German priest who came in 1935 to study Rapa Nui and push for its conservation, the excellent **Museo Antropológico P. Sebastián Englert** (Tahai s/n, tel. 32/2551 020, www.museorapanui.cl, 9:30am-5:30pm Tues.-Fri., 9:30am-12:30pm Sat.-Sun., free) has a worthy collection of artifacts from across the island. One of the most interesting is a rare female *moai;* only 10 have been found on the island.

The museum offers information about the social and political organization of the island, funerary rites and religion, and tattoos and ear stretching. Display cases are filled with the hard basalt and obsidian tools known as *toki,* made in various sizes and used for carving the *moai.* Wooden tablets carved with *rongo-orongo,* an undeciphered glyph system that originated in Rapa Nui, are also on display. A small building at the back contains temporary exhibitions of local art and cultural objects. All the museum's signage is in English and Spanish.

★ Ahu Tahai

For a stunning sunset, head to the large green that houses three restored ceremonial platforms and several *moai.* The site is referred to as **Ahu Tahai,** but this is actually the name of the platform that supports the weathered solitary *moai* in the middle. To the right stands the striking **Ahu Ko Te Riku,** with a red topknot and coral eyes. To its left is the row of five *moai* of the **Ahu Vai Uri.** Notice the gap on the left side, where, presumably, a sixth figure once stood. All were restored 1968-1970 by William Mulloy and Gonzalo Figueroa.

There's a car park at the top of the hill that leads down to the site, although it's an easy and scenic 15-minute walk from Caleta Hanga Roa.

BEACHES

Playa Pea (Policarpo Toro, from Te Pito o Te Henua to Tu'u Maheke) is split by a protruding peninsula on which sits Restaurant Pea. With palm-leaf sun umbrellas, golden sand, and natural rock pools, this beach is a good place for swimming. Green Pacific, leatherback, and hawksbill sea turtles feed on seaweed in the water here. For a better chance of spotting them, go **snorkeling**—but keep your distance, and don't touch the turtles. You can rent gear from the dive operators at Caleta Hanga Roa. This is also a great place for **beginner surfers,** though it's essential you go out with a local surf instructor like **Vai**

Manu Surf Experience (Policarpo Toro s/n, tel. 9/9073 4760), due to the danger posed by hidden rocks.

ENTERTAINMENT

For a lively display of Rapa Nui culture, it's worth attending a show at the **Ballet Cultural Kari Kari** (Atamu Tekena s/n, tel. 9/4280 5388, reservaskarikari@gmail.com, CH$15,000 adults, CH$7,000 children). You'll be treated to a superb selection of traditional Rapa Nui and Polynesian dances with music from traditional wooden and string instruments. Performances are held three times a week at 8:30pm. Book tickets a few days in advance.

Nightlife

Although most visitors opt for early nights to prepare for long days exploring, Hanga Roa has a handful of recommendable bars. The island's clubs aren't ideal for travelers; fights and other rowdy behavior are common.

Just across the airport, **Piroto Henua** (Hotu Matu'a s/n, no phone, 9pm-4am Wed.-Sat.) is a relaxed, divey watering hole with a buzzing atmosphere and eclectic music. Try a locally brewed Mahina beer and test your vocal cords with karaoke on Wednesday and Friday, or live bands on Thursday and Saturday. Like everything in Chile, things only start getting going after 11pm.

A popular spot for visitors, with an extensive dinner menu and bar that opens later than most, **Te Moana** (Policarpo Toro s/n, tel. 32/2551 578, 12:30pm-12:30am daily) has sublime ocean views. Their pisco sours (sample the cucumber and basil one) and Te Moana house cocktail might be the best beverages on the island.

★ Tapati Rapa Nui Festival

The annual **Tapati Rapa Nui Festival** is colorful, competitive, and unmissable. Held the first two weeks of February, it has roots in traditional Rapa Nui demonstrations of skill and physical prowess, although it only dates from the 1970s, when it was introduced to help preserve the island's distinctive culture.

Two candidates for Queen of Tapati, a coveted role that sees the winner representing the island in global appearances, are nominated by two rival clans. Teams of men and women compete in sporting competitions to score points to help their candidate win. The festival's events revolve around these competitions, including a triathlon on the coast of Hanga Roa, swimming, and canoeing. There are energetic dancing and singing events as well as others where the quality of Rapa Nui cuisine and handicrafts are evaluated by judges. Perhaps the most visually spectacular and pain-inducing event is the **Haka Pei,** where male contestants skid down the sides of a volcano on the back of a sled, hitting thrilling speeds of 70km/h.

Activities are held around the island, but the main site is the green at **Hanga Vare Vare** (Policarpo Toro, north of Caleta Hanga Roa), where Polynesian dance routines are performed for droves of spectators. The final two days of the festival see parades through Hanga Roa, with performers donning traditional regalia, culminating in the coronation of the Queen of Tapati.

Visitors are welcome to watch all the events and are often invited to join the final parades by dressing up and adorning themselves with body paint. Be aware that Hanga Roa grinds to a standstill during much of these two weeks. Accommodations must be booked at least six months in advance. The schedule of events is published a few weeks before the festival begins.

SHOPPING

There's a strong wood-carving culture on the island and plenty of places to find a handmade souvenir. The **Feria Artesanal** (Atamu Tekena s/n, 10am-8pm Mon.-Sat.) is a collection of tiny stalls spilling onto the pavement, starting from the municipal building southwest along the main road. You'll see many vendors carving wooden *moai* figurines.

Understanding the *Moai*

WHAT ARE THEY?

The ultimate draw of Rapa Nui is the island's *moai,* singular monolithic figures set on ceremonial platforms called *ahu.* Historically, after a chief or other important community member died, one of these statues would be carved in their honor.

The *moai* were carved from soft volcanic rock with basalt tools. These stylized human figures could weigh up to 180 tons. *Moai* are characterized by long noses, prominent cheekbones, a pointed chin, and large ears. Their arms hang down next to their torsos and join at the stomach, just below the navel. On their back are carvings depicting clothing worn by the Rapa Nui people. A common misconception is that the *moai* face out to sea; in fact, they were positioned to look back over the land, symbolically watching over their people.

Ahu are made of basalt that was cut and fitted together to form walls and a foundation (in many cases filled with the bones of the ancestor depicted by the

moai heads at Rano Raraku

moai above). In front, a ramp leading down to a leveled area now known as the plaza was paved with rounded stones. The space in front of the *ahu* likely had ceremonial functions and was where activities and meetings would take place.

HOW DID THEY GET THERE?

Of the 887 *moai* that have been found on the island, only 288 are located on an *ahu.* Nearly 400 remain in the Rano Raraku quarry; 92 have been found "in transit"—on roads that were used to transport them across the island. The main question that has long perplexed archaeologists is how the local people managed the laborious task of moving the giant figures from the quarry to the *ahu.* Various experiments have demonstrated possible methods; the most famous proved that a wooden sled greased with oil could be used to pull a *moai* on its back.

However, Rapa Nui oral history has always suggested that the *moai* were capable of "walking" to their destination. Czech engineer Pavel Pavel experimented with transporting the *moai* vertically, using ropes to "walk" them along. This theory has recently been confirmed as the most likely method. Finally, the figures were most likely raised onto the *ahu* using tree trunks and piles of stones to leverage them into place.

WHY DON'T SOME OF THEM HAVE EYES?

It was only once they reached their *ahu* that the *moai* would have their eyes carved and installed. (You'll notice that many of the *moai* that aren't on an *ahu* don't have carved eyes.) The eyes were made of white coral and red scoria; their installation was considered a sacred moment. At **Ahu Tahai,** you can see a *moai* with restored eyes. The only original example that has been found on the island was at Ahu Nau Nau, inland from Anakena. It's on display at the **Museo Antropológico P. Sebastián Englert.**

Some are made of stone and were likely made from a mold. Other wooden decorative items include the feather skirts worn by Rapa Nui dancers, part of the traditional dance outfit known as *huru-huru*. Prices tend to be low, but so does the quality.

The much larger and more expensive **Mercado Artesanal** (Ara Roa Rakei s/n, tel. 32/2551 346, 9am-1pm and 5pm-8pm Mon.-Sat.) has an array of items: shell jewelry, stone *moai*, textiles, and carvings of *moai kava-kava* (skeleton-like representations of ancestors). Expect to pay at least CH$20,000 for a carved *moai*. Intricately carved versions can sell for over CH$80,000. Avoid buying items made from coral.

RECREATION
Diving
Scuba diving is popular around Hanga Roa. One spot south of the island has a **replica** *moai* on the ocean floor. You'll need a PADI license to visit this dive site, but there are a number of other locations where scuba experience isn't required. The water is clear (up to 60 meters visibility on a good day), with temperatures of 18-26°C. The marinelife isn't spectacular, but you can see coral and sea caves.

Orca Diving Center (Caleta Hanga Roa s/n, tel. 32/2550 877, www.orcadivingcenter. cl) dates to 1980 and is the island's most recommended operator, with trips to the submerged *moai* (2-hour dive, CH$40,000) and scuba initiations (30min, CH$45,000, photos included). They also offer boat and snorkeling trips to the Motu Nui, Motu Iti, and Motu Kao Kao Islets (2hr, CH$25,000). They don't run trips on Sunday. Strong winds can cause cancelations. Staff and guides speak English.

Surfing
Playa Pea (Policarpo Toro, from Te Pito o Te Henua to Tu'u Maheke) is the most popular bay for surfing. Go with a guide, as the rocks in this bay can make the water treacherous. It's essential to surf only at high tide to avoid them. September-March have the best conditions for surfing; waves can reach up to five meters. Advanced surfers may find that the waves around **Ahu Tahai,** north of Hanga Roa, and the **airport,** in the south of town, present a better challenge.

Vai Manu Surf Experience (Policarpo Toro s/n, at Te Pito O Te Henua, tel. 9/9073 4760) rents gear (wetsuit and board, CH$15,000 per day) and offers private lessons (from CH$45,000 for 2hr) and group classes (from CH$35,000 for 2hr). Students get free equipment rental for the day.

FOOD
Tuna is served at every Hanga Roa restaurant, prepared with local ingredients like *camote* (sweet potato), taro, pineapple, banana, and papaya. Other common seafood includes *rapa rapa* (swordfish), lobster, and mahimahi. In most restaurants, you'll be asked how you like your fish cooked. *Bien cocido* (well done) is the option to choose if you don't like your fish raw in the middle.

Most of the fresh fruit and vegetables on the island are imported by plane from mainland Chile. The daily *feria* (farmers market, Atamu Tekena), in front of the Feria Artesanal (Artisan Market), is an informal affair. Locals sell produce and fish from the backs of their cars in the early morning—a good option for cheap local food. Plenty of mini markets dot Atamu Tekena, but prices can be up to 50 percent more than on the mainland. To save some money, consider packing food in your checked bags if you plan to cook for yourself; you're allowed to bring fresh fruit and vegetables purchased in mainland Chile.

Rapa Nui
An extensive menu with plenty of alternatives to fish and great sea views make **Te Moana** (Policarpo Toro s/n, tel. 32/2551 578, 12:30pm-12:30am daily, CH$15,000-20,000) a good choice for pickier eaters or to watch the sun set with a pisco sour. The restaurant serves beautifully presented dishes in an atmospheric dining room with flickering candles and the crash of the sea below. Don't miss the seared sesame-crusted tuna steak, ceviche

with ginger and coconut milk, or the lobster. They also have a mouthwatering cocktail selection.

The setting at ★ **Kaloa** (Hangaroa Eco Village & Spa, Av. Pont s/n, tel. 32/2553 120, 6:30pm-10:30pm daily, CH$14,000-18,000) is sophisticated and minimalist, and provides the perfect atmosphere for tasting the island's top cuisine. Dishes are similarly priced to most restaurants, but the quality and detail is exceptional, and the menu truly inventive. Sample the sharing platter of pumpkin seed-crusted tuna with caramelized mango, as well as their ceviche duo of octopus and tuna. If you've had enough fish, try the beef loin. You can't go wrong with their expansive Chilean wine selection.

Nothing encompasses the laid-back Rapa Nui vibe better than **Tataku Vave** (Hanga Piko s/n, tel. 32/2551 544, apakomio@hotmail.com, noon-11pm Mon.-Sat., CH$12,000-15,000), where the terrace looks over red volcanic rock and breaking waves just south of Hanga Piko. The huge platters of lightly dressed tuna ceviche with baked sweet potato slices are the main attraction. Relaxed service embraces the general attitude of the island, but servers are effusively friendly. This is a great spot to catch a breeze on a sunny day.

A small open-fronted shack overlooking Playa Pea, ★ **Haka Honu** (Policarpo Toro, tel. 32/2552 260, honurapanui@gmail.com, 12:30pm-10:30pm Tues.-Sun., CH$12,000-15,000) is the spot for lunch, specializing in fresh fish cooked using traditional Rapa Nui ingredients and styles. Delicate flavors include the standout grilled fish dressed with sweet-and-sour papaya chutney and sweet potato mash. Welcoming staff and a partial sea view sweeten the deal. Haka Honu attracts more tourists than locals.

Practically hanging over the crashing waves at the north end of Caleta Hanga Roa, **La Kaleta** (Caleta Hanga Roa, Otai s/n, tel. 32/2552 244, 12:30pm-11pm daily, CH$12,000-18,000) has won awards for freshness. Seafood includes tuna ceviche and fish of the day in a shrimp and bacon bisque with locally grown potatoes. If you're on a budget or looking for a light meal, seafood, beef, and vegetarian sandwiches are available. The restaurant has sensational views through large patio windows that open to allow the breeze in.

Light Bites

★ **Ahi-Ahi** (Policarpo Torre s/n, no phone, 10am-9pm daily, CH$2,000-12,000), the third wooden shack on the southern side of the football field, is nicer inside than it looks from the exterior. Reggaeton plays as you enjoy huge empanadas, which aren't greasy and are undoubtedly the best on the island. Pick from an array of fillings, including tuna with goat cheese and basil.

Huge and comparatively cheap Chilean-style sandwiches at **Club Sandwich** (Atamu Tekena s/n, tel. 32/2550 379, noon-midnight daily, CH$4,000-8,000) are good options for budget-conscious travelers. Burgers, hot dogs, and a smattering of salads round out the menu. Chow down at a sticky plastic table as '80s rock blares.

For ice cream made with local fruit, there's no place like **Mikafe** (Caleta Hanga Roa s/n, no phone, gelateriamikafe@gmail.com, 9am-9pm daily, CH$4,000-6,000) to satisfy your sweet tooth. It's also good for breakfast, with options like omelets and pastries. There's a range of teas, coffees, paninis, and cakes. Outdoor tables offer views across the harbor, adding to this cute café's charm.

ACCOMMODATIONS

If you're going to visit during the Tapati Rapa Nui Festival, book your lodgings at least six months in advance. For the rest of the December-March high season, book three months in advance. Prices are higher than in mainland Chile, although IVA is not charged on the island. Be aware that many lodgings do not accept credit cards, so bring cash.

1: Caleta Hanga Roa **2:** tuna ceviche, a popular dish on the island

Under CH$25,000

Nowhere is fairer in price than budget favorite **Mihínoa Camping** (Av. Pont s/n, tel. 32/2551 593, www.camping-mihinoa.com, CH$8,000-10,000 camping, CH$15,000 dorm, CH$35,000 d private bath). A 15-minute walk from Caleta Hanga Roa with sea views, this well-equipped campsite and guesthouse has three kitchens, a lounge area decked out with lime-green furnishings, and a large grassy garden for tents. The dorms and private rooms are simple but lack fans, which can be a drag on a hot day. The spotty Wi-Fi only works in the lounge area. Showers are heated by solar energy.

CH$25,000-40,000

For utilitarian budget digs, the simple guesthouse **Kona Tau** (Avareipua s/n, tel. 9/7572 5212, konatau@entelchile.net, CH$39,000 d) has 11 rooms that are a bit stuffy without fans, but all have private baths. Kitchen access and a lengthy thatch-roofed terrace are welcome additions. It has the necessary amenities, even if it lacks atmosphere.

CH$40,000-60,000

Nowhere else on the island merits the term "home away from home" more than welcoming guesthouse **Hostal Marari** (Hotu Matu'a s/n, tel. 9/9676 6396, contactomarari@gmail.com, CH$20,000 dorm, CH$45,000 d). English-speaking owners Jessica and Cristian make guests feel like part of the family, offering transport around the island and accompanying you to dance shows. All five rooms are simple but spotless, with private baths and a terrace, plus access to a communal kitchen and living area.

With a hostel feel with modern decoration, ★ **La Casa del Kori** (Paoa s/n, tel. 9/9711 7098, www.lacasadelkori.cl, CH$20,000 dorm, CH$59,000 d) has quickly become a popular hangout for backpackers and budget travelers. Dorms feature sturdy bunk beds in large rooms with lockers. The private rooms are ample in size with spotlessly clean baths. The walls and flooring are on the cheap side, but

the freshness of the facilities and the friendliness of the English-speaking owners, Marcela and Kori, more than make up for it.

CH$60,000-80,000

The simple cabins at **Cabañas Christophe** (Policarpo Toro s/n, tel. 32/2100 826, CH$66,000-98,000 d) are excellently run by helpful English-, Spanish-, and French-speaking Christophe. Cabins include a dining table, a fridge, and a basic kitchenette, plus small terraces with furniture. A breakfast of scrambled eggs, fresh bread, and jam is delivered daily. The cabins are 2.5km south of the main part of Hanga Roa, offering peace and quiet—and poor cell service. Book well in advance.

Over CH$80,000

To dig deep into Rapa Nui culture, the place to stay is ★ **Aukara B&B** (Av. Pont s/n, tel. 32/2100 53 or 9/7709 5711, www.aukara-rapanui.com, CH$85,000 d). Five bungalows amid the property's pretty gardens are large, airy, and decorated with local textiles. There's an on-site museum with traditional wooden carvings and other items crafted by members of the family that owns this place.

Easily the best thing about ★ **Hareswiss** (Te Hoe Manu s/n, tel. 32/2552 221 or 9/9812 5726, www.hareswiss.com, CH$92,000 d) is Swiss expat owner Peter, whose grasp of five languages, knowledge of the island, and superb hospitality make him the perfect host. Three cabins are spotless, with small kitchenettes with a hot plate and a fridge. A superb breakfast is available (additional CH$4,500). The only downside is the 25-minute walk or short taxi ride into town; many guests consider the remote feel and sublime sunset views highlights of their stay. Book well in advance.

U.S.-native Paul Pownall came in 1968 to help restore Ahu Tahai. Nowadays, he runs **Hotel Tekarera** (Tekarera s/n, tel. 9/8134 5757, www.tekarera.com, CH$92,000 d), a clutch of dark but clean bedrooms with private baths, all with access to the hotel's highlight: the wraparound terrace with sea views. Set back from the road and insulated from the surroundings by trees, this eight-hectare plot feels wonderfully remote. Paul also runs tours if you arrange in advance.

If you're curious about the traditional *hare vaka* (boat-shaped houses) of the Rapa Nui people, stay at **Hotel Vai Moane** (Miru s/n, tel. 32/2100 626, www.vaimoana.cl, CH$141,000 d standard, CH$155,000 d *hare vaka*). The 14 *hare vaka* rooms have a traditional design with impressive ecofriendly amenities, such as an air circulation system that precludes the need for air-conditioning. This spot also has a dozen standard rooms in cabins. The grounds contain groves of banana trees, a boardwalk, and a pool and spa. A restaurant and a tour agency are available to guests. Workshops run by locals allow guests to learn how to cook a traditional *umu* or make handicrafts.

A short distance up the coast from Ahu Tahai, within the grounds of a stud farm, ★ **Pikera Uri Lodge** (Tekerera s/n, tel. 32/2100 577, www.pikerauri.com, CH$155,000 d) comprises six stylish one-bedroom bungalows with hardwood terraces. Each high-ceilinged bungalow has been decorated with local art and stays cool even in the midday heat. The breakfast room has spellbinding sea vistas, and a sizeable breakfast incorporates fruit from the extensive gardens. The owners will happily show you around the archaeological remains on the property. Service is attentive and personalized. The owners also run Cabalgatas Pantu, an agency specializing in horseback tours.

Slightly old-fashioned compared with more modern options in town, **Hotel Puku Vai** (Hotu Matu'a s/n, tel. 32/2551 838, www.pukuvaihotel.com, CH$158,000 d) offers large bedroom suites with a TV and spacious sitting areas featuring heavy hardwood furniture and comfortable kings. Each room opens onto a pretty garden of palms, flowering shrubs, and a swimming pool flanked by replica *moai*. It's a 20-minute walk to town but very close to the airport.

The beach-facing **Hangaroa Eco Village & Spa** (Av. Pont s/n, tel. 32/2553 700, www.hangaroa.cl, US$470-650 d, US$605-785 d suite) is what comes to mind when you imagine a luxury hotel on Rapa Nui. Low grass-topped rooms have private terraces and access to the spa, the swimming pool, and the restaurant, **Kaloa** (6:30pm-10:30pm daily), one of the best on the island. The vast bedroom suites mimic the style of traditional Rapa Nui houses and come complete with deep stone tubs, huge king beds, and air-conditioning. Ask for one of rooms 1-44 for a terrace and ocean views. The owners also operate private tours for guests.

The extraordinary service and expertise of the English-speaking guides at ★ **Explora** (tel. 2/2395 2800, www.explora.com, min. 3 nights, US$1,700 d all-inclusive) make this resort a standout choice. Packages are all-inclusive; 30 rooms have been built discreetly into a hillside overlooking the ocean and connect to the main bar and restaurant, which serves gourmet Rapa Nui cuisine using seasonal ingredients from their organic farm. They offer a range of tours for hiking, mountain biking, and other active pursuits.

INFORMATION AND SERVICES

SERNATUR (Policarpo Toro s/n, tel. 32/2551 933, 9am-5:30pm Mon.-Thurs., 9am-4:30pm Fri., 10am-1pm Sat.) has an office overlooking Playa Pea. The English-speaking staff offer advice on transportation, open hours of sites, and events and activities.

The **Hospital Hanga Roa** (Simón Paoa s/n, tel. 32/2100 215) can provide basic emergency attention. The post office, **Correos** (Te Pito o Te Henua s/n, 8:30am-1:30pm and 2pm-5pm Mon.-Fri., 9am-noon Sat.), will stamp your passport with a unique Rapa Nui stamp.

One of the two **Parque Nacional Rapa Nui ticket offices** (Atamu Tekena s/n, no phone, 8:30am-4pm daily) is on the main road through Hanga Roa but isn't well signed. It's a few doors south of Santa Cruz pharmacy. Credit cards are accepted. The other ticket office is in the arrivals hall of the airport.

Entel (Oho Vehi Lane s/n, tel. 32/2100 123, 8:30am-1:30pm and 3:30pm-5:30pm Mon.-Fri.) is the only company that offers cell-phone service on the island; you can buy a SIM card from their office. Coverage is spotty and generally only available around Hanga Roa. The gas station **Puna Vai** (Hotu Matu'a s/n, 7:30am-10pm daily) is 500 meters northwest of the airport and accepts credit cards; queues here are common and can be lengthy in high season.

GETTING THERE

The most common way to get to Rapa Nui is by plane. It's also possible to get here by cruise ship, some of which originate in Tahiti.

Air

Aeropuerto Internacional Mataveri (IPC, Av. Hotu Matu'a, tel. 32/2210 0237) is the island's only airport, with non-stop flights on Boeing 767 aircraft from Santiago. **LATAM** (Tekena s/n, tel. 32/2100 279, www.latam.com) is the only airline that serves Rapa Nui. There are two daily flights January-March; this drops to 10 flights weekly April-December. LATAM offers weekly flights between Rapa Nui and Tahiti's Fa'a'ā International Airport (PPT). Round-trip economy airfares range CH$250,000-800,000.

Passengers disembark on the tarmac and walk to the tiny arrivals hall. On the left before you enter is a **Parque Nacional Rapa Nui ticket office** (hours coincide with flight arrivals). This is one of two locations where you can buy your park entrance ticket, which you must present to enter most sites; credit cards are accepted.

Boat

Cruise ships dock at Rapa Nui October-February each year. Cruises set sail from Papeete, Tahiti, visiting various Polynesian islands, including Mangareva and the Pitcairn Islands, to end at Rapa Nui. Another route begins in Valparaíso and sails six days to the island. There is no harbor big enough for cruise ships to dock, so passengers board smaller boats to reach shore. Strong winds can cause delays.

GETTING AROUND

If you stay on the extremities of Hanga Roa, walking into town can be exhausting due to the heat and lack of shade. For most visitors, vehicle rental is a sensible alternative, although be aware that there is no car insurance on the island; you will be required to foot the bill for any accidents. Rentals normally run for 24 hours. To maximize your time, rent your car at 6pm so you can see the sunset at Ahu Tahai and the sunrise at Ahu Tongariki. Most accommodations on the island can arrange car hire, often for cheaper rates than the official rental agencies. In high season, demand outstrips supply, so request a rental car when you make your hotel reservation.

Oceanic Rapa Nui (Atamu Tekena s/n, tel. 32/2100 985, www.rentacaroceanic.com, 8:30am-8:30pm daily) has 200 rental vehicles, including SUVs with 4WD. Rentals start at CH$50,000 per 24 hours. They also rent out quad bikes (from CH$50,000), scooters (from CH$30,000), and bicycles (from CH$12,000). Be aware that pedaling the length of the island can be exhausting and sunburn-inducing.

For trips around town, you'll find a **taxi service** (tel. 32/2100 211) on the main street, a few doors north of Club Sandwich. Taxi rides are usually a flat rate of CH$2,000 for trips around the island and CH$3,000 to the airport. Most lodgings include airport transfers in their fees; confirm this upon booking.

Parque Nacional Rapa Nui

Covering 7,000 hectares, or 42 percent of the island, **Parque Nacional Rapa Nui** (www.parquenacionalrapanui.cl, most sites 9am-8pm daily Oct.-Mar., 9am-5:30pm Apr.-Nov., CH$54,000 or US$80 adults, CH$27,000 or US$40 children) protects the majority of the island's *moai* as well as other vestiges of a culture that feels like it disappeared overnight.

What makes the park so captivating to its 60,000 annual visitors are the 887 *moai*, 300 *ahu,* and thousands of structures that played a role in Rapa Nui agriculture or housing. All the *moai* were toppled between the late 18th and mid-19th centuries; many have since been restored. Within the park, it's possible to see 15 restored *moai* in a row, as well as sites where *moai* remain facedown.

You are required to present your **entry ticket** at the entrance of most sights. It is not possible to purchase this ticket in the park. Buy your ticket from the **park office** at the airport (in the arrivals hall; hours coincide with flight arrivals) or the Hanga Roa location (Atamu Tekena s/n, no phone, 8:30am-4pm daily) before attempting to enter any sites.

There are **public restrooms** (CH$500, bring change) at major destinations, including Orongo, Rano Raraku, and Anakena. Other than the cafeteria at Rano Raraku and the small fish restaurants at Anakena, there is no food or drink within the park, so stock up on lunch and snacks before heading out. Cell phone service is only available at certain points around the island; connection is spotty.

Treat the park with respect and you'll help with conservation efforts. Don't touch or climb on the monuments, and don't remove any objects from the sites.

PLANTS AND ANIMALS

The flora and fauna of Rapa Nui have faced serious challenges in the last millennium. Birds were likely responsible for introducing most plants. The Polynesians planted banana, sweet potato, pumpkin, and sugarcane. This resulted in the deforestation of the *Jubaea* palms and *toromino* (a species of flowering tree) that once covered the island.

Later, the introduction of 70,000 sheep further degraded native flora and fauna. Fast-growing eucalyptus was introduced to prevent soil erosion, with mixed results. Today, attempts at reforestation in areas such as the Poike peninsula are aimed at restoring native flora.

There is limited fauna on the island. At one time there were 25 species of birds, but their populations have plummeted, likely due to the introduction of the Polynesian rat. Only a few still nest here, including frigates and masked boobies off the coast of Orongo. The Chilean tinamou and Chimango caracara are two of the birds most likely to be spotted. There are no native mammals. Horses, owned by the local people, roam freely.

TOURS AND TRANSPORTATION

Most hotels run their own excursions or can set you up with a tour agency for a half- or full-day tour of the sites. Most agencies follow similar routes, so you will likely find yourself behind large groups of other tourists. For full-day tours, expect to pay CH$40,000-60,000 pp. Transport from the agency's office is included in the cost, but food and park entry are not.

Some of the best-value tours are offered by **Easter Island Travel** (Te Pito O Te Henua s/n, tel. 9/7510 3841, www.easterisland.travel). Tours have a maximum of eight passengers, and their guides are knowledgeable and speak good English. **Mahinatur** (Atamu Tekena s/n, tel. 32/2100 635, www.mahinatur.cl) is one of the largest agencies on the island. It runs group tours of up to 18 passengers (half-day CH$20,000).

To spend some time at Anakena, **Te Ao Tour** (Atamu Tekena s/n, tel. 9/8478 2491) offers **transfer service** (4 daily, CH$7,000 round-trip) in modified trucks that run between Hanga Roa and the beach. They pick up passengers outside their office, as well as various other points in town. The final shuttle back departs Anakena at 7pm.

ORIENTATION

The national park covers large areas of the island stretching north, east, and south of Hanga Roa. The small size of the island means it is possible to visit the main sites in two or three days. Most visitors and tour groups break the park into four general areas for maximum efficiency:

- the **vicinity of Hanga Roa,** with the archaeological sites north and east of Hanga Roa
- **Anakena and vicinity,** the central part of the northern coast
- the **southeastern coast,** including the Poike peninsula and along the coast to Ahu Tongariki
- the **southwestern coast,** including Orongo

VICINITY OF HANGA ROA

North of Hanga Roa are some of the least-explored destinations, including caves, known as *ana*. It's also possible to hike the entire northern coast, connecting Hanga Roa with Anakena, as you circuit the edges of Maunga Terevaka, the island's highest volcano. Most sites have small booths staffed by rangers who check and stamp your national park ticket before allowing you to enter.

Hanga Kio'e

A grassy peninsula 700 meters north of Ahu Tahai, **Hanga Kio'e** is home to two restored *ahu*: **Ahu Akapu,** with a four-meter-tall *moai,* and **Ahu Hanga Kio'e,** with just the torso of its original statue. It's believed that every new *ariki* (king) lived at this site for a

short period. This site receives few visitors and is a good alternative to Ahu Tahai to watch the sunset.

Ana Kakenga

Around 2km north of Hanga Kio'e and only accessible on foot or bicycle due to the poor state of the road, **Ana Kakenga** is one of the island's most interesting caves. From the road, look for the small hole that is the cave opening. It looks like a pile of rubble but has a set of steps descending it; be careful not to hit your head. Inside, the cave widens into a 50-meter-long lava tube. The flow of the lava reached the cliff edge, leaving two holes facing the ocean and giving it the colloquial name "the cave of two windows." This experience is not for claustrophobes.

The cave faces west, making it a beautiful spot for sunset. When you visit, make sure to bring a flashlight and avoid going alone, as the cave floor can be slippery, particularly after rainfall.

Ahu Te Peu

It's 1.2km north of Ana Kakenga along a rough road (only traversable on foot or by bicycle) to **Ahu Te Peu,** an unrestored platform surrounded a well-preserved collection of the archaeological remains of a large village. A short path to the right leads to the foundations of a 43-meter-long *hare paenga* (upside-down boat-style house, also known as a *hare vaka*). It's believed it belonged to Ariki Tu'u Ko Ihu, an important 13th-century Rapa Nui leader, or was used for community meetings.

Ahu Te Peu can be reached by vehicle by driving to Ahu Akivi and continuing along this same road heading west to the coast; note that this road becomes muddy and impassable following heavy rain.

Ana Te Pahu

Two kilometers east of Ahu Te Peu, **Ana Te Pahu** is the largest of the island's caves, formed from lava tubes. It extends a few hundred meters back from the entrance, inside which you'll find a grove of banana plants that have made the most of the cave's protection and humidity. How much rain has fallen recently will affect how far into the cave you can explore, although there are few features of note inside.

You can reach the site by road, an 8-km drive north of Caleta Hanga Roa on Calle Ara Piki as it leaves town, or by walking or cycling from Ahu Te Peu. The road that runs east from Ahu Te Peu is closed to vehicles following heavy rain due to its poor state; if it's dry, it's passable with caution.

Ahu Akivi

On the flanks of Maunga Terevaka (Terevaka Volcano) are the seven *moai* of the 90-meter-long **Ahu Akivi,** the first of the island's *ahu* to be excavated and restored. It features the most substantial group of *moai* that appear to be looking out to sea. A substantial village was once located below the *ahu,* making it more likely that they were actually positioned to look over their descendants, as was common with the *moai.*

Oral history suggests that these *moai* represent the seven explorers who scouted the island as a possible new settlement for the Polynesians who eventually came here. This *ahu* is believed to have played a role in agricultural timekeeping, as it aligns with certain stars on the spring and fall equinoxes.

The site can be reached by vehicle, either along the road that continues north from Puna Pau or the smaller local road north from Calle Ara Piki, on the northeastern edge of Hanga Roa, a 4-km drive. A booth (where you must get your ticket stamped for entry) by the side of the road marks the entrance to the site, and a car park is 150 meters beyond.

Maunga Terevaka

Dominating the northwestern part of the island is **Maunga Terevaka,** the youngest of Rapa Nui's three volcanoes. Its summit marks the highest point on the island, 511 meters elevation, and offers striking views across Rapa Nui, making this a place to get a real sense of its remote and isolated location in the middle of the Pacific Ocean.

The site is reached on the same access road as Ahu Akivi. Around 100 meters past the entry booth (where you need to get your ticket stamped for Ahu Akivi and the volcano), a yellow sign directs you right toward "Maura Tere Vaka." From here, it's a 9km, three- to four-hour out-and-back hike on a well-signed path.

You can also summit the volcano on horseback. **Cabalgatas Pantu** (Tekerera s/n, tel. 32/2001 0557, www.pikerauri.com), which operates from Pikera Uri Lodge, offers a two- or three-hour tour with hotel pickup and drop-off included (CH$40,000).

Puna Pau

Six kilometers east of Hanga Roa, **Puna Pau** is a vent of the Maunga Terevaka volcano and a quarry where red *hani hani* (scoria rock) was excavated for carving the *pukao* (topknots) of the *moai.* Although they resemble enormous millstones or giant marbles, these rocks are believed to represent a hairstyle still worn by Polynesian men: long hair tied in a bun on the top of the head.

There are 20 carved *pukao* at the site, ready to be transported. Archaeologists believe the Rapa Nui people moved the *pukao,* rocks that weigh up to 10 tons, by rolling them, enabling them to be moved over 12km. The quarry gives a sense of the scale of these enormous headpieces and the *moai.* If you look closely at some, it's possible to distinguish weathered carvings of canoes and other important symbols; these are believed to be later additions, crafted after the quarry fell into disuse.

A 400-meter trail leads from the entrance in a loop around the stones to the crater and a *mirador* with views west. You can watch the sun set across Hanga Roa from here. Officially the site is only open until 9pm daily in summer, but you can enter after this time to catch the sunset if there is no one at the entry booth.

The Northern Coast

From Ahu Te Peu, it's possible to hike around

Significant Sites on Rapa Nui

- Largest *ahu:* 220 meters long with 15 *moai,* the restored **Ahu Tongariki** on the northeastern side of the island is officially the largest *ahu.*

- Biggest *moai:* Still attached to the bedrock in the Rano Raraku quarry, **Te Tokanga** or **El Gigante (The Giant)** is 21.6 meters long and weighs 160-180 tons.

- Biggest erected *moai:* The toppled **Paro** *moai* at Ahu Te Pito Kura was 9.8 meters tall and weighed 70-80 tons. Unfortunately, the statue broke in two when it was pushed from its platform.

- Largest basalt *moai:* **Ho'a Hakananai'a** was found at the Orongo ceremonial village in the south of the island. It was taken off the island in 1868 and is on display in the British Museum.

- Largest petroglyph: **Papa Vaka,** on the northern coast, is home to a 12-meter double-hulled canoe carved into the lava flow on the ground.

- Most unusual *moai:* **Tukuturi** in Rano Raraku is the only known *moai* with legs. This statue is more humanistic in style, with rounded facial features.

the edges of the northern coast to Anakena. It's an eight-hour, 18-km, moderate trek that skirts Maunga Terevaka and is best appreciated with a guide, as many of the archaeological sites can be indistinguishable to the untrained eye. **Easter Island Travel** (Te Pito O Te Henua s/n, tel. 9/7510 3841, www. easterisland.travel) runs private hiking excursions of the northern coast (CH$117,000 pp, min. 2 people).

This region is unique: All the *moai, ahu,* and other remains lie as they have for centuries, unaffected by the restoration done in other parts of the island. The area's highlights include **Ahu Poe Poe,** an *ahu* in the shape of a boat, and **Cabo Norte,** the northern tip of the island.

If you plan to do this hike by yourself, start early and take the **transfer service** offered by **Te Ao Tour** (Atamu Tekena s/n, tel. 9/8478 2491) or a taxi to Anakena so you can travel counterclockwise and have the sun behind you for most of the walk. Avoid standing on archaeological remains.

ANAKENA AND VICINITY

Described as the "cradle of Rapa Nui civilization," Anakena, a palm-fringed sandy beach in the middle of the northern coast, is the island's most picturesque and traditionally Polynesian spot. Thanks to the aridity of the sand, it is an archaeologically valuable site, helping experts draw more accurate conclusions about the dates of the Polynesian arrival.

Ahu Nau Nau

The seven well-preserved *moai* of **Ahu Nau Nau** rise out of the grass just inland of Anakena. Surrounded by towering palm trees, the platform was restored in 1978 by Rapa Nui archaeologist Sergio Rapu. The *moai* were protected from the elements by the sand they were in, and they were remarkably preserved. Walk around and look at the *moai* from behind to see the circular carvings on their backs. Two still wear complete *pukao.*

A second *ahu* to the right of the main platform and closer to the sea supports the lone *moai* of **Ahu Ature Huki.** This figure is far more weathered but notable as the first to be re-erected, in 1956 by Norwegian adventurer Thor Heyerdahl and a team of local people. To its right on the hill, scattered rocks indicate a village with remains of *umu pae* (underground ovens) and *hare paenga* (boat-shaped houses), although they're hard to distinguish in the long grass.

Anakena

According to oral history, **Anakena** is where Hotu Matu'a, the first Rapa Nui king, originally set foot on the island. A tropical paradise of white coral sand, warm water, and coconut trees, this beach is where most visitors head to sunbathe or swim. A lifeguard is usually here in high season. The waters are calm and ideal for swimming, with temperatures of 18-24°C. Just above the beach, palm-roofed shacks do a roaring trade in empanadas, ceviche, and fruit juices. There are public restrooms (CH$500) next to the car park.

Just before the main car park, **Camping Ana Tekena** (tel. 9/9690 6941 or 9/5233 9501, CH$12,000 tent site, CH$16,000 tent site and rental equipment) is one of the few lodgings outside Hanga Roa. It has hot showers powered by solar energy and rainwater, huge hammocks, and a warm welcome. To get here, **Te Ao Tour** (Atamu Tekena s/n, tel. 9/8478 2491) runs four daily transfers from Hanga Roa (CH$7,000 pp round-trip).

Ovahe

A rocky cove with white coral sand but notably lacking in tourists, **Ovahe** is equally picturesque as Anakena. Dramatic black-and-red volcanic rock forms a striking cliff above the beach; rockfalls have been known to occur. A sign warns that the water isn't safe for swimming, but you'll see locals doing it anyway. Swim at your own risk; there are no lifeguards.

The rubble of black rocks on an outcrop before you reach the beach marks an ancestral graveyard; don't walk on it. On the way back to the car park, a trail peels left past an abandoned and unrestored *ahu* comprising fragments of broken rock.

Get here via the signposted dirt road 500 meters after the road for Ahu Tongariki. It's accessible in an ordinary car, but the road can be difficult after heavy rain.

Ahu Te Pito Kura

Four kilometers from Ovahe, east along the road to Ahu Tongariki, a small car park grants access to **Ahu Te Pito Kura.** This platform might look like its two *moai* have toppled to lie facedown in the earth, but these two pieces are actually part of one *moai,* **Paro,** the largest to have been erected. Weighing 70-80 tons (the *pukao* next to it weighs 12 tons) and standing 9.8 meters tall, this giant now lies with its head and upper torso cracked from the rest of its body.

To the left of the *ahu* is a circular stone structure protecting five stones, a large one in the center and four smaller ones in a square around it. It's claimed that the central stone, known locally as the **Magnetic Stone,** was brought by Hotu Matu'a, the first Rapa Nui king, from Hiva, his native land. It's believed to contain a high level of spiritual energy, which explains why it causes compasses to lose direction when held above it.

Papa Vaka Petroglyphs

Heading east toward Ahu Tongariki, 1km from Ahu Te Pito Kura, are the remains of the **Papa Vaka petroglyphs,** on the right side of the road. A trail of a few hundred meters passes three petroglyph panels carved into lava flow on the ground.

At the first set of petroglyphs, Papa Mango, you can see *kahi* (tuna), *mango* (shark), and the *mangai kahi* (fishhooks) used to catch them carved into the rock. Farther along the trail, Papa Vaka contains the largest petroglyph on the island, a 12-meter-long double-hulled canoe that likely represents the original canoe of Hotu Matu'a, the first Rapa Nui king.

SOUTHEASTERN COAST

The southeastern coast of Rapa Nui is home to many of the island's most dramatic sites. The restored and well-maintained *ahu* and *moai* of Ahu Tongariki and the Rano Raraku quarry offer contrast with sites that have been left as they were found.

The barely visited Peninsula Poike merits at least half a day of exploration. If you start with sunrise at Ahu Tongariki, it's possible to explore the rest of the sites in a full day, even if you stop every few kilometers for other *ahu* not covered in this guide.

Peninsula Poike

The oldest volcano on the island, Poike, erupted three million years ago and gave its name to **Peninsula Poike,** the plateau that rises to 370 meters and protrudes from the eastern edge of the island with 100-meter cliffs over the ocean. Inside the volcano's main crater, Pua Katiki, is a lush grove of introduced eucalyptus trees.

Some of the peninsula's most interesting sights include the striking three-meter carving of a head in rock, known as **Ma'unga Vai a Hev,** and the **Ana or Keke** (Virgins Cave). This 380-meter cave is decorated with petroglyphs and is believed to be where young female virgins were held to keep their skin pale and prepare them for sexual or religious rites. The *moai* on the peninsula are also of interest. Most were carved from white trachyte from the Poike volcano, perhaps suggesting a divide between these inhabitants and those working at Rano Raraku.

Although it's possible to visit alone, many of the sites are difficult to find, so a guided tour is recommended. **Easter Island Travel** (Te Pito O Te Henua s/n, tel. 9/7510 3841, www.easterisland.travel) offers private six-hour hiking tours of the peninsula, including transportation from their office (CH$110,000 pp). As on most of the island, shade is scarce, so a sun hat and sunscreen are essential.

★ Ahu Tongariki

On the far southeastern coast, just before Peninsula Poike, 15 of Rapa Nui's most famous *moai* line up at dramatic **Ahu Tongariki.** These cliff-side sculptures are striking any time of day, but the mysterious atmosphere is heightened at dawn in summer—specifically on the solstice, when the sun rises directly between the figures.

This ceremonial platform is 220 meters long, the largest built on the island. In 1960, a tsunami caused by a magnitude 9.4 earthquake near Valdivia washed these giants hundreds of meters inland. Restoration work, initiated by Sergio Rapu, archaeologist and former governor of Rapa Nui, was done 1988-1996.

Of the *moai* returned to the platform, only one still has his *pukao*. Seven of the others lie in a row a few hundred meters away. Beneath the platform, the polished circular *poro* stones slope down to what would have been the main ceremonial plaza. Walk around the back of the *ahu;* if you look closely, you'll notice petroglyphs carved into some of the statues' backs.

At the front of the platform you'll also see a large fractured *moai* lying on its back. Its eye sockets have yet to be carved, suggesting that it was never erected on the platform and perhaps was broken upon arrival. At the entrance, a lone *moai* stares toward the car park. It has had an interesting history: In 1982, it was sent to Japan by ship and exhibited in various cities before being returned to the island and dubbed "the traveling *moai*."

This is the best spot to watch the sun rise. The site opens at 7am daily in summer and 7:30am daily in winter to allow visitors to appreciate the dramatic scene. Note that while the event is still dramatic in winter, the sun appears behind Peninsula Poike instead of the *moai*.

★ Rano Raraku

As you approach the lush green slopes of **Rano Raraku,** a volcanic crater and the quarry from which the island's *moai* were carved, the towering heads of in situ *moai* offer a powerful reminder of their sheer scale. It's also hard not to be struck by the sense that the carvers will be back soon to finish the work that seems to have been stopped suddenly.

Just before Ahu Tongariki on the far southeastern coast, Rano Raraku is home to 400 *moai,* many lying on their backs and only partially carved from the rock; others stand vertical and look like decapitated heads. They are actually complete *moai;* in the years since the quarry was abandoned, erosion has caused

---

1: Ahu Tongariki **2:** Rano Raraku

soil to collect around the torsos of these statues, leaving them half buried.

From the entrance, where your ticket is stamped, a path heads toward the crater. Head right, toward the quarry, and climb some steps to the largest *moai* ever attempted, **Te Tokanga** or **El Gigante** (The Giant), still attached to the rock. It's over 21 meters long and weighs 160-180 tons. Continue along the path and down the next set of steps. To the left are a few *moai* still attached to the rock. At the end of the path, a viewpoint grants a spectacular panorama of the northeastern edge of the island, including Ahu Tongariki and Peninsula Poike.

This is also the location of **Tukuturi,** a unique *moai*. His facial features are notably more human than the stylized, sharply carved faces of the traditional *moai,* and he has legs, kneeling with his hands on his thighs. Debate continues as to whether this is an early form of *moai* or a later one. On the path back, don't miss the island's most famous single *moai,* **Hinariru,** a four-meter-tall head and shoulders that looms out of the grass with a slight tilt.

Following the steep path up to the crater, after 10 minutes you'll reach the top to see the remains of 317 *moai,* although only 30 are easily identifiable. Inside the crater is a freshwater lagoon. The site is best photographed in the afternoon, when the sun's rays catch the crater's western slopes. It's better to go with a guide, as many of the *moai* in the rock are hard to identify if you don't know where to look. Just by the car park, there are restrooms, a café, and stalls selling *artesanía*.

As with all the large important sites on the island, you can only visit this part of the island once (a policy presumably to prevent overcrowding). Once your pass is stamped at the entrance booth, you can enter the site.

★ Ahu Akahanga

The southeastern coastal road between Hanga Roa and Peninsula Poike is a dramatic drive with views of the heaving Pacific. Halfway along, **Ahu Akahanga** houses a platform that hasn't been restored, complete with toppled *moai,* along with excellently preserved examples of the islanders' *hare paenga* (boat-shaped houses). Gain insight into the fall of the ancestor cult when the *moai* were toppled.

On the right-hand side after the entrance, you can see the stone foundations of a couple of houses. There are holes in the foundation stones where wooden beams were inserted to support the building's roof, thatched with the native *hau hau* (burweed) plant. The door is on the southern side of the house, facing the *ahu.*

Farther south is the main *ahu.* Its 12 *moai* lie toppled, many looking up at the sky. You'll also see a small *moai* that looks slightly alien in facial structure, thought to be one of the first carved. A short walk west is another unrestored platform known as **Ura Uranga Te Mahina,** with four toppled *moai.*

SOUTHWESTERN COAST

The southwestern coast is easily accessible from Hanga Roa, both by vehicle and on foot, and makes a good half-day or longer excursion.

★ Orongo Ceremonial Village

On the far southern reaches of the island are the 54 restored houses of the **Orongo ceremonial village.** From the village, you can see three islands, the largest of which is Motu Nui.

Around 1,700 petroglyphs adorn the rocks in this area. Many feature a figure with a bird head, known as the birdman. Others depict the creator god Make-make. Unfortunately, erosion means that many are hard to distinguish. The birdman and Make-make are linked with a 17th-century ceremonial event in which locals competed to obtain the egg of the sooty tern in order to choose their newest leader. The on-site **visitors center** provides an excellent overview of the birdman cult.

From the visitors center, a cliff-side path leads to a row of houses, half of which are subterranean to protect them against the fierce wind around this exposed cliff edge. Continue along the trail to the western side of the **Rano**

The Cult of the Birdman

Sometime in the 17th century, the cult of the birdman, *tangata manu*, emerged as a new way to choose the annual ruler. The selection ceremony coincided with the return of the migratory *manutara* (sooty tern) to Motu Nui, an island visible from Orongo. A competitor was selected from each tribe to represent their chief. When the competition began, each competitor would swim through the crashing ocean to Motu Nui and wait until the tern's first egg was laid. The first competitor to claim it would swim back to the main island to present it to their chief, who would become the *tangata manu*, or spiritual leader, of the island for the year.

The competition was linked to the creator god Make-make, who brought marine birds to nest on the island, thus explaining the profusion of petroglyphs of his image on the rocks around Orongo. The competition ended in 1867 because Catholic missionaries on the island considered it pagan. Thanks to the tireless investigations of Katherine Routledge, an archaeologist and anthropologist who interviewed islanders, we know much about the ceremony. Her work preserved the oral history of indigenous Rapa Nui culture.

Kau volcanic crater. Inside the crater is filled with reeds, marsh, and rainwater. From here, you can see the island's other two volcanoes. One kilometer north, along the road back toward Hanga Roa, an overlook offers a viewpoint across Rano Kau. A 2.5-km trail continues around the eastern rim of the crater, offering more views.

As with all the large important sites on the island, you can only visit once, and it's worth spending a few hours exploring its treasures. Your pass must be stamped at the desk just inside the visitors center before you can enter the site. To get here is a 6-km drive along the road that passes west of the airport or a 5-km, two-hour hike.

Ahu Vinapu

Just beyond the eastern tip of the runway, **Ahu Vinapu** is home to some of the island's most intriguing stonework. This *ahu* is interesting for its female statue, one of only 10 found on the island. It's also unusual because it's made of red scoria, the material usually reserved for the topknots of the *moai*.

There are two *ahu* at this site: A few meters north is **Ahu Tahira,** with six *moai* facedown in the earth. The back wall of the *ahu*, formed from a layer of carefully cut basalt rock, resembles the careful masonry seen at Inca cities such as Cusco, leading some archaeologists to wonder if the wall's design was influenced by the Inca.

Background

The Landscape

Chile's land mass covers 756,000 square kilometers, an area slightly larger than France. Its most notable feature is its uniquely narrow form: Chile is 4,270 kilometers long but averages a mere 177 kilometers wide. This land is home to an incredible diversity of geographical forms and climate types.

GEOGRAPHY

On the western edge of South America, Chile is on the convergence of the Nazca and South American tectonic plates, meaning it is subjected

to extensive seismic activity. Of the 7,000 earthquakes annually, 95 percent are too small to be felt. The 1960 earthquake that struck off the coast of Valdivia is the strongest ever recorded; it had a magnitude of 9.5.

Mountains and Valleys

Partitioning Chile from its neighbors are the Andes Mountains, a natural border with Argentina and Bolivia. These peaks reach 6,959 meters elevation at Aconcagua in the Cordillera Occidental, with the range lowering gradually as it snakes south. It becomes the lower Andes Mediterráneos (Mediterranean Andes) at Santiago, then the Cordillera de la Araucanía and the Cordillera Patagónica, which plunges into the Strait of Magellan, resurfacing as the Cordillera Darwin south of the Beagle Channel.

These mountain ranges host 580 volcanoes, of which 90 are considered active—having erupted at least once in the last 10,000 years. Several erupt more regularly, including top attraction Volcán Villarrica, the most active volcano in Chile.

West of the Andes, the land plunges to form the main longitudinal valleys where most of the country's settlement is. A string of coastal mountains in the east of Chile, known as the Cordillera de la Costa, runs parallel to the Andes, and the land tapers from here to the Pacific Ocean. These coastal peaks barely surpass 2,000 meters elevation and run parallel to the ocean for two-thirds the length of the country. They play an integral part in viticulture by trapping moisture from southwesterly winds, allowing for the cultivation of grapes in the Central Valley.

Between these two mountain ranges, the Longitudinal Depression is a narrow valley carved through with river gorges and transverse valleys. Between the Aconcagua River Valley and Puerto Montt, the Central Valley is the most densely populated part of the country. It contains the highest concentration of

agriculture, including fruit plantations and vineyards.

Rivers

Chile's many rivers have long been used to mark territories. The Río Bío Bío was the dividing line between the Spanish and the Mapuche people for 300 years. Modern Chileans reference rivers when discussing the boundaries of the country's 16 regions.

Most rivers originate in the Andes. In the arid north, Río Luta and Río Loa have long been used for irrigation, allowing for fertile oases where tropical fruits and vegetables are grown. Many rivers in the rainy south appeal to white-water rafting enthusiasts, with the Río Futaleufú renowned for its Class V rapids. Other Patagonian rivers, such as the marvelously teal waters of the Río Baker, teem with brown and rainbow trout.

Lakes

Glaciation is responsible for myriad unspoiled lakes dotting the south of the country. One of the most astonishing is the cerulean blue Lago General Carrera, the second-largest lake in South America, which extends from Chile's Aysén region into Argentina. The Los Lagos region also takes its name from its sparkling lakes.

On the border with Bolivia in the north, Lago Chungará is superbly scenic, reflecting the twin peaks of Volcán Parinacota and Volcán Pomerape in its crystal waters. It's also home to breeding colonies of native birdlife.

CLIMATE

The extreme geography of Chile contributes to the country's diverse climates. From its border with Peru and Bolivia, Chile stretches to subantarctic Cabo de Hornos (Cape Horn). Elevation also affects the distinct climates of different regions.

In most of the country, four seasons are notable, in the opposite time of the year to

---

Previous: Parque Nacional Radal Siete Tazas.

Chilean Volcanoes and the Ring of Fire

Almost 3,000 volcanoes stud the Andes from the Atacama Desert to the tip of Tierra del Fuego. The fault line between the South American and Nazca tectonic plates led to the formation of the Andes Mountains and is part of the Ring of Fire, an area around the edges of the Pacific Ocean where seismic activity is common. The constantly moving plates cause Chile's numerous earthquakes as well as regular eruptions of the country's 90 active volcanoes.

In Chile, volcanic eruptions rarely cause loss of life, as alerts and evacuation systems are in place. For adventure seekers, these volcanoes provide a thrilling way to explore the rugged Chilean landscape. Many are home to hiking trails and ski resorts. The most summited volcano in the Lakes District, 2,847-meter **Volcán Villarrica,** regularly puffs smoke, and it's not unusual to see lava bubbling in its crater. Although the skiing conditions are unreliable, the slopes of the volcano are fun to ride down on a sled after you've hiked to the top.

One of Chile's largest volcanoes, 3,125-meter **Volcán Llaima** is the centerpiece of Parque Nacional Conguillío. Its name means "reawakened one" in Mapudungan, an appropriate name for one of the most active volcanoes in the country, with its last major eruption in 1994. It's a challenging climb thanks to the soft ash covering its slopes, but it makes a wonderfully quiet alternative to the busier trails up Volcán Villarrica. There's a small ski resort here.

With some of the best skiable terrain, made even better by a lack of visitors, 2,865-meter **Volcán Lonquimay** in Reserva Nacional Malalcahuello-Nalcas is ideal for winter sports fanatics thanks to good infrastructure at its small ski resort, but there's also a lesser-known trek to its summit, with 360-degree views of seven other volcanoes on a clear day.

those in the northern hemisphere. *Verano* (summer) is December-February, followed by *otoño* (fall) March-May. *Invierno* (winter) is June-August, while *primavera* (spring) is September-November. Unlike other parts of South America, Chile does not have a specific rainy season, although rainfall in the southern half of the country, from Santiago south, is more common in fall and winter. Temperatures throughout the country are warmer during summer.

Norte Grande

Northernmost Norte Grande has a dry climate. Daytime temperature ranges vary on the coast, inland, and in the altiplano. Inland, temperatures average 25°C during summer, although coastal fog makes it feel milder, while at the Pacific temperatures reach 19°C in summer—the hottest beaches you'll find in the country.

In the foothills, in places such as San Pedro de Atacama, temperatures can drop to below freezing at night; snowfall in July-August in the desert is not uncommon. Farther north, in the altiplano of the Arica and Parinacota

region that borders Bolivia, summer rain occurs December-March. Travel in the national parks and reserves can become difficult during these months. Temperatures throughout the year rarely reach above 10°C.

Norte Chico

The Norte Chico has similarly dry weather to the Norte Grande. Heavy rainfall brought by El Niño every 5-7 years along the coast creates the beautiful phenomenon known as the *desierto florido* (flowering desert). Throughout the year, the *camanchaca* (coastal fog) keeps the coast green with low shrubby plants. Temperatures in inland valleys such as the Valle de Elquí can reach beyond 35°C in the peak of summer, with fierce sun making it feel even hotter.

Central Valley

The Central Valley has a Mediterranean climate, with occasional rainfall in winter and average temperatures reaching 31°C in January in the capital, Santiago. The rest of the year, the weather is generally mild, hovering in the low and mid-20s. During summer,

Valparaíso, Viña del Mar, and other coastal towns and cities have welcoming 20°C temperatures regulated by a cooler breeze off the Pacific. The presence of the Humboldt Current keeps ocean temperatures at a refreshing 15°C.

The southern part of the valley is wetter, with rainfall throughout the year. Sunny days aren't uncommon during summer, leading many Chileans to converge on the region in the hottest months.

Patagonia

Patagonia has high levels of precipitation throughout the year, although there is marked reduction in summer, when winds are at their strongest. The western edge, comprising the fjords and the Aysén region, is the wettest part of the country. Heavy rainfall and snowfall in winter can make travel practically impossible. On the eastern side of Patagonia, across the Andes, the landscape is cold steppe, protected by the mountains from the wet westerly winds, although winds from other directions can still be fierce.

ENVIRONMENTAL ISSUES
Pollution

Pollution is an increasing issue in Santiago and other cities in Chile. Vehicle emissions and wood-burning stoves account for 94 percent of fine particulate matter in the cities. Combined with a lack of rainfall or wind, this causes very high levels of smog, thought to contribute to the deaths of 4,000 people per year.

A report on air pollution published by the World Health Organization in 2007 named Coyhaique as the world's most polluted city, beating other South American cities such as Lima and La Paz. Osorno also made it to number 10 on the same list.

Climate Change

Many Chileans view climate change as the biggest external threat to the country, seen in multiple interlinking features of daily life.

Flooding has become increasingly regular across the country. In 2015, uncommonly heavy rainfall wiped out buildings and houses, displacing over 27,000 people and resulting in 31 deaths in towns and cities in the Antofagasta, Atacama, and Copiapó regions. Two years later, the equivalent of a year's worth of rain fell in two days in Copiapó, causing extreme flood damage.

In 2016 and 2017 the worst wildfires in Chilean history destroyed 600,000 hectares of woodland. Increasing annual temperatures make fires more likely. Extreme droughts have also caused serious damage. In the Central Valley, lakes that depend on rainfall have completely dried up.

Climate change is also affecting Patagonia's glaciers. Chile contains 24,133 glaciers, 82 percent of all those in South America. Scientists have measured their retreat at 10 to 100 times faster in the last 30 years than previously. In late 2017, a chunk of ice measuring 350 by 380 meters broke off Glaciar Grey in Parque Nacional Torres del Paine. Climatologists point the finger at the mining industry, claiming that the mining dust that settles onto glaciers means the ice absorbs solar energy more quickly.

Successive Chilean governments have implemented tentative steps to reduce the impact of climate change, although more action is necessary. Schools have introduced lessons discussing the causes and consequences, while the government has committed to reducing greenhouse gas emissions. Reforestation efforts have begun, with 100,000 hectares of mostly native woodland introduced across the country.

Another catastrophe linked to climate change is the increasing regularity of the *marea roja* (red tide), an algal bloom caused by unusually warm sea temperatures that allow toxic algae to proliferate. Bivalve shellfish that have consumed the algae build up toxins that can be fatal to humans if consumed. In 2016, an outbreak wiped out millions of fish and brought loses of US$800 million to Chile's enormous salmon farming industry, the second-largest exporter in the world. Scientists and critics of the powerful and poorly regulated aquaculture industry have laid blame at their feet, with reports alleging that salmon with high levels of the toxins had been thrown back into the ocean, contaminating other fish stocks and compounding the disaster.

Renewable Energy
A 2016 report by the International Renewable Energy Agency put Chile within the top 10 renewable energy markets in the world. Although 58 percent of energy in Chile is made from fossil fuels, 20 percent comes from hydroelectricity. However, this has proven controversial in the past few decades.

Dams have been implemented in the river basins of many parts of the Central Valley, but many have met fierce resistance from local communities.

Chile has long been in a vulnerable situation with energy. Extreme weather events causing droughts and flooding have made hydropower less reliable, with focus now turning to less conventional energy sources such as solar, wind, and geothermal. Much of the new clean energy has come from solar panels installed in the Atacama Desert, followed by wind farms in the Norte Grande and along the coast. South America's first geothermal plant was installed in 2017 near Ollagüe in the Antofagasta region; it's capable of providing 165,000 homes with electricity.

Plants and Animals

The country is home to 4,600 native plant species, including 124 species of ferns. Around 50 percent of these plants are endemic. Chile is also home to around 1,200 species of fish, 43 species of amphibians, 94 species of reptiles, 456 species of birds, and 148 species of mammal. The central Mediterranean zone, Valdivian temperate rainforest, and the high Andean steppe of the Norte Grande have been designated global hot spots for biodiversity.

COASTAL DESERTS
The **Atacama Desert** extends to the border with Peru. Plantlife is mostly in the form of drought-resistant cacti, such as tree-like *Eulychnia,* which can grow to four meters high, and the *Copiapoa* cacti, which produce yellow blooms.

The most extraordinary animal species in the north of Chile are in **Parque Nacional Bosque de Fray Jorge,** a tract of moisture-rich Valdivian temperate rainforest nourished by the fog. Molina's hog-nosed skunks, pumas, and Andean (culpeo) fox are resident, though rare. Also in the park are Chilean tinamous, Magellanic horned owls, and black-chested

buzzard-eagles. You're most likely to spot guanaco here.

The **Reserva Nacional Pampa del Tamarugal** is home to the tamarugo, a native species of tree. It also sustains a wide range of wildlife, including honeybees, the gray tamarugo conebill, as well as small rodents such as Darwin's mouse.

Along the coast, the South American sea lion and the endangered *chungungo* (marine otter) can be sighted, with 25,000 Humboldt penguins, around 80 percent of the global population of the species, arriving to breed during the summer on the islets of **Reserva Nacional Pingüino de Humboldt.** The southernmost colony of bottlenose dolphins also frequents these waters, while a dozen species of whales, including blue, fin, sei, humpback, and minke as well as orcas can be sighted in the waters farther north, off the coast of **Chañaral de Aceituno.**

HIGH ANDEAN STEPPE
The high Andean steppe comprises the altiplano and the puna, two sets of high mountain plateaus at 4,000 meters elevation and ringed

by high-altitude volcanoes and snowcapped mountains. Despite the seemingly barren landscapes, they support over 160 plant species, mostly perennial grasses and resinous shrubs known as *tola*. Wildflowers bloom March-May following rainfall, and candelabra cacti grow in ravines leading up to the steppe.

The most notable plant species is the bright green *llareta*. It forms solid, dense mounds that resemble cushions. On these deserted plains, watch for animals such as the ostrich-like Darwin's rhea or *ñandú,* often spotted around the delicate vicuña, the wild ancestor of the alpaca. Viscachas are rife in rocky outcrops by the side of the road in **Parque Nacional Lauca,** home to 130 bird species, including large numbers of giant coots, silvery grebes, and yellow-billed pintails. The neighboring **Monumento Natural Salar de Surire** is also home to 15,000 Andean, Chilean, and James's flamingos, which arrive February-March to breed.

MEDITERRANEAN SCRUB

From La Serena south through the Central Valley to the Río Bío Bío, the native flora is mostly composed of *matorral* scrubland. It grows alongside sclerophyll forests (shrubs with hard leaves). Chilean palms, which can grow to 25 meters, were once native but are now rare. Forests of palms still exist in **Parque Nacional La Campana.** In the highlands of the Central Valley, oak species are prevalent, including evergreen *coigüe* and deciduous roble, *lenga,* and *ñirre.*

Birdlife is perhaps most notable in this part of Chile. The **Reserva Nacional Río de los Cipreses** is home to a breeding colony of burrowing parrots, Chile's largest parrot species. Andean condors and black-chested buzzard-eagles are also present. In parks and green spaces in Santiago, monk parakeets, escaped cage birds that have adapted to their urban home, can be heard if not seen. The best place to spot mammals is in the **Reserva National Radal Siete Tazas,** where rarer species such as the nocturnal *gato colocolo* and the

Molina's hog-nosed skunk exist, alongside the bolder red-coated Andean fox and the slightly smaller South American *chilla* (gray fox).

SOUTHERN BEECH AND CONIFEROUS FORESTS

South of the Río Bío Bío, southern beeches are the dominant fauna, comprising perennial *Nothofagus* (false beech) species such as *coigüe* in higher elevations, while roble and *hualo* are found in the Andean foothills. The most iconic tree of this region is the *araucaría* (monkey puzzle) tree, also known as the *paraguas* (umbrella) for its unique shape. They grow on lava fields or poor soil and in areas of high precipitation, with **Parque Nacional Laguna del Laja** and **Parque Nacional Conguillío** the best places to see them. They are threatened by illegal logging that has led to near-extinction.

The male Magellanic woodpecker, with its gorgeous red head, can more often than not be heard in these woodlands. Yellow-billed pintails, four types of egrets, and the ringed kingfisher are present around waterways. Mammals such as pumas and the near-threatened *pudú,* the world's smallest deer species, are present, as are a range of lizards and one of the country's handful of snakes, the Chilean slender snake. Like all snakes in the country, it does not pose any threat to humans.

VALDIVIAN TEMPERATE RAINFORESTS

The country's lushest landscapes span from the Río Bío Bío to the southern tip of Chiloé. Dense forests of evergreen broadleaf trees and low shrubs with waxy leaves have adapted to the significant rainfall that the region experiences—up to 400 centimeters in mountain areas. Trees such as *canelo* and *ulmo* combine with a thick understory of ferns, bamboo, and epiphytes. The unmissable giant *nalca* (Chilean rhubarb), a vast plant with tough fine-haired leaves that grows up to two meters tall, lines much of the **Carretera Austral.** These forests are also home to the

Chilean national flower, the delicate, pink-hued *copihue*.

Sections of ancient conifers such as Guaitecas cypress, the world's second-oldest living tree species, and towering *alerce* exist in small pockets. **Parque Nacional Pumalín** and **Parque Nacional Vicente Pérez Rosales** contain some of the oldest and most accessible ancient *alerce*, which is protected by law. **Parque Tantauco** in Chiloé contains trees as old as 2,000 years.

Similar to southern beech and coniferous forests, the Valdivian temperate rainforest is home to small mammals such as the *pudú*—surprisingly commonly seen on northern stretches of the Carretera Austral and rural areas of Chiloé, although you're far less likely to see the rare *monito del monte (colocolo* opossum) and silvery-gray Geoffroy's cat.

The entire region is rich in birdlife, with the Golfo de Quetalmahue, west of Ancud, and bays along the eastern coast of the island providing important breeding grounds for birds such as sooty shearwaters, black-browed albatross, and southern giant petrels. Blue, southern right, humpback, and pygmy whales are a common sight off of the west coast of the island, while the *huillín* (southern river otter) inhabits rivers, lakes, and rocky coasts, although you're most likely to spot them on the rivers in Chepú and Cucao in Chiloé.

EVERGREEN AND MAGELLANIC FORESTS

The temperate *siempreverde* (evergreen) forest dominates the coast at elevations below 1,000 meters from Temuco south of Chiloé and the Península de Taitao near Caleta Tortel. It comprises a multiple-canopy forest of *coigüe* alongside the smaller *ulmo* and the *tineo,* whose fruit capsules turn red in fall. The flowering *tepa, luma,* and *canelo* grow beneath.

This transitions into the similarly temperate Magellanic rainforest in the wetter foothills of the Patagonian Andes and the fjords along the western coast, where the dominant species is Magellanic *coigüe*. It grows alongside Magellanic *maitén*. The trees are draped with lichens such as old man's beard, mistletoe, and *pan de indio* (Darwin's bread), an edible fungus that was a staple of the indigenous Yaghan people.

Magellanic fuchsias are also common, blooming in vast bushes by waterways and feasted on by green-backed firecrown, the southernmost hummingbird on earth. Magellanic woodpeckers and austral parakeets are present in Magellanic forests. Marine birds are extensive, with common diving petrels and flightless steamer-ducks commonly seen off the coast. The majestic black-browed albatross is present around the fjords and farther out to sea. In the waters plied by ferries that break up the Carretera Austral, Peale's dolphins swim, while rocky coastlines are home to Guanay, red-legged, and imperial cormorant species.

Back on land, the *pudú* and the *huemul,* the endangered South Andean deer, can be spotted with luck in wilder, more southern sections of the Carretera Austral and around Lago Cochrane in the **Reserva Nacional Tamango.** The *huemul* is the national animal of Chile and appears on the country's coat of arms. The *ñandú* has been reintroduced in the park. It's also a good place for spotting pumas and Andean condors, also present in **Parque Nacional Torres del Paine.** This park is also home to 118 species of birdlife on various lakes and woodlands, including the flying steamer-duck, the distinctive black-necked swan, and the Andean duck. There are also white-tufted, silvery, and great grebes, plus black-faced ibis, often found probing the ground with their long, curved bills or calling noisily—although they're decidedly quieter than the southern lapwing and its sharp, piercing call.

Magellanic horned and austral pygmy owls can be spotted with luck in the trees, while in the skies, the Andean condor, with its vast wingspan and white collar, can be seen. Two types of caracara, southern crested and Chimango, are also resident here and farther south.

PATAGONIAN STEPPE

On the eastern edges of the Andes and across Tierra del Fuego, extensive grasslands exist alongside plants such as the Calafate bush, a Magellan barberry that produces rich fruit. Intensive sheep farming has eliminated much of the landscape, but occasional wildflowers survive, most commonly the *zapatillas de la virgen,* named after its slipper-like shape, and even the occasional *pico de loro* orchid, found on the edges of marshes.

On these vast plains and inside **Parque Nacional Pali Aike,** the guanaco, the elegant wild ancestor of the llama and cousin of the vicuña, is plentiful, often accompanied by the *ñandú.* Puma sightings in this park are surprisingly common, with those of the Humboldt's hog-nosed skunk and the big hairy armadillo less so.

Wetlands and lakes are home to Chilean flamingos, the southernmost species in the world. The western edge of **Tierra del Fuego** at Bahía Inútil contains a 60-strong king penguin colony. Magellanic penguins are also on **Isla Magdalena** in the Strait of Magellan as well as outlying islands, which are also home to South American sea lions and southern fur seals. Humpback whales feed off the coast of the **Parque Marino Francisco Coloane** in the Strait of Magellan.

In Tierra del Fuego, an invasive beaver population, introduced from Canada to foster a fur industry, has ransacked the island. Without natural predators to regulate their numbers, 20 beavers have become 100,000 since their introduction in 1946. Bold South American gray foxes are also very common here, particularly in montane forests deeper in the island.

RAPA NUI

Rapa Nui is believed to have been covered in low scrub and large *Paschalococos disperta,* a species of palm similar to the Chilean palm. A combination of deforestation caused by humans, the introduction of Polynesian rats, and the arrival of sheep and other domesticated animals to the land in the mid-1800s has resulted in the barren landscapes of today.

There are 30 flowering plants and 16 ferns on Rapa Nui, mostly in the peat bogs of the two main volcanic craters, Rano Kau and Rano Raraku. Introduced bananas, yams, and guavas grow in small plantations. Tropical seabirds, such as the great frigate bird, the yellow-billed masked booby, and the red-tailed tropicbird, with its delicate red tail, can be seen at the Rano Raraku volcano, while sooty tern featured in the annual egg hunt that was part of the birdman cult. In the waters around the island, the critically endangered hawksbill turtle and endangered green turtle are spotted from time to time.

History

ANCIENT CIVILIZATION

The first inhabitants of Chile are believed to have entered from the north, either across the Atacama Desert or the Andes Mountains that divide the country from modern-day Bolivia. The exact date that humans first arrived in Chile remains extremely controversial. Monte Verde, an archaeological site southeast of Puerto Montt, has been claimed as the country's oldest evidence of human settlement. Radiocarbon dating has marked human occupation there to 14,500 years ago.

Other early inhabitants of Chile are known to have been hunter-gatherers, with evidence of human settlement in the very north of Chile dating to 10,000 years ago. They inhabited caves and fertile ravines in the high-altitude plains of the puna of the Norte Grande and began to establish more stable settlements in ravines and oases. At some point, they domesticated guanacos and vicuñas, which allowed the formation of more complex settlements centered on agriculture.

Hunter-gatherer cultures moved up and down the coast, stopping at oases along the Pacific to gather seafood. Later groups such as the Chinchorro (5500-2000 BC) settled along the coast of southern Peru and Chile. They formed small groups and were expert fishers. Mummies uncovered on Playa Chinchorro in Arica have been dated to 5050 BC, which is 2,000 years older than the oldest in Egypt.

In Patagonia, humans arrived somewhere around 12,000 BC, using rock shelters to support a nomadic way of life. In the fjords, sometime around 6000 BC, small nomadic groups began making canoes from tree bark to traverse the rugged coastlines of the region. These southernmost indigenous groups developed into four distinct peoples: the land-dwelling Tehuelche people (the Günakëne and the Aónikenk), the Selk'nam, the seafaring Yaghan, and the Chonos. All had complex spiritual belief systems and hardy oral traditions. They survived some of the world's most extreme conditions until the arrival of the Europeans.

PRE-COLOMBIAN HISTORY AND CIVILIZATION

Hunter-gatherer communities continued to develop along the coast of the Norte Grande and into the Norte Chico. The term *chango* was first used in the 17th century by the Spanish to describe the seafaring people living on the coast between Coquimbo and Copiapó, with the term broadly referring to all maritime groups. Many are thought to descend from the Chinchorro people. These disparate fishing communities subsided on marine resources such as fish, mollusks, and seabirds. They supplemented their diet with land mammals and plants from the coast.

A system of trade operated between the coast and the inland agricultural San Pedro communities (500 BC-AD 1535), who used irrigation systems to grow maize, beans,

quinoa, and squash. They employed llama caravans to traffic goods between the coast and the mountains. They began trading with the Tiwanaku (500 BC-AD 1000), an empire whose political center was the eponymous city on the high-altitude shores of Lake Titicaca in modern-day Bolivia.

During this period, other cultures such as El Molle people (AD 1-600) inhabited fertile valleys south from Copiapó to the Valle de Limarí and developed expertise in stonework. They left behind *piedras tacitas,* stone boulders with cups used as mortars to grind flour from the seeds of the algaroba and *chañar* plants. They were followed by Las Ánimas (AD 600-1000), known as expert metallurgists, using copper to create complex jewelry, and the Diaguita (900-1500), recognized for their symmetrical, geometrical pottery painted in red, black, and white.

Farther south, culture developed throughout the forested Central Valley. The horticultural societies of Pitrén (AD 100-1100) and El Vergel (1100-1450) were the ancestors of the Picunche and the scattered Mapuche. They are thought to have lived a semi-sedentary lifestyle in agricultural settlements and existed alongside the Pehuenche, the Huilliche, and the Puelche. The groups south of the Río Maule resisted being absorbed into the Inca Empire that expanded rapidly through the north of Chile from AD 1470.

Thousands of kilometers from the Chilean mainland, the first settlers of the volcanic island of Rapa Nui arrived by canoe in AD 1200—although this date remains contested, with some scientists arguing it was 400 years earlier. Their journey was long: 2,000 km from other Polynesian islands across the Pacific, perhaps Mangareva or the Marquesas Islands. Using the stars to navigate, they likely located Rapa Nui by following marine birds.

SPANISH COLONIZATION

Portuguese sailor Ferdinand Magellan sailed through the strait that separates mainland South America from Tierra del Fuego in 1520, naming it Todos Los Santos—although it would later come to be called the Strait of Magellan.

Francisco Pizarro arrived in Peru in 1532 with just 200 men and began a prolonged but ultimately successful conquest of the Inca. On the hunt for more gold, his partner, Diego de Almagro, and a 500-strong army of Spaniards and enslaved indigenous people led the first expedition into Chile in 1535. Pedro de Valdivia, a distinguished officer in Pizarro's army, made the second and ultimately successful attempt at colonizing the territory, becoming the governor of Chile in the process. In January 1540, Valdivia and his men set out from Peru and crossed the Atacama Desert, continuing south to reach the banks of the Río Mapocho, where they founded the city of Santiago de la Nueva Extremadura on February 12, 1541. The next nine years saw La Serena and Concepción built along with a handful of forts farther south.

Mapuche Resistance and the *Encomienda* System

Although the Spanish appeared to have pacified the indigenous Mapuche people (dubbed the Araucana by the Spanish), the conquest had yet to be won. The Mapuche, pushed south, were plotting resistance, led by their youthful and fearless leader Lautauro. The Mapuche staged regular attacks on Spanish settlements, but Lautaro was eventually defeated in battle. García Hurtado de Mendoza, governor following the death of Valdivia, flattened much of the Mapuche resistance.

As the suppression of indigenous resistance continued, the Spanish established the *encomienda* system. An *encomienda* was the grant to a conquistador of indigenous people, from whom he could extract labor as payment in return for protecting them. In practice, workers were overworked in a system that was effectively slave labor, particularly as diseases brought by the conquistadores from Europe wiped out thousands of indigenous people.

As the indigenous population declined, the mestizo population, those born of mixed indigenous and Spanish blood, began to grow.

These people were often granted the status of *inquilinos,* granted land to farm while also providing labor as part of the *encomienda.* Later, these developed into self-contained haciendas, estates owned by rich families who continued the use of enslaved indigenous people to provide farm labor.

The system of *encomiendas* was outlawed in 1791 by Governor Ambrosio O'Higgins, who successfully settled indigenous people in small settlements with parcels of land for subsistence farming. Of the estimated 500,000 indigenous residents when the Spanish arrived, only 2,000 are thought to have remained in the Chilean heartland.

Growth of an Economy

During this period, primeval forests were cleared for agricultural land. Chile remained an economic burden to Spain due to its apparent lack of precious minerals. Growth of the new colonies remained modest, but the 17th century saw increasing arrivals of Spanish immigrants. By the end of the century, the population of Chile was 100,000. Charles III's reign (1759-1788) finally allowed direct trade among Chile, Peru, and Spain as well as across the border with what would become Argentina. The United States and Britain followed the French in allowing trade, helping Chile's economy to develop its agricultural and mining industries.

The Role of the Church

As the conquistadores had arrived in Chile, so had Roman Catholic missionaries, set on converting the local population. The Church had major success, although many of those who did convert adopted a syncretistic assimilation of Catholic and indigenous belief systems that remain evident in religious communities in northern Chile.

The Struggle for Independence

The start of the 19th century brought growing discontent among the elite. Revolutionary texts sparked ideas that had been planted after the declaration of independence by the United

States in 1776 and the French Revolution of 1789. The colony's geographical isolation from Spain generated strong national pride, supported by a belief in the richness of the terrain and its potential. This helped to create an increasing sense of national identity among the *criollos*.

Wealthy sergeant major José Miguel Carrera, recently returned from Spain, held revolutionary ideas that prosperity could only be achieved through independence, and so used his family's wealth and connections to stage a military coup in September 1811, installing himself as leader. Among the immediate reforms were widely expanded access to education across the country, the country's first constitution in 1812, and a new Chilean flag.

The Spanish government sent troops to strengthen the defenses in Chiloé and Valdivia with the plan to advance on Santiago and reclaim power. Carrera caused a full-blown civil war when General Bernardo O'Higgins refused to accept the legitimacy of the Carrera military dictatorship. As chaos ensued, the Royalists recaptured the capital. Those in favor of independence were removed and exiled to the remote Juan Fernández Islands.

These decisions were the foundations of the Spanish crown's ultimate downfall, with the brutal reinstatement of Spanish rule convincing Chile's elite to back the cause of independence. They were not alone: Farther north, Simón Bolívar was preparing his army to force independence in Venezuela, a movement that would later spread to the rest of the north of the continent. Across the border in Mendoza, Argentinean general José de San Martín was preparing to embark on his campaign against Spanish forces in Chile and Peru.

In 1817, San Martín sent his troops across the border into Chile, uniting with forces led by O'Higgins, and defeated the Spanish troops at the Battle of Chacabuco on February 12, 1817. Independence was officially declared on the first anniversary of the Battle of Chacabuco, and O'Higgins was sworn in as head of a new government.

INDEPENDENT CHILE
Conservative Rule and Rapid Economic Growth

The success of the years 1830-1870 is generally assigned to Diego Portales, an important tactical figure behind the scenes of the Conservative Party, helping to install authoritarian rule through a series of presidents chosen by the political elite despite the appearance of free elections. Portales's power came to an end when he pushed Chile into war against the newly formed confederation of Bolivia and Peru; he was assassinated by an army battalion in 1837.

Political stability was accompanied by substantial economic progress. Copper and silver mining became the most important sector of the economy. Agriculture in the central heartlands was another key form of employment. Here, wealthy landowners controlled haciendas worked by seasonal laborers. Thanks to this sudden prosperity, rapid developments were seen in transportation, with steamer ships cutting the journey to Europe from three months to 40 days. By 1882 there were 1,900 km of railway.

The War of the Pacific

The collapse of the silver boom in 1873, coupled with that of wheat and copper, threatened to destabilize the government. A fortuitous opportunity presented itself in the form of rapidly increasing nitrate exploitation in the Atacama Desert. However, the nitrate fields were across the border in Peruvian and Bolivian territory, mostly around present-day Antofagasta, then part of Bolivia.

In a treaty, Chile and Bolivia had agreed to share export taxes on nitrate. The treaty was later revised to drop Chile's right to the taxes on the exports; in exchange, Bolivia would not raise taxes on the Chilean companies working in Bolivian territory for 25 years. Bolivia reneged on the deal, increasing taxes in 1878. With Chilean interests at risk, the country occupied the port city of Antofagasta on February 14, 1879, forcing

Bolivia to declare war and bring into the conflict its ally Peru, with whom it had a preexisting alliance.

Chile had the upper hand with superior naval forces and soon took Bolivia's only port, Antofagasta, and continued north, taking the provinces of Tarapacá, Arica, and Tacna, claiming as Chilean territory all of the nitrate fields. Despite attempted mediation by the United States in October 1880, the Chileans pushed farther north, capturing Lima in January 1881. What's now known as the War of the Pacific continued for another two years, with high losses to human life on both sides before it ended on October 20, 1883, when the two nations signed the Treaty of Ancón. This officially ceded control of the province of Tarapacá to Chile, while Bolivia was forced to concede all access to the ocean. At the end of the war, Chile had expanded its territory by a third and gained possession of the nitrate fields, which would account for half of government revenue for the next 40 years.

European Immigration and Civil War

The 1880s saw the election of Domingo Santa María, whose liberal administration oversaw ambitious changes that secularized the government, a decisive reduction in the power of the church. Santa María's presidency also introduced great changes in the ethnic and social makeup of the country. The government began to recruit immigrants to southern Chile to populate areas previously inhabited by hostile Mapuche forces. The area had been "pacified" in the previous 20 years, a euphemism for the brutal massacre of around 100,000 Mapuche people in both Chile and Argentina. Some estimates suggest that around 90 percent of the Mapuche population died during these campaigns. Those who remained were thrown off their land; Mapuche society began to fragment and disintegrate. Immigrants, mostly from Germany, arrived to colonize the land south of the Río Bío Bío, with an average of around 1,000 immigrants yearly in the 1880s. Sheep farmers from England and Scotland colonized the Magallanes and Tierra del Fuego regions.

Reformist José Manuel Balmaceda took office in 1886 and began an ambitious program of construction and social investment. His authoritarian style of rule was increasingly objectionable to the congress, however, especially when he intervened in congressional elections. This act culminated in civil war. The army backed Balmaceda, while the navy backed the congress during a series of battles in Valparaíso, in which the congress would emerge victorious.

The Parliamentary Republic

World War I dramatically disrupted Chile's international trade, which relied heavily on Germany. In the postwar years, the economy fared no better; nitrate mines began to close once synthetic nitrate was invented. Alongside economic stagnation, the growth in the Chilean working class began to pose problems for the congress, which represented only the wealthiest members of society.

Arturo Alessandri Palma was elected president in 1920. He tried to impose ambitious social and economic reform, but the congress resisted, with the government practically grinding to a halt for the next four years. In 1924, a military junta demanded that Alessandri appoint members of the military to the congress, which swiftly passed new legislation to improve the salaries of the military, alongside other social reform legislation that, until then, had been vetoed by the congress. Alessandri resigned and fled to Argentina.

The following year, another coup was sprung, this time headed by General Carlos Ibáñez. Ibáñez sought radical social, economic, and political change. Alessandri was invited to return as president, and he finished his term by drafting a new constitution, which was ratified by the populace. The new constitution legally separated the church and state and included extensive social reform. Animosity between Alessandri and Ibáñez arose; Alessandri once again resigned, and Ibáñez was elected president.

Ibáñez strictly curtailed freedom of the press while embarking on an ambitious program of economic and social reform. This featured progressive themes such as recognizing workers' rights to organize and strike, which brought about a higher standard of living than the country had yet seen. The Wall Street crash of 1929 flattened national prosperity, resulting in high unemployment rates, particularly in the mining industry. Street demonstrations and strikes in Santiago finally precipitated Ibáñez's resignation on July 26, 1931.

Electoral Democracy and Multiparty Governments

The Chilean political system developed into a kaleidoscope of ideologies, with new governments formed by an array of parties spanning extreme left to extreme right. The economy was heavily dependent on the United States, which quickly became Chile's premier trading partner and a key figure in the mining industry.

New political parties developed to reflect the new social makeup. A burgeoning professional middle class saw themselves represented in the Popular Front, a center-left coalition that swept into power in 1938 and focused on industrialization. This was followed by elections of the Radical Party in 1942, who promoted similar policies, plus expansive educational, social welfare, and urban labor reforms. Few of these changes directly improved the lot of most Chileans, who continued to toil in low-paying jobs.

In the 1958 election, faced with the choice between Conservative candidate Jorge Alessandri Rodríguez and Marxist candidate Salvador Allende, the electorate narrowly voted for pro-business Alessandri, who advocated reduced state control over the economy. His policies resulted in rising devaluation and crippling debt, followed by strikes of white-collar workers in 1960.

The election of 1964 saw compulsory voting introduced and the ascendance of the center-right Christian Democrats fronted by Eduardo Frei. Frei pursued a surprisingly progressive program in which he sought to improve efficiency in the copper industry. He granted the Chilean government a 51 percent share of the country's copper companies, beginning a process of nationalization. He also set to work on agrarian reform, seeking to break up unequal land distribution. Over half the land was privately owned agricultural estates farmed by employed peasants; Frei began returning large farms to rural working-class people, significantly reducing poverty.

The direction of Frei's policies began to worry industrialists, while the working class felt like the pace of change was not enough. Into this increasingly fractured sea of political allegiances, Socialist Party nominee and leader of the Popular Unity party Salvador Allende was elected in 1970.

CONTEMPORARY CHILE
Salvador Allende

The election of Allende sent shockwaves throughout the international political system; he was the first Marxist to be elected president of a liberal democracy. The first year of Allende's presidency saw bold socialist reforms aimed at bringing the working classes out of entrenched poverty. He set about raising minimum wages and establishing an ambitious program of investment in public housing, education, and health.

Allende continued the agrarian policies implemented under Frei, but the threat of expropriation caused a decline in agricultural investment and, subsequently, production. Allende fully nationalized the copper mines, but it wasn't enough to counteract the rapid increases in government expenditures. The government deficit soared, leading to inflation that hit 304 percent in August 1973.

Fidel Castro's visit to Chile in 1971 raised fears that the country was beginning a steady descent into communism. As the economy faced dire straits, public protests and labor strikes began in Santiago. Vocal opposition from across the political spectrum grew, amid increasing political polarization and eruptions of violence throughout the electorate.

The Military Dictatorship

On September 11, 1973, under the auspices of General Augusto Pinochet, a military coup deposed Salvador Allende. Official reports claim that when the military forces stormed the building at around 1:30pm that afternoon, they found the body of Allende, who had shot himself; supporters of Allende have long claimed it was an execution at the hands of the military.

No one could have predicted the brutality of the 1973 coup. The immediate aftermath saw thousands of Allende supporters rounded up and detained in places such as the National Stadium in Santiago, which became torture centers. Although exact numbers have never been identified, in the first four months of the coup, 80,000 to 250,000 political prisoners were rounded up by the Dirección de Inteligencia Nacional (DINA, National Intelligence Directorate); many were tortured, imprisoned, forced into exile, or executed. DINA was a secret police service used as a means of political control. The media was used as a propaganda machine for the new regime. Directly following the coup, the congress was dissolved, curfews and restrictions on movement were imposed on the populace, and thousands fled the country.

General Pinochet, who stood as commander in chief of the army, quickly positioned himself as head of state. Pinochet believed that he could save the country from the changes imposed under Allende and reconstruct Chile. His economic policies were led by the Chicago Boys, a group of economists that sought to completely reconstruct the economy.

Between 1974 and 1976, the Chicago Boys' shock treatment policies were implemented. State spending was cut, and tariffs on imports were slashed. The state began dismantling the nationalization enacted under Allende. The consequence of this was the concentration of economic power in a handful of companies; following the sell-off of the state companies, five economic conglomerates controlled over half of the assets of Chile's 250 largest private enterprises.

The impact on the Chilean people was drastic. Wages dropped to half their 1970 level; one-third of the workforce became unemployed. Public investment fell by half, with social welfare becoming increasingly underfunded. But as the 1970s came to a close, high growth rates were recorded, inflation dropped dramatically, and the fiscal deficit was eliminated.

During this period, Pinochet sought to entrench his authority. A referendum asked the populace to vote on whether they supported the regime; officials claimed that 75 percent voted yes. A second referendum was held in 1980 to allow Pinochet to remain in power until 1988, when another referendum would determine whether he continued in power, or whether democratic elections would be called. Officials again claimed that the electorate voted in favor.

Protest and the 1988 Plebiscite

By the early 1980s, a financial crisis and deep depression gripped the country. Social discord and a gathering demand for a return to democracy fueled protests throughout the 1980s, starting with the reformation of political parties in the first half of the decade, giving momentum to the "No" campaign in the national referendum on Pinochet's rule, dutifully held in 1988. Pinochet and his advisers never believed that they might lose. The opposition was victorious, winning 55 percent of a vote that saw 97 percent of the registered electorate participating.

The referendum gave a year until democratic elections would be held. During this time, Pinochet passed a series of laws that altered the composition of the congress and the supreme court and made it impossible for the president to dismiss the commander in chief of the armed forces—a role that Pinochet held until 1998. He also passed laws that would protect him and other members of the military from charges relating to the human rights abuses enacted under his rule.

On December 14, 1989, Patricio Aylwin stood as the candidate for the Christian Democrat party and was backed by parties across the political spectrum under a coalition known as the Concertación de Partidos por la Democracia. He defeated the military-backed candidate Hernán Büchi to be elected president of Chile.

The Return of Democracy

Aylwin took office and began to deal cautiously with the transition back to democracy. He instigated no change to the economic policies that had been pursued over the past 17 years. He was aware of the necessity of managing a delicate balance to prevent the military from interfering in the process of democratic return. Congress prevented him from making sizable changes to the constitution.

One of the first reforms he made was setting up the Comisión de la Verdad y de la Reconciliación (National Commission for Truth and Reconciliation). This independent body sought to investigate the truth of the human rights abuses enacted under the Pinochet regime. Bringing the guilty parties to justice was an entirely different matter, exacerbated by the laws Pinochet had implemented in his final year as head of state.

In October 1998, Pinochet, who was in the United Kingdom for surgery, was arrested on a warrant signed by Spanish judge Báltazar Garzón, issued as part of an investigation into the deaths of Spanish nationals under the dictatorship. The struggle to extradite Pinochet to Spain for trial continued for 15 months, until a British medical team declared him unfit on health grounds to do so.

Returned to Chile, Pinochet was stripped of his immunity for trial by the supreme court and was placed under house arrest in January 2001 on charges of murder and kidnapping. He died in 2006 at age 91, never convicted for any of the crimes he was accused of.

Present-Day Chile

In the early 2000s, a number of right-wing politicians and former military members publicly apologized for their role in the coup. In 2006, Chile gained its first female president, Michelle Bachelet. Bachelet's election was applauded internationally, while her personal history as the daughter of an air force general who was tortured to death in the early years of regime, and who also experienced torture herself, bolstered her image.

In the 2010 presidential election, right-wing billionaire businessman Sebastián Piñera was voted into the presidency. He allegedly invested US$13.6 million in his campaign and became the first elected right-wing leader in 52 years. The first year of his presidency was marked by a series of dramatic natural disasters. On February 27, 2010, an 8.8-magnitude earthquake caused widespread damage in Concepción and a death toll of 500. In August 2010, near Copiapó, 33 miners became trapped in a copper and gold mine. The news garnered international headlines as the struggle to reach and rescue the miners was miraculously achieved after 69 days.

Michele Bachelet was elected for a second term in 2013. She legalized same-sex civil unions in 2015, modified the repressive Pinochet-era abortion laws, and introduced legislation to legalize gay marriage in the final few months of her presidency.

In the 2017 elections, Piñera was elected for a second term. In 2019, an increase in metro ticket prices led to the largest protests since the dictatorship, with over a million people marching on the capital. Issues raised included decades of growing inequality and the constitution, unchanged since Pinochet's rule. Following a month of unrest across the country, in which the government was accused of human rights abuses and investigated by the United Nations, Piñera agreed to hold a referendum on writing a new constitution in April 2020.

Government and Economy

Since the country's first constitution, enacted in 1811, Chile has moved from a presidential authoritarian government to a republic with three branches of power—the executive, the legislative, and the judicial. As of the 1925 constitution, the president, who is head of state and head of government, is elected by popular vote every four years, and this has been the case except for the period following the 1973 coup, when elected president Salvador Allende was removed from office by military leader General Pinochet, whose dictatorship lasted until 1990.

The president can serve a four-year term without the possibility of immediate reelection, but can run for president in the subsequent election. Presidential voting is held with the first round in November, where candidates must secure an absolute majority of over 50 percent of the vote to win. A second round of voting follows in December if no candidate has achieved this, with the newly elected president taking office in March.

The government is highly centralized in Santiago. The Supreme Court, which operates from the Palacio de Tribunales de Justicia in Santiago, is the ultimate judicial authority in the country, with 21 judges appointed by the president following a Senate vote.

The voting age is 18, with all Chileans, except those who have served over three years of prison time, allowed to vote. As of 2014, Chileans living abroad are able to vote in presidential elections. Women gained the right to vote in 1949, while the people of Rapa Nui were only given Chilean citizenship—and thus the legal right to the vote—in 1966.

POLITICAL PARTIES

Following the return to democracy, two main coalitions have formed. These are center-left Nueva Mayoría, which was called Concertación para la Democracia (Consensus for Democracy) until 2010, and the center-right Chile Vamos, known as Alianza por Chile (Alliance for Chile) until 2017. In the 2017 elections, a group called Frente Amplio made political headway, threating to break up the traditional two-coalition system, winning 20 percent in the first round of voting as well as 20 seats in the Chamber of Deputies.

ELECTIONS

The country is divided into 16 regions, denoted by a number. Each region is run by a government-appointed *intendente* (administrator). The regions are subdivided into 56 provinces, administered by a government-appointed *gobernador* (governor). Each province is then divided into *municipalidades* (municipalities) or *comunas* (boroughs), run by an elected mayor and councilors. Each region is divided into electoral districts and senatorial constituencies, which directly elect two deputies and two senators.

The bicameral National Congress is home to 50 members of the Senado (Senate) and 155 members of the Cámara de Diputados (Chamber of Deputies). *Diputados* (deputies) are elected every four years, while *senadores* (senators) have eight-year terms, with all deputies and half the senators elected every four years. A gender quota law was implemented during Bachelet's second term, increasing representation of women in the Chamber to 23 percent and the Senate to 18 percent. Indigenous people, including the Mapuche and Rapa Nui, are poorly represented in both chambers; Rapa Nui has no representatives.

Until 2012, voting was a legal obligation for Chileans on the electoral register, and enrollment was not automatic. Now, all Chileans are automatically registered to vote and voting is voluntary.

POLITICAL ACTIVISM AND PROTEST

Chile has a long tradition of student protest and activism, which paved the way for the return to democracy during the final decade of the military dictatorship. More recently, student protests began in Santiago in 2006, drawing 600,000 to 1 million high school-age student protestors across the country. Their protests called for an increase in the caliber of teaching in high schools. A huge gap in quality between free public schools and private schools continues to exist.

By 2011, these teenagers had forced some political change, with an increase in government scholarships, but led further protests following the election of right-wing president Sebastián Piñera. They marched for free university education. Transport workers and public service workers joined the students in protest; peaceful protests sometimes descended into violent skirmishes with police.

At the heart of these protests were student leaders such as Camila Vallejo, president of the Students Federation of the University of Chile (FECH), who has been compared to the folkloric figureheads previously seen in Chile, such as folk singer and Communist Party activist Víctor Jara.

The 2011 student protests have led to a new wave of left-wing Deputies being elected to congress, with four leaders, including Vallejo, plus Karol Cariola, Giorgio Jackson, and Gabriel Boric, elected in 2013. Jackson and Boric also led the formation of the Frente Amplio, a new political coalition that became the third largest in congress in the 2017 elections.

In October 2019, following a 3 percent hike in subway fares for the Santiago metro, students led a series of protests, which later broke out into mass country-wide demonstrations involving citizens across the entire political spectrum. After 25 days of protests, President Piñera was forced to offer a referendum on writing a new constitution in April 2020, an act that could radically alter the economic and political landscape of Chile. During the protests, 24 citizens were killed and the UN launched an investigation into human rights abuses due to the use of excessive police force.

ECONOMY

The Chilean economy has often been held up as an example of development across Latin America, regarded as one of the region's most stable. Following the return to democracy in 1990, the country has presided over two decades of uninterrupted growth, making it one of the fastest-growing economies in the region.

The country's GDP in 2017 was US$277 billion; it's considered a high-income country. It became the first Latin American country to join the Organisation for Economic Co-operation and Development (OECD) in 2010. Inflation has averaged 3.36 percent in the past five years, while unemployment rates have remained around 6.6 percent in the same period.

Chile has the widest income gap of countries in the OECD, according to a report released in 2015, with the income of the richest 25 times that of the poorest. The minimum wage is exceptionally low, set at $276,000 (around US$410) per month. Between 2000 and 2015, poverty levels dropped from 26 percent to 7.9 percent. Poverty is geographically distributed, with the lowest levels found in Santiago and the Metropolitana region, the thinly populated Aysén and Magallanes regions, as well as mining hubs such as Antofagasta and Tarapacá. The region experiencing the highest levels of poverty is Araucanía, with 17.2 percent living in poverty, almost double the national average, followed by Ñuble (16.1 percent) and Maule (12.7 percent). All are home to large indigenous Mapuche populations.

Saltpeter mining in the territory gained from Peru and Bolivia in the War of the Pacific was an integral feature of the Chilean economy, although the economy suffered a huge shock after artificial nitrate was developed in 1918. Copper mining helped fill the gap in nitrate revenue. It is now the country's largest export, around 50 percent of global exports, with Chile home to three of the six largest copper mines in the world. Mining occurs in 12 of the 16 regions in Chile, with the largest mines in the vicinity of Copiapó in the Norte Chico, around Rancagua in the O'Higgins region, and Concepción in the Bío Bío region. The country is also the largest producer of lithium, with Chile thought to contain 39 percent of South American reserves of the metal.

Modern-day agriculture accounts for 18 percent of GDP in Chile and directly employs 8.3 percent of the country's population. Most output is in the agricultural heartland of the Central Valley. Grapes for eating and for wine as well as cereals and tree and berry fruits such as plums, apples, cherries, nectarines, and blueberries are grown here, accounting for nearly 60 percent of southern hemisphere exports.

Wine is a rapidly growing export market. The first vines were planted in colonial times, but it's only in the past few decades that exports have boomed. Chile has made massive inroads in wine production, with 75 percent of all exported wine now sustainably produced.

Fishing is another industry that has grown substantially in the last few decades. Exports have boomed, particularly from salmon farming, for which Chile is the second biggest producer behind Norway. Around 70,000 Chileans are employed in the industry. Intensive salmon farming takes place in ocean bays in the Lakes region, Chiloé, Aysén, and Magallanes. The 2016 outbreak of *marea roja* (red tide), a toxic algal bloom that impacts bivalve shellfish and poses a deadly risk to human life if affected fish are consumed, lost the industry US$800 million. The industry has also faced criticism for its liberal use of antibiotics, with concerns raised that this could lead to antibiotic-resistant super bacteria.

Tourism is a growing industry in Chile, with revenues reaching US$2.9 billion in 2015; it comprised 10.1 percent of the country's GDP in 2016. Around 9.8 percent of all Chileans are employed in the industry. According to statistics released by the Ministry for Tourism, the number of foreign visitors to Chile reached 6.4 million in 2017, an increase of 900,000 from the previous year. Half of all visitors come from Argentina, but Brazil, Bolivia, and Peru are also key markets. Visitors from the United States make up the next largest group, along with European countries such as France, Spain, and Germany, followed by the United Kingdom, Australia, and Canada. Key destinations receive the lion's share of tourists, including San Pedro de Atacama, plus Parque Nacional Torres del Paine and Rapa Nui.

People and Culture

DEMOGRAPHY

The population of Chile was 17,574,000 in the 2017 census, making it the seventh-most populated country in Latin America. Life expectancy is highest in South America at 79.1 years, with 69 percent of the population of working age. The percentage over 65 has steadily increased over the past three decades and will pose significant problems in health care and pensions in coming years.

The urban population is high, at 87.8 percent, and 40 percent, some 7,400,000 people, live in the Metropolitana region of Santiago, three times the size of the Valparaíso region and the Viña del Mar and Valparaíso conurbation. The rest of the population is mostly directly south, within the O'Higgins, Maule, and Bío Bío regions that form the Central Valley. The most scarcely populated regions are Aysén, with just 103,000 inhabitants, and Magallanes, with 166,000—jointly 1.5 percent of the population on land that makes up a third of Chilean territory.

Chilean society is based around close-knit

family units. Most Chileans view themselves as separate from Latin America, particularly as so many claim European descent, while the relative modernity and European tastes of the country make it feel more European than Latino in many ways.

In the capital and most large cities, time frames are decidedly un-Latin American: Expect transport to always leave on time, and business meetings to be generally timely. In the social sphere, however, fluid timekeeping is normal, and it's not unusual for Chileans to arrive an hour late to a social event.

Chile is a mishmash of ethnicities. In 1882, the Chilean government invited Europeans to populate the southern parts of the country. Waves of Germans came to Osorno, Valdivia, and Lago Llanquihue. They were followed by sheep farmers from England and Scotland, who settled in Magallanes and Tierra del Fuego. Later came people from Croatia, Ireland, Poland, Greece, and Italy. Chilean surnames today bear testament to the wave of immigration.

Indigenous Groups

The population of Chile is predominantly mestizo, of mixed Spanish and indigenous descent. In the 2017 census, respondents were asked if they "identified as indigenous," with 12.8 percent of the Chilean population responding in the affirmative. Of this number, 79.8 percent (some 1,745,000 people) identify as having Mapuche origins. The next largest indigenous populations are Aymara (7.2 percent) and Diaguita (4.1 percent).

CHILEAN MAPUCHE

The Mapuche people of Chile survived the brutal "pacification" campaign of 1861-1883, when an estimated 100,000 people in both Chile and Argentina, 90 percent of the Mapuche population, were killed in efforts to bring the region under Chilean rule. As a result, the community lost most of its ancestral lands.

A 1979 law encouraged the Mapuche to divide communal lands into private plots, but this resulted in many selling their land to agribusinesses. Now, one-third of the Chilean Mapuche population lives in Santiago. Small, rural Mapuche communities also exist in pockets in the foothills of the Andes and along the coast in the Bío Bío, Araucanía, and Los Lagos regions, some of the country's poorest areas. Levels of poverty in Mapuche communities are higher than the Chilean average.

Mapuche communities in rural areas are primarily patrilineal groups of kin living on private land through subsistence farming. Some communities are opening to tourism, while others focus on cultivating crops to be sold at local markets. The community is organized around the *lonko,* an elected chief, who leads decision making in political and day-to-day spheres, while the *machi,* a shaman, leads in areas of religion and medicine.

The Mapuche are known for their expertise with livestock, emerging as leading horse and cattle traders during the 17th-18th centuries. They are also expert silversmiths.

OTHER INDIGENOUS GROUPS

The **Aymara** people are another of Chile's major indigenous groups, inhabiting the northernmost regions of Arica and Parinacota, Tarapacá, and Antofagasta, from the lowland valleys to the high-altitude altiplano. They are directly descended from the Tiwanaku people (AD 500-1000), who were incorporated into the Inca Empire. Their religious beliefs assimilated Christianity into their existing religion, which is particularly visible during religious festivities held throughout the Norte Grande.

The **Diaguita** people inhabit the Huasco and Choapa river valleys of the Coquimbo region in Norte Chico, mostly in rural settlements. The Diaguita primarily work in agriculture, growing surpluses that are sold at local markets. Similar to the Aymara, they celebrate hybrid Catholic-indigenous religious festivities, which feature traditional deities such as Yastay, the guardian spirit of animals that is believed to appear as a guanaco.

Farther south, tiny populations of **Yaghan** and **Kawésqar** peoples still remain. Their languages and history are being preserved in sensitive museums about the original Patagonian cultures, such as the Museo Martín Gusinde in Puerto Williams.

Across the Pacific, the **Rapa Nui** people number around 9,000, most of whom live on Rapa Nui (Easter Island). After being annexed by Chile in 1888, Rapa Nui was used for sheep grazing; the indigenous population was forced to live on only a small portion of the island until 1953. It took until 1966 for the Rapa Nui to be granted Chilean citizenship.

WOMENS' RIGHTS

Chile is often held up as the most progressive Latin American country when it comes to attitudes toward women. In many ways, however, attitudes remain highly conservative, with women allowed few rights within marriage and in the workplace.

Feminist movements grew during the 1980s under the slogan *"democracia en le país y en la casa"* (democracy in the country and in the house) and sought to challenge traditional patriarchal power in politics and society. Women earn, on average, a third less than men. Many of the largest industries in Chile (mining, finance, and construction) remain dominated by men. The burden of child-raising and caring for the elderly falls to women.

Chilean laws against abortion remain among the most punitive in the world. Reform to allow for abortion in the case of rape or when the mother's or fetus's life is at risk was introduced in 2017 by President Michele Bachelet.

New bills protecting women against violence and defining sexual violence as a form of torture were introduced during Bachelet's second term as president. High-profile student protests led by women such as Camila Vallejo, president of the Students Federation of the University of Chile (FECH), have helped to forward the cause of gender equality. Over half of all university admissions are

women, and a growing range of women are participating in political and other public positions.

IMMIGRATION

Immigration has increased steadily in the last two decades, at a faster rate than in any other Latin America country, with a third of all immigrants undocumented. Chile's relative stability and prosperous economy have attracted immigrants from Peru and Bolivia, while the last decade has also seen a growing number of Colombian, Venezuelan, and Haitian immigrants, the latter following the 2010 Haitian earthquake, when Chile offered residency permits and visas to those fleeing the catastrophe. Sadly, Haitian immigrants face increasing hostility and racism from Chileans.

In the final few months of her second presidential term, Michele Bachelet attempted to loosen Chile's restrictive immigration policies, but few of her plans were ultimately implemented. An increasing politicization of immigration fueled anti-immigrant sentiments in the 2017 presidential election, with far-right independent candidate José Antonio Kast calling for physical barriers along the borders with Peru and Bolivia. After his election, President Piñera stated that he favored tighter border controls.

The government has also faced criticism for offering free flights to Haitian immigrants in 2018, under the stipulation that they cannot return to Chile within the following nine years and must take their family with them—an act that migrant groups labeled as "forced deportations."

LGBTQ RIGHTS

Homosexuality has been legal in Chile since 1993, although in reality attitudes toward gay people have only begun to change noticeably in the past decade. Same-sex civil unions have been legal since 2015. Michele Bachelet sought to legalize gay marriage and the rights of gay couples to adopt children in the final few months of her presidency, although the bill has yet to be passed by the congress.

Discrimination against gay people is illegal in Chile. Laws came into place following the murder of a young gay man in March 2012, which sparked protests and forced the country to face up to its conservative attitudes. However, discrimination and acts of violence against gay people remain common.

RELIGION

Roman Catholicism arrived with Pedro de Valdivia and his men in the 16th century, shaping both the architectural and social geography of the country. The wooden churches of Chiloé, a product of the Jesuits and Franciscans, are matched in beauty by the stunning colonial churches of Santiago and those in other towns and cities throughout the country.

Religion has had a strong influence on social norms. Divorce was only permitted in 2004, while reform of the abortion laws in 2017 faced fierce religious backlash. Religious belief in Chile has dropped in the last two decades: 64 percent of Chileans identified as Catholics in 2017, compared with 74 percent in 1995. Those who define themselves as atheists now comprise 25 percent.

Despite the falling number of believers, Catholic festivals still pull large audiences, with pilgrims advancing on Andacollo in the Coquimbo region for the Fiesta de la Virgen de Andacollo December 24-26, and the largest religious pilgrimage and festivity in the country, Fiesta de La Tirana, July 12-16 in the Tarapacá region. Unlike other Catholic countries in Latin America, Semana Santa (the week before Easter) is not an important religious festival.

Indigenous Religious Beliefs

Chile's indigenous populations maintain their own religious beliefs. The Mapuche people are noted for their focus on a supreme being known as Nguenechén, the main creator god, although four other main deities are often invoked in Mapuche rituals, led by *machi* (Mapuche shamans), who are generally female.

In the north of the country, Andean pantheistic beliefs of the Aymara are still present, although syncretism prevails, with many indigenous and Catholic traditions and belief systems now mixed, as seen in the dances of the pilgrims to the religious festivals held in Andacollo and La Tirana.

LANGUAGE

Spanish is the official language of Chile, although many words show roots in other languages, including Aymara, Quechua, Mapudungun, and English, reflecting the country's varied ethnic and linguistic makeup. Many of the indigenous people in Chile are bilingual. Communities such as the Mapuche now offer bilingual Spanish-Mapudungun schools to ensure the survival of the language. Schools nationwide with more than 20 percent indigenous students must include indigenous languages in their curriculum. On Rapa Nui, many people also speak their native Polynesian-influenced language, also called Rapa Nui.

THE ARTS

The Chilean arts scene is best known for its contributions to poetry through two Nobel Prize-winning poets, Gabriela Mistral and Pablo Neruda.

Literature

Chile has a strong tradition of poetry, starting with conquistador Alonso de Ercilla y Zúñiga (1533-1592), who described the war against the indigenous Mapuche people and the bravery of the chieftain Caupolicán in his epic poem *La Araucana*.

The Chilean poetry scene rose to prominence four centuries later with Gabriela Mistral (1889-1957), the country's first Nobel laureate in 1945. Her lyric poetry was associated with the aspirations of the Latin American working class. Despite being an influence on Chile's second Nobel laureate, the markedly more famous Pablo Neruda, Gabriela Mistral has been comparatively ignored by the Chilean populace. This could be due to her status as a woman or the fact that her work as an educator and her quiet, modest lifestyle less captured the imagination of the country than the more provocative Neruda.

Pablo Neruda (1904-1973) is Chile's most famed poet, winning recognition in 1971 for his work that includes *Cien sonetos de amor* (*One Hundred Love Sonnets,* 1959)—written to his third wife, Matilde Urruti—and the epic poem *Canto General* (*General Song,* 1950).

Born into a coal-mining family in the Bío Bío region, Gonzalo Rojas (1917-2011) is another Chilean poet that has risen to greater international prominence in the past few decades. His lyrical poetry focused on sensuality and eroticism, as well as the plight of women and others affected by the 1973 military coup. He was awarded the Chilean National Literature Prize in 2002 and the Cervantes Prize in 2003.

The most famous Chilean author is Isabel Allende, who was born in 1942 in Peru to Chilean parents and later worked as a journalist in Chile before being forced to flee to Venezuela after the death of her uncle, Chilean president Salvador Allende, in 1973. Her best-known work is *La casa de los espiritus* (*The House of Spirits,* 1982), a novel in the magic realist tradition that touches on the political and social history of Chile and which propelled her into the spotlight. She is the world's best-selling author in Spanish.

Perhaps the most notable of contemporary Chilean authors, having garnered attention in New York and international literary circles, is Roberto Bolaño (1953-2003), who won various prizes for his novels *Los detectives salvajes* (*The Savage Detectives,* 1998) and *2666,* published posthumously in 2004 and now considered a modern masterpiece. He has been described as the leading Latin American writer of his generation.

Antonio Skármeta won the Premio Iberoamericano Planeta-Casa de América for his novel *Los días del arco iris* (*The Days of the Rainbow,* 2011). His unpublished play *El Plebiscito* was the basis of Pablo Larrain's 2012 film *No,* about the success of the "No" campaign in the 1988 referendum on the Pinochet dictatorship.

Visual Arts

The earliest visual art in Chile is found in the preserved remains of pre-Columbian ceramics, such as the *jarro pato* (duck-shaped pitcher) and tricolored geometric pottery of the Diaguita people in the Norte Chico, now found in the Museo Arqueológico de La Serena and the Museo Chileno de Arte Precolombino. Scattered cave paintings and petroglyphs also survive thanks to the aridity of the Atacama Desert in the Norte Grande.

Ecclesiastic art followed the arrival of the conquistadores. Examples of early Jesuit artistry can be found at the Museo de Arte Colonial inside the Iglesia de San Francisco in Santiago.

Prominent foreign artists whose work influenced Chilean art include Afro-Peruvian José Gil de Castro (1785-1841), who painted portraits of many of Latin America's independence heroes, such as Bernardo O'Higgins and Ramón Freire, and portrayed the transformation from colony to independence. English landscape and seascape painter Thomas Somerscales (1842-1927) also contributed work detailing the War of the Pacific during his 23 years in Valparaíso.

The most internationally recognized Chilean artist is the late surrealist painter Roberto Matta (1911-2002). Of the same era, Carlos Sotomayor (1911-1988) stood at the forefront of South American neocubism. Sculptor Rebeca Matte (1875-1929) is prominently featured, alongside Matta, in the Museo de Bellas Artes in Santiago.

The capital has more museums dedicated to contemporary art than fine art, including the Museo de Artes Visuales and the two branches of the Universidad de Chile-run Museo de Arte Contemporáneo. Also in Santiago are graffiti murals with roots in the 1940s murals of Mexican muralist David Alfaro Siqueiros in the Escuela México in Chillán and 1960s-1970s political protests. Neighboring Valparaíso is even better known for its strong tradition of graffiti, with the cobbled streets of Cerro Alegre and Cerro Bellavista a product of the Museo a Cielo Abierto, an open-air museum of murals featuring Roberto Matta and other modern Chilean artists.

Art has also found it ways onto streets in Chile. Calle Bandera, a pedestrianized street in downtown Santiago, was transformed by Chilean visual artist Dasic Fernández and architect Juan Carlos López with the installation of a four-block-long mural painted onto the asphalt in 2017, depicting the history of Chile from pre-Colombian times to the future. Art installations in other parts of the country include Mario Irarrázabal's *Mano del Desierto (Hand of the Desert)* outside Antofagasta.

Architecture

The country's oldest buildings reflect its colonial roots, with those in downtown Santiago evidencing the 16th-century neoclassical style of the period. Many, such as the Palacio de la Moneda and the Catedral Metropolitana, were the work of Italian architect Joaquín Toesca. Famed French architect Gustave Eiffel left his mark in the Gothic cast-iron Catedral de San Marcos in Arica.

The Norte Grande is further influenced by foreign architecture, most evident in the use of Oregon pine, brought by boat from the United States to construct elegant balconied Georgian and Victorian mansions in late 19th- and early 20th-century Iquique.

In the Bío Bío and Araucanía regions, traditional Mapuche architecture is experiencing a revival, with thatched *rukas* (traditional Mapuche house) finding new life as overnight lodgings for curious travelers. Farther south, in Puerto Varas and Frutillar, German influences can be noted in the shingled *alerce* housing.

Jesuit missionaries reached Chiloé in 1608 and traveled extensively among the archipelago's inhabited islands, building shingled wooden churches that fused European architectural styles and Chilote building techniques. Of the original 150 structures, 16 are now UNESCO World Heritage Sites. On the same islands, *palafitos* (stilted houses), built precipitously over the edges of bays and harbors, also reflect a unique feature of Chilote architecture. Many have been restored and repurposed as boutique hotels and restaurants.

Santiago reflects a fusion of modern and historic architecture. Many contemporary buildings in the city center are utilitarian in style, although green and sustainable buildings using cutting-edge technology are beginning to appear, particularly in the financial district. Chilean architect Alejandro Aravena has made waves for his approach to reinventing social housing in cities such as Iquique, for which he won the prestigious Pritzker Prize in 2016.

Music and Dance

Chile's musical tradition is in the folkloric Andean-influenced music of Nueva Canción Chilena (New Chilean Song Movement) of the 1950s and 1960s, a reflection of the rural-urban migration across the country, which saw indigenous and other rural people mixing their distinctive musical traditions with those rooted in European culture.

This movement was spearheaded by folk singer Violeta Parra, joined by her son Ángel Parra, Víctor Jara, Patricio Manns, and Rolando Alarcón, and spread throughout Argentina, Uruguay, and the United States. The genre became an outlet for protesting political oppression and was formative in the emergence of *peñas,* cultural centers where folk music was performed. The folk band Inti-Illimani ranks as the most internationally famous of the Nueva Canción, incorporating traditional Andean instruments such as panpipes, the Andean flute, and *charango* (a string instrument similar to the mandolin). The dictatorship gave birth to a new genre of protest music, spearheaded by 1980s punk group Los Prisoneros, who courted controversy by criticizing the socioeconomic structures of the dictatorship.

More contemporary Chilean bands include the hugely successful rock band La Ley, who won a Latin Grammy Award for best group album in 2001, while their contemporaries Los Tres experienced popularity across Latin America. Hip hop artist Ana Tijoux was nominated for a Grammy in 2010 for her album *1977*. Classical performers have included child prodigy Claudio Arrau (1903-1991), a classical pianist who studied at the Stern Conservatory of Berlin and went on to perform throughout Europe and the United States.

With roots in colonial rural Chile, the *cueca* is the ubiquitous Chilean dance. It depicts the courtship of a rooster and a hen, as the two dancers—one male, one female—move in circles around one another, their gazes fixed. It was adopted under the dictatorship, making it, for many years, inexorably associated with repression. Women who lost a son or partner to the dictatorship would create the *cueca sola*, a solitary version of the dance performed in protest, often without music.

Cinema and Theater

The Chilean film industry first found its feet in the 1960s, with the first ever Festival del Nuevo Cine Latinoamericano (Festival of New Latin American Cinema) held in Viña del Mar in 1967. It was followed by integral films from the new genre, including urban drama *Tres tristes tigres* (*Three Sad Tigers*, 1968) by Raúl Ruiz, experimental social drama *El xhacal de Nahueltoro* (*The Jackal of Nahueltoro*, 1968) by Miguel Littín, and the social realist *Valparaíso mi amor* (*Valparaiso, My Love*, 1969) by Aldo Francia.

Following the fall into military rule, many Chilean filmmakers were forced underground or into exile. The documentaries of Patricio Guzmán chronicled the violent overthrow of the Allende government, finding international acclaim with the three-part *La batalla de Chile* (*The Battle of Chile*, 1975-1979). This was later followed by *El caso de Pinochet* (*The Pinochet Case*, 2001), about Pinochet's detention in London, and *Salvador Allende* (2004), which followed the president from his election campaign to the military coup that saw him lose his life. The return to democracy allowed the industry to flourish once more, although it took until 1995 before the creation of the Film School of Chile provided training to would-be filmmakers.

Among the most prolific of recent years is Oscar-nominated director Pablo Larraín, whose film *No* (2012) charted the role of the "No" campaign in the 1988 referendum that removed Pinochet from power. His first foray into English-language film was *Jackie* (2016), a biographical drama about Jackie Kennedy. His anti-biopic of poet Pablo Neruda, *Neruda* (2016), was also nominated for a Golden Globe.

Other important films produced in recent years include the black-humor *Taxi para tres* (*Taxi for Three*, 2001) by Orlando Lübbert; Andrés Wood's *Machuca* (2004), which follows the social turmoil and repression in the wake of the military coup; and the tragicomedy *Mi mejor enemigo* (*My Best Enemy*, 2005), by Alex Bowen, which explores the 1978 Patagonia conflict between Argentina and Chile. *Una mujer fantástica* (*A Fantastic Woman*, 2017), directed by Sebastián Lelio, about a transgendered woman living in Santiago, won the Academy Award for Best Foreign Language Film in 2018 among a string of other international accolades.

Chile's theatrical history is far longer than its cinematic, although the industries suffered the same repressive fates under the dictatorship. Theaters were widespread during the 19th-20th centuries, built in the nitrate towns of the Norte Grande by the entrepreneurial British owners of the fields. The 21st century saw vanguard and experimental theater in the works of playwrights Luis Alberto Heiremans and Egon Wolff. During the military regime, the satirical group Ictus continued to perform.

The return to democracy has allowed Chilean theater to flourish, in the form of puppetry company La Troppa and the Gran Circo Teatro, influenced by founder Andrés Pérez's time working for the prestigious French theater company Théâtre du Soleil. Santiago A Mil is an annual performing arts festival that attracts national and international acts.

Handicrafts

Chile has a strong tradition of handicrafts, many with deep roots in indigenous traditions. One of the best places for an introduction to the myriad artisanal styles across the country is at the Museo de la Artesanía Chilena in Lolol in the O'Higgins region. This museum showcases typical crafts, most of which you can only find in the small communities that make them.

The Mapuche people are known for their exceptional silverwork. Thick llama and alpaca wool sweaters are made by Aymara weavers in the altiplano of the Norte Grande. Artisans on Rapa Nui make an extensive selection of hand-carved stone and wood *moai.*

Delicate dyed *crin* (horsehair) is fashioned into jewelry and ornaments in the hamlet of Rari in the Maule Region, while *mimbre* (wicker) furniture and baskets are more widespread, encountered in various communities in the O'Higgins region and the Mapuche communities of the Central Valley. Lapis lazuli, a metamorphic rock prized for its intense blue color and only found in a handful of sites on earth, is featured in jewelry and sold in craft markets around the capital. Pottery also takes many forms, reflecting the continent's long-held ceramic traditions, with Pomaire near Santiago famed for its earthenware tableware and lucky three-legged piggy banks. Combarbalá in the Coquimbo region is the only place in the world where you can find the semiprecious volcanic *combarbalita.* Artisans carve ornaments out of the stone.

SPORTS

The country is dominated by a love of football (soccer). The international squad, known as La Roja (The Reds) won the Copa América in 2015, although they failed to qualify for the 2018 World Cup. Chile hosted the World Cup in 1962 and came in third, behind Czechoslovakia and winner Brazil.

All cities and towns have their own clubs. Colo Colo from the Santiago area of Macul, named after a Mapuche leader, are the country's most successful football team, having won the Copa Libertadores de América in 1991, with another Santiago team, Universidad de Chile, biting at their heels. Deportes Puerto Montt, the team based in Puerto Montt, is the world's southernmost professional football team.

The Chilean rodeo is a national sport that takes place in rural parts of the Central Valley in corrals known as *medialunas.* Chilean cowboys, known as *huasos,* herd calves before audiences as large as 50,000 during the annual Campeonato Nacional de Rodeo in Rancagua.

The Chilean polo team has seen a successful few years, defeating the U.S. national team to become world champions in 2015. The Chilean team features members of the prominent viticulture family Silva, who own the Casa Silva wine empire in the Valle de Colchagua.

Tennis is an increasingly important sport in Chile, thanks to the inroads achieved by Marcelo Ríos, who became the first Latin American player to be ranked number one in the ATP rankings. He is followed by Nicolás Massú, who won gold in singles at the 2004 Olympic Games alongside silver medalist Fernando González, who went on to win gold in the doubles, plus silver again in Beijing four years later. Rowing is also becoming an important sport, with strong rowing programs in Santiago as well as cities such as Concepción, Valdivia, and Valparaíso. The 2007 Pan American Games in Río de Janeiro saw the country win a gold medal in the sport.

Indigenous sports still prevail in Mapuche communities. The traditional Mapuche game *palín* is similar to hockey, using a curved wooden stick and ball. It is played alongside ritual celebrations and ceremonies and was declared a national sport in 2004.

Essentials

Transportation

GETTING THERE
Air

Most visitors land in Chile at **Aeropuerto Internacional Arturo Merino Benítez** (SCL, tel. 2/2690 1752, www.nuevopudahuel.cl) in Santiago, which has extensive domestic connections. There are also some flights from neighboring South American countries to **Aeropuerto Internacional El Tepual** (PMC, V-60, tel. 65/2294 161, www.aeropuertoeltepual.cl) in Puerto Montt and **Aeropuerto Internacional Presidente Carlos Ibáñez del Campo** (PUQ, Km

20.5 Ruta 9, tel. 62/2238 282) in Punta Arenas. Planes from Tahiti in French Polynesia fly weekly to **Aeropuerto Internacional Mataveri** (IPC, Av. Hotu Matu⬚a, tel. 32/2210 0237) on Rapa Nui (Easter Island).

For the best deals on flights, avoid the Christmas-New Year period, when many Chileans fly to North America and Europe for the holiday season. The week leading up to and after Independence Day celebrations (Sept. 18-20) is also a peak period for flights and sees increased airfares. Flying just before holiday seasons, or during the shoulder seasons of November and March, can lead to much cheaper deals.

FROM NORTH AMERICA

American Airlines has nonstop flights to Chile from Dallas-Fort Worth, Miami, and Los Angeles. **LATAM** has the most nonstop flights between the United States and Santiago, from Chicago, New York City's JFK, Los Angeles, San Francisco, and Miami. **Delta** operates nonstop flights from Atlanta. **Avianca** has flights via its Colombian hub, Bogotá, from Boston, Fort Lauderdale, Miami, New York, Orlando, and Washington DC. **Air Canada** operates a flight from Toronto to Santiago via Buenos Aires.

FROM CENTRAL AMERICA

Aeroméxico operates nonstop flights from Mexico City. Panama-based **COPA** flies nonstop to Santiago from Panama City.

WITHIN SOUTH AMERICA

LATAM has 10 daily flights from Lima and a daily flight from Cusco, both in Peru; there are also multiple daily flights from Buenos Aires and Mendoza, plus daily departures from Córdoba, in Argentina. LATAM also operates nonstop flights from São Paulo and Rio de Janeiro in Brazil and La Paz, Bolivia. **Sky Airline** operates similar, less frequent flights to the same destinations,

except Peru. Budget carrier **JetSmart** has irregular flights to Mendoza, Buenos Aires, Córdoba, and Lima. **COPA** also has a variety of Santiago-bound flights, departing various cities in Colombia, including Bogotá, as well as Quito, Ecuador. Colombia's **Avianca** operates direct flights from Bogotá. Using 19-passenger Twin Otter light aircraft, **Aeriovías DAP** have flights between Ushuaia, Argentina, and Punta Arenas and Puerto Williams.

FROM EUROPE

Most flights from Europe operate through Madrid via **Iberia** or **LATAM. Air France** flies nonstop from Charles de Gaulle in Paris to Santiago, while **Alitalia** flies nonstop from Rome. **KLM** serves Santiago nonstop from Amsterdam, while **British Airways** flies from London's Heathrow. **Air Europa** flies to Santiago from Madrid with a connection in Buenos Aires, while **Lufthansa** runs flights from Frankfurt, connecting in São Paulo.

Overland

Arriving overland is an easy option for travelers thanks to frequent good-quality bus service crossing the border between Argentina and Chile, with a handful from Peru and Bolivia. One of the most common entry points to Chile is one of the five daily buses between Mendoza, Argentina (9hr), and Santiago via Los Libertadores tunnel.

Other popular border crossings from Argentina include Salta to San Pedro de Atacama (12hr) via the Paso Jama in the Norte Grande; the scenic journey from Bariloche to Pucón (5hr) or Temuco (9hr) via San Martín de los Andes at Paso Mamuil Malal; and the bus between El Calafate and Puerto Natales (5-8hr) via Paso Río Don Guillermo. There are also private minibus services that connect El Calafate directly with Parque Nacional Torres del Paine. Small minibuses also operate between Esquel and Futaleufú via the

Paso Futaleufú, although service drops significantly outside summer.

The northernmost entry point is via the Paso Chacalluta (24 hr daily) from Tacna in Peru, arriving either by bus, shared taxi, or the scenic twice-daily **Ferrocarril Arica-Tacna** (Av. Comandante San Martín 799, no phone) passenger train (1.25hr). Shared taxis, which leave when full from Tacna's **Terminal Terrestre Internacional** (Hipólito Unanue s/n, tel. 052/427 007), are the most efficient, if marginally more expensive, method.

From Bolivia, buses leave La Paz for Arica for the scenic high-altitude route through the Paso Chungará and Parque Nacional Lauca. Don't underestimate the impact of high elevation; consider breaking up the journey with a few days in Putre.

Fit cyclists with minimal luggage should have few issues crossing most borders, but keep in mind that many of the central and northern border crossings are at high elevation. The crossing between El Chaltén in Argentina and Villa O'Higgins, both in Patagonia, is only passable by bicycle or on foot.

You can find information about the state of the roads, plus open hours of border crossings (many of which close overnight), on the up-to-date government border crossing website (www.pasosfronterizos.gov.cl).

Sea

A handful of cruise ships dock at Chilean ports, primarily in Valparaíso and farther south in San Antonio. **Australis** (Av. Bosque Norte 440, Santiago, tel. 2/2840 0100, US tel. 800/743-0119, www.australis.com) operates adventure cruises that pick up and drop off passengers in Punta Arenas and Ushuaia, Argentina. Speedboats from Ushuaia connect daily with Puerto Williams, across the Beagle Channel on Isla Navarino.

GETTING AROUND
Air

For those with time constraints, Chile's extensive domestic air service is the most efficient,

and increasingly the most economical, means of covering large distances, with internal flights all under three hours. International and domestic carrier **LATAM** continues to dominate the field and flies the most modern planes; budget carriers **Sky Airline** and extremely low-cost **JetSmart** offer excellent affordable flights. Most trips between the south and the north of the country require a layover in the capital.

Santiago is the country's major international and domestic hub. Internal flights operated by domestic carriers LATAM, Sky Airline, and JetSmart depart from the domestic wing of the airport. Domestic departures generally only require you to be in the airport 1.5 hours before takeoff.

Within Patagonia, **Aeriovías DAP** operates flights between Punta Arenas and Porvenir, Puerto Williams, and Coyhaique. Rapa Nui is only accessible by air; all domestic flights are operated by LATAM.

If you visit San Pedro de Atacama, Puerto Natales, or Rapa Nui during the December-February high season, it's essential to book flights well in advance, as seats sell out and prices rise significantly. Outside these months, flights can be booked only a couple of days in advance, although prices are generally cheapest a few weeks out.

Bus

For destinations within 6-8 hours of Santiago, long-distance buses can save you hassle and are often faster than flying. These buses are surprisingly comfortable. Taking overnight buses can save on lodging costs.

Long-distance travel is normally in spacious buses, with the vehicle's speed displayed on an electronic screen at the front of the bus, tagged to a buzzer that sounds if the driver goes over the speed limit. Bus crashes in Chile are rare but occasionally occur, and the Chilean police pull over buses for impromptu security checks.

Recommended companies include **EME Bus** (http://emebus.cl), **Buses ETM** (http://etm.cl), **Cruz del Sur** (www.busescruzdelsur.

cl), and **Turbus** (http://turbus.cl). Turbus has the widest range of destinations. Most cities have a central *terminal de buses* (bus terminal), also known as the *terminal rodoviario*, although many cities have multiple terminals from where different regional, long-distance, and even rural services depart. Larger bus companies sometimes have their own terminals.

When you arrive at a bus terminal, you'll likely be surrounded by touts hoping to entice you into buying a seat on their bus, but you should continue to the official ticket booths to buy your ticket. Aim to buy a ticket a few hours in advance or the day before. Fares are normally fixed and generally rise on weekends and during national holidays, such as the Independence Day celebrations in mid-September, Christmas-New Year, and Semana Santa (Easter Week).

When buying a ticket, you have the option to choose between *semi-cama* (seats with a 140-degree recline), *salón cama* (seats with a 160-degree recline and a retractable leg and foot rest), and, increasingly, *salón premium* (seats that lie fully flat, occasionally with an individual screen). *Salón cama* and *premium* seats are wider and more spacious; cushions and a blanket are often included. For some overnight buses, an evening meal of a sandwich and a drink, plus a simple breakfast, are included in the fare; double-check when you purchase your ticket to see what's included.

All buses should have a working restroom and television screens—although you have no choice in the movie, and it's more than likely that it'll be dubbed into Spanish. The films are switched off at some point to allow you to sleep. Eye masks and earplugs can help guarantee a good sleep, and you'll want a layer or two in case the air-conditioning is on full blast. Bring snacks and water, as the bus won't stop for provisions during the journey.

In the bus terminal, keep a firm eye—and hand—on all of your belongings. On the bus, bulky items will be checked into the luggage storage underneath, and you should receive a bag claim ticket that you'll need to show when you arrive at your destination. Never place any valuables in your checked luggage, and don't put your onboard items in the overhead compartment; keep all valuables in a bag either underneath your feet or attached to your person to ensure that nothing gets stolen while you sleep.

Local buses that shuttle between rural destinations often depart from the *terminal rural*. They are often crammed with people, produce, and occasionally livestock. Pay for your ticket on the bus; a card in the window should indicate the bus's destination.

Rail

From its heyday of 1,900km of railway in the late 1800s, Chile now has a massively reduced rail network that's used by increasingly fewer people. A handful of commuter trains operate in the Central Valley, connecting Santiago with Rancagua and towns all the way to Chillán, with the antique **Buscarril,** the final remaining narrow-gauge *ramal* train in the country, running from Talca to Constitución at the coast. All are operated by the Empresa de los Ferrocarriles del Estado (EFE), also called **Tren Central** (http://trencentral.cl). While the route is scenic, the speed of the service doesn't compare with the myriad bus companies running the same routes.

Public Transportation

Within cities, public transport is often the fastest way of getting around. In Santiago, the **metro** (http://metro.cl) is an exceptionally efficient and cheap means of traveling around the capital, although it can become unpleasantly crowded during peak hours (7:30am-9am and 6pm-8pm Mon.-Fri.), particularly along Línea 1. Keep belongings zipped away and bags where you can see them; pickpockets are rife, especially when the metro is full. To ride the metro, you need a rechargeable **Tarjeta BIP** (http://tarjetabip.cl) that can be purchased for a small fee and refilled at the booths inside the metro and around the city at convenience stores with "BIP" signs, or you buy single-use tickets.

BIP cards also work for public buses. Plan to use Google Maps for route planning, as there's rarely any information at bus stops indicating where they go. In Santiago, many of the bus drivers go very fast; the driving in other cities across the country can be decidedly worse. Everywhere but Santiago, you pay the bus fare directly to the driver upon boarding. Bring small change and plan on paying the exact fare.

Taxis colectivos are shared taxicabs that drive a set route along which they pick up passengers; they are often faster than the bus, costing a few hundred pesos per journey. Their route is generally indicated on a sign on the roof. The free **Moovit** app and **Google Maps** can help with route information in most cities in Chile.

Car and Motorcycle

Driving in Chile is very safe by South American standards. Motorists in the capital drive aggressively; you'll need nerves of steel to survive Santiago's roads. Access roads connecting the city's main arteries are rarely well signed, and it's easy to miss a turn because you're in the wrong lane. Be aware of one-way streets, which can pose a navigation headache.

Getting around Santiago and other busy urban areas is significantly easier with the use of a navigation app like Waze. Parking on streets is normally permitted and administered by attendants in high-visibility jackets carrying portable ticket machines.

ROAD RULES

For any of the biggest highways in Santiago, a complex toll system is in place, and charges are made through a TAG transponder attached to your windshield. Rental cars picked up from the capital should have this preinstalled, although you'll need to confirm whether the charges are included in your rental fee. Using your own vehicle with foreign plates, you can buy a day pass online through **COPEC** (http://pdu.prontocopec.cl) for CH$6,800 or at COPEC gas stations on the approach to the city. You can buy day passes up to 20 days after your journey.

Peajes (tolls) are imposed at regular intervals along the Pan-American Highway and other major highways. They can cost up to CH$5,000, so be sure to bring plenty of cash; credit cards are not accepted, but large bills are fine. Fuel pumps and service stations exist at regular intervals and offer modern restrooms, snack shops, and fast-food restaurants.

The speed limit on expressways is 100-120km/h. *Carabineros* (police) armed with radar guns are common. If caught speeding, you can be fined (CH$35,000) and have your driver's license confiscated, with the requirement to attend a court hearing in the region where you received the fine.

Carabineros checking for speeding and erratic driving are very commonplace in the wine region. Note that there is zero tolerance on drinking and driving; you are not permitted any alcohol in your system, and it's not worth the risk of being caught.

The *carabineros* often stop drivers for routine document checks. Always pull over if requested. Make sure to have a copy of your passport, the *permiso de circulación* (vehicle registration document), and driver's license handy. It is advisable to bring an International Driving Permit. Be friendly and do as you're asked. Don't try to bribe a police officer.

During winter in Santiago, to combat high levels of air pollution, *restricciónes vehicular* (vehicle restrictions) are imposed to stop a certain portion of the city's vehicles from running for a day. This is determined by the final digits of the vehicle's license plates. Restrictions are announced the day before on the website www.uoct.cl.

CAR RENTAL

Rental cars are relatively inexpensive in Chile compared with other South American countries. You'll find the cheapest places to rent cars are hubs such as Santiago, Puerto Montt, Punta Arenas, and Antofagasta. International rental companies have offices throughout the country. Smaller companies can occasionally offer cheaper deals, but they tend to be less reliable. Always shop around for prices. You must be minimum age 25, although some companies allow as young as 21.

Prices start at CH$22,000 per day for a compact car; always confirm that the price includes the 19 percent IVA (value-added tax), insurance, and unlimited mileage. Rental cars from more remote destinations such as Coyhaique on the Carretera Austral and San Pedro de Atacama can start at CH$100,000 per day. One-way fees, where you return the car to a different office than where you picked it up, can end up costing as much as the basic rental price.

Your insurance will likely require you to pay a substantial deductible in the event of an accident, which can range US$500-2,000. You will generally be required to pay a deposit using a credit card, ranging CH$500,000-800,000. Most international companies offer roadside assistance; this is rarely the case for smaller local companies. Along the Carretera Austral, you may struggle to get insurance for cars that aren't 4WD—double-check this when you rent. There is no insurance available for vehicles on Rapa Nui; you must pay for any damage sustained to the vehicle or inflicted on another vehicle.

Ensure that the car comes with its *permiso de circulación* (vehicle registration document) and the *revisión técnica* (MOT certificate), generally stored in the glove compartment. If crossing into Argentina with a rental vehicle, you need the necessary paperwork and insurance; this should be organized through your rental company at least 10 days in advance and generally costs CH$80,000.

The **Automóvil Club de Chile** (http://automovilclub.cl) can provide services such as roadside assistance to members of its foreign counterparts, such as the American Automobile Association (AAA) and the British Automobile Association (AA).

You can rent camper vans from a number of companies across the country, including Pucón-based **Chile Campers** (www.chile-campers.com), Punta Arenas-based **Andes Campers** (tel. 9/4237 4562, http://andescampers.com), and Santiago-based **Condor Campers** (tel. 9/5675 6432, http://condorcampers.com). For RVs, look up Santiago company **Holiday Rent** (Santa Marta de Liray 15-2, tel. 2/2409 4185, http://holidayrent.cl) and Santiago- and Punta Arenas-based **Chile Motor Homes** (tel. 9/9743 3141, http://chilemotorhomes.cl).

ROAD CONDITIONS

Roads are well maintained throughout the country. The Pan-American Highway, also known as *La Panamericana,* Ruta 5, or *El Longitudinal,* offers a speedy and efficient means of getting from the very north of the country down to the southern end of Chiloé in the Lakes region.

Potholes can be a serious issue on smaller rural roads, many of which become *ripio* (compacted gravel) or even dirt as you get farther from Ruta 5. Many don't require a 4WD vehicle, although heading into the mountains or the altiplano, it's a wise investment, as river crossings or dreadfully potholed roads can present serious concerns to drivers. Make sure you have a spare tire. Fortunately, most towns and villages have workshops dedicated to tire repair, and you'll likely be able to find a local mechanic who can get you back on the road. Look for signs reading *"Vulca"* or *"Vulcanización."*

The annually updated Rutas de Chile map, published by COPEC and available in most of their gas stations, indicates—with general accuracy—the current state of roads throughout the country. Always carry extra fuel or a *bidón* (fuel container) if heading into remote areas, such the Carretera Austral in Aysén and the Norte Grande, as gas stations can be few and far between; you can normally ask for one from your rental company. Extra water and warm layers are also a good idea.

Within towns and cities, keep an eye out for *lomos de toro* (speed bumps), which can be poorly signposted and can cause significant damage if hit at full speed. Be aware of livestock when driving at night in rural areas; stray dogs appear regularly on main roads.

Boat

A truly Patagonian experience is journeying on one of the local ferries that carve their routes through the disjointed network of fjords in the south of Chile, with some sections of the discontinuous Carretera Austral linked by boat connections. Farther north in the Lakes region, a number of passenger ferries offer scenic transport through narrow lakes to connect with the Argentinean border, including Lago Pirihueico and Lago Todos Los Santos, as well as the scenic one across Lago General Carrera between Puerto Ibáñez and Chile Chico in Aysén.

One of the finest ways to see Chilean Patagonia is by boat. The comfortable **Navimag** (Diego Portales 2000, Puerto Montt, tel. 2/2869 9900, www.navimag.com) has twice-weekly passenger and vehicle transport from Puerto Montt to Puerto Chacabuco (24hr) and to Puerto Natales (3 days). The no-frills **Naviera Austral** (Empresa Portuaría, Agelmí 1673, tel. 600/4019 000, www.navieraustral.cl) runs different routes, including Puerto Montt to Chaitén (12hr) and Quellón to Puerto Chacabuco (31hr).

More remote routes include the *Yaghan* from Punta Arenas to Puerto Williams via the desolate, wildlife-rich channels surrounding Tierra del Fuego and the glacier-hung Beagle Channel operated by **Transbordadora Austral Broom** (Terminal de Ferry Tres Puentes, Punta Arenas, tel. 61/2728 100, www.tabsa.cl) and the similarly isolated route between Puerto Natales and Caleta Tortel, also operated by **Transbordadora Austral Broom** (Av. Pedro Montt 605, Puerto Natales).

Bicycle

Adventurous cyclists covering the length of Chile on two wheels are an increasingly common sight on the country's roads. In Patagonia, it's easy to set up camp on any unattended land—although if you do see the owners, be courteous and ask for their permission. In other parts of the country, you can generally find campsites or hostels where you can pitch your tent for a minimal fee.

Cyclists will want to avoid cities, where there are rarely cycling lanes (except in Santiago, where a network is developing), as well as the Pan-American Highway, particularly on stretches on the outskirts of Santiago, which can see high volumes of aggressive traffic; high-visibility clothing and lights are essential, as is a good helmet.

Along the Carretera Austral, one of the country's most popular cycling routes, both touring bikes with fat tires and mountain bikes work well on the gravel roads. Any of the smaller side roads in other parts of the country also demand thick tires. Stock up on water and food at every possible opportunity. A tent is essential, as you cover many long stretches of road without the prospect of finding lodging.

Calle San Diego in Santiago sells inexpensive, reasonable-quality used bikes; for new bikes, **Mall Sport** (Av. Las Condes 13451, http://mallsport.cl) is a good option. Companies rent bikes in Santiago, and there are plenty of new and used bike sellers in Coyhaique in Aysén for the Carretera Austral. You will struggle to find spare parts outside Santiago and other large cities, so bring a repair kit with you from home.

Some bus companies allow you to transport your bike, although many don't. It's sometimes possible to include them as luggage for free on airlines.

Hitchhiking

Hitchhiking is the transport method of choice for most young Chileans, as it's the cheapest means of travel, used by many people in remote communities with little public transport. Hitchhiking is generally considered safe in Patagonia and particularly along the Carretera Austral. It has become so popular here that, December-February, there is stiff competition among backpackers for a lift, and many find themselves waiting for hours.

Preparing for a Chilean Road Trip

With its sprawling network of roads and marvelous diversity of terrain, a road trip is a fine way to explore Chile, particularly as some of the country's most beautiful spots can be laborious to reach on public transport.

- Check that the car comes with a *permiso de circulación* (vehicle registration document) and the *revisión técnica* (MOT certificate). These are normally stored in the glove compartment, and the rental company should indicate them to you during the initial vehicle inspection.

- If you cross the border, make sure you have a copy of all insurance policies for the car (this includes mandatory third-party insurance). Also, rental cars need a special permit to be taken abroad, organized by the rental company at least 10 days in advance.

- If you pass through Santiago, check that your car has a working TAG transponder. If not, you can buy a Pase Diario online or in big COPEC stations when approaching the city. This can be bought up to 20 days *after* you used automatic toll roads.

- Try to avoid Chilean holidays or high season. Traffic will increase considerably, and airports and bus terminals are much busier.

- If you travel to the mountains, it is mandatory to bring tire chains. On the most popular roads in fall-winter, there are *carabineros* checking that you have them. Although you may think you don't need them, weather can change dramatically in the Andes, and a sunny day can turn into a snowstorm quickly. Ski rental shops offer chains for rent, and it is also safe to rent them from the opportunistic entrepreneurs on the sides of mountain roads. Usually, their presence means there will be a police control farther up.

- If you cross the Andes to Argentina or Bolivia, check the working hours of the border stations, as they may close without warning if there is bad weather, particularly June-September. The busiest stations have Twitter accounts that update on the condition of the roads.

- A GPS receiver or a downloadable map that doesn't require an internet connection, such as Maps.me, is essential for navigation.

- Bring a phrase book to help communicate with local people, who probably won't speak much English; the *carabineros* definitely won't.

- Ensure your vehicle has a spare tire, as flat tires can be common on unpaved roads.

- Avoid picking up a car in one place and dropping it off in another; one-way fees can double the cost of the rental.

- Your insurance will likely require you to pay a substantial deductible as liability in the event of an accident, such as damage, theft, or write-off, which can be US$500-2,000. Before departing your home country, you can find insurance policies that cover your deductible in the event that you have an accident.

- Keep warm clothes, spare food and water, and extra fuel in your car at all times, particularly if you're heading into the mountains or remote areas. A cell phone with a local or international SIM card is a good idea in case of emergency.

The Valle de Elqui is another top hitchhiking destination.

If you hitchhike, it's best to do so in groups of two, and no more than three. It is generally not an issue to hitchhike as a woman alone, but it's best to travel with a companion.

Always get out of the vehicle if you ever feel unsafe. Attempt to get rides as early as possible in the day so that you don't find yourself stuck in the middle of nowhere as night falls. Always bring plenty of food, water, and warm clothing. It may be worth bringing a tent in case you wind up on the side of the road overnight. Drivers don't expect payment, but appreciate conversation in return for the lift.

BORDER CROSSINGS

Crossing between Argentina, Peru, or Bolivia and Chile is generally very straightforward. On each side of the border are offices where officials process passports and, upon entry into Chile, provide you with a PDI receipt, indicating the date and time of your arrival. You must keep this paper slip, as it is required to exit the country. If you lose it, you can get another copy for free at the office for the **Departamento de Extranjería y Migración** (Eleuterio Ramírez 852, Santiago, tel. 600/4863 000, http://extranjeria.gob.cl, 8am-2pm Mon.-Fri.); take your passport.

Crossing with your own vehicle or rental car, be sure to have all the necessary documents at hand and be aware that you can't cross into Argentina or into Chile with fresh fruit, vegetables, or meat and dairy. If you don't declare such items, you can receive hefty fines. Be aware that most borders close overnight.

Bad weather, particularly in winter, can close the high-elevation Andes border crossings. Many stay open throughout the year. This information can be found on the Chilean government's border crossing website (www.pasosfronterizos.gov.cl).

Visas and Officialdom

PASSPORTS AND VISAS

Entering Chile is straightforward, and citizens of the United States, Canada, European countries, Australia, and New Zealand do not need a visa for visits of fewer than 90 days. You may be asked to show a return ticket when checking in for your flight.

As of 2014, the *tasa de reciprocidad* (reciprocity fee) previously imposed on citizens of Canada and the United States has been withdrawn. However, Australians must still pay US$117, and Mexicans US$27, in U.S. or Chilean cash on arrival at the international airport in Santiago. The desk is before you reach immigration and customs.

If you overstay, you will be charged a fee per day, and you will not be allowed to leave the country until it has been paid. It's not a great idea to do this if you plan to return to Chile someday; you may be prohibited from future entry. Far easier is to cross the border into a neighboring country and return the next day, a practice known as "border hopping," or to extend your 90-day entrance permit by another 90 days with a visit the **Departamento de Extranjería y Migración** (Matucana 1223 or Fanor Velasco 56, tel. 600/4863 000, http://extranjeria.gob.cl, 8:30am-4pm Mon.-Fri.). You'll need to make a reservation for an appointment online (http://reservahora.extranjeria.gob.cl/ingreso) and should take your passport (and a photocopy) and the PDI slip given to you at the border, plus US$100 in Chilean pesos.

CUSTOMS

Upon arrival at Santiago's airport and at all land border crossings, customs agents scan and search bags to check for illegal drugs and edible products of animal origin, as well as flowers, fruits, and vegetables. There are often drug- and food-sniffing Labradors in operation, which you should avoid petting, regardless of how cute they are. You must declare if you are carrying in excess of US$10,000 in cash. You are permitted to bring duty-free items of up to US$500 value.

EMBASSIES AND CONSULATES

The **United States Embassy** (Av. Andrés Bello 2800, Las Condes, tel. 2/2330 3716, outside office hours tel. 2/2330 3000, http://cl.usembassy.gov, 8.30am-5pm Mon.-Fri.)

is in Las Condes in Santiago, a few blocks northeast of the Costanera shopping mall. Nonemergency services require an appointment, which can be scheduled online through its website. For updates on security or emergency situations in Chile, sign up for the Smart Traveler Enrollment Program (STEP) on the **Bureau of Consular Affairs website** (http://step.state.gov).

The **Canadian Embassy** (Nueva Tajamar 481, Torre Norte, Piso 12, Las Condes, tel. 2/6523 800, http://chile.gc.ca, 8:30am-12:30pm and 1:30pm-5:30pm Mon.-Thurs., 8:30am-1pm Fri.) is in Santiago. In an emergency,

call the **Emergency Watch and Response Center** (tel. 613/996 8885) in Canada collect.

The **British Embassy** (Av. El Bosque Norte 125, Las Condes, http://gov.uk/world/organisations/british-embassy-chile, tel. 2/2370 4100, 9am-1pm and 2pm-5:30pm Mon.-Thurs., 9am-1pm Fri.) is two blocks north of the Tobalaba metro station in Santiago. The **Australian Embassy** (Isidora Goyenechea 3621, 12th-13th Fl., tel. 2/2550 3500, http://chile.embassy.gov.au, 8:30am-12:30pm Mon.-Fri.) is also in Santiago; 24-hour assistance is available by calling the **emergency helpline** (tel. 2/6261 3305).

Recreation

NATIONAL PARKS AND RESERVES

Chile's protected areas cover 15 million hectares, around 21 percent of the country's territory. Some of the 39 national parks, 48 national reserves, and 16 national monuments are hard to reach and understaffed by the Corporación Nacional Forestal (CONAF), the private not-for-profit agency partially funded by the government, which administers them. Most are well connected with public transportation and roads for private vehicles.

Admission fees are charged on entry and always in cash; credit cards and foreign currency are not accepted. Children pay a reduced fee. Parks are generally open year-round with reduced hours during winter and occasional closures for poor weather at high elevation, such as Parque Nacional Nevado Tres Cruces in the Atacama Region, or those with high levels of snow such as Parque Nacional Radal Siete Tazas and Reserva Nacional Altos de Lircay. Parque Nacional Torres del Paine, home to the popular W and O treks, is open during the winter, but visitors must enter with a registered guide to do any hiking.

Some parks have campgrounds administered by CONAF or by a concessionaire.

Except at Torres del Paine, it is easy to turn up without booking in advance, although some popular parks, such as Parque Nacional Huerquehue near Pucón and Parque Nacional Pumalín Douglas Tompkins near Chaitén on the Carretera Austral, should be reserved in advance in January-February, as they are popular during these months with Chilean tourists.

Visitor numbers to Parque Nacional Torres del Paine have skyrocketed from 144,000 in 2010 to 265,000 in 2017. Those planning on camping in the park at an official campground must make online reservations in advance, at least three months ahead for December-March. At the time of writing, the park was also trialing an online system for purchasing entrance tickets; this may well become the norm for all visitors.

Fires are not permitted in national parks or reserves, so bring a gas stove if you plan to cook. Stoves are sometimes restricted to certain areas to prevent wildfires. Parks work on leave-no-trace principles, so take all rubbish out with you.

Offices with CONAF rangers are in cities across Chile, while park headquarters staffed by rangers are in each of the parks and reserves. Staff are generally very helpful and can offer maps, detailed hiking routes, and other information.

The **Santiago CONAF office** (Paseo Bulnes 265, 1st Fl., tel. 2/2663 0125, www. conaf.cl, 9:30am-5:30pm Mon.-Thurs., 9:30am-4:30pm Fri.) can provide information about regional offices. The website (in Spanish) has detailed information about open hours, costs, and logistics of getting to each of the different parks and reserves.

SURFING

With 4,270km of coastline along the brusque, chilly Pacific Ocean, it is no surprise that Chile is a surfing destination. Some of the most popular waves are at the chilled surfing hangout of Pichilemu, three hours south of Santiago; these include Chile's longest wave, the 800-meter break at Playa La Puntilla, best March-November, and six-meter swells at the steep left point break at Punta de Lobos, widely regarded as one of the country's best surfing spots.

The north of the country has warmer waters and sizeable waves. La Serena is home to beginner waves on its long, sandy main beach, plus a right-hand point break at **Punta de Teatinos,** 7km north. Nearby **Totoralillo** is best for advanced surfers March-June.

Iquique is a spot for beginners at **Playa Brava** and pros at **El Colegio** and **La Bestia.** Arica also has its share of top surf. **Playa Brava** promises consistent surf, while **El Gringo** vies with Punta de Lobos for the best surfing spot in the country.

RAFTING AND KAYAKING

Southern Chile is characterized by gushing rivers, feeding both agriculture and kayak and rafting enthusiasts. The Futaleufú River beside Futaleufú in the Aysén Region has 47 rapids and world-class status, plus plenty of excellent rafting outfits, many operated by U.S. expats. The nearby River Espolón has excellent conditions for kayaking, particularly for beginners. The main season for both

is November-March; the highest water levels and most hair-raising rapids are in March.

Farther south, kayaking on Río Cochrane or Lago General Carrera through the kaleidoscopic-hued marble caves is also an option. There is also kayaking and rafting along Río Petrohué, just above the Saltos del Petrohué near Puerto Varas, and Río Liucura, just outside Pucón. You can also kayak to the foot of glaciers in both Parque Nacional Torres del Paine in Magallanes and Parque Nacional Los Glaciares across the border in Argentina, or paddle on unique multiple-day kayaking expeditions downstream from Lago Grey in Torres del Paine to Puerto Natales. Most operators only function November-April, closing for winter. Year-round you can kayak through the sunken forest of Chepú in Chiloé while bird-watching and spotting giant river otters.

There are various spots across the country for sea kayaking, including to visit sea lion colonies close to Chaitén in Aysén and in the Beagle Channel with agencies in Puerto Williams.

SCUBA DIVING

Scuba diving is done off Rapa Nui, where a replica *moai* lies on the ocean floor and you can swim to coral and caves. Visibility is up to 60 meters on a very good day, but the marinelife isn't spectacular, although the region is known for its wealth of fish species and the chance to spot leatherback and hawksbill turtles.

FISHING AND FLY-FISHING

Chile is one of the world's foremost destinations for freshwater fly-fishing, with serpentine rivers teeming with trophy-size rainbow, brown, and brook trout, heavy chinook salmon, and sea-run varieties. Due to the remoteness of many rivers, fish are plentiful and it's relatively easy for beginners. Fish rise for dry flies such as mayflies, caddis, and stoneflies, all of which are similar to those used by anglers in the western United States, meaning it's not necessary to invest in new equipment.

Patagonia's abundant waters offer world-class fly-fishing mid-November-mid-April, with optimal conditions for dry fly-fishing January-mid-March. Top locations include lodges along the Carretera Austral for rivers such as the Palena, Rosselot, Figueroa, and Yelcho, plus Lago Rosselot and Lago Yelcho, all near La Junta. On the outskirts of Coyhaique, the Simpson, Mañihuales, Ñirehuao, and Cisnes Rivers guarantee extensive catches. In Tierra del Fuego, the rivers surrounding Lago Blanco and Lago Fagnano, such as the gushing Río Grande, are also considered strong destinations for fly-fishing, with even less competition from other anglers.

Independent fishing guides can be organized from nearby towns such as La Junta and Coyhaique, as well as in a handful of other destinations in the Lakes District, but most anglers opt to stay in fishing lodges, which general cater to a moneyed crowd; expect to spend US$4,500-7,000 for a week-long package that includes your guide, lodging, meals, an open bar, and transfers.

Fishing is on a catch-and-release basis and you'll need a license (CH$35,000 per year). Lodges can help you obtain one or buy it online, or find a full list of shops selling them on the **Servicio Nacional de Pesca** (http://pescarecreativa.sernapesca.cl).

WILDLIFE-WATCHING

Despite lack of access to the Amazon rainforest, Chile has a surprising wealth of endemic wildlife and opportunities to observe it. In the far northern Arica and Parinacota region, a popular day trip (although a few nights' stay in Putre is far better for acclimatization) is to the high-elevation Parque Nacional Lauca on the border with Bolivia. Flocks of flamingos are here year-round, although February-March is when the birds arrive to breed, along with 130 other bird species. On the arid plains of the Reserva Nacional Las Vicuñas, Darwin's rheas and rust-colored vicuñas live alongside chinchilla-like viscachas.

Off the shores of Punta Choros, northeast of La Serena, 25,000 Humboldt penguins, 80 percent of the global population, breed during the summer on the islets of the Reserva Nacional Pingüino de Humboldt, with observation boats leaving regularly from two harbors in Punta Choros. It's also likely to spy bottlenose dolphins here. Farther north at Chañaral de Aceituno, a dozen species of whale frequent the waters November-mid-April, although local tour agencies such as **Orca Turismos** (tel. 9/9640 4844, turismosorca.cl) that take you on the water claim 90 percent likelihood of spotting a whale mid-January-March.

In Chiloé, kayaking tours through the sunken waterways of Río Chepú with **13 Lunas** (Los Carrera 855, Ancud, tel. 65/2622 106, http://13lunas.cl) or the brackish waters of Lago Cucao with **Palafito Trip** (tel. 9/9884 9552, http://palafitotrip.cl) offer the opportunity to spy southern river otters.

Despite being the country's most visited protected area, Parque Nacional Torres del Paine remains one of the best places to spot pumas. Luxury lodge **Awasi Patagonia** (tel. 2/2233 9641, US tel. 1/888 880 3219, www.awasipatagonia.com) leads puma-spotting tours in the park and in the newly inaugurated **Awasi Puma Foundation,** with restored grasslands for pumas to roam. Wildlife experts **Far South Expeditions** (Manuel Señoret 610, Punta Arenas, tel. 61/2615 793, www.farsouthexp.com) also lead puma- and bird-spotting tours in the park as well as extensive bird and wildlife tours throughout the Magallanes region. Most operate November-April, although trips to the remote, bird-rich Juan Fernández Islands leave year-round.

From Punta Arenas, **Transbordadora Austral Broom** (Terminal de Ferry Tres Puentes, Punta Arenas, tel. 61/2728 100, www.tabsa.cl) operates 220-passenger ferries to Isla Magdalena, home to a 120,000-strong Magellanic penguin colony that breeds here November-March; **Solo Expediciones** (José Nogueira 1255, Punta Arenas, tel. 61/2710 219, www.soloexpediciones.com) has smaller boats and lands at alternative times to the big crowds.

On the western shore of Chilean Tierra del Fuego, Bahía Inútil is home to a small king penguin colony, best visited by rental car or through operators based in Punta Arenas. Humpback whales feed in the waters of Parque Marino Francisco Coloane in the Strait of Magellan and can be reached with the marathon 12- to 14-hour tour operated by **Solo Expediciones** (José Nogueira 1255, Punta Arenas, tel. 61/2710 219, www.soloexpediciones.com) from Punta Arenas. A more leisurely option is a three-day trip with experts **Fitz Roy Expediciones** (Roca 825 Oficina 3, Punta Arenas, tel. 61-2613932, www.expedicionfitzroy.com) or **Far South Expeditions** (Manuel Señoret 610, Punta Arenas, tel. 61/2615 793, www.farsouthexp.com) November-late April.

Food

If you don't consider Chile among South America's top culinary destinations, Santiago and other places will come as a surprise. Chile's modest culinary culture is characterized by homemade or bistro-style cooking rather than extravagant gourmet cuisine. While the standard of food is generally good, you need to know where to go to avoid getting a dud meal.

Santiago is awash with increasingly high-end dining options, and you can easily find prices comparable with Europe and pricier U.S. cities. That said, tiny local-frequented eateries remain a firm feature of Santiago's dining culture, and it's possible to find undiscovered no-frills options serving excellent food.

Meals

Breakfast consists of *marraqueta* bread, cheese, ham, avocado, and in parts of the Lakes region and Aysén with German roots, *kuchen* (fruit crumble tarts), plus instant coffee and tea. Milk is often a luxury addition, while fresh fruit is not common.

Once is a light meal comparable to supper, sometimes eaten in late afternoon. Cafés get packed in late afternoon for cakes, coffee or tea, and sandwiches or toast with avocado—a meal that looks similar to a standard Chilean breakfast.

Lunch is normally available noon-3pm, and dinner 7:30pm-11pm. In most restaurants, a two- or three-course *menú del día* (lunch menu), occasionally with a drink included, is the most affordable means of dining out and normally allows you to sample traditional dishes.

In rural areas, a typical lunch menu will include a starter of soup followed by beef, chicken, or fish with rice and a salad. A staple on the table in most restaurants and offered with bread to start is *pebre,* a spicy salsa normally made from pureed herbs and chopped tomatoes, onion, garlic, and chili peppers, although it rarely carries much heat.

Traditional Chilean Food

Picadas are a Chilean institution and a solid option for lunch or an evening meal. These small family-run restaurants, normally down a backstreet, are frequented by locals from all walks of life. The appeal is the focus on good-quality and affordable traditional Chilean dishes. *Picadas* are usually famed for a specific type of food or drink. You can find them throughout towns and cities.

TYPICAL DISHES

Heavy seafood stews and delicately grilled fish are the norm along the coast. Inland, beef and chicken *cazuelas* (stews made with chicken or beef mixed with vegetables and potatoes) are common. A traditional campesino dish throughout the Central Valley is *pastel de choclo* (minced beef and potato casserole topped with corn), but be aware that in some parts of the country, it's finished with a heavy sprinkle of sugar—an acquired taste.

SANDWICHES

Churrascos (thinly sliced steak sandwiches) are a popular lunchtime meal, with many *sangucherías* (sandwich shops) specializing almost exclusively in them. They are usually served in *pan amasado* (homemade bread) or *marraqueta* (crispy bread roll), with additional fillings of *palta* (avocado), tomatoes, *porotos verdes* (green beans), and even sauerkraut.

The **lomito** is another popular type of sandwich made with sliced pork, avocado, tomato, and mayonnaise. **Fuentes de soda,** small typical restaurants with limited seating, normally around a horseshoe-shaped bar where the food is prepared, are the conventional homes of these two traditional dishes.

MEAT

Widespread across the country, **parrillas** or **asados** are steak houses, where Argentinean or U.S. cuts of meat are seared over an open grill or barbecue. The cuts are different than you might be accustomed to; the best are *ojo de bife* (rib-eye), *entrañas* (thin, tender skirt steak served *a punto*, medium rare), and, if available, *lomo vetado* (rib-eye off the bone). Meat is normally served alone, with sides available that include *puree de papa* (mashed potato, sometimes mixed with *merkén*), *papas fritas* (fries), or salads. Steak is usually consumed *tres cuartos* (pink).

In Patagonia, the most traditional dish is *cordero asado* or *cordero al palo* (spit-roasted lamb) cooked over an open wood fire, with some restaurants having specially designed areas where you can watch the lamb being roasted.

Longanizas, dense sausages similar in texture to Spanish chorizo, are the sausage of choice in Chile and originate from Chillán, although they are normally available in steak houses up and down the country.

SEAFOOD

Caletas (harbors) are a great place to sample fish and shellfish dishes, although high-end restaurants serving primarily fish are found in most coastal towns and cities. Traditional dishes include *pastel de jaiba* (crab casserole with breadcrumbs and parmesan), sometimes made with *centolla* (king crab) in Chiloé, Punta Arenas, and Puerto Williams, as well as *machas a la parmesana* (razor clams baked in their shells with grated parmesan). *Reineta* (southern ray bream), *congrio* (conger eel), and corvina, all with white meat, are the fish usually found on menus, most often grilled, or in the case of *congrio,* deep-fried and served with rice, salad, or fries, and sometimes all three. It's conventional to enjoy seafood with a pisco sour aperitif, followed by a glass of sauvignon blanc or chardonnay.

Reineta is the most commonly used in ceviche, a dish similar in taste to Peruvian ceviche but with blanched red onions, finely diced chilis, *merkén* (Chilean smoked chili pepper), and lemon juice; you can find it sold in small plastic containers at fish markets or down by the harbor.

Chiloé also has its own regional dishes, mostly seafood, including **curanto,** as well as *longanizas* and dumplings, the region's most famous dish, traditionally cooked in a hole in the ground to feed a dozen or more; you're more likely to find it cooked in a large pot known as an *olla*. For the best experience, try the traditional cooking method on a tour with a local company or at one of the restaurants in Chiloé, most only open January-February. They also make delicious fried *milcao* (potato dumplings filled with pork rinds), which serve as a snack or even for breakfast, smeared in honey.

SNACKS

Empanadas are a favorite among Chileans, normally for a light lunch or afternoon snack. The most traditional is *empanada de piña* (short-crust pastry shell filled with minced beef, gravy, onions, a solitary olive, and half a boiled egg); *empanada de queso* (short-crust pastry filled with cheese) is also popular. Deep-fried *empanadas fritas* are delicious and come filled oozing with cheese *(empanada de queso)* or shellfish *(empanada de* *mariscos).* Find street vendors selling empanadas throughout the big cities and at most corner shops; in Santiago, the best are from Tomás Moro, widely sold throughout the city. For shellfish empanadas, *caletas* (harbors) along the coast are where you'll find the freshest, juiciest ones.

BEVERAGES

Common drinks include *mote con huesillo,* a sugary, clear, nonalcoholic nectar flavored with cinnamon and a dried peach and mixed with *mote* (husked wheat), sold by street vendors in summer. Pisco sours are popular, made from Chilean **pisco** (grape brandy) and mixed with sugar syrup, lemon juice, and ice—unlike in Peru, they don't add egg whites, which means less risk of contracting salmonella.

Chicha, generally made from apples, tastes similar to noncarbonated cider, although it is normally nonalcoholic. Chilean craft beer or *cerveza* is increasingly popular, with small microbreweries and gastropubs around Santiago, in cities in the Lakes District such as Valdivia, along the Carretera Austral, and in Patagonia. Wine, produced in the country's dozen wine regions, is on the menu at all restaurants, although the best selection is at high-end restaurants or those specializing in wine. Sweet wine is also mixed into the lethal *terremoto,* which translates directly as "earthquake" and combines *pipeño* (sweet wine) with grenadine, pineapple ice cream, and occasionally a slug of extra pisco or fernet. It's enthusiastically consumed during the Independence Day celebrations in September.

A decent cup of coffee is hard to find, as most hotels, even high-end ones, use instant. There is a burgeoning coffee movement spearheaded by small specialty coffee shops in hip hubs such as Santiago, Puerto Varas, and Castro. To get coffee with milk, ask for *café con leche.* In the south of the country, some Chileans drink *mate,* the more traditionally Argentinean caffeinated drink.

Vegetarian Options

Vegetarian food is growing in presence across the country, and you're now more than likely to find entirely vegetarian—and occasionally even vegan—restaurants in the cities and even some towns. Most restaurants have vegetarian dishes as an option, although these can sometimes be as uninspired as iceberg lettuce salad with a handful of vegetables. *Menús del día* rarely include vegetarian options.

Accommodations

Lodging standards in Chile are generally very high compared with the rest of the continent. That said, smaller towns and villages often have very basic shoestring lodgings. Practically all hotels include free wireless internet, although in rural areas the signal strength can be variable. A small selection of the most luxurious hotels in remote locations have opted for full internet detox or only offer connection in communal areas rather than bedrooms. Breakfast is generally included, although the quality and scope vary significantly; hotels generally offer a buffet, while in very low-budget accommodations, expect bread, butter, and jam.

English-speaking front desk staff are the standard in most lodgings in Santiago and other tourist hot spots such as San Pedro de Atacama, Puerto Natales, Pucón, and Rapa Nui. Outside these areas, it is the exception. Rates are generally charged per room, although you can occasionally ask for discounts for single travelers in a double room.

Central heating is rare. Even in the coldest parts of the south, electric, kerosene, or gas heaters tend to be the only means of keeping rooms warm; others rely on the warmth of woodstoves in other parts of the building. International chains and top-end hotels and an increasing number of midrange options include air-conditioning units, some of which double as heating in winter.

Note that *moteles* are sex hotels, and are not geared toward travelers.

VALUE-ADDED TAX EXEMPTION

Theoretically, all visitors to Chile for fewer than 60 days are exempt from paying the Impuesto al Valor Agregado (IVA, value-added tax), the 19 percent normally applied to hotel rates. If you pay in foreign currency (usually U.S. dollars) or with a foreign-issued credit card, you should be exempt from the tax. In practice, your lodging must be registered with the Servicio de Impuestos Internos (Internal Tax Service) for this to be the case; many small and medium-size accommodations are not, and so you won't get this exemption. Many accommodations only accept foreign currency, not credit cards, for you to be exempt.

Either way, the system is complicated, and there's no guarantee that the lodging you've booked—unless they make it very clear on their website—is playing by the rules. Always ask whether IVA is included in your rate, and ask for a discount if you are paying with a credit card or foreign currency. You will need to prove you are a foreigner by showing your passport and the PDI slip issued when you entered the country; most lodgings accept a photocopy of these two items for their records.

MAKING RESERVATIONS

Reservations are essential for travel December-February, when prices rise and Chileans—and foreign tourists—descend on popular destinations such as Southern Patagonia, the Valparaíso coast, Pucón, Puerto Varas, San Pedro de Atacama, and Rapa Nui.

National holidays such as Semana Santa (Easter Week), the winter school holidays (mid-July), and Independence Day celebrations in mid-September also inflate prices and make reservations essential.

If you book directly with the lodging rather than a third-party booking website, rates are invariably cheaper and allow you to confirm whether IVA is exempted. Many travelers booking through international websites later find that IVA must be paid in addition to the quoted rate.

HOTELS

Midrange hotels are generally of a good standard in Chile, with TVs and en suite baths standard, commonly with ceiling fans or air-conditioning. The size of the bedroom and the modernity of the decor can vary. More than basic English is rarely spoken by staff, and properties may lack parking. Rates range CH$50,000-80,000.

Plenty of high-end hotels in Santiago have restaurants, swimming pools, and gym facilities, with rates beginning at CH$80,000. Outside the capital, a few upscale options exists in remote destinations such as Parque Nacional Torres del Paine, San Pedro de Atacama, and Rapa Nui, many of which focus on offering adventure tours with luxury accommodations. Chilean chains such as Awasi, Terra, and Explorer are the top options in this category; expect to pay upward of CH$600,000 per night all-inclusive.

The word "boutique" means little more than "small hotel," and this label bears no reference to the quality of the lodging or the decor, but you can find a handful of lovely boutique options in Santiago, included in this guide.

HOSTELS

A profusion of hostel-style lodging targeted at budget travelers and backpackers is found throughout Chile's tourism hot spots, offering affordable dormitory and private rooms plus communal kitchens and shared areas, and occasionally even swimming pools. They provide an excellent forum to meet like-minded travelers and often have a strong community feel.

Expect to pay upward of CH$10,000 per dorm bed and CH$20,000 per private double room. They're also a great way to get reliable information about local activities and public transportation—information you rarely find at hotels or any of the other types of budget lodging. Many hostels have a website where you can book directly, or they maintain an active Facebook page.

OTHER BUDGET ACCOMMODATIONS

The many other forms of budget accommodations vary from dirty, uninviting digs to clean, well-run operations. *Pensiones* are generally family-run guesthouses used by longer-term transient workers who pay for meals in the rates. *Hospedajes* and *residenciales* are interchangeable terms that refer to accommodations in a family house expanded to provide lodging, sometimes with en suite bathrooms. *Hosterías* are normally larger and slightly more formal than *hospedajes* and *residenciales*, with a range of en suite and shared baths.

All usually include breakfast, and other meals can sometimes be arranged for an additional fee. Most will include TVs and the use of gas heaters; air-conditioning and even fans are rarely available. You are expected to bring your own towel, and in the more basic options, warm clothing or a sleeping bag, as many are in poorly insulated wooden houses that can feel chilly even in summer.

Not to be confused with hostels, *hostal* doesn't have the same meaning as in English. In smaller towns and less touristed areas, *hostal* can mean budget accommodations with private bedrooms, normally with en suite baths, and no dormitories. Kitchen access is often not included, and the price is generally only a little more than staying in a hostel, although it's unlikely you'll be surrounded by other foreign tourists. Expect to pay CH$20,000-35,000 for a double room. *Hostales* are a great alternative economical lodging option and are frequented by locals; be aware that some in the Norte Chico and Norte Grande are predominantly for mine workers, while others have contracts with other nearby industry workers, all of whom will be male. Solo female travelers might find the experience of staying in these places a little intimidating, although always safe.

All these are affordable alternatives on a budget and grant more interaction with local people. Many of the owners are very chatty with guests—although you'll need some Spanish, as the chances of them speaking any English are practically zero. Some have a Facebook page or website, but most have no social media or internet presence and are searchable purely by scouring the information for a destination on Google Maps. More often than not, a brief search brings up a telephone number.

CABAÑAS

Chilean tourists conventionally book *cabañas*: rustic (or sometimes more luxurious) wood cabins, often on the outskirts of town or in a picturesque rural location. Most are designed for groups or families of 4 to 8 or 10, although there are many 2-person cabins. Traveling as a couple or small group, it's often possible to secure a discount on a larger cabin, particularly outside high season. Cabins are the equivalent of a small fully contained house, with a kitchen, bathroom, separate bedrooms, and a living area; some include terraces and hot tubs. They can work out cheaper than the comparable bedrooms at a hotel and provide additional flexibility.

Geodesic domes are also becoming popular, although they rarely have kitchens and normally can only accommodate 2-3 people.

CAMPING

A growing number of campgrounds are being established across Chile, although most are in the Lakes region and south in Patagonia, as well as in many national parks. They offer the most inexpensive lodging and generally include hot showers and communal barbecue areas. Note that many campsites are charged per site for up to six people, which can increase costs and make it a less affordable option for couples or single campers. In this case, budget accommodations are a good alternative.

Conduct and Customs

Chileans are polite to foreigner visitors, and a general timidity can often be misinterpreted as rudeness—but this is rarely the case. When you get to know local people, you'll find they are warm and happy to help. Knowing some Spanish, as the general populace rarely speaks more than a handful of words of English, goes a long way. In rural areas, local people are very inquisitive, particularly toward solo travelers.

Greeting people with a friendly *Buenos días* (Good morning), *Buenos tardes* (Good afternoon), or *Buenas noches* (Good evening) and *¿Cómo está?* is the key to a friendly response in most shops, restaurants, and hotels. It is customary if meeting social or business acquaintances to greet each person individually with a handshake and a brief one-armed hug (between men) or an air kiss on the right cheek (for women), sometimes including a hug in more informal circumstances. In situations where you don't know the person, a handshake often suffices for women too.

Women travelers are often asked about their husbands, boyfriends, and children; more often than not, it's out of curiosity rather than any forward gesture. In formal restaurants and bars in Santiago and other cities, trousers for men and nice shoes are expected. In churches and sacred sites, both women and men should wear clothing that covers their legs.

When taking photographs, avoid conspicuously including a local person in the image unless you have their consent. One of the easiest ways to achieve this is to strike up a conversation before you pull out your camera. In markets, purchasing an item before asking to photograph the scene is also likely to achieve success. A respectful option is to offer to send the person a copy of the photo.

Note that, while somewhat more timely than other South American nations, Chileans are not usually punctual. If you organize to meet a Chilean person at a specified time, they might arrive anywhere up to an hour late, although this is generally less the case in Santiago and among the younger generation. To be sure of their arrival time, agree to operate on *hora inglesa* (English time), and they should arrive around the hour you agreed. Tours and other events organized through agencies are generally punctual.

CHILEAN SPANISH

A complicated feature of traveling in Chile for those with basic Spanish learned elsewhere is that the local Spanish sounds unlike what you've heard before. Chileans are notable fans of *jerga* (slang terms), and while Chilean Spanish is spoken with great speed, confusion is often more due to pronunciation and dropping consonants at the end of words.

¿Cómo estai? (with a long emphasis on the final *i*) is the Chilean form of the conventional *¿Cómo está?* (How are you?), while *cachai*, a distortion of the verb *cachar* (to catch), means "Do you understand?" The word *weón* (also spelled *hueón, güeón, weon*) has a litany of meanings depending on the context, ranging from "thing" to "mate" or "dude" to offensive expletives. You might also notice the liberal use of the word *po*, which has no translatable meaning but is used at the end of sentences as a form of emphasis.

While struggling to understand the words themselves might feel like the biggest challenge, accents in rural areas can also be problematic. Ask for people to speak more slowly by saying *"Habla más lento, por favor."* (Speak more slowly, please.) Outside the cities and tourism hot spots, few Chileans speak much English, so it's worthwhile bringing a phrase book.

TIPPING

At restaurants with table service, a 10 percent tip is included in bills, and the server should ask if you want to pay it: *"¿Quiere incluir la propina?"* (Would you like to include the tip?). It's standard to pay this fee, although you are within your rights to opt not to if service was truly awful. It's not usual to tip taxi drivers, but you can always round up to the nearest CH$1,000 to make life easier. In high-end hotels, tipping the cleaning staff is appreciated.

Health and Safety

EMERGENCY SERVICES

To reach emergency services anywhere in the country, dial 131. In case of fire, dial 132. To reach the police, dial 133.

VACCINATIONS

No vaccinations are required for travel to Chile, although it is recommended that your routine vaccinations for tetanus, diphtheria, and hepatitis A are up to date. The U.S. Centers for Disease Control and Prevention (CDC) recommends vaccinations against typhoid and hepatitis B if you plan to work with children or in a hospital. Rabies vaccination, which requires a course of three injections, is also recommended for those traveling to remote destinations due to the country's sizeable stray dog population, although the virus can also be carried by cats and bats.

There is officially no yellow fever in Chile; you do not need to show proof of a yellow fever vaccination, even if you're entering from an area with yellow fever.

DISEASES AND ILLNESSES
Insect-Borne Diseases and Animal Bites

Malaria is not present in Chile, although there are mosquitoes on Rapa Nui. Preventative measures of wearing long clothing to cover skin and using insect repellent are recommended to avoid being bitten.

Pregnant women are not at risk of Zika on mainland Chile. There have been reported cases of Zika spread by mosquitoes on Rapa Nui, although scientists have since confirmed that the virus is no longer present. The World Health Organization does not expect the virus to reach mainland Chile or to return to Rapa Nui, so the risk of being infected is exceptionally low. The mosquitoes that carry Zika tend to bite during daylight hours.

A viral infection, dengue is found in areas with standing water and is transmitted through mosquito bites, particularly during the rainy season. It causes fever, headaches, muscle and joint pain, nausea, and skin rashes, although symptoms can take 4-7 days to show, and some people who have contracted the infection exhibit no symptoms. Dengue hemorrhagic fever is a complication that can prove deadly and which manifests as a high fever, vomiting, diarrhea, and uncontrolled bleeding. It is more likely to occur in people who have been infected previously. Cases of dengue are occasionally reported on Rapa Nui, and prevention in the form of insect repellent with 20-30 percent DEET, long-sleeved light-colored garments, and applying sunscreen can help avoid contracting the disease. The mosquitoes that carry dengue tend to bite during daylight hours.

Chagas disease, also known as trypanosomiasis, is an incurable disease spread by the bite and subsequent infection of the bite of the *vinchuca* (assassin bug, also known as the kissing bug), which lives in the roofs and walls of adobe buildings, primarily in the north of Chile. The initial symptoms including skin lesions and purple swelling on the eyes, which can be accompanied by fever, headaches, and difficulty breathing. This disease stays in the body in the form of parasites; in later years, these can cause intestinal problems or heart damage resulting in heart failure. Avoid staying in adobe buildings when possible, and if you do, sleep away from the walls and use a net to cover your bed while sleeping, as the bugs normally come out at night.

Chile has a handful of venomous snakes, but none that pose any serious risk to visitors. The *araña del rincón* (recluse spider) lives in homes across the country, and a bite can prove fatal. The antidote works up to six hours after contact, so if you believe you've been bitten, get yourself to a hospital as soon as possible. Even remote clinics have access to the antidote.

Hantavirus

Hantavirus is a rare but fatal disease transmitted through the urine and feces of the long-tailed mouse, mostly in the rural south of Chile. Avoid touching food that may have been in contact with a rodent, and when camping, hang food in trees so that it is less likely to be reached. Avoid abandoned huts and buildings or those that have been closed for the winter, particularly when hiking in forests and other rural areas.

The virus produces fatigue, muscle pains, headaches, and shortness of breath and can result in heart failure. There is no specific cure, but if you think you may have been infected, it is essential to seek hospital treatment immediately.

Rabies

Chile's large stray dog population means that rabies is a real concern. The virus causes inflammation of the spiral cord and the brain and is transmitted through the bites or scratches of infected mammals, usually dogs and cats as well as bats. Symptoms usually show 20-60 days after exposure and include headache, fever, and a tingling around the wound. By the time symptoms have developed, rabies is fatal.

To avoid contracting the virus, stay away from stray animals, and if bitten or even scratched, immediately wash the affected area with soap and water and then with an iodine solution or 40-70 percent alcohol. Try to catch the animal for identification purposes, but not

if putting yourself at further risk of bites. Go directly to a hospital for treatment.

Before travel, a three-dose pre-exposure vaccine can be administered over a period of three to four weeks. It has two benefits: It reduces the numbers of postexposure vaccinations required in the event of infection, and it means that if you're in a remote place without access to medical assistance, the delay it takes for you to receive treatment is less likely to prove fatal.

Altitude Sickness

Travelers visiting the Andes Mountains in the north of the country or any elevation over 2,500 meters are at risk of contracting *soroche:* altitude sickness or acute mountain sickness (AMS). Your age, gender, and physical fitness have no impact on your likelihood of experiencing altitude symptoms, and even those who haven't suffered from it before are at risk.

It's most likely to be experienced after a rapid ascent from sea level to the altiplano and can cause symptoms such as headaches, nausea and vomiting, dizziness, tiredness, loss of appetite, and shortness of breath.

If these symptoms are ignored, it can quickly develop into high altitude cerebral edema (HACE), which causes swelling of the brain, after which high altitude pulmonary edema (HAPE) can develop, characterized by a blue tinge to the skin, breathing difficulties, a tight chest, and coughing that brings up pink or white liquid; both can be fatal if not treated.

For those experiencing mild symptoms, rest and not going any higher for 24-48 hours, while drinking plenty of water and taking ibuprofen or acetaminophen to combat headaches will help your body acclimatize to the altitude. Acclimatizing can take up to 2-3 days, after which it is possible to ascend again. You should also avoid alcohol and exertion. If symptoms don't improve after 24 hours, drop altitude by at least 500 meters, and see a doctor if the symptoms do not disappear after 2-3 days.

Acetazolamide (Diamox) can be prescribed by a doctor and taken before ascending to high altitudes, as it helps your body to acclimatize more quickly, but you should still practice slow ascent.

Be aware that high elevation has greater exposure to UV radiation, so use sunscreen with a high sun protection factor (at least SPF 15), wear a hat to protect your head and long-sleeved clothing for your body, and use sunglasses with lenses that filter UV light.

Traveler's Diarrhea

The risk of succumbing to traveler's diarrhea is always a possibility in Chile, although the risk is generally considered moderate and much lower than in the rest of South America. Traveler's diarrhea is most typically caused by a lack of basic hygiene, with those preparing food not washing their hands properly and so passing the infection through food and water.

Raw, undercooked, or unwashed food is a particular risk, and you should be careful with buffets and any food that sits for prolonged periods at lukewarm temperatures, or at street food stalls where basic hygiene practices may not be followed sufficiently. Avoid meat products not well-cooked and dairy products that appear to have been outside the refrigerator for an extended period.

In general, restaurants in Chile follow acceptable hygiene standards, and you shouldn't have any problems, but a rule of thumb is to avoid restaurants and market stalls with few customers. Following the rule of "Boil it, cook it, peel it, or forget it" can help prevent getting ill. Always wash your hands thoroughly after using the restroom with soap and hot water (if available). If not available, use an alcohol-based hand sanitizer with 60 percent alcohol content.

If suffering from the ailment, loperamide (Imodium) or bismuth subsalicylate (Pepto-Bismol) can be taken to reduce the frequency of diarrhea, while sachets of oral rehydration solution can make you feel significantly better and help replenish essential electrolytes in your body.

Cholera

Spread by infected water supplies and contaminated food resulting from poor hygiene, cholera can cause diarrhea that leads to rapid dehydration and ultimately death. In September 2018, there were 29 cases confirmed in Santiago, although no deaths were reported, and while the disease is uncommon, preventative steps similar to those recommended for avoiding traveler's diarrhea should be followed.

Tap Water

Tap water, except in some parts of the Atacama Desert, is potable. The high mineral content of the water can, however, cause an upset stomach. For those affected by the water, boil it for one minute (or three minutes at 3,000 meters or above), invest in a portable water filter that removes heavy minerals, or stick to bottled water. In the Atacama Desert, water sources have levels of arsenic above the World Health Organization's safe limits, which means you should always drink bottled water.

Marea Roja

Caused by the accumulation of alga-produced toxins in bivalve shellfish, *marea roja* (red tide) can prove fatal to humans and mostly affects the waters around Chiloé and other parts of southern Chile. It has also been detected in the waters around Caldera. Government regulations on the cooking and sale of seafood potentially infected with the toxins mean there is minimal likelihood that you will be served infected shellfish at restaurants or markets. Always confirm the latest situation with local fishermen if collecting any to cook yourself.

MEDICAL SERVICES

Chile has excellent medical facilities, with the majority concentrated in Santiago. The **Clínica Alemana** (Vitacura 5951, Vitacura, tel. 2/2210 1111, www.clinicaalemana.cl) is considered second best on the continent, according to *AméricaEconomía* magazine's listing of Latin America's top 40 hospitals. It is very expensive, but excellent in an emergency.

The cheaper **Clínica Santa María** (Av. Santa María 500, Providencia, tel. 2/2913 0000, http://clinicasantamaria.cl) also provides swift assistance in an emergency. Private clinics are generally open 24 hours, can provide the swiftest attention in an emergency, and are more likely to have doctors that speak English.

Most villages have *postas medicas* (clinics) that provide basic immediate assistance in an emergency, but often lack supplies. Serious incidents may require transfer to the hospital in the nearest city, which can be a few hours away.

Insurance

Investing in health insurance before traveling is strongly recommended, as private medical treatment can prove expensive, particularly if transportation to a hospital or to Santiago is required; you want coverage that includes evacuation in an emergency. You may be required to pay first and claim back on insurance later; confirm with your insurance company the exact protocol, as many avoid payout if medical services haven't been agreed to by their representatives *before* being used. You can find a list of insurance companies on the **U.S. State Department's website** (http://travel.state.gov).

Pharmacies

You're rarely more than a few meters from a pharmacy in Chile, and they can provide over-the-counter medications and some medical advice. Be aware that they may prescribe incorrect medications through misdiagnosis of symptoms or because of the language barrier. It's always better to attend a walk-in clinic or book a doctor's appointment for any serious issues. Cities normally have at least one pharmacy open 24 hours on a rotating basis; this is indicated by a sign in the door of other pharmacies, with the address for the *farmacia de turno*.

CRIME

Chile is generally a safe county for travel, and few visitors face problems during their stay.

Most crimes are opportunistic, with pick-pocketing a real issue in cities, particularly on public transport and at bus stations. Store your passport and valuables in your hotel safe and always travel with your backpack or bag on your front and wallets where you can see or feel them when taking the metro or other busy public transport in Santiago. Muggings are rare but do happen, and they are on the rise in the tourist area of Bellavista in Santiago. If you are accosted, it's not worth fighting; give up your belongings. At night, be alert to your surroundings.

Cell phone theft is a real issue in the capital and other cities, with theft normally occurring when victims are waiting at road crossings and thieves on motorcycles speed by and snatch the device from their hands. Don't leave cell phones out on tables at restaurants, particularly if you're on an outdoor terrace where distraction techniques can be employed to steal the item. Hooks on the underside of tables in restaurants and bars are there for hanging handbags, as theft of bags from restaurants is reasonably common, and waiters will remind you to keep an eye on your belongings. Never allow your credit card to be taken out of view, as card skimming can occur. Avoid carrying lots of cash, and bring a photocopy of your passport. If your clothes are splashed with a brown substance (normally mustard or a type of sauce), do not accept help from bystanders: this is a type of diversion theft and normally results in your valuables being stolen. On buses, never place valuables in the overhead lockers—keep items by your feet or attached to your person.

Taxi crimes are on the rise, particularly with unlicensed cabs from the airport in Santiago charging inflated fees and using devices to steal money from your credit card after you have extracted money from an ATM. Always book via official taxi firms and ask for proof of booking if you are approached by someone claiming to be your driver. If in doubt, go to the official desk for the taxi company in the airport.

Nationwide protests take place on a number of days, including September 11 (anniversary of the Pinochet military coup), March 29 (Day of the Young Combatant, which recognizes the assassination of two brothers during the dictatorship), May 1 (Labor Day), and June 1 (the Chilean president's State of the Union address, held in Valparaíso). Protests are a regular occurrence in Plaza Italia in Santiago, often closing off the entire square and continuing west along Avenida O'Higgins to La Moneda. Tear gas and water cannons known as *guanacos* are used against protestors, and despite starting out peaceful, demonstrations can quickly become violent. It's strongly recommended to avoid getting caught up in demonstrations.

For up-to-date travel advisories, visit the website for the U.S. Department of State's **Bureau of Consular Affairs** (http://travel.state.gov) or the corresponding body in your home country.

NATURAL DISASTERS
Earthquakes are always a risk in Chile, but be reassured that all new buildings are constructed using strict regulations on seismic risk. Always read safety information inside your hotel; if there is none, speak with the front desk about the safest location in an earthquake. Generally, you should drop to the floor and cover your head; avoid being next to heavy items that aren't attached to the wall, such as televisions or cabinets. You are safer inside than out and should stay there until the shaking stops. Don't use elevators during an earthquake. In a vehicle, stop the car away from buildings, trees, overpasses, utility wires, or any street furniture that could collapse.

Earthquakes can spark tsunamis, which can cause catastrophic damage to coastal settlements. If you are staying in a coastal town during an earthquake, an alert should indicate whether a tsunami is predicted, and signs around towns show the direction you should travel to reach higher ground.

Volcanic eruptions are an additional threat in Chile. Stringent monitoring systems generally pick up increased volcanic activity in the country's 90 active volcanoes, allowing plenty of time for evacuation, but this isn't always the case. In 2008, Chaitén, not previously identified as a volcano, erupted and produced lahars that practically wiped out the nearby town—although all the villagers were successfully evacuated. In the event of a volcanic evacuation, follow instructions issued by the *carabineros*.

Any emergency in the country will trigger an alert on the official government website (www.onemi.cl).

Travel Tips

WHAT TO PACK
Regardless of the season, if you plan to head into the rainy Lakes region or farther south into Chiloé and Patagonia, a lightweight waterproof jacket is essential, particularly as fierce winds in the south can break umbrellas within seconds of stepping outside. Waterproof pants are also good for hikers, particularly for Parque Nacional Torres del Paine and any of the routes in the south, as they can be useful in keeping you dry during the day and around camp in the evening. Camping in Patagonia, long underwear can keep you warm at night, as even in summer the temperature can drop, and during shoulder seasons it can be quite cold. Heading up into the altiplano in the Atacama Desert, temperatures can go below freezing at night, even during summer, and those on stargazing tours will be thankful for the layers to keep out the chill.

Layers of clothing are an excellent idea for any trip in Chile. Layer up or strip down depending on the weather, particularly in the south, where the weather can pass through four seasons in a day. A wide-brimmed hat for sun protection is essential in both the north and south to protect from harmful UV rays, particularly around Patagonia, where the ozone layer is thinning.

Lightweight hiking boots are strongly recommended for Patagonia and will work well on other trails throughout the country. Before you leave for Chile, treat them with a water-resistant wax or spray to ensure they keep your feet dry.

A small 20- to 40-liter day pack is sensible for day excursions, whether in cities or out on the trail. For multiple-day trekking and camping, such as the W or O treks in Torres del Paine, a 50- to 60-liter pack is a suitable size. Camping gear can be rented in hiking hot spots such as Pucón, Puerto Varas, Coyhaique, and Puerto Natales, and buying gear is also possible, but you can expect to pay at least 30 percent more than at home or settle for poor-quality locally produced brands such as Doite. If you plan to do more than one multiple-day trek, it may be easier to bring your own camping gear and a lightweight tent with durable fly that can withstand the gale-force squalls in Patagonia. A three-season sleeping bag should be suitable, although a four-season bag is sensible for trekking at higher altitudes in the Andes.

Tap water is drinkable, and water can be taken from streams without problems in more remote parts of Patagonia; elsewhere, you'll want a portable water filter or iodine tablets and a water bottle. Toilet paper is generally included at all lodgings, but on long bus journeys and in public restrooms, you may struggle to find any. Earplugs and eye masks are essentials for overnight bus travel and thin-walled lodgings, while a padlock will keep your belongings safe in hostel dorm lockers. A money belt can make you feel safer with valuables such as your passport and money, but be aware that would-be thieves are getting wise to their existence.

A pair of binoculars can be invaluable for wildlife spotting across the country, while a GPS receiver or mobile phone with a map that doesn't require internet access is essential for road trips into rural areas or hiking in the less-visited national parks.

MONEY

Chile's official currency is the Chilean peso (CH$, also CLP). This comes in bills denominated 1,000, 2,000, 5,000, 10,000, and 20,000. Bills smaller than CH$10,000 are made from a polymer material. Coins are in denominations of 5, 10, 20, 50, 100, and 500 pesos, although 5-peso coins are gradually being removed from use. There are two versions of the 100-peso coin. In Chile, 1,000 pesos is known colloquially as a *luca*.

The Chilean peso has remained stable over the past few years, and the country is still quite expensive for international visitors, particularly when compared to other South American nations. Be aware that bargaining is not common in Chile.

Counterfeit bills can be a problem, and the biggest culprits are taxi drivers, who accept a legitimate bill from you, swap it while you're not watching, and then present it back to you, telling you that you gave them a fake. Always keep an eye on the money you pay with, and double-check the change you receive to ensure you've not been palmed off with counterfeit bills.

Exchange Rates

You can exchange money at some banks, but you'll get a better rate using one of the *casa de cambio* (exchange houses) in most cities; many banks only exchange money for those with a local account. Exchange houses are very particular about the bills they will exchange, so bring crisp new bills, as any that are dirty, torn, or marked will be rejected. You will need your passport for the transaction. Few accept euros and British pounds; you will get the best rates for U.S. dollars. You do not generally see money changers on the streets, and it is not safe to use them. You can expect *casas de cambio* to be closed on Saturday afternoon and Sunday.

Traveler's checks are not recommended, as they are difficult to cash. Instead, it's easier to wire yourself cash through Western Union, which has branches in most major cities. All **Tur Bus** (http://turbus.cl) offices also operate as Western Union branches and can be used to send and receive money.

ATMs and Cash Withdrawal

ATMs are a very reliable way to get currency in Chile, and there are *cajeros* (ATMs) for a variety of different banks in cities and towns across the country, with most open 24 hours. Even some small remote towns will have one ATM, although it is generally operated by Banco del Estado, whose ATMs sometimes do not work with all cards. In rural destinations, ATMs can run out of money during busy holiday periods of long weekends. Bring plenty of cash if you enter the country at a remote border crossing such as those along the Carretera Austral, where banks are only located in Cochrane, Chile Chico, Coyhaique, Chaitén, and Futaleufú.

You must select the *tarjeta extranjera* (foreign card) option on the ATM to be able to withdraw cash. All ATMs have an English language option. Withdrawal fees are painfully expensive, generally CH$4,000-6,000 to withdraw money and only allowing up to CH$200,000 per withdrawal, which can wind up being very costly. Scotiabank, which has branches only in the cities, and Banco International, with branches only in Santiago, do not charge fees for withdrawals at the time of writing. Always complete the transaction in Chilean pesos, not your home currency, to avoid getting ripped off through exorbitant exchange rates.

ATMs will often give you CH$20,000 bills, which can be a pain to pay with; even CH$10,000 bills can cause problems in rural areas. Supermarkets and gas stations are good places to ask for *sencillo* (change).

Using Dollars

Throughout the country, to be eligible for the IVA (value-added tax) discount of 19 percent from your lodging bill, which is available to foreigners staying fewer than 60 days in the country, you must pay in a foreign currency and show your passport and PDI slip that was issued when you arrived. Most medium and large hotels allow you to do this using your credit card; smaller establishments expect you to pay in U.S. dollars. This is especially the case in Patagonia, so it's worth bringing some U.S. dollars if you plan to stay at midrange accommodations.

We have tried to indicate where IVA discounts can be received through paying with a foreign credit card, although this information can change. It is therefore essential to confirm upon booking which payment methods are available to you so you can avoid being made to pay an additional 19 percent.

Credit and Debit Cards

Most foreign cards are accepted, with Visa, MasterCard, and American Express accepted almost universally. Paying hotel fees with a foreign credit card is useful in that it can save you from paying the IVA (value-added tax), but always do the math, as sometimes the U.S. dollar rate can wind up being more expensive than the rate in Chilean pesos, even with IVA included.

At businesses in smaller towns and rural areas, a 2-4 percent surcharge might be imposed by the merchant, so bringing cash when traveling outside the cities is essential; many places do not accept credit cards anyway.

Value-Added Tax

A 19 percent IVA (value-added tax) is levied on goods and services throughout Chile and is generally included in the price. The only tax breaks available to tourists are on hotel rates.

COMMUNICATIONS AND MEDIA

Internet Access

A Wi-Fi connection is available at practically all hotels, cafés, and many restaurants across Chile, with free internet access also available in some shopping malls. Many

Managing Money in Argentinean Patagonia

Argentina's economy has suffered rapid inflation and devaluation since 2017 and has become a far more affordable destination for travelers than in recent years. However, the volatile nature of the Argentinean economy means that there can be no predicting what will happen in the future.

The official currency is the Argentinean peso (ARS$). Bills come in denomination of 2, 5, 10, 20, 50, 100, 200, 500, and 1,000 pesos. One peso is the equivalent of 100 *centavos* (cents), which come in coin denominations of 5, 10, 20, and 50. Pesos also come in coins of 1, 2, and 5.

Bills in Argentina are normally tatty but should be accepted regardless. Be on the lookout for counterfeit notes, which are rampant: Always watch carefully what the driver does with your money when paying for a taxi, and check that the returned bill is not a fake: It should have a watermark or a shiny security thread weaving in and out of the bill that should show as a full line when held up to the light.

ATMS AND CASH WITHDRAWAL

Withdrawing money in Argentina can be a real hassle, and you can spend hours trying to do so. *Cajeros automáticos* (ATMs) can often run out of cash or stop working for hours, and many bank cards are not accepted. Bring a couple of different cards to ensure that you don't get stuck. Visa-branded cards work best, followed by MasterCard.

ATMs also charge a transaction fee of ARS$180 every time you withdraw and impose a limit of ARS$4,000 (around US$104) per transaction, meaning the cost of withdrawing money can quickly add up. ATMs in El Chaltén and El Calafate run out of money regularly in summer, while those in Ushuaia have been known to stop working for extended periods. In El Chaltén, withdrawals are often fixed lower than the normal ARS$4,000 limit, and the ATM is frequently empty, so it's better to withdraw money in El Calafate.

Big bills can be very difficult to use in Argentina. Withdraw money in amounts ending in 80 or 90 (for example ARS$3,980) to be given smaller denominations. You can often exchange large bills for smaller ones in supermarkets.

EXCHANGING MONEY

Until 2016, changing money in Argentina was simple thanks to the Blue Dollar, a black-market exchange rate that was 40 percent better than the official rate set by the government. It is no longer recommended to exchange money using unofficial money changers due to the prevalence of counterfeit bills.

Instead, banks and exchange houses are the best bet and will readily accept US$50 and US$100 bills. Exchanging Chilean pesos will get a poor rate, if you're even successful. You will need your original passport to exchange money. Traveler's checks are rarely accepted.

PAYING WITH CREDIT CARDS AND DOLLARS

Credit cards are generally accepted across Argentina, but you may find smaller hotels and many tour agencies only work with cash, while many of the restaurants, hotels, and shops in El Chaltén do not have a consistent internet connection and so do the same. When paying with a credit card, a photo ID (your passport) is often required. Crisp, new US$100 bills are an excellent thing to bring with you, as they can be used to pay for higher-priced goods (including tours and hotels) and can often result in a discounted price. In restaurants, you can generally pay in U.S. dollars and get change in Argentinean pesos, which may not offer the best exchange rate but is useful if you only have a few days in the country and don't want to withdraw money.

Paying with a card, you may be charged a surcharge of 6-10 percent. A discount to pay in cash, even pesos, rather than with a credit card is sometimes offered.

plazas across the country have free Wi-Fi connections too. Wi-Fi speeds in Santiago are excellent, although rainfall and storms can cause downtime, while speeds in rural locations and most of Patagonia can be painfully slow, but normally sufficient for downloading emails. A useful expression to know is *"¿Cuál es la clave del Wi-Fi?"* (What is the Wi-Fi password?).

Phones and Cell Phones

Cell phone service covers practically all of the country, except remote high-elevation locations and most of the isolated Chilean fjords—although you will find signal with the cell phone provider Entel at the marvelously secluded Puerto Edén. A prepaid SIM card or *chip* is easy to buy and use in your cell phone, and can be purchased from booths in most shopping malls operated by the main companies Entel, Movistar, Claro, and Wom. You can expect 4G connectivity in most cities. For stays longer than 30 days, a law introduced in 2017 means that you must register your cell phone at one of the companies listed on the **Subsecretaría de Telecomunicaciones** website (http://multibanda.cl). When you first put your SIM card in your phone, an automatic text message should guide you through the process.

Unhelpfully, shops operated by the different telecommunication companies do not actually sell SIM cards or provide refill services; they can sometimes provide assistance with connectivity issues. For trips where you plan on visiting remote areas such as Patagonia, Entel has the best coverage, and 3G speeds are not unusual, even outside large cities. Phone calls in Chile are expensive, while buying data add-ons is not; expect to pay around CH$7,000 for 3 GB of data. Adding value to the SIM is possible at some kiosks and all pharmacies; ask to *recargar* (top up or buy credit). Call centers and public telephones are becoming less common, so it's best to buy a SIM or opt to use an internet calling service such as Skype.

Note that many restaurants and tour agencies can be contacted through Facebook or WhatsApp, the latter often being the communication of choice.

The telephone code for Chile is 56. Cell phone numbers are nine digits long and always start with the number 9. Landlines are seven or eight digits and are preceded by an area code. For Santiago, the area code is 2; for the rest of the country, the area code is two digits. To make calls, you should just need to input the number and press Call; if you're using a foreign SIM, you need to add +56 before dialing.

Because the whole telephone system changed in 2016, you may find that people who give you their phone number forget to convert it to the new format. In this case, if it's a mobile number, you need to add 9 to the beginning. If it's a landline, add 2.

Postal Service

Correos de Chile (http://correos.cl), the Chilean postal service, is generally very reliable—if you're happy to wait a few months for packages to arrive. On the way into Chile, items tend to get caught up in customs and can stay there for what feels like decades. Post leaving the country is generally far more efficient and shouldn't take more than a few weeks to reach its destination.

A speedier alternative is **DHL** (http://dhl. cl) or another courier service. These are also an excellent means of sending post within the country and allow you to pick up an item from one of their branches, located in all cities and even some towns. For locations without a courier office, **Turbus** (http://turbus. cl) offers a cargo service, with cargo offices often in their passenger ticket offices. They can send items to Tur Bus offices throughout the country. For valuable items, a courier service is recommended.

Newspapers and Magazines

The Santiago Times (http://santiagotimes. cl) is the only English-language option in Chile and is accessible online.

WEIGHTS AND MEASURES
Electricity

Outlets are generally 220 volts at 50 Hz. Most plug sockets take two rounded pins, known as Type C plugs, and it is easier to buy a plug adapter before arriving. That said, you can generally find plug adapters for U.S. and some European plugs in hardware shops and many shopping malls, although this is harder outside Santiago. In Argentina, Type C and Type I (two or three flat pins) are the norm, and outlets are also 220 volts, 50 Hz.

For both countries, you may need a power converter, but most common appliances, such as laptops, are now dual voltage and can work with both 110-120 volts (standard in the United States and Canada) and 220-240 volts.

Time Zones

Chile is usually on UTC-3, meaning three hours earlier than Coordinated Universal Time (UTC), but winter time, which is four hours earlier than UTC, is used from the second Sunday in April until the first Sunday in September. As of 2017, the Magallanes region uses UTC-3 year-round. Rapa Nui is UTC-5 but adopts UTC-6 during winter, making it always two hours earlier than most of mainland Chile. Be aware that while Chile has been using winter time since 2010, the date of its adoption each year is prone to change. Keep an eye on newspapers or consult a local if traveling during these months. You can also confirm the exact time on the website www.horaoficial.cl.

Measurements

The metric system is the official system in Chile.

OPPORTUNITIES FOR STUDY AND VOLUNTEER WORK

Although Chilean Spanish isn't the easiest, some visitors choose to spend a few weeks learning Spanish before they travel. The easiest place to do this is in Santiago, where there is the widest selection of Spanish language schools. That said, living costs are considerably higher than in most places across the country. Fees start at US$190 per week for four hours of group instruction per day, with longer stays often cheaper; private tuition is around double the cost. Packages including hostel or flat accommodations, or a homestay with a Chilean family, can be arranged.

There is a growing network of Chilean hostels, businesses, and sustainable and ecotourism ventures looking for volunteers for stays of anywhere from a week to several months, and most are found online on websites such as **Workaway** (http://workaway.info) and **Helpx** (http://helpx.net). Both require a small annual sign-up fee.

ACCESS FOR TRAVELERS WITH DISABILITIES

Facilities for travelers with disabilities are not common in Chile, and only large international chains and higher-end hotels generally have accessible facilities, although there are some exceptions.

Public transport, such as long-distance buses, is practically impossible to use for anyone in a wheelchair. According to the law, Santiago's metro ought to be fully accessible, but not all stations on Líneas 1 and 5 have wheelchair-accessible lifts, although the metro is in the process of installing new facilities. Newer intercity buses often have ramps and spaces designated for wheelchair users.

Throughout Santiago, ramps make sidewalks generally wheelchair accessible. In other cities and towns, this varies, with uneven and potholed sidewalks. Pedestrian crossings are obeyed by motorists, but it's worth noting that cars can still turn on a red light. There are often wheelchair-accessible restrooms in modern shopping malls.

Chilean-based **Wheel the World** (US tel. 510/9432 853, http://gowheeltheworld.com) has highly trained guides that organize wheelchair-accessible adventure expeditions to some of the country's adventure hot spots, including Parque Nacional Torres del Paine and other parts of Patagonia, Rapa Nui, and San Pedro de Atacama.

TRAVELING WITH CHILDREN

Chile is both child- and family-friendly, with plenty to keep young travelers occupied. The extreme landscapes and wildlife can really bring geography to life. Children are generally charged a discounted entry to museums and other activities, and efforts have been made to transform dusty old museum displays into more interactive and appealing exhibits for the whole family.

Restaurants often have a children's menu, although be aware that outside Santiago, restaurants often only open at 7pm or later. *Cabañas,* wooden cabins with multiple bedrooms, a bathroom, kitchen, and living space, are designed for families and can generally work out as far more affordable than two or more rooms in a hotel. Hotel family rooms, normally with a double bed and three single beds, can also be economical for families and are common throughout the country, reflecting the fact that most Chileans travel in family units. Many accommodations do not have portable extra beds, however.

Strollers can be useful in cities, although narrow sidewalks can make movement difficult. In the national parks or on trails, a baby carrier is very useful. When you arrange a rental car, be sure to request a child seat, as it is a legal requirement for children to use them. In buses, younger children can be exempt from buying a ticket if they sit on the parent's lap; you need to pay for a ticket if you want them to have their own seat.

WOMEN TRAVELING ALONE

Despite the misogynistic attitudes toward women found predominantly among older members of the population, Chile is a safe place for solo female travelers. Wolf-whistling and catcalling is unfortunately a fact of life in practically all cities and towns, and you tend to attract more attraction if your legs are bare—although just being identifiably foreign is normally enough to invoke this type of response from men. Taxis, mostly outside the capital, also have a secondary horn that sounds like a wolf-whistle and is used against female pedestrians. The best way to handle any form of catcalling is to ignore it, as responding can sometimes put you in a more dangerous situation. Wearing a wedding ring can curb would-be suitors.

General caution should be applied: At night, it's best to avoid quiet streets when you're alone, and it's advisable to call a taxi rather than flagging one down on the street. The free **Easy Taxi** app is a good option; **Uber** is illegal but still widely used and preferred over a normal cab.

LGBTQ TRAVELERS

Homosexuality has been legal in Chile since 1993, while discrimination against gays and lesbians was ruled illegal in 2012. The reality, however, is that attitudes toward LGBTQ people are only slowly changing. Santiago demonstrates the most liberal attitudes, and it's not unusual to see gay couples in the city. It also has one of the country's only thriving gay scenes, centered on Barrio Bellavista, although there are clubs in Viña del Mar. All clubs cater to both men and women, regardless of sexual orientation. Attitudes are not as liberal in more rural parts of the country.

Transgender rights are gradually developing, with a landmark bill signed into law in November 2018 recognizing the right of people over age 18 to legally change their gender.

The **International Gay & Lesbian Travel Association** (http://iglta.org) has a list of LGBTQ-friendly hotels and tourism facilities on their website. **Pride Tours** (tel. 9/8149 3602, http://pridetours.cl) is a gay tour operator that runs tours throughout Chile, including visits to Santiago's gay nightlife.

Not-for-profit **Movilh** (www.movilh. cl) has been working since 1991 to support LGBTQ Chileans with chapters around the country. **Iguales** (http://iguales.cl), Chile's largest human rights organization, fights for the rights of LGBTQ people, while **Pride Connection** (http://prideconnection.cl) works with businesses to make them more inclusive. LGBTQ Pride events are held in Santiago in June.

TRAVELERS OF COLOR

There is entrenched racism in Chile that has become more visible with the new wave of immigration from countries such as Colombia and Haiti. While travelers of color will unlikely experience discrimination, they will face constant staring, even in cities like Santiago. You may face hostility until it becomes clear that you are not from Colombia or Haiti. People from those countries have experienced a rise in anti-immigrant sentiment that has been stoked by the right-wing media and extreme right-wing politicians.

VISITOR INFORMATION
Tourist Offices

All cities have an office of Servicio Nacional de Turismo (SERNATUR), the national tourism board, generally open 6-7 days per week and well stocked with maps, logistical information, and English-speaking staff. Cities and some towns also have a municipal-run tourist information office; these are more variable in terms of resources and how helpful they can be. Few speak English, and most are only open weekdays or only during the summer months of January-February.

Maps

Publishing detailed topographical maps, the **Instituto Geográfico Militar** (IGM, Dieciocho 369, Santiago, tel. 2/2410 9363, www.igm.cl) also sells road atlases and city maps. The excellent **Chiletur Copec** series comprises a selection of guidebooks (in Spanish only) with useful city maps and the Rutas de Chile road map, which covers the entire country and is invaluable for road trips. All are updated annually and can be purchased from most COPEC gas stations across the country.

Trekking Chile (http://trekkingchile. com), a tour agency and mapmaker, produces detailed hiking maps covering San Pedro de Atacama, Parque Nacional Torres del Paine, the Carretera Austral by bike, as well as hiking routes in the protected areas east of Santiago and a city map of Valparaíso, plus guidebooks with information about treks across the country. Their free smartphone app, **Trekking Chile,** works offline and has various routes and trail guides.

At the entrance to most national parks, **CONAF** provide visitors with maps that have the parks' trails marked on them. The quality and usefulness of these maps varies, with a lack of contour lines and other geographical markers often making them difficult to follow.

SIG Patagon also draws topographical hiking maps to a scale of 1:100,000 of Parque Nacional Torres del Paine, Isla Navarino and the Dientes de Navarino trail, as well as other destinations in Patagonia; they can be bought online and downloaded to a phone through **Avenza Maps** (http://avenzamaps.com).

AndesProfundo (http://andesprofundo. com) also produces topographical maps at a scale of 1:25,000 for various national parks and volcanoes, and sells maps in camping equipment shops in Santiago and in some hostels and hotels across the south of the country.

Chaltén Out Door produces 1:100,000 and 1:60,000 topographical maps that cover Patagonia, including Chaltén, Torres del Paine, around Villa O'Higgins, and the Carretera Austral. You can buy their maps in shops in Chaltén and a handful of other places in Patagonia. Check out their Facebook page for more information.

Tour Operators

Chiloé-based **Austral Adventures** (Av. Costanera 904, Ancud, Chiloé, tel. 65/2625 977, www.austral-adventures.com) operates tailored tours in Chiloé, Patagonia, and Rapa Nui, plus self-drive tours in and around Chiloé.

French-operated **Azimut 360** (José Manuel Infante 1190, Providencia, Santiago, tel. 2/2235 1519, http://azimut360.com) caters to adventure travelers, with expeditions up Volcán Licancabur and Cerro Aconcagua to trekking routes through Patagonia and the Norte Grande and self-drive adventures along the Carretera Austral.

Cascada Expediciones (Don Carlos 3227 C, Las Condes, US/Can. tel. 888/232-3813, http://cascada.travel) covers most of the country with activity-oriented excursions such as skiing in the Central Valley, kayaking in the Lakes District, or hiking in Parque Nacional Torres del Paine, where their trademark geodesic lodgings, EcoCamp, is based.

Specializing in bird-watching and wildlife tours, the superb **Far South Expeditions** (Manuel Señoret 610, Punta Arenas, tel. 61/2615 793, www.farsouthexp.com) has expert naturalist guides and leads an extensive array of tours in the Magallanes region and throughout the country. Most run November-April, with trips such as the remote, bird-rich Juan Fernández Islands leaving year-round.

Puerto Natales-based **Skorpios** (Camino Puerto Bories s/n, Puerto Natales, tel. 61/241 2714, US tel. 305/285-8416, www.skorpios.cl) leads cruises exploring the fjords of remote Parque Nacional Bernardo O'Higgins, Laguna San Rafael, and the Chiloé archipelago.

Covering the full length of the country with an array of unique tours that work predominantly with indigenous communities and guides, the fantastic **Travolution** (http://travolution.travel) is spearheading sustainable and sensitive indigenous tourism in Chile. They also work as the nonprofit Travolution. org, which leads annual conferences for indigenous and community-led tourism initiatives across South and Central America.

Talca-based **Trekking Chile** (Viña Andrea s/n, tel. 71/1970 097, www.trekkingchile.com), along with offering their own guided trekking and mountaineering activities, has a registry of 600 tour guides from across Chile that you can use to book your own trip.

The Santiago-based **Upscape Travel** (http://upscapetravel.com) operates high-end trips throughout Chile, including food and wine tours in the Central Valley and backcountry destinations in Patagonia.

Chile Off Track (tel. 9/7749 6815, http://chileofftrack.com) runs hiking and horseback tours in the Andes as well as winery, dining, and coastal tours from Santiago. **Uncorked Wine Tours** (tel. 2/2981 6242, www.uncorked.cl) visits wineries in Casablanca and Colchagua, and offers customizable tours as well as cooking classes.

Resources

Glossary

á dedo: hitchhiking

altiplano: a mountain plateau

araucaría: monkey puzzle tree

artesanía: handicrafts

asado: barbecue

ascensor: literally "elevator," but normally used in reference to the funiculars in Valparaíso

ahu: stone ceremonial platforms onto which the *moai* of Rapa Nui were placed

buena onda: good vibes; normally used to refer to a person or the atmosphere of a place

cabañas: rustic wood cabins

cama/semi-cama: reclining/half-reclining seat on a bus; *cama premium* refers to a lie-flat seat

camanchaca: coastal fog

campesinos: people from rural areas

campo: rural area, countryside

Carabineros: Chilean national police force

Carretera Austral: popular name for the Pan-American Highway/Ruta 5

colectivo: shared taxi with a set route; also called a *taxi colectivo*

CONAF: Chilean national park service

crin: horsehair

curanto: a dish typical to Chiloé that's made of chicken, shellfish, sausages, and dumplings and cooked underground

desierto florido: literally "flowering desert," this phenomenon occurs after periods of high rain

El Longitudinal: alternate name for the Pan-American Highway/Ruta 5

empanada: a flaky pastry stuffed with minced beef and onions, cheese, or shellfish and served as a snack

estancía: ranch, normally for raising sheep, in Patagonia

guanaco: South American mammal that's related to camels and llamas

guardería: national park ranger station

huemul: a type of South American deer that features on the Chilean coat of arms

La Panamericana: alternate name for the Pan-American Highway/Ruta 5

luca: 1,000 Chilean pesos

menu del día: daily fixed price menu, normally offered at lunch

merquén: seasoning made from smoked chili pepper and added to dishes such as ceviche and empanadas

mestizo: person of mixed indigenous and Spanish descent

micros: small public buses

moai: monolithic statues of Rapa Nui

nalca: the Chilean rhubarb, a plant with tough leaves that grow up to two meters tall; visible along the Carretera Austral

once: afternoon tea; usually a light meal

palafitos: houses built on stilts in Chiloé

parrilla: a grill used for barbecuing meat

picada: small, family-run restaurant serving traditional Chilean food

porteño: name for a resident of Valparaíso, a port city

pudu: pygmy deer

quincho: covered outdoor cooking area, normally containing a grill

Santiaguinos: name for people who live in Santiago

SERNATUR: Chilean national tourism organization

Spanish Phrasebook

Spanish commonly uses 30 letters—the familiar English 26, plus four straightforward additions: ch, ll, ñ, and rr, which are explained in "Consonants," below.

PRONUNCIATION

Once you learn them, Spanish pronunciation rules—in contrast to English—don't change. Spanish vowels generally sound softer than in English. (*Note:* The capitalized syllables below receive stronger accents.)

Vowels

a like ah, as in "hah": *agua* AH-gooah (water), *pan* PAHN (bread), and *casa* CAH-sah (house)

e like ay, as in "may:" *mesa* MAY-sah (table), *tela* TAY-lah (cloth), and *de* DAY (of, from)

i like ee, as in "need": *diez* dee-AYZ (ten), *comida* ko-MEE-dah (meal), and *fin* FEEN (end)

o like oh, as in "go": *peso* PAY-soh (weight), *ocho* OH-choh (eight), and *poco* POH-koh (a bit)

u like oo, as in "cool": *uno* OO-noh (one), *cuarto* KOOAHR-toh (room), and *usted* oos-TAYD (you); when it follows a "q" the **u** is silent; when it follows an "h" or has an umlaut, it's pronounced like "w"

Consonants

b, d, f, k, l, m, n, p, q, s, t, v, w, x, y, z, ch pronounced almost as in English; **h** occurs, but is silent—not pronounced at all

c like k as in "keep": *cuarto* KOOAR-toh (room), Tepic tay-PEEK (capital of Nayarit state); when it precedes "e" or "i," pronounce **c** like s, as in "sit": *cerveza* sayr-VAY-sah (beer), *encima* ayn-SEE-mah (atop)

g like g as in "gift" when it precedes "a," "o," "u," or a consonant: *gato* GAH-toh (cat), *hago* AH-goh (I do, make); otherwise, pronounce **g** like h as in "hat": *giro* HEE-roh (money order), *gente* HAYN-tay (people)

j like h, as in "has": *Jueves* HOOAY-vays (Thursday), *mejor* may-HOR (better)

ll like y, as in "yes": *toalla* toh-AH-yah (towel), *ellos* AY-yohs (they, them)

ñ like ny as in "canyon": *año* AH-nyo (year), *señor* SAY-nyor (Mr., sir)

r is lightly trilled, with tongue at the roof of your mouth like a very light English d, as in "ready": *pero* PAY-doh (but), *tres* TDAYS (three), *cuatro* KOOAH-tdoh (four)

rr like a Spanish r, but with much more emphasis and trill. Let your tongue flap. Practice with *burro* (donkey), *carretera* (highway), and Carrillo (proper name), then really let go with *ferrocarril* (railroad)

Note: The single small but common exception to all of the above is the pronunciation of Spanish **y** when it's being used as the Spanish word for "and," as in "Ron y Kathy." In such case, pronounce it like the English ee, as in "keep": Ron "ee" Kathy (Ron and Kathy).

Accent

The rule for accent, the relative stress given to syllables within a given word, is straightforward. If a word ends in a vowel, an n, or an s, accent the next-to-last syllable; if not, accent the last syllable.

Pronounce *gracias* GRAH-seeahs (thank you), *orden* OHR-dayn (order), and *carretera* kah-ray-TAY-rah (highway) with stress on the next-to-last syllable.

Otherwise, accent the last syllable: *venir* vay-NEER (to come), *ferrocarril* fay-roh-cah-REEL (railroad), and *edad* ay-DAHD (age).

Exceptions to the accent rule are always marked with an accent sign: (á, é, í, ó, or ú), such as *teléfono* tay-LAY-foh-noh (telephone), *jabón* hah-BON (soap), and *rápido* RAH-pee-doh (rapid).

BASIC AND COURTEOUS EXPRESSIONS

Most Spanish-speaking people consider formalities important. Whenever approaching anyone for information or some other reason, do not forget the appropriate salutation—good morning, good evening, etc. Standing alone, the greeting *hola* (hello) can sound brusque.

Hello. *Hola.*
Good morning. *Buenos días.*
Good afternoon. *Buenas tardes.*
Good evening. *Buenas noches.*
How are you? *¿Cómo está usted?*
Very well, thank you. *Muy bien, gracias.*
Okay; good. *Bien.*
Not okay; bad. *Mal or feo.*
So-so. *Más o menos.*
And you? *¿Y usted?*
Thank you. *Gracias.*
Thank you very much. *Muchas gracias.*
You're very kind. *Muy amable.*
You're welcome. *De nada.*
Goodbye. *Chao.*
See you later. *Hasta luego.*
please *por favor*
yes *sí*
no *no*
I don't know. *No sé.*
Just a moment, please. *Momentito, por favor.*
Excuse me, please (when you're trying to get attention). *Disculpe* or *Con permiso.*
Excuse me (when you've made a boo-boo). *Lo siento.*
Pleased to meet you. *Mucho gusto.*
How do you say ... in Spanish? *¿Cómo se dice ... en español?*
What is your name? *¿Cómo se llama usted?*
Do you speak English? *¿Habla usted inglés?*
Is English spoken here? (Does anyone here speak English?) *¿Se habla inglés?*
I don't speak Spanish well. *No hablo bien el español.*
I don't understand. *No entiendo.*
My name is ... *Me llamo...*
Would you like ... *¿Quisiera usted ...*
Let's go to ... *Vamos a...*

TERMS OF ADDRESS

When in doubt, use the formal *usted* (you) as a form of address.

I *yo*
you (formal) *usted*
you (familiar) *tu*
he/him *él*
she/her *ella*
we/us *nosotros*
you (plural) *ustedes*
they/them *ellos* (all males or mixed gender); *ellas* (all females)
Mr., sir *señor*
Mrs., madam *señora*
miss, young lady *señorita*
wife *esposa*
husband *esposo*
friend *amigo* (male); *amiga* (female)
sweetheart *novio* (male); *novia* (female)
son; daughter *hijo; hija*
brother; sister *hermano; hermana*
father; mother *padre; madre*
grandfather; grandmother *abuelo; abuela*

TRANSPORTATION

Where is ...? *¿Dónde está ...?*
How far is it to ...? *¿A cuánto está ...?*
from ... to ... *de ... a ...*
How many blocks? *¿Cuántas cuadras?*
Where (Which) is the way to ...? *¿Dónde está el camino a ...?*
the bus station *la terminal de autobuses*
the bus stop *la parada de autobuses*
Where is this bus going? *¿Adónde va este autobús?*
the taxi stand *la parada de taxis*
the train station *la estación de ferrocarril*
the boat *el barco*
the launch *lancha; tiburonera*
the dock *el muelle*
the airport *el aeropuerto*
I'd like a ticket to ... *Quisiera un boleto a ...*
first (second) class *primera (segunda) clase*

roundtrip *ida y vuelta*
reservation *reservación*
baggage *equipaje*
Stop here, please. *Pare aquí, por favor.*
the entrance *la entrada*
the exit *la salida*
the ticket office *la boletería*
(very) near; far *(muy) cerca; lejos*
to; toward *a*
by; through *por*
from *de*
the right *la derecha*
the left *la izquierda*
straight ahead *derecho; directo*
in front *en frente*
beside *al lado*
behind *atrás*
the corner *la esquina*
the stoplight *la semáforo*
a turn *una vuelta*
right here *aquí*
somewhere around here *por acá*
right there *allí*
somewhere around there *por allá*
road *el camino*
street; boulevard *calle; avenida*
block *la cuadra*
highway *carretera*
kilometer *kilómetro*
bridge; toll *puente; peaje*
address *dirección*
north; south *norte; sur*
east; west *oriente (este); poniente (oeste)*

ACCOMMODATIONS

hotel *hotel*
Is there a room? *¿Hay cuarto?*
May I (may we) see it? *¿Puedo (podemos) verlo?*
What is the rate? *¿Cuál es el precio?*
Is that your best rate? *¿Es su mejor precio?*
Is there something cheaper? *¿Hay algo más económico?*
a single room *un cuarto sencillo*
a double room *un cuarto doble*
double bed *cama matrimonial*
twin beds *camas gemelas*
with private bath *con baño*

hot water *agua caliente*
shower *ducha*
towels *toallas*
soap *jabón*
toilet paper *papel higiénico*
blanket *frazada; manta*
sheets *sábanas*
air-conditioned *aire acondicionado*
fan *abanico; ventilador*
key *llave*
manager *gerente*

FOOD

I'm hungry *Tengo hambre.*
I'm thirsty. *Tengo sed.*
menu *carta; menú*
order *orden*
glass *vaso*
fork *tenedor*
knife *cuchillo*
spoon *cuchara*
napkin *servilleta*
soft drink *refresco*
coffee *café*
tea *té*
drinking water *agua pura; agua potable*
bottled carbonated water *agua con gas*
bottled uncarbonated water *agua sin gas*
beer *cerveza*
wine *vino*
milk *leche*
juice *jugo*
cream *crema*
sugar *azúcar*
cheese *queso*
snack *snack*
breakfast *desayuno*
lunch *almuerzo*
daily lunch special *el menú del día*
dinner *cena*
the check *la cuenta*
eggs *huevos*
bread *pan*
salad *ensalada*
fruit *fruta*
mango *mango*
watermelon *sandía*

papaya *papaya*
banana *plátano*
apple *manzana*
orange *naranja*
lime *limón*
fish *pescado*
shellfish *mariscos*
shrimp *camarones*
meat (without) *(sin) carne*
chicken *pollo*
pork *puerco*
beef; steak *res; bistec*
bacon; ham *tocino; jamón*
fried *frito*
roasted *asada*
barbecue; barbecued *asado a la parrilla*

SHOPPING

money *dinero; plata*
money-exchange bureau *casa de cambio*
I would like to exchange traveler's checks. *Quisiera cambiar cheques de viajero.*
What is the exchange rate? *¿Cuál es el tipo de cambio?*
How much is the commission? *¿Cuánto es la comisión?*
Do you accept credit cards? *¿Aceptan tarjetas de crédito?*
money order *giro*
How much does it cost? *¿Cuánto cuesta?*
What is your final price? *¿Cuál es su último precio?*
expensive *caro*
cheap *barato; económico*
more *más*
less *menos*
a little *un poco*
too much *demasiado*

HEALTH

Help me please. *Ayúdeme por favor.*
I am ill. *Estoy enfermo.*
Call a doctor. *Llame un doctor.*
Take me to ... *Lléveme a ...*
hospital *hospital; sanatorio*
drugstore *farmacia*

pain *dolor*
fever *fiebre*
headache *dolor de cabeza*
stomach ache *dolor de estómago*
burn *quemadura*
cramp *calambre*
nausea *náusea*
vomiting *vomitar*
medicine *medicina*
antibiotic *antibiótico*
pill; tablet *pastilla*
aspirin *aspirina*
ointment; cream *pomada; crema*
bandage *venda*
cotton *algodón*
sanitary napkins use brand name, e.g., Kotex
birth control pills *pastillas anticonceptivas*
contraceptive foam *espuma anticonceptiva*
condoms *preservativos; condones*
toothbrush *cepillo dental*
dental floss *hilo dental*
toothpaste *pasta de dientes*
dentist *dentista*
toothache *dolor de muelas*

POST OFFICE AND COMMUNICATIONS

long-distance telephone *teléfono larga distancia*
I would like to call ... *Quisiera llamar a ...*
collect *por cobrar*
station to station *a quien contesta*
person to person *persona a persona*
credit card *tarjeta de crédito*
post office *correo*
general delivery *lista de correo*
letter *carta*
stamp *estampilla, timbre*
postcard *tarjeta*
aerogram *aerograma*
air mail *correo aereo*
registered *registrado*
money order *transferencia*
package; box *paquete; caja*
string; tape *cuerda; cinta*

AT THE BORDER

border *frontera*
customs *aduana*
immigration *migración*
tourist card *tarjeta de turista*
inspection *inspección; revisión*
passport *pasaporte*
profession *profesión*
marital status *estado civil*
single *soltero*
married; divorced *casado; divorciado*
widowed *viudado*
insurance *seguros*
title *título*
driver's license *licencia de manejar*

AT THE GAS STATION

gas station *gasolinera*
gasoline *bencina*
unleaded *sin plomo*
full, please *lleno, por favor*
tire *neumático*
tire repair shop *vulcanización*
air *aire*
water *agua*
oil (change) *aceite (cambio)*
grease *grasa*
My . . . doesn't work. *Mi . . . no funciona.*
battery *batería*
radiator *radiador*
alternator *alternador*
generator *generador*
tow truck *grúa*
repair shop *taller mecánico*
tune-up *afinamiento*
auto parts store *tienda de repuestos*

VERBS

Verbs are the key to getting along in Spanish. They employ mostly predictable forms and come in three classes, which end in *ar, er,* and *ir,* respectively:

to buy *comprar*
I buy, you (he, she, it) buys *compro, compra*
we buy, you (they) buy *compramos, compran*

to eat *comer*
I eat, you (he, she, it) eats *como, come*
we eat, you (they) eat *comemos, comen*

to climb *subir*
I climb, you (he, she, it) climbs *subo, sube*
we climb, you (they) climb *subimos, suben*

Here are more (with irregularities indicated):

to do or make *hacer* (regular except for *hago,* I do or make)
to go *ir* (very irregular: *voy, va, vamos, van*)
to go (walk) *andar*
to love *amar*
to work *trabajar*
to want *desear, querer*
to need *necesitar*
to read *leer*
to write *escribir*
to repair *reparar*
to stop *parar*
to get off (the bus) *bajar*
to arrive *llegar*
to stay (remain) *quedar*
to stay (lodge) *hospedar*
to leave *salir* (regular except for *salgo,* I leave)
to look at *mirar*
to look for *buscar*
to give *dar* (regular except for *doy,* I give)
to carry *llevar*
to have *tener* (irregular but important: *tengo, tiene, tenemos, tienen*)
to come *venir* (similarly irregular: *vengo, viene, venimos, vienen*)

Spanish has two forms of "to be":

to be *estar* (regular except for *estoy,* I am)
to be *ser* (very irregular: *soy, es, somos, son*)

Use *estar* when speaking of location or a temporary state of being: "I am at home." *"Estoy en casa."* "I'm sick." *"Estoy enfermo."* Use *ser* for a permanent state of being: "I am a doctor." *"Soy doctora."*

NUMBERS

zero *cero*
one *uno*
two *dos*
three *tres*
four *cuatro*
five *cinco*
six *seis*
seven *siete*
eight *ocho*
nine *nueve*
10 *diez*
11 *once*
12 *doce*
13 *trece*
14 *catorce*
15 *quince*
16 *dieciseis*
17 *diecisiete*
18 *dieciocho*
19 *diecinueve*
20 *veinte*
21 *veintiuno*
30 *treinta*
40 *cuarenta*
50 *cincuenta*
60 *sesenta*
70 *setenta*
80 *ochenta*
90 *noventa*
100 *ciento*
101 *ciento y uno*
200 *doscientos*
500 *quinientos*
1,000 *mil*
10,000 *diez mil*
100,000 *cien mil*
1,000,000 *millón*
one half *medio*
one third *un tercio*
one fourth *un cuarto*

TIME

What time is it? *¿Qué hora es?*
It's one o'clock. *Es la una.*
It's three in the afternoon. *Son las tres de la tarde.*
It's 4 a.m. *Son las cuatro de la mañana.*
six-thirty *seis y media*
a quarter till eleven *un cuarto para las once*
a quarter past five *las cinco y cuarto*
an hour *una hora*

DAYS AND MONTHS

Monday *lunes*
Tuesday *martes*
Wednesday *miércoles*
Thursday *jueves*
Friday *viernes*
Saturday *sábado*
Sunday *domingo*
today *hoy*
tomorrow *mañana*
yesterday *ayer*
January *enero*
February *febrero*
March *marzo*
April *abril*
May *mayo*
June *junio*
July *julio*
August *agosto*
September *septiembre*
October *octubre*
November *noviembre*
December *diciembre*
a week *una semana*
a month *un mes*
after *después*
before *antes*

(Based on text provided by Bruce Whipperman, author of *Moon Pacific Mexico*.)

Suggested Reading

HISTORY AND CULTURE

Bethell, Leslie, ed. *Chile since Independence.* Cambridge, UK: Cambridge University Press, 1993. A systematic, if somewhat dry, look at Chile's economic and social fortunes from the mid-1830s through to the return to democracy.

Collier, Simon, and William F. Sater. *A History of Chile, 1808-2002.* Cambridge, UK: Cambridge University Press, 2004. A thorough chronicle of the country's history, focusing largely on the economic and social development of the two centuries. It's an impressively objective analysis of a thoroughly controversial period.

Galeano, Eduardo. *Open Veins of Latin America: Five Centuries of the Pillage of a Continent.* New York: Monthly Review Press, 1997. A challenging read offering a crash course in Latin American economic history and policies over the last half millennium, it discusses how Chile and other Latin American countries have been exploited for their mineral and agricultural wealth and the creation of a widely unequal society as a result.

Hunt, Terry, and Carl Lipo. *The Statues That Walked: Unravelling the Mystery of Easter Island.* New York: Free Press, 2011. A gripping read from two archaeologists involved in digs in the early 2000s that unpicks the fallacies associated with the mysterious island and proposes an answer to the question that has plagued researchers for decades: How did the islanders move the *moai*?

Moss, Chris. *Patagonia: A Cultural History (Landscapes of Imagination).* Oxford, UK: Signal Books, 2008. Regional expert and travel writer Chris Moss unpacks the myths and legends of Patagonia, grounding them in a compelling and often violent history of indigenous survival against the elements.

The Dictatorship

Beckett, Andy. *Pinochet in Piccadilly: Britain and Chile's Hidden History.* London: Faber and Faber, 2002. A fascinating book that examines in painstakingly researched detail the shared history of Britain and Chile, which culminated in General Pinochet's arrest on British soil in 1998.

Constable, Pamela, and Arturo Valenzuela. *A Nation of Enemies: Chile under Pinochet.* New York: W. W. Norton, 1993. A riveting journalistic and academic undertaking that explores the Chilean coup and its implications for ordinary Chileans, particularly following the return to democracy.

Márquez, Gabriel García. Translated by Asa Zatz. *Clandestine in Chile.* New York: New York Review of Books, 1986. The Nobel Prize-winning Colombian author takes on the gripping story of exiled film director Miguel Littín, who returned to Chile in 1985 to secretly put together a film to expose the truth of the Pinochet dictatorship.

NATURAL HISTORY

Chester, Sharon. *A Wildlife Guide to Chile.* Princeton, NJ: Princeton University Press, 2008. The first comprehensive field guide to the flora and fauna of Chile and its island territories. A must for would-be naturalists or those interested in fully appreciating the country's biodiversity.

TRAVELOGUES

Chatwin, Bruce. *In Patagonia.* New York: Penguin Classics, 1988. Although there are elements embellished by the author, this classic tale of Chatwin's trip through the fabled land has charmed and inspired travelers for decades with its evocative description of a wild land.

Darwin, Charles. *The Voyage of the Beagle.* London: Penguin Books, 1989. A groundbreaking narrative covering 22-year-old Darwin's five-year 19th-century voyage around South America that vividly recreates his interactions with the people of Chile and its flora and fauna. His journey would later inform his groundbreaking book *On the Origin of Species.*

Guevara, Ernesto. *The Motorcycle Diaries: A Journey through South America.* New York and London: Verso, 1995. Written during the period of travel that shaped his revolutionary tendencies, this travelogue charts Che's journey by motorbike around South America, with time spent in early 1950s Chile.

Jacobs, Michael. *Ghost Trail through the Andes: On My Grandfather's Trail in Chile and Bolivia.* London: John Murray, 2006. The travel writer sets out to Chile in the footsteps of his grandfather, who'd worked as an engineer on the British-built Chilean and Bolivian railways. This entertaining narrative grants fascinating insights into Valparaíso and the northern desert in the early 1900s.

TRAVEL GUIDES

Grant-Peterkin, James. *A Companion to Easter Island.* Chile: James Grant-Peterkin, 2014. Written by a long-time Scottish resident of the island, this guide contains plenty of practical information, including color photos and maps, plus snippets of fascinating local history.

Sinclair, Hugh, and Warren Houlbrooke. *Chile: The Carretera Austral.* Guilford, CT: Globe Pequot Press, 2016. A well-researched and detailed guidebook dedicated to travel along the mystical route of the Carretera Austral.

Internet Resources

GENERAL INFORMATION
Departamento de Extranjería y Migración
http://extranjeria.gob.cl
The Chilean Ministry for Migration and Foreign Affairs has information about visas and how to extend a 90-day tourist visa.

Dirección Meteorológica de Chile
www.meteochile.gob.cl
This Spanish-language site has up-to-date weather forecasts and information about the status of border crossings from the Chilean meteorological office.

Latin American Network Information Center (LANIC)
http://lanic.utexas.edu
Although it's no longer updated, this database, created by the University of Texas, has links to an array of useful information relating to history, politics, economics, and tourism in Chile.

U.S. Embassy in Santiago
http://cl.usembassy.gov
Find regularly updated security information for visitors to the country.

ENTERTAINMENT

Cívico
http://civico.com
This website has up-to-date cultural, musical, and gastronomic events listings in Santiago.

TRANSPORTATION

Recorrido
http://recorrido.cl
A comparison site with timetables and fares for journeys with some of the largest bus companies in the country. You can also book tickets here.

HISTORY

Chile Precolombino
http://chileprecolombino.cl
The website of the Museo Chileno de Arte Precolombino contains extensive historical information about indigenous people throughout Chile, including contemporary indigenous groups. English translation is available.

Memoria Chilena
http://memoriachilena.cl
The archives of Chile's Biblioteca Nacional (National Library) are rich in information regarding historical, cultural, and social themes.

TRAVEL INFORMATION

Chile Travel
http://chile.travel
The official website of the Chilean tourism board, SERNATUR, with information detailing tourism activities across different regions of Chile and some historical information.

SERNATUR
http://serviciosturisticos.sernatur.cl
Find the tourism board's interactive database of all registered tour operators and hotels.

INDIGENOUS TOURISM

Travolution
http://travolution.travel
This company leads unique tours almost exclusively in conjunction with indigenous Chilean communities. They also run the nonprofit Travolution.org, which runs annual conferences for indigenous and community-led tourism initiatives across South and Central America.

BIRDING

Aves Chile
http://avesdechile.cl
This is a great resource for birders, with a comprehensive directory of birds, complete with photos and their English-language names.

NATIONAL PARKS AND CONSERVATION

Corporación Nacional Forestal
www.conaf.cl
The official website of the quasi-governmental body that administers all Chilean national parks and reserves, with information (in Spanish only) on operating hours and logistics for getting to each.

Conservación Patagónica
http://conservacionpatagonica.org
Spanish- and English-language information about the projects implemented in Chile and South America by philanthropic billionaires Kristine McDivitt and the late Douglas Tompkins.

RECREATION

Andes Handbook
http://andeshandbook.org
This not-for-profit publishes guidebooks and plenty of community-posted online content with detailed trail descriptions for hiking in the Andes, with a strong focus on Chile. Mostly in Spanish.

Escalando
http://escalando.cl
Provides Spanish-language information on hiking and climbing routes in Chile.

NEWS AND MEDIA

El Mercurio
http://elmercurio.com
The country's leading right-wing newspaper covers business, culture, and travel.

The Santiago Times
http://santiagotimes.cl
The only English-language news website in Chile.

La Tercera
http://latercera.com
This conservative tabloid is the closest competitor of *El Mercurio.*

SMARTPHONE APPS

Moovit
A useful app with public transportation information for Santiago and other Chilean cities.

Maps.me
This app uses OpenStreetMap data to produce off-line hiking and driving maps for the whole country.

Index

N

List of Maps

Photo Credits

Acknowledgments

Thanks to all of the companies in Chile and Patagonia who supported me with the research for this book. The biggest *gracias* go to Terrace Lodge and Tours for the memorable and altitude sickness-inducing tour; Paul and Annie for a plethora of Conce recommendations; Julien and Amalia at Refugio Pullao and Francisco and Marie at Isla Bruja for information and *buena onda;* Bianca and Karin for accompanying me as I ate my way around Santiago; and the numerous others who gave invaluable information and the best of Chilean hospitality. I also raise my glass to Olivia, for her constant help in keeping me focused when endless days on the road got too much, and Gonzalo for his love, mental support, and dedicated fact-checking.

MOON

BAJA
Tijuana to Los Cabos
JENNIFER KRAMER

MOON

CANCÚN &
COZUMEL
With Playa del Carmen,
Tulum & the Riviera Maya
LIZA PRADO & GARY CHANDLER

MOON

MEXICO
CITY
JULIE MEADE

MOON

OAXACA
Andy Copeland

MOON

PUERTO
VALLARTA
With Sayulita, the Riviera Nayarit
& Costalegre
MADELINE MILNE

MOON

SAN MIGUEL
DE ALLENDE
with Guanajuato & Querétaro
JULIE MEADE

MOON

TIJUANA, ENSENADA &
VALLE DE GUADALUPE
WINE COUNTRY
JENNIFER KRAMER

MOON

YUCATÁN
PENINSULA
LIZA PRADO & GARY CHANDLER

More Mexico & Latin America from Moon

MOON

BELIZE
LEBAWIT LILY GIRMA

MOON

CARTAGENA
& COLOMBIA'S
CARIBBEAN COAST
ANDREW DIER

MOON

CHILE
With Easter Island
STEPH DYSON

MOON

COSTA RICA
NIKKI SOLANO

MOON

ECUADOR
& THE GALÁPAGOS ISLANDS
BETHANY PITTS

MOON

GALÁPAGOS
ISLANDS
LISA CHO
TRIP OF A LIFETIME

MOON

MACHU
PICCHU
With Lima, Cusco & the Inca Trail
RYAN DUBÉ
TRIP OF A LIFETIME

MOON

PATAGONIA
Including the Falkland Islands
WAYNE BERNHARDSON
TRIP OF A LIFETIME

Craft a personalized journey through the top national parks in the U.S. and Canada with Moon Travel Guides.

MOON

USA NATIONAL PARKS

THE COMPLETE GUIDE TO ALL 59 PARKS

BECKY LOMAX

MOON
ACADIA NATIONAL PARK
HILARY NANGLE

MOON
ARCHES & CANYONLANDS NATIONAL PARKS
W. C. MCRAE & JUDY JEWELL

MOON
BANFF NATIONAL PARK
HIKE · CAMP · KAYAK
ANDREW HEMPSTEAD

MOON
DEATH VALLEY NATIONAL PARK
JENNA BLOUGH

MOON
GLACIER NATIONAL PARK
BECKY LOMAX

MOON
GRAND CANYON
HIKE · CAMP
RAFT THE COLORADO RIVER
TIM HULL

MOON
GREAT SMOKY MOUNTAINS NATIONAL PARK
HIKE · BIKE · CAMP
JASON FRYE

MOON
MOUNT RUSHMORE & THE BLACK HILLS
Including the Badlands
LAURAL A. BIDWELL

MOON
ROCKY MOUNTAIN NATIONAL PARK
HIKE · CAMP
SEE WILDLIFE
ERIN ENGLISH

MOON
SEQUOIA & KINGS CANYON
HIKE · CAMP
SEE REDWOODS
LEIGH BERNACCHI

MOON
YELLOWSTONE & GRAND TETON
HIKE · CAMP
SEE WILDLIFE
BECKY LOMAX

MOON
YOSEMITE
SEQUOIA & KINGS CANYON
ANN MARIE BROWN

MOON
ZION & BRYCE
Including Arches, Canyonlands, Capitol Reef, Grand Staircase-Escalante & Moab
W. C. MCRAE & JUDY JEWELL

MAP SYMBOLS

▬▬▬	Expressway	○	City/Town	✈	Airport	⚓	Golf Course
▭▭▭	Primary Road	◉	State Capital	✗	Airfield	🅿	Parking Area
▭▭▭	Secondary Road	⊛	National Capital	▲	Mountain	⬭	Archaeological Site
▯▯▯	Unpaved Road	✪	Highlight	✦	Unique Natural Feature	⬙	Church
- - - -	Trail	★	Point of Interest			⚱	Gas Station
··········	Ferry	•	Accommodation	⌇	Waterfall	⬭	Glacier
▰▰▰	Railroad	▾	Restaurant/Bar	♠	Park	▨	Mangrove
▭▭▭	Pedestrian Walkway	▪	Other Location	🆃🅷	Trailhead	▤	Reef
⬚⬚⬚	Stairs	⋀	Campground	⛷	Skiing Area	▥	Swamp

CONVERSION TABLES

°C = (°F − 32) / 1.8
°F = (°C x 1.8) + 32
1 inch = 2.54 centimeters (cm)
1 foot = 0.304 meters (m)
1 yard = 0.914 meters
1 mile = 1.6093 kilometers (km)
1 km = 0.6214 miles
1 fathom = 1.8288 m
1 chain = 20.1168 m
1 furlong = 201.168 m
1 acre = 0.4047 hectares
1 sq km = 100 hectares
1 sq mile = 2.59 square km
1 ounce = 28.35 grams
1 pound = 0.4536 kilograms
1 short ton = 0.90718 metric ton
1 short ton = 2,000 pounds
1 long ton = 1.016 metric tons
1 long ton = 2,240 pounds
1 metric ton = 1,000 kilograms
1 quart = 0.94635 liters
1 US gallon = 3.7854 liters
1 Imperial gallon = 4.5459 liters
1 nautical mile = 1.852 km

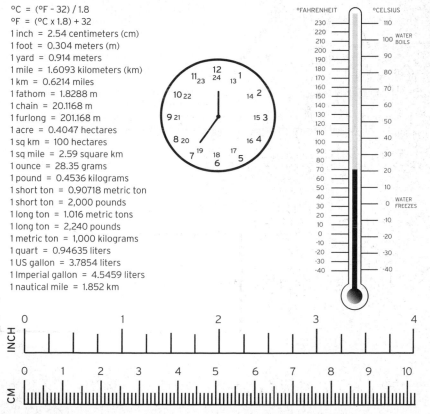

MOON CHILE

Avalon Travel
Hachette Book Group
1700 Fourth Street
Berkeley, CA 94710, USA
www.moon.com

Editor: Leah Gordon
Acquiring Editor: Nikki Ioakimedes
Series Manager: Kathryn Ettinger
Copy Editors: Christopher Church, Brett Keener
Graphics Coordinator: Rue Flaherty
Production Coordinator: Rue Flaherty
Cover Design: Faceout Studios, Charles Brock
Interior Design: Domini Dragoone
Moon Logo: Tim McGrath
Map Editor: Kat Bennett
Cartographers: Brian Shotwell, John Culp,
   Kat Bennett
Indexer: Rachel Kuhn

ISBN-13: 9781640492752

Printing History
1st Edition — July 2020
5 4 3 2 1

Front cover photo: Torres del Paine National Park
   © Santiago Urquijo / Getty Images
Back cover photo: Marble Caves © Mikhail Dudarev
   | Dreamstime.com

Printed in China by RR Donnelley

Avalon Travel is a division of Hachette Book Group,
Inc. Moon and the Moon logo are trademarks of
Hachette Book Group, Inc. All other marks and logos
depicted are the property of the original owners.